D1526559

HISTORICAL DICTIONARY

The historical dictionaries present essential information on a broad range of subjects, including American and world history, art, business, cities, countries, cultures, customs, film, global conflicts, international relations, literature, music, philosophy, religion, sports, and theater. Written by experts, all contain highly informative introductory essays of the topic and detailed chronologies that, in some cases, cover vast historical time periods but still manage to heavily feature more recent events.

Brief A–Z entries describe the main people, events, politics, social issues, institutions, and policies that make the topic unique, and entries are cross-referenced for ease of browsing. Extensive bibliographies are divided into several general subject areas, providing excellent access points for students, researchers, and anyone wanting to know more. Additionally, maps, photographs, and appendixes of supplemental information aid high school and college students doing term papers or introductory research projects. In short, the historical dictionaries are the perfect starting point for anyone looking to research in these fields.

HISTORICAL DICTIONARIES OF RELIGIONS, PHILOSOPHIES, AND MOVEMENTS

Jon Woronoff, Series Editor

Orthodox Church, by Michael Prokurat, Alexander Golitzin, and Michael D. Peterson, 1996

Civil Rights Movement, by Ralph E. Luker, 1997

North American Environmentalism, by Edward R. Wells and Alan M. Schwartz, 1997

Taoism, by Julian F. Pas in cooperation with Man Kam Leung, 1998

Gay Liberation Movement, by Ronald J. Hunt, 1999

Islamic Fundamentalist Movements in the Arab World, Iran, and Turkey, by Ahmad S. Moussalli, 1999

Cooperative Movement, by Jack Shaffer, 1999

Kierkegaard's Philosophy, by Julia Watkin, 2001

Slavery and Abolition, by Martin A. Klein, 2002

Prophets in Islam and Judaism, by Scott B. Noegel and Brannon M. Wheeler, 2002

Lesbian Liberation Movement: Still the Rage, by JoAnne Myers, 2003

Descartes and Cartesian Philosophy, by Roger Ariew, Dennis Des Chene, Douglas M. Jesseph, Tad M. Schmaltz, and Theo Verbeek, 2003

Unitarian Universalism, by Mark W. Harris, 2004

New Age Movements, by Michael York, 2004

Utopianism, by James M. Morris and Andrea L. Kross, 2004

Feminism, Second Edition, by Janet K. Boles and Diane Long Hoeveler, 2004

Jainism, by Kristi L. Wiley, 2004

Wittgenstein's Philosophy, by Duncan Richter, 2004

Schopenhauer's Philosophy, by David E. Cartwright, 2005

Seventh-day Adventists, by Gary Land, 2005

Methodism, Second Edition, by Charles Yrigoyen Jr. and Susan E. Warrick, 2005

Sufism, by John Renard, 2005

Sikhism, Second Edition, by W. H. McLeod, 2005

Kant and Kantianism, by Helmut Holzhey and Vilem Mudroch, 2005

Olympic Movement, Third Edition, by Bill Mallon with Ian Buchanan, 2006

Anglicanism, by Colin Buchanan, 2006

Welfare State, Second Edition, by Bent Greve, 2006

Feminist Philosophy, by Catherine Villanueva Gardner, 2006

Logic, by Harry J. Gensler, 2006

Leibniz's Philosophy, by Stuart Brown and Nicholas J. Fox, 2006

Historical Dictionary of Human Rights

Jacques Fomerand

ROWMAN & LITTLEFIELD
Lanham • Boulder • New York • Toronto • Plymouth, UK

Published by Rowman & Littlefield
4501 Forbes Boulevard, Suite 200, Lanham, Maryland 20706
www.rowman.com

10 Thornbury Road, Plymouth PL6 7PP, United Kingdom

British Library Cataloguing in Publication Information Available

Library of Congress Cataloging-in-Publication Data
Fomerand, Jacques.
  Historical dictionary of human rights / Jacques Fomerand.
      pages cm. — (Historical dictionaries of religions, philosophies, and movements)
  Includes bibliographical references.
  ISBN 978-0-8108-5845-9 (cloth : alk. paper) — ISBN 978-0-8108-8035-1 (ebook)
  1. Human rights—History—Dictionaries. I. Title.
  JC571.F59 2014
  323.03—dc23   2013033859

∞™ The paper used in this publication meets the minimum requirements of American
National Standard for Information Sciences—Permanence of Paper for Printed Library
Materials, ANSI/NISO Z39.48-1992.

Printed in the United States of America.

Contents

Editor's Foreword

The field of human rights has quickly become the center of international affairs and, although still far from achieving its many goals, it is a definite reality. What has been done and what remains to be completed will become clear in this extraordinary *Historical Dictionary of Human Rights*. The most important section and the core of the book is the dictionary, which lists and describes in alphabetical order the many conventions, treaties, and other related documents; the increasing number of intergovernmental organizations in the UN family or regional bodies; the constantly expanding universe of nongovernmental organizations; pioneers and defenders; and often intricate and confusing terminology. The chronology indicates that the number of annual events continues to grow as the process accelerates, the list of acronyms identifies the players, and the introduction provides an overview of the field. Finally, the bibliography is detailed and comprehensive.

This book was written by Jacques Fomerand, who worked for the United Nations in the Department of Economic and Social Affairs, beginning in 1977. From 1992 to 2003, he was the director of the United Nations University Office in North America. Now he teaches at the United Nations Program of Occidental College and the John Jay College of Criminal Justice, as well as writing on many of the issues raised in this book. Given the role of the UN and other organizations in regard to human rights, it would have been impossible to write about the events of recent decades without understanding how the organization operates. In addition to the current volume, Dr. Fomerand has written the thorough and equally insightful *Historical Dictionary of the United Nations*. Both of these books provide a wealth of useful information.

Jon Woronoff
Series Editor

Preface

This book explores the *praxis* of human rights norms, standards and treaties by states and nonstate actors in the contemporary world. I seek in the first place to identify the actors involved in these processes (i.e., governments, civil society organizations and individuals) as well as the ubiquitous "spoilers." I also investigate their interactions through a number of mechanisms that have developed incrementally in the past half century pertaining to the norm-making process, the rise of judicialization, the development of transitional retributive, reparative and restorative justice tools, and the enforcement instruments, which range from benign neglect to naming and shaming to sanctions, peace operations and the use of force. On balance, I conclude this overview with the feeling that, while much remains to be done to perfect the architecture and operation of the human rights landscape, the incremental and disjointed achievements of the past decades since the end of the World War II have spawned a world that is far more aware of and vigilant about the need to punish and prevent human rights abuses than it was a half century ago.

I would like to acknowledge my debt of gratitude to my human rights and international law students whose feedback has been invaluable. Very special thanks to my editor, Jon Woronoff, who, with incomparable dexterity and effectiveness, was able to resolve the string of unending editorial problems that I inflicted upon him.

I dedicate this work to my companion, Marianthi, and to my sons, Ross and Thierry, who had to bear my estrangement. This book is homage to my parents, whom, I found out, knew better all along.

Acronyms and Abbreviations

AAWORD	Association of African Women for Research and Development
ACHPR	African Charter on Human and People's Rights
ACHR	(Inter) American Convention on Human Rights
ACLU	American Civil Liberties Union
ACmHPR	African Commission on Human and People's Rights
ACRWC	African Charter on Rights and Welfare of the Child
ACterHR	Asian Center for Human Rights
ACtHPR	African Court on Human and People's Rights
ACTSA	Action for Southern Africa
ACtteeRWC	African Committee on the Rights and Welfare of the Child
ADL	Anti Defamation League
AHRC	Asian Human Rights Commission
AI	Amnesty International
AISA	Africa Institute of South Africa
AJC	American Jewish Committee
ALU	Arab Lawyers Union
AMIS	African Union in Sudan
AOHR	Arab Organization for Human Rights
APT	Association for the Prevention of Torture
ArCHR	Arab Charter on Human Rights
ARIS	Anti Racism Information Service
ASIL	American Society of International Law
ATS	Alien Tort Statute
AU	African Union
AWID	Association for Women's Rights in Development
BIHR	British Institute of Human Rights
BW	Biological Weapons
BWIs	Bretton Woods Institutions
CAJ	Committee on the Administration of Justice
CATW	Coalition Against Trafficking in Women
CCR	Center for Constitutional Rights

CCS	Committee of Concerned Scientists
CEDHA	Center for Human Rights and the Environment
CEJIL	Center for Justice and International Law
CEMIRIDE	Center for Minority Rights Development
CESR	Center for Economic and Social Rights
CETIM	Europe Third World Center
CGRS	Center for Gender and Refugee Studies
CHRI	Commonwealth Human Rights Initiative
CI	Consumers International
CIA	Central Intelligence Agency
CICC	Coalition for the International Criminal Court
CIDCM	Center for International Development and Conflict Management
CIFEDHOP	International Training Centre on Human Rights and Peace Research
CIHRA	Cairo Institute for Human Rights
CIJ	Coalition for International Justice
CIL	Customary International Law
CIS	Commonwealth of Independent States
CJ	Court of Justice
CJA	Center for Justice and Accountability
CMS	Center for Migration Studies
CODESRIA	Council for the Development of Social Science Research in Africa
COHRE	Center on Housing Rights and Evictions
COMIR	Consortium of Minority resources
CONGO	Conference of Non Governmental Organizations in Consultative Relationship with the United Nations
CPT	European Committee for the Prevention of Torture
CRIN	Child Rights Information Network
CSR	Corporate Social Responsibility
CtteeRWR	Committee on the Rights and Welfare of the Child
CVT	Center for Victims of Torture
DCI	Defense for Children International
DIHR	Danish Institute for Human Rights
DoCip	Indigenous Peoples' Center for Documentation, Research and Information
DPI	Disabled Persons International
DRC	Democratic Republic of the Congo
EChFR	European Charter of Fundamental Rights of the European Union

ECHR	European Convention on Human Rights and Fundamental Freedoms
ECJ	European Court of Justice
ECOWAS	Economic Community of West African States
ECPT	European Convention for the Prevention of Torture
ECRI	European Commission Against Racism and Intolerance
ECRML	European Charter for Regional or Minority Languages
ECtHR	European Court of Human Rights
EDF	European Parliament
EITI	Extractive Industries Transparency Initiative
EMHRN	Europe-Mediterranean Human Rights Network
EP	European Parliament
ERCOMER	European Research Centre on Migration and Ethnic Relations
ERI	Earthrights International
ERRC	European Roma Rights Center
ESC	European Social Charter
ESCR-Net	International Network for Economic, Social and Cultural Rights
EU	European Union
FAO	Food and Agriculture International
FCI	Family Care International
FEWER	Forum on Early Warning and Early Response
FFDA	Forum for Fact Finding Documentation and Advocacy
FGM	Female Genital Mutilation
FIAN	Food First Informational and Action Network
FIDH	International Federation for Human Rights
FOEI	Friends of the Earth International
GAATW	Global Alliance Against Traffic in Women
GC	Geneva Conventions
GCR2P	Global Center for the Responsibility to Protect
GDI	Gender Development Index
GEM	Gender Empowerment Measure
GIRCA	Gypsy International Recognition and Compensation Action
GJC	Global Justice Center
GPF	Global Policy Forum
GW	Global Witness
HDR	Human Development Report
HIC	Habitat International Coalition
HRBA	Human Rights Based Approach to Development
HRDs	Human Rights Defenders

HREA	Human Rights Education Associates
HRF	Human Rights First
HRI	Human Rights Internet
HRW	Human Rights Watch
HURISA	Human Rights Institute of South Africa
IA	International Alert
IACAT	Inter-American Convention to Prevent and Punish Torture
IACDAPD	Inter-American Convention on the Elimination of All Forms of Discrimination Against Persons with Disabilities
IACFD	Inter-American Convention on Forced Disappearances of Persons
IACmHR	Inter-American Commission on Human Rights
IACPPT	Inter-American Convention to Prevent and Punish Torture
IACtHR	Inter-American Court of Human Rights
IACVAW	Inter-American Convention on the Prevention, Punishment and Eradication of Violence Against Women
IACW	Inter-American Commission of Women
IADL	International Association of Democratic Lawyers
IAII	Inter-American Indian Institute
IALANA	International Association of Lawyers Against Nuclear Arms
IAP	International Accountability Project
IARF	International Association for Religious Freedom
IARLJ	International Association of Refugee Law Judges
IAWJ	International Association of Women Judges
IBA	International Bar Association
IBAHARI	International Bar Association Human Right Institute
IBCR	International Bureau for Children Rights
IBRD	International Bank for Reconstruction and Development
ICAN	International Civil Society Action Network
ICBL	International Campaign to Ban Landmines
ICC	International Criminal Court
ICCLR	International Center for Criminal Law Reform and Criminal Justice Policy
ICCPR	International Covenant on Civil and Political Rights
ICCR	Interfaith Center on Corporate Responsibility
ICERD	International Convention on the Elimination of All Forms of Racial Discrimination
ICESCR	International Covenant on Economic, Social and Cultural Rights

ICFTU	International Confederation of Free Trade Unions
ICG	International Crisis Group
ICISS	International Commission on Intervention and State Sovereignty
ICJ	International Commission of Jurists
ICJ	International Court of Justice
ICL	International Criminal Law
ICLR	International Commission for Labor Rights
ICPED	International Convention for the Protection of All Persons from Enforced Disappearances
ICRC	International Committee of the Red Cross
ICRD	International Convention on the Elimination of All Forms of Racial Discrimination
ICRMW	International Convention on the Protection of the Rights of All Migrant Workers and Their Families
ICR2P	International Coalition for the Responsibility to Protect
ICTJ	International Center for Transitional Justice
ICTR	International Criminal Tribunal for Rwanda
ICTUR	International Center for Trade Union Rights
ICTY	International Criminal Tribunal for the Former Yugoslavia
ICW	International Council of Women
IDA	International Disability Alliance
IDMC	Internal Displacement Monitoring Centre
IDPs	Internally Displaced Persons
IDS	Institute of Development Studies
IFES	International Foundation for Electoral Systems
IFEX	International Freedom of Expression Exchange
IFHR	International Federation for Human Rights
IFJ	International Federation of Journalists
IFRC	International Federation of Red Cross and red Crescent Societies
IFTDH	International Federation Terre des Hommes
IGC	Institute for Global Communications
IGLHRC	International Gay and Lesbian Human Rights Commission
IHL	International Humanitarian Law
IHRB	Institute for Human Rights and Business
IHRDA	Institute for Human Rights and Development in Africa
IHRLI	International Human Rights Law Institute
II	Inclusion International
IIDH	Inter-American Institute of Human Rights
IIHL	International Institute of Humanitarian Law

IILHR	Institute for International Law and Human Rights
IILJ	Institute for International Law and Justice
IIN	Inter-American Children Institute
ILA	International Law Association
ILC	International Law Commission
ILHR	International League for Human Rights
ILI	International Law Institute
ILO	International Labour Organization
IMADR	International Movement Against All Forms of Discrimination and Racism
IMF	International Monetary Fund
INTERIGHTS	International Centre for the Legal Protection of Human Rights
IOM	International Organization for Migration
IPEC	International Programme on the Elimination of Child Labor
IPI	International Peace Institute
IPPF	International Planned Parenthood Federation
IPU	Inter-Parliamentary Union
IRC	International Rescue Committee
IRCT	International Rehabilitation Council for Torture Victims
ISHR	International Service for Human Rights
ISHR	International Society for Human Rights
ITEM	Third World Institute (Instituto del Tercer Mundo)
ITUC	International Trade Union Confederation
IWGIA	International Work Group for Indigenous Affairs
IWPR	Institute for War and Peace Reporting
IWRAW	International Women's Rights Action Watch
KHR	Kurdish Human Rights Project
KPCS	Kimberley Process Certification Scheme
LAS	League of Arab States
LRA	Lord's Resistance Army
MAR	Minorities at Risk Project
MDGs	Millennium Development Goals
MINUGUA	United Nations Verification Mission in Guatemala
MINURCA	United Nations Mission in the Central African Republic
MINURCAT	United Nations Mission in the Central African Republic and Chad
MINURSO	United Nations Mission for the Referendum in Western Sahara
MINUSTAH	United Nations Stabilization Mission in Haiti

MONUC	United Nations Organization Mission in the Democratic Republic of the Congo
MONUSCO	United Nations Stabilization Mission in the Democratic Republic of the Congo
MPG	Migration Policy Group
MRG	Minority Rights Group International
MRI	Migrant Rights International
MSF	Médecins Sans Frontières (Doctors Without Borders)
NATO	North Atlantic Treaty Organization
NED	National Endowment for Democracy
NGOs	Non-Governmental Organizations
NGOWG	NGO Working Group on Women, Peace and Security
NHRIs	National Human Rights Institutions
NPWJ	No Peace Without Justice
OAS	Organization of American States
OAU	Organization of African Unity
OECD	Organization for Economic Cooperation and Development
OIC	Organization of Islamic Cooperation
OMTC	World Organization Against Torture
ONUB	United Nations Operation in Burundi
ONUMOZ	United Nations Operation in Mozambique
ONUSAL	United Nations Observer Group in El Salvador
ORCI	Office for Research and the Collection of Information
OSCE	Organization for Security and Cooperation in Europe
PBI	Peace Brigades International
PCHR	Palestinian Center for Human Rights
PCIJ	Permanent Court of International Justice
PDHRE	The People's Movement for Human Rights Education
PGA	Parliamentarians for Global Action
PGI	Prevent Genocide International
PHR	Physicians for Human Rights
PICT	Project on International Courts and Tribunals
PICUM	Platform for International Cooperation on Undocumented Migrants
PMCs	Private Military Companies
R2P	"Responsibility to Protect"
RAN	Rainforest Action Network
RI	Refugees International
RI	Rehabilitation International
RPF	Rwandan Patriotic Front
RWB	Reporters Without Borders

RWI	Raoul Wallenberg Institute
SAARC	South Asian Association for Regional Cooperation
SADC	Southern African Development Community
SAPs	Structural Adjustment Programmes
SCSL	Special Court for Sierra Leone
SI	Survival International
SI	Survivors International
STL	Special Tribunal for Lebanon
TANs	Transnational Advocacy Networks
TI	Transparency International
TNCs	Transnational Corporations
TRCs	Truth and Reconciliation Commissions
TRIPS	Agreement on Trade Related Aspects of Intellectual Property Rights
UDBHR	Universal Declaration on Bioethics and Human Rights
UDHR	Universal Declaration of Human Rights
UN	United Nations
UNAMA	United Nations Assistance Mission in Afghanistan
UNAMID	African Union-United Nations Hybrid Operation in Darfur
UNAMIR	United Nations Assistance Mission for Rwanda
UNAMSIL	United Nations Mission in Sierra Leone
UN-CAT	United Nations Convention Against Torture and Other Cruel, Inhuman or Degrading Treatment
UN-CBD	United Nations Convention on Biological Diversity
UN-CCD	United Nations Convention to Combat Desertification
UN-CEDAW	United Nations Convention on the Elimination of All Forms of Discrimination Against Women
UN-CHR	United Nations Commission on Human Rights
UN-CPPCG	United Nations Convention on the Punishment and Prevention of the Crime of Genocide
UN-CPRD	United Nations Convention on the Rights of Persons with Disabilities
UNCTAD	United Nations Conference on Trade and Development
UN-CRC	United Nations on the Rights of the Child
UN-CSW	United Nations Commission on the Status of Women
UN-CtteeCAT	United Nations Committee Against Torture
UN-CtteeEDAW	United Nations Committee on the Elimination of Discrimination Against Women
UN-CtteeERD	United Nations Committee on the Elimination of Racial Discrimination

UN-CtteeESCR	United Nations Committee on Economic, Social and Cultural Rights
UN-CtteeRC	United Nations Committee on the Rights of the Child
UN-CtteeRMW	United Nations Committee on the Protection of the Rights of All Migrant Workers and their Families
UNDP	United Nations Development Programme
UN-ECOSOC	United Nations Economic and Social Council
UNESCO	United Nations Educational, Scientific and Cultural Organization
UNFCC	United Nations Framework Convention on Climate Change
UNFPA	United Nations Population Fund
UN-GA	United Nations General Assembly
UN-HABITAT	United Nations Human Settlements Programme
UN-HCR	United Nations High Commissioner for Refugees
UN-HRC	United Nations Human Rights Council
UN-HRCttee	United Nations Human Rights Committee
UNICEF	United Nations Children's Fund
UNMBIH	United Nations Mission in Bosnia and Herzegovina
UNMIH	United Nations Mission in Haiti
UNMIK	United Nations Interim Administration Mission in Kosovo
UNMISET	United Nations Mission of Support in East Timor
UNMISS	United Nations Mission in the Republic of South Sudan
UNMIT	United Nations Integrated Mission in Timor Leste
UNMSIL	United Nations Mission in Sierra Leone
UNOCI	United Nations Operation in Cote d'Ivoire
UN-OHCHR	United Nations Office of the High Commissioner for Human Rights
UNOMIG	United Nations Observer Mission in Georgia
UNOMIL	United Nations Observer Mission in Liberia
UNOSOM	United Nations Operation in Somalia
UN-PCB	United Nations Peace Building Commission
UNPO	Unrepresented Nations and Peoples Organization
UNPRI	United Nations Principles for Responsible Investment
UNPROFOR	United Nations Protection Force
UN-SC	United Nations Security Council
UN-SG	United Nations Secretary-General
UNTAC	United Nations Transitional Authority in Cambodia
UNTAET	United Nations Transitional Administration in East Timor
UNTAG	United Nations Transition Assistance Group
UN-TOC	United Nations Convention Against Transnational Organized Crime

UNWRA	United Nations Relief and Works Agency for Palestine Refugees in the Near East
UPR	Universal Periodic Review
USIP	United States Institute of Peace
WBCSD	World Business Council for Sustainable Development
WBU	World Blind Union
WCC	World Council of Churches
WCED	World Commission on Environment and Development
WCL	World Confederation of Labor
WFD	World Federation of the Deaf
WFDB	World Federation of the Deafblind
WFM	World Federalist Movement
WFN	Women's Funding Network
WFTU	World Federation of Trade Unions
WFUNA	World Federation of United Nations Associations
WHO	World Health Organization
WILPF	Women's International League for Peace and Freedom
WJP	World Justice Project
WMD	Weapons of Mass Destruction
WSF	World Social Forum
WSIS	World Summit on the Information Society
WTO	World Trade Organization

Chronology

1493 Colonization of the Western Hemisphere begins resulting in the demise of indigenous populations and challenges by Christian theologians regarding means employed to enforce the laws of God.

1648 Treaty of Westphalia.

1755–1763 Acadian expulsion.

1776 **4 July:** United States Declaration of Independence proclaims that all men are created equal and endowed with certain inalienable rights.

1787 **17 September:** U.S. Constitution adopted.

1789 **26 August:** National Assembly adopts French Declaration of the Rights of Men.

1791 **15 December:** U.S. Bill of Rights incorporating notions of freedom of speech, press and fair trial in U.S. Constitution enters into effect.

1807 **25 March:** The British Parliament bans the slave trade.

1815 **8 February:** Major European powers issue declaration relative to the Universal Abolition of the Slave Trade. **8 June:** Congress of Vienna proclaims that the slave trade should be abolished as soon as possible.

1822–23 Some 68,000 Greeks killed in revolt against Turkey.

1824–1908 Killing or removal of Aborigines in Australia.

1830 **28 May:** U.S. Congress passes Indian Removal Act to free land for settlement, forcing 70,000 Native Americans to relocate in what came to be known as the Trail of Tears.

1834 **1 August:** Slavery officially abolished in most of the British Empire.

1840s–50s Some 20,000 Baha'is put to death in Iran.

1841 **20 December:** Russia, France, Prussia, Austria, and Great Britain sign Treaty of London, first multilateral instrument proclaiming the trade in slaves an act of piracy.

1850–64   Some 12 million killed during the Taiping Rebellion in China.

1855–73   Mass killings during Muslim rebellion in China.

1860   10,000 Christians massacred in Lebanon and Syria.

1860s   3 million killed during Triad Rebellion against Manchu dynasty of China.

1863   **1 January:** U.S. President Abraham Lincoln issues the Emancipation Proclamation. **9 February:** Henri Dunant takes first steps toward establishment of the International Committee of the Red Cross (ICRC). **24 April:** Instruction issued by President Lincoln spelling out norms of conduct by soldiers of the Union in wartime. **26–29 October:** International conference endorses foundation of national relief societies sets up ICRC.

1864   **22 August:** Convention for the Amelioration of the Condition of the Wounded in Armies in the Field adopted in Geneva. This is the first Geneva Convention.

1868   **11 December:** Declaration renouncing the use of certain explosives projectiles is adopted in St. Petersburg.

1871   Gustave Moynier, co-founder of the ICRC, suggests the establishment of a Universal Criminal Court. **May:** Some 15,000 summarily executed during Paris Commune.

1873–1913   Between 30,000 and 100,000 massacred by Indonesians in occupation of Sumatra.

1876–79   Some 15,000 Bulgars massacred.

1881–82   Wave of anti-Jewish pogroms in Russia.

1885   King Leopold of Belgium acquires Congo Free State as his personal property.

1891   **15 May:** Pope Leo XIII issues "Rerum Novarum" calling for amelioration of "the misery and wretchedness pressing so unjustly on the majority of the working class."

1894–96   200,000 Armenians massacred by Turks and Kurds.

1897   Brazilian army suppresses Canudos settlers in state of Bahia.

1899   **19 July:** International Peace Conference held at The Hague gives birth to Laws and Customs of War on Land.

1899–1913   Some 250,000 to 1 million civilians perish during the Philippine-American War.

1903   Ottomans subdue Macedonian rebels (20,000 dead).

1903–06   Some 3,000 Jews killed in new wave of pogroms in Russia.

1904   Germany puts down indigenous rebellion in South West Africa (now Namibia) with 65,000 fatalities.

1906   Finnish women granted right to vote.

1909   An estimated 25,000 Armenians massacred in Adana.

1910–20   250,000 believed to perish during Mexican revolution.

1911   Some 2.4 million die during Chinese Revolution.

1914–18   Millions displaced in aftermath of World War I.

1915–18   Some 1.5 million Armenians massacred in Turkey.

1916   Some 120,000 die in Kyrgyz revolt against Russia.

1917   **2 November:** British government issues Balfour Declaration which "views with favor the establishment in Palestine of a national home for the Jewish people."

1917–21   Some 5 million die during Soviet Revolution.

1918   **8 January:** In a speech delivered to the U.S. Congress, President Woodrow Wilson outlines his Fourteen Points as the basis for the terms of a postwar settlement.

1919   **29 April:** Covenant of the League of Nations enters into force. **28 June:** Versailles treaty requires Kaiser Wilhelm II to be placed on trial for a "supreme offense against international morality and the sanctity of treaties." Other peace treaties stress minorities' rights, including right to life, liberty, freedom of religion, nationality and exercise of civil and political rights. **29 October:** First annual conference of the International Labour Organization (ILO) with mandate to promote labor rights encompassing employment, discrimination, forced labor and worker safety.

1920   **10 January:** Covenant of League of Nations enters into force calling upon members to "endeavor to secure and maintain fair and humane conditions of labor for men, women and children, secure just treatment of the native inhabitants of territories under their control, and take measures for the prevention and control of disease." **April:** 45,000 Terek Cossacks deported from North Caucasus to Ukraine and northern Russia.

1920–49   Some 14 million die in Chinese civil war.

1921   23 May–6 July: Leipzig War Crimes Tribunal, first attempt to devise a comprehensive system for prosecution of violations of international law. ILO adopts Right of Association Convention.

1922   Forced population exchange between Turkey and Greece. Some 30,000 Christians (mostly Greeks) massacred. First Nansen passports for stateless persons issued. **September:** Roughly 18,000 "socially dangerous" sent from Western border of Ukraine and Byelorussia to Western Siberia and Far East.

1922–41   Cleansing of bourgeoisie, aristocracy and kulaks in Soviet Union.

1924   League of Nations adopts Geneva Declaration recognizing and affirming for the first time the existence of rights specific to children.

1924–27   As many as 30,000 killed in anti-Kurdish campaign by Turkey.

1926   26 September: Slavery Convention adopted.

1927   27 August: Kellogg-Briand Pact outlawing war signed.

1928   13 September: Permanent Court of International Justice (PCIJ) rules that reparations for an unlawful act is a general principle of international law.

1928–37   Some 2 million die during that phase of Chinese civil war.

1930   28 June: ILO adopts Convention Concerning Forced or Compulsory Labor requiring states parties "to suppress the use of forced or compulsory labor in all its forms within the shortest possible period."

1930–36   Some 6.5 million kulaks cleansed of which 2.3 million resettled to Northern Russia, Urals, Siberia and Caucasus.

1932   1 May: ILO Convention on forced labor comes into force. **November–December:** An estimated 45,000 peasants forcibly removed from Krasnodar Krai (Russia) to Northern Russia.

1932–33:   Some 5 to 7 million peasants (mostly Ukrainians) die in artificially induced famine.

1933   Some 200,000 nomadic Kazakhs transferred to China, Mongolia, Iran, Afghanistan and Turkey. **30 January:** Adolf Hitler's Nazi regime comes to power in Germany.

1933–39   Discriminatory laws passed in Germany (so-called Nuremberg Laws).

1933–45   Some 6 million Jews are exterminated. Millions of other civilians (communists and other internal dissidents, Poles, Ukrainians, Soviet prisoners of war, Roma, disabled, homosexuals) are killed in Germany and occupied Europe.

1934 Some 170,000 die during Mao Zedong's Long March.

1935 **February–March:** Some 412,000 Germans and Poles removed from Central and Western Ukraine to Eastern Ukraine. **February–May:** 30,000 Ingrian Finns removed from Leningrad Oblast to Western Siberia, Kazakhstan and Tajikistan. **15 April:** Treaty on the protection of Artistic and Scientific Institutions and Historic Monuments called the Roerich Pact is adopted in Washington. **May:** 45,000 Germans and Poles deported from border regions of Ukraine to Kazakhstan.

1935–39 Between 3 and 10 million Chinese massacred by Japan, including the "rape of Nanking" (December 1937) at the beginning of the Second Sino-Japanese War.

1935–45 20,000 Indonesian civilians killed by Japanese occupiers.

1936–37 13 million perish in Stalin's purges.

1936–39 Close to a half million die in Spanish civil war.

1937 Some 30,000 Ethiopians executed by Italians after failed assassination attempt against Graziani. **September–October:** 172,000 Koreans deported from Far East to Northern Kazakhstan and Uzbekistan.

1938 League of Nations High Commissioner Office established superseding Nansen International Office. International Law Association approves Draft Convention for the Protection of Civilian Populations against New Engines of War produced by one of its committees.

1940 **June:** 276,000 Poles forcibly moved from Western Ukraine and Western Byelorussia to Northern Russia, Ural, Siberia, Kazakhstan and Uzbekistan.

1940–53 Antinationalist deportations of Balts in Estonia.

1941 **6 January:** U.S. President Franklin D. Roosevelt, in speech before the United States Congress, identifies "Four Freedoms" as essential for all people: freedom of speech, freedom of religion, freedom from want and freedom from fear. **10 April:** Independent State of Croatia comes into existence with support of Adolf Hitler and Benito Mussolini, leading to massacres of Serbs, Jews, and Gypsies throughout the war. **May–June:** Over 100,000 "counter-revolutionaries and nationalists" taken away from Ukraine, Byelorussia, Moldova, and Baltic states to Siberia, Kirov, and Kazakhstan. **14 August:** President Roosevelt and Prime Minister Winston Churchill adopt

Atlantic Charter, in which they state their hope, among other things, "that all men in all the lands may live out their lives in freedom from want and fear." **September (until March 1942):** More than 780,000 Germans deported from Caucasus, Crimea, Ukraine, Moscow and central Russia to Siberia and Kazakhstan. **September:** 91,000 Germans and Ingrian Finns removed from Leningrad Oblast to Kazakhstan, Siberia and Far East. **7 December:** Japanese attack Pearl Harbor, triggering U.S. entry into the war and forcible removal of some 120,000 Japanese Americans from the western United States into detention camps.

1942 Rene Cassin of France urges that an international court be created to punish those guilty of war crimes.

1943 August: 70,000 Karachais transferred to Kazakhstan and Kyrgyzstan for "banditism." **October:** United Nations War Crimes Commission established in London in preparation of Nuremberg trials. **December:** 93,000 Kalmyks deported to Kazakhstan and Siberia.

1943–47 Some 500,000 to 1.1 million repatriated Soviet nationals murdered.

1943–57 Some 230,000 Chechens, Ingushi, Karachai, and Balkars murdered.

1944 February: Some 522,000 Chechens, Ingushes and Balkars removed from North Caucasus to Kazakhstan and Kyrgyzstan. **May:** An estimated 182,000 Balkars moved from Crimea to Uzbekistan. **May–June:** Some 42,000 Greeks, Bulgarians, Armenians and Turks deported from Crimea. **August–September:** Some 30,000 Poles removed from Urals, Siberia and Kazakhstan to Ukraine, Kazakhstan and Kyrgyzstan. **November:** Some 92,000 Meskhetian Turks, Kurds, Hamshenis, and Karapapaks deported from southwestern Georgia to Uzbekistan, Kazakhstan and Kyrgyzstan.

1944–50 At least half a million perish as some 12 to 14 million Germans are removed from Czech Republic, Poland, Russia and other Central and Eastern European countries and resettled in Germany. 36,000 to 60,000 killed in Albanian resistance to Serbian rule in Kosovo.

1944–68 57,000 to 175,000 Meskhetians and Crimean Tatars murdered.

1945 8 May: French army puts down Muslim demonstrations in Setif, Algeria, unleashing a wave of killings by settler population. **26 June:** UN Charter signed in San Francisco. One of its purposes is to promote "respect for human rights and for fundamental freedoms for all without distinction as to race, sex, language or religion." **2 August:** Potsdam Agreement calls for "orderly population transfers." **8 August:** Charter establishing International Military Tribunal at Nuremberg signed. **20 November:** Trial of major Nazi war criminals opens in Nuremberg.

1945–53 Cleansing of Jews and intelligentsia in Soviet Union.

1946 January 19: Allied Powers of World War II announce the establishment of a second war crimes court, the Military Tribunal for the Far East, to prosecute Japanese war criminals. **5 May:** International Military Tribunal for the Far East starts prosecution of Japanese officials and soldiers for war crimes, crimes against peace and crimes against humanity. **21 June:** UN-Economic and Social Council (UN-ECOSOC) establishes Commission on Human Rights and Commission on Status of Women. **11 December:** UN-General Assembly (UN-GA) determines that the Principles of International Law recognized by the Charter of the Nuremberg Tribunal are an integral part of international principles.

1946–47 Communal violence prevails through the process of partitioning the Indian subcontinent involving 500,000 massacred and massive postwar transfers of population.

1946–49 Last phase of China's civil war kills 1.2 million. Greek civil war (50,000 fatalities).

1946–54 France-Vietnam War (600,000 dead).

1947 Mass murder of Ukrainian nationalists. Kuomintang suppresses uprising by Taiwanese (30,000 fatalities). **March:** Madagascar nationalist revolt quelled with great loss of life.

1948 May: 49,000 Kulaks deported from Lithuania to Eastern Siberia for "banditism." **2 May:** Ninth International Conference of American States in Bogotá, Colombia, adopts American Declaration of the Rights and Duties of Man, the world's first international human rights instrument of a general nature. **June:** 58,000 Greeks and Armenians removed from the Black Sea coast of Russia to southern Kazakhstan. **9 July:** ILO passes Convention on Freedom of Association and Protection of the Right to Organize. **12 November:** Tokyo tribunal adjourns. **9 December:** UN-GA adopts Convention on the Prevention and Punishment of the Crime of Genocide (entered into force in 1951). In the same resolution, the UN-GA invites its International Law Commission "to study the desirability and possibility of establishing an international judicial organ for the trial of persons charged with genocide." **10 December:** UN-GA adopts Universal Declaration of Human Rights, first international agreement proclaiming the fundamental and inalienable rights of all human beings.

1948–58 Colombian civil war (250,000 dead).

1949 May: Council of Europe statute adopted. **12 August:** Diplomatic conference adopts four Geneva Conventions on the treatment of members of armed forces in the field and at sea, the treatment of prisoners of war and the protection of civilians in wartime (entered into force in 1950). **2 December:** General Assembly adopts Convention for the Suppression of the Traffic in Persons and of the Exploitation of the Prostitution of Others.

1949–52   78,000 Kulaks deported from Moldavia, the Baltic states, Byelorussia and Ukraine to Siberia, Kazakhstan and Far East.

1949–54   International Law Commission of the UN drafts statutes for an international criminal court but opposition from powerful states on both sides of the Cold War stymies the effort and the UN General Assembly effectively abandons the effort pending agreement on a definition of the crime of aggression and an international Code of Crimes.

1950   **7 April:** ILO convention on freedom of association and rights to organize enters into force. **11 July:** International Court of Justice (ICJ) hands down first in a series of advisory opinions finding that the League of Nations mandate agreement over South West Africa is still binding on South Africa and that the UN has the authority to exercise the same supervisory functions as had the League. **7 October:** Chinese troops enter Tibet. **4 November:** Council of Europe endorses the Convention for the Protection of Human Rights and Fundamental Freedoms (European Convention on Human Rights [ECHR]). **1 December:** UN-GA creates Committee on Crime Prevention and Control and authorizes quinquennial crime congresses.

1951   **January:** UN High Commissioner for Refugees (UN-HCR) begins operation. **12 January:** Convention on the prevention of the crime of genocide adopted. **8 May:** ICJ issues advisory opinion rejecting the contention that parties to the Genocide Convention can stipulate reservations to any provisions they dislike. **18 July:** ILO convention on right to organize and collective bargaining enters into force. **29 June:** ILO adopts convention on equal remuneration for men and women. **28 July:** United Nations conference adopts Convention Relating to the Status of Refugees.

1952   **20 December:** UN-GA adopts Convention on the Political Rights of Women.

1952–59   British suppress Kenya's Mau Mau insurrection (20,000 dead).

1952–72   Half-million Southern nationalists murdered in Sudan.

1953   **23 May:** ILO convention on equal remuneration comes into force. **23 October:** UN-GA adopts protocol amending 1926 Slavery Convention.

1953–54   15,000 Catholic landlords and rich peasants killed in Vietnam.

1954   May: United Nations Educational, Scientific and Cultural Organization (UNESCO) adopts Convention for the Protection of Cultural Property in the Event of Armed Conflict. **17 May:** U.S. Supreme Court rules in *Brown vs. Board of Education* that racial segregation in public schools is unconstitutional. **28 September:** Conference of Plenipotentiaries adopts Convention Relating to the Status of Stateless Persons. **November:** Battle of Algiers grips the capital of Algeria in its struggle for independence until December 1960, pitting insurgents against the French army.

1954–62   700,000 die and 2 million are uprooted in the course of the Algerian war of independence.

1955   30 August: First United Nations Congress on the Prevention of Crime and the Treatment of Offenders endorses Standard Minimum Rules for the Treatment of Prisoners.

1956   1 August: UN-ECOSOC calls for periodic reports on human rights and studies of specific rights or groups of rights, foreshadowing the reporting requirements of many subsequent human rights treaties. **7 September:** Supplementary Convention on the Abolition of Slavery, the Slave Trade, and Institutions and Practices Similar to Slavery adopted by Conference of Plenipotentiaries.

1957   29 January: UN-GA adopts Convention on the Nationality of Married Women. **25 June:** ILO adopts Convention on the Abolition of Forced Labor.

1958   11 August: UN Convention on Nationality of Women enters into force.

1958–61   Some 38 million die during Mao's "Great Leap Forward."

1958–2003   Tamil-Sinhalese conflict in Sri Lanka. An estimated 80,000 to 100,000 die during its course.

1959   17 January: ILO adopts abolition of forced labor convention. **21 January:** European Court of Human Rights established. **30 July:** UN-ECOSOC authorizes Commission on Human Rights to exert certain responsibilities with regard to the treatment of communications. **20 November:** UN-GA adopts Declaration of the Rights of the Child.

1959–75   Mass murder of Kurdish nationalists in Iraq.

1959–94   Massacres during Hutu-Tutsi conflicts in Rwanda culminating in 1994 genocide.

1960   1 April: UN Security Council (UN-SC) demands an end to apartheid and racial discrimination in South Africa, which it deems to be a threat to international peace and security. **6 June:** Convention relating to the Status of Stateless Persons enters into force. **15 June:** ILO discrimination in employment convention enters into force. **30 June:** Belgian Congo achieves independence. Civil war breaks out almost immediately, lasting for five years. **14 December:** UN-GA adopts Declaration on the Granting of Independence to Colonial Countries and Peoples. UNESCO approves convention banning discrimination in education.

1960–96 Mass murder of indigenous peoples and leftists in Guatemala's civil war.

1961 Inter-American Commission on Human Rights (IACmHR) begins operations. **30 August:** Convention on the Reduction of Statelessness agreed to by Conference of Plenipotentiaries. **18 October:** Council of Europe adopts European Social Charter proclaiming rights of men and women to just, safe, fairly remunerated conditions of work (in force in 1965). **19 December:** UN-GA proclaims the inalienable right of self-determination of the people of South West Africa to independence and national sovereignty.

1961–62 Some 40,000 Bakongo massacred during nationalist uprising in Angola.

1961–98 An estimated 100,000 are killed in West Papua/Irian insurrection.

1962 **July:** Mass murder of Muslim Algerians who served as auxiliaries with the French army during the Algerian war of independence. **6 November:** UN-GA calls for a boycott of South Africa and sets up a special committee to monitor and report on developments. **7 November:** UN-GA adopts Convention on Consent to Marriage, Minimum Age for Marriage and Registration of Marriage. **December:** UNESCO adopts Declaration on Permanent Sovereignty over Natural Resources. **14 December:** Adoption by UN-GA of Resolution 1803 (XVII) on permanent sovereignty over natural resources. **21 December:** ICJ dismisses case brought by Ethiopia and Liberia against South Africa over its administration of South West Africa finding that it had no jurisdiction to adjudicate upon the merits the dispute.

1962–64 6,000 to 16,000 Tutsis ruling class murdered in Rwanda.

1962–75 Mozambique's war of independence.

1963 Mass murder of Meo tribesmen in Lao People's Democratic Republic. **7 August:** UN-SC condemns apartheid and calls for a voluntary arms embargo. **20 November:** UN-GA adopts Declaration on the Elimination of All Forms of Racial Discrimination.

1964 **2 July:** U.S. President Lyndon Johnson signs into law Civil Rights Act outlawing major forms of discrimination against blacks and women, which ended racial segregation in the United States. **9 December:** UN Convention on Consent to Marriage enters into force.

1964–73 Some 3 million die in Vietnam War.

1965 **11 November:** White minority of Rhodesia unilaterally proclaims its independence. **21 December:** International Convention on the Elimination of All Forms of Racial Discrimination approved by UN-GA (enters into force in 1969).

1965–67 500,000 to 1 million perish in anticommunist/anti-Chinese massacres in Indonesia.

1966 **16 May:** Cultural Revolution launched in China. **18 July:** ICJ rules against Ethiopian and Liberian claims against South Africa continued rule in South West Africa on the grounds that they have no legal rights or interest in the subject. **7 October:** UN-GA revokes South Africa mandate over South West Africa. **16 December:** UN-GA approves International Covenants on Civil and Political Rights and Economic, Social and Cultural Rights. Agreement also reached on a Protocol to the Covenant on Civil and Political Rights allowing individuals to charge violations of human rights (in force in 1976). Human Rights Committee established. **16 December:** UN-GA labels and condemns apartheid as a "crime against humanity."

1966–69 Over 10 million die during Mao Zedong's Cultural Revolution.

1966–70 1 million Igbos are believed to die in attempt by Biafra to secede from Nigeria.

1967 **6 June:** UN-ECOSOC authorizes Commission on Human Rights and Subcommission on Prevention of Discrimination and Protection of Minorities to examine information relating to gross violations of human rights and fundamental freedoms (Resolution 1235 [XLII]). **8 August:** Association of Southeast Asian Nations (ASEAN) founded. **7 November:** UN-GA approves Declaration on the Elimination of Discrimination against Women. **15 November:** Russell-Sartre Tribunal constituted.

1968 **4 April:** Martin Luther King assassinated. **13 May:** First World Conference on Human Rights takes stock of failures and successes of human rights promotion since the adoption of the Universal Declaration of Human Rights and adopts Proclamation of Tehran. **26 November:** UN-GA approves Convention on the Non-Applicability of Statutory Limitations to War Crimes against Humanity (in force in 1970) stipulating that there can be no statute of limitations to war crimes and crimes against humanity.

1968–80 Rhodesian civil war.

1969 New People's Army leads insurgency in the Philippines. United Nations Fund for Population Activities (UNFPA) established. **22 November:** American Convention on Human Rights (ACHR) approved (entered into force in 1978). **11 December:** UN-GA adopts Declaration on Social Progress and Development.

1970 **27 May:** UN-ECOSOC authorizes UN Commission on Human Rights (UN-CHR) and its Sub-Commission on the Prevention of Discrimination and Protection of Minorities to hold private meetings to review communications relating to violations of human rights. **24 October:** UN-GA adopts resolution describing apartheid as "a crime against the conscience and dignity of mankind."

1971 **26 March:** Outbreak of Bangladesh Liberation War followed by widespread killings and atrocities. 10 million Bengali refugees flee to India. **21 June:** ICJ issues advisory opinion ruling that the continued presence of South Africa in Namibia is illegal and it should withdraw immediately. **20 December:** UN-GA adopts Declaration of the Rights of Mentally Retarded Persons and Declaration of the Rights of the Elderly.

1971–86 50,000 to 100,000 die in tribal killings in Uganda.

1972 Muslim separatists battle government forces in Philippines. **6–16 June:** United Nations Conference on the Human Environment convened under United Nations auspices in Stockholm, Sweden.

1973 **11 September:** Military junta seizes power in Chile. **30 November:** UN-GA adopts International Convention on the Suppression and Punishment of the Crime of Apartheid (in force in 1976).

1974 **25 January:** Council of Europe adopts European Convention on the Non-Applicability of Statutory Limitation to Crimes against Humanity and War Crimes. **20 July:** Turkish invasion of Cyprus triggers displaced persons crisis. **30 September:** UN-GA does not accept the credentials of the South African representative. **25 October:** First of three reports of the IACmHR on the spot visit to Chile documenting serious violations of human rights by the Augusto Pinochet regime and calling for remedies. **14 December:** UN-GA adopts resolution defining aggression. UN-GA endorses Declaration on the Protection of Women and Children in Emergency and Armed Conflict.

1974–91 1 million killed in Ethiopian civil war.

1975 **24 June:** ILO adopts convention concerning migrations in abusive conditions and the promotion of equality of opportunity and treatment of migrant workers. **1 August:** Final Act of the Conference on Security and Cooperation in Europe establishes Organization for Security and Cooperation in Europe (OSCE) as framework for East-West communication on human rights and humanitarian issues. **16 October:** ICJ delivers advisory opinion finding that it had not found legal historical ties justifying the Moroccan and Mauritanian claims of sovereignty over Western Sahara and the question of historical claims should in no way be seen as detracting from the fundamental right of self-determination of the people of Western Sahara. **7 December:** Indonesian invasion of East Timor begins. **9 December:** UN-GA proclaims Declaration on the Protection of All Persons from Being Subjected to Torture and Other Cruel, Inhuman or Degrading Treatment or Punishment. UN-GA approves Declaration on the Rights of Disabled Persons. UN GA adopts Declaration on the Protection of All Persons from Being Subjected to Torture and Other Cruel Inhuman or Degrading Treatment. **13 December:** Convention on the Reduction of Statelessness enters into force.

1975–78 Some 1.5 million killed under Haile Mariam Menghitsu's rule in Ethiopia.

1975–79 Genocidal rule of Khmer Rouge in Cambodia kills 1.7 million.

1975–87 About 250,000 Vietnamese and Chinese "boat peoples" perish.

1975–2002 Angolan civil war kills approximately half a million people.

1976 23 March: Covenants on Civil and Political Rights and Economic, Social and Cultural Rights enter into force. **24 March:** Military seizes power in Argentina and masterminds the extrajudicial killing of 9,000 to 30,000 leftists until the end of its rule in 1983. **31 May–11 June:** UN convenes conference on human settlements. **19 June:** ILO convention on the elimination of child labor comes into force. **September:** Secret police officials trials begin in Portugal. **26 October:** UN-GA declares "invalid" South Africa's creation of Transkei.

1976–99 Indonesia annexes East Timor. Roughly 100,000 to 145,000 people killed during Indonesian occupation which the United Nations never recognized.

1976–2005 Indonesia-Aceh civil war brought to an end by the devastating 2004 tsunami.

1977 8 June: Additional Protocols of the Geneva Conventions are approved. **4 November:** UN-SC imposes mandatory arms embargo on South Africa with a view to forcing it to grant Namibia independence. **11 December:** Amnesty International awarded Nobel Peace Prize.

1978   Myanmar mass murder of Muslims in border region. **18 January:** In *Ireland v. United Kingdom*, European Court of Human Rights (ECtHR) rules that wall standing, hooding, subjection to noise and deprivation of sleep and food amount to a practice of inhumane and degrading treatment. **18 July:** ACHR enters into force. **27 November:** UNESCO General Conference adopts Declaration on Race and Racial Prejudice.

1979   Civil war in El Salvador begins. Idi Amin forced into exile from Uganda. **3 September:** Inter-American Court Human Rights (IACtHR) formally inaugurated in San Jose, Costa Rica. **20 September:** First onsite visit of the IACmHR in Argentina. **17 December:** UN-GA adopts Code of Conduct for Law Enforcement Officials. **17 December:** UN-GA adopts UN Hostage Convention. **18 December:** UN-GA endorses Convention on the Elimination of All Forms of Discrimination against Women (in force in 1981). **25 December:** Soviet Union invades Afghanistan and installs puppet regime.

1979–86   Mass murder of indigenous H'mong in Lao People's Democratic Republic.

1980   **29 February:** UN-CHR sets up Working Group on Enforced or Involuntary Disappearances, first UN human rights thematic mechanism established with a global mandate.

1980–92   75,000 killed in El Salvador's civil war. 69,000 perish in Peru's civil war.

1981   UN-HCR receives second Nobel Peace Prize. **26 June:** African Charter on Human and People's Rights (ACHPR) approved by heads of states of Organization of African Unity (OAU) (entered into force in 1986). **22 October:** ECtHR invalidates 19th-century legislation criminalizing male homosexual acts in England (*Dudgeon v. United Kingdom*). **25 November:** After 20 years of negotiations, UN-GA votes on Declaration on the Elimination of All Forms of Intolerance and of Discrimination Based on Religion or Belief.

1981–?   10,000 to 20,000 Kurds, Baha'is and Mujahideen murdered in Iran.

1982   **16–18 September:** Sabra and Shatila massacre of refugees by Christian Phalangists in Lebanese area under Israeli control. **3 December:** UN-GA adopts declaration endorsing women's participation in international peace and cooperation. **18 December:** UN-GA adopts resolution on principles of medical ethics on the role of health personnel in protection of prisoners and detainees against torture.

1982–90   Dictatorial rule of Hissene Habre kills 40,000 in Chad.

1983   15 December: UN-GA condemns nuclear war as a violation of right to life.

1983–2002   2 million perish in Sudanese civil war.

1984   Anti-Sikh violence in India kills 5,000 to 10,000 Sikhs. **June:** UN-GA and UN-ECOSOC endorse Nairobi Forward-Looking Strategies for the Advancement of Women. **17 August:** UN-SC rejects South Africa's new constitution. **23 October:** UN-SC endorses UN-GA determination that apartheid is a crime against humanity and declares South Africa's new constitution "null and void." **12 November:** Adoption by UN-GA of the Declaration on the Rights of Peoples to Peace. **10 December:** UN-GA approves Convention against Torture (in force in 1987).

1985   28 May: UN-ECOSOC establishes United Nations Committee on Economic, Social and Cultural Rights (UN-CtteeESCR), responsible for monitoring the implementation of the International Covenant on Economic, Social and Cultural Rights (ICESCR). **26 July:** UN-SC recommends voluntary economic sanctions against South Africa. **29 November:** UN-GA adopts United Nations Standards Minimum Rules for the Administration of Juvenile Justice and Declaration of Basic Principles of Justice for Victims of Crime and Abuse of Power. United Nations Congress on the Prevention of Crime and the Treatment of Offenders adopts Basic Principles on the Independence of the Judiciary. **9 December:** OAS adopts Inter-American Convention to Prevent and Punish Torture (IACAT). **10 December:** UN-GA approves International Convention against Apartheid in Sports. **13 December:** UN-GA adopts Declaration on the Human Rights of Individuals Who Are Not Nationals of the Country in Which They Live.

1986   16–20 June: Third Conference on Sanctions against Racist South Africa in Paris. **4 December:** UN-GA adopts Declaration on the Right to Development.

1987   26 November: Council of Europe adopts European Convention for the Prevention of Torture and Inhuman or Degrading Treatment or Punishment.

1987–93   First Intifada, Palestinian uprising against Israeli rule.

1988   22 February: First direct confrontations between Azeris and Armenians in Soviet province of Nagorno-Karabakh. **8 April:** International Convention against Apartheid enters into force. **29 July:** IACtHR finds Honduras government responsible for two cases of forced disappearances. **22 September:** Vienna Convention on Ozone layer enters into force. **11 November:** OAS adopts protocol to ACHR relating to economic, social and cultural rights. **9 December:** UN-GA adopts Body of Principles for the Protection of All Persons under Any Form of Detention or Imprisonment.

1988–2001   Civil war kills 400,000 in Afghanistan.

1989   15 February: Soviet government announces that its troops have withdrawn from Afghanistan. **16 February:** UN-SC sets up United Nations Transition Assistance Group (UNTAG) to transition Namibia toward independence. **15 April:** Demonstrators gather in Tiananmen Square in China protesting against high inflation, low wages and poor housing, and demand more democracy. **24 May:** UN-ECOSOC adopts Principles on the Effective Prevention and Investigation of Extralegal, Arbitrary and Summary Executions. **June:** Trinidad and Tobago resurrects proposal for an International Criminal Court and UN-GA asks the International Law Commission to prepare a draft statute. **2 June:** Chinese Communist Party approves plan to put down Tiananmen Square demonstrators. **27 June:** ILO adopts new Convention Concerning Indigenous and Tribal Peoples in Independent Countries. **7 July:** Landmark judgment of the ECtHR establishing that extradition of a young German national to the United States to face charges of capital murder violated the European Convention guaranteeing the right against inhuman and degrading treatment (*Soering v. United Kingdom*). **20 November:** UN-GA adopts UN Convention on the Rights of the Child (UN-CRC) (into force in 1990); UN Committee on the Right of the Child (UN-CtteeRC) established. **4 December:** UN-GA adopts International Convention against the Recruitment, Use, Financing and Training of Mercenaries. **15 December:** Second Optional Protocol to the International Covenant on Civil and Political Rights (ICCPR) aiming at the abolition of the death penalty adopted by the UN-GA. ICJ delivers advisory opinion confirming privileges and immunities of UN special rapporteurs.

1989–96   First Liberian civil war.

1990   8 June: Second Protocol to the American Convention on Human Rights to Abolish the Death Penalty prohibiting capital punishment adopted. **13 April:** USSR expresses "profound regret" and admits Soviet secret police responsibility in Katyn massacre. **5 August:** Organization of Islamic Conference issues Cairo Declaration on Human Rights in Islam. **25 September:** UN-SC condemns treatment by Iraqi forces of Kuwait nationals. **30 September:** UN-sponsored World Summit for Children adopts World Declaration on the Survival, Protection and Development of Children. **21 November:** Summit meeting of European governments joined by Canada, United States and USSR approved Charter of Paris for a New Europe. **14 December:** UN-sponsored meeting endorses Basic Principles for the Treatment of Prisoners.

UN-GA adopts resolution recognizing need to ensure a healthy environment for the well-being of individuals. **18 December:** UN-GA adopts International Convention on the Protection of the Rights of All Migrant Workers and Their Families.

1991   Ethnic cleansing of Kurds in Iraq brought to an end by the establishment of no-fly zones. **5 April:** In resolution 688 on Iraq, UN-SC declares that repression against civilian population within a state had consequences that could "threaten international peace and security in the region." **29 April:** UN-SC establishes United Nations Mission for the Referendum in Western Sahara (MINURSO). **20 May:** UN-SC establishes United Nations Observer Mission in El Salvador (ONUSAL). **5–21 June:** South African Parliament repeals Apartheid legislation. **25 June:** Croatia proclaims independence from Yugoslavia. **8 December:** Establishment of the Commonwealth of Independent States (CIS). **10 December:** In a referendum boycotted by local Azerbaijanis, Armenians in Nagorno-Karabakh approve the creation of an independent state.

1991–95   About 200,000 Muslims and Croats killed in Bosnia during Bosnian war.

1991–97   Some 800,000 killed in the Democratic Republic of the Congo's civil war.

1991–2000   An estimated 200,000 are killed in Sierra Leone war.

1992   **January–March:** Ethnic conflict breaks out in Nagorno-Karabakh following dissolution of Soviet Union. **23 January:** UN-SC imposes general and complete arms embargo on Somalia. **7 February:** Maastricht Treaty signed. **21 February:** UN-SC establishes United Nations Protection Force (UNPROFOR). **28 February:** UN-SC sets up United Nations Transitional Authority in Cambodia (UNTAC). **24 April:** UN-SC establishes United Nations Operation in Somalia (UNOSOM) to protect delivery of humanitarian assistance. **5 May:** Basel Convention enters into force. **30 May:** UN-SC imposes sanctions on Federal Republic of Yugoslavia and demands that the parties to the Bosnian conflict allow the unimpeded delivery of humanitarian supplies. **June:** Conference for Cooperation and Security in Europe creates 11-country Minsk Group to find solution to Nagorno-Karabakh situation. **3–14 June:** Earth Summit held in Rio de Janeiro. **25 June:** European Charter for Regional or Minority Languages signed. **17 August:** UN-SC authorizes stationing of United Nations Observer Mission in South Africa. **14 September:** UN-SC enlarges UNPROFOR's mandate. **16 November:** UN-SC Council condemns "ethnic cleansing" in Bosnia and Herzegovina. **3 December:** UN-SC authorizes use of force to create a "secure environment" in order to provide humanitarian assistance to Somalia's civilian population. **8 December:** Declaration on the Rights of Persons Belonging to National or Ethnic, Religious and Linguistic Minorities adopted by the UN-GA. **10 December:** Rigoberta Menchú Tum awarded Nobel Peace Prize. **16 December:** UN-SC sets up United Nations Operation in Mozambique (UNOMOZ). **18 December:** UN-GA adopts Declarations on the Protection of All Persons from Enforced Disappearances and Rights of National, Ethnic, Religious, Linguistic Minorities.

1992–96 Civil war in Tajikistan kills 50,000. Breakup of Yugoslavia results in 260,000 deaths.

1992–99 Algerian civil war kills 150,000.

1993 **25 February:** ECtHR rules that the concept of a fair trial enshrined in the European Convention grants to persons facing criminal charges the right to remain silent and the right against self-incrimination (*Funke v. France*). **29 March:** Asian ministers adopt Bangkok Declaration. **20 April:** UN-GA authorizes participation of the United Nations jointly with the Organization of American States in an international Civilian Mission to Haiti (MICIVIH). **25 May:** UN-SC establishes the International Criminal Tribunal for the Prosecution of Persons Responsible for Serious Violations of International Humanitarian Law Committed in the Territory of the Former Yugoslavia (ICTY) since 1991, the first international war crimes tribunal since the Nuremberg Trials. **14 June:** At the opening of UN-sponsored World Conference on Human Rights in Vienna, the United Nations Secretary-General (UN-SG) describes human rights as "the quintessential values through which we affirm together that we are a single human community." **22 June:** UN-SC establishes United Nations Observer Mission Uganda-Rwanda. **25 June:** UN Conference on Human Rights adopts Vienna Declaration and Programme of Action reaffirming the universality of human rights. **24 August:** UN-SC establishes United Nations Observer Mission in Georgia (UNOMIG). **September:** UNTAC terminated upon completion of its mandate. **15 September:** UN-SC imposes embargo on sale or supply of oil to Angola. **22 September:** UN-SC sets up United Nations Observer Mission in Liberia (UNOMIL) with mandate to monitor cease-fire agreement and to report on human rights violations. **23 September:** United Nations Mission in Haiti (UNMIH) established. **5 October:** UN-SC sets up United Nations Assistance Mission for Rwanda (UNAMIR). **9 October:** European Commission against Racism and Intolerance established. **20 December:** UN-GA establishes post of United Nations High Commissioner for Human Rights (UN-HCHR). UN-GA adopts Declaration on the Elimination of Violence against Women. UN-GA proclaims Third Decade to Combat Racism and Racial Discrimination. International

Decade of the World's Indigenous Peoples launched by UN-GA. **29 December:** Biodiversity Convention enters into force.

1993–2005   Civil war in Burundi kills an estimated 300,000 people.

1994–96   First Chechen war.

1994   11 January: Military commander of UNAMIR informs UN headquarters of reports that Hutu militias are plotting to kill large numbers of Tutsis. **23 February:** UN-SC establishes civil police component of United Nations Operation in Mozambique. **18 March:** OAS adopts Inter-American Convention on International Traffic in Minors. **5 April:** José Ayala Lasso of Ecuador assumes the newly created post of United Nations High Commissioner for Human Rights. **6 April:** Airplane carrying Rwandan president shot down, triggering Rwandan genocide. **21 April:** UN-SC votes to reduce UNAMIR's strength and imposes arms embargo on Rwanda. **26–28 April:** First nonracial democratic elections held in South Africa. **29 April:** UN-SG urges UN-SC to consider use of force to restore law and order in Rwanda and put an end to massacres. **16 May:** International group of experts on human rights and environmental protection convened at the United Nations in Geneva issues first-ever declaration of principles on human rights and the environment. **17 May:** UN-SC expands UNAMIR to 5,500 troops. **24–25 May:** At Canada's request, UN-CHR meets in emergency session to discuss genocide in Rwanda and dispatches special rapporteur to visit and report on the scope of the genocide. **25 May:** UN-SC lifts sanctions against South Africa. **9–20 June:** Special rapporteur of UN-CHR conducts field mission in Rwanda. **22 June:** UN-SC authorizes Operation Turquoise. **Mid-July:** Over a two-week period, 1.5 million Rwandan refugees cross into Zaire. **26 August:** UN-GA adopts draft United Nations Declaration on the Rights of Indigenous Peoples. **5–13 September:** UN-sponsored International Conference on Population and Development held in Cairo. **15 September:** Declaration of the Arab Charter on Human Rights. **19 September:** UN-GA establishes United Nations Mission for the Verification of Human Rights and of Compliance with the Commitments of the Comprehensive Agreement on Human Rights in Guatemala (MINUGUA). **23 September:** UN-SC reiterates that "ethnic cleansing" constitutes a clear violation of international humanitarian law. **1 October:** UN Commission of Experts set up by UN-SC concludes that both sides have perpetrated serious breaches of international humanitarian law and recommends expansion of jurisdiction of ICTY to cover international crimes committed in Rwanda. **7 November:** ICTY issues its first indictment, against commander of Sušica camp in eastern Bosnia and Herzegovina, for crimes committed against non-Serbs in 1992. **8 November:** UN-SC establishes International Criminal Tribunal for the Prosecution of Persons Responsible for

Genocide and Other Serious Crimes against Humanitarian Law Committed in Rwanda (ICTR) during 1994. **9 December:** International Law Commission (ILC) presents a final draft Statute on the International Criminal Court (ICC) to the UN-GA. An ad hoc committee is appointed to work on establishing the court. Commission of experts issues final report, concluding that there is overwhelming evidence that Hutu elements committed genocide against Tutsis in Rwanda. **23 December:** UN-GA proclaims United Nations Decade for Human Rights Education (1995–2004).

1995   22 February: UN-SC adopts resolution accepting proposal of UN-SG to select Arusha as the seat of ICTR. **3 March:** UN-CHR establishes a working group to elaborate a draft declaration on the rights of indigenous peoples. **26 May:** CIS Convention on Human Rights and Fundamental Freedoms signed. **7 July:** Fall of Srebrenica. **4–15 September:** World Conference on Women declares that women's rights are human rights. **11 December:** UN-GA establishes Preparatory Committee for the establishment of a permanent International Criminal Court. **12 December:** ICTR issues its first indictment.

1996   Traditional community courts (*gacaca*) begin trying people accused of involvement in 1994 Rwanda genocide. **13 February:** Nepali civil war breaks out. **8 July:** Advisory ruling of the ICJ determines that while there is no comprehensive and universal prohibition of the threat or use of nuclear weapons in international law, the threat or use of nuclear weapons would generally be contrary to the rules of international law applicable in armed conflict, and in particular the principles and rules of humanitarian law. **6 September:** Graça Machel presents her report on the impact of armed conflicts on children to UN-GA. **18 December:** Landmark case of the ECtHR finding that Turkey had committed a continuing violation of the rights of a Greek Cypriot by preventing her from going to her property located in northern Cyprus. **26 December:** UN Convention on Desertification (UN-CCD) enters into force.

1996–97   50,000 to 100,000 Hutu refugees from Rwanda and Burundi in Congo killed by Tutsi army from Rwanda.

1997   20 February: UN-GA recommends appointment of a special representative of the UN-SG on children and armed conflict. **12 September:** Mary Robinson, former president of Ireland, becomes second UN High Commissioner for Human Rights. **18 September:** Diplomatic conference approves Convention on the Prohibition of the Use, Stockpiling, Production and Transfer of Anti-Personnel Mines and On Their Destruction. **8 October:** UN-SC imposes embargo on the sale or supply of oil to Sierra Leone. **11 November:** UNESCO endorses Universal Declaration on Human Genome and Human Rights.

1998 1 February: Framework Convention for the Protection of National Minorities in Europe enters into force. **8 March:** UN-GA proclaims Declaration on the Right and Responsibility of Individuals, Groups and Organs of Society to Promote and Protect Universally Recognized Human Rights and Fundamental Freedoms. **26 March:** U.S. Senator Jesse Helms, chairman of the Foreign Relations Committee, declares any International Criminal Court "dead on arrival" in the U.S. Senate unless the United States is given control over the court. **13 April:** UN-SG issues report on causes of conflict in Africa that addresses for the first time the protection of civilians in armed conflicts. **12 June:** UN-SC imposes embargo on diamonds from Angola. **29 June:** Issue of children and armed conflict formally placed on agenda of the UN-SC for the first time. **17 July:** Diplomatic conference in Rome adopts statute establishing the International Criminal Court (ICC) with its seat in The Hague to try individuals responsible for genocide, crimes against humanity and other serious breaches of human rights. **4 September:** ICTR hands down first conviction finding former Rwandan Prime Minister Jean Kambanda guilty of genocide and crimes against humanity and condemning him to life imprisonment. **2 October:** ICTR sentences former teacher and mayor to life imprisonment for genocide, direct and public incitement to commit genocide and crimes against humanity (extermination, murder, torture and rape). **16 October:** British authorities arrest former Chilean dictator Pinochet on an extradition request from a Spanish judge who brought charges of genocide, torture, and other crimes during his rule in the 1970s and 1980s. **28 October:** The Truth and Reconciliation Commission is set up in South Africa to address violations of human rights under Apartheid issues its report condemning all parties for committing atrocities.

1998–99 Large numbers of Albanian Muslims "cleansed" by Serbians during Kosovo war.

1999 Second Chechen war. **12 January:** Council of Europe adopts European Convention on Human Rights and Medicine. **31 January:** UN-SG introduces Global Compact at the World Economic Forum in Davos. **12 February:** UN-SC adopts presidential statement addressing the protection of civilians in armed conflicts. **16 March:** Group of UN-SG appointed experts recommends that an ad hoc tribunal be established by the United Nations in an Asian city to prosecute Khmer Rouges. **23 March:** North Atlantic Treaty Organization (NATO) authorizes the commencement of air strikes on Kosovo and Belgrade. **24 March:** British House of Lords rules that Pinochet can be prosecuted for crimes committed after 1988 and should be extradited. **1 April:** Second Protocol to the 1954 Hague Convention for the Protection of Cultural Property in the Event of Armed Conflict adopted by UNESCO.

29 April: Building upon the earlier 1989 case, ICJ advisory opinion confirms that a Malaysian jurist, who was appointed special rapporteur on the independence of judges and lawyers by the UN-CHR in 1994, is "entitled to immunity from legal process." **1 May:** Amsterdam Treaty enters into force. **7 May:** Council of Europe establishes Commissioner for Human Rights post. **13 May:** Coalition for the International Criminal Court launches a campaign from The Hague calling for the worldwide ratification of the ICC statute. **21 May:** ICTR finds a businessman and a former prefect guilty on charges of genocide (*Prosecutor v. Kayishema and Ruzindana*). **24 May:** ICTY indicts five Serbian leaders including President Slobodan Milosevic of four criminal counts arising out of events in Kosovo and Metojija. **10 June:** UN-SC places Kosovo under authority of United Nations Interim Administration in Kosovo (UNMIK). **17 June:** ILO adopts convention prohibiting worst forms of child labor, including child soldiering. **6 August:** UN-SG promulgates fundamental principles and rules of international humanitarian law applicable to UN forces conducting military operations under UN command and control in situations of armed conflict. Swedish Prime Minister Goran Persson announces establishment of Independent International Commission on Kosovo. **30 August:** UN-SC adopts first resolution on children and armed conflict. In a UN-sponsored referendum, an overwhelming majority of East Timorese vote for independence from Indonesia. **6 September:** Israel Supreme Court rules that enhanced interrogation methods used by General Security Service are illegal. **16 September:** UN-HCHR invited for the first time to address UN-SC (on the protection of civilians in armed conflicts). **15 October:** UN-SC adopts Resolution 1267 imposing an air embargo and an assets freeze on the Taliban, which was then the de facto Afghan government, for refusing to extradite Osama bin Laden in connection with the 1998 bombings of U.S. embassies in Kenya and Tanzania. Médecins Sans Frontières awarded Nobel Peace Prize. **25 October:** UN-SC establishes the United Nations Transitional Administration in East Timor (UNTAET) to administer territory until achievement of self-government and to achieve accountability for murders and destruction associated with termination of Indonesian rule. **16 November:** Additional Protocol to the American Convention on Human Rights in the Area of Economic, Social, and Cultural Rights enters into force 11 years after its signature. **19 November:** ILO Convention on Worst Forms of Child Labor comes into force. **1 December:** European Convention on Human Rights and Biomedicine enters into force.

1999–2003 Second Liberian civil war.

2000 **27 January:** ICTR convicts Alfred Musema of genocide and of crimes against humanity (extermination and rape). **31 January:** A UN commission recommends that the Security Council establish a tribunal to prosecute war crimes in East Timor, but member nations ignore the recommendation and instead ask the Indonesian government to mete out justice. **14 March:** UN-sponsored report (Fowler report) detailing links between illicit diamond trade and Third World conflicts published. **11 April:** ICJ rules that Belgium arrest warrant of Congo foreign minister fails to respect his immunity from criminal jurisdiction. **16 May:** Optional Protocol to the Convention on the Rights of the Child opens for signature. **1 June:** ICTY convicts Belgian citizen working as journalist for Radio Television Libre des Mille Collines of direct and public incitement to commit genocide in Rwanda. **3 June:** ICTY prosecutor concludes that there is no sufficient basis to proceed with investigation of allegations of serious violations of international humanitarian law by senior NATO figures during air bombing of Yugoslavia. **15 June:** ILO adopts Maternity Protection Convention. **21 June:** Working paper prepared by expert for UN-HRC Sub-Commission on the Promotion and Protection of Human Rights argues that the right to impose sanctions is not unlimited as sanctions may directly or indirectly cause deaths. **27 June:** Organization for Economic Cooperation and Development (OECD) recommends set of voluntary guidelines for responsible business conduct. **5 July:** UN-SC imposes embargo on all rough diamonds from Sierra Leone. **28 July:** UN-ECOSOC establishes Permanent Forum on Indigenous Issues. **14 August:** UN-SC requests UN-SG to negotiate an agreement with Sierra Leone to try those bearing the greatest responsibility for crimes against humanity, war crimes and other serious violations of international humanitarian law committed in the civil war. **8 September:** World leaders assembled at United Nations adopt Millennium Declaration. **23 October:** Independent international commission on Kosovo issues its report. **31 October:** UN-SC adopts Resolution 1325 calling for gender mainstreaming in UN peace operations. **1 December:** UN-GA approves Kimberley scheme. **15 November:** UN-GA adopts UN Convention against Transnational Organized Crime (UN-TOC) and supplementary protocols. **7 December:** European Union (EU) leaders sign Charter of Fundamental Rights of the European Union.

2000–05 Second Palestinian Intifada.

2001 **3 January:** Cambodian National Assembly passes legislation establishing a tribunal in conjunction with the United Nations to prosecute "senior leaders" of the Khmer Rouge for atrocities from 1975 to 1979. **15 January:** ECtHR upholds government right to require a teacher to remove her headscarf in the performance of her teaching duties (*Dahlia v. Switzerland*). **1 February:** Mass rape ruled as war crime in ICTY landmark case against three Bosnian Serbs. **27 June:** UN-GA special session endorses Declaration of Commitment on HIV/AIDS. **2 August:** UN-SC holds first open debate on small arms. ICTY finds former Bosnian Serb General-Major Radislav Krstic guilty of genocide in the 1995 Srebrenica massacre and sentences him to 46 years in prison. **31 August:** UN-sponsored World Conference opens in South Africa, amid political controversies about southern claims of reparations for slavery and colonialism and criticisms of Israel occupation policies in Palestinian occupied territories. Inter-American Court of Human Rights (IACtHR) rules that Nicaragua violated an indigenous people's right to own their ancestral land and natural resources when it granted concessions to a Korean firm. **6 September:** OAS adopts charter declaring that the peoples of the Americas had a right to democracy and their governments had an obligation to promote and defend it. **28 September:** UN-SC declares terrorism a threat against all members of the United Nations and imposes obligation on all states to combat international terrorism. **20 October:** International Convention against the Recruitment, Use, Financing and Training of Mercenaries enters into force. **2 November:** UNESCO's General Conference adopts Universal Declaration on Cultural Diversity. **3 November:** UNESCO General Conference adopts Convention on the Protection of the Underwater Cultural Heritage. **10 December:** UN-SG Kofi Annan and the United Nations jointly awarded Nobel Peace Prize "for their work for a better organized and more peaceful world." **18 December:** Annan receives Responsibility to Protect report.

2002   **5 January:** South Asian Association for Regional Cooperation adopts convention on preventing and combating trafficking in women and children. **12 January:** United Nations concludes agreement with Sierra Leone establishing Special Court for Sierra Leone. **12 February:** Optional Protocol to the Convention on the Rights of Children enters into force. **21 February:** Amendment to European Convention of Human Rights provides for full abolition of the death penalty. **1 March:** Special rapporteurs of the IAComHR and the ACHPR issue joint declaration calling for an end to impunity in cases of violence against women. **28 March:** UN-SC sets up United Nations Assistance Mission in Afghanistan (UNAMA). **6 May:** U.S. government under President George W. Bush formally announces its intention not to ratify the ICC Rome Statute. **20 May:** East Timor internationally recognized as an independent state under the name of Timor-Leste. United Nations Mission of Support to East Timor (UNMISET) established. **3 June:** OAS adopts Inter-American Convention against Terrorism. **1 July:** ICC Rome Statute enters into force. **11 July:** ECtHR rules that to not legally recognize a gender reassignment of a British transsexual is a violation of the ECHR. **15 July:** After intense U.S. pressure, UN-SC adopts resolution in effect granting peacekeepers immunity from investigations by the ICC for a renewable one-year period. **3–10 September:** Historic first meeting of the ICC Assembly of

States Parties. **12 September:** Sergio Vieira de Mello appointed UN-HCHR. **19 September:** Cote d'Ivoire sinks into civil war, splitting the country. **5 November:** Kimberley Process Certification Scheme adopted after almost two years of negotiations. **18 December:** UN-GA adopts Optional Protocol to Convention against Torture providing for onsite visits.

2003 Genocide in "slow motion" in Darfur starts. **28 January:** UN-SC endorses Kimberley process. **30 January:** UN-SC adopts resolution on children and armed conflict expressing concern about reports of sexual exploitation of children. **12 February:** Belgium Court of Appeals rules that the presence of Ariel Sharon, accused of grave violations of international law for his alleged involvement in the Shabra and Shatila massacres, is not necessary for the prosecution to proceed. **25 February:** Spain's Supreme Court rules that Spanish court could exercise jurisdiction over the investigation of acts of torture committed in Guatemala in 1980 by former Guatemalan officials against Spanish nationals. **27 February:** ICTR sentences former postwar president of Republika Srpska to prison term for crimes against humanity. (*Prosecutor v. Plavsi*). **11 March:** First 18 judges of the ICC are sworn in. **17 March:** Agreement reached between the United Nations and Cambodian government for an international criminal tribunal to try former Khmer Rouge leaders. **20 March:** Iraq invaded. Civil war breaks out. **20 May:** Supreme Court of Spain rules that Spanish courts could not at the present time exercise universal jurisdiction over claims of genocide, terrorism, torture and illegal detention alleged to have been committed by Peruvian ex-presidents Alan García and Alberto Fujimori. **6 June:** United Nations and Cambodia reach agreement on prosecuting under Cambodian law crimes committed during Khmer Rouge rule. **16 June:** First ICC prosecutor, Luis Moreno-Ocampo, sworn in. **27 June:** European Convention on Non-Applicability of Statutory Limitations enters into force. **1 July:** International Migrant Workers Convention enters into force. **11 July:** African Union (AU) adopts Maputo Protocol prohibiting violence against women. **6 August:** United Nations Human Rights Committee (UN-HRCttee) finds that the government of Australia discriminated against a homosexual man by denying him pension benefits following the death of his male partner (*Young v. Australia*). **13 August:** UN Sub-Commission on the Promotion and Protection of Human Rights adopts draft of Norms on the Responsibilities of Transnational Corporations and Other Business Enterprises with Regard to Human Rights. UN-HRCttee finds that Canada violated right to life guaranteed by ICCPR by deporting a person to the United States who would face the death penalty. **19 August:** Bertrand Ramcharan appointed as acting high commissioner for human rights after the death of Sergio Vieira de Mello during the attack on the UN headquarters in Baghdad. **18 September:** UN-HRCttee finds that Australia violated the rights of two

Kurdish Iraqi nationals for having detained them in immigration for almost two years without justification and review of their case under the Optional Protocol to the ICCPR. **24 September:** UN-SC adopts presidential statement on the role of the United Nations in promoting justice and the rule of law. **30 September:** UN-SC holds open debate on the theme of "Justice and the Rule of Law: The United Nations Role." **10 October:** Journalistic reports cite Red Cross officials in Washington, D.C., as saying that it was unacceptable that detainees should be held indefinitely at Guantanamo Bay without legal safeguards. **17 October:** UNESCO General Conference adopts Convention for the Safeguarding of the Intangible Cultural Heritage. **31 October:** UN-GA adopts Convention against Corruption. **5 December:** ICTY convicts Serb general of violations of the laws of war for conducting a campaign of sniping and shelling attacks on civilian population of Sarajevo (*Prosecutor v. Galic*). **9 December:** UN Convention against Corruption (UN-TOC) opens for signature. **10 December:** Coalition Provisional Authority concludes statute establishing the Iraqi Special Tribunal for Crimes against Humanity. **13 December:** Saddam Hussein captured, prompting worldwide debate about how best to try him and other top Baath Party leaders. **25 December:** UN-TOC's optional protocol on trafficking in persons enters into force.

2004 8 January: ECHR finds that Turkey violated the European Convention for failing to carry out an effective investigation into allegations of police torture (*Sadik Önder v. Turkey*). **22 January:** ICTR convicts Rwanda's former minister of higher education of genocide. **26 January:** UN-SC holds open debate on postconflict national reconciliation, with speakers stressing the need to avoid impunity as an element of national reconciliation. **27 February:** UN-SC establishes UN Operation in Cote d'Ivoire (UNOCI). **8 March:** Spain's Supreme Court upholds jurisdiction over claims of torture of Spanish nationals committed by Chilean defense minister. **31 March:** ICJ rules that United States breached Vienna Convention on Consular Relations for failing to inform Mexican nationals of their rights under the convention upon their detention. **7 April:** Dutch court finds army officer of former dictator Mobutu Sese Seko of the Democratic Republic of the Congo guilty of torture under national law implementing UN Convention Against Torture (UN-CAT). **19 May:** ECtHR determines that France had violated the prohibition of inhuman or degrading treatment when French police detained applicant in a psychiatric infirmary for an unnecessary period of time. **21 May:** UN-SC authorizes deployment of United Nations Operation in Burundi (ONUB). **22 May:** Arab Charter on Human Rights adopted by League of Arab States. **31 May:** Special Court for Sierra Leone rules that Charles Taylor, former Liberian president, is subject to criminal proceedings before the court. The Appeals Chamber of the Special Court for Sierra Leone holds that the recruitment of child soldiers is a crime and a violation of international law. **1 June:** United Nations Stabilization Mission in Haiti (MINUSTAH) established. **8 June:** OAS adopts Declaration on Democracy and Development, emphasizing the negative impact of corruption. **17 June:** ICTR convicts former mayor of genocide and extermination and rape as crimes against humanity (*Prosecutor v. Sylvestre Gacumbitsi*). **28 June:** U.S. Supreme Court rules that the government can detain individuals involved in the war on terror indefinitely but U.S. nationals must have an opportunity to challenge their detention (*Hamdi v. Rumsfeld*). **1 July:** Louise Arbour appointed high commissioner for human rights. **8 July:** ECtHR rules that France did not violate right to life by failing to punish the unintentional killing of a fetus (*Vo v. France*). **9 July:** ICJ rules that Israel's security barrier in the West Bank is illegal and should be pulled down immediately. **13 July:** UN-CHR distances itself from controversial binding "norms" on business and human rights first proposed by one of its advisory groups. **21 August:** Argentina's Senate annuls amnesty laws enacted in 1986 and 1987. **24 August:** Supreme Court of Argentina confirms nonapplicability of statutory limitations to crimes against humanity. **26 August:** Supreme Court of Chile lifts immunity of Pinochet. **9 October:** UN-SG issues policy bulletin on special measures for protection from sexual exploitation and abuse. **6 October:** UN-SC adopts presidential statement on justice and the rule and transitional justice in conflict and postconflict societies. **15 November:** UN-SC imposes sanctions on Cote d'Ivoire. **17 November:** Supreme Court of Chile confirms the prison sentences of a number of defendants convicted for their participation in forced disappearances. **1 December:** ICTR convicts bourgmestre of Mukingo commune in Rwanda of genocide. **10 December:** UN-GA proclaims World Programme for Human Rights Education. **15 December:** ICJ rules that it has no jurisdiction to determine whether Serbia and Montenegro had a valid legal claim against NATO countries that participated in the intervention in Kosovo in 1999 because Serbia and Montenegro were not recognized as UN member states until 2000.

2005   8 February: Independent expert submits Set of Principles for the Protection and Promotion of Human Rights Through Action to Combat Impunity to UN-CHR. **24 February:** ECtHR rules that in six cases concerning incidents which occurred in Chechnya from 1999 to 2000 Russia had violated the applicants' rights to life and to an effective remedy. **8 March:** UN-GA adopts declaration banning human cloning by recorded vote of 84-34-37. **21 March:** Accused of forced labor, rape and murder by Burmese villagers, UNOCAL Corporation reaches settlement following litigation brought under the Alien Tort Statute. **24 March:** Special representative of the UN-SG issues report documenting widespread patterns of sexual abuse in peacekeeping operations. UN-SC authorizes the deployment of 10,000 troops "to protect civilians under imminent threat of physical violence" in Sudan and calls for an immediate increase in human rights monitors in Darfur. **31 March:** UN-SC refers Darfur situation to the ICC. **18 April:** UN-SC imposes assets freeze and travel restrictions on persons acting in violation of the UN arms embargo. **19 April:** UN-CHR approves Basic Principles on the right to a remedy and reparations for victims of gross violations of international human rights law. **20 April:** UN-CHR requests UN-SG to appoint special representative on human rights and business enterprises. **12 May:** In a case involving the former leader of Kurdistan Workers Party, ECtHR finds Turkey in violation of the plaintiff's right to a fair trial (*Öcalan v. Turkey*). **16 May:** Council of Europe adopts Convention on Prevention of Terrorism, defining crimes of terrorism and underlining the need to protect freedom of expression, freedom of association, and freedom of religion. Council of Europe Convention on Action against Trafficking in Human Beings opens for signature. **31 May:** UN-SC holds first open meeting on sexual exploitation and abuse in peacekeeping. **6 June:** ICC prosecutor opens investigation in Darfur. **14 June:** Argentine Supreme Court declares all previously adopted immunity laws null and void. **29 June:** Belgian court sentences two Rwandan nationals for involvement in Rwandan genocide. **3 July:** UN-TOC's protocol on illicit manufacturing and trafficking in firearms enters into force. **26 July:** UN-SC establishes monitoring and reporting mechanism on use of child soldiers. **27 July:** Commission of Experts' review of serious crimes in Timor-Leste in 1999 recommends that Indonesia strengthen its legal capacity. **3 August:** UN-GA adopts United Nations Declaration on Human Cloning in recorded vote. **11 August:** Iraqi Transitional National Assembly approves establishment of a war crime tribunal. **8 September:** IACtHR finds Dominican Republic in violation of American Convention on Human Rights for practices which deprived two migrants' children of their right to a nationality (*Girls Yean and Bosico v. The Dominican Republic*). **15 September:** Israel's Supreme Court requests government to reconsider separation wall route because it injures the fabric of life in a number of villages. **6 October:** ECtHR finds that restriction of voting rights of all convicted prisoners in Great Britain is a violation of the ECHR. **19 October:** UNESCO approves Universal Declaration on Bioethics and Human Rights. **20 October:** UNESCO's Convention on the Protection and Promotion of the Diversity of Cultural Expressions adopted by recorded vote. **28 October:** IACmHR requests that the United States take immediate measures necessary to have the legal status of the detainees at Guantanamo Bay effectively determined by a competent tribunal. **31 October:** UN-SC adopts travel and financial sanctions in relation to Lebanon in response to killing of Prime Minister Rafic Hariri and 22 others. **8 December:** House of Lords unanimously rules that that evidence obtained by torture by officials of a foreign state without the participation of British authorities is not admissible. **9 December:** UN-SC holds one-day open debate on protection of civilians in armed conflict. **14 December:** UN Convention against Corruption enters into force. **15 December:** UN-SC imposes embargo on all rough diamonds from Cote d'Ivoire and mandates UNOCI to continue the application of the sanctions. **16 December:** UN-GA adopts Basic Principles and Guidelines on the Right to a Remedy and Reparation for Victims of Gross Violations of International Human Rights Law and Serious Violations of International Humanitarian Law. **19 December:** ICJ finds Ugandan state liable for violating the Democratic Republic of the Congo's (DRC) territorial integrity between 1998 and 2003 and orders Uganda to make substantial financial amends to the DRC for humanitarian wrongs.

2006   13 February: India's Supreme Court decides that a French carrier must stay outside of Indian waters because it contains hazardous toxic material. **15 February:** Five UN special rapporteurs issue report critical of U.S. practices in Guantanamo. **22 February:** OECD adopts guidelines for the licensing of genetic inventions. **26 February:** ILO adopts Maritime Labor Convention. **7–10 March:** U.S. Food and Agriculture Organization (FAO) sponsors International Conference on Agrarian Reform held in Porto Alegre. **15 March:** UN-GA sets up United Nations Human Rights Council (UN-HRC) that replaces Commission of Human Rights. **29 March:** Responding to a request of the Lebanese government, the UN-SC establishes an international tribunal to try those found responsible for the 2005 terrorist attack that killed Prime Minister Hariri. Charles Taylor, former president of Sierra Leone, is apprehended and surrendered to the Special Court for Sierra Leone. **28 April:** UN-SC adopts omnibus resolution on protection of civilians in armed conflicts, reaffirming the "responsibility to protect" concept as formulated by 2005 World Summit Outcome Document. UN-SC imposes sanctions on four individuals involved in the fighting in Darfur. **18 May:** UN-CAT determines that Senegal had violated its obligations under the UN-CAT for failing to either prosecute former Chad leader Hissene Habre or comply with Belgium's request for his extradition. Ten independent experts comprising members of UN-CAT urge an end to Guantanamo detention. **30 May:** European Court of Justice (ECJ) rules that the European Union overstepped its authority by agreeing to give the United States personal details about airline passengers on a flight to America. **2 June:** UN-GA adopts Political Declaration on HIV/AIDS. **12 June:** ICTR convicts former member of the governing board of Radio Television Libre des Mille Collines's complicity to commit genocide and direct and public incitement to commit genocide (*Prosecutor v. Joseph Serugendo*). Special rapporteur of the Council of Europe's Parliamentary

Assembly issues report critical of the U.S. Central Intelligence Agency's (CIA) secret rendition program. **14 June:** Great Britain's House of Lords rules that British courts have no jurisdiction in a case of alleged torture against Saudi Arabia because a serving foreign minister is immune from suit and the UN-CAT does not grant universal jurisdiction. **22 June:** Optional Protocol to UN-CAT establishing monitoring mechanism of visits to detention centers by independent international and national independence expert bodies takes effect. **26 June:** UN-GA begins review of its program to prevent and eliminate small arms trade. **29 June:** U.S. Supreme Court rules that military tribunals set up by the Bush administration to try terrorist suspects at Guantanamo Bay are unlawful under U.S. and international law and that inmates are protected by the Geneva Conventions (*Hamdan v. Rumsfeld*). **29 June:** UN-HRC adopts Draft Declaration on the Rights of Indigenous Peoples. **2 July:** African Court on Human and People's Rights (ACtHPR) constituted. **23 July:** Former Mexican president Luis Echeverría indicted for allegedly ordering the killing of student demonstrators in 1971. **24 July:** In unprecedented decision, IACtHR condemns Brazil for human rights violations in a case related to people with mental disabilities. **11 August:** UN-HRC meeting in special session condemns Israeli violation of human rights and breaches of international humanitarian law in Lebanon and sets up "high level inquiry commission." **27 August:** After five years of negotiations, countries agree on a new treaty to protect the rights of persons with disabilities. **28 August:** ICC prosecutor formally charges Thomas Lubanga, a former militia leader in the DRC, with enlisting and conscripting children under the age of 15 and using them to participate actively in hostilities. **31 August:** Inviting the consent of the Sudanese government, UN-SC agrees to deploy a UN peacekeeping force of more than 17,000 in Darfur. **1 September:** UN-HRC names three members of a High-Level Commission of Inquiry to probe what the Geneva-based body termed "systematic targeting and killings of civilians by Israel" in Lebanon. **12 October:** ECtHR finds Russian forces responsible for summary execution of Chechnyan civilians in 2000 Novye massacre and faults government for failing to adequately investigate the matter. **26 October:** UN-SC holds open debate on women, peace and security focused on the role of women in peacekeeping and postconflict situations. **5 November:** Iraqi court finds Saddam Hussein guilty of 1982 mass killing of villagers in the Shia town of Dujayl and related atrocities and sentences him to death. **8 November:** Government of Nepal and Maoist rebels reach peace agreement after 10 years of civil conflict. **14 November:** Criminal complaint filed in German court against former U.S. secretary of defense Donald Rumsfeld and former CIA director George Tenet alleging torture and war crimes at Guantanamo Bay Prison Camp and Abu Ghraib prison. **23 November:** UN-SC backs Special Tribunal for Lebanon to try alleged perpetrators of 2005 assassination of Lebanese prime minister. **28 November:** Third Committee of the UN-GA adopts Declaration on the Rights of Indigenous Peoples by recorded vote (83-0-91). **30 November:** ICTY sentences former Bosnian Serb general to life in prison for violating the laws of war and crimes against humanity, murder and inhumane acts committed in the campaign of daily shelling and sniping which he organized during the siege of Sarajevo. **6 December:** ICTR convicts former pastor of aiding and abetting extermination in Rwandan genocide. **12 December:** UN-HRC holds inconclusive special session on human rights situation in Darfur. **16 December:** Israeli Supreme Court rules that preventative strikes targeted at terrorists are not always illegal but must be examined in the context of the law of armed conflict and with respect to the international law norm of proportionality. **19 December:** UN-SC requests the UN-SG to establish a focal point within the UN Secretariat to receive delisting requests of individuals suspected of terrorist activities. **20 December:** Adopted by UN-GA, treaty outlawing enforced disappearances opens for signature. **30 December:** Saddam Hussein executed.

2007   12 January: China and Russia veto resolution calling for release of political prisoners in Myanmar and an end to human rights abuses against ethnic minorities. **29 January:** ICC decides to try Congolese militia leader for war crimes involving recruiting children as soldiers in what is the court's first trial. **30 January:** AU adopts African Charter on Democracy, Elections, and Governance. **7 February:** UN-GA adopts resolution calling for the elimination of rape and other forms of sexual violence in conflict and related situations. **26 February:** ICJ clears Serbia of direct involvement in genocide during the 1992 to 1995 Bosnian war as the Bosnian government had charged but also concludes that Belgrade violated international law by failing to prevent the Srebrenica massacre and by not earnestly committing to capturing high-profile fugitives. **7 March:** Under South Africa's presidency, UN-SC adopts presidential statement reiterating language contained in its Resolution 1325 of 2000. **18 March:** Convention on the Protection and Promotion of the Diversity of Cultural Expressions enters into force. **26 March:** Group of human rights experts including Mary Robinson and UN special rapporteurs issue set of principles on the application of international human rights law with respect to sexual orientation and gender identity. **31 March:** UN-SC adopts resolution imposing sanctions against individuals involved in serious violations on international law including sexual violence in the DRC. **10 April:** A Serbian war crimes court convicts four former paramilitary officers in the July 1995 killings of Bosnian Muslims from Srebrenica. **27 April:** ICC pretrial chamber determines that there are reasonable grounds to believe that Ahmad Harun, former minister for the interior, and a Janjaweed leader Ali Kushayb are criminally responsible for crimes against humanity and war crimes. **15 May:** UN-SC recognizes the specific link between illicit exploitation and trade of natural resources and the proliferation of arms trafficking in the DRC in a resolution renewing the mandate of UN Organization Mission in the Democratic Republic of the Congo (MONUC). **21 May:** U.S. Court of Appeals dismisses an Alien Tort Statute suit that the crime of statutory rape did not constitute a violation of the law of nations. **22 May:** ICC opens investigation in Central African Republic. **30 May:** Acting under Chapter 7, UN-SC authorizes establishment of Special Tribunal for Lebanon (STL). **4 June:** War crime trial of Charles Taylor opens in Special Court for Sierra Leone (SCSL). **18 June:** UN-HRC adopts "Institution Building package" as framework for its future activities. **20 June:** SCSL finds three suspects guilty of war crimes, including acts of terrorism, collective punishments, extermination, murder, rape, outrages upon personal dignity, conscripting or enlisting children under the age of 15 into armed forces, enslavement and pillage. **21 June:** ECtHR rules that Russia was responsible for the illegal detention and killing of a human rights activist (*Bitiyeva and X v. Russia*). **25 June:** UN-SC adopts presidential statement recognizing the role that the exploitation, trafficking and illicit trade of natural resources can play in armed conflict and postconflict situations. **31 July:** UN-SC authorizes deployment of African Union-United Nations Hybrid Operation in Darfur (UNAMID) with a mandate to take necessary action to protect civilians and ensure security and freedom of movement of humanitarian workers. **7 September:** UN-GA adopts nonbinding Declaration on the Rights of Indigenous Peoples. **21 September:** UN-HRC adopts calendar for first round of Universal Periodic Review (UPR) for 2008 to 2011. **25 September:** UN-SC authorizes United Nations Mission in the Central African Republic and Chad (MINURCAT) with mandate to increase security in refugee camps and take all necessary measures to protect civilians. **28 September:** UN-HRC establishes Forum on Minority Issues. **2 October:** UN-HRC concludes special session strongly deploring continued violent repression of peaceful demonstrations in Myanmar. **25 October:** Council of Europe adopts Convention on the Protection of Children against Sexual Exploitation and Sexual Abuse. **20 November:** ASEAN Charter endorsed at organization's summit. **24 November:** Spanish Supreme Court affirms conviction of Argentine former naval officer for crimes against humanity. **18 December:** UN-GA votes on controversial resolution expressing deep concern about the negative stereotyping of religions and manifestations of intolerance and discrimination in matters of religion or belief. **21 December:** UN-SC adopts resolution requesting MONUC to pursue a missionwide strategy to strengthen prevention, protection and response to sexual violence.

2008 **16 January:** European Parliament passes resolution condemning use of rape as weapon of war. **24 January:** Human Rights Arab Charter enters into force. **24 January:** UN-HRC concludes special session expressing concern about Israeli military attacks in Gaza Strip. **1 February:** European Convention against Trafficking in Persons enters into force. **13 February:** Australian Prime Minister Kevin Rudd apologizes to Aboriginal people for past policy of forced assimilation. **17 February:** Kosovo proclaims its independence. **22 February:** U.S. court dismisses claim of a group of Vietnamese nationals against multinational corporations under the Alien Tort Statute because they failed to demonstrate violation of international law. **28 February:** ECtHR reasserts absolute prohibition on *nonrefoulement* in terrorism extradition cases (*Saadi v. Italy*). **25 March:** U.S. Supreme Court holds ICJ decisions under Consular Convention not binding federal law (*Medellin v. Texas*). **28 March:** UN investigation commission issues report on assassination of former Lebanese Prime Minister Rafik Hariri. UN-HRC asserts that climate change poses an immediate and far-reaching threat to peoples and communities. **3 April:** ICTY acquits Ramush Haradinaj, former guerrilla leader and prime minister of Kosovo, of war crimes and crimes against humanity during the 1999 Kosovo war. **4 April:** British High Court of Justice rules in favor of five men who challenged government's orders to implement the assets freeze of UN-SC Resolution 1267 on the grounds that the suspects had no opportunity to challenge the listing. **4 April:** Study commissioned by UN-HCHR critically assesses how current UN treaty framework addresses national laws discriminating against women. **6 April:** U.S. Department of Justice releases classified memos providing legal guidance on the permissibility of aggressive interrogation techniques. **7 April:** UN-HRC begins UPR process. **12 April:** ECtHR upholds decision of a French school to expel students for covering their heads during physical education classes (*Dogru v. France*). **3 May:** Convention on the Rights of People with Disabilities (UN-CPRD) and its Optional Protocol come into force. **22 May:** UN-HRC holds first ever special session devoted to the negative impact of world food crisis on enjoyment of right to food. **3 June:** UN-SG special representative on Human Rights and Transnational Corporations issues his final report. **10 June:** ILO adopts Declaration on Social Justice for a Fair Globalization. **11 June:** Israeli Supreme Court upholds the constitutionality of the incarceration of "unlawful combatants." **12 June:** U.S. Supreme Court rules that noncitizens detained at Guantanamo Bay have a constitutional right to habeas corpus review by federal civilian courts (*Boumediene v. Bush*). **18 June:** UN-HRC endorses policy framework proposed by special representative of the secretary-general on business and human rights. **19 June:** UN-SC holds open debate at the ministerial level and adopts statement stressing that sexual violence as a tactic of war can significantly exacerbate situations of armed conflict. **30 June:** UN-SC reaffirms that acts of terrorism are criminal and unjustifiable and adopts revised rules of the listing process of individuals and entities suspected of terrorism. **12 July:** Russian and Chinese vetoes squash UN-SC sanctions on Zimbabwe. **14 July:** ICC prosecutor indicts sitting president of Sudan Omar Hassan Ahmad al-Bashir on charges of genocide, crimes against humanity and war crimes in Darfur. **17 July:** UN-SC condemns violations against children in conflict. **21 July:** Radovan Karadzic arrested in Belgrade after 13 years as a fugitive. **6 August:** Algerian detained in Guantanamo Bay files complaint with the IACmHR. **6 August:** UN special rapporteur on the Promotion and Protection of Human Rights and Fundamental Freedoms issues report focused on the fundamental right to a fair trial in the specific context of prosecuting terrorism suspects. **1 September:** South African judge Navanethem Pillay begins her tenure as UN Commissioner for Human Rights. **3 September:** European Court of Justice annuls EU Council's regulation freezing the assets of two persons blacklisted by the UN-SC on suspicion of links with terrorism on the grounds that it infringed on their civil rights. **17 September:** Karadzic trial by ICTY opens. **8 October:** At Serbia's prodding, UN-GA asks ICJ advisory opinion on Kosovo unilateral declaration of independence. **20 October:** UN special rapporteur on the Promotion and Protection of Human Rights and Fundamental Freedoms briefs UN-SC on options to address human rights challenges in the 1267 sanctions regime. **27 October:** Economic Community of West African States (ECOWAS) court finds Niger guilty of failing to protect a woman from slavery. **29 October:** UN-HRCttee declares that Belgium violated ICCPR by restricting an applicant's right to travel when it assisted the UN-SC in placing names on the Consolidated List of UN Sanctions Committee. **18 November:** ICJ decides to hear Croatian genocide claim against Serbia. **1 December:** UN-HRC expresses serious concern at the deteriorating human rights and humanitarian situation in North Kivu of the Democratic Republic of the Congo. **10 December:** Optional Protocol to Covenant of Economic, Social and Cultural Rights, allowing for individual complaints, adopted by the UN-GA and opens for signature. **15–16 December:** Inaugural session of the UN Forum on Minority Issues.

2009   9 January: UN-HRC condemns Israeli military operations in Gaza Strip and sets up fact-finding mission. **22 January:** President Barack Obama issues executive orders changing U.S. policy on detention and interrogation of individuals held in custody for suspected acts of terrorism. **30 January:** Four non-governmental organizations (the American Civil Liberties Union, Amnesty International, and Human Rights Watch) and Human Rights First (HRF) write to President Obama requesting full access to Guantanamo Bay detention camps. **17 February:** Trial of Khmer Rouge commander of Tuol Sleng prison opens on charges of murder, extermination, enslavement, imprisonment torture, rape, persecutions on political grounds and other inhuman acts. **19 February:** Belgium files a case with the ICJ demanding that Senegal prosecute or extradite Habre to Belgium in accordance with its obligations under UN-CAT. **20 February:** UN-HRC meets in special session on impact of world economic crisis on human rights and international community to support national efforts to establish and preserve social safety nets for the protection of the most vulnerable segments of their societies. **1 March:** STL officially opens. **3 March:** UN-SC imposes an assets freeze and travel ban on three individuals identified in 2008 by the Expert Group report as responsible for sexual violence in DRC. **4 March:** ICC issues arrest warrant for Sudanese president. **26 March:** Charges of genocide against former Mexican president Luis Echeverria dismissed by a federal court. **8 April:** U.S. court dismisses claim under Alien Tort Statute alleging that transnational corporations aided and abetted the Apartheid regime in South Africa. **8 April:** IACmHR rules that amnesties and statutes of limitations cannot be applied to crimes against humanity committed during Brazil's military dictatorship. **30 April:** Fact-finding committee established by League of Arab States finds "sufficient evidence" of human rights and humanitarian law violations in the December 2008 Israeli offensive in Gaza Strip. **27 May:** UN-HRC concludes special session on Sri Lanka, ignoring calls for an international investigation of human rights abuses at the end of the civil war. **9 June:** In a case of domestic violence, ECtHR finds that Turkey failed to protect the victims and violated protection of life and prohibition of torture provisions of the European Convention. **15 June:** Russia vetoes extension of UN Mission in Georgia. **22 June:** Panel of judges finds former Peruvian president Alberto Fujimori guilty of ordering murders committed by death squads supervised by government. **11 June:** ECJ issues another ruling similar to its Kadi decision (*Omar Mohammed Othman v. Council and Commission*). **18 June:** U.S. Senate adopts resolution apologizing to Afro-Americans for slavery and segregation. **19 June:** United Nations announces independent probe into former Pakistani Prime Minister Benazir Bhutto's killing. **19 June:** UN-SC meets at ministerial level to discuss sexual violence in armed conflict. **22 June:** ICTR sentences former Rwandan interior minister to 30 years in prison for genocide and complicity to commit genocide. **2 July:** ECtHR rules Russia violated European Convention of Human Rights in a disappearance case which took place in Chechnya (*Pukhigova v. Russia*). **4 July:** Invoking the Inter-American Democratic Charter, OAS General Assembly terms the Honduras coup an "unconstitutional alteration of the constitutional order" and suspends Honduras from participation in the OAS. **10 July:** AU ceases cooperation with ICC, refusing to recognize the international arrest warrant it had issued against Sudan's leader. **14 July:** ICTR jails for life former Kigali governor convicted of genocide, rape and murder. **19–20 July:** ASEAN adopts terms of reference for Intergovernmental Commission on Human Rights. **4 August:** UN-SC adopts resolution strongly condemning all violations of applicable international law involving the recruitment and use of children by parties to armed conflict (Resolution 1882). **7 August:** UN-SC holds open debate on sexual violence in armed conflict. **12 August:** Inter-American Juridical Committee adopts nonbinding resolution on essential elements of representative democracy. **14 September:** UN-GA votes to create a new agency for women, merging four existing offices into a single body. **15 September:** Judge Richard Goldstone report on Gaza war issued. Finds strong evidence of war crimes and crimes against humanity during the conflict and calls for end to impunity. **5 October:** UN-SC reaffirms its Resolution 1325 of 2000 and condemns violations of international law committed against women and girls in situations of conflict and postconflict. **23 October:** AU approves the Convention for the Protection and Assistance of Internally Displaced Persons in Africa. **23 October:** ASEAN Intergovernmental Commission on Human Rights formally established. **29 October:** Quebec Supreme Court convicts Rwandan national of genocide, crimes against humanity and war crimes committed in 1994. **16 November:** IACtHR rules that Mexico violated several human rights obligations, including the rights to life, personal integrity, and personal liberty, when it failed to protect the life of three young women, two of whom were minors *("Cotton Field" v. Mexico)*. **18 November:** ECOWAS court finds that Hissene Habre may only be tried by an "ad hoc special tribunal of an international character." **30 November:** UN-SC exchange views on ways to improve respect for human rights while strengthening the international response to terrorism. **1 December:** Lisbon treaty enters into force making EU Charter of Fundamental Rights legally binding. **10 December:** IACtHR issues landmark decision holding Mexico responsible for unsolved disappearances and murders in Cuidad Juarez. **15 December:** African Court on Human and People's Rights issues its first decision dismissing an individual's application against the Republic of Senegal for lack of jurisdiction. **17 December:** UN-SC approves significant changes in the administration of the 1267 regime and creates an office of the ombudsman to serve as a point of contact for individuals and entities requesting to be removed from list of suspected terrorists. **22 December:** UN-SC imposes arms embargo on Eritrea, travel bans on Eritrean leaders, and asset freezes on Eritrean officials. **31 December:** U.S. Federal court dismisses charges of voluntary manslaughter and firearms violations committed in Iraq against five private security guards.

2010 4 January: Peru's Supreme Court upholds 25-year prison term for Alberto Fujimori for death squad killings and kidnapping during his 1990 to 2000 presidency. **7 January:** ECtHR rules that that Cyprus and Russia violated Article 4 (prohibition of slavery and forced labor) of the ECHR for neither preventing nor investigating the trafficking of a young Russian woman to Cyprus (*Rantsev v. Cyprus & Russia*). **12 January:** ECtHR rules that random stops and searchs of two British citizens under the United Kingdom Terrorism Act 2000 is a violation of the right to privacy guaranteed by the ECHR. **2 February:** UN-SG appoints Margot Wallström of Sweden as his special representative on sexual violence in conflict. **10 February:** African Commission on Human and People's Rights orders Kenya to return ancestral land originally belonging to the Endorois, an indigenous community living in Kenya, and to pay compensation for losses suffered due to unlawful eviction. **25 February:** ECtHR rules that products originating in the West Bank are outside the scope of the EC-Israel Association Agreement, thus implying that the occupied territories are not part of Israel (Case C-386/08, *Brita GmbH v. Hauptzollamt Hamburg-Hafen*). **5 March:** Former president of Uruguay Juan Maria Bordaberry sentenced to 30 years in prison for murder. **10 March:** Serbian Parliament condemns 1995 Srebrenica massacre. **17 March:** IACmHR accepts petition of residents of Louisiana community alleging that they "suffer or are put at risk of various health problems caused by dumping of industrial toxic wastes." **17 March:** AU imposes penalties on Madagascar president Andri Rajoelina and other public officials until government returns to internationally mediated power sharing talks. **18 March:** ECtHR Grand Chamber overturns earlier 2009 ruling that it was justifiable for publicly funded schools to continue displaying crucifixes on class rooms walls (*Lautsi v. Italy*). **31 March:** Argentinian court convicts former general Eduardo Cabanillas of murder, torture and illegal imprisonment when he ran a detention center during his 1976 to 1983 military rule. **7 April:** ASEAN Commission for the Promotion and Protection of the Rights of Women and Children established in Hanoi. **10 April:** ECtHR issues seven judgments finding Russia responsible for unlawful disappearances and deaths in Chechnya and Dagestan. **15 April:** Croatian President Ivo Josipovic apologizes for crimes committed in Bosnia and Herzegovina during the 1990s. **27 April:** UN-SC holds open debate on women's peace and security. **29 April:** House of Representative of Belgium approves burqa ban. **1 June:** UN-SC issues a presidential statement condemning the loss of life and expressing deep regrets regarding the use of force by Israel against ships carrying humanitarian aid to Gaza. **10 June:** ICTY convicts seven former Bosnian Serb army members of genocide and crimes against humanity for their involvement in the 1995 Srebrenica massacre (*Prosecutor v. Popovic et al.*). **11 June:** States parties of the ICC statute agree on definition of aggression allowing court to exert jurisdiction over crimes against peace. **24 June:** ECtHR rules that there is no requirement under the ECHR to grant same-sex couples access to marriage (*Schalk & Kopf v. Austria*). **29 June:** UN-SC holds open debate on justice and the rule of law. **21 July:** Ramush Haradinaj arrested again for a partial retrial by ICTY. **22 July:** ICJ releases advisory opinion stating that Kosovo's declaration of independence does not violate international law. **28 July:** UN-GA acknowledges right to water. **1 August:** Convention on Cluster Munitions enters into force. **16 September:** Cambodia special court indicts four senior Khmer Rouge figures including the former head of state of Kampuchea, the foreign minister and the social action minister. **17 September:** U.S. Circuit Court dismisses class action brought under Alien Tort Statute by Ogoni plaintiff. UN-SC adopts presidential statement in response to mass rape in DRC. **24 September:** UN-HRC adopts resolution affirming the human right to safe drinking water and sanitation. **27 September:** Panel of inquiry set up by UN-HRC finds that Israel demonstrated "totally unnecessary violence" during its interception of Gaza bound flotilla on 31 May. Committee on Legal Affairs of Parliamentary Assembly of Council of Europe issues report on corporate responsibility in the area of human rights, stressing that "private individuals and legal persons, including businesses, have responsibilities." **1 October:** Panel of experts set up by the UN-SG releases a report documenting gross violations of human rights and international crimes in DRC between 1993 and 2002. **7 October:** Constitutional Court in France rules that the bill making it illegal to wear full face veils in public is constitutional. **8 October:** Fifty-eight private military companies sign the International Code of Conduct for Private Security Service Providers, committing to adhere to numerous international human rights principles. **21 October:** ECtHR rules that Russia wrongfully denied numerous petitions by the applicant to organize a gay pride parade in Moscow (*Alekseyev v. Russia*). **9 November:** The EU Court of Justice rules that member states, in determining whether to grant refugee status to persons who were members of terrorist organizations, must consider each applicant's situation on a case-by-case basis (Joined Cases C-57/09 and C-101/09, *Germany v. B, and Germany v. D*). **11 November:** Eighteen Latin American countries approve the Declaration on the Protection of Refugees and Stateless Persons in the Americas. **22 November:** Trial of former vice president of DRC opens at ICC on charges of torture, murder and rape committed in 2002 and 2003 in Central African Republic. **22 November:** UN-SC holds open debate on protection of civilians in armed conflict. **24 November:** IACtHR invalidates Brazil's 1979 Amnesty Law (Gomes Lund v. Brazil). **26 November:** Russia's Parliament approves statement holding Stalin responsible for ordering the 1940 Katyn massacres. **30 November:**

ICJ finds that in carrying out the arrest, detention and expulsion of a Guinean businessman, the DRC had violated his fundamental rights under the ICCPR and the African Charter of Human and People's Rights (Ahmadou Sadio Diallo). **15 December:** UN-SC terminates Oil for Food program. **16 December:** UN-SC votes unanimously to name and shame individuals who are "credibly suspected" of committing rape or other forms of sexual violence. ECtHR rules that Ireland's constitutional ban on abortion violates pregnant women's right to receive proper medical care in life-threatening cases. Council of Europe commissioned report concludes that Khasim Thaçi, prime minister of Kosovo, led a clan of criminal entrepreneurs involved in organ trafficking during the Kosovo conflict in 1999. **17 December:** Popular demonstrations begin in Tunisia. **22 December:** UN-SC sets up new body to complete tasks of ICTY and ICTR while calling on them to conclude their work by the end of 2014. **23 December:** Landmark treaty to deter enforced disappearances enters into force. **23 December:** UN-HRC meets in special session and condemns violations of human rights in Cote d'Ivoire.

2011 11 January: ECtHR rules that both Greek and Belgian governments violated the European Convention of Human Rights when applying the Dublin Regulation on asylum seekers. **21 January:** ECtHR rules that Greece violated the European Convention for failing to provide adequate detention facilities and living conditions to an asylum seeker from Afghanistan (*M.S.S. v. Belgium & Greece*). **24 January:** Tunisian president toppled. **25 January:** Dissent spreads to Egypt. **11 February:** President Hosni Mubarak steps down. **18 February:** United States vetoes resolution condemning Israel's settlement policy. **23 February:** Former Serbian police chief jailed for 27 years for his role in murder of 700 ethnic Albanians in Kosovo in 1999. ICTY convicts former assistant minister of the Serbian Ministry of Internal Affairs of crimes against humanity and war crimes committed against Kosovo Albanians in 1999 (*Prosecutor v. Djordjevic*). **25 February:** Citing "indiscriminate armed attacks against civilians, extrajudicial killings, arbitrary arrests, detention, and torture" of demonstrators, UN-HRC decides to "urgently dispatch an independent international commission of inquiry to investigate all alleged violations of international human rights law" in Libya. **26 February:** In swift action, the UN-SC demands an end to the violence and refers Libyan situation to the ICC while imposing an arms embargo on the country, a travel ban, and assets freeze on the family of Muammar Al-Gaddafi and a number of government officials. **March:** Protests spreading throughout Syria are met by government crackdown. **1 March:** At the urging of UN-HRC, UN-GA suspends Libya's membership from the council. **2 March:** ICC prosecutor opens investigation into alleged crimes against humanity committed in Libya.

3 March: The African Commission on Human and People's Rights institutes proceedings against Libya before the ACtHPR "for serious violations" of the African Charter on Human and People's Rights. **7 March:** Nagoya Protocol is adopted which provides international rules and procedure on liability and redress for damage to biodiversity resulting from living modified organisms. **10 March:** ECtHR rules that Russia violated Article 14 (prohibition of discrimination) and Article 8 (right to private and family life) of the ECHR by denying an applicant a residence permit on the basis of his HIV-positive status (*Kiyutin v. Russia*). **15 March:** Popular demonstrations start in Syria and rapidly grow nationwide. **17 March:** UN-SC approves no-fly zone and bans all flights within the Libyan airspace except for those whose purpose is solely humanitarian and for the benefit of the Libyan people. NATO airstrikes start two days later. **18 March:** ECtHR rules that the presence of crucifixes in state-school classrooms in Italy does not violate the European Convention. **21 March:** UN-HRC appoints special rapporteur on Iran. **21 April:** UN-HRC sets up investigative mission to Syria. **25 March:** For the first time in its history, the ACtHPR orders provisional measures against Libya. **31 March:** Argentinian court sentences former general to life in prison for running a notorious detention center during military rule. **1 April:** ICJ dismisses Georgia's claim alleging that Russia violated the International Convention on the Elimination of All Forms of Racial Discrimination. **5 April:** European Commission proposes EU Framework for National Roma Integration Strategies for consideration by Council and Parliament. **12 April:** UN torture investigator asserts that he has been denied unmonitored access visit to U.S. army private suspected of giving classified material to WikiLeaks. **25 April:** UN-SG fact-finding panel issues report concludes that Sri Lankan government and Tamil Tigers committed abuses at the end of the civil war. **29 April:** UN-HRC meeting in special session condemns violence in Syria and requests UN-HCHR to investigate alleged violations of human rights. **17 May:** ICTR convicts former chief of staff of Rwandan armed forces of genocide, crimes against humanity for murder, extermination and rape and violations of the Geneva Conventions. **21 May:** ECtHR rules that Russia violated the right to life of Chechnyan residents whose relatives were killed in air strikes carried out by Russian forces in 1999 as part of counterterrorism operation. **25 May:** OECD adopts updated version of its Guidelines for Multinational Enterprises. **26 May:** Ex-Bosnian Serb army commander Ratko Mladic arrested on war crimes charges. **30 May:** Spanish judge indicts 20 Salvadoran military officials in 1989 murders under universal jurisdiction doctrine. **31 May:** UN expert issues global standards for human rights in business world. **10 June:** President Juan Manuel Santos of Colombia signs law compensating victims of human rights abuses and violations. **10 June:** Special Tribunal for Lebanon indicts four individuals charged in the killing of former Lebanese prime minister Rafiq Hariri. **16 June:** ILO adopts Convention Concerning Decent Work for Domestic Workers. UN-HRC endorses "Guiding Principles on Business and Human Rights: Implementing the United Nations 'Protect, Respect and Remedy' Framework." **17 June:** UN-HRC adopts optional protocol to the Convention on the Rights of the Child, instituting a communication procedure. UN-HRC adopts resolution supporting equal rights for all, regardless of sexual orientation. **23 June:** ICC prosecutor requests authorization to open investigation into war crimes and crimes against humanity allegedly committed in Cote d'Ivoire following the presidential runoff. **24 June:** First woman, former Rwandan government minister of family and women's development, convicted of genocide and sentenced to life in prison by ICTR. **27 June:** Joint trial of the four most senior surviving leaders of Khmer Rouge regime gets under way in UN-backed tribunal. **28 June:** ICC prosecutor issues warrants for the arrest of Gaddafi, his son and the head of Libyan intelligence forces for crimes against humanity. **30 June:** UN-backed Lebanon tribunal issues four arrest warrants. **6 July:** Dutch court rules that the Netherlands is responsible for the deaths of three Muslim men executed by Bosnian Serb troops in the massacres at Srebrenica and orders the government to compensate the men's relatives. **7 July:** ECtHR issues landmark judgment ruling that Great Britain is obligated to uphold the European Convention in the southeast region of Iraq which it controls. **8 July:** UN-SC establishes multitask peace operation in South Sudan. **21 July:** IACmHR finds United States in violation of American Declaration of Rights and Duties of Man for failing to provide sufficient protection to victims of domestic violence. **22 July:** Last remaining fugitive, former president of self-proclaimed Republic of Serbian Krajina, taken into custody by ICTY. **23 August:** Meeting in special session, UN-HRC orders an investigation into violations committed by Syrian security forces during crackdown on dissent. **7 September:** ICTY convicts Serbian army's ex-chief of staff of crimes against humanity and war crimes in Bosnia and Herzegovina. **22 September:** High level UN-GA meeting marks 10th anniversary of the adoption of the Durban Declaration and Programme of Action. **25 September:** Saudi Arabia gives women the right to vote and run in local elections in 2015. **30 September:** African Committee of Experts on Rights and Welfare of the Child finds Kenya in violation of the rights of Nubian children to nondiscrimination. **3 October:** ICC authorizes probe into postelection violence in Cote d'Ivoire. Two former government ministers in Rwanda convicted for conspiracy to commit genocide. **13 October:** UN completes first cycle of Universal Periodic Review. UN welcomes Mexico's promulgation of constitutional reform recognizing right to food. **20 October:** Colonel Gaddafi killed. **18 November:** Brazilian government establishes truth commission to look into human rights abuses during military rule. **23 November:** UN Commission of Inquiry blames Syrian government military and security forces for human rights violations and crimes against humanity. **25 November:** Egyptians go to polls. **27 November:** Arab League approves sanctions against Syria. **15 December:** UN-HCHR issues first ever report documenting human rights violations against lesbian, gay, bisexual, transgender and intersexual individuals. **19 December:** Obama administration releases National Action Plan on Women, Peace and Security.

2012   11 January: ECtHR orders Turkey to pay more than 20 million euros in compensation for loss of home and property by 13 Cypriot nationals caused by Turkish troops stationing in Northern part of the island. **13 January:** UN Human Rights Committee rules that France violates Sikhs' religious freedom by forcing them to remove their turbans when having photos taken for passports and ID cards. **14 January:** Aung San Suu Kyi of Myanmar allowed to seek elected office for the first time since 1990. **16 January:** Citing concerns about the use of torture on suspects in Jordan, the ECtHR rules that Great Britain cannot deport radical Islamic preacher. **23 January:** ICC rules that four prominent Kenyans, including Uhuru Kenyatta, are to stand trial for crimes against humanity and other offenses allegedly committed following the general elections in late 2007. French Parliament adopts law making genocide denial a crime. **1 February:** Trial Chamber of Special Tribunal for Lebanon decides to start trial against four men in absentia. Arab League calls for UN-SC action on Syria. **3 February:** ICJ rules that Italy had violated its obligation to respect Germany's immunity under international law by allowing civil claims seeking reparations for Nazi war crimes to be brought against it in Italian courts. **5 February:** Russia and China veto UN-SC resolution calling for peaceful transfer of power in Syria. **7 February:** Arria Formula meeting of the UN-SC on human rights components in UN peace missions. **16 February:** UN-GA adopts resolution by 137 to 12 vote calling upon Syrian regime to halt its crackdown and comply with Arab League's demand for transition to power. **1 March:** ICC issues arrest warrant against Sudanese defense minister Abdel Rahim Mohamed Hussein on 41 counts of crimes against humanity and war crimes allegedly committed in Darfur. **14 March:** ICC issues its first ruling convicting former Congolese warlord of conscripting child soldiers. **16 March:** Brazil starts prosecution of retired colonel for abuses during military rule. **21 March:** UN-SC backs UN-Arab League envoy Kofi Annan's peace plan. **30 March:** IACtHR accepts jurisdiction over a case of a man detained in Guantanamo Bay. **2 April:** National League for Democracy of Aung San Suu Kyi claims landslide victory in parliamentary by-elections. **3 April:** ICC rejects Palestinian petition to prosecute Israel for alleged violations in West Bank and Gaza Strip. AU imposes travel ban and asset freeze on leaders of military coup against civilian government in Mali. **14 April:** UN-SC authorizes the deployment of 30 military observers to Syria. **16 April:** ECtHR rules that Russian Federation violated the rights of relatives of Poles murdered in Katyn and that the massacre was a war crime. **17 April:** AU suspends membership of Guinea-Bissau in wake of military coup. **21 April:** UN-SC establishes United Nations Supervision Mission in Syria (UNSMIS) to monitor a cessation of armed violence in all its forms by all parties and to monitor and support the full implementation of the special envoy's six-point plan to end the conflict in Syria. **26 April:** SCSL hands down a guilty verdict against Charles Taylor for planning, aiding and abetting war crimes and crimes against humanity. **30 May:** Charles Taylor sentenced to 50 years' prison term. **31 May:** ICTR convicts former Rwandan minister of youth of genocide, conspiracy to commit genocide, direct and public incitement to commit genocide and extermination as a crime against humanity and sentences him to life imprisonment. **6 July:** HRC condemns gross violation of human rights and indiscriminate targeting of civilians in Syria. **18 July:** Russia and China veto UN-SC draft resolution that would have threatened further sanctions against Syria. **20 July:** ICJ rules that Senegal must prosecute ex-Chadian leader or extradite him. **15 August:** Commission of inquiry set up by UN-HRC reports state policy to commit war crimes and blames insurgents for similar offences. **19 August:** UNSMIS mandate terminated by UN-SC. **6 September:** Venezuela gives notice of its denunciation of the ACHR. **29 September:** ECtHR refuses to block extradition of radical Muslim cleric and four others on terrorism charges. **14 November:** UN internal review concludes that the organization's response to the bloody final months of Sri Lanka's civil war was "a grave failure." **22 November:** UN-GA accords Palestine non-member state status. **6 December:** World's first regional treaty on internal displacement (Kampala treaty) comes into force. U.S. Senate fails to ratify UN Disabilities Convention. **20 December:** ICTR convicts former government minister of planning in Rwanda of genocide and rape as a crime against humanity.

2013 **24 January:** UN special rapporteur initiates investigation to ascertain lawfulness of drone strikes used in counterterrorist operation. **28 January:** Guatemala judge authorizes public trial of former dictator Efrain Rios Montt on charges of genocide and crimes against humanity. **1 February:** Italy convicts in absentia a former CIA station chief and two other Americans for their role in the kidnapping of an Egyptian cleric as part of the CIA's rendition program for terrorism suspects. **5 February:** Open Society Justice Initiative publishes a report documenting CIA secret detention, rendition and interrogation programs. **5 February:** Press makes public U.S. Justice Department's confidential memorandum about the legality of killing U.S.

nationals suspected of terrorism in drone strikes. 25 defendants accused of human rights abuses during operation Condor go on trial in Buenos Aires. **8 March:** Uhuru Kenyatta, charged of crimes against humanity by ICC, wins presidential election. **14 March:** Ieng Sary, former official of Khmer Rouge, dies before completion of his trial by Special Court on Cambodia. **15 March:** United Nations Commission on the Status of Women adopts declaration to combat violence against women. **19 March:** UN-GA endorses document condemning and calling for prevention of violence against women and girls. **21 March:** UN-HRC sets up three-person commission to investigate allegations of human rights violations in North Korea, including deprivation. **April:** Arms trade treaty approved by UN-GA opens for signature and ratification. **10 April:** UN-GA holds controversial two-day meeting on the role of international criminal justice. **12 April:** U.S. Justice Department makes public a 2012 U.S. immigration judge ordering deportation of former defense minister of El Salvador for his role in the 1980 rape and killing of four American churchwomen. **16 April:** A nonpartisan review, sponsored by the Constitution Project, a legal and advocacy group, concludes that the United States engaged in torture after the terror attacks in the United States on 11 September 2001. **17 April:** U.S. Supreme Court (*Kiobel v. Royal Dutch Petroleum Co.*) rules that claims in U.S. courts will generally not be allowed under the Alien Tort Statute. **9 May:** Kenya asks United Nations to halt ICC charges against Kenyatta. **10 May:** A Guatemalan national court finds Efrain Rios Montt, the former dictator who ruled the country during a period of civil war, guilty of genocide and crimes against humanity. **10 May:** A Bangladesh tribunal convicts and sentences to death an Islamist party leader for atrocities in the country's war of independence. **15 May:** UN-GA adopts nonbinding resolution encouraging the UN-SC to "consider appropriate measures" that would ensure accountability for the ongoing violence and human rights violations in Syria and expressing support for a political transition through the establishment of the Syrian National Coalition. **20 May:** Constitutional Court of Guatemala overturns genocide conviction of Rios Montt. **24 May:** Declaring the United States was "at a crossroads" in its fight against terrorism, President Obama announces that he would curtail the use of drones, recommit to the closing of the prison at Guantanamo Bay and seek new limits on his own war power. **29 May:** UN-HRC condemns intervention of foreign combatants on the government side in Syrian civil war. **30 May:** A Spanish judge issues international arrest warrants for 20 Salvadoran military officials in connection with the slaying of eight people, including six Jesuit priests. **June–August:** British newspaper *The Guardian* publishes top secret U.S. and British governments' mass surveillance programs leaked by a former intelligence analyst working for the U.S. National Security Agency. **7 June:** Britain announces that it will compensate more than 5,000 victims of abuse by British colonial forces in Kenya during the Mau Mau uprising. **7 June:** Cambodia passes law making denial of Khmer Rouge genocide illegal. **13 June:** United Nations declares 96,000 killed in Syrian civil war since March 2011. **4 July:** The ICC Legal Tools Database makes available "virtually all of the unrestricted records of the United Nations War Crimes Commission from 1943 to 1948." **13 July:** Mohamed Morsi is deposed as president of Egypt in a military coup d'état amid mass protests. **18 July:** Court of Justice of the European Union invalidates EU regulation reinstating UN counter-terrorism measure against Mr. Kadi. **28 August:** UN Special Rapporteur on the Promotion of Truth issues report assessing functioning of truth and reconciliation commissions. **5 September:** Domestic Workers Convention of ILO enters into force. **6 September:** Netherlands Supreme Court finds the Dutch States responsible for the death of a number of Muslims in the UN-protected Srebrenica enclave. **10 September:** Venezuela submits formal notice of denunciation of the American Convention on Human Rights. **27 September:** UN Human Rights Council sets up fact-finding commission to investigate torture and detention camps in North Korea. **22 October:** ECtHR rules that, while Russia had failed to adequately investigate the 1940 Katyn massacre of Polish prisoners of war, it had no jurisdiction over the massacre itself and did not find that the suffering of the families of the disappeared constituted a form of inhuman or degrading treatment. **8 November:** Nine imprisoned Basque militants ordered freed after European Court of Human Rights rules that Spain had acted illegally in retroactively extending their prison terms. **8 November:** European Court of Human Rights orders Greece to open civil unions to same-sex couples.

Introduction

If the sheer number of references to human rights in media headlines or government statements is of any guidance, human rights concerns now appear virtually at the center of the framework of the norms, principles and obligations that shape relations within the international community both among and within states. That political journey began, perhaps arbitrarily, on 10 December 1948 when the United Nations General Assembly (UN-GA) embraced and proclaimed the Universal Declaration of Human Rights (UDHR), a ringing endorsement and advocacy of the notion that regardless of race, religion or nationality, all men and women, everywhere in the world, are entitled to the human rights and fundamental freedoms simply because they are human.

At that time, none of UDHR's progenitors would have been able to foresee the contours of the international human rights landscape that emerged in subsequent decades. The UDHR itself is not a binding treaty and makes no provisions for enforcement, but it has acquired a status roughly equivalent to customary international law and spawned over 250 multilateral human rights and humanitarian conventions and treaties. These legally binding international instruments are monitored by a multiplicity of global and regional actors, notably "special rapporteurs" and "expert" bodies, judicial institutions and vigilant non-governmental organizations (NGOs) which rarely shy away from loudly denouncing and mobilizing public opinion against violations of human rights. At the same time, numerous states have enacted legislation incorporating internationally recognized human rights norms into their municipal laws.

The progressive expansion and development of this imposing normative framework and the proliferation of human rights actors in the second half of the 20th century has, if not eroded, certainly transformed traditional notions of sovereignty. International law, which until recently focused exclusively on rules governing the external relations of states and their representatives, now imposes substantial restrictions on the domestic affairs of states and protects ordinary persons against mistreatment by their own government. The principle of state sovereignty which prohibits any interference into the domestic affairs of nations appears to be questioned by the notion of a "responsibility to protect," an "emerging norm" which would invalidate the principle of nonintervention and sanction armed interventions against states committing or not preventing acts of genocide, ethnic cleansing or systematic rape.

The long-standing notion that government authorities are beyond the reach of justice for acts performed in their official state capacity was breached by the Nuremberg and Tokyo trials of the 1940s and has since been further eroded with the creation of ad hoc criminal tribunals by the United Nations Security Council (UN-SC) and, more importantly, the establishment in 2002 of a permanent tribunal, the International Criminal Court (ICC), to prosecute individuals for genocide, crimes against humanity and war crimes. It is not uncommon now for states, governments, local officials and military commanders to find themselves in the docks of the accused and to be sentenced to prison terms for human rights abuses. Meanwhile, individuals have been granted access to the enforcement mechanisms set up by international human rights conventions. In steps toward a universal approach to human rights law, there have been investigations or prosecutions in such countries as Argentina, Australia, Austria, Belgium, Canada, Denmark, Finland, France, Germany, Great Britain, Israel, Netherlands, Norway, Spain, Sweden, Switzerland and the United States based on the principle of "universal jurisdiction," a notion which posits that every country has an interest in bringing to justice the perpetrators of grave crimes, no matter where the crime was committed and regardless of the nationality of the perpetrators or the victims. In the United States, human rights groups have used the dormant provision of an obscure 1789 Alien Tort Statute to hold state officials and multinational corporations liable for violations of human rights norms.

The growing salience of human rights issues in internal politics further underlines the normative power that the human rights discourse has acquired. In the United States, the release of internal governmental memoranda which justified the use of techniques euphemistically dubbed "enhanced interrogation techniques" like water boarding, sleep deprivation and isolation provoked a storm of controversies and a political debate that still resonates today. The long-standing practice of female genital mutilation has become the focus of intense debates within countries where the practice has deep historical and cultural roots. Attempts by national or local legislatures to label as genocide the World War I massacres of Armenians by the Ottoman regime provoke indignation and outrage in Turkey. The recent Spanish government decision to enact legislation requiring local authorities to search for mass graves of victims of the civil war and mandating the removal of all symbols of the fascist regime from public buildings infuriated the right-wing opposition and prompted the Catholic Church to beatify some 500 "martyrs" killed by republican militias. When the Israeli government announced that it planned to cut the energy supply to the Gaza Strip, several human rights groups requested an injunction from Israel's Supreme Court arguing that such a decision would create a humanitarian crisis leading to human rights violations. The UN Security Council practice of blacklisting suspected terrorists has triggered intense criticism centering on issues of denial of due process.

There is also a darker side to the story though. An American political scientist calculated that, in the 20th century, 262 million persons had been killed by their own governments, victims of what he called "democide." More recently, another political scientist documented no less than 50 genocides and political mass murders in the 50 years following the end of World War II with a death toll ranging from a conservative 12 million to a high of 22 million people. Civilian casualties amounted to about 25 percent of all casualties during World War I. Because of changes in the nature of armed conflict, that ratio rose to around 65 percent in World War II and often exceeds 90 percent of casualties today. Traditional forms of slavery and the slave trade are no longer legally acceptable, but such slave-like practices as the trafficking of women and children, the use of children in armed conflicts, exploitative labor conditions, debt bondage and the sale of human organs still persist. Between 10 and 20 million people are subjected to debt bondage today and it is believed that some 200,000 to 300,000 children are involved in armed conflicts in the world. There are up to 25 million internally displaced persons around the world who have been forced to leave their homes because of war and human rights abuses. Indigenous peoples which number 300 to 350 million people spread over 70 countries face widespread and deeply entrenched discrimination and racism.

Against this background, the purpose of this historical dictionary is to explore both the theory and the practice of international human rights. "Practice" in this book means examining the norms and institutions that make up the "architecture" of the global human rights regime and the processes and procedures through which such norms are "enforced." In this regard, an attempt is made to strike a balance between a narrowly focused "hands-on" "how-to" "toolbox" approach and an exceedingly broad methodology that would center on scholarly theoretical speculations. Addressed primarily to interested laymen, practitioners and students of human rights, the volume provides a broad overview of the mechanisms involved in the emergence, spread and implementation of international human rights norms. Particular attention is also given to the political and sociological factors that shape and constrain the operation and functioning of international human rights institutions.

Readers will find here factual answers and policy-oriented interpretations that will assist in identifying the tasks, actions and steps involved in engaging, applying, exercising and realizing human rights standards and norms in their political context. To comprehend how human rights ideas turn into "praxis" thus requires an appreciation and understanding of the actors involved in the recognition, production and dissemination of human rights norms and standards. This also entails the identification of the tools used in measuring and tracking respect for or breaches of rights. Finally, the task involves a mapping of the instruments which can be relied on in the enforcement of human rights norms. Appropriate references to international humanitarian law practice will be made whenever it intersects with human rights law.

THE ACTORS

A handful of experts and government officials prepared the UDHR in 1948. More than 150 government delegations and hundreds of individuals, officials of international organizations and NGOs participated in the drafting of the Rome Statute of the International Criminal Court in 1998. As is the case for other international human rights instruments, not all of these actors weighed equally in the final outcome. The modalities of their involvement varied considerably and so did their incentives and motivations. In the world of legal and *realpolitik* fictions, states ultimately determine what will be adopted. In practice, the process of standards' setting is a coalition-building exercise entailing cooperation, bargaining and acquiescence by a wide-ranging number of state and non-state actors. The human rights field is not now—if it ever was—the exclusive preserve of governments. It is also populated by a wide range of "non-state actors," a broad category encompassing such disparate entities as NGOs, transnational corporations, think tanks, "epistemic communities" as well as international organizations and "norm entrepreneurs." The list is not exhaustive. A key determinant of success in multilateral diplomacy is the emergence of "lead" countries that bring together "friends" or "like-minded" states, coalitions of NGOs and international civil servants which coalesce around a given issue and secure its approval.

States

As crowded, vibrant, disorderly and confusing as the international human rights field may be, it is still overshadowed by sovereign states and the governments which claim to represent them. Non-state actors influence and shape its contours, but they do not make human rights law nor do they enforce it. Ultimately, states do both. Under international law, the sovereignty of states implies that each state is free to independently determine its policies, that it can participate in the international arena on an equal footing with other states and that it can enter into treaties limiting its sovereignty on the basis of its consent. Sovereignty also enjoins states not to intervene into the domestic affairs of other states. Of course, in practice, the capacity of states to act autonomously varies considerably and hinges on their capabilities and the distribution of power between them. But under the doctrine of sovereignty and the principles of equality, non-intervention, non-interference and exclusive control over one's internal affairs that flow from it, it is states that ultimately determine what multilateral treaties—the main source of international human rights law—they will be bound by. Respecting, protecting and fulfilling human rights obligations hinges on the consent of states; they have the sole and final authority to embrace and eventually implement and enforce human rights tenets and injunctions within their boundaries.

In this regard, it should be emphasized that governments are not monolithic entities. Normally, ministries of foreign affairs staff conduct norm-setting negotiations and they may seek the advice and the views of other ministries (most frequently Justice and Interior) back home. But it is by no means unusual for different ministries in a country to take different positions on a particular human rights issue, a situation which provides lobbying opportunities for other actors. Changes in governments, ministers and representatives may also affect national negotiating positions.

Be it as it may, the centrality of the state in human rights practice underlines the contradictions that constrain the international human rights system and the eminently political nature of human rights practice. On the one hand, the norm of sovereignty posits that the participation of states in any international human rights regime is purely voluntary. On the other hand, human rights law seeks to place limits as well as conditions on the exercise of state sovereignty. In the human rights discourse, states are "duty bearers" that have the obligation to meet the claims of "rights holders." From this standpoint, the entitlement of individual rights generates the corresponding legal duty of states to protect against, prevent, and remedy human rights violations and state governments may thus become accountable to international authorities for domestic acts affecting human rights. The practice of human rights institutions cannot be understood without comprehending the state-driven nature of international human rights norms and standards and the political dynamics through which rights can be reconciled with and accommodate state sovereignty. Human rights law does not necessarily trump sovereignty but, at one and the same time, it does accommodate state sovereignty while placing constraints on its exercise. For example, most human rights treaties allow states to temporarily limit some human rights protections in times of "public emergencies" for the purpose of protecting the safety and well-being of everyone. But human rights law does not allow them to suspend so-called nonderogable rights." In addition, human rights law underlines a number of procedural conditions under which derogations from rights may be permitted. In the same vein, individuals may lodge complaints against their governments in a number of international judicial or quasi-judicial bodies. But before bringing their claims to these international bodies they must first have exhausted all available domestic remedies.

Interstate Organizations

There is considerable controversy among scholars and laymen as to the "actorness" of international organizations. To what extent can they be differentiated from their constituting environment, enjoy a degree of identity, structural and functional autonomy and have the capacity to influence the statist environment they spring from? So-called realists take the view that international organizations are simply creatures and servants of their principals. At the other side of the academic divide, "constructivists" argue that states' identities, interests and their sovereignty are "constructed" through social practice, socialization and interaction of a multiplicity of actors. Because such ideas and processes form a structure of their own which in turn impacts on international actors, international organizations enjoy a significant though not necessarily complete autonomy in relation to their principals and can have a conditional role in international political processes. Studies have indeed shown in this regard that international organizations can acquire a life of their own deviating from and expanding on their original mandates in ways dictated not by states but by the "constitutive" nature of bureaucracies and their culture. Interstate organizations (IOs) can thus variously be "managers," "enforcers," and "authorities." From a public policy perspective, they can produce "norm-making" policies or "distributive," "regulatory," and "redistributive" policies which have distinct implications for the practice of human rights.

Normative policies may be viewed as prescriptive statements of action in support of desirable goals and aspirational ways of doing things. In the field of human rights, the United Nations "legislative bodies" produce non-binding "resolutions," recommendations," "directives" and the like which carry with them a seal of approval (or disapproval) or of "collective legitimization" of broad aims and objectives supported by a majority of states and non-state actors in the international community. A number of intergovernmental organizations, primarily the specialized agencies of the United Nations, have been involved in distributive policies providing services and defining international rules to govern a steadily expanding set of transnational transactions which have been portrayed as "the soft infrastructure" of the world economy.

Regulatory policies place restrictions on individuals and institutions and may entail a degree of coercion by prohibiting unacceptable forms of behavior and requiring mandatory alternate ones. Instances of regulatory policies include the sanction regimes adopted by the UN Security Council which entail such measures as arms, commodities and oil embargoes, travel bans, partial asset freezes to economic blockades and more comprehensive measures. Their purpose has widely varied over time depending on whether they were designed to contain a conflict, to encourage compromise by parties to a conflict, to force a state to withdraw from a territory, to hand over suspects or to cease active hostilities. They have increasingly been framed in a human rights language and designed to achieve human rights objectives.

The adjudicatory functions of international courts are another long-standing and expanding variety of the IO's regulatory policies extending back to the unheralded and underestimated advisory and compulsory rulings of the Permanent Court of International Justice (PCIJ) and now reflected in the jurisprudence of the UN International Court of Justice (ICJ). A related striking postwar development has been the emergence of human rights regional courts. In interpreting and applying their mandates, these bodies have not shied away from confronting states in sensitive areas long held to belong to their "domestic jurisdiction." In so doing and with varying degrees of effectiveness, their interpretation and application of human rights norms procedural requirements and remedies have in no negligible manner impacted national constitutions, law, policies and societies, and enhanced the principle of accountability.

Typically, redistributive policies involve the transfer of goods and services from one social group to another, most frequently by means of taxation. The Bretton Woods Institutions—the World Bank and the International Monetary Fund (IMF)—enjoy a strong executive capacity and have acted as resource-transfer mechanisms channeling large discretionary powers' assessed or voluntary state contributions to public or semipublic recipients. From that standpoint, the World Bank and the IMF exert considerable influence on the economic predicament of many countries and may thus hinder or foster the realization of human rights.

The role of the secretariats of international organizations in standards' setting should not be underestimated. To be sure, international civil servants like to portray themselves as the mere servants of their state masters. There is truth in this assertion and many states are indeed reluctant if willing at all to allow them to play—at least publicly—active and independent roles.

But beyond collecting and collating comments and convening and servicing intergovernmental or expert meetings, international bureaucrats often shape and influence interstate negotiations through the backstage provision of information, expertise and informal advice. Not infrequently, they may become "norm entrepreneurs," a point that shall be revisited below.

Civil Society Organizations

The emergence of NGOs advocating and promoting human rights internationally is probably the most important postwar development that has reshaped the international human rights arena. The heading of NGO encompasses disparate entities in terms of leadership, internal structures, modalities of action, sources of funding and policy objectives as evidenced by the proliferation of acronyms such as CSO (for civil society organizations), GONGO (for government-operated NGOs), INGO (for international NGOs), TANGO (for technical assistance NGOs), GSOs (for grassroots support organizations) and MANGO (for market advocacy NGOs). Focusing on their organizational makeup, practitioners and observers also talk about "caucuses," "coalitions," "networks, "movements," and "umbrella organizations." Some NGOs assign themselves a broad spectrum of tasks ranging across the entire spectrum of internationally recognized human rights, others concentrate on the substantially or geographically limited human rights sector and still others may pursue single issue objectives. A number of them act primarily as lobbyists while others provide technical services.

Whatever the label used, NGOs are essentially independent, non-profit entities situated between government and business which mobilize individuals coalescing around shared interests, purposes and values and seeking to influence public policy. Normally registered as associations under domestic law, they are endowed with some very limited and circumscribed rights under international law. Many are perennially understaffed and underfinanced and their lifespan may be short, thus prompting questions about their accountability to the public at large and toward their own membership. NGOs have no coercive power, military or economic; only the capacity "to orchestrate shame." For this reason, their activities often elicit reticence not to say outright hostility on the part of governments.

Yet, in spite of these obstacles, driven by a global consciousness and beliefs in the basic tenets of human rights and further empowered by revolutionary changes in information technology, in particular e-mail, faxes and now social media, NGOs have become prominent actors in the field of human rights and are variously portrayed as "paradigm shifters," "monitors" and "law makers." Combining domestic with international action, NGOs gather information, investigate, advocate, name and shame, lobby government and international organizations, litigate, educate and fundraise. At the international level, NGOs may channel humanitarian appeals on behalf of individual victims of human rights violations or persons in immediate danger by bringing them to the attention of the UN High Commissioner for Human Rights (UN-HCHR), the special rapporteurs and working groups operating under the authority of the UN Human Rights Council or the secretariats of the Inter-American Commission on Human Rights and the European Court of Human Rights. They may file complaints to UN treaty bodies, the International Labour Organization (ILO) under its relevant conventions, the UN Human Rights Council under the 1503 Procedure or petition regional human rights bodies such as the Inter-American Commission on Human Rights.

In regard to large-scale violations of rights, NGOs frequently seek to mobilize public opinion to influence the policies of foreign governments and international organizations through the publication of reports, dispatchs from fact-finding missions and the publication of eyewitness accounts or recourses to formal international mechanisms. NGOs domestic initiatives range from letter-writing campaigns and exposing human rights violations in the media to engaging all available local remedies, initiating legal challenges and pressing governments to take "urgent actions."

The impact of these activities varies considerably depending on the nature of the issue at hand and its political implications. Much also hinges on the credibility, reputation and legitimacy of the groups involved. The end of the Cold War, the restoration of democracy in Eastern Europe, the democratic transitions in Latin America and the current battles against executives breaches in civil liberties in the post–September 11 era cannot be understood without reference to the political activism of NGOs. More specifically, the UN Convention against Torture is very much a by-product of a campaign orchestrated by Amnesty International (AI). The Ottawa Treaty on antipersonnel landmines and the Rome Statute of the ICC were both driven by large NGO coalitions which generated public support and political momentum.

Indeed, the contributions of NGOs to the promotion and protection of human rights cannot be underestimated. For all intents and practical purposes, they have become an essential part of the international human rights protection and monitoring architecture, and the argument can be reasonably made that human rights are enforced more by activist NGOs than state officials or international lawyers. The reader may get a better sense of the weight of civil society knowing that Human Rights Watch has an annual budget exceeding $60 million, a staff of 330 and a presence in 90 countries. AI is by and large made up of volunteers but its International Secretariat boasts 500 professional staff members loosely overseeing the activities of over 50 sections worldwide.

NGOs have achieved a significant degree of (grudging) recognition as participants of international intergovernmental meetings. They are involved in UN global conferences and their preparations. Under the terms of Article 71 of the UN Charter, they have "consultative status" with the Economic and Social Council (ECOSOC). NGOs also sit as observers in the UN Human Rights Council and have been granted a degree of participation in its Universal Periodic Review Process. They can even contribute to the proceedings of the UN Security Council under a special formula approved by the Council in the early 1990s. Regional organizations such as the Council of Europe have issued rules similar to those of the ECOSOC. International judicial and quasi-judicial bodies including the European Court of Human Rights (ECtHR), the Inter-American Commission of Human Rights (IACmHR), the African Commission for Human and People's Rights (ACmHPR) and the recently established African Court (ACtHPR) and, to a certain extent, the European Court of Justice all grant legal standing to NGOs. The overall trend is definitely toward the development of informal and, to a lesser extent, formal arrangements and mechanisms for NGOs' consultation and engagement in human rights practice.

Experts

Think tanks, "special rapporteurs" working for international entities involved in human rights, charitable foundations, academic institutions and other individuals all play a vital role in standards' setting. Their authority and influence derives, in large part, from their claims of independence and objectivity, expertise and technical knowledge.

Public policy research and analysis institutions, commonly called think tanks, have proliferated in recent decades and acted as a link between civil society and governments at the national, regional and global levels. As not-for-profit organizations, think tanks differ widely from one another in their ideological perspectives, degree of independence, sources of funding, issue focus and prospective audience. Some receive direct government support; others rely on private individuals, advocacy groups or corporate donors. Some are politically non-partisan; others are in effect special interest groups promoting their own political agenda or providing intellectual support to politicians or political parties. But they all essentially generate public policy and problem-solving–oriented research, analysis and advice for national and international policymakers. There are currently 6,300 think tanks, two-thirds of them located in North America and Western Europe. Among those, think tanks concerned with human rights issues continue to grow in number and size and have become more transnational through cross-border collaborative activities. Such is the case, for instance, of the Global Center for the Responsibility to Protect, an entity which, in close cooperation with NGOs, governments and academia, engages in advocacy, conducts research designed to further understanding of Responsibility to Protect and recommends and supports strategies to consolidate the norm. Regional and global intergovernmental organizations have come to recognize the usefulness of the role think tanks play in the policy- and norm-making processes as illustrated by the close interaction between UN civil servants, government representatives and think tanks all brought together under the umbrella of the policy research–oriented activities of the International Peace Institute.

Lurking below the radar screen of most observers, private and public foundations through their charitable giving exert a significant influence on the process of instituting international norms and policymaking. Their numbers have increased exponentially in recent decades. The Foundation Center, a leading source of information about philanthropy worldwide based in New York with branches in four other American cities, estimates that there are some 76,000 foundations in the United States. Their size varies considerably and their resources are enormous. The top-30 most wealthy foundations, based in the United States, the Netherlands, Great Britain, the United Arab Emirates, Hong Kong, Germany, Sweden, Denmark and Portugal, have combined endowment assets close to $260 billion. Total grant giving by U.S. foundations alone amounted to $45 billion in 2010 and, in 2012, U.S. Foundation International giving exceeded $10 billion to 20,000 recipients for over 50,000 grants. Exactly how this grant giving translates in terms of promoting human rights remains clouded with uncertainty. A recent survey of European foundations found that over one-third of them gave grants or operated programs intended to benefit women and girls. It is also known that foundations such as the network of Open Society Foundations seek to promote democratic governance, the rule of law and the development of independent media, education, public health, economic, legal and social reform. They channeled more than $8 billion between 1979 and 2010 into local human rights organizations throughout Eastern Europe, Africa and Asia, thus helping to launch such NGOs as Physicians for Human Rights and the Lawyers Committee, Global Rights. The Ford Foundation also devoted resources to build the infrastructure of civil society organizations assisting, for instance, in the "incubation" of Human Rights Watch, and more recently, the International Center for Transitional Justice.

Many universities include variously called "centers" or "institutes" which offer interdisciplinary educational programs, carry out research on human rights issues and engage in promotional activities to advance respect for human rights. A number of university institutions have played a key role in standards' setting. To cite one particular but telling instance, several expert initiatives were launched by Maastricht University in the Netherlands which led to the formulation of early versions of the Optional Protocol to the Convention on the Elimination of All Forms of Discrimination against Women, the 1986 Limburg Principles on the Implementation of the International Covenant on Economic, Social and Cultural Rights and the 1997 Maastricht Guidelines on Violations of Economic, Social and Cultural Rights.

Individuals can also make a difference. Deservedly labeled "norm entrepreneurs" and acting singly, or through ad hoc bodies, NGOs or international organizations, these individuals draw attention to a problem while offering a solution or a norm which provides an alternative understanding and appreciation of the problem embedded in well-known principles enshrined in international human rights instruments. They also participate in the process of agenda setting and law making as they seek to engage the participation and support of other national or international actors. The drafters of the Universal Declaration of Human Rights may be portrayed as norm entrepreneurs. President Oscar Arias, Cherif Bassouini, Jan Herman Burgers, Juan Mendez Aryeh Neir, Peter Berenson, Jody Williams, among many others, led human rights activities warranting their being labeled norm entrepreneurs. UN secretaries-general often play a similar role from their bully pulpits (Boutros Ghali in regard to "democracy," Kofi Annan to corporate "social responsibility"). Development economists in the United Nations Development Programme (UNDP) were instrumental in the development and "cascading" of the norm of "human development." International Commissions that bring together eminent personalities have also produced influential norms. Sustainable development and the "responsibility to protect," for instance, were initiated by the Brundland Commission and the International Commission of State Sovereignty and Intervention, respectively.

Special rapporteurs, individuals working on behalf of the regional organizations or the United Nations within the scope of "Special Procedures" mechanisms established by the United Nations Human Rights Council, examine, monitor, advise and publicly report on human rights problems, respond to individual complaints, conduct studies, provide advice on technical cooperation at the country level, and engage in general promotional activities. The UN Special rapporteur on torture, for example, discreetly participated in the elaboration of the Optional Protocol to the Convention against Torture by providing expert opinion and advice to the drafting committee. The landmark studies and recommendations emanating from the experts sitting in the "working groups" of the UN Sub-Commission on the

Promotion and Protection of Human Rights have in no small way contributed to creating conditions favoring the adoption of new human rights standards on minorities, the administration of justice, the rights of non-citizens and contemporary forms of slavery among other subjects.

In fact, numerous important "soft law" instruments originate from the Sub-Commission including the Basic Principles and Guidelines on the Right to a Remedy and Reparation for Victims of Gross Violations of International Human Rights Law and Serious Violations of International Humanitarian Law, the Set of Principles for the Protection and Promotion of Human Rights through Action to Combat Impunity, and the Norms on the Responsibilities of Transnational Corporations and Other Business Enterprises. Collectively and often with the assistance of NGOs or the financial support of international organizations, victims or those who were affected by human rights violations may be brought into the standards' setting process. Special funds set up in the United Nations have enabled representatives of indigenous communities, peoples with disabilities and relatives of disappeared persons to attend intergovernmental meetings where international human rights instruments of concern to them were being negotiated.

STANDARDS' SETTING: THE ISSUE OF RECOGNITION

Given the centrality of the state, the practice of human rights involves intricately linked matters of sovereignty, law, power and values. Taking also into account that human rights norms can be used as benchmarks for conferring or withholding authority and legitimacy and as the basis for value claims by individuals or groups, it is hardly surprising that the production of human rights norms should constantly be a politically contested process.

The adoption of the UN Charter in 1945 and of the Universal Declaration of Human Rights three years later were the first breaches in the hitherto universally shared legal and political view that international law did not place limits on the right of sovereign states to oppress their nationals. The idea that "every human being, in every society, is entitled to have basic autonomy and freedoms respected and basic needs satisfied" and that he or she may "make a fundamental claim that an authority, or some part of society do—or refrain from doing—something that affects significantly one's human dignity" has been expanded to a widening range of personal, legal, civil political, economic and social and cultural rights enshrined in global and regional multilateral treaties.

This process, by and large, has been a state-controlled and highly politicized one that has generated a fuzzy and shifting line between the territorial claims of state jurisdiction and the universalist or cosmopolitan prescriptions of human rights norms. Disputes over exactly what those matters are which, under Article 2.7 of the Charter, constitute "matters which are essentially within the jurisdiction of states" prohibiting any UN intervention have flared up and simmered since the inception of the organization when India and South Africa clashed over the question of determining whether the treatment of Indians in the Union of South Africa could be included in the agenda of the first session of the General Assembly. They continue to erupt as evidenced by more recent contentious debates about the implementation of a "responsibility to protect" or a right of "humanitarian intervention."

A related controversial issue is that states differ on the nature of the rights that must be protected. Human rights scholars, in a nod to the 1789 French Revolution motto of "Liberty, Equality, Fraternity," generally refer to three "generations" of rights with "first-generation" rights deriving from the principle of "liberty." They are also known as "negative" rights in the sense that they focus on the civil and political rights that states may not encroach upon. Such rights are enshrined in the International Covenant on Civil and Political Rights and include the right to life and personal integrity, due process of the law, freedom of expression, religion and conscience, the right to participate in free elections and government, the right to marry, the right to equality and freedom from discrimination. "Second-generation" rights are based on the principle of equality. They are also referred to as "positive" rights because states have an obligation "to take steps" "to the maximum of available resources" to "achieving progressively" their "full realization" (Art. 2, 1 of the International Covenant of Economic, Social and Cultural Rights [ICESCR]). These include under the ICESCR, the right of work, to join trade unions, the right to social security, to protection for the family, mothers and children, the right to be "free from hunger," to have an adequate standard of living, including food, clothing and housing, health and education. Based on the principle of fraternity, "third-generation" human rights are "solidarity" or "collective" rights among states such as the right to development, to a healthy environment, to peace, to the sharing of a common heritage and humanitarian assistance.

First-, second-, and third-generation rights are deemed to be "universal," "indivisible" and "interdependent," that is to say they are coequal in importance, form an integrated whole and require the same degree of protection and promotion because the improvement of one right facilitates the enjoyment of the others and, conversely, the abridgement or curtailment of a right adversely affects the others. As an AI document asserts, "Freedom from fear and want can only be relieved if conditions are created where everyone may enjoy his or her economic, social, and cultural rights and his or her civil and political rights." The right to life, for instance, has been traditionally considered as offering protection against killing by state actors. But it can also be linked to positive measures by governments to reduce infant mortality and foster life-expectancy. The right to health relates to the availability of basic health services but also to other underlying preconditions for health such as access to safe water and sanitation, environmental and occupational health, health education and adequate nutrition. In turn, the right to food can be considered part of the right to health. The right to adequate housing links with the availability of basic services such as drinking water, the availability of health care services and freedom from health-related environmental health hazards.

In a 2004 advisory opinion, the ICJ stated that the construction and establishment of a "security" wall separating Israel and the Occupied Palestinian territory constrained freedom of movement and by the same token infringed upon the enjoyment of social and economic rights. One can also make the case that debt servicing by developing countries locks people in poverty and blocks the practical realization and full enjoyment of human rights to the extent that the elimination of government-funded social services that provide food, shelter, health and education services threatens the lives of vulnerable population groups. In the same vein, it has been argued that the conditionalities imposed by the Bretton Woods Institutions in their structural adjustment programs erode the capacity of individuals to enjoy their rights.

This integrated approach to the practice of human rights has been the mainstay of NGOs and UN human rights bodies. Opponents contend that economic, social and cultural rights are fundamentally different from civil and political rights and require completely different approaches. The former are resource intensive, non-justiciable and difficult to measure quantitatively. They require the active provision of entitlements beyond the financial means and capacity of most states. At best, they are aspirations or goals rather than legally grounded claims. Conversely, civil and political rights are cost-free, immediate, precise, and justiciable.

The contrast may be overdrawn but in practice, states select from first-, second-, and third-generation rights and give priority to one category instead of another depending on their traditions, cultures and politics. An early casualty of this pattern of cherry picking was the Universal Declaration of Human Rights which, because of the ideological split between East and West, spawned two binding covenants rather a single document. But politics continues to collide with the rhetoric of indivisibility. Western states tend to give priority to civil and political rights over economic, social and cultural rights, while countries of the Global South (and previously, socialist countries during the Cold War) have embraced economic, social and cultural rights and solidarity rights. Such competing and mutually exclusive conceptions of human rights provide fertile ground for mutual recriminations and suspicions. For Southern states, the emphasis on civil and political rights under the guise of universality is yet another instance of Western imperialism and hardly veiled justification for intrusion, domination and control. For Northern states, the focus on socioeconomic and collective rights is an attempt to inject an inappropriate element of obligation into international development cooperation practices.

Be that as it may, while a case can be made that there are solid reasons to believe that there is a "structural indivisibility" of the whole gamut of human rights, there is little political commitment behind the idea. It is striking in this regard that neither the IMF nor the World Bank (to a lesser extent) have acknowledged or clarified their human rights obligations or carried out human rights impact evaluations of their work. Likewise, there is little quarreling about the substantive objectives of the Millennium Development Goals, but member states of the United Nations have deliberately refrained from contextualizing them into a human rights framework.

To add another layer of complexity, some states deny the universality of rights altogether on the grounds of "cultural relativism." That view, forcefully articulated by Southeast Asian countries in the 1990s and more recently by Muslim states, draws on the anthropological notion that human rights like any other beliefs and activities are embedded in the local context of a person's own culture. Insofar as cultures vary in place and time, they all are equally valid and so are the "rights" that they nurture. Under these conditions, the focus of Western attention on individual civil and political rights may be appropriate for that region of the world. To extend their scope beyond that region in effect violates respect for other cultures and the norms that they value, notably, communal and group ties and the importance of the duty of obedience to authority. The argument of cultural relativism frequently includes or leads to the assertion that the universalist discourse of the North and its selective set of priorities on civil and political rights is a barely hidden attempt to give moral legitimacy to a liberal economic agenda which in turn supports economic programs such as the structural adjustment programs of the Bretton Woods Institutions.

The claims of cultural relativism pose the logically awkward and politically intractable question of how universal human rights can exist in a culturally diverse world. The universalist theory of human rights with its emphasis on the value and primacy it places on the individual is indeed, historically speaking, a by-product and a reflection of the Western political and cultural experience. In this context, the argument that the universal human rights discourse could disguise a hidden agenda is not altogether implausible.

But that does not make the cultural relativist discourse agenda-free either. Looking back, the preparatory work on drafting the Universal Declaration of Human Rights amply demonstrates that its drafters did indeed seek to reflect and accommodate differing cultural and religious traditions in the world in the language that they eventually agreed upon. More disquieting, however, is the fact that all too often the argument that traditional cultures are sufficient to protect human dignity is used to reassert state discretion to determine the scope of their treaty obligations or to stymie international scrutiny of their human rights practices. Cultural traditions then trump international law and standards and are deemed to govern state compliance. In that sense, cultural relativism poses an existential challenge to the effectiveness of the international legal system of human rights that has been so painstakingly constructed over the decades.

Norm Making: The Uncertain Contours of Treaty-Based Human Rights Law

Individual and group rights are recognized in international human rights law which, like international law, is grounded on treaties, state practice ("custom") and "soft law" instruments. Treaties are the most important source of human rights law. Such treaties may focus on a single right (life), a theme (civil and political rights, disappearances) or protect a particular group (women, children, migrants). They may be global or regional in scope. International instruments produced under the auspices of the United Nations—the so-called "core" international treaties and their optional protocols—address economic, social and cultural rights, civil and political rights, the elimination of racial and gender discrimination, protection against torture and forced disappearance and the rights of women, children, migrants and persons with disabilities.

Instances of regional instruments include in Africa, the African Charter on Human and People's Rights and the African Charter on the Rights and Welfare of the Child; in Latin America, the American Convention on Human Rights, the Inter-American Convention to Prevent and Punish Torture, the Inter-American Convention on Forced Disappearance of Persons, the Inter-American Convention on the Prevention, Punishment, and Eradication of Violence against Women; and in Europe, the Charter of Fundamental Rights of the European Union, the Convention on Action against Trafficking in Human Beings, the European Charter for Regional or Minority Languages, the European Convention on Human Rights, the European Convention for the Prevention of Torture and Inhuman or Degrading Treatment or Punishment, the European Social Charter, and Revised Social Charter and the Framework

Convention for the Protection of National Minorities. United Nations human rights treaties have the most universal coverage but the weakest accountability provisions as their implementation is monitored by committees of experts, the so-called treaty bodies (discussed below), which have only a power of recommendation. In contrast, regional systems (especially the European system) have stronger oversight bodies endowed with quasi-judicial or judicial powers.

International human rights law assigns rights to individuals and negative as well as positive responsibilities and duties to states: respect, protect, fulfill. Thus states should not take measures that would adversely impact human rights protections. States must have long-term strategies to "realize" rights. They may be responsible for the action of third parties if they act negligently in preventing rights violations over which they have jurisdiction. States may take exceptional measures and derogate from some rights in emergency situations such as armed conflict, civil and violent unrest or environmental and natural catastrophes. But these measures are permissible and valid subject to fulfilling a number of procedural and substantive requirements set by treaty law such as qualifications of severity, temporariness, proclamation and notification, legality, proportionality, consistency with other obligations under international law and non-discrimination. Certain rights—peremptory norms—should be protected all the time and may not be suspended even for reasons of national security. They include the right to life and the prohibition of slavery, torture or cruel, inhuman or degrading treatment or punishment and retroactive penal measures.

The participation of states in the treaty-making process is entirely voluntary. Likewise, the obligations arising from human rights treaties as well as the limitations they place on their sovereignty, one can presume, are equally freely assumed. From this perspective, the international human rights treaty system seeks to engage states in adhering to global standards and obligations by spelling out benchmarks for assessment, providing a remedial forum for individual complaints and encouraging a credible national process of review and reform. Human rights treaties have reshaped domestic legal systems and numerous instances of legal reform inspired by treaty obligations can be cited. National courts invoke international standards in their rulings. Special rapporteurs, country-specific rapporteurs, fact-finding missions and working groups, treaty-monitoring bodies, human rights courts and NGOs have done much in the way of concretizing these lofty aspirations by applying them to concrete situations and providing means of redress to victims of human rights violations.

This being said, neither the legal character of these treaty-sanctioned rights nor the expanding number of state ratifications should conceal the fact that these global proclamations of entitlements ultimately remain subject to the acquiescence of governments. State discretion remains of the essence. Practitioners seeking to measure degrees of state acceptance may rely on a variety of "indicators," notably the number of ratifications. This criterion, however, is not necessarily a reliable measure of state capacity or consent. Reservations entered by state parties to human rights treaties are far more revealing. For instance, the UN Convention on the Elimination of All Forms of Discrimination against Women has achieved near universality in the number of ratifications that it has received. It has also the dubious distinction of having drawn the highest number of reservations. Some relate to ancillary and relatively unimportant matters of procedure. Others like those of Muslim states which emphasize the primacy of Sharia Law in the implementation of treaty obligations, in essence undercut the norm of gender equality which guides the Convention. In the same vein, the reservations adopted by the U.S. Senate labeling human rights treaties "non-self-executing" simply make them toothless.

Norm Making: Other Sources of Human Rights Law

Another important source of human rights law is "custom" which international legal scholars define as "an established state practice, accepted by many nations." Custom has a long and rich history in the relations among states largely because treaties use a vague language and many international obligations are not expressed in treaties. In the field of human rights, for instance, it is now generally acknowledged that states have a duty to respect international human rights, to ensure them and to prevent their violations. In a similar vein, it is recognized that the breach of any international obligation by a state or organ of a state constitutes an international tort whose commission involves a corresponding duty to make reparations. Having been repeatedly and consistently affirmed in the decisions of international judicial bodies, national human rights courts and through national and regional law and practice, the idea may be understood to have attained the status of customary law.

The 1948 Universal Declaration of Human Rights (UDHR) technically speaking is merely a recommendation of the UN General Assembly. Many of its provisions, however, have become statements of customary law. The UDHR has also formed the basis of legally binding global treaties such as the Convention on the Rights of the Child, and the Convention against Torture or regional instruments like the European Convention of Human Rights. Individual states have incorporated its provisions into their constitutions and they are widely cited by governments, academics, advocates and constitutional courts and individuals who appeal to its principles for the protection of their recognized human rights.

Custom, however, can also lend itself to endless controversies: When is custom binding? Whose practice qualifies? How can it be identified? Practitioners and commentators do not always sing in unison on these questions. The slow and jerky pace of formation of international customary law is another problem which in addition to the unwillingness of states to commit themselves in controversial areas through the treaty-making process and the sharp divisions among states over a broad range of human rights issues all account for the ever broadening of the scope and coverage of "soft law" in the field of human rights. "Soft law" essentially refers to a wide range of quasi-legal instruments created by the state organs of international organizations and other non-state actors. Instances of soft law include most resolutions and declarations of the UN General Assembly, the action plans and programs of action adopted by international conferences, the interpretative "comments" of UN treaty bodies, the pronouncements of the UN Security Council, the "codes of conduct," "Guiding Principles," and "Minimum Standards" dealing with indigenous peoples, minorities, the treatment of prisoners, juvenile offenders and the administration of justice, internally displaced persons, the environment, development, transnational corporations (TNCs), among others.

None of these instruments can be said to have the force of conventional law (the so-called "hard law," although soft law is often used to evidence *opinio juris* on applying or interpreting a treaty). But they carry with them an aspirational and normative weight which, with the passage of time and through repetition, in spite of their weak or nonexistent formal enforcement mechanisms, may translate into the emergence of a sense of obligation and commitment of sort. As noted above, the UDHR is a case in point of soft law evolving into a customary norm. Many declarations of the United Nations have in fact been the first step paving the way toward the adoption of binding treaties as was the case of the two covenants on civil and political and socioeconomic rights, women, children, the disabled, migrant workers and enforced disappearances. But not all soft law instruments morph into hard law. Efforts to turn the 1986 UN Declaration on a Right to Development into a binding treaty are in effect stalled. In the same vein, soft law in the shape of the Global Compact and the so-called Respect and Remedy Framework and "guiding principles" for multinational corporations have provided the way out of the stalemate that had emerged in the 1970s in North-South negotiations over the formation of binding codes of conduct for multinational corporations.

Notwithstanding the pressures of civil society organizations and its appeal in the international academic community, it is doubtful that the so-called emerging norm of a "responsibility to protect" will ever gel into a binding rule. Be that as it may, any assessment of the possible evolution of legal human rights norms requires weighing the respective roles of governments, national and international courts, civil society, business, affected individuals and groups and analyzing how their interaction and dynamics over the long term may affect policy outcomes. Understandably, fact finding and monitoring have become the most salient features of human rights practices.

FACT FINDING

As part of the broader process of human rights monitoring, fact finding involves the gathering and analysis of evidence about circumstances related to situations of concern or violations of human rights that have allegedly been committed by state or non-state actors. In its more formal and institutional modalities, fact finding results in the issuance of reports and publications which may include recommendations for corrective measures. A follow-up phase may then involve procedures established for monitoring the implementation of remedial measures giving effect to the recommendations. Fact finding may be carried out by single individuals, "panels," or "commissions" and may take several forms: investigations, on-site inspections, data gathering that can be gleaned from states reporting to treaty bodies and individual complaints, among others.

So defined, fact finding has a long history extending back to the propagandist attempts of the British government to investigate the German invasion of Belgium at the outset of World War I to the ill-fated missions undertaken by the League of Nations in the wake of Japan's invasion of Manchuria in 1931 and Italy's attack on Abyssinia in 1934. Nowadays, fact finding is practiced by virtually all human rights actors. International organizations—the United Nations, the Organization of American States (OAS), and the Council of Europe—regularly engage in the dispatch of fact-finding missions. The ILO conducts its fact-finding work in the context of its supervisory role in the monitoring of its conventions and complaint procedures. All the principal organs of the United Nations—the Security Council, the General Assembly, and the Human Rights Council—have dispatched fact-finding missions. Virtually all UN peace operations have a human rights component tasked with monitoring, investigating and analyzing human rights situations. The UN secretary-general has extensively used his authority under Article 99 of the Charter to bring to the attention of the Security Council any matter which in his opinion may threaten the maintenance of international peace and security to send fact-finding missions with or without a mandate from the Assembly or the Council.

The UN-HCHR can also conduct fact-finding missions or provide logistical and substantive support to missions established by the Human Rights Council (UN-HRC). In this regard, the office with the assistance of international experts has developed matrices of human rights indicators for use in state party reports to treaty monitoring bodies. The mandate of all special rapporteurs is to examine, monitor, advise and publicly report on human right problems, for instance, by responding to individual complaints and conducting studies. In 2010, with the logistical support of the UN-HCHR, special rapporteurs carried out 67 country visits to 48 countries and territories and sent 604 "communications" to 110 states relating to allegations of human rights violations by some 1,400 individuals or groups of individuals. UN treaty bodies, when they review state reports or act on individual complaints, inevitably embark on fact finding. A singular instance of fact finding and inquiries combined with a preventive mandate is the system of regular visits to places of detention called for in the Optional Protocol to the Convention against Torture which became effective in 2006.

Regional human rights regimes make ample room for fact finding. The European Committee for the Prevention of Torture offers an interesting instance of fact finding which goes deep into the usually well-protected domestic jurisdiction of sovereign states. Small teams of the committee's members assisted by experts are allowed to make unannounced visits to all places of detention (i.e., jails, prisons, psychiatric institutions, people's homes) of the members' states of the Council of Europe. Their findings and recommendations are contained in reports which are confidential but can always be made public by the committee. (It was this European model that was used as a template for the 2006 Optional Protocol to the UN Convention against Torture; not surprisingly, the protocol has been ratified by only 63 states.)

International human rights courts have developed methodologies to collect data that can be adduced as evidence in international courts for the purpose of criminal prosecution. The Inter-American Court of Human Rights has broad evidence-gathering powers including hearing witnesses and experts, requesting the production of evidence by the parties involved and calling for a report or an opinion from a third party. The African Commission of Human Rights has conducted fact-finding missions to report on overall human rights situations and, more rarely, for the purpose of investigating individual complaints. The European Court of Human Rights dispatches judicial delegations to hear witnesses or conducts on-the-spot investigations.

Financial constraints often limit their capacity to carry out on-site investigations, but a common characteristic of all NGOs is that they engage in some form of fact finding. In so doing, they rely in part on the wide variety of socioeconomic statistics produced by governments and international organizations. These data on per capita income, infant mortality, life expectancy, literacy and the like, translated into "indexes" (i.e., the Physical Quality of Life Index [PQLI] developed by the Overseas Development Council and the Human Development Index of the UN Development Programme), inform about the distribution of benefits among countries and within countries between sexes, among ethnic groups and by region and sector which can be used as approximate measures of human rights. NGOs devote the bulk of their resources to counting and charting acts of violations committed against individuals and groups, be they extrajudicial killings, arbitrary arrests, cases of torture or attacks on human rights defenders, the capacity and efforts of states for the progressive realization of socioeconomic rights (Centre for Economic and Social Rights), the causes of violence (World Organization against Torture) or the causes and consequences of corruption (International Council for Human Rights Policy). Universities have developed databases measuring violations committed by governments within their territorial jurisdiction.

Some NGOs rely on increasingly sophisticated forms of measurement and analyses. For instance, Human Rights Watch has conducted investigations of government and army actions relying in part on satellite imagery. The Human Rights Data Analysis Group of the American Association for the Advancement of Science in Washington, D.C., has assisted the work of truth commissions by developing advanced statistical techniques for the analysis of mass atrocities. In recurrent flagship reports such as Human Rights Watch's World Report or Amnesty International's State of the World, NGOs disaggregate events-based data at the level of victims, perpetrators and witnesses and seek to identify broad patterns of violations within and across countries or different groups of countries.

On the basis of standard-based measurements, some NGOs apply ordinal scales to qualitative information and rank and/or categorize countries in terms of the degree to which states respect, protect and fulfill human rights. Freedom House, for example, has drawn up a scale of civil and political liberties against which it plots states on a scale ranging from "full protection" to "full violation." In close cooperation with "epistemic communities," NGOs have used survey data to map out national experiences and perceptions of rights protection within countries, to measure support for democracy, to identify patterns of corruption, to survey "at risk population," among others.

Fact finding may sometimes relate to truth seeking. As a tool, however, it has no purposes of its own. It is above all an instrument with possibilities and limitations in regard to its uses. Those individuals and organizations that monitor human rights, however, do have purposes and those vary widely.

Fact finding can be used for alerting the international community about egregious violations and, as such, is an essential tool for impact assessment and prevention. Knowledge and awareness of the "facts," however, do not necessarily trigger policy actions as evidenced by the low rate of governments' responses to the "urgent appeals" of UN special rapporteurs and, more dramatically, by the failure of the international community to intervene in such tragedies as the breakup of the former Yugoslavia, the Rwanda genocide and the ongoing slow-motion killing in Darfur and Syria. NGOs use fact finding as advocacy tools at the domestic and international levels to "name and shame," to demand additional standards' setting and to mobilize different constituencies around particular human rights issues.

Fact finding in the context of international prosecutions is intended to prove "beyond a reasonable doubt" that the defendants have committed specific acts that qualify as crimes under the law. In the cases of truth and reconciliation commissions, fact finding documents human rights abuses as part of a broader process designed to help foster a climate of national reconciliation. In this respect, fact-finding investigations are sometimes more akin to public relations missions intended to reduce tensions or abate violence and restore peace as in the case of high-level appointments by the UN secretary-general of "personal representatives" or the missions undertaken by the high commissioner on human rights and the high commissioner on refugees themselves.

Whatever the objective assigned to fact finding, in all circumstances, the credibility (and impact) of the process hinges on sound good practices eliminating possibilities of bias. It is in this spirit that the UN secretary-general issued the Draft Model Rules of Fact Finding Procedure for UN bodies in 1970 dealing with violations of human rights. More recently, two U.S. NGOs (the International Bar Association's Human Rights Institute and the Raoul Wallenberg Institute) have adopted "Guidelines on International Human Rights Fact-Finding Visits and Reports" which outline procedural methods designed to enhance the reliability of fact finding by NGOs. But even when conducted in the most rigorous conditions, fact finding often collides with politics.

This is particularly true when fact finding serves as a basis for the continued development of human rights policies. Governments' monitoring of human rights situations in the world in particular should be treated with caution because such practices may rest on selective conceptions of rights and serve unstated political agendas. The Country Reports on Human Rights Practices which are submitted annually by the U.S. Department of State to the U.S. Congress, for instance, by and large ignore socioeconomic rights. Human rights measures have been in great demand by bilateral donor agencies such as the U.S. Agency for International Development and the Canadian International Development Agency. This development has been lauded by some as a welcome effort to integrate human rights assessments into overall policy formulation and aid allocation strategies. Others have decried it as another form of conditionality, tying the allocation of aid to those countries that can demonstrate improvements in human rights policies and practices.

Likewise, one may recall here the controversies triggered by the Goldstone report which had been mandated by the UN Human Rights Council to investigate "all violations of international human rights law and international humanitarian law that might have been committed at any time in the context of the military operations that were conducted in Gaza during the period from 27 December 2008 to 18 January 2009, whether before, during or after." The report released in 2009 concluded that Israel and Hamas had committed violations of the laws of war and was endorsed by the Human Rights Council by a 25-6-11 vote. Both Hamas and Israel rejected its findings and recommendations, the former because they were "unbalanced," the latter because they embodied an effort to delegitimize the existence of the State of Israel. The report of the panel of experts set up by the UN secretary-general to investigate violations of humanitarian laws in the final months of the Sri Lankan civil war met a similar fate. The panel, consisting of three internationally recognized experts in international law, conducted a rigorous investigation. It examined "reports, documents and other written accounts by the various agencies, departments, funds, offices and programmes of the United Nations and other inter-governmental organizations, [nongovernmental organizations] and individuals, such as journalists and experts on Sri Lanka," as well as satellite imagery, photographs, and video materials. The panel also reviewed submissions received in response to notifications on the UN website, and consulted a number of individuals with expertise or experience related to the armed conflict. The report's main conclusion was that government forces and the separatist Liberation Tigers of Tamil Eelam had conducted military operations "with flagrant disregard for the protection, rights, welfare and lives of civilians and failed to respect the norms of international law." The Sri Lankan government dismissed the report as "illegal, biased, baseless and unilateral."

On the other hand, cases (albeit much rarer) can be mentioned where fact finding had a major impact. Perhaps the most significant fact-finding operation in UN history was the work of the Commission established by the UN Security Council in 1992 to investigate war crimes in the former Yugoslavia. In the course of its two-year-long operations, the Commission conducted extensive field investigations and created an extraordinarily rich database of evidence and information about violations of humanitarian law, places of detention, cases of torture and violent death, displacement and rapes. It was on the basis of this work that the Security Council established the International Criminal Tribunal for the Former Yugoslavia (ICTY).

State Reporting

On a practical level, fact finding remains a politically driven process where ad hocism prevails. Establishing the facts does not mean that the facts will speak for themselves. Much the same could be said about state reporting (i.e., the formal procedures established by treaty or intergovernmental bodies to oversee and promote state compliance with their international human rights obligations). Four types of procedures have emerged over time. Under a number of global and regional human rights treaties, committees of independent experts monitor the implementation of treaty provisions by their state's parties on the basis of reports that they submit at more or less regular intervals of time. A new mechanism put in place in 2006 by the Human Rights Council of the United Nations, the so-called Universal Periodic Review (UPR), modeled after the preceding system scrutinizes all members of the United Nations every four years on the fulfillment of their human rights obligations. The process also begins with the submission of state reports. The other two procedures triggering reviews of states adherence to human rights norms are complaints lodged by individuals against their government or by one government against another.

Interstate complaints have been few and far between and warrant only a brief reference here since states have consistently proved to be reluctant to use the procedure. Only isolated instances may be found, for example, in the European human rights regime. In 1956, Greece filed an interstate complaint concerning British practices in Cyprus. Ireland lodged a complaint against Great Britain in relation to its interrogation techniques in Northern Ireland from 1971 to 1975. The Convention on the Elimination of Discrimination calls upon the ICJ to resolve disputes among its parties concerning the interpretation and application of the Convention. The procedure has been recently invoked by Georgia against Russia but the ICJ ruled that Georgia had not fulfilled the preconditions required for the Court to seize the case and declined to answer the more substantive issues of violations of human rights and humanitarian law that Georgia accused Russia of committing during their brief war in August 2008.

Of far greater significance is the reporting system most commonly found in the United Nations and some of its specialized agencies, notably the ILO and United Nations Educational, Scientific and Cultural Organization

(UNESCO). The Latin American and African human rights regimes also make provision for a reporting system. State reports are not used under the European Convention of Human Rights but they are required by the European Charter for Regional or Minority Languages, the Framework Convention for the Protection of National Minorities and the European Social Charter. Under these treaties—for the United Nations, the two covenants and the Conventions and their optional protocols concerned with racial discrimination, discrimination against women, torture, migrant workers, persons with disabilities and enforced disappearances; for the ILO, its conventions on basic labor rights; and for UNESCO, its conventions against discrimination in education—committees of experts (the so-called treaty bodies) examine recurrent government reports documenting the legal, administrative and judicial measures they have taken as well as the difficulties they face in the implementation of the treaty provisions. The number of experts serving on these bodies varies widely (10 to 23). They are elected for renewable terms of a varying number of years (four years for the United Nations) and meet periodically. They are expected to be knowledgeable, independent and of high moral standing. Although nominated by their governments and not infrequently employed in some capacity by the same governments, they have displayed a remarkably consistent degree of independence. Their consideration of state reports ends with the publication of findings ("concluding observations" or "concluding comments") which identify specific shortcomings and obstacles to the implementation of treaty provisions and call for remedial measures

The quality and impact of the process on human rights situations hinges on the willingness of states being reviewed to cooperate. Not infrequently, states do not report or are late in their submissions, most of the time because of a lack of adequate internal specialist administrative capacity. In virtually all instances, national reports tend to be reassuringly formal and self-congratulatory, primarily reproducing an impressive array of instruments enacted in implementation of the treaties' injunctions. The treaty bodies have no means to sanction a delinquent state ignoring their recommendations other than persuasion and prodding. Over time, the system, especially in the United Nations, has developed increasingly acute structural problems. The backlog in reports has prompted calls for changes in the frequency and modalities of reporting and shorter and consolidated documents. The proliferation of treaty bodies has also led to overlap and duplication in their work, contributing to conflicting recommendations while placing increased workloads on financially strapped secretariats. The work of the treaty bodies still needs to more effectively linked to the field presence of the UN programs and funds and the specialized agencies of the United Nations. The response of the system to these challenges has been incremental and overwhelmingly focused on micromanagerial remedial measures. That being said, the merits of the system should not underestimated.

UN treaty bodies have been able to assert their institutional identity and autonomy in their tailored assessments of national human rights situations. The shortcomings of national state reports have been compensated by the issuance of more informative and reliable reports produced by international organizations and the "shadow reports" issued by NGOs. Treaty bodies have no means of coercion but the publication of their findings has prompted compliance and changes in national human rights policy and practices. Owing perhaps to the tripartite nature of the organization membership and its targeted programs of technical assistance, the ILO supervisory system has yielded significant results in the long term. At the regional level, the American practice of dispatching state visits for on-site observation in conjunction with the review of country reports has had in some cases a visible impact.

Prima facie, the UPR of the UN Human Rights Council, which started operating in January 2008, is a remarkably innovative state reporting mechanism whereby the human rights standards and performance of all members of the United Nations are reviewed by the Council every four years. One of its stated purposes is to respond to accusations of inconsistencies and double standards that have been addressed at the Commission on Human Rights, the Council's predecessor body, for its unbalanced treatment of national human rights situations. In the longer term, the UPR is intended to improve the human rights situation in all countries. The review is mandatory and a state's human rights records is based on a compendium of documents including a national report submitted by the state under review; information contained in the reports of the special procedures, human rights treaty bodies, and other UN entities; and information from other interested parties, notably NGOs and national human rights institutions.

The criteria used to measure the extent to which states respect their human rights obligations are based on the UN Charter and the Universal Declaration of Human Rights; the human rights treaties ratified by the state concerned; and voluntary pledges and commitments made by the state and applicable international humanitarian law. Each review may not exceed three hours. In the course of this "interactive dialogue," states may ask questions and make recommendations. NGOs have been granted the ability to participate in these proceedings. The final stage of the review entails a half-hour examination and subsequent adoption by the full Council of an "outcome report" which summarizes the discussions and enumerates the questions, comments and recommendations made by states to the country under review, as well as the responses provided by the reviewed state. The reviewed state is given an opportunity to make preliminary comments on the recommendations and in particular to indicate whether it accepts or rejects them.

All members of the United Nations have been reviewed and the Council has just embarked on its second four-year round of reviews. If size, quality and levels of delegations are reliable indicators, states appear to have taken their first UPR seriously. Virtually all states members of the Council as well as the "observers" were actively involved as measured by the frequency of their floor interventions. Participation of the member states was high, although the level varied from one session to another. The first cycle of state reviews has yielded more than 15,000 recommendations! And the process has generated a gold mine of information on national human rights situations and practices. Also, the UPR process has provided new political space for civil society as states under review are mandated to prepare their reports in consultation with "all relevant stakeholders." NGOs can also send submissions to the Office of the High Commissioner for Human Rights (OHCHR) which are subsequently distilled by the OHCHR into a "Summary of Stakeholders Information" that is part of the documentation used by the Council for its reviews. In addition, NGOs may also take the floor during the plenary before the adoption of the UPR outcome document.

That being said, the UPR practice has not taken the human rights community to nirvana. The process is and remains a state-driven and -controlled process where achieving consensus and deferring to the norm of sovereignty are more valued than protecting rights. National reports are rarely self-critical or do not genuinely seek to identify areas requiring further government action. Complacency and self-righteousness are artfully packaged in vast amounts of factual information on constitutional arrangements with formal legislative or administrative instruments having little or only a remote connection with the sobering realities of practice and implementation. Nor are national reports always transparent about the consultations that states are supposed to organize with civil society organizations. The quality of the "interactive dialogues" cast in the format of public hearings varies considerably. A bloc mentality prevails as "friendly states" or states from the same region take the floor alternately praising the human rights record of the country under review or blaming lapses on the burden of foreign debt, poverty, vulnerability to natural disasters and other extraneous factors beyond the reach of national governments. This means that, on the whole, many questions and recommendations on sensitive issues are not properly addressed or simply eluded. More credible comments of substance originate primarily from civil society organizations, but some countries, blaming them for "abusing their influence," have sought to limit their floor interventions. Far more disquieting is the fact that by the end of the UPR process, countries under review are free to accept or reject recommendations made regarding them. Rates of acceptance vary widely but they are stark reminders of the long shadow of the norm of sovereignty hanging over the UPR work of the Council. In any case, the true test lies in the follow-up and implementation on the ground. Of particular significance here is the fact that there is no mechanism to measure the implementation of recommendations

Another mechanism used to realize human rights under the broad heading of "state reporting" is individual complaints. The names vary: "applications," "petitions," or "communications," but in all cases, the terms refer to procedures enabling individuals who cannot effectively access justice in their home countries to seek an international review of their case in the same quasi-judicial supervisory bodies reviewing the reports of states parties referred to above. This individual complaint system should not be confused with the 1503 Procedure in place in the Human Rights Council since 1970 which is a confidential process concerned with "consistent patterns of gross and reliably attested violations of human rights and fundamental freedoms." (The Commission on the Status of Women also has its own complaint procedure.) It is also distinct from the regional judicial courts (discussed below) and unrelated to the complaints (over 100,000 a year) which are addressed to the UN-HCHR.

The novelty, significance and impact of the system cannot be underestimated as it is designed "to operate as an instrument of enforcement by which individual victims can seek international protection against their defaulting governments occurring in any part of the world and under any circumstances." An increasing number of states have accepted (albeit not uniformly) the jurisdiction of treaty-monitoring bodies (from a high of 114 states under the International Covenant on Civil and Political Rights to 65 under the Convention against Torture to five under the Migrant Workers Convention!!). Findings of treaty violations may spur delinquent governments to take remedial or corrective actions. Adverse publicity generated by negative findings may shame states into compliance. The complaint procedure, as it progresses, may also trigger "a positive dialogue, resulting in an amicable resolution between the complainant and the state concerned, which remedies the prejudice complained of." The rulings of treaty-monitoring bodies—notably the Human Rights Committee—have built a large body of jurisprudence that is cited in national courts and scholarly writings and can guide governments, international organizations and NGOs.

On the downside, complainants must fulfill rigorous criteria to gain a hearing of their cases. Each reviewing body has its own specific requirements, but all of them require that the state against which a complaint has been lodged must be a party to the relevant treaty and have explicitly recognized the competence of the treaty body to receive communications. Complainants must have exhausted all domestic remedies. The violation must be covered by the treaty and must have been committed while the treaty was in force on the territory of the violating state. Additional criteria of admissibility eliminate complaints which are "manifestly politically motivated" or "inconsistent" with international human rights law or lack "clear evidence." The demanding character of these admissibility criteria explains in part why a large number of complaints are deemed inadmissible. Between 1997 and 2010, the Inter-American Commission of Human Rights (IACHR) accepted only 1,926 of 14,880 complaints. The non-exhaustion of domestic remedies and inadequate proof of a violation are the two most commonly cited reasons for rejection.

The system is slow moving and plagued by considerable backlogs. Since 1977, when the first cases were decided, UN treaty bodies have adopted decisions on only approximately 2,000 communications. Violations were found in one-third of the cases. At the time of writing some 500 cases were pending. The number of cases and petitions pending in the IACHR exceeds 1,500. On average, the processing time for the Committee against Torture is 30 months. UN-HRC spends an average of 47 months per case. A disproportionate percentage of claims emerge from and are settled against countries of the developed world. Far fewer complaints are registered against blatant violators of rights from other parts of the world.

Finally, all the supervisory bodies enjoy only powers of recommendation. Their rulings are not legally binding and rely on moral persuasion. The remedies they provide for are essentially political, the expectation being that the public impact of negative findings will provide sufficient impetus for state authorities to change their human rights practices. But this is clearly not always the case and states may always choose to ignore or flaunt the rulings of treaty bodies.

JUDICIALIZATION

The term "judicialization" refers to the growing practice of victims of human rights violations bring their cases to and seeking remedies from an international court of law against state or non-state authorities (criminal actions and proceedings are discussed below). Litigation may also be part of a broader advocacy strategy by NGOs, but it must always begin in national courts as international judicial bodies are institutions of last resort, playing, by law, only a residual and complementary role to national courts.

Raising legal claims requires institutions. By the end of the 1940s, there were none in place to give effect to the lofty aspirations of the UDHR. An intense process of institution building unfolded in subsequent years and decades which started in Europe and Latin America, then spread to Africa, and is only now beginning to mobilize Asian and Middle Eastern countries. All of the structures which emerged from this incremental and disjointed process appear to have stemmed from the multitier model that was first initiated in Europe whereby individual complaints are filtered, disposed of or referred to a higher court by a body of government officials all selected by the decision-making bodies of the Council of Europe. The institutions that subsequently sprang out of this common trunk vary widely and the evolving scope of their political autonomy and authority reflects each region's peculiar historical and cultural experience. Undoubtedly, the strongest system of rights protection is in Europe, the weakest in Asia and the Middle East with Latin America and Asia in between. But notwithstanding these variations, regional judicial systems for the protection of human rights have become an important part of the international system for the protection of human rights and a rich source of remedial jurisprudence on human rights issues at the domestic level.

A parallel striking development in recent decades has been the growing recognition that past abuses of human rights cannot be left unpunished. Gingerly and in an equally disconnected incremental manner, practitioners of human rights have created and progressively enlarged the space of "transitional justice," a broad approach to confronting legacies of past human rights violations through a combination of judicial and non-judicial tools including the use of investigation, the prosecution of perpetrators, the establishment of truth and reconciliation commissions and the reform of public political, military and judicial institutions.

The European Regime

The spectacular expansion of the European system has been enhanced by the end of the Cold War and the breakup of the former Soviet bloc which triggered a wave of new entrants into the Council of Europe. Membership in the Council has in fact turned into providing a collective stamp of approval on a nation's human rights credentials and, for some, a gateway to the European Union. In this regard, mention must be made of the role and impact of the European Court of Justice (ECJ), the judicial arm of the European Union. The ECJ's prime concerns are economic integration-related matters but in many ways its rulings have touched on human rights issues. The ECJ has thus articulated a set of fundamental rights which it considers to be at the core of European Community values. In turn, these norms have strengthened the legal rationale of the rulings of the European Court on Human Rights (ECHR), the human rights judicial arm of the Council of Europe.

For example, the ECJ has established that freedom of movement entails the elimination of any discrimination based on nationality between workers as regards employment, remuneration and other conditions of work. Perhaps more importantly, the ECJ has relied in its rulings on the fundamental principle of the supremacy of community law over national law and the idea that member states are bound directly by community law (i.e., not through their governments). Long-standing concerns about consistency in case law between the ECJ and the ECHR should be alleviated by the fact that, in accordance with the Lisbon Treaty, the European Union has acceded to the Convention. This should make the ECJ fully bound by the judicial precedents of the ECHR.

The European human rights regime is embedded in the Council of Europe where the ECHR was negotiated and agreed on in 1953. Member states of the Council of Europe cannot be admitted if they do not subscribe to the ECHR and most states have by now incorporated the ECHR into their domestic law. From 1954 to 1998, individuals first applied to the European Commission of Human Rights, a body of government officials, which decided upon the admissibility of their complaints. In cases that it deemed admissible, the Commission then could mediate or refer them to the ECHR if mediation failed to produce friendly settlement. The Commission was abolished in 1998 and since then all nationals of the states members of the Council of Europe have direct access to the Court which decides on the admissibility and merits of the cases.

In this regard, the European system is unique. It is the only regional human rights regime that gives the possibility to any one claiming to be a victim of a violation of a right recognized in the Convention or its optional protocols to lodge an application before a court which enjoys compulsory jurisdiction and may resolve the complaint through a legally binding judgment. Almost all complaints have been lodged by individuals, the remainder by groups of individuals, NGOs or one state against another. Since it was established in 1959, the Court has delivered more than 15,000 judgments. Nearly half of them concerned four member states: Turkey (2,747), Italy (2,166), Russia (1,212) and Poland (945). As of 2011, Russia had been convicted 160 times for gross human rights violations in the North Caucasus.

In its judgments, the Court has not hesitated to deal with such major issues of social concern as abortion, assisted suicide, the rights of prisoners and mental patients, torture, domestic slavery, prisons rules, sexual orientation, the wearing of the Islamic headscarf in schools and universities, the protection of journalists, discrimination against Roma and the environment. The Court's judgments have generally been accepted though not always welcome. Accused at one and the same time of being reluctant to find violations in sensitive matters affecting the interests of states parties or unduly intrusive (a "small claims court" as British Prime Minister David Cameron recently dismissively put it), the Court's reach probably suggest that it is doing something right.

The Court's work has indeed become a beacon of light for human rights advocates. But its story also has a flipside as the Court appears to be a victim of its own success. The Court is clearly overburdened, primarily as a result of a dramatic surge in individual complaints from the countries of East and Central Europe which joined the Council of Europe after the demise of the Cold War. The original division of labor between the Court and the Commission worked well in spite of the fact that the caseload of the Court increased significantly from 16 cases between 1960 and 1975 to 119 in 1997 alone. This in effect meant that a great majority of complaints failed the test of admissibility. Indeed, between 1959 and 1998, the Court received 45,016 applications and issued 837 judgments. The 1998 reform has compounded the problem to seemingly unmanageable proportions. The number of applications has steadily increased from 8,408 in 1999, to 28,201 in 2002, to 42,376 in 2008. The number of judgments of the Court for these years were 177,844 and 1,205, respectively. Ten years after the reform, the Court delivered its 10,000th judgment. Ninety percent of its output since its creation was produced between 1998 and 2011!

Now the Court receives over 50,000 new applications every year. More than 80 percent of applications are declared inadmissible because they are "manifestly ill-founded," the applicants did not exhaust domestic remedies or wanted the Court to quash, rehear or revise decisions taken by domestic courts or were incompatible with the provisions of the Convention and its protocols. The Court at the time of writing had a backlog of some 150,000 complaints from individuals seeking redress for alleged violations of the ECHR. If the Court continues to work at its present pace, it would take half a century to clear pending cases. In 2010, the Council of Europe approved amendments to the ECHR designed to maintain and improve the Court's efficiency, including procedures for speeding up the process for determining the admissibility of new complaints. Additional proposals are under considerations within the Council of Europe prompted by the fact that under the terms of the 2009 Lisbon Treaty the European Union has acceded to the ECHR.

The Latin American System

The Latin American regime is roughly identical to the pre-1998 European arrangements but it has its own particular characteristics and by and large is far more state driven. The system retains the two-tier structure that prevailed in Europe until 1998 of a Commission and a Court where individuals have no standing and are entitled to bring cases only to the former which will rule on their admissibility, make recommendations to states for redress and remedies and refer the case to the Court if it fails to resolve the matter in a non-contentious manner. The mandate of the IACmHR is prescribed in the charter of the OAS and the IACHR. The Commission was created in 1959 and met for the first time in 1960. In 1965, it was authorized to examine complaints or petitions regarding specific cases of human rights violations. The Inter-American Court of Human Rights (IACtHR) was established later in implementation of the 1969 American Convention on Human Rights which came into force in 1978. In its adjudicatory function, the Court hears and rules on specific cases of human right violations referred to it by the Commission. It may also issue advisory opinions brought to its attention by OAS bodies or member states. OAS members have the discretion whether to ratify the Convention and are therefore free to accept and be bound by the Court's contentious jurisdiction (as of now the Convention has 24 state parties and there have been cases of acceptances withdrawn and then reinstated).

The applicable standards and techniques used by the Commission and the Court are on the whole similar to the practice of the European Court of Human Rights. For instance, the 1990 second protocol of the American Convention on Human Rights requires states parties to refrain from using capital punishment in any peacetime circumstances. On the other hand, the 1988 additional protocol to the Convention extends the range of rights protected by the IACtHR to socioeconomic rights to work, to health, to food, and to education. Also, the conditions under which the Latin American system came into existence and functioned for a number of years were vastly different. In contrast to Europe's postwar historical background of regulated democracies, the experience of the Latin American continent was one of sharp social and economic cleavages, political violence and terrorism and repression by military dictatorships or authoritarian governments. In the wake of the political transformations of the continent and the return of democratic regimes, the Commission and perhaps even more so the Court have slowly gained recognition and acceptance.

These data illustrate the growing pains and evolving trends. The Commission disposes of 100 cases on average each year. Between 1979 and 2006, the Court issued 19 advisory opinions, 162 judgments and 71 provisional measures and solved 85 cases. In 1997, two cases had been submitted to the Court. In 2010, 16 cases had been referred to it. This relatively modest quantitative output should be measured against the remarkable quality of the jurisprudence of the Commission and the Court. Both have had to deal with issues involving existential right-to-life issues, summary executions, killings, torture, disappearances, and arbitrary detentions. Their rulings, driven by the claims of victims, the vigilance of the Commission and creative jurists, have established influential groundbreaking doctrinal precedents. For instance, in a 1988 case of enforced disappearances involving Honduras, the IACtHR determined that the government was required to "take reasonable steps to prevent human rights violations and to use the means at its disposal to carry out a serious investigation of violations committed within [its] jurisdiction, to identify those responses, to impose the appropriate punishment and to ensure the victim adequate compensation."

In other cases, the Court has established the right of individuals to receive information about themselves that appears in government files. Also notable are rulings made in defense of the rights of indigenous peoples and in support of the provision of extensive reparations by states found in violation of human rights. In 2001, 2006 and 2010, the court invalidated amnesty laws adopted by Peru, Chile and Brazil protecting perpetrators of human rights violations committed when the military was in power on the grounds that they were incompatible with the right to the truth and impeded investigations of grave human rights violations.

The African System

The African regime of human rights is the latest newcomer in the regional human rights architecture. It developed under the auspices of the Organization of African Unity (OAU) which in 1981 adopted the African Charter on Human and People's Rights. Like other regional instruments, the Charter includes a fairly extensive catalogue of civil and political individual rights. It differs from them in its provisions, no doubt inspired by the continent's long history of slavery and colonialism, on "people's" rights, which comprise the rights to equality, to self-determination, to freely determine their political status and economic development, to "national and international security" and to "a general satisfactory environment favorable to their development." Under the Charter, states are obligated to ensure the protection of the rights of women and children as stipulated in international declarations and conventions, to eliminate all forms of foreign and domestic economic exploitation of natural resources, and to "assist the family which is the custodian of morals and traditional values recognized by the community." The Charter also spells out a number of duties that individuals incur "towards his family and society, the state and other legally recognized communities and the international community."

The normative regime thus instituted provided for the establishment of a protective body, the African Commission on Human Rights and People's Rights which became operational only in 1987. The basic functions of the

Commission were patterned along the model of the UN Human Rights Committee as it was tasked to examine state reports, consider individual communications alleging violations and interpreting the African Charter at the request of a state party to the OAU, the OAU or any organization recognized by the OAU. The Commission was also empowered to "collect documents, undertake studies and researches on African problems in the fields of human rights and peoples rights, organize seminars, symposia and conferences, disseminate information, encourage national and local institutions concerned with human rights and peoples rights and, should the case arise, give its views or make recommendations to governments."

This all-encompassing but state-driven agenda has collided with the political realities of the African continent. Only a handful of states could at the time of the establishment of the Commission claim to have democratic credentials. The first wave of leaders emerging from decolonization gave priority to the sanctity of the territorial integrity of states over the self-determination of the people and in that process frequently closed ranks behind abusive governments. All throughout the 1990s, civil wars broke out here and there on the continent accompanied by widespread and massive violations of human rights.

Against this background, the Commission's record has been less than impressive. Underutilized, strapped by lack of financial resources and constrained by rigorous rules of admissibility, it decided on average 10 cases a year. Some of these rulings were groundbreaking. Among other things, the Commission has made significant strides in legitimizing the idea that socioeconomic and group rights are justiciable rights. For example, in a 1992 case involving indigenous groups seeking autonomy in Zaire, the Commission established the precedent that self-determination could be achieved in a manner consistent with the sovereignty and territorial integrity of the country. In a subsequent decision, the Commission found that Sudan was responsible for large-scale evictions and violations of the rights to life, housing, food, health and judicial remedies. In a more recent ruling against Kenya, the Commission recognized the rights of an indigenous community over traditionally owned land and found that the Kenyan government had violated their right to their ancestral land by evicting them to make way for a wildlife reserve.

But compliance has not been the most striking characteristic of the system. The checkered record of the Commission and the spread of democratic institutions in many African countries all pointed to the need for change. A 1998 protocol to the African Charter which became effective in 2006 provided for a Court on Human and People's Rights. A particularly innovative stipulation of the protocol is that legal actions against a state can be brought to the Court on the basis of any international human rights treaty that it signed thus potentially making the Court the judicial arm of any regional or global human rights instrument. But the system now in place still does not provide for the direct right of individual petition. The African Commission, any state party whose citizen is a victim of a human rights violation, African intergovernmental organizations and with the Court's permission non-governmental with observer status and individuals can make submissions of cases before the Court. But NGOs and individuals acquire standing only after a state party delivers a declaration specifically allowing them to do so.

Practice will tell how these seemingly apparent contradictory arrangements will be resolved and whether there is sufficient political will among the members of the African Union (which replaced the OAU in 2001 and whose Constitutive Act uniquely provides for a right to humanitarian intervention in member states of the Union) to allow for the growth and development of the system. So far only one case has been adjudicated by the African Court. In March 2011, the Court took the unprecedented step of ordering provisional measures against Libya requiring the country to "immediately refrain from any action that would result in loss of life or violation of physical integrity of persons, which could be a breach of the provision of the African Charter." Almost at the same time, the African Committee of Experts on the Rights and Welfare of the Child, a watchdog body similar to UN treaty bodies established under the African Charter on the Rights and Welfare of the Child, issued its first decision on a communication submitted by the Institute for Human Rights and Development in Africa which found Kenya in violation of the rights of Nubian children to non-discrimination. Political winds in Africa may be shifting.

Other Regions of the World

Institutional ferment also seems to have reached, albeit in muted ways, the hitherto dormant Asian region whose claim for human rights fame lies primarily in its extreme deference to state sovereignty. Following the 1993 UN World Conference, the members of the Association of South East Asian Nations (ASEAN) signaled their support for the Vienna Declaration and indicated that they could consider the establishment of an appropriate regional mechanism on human rights. In 2007, they agreed on an Asian Charter, one purpose of which is to promote and protect human rights. Two years later, they established an ASEAN Intergovernmental Commission on Human Rights, which formally met for the first time in 2010. The UN High Commissioner for Human Rights welcomed the creation of the first Asian regional body in the region but expressed her disappointment at its "lack of a real protection mandate" while expressing the hope that its role would expand after its launch. At the same time, other developments are unfolding. In 2010, an ASEAN Commission for the Promotion and Protection of the Rights of Women and Children was inaugurated in Hanoi, Vietnam. An ASEAN instrument on the protection and promotion of the rights of migrant workers is being drafted.

Likewise the "Arab Spring" of 2011 may lead to some improvements in the future. But for the time being, there is no bona fide human rights machinery in the Middle East region. The League of Arab States did set up a Permanent Commission on Human Rights in 1968. The move was intended to be a response to the occupation of Palestinian territories in the wake of the 1967 Arab military debacle, but the Commission has refrained from scrutinizing the practices of member states. Under the terms of the 2005 Arab Charter of Human Rights, an Arab Human Rights Committee has come into existence. Its prime function is to review state reports. It is far too early to assess its effectiveness and impact, although it may be noted that most of the members of the Commission hold government positions.

The International Court of Justice

A few words about the International Court of Justice are warranted before closing this section. As the judicial organ of the United Nations, the ICJ's mandate is to settle legal disputes submitted to it by states and to issue advisory opinions at the request of governments, the specialized agencies of the UN and the General Assembly. It can exert its compulsory jurisdiction only when both parties have consented to its jurisdiction. Individuals have thus no access to it. Nor should the Court be considered a human rights institution. The logic of its rulings is grounded more on international legal and procedural concerns than substantive human rights instruments. In addition, the Court's organizational culture has made it reluctant to get embroiled in political disputes and to openly challenge the norm of sovereignty. In the 1960s, for instance, the Court determined that neither Liberia nor Ethiopia had legal standing to challenge the Apartheid regime in South West Africa.

Asked for guidance by the UN General Assembly as to whether the use of nuclear weapons by a state in war or other armed conflict was a breach of its obligations under international law, the Court rejected the argument that the use of nuclear weapons would unlawfully violate the right not to be arbitrarily deprived of life under Article 6 of the Covenant on Civil and Political Rights. Instead, while affirming the applicability of international human rights law during armed conflicts, it contended that there is in neither customary nor conventional international law any specific authorization of the threat or use of nuclear weapons or any comprehensive and universal prohibition of the threat or use of nuclear weapons as such. On that basis, the Court concluded that "the threat or use of nuclear weapons would generally be contrary to the rules of international law applicable in armed conflict, and in particular the principles and rules of humanitarian law; however, in view of the current state of international law, and of the elements of fact at its disposal, the Court cannot conclude definitively whether the threat or use of nuclear weapons would be lawful or unlawful in an extreme circumstance of self-defense, in which the very survival of a State would be at stake."

In 2002, the ICJ ruled that Belgium had failed to respect the immunity from criminal jurisdiction which incumbent state officials enjoy under international law when it issued a warrant for the arrest of the foreign minister of the Congo under the doctrine of universal jurisdiction. In a judgment delivered in 2008, the Court found that because Georgia had not used or first attempted to use the mode of dispute resolution contained in the Convention on the Elimination of Racial Discrimination, it had no jurisdiction to entertain a complaint filed by Georgia against Russia for its alleged ethnic cleansing by its forces in South Ossetia and Abkhazia in violation of the Convention.

On the other hand, the Court has increasingly accepted cases with human rights dimensions. Rulings can be cited which have strengthened the applicability and broadened the reach of human rights law. Thus, the ICJ confirmed on two occasions that UN special rapporteurs enjoy the privileges and immunities of UN experts on mission under the UN Convention on Privileges and Immunities. In a 2004 advisory opinion, the Court validated the applicability of international human rights law to situations of military occupation and determined that Israel's construction of a wall in the Occupied Palestinian Territories and in East Jerusalem impeded the exercise by Palestinians of their rights to work, health and self-determination. A year later, in a binding judgment, the Court ruled that the presence of Ugandan troops in the Ituri province of the Democratic Republic of the Congo was a breach of the principle of non-use of force. The Court also asserted that, as an occupying power, Uganda had failed to respect human rights and humanitarian law. In another 2007 binding judgment, the ICJ confirmed the ICTY's determination that the Srebrenica massacre was an act of genocide. It could not find enough evidence of direct Serbian responsibility for it, but it did rule that Serbia was in breach of the Convention against Genocide when it failed to prevent the massacre and did not cooperate with the ICTY in apprehending and punishing the perpetrators. In 2012, the ICJ found Senegal in breach of the UN Convention against Torture and ordered it to prosecute or extradite Hissene Habre in connection with political killings and acts of torture committed when he was president of Chad from 1982 to 1990.

TRANSITIONAL JUSTICE

The exact modalities of transitional justice have varied widely from one case to another, but its underlying assumption—the linkage between justice and transition—is a common thread in all national experiences. Basically, the purpose of transitional justice is to promote political transformations from authoritarian dictatorial and conflictual regimes to sustainable peaceful and democratic state citizens relations. The first experiments in transitional justice can be traced back to the Nuremberg and Tokyo trials, the investigation, prosecution, denazification and democratization programs carried out by the occupying powers in Germany and Japan and the trials conducted by West Germany and formerly occupied states. Although overshadowed by criticisms of "victors' justice and selective retribution," these developments were more satisfactory than the prevailing pattern of impunity that had emerged from the previous global conflict. In any event, the Cold War brought them to an end. General amnesties and the release of a large number of convicted perpetrators followed. In other parts of the world, notably Latin America, the strategic rivalries of the United States and the Soviet Union empowered authoritarian regimes which, in the name of national security and the survival of the nation, gave them license to indulge in grievous violations of rights.

The postwar precedents in transitional justice were given a new lease on life by networks of human rights activists, NGOs and their allies in some governments and international organizations who anchored their efforts in the human rights institutions and the body of international human rights and humanitarian laws and conventions that had progressively emerged in the preceding decades. Thus, in an ironic twist of events, the Cold War refocused the search for accountability onto states within the confines of their domestic jurisdiction. Several countries enacted piecemeal domestic legislation which incorporated the Nuremberg principles or extended or abolished limitation statues. On that basis, some of them—Israel, France, Canada, Australia and West Germany—conducted domestic trials with varying degrees of effectiveness and equity.

The turning points were the trials of former members of the military juntas in Greece (1975), Portugal (1976) and Argentina (1983) followed by the establishment of truth commissions in Chile and Uruguay (1990) and South Africa (1995) among others, notably East Timor, Ghana, Peru, and Sierra Leone. After the collapse of the communist regimes across Central and Eastern Europe in the late 1980s and early 1990s, several states dealt with the trauma of their communist past by enacting programs of "lustration" or "vetting" which entailed either the dismissal of politically discredited individuals or their integration in the new society in exchange for truth.

Transitional justice practices have been integrated into most recent United Nations peace operations. The United Nations Organization Stabilization Mission in the Democratic Republic of the Congo, the African Union/UN Hybrid Operation in Darfur, the United Nations Mission in South Sudan (UNMISS), the United Nations Mission in Cote d'Ivoire, the United Nations Stabilization Mission in Haiti and the United Nations Assistance Mission in Afghanistan all have peace-building and democratization mandates. Now, typical UN peace missions have extensive built-in human rights activities ranging from monitoring and investigating human rights, operating mission-wide early warning mechanisms, responding to violations of human rights, advising on institutional reform and capacity building and strengthening the rule of law through legal and judicial reform, security sector reform and prison system reform.

Other multilateral organizations have developed extensive transitional justice programs. A case in point is the World Bank which devoted its 2011 World Development Report to the linkages between conflict, security and development. NGOs have jumped on the bandwagon, some of them, such as the International Center for Transitional Justice, specializing exclusively on the subject. Think tanks and academic institutions and scholars are also devoting increasing attention to the question.

While not specifically designed to strengthen transitions toward democracy, the establishment of ad hoc tribunals after the end of the Cold War and, above all, the International Criminal Court in 1998, have been significant steps toward greater accountability. The "reinternationalization" of retributive justice for human rights abuses, in part, reflects the failure, reluctance or incapacity of national governments to prosecute their own nationals which resulted either in patterns of persisting continuing impunity or long delays in addressing the Commission of Human Rights violations. The prosecutions carried out by Turkey and Germany under pressure of the victorious Allies were notable for being the first in history involving the use of national law for what are now recognized international crimes. But only a handful of Ottoman former senior officials were held to account, and to this day, Turkish authorities still deny that the deportation and mass killing of Armenians constitute forms of genocide.

The idea of an international tribunal proposed after the signing of the Versailles Treaty by a Commission on the Responsibility of the Authors of the War and on Enforcement of Penalties quickly fizzled out. Eventually, only 12 individuals among a list of some 895 individuals identified by the Commission were prosecuted by German tribunals and six were convicted to light sentences. Between 1945 and 1995, more than 100,000 individuals were investigated by the Federal Republic of Germany for crimes committed during World War II resulting in less than 7,000 convictions (the Auschwitz concentration camp alone employed 6,000 staff, only 22 of whom were brought to trial). European countries that had been occupied during the war enacted domestic legislation enabling them to prosecute individuals suspected of war crimes or crimes against humanity perpetrated on their territory or by their own nationals. But prosecutions in Eastern Europe and the Soviet Union were clouded by allegations of the use of torture to obtain evidence. Others, as is the case for France, were inordinately delayed by the dynamics of domestic politics. The trial of Adolf Eichmann in 1961 received much public attention and triggered controversy about Israel's jurisdiction, but its proceedings remained silent over the fact that a number of high-level officials in the German government had served the Nazis during the war. Somewhat later, war crimes committed during the Vietnam War, such as the 1968 murder of civilians in My Lai, by and large, remained unpunished. Throughout the 1980s and 1990s, Latin American countries enacted amnesty laws under the guise of promoting national reconciliation which reduced or eliminated altogether all forms of liability for crimes committed by the previous authoritarian or military regime. Domestic prosecutions of major crimes in Bosnia and Herzegovina have been vetted by the ICTY, thus establishing international standards for their conduct, but only a few of them have reached the trial stage, and domestic courts have primarily dealt with defendants belonging to an ethnic minority within that state.

To a considerable extent, the establishment of war crime tribunals in the post-Cold War era has filled this national impunity gap. By holding individuals accountable regardless of their official positions, war crime tribunals have blown away the hitherto legally sanctioned tradition of state immunity. In their jurisprudence, war crime tribunals have indicted heads of state, prime ministers, army chiefs-of-staff, government ministers and many other leaders from various parties. The ICTY has indicted 161 accused for crimes committed against many thousands of victims during the conflicts in Croatia (1991–95), Bosnia and Herzegovina (1992–95), Kosovo (1998–99) and the former Yugoslav Republic of Macedonia (2001). So far, the International Criminal Tribunal for Rwanda (ICTR) has finished 69 trials convicting 42 accused persons and acquitting 10 while 17 cases are in appeals. The prosecutor intends to transfer three to national jurisdiction for trial and nine others are still at large, some suspected to be dead.

By establishing the facts through testimonies of eyewitnesses, survivors and perpetrators, forensic data, and other documentary evidence, the judgments of war tribunals have contributed to the creation of a historical record which may make denials of human rights atrocities less credible. Equally significant are the contributions of war crime tribunals to the development of international humanitarian and criminal law with regard to boundary definition, substance and procedure. In their jurisprudence, they have clarified and expanded on the body of law which had been incubating throughout the Cold War period. Legal precedents can now be cited establishing that enslavement and persecution constitute crimes against humanity, that rape and the instigating of genocide through the media are crimes of genocide, that the general prohibition of torture in international law cannot be derogated from a treaty, internal law or otherwise, and that in regard to the so-called doctrine of command responsibility, a formal superior-subordinate relationship is not necessarily required for criminal responsibility.

While early detractors like China and Brazil no longer question the legal propriety of the existence of war crime tribunals, their operation has elicited a wide range of criticisms. Their costs are fairly high especially in relation to their modest judicial output: For the biennium 2010 to 2011, the UN General Assembly approved appropriations for the ICTY in the amount of $301 million and for the ICTR of $245 million. Reliance on plea bargaining has led to inconsistencies in the punishments received by defendants. Many also argue that the deterrence value of war crimes tribunals is negligible, that they focus primarily on middle-ranking officers, soldiers, and politicians and that they neither address nor alleviate the underlying causes of the conflicts that led to massive violations of rights. More disturbing perhaps is the argument that war crimes tribunals offer only yet another modality of victors justice, this time dressed in multilateral blue garb. This line of reasoning, of course, places center stage the potential role of the International Criminal Court, the "permanence" of which as an international criminal justice institution, stands in stark contrast with the ad hoc and time-bound nature of the ICTY, the ICTR or "hybrid courts" such as the Extraordinary Chambers in the Courts of Cambodia or the Special Court for Sierra Leone.

The establishment of a permanent international court, which owes much to the lobbying and advocacy efforts of NGOs, cannot be underestimated. Its creation fulfills the long-held aspiration of bringing perpetrators to justice and providing redress to victims when governments are unwilling or unable to do so. The Court can prosecute individuals for genocide, crimes against humanity, war crimes and (not before 2017) the crime of aggression. It has received complaints alleging crimes in at least 139 countries and is conducting preliminary reviews of "situations"—a potential preliminary step to a full-fledged investigation—in Afghanistan, Georgia, Guinea, Colombia, Palestine, Honduras, Korea and Nigeria. To date, it has opened investigations in only seven "situations," three of them referred to the Court by states parties to its statute (Democratic Republic of the Congo [DRC], Uganda, and Central African Republic), two by the UN Security Council (Darfur and

Libya) and two initiated by the prosecutor Kenya and Cote d'Ivoire). The Court has indicted 28 people and issued arrest warrants for 19 individuals and summonses to nine others. Five individuals are in custody and four of them are being tried. In 2012, the Court delivered its first verdict against a Congolese national who was found guilty of having committed the war crime of enlisting and conscripting children under the age of 15 years and using them to participate actively in hostilities.

The ICC still faces serious challenges. First, while over 120 states have ratified its statute and a further 32 have signed it, key members of the United Nations are not on board, notably China, India and the United States. At the ICC's 2010 review conference, the present U.S. administration of Barack Obama—in a reversal of the Bush administration—asserted that the United States intended to give diplomatic and informational support to ICC prosecutions on a case-by-case basis. But congressional legislation adopted in 2002 prohibits the U.S. government from providing material assistance to the Court. Also, the ICC jurisdiction is constrained in at least two related respects. Like all other international judicial or quasi-judicial bodies, it is a court of last resort. It is designed to investigate and prosecute only when national courts have failed or are unable to do so. Individual states still retain the primary responsibility for prosecuting individuals suspected of rights violations. Although many states and non-state actors pressed for the idea when the Rome Statute was negotiated, the ICC is not allowed to exercise universal jurisdiction. In only three types of situations is the court empowered to exercise jurisdiction: when the accused is a national of a state party, if the alleged crime took place on the territory of a state party, or if a situation is referred to the Court by the Security Council of the United Nations. To those constraints must be added the ever-present problem of the tradeoffs between securing justice and mending the societal divisions that led to civil strife. Some regard the outstanding arrest warrants of four leaders of the Lord's Resistance Army as an obstacle to ending the conflict in Uganda. The prosecution of four prominent Kenyans ordered by the Court on charges of crimes against humanity in connection with the violence which followed the 2007 disputed elections has met with objections of the Kenyan government whose officials contend that the involvement of the Court could destabilize the country.

These politically charged debates are not likely to come to a close in the near or foreseeable future. In the meantime, the ICC faces the same political difficulties that have baffled other international judicial bodies: without an executive arm of its own, it must rely, like the ICTY, the ICTR and other "hybrid courts," on the willingness of all states to assist in the collection of evidence, the arrest of suspected criminals and the imprisonment of those who have been convicted. Such cooperation can never be taken for granted at any stage of the judicial process. Contentious negotiations between the United Nations and Cambodia over the law to be applied, the composition of the Court and the defendants to be charged delayed the launch of the Special Court of Cambodia for years and the tribunal today still remains mired in persisting allegations of corruption and intrusions by the government of Cambodia. Indonesian stonewalling and delaying tactics hampered the functioning of the East Timor mixed panels. African countries provided a safe haven to Charles Taylor before he was surrendered to the Special Court for Sierra Leone. Notorious suspected war criminals of the Balkans wars were able to elude arrest, thanks to the tacit and discreet support they received from states in the region.

Be that as it may and bearing in mind that all ad hoc tribunals are expected to disappear in the next few years as part of now agreed "completion strategies," the International Criminal Court, in spite of its built in limitations, is likely to remain the judicial template for the future in the constellation of policy instruments falling under the umbrella of transitional justice. Criminal punishment is increasingly viewed as a necessary element of human rights protection. In this regard, the long-standing separation of national and international laws has considerably eroded as domestic courts and legislation become increasingly internationalized. But it is also widely understood that prosecution is only one of the components of broader strategies in postconflict situations; amnesties, reparations, truth and reconciliation commissions were all designed to confront past human rights abuses, put an end to impunity, heal societal wounds and reconstruct an inclusive political space.

Transitional justice situations involve regime change and long-term social and economic transformations fraught with uncertainties as to the proper mix of retributive and reparative measures to achieve the not always converging objectives of democracy, stability, equity and fairness to victims. The most daunting challenges include legal or constitutional limitations such as amnesties which constrain prosecutorial capacities, the continuing influence of former power brokers and other "spoilers," weak, corrupt or ineffective institutions and the sheer number of victims. In this respect, one of the most striking development since the mid-1970s was the emergence of temporary, government-sanctioned or independent truth commissions, particularly following internal conflict to investigate, document and report on past human rights violations committed over a specified period of time.

The assumption underlying these practices is that finding the truth will help pave the way toward reconciliation, prevent violations of human rights in the future, and strengthen the transition to democratic rule. The benefits of truth commissions over retributive mechanisms are still hotly debated. Recent research does show that trials and truth commissions neither destabilize nor foster animosity, and in Latin America, there is some evidence that truth commissions and prosecution can contribute to lessening repression, but overall, studies of the effects of truth commission have yielded inconsistent results. In any case, it is too early to aver that there is an emerging right to demand punishment for violations of rights but, as the currently unfolding drama in Darfur and Syrian emphasizes, the way national leaders treat their nationals is no longer an exclusively domestic matter. Whether this is a trend that is likely to continue and spread to more powerful countries remains to be seen and in part hinges on questions which by and large warrant further reflection and study.

ENFORCEMENT

The prevailing pattern of what is labeled here as "enforcement" of human rights norms is through monitoring, supervision, dialogue, confrontation and exposure and condemnation. Ultimately, voluntary government compliance is of the essence. Compelling adherence to human rights standards or changes in government human rights policies through coercive tools remains the exception. But recourse to such practices—sanctions, peace operations by the United Nations or regional organizations and collective armed interventions for humanitarian or human rights purposes—has become more frequent in the past two decades.

Sanctions

The United Nations Charter confers upon the Security Council the power to decide, when all other peaceful means of conflict resolution have failed, what measures short of the use of armed force are to be employed to give effect to its decisions. The Council may thus call upon all members of the organization to apply such measures to maintain or restore international peace and security. It is in this context that the Council can order, in the quaint language of the Charter, the "complete or partial interruptions of economic relations and of rail, sea, air, postal, telegraphic and other means of communication and the severance of economic relations." In practice, the Council has resorted to a wide variety of sanctions such as comprehensive economic and trade sanctions and more recently more targeted measures such as arms embargoes, travel bans, and financial and diplomatic restrictions. It has not had recourse to its powers of suspension and exclusion spelled out in Article 5 of the Charter.

The Charter does not clarify what kind of state behavior should be censored by the Council nor does it define the terms "peace and security." It simply asserts that these "measures" may be taken in response to "threats to the peace" or "breaches of the peace and acts of aggression," the existence of which is determined by the Council. Presumably, most delegations involved in the drafting of the Charter conceived of "threats to the peace" as conventional security threats such as "armed attacks," a term explicitly referring to the right of states to individual and collective self-defense. The idea that violations of human rights constitute a "threat to the peace" only began to surface gingerly and incrementally against the background of decolonization.

The 1965 Unilateral Declaration of Independence by the white minority in Southern Rhodesia was a widely perceived move designed to avoid a system of shared powers laid down as one of the conditions for granting independence. In 1965 the Security Council adopted a non-binding resolution calling for a voluntary embargo on oil shipments. A year later, the Council characterized the situation as "a threat to international security" and prohibited the import and export of specific products. Noting the increasing number of violations of human rights, the Council subsequently stiffened the sanctions regime imposed on Southern Rhodesia, making it comprehensive and mandatory in scope with the exception of medical and humanitarian goods. Early on, the Apartheid regime in South Africa had become the target of non-binding sanctions adopted by the General Assembly. Opposition by France, Great Britain and the United States prevented the Security Council until 1963 from approving a mandatory arms embargoes on the sale and shipment of equipment and materials for armaments production. Eventually, in 1977, the Council determined that "the acquisition by South Africa of arms and related material constitute(d) a threat to the maintenance of international peace and security" and imposed a second mandatory arms embargo.

With the end of the Cold War and the growing involvement of the international community in civil conflicts characterized by gross violations of human rights—massacres, indiscriminate attacks on civilians, extra-judicial killings, torture, disappearances and wanton sexual violence—the Security Council has with increasing frequency exercised its powers under Chapter VII of the UN Charter to use sanctions in cases of gross human rights violations. In the wake of Iraq's invasion of Kuwait, the Council imposed a comprehensive range of economic sanctions on Iraq. These were tightened on 25 September 1990 in a resolution which condemned "the treatment by Iraqi forces of Kuwait nationals, including measures to force them to leave their own country and mistreatment of persons and property . . . [and] its holding of third-state nationals against their will." The economic sanctions against the Federal

Republic of Yugoslavia that the Council adopted in 1992 were in part prompted by its concern for the continued forced displacement of non-Serb civilians.

The Council's general and complete arms embargo on Somalia in 1992 reflected its apprehensions about "the rapid deterioration of the situation in Somalia and the heavy loss of human life and widespread material damage resulting from the conflict in the country." Belatedly, the Council condemned the genocide which had taken place in Rwanda and imposed a complete arms embargo on the county. The continued violence, loss of life and aggravated human rights conditions following the military coup in Sierra Leone prompted the Council to adopt economic sanctions including an arms embargo on non-state actors and a travel ban.

Beginning in 1995 and in response to a disastrous humanitarian situation, the Council adopted several resolutions imposing sanctions on Liberia including an arms embargo, a travel ban and an assets freeze. To prevent the financing of armed groups responsible for human rights violations through the illegal exploitation of natural resources, the Council put in place an increasingly stringent arms embargo on all foreign and Congolese armed groups operating in the eastern part of the DRC. The human rights situation in Cote d'Ivoire and in particular, the use of the media, in the northern part of the country to incite hatred and violence against foreigners in Côte d'Ivoire led the Council to put in place an arms embargo, a travel ban, an assets freeze and diamond sanctions. In a 2004 resolution that reminded the Sudanese government of its responsibility to maintain law and order and to protect its population within its territory, the Council adopted sanctions, including an arms embargo on all non-governmental entities and individuals suspected of indiscriminate attacks on civilians, rapes, or forced displacements in Darfur.

Regional organizations have emulated the UN Security Council and followed suit. First and foremost among them is the European Union which applies what it describes as "restrictive measures" in pursuit of specific objectives within the framework of its Common Foreign and Security Policy and in implementation of UN Security Council resolutions. Additionally, the European Union has also implemented embargoes imposed by the Organization for Security and Cooperation in Europe. Among them is the objective of developing and consolidating democracy, the rule of law and respect for human rights and fundamental freedoms. Possible restrictive measures include diplomatic sanctions (expulsion of diplomats, severance of diplomatic ties, suspension of official visits), trade sanctions, arms embargoes and a wide range of financial sanctions (i.e., freezing economic resources, prohibiting financial transactions, restrictions on export credits or investment, flight bans and restrictions on admission into the European Union). In effect, EU sanctions seek to promote human rights by linking respect for them to preferential economic relations. When targeted to its geographic proximity, EU economic sanctions, which must be approved by the Council of Ministers, have been driven primarily by security considerations. In contrast, sanctions with regard to the rest of the world are grounded in international law and value-based motives. The majority of sanctions have been imposed to protect democracy and human rights as was the case in South Africa, China, Myanmar, Yugoslavia, DRC, Nigeria, Sudan, Afghanistan, Belarus, Eritrea, Indonesia and Zimbabwe.

The 1951 Founding Charter of the Organization of American States contains a "democracy clause" enjoining OAS member states to maintain democratic systems as a sine qua non-condition for being part of the organization. The clause remained dormant or was used sparingly and selectively owing to the realities of the Cold War, United States regional hegemony and the proliferation of military regimes in the 1970s and 1980s as illustrated by OAS sanctions on the Dominican Republic in 1960 and Cuba in 1962. Since the early 1990s, the OAS has increasingly been willing to intervene in support of the protection of democratic systems, especially in countries where periods of dictatorship had recently ended. Thus the OAS took the lead in condemning the 1990 military overthrow of Jean-Bertrand Aristide, adopting diplomatic and economic sanctions against the regime and urging the United Nations to follow suit. Subsequently adopted normative instruments, notably the 2001 Inter-American Democratic Charter and the Additional Protocol to the Constitutive Treaty of the Union of South American Nations, have given added legitimacy to the region to address cases of a "rupture" or "threat of a rupture" in the democratic order. The Inter-American Democratic Charter thus recognizes democracy as a right of the people and establishes the elements considered essential for democracy, including respect for human rights and fundamental freedoms; access to and exercise of power in accordance with the rule of law; holding of periodic, free, and fair elections based on secret balloting and universal suffrage as an expression of the sovereignty of the people; pluralistic systems of political parties and organizations; and separation of powers and independence of the branches of government. These normative injunctions have provided the basis for more or less "muscled" interventions in Paraguay (1996 and 1999), Honduras (2009) and Ecuador (2010).

For most of its existence, the members of the Organization of African Unity were more deferential to the sanctity of territorial boundaries inherited from their colonial past than to human rights norms and principles. Its successor organization, the African Union (AU), has since its establishment in 2002 considerably changed this pattern. The promotion of democratic institutions, good governance and human rights is one of the key objectives of the AU.

Under the terms of its Constitutive Act, members of the AU also recognize the right of the organization to intervene in member states in circumstances of war crimes, genocide and crimes against humanity. The African Charter on Democracy, Elections, and Governance of 2007 provides for penalties in cases of unconstitutional changes of government including trial by competent bodies of the AU and the possibility for the AU Assembly to apply economic sanctions. The AU has thus been active in the Comoros, Darfur, Somalia, the DRC, Burundi and Cote d'Ivoire. It has also imposed sanctions against Mauritania, Guinea, Guinea Bissau, Mali and Madagascar.

All of this is not meant to suggest that regional organizations—and for that matter the UN Security Council—have been consistent in their practice. Vetoes (and sometimes double vetoes) have paralyzed the Council. The African Union and the European Union have remained silent or muted in a number of cases. Nor could it be safely concluded that sanctions necessarily bolster respect for fundamental human rights or deter or stop violations of rights. The story of multilateral sanctions is in fact a rather checkered one. There are indeed a few notable success stories. Under sanctions and multilateral and bilateral pressures, the government of Muammar Qaddafi admitted to responsibility for the 1988 Lockerbie bombings and renounced its weapons of mass destruction program. Sanctions weakened the regime of Slobodan Milosevic and pushed it toward accession to the 1995 Dayton Accords. Some observers believe that UN sanctions on Liberia's timber trade contributed to the downfall of Charles Taylor. On the other hand, inordinate delays and faulty implementation rendered sanctions against Somalia and Rwanda toothless in the early 1990s. In spite of strict UN sanctions, the Taliban regime in Afghanistan did not change its policies until its removal by the use of force. In Darfur, sanctions have constrained but not swayed the course of the Sudanese government actions.

Sanctions can also be destructive to the targeted societies while being ineffective in terms of their stated objectives. This much was learned from the experience of the tough UN sanctions against Iraq which neither reined in nor dislodged the Saddam Hussein regime. At the same time, as documented by UNICEF and other United Nations bodies and officials, they triggered severe humanitarian problems in the early 1990s which were partially offset by the creation of the Oil for Food Program. In response to these criticisms, "targeted," "smart" sanctions, especially those related to counterterrorism, have been developed. But in turn, these practices have elicited novel objections for being inconsistent with due process rights. A case in point is the designation of individuals and entities suspected of terrorism whose financial assets were to be frozen in implementation of the Security Council sanctions regime imposed on the Taliban in 1999.

The impact of sanctions on the enjoyment of human rights remains clouded by political as well as scholarly controversy. What is clear, however, is that a crucial connection has emerged from practice between the maintenance of international peace, the protection and promotion of rights and the rule of law in the broader context of democratization and development. Normatively speaking, human rights violations are now understood to be one of the root causes of conflict and humanitarian crises and not merely a consequence of insecurity and instability. From this vantage point, addressing human rights violations is a precondition of peace that requires the integration of human rights functions into peace operations.

The trend is apparent in the increasing frequency of senior human rights officials' interventions in the Council proceedings which started back in 1999 with the participation of the High Commissioner for Human Rights in an open debate of the Council on the protection of civilians in armed conflicts and East Timor in particular. Also noticeable has been the Council's growing willingness to consider a wide range of factors for their bearing on the maintenance of international peace and security including health issues such as HIV/AIDS, gender, transnational organized crime, climate change, breaches of the rule of law, the protection of civilians and the use of child soldiers and rape as weapons of war. In the fall of 2011, the Security Council held a high-level briefing on interrelated issues constituting "New Challenges to International Peace and Security." The Council took no action but this was the first time that it addressed these "new challenges" together under the broad rubric of the maintenance of international peace and security. In the same vein, in 2003 when the European Council adopted the European Security Strategy, it underlined the fact that "establishing the rule of law and protecting human rights" in combination with other instruments "are the best means of strengthening the international order." Another instance of a major international organization factoring non-traditional security threats into its security agenda would include the Arab League which, in the wake of the Arab Spring, backed UN action against Libya in 2011 and sanctioned Syria in 2012.

Peace Operations

The evolution of peace-keeping operations into what is now known as multifunctional "peace operations" provides further evidence of the growing recognition that the protection of human rights is an essential ingredient of peace and security. Originally, peacekeeping was a rather modest undertaking involving the stationing of military infantry–based forces observing ceasefire arrangements between consenting states. Their primary purpose, in Kashmir,

Cyprus, Southern Lebanon and the Sinai desert, was political (i.e., to create conditions for political negotiations conducive to a peaceful settlement of disputes). They were sometimes assigned human rights functions—the protection of civilians, the delivery of humanitarian assistance and the maintenance of law and order —as is the case in Cyprus where civilian police monitors have carried out searches for those reported missing. But these tasks were secondary and, in any case, could not be too overtly clarioned because of the Cold War.

The establishment of the United Nations Observer Group in El Salvador was the key precedent in the process that morphed UN peacekeeping into peace operations. The agreement brokered by the United Nations between the government and the insurgents stipulated that civilian monitors would be placed around the country to carry out the work of "active verification" of the human rights situation. It also provided for the dismantlement of existing security and police structures and the creation of a civilian national police. Thereafter, the UN Transition Assistance Group in the former South West Africa oversaw the repeal of discriminatory and restrictive legislation, the release of political prisoners, and the return of 42,000 exiled Namibians. The United Nations Transitional Authority in Cambodia virtually ruled the country during a transitional period leading to the 1993 national elections and was empowered to investigate and police human rights complaints and to take "corrective action." While attempting to broker a political settlement, the 1992 United Nations Operation in Somalia and the United Nations Protection Force (UNPROFOR) used military personnel to ensure the delivery of humanitarian assistance.

In current parlance, "peace operations" are no longer serving simply as a passive barrier between fighting forces. They are also deeply involved in a wide range of tasks allotted to specialized components, military observers, civilian police monitors, civilian human rights observers, refugee protection officers, electoral monitors, judicial or legislative advisers, development and technical development experts, and political and administrative personnel. Now virtually all UN peace operations incorporate human rights prevention, promotion and protection functions into their mandated work. In Afghanistan, Burundi, Central African Republic, Cote d'Ivoire, Darfur (Sudan), the Democratic Republic of the Congo, Guinea-Bissau, Haiti, Iraq, Liberia, Sierra Leone, Somalia, Sudan and Timor-Leste, peacekeepers monitor, issue public reports, assist in building capacity, provide technical assistance and financial support, and carry out training and sensitization activities.

One of the biggest human rights units deployed to date was the Human Rights Division of the United Nations Mission in the Democratic Republic of the Congo which provided advice and assistance concerning essential human rights legislation and fundamental freedoms, monitored, documented and reported on human rights violations and facilitated the protection of individuals under imminent threat of physical violence. The Human Rights Section of the recently established United Nations Integrated Peace Building Office in Sierra Leone advocates for the implementation of the recommendations of a truth and reconciliation commission and supports the newly established Human Rights Commission of the country and civil society in their efforts to advance human rights in the country. The UN/EU Mission in the Central African Republic and Chad monitors and investigates cases and incidents of sexual and gender-based violence and the recruitment and use of children as combatants by armed groups. The Human Rights Section of the AU/UN Hybrid Operation in Darfur provides human rights training for the police, prosecutors and judicial authorities and is empowered to visit places of detention to assess the legality of detentions, detained persons' access to justice, and monitoring any alleged ill-treatment or torture of detained persons.

Since the adoption in 2000 of Resolution 1325 by the UN Security Council, UN peace operations have increasingly incorporated gender advisers, units and focal points whose core function is to integrate gender perspectives into peace operations. The Gender Unit of the UN Mission in Liberia, for instance, is involved in disarmament, demobilization, reintegration processes, security sector reform, and the electoral process and legislative reforms. One of the tasks assigned to the UNMISS is to support the government in developing strategies for security sector reform, rule of law and justice sector including human rights capacities and institutions.

The Use of Force

The collective use of force is the most coercive and least frequently utilized instrument of coercion for the protection of human rights. Under the terms of the UN Charter, the recourse to force should receive the approval of the Security Council. Thus, on the basis of a council resolution, the United States, Great Britain, France and Turkey established a no-fly zone in 1991 in which Iraqi aircraft were prevented from flying. Its purpose was to prevent possible bombing or chemical attacks against the Kurdish population by the Iraqi regime. In 1992, the North Atlantic Treaty Organization (NATO) was authorized by the UN Security Council to prohibit unauthorized military flights over Bosnia. In 2011, and with a view to prevent further attacks against civilian targets, the Council approved a no-fly zone over Libyan territory.

The 1999 NATO bombing against Yugoslavia during the Kosovo war did not receive the endorsement of the Council, and for that reason it remains controversial (in addition to being criticized for the number of civilian casualties that it provoked). But the stated purpose of the campaign was to bring to an end the ethnic cleansing and other repressive activities carried out by Serbian forces against Albanian Kosovars. The latest instance of the use of coercion for human rights purposes may be found in the actions of the Council in relation to Libya. In response to "gross and systematic violation of human rights, including the repression of peaceful demonstrations, the deaths of civilians and the incitement of hostility and violence against the civilian population made from the highest level of the Libyan government," the Council first imposed travel bans on key Libyan leaders, froze their assets and referred the whole issue to the International Criminal Court. It subsequently authorized member states "to take all necessary measures . . . to protect civilians and civilian populated areas under threat of attack in the Libyan Arab Jamahiriya," a code word for the use of collective armed force.

In so doing the Council was drawing from a set of principles known as the "responsibility to protect" (R2P) which had emerged from the work and recommendations of a panel of former government officials, international relations experts and academics and received a nod of approval in non-binding resolutions of the General Assembly and the Security Council. But invocation of this "emerging norm" has triggered another intense round of controversies. Proponents of R2P—primarily NGOs—maintain that the principle is meant to be applied only when a state is no longer upholding its responsibilities as a sovereign by allowing and committing atrocities or being unable to prevent them. Only then can the international community "intervene" without state consent, it being understood that the final authority to employ force as a last resort still belongs to the UN Security Council. Critics object that R2P infringes on national sovereignty. They also argue that in practical terms, R2P is a tool of powerful nations—especially Western nations—to justify interventions driven by security interests dressed in human rights and humanitarian garb.

The debate still rages on and its intensity has been further intensified by the demise of the Libyan regime, an outcome which was not intended in the Council's enabling resolutions. In fact, the feeble, halting and incremental response of the international community to the Syrian crisis can also be viewed as a consequence of the demise of the Libyan regime in the wake of the NATO armed intervention. The Arab League, the European Union, the secretary-general of the United Nations and many governments have condemned the violence which has triggered a massive humanitarian crisis. Sanctions have been imposed but more decisive actions have been stymied by Russian and Chinese vetoes in the Security Council and military intervention has been ruled out by most countries, notwithstanding the fact that the human and humanitarian toll far exceeds that of the Libyan crisis.

These latest developments once again underline how differential human rights policy outcomes may be determined by the highly politicized nature of human rights issues and the contradictory pulls and pushes of the conflicting imperatives of sovereignty, national security and human rights. The international community did intervene with more or less resolve and vigor in Iraq (1991), Somalia (1992), Bosnia (1992), Kosovo (1999), East Timor (1999), Sierra Leone (2000), the DRC (2003), and Darfur (2004). But prior to the end of the Cold War, the UN Security Council had hardly invoked Chapter VII of the Charter to come to the rescue of human rights causes. Cases of omission include the Soviet invasion of Hungary in 1957, the French and English armed intervention in Egypt in 1956, the Indonesian occupation of East Timor beginning in 1975, the U.S. invasion of Granada in 1983, and what many view as genocidal acts against the Ache Indians in Paraguay, the Bengalis in East Pakistan, the Bangsa Moro in the Philippines and the Ibos in Nigeria. In the same vein, the Security Council remained silent over the blanket bombings, systematic burning of villages and use of napalm throughout the Vietnam War. Likewise, it did not act when chemical weapons were used in northern Iraq against the Kurds in the late 1980s. Perhaps the most jarring and disturbing instance of incoherence and double standards may be found in the fact that after being overthrown by a Vietnamese military intervention, representatives of the genocidal Khmer Rouge regime were voted in each year until 1993 by the UN General Assembly as the sole legal representatives of Cambodia in the organization!

In their own rights, peace operations have justifiably been praised as a cost-effective and relatively efficient multilateral response to the prevention, management, control and resolution of intrastate conflicts. From a human rights perspective, however, peace operations have a darker side. The effectiveness of the use of force is one issue. In essence, peace operations have at least three interrelated goals: to reduce or eliminate armed violence; to contain internally and externally the spread of armed violence; and to pave the way to the settlement of the conflict. It is against this background, for instance, that peace operations are assigned the task of protecting civilian populations in conflict situations through the creation of buffer zones or enclaves as they can be subjected to widespread human rights violations by government or insurgent forces. Looking at the experience of UNPROFOR and its failure to protect "safe areas," one might be prompted to reach the pessimistic conclusion that collective interventions may save a few lives but extend the war and increase human suffering in the longer term. More generally, while much has been said and written about the reasons accounting for particular human rights policy outcomes, not much has been done to evaluate in a rigorous and reliable manner the "success" (or lack thereof) of peace operations on the basis of consistent and reliable standards, indicators and tools of measurement.

Another neglected area of peace enforcement is that coercive measures may take a heavy human toll constituting or amounting to de facto massive violations of human rights. Estimates of the impact of the sanctions imposed on Iraq in 1990 vary widely, but it is believed that the sanction regime imposed on the country contributed to a shrinking of its GNP on the order of 50 percent, extraordinary declines in per capita income, dramatic increases in child mortality, water-borne diseases and malnutrition and losses in economic opportunities in the amount to $265 billion for 1990 to 1995.

Equally troublesome are the consequences of the proliferation of non-state armed groups (NSAGs) which has accompanied the fragmentation of states into smaller virtually self-governing entities and the augmented privatization of warfare. For instance, governments, private companies, NGOs and the United Nations take advantage of the services offered by NSAGs which undertake a growing range of activities in an increasing number of countries from drug-eradication programs to postconflict reconstruction work. Of particular concern is the use of private military and security companies, which raises issues of regulation, legitimacy, and practical operability that are imperfectly met by existing international human rights instruments and underline the need for a revamped regulatory regime in regard to the legal definition of mercenaries, their international treatment and the nature of their activities which requires criminalization.

Finally, the presence and activities of a large number of soldiers, police officers and civilian personnel have had unintended and harmful consequences on the host countries, leading notably to sexual abuse and exploitation, corruption, the creation of a parallel or illegal economy and the siphoning off of local entrepreneurial talent. Cases of sexual violence have received particular attention as they surfaced in such countries as Burundi, the Democratic Republic of the Congo, Sudan, Haiti, Liberia and Cote d'Ivoire. Most of these allegations are investigated but few lead to convictions or sanctions. All peacekeeping troops enjoy legal immunity. The UN and the host country both lack jurisdiction. Only troop-contributing countries have the authority to try and punish such wrongful acts and they have little incentive to do so. The result is a political or legal vacuum together with a general pattern of impunity.

CONCLUDING THOUGHTS: HALF EMPTY OR HALF FULL?

Over the past half century, human rights have moved to center stage throughout the world mobilizing a wide array of state and non-state actors.

The idea that human rights must be respected and defended—revolutionary a few decades ago—has become "conventional wisdom." Marked advances have been made in the codification of human rights laws and norms as reflected in the large body of international legal instruments that has steadily emerged and expanded since the end of World War II. No part of the world is immune to the scrutiny of international bodies monitoring state compliance with human rights norms. Dictators, military rulers and other perpetrators of gross human rights violations have been or are being held accountable for the atrocities committed in their name in courts of law. The contrast with the pattern of benign neglect, tolerance and accommodation to evil that prevailed during the interwar period is striking.

For all intents and purposes, international human rights standards have deeply transformed the relation between governments and the governed. Domestic legal systems have been reshaped by international human rights norms and treaties. Most states have written constitutions, many of which enshrine values inspired and guided by international human rights instruments. When treaties are incorporated into national law, the process triggers legal reforms. In the past decade or so, many states have introduced laws addressing various forms of violence against women such as domestic violence, marital rape, sexual harassment, trafficking in human beings, and female genital cutting. National courts' interventions are intended to review whether national laws are consistent with the spirit and letter of international human rights treaties. NGOs and national human rights institutions invoke treaty standards in relation to proposed government legislation and policies. So-called human rights defenders, whether journalists, lawyers, trade unionists, women, environmentalists or social workers, community organizers and other human rights "activists," expose human rights violations, teach, promote and spread international human rights norms.

Normative Gaps: What "Self-Evident Truths"?

The human rights revolution is still a work in progress. The axiomatic principles which all human rights advocates take for self-evident—participation and inclusion, equality and non-discrimination, accountability and the rule of law, and above all, the universality, indivisibility and interrelatedness of human rights—remain or have become the subjects of intense debate. Human rights—civil and political, economic, social and cultural—are interrelated, a point that has been repeatedly emphasized by UN treaty bodies in the comments and observations. However, in practice and for widely differing reasons, such connections are not made. Most national constitutions and legislative systems at least formally do recognize all human rights but rarely endow economic, social and cultural rights with the same mechanisms for review and enforcement as civil and political rights, the former being viewed as non-justiciable and aspirational policy-oriented rights. At the international level, cherry-picking remains the dominant pattern.

If anything, the demise of the Cold War has further underlined the elusiveness of the notion of the indivisibility of rights by adding other layers of complexity to the debate. A case in point are the recent acrimonious discussions over "defamation of religion" in which an Islamic coalition of states clashed with the West when it denounced "the intensification of the campaign to defame religions and the ethnic and religious profiling of Muslim minorities in the aftermath of the tragic events of 11 September 2001" and called for limitations on the right of freedom of expression.

Meanwhile, the North-South split over economic and social rights has not dissolved, thus perpetuating the tensions and disconnect between human rights and development. Poverty eradication and development undoubtedly contribute to the realization of human rights or create the conditions under which human rights can be realized. Likewise, there is merit in stressing the convergence of the broad principles underlying development and human rights: participation and consultation, inclusiveness, equality, empowerment, good governance and equity, among others. But the human rights language carries with it a polarizing dimension of duty and legal obligation. The South perceives the "imposition" of human rights standards in trade arrangements, bilateral development assistance or the lending policies of multilateral organizations as new modalities of conditionalities, intrusions in their national sovereignty and outright manifestations of double standards and hypocrisy by powerful countries. Conversely, Northern states hotly contest the Southern assertion that there is some sort of transnational obligation on the part of wealthy states to provide assistance to developing states in order to enable them to achieve their right to development. Not surprisingly, multilateral development agencies, with the possible exceptions of a handful of organization such as the ILO, the United Nations Development Programme and the United Nations Children Fund, have either ignored the human rights language (a case in point being the IMF) or very gingerly or very superficially "mainstreamed" human rights considerations in their activities. The Millennium Development Goals is a typical instance of a multilateral development scheme which purports to be a "framework of accountability" but refrains from expressly referring to rights.

The disconnect between human rights and development is all the more regrettable in light of the growing role and unprecedented power of multinational corporations. The impact of TNCs on human rights is widely debated, some arguing that their presence enhances security rights, but others that they reinforce state coercion and labor suppression. Good or bad, it is clear that TNCs are major influences in the daily life of millions of people and that the realization of their rights increasingly depends on the activities and practices of these global actors. The legal duties of TNCs can be readily identified in the context of domestic criminal laws, civil rights laws, and consumer protection laws. There are also a few cases, mainly before the European Court of Human Rights, grounded in the doctrine of the state's responsibility to ensure that private entities or individuals over which they exercise jurisdiction do not deprive individuals of their economic, social and cultural rights.

But whether TNCs should or could be held legally responsible for not observing international human rights norms remains by and large an unresolved legal puzzle. Most international law documents regarding corporate human rights duties are not legally binding and efforts to go beyond voluntary guidelines have grounded or are grinding to a halt. The expectations raised by the initial cases brought in the United States against corporations under the Alien Tort Claims Act (ACTA) for alleged violations by transnational corporations of human rights protected by the laws of nations have yielded to disappointment and skepticism. None of these cases has been settled on its merits and the jurisdiction of U.S. courts has been contested with increasing success. In any case, while it is plausible—though highly improbable—that ACTA could lead to rulings prohibiting the abuse of rights recognized as non-derogable under international customary law, breaches of less universally recognized rights such as a right to the environment or the right to trade unions might not necessarily lead to rulings unfavorable to transnational corporations. Clarifying private sector responsibility in the human rights sector and where TNCs' responsibilities begin and end remain clouded in normative uncertainty as there is no agreement about who should define acceptable human rights standards for TNCs, monitor their behavior, make judgments about transgressions and enforce sanctions.

Institutional Gaps

As noted earlier, the number of human rights institutions that have emerged in the postwar period is truly extraordinary. But that pattern of politically driven institutional growth has proceeded in an unbridled, ad hoc and disjointed manner, contributing to fragmentation, redundancies and glaring dysfunctions. The uncontrolled proliferation of judicial and quasi-judicial bodies, in particular, has led to inconsistencies and contradictions in practice and jurisprudence. Some of the shortcomings of the UN treaty body system—the superficiality of state reports and the inordinate delays in their submission—have already been noted. Observers have also raised questions about the level of expertise and independence of their members, the frequently exceedingly broad and general nature of their comments on states reports and the generally inadequate follow up to recommendations made to governments.

Of course, governments rarely display great enthusiasm in facilitating debate about their period reports. But the growing number of states ratifications has been accompanied by burdensome and duplicative reporting obligations and backlogs in the consideration of reports and individual complaints. Even cooperative states have become more reluctant to be subjected to new monitoring. The multiplication of monitoring bodies that by and large act independently from one another has led to diverging normative injunctions and different levels of protection. The International Covenant on Civil and Political Rights, for example, allows for derogation from the right to join and form trade unions, while the International Covenant on Economic, Social and Cultural Rights does not. This pattern of fragmentation undermines the capacity of states—whenever they are willing to do so—to translate these inconsistent rulings into integrated cross-sectoral national planning and programming.

There is clearly a need to consolidate and streamline the work of UN treaty bodies, and discussions about reform have been ongoing for some year involving the UN's human rights commissioner, current and former members of the treaty bodies, a number of national human rights institutions and several NGOs. Reforms have been primarily incremental, focusing on the harmonization of working methods and encouraging states to submit wide-ranging common core documents with information relevant to the work of all treaty bodies as well as targeted reports pertaining to the obligations specific for each of the treaties. Suggestions for more drastic steps such as the creation of a unique standing treaty body initially put on the table by the high commissioner has not elicited much enthusiasm. But interestingly enough, the issue is specifically addressed in the International Convention for the Protection of All Persons from Enforced Disappearance, which calls on its committee to consult other treaty bodies with a view toward ensuring the consistency of their respective observations and recommendations.

But even such modest proposals would hardly make a dent in the broader issue of bringing consistency to the normative outputs of different organizations. The United Nations, ILO, Council of Europe, and European Union have each developed standards on social security and discrimination that offer different forms and degrees of protection. In 2012, the UN-HRC ruled that France was violating Sikhs' religious freedom by forcing them to remove their turbans when having photos taken for passports and ID cards.

In 2008, the ECHR had dismissed a similar appeal on grounds of security. Another layer of complexity is the uneasy relationship between organizations which have mainstreamed human rights considerations into their programs of work and those which claim that their primary mandate has only a remote connection with human rights.

The problem arises in particular in regard to the World Trade Organization (WTO) norms of most favored nation and national treatment and like product rules which constrain the capacity of national policymakers to protect or advance particular human rights. For instance, all WTO member governments have officially committed to observe the narrow set of internationally recognized "core" labor standards embraced by the ILO from the use of child labor and forced labor, to the right to organize trade unions and strike, and for minimum wages, health and safety conditions, and working hours. How to reconcile these normative principles with the trade liberalization mandate of the WTO under the banner of "coherence" remains a contentious issue: Should the WTO as an international organization be bound by international human rights? Should the existence of low labor standards in some countries be a signal for all countries to lower their higher standards? Should countries only trade with those with similar labor standards? Should WTO rules allow governments to use trade as a vehicle for putting pressure on other countries to comply? Where should these matters be discussed? In the ILO? In the WTO? The debate is still unfolding.

The Enforcement Gap

As it has developed over the past decades, the human rights system has generated a complex structure comprised of numerous institutions enjoying a wide spectrum of decision-making authority, enforcement capacities and mechanisms. But if "enforcement" means to describe vertical "top down" "authoritative mechanisms designed and expected to compel direct consequences, such as changes in governmental policy, payment of civil compensation, or criminal penalties, under the threat of meaningful sanction," then the enforcement of human rights norms is, to put it blandly, "anemic." The prevailing mode of enforcement, as provided for in most multilateral treaties, remains implementation of international human rights norms through domestic institutions supplemented by weak international institutions with the limited authority to monitor state compliance and encouraging states to voluntarily change their behavior through dialogue, confrontation, disclosure and technical assistance.

With some minor exceptions, global human rights institutions essentially provide for public condemnation of states guilty of a "consistent pattern of gross violations." They have neither the authority to provide individual redress nor the legal and de facto capacity to give effect to their decisions. Even international criminal law institutions have to rely on national instruments of enforcement. The unavoidable consequence of this state of affairs is delay and selectivity in the application of international human rights norms. Thus, the relative success of the ILO's and ECHR's petitioning systems in securing state compliance stands in sharp contrast to the relatively modest record of the inter-American system and the UN Human Rights Committee. The "reform" of the UN Human Rights Council failed to bring an end to the "politicization" which had plagued its predecessor body.

Some governments have no qualms in refusing to grant access to special procedures mandate holders. When they do not, they may hamper their work on the ground or continue to victimize the human rights defenders who collaborate with them. As a recent global survey underlines, National Human Rights Institutions (NHRIs) have an uneasy relationship with public bodies, such as the executive, the parliament, the judiciary or the police, which they believe attach little value to their work or ignore or do not follow up on their recommendations. The survey also found that governments seek to control NHRIs through the provision of budget allocation. Cases have been brought to the European Court of Human Rights, the Inter-American Commission of Human Rights and national courts by human rights lawyers and activists who sought to apply human rights norms to military conduct in international and internal conflicts and to situations of belligerent occupations. This type of litigation can in part be explained by the fact that there are no judicial bodies that can hear claims of violations of international humanitarian law. But by and large governments have resisted such attempts essentially because they feel that human rights norms place greater constraints on their conduct of hostilities, detention and administration practices in occupied territories.

The prohibition of genocide, crimes against humanity and war crimes is a commonly accepted "peremptory" norm of international human rights law. Yet, even when they are not complicit, the states involved are often reluctant to prosecute such crimes. Brazil is only now beginning to prosecute human rights violations committed during the military dictatorship in the 1970s. Previous attempts have been blocked by interpretations of a 1979 amnesty law which was ruled invalid under international human rights law in 2010 by the Inter-American Court of Human Rights. While the International Criminal Tribunal for the Former Yugoslavia, the International Criminal Tribunal for Rwanda and the Special Court of Sierra Leone have successfully tried and convicted a large number of defendants, their work has been slowed by the unwillingness of governments to promptly hand over suspected high-ranking fugitives.

A quarter of the population died as a result of torture, starvation, disease, exhaustion or outright killing in the experiment in social engineering launched by the Khmer Rouge between 1975 to 1979. Only a handful of aging Khmer Rouges are now facing war crimes and crimes against humanity in a mixed international tribunal laboriously constituted 35 years later. More than 20,000 ex-Khmer Rouge soldiers and workers are believed to live freely in the country and the government includes many former Khmer Rouge cadres. Not surprisingly, the Cambodian prime minister lambasted the tribunal when an international prosecutor recommended to investigate five more suspects, and several international investigating judges have resigned, citing government interference. Under international pressure, Indonesia set up a special court to try those responsible for the orchestrated violence which left 1,500 people dead and displaced more than a third of the population when East Timor, under UN supervision, won its independence from Indonesia between 1999 and 2002. All the Indonesians were acquitted on appeal, prompting advocacy groups to deride the process as a "farce." An estimated 3,000 to 5,000 people have disappeared in Chechnya since 2000, but the Russian government has neither properly investigated these abuses nor taken effective steps to end them.

The fight against terrorism has also taken a heavy toll. UN treaty bodies, in their concluding observations on states reports or in their jurisprudence, have repeatedly enjoined governments to ensure that counterterrorism measures should be fully consistent with human rights standards and the rule of law. The European Court of Justice and the European Court of Human Rights have invalidated national and EU counterterrorism legislative measures, reasserted the absolute nature of the prohibition of torture and *non-refoulement* and reaffirmed the need to balance human rights and security interests. Yet, a 2009 comprehensive survey of the International Commission of Jurists "Assessing Damage, Urging Action" still found extensive evidence of grave human rights abuses perpetrated under the banner of combating terrorism, including torture, inhuman and degrading treatment, enforced disappearances, arbitrary detentions, racial profiling, breaches of privacy rights, violations of due process rights, denial of effective remedies and criminalization of protest and dissent. Executive attacks on civil liberties bolstered by acquiescing majorities can also take place in democratic regimes.

The other side of the coin, which receives less public attention, is that while governments undoubtedly commit abuses in the struggle against terrorism, "insurgents," "irregulars," "freedom fighters" or "terrorists"—whatever label may be used—do display a sometimes more striking and objectionable lack of concern of human rights. Investigations and fact-finding missions carried out by human rights groups or officials of international organizations repeatedly show that non-state armed opposition groups are also involved in such grievous human rights as unlawful killing, torture and ill-treatment, kidnapping and hostage taking. Typical instances include the armed conflict which pitted Islamic rebel groups against the government throughout the 1990s and the still unfolding civil war in Syria.

The Financial Gap

The language of international organizations concerned with human rights frequently takes on messianic overtones. For instance, the latest budget documents of the United Nations aver that "the over-arching objective of the United Nations human rights programme is to promote and protect the effective enjoyment by all of *all human rights*" (author's emphasis). In that context the Office of the High Commissioner will continue to give priority "to emphasizing the importance of human rights in international and national agendas, combating poverty and countering discrimination on all internationally recognized grounds, including race, sex, language or religion, advancing the rights of children and women, raising awareness of human rights at all levels of education, responding to the needs of the vulnerable for protection and addressing situations of international concern, in particular, gross and systematic violations of human rights, as identified by the Human Rights Council and other relevant United Nations organs." Similarly lofty and sweeping language can be found in EU documents. Launched in 2006, the European Instrument for Democracy and Human Rights is tasked with providing "support for the promotion of democracy and human rights in non-EU countries." Its "key objectives" are to enhance respect for human rights and fundamental freedoms in countries and regions where they are most at risk; to strengthen the role of civil society in promoting human rights and democratic reform, to support actions in areas covered by EU guidelines (i.e., "dialogues" on human rights, human rights defenders, the death penalty, torture, children and armed conflicts and violence against women); to strengthen the international and regional framework for the protection of human rights, justice, the rule of law and the promotion of democracy; and to enhance the reliability and transparency of democratic electoral processes.

These exalted objectives, however laudable they may be, stand in sobering contrast with the financial resources made available to both organizations by their member states. The UN secretary-general's proposals for the 2012 to 2013 biennium earmarked some $147 million for the Office of the High Commissioner, a sum that represents a puny 2.6 percent of the total UN budget. If voluntary contributions to the Office of the High Commissioner are factored in against all extrabudgetary resources made available to the

UN system (they amount to close to $240 million), then the 2 percent ratio plunges to an infinitesimal proportion. For the period 2007 to 2013, the European Union has a budget of over 1 billion euros for human rights projects, programs and grants. For a single year (2011), the overall EU budget was 141 billion euros! The disparity between public statements and actual deeds and, some would add, between rhetoric and engagement needs no further highlighting. If anything, it is yet another manifestation of the ambivalence of governments.

Changing Tectonic Trends and Looming Challenges

Counterterrorism relates to the short and medium term. Other tectonic transformations will influence and continue reshaping human rights practices. Revolutions in demography, science and technology, especially information technology, the globalization and liberalization of the world economy, the growing significance of non-state actors in international relations and transnational threats to human security are posing new problems and challenges, altering the frontiers of human rights protection and accountability and introducing a degree of uncertainty and unpredictability into the international human rights system.

Demographic shifts, especially changes in the size, age structure and geographic distribution of the world population, will have critical implications for policy and the realization of human rights. Social institutions such as marriage, the family and other civic partnerships and gender relations will be affected. The expected aging of all societies implies that human rights issues associated with age—the access to opportunities to resources and entitlements of the elderly and of emerging new generations—will likely become more prominent. Population decline in the North and the "youth bulge" in the South will intensify migration movements with the more than probable consequence that questions of recognition and entitlement of rights, residence naturalization and citizenship will acquire further salience on governmental public policy agenda in host countries.

Dramatic scientific advances and innovations in the past decades in biology—notably in biomedicine and biotechnology—and their applications in health care have raised and will pose a growing number of ethical and human rights concerns related to identity, privacy, the structure of the family, access to health care and protection against discrimination, among others. Some international organizations—the United Nations, the United Nations Educational, Scientific and Cultural Organization, and in particular, the Council of Europe—have made significant efforts over the past few years to establish common standards that can be regarded as the beginning of an international biomedical law embedded in human rights principles. But most of this body of law is soft law, reflecting the fact that beyond the urgency of preventing human germ-line interventions and human reproductive cloning, there is no universal consensus on a host of issues. For example, what is the moral status of embryos and stem cells? Is their use in research or their potential contribution to improving or harming human health permissible? Could reproductive cloning and genetic enhancement be classified as a new category of "crimes against humanity"? Could scientists developing such technologies be deemed to potentially commit terrorist acts? Could the human use of genetic technology and information result in breaches of privacy and new inequalities between individuals in regard to access to medical treatment, employment and insurance? Should the mapping of the human genome belong to the "global commons"? Is a human rights framework with its universalist or cosmopolitan claims the proper approach to dealing with these issues?

The more visible breakthroughs in global communications technology—web-based publishing satellite television, Voice over Internet Protocol, transnational broadcasting, among others—are transforming the way people live and how they relate to one another. They are generating new layers of legal entitlement as the focus of public debate is increasingly on "Internet freedom" (i.e., the right to have access to and to use the Internet as a means to exercise such freedoms). The UN special rapporteur for the promotion and protection of freedom of information and expression has acknowledged Internet access as a basic right. The European Court of Justice has condemned Internet filtering, and the UN High Commissioner for Human Rights has publicly deplored restrictions on the Internet and the arrests of bloggers in some countries. By virtually eliminating the transaction costs of collective action, the Internet provides a platform for easy group forming and has begun to change existing prevailing modes of advocacy. It is also easier for human rights organizations to monitor state compliance with human rights standards. The rapidity with which protest movements have spread in the Middle East and North Africa is to a large extent a consequence of the use of social media. These upheavals are also reminders of the direct links between economic and social rights and civil and political rights. As a recent UN study demonstrates, these popular movements are a manifestation of poverty, unemployment, inequality and exclusion which, in turn, is the result of a long-term deficit in democratic governance.

But the vast potential of cyberspace is a double-edged sword as this has also rekindled old debates about the parameters of human rights—freedoms of expression, opinion and association—protected by international human rights instruments. The modern world is increasingly monitored through more and more ubiquitous and powerful techniques of surveillance such as video cameras, mobile phone monitoring, control of financial transactions, and satellite and drone observation. Independent UN experts and NGOs like Reporters without Borders have warned that governments, under the guise of "Internet sovereignty," are giving priority to internal security, the war on terrorism and cybercrime and even the protection of intellectual property over the free flow of news and information online by restricting even more the flow of information on the Internet, censoring Internet content, using information obtained from the Internet against dissidents, and engaging in cyberattacks against political opponents.

The 1972 Stockholm Declaration established a foundational link between human rights and environmental protection and declared that man has a "fundamental right to freedom, equality and adequate conditions of life, in an environment of a quality that permits a life of dignity and well-being, and he bears a solemn responsibility to protect and improve the environment for present and future generations." The idea that human rights, and especially the right to life, are threatened by a degraded or polluted environment has gained political traction in multilateral fora in recent years. The long-term potential consequences of changes associated with climate change—sea level rises, more intense and longer droughts, more intense tropical storms and heat waves—include food and water shortages, population shifts, economic losses and heightened security risks. Some economies may wither and collapse, impoverishing affected communities, causing large movements of population and generating numerous inequities and tensions especially in relation with burden sharing and risk allocation.

It is understood that climate change does pose a direct potential threat to a wide range of economic and social rights and is likely to affect the enjoyment of human rights, most particularly of vulnerable groups. For example, environmental problems—desertification, lack of water, salination of irrigated lands and the depletion of biodiversity—have already contributed to large permanent migrations and the number of "environmental migrants," "environmental refugees," "climate refugees" and "climate migrants" may grow exponentially, possibly reaching 150 to 200 million by 2050. These figures are contested and controversial but some observers have argued that "environmental persecution" as a new category of "refugees" needs to find a place in international agreements. Should the 1950 Refugee Convention be accordingly amended or is a new human rights treaty required to address this type of human vulnerability to climate change? Who are the "duty holders" vis-à-vis the "rights bearers": Governments? Private companies? In any event, and this is not surprising in light of the complexity of the stakes and issues involved, international negotiations on climate change mitigation and adaptation have taken place with little if any account being taken of their human rights implications. Equally disquieting is the fact that current prevailing human rights remedial mechanisms are ill equipped to respond to the climate change challenge. Assuming that global warming may infringe on certain fundamental human rights, having recourse to litigation as a means of redress poses virtually unanswerable questions about the kind of admissible evidence that could establish a causal link between greenhouse gas emissions to specific climate change–related effects and direct implications for the enjoyment of a particular right.

The evidence available on the overall human rights impact of the globalization of trade, money, finance and technology is contradictory but it underlines the need for new mechanisms and modalities of human rights accountability. The wave of privatization and the emergence of private public partnerships that have accompanied globalization in the past decades in the name of market efficiency have altered in significant ways our understanding of the role and function of the state in the provision of public goods and basic services. The problem directly feeds into human rights concerns to the extent that, both in theory and practice, the state is considered the sole source of responsibility and accountability. Globalization has eroded the validity of this assumption while raising questions about what constitutes the public interest, who should determine it, and who should be accountable: states or the private sector? These questions are all the more pertinent in light of the persistence of mass poverty and growing inequalities within countries and between North and South. More than 1 billion people across the globe currently live on the U.S. equivalent of less than $1 per day. Lack of income is not necessarily a human rights violation. But lack of income does imply low life expectancy, lack of access to education, health and social services, housing and employment, in effect, social exclusion and de facto enslavement and blatant violations of the International Bill of Rights.

To be more specific, globally induced economic adjustments may erode the capacity of states to protect human rights or produce state policies that trigger violations of social and labor rights and intensify poverty and protest. The Asian financial crisis of the 1990s brought home the reality of the impact of the unbridled functioning of financial and monetary markets and policies on the economic and social security of large segments of the population who are not protected against their vicissitudes. The still currently unfolding debt crisis that has engulfed Europe and America has been accompanied by a wave of social cuts and a worrisome trend of legal reforms to contain budget deficits, which carry the risk of potential regressions in the levels of achievement of economic, social and cultural rights. The deregulation and privatization of the social means of production have led to increased reliance on subcontractors by private and public sector corporations whose workers enjoy significantly fewer rights and benefits.

At the same time, a growing number of individuals do not enjoy full citizenship. Recent data issued by the ILO show that more than 20 million people worldwide are victims of forced labor, the bulk of them being exploited in the private economy. According to UN-HCR estimates, right now there are about 42 million displaced people in the world. One-third of them are officially recognized as refugees because they crossed an international border. The others are internally displaced persons, a category that includes undocumented "economic migrants" without civil rights. In this respect, observers have drawn attention to the fact that within the same state there may be varying configurations of citizenship with limitations on movement, speech and assembly. In China alone there are now over 100 million economic migrants and this number is expected to rise by another 243 million by 2025. In many countries, internal migration produces rural to urban migrants who are often illiterate, lack civil status and experience discrimination.

Depending on the definition used, many states cumulatively host around 350 million indigenous people in a de facto tutelary political and civic status and whose lifestyle and land rights are threatened by environmental degradation and external intrusions. More generally, unequal ownership of agricultural land and lack of access to income from land have been and remain flashpoints conducive to economic exploitation and social unrest. The UN independent expert on the right to food recently bemoaned the growing practice of contract farming arrangements with processing or marketing companies by smallholder farmers and warned that it "left the door open for produce to be summarily rejected, for farm debt to spiral, for labor to be sub-contracted without regulatory oversight, and for a region's food security to be undermined by production of export-oriented cash crops at the expense of all else."

There is no consensus on the human rights impacts of trade liberalization and trade agreements. But, as discussed earlier, human rights advocates have often expressed concern about the human rights implications of the work of WTO, which they accuse of either not paying enough attention to human rights or of facilitating and perpetuating human rights abuses. One prominent and continuing instance of the tensions between human rights and trade law is the shrill and contentious debate over international patent law and access to medication for AIDS, bird flu, and anthrax, among others, which pits less-developed countries against Northern states and drug companies. Another related contentious issue involves the practice by international agricultural and biotech companies which patent local agricultural methods and seed types, thus becoming the owners of what was once considered part of a cultural heritage. Higher tariffs, temporary import restrictions, state purchase from smallholders, active marketing boards, safety net insurance schemes, and targeted farm subsidies are increasingly acknowledged as vital measures to rehabilitate local food production capacity in developing countries. But WTO rules leave little space for developing countries to put these measures in place, leading a UN right to food expert to lament the fact that food security was held hostage to trade in current WTO negotiations. Another troubling issue is the notorious "race to the bottom," a phenomenon triggered by deregulation measures designed to gain a comparative advantage and attract foreign investment, which may lead to a deterioration in working conditions and wages. In the final analysis, the key problem is that the human rights and trade legal regimes have developed separately and need to be reconciled and made mutually supportive rather than contradictory.

One last observation on the subject of globalization. The transnationalization of markets has nurtured the emergence of a number of transnational organized crime threats ranging from trafficking in persons, to the smuggling of migrants and natural resources, to drug and arms trafficking, to the illicit trade in counterfeited goods, to maritime piracy, which, in turn, have spawned human rights abuses affecting countries of supplies, trafficking, or demand and undermining the rule of law and good governance. The indiscriminate violence that accompanies the activities of transnational criminal networks not only threatens the safety and rights of individuals, it also casts a long shadow over the capacity of states to cope with the threats they pose. So far, these issues have been dealt with primarily in terms of criminalization. They also raise by and large unresolved questions of liability and culpability for both state and non-state actors.

More Rights?

In a recently published work, an expert in psycholinguistics argued that the world is becoming less violent and he attributes that trend to a variety of factors including the rise of the modern centralized states and the impact of human rights. The present study is perhaps unduly and overly concerned with the short and medium term. But like so many others, it must conclude that the practice of upholding and giving effect to the human dignity of groups and individuals in a world order still overshadowed by sovereign states is yet another variation on the proverbial theme of the half full–half empty glass. True enough, as an Italian academic opined, "the struggle for human rights is like an overflowing river that floods down across the valley making the fields ever more fertile." The human rights movement has indeed been an expanding force covering new areas. And improvements there have been seen, but they are uneven. In addition, reliance on voluntarism for enforcement in effect means that human rights protection mechanisms are most needed where they are likely to be the least effective and, conversely, most effective where they are (most of the time) less needed! As societies evolve constantly, new standards can be expected to be developed to fill emerging gaps in protection. There are, for example, spirited discussions in multilateral forums about the desirability of legalizing a human right to international solidarity, a human right to peace or of developing soft law mechanisms for the protection of victims of terrorism.

But, critics counter, why elaborate new standards if they cannot be enforced, if they have not been meaningfully incorporated into domestic law or if the global machinery put in place to monitor them has been hijacked by governments? For these critiques, the gap between the ideals of the human rights movement and the reality on the ground requires that priority be given to achieving practical results and tangible improvements, in brief, to implementation (i.e., to translating agreed upon norms into practice). They also make the additional argument that standards' setting is a slow, protracted and contentious process fraught with uncertainty as to outcomes in light of the difficulty to achieve a bona fide consensus among countries with different sociocultural backgrounds and political agendas. In all likelihood, the debate—standards' settings versus implementation—like all other policy debates about the praxis of human rights, will continue to evolve in an incremental, disjointed, and chaotic manner fed by the uncoordinated interplay of doctrinal disputes, intellectual debates, clashing political interests, the implausible premise of voluntary state compliance, and the actions of state and non-state actors. As a thoughtful observer of the human rights movement aptly put it in a recent assessment of the work of the Human Rights Watch, "Victories in human rights are always a reprieve, not a harbinger of radiant tomorrows."

1235 PROCEDURE. *See* 1503 PROCEDURE.

1503 PROCEDURE. One of the "**Special Procedures**" utilized by the United Nations Council on Human Rights (previously, the **United Nations Commission on Human Rights**) for the redress of human rights **violations**. Named after Resolution 1503 adopted in 1970 by the **United Nations Economic and Social Council** (UN-ECOSOC) by which it was established, this procedure is set in motion when the Council receives an individual complaint (in UN parlance, a "**communication**") about gross human rights violations by their governments. Targeted states appear before the full Council, which then decides whether to keep the situation under review and wait for further information, appoint an expert to make investigations or discontinue consideration of the complaint. If the human rights violations continue, the Council may have recourse to another procedure (the so-called 1235 Procedure, also named after a 1967 enabling resolution of UN-ECOSOC) under which it can hold an annual public debate on them. Eventually, the Council may recommend to the UN-ECOSOC the adoption of a resolution condemning the delinquent state, a step deemed to tarnish the reputation and prestige of the ruling authorities. Between 1989 and 2005, 106 states were targeted (86 under the 1503 Procedure, 53 under the 1235 Procedure and 32 under both). *See also* UNITED NATIONS SUB-COMMISSION ON THE PROMOTION AND PROTECTION OF HUMAN RIGHTS.

1969 ORGANIZATION ON AFRICAN UNITY CONVENTION GOVERNING THE SPECIFIC ASPECTS OF REFUGEE PROBLEMS IN AFRICA. Regional instrument adopted by the **Organization of African Unity** extending the meaning of the term **refugee** to every person who, owing to external aggression, occupation, foreign domination or event seriously disturbing public order in either part or the whole of his country of origin or nationality, is compelled to leave his place of habitual residence in order to seek refuge in another place outside his country of origins or nationality. *See also* CARTAGENA DECLARATION OF REFUGEES; UNITED NATIONS CONVENTION RELATING TO THE STATUS OF REFUGEES.

ABACHA, SANI (1943–1998). Nigerian military leader and politician who took power in 1993 and ruled Nigeria until his sudden death. Under his rule, numerous **violations of human rights** were committed, ranging from the banning of political activities to the jailing of political opponents to the hanging in 1995 of Ogoni activists opposed to the exploitation of Nigerian land by transnational oil corporations. Portrayed after his death as a traitor and looter of the Nigerian treasury by the successor government, he is accused of having stolen US$3 to $4 billion in public funds. In 2004, **Transparency International** listed Abacha as the world's fourth most corrupt leader in recent history. *See also* CORRUPTION.

ABDUCTION. *See* FORCED DISAPPEARANCES.

ABKHAZIA. Breakaway region of northwest Georgia bordering on Russia and the Black Sea which proclaimed its independence in 1992, a year after Georgia proclaimed its own independence with the breakup of the Soviet Union. After the 1917 Russian Revolution, Abkhazia was made an autonomous republic within Soviet Georgia. After **Josef Stalin**'s death, the province was granted a considerable degree of political and cultural autonomy which was all the more significant as ethnic Abkhaz made up only 18 percent of the population of Abkhazia and ethnic Georgian 46 percent. Ethnic tensions between Abkhaz and Georgians thus rapidly built up with the disintegration of the Soviet Union at the end of the 1980s and Georgia's move toward independence. In response to Georgia's independence in April 1991, which many Abkhaz construed as the abolition of their autonomous status, the Abkhazia government seceded from Georgia. After a yearlong war, Georgian troops were forced to withdraw from the region.

Both sides committed gross **violations of human rights** during the war as combatants targeted and indiscriminately attacked civilian populations and structures. Virtually all ethnic Georgians fled the region, escaping an ethnic cleansing initiated by the victors. Some 250,000 to 300,000 people (half of the prewar population) were thus forcibly displaced. The Georgian-Abkhaz conflict remains intractable. A 1994 agreement facilitated by Russia and signed under United Nations auspices provides for a ceasefire, separation of forces and the deployment of a **Commonwealth of Independent States (CIS)** peacekeeping force, made up entirely of Russian troops. In 1993, the **United Nations** set up an observer mission, the **United Nations Observer Mission in Georgia**, to monitor the observance of the ceasefire, the activities of the CIS force and the facilitation of the return refugees and **internally displaced persons**.

Periodic meetings under the auspices of the United Nations between Georgian and Abkhaz representatives have yielded no political settlement and negotiations are stalled. The Abkhaz claim a right to statehood based on national **self-determination**, while Georgia argues that de facto authorities who won the armed struggle and forcibly displaced a majority of the population lack the democratic legitimacy which would otherwise give them a right to control Abkhazia. Georgia also blames the Russian Federation for providing military, economic and political support to the Abkhaz as part of broader territorial and hegemonic ambitions. Conversely, Russia retorts that it is only playing a humanitarian and restraining role. Meanwhile, neither side to the conflict has seriously investigated, let alone punished, criminal offenses committed during the conflict. A quarter million ethnic Georgians live in precarious conditions as they are unable to return to their prewar homes and cannot or are not willing to settle in Georgia. *See also* SOUTH OSSETIA.

ABORIGINAL PEOPLES IN CANADA. Term used to describe **indigenous peoples** in Canada who were recognized in the 1982 Canadian Constitution as Indians. According to a 2001 census, there are over 900,000 Aboriginal peoples in Canada, including 600,000 of First Nations descent, 290,000 metis and 45,000 Inuit. They assert that their sovereign rights were extinguished by a 1763 Royal Proclamation and that these collective rights come with a social order that existed prior to European contact and land occupation. Most Aboriginals consider this their right to self-determined independence when it comes to their culture, land, governance and resources. Canada's relationship with its Aboriginal peoples has many similarities with Australia's as both countries moved from segregation to assimilation policies to relative benign neglect and greater acceptance of pluralism. A Royal Commission on Aboriginal Peoples assessed past government policies and made a number of meliorative recommendations, most of which remain to be implemented by the Canadian government. *See also* SELF-DETERMINATION.

ABORTION. According to the **World Health Organization**, more than 45 million abortions—legal and illegal—take place each year in the world. At the same time, some 65,000 women die from the complications of unsafe abortion. Abortion was viewed until the mid-1980s as an acceptable means of population control. Criticized for its narrow focus and for leading to coercion and decreased quality of care, the abortion debate has morphed into a reproductive justice debate in which "access to safe abortion is a matter of human rights, democracy and public health, and the denial of such access is a major cause of death and impairment, with significant costs to [international] development." This was a contentious issue at the 1994 **International Conference on Population and Development** (ICPD). The program of action adopted by the ICPD does not recommend the legalization of abortion but it simply advises governments to provide proper postabortion care and to invest in programs which would contribute to a decrease in the number of unwanted pregnancies. The matter remains politically divisive both within and among nations. Access to legal abortions varies considerably from the relatively permissive countries of Western Europe to the highly restrictive practices of Latin American and Muslim countries.

The **American Convention on Human Rights** is the only international human rights instrument that explicitly provides for the **right to life** from the moment of conception. In 2008, the Parliamentary Assembly of the **Council of Europe** adopted a non-binding resolution calling for the decriminalization of abortion within reasonable gestational limits and guaranteed access to safe abortion procedures. The **European Court of Human Rights** has issued rulings suggesting that there is no absolute right to life from conception and that the life of the fetus and embryo protection are linked to the protection of the mother. It deemed inadmissible the complaint of a man who had sought to prevent his estranged wife from having an abortion. In a 2010 landmark ruling, the Court found that Ireland had violated the **European Convention for the Protection of Human Rights and Fundamental Freedoms** by failing to provide accessible and effective procedures enabling a woman to determine whether her condition qualifies for a legal abortion under Irish law. At the same time, the Court stated that the Convention did not contain a right to abortion.

ABROGATION OF RIGHTS. The failure to honor human rights by means of an official or legal act of cancellation, annulment or repeal. As such, the idea is inconsistent with the principle of the inalienability of rights. In this regard, the **Universal Declaration of Human Rights** asserts that "in the exercise of his rights and freedoms, everyone shall be subject only to such limitations as are determined by law solely for the purpose of securing due recognition and respect for the rights and freedoms of others and of meeting the just requirements of morality, public order and the general welfare in a democratic society" (Art. 29.1). The **International Covenant on Civil and Political Rights** allows for the temporary suspension of human rights in times of **"public emergencies"** and rules out any derogation in regard to the **right to life, torture** and **slavery** (Art. 4). In the same vein, the **International Covenant on Economic, Social and Cultural Rights** stipulates that states may impose limitations on the enjoyment of economic, social and cultural rights only in as much as they are "determined by law" and remain "compatible with the nature of these rights and solely for the purpose of promoting the general welfare in a democratic society" (Art. 4). *See also* UNALIENABLE RIGHTS.

ABU GHRAIB PRISON (IRAQ). Detention facility built in the early 1960s where political dissidents to the **Saddam Hussein** regime were incarcerated, tortured and executed. The prison is believed to have held as many as 15,000 inmates in 2001. Abandoned prior to the 2003 invasion of Iraq, it was used by the **United States**–led coalition occupying Iraq until 2006 when it was again closed down and handed over to the Iraqi government. It was during that period that cases of **torture** and abuse of Iraqi inmates by American soldiers came to light in April 2004 in U.S. media. Several soldiers have been convicted of various charges relating to the incidents, including dereliction of duty, assault and maltreatment of prisoners. The U.S. commanding officer of the prison was demoted. The U.S. government has characterized the incidents as isolated cases involving inexperienced interrogators atypical of American actions and policies in Iraq. This view has been disputed by **nongovernmental organizations** like the **International Committee of the Red Cross** which says that, for more than a year, it had made representations to the U.S. administration about prisoner abuse inconsistent with the obligations of the United States under the provisions of the **Geneva Conventions**. *See also* CENTER FOR JUSTICE AND ACCOUNTABILITY; UNITED NATIONS CONVENTION AGAINST TORTURE AND OTHER CRUEL, INHUMAN OR DEGRADING TREATMENT AND PUNISHMENT.

ABUSE. *See* VIOLATION OF HUMAN RIGHTS.

ACCESS TO JUSTICE. The right to a **remedy** implies the existence of remedial institutions and procedures that can provide a fair hearing for individuals asserting a claim that their rights have been infringed upon. The nonexistence of such institutions, inordinate delays in their work or outright denial of access to them all may constitute denials of justice. Under international human rights law, access to justice as a human right remains exceptional and narrowly circumscribed as it derives from specific **treaty**

arrangements regulating individuals' access to such bodies as the **United Nations Human Rights Committee** and the **European Court of Human Rights**. Other legal norms may also further constrain individual access to justice, notably the legal doctrine of **sovereign immunity** and the non-reviewability of **United Nations Security Council** measures affecting individuals.

Recent developments have nevertheless considerably broadened the conventional and basic meaning of the term, which entails access to procedures that can investigate, prosecute and punish. The jurisprudence of regional human rights courts has recognized that states have a duty to prosecute crimes against individuals' **right to life** and security. There is also a move toward including victims in international criminal proceedings, which is now sanctioned in the statute of the **International Criminal Court**. From a developmental perspective, access to justice has been linked to the strengthening of the capacity of the poor to secure access to formal or informal justice mechanisms and to ensure that judicial outcomes are just and equitable. From this standpoint, advocated in particular by the **United Nations Development Programme** for crisis or postconflict countries, access to justice requires the provision of legal standing in formal or traditional law for disadvantaged peoples, disseminating information about their rights and entitlements, providing legal aid and counsel and strengthening the adjudicative and enforcement capacities of remedial institutions. *See also* AD HOC INTERNATIONAL COURTS; ADMISSIBILITY REQUIREMENTS; REDRESS; SECURITY, RIGHT TO; "WAR ON TERROR."

ACCESSION. This term is generally used to refer to states expressing their consent to be bound by a **treaty** where the deadline for signature has passed. *See also* OPTIONAL PROTOCOL; RATIFICATION.

ACCOUNTABILITY. Global network of business, public and civic institutions founded in 1995 describing itself as "working to build and demonstrate the possibilities for tomorrow's global markets and governance through thought-leadership and advisory services." At a 2007 meeting sponsored by the **United Nations Global Compact**, AccountAbility issued a report on the "State of Responsible Competitiveness" assessing countries' efforts in advancing competitiveness based on responsible business practices. This **think tank** has also developed a "responsible competitiveness index" ranking over 100 countries in terms of their efforts in advancing responsible business practices in their competitiveness strategies and practices. *See also* CORPORATE SOCIAL RESPONSIBILITY.

ACCOUNTABILITY. Concept of **governance** implying the idea of an assumption of responsibility for actions, decisions and policies together with an obligation to report, explain and be answerable for resulting consequences. In regard to human rights, accountability means that states, governments and other so-called **duty bearers** should comply with legal norms and standards set in international human rights treaties. Aggrieved rights holders should be entitled and have access to **remedies** provided by law.

See also ACCESS TO JUSTICE; ARMED GROUPS; DRONES; HUMAN RIGHTS PRINCIPLES; IMPUNITY; INSTITUTE FOR INTERNATIONAL LAW AND JUSTICE; LITIGATION; NON-STATE ACTORS; PRIVATE MILITARY COMPANIES; PRIVATIZATION; REDRESS; REVENUE WATCH; RULE OF LAW; UNITED NATIONS DEVELOPMENT PROGRAMME.

ACEH (1976–2005). "Special territory" of **Indonesia** located at the northern tip of the island of Sumatra. Ethnically and culturally different from the remainder of the island population, Aceh never came under full Dutch control during the colonization era and its amalgamation within the province of Sumatra, when Indonesia won independence, triggered recurring armed conflicts with the central government. Since the 1970s, a separatist insurgency led by the Free Aceh Movement fought against Jakarta. The conflict, largely unnoticed by the international community, was fed not only by long-standing cultural values' differences but also disputes over the control and disposition of substantial natural resources (oil and gas in particular). Some 15,000 people—mostly noncombatants—are believed to have been killed since hostilities began. In addition, 1.4 million were internally displaced between 1992 and 2002. Aceh was struck on 26 December 2004 by a devastating tsunami. Approximately 230,000 people perished and half a million were left homeless. One of the unexpected consequences of the tragedy was to bring about a peace settlement between the rebel movement and the government of Jakarta on 15 August 2005. The peace accord seems to be holding. *See also* MINORITIES; SELF-DETERMINATION.

ACT OF STATE DOCTRINE. Legal principle asserting that the domestic actions of a sovereign state may not be questioned or invalidated by the courts of another state. Recognized by British courts since the 17th century, the doctrine has been used broadly and with more frequency by the **United States** than in other countries as it is recognized and understood by American federal courts not to protect the **state sovereignty** of other nations but to protect the constitutionally recognized power of the executive to conduct foreign relations without interference by U.S. courts. In this context, the doctrine has been used in **litigation** cases involving the expropriation of private property by a foreign sovereign. U.S. federal courts have also addressed the question of whether the act of state doctrine overrode the **jurisdiction** of U.S. courts over cases brought to them under the **Alien Tort Statute** involving human rights abuses by foreign officials and the responsibility of U.S. companies cooperating with foreign government in projects in which such abuses are alleged to have occurred. *See also* EICHMANN, ADOLF; SOVEREIGN IMMUNITY.

ACTION FOR SOUTHERN AFRICA (ACTSA). Not-for-profit successor organization to the Anti-Apartheid Movement which conducts **advocacy** campaigns through media and reports and lobbies governments in Europe on policies affecting the countries of the Southern African region. ACTSA's major activities since its inception in 1994 have focused on promoting stronger **sanctions** against the illicit diamond trade, greater access to vital treatments for the **HIV/AIDS** pandemic and fairer trade for southern African producers. *See also* CONSUMERS INTERNATIONAL; CORPORATE RESPONSIBILITY REPORTING.

ADEQUATE STANDARDS OF LIVING, RIGHT TO. A right enshrined in Article 25 of the **Universal Declaration of Human Rights** which posits that "everyone has the right to a standard of living adequate for the **health** and well-being of himself and of his family, including **food**, clothing, **housing** and medical care and necessary social services, and the right to security in the event of unemployment, sickness, disability, widowhood, old age or other lack of livelihood in circumstances beyond his control." Drawing from the Declaration, Article 11 of the **International Covenant on Economic, Social and Cultural Rights** enjoins its states parties "to recognize the right to an adequate standard of living for himself and his family, including adequate food, clothing and housing, and to the continuous improvement of living conditions." Article 14 of the **United Nations Convention on the Elimination of All Forms of Discrimination against Women** calls upon its signatories to take all appropriate measures to eliminate discrimination against women in rural areas and in particular to ensure to such women the right to enjoy adequate living conditions, particularly in relation to housing, sanitation, electricity and water supply, transport and communications. Article 27 of the United Nations Convention on the Rights of the Child mandates states to recognize the right of every child to a standard of living adequate for the child's physical, mental, spiritual, moral and social development. In reviewing state reports, the **United Nations Committee on Economic, Social and Cultural Rights** assesses progress (or lack of) in relative standards of living by examining income distribution patterns and the overall condition of vulnerable groups such as landless peasants, rural workers, urban unemployed, **migrant workers** and **indigenous peoples**. *See also* WORK, RIGHT TO.

AD HOC INTERNATIONAL COURTS. Unlike standing, permanent institutions such as the **International Court of Justice** and the **International Criminal Court** at the global level or the **African Court on Human and People's Rights** in the African region, the **Inter-American Court of Human Rights** in the Latin American region and the **European Court of Human Rights** and the **Court of Justice** in Europe, ad hoc courts or tribunals are set up for a limited duration to try individuals accused of crimes recognized under international humanitarian law that were committed in a specific place and at a particular time. They are established under the authority of an international organization such as the **United Nations Security Council** as was the case for the **International Criminal Tribunal for the Former Yugoslavia** and the **International Criminal Tribunal for Rwanda**. These courts exist independently from the national justice systems in the affected countries. They have international judges and they are funded by the international community. New criminal justice bodies have emerged around 2000 such as the crimes panels constituted in Kosovo, the **Special Court for Sierra Leone**, the **Special Tribunal for Cambodia** and the **Special Panels of the Dili District Court** of East Timor.

Like all other international judicial bodies, hybrid courts are composed of independent judges rendering binding decisions on the basis of predetermined rules of procedures and principles (**due process**, impartiality). Their purposes are similar—to sanction grievous violations of **international human rights law** and **humanitarian intervention**. They differ from other judicial bodies because of their mixed nature that incorporates international as well as national features. For example, they are composed of international as well as local judges, prosecutors and servicing staff. The law that they apply is a mix of international and national instruments. *See also* SPECIAL TRIBUNAL FOR LEBANON; UNITED NATIONS INTERIM ADMINISTRATION MISSION IN KOSOVO.

ADJUDICATION. Methods of resolving disputes, legislating and enforcing international human rights law by judicial means. Major advances have been made in the 20th century in the establishment of judicial bodies dealing with human rights (hence the term "judicialization" is also used to refer to this phenomenon). Estimates by **non-governmental organizations** (some of them are intimately involved in these court proceedings) count more than 20 permanent bodies set up as international courts and tribunals and three times as many other international institutions exercising judicial or quasi-judicial functions. The extent to which this proliferation of international, regional and specialized courts constitutes a "system" involving a recognized hierarchy similar to national court systems remains an open question.

See also AD HOC INTERNATIONAL COURTS; ADMISSIBILITY REQUIREMENTS; AFRICAN COURT ON HUMAN AND PEOPLE'S RIGHTS; AMICUS CURIAE; COURT OF JUSTICE; EAST AFRICAN COURT OF JUSTICE; EUROPEAN COURT OF HUMAN RIGHTS; INTER-AMERICAN COURT OF HUMAN RIGHTS; INTERNATIONAL COURT OF JUSTICE; INTERNATIONAL CRIMINAL COURT; INTERNATIONAL CRIMINAL TRIBUNAL FOR RWANDA; INTERNATIONAL CRIMINAL TRIBUNAL FOR THE FORMER YUGOSLAVIA; PERMANENT COURT OF INTERNATIONAL JUSTICE; SPECIAL COURT FOR SIERRA LEONE; SPECIAL TRIBUNAL FOR CAMBODIA; SPECIAL TRIBUNAL FOR LEBANON.

ADMISSIBILITY REQUIREMENTS. The initial prerequisites which must be met by a complainant before being allowed to submit a claim to a particular human rights monitoring **treaty** body such as the **United Nations Human Rights Committee** or other judicial bodies like the **European Court of Human Rights**. Such requirements vary widely from one treaty to another but the most common ones are: (a) the **complaint** must be made by an individual or, under certain circumstances, a group of individuals; (b) the complainant must have been personally affected by the **violation**; (c) the complaint must not be anonymous; (d) the victims must have been subjects to the jurisdiction of the alleged violating state party when the violation occurred; (e) the victims must have exhausted all domestic **remedies**; (f) the same complaint must not be pending before another international forum; and (g) the victim's claim must be sufficiently substantiated.

See also 1503 PROCEDURE; ACCESS TO JUSTICE; AFRICAN COMMISSION ON HUMAN AND PEOPLE'S RIGHTS; AFRICAN COURT ON HUMAN AND PEOPLE'S RIGHTS; COMPLEMENTARITY PRINCIPLE; COURT OF JUSTICE; EAST AFRICAN COURT OF JUSTICE; INTER-AMERICAN COURT OF HUMAN RIGHTS; INTERNATIONAL CRIMINAL COURT; LITIGATION.

ADOPTION. Under the **international law** of treaties, adoption usually refers to the initial diplomatic stage at which a state gives its acceptance to a **treaty**. To become effective after adoption, however, a treaty must be ratified by the constitutionally defined national appropriate body (normally, a legislature). The **United Nations General Assembly** frequently "adopts" multilateral treaties which become binding on its states parties only after their **ratification**. *See also* ACCESSION; INCORPORATION; RESERVATIONS TO TREATIES.

ADVISORY OPINION. Formal pronouncement by a judicial body advising on the constitutionality or interpretation of a point of law. Advisory opinions do not resolve legal cases. They are not binding but may have significant legal effects. At the request of some of the organs and agencies of the **United Nations**, the **International Court of Justice** (ICJ) may give advisory opinions. The ICJ has thus issued advisory opinions on a number of human rights–related issues, notably on the validity of **reservations** to the **Genocide** Convention (1951), the legality of the use or threat of **nuclear weapons** (1996) and the legal consequences of the construction of a wall in the Palestinian Occupied Territories (2004). Likewise, the **Inter-American Court of Human Rights** may give advice to the states members of the **Organization of American States** on the compatibility of their domestic laws and proposed legislation with the American Convention of American States. *See also* INTERNATIONAL LAW; PERMANENT COURT OF INTERNATIONAL JUSTICE.

ADVISORY SERVICES. Broad range of activities delivered by donor governments, international organizations and **non-governmental organizations** involving the provision of expert advice and technical assistance in the form of projects and programs designed to establish or strengthen national and regional institutions and infrastructures which are expected to improve the incorporation and implementation of international human rights norms and standards. The focus of these programs varies widely from constitutional assistance and legislative reform to the organization of free and fair elections and the strengthening of independent judiciaries and decent penal institutions to enhancing the effectiveness of parliaments and fostering independent national institutions and strong civic society organizations.

See also CAPACITY BUILDING; INTERNATIONAL CENTRE FOR CRIMINAL LAW REFORM AND CRIMINAL JUSTICE POLICY; INTERNATIONAL CENTRE FOR TRADE UNION RIGHTS; INTERNATIONAL CENTER FOR TRANSITIONAL JUSTICE; UNITED NATIONS OFFICE OF THE HIGH COMMISSIONER FOR HUMAN RIGHTS; UNREPRESENTED NATIONS AND PEOPLES ORGANIZATION.

ADVOCACY. Broadly understood, the term refers to individual or collective actions seeking to shape public policy and resource allocation decisions affecting people's lives. As such, advocacy is one of the most important activities carried out by human rights **non-governmental organizations** (NGOs). So-called advocacy NGOs generally identify, articulate, raise and mobilize public awareness, acceptance and knowledge of particular human rights issues. They defend and promote policies or actions that seek to resolve them or endeavor to influence the priorities, policies and practices of governmental decision-making at the local, national and international levels. In so doing, advocacy groups rely on a wide variety of instruments ranging from policy research and analysis and information dissemination to **lobbying** political officials, corporations, international financial institutions and intergovernmental organizations to organizing media campaigns. With increasing frequency, advocacy NGOs have formed informal transnational networks linking national groups through the Internet which may occasionally evolve into global campaigns such as the **International Campaign to Ban Landmines**, the **Coalition for the International Criminal Court**, the **Coalition for International Justice** and the **Coalition to Stop the Use of Children**.

See also ACTION FOR SOUTHERN AFRICA; ADVOCATES FOR HUMAN RIGHTS; AL HAQ; ALAN GUTTMACHER INSTITUTE; AMERICAN JEWISH COMMITTEE; AMNESTY INTERNATIONAL; ANTI-SLAVERY INTERNATIONAL; ARAB ASSOCIATION FOR HUMAN RIGHTS; ARTICLE 19, THE INTERNATIONAL CENTRE AGAINST CENSORSHIP; ASSOCIATION OF AFRICAN WOMEN FOR RESEARCH AND DEVELOPMENT; CENTER FOR ECONOMIC AND SOCIAL RIGHTS; CENTER FOR HUMAN RIGHTS AND THE ENVIRONMENT; CENTER FOR MINORITY RIGHTS DEVELOPMENT; CENTER FOR REPRODUCTIVE RIGHTS; CENTRE ON HOUSING RIGHTS AND EVICTIONS; CHILD RIGHTS INFORMATION NETWORK; COALITION AGAINST TRAFFICKING IN WOMEN; COALITION FOR INTERNATIONAL JUSTICE; COALITION FOR THE INTERNATIONAL CRIMINAL COURT; COALITION TO STOP THE USE OF CHILDREN; CONGO REFORM ASSOCIATION; CONSORTIUM OF MINORITY RESOURCES; EARTH RIGHTS INTERNATIONAL; EQUALITY NOW; GLOBAL CENTER FOR THE RESPONSIBILITY TO PROTECT; EURO-MEDITERRANEAN HUMAN RIGHTS NETWORK; EUROPEAN ROMA RIGHTS CENTER; FOOD FIRST INFORMATION AND ACTION NETWORK; FORUM FOR FACT-FINDING DOCUMENTATION AND ADVOCACY; GLOBAL POLICY FORUM; GLOBAL RIGHTS; GRASSROOTS INTERNATIONAL; HUMAN RIGHTS FIRST;

HUMAN RIGHTS INSTITUTE; HUMAN RIGHTS INSTITUTE OF SOUTH AFRICA; HUMAN RIGHTS WATCH; INSTITUTE FOR INTERNATIONAL LAW AND HUMAN RIGHTS; INTERNATIONAL ACCOUNTABILITY PROJECT; INTERNATIONAL ALERT; INTER-NATIONAL ALLIANCE TO END GENOCIDE; INTERNATIONAL ASSOCIATION OF DEMOCRATIC LAWYERS; INTERNATIONAL BUREAU FOR CHILDREN'S RIGHTS; INTERNATIONAL CAMPAIGN TO BAN LANDMINES; INTERNATIONAL CENTRE FOR HUMAN RIGHTS AND DEMOCRATIC DEVELOPMENT; INTERNATIONAL CIVIL SOCIETY ACTION NETWORK; INTERNATIONAL COALITION FOR THE RESPONSIBILITY TO PROTECT; INTERNATIONAL COMMISSION FOR LABOR RIGHTS; INTERNATIONAL CRISIS GROUP; INTERNATIONAL DISABILITY ALLIANCE; INTERNATIONAL FEDERATION FOR HUMAN RIGHTS; INTERNATIONAL FEDERATION TERRE DES HOMMES; INTERNATIONAL FOUNDATION FOR ELECTORAL SYSTEMS; INTERNATIONAL GAY AND LESBIAN HUMAN RIGHTS COMMISSION; INTERNATIONAL HUMAN RIGHTS LAW INSTITUTE; INTERNATIONAL MOVEMENT AGAINST ALL FORMS OF DISCRIMINATION AND RACISM; INTERNATIONAL NGO COALITION FOR AN O.P. TO THE ICESCR; INTERNATIONAL PEACE INSTITUTE; INTERNATIONAL RESCUE COMMITTEE; INTERNATIONAL SAVE THE CHILDREN ALLIANCE; INTERNATIONAL SOCIETY FOR HUMAN RIGHTS; INTERNATIONAL WOMEN'S RIGHTS ACTION WATCH; INTERNATIONAL WORK GROUP FOR INDIGENOUS AFFAIRS; KURDISH HUMAN RIGHTS PROJECT; MIGRANT RIGHTS INTERNATIONAL; MINORITY RIGHTS GROUP INTERNATIONAL; OXFAM INTERNATIONAL; PREVENT GENOCIDE INTERNATIONAL; REFUGEES INTERNATIONAL; ROBINSON, MARY; SIERRA CLUB; SOROS, GEORGE; SPECIAL RAPPORTEURS; SURVIVAL INTERNATIONAL; THINK TANKS; TRANSNATIONAL ADVOCACY NETWORKS; TRANSNATIONAL INSTITUTE; UNITED NATIONS ASSISTANCE MISSION IN AFGHANISTAN; UNITED NATIONS CHILDREN'S FUND; UNITED NATIONS OFFICE OF THE HIGH COMMISSIONER FOR HUMAN RIGHTS; WOMEN'S REFUGEE COMMISSION; WORLD BLIND UNION; WORLD FEDERATION OF UNITED NATIONS ASSOCIATIONS.

ADVOCATES FOR HUMAN RIGHTS. United States **non-governmental organization** (NGO) dedicated to promoting and protecting human rights through **research, education** and **advocacy**. Founded in 1983, this NGO has produced numerous reports documenting human rights practices in some 25 countries. One of its earliest and notable accomplishments was the publication of a Manual on the Effective Prevention and Investigation of Extra-Legal, Arbitrary and Summary Executions which details still widely used proper forensic procedures in conducting investigations and autopsies in cases of politically motivated homicide. Its current work deals with **refugees**, immigrants, women, ethnic and religious **minorities**.

AFFIRMATIVE ACTION. Policies undertaken by governments, educational institutions, businesses and other bodies to eliminate existing **discrimination** or inequalities, provide immediate remedies for past and current discrimination and prevent its reoccurrence. Typical "affirmative" steps range from measures to promote access to education and employment to the targeted recruitment of socioeconomic disadvantaged groups to preferential treatment given to these groups. The latter practice is known as "reverse discrimination" and is permitted under certain conditions under the **International Convention on the Elimination of All Forms of Racial Discrimination** and the **United Nations Convention on the Elimination of All Forms of Discrimination against Women**.

AFGHANISTAN. Landlocked Islamic country inhabited by a mosaic of peoples which speak some 30 languages and dialects that regained independence in 1919. The overthrow of the monarchy and, in 1978, the installation in power of communist rulers opened a still unfolding phase of bloody internal struggles and foreign interventions. In response to the **United States**'s covert funding and training of anti-government Mujahideen forces opposed to the Marxist regime, 110,000 to 150,000 Soviet troops intervened in December 1989 to bolster the government. Unable to overwhelm local resistance, faced with mounting international condemnation and reeling over the loss of over 15,000 soldiers, the Soviets withdrew from the country in 1989. The political vacuum created by the downfall of the Soviet-backed communist regime gave way to a fratricidal civil war out of which rose the Taliban, a politico-religious force bent on restoring stability and enforcing strict interpretation of Islam. By the end of 2000, the Taliban had captured and controlled most of the country. Accusing the Taliban of harboring networks of terrorists, the United States, with the support of the Afghan Northern ethnic groups, launched a military campaign which resulted in the quick removal of the Taliban in November 2001. Peacekeeping troops began arriving in January 2002 under a **United Nations** mandate. In 2004, the country adopted a new moderate Islamic constitution and elected a president and in 2005 a national assembly and regional councils were elected.

For more than a quarter of a century, Afghanistan has thus been at war with itself or against foreign aggressors. From this standpoint, the human rights situation emerging from this history of violence is grim. In 10 years of Soviet occupation, 1 million died and 5 million, a third of the population, were forced to flee Afghanistan. The Soviet occupation also resulted in a mass exodus of over 5 million Afghans who moved into refugee camps in neighboring Pakistan, Iran and other countries. Between 1979 and 2001, a total of 1.5 million people are estimated to have died as a direct result of the conflict. From 2007 when the United Nations began reporting statistics to the end of 2011, some 12,000 civilians had been killed.

Throughout the war, all of the major factions have been guilty of grave breaches of **international humanitarian law** and **human rights principles**. While in power, the Taliban committed other serious internationally recognized **violations of human rights**. **Minorities** were discriminated against and were subjected to arbitrary arrest and torture. **Discrimination** against women became a matter of official policy. Suspected criminals were tried in summary proceedings, frequently resulting in harsh sentences inspired from strict interpretations of Islamic law. Since the beginning of the UN involvement, there have been accusations and sometimes evidence of human rights violations by Western powers. Postconflict recovery of Afghanistan remains precarious. Security, good governance, the **rule of law** and human rights and social and economic development are the critical and interdependent pillars of activity that have been agreed upon by the international community and Afghan authorities to guide the reconstruction of the country.

The assumption of security has been undercut by an increasingly bold insurgency led by the Taliban in the southern and eastern provinces. In the north, a few semi-independent warlords cling to power beyond the reach of the central government. Opium cultivation and trafficking involving state officials and non-state actors have dominated the economy. The government has been unwilling (or unable) to tackle the issue of accountability for grievous violations of human rights committed in the course of the conflict for the sake of preserving a modicum of stability among the fractious factions that make up the kaleidoscopic political landscape of the country. The future of the country remains clouded with uncertainty. A number of Western powers are withdrawing, with others, notably the United States and Great Britain, already phasing out. The chances that the Afghan government can control the country are remote, and the Taliban could indeed make a comeback.

AFRICA. *See* 1969 ORGANIZATION OF AFRICAN UNITY CONVENTION GOVERNING THE SPECIFIC ASPECTS OF REFUGEE

PROBLEMS IN AFRICA; ABACHA, SANI; ACTION FOR SOUTHERN AFRICA; AFRICA INSTITUTE OF SOUTH AFRICA; AFRICAN CHARTER ON HUMAN AND PEOPLE'S RIGHTS; AFRICAN CHARTER ON THE RIGHTS AND WELFARE OF THE CHILD; AFRICAN COMMISSION ON HUMAN AND PEOPLE'S RIGHTS; AFRICAN COMMITTEE ON THE RIGHTS AND WELFARE OF THE CHILD; AFRICAN COURT ON HUMAN AND PEOPLE'S RIGHTS; AFRICAN UNION; AFRICAN UNION-UNITED NATIONS HYBRID OPERATION IN DARFUR; AMIN, IDI; ANGOLA; APARTHEID; ASSOCIATION OF AFRICAN WOMEN FOR RESEARCH AND DEVELOPMENT; BIAFRA; BOKASSA, JEAN-BEDEL; BURUNDI; CODESRIA; COMMITTEE ON THE RIGHTS AND WELFARE OF THE CHILD; CONGO FREE STATE; CONVENTION FOR THE PROTECTION AND ASSISTANCE OF INTERNALLY DISPLACED PERSONS IN AFRICA; CONVENTION GOVERNING THE SPECIFIC ASPECTS OF REFUGEE PROBLEMS IN AFRICA; COTE D'IVOIRE; DARFUR CONFLICT; DENG, FRANCIS; EAST AFRICAN COURT OF JUSTICE; ECONOMIC COMMUNITY OF WEST AFRICAN STATES; HABRE, HISSENE; HUMAN RIGHTS INSTITUTE OF SOUTH AFRICA; INSTITUTE FOR HUMAN RIGHTS AND DEVELOPMENT IN AFRICA; INTER-AFRICAN COMMITTEE ON TRADITIONAL PRACTICES AFFECTING THE HEALTH OF WOMEN; NIGER DELTA CONFLICT; PROTOCOL TO THE AFRICAN CHARTER ON HUMAN AND PEOPLE'S RIGHTS ON THE RIGHTS OF WOMEN IN AFRICA; SIERRA LEONE CIVIL WAR; SOUTHERN AFRICAN DEVELOPMENT COMMUNITY TRIBUNAL; SPECIAL COURT FOR SIERRA LEONE; UNITED NATIONS ASSISTANCE MISSION IN RWANDA; UNITED NATIONS MISSION IN SIERRA LEONE; UNITED NATIONS MISSION IN THE CENTRAL AFRICAN REPUBLIC AND CHAD; UNITED NATIONS MISSION IN THE REPUBLIC OF SOUTH SUDAN; UNITED NATIONS OBSERVER MISSION IN LIBERIA; UNITED NATIONS OPERATION IN BURUNDI; UNITED NATIONS OPERATION IN COTE D'IVOIRE; UNITED NATIONS OPERATION IN MOZAMBIQUE; UNITED NATIONS OPERATION IN SOMALIA.

AFRICA INSTITUTE OF SOUTH AFRICA. Think tank established in 1960 doing **research** and **capacity building** on contemporary African affairs with particular emphasis on sustainable development, peace and security, Africa and the Diaspora, **democracy**, **governance** and **health** and social development.

AFRICAN CHARTER ON HUMAN AND PEOPLE'S RIGHTS. International regional human rights instrument adopted by the Organization of African Unity in 1981. In force since 1986, the Charter enumerates basic rights and freedoms to be protected on the African continent. It is notable for its emphasis on community and **group rights** and duties. As is the case in other regional human rights systems, it also established a safeguard mechanism in 1987, the **African Commission on Human and People's Rights.** A 1998 Protocol to the Charter provided for the creation of an **African Court on Human and People's Rights** which came into effect in 2004. The first judges of the Court were elected a year later. *See also* CULTURAL RIGHTS; EAST AFRICAN COURT OF JUSTICE; INTERNATIONAL COMMISSION OF JURISTS.

AFRICAN CHARTER ON THE RIGHTS AND WELFARE OF THE CHILD (ACRWC). First comprehensive regional treaty adopted by the Organization of African Unity in 1990 covering the rights of children in Africa. By and large, the Charter is modeled after the **United Nations Convention on the Rights of the Child** (UN-CRC) and shares its basic principles, notably its underlying principles for the need to be guided by the best interests of children and to protect and promote their rights to life, survival and development. The ACRWC defines a "child as a human being below the age of 18," acknowledges that children are entitled to the enjoyment of freedom of expression, association, peaceful assembly, thought, religion, and conscience and aims at protecting the private life of the child. The Charter set up an African expert committee on the rights and well-being of the child (the **African Committee on the Rights and Welfare of the Child**) with the mission to promote and protect the rights established by the Charter by its state parties.

The ACRWC places greater emphasis than the UN-CRC on specifically African cultural and socioeconomic issues which were overlooked in the drafting of the Convention such as the role of the extended family in matter of adoption and fostering, the practice of **female genital mutilation** and the severe socioeconomic conditions of the African continent. Thus, the ACRWC provides for the protection of children against harmful and potentially dangerous cultural practices with an emphasis on "customs and practices prejudicial to the health or life of the child and those customs and practices discriminatory to the child on the grounds of sex and others status" (Art. 21.1). The Convention also obliges states to establish 18 as the minimum age for marriage and to make registration of all marriages compulsory with the aim of combating the practice of early marriage or forced child marriage. In addition, it calls for safeguards against all forms of economic exploitation and against work that is hazardous, interferes with the child's education, or compromises his or her health or physical, social, mental, spiritual, and moral development. *See also* CHILDREN IN ARMED CONFLICT; CULTURAL RELATIVISM.

AFRICAN COMMISSION ON HUMAN AND PEOPLE'S RIGHTS. Set up in 1987, the African Commission was, until the creation of the **African Court on Human and People's Rights**, the only enforcement or supervisory institution of the **African Charter on Human and People's Rights**. Tasked with promoting and protecting human rights throughout the African continent, the Commission is empowered to receive state **complaints** against other states believed to have breached their human rights obligations under the Charter. It may also receive complaints from individuals and **non-governmental organizations** (NGOs) about state conduct and study or investigate "situations" involving **violations of human rights**. States' parties to the Charter are also required to submit a report every two years on the legislative or other measures they have taken to give effect to the rights and freedoms recognized and guaranteed by the Charter. The Commission's members serve in their personal and individual capacities and enjoy full independence in the discharge of their duties. But they are selected by the Assembly of Heads of States and Government of the Organization of African Unity (now the African Union [AU]) to which it also reports. The subordination of the Commission to the political organs of the AU (comparable to the institutional arrangements made for the 1994 Framework Convention on the Protection of National Minorities set up by the Council of Europe) and the long-standing preoccupation of African states with political unity and noninterference in addition to strict rules of confidentiality all explain why the Commission has for a long time been reluctant to challenge the human rights record of governments.

Beginning in the early 1990s, however, the Commission became more pro-active and accessible and, in prominent cases, it has made pronouncements recognizing "peoples" rights to existence and self-determination and to freely dispose of their wealth and natural resources. It has developed close ties with NGOs which are often instrumental in bringing cases to the Commission, submitting "shadow reports" and proposing agenda items. It has also evolved a network of special rapporteurs on freedom of expression, prison conditions, the death penalty, economic, social and cultural rights, extrajudicial refugees and internally displaced persons, indigenous peoples and women. To date, however, the Commission has not received any interstate communications. Like most other treaty bodies, the Commission is also faced with the chronic failure of state parties to meet their reporting obligations in a timely fashion. Its modalities of interaction and scope of responsibilities relative to the newly established African Court are still to be clarified. In 2011, the Commission filed a complaint against Libya before the African Court. *See also* ARBITRARY DETENTION; FOOD, RIGHT TO; NIGER DELTA CONFLICT; RIGHTS AND DEMOCRACY; RIGHTS INTERNATIONAL.

AFRICAN COMMITTEE ON THE RIGHTS AND WELFARE OF THE CHILD. Established in pursuance of the **African Charter on the Rights and Welfare of the Child**, this group of experts, elected in their personal capacity by the Assembly of Heads of States of the **African Union**, monitors the implementation of the Charter by its states' parties. Under the terms of the Charter, the Committee exerts its oversight on the basis of periodic states' reports and "**communications**" from individuals, groups of **non-governmental organizations** and states members of the African Union or the **United Nations** concerning any relevant issue. The Committee may also use any appropriate **investigation** procedures in relation to any issue covered by the Charter. Notwithstanding this promising legal framework, the work of the Committee has been hampered by the slow pace of ratifications of the Charter (the Committee met for the first time only in 2001) and lack of funding.

AFRICAN COURT ON HUMAN AND PEOPLE'S RIGHTS. The latest addition to the regional human rights judicial bodies already in existence in Europe and Latin America. The African Court came into existence in 2005 when a 1998 protocol to the **African Charter on Human and People's Rights** laboriously negotiated within the Organization of African Unity came into effect. The Court is based in Arusha, Tanzania, utilizing the facilities developed for the **International Criminal Tribunal for Rwanda**. In many ways, the establishment of the Court may be viewed as a watershed moment in the history of human rights in Africa. Until its creation, there was no enforcement mechanism of human rights obligations in the continent since supervisory functions of the **African Commission on Human and People's Rights** were limited to investigations and **communications** resulting in nonbinding decisions. Individuals and **non-governmental organizations** have the right to bring cases, and the Court may apply any instrument or source of law concerning human rights that is ratified by the states concerned, thus potentially extending the scope of its jurisdiction beyond the provisions of the African Charter. In effect, the African Court could conceivably become the judicial arm of human rights instruments set up in accordance with agreements concluded under the aegis of the **United Nations** and regional organizations such as the **International Covenant on**

Civil and Political Rights, the conventions of the **International Labour Organization** or any **international humanitarian law** treaties that have no judicial mechanisms to ensure implementation of their decisions. However, the Court has yet to become operational as its judges were selected only in 2006 and it has not received a single case to adjudicate. It is strictly speaking an organ of the **African Union** (AU) reporting to the political bodies of the AU and compliance with its rulings, under the terms of the Protocol, is still in effect voluntary. Only individuals and groups of individuals and NGOs that have been recognized as having observer status in the AU may bring cases to the Court. Finally, if the Court is meant to complement the functions of the Commission, their respective responsibilities and roles remain to be agreed upon.

AFRICAN UNION (AU). Successor organization of the Organization of African Unity (OAU) established in 2001 whose main objectives are to promote unity and solidarity among African states, encourage development cooperation among them, notably through the **United Nations**, bring an end to intra-African conflicts, help support democratic principles and institutions, popular participation and good **governance**, and protect human and people's rights in accordance with the **African Charter on Human and People's Rights** and other international human rights instruments. The AU faces the same wide array of challenges which confronted the OAU, ranging from controlling and resolving the continent's recurrent civil wars, improving the standards of living of millions of impoverished and uneducated people, halting and reversing the spread of deadly pandemics, achieving ecological sustainability and overcoming economic dependence and marginality. It is equally divided politically about the ways and means to deal with these issues, especially when questions of sovereignty, territorial integrity and national unity creep into the debates. Reports of the **African Commission on Human and People's Rights** on the situation in Zimbabwe, for example, have triggered intense controversies in the intergovernmental bodies of the AU. But the AU has been more inclined than the OAU was to support human rights norms and democratic principles. In particular, it has occasionally intervened in internal conflicts. In 2003, the AU thus deployed a peacekeeping force in **Burundi** to oversee the implementation of a ceasefire agreement. Likewise, the AU has dispatched troops in Somalia and Sudan in Darfur. *See also* AFRICAN CHARTER ON THE RIGHTS AND WELFARE OF THE CHILD; AFRICAN COMMITTEE ON THE RIGHTS AND WELFARE OF THE CHILD; AFRICAN COURT ON HUMAN AND PEOPLE'S RIGHTS; AFRICAN UNION-UNITED NATIONS HYBRID OPERATION IN DARFUR.

AFRICAN UNION-UNITED NATIONS HYBRID OPERATION IN DARFUR (UNAMID). Joint **African Union-United Nations peace operations** which in 2007 took over from and absorbed the 7,000 African Union force which had failed to stop the violence in Darfur. UNAMID's core functions are to protect civilians and provide security in camps, to secure access for humanitarian assistance, to promote human rights and the rule of law, to monitor the situation along the borders with Chad and the Central African Republic and to implement disarmament, demobilization and reintegration. UNAMID's peacekeeping efforts have been hindered by infrastructure and resources inadequacies, Sudanese government interferences that have curtailed the freedom of movement of both peacekeepers and humanitarian aid workers, on and off violence targeted at civilians and intertribal infighting.

AGGRESSION. In **international law**, the idea of aggression refers to the use of force by one state against another, which is not justified by defensive necessity or has not received the approbation of the **United Nations Security Council.** A 1974 resolution of the **United Nations General Assembly** avers that "the first use of armed forces by a state in contravention of the Charter" constitutes aggression. The same resolution also provides an illustrative list of acts of aggression including invasions, attacks, occupations, bombardments; blockades; attacks on another state's armed forces; and allowing territory to be used by armed groups to carry out cross-border attacks. Attempts to define aggression with greater specificity and to apply it with consistency have proved elusive and generated endless political debates. All throughout the decolonization process, subjected groups and developing countries argued that this definition did not prejudice the right of non-self governing peoples to seek and receive political and military support in their efforts to achieve **self-determination** and independence.

More recently, the issue of definition has become even more intractable as a result of the spread of international **terrorism** and the evolving nature of warfare and the proliferation of internal wars spilling over national borders. Easily recognizable acts of aggression such as the 1950 and 1990 invasions of South Korea and Kuwait by North Korea and Iraq, respectively, are indeed uncommon. Even more controversial is the idea enshrined in a 1970 UN General Assembly Declaration on Principles of International Law Concerning Friendly Relations among States asserting that "a war of aggression constitutes a **crime against the peace**, for which there is responsibility under international law." So-called crimes against the peace were the chief offense of the German and Japanese nationals brought to trial in 1945 and 1948 and fierce debates continue to this day as to whether the victorious Allies applied international criminal law retroactively insofar as starting a war had not until then been considered a criminal act.

Persisting doctrinal and political disputes about what exactly constitutes aggression explain why the UN Security Council did not authorize the **International Criminal Tribunal for the Former Yugoslavia** to deal with crimes against peace. The Rome Statute of the **International Criminal Court** gave jurisdiction to the Court over crimes against peace only after the states' parties had agreed on a definition of aggression. In June 2010, a review conference agreed on an amendment of the Rome Statute specifying the crime of aggression. The Court, however, will only have jurisdiction over the crime of aggression after the amendment has been ratified by 30 states and is subject to a decision by the Assembly of States Parties to the statute after 1 January 2017. *See also* INTERNATIONAL MILITARY TRIBUNAL FOR THE PROSECUTION AND PUNISHMENT OF THE MAJOR WAR CRIMINALS OF THE EUROPEAN AXIS; NUREMBERG PRINCIPLES; RUSSELL-SARTRE TRIBUNAL.

AGRARIAN REFORM. Narrowly defined, agrarian reform refers to the redistribution of land among the farmers of a country at the initiation or with the support of the government. More broadly, it may refer to a redirection of the whole system of agriculture thus involving not only reform of land tenure, production and supporting support structures but also the reform and development of complementary supportive institutional framework such as the establishment of administrative governmental agencies, credit measures, rural educational, training and special welfare institutions. Agrarian reform policies are generally viewed as a major tool in the protection of the environment, **poverty** reduction, the enhancement of inclusive economic development and, by the same token, the **realization of human rights** and in particular of the **right to food, food sovereignty** and **food security**. *See also* INTERNATIONAL CONFERENCE ON AGRARIAN REFORM AND RURAL DEVELOPMENT; LAND RIGHTS.

AGREEMENT ON TRADE-RELATED ASPECTS OF INTELLECT-UAL PROPERTY RIGHTS (TRIPS). International agreement reached in 1994 in the General Agreement on Tariffs and Trade (GATT) and now implemented by the **World Trade Organization** (WTO), GATT's successor organization. TRIPS enjoins members of the WTO to enact legislation protecting the intellectual property rights of producers and users of technological knowledge. It also specifies enforcement procedures, remedies, and dispute resolution procedures. Developing countries have been granted extra time to change their national laws, because most of them are net importers and payers of copyrights, patents, and trademark-related royalties. The TRIPS agreement has been criticized by developing countries, academics and **non-governmental organizations** for its wealth redistributive effects (especially in regard to access to technology) and its imposition of relative scarcity on already deprived populations. The TRIPS agreement is thus presented as an obstacle not only to the overall development of Southern countries but also to the enjoyment of basic socioeconomic rights such as the **right to food, health, work** and adequate **housing**. Critics also argue that it hinders access to and the fair and equitable sharing of benefits arising from the utilization of genetic resources and the preservation of and respect for the knowledge, innovations and practices of **indigenous peoples** granted to local communities in the **United Nations Convention on Biological Diversity**.

In 2000, the **United Nations Sub-Commission on the Promotion and Protection of Human Rights** under the **United Nations Commission on Human Rights** did question the balance of rights between those promoted by the TRIPS agreement and the broader human rights of peoples. In 2001, the WTO adopted a declaration stating that TRIPS should not prevent states from dealing with public health crises, but it has not been heeded by most Northern governments and multinational corporations. Not surprisingly, UN **special rapporteurs** keep stressing in their reports that the TRIPS agreement has an adverse impact on prices and availability of medicines, making it difficult for countries to comply with their obligations to respect, protect and fulfill basic human rights.

AKAYESU CASE (1998). Landmark ruling of the **International Criminal Tribunal for Rwanda** convicting a former schoolteacher and local mayor of **genocide** and **crimes against humanity**. The court held that "sexual assault formed an integral part of the process of destroying the Tutsi ethnic group and that the rape was systematic and had been perpetrated against Tutsi women only, manifesting the specific intent required for those acts to constitute genocide." In effect, the Court established the precedent that rape can be prosecuted as genocide. In the words of judge **Navanethem Pillay**, the presiding officer, "From time immemorial, rape has been regarded as spoils of war. Now it will be considered a war crime. We want to send out a strong message that rape is no longer a trophy of war." It was also the first time that an internationally constituted court was enforcing the 1948 **United Nations Convention on the Punishment and Prevention of the Crime of Genocide**. *See also* SEXUAL VIOLENCE.

AL-ANFAL CAMPAIGN. Military campaign mounted by Iraq in the Northern area of the country against its Kurdish minority in the course of and just after the 1980–88 Iran-Iraq war. The campaign involved indiscriminate willful killings, forced relocations, summary executions, enslavement, **forced disappearances** and the use of chemical weapons on civilian populations. It resulted in the killing of at least and possibly more than 100,000 Kurds. After extensive investigations in the field, a **Human Rights Watch** team concluded that Al-Anfal constituted **genocide** and sought, in vain, to persuade several governments to bring a case against Iraq under the **United Nations Convention on the Punishment and Prevention of Genocide**. The charge of war crimes committed in the course of the Al-Anfal campaign was one that was brought against **Saddam Hussein** by the **Supreme Iraqi Criminal Tribunal**. *See also* KURDISH QUESTION; MINORITIES.

AL HAQ. Established in 1979 by Palestinian lawyers concerned with the lack of human rights protection mechanisms in the Occupied Palestinian Territories (OPTs), Al Haq is one of the first human rights organizations in the Arab world. While considerably evolving over time under the impact of the tribulations of local and international Middle Eastern politics, its **advocacy**, **research** and documentation work has generally focused on the status of the OPTs and legal analyses of human rights and humanitarian law violations within them. Al Haq has consultative status within the **United Nations Economic and Social Council**. It is also the West Bank affiliate of the **International Commission of Jurists** and a member of the **International Federation for Human Rights** and the **World Organization against Torture**. *See also* ARAB ISRAELI CONFLICT.

AL MEZAN CENTER FOR HUMAN RIGHTS. Palestinian **non-governmental organization** based in the Gaza Strip intended, under the terms of its charter, "to promote, protect and prevent violations of human rights in general and economic, social and cultural . . . rights in particular, to provide effective aid to those victims of such violations, and to enhance the quality of life of the community in marginalized sectors of the Gaza Strip." In effect, the bulk of the Center's work focuses of what it alleges to be the **violations** of basic civil and human rights by the Israeli Defense Forces (i.e., military attacks resulting in widespread civilian casualties, imprisonments without trial, political assassinations and official policies condoning brutality and torture). Israeli perceptions of the Center vary considerably, with some observers arguing that its activities encapsulate a virulently anti-Israel political agenda which entirely ignores Palestinian **terrorism**. *See also* ARAB ISRAELI CONFLICT.

ALAN GUTTMACHER INSTITUTE. American independent, not-for-profit corporation founded in 1968 which seeks to promote sound sexual and

reproductive rights policies in the **United States** and developing countries through social science research, policy analysis and public education. The Institute has an annual budget of some $12 million derived largely from private foundations and individual contributions, U.S. government grants, international governments, global organizations and the sale of special reports and its peer-reviewed journals such as *Perspectives on Sexual and Reproductive Health* and *International Family Planning Perspectives.*

ALGERIA. North African country originally settled by **Berbers**. The land came under the influence of the Carthaginians from 1000 BC onward, fell under Roman domination in the third century BC and then the Byzantine empire until the coming of the Arabs in the eighth century. Algeria was brought into the Ottoman Empire in the 15th to 16th centuries and became a French colony from 1930 to 1962. In November 1954, Algerian nationalists launched urban and rural warfare which climaxed in independence in July 1962 and the exodus of over a million people of European descent and some 100,000 Algerian Muslims who had served as auxiliaries in the French army in the remainder of the year. Under the hardly veiled tutelage of the army, Algeria was ruled for three decades by the Front de Libération National which had led the insurrection against France. Building on its oil and gas resources, the country experienced rapid modernization and demographic and social change which, in turn, triggered Berber identity movements and demands for the abolition of one-party rule and broader political participation. The first round of the country's multiparty elections were held in December 1991, resulting in the victory of the Front Islamique du Salut (FIS), a loose coalition of groups with varying degrees of allegiance to Islam. The army cancelled the second round of the elections, forced the president to resign and drove the FIS underground. Algeria was then engulfed in a brutal civil war which began to wane only in the late 1990s. Relatively open legislative and presidential elections have been held since 1995, and the government has made some concessions to the Berber minority. *See also* ALGERIAN CIVIL WAR; ALGERIAN WAR OF INDEPENDENCE; HARKIS; MINORITIES.

ALGERIAN CIVIL WAR (1992–2002). Internal armed conflict that pitted the Algerian government against a coalition of groups embracing a broad spectrum of Islamic beliefs. Originally triggered by demands for multiparty rule and fed by increasing levels of poverty, the conflict became increasingly violent as the government declared a state of emergency, suspended constitutional rights and held suspects without charge. Human rights organizations also charge that the government had recourse to **extra-judicial executions** and **torture**. In response, rebel groups targeted security forces as well as government employees, journalists, intellectuals and unveiled women. The reports of **investigations** carried out by the **European Union** also condemned the insurgents for large-scale massacres of civilian populations in entire rural villages and urban neighborhoods.

The muscled response of the government and skillful liberalization of the regime as well as sheer revulsion against the atrocities committed by all parties involved led to an uneasy end of the civil war. An **amnesty** proposed by the government that provided for immunity against prosecution of ex-guerrillas who had surrendered and army personnel "safeguarding the nation" was endorsed in a 2005 national referendum. Human rights **nongovernmental organizations** have criticized the amnesty because, in effect, it prevents the victims of abuses from seeking **redress** through Algerian courts. A 2006 decree provides for punishment of up to five years in prison for anyone "who by speech or in writing exploits the wounds of the 'National Tragedy,'" to tarnish the image of Algeria or "the good reputation of its agents." It is estimated that the conflict cost over 150,000 lives. *See also* ARMED CONFLICT; DEATH SQUADS; GENEVA CONVENTIONS.

ALGERIAN WAR OF INDEPENDENCE (1954–1962). One of the bloodiest wars of decolonization which involved **terrorism** against civilians and large-scale atrocities by both sides. The struggle was touched off on 1 November 1954 by guerrilla attacks throughout the Algerian territory. For Muslim nationalists, the purpose of the struggle was the "restoration of the Algerian state, sovereign, democratic and social, within the framework of the principles of Islam." But from the outset, the French government took the position that Algeria was a French territory and that "the internal peace of the nation" was at stake. Algerian nationalists were accordingly never granted the status of belligerents, and France refused to consider the legitimacy of the application of the **Geneva Conventions** to them or to civilian populations. In a similar vein, France strenuously resisted attempts by developing countries to place the "Algerian question" on the agenda of the **United Nations**. The notion that the task on hand was merely one of maintaining order against undefined "outlaws," "rebels" and "suspects" thus provided fertile grounds for the commission of **war crimes**, especially when the struggle spread from the countryside to the cities where Algerian nationalists unleashed in 1956 a wave of indiscriminate shootings and bombings targeted at civilian populations.

By then, France had committed more than 400,000 troops to Algeria, and in subsequent years a regime of "exceptional circumstances" superseded international humanitarian law. The principle of collective responsibility was ruthlessly applied. "Terrorist acts" were attributed to groups of population and the nearest villages suspected of any assistance to guerrillas were indiscriminately bombed. Hostage taking, vigilante reprisals and **extrajudicial executions** became commonplace and large segments of the rural population (2 million according to most estimates) were removed and resettled in military-supervised camps or forced to flee to Morocco, Tunisia, and into the Algerian hinterland in order to prevent villagers from aiding the rebels. At the same time, the continual search for intelligence led to the widespread utilization of **torture** not only against Algerian combatants but also civilians suspected of providing them with any form of assistance. In spite of insurrections staged in January 1960 and April 1961 by elements of the French army and portions of the French population, rising opposition to the conflict within French society and increasing international pressure on France to grant Algeria independence brought the conflict to a tumultuous end. According to Algerian sources, eight years of revolution cost 1.5 million lives. French officials use a figure of 350,000 dead. The ceasefire agreement negotiated by French and Algerian authorities provided for a reciprocal **amnesty** for "acts committed in the context of operations designed to maintain order in response to the Algerian insurrection" on the one hand and "acts relating to the participation in the insurrection and aid to the FLN [Front de Libération National]" on the other. See also AUSSARESSES, PAUL; *BATTLE OF ALGIERS*; COLONIALISM; HARKIS; PUBLIC EMERGENCIES.

ALIEN TORT STATUTE (ATS). Federal law adopted by the **United States** Congress in 1789 which simply asserted that American "district courts shall have original jurisdiction of any civil action by an alien for a tort only, committed in violation of the law of nations or a treaty of the United States." For almost two centuries, the statute lay relatively dormant, and it was widely assumed that it was intended to deal with torts occurring during such acts as piracy or interference with the rights of ambassadors. As a result of increasing international concern with human rights issues, foreign nationals have in recent years utilized the statute to sue American government officials, military and corporate leaders for human rights abuses committed as a result of their presence or activities in their country. Over 100 suits have been filed under ATS since a 1980 case involving the relatives of a Paraguyan who was kidnapped and tortured to death by a Paraguayan.

Since then, the law has been used with mixed results for the plaintiffs in cases involving **torture** (including rape), **extra-judicial executions, crimes against humanity, war crimes**, and **arbitrary detention**. For instance, in December 2004, the energy company Union Oil Company of California agreed to settle a suit brought against it under the statute by Burmese villagers alleging human rights violations, including **forced labor**, in the construction of a gas pipeline in **Myanmar**. In a related vein, the Torture Victim Protection Act, passed in 1991 and signed into law by President **George W. Bush** in 1992, gives similar rights to U.S. citizens and noncitizens alike to bring claims for torture and extrajudicial killing committed in foreign countries. The perpetrator generally must be served with the lawsuit while he also is present in the United States in order for the court to have **jurisdiction**. Recent jurisprudence suggests that **transnational corporations** may no longer be subject to suit under the act. *See also* ACT OF STATE DOCTRINE; CENTER FOR CONSTITUTIONAL RIGHTS; CENTER FOR JUSTICE AND ACCOUNTABILITY; RUMSFELD, DONALD; UNIVERSAL JURISDICTION.

ALIENS, TREATMENT OF. The protection of foreign nationals against personal injury or damage to their property is one of the central questions of the law of state responsibility and diplomatic relations. The compensation of private investors in cases of political and economic disturbances and nationalization, in particular, has been an ongoing subject of controversy. From a human rights perspective, the rights and obligations of aliens— **asylum seekers**, immigrants, **migrant workers**, **refugees**, stateless persons, and trafficked persons—vary considerably depending on bilateral and multilateral agreements and the particulars of national legislation. In 1985, the **United Nations General Assembly** adopted a resolution proclaiming that non-citizens should be free from **arbitrary detention**, child labor, **forced labor**, inhuman treatment, invasions of privacy and *refoulement*. They should also have a right to consular protection, equality of treatment before the law, **freedom of religion**, peaceful association and assembly and social economic and cultural rights. Non-citizens can be confronted with institutional and endemic discrimination and suffering. These broad provisions have been strengthened by several global and regional human rights treaties. In the **European Union**, nationals of member states have virtually the same rights and obligations as citizens of the states they reside in. In practice, non-citizens often face hardship and institutional and endemic **discrimination**.

ALSTON, PHILIP (1950–). Prominent international law scholar and human rights practitioner who served in various capacities in senior **United Nations** positions for more than two decades. Actively involved in the field of children's rights and as legal adviser to the **United Nations Children's Fund**, he played an important role in the drafting of the **United Nations Convention on the Rights of the Child**. Through a series of reports spanning over almost a decade from 1989 to 1997, he spearheaded the efforts of the

United Nations Office of the High Commissioner for Human Rights and the **United Nations Commission on Human Rights** to streamline the UN human rights treaty **monitoring** system. Since 2004 he has been the United Nations **special rapporteur** on extrajudicial, summary or arbitrary executions. In that capacity, he has dealt with and commented on such politically sensitive issues as the activities of national-level commissions of inquiry dealing with unlawful killings, the need to regulate the use of lethal force by law enforcement officers, mercy killings in times of armed conflict, the need to make military justice systems human rights compatible and, in regard to **capital punishment**, the unacceptability of the mandatory death penalty under international law and the definition of the "most serious crimes" for which capital punishment may be imposed.

AMERICAN CIVIL LIBERTIES UNION (ACLU). Founded in 1920 by a handful of civil liberties activists, the ACLU has grown to more than 500,000 members and supporters. Now one of the most important human rights organization in the **United States**, the ACLU works in the courts, legislatures and communities to defend and preserve the individual rights and liberties guaranteed by the Constitution and the laws of the United States—freedom of speech, **association** and assembly; freedom of the press, and **freedom of religion**, the right to **due process** and equal protection under the law—equal treatment regardless of race, sex, religion or national origin. The ACLU has maintained that these civil liberties must be respected, even in times of national **public emergencies** and, for this reason, has taken the position that the Patriot Act passed by the U.S. Congress in response to the 11 September 2001 terrorist attacks needed to be amended and realigned with key constitutional protections because it unduly expanded the government's power to spy on its citizens and reduced checks and balances on those powers. The ACLU has also focused its work on segments of the population that have traditionally been denied their rights, including Native Americans and other people of color; lesbians, gays, bisexuals and transgendered people; women; mental-health patients; prisoners; people with disabilities; and the poor. The ACLU handles nearly 6,000 court cases annually. The bulk of its income (the annual budget exceeds $100 million) derives from annual dues and contributions from its members. The ACLU does not receive any government funding.

AMERICAN CONVENTION ON HUMAN RIGHTS. International human rights instrument which was adopted by Latin American countries in 1969 and entered into force in 1978. The objective of the Convention is "to consolidate in this hemisphere, within the framework of democratic institutions, a system of personal liberty and social justice based on respect for the essential rights of man." It enjoins state parties to uphold and incorporate into their domestic law the individual **civil and political rights** due to all persons set forth in the Convention, including the **right to life** "in general, from the moment of conception," to humane treatment, to a fair trial, to privacy, to freedom of conscience, freedom of assembly, **freedom of movement**, among others. Only one article of the Convention deals with **economic, social and cultural rights** but it was considerably strengthened by an additional 1999 Optional Protocol which covers such areas as the **rights to work**, to **health**, to **food**, and to **education**. A second Protocol places restrictions on the imposition of **capital punishment** which may be applicable to only the most serious crimes, may not be reinstated if previously abolished, may not be used for political offenses and against individuals aged under 18 and over 70 or against pregnant women. The implementation of the Convention is overseen by the **Inter-American Commission on Human Rights** and the **Inter-American Court of Human Rights**. *See also* ABORTION; AMERICAN DECLARATION OF THE RIGHTS AND DUTIES OF MAN; COMPLAINTS; DEMOCRACY.

AMERICAN DECLARATION OF THE RIGHTS AND DUTIES OF MAN. Aspirational, normative statement of a general nature adopted by the **Organization of American States** (OAS) in April 1948 for the countries of the Latin American region. Like the United Nations **Universal Declaration of Human Rights** (UDHR) issued six months later by the **United Nations General Assembly** (whose scope is universal rather than regional), the Declaration first sets forth a catalogue of **civil and political rights** and **economic, social and cultural rights** to be enjoyed by the citizens of countries of the region. In contrast to the UDHR, which is silent on the subject, the American Declaration contains a section spelling out the corresponding duties of states. As stated in the preamble of the Declaration, "The fulfillment of duties by each individual is a prerequisite to the rights of all. Rights and duties are interrelated in every social and political activity of man. While rights exalt individual liberty, duties express the dignity of that liberty."

Formally, the Declaration is not a treaty and therefore is not binding. It has been used, however, as a source of jurisprudential guidance by the **Inter-American Court of Human Rights** and the **Inter-American Commission on Human Rights** set up in accordance with the treaty-based **American Convention on Human Rights**. The Inter-American Court has taken the view that the member states of the OAS have signaled their agreement that the Declaration defines the human rights referred to in the OAS Charter. The argument has also been made that insofar as the Declaration incorporates many of the same rights expressed in the UDHR, it may be considered customary international law and may be a source of obligation for those states like **Cuba** and the **United States** that have not signed the American Convention on Human Rights. *See also* CULTURAL RIGHTS.

AMERICAN JEWISH COMMITTEE (AJC). Non-profit international and **advocacy think tank** and **non-governmental organization** (NGO) set up in 1906 to promote pluralistic and democratic societies and the protection of minorities worldwide as a means to protect Jewish populations. Headquartered in New York, the AJC operates a network of offices in the **United States** and overseas. Dedicated to combating anti-Semitism and supporting Israel's quest for peace and security, the AJC's human rights concerns have focused on religious intolerance, **torture, discrimination, crimes against humanity, war crimes** and the prevention of **genocide**. AJC members were official NGO consultants to the U.S. delegation at the founding conference of the **United Nations** in 1945 and successfully pressed for the inclusion of human rights provisions in the UN Charter.

   The AJC has supported U.S. ratification of major human rights instruments including the **United Nations Convention on the Punishment and Prevention of the Crime of Genocide**, the **International Covenant on Civil and Political Rights**, the **International Convention on the Elimination of All Forms of Racial Discrimination**, and the **United Nations Convention against Torture** and called for U.S. ratification of the **United Nations Convention on the Elimination of all Forms of Discrimination against Women** and the Rome treaty establishing the **International Criminal Court**. The AJC's human rights agenda is pursued primarily through its Jacob Blaustein Institute for the Advancement of Human Rights which also conducts **research** on the effectiveness of international human rights mechanisms and institutions, **human rights defenders, terrorism**, torture, the prevention of genocide, religious intolerance, the protection of civilians in armed conflicts and the rights of women.

AMERICAN SOCIETY OF INTERNATIONAL LAW (ASIL). Nonprofit educational membership organization founded in 1906 for the purpose of advancing **international law** scholarship and education through meetings, publications, information services and outreach programs. Some of the material produced by the Society—notably its inventory of electronic resources for international law research and its cogent briefs on legal topical issues—are an excellent source of information. The Society has 4,000 members from nearly 100 nations including attorneys, academics, corporate counsel, judges, representatives of governments and **non-governmental**

organizations, international civil servants, students and others interested in international law. ASIL is located in Washington, D.C., and has consultative status to the **United Nations Economic and Social Council**.

AMICUS CURIAE. Latin phrase meaning "friend of the court" referring to individuals or **non-governmental groups** that are not parties to a legal case but can assist a court or a quasi-judicial body in deciding a matter before them. The information provided may be in the form of testimonies or briefs offering a legal opinion. Amicus briefs by international human rights groups have become a widespread practice in **United Nations** treaty bodies and regional courts of human rights. *See also* ADJUDICATION.

AMIN, IDI (c. 1924–2003). Army officer who seized power in a coup d'etat in 1971. Initially welcomed both within **Uganda** and by the international community, his rule soon turned violent and bloody. Ugandan tribal groups which had not supported his coup were persecuted and Uganda's 50,000 Asians were expelled from the country. Ugandan exiles aided by Tanzanian military forces drove Amin out of power in 1979. The new government did make it known that Amin would face **war crime** charges if he ever returned to Uganda, but eventually allowed him to stay in exile in Saudi Arabia where he found asylum until his death (Amin had converted to Islam). Human rights organizations believe that as many as half a million people were killed or disappeared under Amin's rule. *See also* IMPUNITY; INTERNATIONAL COMMISSION OF JURISTS.

AMNESTIES. Government official actions whereby persons having committed a criminal offense (usually of a political nature) are granted immunity from prosecution. Their underlying rationale is that punishing offenders is deemed to be less important than preserving a fragile peace, ensuring the survival of a transitional government or promoting long-term reconciliation in a fractured society. For example, amnesty was used in South Africa, during the 1990s, as part of a truth and reconciliation process. Amnesties, however, can also be a source of controversy as they may, for the sake of political expediency, in effect lead to **impunity** in cases of serious human rights violations. Civilian authorities in countries emerging from conflict such as **Algeria**, **Argentina**, **Brazil**, **Chile**, **El Salvador**, **Guatemala**, Haiti, **Honduras**, Nicaragua, **Peru**, Spain, **Uganda** and **Uruguay** have issued broad amnesties or were compelled to accept amnesties previously enacted by the outgoing military. Regional human rights courts in their jurisprudence, notably the **Inter-American Court of Human Rights** and the **Inter-American Commission on Human Rights**, have determined that a number of national amnesties were inconsistent with the **American Convention on Human Rights** and the **American Declaration of the Rights and Duties of Man**. Other judicial or quasi-judicial bodies like the **European Court of Human Rights**, the **African Commission on Human and People's Rights**, the **United Nations Committee Against Torture** and the **United Nations Human Rights Committee** have clarified the conditions for lawful amnesties in some of their **General Comments**. *See also* ALGERIAN CIVIL WAR; AUSSARESSES, PAUL; BOKASSA, JEAN-BEDEL; IENG SARY; PINOCHET, AUGUSTO; TRANSITIONAL JUSTICE; VIDELA, JORGE RAFAEL.

AMNESTY INTERNATIONAL (AI). Advocacy international **non-governmental organization** with the broad purpose of laying down the foundations of "a world in which every person enjoys all the human rights enshrined in the **Universal Declaration of Human Rights** and other international standards." The brainchild of a British lawyer **Peter Benenson**, AI was founded in 1961 and modestly began its activities in the early 1960s focusing on prisoners of conscience. It subsequently expanded its programs to include work on **torture, extra-judicial executions**, "**forced disappearances**" (especially under military dictatorships in Latin America), **capital punishment** and the rights of **refugees**. More recently, in deference to the principle of the **indivisibility** of human rights and increasingly aware of the pace of **globalization**, AI has widened the scope of its work to include economic, social and cultural rights. To achieve its goals, AI investigates claims of human rights abuses, publicizes its findings, and mobilizes its membership (now close to 2 million) to lobby against such abuses by letter writing, protesting, demonstrating, organizing fund-raising campaigns and educating the public at large.

Over the years, AI has pressed for the application of the **United Nations Standard Minimum Prison Rules**, the ratification of the International Covenant on Civil and Political Rights and the International Covenant on Economic, Social and Cultural Rights, the creation of a **United Nations Office of the High Commissioner for Human Rights** and the establishment of an **International Criminal Court**. AI describes itself as "independent of any government, political ideology, economic interest or religion. It does not support or oppose any government or political system, nor does it support or oppose the views of the victims whose rights it seeks to protect. It is concerned solely with the impartial protection of human rights."

AI has, however, been the target of criticism by governments for "one-sided reporting" or failures to treat threats to security as mitigating factors. Thus, critics have pointed to a disproportionate focus on allegations of human rights **violations** in relatively more democratic and open countries such as Israel. AI's 2005 annual report, which referred to the **Guantanamo Bay Detention Camp** as "the gulag of our times, entrenching the practice of arbitrary and indefinite detention in violation of international law," was labeled as "reprehensible" and "absurd" by **United States** government officials. *See also* BURGER, JAN HERMAN.

AMSTERDAM TREATY. A treaty of 1997 which entered into force in 1999 and was designed to further democratize the **European Union** (EU) in preparation for its eastward enlargement. The **European Parliament** was given powers to legislate in concert with the Council of Ministers on a range of new issues including employment, social policy, health, transport and the environment. In the Council of Ministers, unanimity was replaced with qualified majority voting on employment, social exclusion and customs. The Union members also agreed to coordinate their approach to **asylum** and immigration as well as increasing cooperation on police and law enforcement. The overall objective of the treaty was to underline the centrality of the principles of respect for human rights and fundamental freedoms in the process of European integration. The provisions of the Amsterdam Treaty thus include a procedure for dealing with cases where a member state has committed a breach of the principles on which the EU is based. It calls for more effective action to be taken to combat not only **discrimination** based on nationality but also discrimination based on sex, racial or ethnic origin, religion or belief, disability, age or sexual orientation. The Final Act was accompanied by declarations on the abolition of **capital punishment** and respect for the status of churches. The provisions of the treaty have been amended and expanded by the **Lisbon Treaty**.

ANGOLA. Former Portuguese colony which plunged into civil war shortly after gaining independence as rival factions reflecting deep-seated ethnic divisions fought for political control of the country. The conflict, which lasted from 1975 to 2002 with an uneasy interlude between 1994 and 1998, was driven by **Cold War** regional and global geopolitics as the **United States** and the Soviet Union and **Cuba** threw their political and military weight in support of their respective political clients. The war was also prolonged by one of the factions refusal to adhere to a 1994 political agreement and its control of diamond mining and sale despite international sanctions. By the end of the war, an estimated 1.5 million people had lost their lives and over 4 million, one-third of Angola's population, had been displaced. **Non-governmental organizations** (NGOs) also reckon that some 10,000 child soldiers—some of them forcibly impressed—participated in the conflict. Several thousands of underage girls are also believed to have been coerced into forms of sexual slavery.

A peace agreement concluded in 2006 brought to an end an on-and-off separatist insurgency in the oil-rich northern exclave of Cabinda. Since the end of the civil war, more than 400,000 Angolan **refugees** living in camps and settlements in neighboring countries have been brought back home with the assistance of the **United Nations Office of the High Commissioner for Human Rights** and NGOs. Most **internally displaced persons** have returned home. But the country still faces an unfinished reintegration agenda. Operations to neutralize the 15 million landmines laid in the course of the conflict are expected to be completed sometime between now and 2014. Against a background of continuing **poverty** and deprivation (Angola has one of the lowest Human Development Indices), political violence, media restrictions and **violations** of human rights are still not uncommon. *See also* SELF-DETERMINATION; KIMBERLEY PROCESS CERTIFICATION SCHEME.

ANNAN, KOFI (1938–). Ghanaian diplomat who rose from the rank and served as assistant secretary-general for human resources, management and security coordinator (1987–90); program planning, budget and finance, and controller (1990–92); and peacekeeping operations (March 1993–February 1994) before being elected secretary-general of the **United Nations** for two consecutive terms from 1997 to 2006. He was criticized for failing to provide logistical and material support to the UN force commander in Rwanda on the eve of the **genocide**, and in 2004, he did acknowledge that he "should have done more to sound the alarm and rally support." Often portrayed as a **"norm entrepreneur**," he gave priority throughout his tenure at the helm of the United Nations to strengthening the role of the organization in the areas of development and the maintenance of international peace and security while seeking to "bring it closer to the people." He was a strong advocate of mainstreaming human rights in the activities of the United Nations. In 2001, Annan and the United Nations were jointly awarded the **Nobel Peace Prize** for "for their work for a better organized and more peaceful world."

ANTI-DEFAMATION LEAGUE (ADL). Founded in 1913 "to stop the defamation of the Jewish people and to secure justice and fair treatment to all," its stated mission is to fight **anti-Semitism** and all forms of bigotry, defend democratic ideals and protect civil rights for all. Toward these ends, the ADL scrutinizes and exposes extremists and hate groups, monitors hate on the **Internet**, provides expertise on domestic and international **terrorism**, develops educational programs, fosters interfaith and intergroup relations and mobilizes communities to stand up against bigotry.

ANTI-RACISM INFORMATION SERVICE (ARIS). Non-governmental organization (NGO), founded in 1992 in Geneva, Switzerland, and enjoying since 1997 consultative status with the **United Nations Economic and Social Council**. ARIS serves national and regional NGOs, human rights groups and individuals who are not represented at the United Nations by facilitating their access to the proceedings of the **United Nations Committee on the Elimination of All Forms of Racial Discrimination**.

ANTI-SEMITISM. The term refers to all forms of hostility and violence or denotes discriminatory beliefs or practices against Jews as a religious, ethnic, or racial group. Anti-Semitism is an age-old phenomenon that initially may have originated from tensions between Judaism, early Christianity and Islam. Since then, nurtured by political, economic, religious, nationalistic and racial motifs, anti-Semitism has evolved over time into various forms of violence ranging from individual prejudice and discrimination in employment and access to residential areas, to accusations of deicide, to institutionalized persecutions such as the Spanish Inquisition, the eviction of Jews from Spain and Portugal in 1492 and 1497, respectively, to recurrent pogroms throughout Europe and the Muslim world culminating in the infamous **Holocaust** of Adolf Hitler's Germany. More recently, criticisms of **Israel** and Zionism have been portrayed by some as a new variety of anti-Semitism, while others took the position that the argument was designed to stifle debate and deflect attention from legitimate criticism of Israel's policies in regard to Palestinians. Incidents involving verbal attacks, physical assaults, vandalism, desecration of synagogues and cemeteries and fire bombings are not infrequent in many countries, especially in Europe, in spite of preventive or corrective administrative legislative measures.

At the multilateral level, after decades of frosty relations between Israel and the **United Nations** (in 1975, the **United Nations General Assembly** [UN-GA] adopted a resolution branding Zionism as a form of racism which it subsequently repealed in 1991), the **United Nations Commission on Human Rights** formally condemned anti-Semitism in a 1994 resolution and requested its **special rapporteur** on contemporary forms of racism to investigate and report on anti-Semitic incidents worldwide. On 24 January 2005, the UN-GA held a commemoration of the 60th anniversary of the liberation of the Nazi **concentration camps**. In November 2005, the UN-GA designated 27 January as Holocaust Remembrance Day at the United Nations, called on member states to include the Holocaust in their educational curriculums and condemned manifestations of Holocaust denial. The **Organization for Security and Co-operation in Europe** organized conferences in 2003 and 2004 which focused high-level political attention on the problem of anti-Semitism, identifying it as a human rights issue and leading to the establishment of a system of information gathering on hate crime legislation and promotion of "best practices" in the areas of law enforcement, combating hate crimes, and education. *See also* AMERICAN JEWISH COMMITTEE; ANTI-DEFAMATION LEAGUE.

ANTI-SLAVERY INTERNATIONAL. London-based **non-governmental organization** tracing its origin to 19th-century abolitionist movements which campaigned against the transatlantic **slave trade** in 1807 and fought for Britain's abolition of **slavery** in 1833. Formally established in 1839 under the name of British and Foreign Anti-Slavery Society, the Society played a key role in campaigning for and drafting the 1926 **Convention on the Abolition of Slavery** and the 1956 Supplementary Convention on the Abolition of Slavery, the Slave Trade and Practices Similar to Slavery. It also contributed to the creation in the mid-1970s of the United Nations Working Group on Contemporary Forms of Slavery, a group of experts functioning under the authority of the **United Nations Commission on Human Rights**. In 1990, the Society changed its name to Anti-Slavery International. It currently seeks to eradicate all forms of slavery, including **forced labor**, child labor and trafficking in human beings by exposing current cases of such abuses, supporting local initiatives to release people and pressing for more effective implementation of international laws against slavery. *See also* LABOR BONDAGE.

APARTHEID. Legal system of **racial discrimination** and separation of races enforced in South Africa from 1948 until its abolition in 1994. Under it, access to education, medical care, public services and housing and the scope of civil and political rights all hinged on whether persons were classified white, Bantu (black), colored (mixed race), or Asian. In effect, the system served to preserve and solidify the political, socials and economic domination of the white minority. Racial **discrimination** in South Africa was discussed early on in the **United Nations** as India brought the question of the treatment of the Indian minority in the country to the **United Nations General Assembly**. As the number of **developing countries** grew in subsequent years, the pressure on South Africa to dismantle racial laws and apartheid accordingly intensified. On 6 November 1962, the UN-GA adopted a resolution condemning South African Apartheid policies. On 7 August 1963, the **United Nations Security Council** decreed a voluntary arms embargo against South Africa. Following the brutal suppression of a popular uprising in 1976, the arms embargo was made mandatory by the Council in 4 November 1977. UN-sponsored world conferences on racism also condemned apartheid in 1978 and 1983.

Concurrently, a significant divestment movement started pressuring investors to refuse to invest in South Africa.

The intent of the United Nations **International Convention on the Suppression and Punishment of the Crime of Apartheid**, which came into force in 1976, was to empower state parties to apply sanctions to press South Africa to change its policies. Additional Protocol I to the 1949 **Geneva Conventions** lists apartheid and other inhuman and degrading practices as grave breaches. The 2002 Statute of the **International Criminal Court** also criminalizes apartheid defining it generically as one of 11 **crimes against humanity** "committed in the context of an institutionalized regime of systematic oppression and domination by one racial group over any other racial group or groups . . . with the intention of maintaining that regime." Groups such as the Kurds, the Tamils, the South Sudanese, or other **indigenous peoples** do suffer systematic discrimination that might be akin to this definition of apartheid. But neither victims nor their advocates use the term, which remains associated solely to the South African experience. In any case, many of the inequalities created and maintained by apartheid still subsist in South Africa. *See also* EQUALITY; GOLDSTONE, RICHARD; INTERNATIONAL CONVENTION AGAINST APARTHEID IN SPORTS; KURDISH QUESTION; MINORITIES; TRUTH AND RECONCILIATION COMMISSIONS; TUTU, DESMOND; WORLD CONFERENCE AGAINST RACISM.

APOLOGIES. Reparative justice mechanism whereby the perpetrator(s) of human rights violations (or a representative on their behalf if generations have elapsed since the abuse took place) admit responsibility and express regret for them. Through the acknowledgment and vindication of the suffering of the victims, the purpose of apologies is to advance intergroup reconciliation and restore national social harmony. There is considerable debate as to whether apologies are genuine in the first place or constitute cynical attempts to avoid more costly forms of **reparations** or **restitution**. There are widespread doubts, for example, about the sincerity of Prime Minister Shinzo Abe's apologies in 2007 about Japan's World War II role in regard to **"comfort women."** Cases of outright denials are perhaps more numerous. Pakistan has resisted calls to apologize to Bangladesh for acts of **genocide** committed during the 1971 **Bangladesh Liberation War**. But official apologies (and **truth and reconciliation commissions**) have been increasingly used in recent years as a form of partial **redress** for past human rights abuses. Thus, Canada, Australia, Peru, and Guatemala have made apologies to their **indigenous peoples** communities. In 2009, the **United States** Senate unanimously passed a resolution apologizing to African

Americans for **slavery** and segregation. Following the issuance of reports that he commissioned, **United Nations Secretary-General Kofi Annan** publicly apologized for the inaction of the United Nations in **Srebrenica** and the **Rwandan genocide**. *See also* COLONIALISM; KOREMATSU, FRED TOYOSABURO.

APPLICATION. Term used notably by the **European Court of Human Rights** to refer to a **complaint** lodged by an individual alleging **violations** of his or her rights by one of the states parties to the **European Convention for the Protection of Human Rights and Fundamental Freedoms**. *See also* COMMUNICATION.

ARAB ASSOCIATION FOR HUMAN RIGHTS. Advocacy human rights group established in 1988. Registered as a non-profit organization in Israel in 1990 and based in Brussels, this **non-governmental organization** focuses its activities on the promotion and protection of international human rights standards for the Palestinian Arab minority in Israel. It has submitted alternative reports on **housing** and conditions and gender issues affecting the Palestinian Arab minority in Israel to the **United Nations Committee on Economic, Social and Cultural Rights** and the **United Nations Committee on the Elimination of All Forms of Discrimination against Women.**

ARAB CHARTER ON HUMAN RIGHTS. Draft aspirational human rights statement adopted by the governing council of the **League of Arab States** in 1994 and subsequently revised in 2003. Drawing from principles contained in the **United Nations Charter**, the **Universal Declaration of Human Rights**, the **International Covenant on Civil and Political Rights**, the **International Covenant on Economic, Social and Cultural Rights** and the **Cairo Declaration on Human Rights in Islam,** the Charter acknowledges a number of traditional human rights, notably the right to liberty and **security** of persons, **equality** of persons before the law, protection of persons from **torture**, the right to own private property, freedom to practice religious observance and freedom of peaceful assembly and **freedom of association.** The Charter, which entered into force in 2008, has been criticized by human rights advocates for failing to recognize a number of important rights such as the right not to be held in servitude or **slavery**, the prohibition of **capital punishment**, the **freedom of religion** and **expression** and the right to vote. Critiques have also censured the Charter for subordinating the principle of equality between women and men to Islamic law and for not providing a monitoring mechanism of state implementation. *See also* CULTURAL RELATIVISM.

ARAB COMMISSION ON HUMAN RIGHTS. Founded in 1998 by a group of human rights advocates from different Arab countries, this **non-governmental organization** seeks to protect human rights and fundamental freedoms throughout the Arab world through research and studies and the dissemination of information.

ARAB ISRAELI CONFLICT. A wide array of interrelated issues and tensions which can be traced back to the 1917 Balfour Declaration making public the British government support of a Jewish homeland in Palestine, the circumstances of the creation of the State of **Israel** in 1948, the outcomes of the 1967 and 1973 wars, and the stymied aspirations of Palestinian nationalism. One set of issues relates to the legal borders between Israel and a Palestinian state and, in particular, the status of the territories seized by Israel in the wake of the 1967 war is in dispute. These include the West Bank and Gaza Strip (which are now under the nominal control of the Palestinian Authority), East Jerusalem, and the Sinai Peninsula (until 1982 when Egypt and Israel signed a peace agreement returning it to Egyptian sovereignty).

There is a broad consensus sanctioned by the **United Nations Security Council** and the **International Court of Justice** (ICJ) that these territories are under **occupation**, a designation that triggers the application of the **Geneva Conventions** which provide for special protection of civilian populations, limitations on the use of land and access by international relief agencies. Israel disputes this approach, uses the terminology of "disputed" territories, and, in 1980 to 1981, annexed East Jerusalem and the Golan Heights. These annexations have not been recognized by any country nor has Israel's unilateral declaration that it was no longer in occupation of the Gaza Strip when it withdrew its forces in 2005. In effect, Israel controls Gaza's airspace and coastline, and some countries and human rights organizations continue to refer to it as an occupying power.

Another contested issue is Israel's settlement policy in the territories. The UN Security Council, the ICJ and the **International Committee of the Red Cross** have taken the position that the settlements have no legal validity and are inconsistent with the Fourth Geneva Convention. The Israeli government is of the view that the Conventions do not apply because "the West Bank and Gaza Strip were not under the legitimate and recognized sovereignty of any state prior to the Six Day War, [so] they should not be considered occupied territories." The stretches of barriers constructed by Israel within the West Bank as a means to prevent terrorist attacks were declared contrary to international humanitarian law and international law by the ICJ. Perhaps the most explosive unresolved issue is the fate of the 5 million Palestinian refugees registered with the **United Nations Relief and Works Agency**

for Palestinian Refugees in the Near East dispersed primarily in Syria, Lebanon, the West Bank and Jordan who trace their origin to the 1948 exodus and the 1967 displacements and claim a right of return.

Whether the creation of this refugee population was an example of **ethnic cleansing** by Jewish armed groups or of willful displacement induced by neighboring Arab states is still hotly contested. But setting aside questions of right and wrong, or practicality and moral justice, the fate of Palestinian refugees has by and large been ignored in Mideast diplomacy. So has the brewing question of access to **water** which may in the future prove to be a major obstacle to a peace accord in the region. According to a recent UN survey, Palestinians have increasingly lost access to water sources in the West Bank as a result of the growing presence of Israeli settlers.

See also AL HAQ; AL MEZAN CENTER FOR HUMAN RIGHTS; ARAB ASSOCIATION FOR HUMAN RIGHTS; ARAB LAWYERS UNION; ARAB ORGANIZATION FOR HUMAN RIGHTS; EURO-MEDITERRANEAN HUMAN RIGHTS NETWORK; GOLDSTONE REPORT; INTIFADA; PALESTINIAN CENTRE FOR HUMAN RIGHTS; SABRA AND SHATILA MASSACRE.

ARAB LAWYERS UNION. One of the oldest **non-governmental organizations** in the Arab world. Founded in 1983 and devoted to the defense of human rights in the Arab world, the Union focuses its activities on the release of political prisoners, receives complaints from individuals, groups and organizations, offers legal assistance and provides financial help to families of victims. *See also* ARAB ISRAELI CONFLICT; ARAB ORGANIZATION FOR HUMAN RIGHTS.

ARAB LEAGUE. *See* LEAGUE OF ARAB STATES.

ARAB ORGANIZATION FOR HUMAN RIGHTS (AOHR). Regional **non-governmental organization** created in 1983 to defend citizens and residents of the Arab world subjected to **violations** of civil and political human rights. Based in Cairo, the AOHR has branches in Algeria, Egypt, Jordan, Kuwait, Lebanon, Morocco, Tunisia and Yemen. Its activities include **fact-finding** field missions, legal assistance, financial support and the dissemination of information through conferences and seminars, press releases, newsletters and books. The AOHR has consultative status with the **United Nations Economic and Social Council** and observer status in the **African Union**. *See also* ARAB LAWYERS UNION; PALESTINIAN CENTRE FOR HUMAN RIGHTS.

"ARAB SPRING." Shorthand expression (coined perhaps in reference to the revolutions which shook Europe in 1848, the Prague demonstrations crushed by the Soviet Union in 1968 and regime change in Eastern Europe in 1989) that has gained currency to denote the wave of demonstrations and protests that swept the Arab world since December 2010. While there have been numerous instances of protests in the past in the Arab world, it is the first time that strikes, demonstrations and rallies sustained by the effective use of social media have forced rulers from Tunisia, **Egypt**, **Libya** and Yemen and triggered an ongoing civil war in **Syria**. The phenomenon is understood to be the product of such long-standing issues as social inequalities and widespread poverty, economic decline or stagnation and unemployment, government **corruption** and violations of human rights. Whether social and political unrest will lead to improvements in human rights conditions remains an open question, as suggested by the recent tribulations experienced by such countries as Egypt and Libya. *See also* INTERNET.

ARBITRARY DETENTION. The idea of "detention" may encompass a wide range of issues related to arrests, pretrial imprisonment, the physical conditions of confinement, the incarceration of foreigners as illegal immigrants awaiting extradition or deportation and the like. What all these have in common is the notion of deprivation of **liberty**. With a view to protecting the right to liberty, the **Universal Declaration of Human Rights** (Art. 9) asserts that no one may be subjected to arbitrary arrest, detention or imprisonment.

International human rights law as enshrined in the **International Covenant on Civil and Political Rights** (ICCPR, Art. 9), the **American Convention on Human Rights** (Art. 7), the **African Charter on Human and People's Rights** (Art. 6), the **European Convention for the Protection of Human Rights and Fundamental Freedoms** (Art. 5) and the **International Criminal Court** all prohibit arbitrary detention and set forth core entitlements of protection against arbitrary forms of deprivation of liberty. These include the principles that persons may be arrested or detained only on grounds established by law, that they must be promptly informed of the reasons of their arrest and brought before a judicial authority, that they should be charged and brought to trial (or released) and that they have a right to compensation if they have been wrongfully deprived of their freedom. Keeping someone in detention without taking steps to prosecute or releasing or holding someone indefinitely or for an unjustifiably and unreasonably longtime without charge and criminal prosecution constitute arbitrary detention.

In this respect, in some of its **General Comments**, the **United Nations Human Rights Committee** has commented that the term "arbitrary" in the

ICCPR is to be interpreted broadly to include elements of inappropriateness, injustice and lack of predictability. The **African Commission on Human and People's Rights** has also expressed the view that detaining a person beyond the expiry of the sentence constitutes a violation of the African Charter. The **Inter-American Commission on Human Rights** identified three forms of arbitrary detention: extra-legal detention (detention without legal basis or which has been carried out by paramilitary groups with the consent or acquiescence of the government officials); detention which violates the law; and detention as an abuse of power.

See also ALIEN TORT STATUTE; AUNG SAN SUU KYI; COUNCIL OF EUROPE; ETHNIC CLEANSING; FORCED DISAPPEARANCES; GUANTANAMO BAY DETENTION CAMP; INTERNATIONAL CONVENTION FOR THE PROTECTION OF ALL PERSONS FROM ENFORCED DISAPPEARANCE; TERRORISM; TRUTH, RIGHT TO THE; TURKEY; UNITED NATIONS WORKING GROUP ON ARBITRARY DETENTION; WORLD ORGANIZATION AGAINST TORTURE.

ARBOUR, LOUISE (1947–). Former Supreme Court of Canada justice and, currently, since 2004, **United Nations** high commissioner for human rights. From 1996 to 1999, she was chief prosecutor of **war crimes** for the **International Criminal Tribunal for the Former Yugoslavia**. It was in that capacity that she indicted then-President **Slobodan Milosevic** for war crimes, the first time a serving head of state was asked to respond regarding his actions before a standing international tribunal. During the 2006 Israel-Lebanon war, in a statement interpreted to be directed at **Israel**, she opined that "those in positions of command and control" could be subject to "personal criminal responsibility" for their actions in the conflict. Her term in office, which ended in 2008, was not renewed. Since 2009, she has been president of the **International Crisis Group**.

ARGENTINA. Latin American country which was gripped by a bloody civil war culminating in state-sponsored violence carried out by the military dictatorship which ruled the country from 1976 until the return to civilian rule in 1983 with the self-assigned objective supported by the **United States** to defend against international communism. Estimates of the number of people who were killed, tortured or disappeared vary from 9,000 (according to a national commission which investigated the matter) to 30,000 (according to Argentinian human rights groups). Most victims were guerrilla fighters who had battled the previous defunct Peronist regime, trade union members, students and people reputed to have left-wing views. Following elections held in the wake the disastrous Malvinas/Falkland war, the junta relinquished power.

A National Commission on the Disappearance of Persons revealed documented evidence of the atrocities committed under military rule, and all nine members of the junta were tried and convicted of **violations of human rights** in 1985. Their prison sentences, however, were extinguished by **amnesty** laws, which remained in force until the Argentinian Supreme Court overturned them in 2005. The Court's decision reopened the door for prosecution of former junta officials. Most of them are either on trial or serving jail sentences.

See also COLD WAR; DEATH SQUADS; "DIRTY WAR"; MOTHERS OF THE PLAZA DE MAYO; OPERATION CONDOR; STATE TERRORISM; TRUTH AND RECONCILIATION COMMISSIONS; UNIVERSAL JURISDICTION; VIDELA, JORGE RAFAEL.

ARIAS, OSCAR (1940–). Costa Rican politician who served two non-consecutive terms as president of his country (1986–90 and 2006–10). He was awarded the **Nobel Peace Prize** for his efforts to bring to an end to the civil wars in **El Salvador** and **Guatemala** and to strengthen democratic institutions in Central America.

ARMED CONFLICT. International humanitarian law recognizes three types of armed conflict: international armed conflicts which occur between the legal armed forces of two different states (wars of national liberation against a colonial power, foreign **occupation** or racist regimes all qualify as international armed conflicts); internationalized armed conflicts which take place between two different factions fighting internally with the support of two states (it is now understood that the stationing of a multinational peacekeeping force on the territory internationalizes the conflict); and non-international armed conflicts or civil wars, which take place in the territory of one state between its armed forces and dissident armed forces or other organized groups. Problems arise in regard to non-international armed conflicts, as they need to be distinguished from internal disturbance or tensions such as riots, isolated and sporadic acts of violence which are not considered armed conflicts. In such situations, the principles of Common Article 3 of the **Geneva Conventions** as well as the protection of **non-derogable rights** remain in force.

According to the Geneva Conventions, two conditions must be fulfilled for a conflict to be labeled a non-international armed conflict: the level of intensity of the fighting and the degree of organization of armed groups. Applying these ambiguous and vague criteria has proved a challenge as governments involved are generally loath to regard insurgents as legal contestants rather than mere criminals and law breakers. Further difficulties in the application of international humanitarian law have surfaced from the involvement of new actors in zones of conflicts such as **private military companies**, **transnational corporations** and transnational armed groups. For example, there are still ongoing controversies as to whether the "**war on terror**" is an armed conflict, whether **terrorism** should be viewed as a form of **aggression** and whether terrorists can be considered combatants subject to the laws of war. *See also* ALGERIAN CIVIL WAR; CHECHNYA; DECLARATION ON THE PROTECTION OF WOMEN AND CHILDREN IN EMERGENCY AND ARMED CONFLICTS; "DIRTY WAR"; FUNDAMENTAL GUARANTEES; INTERNAL DISTURBANCES; NUCLEAR WEAPONS; PROTECTED PERSONS; PUBLIC EMERGENCIES; SELF-DETERMINATION; WOMEN IN PEACE AND SECURITY.

ARMED GROUPS. Groups also known as "irregulars" or "paramilitaries" that use force to achieve their objectives and operate beyond state control. They include a wide variety of actors, including opposition and insurgent movements, pro-government militias, religious fighters, large-scale predatory transnational organizations, organized drug cartels and community-based vigilante groups, among others. The line between groups that pursue political objectives as opposed to criminal objectives is often blurred. The types and motivations of these groups have become increasingly diverse, complex and complicated. They are considered "terrorists" by some and "liberation fighters" by others. In many internal conflicts, armed groups control territory where they deploy state-like structures providing education, health, humanitarian relief and law and order services. In some instances, they have partially integrated into the national governance structure while retaining control over their local military power. Their proliferation is associated with the fragmentation of states into smaller quasi-self-governing entities, the privatization of warfare, vastly improved means of communication and the **globalization** of business and finance. Their involvement in **armed conflicts** has led to massive and systematic **violations of human rights** and humanitarian norms and posed baffling issues as to how they should be engaged by the international community for purposes of **prevention** and **accountability** in regard to such matters as the protection of **civilians** and children, respect for human rights and humanitarian law and disarmament, demobilization and reintegration programs. *See also* CENTRAL INTELLIGENCE AGENCY; COLOMBIA; GUATEMALA; LORD'S RESISTANCE ARMY; MERCENARY; PARAMILITARIES; PERU; PHILIPPINES; PRIVATE MILITARY COMPANIES; STATE TERRORISM; TERRORISM.

ARMENIAN GENOCIDE. This refers to the atrocities committed on orders of the government of the Young Turks from 1915 to 1917 in the Ottoman Empire against the Armenian minority. After a lull, **massacres** and brutalities resumed between 1920 and 1923, leading to the expulsion of most remaining Armenians. Out of an estimated 2 million Armenians living in the Ottoman Empire on the eve of World War I, 1 million to 1.5 million perished as a result of **deportation**, **torture**, starvation and summary mass killings. The 1920 Treaty of Sevres between the Allies and the Ottoman Empire recognized the existence of a "Democratic Republic of Armenia" and committed the Ottoman Empire to hand over for international trial to the Allied Powers anyone complicit in the Armenian massacres. Domestic courts-martial set up in November 1918 established the **command responsibility** and culpability of several government ministers in the slaughter and sentenced them to death in absentia as they had escaped abroad.

National and international efforts to hold Turkish authorities accountable foundered as a result of dissentions among the Allies and the rise of Turkish nationalist leader Mustapha Kemal. Having consolidated his power over **Turkey**, Kemal swiftly denounced the Sevres Treaty and secured the release of suspected Ottoman war criminals held in custody by the British as part of a prisoner of war exchange. The 1923 Treaty of Lausanne, which superseded the Sevres Treaty, made no mention of the criminal treatment of the Armenians. To this day, while acknowledging that large-scale killings did occur as a result of inter-ethnic strife, disease and famine during the upheaval of World War I, Turkey rejects labeling them as "**genocide**" or part of a systematic and organized state-sponsored plan to exterminate the Armenian minority. Under the Turkish penal code, recognition of the Armenian genocide is a criminal offense and may lead to "prosecution for anti-national plots." *See also* PASHA, TALAT; UNITED NATIONS CONVENTION ON THE PUNISHMENT AND PREVENTION OF THE CRIME OF GENOCIDE.

ARTICLE 19, THE INTERNATIONAL CENTRE AGAINST CENSORSHIP. Human rights **non-governmental organization** concerned with the defense and promotion of **freedom of expression** and freedom of information worldwide. Article 19 monitors threats to freedom of expression in different regions of the world, runs **advocacy** campaigns and **lobbies** governments for legal and judicial change and produces legal analyses and critiques of national laws for the development of appropriate national standards of protection. The group also undertakes **litigation** in international and domestic courts on behalf of individuals or groups whose rights have been violated and provides legal and professional training. Its research work has produced useful insights into the connections between freedom of expression and development, censorship with **environmental rights**, access to information for the exercise of **reproductive rights** and analyses of the role of broadcast media in the **Rwandan genocide** and of the media in the former Yugoslavia conflict. *See also* MONITORING OF HUMAN RIGHTS; REPORTERS WITHOUT BORDERS.

ARTICLES ON THE RESPONSIBILITY OF STATES FOR INTERNATIONALLY WRONGFUL ACTS. *See* STATE RESPONSIBILITY.

ASIA. *See* ASIAN CENTER FOR HUMAN RIGHTS; ASIAN HUMAN RIGHTS COMMISSION; ASIAN VALUES; BANGLADESH LIBERATION WAR; BANGKOK DECLARATION; BANGKOK PRINCIPLES ON STATUS AND TREATMENT OF REFUGEES; BOAT PEOPLES; SOCIAL MOVEMENTS.

ASIAN CENTER FOR HUMAN RIGHTS. **Non-governmental organization** headquartered in New Delhi. The Center seeks to promote and protect human rights in the Asian region, notably in India, Sri Lanka, Bangladesh, Nepal and the **Philippines** by providing information and complaints to national human rights institutions and **United Nations** bodies, conducting **investigations** and **research**, **campaigns** and **lobbying** on country situations or individual cases and increasing the capacity of **human rights defenders** and **civil society** groups through training in the use of national and international human rights procedures. **Gender-based violence** is an important component of the Center's activities.

ASIAN HUMAN RIGHTS COMMISSION. Independent **non-governmental organization** established in 1986 by a prominent group of jurists and human rights activists in 1986 to promote greater awareness and realization of human rights in the Asian region, mobilize Asian and international public opinion to obtain relief and redress for the victims of human rights violations. The Commission monitors the human rights situation in the 15 countries of the South Asia, South East Asia, and East Asia region and carries out **investigations** of allegations of **violations of human rights**. It also produces analytical work on selected human rights issues and maintains several websites to enhance its information and education aims. *See also* INTERNET.

ASIAN VALUES. Political viewpoint articulated in the 1990s by a number of Asian governments, notably China, Indonesia, Malaysia and Singapore, which highlights the uniqueness of the region's historical experience, culture and institutions. Such values allegedly shared by the region's countries include a preference for social harmony and consensus, a deference to strong leadership and state institutions and priority given to the socioeconomic welfare of the community over individual rights. Critics have drawn attention to the religious and cultural diversity of the region, counter-arguing that the advocacy of "Asian values" is a scarcely veiled attempt to justify authoritarian rule, delegitimize the defense of civil liberties and negate the universality of human rights. *See also* BANGKOK DECLARATION; BANGKOK PRINCIPLES ON STATUS AND TREATMENT OF REFUGEES; CULTURAL RELATIVISM; INDIVISIBILITY; SHARIA LAW; UNIVERSALITY OF RIGHTS.

ASSOCIATION. *See* FREEDOM OF ASSOCIATION.

ASSOCIATION FOR THE PREVENTION OF TORTURE (APT). Swiss-based independent **non-governmental organization** (NGO) founded in 1977 whose activities are designed to prevent **torture** and other forms of ill-treatment. To achieve this objective and in cooperation with governments, **United Nations** bodies, regional bodies, national human rights institutions, prison authorities, and police services concerned about torture prevention, the APT supports national implementation of international standards, develops training programs for professionals dealing with detainees (e.g., police, NGOs, national institutions, judges and prosecutors) and provides practical guides and relevant legal advice. A key focus of its work is the promotion of preventive control mechanisms such as visits to places of detention. The APT played an important role in the adoption of the Optional Protocol to the **United Nations Convention against Torture and Other Cruel, Inhuman or Degrading Treatment and Punishment**. *See also* CAPACITY BUILDING; PREVENTION; RIGHTS INTERNATIONAL.

ASSOCIATION FOR WOMEN'S RIGHTS IN DEVELOPMENT (AWID). This **non-governmental organization** is a membership entity bringing together over 5,000 researchers, academics, students, educators, activists, business people, policymakers and development practitioners. Set up in the early 1980s, AWID initially focused its work on sustainable development and gender equality and the role of women as agents and beneficiaries of the development process. It has since considerably broadened the scope of its activities and now aims at strengthening the voice, impact and influence of women's rights advocates, organizations and movements internationally to effectively advance the rights of women.

ASSOCIATION OF AFRICAN WOMEN FOR RESEARCH AND DEVELOPMENT (AAWORD). Pan-African **non-governmental organization** based in Dakar, Senegal, which carries out and supports multidisciplinary **research, capacity building** and **advocacy** projects designed to promote the economic, political and social rights of African women. Created in 1977, the AAWORD has steadily grown and evolved into a network of national chapters located primarily in Africa. AAWORD's priority concerns focus on gender equality and the transformation of economic and social policies in Africa; women's entry into sexual life; governance, democratization and women's political empowerment; **gender-based violence**, notably the traditional practices associated with widowhood, postconflict peacebuilding and youth leadership.

ASYLUM, RIGHT OF. This is an ancient practice whereby a person persecuted for political opinions or religious belief in his own country may be protected by another state which has now been codified in Article 14 of the **Universal Declaration of Human Rights** asserting that "everyone has the right to seek and to enjoy in other countries asylum from persecution." The 1951 **United Nations Convention Relating to the Status of Refugees** and its 1967 protocol are supposed to guide national legislation concerning political asylum. The exercise of the right of asylum is a discretionary act of sovereignty. As such, it is a source of recurring political frictions between states, even in situations regulated by bilateral extradition treaties to the extent that it may lead to decisions that could be perceived as unfriendly or inimical to one of the states involved. For instance, governments may grant asylum to individuals who are considered by other states criminals or terrorists.

See also ALIENS, TREATMENT OF; ASYLUM SEEKERS; BANGKOK PRINCIPLES ON STATUS AND TREATMENT OF REFUGEES; CENTER FOR EUROPEAN POLICY STUDIES; CENTER FOR GENDER AND REFUGEE STUDIES; DECLARATION ON TERRITORIAL ASYLUM;. EUROPEAN CHARTER OF FUNDAMENTAL RIGHTS OF THE EUROPEAN UNION; GENDER-SPECIFIC CLAIM; NON-*REFOULEMENT*; PERSECUTION; REFUGEES; RIGHTS INTERNATIONAL.

ASYLUM SEEKERS. Individuals whose claim for **refugee** status has not yet been finally decided by the host country. According to data issued by the United Nations Office of the High Commissioner for Refugees (UNHCR), more than 839,000 people submitted an individual application for **asylum** or refugee status in 2008. The practical determination of whether a person is or is not a refugee ultimately remains the prerogative of the receiving country and the UNHCR has issued non-binding guidelines on "Applicable Criteria and Standards Relating to the Detention of Asylum-Seekers." In addition, Article 31 of the 1951 Refugee Convention states that refugees should not be penalized for having entered a country illegally if they came directly from a place where they were in danger and have made themselves known to the authorities. In practice, many countries detain asylum seekers upon arrival, during the asylum process or while waiting for deportation. Human rights **non-governmental organizations** have documented a growing number of cases of asylum seekers being detained, maltreated and forcibly returned to their home countries after long periods of detention in confined camps. Also, host countries may not recognize the refugee status of asylum seekers and may refuse to treat them as legitimate **migrants**, thus turning them into de facto illegal aliens. *See also* DEPORTATION; DUBLIN CONVENTION; ENVIRONMENTALLY INDUCED MIGRANTS; INTERNALLY DISPLACED PERSONS; RIGHTS INTERNATIONAL; WOMEN'S REFUGEE COMMISSION; WORLD CONFERENCE AGAINST RACISM.

AUNG SAN SUU KYI (1945–). In 1947, following the assassination of her father—a popular hero who helped establish national independence—Suu Kyi left Burma (now known as **Myanmar**) and lived and studied in India and Great Britain. She returned to Burma in 1988 and gained prominence as the leader of democratic opposition to the ruling military regime. Placed under house arrest in 1989, she nevertheless won popular elections held in 1990. The ruling junta did not recognize the outcome of the elections and kept her under house arrest until 1995. Guided by the non-violent practices of Gandhi and **Martin Luther King, Jr.**, she has since become an iconic symbol of pro-democracy activism and a prisoner of conscience. She won the **Nobel Peace Prize** in 1991, was imprisoned again from 2000 to 2002 and, until 2010, was placed under house arrest. The **United Nations Working Group on Arbitrary Detention**, one of the "**Special Procedures**" of the organization, has issued several opinions (in 1992, 2002 and 2004) determining that her deprivation of liberty was arbitrary and in contravention of Article 9 of the **Universal Declaration of Human Rights**. Suu Kyi was freed as part of broader **amnesty** initiated by the government and has since been elected to parliament. *See also* ARBITRARY DETENTION; FREEDOM NOW.

AUSSARESSES, PAUL (1918–). Retired French general who served in the army's intelligence services, notably in Indochina from 1946 to 1948, and in the **Algerian war of independence**. He was one of the main architects and executioner of the repressive measures used by the French army during the

Battle of Algiers and, in memoirs published in 2001, he gave a graphic account of his actions, defending and justifying unapologetically the systematic use of **torture** and summary executions. It was the first time that a senior military commander publicly asserted that torture and killings were tacitly condoned if not ordered by civilian authorities at the highest governmental levels. If General Aussaresses' allegations were correct, French government officials could then conceivably be criminally prosecuted for **crimes against humanity** under the provisions of Common Article 3 of the **Geneva Conventions** which France ratified in 1951. Earlier **amnesty** laws, however, barred French courts from dealing with charges arising from the conduct of the Algerian war. General Aussaresses was thus not tried for crimes against humanity but for "complicity in apologetics for war crimes." Found guilty (together with his publisher), he was fined and suspended from the Legion d'Honneur and expelled from the army. To this day, no independent inquiry or official reexamination of the allegations of General Aussaresses and, more generally, of the war has been initiated. The French military archives on the Algerian war remain closed. At the same time, in an interesting twist of events, some have argued that Aussaresses' conviction stands as a troubling encroachment on free speech principles. *See also* IMPUNITY.

AZERBAIJAN. Former Soviet Republic of approximately 8 million—in their majority Muslim—which declared its independence from the collapsing Soviet Union in 1991. Since its independence, the country has undergone rapid privatization and has been the recipient of a large infusion of Western investments in its oil resources. Nominally a representative democracy and since 2001 a member of the Council of Europe, Azerbaijan has been criticized by independent bodies such as **Human Rights Watch** and **Reporters Without Borders** for its poor human rights record. Elections have repeatedly been contested as fraudulent and "seriously flawed." The government has placed restrictions on media freedom, freedom of assembly, and political participation. Allegations of **torture** and ill-treatment by law enforcement officials and cases of arbitrary arrest and detention, particularly of individuals considered by the government to be political opponents, and lengthy pretrial detention continue to surface. As a result of the **Nagorno-Karabakh** war, Azerbaijan has had to support a half million **internally displaced persons.** *See also* CHEMICAL WEAPONS.

B

BAHA'IS. Religious faith founded in 19th-century Persia with around 6 million followers worldwide. Regarded as infidels and apostates by Muslims, Baha'is have met considerable hostility from Islamic governments, especially in **Iran** where some 300,000 live, constituting the country's largest minority religion. The **United Nations Commission on Human Rights** and its **special rapporteur** on freedom of religion or belief, the **European Union** and **non-governmental organizations** such as **Amnesty International** have issued frequent statements drawing attention to and expressing concern about instances of **arbitrary detention** and arrests, unjustified executions, confiscations of property, destruction of religious sites, denial of employment and other forms of **discrimination**. *See also* MINORITIES.

THE BALKANS. *See* BLASKIC CASE; BOSNIA-HERZEGOVINA WAR; CELEBICI, FURUDZINA, DEALALIC CASES.

BANGKOK DECLARATION (1993). Policy statement adopted by the ministers and representatives of Asian states in preparation of the 1993 World Conference on Human Rights reiterating their opposition to the universality of human rights on the grounds that they are not consistent with "**Asian values**." In the language of the Declaration, the participants recognized that "while human rights are universal in nature, they must be considered in the context of a dynamic and evolving process of international norm-setting, bearing in mind the significance of national and regional particularities and various historical, cultural and religious backgrounds." *See also* CULTURAL RELATIVISM.

BANGKOK PRINCIPLES ON STATUS AND TREATMENT OF REFUGEES (1966, 1987). The Asian region has for a long time had a high number of "persons of concern." Yet, most Asian states have not acceded to international refugee law instruments, especially the 1950 **United Nations Convention Relating to the Status of Refugees** and its 1967 Protocol. Their argument is that these treaties were crafted at a time when most Asian states had yet to attain independence and that they contain definitions, concepts and mechanisms which are not consistent with **Asian values**. The vast majority of Asian states has thus opted to embrace a set of principles which they formally adopted in 1966 and reaffirmed in 1987. The so-called Bangkok Principles do acknowledge the legal existence of **refugees**, endorse the principle of non-*refoulement* and call upon states parties to provide **asylum** to refugees. But the exercise of these rights is limited to cases which do not threaten the security of states. Furthermore, the Principles do not create multilateral obligations on the treatment of refugees nor do they create any enforcement of monitoring system. In effect, each state remains free to decide whether the Principles should be applied to a particular circumstance. *See also* CULTURAL RELATIVISM.

BANGLADESH LIBERATION WAR (1971). British India was partitioned in 1947, giving birth to secular India and Islamic Pakistan, the latter comprising two geographically separate areas to the east and west of India. Rising political discontent in East Pakistan, fed by cultural nationalism and perceptions of economic exploitation, led to the outbreak of war in March 1971. The war started with a violent crackdown by West Pakistani forces and ended in December when India intervened and decisively beat Pakistani forces. Bangladesh declared its independence shortly thereafter. During the nine months' duration of the war, there were widespread grievous **violations of human rights** perpetrated by West Pakistani forces with the support of local and religious East Pakistani collaborators, especially against Hindus. Students, political and military opposition were eliminated and 1,000 pro-liberation intellectuals were systematically executed. Bangladeshi authorities claim that 3 million people were killed during the conflict. There was widespread violence targeted at women and the Hindu minority; some 200,000 Bengali women and girls are said to have been raped by Pakistani soldiers with an estimated 25,000 allegedly forcefully impregnated and many held captive as sex slaves. Although both Pakistan and the **United States**, its primary ally, publicly denied **genocide** allegations, many atrocities committed during the war have come to be viewed by observers as acts of genocide.

Efforts by the **United Nations Security Council** to deal with the civil war were stymied by Soviet vetoes. Concerned about India's close relations with the Soviet Union and determined to develop better ties with China which supported Pakistan, the Richard Nixon administration ignored or downplayed warnings by U.S. officials in West Pakistan about a possible "selective genocide" or genocide. A war crimes tribunal was set up in Bangladesh in 1973 to try Bangladeshi nationals accused of collaborating with the West Pakistanis (the Bangladeshi government made it clear from the outset that it would not prosecute Pakistanis who fought against East Pakistani separatists). The tribunal however remained inactive and an International Crimes Tribunal was set up in 2008 to investigate and prosecute suspects for the 1971 genocide. The first indictments were issued in 2010 and the tribunal has convicted a number of Islamist party leaders for atrocities committed in the country's war of independence. Rights groups such as Human Rights Watch have criticized the tribunal for failing to adhere to international due process and safeguards standards. *See also* COLD WAR; IMPUNITY; INDIA, PARTITION OF; KISSINGER, HENRY.

BARAYAGWIZA CASE (2003). One of the so-called media cases adjudicated by the **International Criminal Tribunal for Rwanda**. The case concerned Jean Bosco Barayagwiza, who broadcasted messages of ethnic hatred and incitement to violence on national radio between 1990 and 1994. In 2003, he was convicted on the counts of instigating the perpetration of acts of **genocide**, for planning, ordering or instigating the commission of a **crime against humanity** (extermination) and for instigating the perpetration of a crime against humanity (persecution). Barayagwiza died in 2010 while serving his 32-year prison sentence.

BARBIE, KLAUS (1913–1991). Midlevel German intelligence and security service agent during World War II. He first served in the Netherlands and then in France. As head of the Gestapo in Lyon, he personally tortured prisoners and is blamed for the death of 4,000 people. In April 1944, he ordered the **deportation** to Auschwitz of a group of 44 Jewish children. After the war, Barbie took part in intelligence activities working for British and the American agencies. He went into hiding in Bolivia in 1955. Extradited to France in 1983, he was tried in a 1987 trial for crimes committed while he was in charge of the Gestapo in Lyon between 1942 and 1944, found guilty of **crimes against humanity** and sentenced to life imprisonment. He died in prison four years later. His lead defense attorney claimed that because Barbie's actions were no worse than the ordinary actions of French colonialists, his trial was an instance of selective prosecution and French courts were in no position to try him. Legislation adopted to protect people accused of crimes under the Vichy regime and in the course of **Algeria's war of independence** led to the dismissal of many of the charges against Barbie. *See also* HOLOCAUST; INTERNATIONAL LEAGUE AGAINST RACISM AND ANTISEMITISM; TOUVIER, PAUL.

BASEL CONVENTION ON THE CONTROL OF TRANSBOUNDARY MOVEMENTS OF HAZARDOUS WASTES AND THEIR DISPOSAL. International treaty aimed at reducing to a minimum the movement of hazardous waste between nations and, in particular, from developed to developing nations. It obligates parties to ensure that such wastes are managed and disposed of in an environmentally sound manner, as close as possible to their source of generation; and to reduce to a minimum the generation of hazardous wastes at the source. *See also* ENVIRONMENT, RIGHT TO A HEALTHY.

BASIC PRINCIPLES AND GUIDELINES ON THE RIGHT TO A REMEDY AND REPARATION FOR VICTIMS OF GROSS VIOLATIONS OF INTERNATIONAL HUMAN RIGHTS LAW AND SERIOUS VIOLATIONS OF INTERNATIONAL HUMANITARIAN LAW (2005). Procedural and substantive non-binding rules adopted after 15 years of negotiations by the **United Nations Commission on Human Rights** recognizing that all victims of gross **violations of human rights** and fundamental freedoms should be entitled to **restitution**, fair and just compensation and the means for as full a rehabilitation as possible for any damage suffered. The obligations of states in cases of gross violations of **international human rights law** entail the duties to investigate and submit to prosecution the person allegedly responsible for the violations; in cases where there is sufficient evidence, to punish the person, and if found guilty, to cooperate with one another in the investigation and prosecution of such violations and to make adequate, effective and prompt **reparation** available to the victims. The Principles are not binding and do not create any new international law but they attempt to structure the multiplicity of standards, principles and interpretations regarding the right to a **remedy** and reparation. They were nevertheless adopted by a recorded vote by the **United Nations General Assembly** acting on a recommendation of the **United Nations Human Rights Council.** The **United States** opposed the Principles because they included the right to victim compensation for violations of international humanitarian law and human rights law. Other governments objected on the grounds that they provided a right to collective action or class action civil suits, a procedure unknown in their legal systems. *See also* SOFT LAW; VAN BOVEN, THEO.

BASSIOUNI, CHERIF. Distinguished **international criminal law** scholar who served **United Nations** human rights bodies in various capacities. He played a major role in the establishment of the **International Criminal Tribunal for the Former Yugoslavia** and the **International Criminal Court.**

BATTLE OF ALGIERS **(1966).** Film commissioned by the Algerian government which narrates the urban guerrilla warfare waged by insurgent Algerian nationalists in Algiers in the 1950s and the French army's efforts to hunt them down and wipe them out through intimidation, arrests, **torture** and summary executions. The terrorist tactics of the insurgents and the French **counterterrorism** response are both portrayed in realistic newsreel and documentary style with a closing suggesting that the French army may have gained a tactical victory but lost the war as Algeria won its independence in 1962. Released in the midst of the process of decolonization and the rise of left-wing radical movements in the West, the film immediately triggered intense political controversies in France where it was banned for several years. It has also gained the dual reputation of being a source of inspiration for urban guerrilla groups and a model to emulate for counterterrorism government services. *See also* ALGERIAN WAR OF INDEPENDENCE; AUSSARESSES, PAUL.

BEIJING DECLARATION AND PLATFORM OF ACTION (1995). Nonbinding consensus documents emerging from the 1995 **Fourth World Conference on Women** in Beijing, China. The **United Nations** had held three previous world conferences on women in Mexico City (1975), Copenhagen (1980) and Nairobi (1985). The conference was a major step in consolidating the global norm of equality between men and women and establishing the responsibility of governments to protect and promote the human rights of women, especially their **reproductive rights**. *See also* SOFT LAW; WOMEN BUILDING PEACE.

BELO, BISHOP CARLOS-FELIPE XIMENES (1948–). East-Timorese Roman Catholic bishop who shared the **Nobel Peace Prize** with his compatriot Jose Ramos Horta for their efforts to secure independence of East Timor on the basis of the principle of **self-determination**.

BENCHMARKING. Points of reference or minimum conditions against which the implementation and fulfillment of human rights policies and practices may be measured by means of systematic applied indicators. Benchmarks have a normative content. They relate to outcomes and shed light on such issues as whether women are included in decision-making processes, whether legislative reforms incorporate freedom rights, changes in political behavior, civic engagement and participation, and whether there are measurable decreases or increases of human rights abuses and **violations of human rights**. Indicators simply signal changes in direction or illuminate trends. Structural or quantitative indicators collect and summarize information, for example, about the number of state ratifications of human rights treaties and the incidences of arbitrary imprisonment and involuntary disappearances. Process or qualitative indicators measure levels of acceptance of individual complaint procedures, poverty rates, access to educational institutions, levels of responsiveness of judicial institutions and the like. *See also* EVENTS-BASED DATA; INVESTIGATION; MONITORING OF HUMAN RIGHTS; STANDARD-BASED MEASURES; SURVEY DATA.

BENENSON, PETER (1921–2005). British lawyer who founded **Amnesty International** in 1961. He pioneered a new type of political action which proved highly effective in the long term. Focusing on political prisoners in the Soviet Bloc, Western states and non-aligned countries, the so-called "prisoners of conscience," Benenson initiated letter-writing **campaigns** to secure their release. *See also* NORM ENTREPRENEURS.

BERBERS. Cultural and ethnic groups indigenous to northwest Africa which now form substantial parts of the populations of Libya, **Algeria** and Morocco. There are roughly 12 million speakers of Berber languages, which together form a branch of the Afro-Asiatic linguistic family. Berbers have been Islamized since their conquest by Muslim Arabs in the seventh century. They have, however, retained their culture and traditions, particularly in inaccessible mountain regions. By and large, their history is one of rebellion against Arab rule and current relations between Berbers and Arabs are fraught with tensions, notably in Algeria where they rebelled against Arab rule immediately after independence in 1963–65 and have since repeatedly demonstrated and rioted against Arab **discrimination**. *See also* MINORITIES.

BIAFRA (1967–1970). Short-lived and failed attempt by the largely Christian Igbo populations (then estimated to number 11 million) to secede from the Nigerian Federation and create an independent Republic of Biafra in the southern part of Nigeria. The insurgency was triggered by mass killings of Igbo migrants living in the predominantly Muslim northern Nigeria. After initial successes by the insurgents, federal forces quickly regained the offensive, cut off Biafra from direct access to the sea by the end of 1967 but stalled in the face of stiff resistance in the Igbo heartland. The military stalemate that lasted until Biafran resistance eventually collapsed in the face of overwhelming force created a major humanitarian crisis within the embattled region. Food and medical supplies became scarce in spite of the efforts of international relief organizations and private and religious groups, thus prompting charges of **genocide** by the Nigerian government.

The Biafran independence cause mobilized little international support. Biafra's independence was recognized only by a handful of countries (Israel, Ghana, Gabon, Haiti, **Cote d'Ivoire**, Tanzania and Zambia) and the approval and military assistance of **South Africa**, **Southern Rhodesia** and Portugal further discredited the Biafran cause in the eyes of most other African states, which were more concerned about the sanctity of territorial boundaries inherited from colonial powers than the potentially destabilizing norms of **self-determination** and respect of **minority** rights. The Soviet Union became an important source of military equipment for Nigeria, while the **United States** opted for a policy of neutrality. Appeals for **United Nations** mediation for a ceasefire floundered against the bedrock of sovereignty and **domestic jurisdiction** claimed by the Nigerian government. At the end of the 30-month-long civil war, estimates of casualties resulting from hostilities, disease and starvation ranged from 1 million to 3 million and more than 3 million Igbo **refugees** crowded the Biafran enclave. The government's subsequent "no victor, no vanquished" policy nevertheless helped pave the way toward national reconciliation.

BILL OF RIGHTS, UNITED STATES (1791). The 1787 U.S. Constitution embodied an effort to achieve two objectives simultaneously in the newly independent **United States** of America: one was to centralize and strengthen government and the other was to limit its power sufficiently to guarantee individual liberty. The first 10 Amendments to the Constitution sought to enhance the latter. Drawing on the human rights philosophy of the 1776 **Declaration of Independence**, they guaranteed a number of individual civil liberties: freedom of speech and of the press, **due process** of law and the right to privacy and to bear arms. The determination of the proper balance between government power and government restraint required to protect individual civil liberties has ever since been a constant source of political controversy within the United States.

BINDING. A human rights norm or principle may be said to be binding when it acquires the quality of constituting a duty or obligation which requires adherence. International human rights treaty bases its law like international law as opposed to **soft law** and derives its binding force primarily from the actual or tacit consent of states.

BIOETHICS. Field of study concerning the ethical issues arising from advances in life sciences, biotechnology and medicine as they intersect with politics, law and philosophy. Specific issues that have triggered controversies include inconclusive and ongoing debates about the boundaries of life (e.g., abortion and euthanasia), the allocation of scarce health resources (organ donation, health care rationing) and the impact of biotechnology on social institutions such as the family.

See also CONVENTION FOR THE PROTECTION OF HUMAN RIGHTS AND DIGNITY OF THE HUMAN BEING WITH REGARD TO THE APPLICATION OF BIOLOGY AND MEDICINE; EUROPEAN CONVENTION ON HUMAN RIGHTS AND BIOMEDICINE; UNITED NATIONS DECLARATION ON HUMAN CLONING; UNIVERSAL DECLARATION ON BIOETHICS AND HUMAN RIGHTS; UNIVERSAL DECLARATION ON THE HUMAN GENOME AND HUMAN RIGHTS.

BIOLOGICAL WEAPONS (BW). Type of weapons that can be developed from pathogenic living organisms or toxins obtained from these organisms. BW are particularly lethal: studies have shown that a missile delivering 30 kilograms of anthrax spores could kill 80,000 to 100,000 people within a 10-square-kilometer urban area. The Hague Conventions of 1899 and 1907, the 1925 Geneva Protocol and the **Geneva Conventions** prohibit the use of such weapons. In addition, the 1975 Biological Weapons Convention bans the research, development, production, stockpiling, or acquisition of biological and toxin weapons. Some observers have argued that there is now an absolute ban on biological weapons as a matter of customary law. Others maintain that they have not been widely used because of their unpredictable effects. Recent advances in biotechnology in civil industry, mainly in the pharmaceutical and veterinary medicine sectors have raised concern about their possible used by non-state actors. A number of states are known to be or suspected of running BW programs. See also CHEMICAL WEAPONS; CIVILIANS, PROTECTION OF; WAR CRIMES; WEAPONS OF MASS DESTRUCTION.

BLASKIC CASE (1997–2004). Case involving a former Croatian commander who was charged with **persecutions**, unlawful attacks against the civilian population, willful killing, taking civilian hostages and using them as human shields and crimes committed against Bosnian Muslims in central Bosnia and Herzegovina between 1 May 1992 and 31 January 1994. In 2000, the trial Chamber of the **International Criminal Tribunal for the Former Yugoslavia** convicted Blastic to 45 years of imprisonment after finding him guilty of committing, ordering, planning, or otherwise aiding and abetting various crimes against the Bosnian Muslim population in central Bosnia. In appeals, several findings were reversed and his sentence was reduced to nine years. Blaskic was granted an early release in 2004. See also COMMAND RESPONSIBILITY.

BLASPHEMY. Vague term variously referring to "imperious utterance(s) or action(s) concerning God or sacred things" or "irreverent behavior toward anything held sacred." In some countries with a state religion, blasphemy is a criminal offense and, conversely, such laws are viewed by others as discriminatory. Blasphemy has become a contentious issue at the **United Nations** as the **United Nations General Assembly** and the **United Nations Human Rights Council** have adopted resolutions prohibiting the "defamation of **religion**." *See also* FREEDOM OF EXPRESSION.

BOAT PEOPLES. Originally, the term was coined to refer to Vietnamese **refugees** who fled communist rule after the **Vietnam War** (1975) in small crudely made and overcrowded boats. Later, it was applied to waves of refugees seeking to reach Australia from **Afghanistan** or the **United States** from **Cuba** and Haiti. The expression is now commonly understood as referring to illegal immigrants seeking to escape oppression or poverty. More than 1 million people left Vietnam in the second half of the 1970s, thus creating a major humanitarian crisis which came to an end only in 2005 when the remaining refugees in the Philippines (around 200) were granted **asylum** in Canada, Norway and the United States (most of them were slowly absorbed into Western European and North American countries, Australia and Hong Kong). The United Nations Office of the High Commissioner for Refugees won the 1981 Nobel Peace Prize for its work in support of the refugees and, in particular, for setting up and running camps in Malaysia, Thailand, the Philippines, Hong Kong and Indonesia where they could seek first aid and protection while their cases were processed. The camps closed in the mid-1990s.

BOER WARS (1880–1881 and 1899–1902). Wars fought by the British and the descendants of the Dutch settlers (Boers) in South Africa who feared being outnumbered by the arrival of thousands of English settlers and prospectors triggered by the discovery of gold in Transvaal. After a protracted war, the two independent Boer republics of the Orange Free State and the Transvaal Republic were absorbed into the British Empire. In the last two years of the conflict, unable to match superior British forces, the Boers had recourse to guerrilla warfare. The British reacted by switching from conventional warfare to counterinsurgency techniques (i.e., "scorched earth" policies involving the destruction of Boer farms and homesteads and the forcible removal of civilians, most of them women and children, into **concentration camps**). Overcrowding, unhealthy conditions, meager food rations and inadequate medical facilities led to a large number of deaths. The precise number of deaths is not known, but a postwar report concluded that over 27,000 Boers (25 percent of the Boer inmates and 50 percent of the total Boer child population) and 14,000 black Africans (12 percent of African inmates) perished in the camps. The latter figure is probably vastly underestimated and the actual total killed is believed to possibly be as high as 600,000.

BOKASSA, JEAN-BEDEL (1921–1996). Military ruler of the Central African Republic (1966–1977) and self-styled and self-proclaimed emperor of the "Central African Empire" until his overthrow in 1979. Under his rule, political dissent was ruthlessly suppressed and **torture** was said to be rampant. French political support and his close personal ties with French President Valery Giscard d'Estaing enabled Bokassa to remain in power. But his extravagant and egotistical style (his "coronation" as emperor modeled upon that of Napoleon I was rumored to have cost $200 million) and his participation in the massacre of 100 school children who had protested mandatory school uniforms eroded French support. With French military assistance, his opponents overthrew him and forced him into exile in 1979. Bokassa returned home in 1986 and was tried and found guilty of murder and embezzlement. His death sentence was commuted to life imprisonment. With the country's return to democracy in 1993, he was one of the beneficiaries of a general **amnesty** declared for all prisoners.

BOLIVIA. In spite of vast mineral resources, Bolivia remains one of the poorest countries in Latin America. Over half of its multiethnic population is of Amerindian origin, the remaining 30 percent are mestizo and 15 percent white, thus contributing to the persistence of public unrest and polarized politics overshadowed by unmet **indigenous peoples'** demands, land disputes and occupations by landless groups. Compounding these issues is the fact that Bolivia is also the world's third-largest producer of coca leaf. The crop has many harmless traditional uses. But it is also an ingredient for the manufacture of cocaine, and there are recurrent reports of allegations of human rights abuses by Bolivian security agents in areas targeted for forcible coca eradication. In the 1960s and 1970s the country was ruled by a succession of military regimes which committed widespread **violations of human rights**, the most serious ones taking place in 1980–82. Some progress has been made in prosecuting these abuses. But overall, lack of accountability remains a problem as the fate of many who "disappeared" before the restoration of democracy in 1982 is still unresolved and trials have been impeded by long delays. When Bolivia's human rights record was assessed under the United Nations **Universal Periodic Review**, concerns were raised around the independence of the judiciary, **impunity** and access to justice, the rights of women, and discrimination on grounds of sexual orientation. *See also* TRUTH AND RECONCILIATION COMMISSIONS.

BONDED LABOR. Also known as debt bondage, this practice is now considered a form of **slavery** occurring when a person pledges themselves against a loan, the services required to repay the debt and the duration of those services remaining undefined and possibly passing from one generation to the next. Bonded labor was a widely accepted practice in American colonies as a means to pay one's passage to the New World. It was prohibited by the 1956 Supplementary Convention to the **Convention on the Abolition of Slavery** but still persists, especially in developing countries where credit security mechanisms do not exist and where few people have formal title to land or possessions. Researchers estimate that the number of debt bondage slaves is approximately 18 million in the world and has increased in recent years as a result of the world economic crisis. *See also* PEONAGE SYSTEM.

BORDABERRY, JUAN MARIA (1928–). President of **Uruguay** from 1972 to 1973. He gave a free hand to the military to defeat a leftist urban guerrilla insurgency. In 1973, he dissolved Congress, suspended civil liberties, banned left-wing labor unions and continued to rule as dictator until 1976 when the military removed him from power. Uruguay remained under military rule until 1985 when democratic elections were held, leading to the election of a new president. Numerous human rights violations were observed during the Bordaberry regime and by the military in subsequent years. In November 2006, a judge ordered that Bordaberry and his former foreign minister be placed under arrest for their role in the abduction and assassination of two congressmen, the prosecution arguing that they had been part of **Operation Condor.** On 5 March 2010, Bordaberry was sentenced to 30 years in prison (the maximum allowed under Uruguayan law) for murder, becoming the second former Uruguayan dictator sentenced to a long prison term. *See also* COLD WAR.

BOSNIA-HERZEGOVINA WAR (1992–1995). The territory of today's Bosnia-Herzegovina was part of an independent medieval Bosnian state which emerged at the end of the 12th century until its conquest by the Ottoman Empire in 1463. Ottoman rule lasted until 1878 when the province was attached to and then annexed by the Austro-Hungarian empire. At the end of World War II, Bosnia-Herzegovina was incorporated into the newly created Serbian-dominated Yugoslav kingdom. Assigned to the Axis-supported independent state of Croatia during World War II, Bosnia-Herzegovina returned to Yugoslav sovereignty under Marshall Tito's postwar regime as a republic of the now defunct Federation of Yugoslavia, its Muslim inhabitants enjoying the status of a "nationality" equal to that of the Serbs, Croats and Slovenes.

War with Serbia and Croatia broke out as soon as Bosnia-Herzegovina, where a Serb minority made up over a third of the population, followed the path taken by Slovenia and Croatia and proclaimed its independence in 1992. Bosnian Muslims were for a long time hopelessly outgunned by local Serbian military forces under the leadership of **Radovan Karadzic** supported by Yugoslav regular army units dispatched by **Slobodan Milosevic**. A massive air bombing campaign launched by the **North Atlantic Treaty Organization** (NATO) redressed the military balance and the war came to an end in November 1995 with the conclusion of the U.S. brokered Dayton Agreements. Under the terms of the peace treaty, Bosnia-Herzegovina was in effect partitioned into two main portions known as the Bosnian Serb Republic and Muslim Croat Federation. The agreement also called for democratic elections, stipulated that war criminals would be handed over to the **International Criminal Tribunal for the Former Yugoslavia** (ICTY) and provided for the deployment of NATO forces to oversee and maintain the ceasefire.

Atrocities were committed by all sides and against all segments of the population as 300,000 people were killed during the war, about 8 percent of the total prewar population in Bosnia. But the Serb strategy of **ethnic cleansing**—actions including the destruction of property, forced resettlement, summary executions and massacres of civilians and rape—targeted at Muslim residents of Bosnia for the purpose of seizing as much territory as possible was the most severe. One of the worst massacres of the war occurred in **Srebrenica** (proclaimed a "safe haven" by the **United Nations Security Council**) where Serbian forces under the command of General **Ratko Mladic** systematically selected and then killed nearly 8,000 men and boys. In a 2001 ruling, the ICTY found former Bosnian Serb General Major Radislav Krstic guilty of **genocide** in the massacre. Wanted by the ICTY, General Mladic remained at large sheltered by Serb security forces for nearly 16 years until his arrest in 2011. His capture was one of the preconditions for Serbian membership in the European Union. *See also* DEPORTATION; GENEVA CONVENTIONS; NO-FLY ZONE; SAFE ZONES; TADIC, DUSAN.

BRAZIL. Human rights are legally protected by the federal constitution. According to numerous **non-governmental organizations** and **United Nations special rapporteurs'** practice, however, Brazil, particularly at the state level, shows the persistence of serious problems including abusive and excessive police responses to widespread violent crime, harsh prison conditions, **gender-based violence**, **forced labor** and child labor in the informal sector, and **discrimination** against black and **indigenous peoples**. After a long hiatus, the country is beginning to confront human rights abuses committed by the military regime between 1964 and 1985, which included **extra-judicial executions**, **forced disappearances**, **torture**, **arbitrary detention**, and the curtailment of free expression. The total number of those who perished or disappeared during the military dictatorship is not as high as the thousands who died in **Chile** or **Argentina**. It is believed that at least 475 people were killed or forcibly disappeared during that period, and a 1985 report released by the Sao Paulo Archdiocese that used the archives of Brazil's military justice system described 1,918 accounts of torture from 1964 to 1979. To date, more than 12,000 victims of these abuses have been granted financial compensation by the government, but a 1979 **amnesty** law, until recently, in effect barred criminal prosecutions.

In response to a petition brought by relatives of 70 people who forcibly disappeared, the **Inter-American Commission on Human Rights** determined in 2009 that amnesties and statutes of limitations cannot be applied to crimes against humanity that were committed during Brazil's military dictatorship. A year later, the **Inter-American Court of Human Rights** issued a judgment endorsing the Commission's view. In October 2011, the Brazilian Congress approved a law expanding public access to government information, thus implementing a recommendation accepted by the government Brazil during its **Universal Periodic Review** in the **United Nations Human Rights Council**. Congress also set up a **truth and reconciliation commission** which will examine and clarify human rights abuses committed between 1946 and 1988. Two criminal cases have been filed against military and police officials for human rights crimes committed in the 1970s in Sao Paulo. *See also* SEX TOURISM.

BRETTON WOODS INSTITUTIONS. Term referring to the **International Bank for Reconstruction and Development** and the **International Monetary Fund** which were set up at the 1944 Bretton Woods conference in New Hampshire (United States). Both institutions wield considerable economic and financial power and have been criticized for promoting liberal, market-based policies harmful to human rights and for their lack of accountability and transparency. *See also* GLOBALIZATION; PRIVATIZATION; STRUCTURAL ADJUSTMENT PROGRAMS.

BRITISH INSTITUTE OF HUMAN RIGHTS. British **non-governmental organization** established in 1974 and concerned with human rights protection and the promotion of public awareness about human rights at home and abroad.

The activities of the Institute include community outreach programs designed to help those who are socially and economically isolated to understand more about human rights, the provision of **human rights education** and capacity building and the undertaking of human rights policy-oriented research.

BRODY, REED (1953–). International human rights activist who directed the intervention of **Human Rights Watch** (HRW) in the **Augusto Pinochet** case in the British House of Lords and initiated and coordinated the prosecution of the exiled dictator of Chad, **Hussene Habre**. Before joining HRW, Brody led UN teams investigating massacres in the **Democratic Republic of the Congo** and observing human rights in **El Salvador**. He is the author of three HRW reports on **United States'** mistreatment of prisoners in the "**war on terror**." *See also* INVESTIGATION.

BRUNDTLAND COMMISSION. *See* WORLD COMMISSION ON ENVIRONMENT AND DEVELOPMENT.

BURGER, JAN HERMAN (1926–). Dutch government foreign ministry official who from 1965 to 1972 was closely involved in the non-proliferation treaty negotiations. Thereafter he worked on human rights issues and played an important role in the drafting and adoption of the **United Nations Convention against Torture and Other Cruel, Inhuman or Degrading Treatment and Punishment**. Subsequently a member of **Amnesty International**, he advocated the use of the Convention as a tool for the prosecution of perpetrators of torture. *See also* LITIGATION.

BURMA. *See* MYANMAR.

BURUNDI. Former Belgian colony which became independent in 1962. Eighty percent of the population is of Hutu ethnic stock, but the country is politically dominated by the Tutsi minority. Ethnic conflicts between the two communities have been the reason for the deaths of thousands of people and displaced of a million more. The 1972 mass killing of Hutus by the Tutsi army deserves, in the eyes of many observers, the designation of **genocide**. The 1993 mass killings of Tutsi civilians by Hutu insurgents was more sporadic and unorganized. International efforts to end the conflict in the past decade and a half have focused on measures including the establishment of a mediation process, the threat of the use of force, the deployment of a **United Nations** peacekeeping force and the authorization of economic **sanctions** by the **United Nations Security Council**, the adverse effects of which have been borne out by the poverty-stricken population and alienating large segments

BUSINESS AND HUMAN RIGHTS RESOURCE CENTRE • 139

of them. By and large, these measures have been focused on the creation of conditions for long-term stability (Burundi is one of the few countries that are on the agenda of the **United Nations Peacebuilding Commission**) rather than preventing mass atrocities. The incidences of mass crime and **crimes against humanity** have significantly declined, but the precarious calm which prevails may not last and the threat of another genocide remains a distinct possibility. *See also* UNITED NATIONS OPERATION IN BURUNDI.

BUSH, GEORGE W. (1946–). Forty-third president of the **United States** from 2001 to 2009 whose policies and practices in the "**war against terror**" triggered highly controversial human rights controversies both at home and abroad centered on the government's reliance on electronic surveillance programs of suspected terrorists, the detention of "unlawful enemy combatants" without due process and the use of so-called "enhanced interrogation techniques." *See also* COMMAND RESPONSIBILITY; COUNTERTERRORISM.

BUSINESS AND HUMAN RIGHTS. *See* ALIEN TORT STATUTE; BUSINESS and HUMAN RIGHTS RESOURCE CENTRE; CORPORATE SOCIAL RESPONSIBILITY; ENVIRONMENT, RIGHT TO A HEALTHY; TRANSNATIONAL CORPORATIONS.

BUSINESS AND HUMAN RIGHTS RESOURCE CENTRE. International, independent nonprofit organization registered in Great Britain and the **United States** operating in collaborative partnership with **Amnesty International** and leading academic institutions. Its stated purposes are to encourage companies to respect human rights, to avoid harm to people, to maximize their positive contribution, to provide easy access to information for companies and **non-governmental organizations** (NGOs), and to facilitate constructive, informed decision making and public discussion. The Centre has evolved into a major resource center on the activities of private business companies as they relate to such human rights issues as **discrimination**, **environment**, **poverty** and development, labor, access to medicines, **health** and safety, security and trade. The website covers over 4,000 companies over 180 countries. It is linked to a wide range of materials published by governments, the **United Nations**, the **International Labour Organization**, business organizations, NGOs, journalists, social investment analysts, policy experts and academics and universities. The Resource Centre also hosts a portal for the United Nations Special Representative on Business and Human Rights. *See also* UNITED NATIONS "PROTECT, RESPECT AND REMEDY" FRAMEWORK FOR BUSINESS AND HUMAN RIGHTS.

C

CAIRO CONFERENCE ON POPULATION AND DEVELOPMENT (1994). **United Nations global conference,** attended by some 20,000 delegates from governments, UN agencies, **non-governmental organizations** and the media, which dealt with a variety of population issues from a development perspective including **immigration,** infant mortality, birth control, family planning and the **education** of women. In spite of resistance from the Holy See and several Islamic nations and Latin American countries, the Programme of Action endorsed by the conference was a major step forward in consolidating the norm of a right to access to reproductive and sexual **health** services. It also contains quantitative targets aimed at providing wider access to women for secondary and higher level education, reducing the incidence of infant and child mortality and maternal mortality. *See also* MILLENNIUM DEVELOPMENT GOALS; FEMALE GENITAL MUTILATION; REPRODUCTIVE RIGHTS; SOFT LAW.

CAIRO DECLARATION ON HUMAN RIGHTS IN ISLAM. Broad statement of principles adopted by the **Organization of the Islamic Cooperation** in 1990 to guide its state members in human rights matters. To the extent that it subordinates individual rights to the **Sharia Law,** the Declaration is widely viewed in the West as a challenge to the **Universal Declaration of Human Rights** and the intercultural consensus on which international human rights treaties are based. For example, in respect to **freedom of expression,** the Declaration states that "Everyone shall have the right to express his opinion freely in such manner as would not be contrary to the principles of the Sharia." In the same vein, the Declaration guarantees equal dignity between men and women but not in other civil and political matters. Critics of the Declaration also draw attention to the fact that, in addition to restricting certain fundamental rights and freedoms, it may contribute to discrimination against non-Muslims and be used to legitimize practices such as **corporal punishment** which are inconsistent with the **dignity** of the human being. *See also* CULTURAL RELATIVISM.

CAIRO INSTITUTE FOR HUMAN RIGHTS STUDIES. Regional research-oriented **non-governmental organization** founded in 1995 to promote respect for the principles of **human rights**, enhancing the capacity of Arab societies to achieve democratization, and disseminating human rights norms in the Arab region through **education**. The Institute has consultative status with the **United Nations Economic and Social Council** and observer status with the **African Commission on Human and People's Rights**. It is also a member of the Euro-Mediterranean Human Rights Network and the Human Rights Education Network.

CAMBODIA. *See* DEMOCRATIC KAMPUCHEA.

CAMPAIGNS. Originally a military term now used in the field of human rights to refer to connected operations orchestrated by **civil society** organizations and grassroots groups to create awareness of, mobilize public opinion about and generate support for a particular human rights–related cause.

See also ASIAN CENTER FOR HUMAN RIGHTS; BENENSON, PETER; CCJO RENE CASSIN; COALITION FOR INTERNATIONAL JUSTICE; INTERNATIONAL CAMPAIGN TO BAN LANDMINES; INTER-NATIONAL CAMPAIGN TO END GENOCIDE; INTERNATIONAL CRIMINAL COURT; JUBILEE DEBT COALITION; SURVIVAL INTERNATIONAL; TRANSNATIONAL ADVOCACY NETWORK; WORLD SOCIAL FORUM.

CANADA. *See* ABORIGINAL PEOPLES IN CANADA; APOLOGIES; COUNTERTERRORISM; CULTURAL RIGHTS; DISABLED PEOPLE'S INTERNATIONAL; EQUITAS—INTERNATIONAL CENTER FOR HUMAN RIGHTS EDUCATION; FINTA, IMRE; FRASER INSTITUTE; INTERNATIONAL COMMISSION ON INTERVENTION AND STATE SOVEREIGNTY; *LOVELACE V. CANADA*; ORGANIZATION OF AMERICAN STATES; REPARATIONS; RESTITUTION; RIGHTS AND DEMOCRACY; UNIVERSAL JURISDICTION; WOMEN IN PEACE AND SECURITY.

CAPABILITY APPROACH. Development-economic paradigm developed initially by **Amartya Sen** and then other scholars which focuses on an individual's functional capabilities or "positive freedoms" (i.e., his or her actual ability to do something, rather than his or her "negative freedoms" which protect his or her autonomy from intrusions by the state). From this perspective, **poverty** is no longer understood as income deprivation but as capability deprivation. One such capability, among others, is life (i.e., being able to live a human life of normal length and not dying prematurely); others being bodily **health** (i.e., being able to have good health, including **reproductive** health); to be adequately nourished and to have adequate shelter; and bodily integrity (i.e., being able to move freely in a safe environment, secure against violent assault, including sexual assault and domestic violence). Choice and opportunities are of the essence, and the prime business of government is to remove obstacles that hinder or thwart an individual's capacity for choice. The approach has gained wide currency in the development community and has shaped the contents of such major studies as the **United Nations Development Programme**'s **Human Development Report**. *See also* HUMAN SECURITY.

CAPACITY BUILDING. Conceptual approach to development derived from the notions of institutional building and organizational development which prevailed in the 1950s and 1960s. The concept that was developed and promoted by the **United Nations Development Programme** grew out of changes in development thinking which refocused attention on the obstacles inhibiting individuals, governments, international organizations and **nongovernmental organizations** (NGOs) from realizing their development goals. Capacity building has now been mainstreamed into the activities of most developmental international organizations, and the term is widely understood as referring to activities designed to "strengthening the skills, competencies and abilities of people and communities in developing societies so they can overcome the causes of their exclusion and suffering." The approach now guides international cooperation programs in support of human rights and focuses attention on the development of individual knowledge, skills and values, structures and practices in public and private sector institutions—government ministries, local authorities, NGOs, professionals, community members—conducive to and supportive of more effective protection and promotion of human rights.

See also AFRICA INSTITUTE OF SOUTH AFRICA; ASIAN CENTER FOR HUMAN RIGHTS; ASSOCIATION FOR THE PREVENTION OF TORTURE; ASSOCIATION OF AFRICAN WOMEN FOR RESEARCH AND DEVELOPMENT; BRITISH INSTITUTE OF HUMAN RIGHTS; CENTER FOR GENDER AND REFUGEE STUDIES; CENTER FOR HUMAN RIGHTS AND THE ENVIRONMENT; CENTRE ON HOUSING RIGHTS AND EVICTIONS; EQUITAS—INTERNATIONAL CENTER FOR HUMAN RIGHTS EDUCATION; EURO-MEDITERRANEAN

HUMAN RIGHTS NETWORK; EUROPEAN RESEARCH CENTRE
ON MIGRATION AND ETHNIC RELATIONS; EUROPEAN ROMA
RIGHTS CENTER; GLOBAL POLICY FORUM; GRASSROOTS
INTERNATIONAL; HABITAT INTERNATIONAL COALITION; HU-
MAN RIGHTS INSTITUTE; HUMAN RIGHTS INSTITUTE OF SOUTH
AFRICA; HUNGER PROJECT; INSTITUTE FOR HUMAN RIGHTS AND
BUSINESS; INSTITUTE FOR HUMAN RIGHTS AND DEVELOPMENT
IN AFRICA; INSTITUTE FOR INTERNATIONAL LAW AND HUMAN
RIGHTS; INSTITUTE FOR WAR AND PEACE REPORTING; INTER-
AMERICAN INDIAN INSTITUTE; INTERNAL DISPLACEMENT
MONITORING CENTRE; INTERNATIONAL CENTRE FOR HUMAN
RIGHTS AND DEMOCRATIC DEVELOPMENT; INTERNATIONAL
CENTRE FOR CRIMINAL LAW REFORM AND CRIMINAL JUSTICE
POLICY; INTERNATIONAL CENTRE FOR THE LEGAL PROTECTION
OF HUMAN RIGHTS; INTERNATIONAL CIVIL SOCIETY ACTION
NETWORK; INTERNATIONAL FEDERATION FOR HUMAN
RIGHTS; INTERNATIONAL FOUNDATION FOR ELECTORAL
SYSTEMS; INTERNATIONAL ASSOCIATION OF REFUGEE LAW
JUDGES; INTERNATIONAL HUMANITARIAN LAW INITIATIVE
RESEARCH; INTERNATIONAL HUMAN RIGHTS LAW INSTITUTE;
INTERNATIONAL LAW INSTITUTE; INTERNATIONAL LABOUR
ORGANIZATION; INTERNATIONAL PROGRAMME ON THE
ELIMINATION OF CHILD LABOUR; INTERNATIONAL SERVICE
FOR HUMAN RIGHTS; INTERNATIONAL TRAINING CENTRE
ON HUMAN RIGHTS AND PEACE TEACHING; INTERNATIONAL
WOMEN'S RIGHTS PROJECT; INTERNATIONAL WORK GROUP
FOR INDIGENOUS AFFAIRS; KURDISH HUMAN RIGHTS PROJECT;
PEACE OPERATIONS; PROJECT ON INTERNATIONAL COURTS
AND TRIBUNALS; RAOUL WALLENBERG INSTITUTE; UNITED
NATIONS HUMAN SETTLEMENTS PROGRAMME; UNITED NATIONS
OFFICE OF THE HIGH COMMISSIONER FOR HUMAN RIGHTS;
UNREPRESENTED NATIONS AND PEOPLES ORGANIZATION;
WORLD BLIND UNION.

CAPITAL PUNISHMENT. Long-accepted sanctioned right by state
authorities to take life as the ultimate punishment for the severest crimes. That
right, however, has come under increasing challenge with the development
of international human rights law. Article 6 of the **International Covenant
on Civil and Political Rights** calls upon governments which have not
abolished the death penalty to exercise caution in carrying it out. A Second
Optional Protocol to the Covenant adopted in 1990 and now in force requires

states to cease executions and take all necessary measures to abolish capital punishment. States parties to the Protocol may not enter **reservations to treaties**, although states may reserve the right to use the death penalty in time of war "pursuant to conviction for a most serious crime of a military nature committed during wartime." Provisions found in the **European Convention for the Protection of Human Rights and Fundamental Freedoms**, the **American Convention on Human Rights**, the **Arab Charter on Human Rights** and the Convention of the **Commonwealth of Independent States** confirm the evolving trend toward the abolition. There are few retentionist states today and the death penalty for juvenile offenders has become increasingly rare. A number of international organizations, notably the **Council of Europe** and the **European Union**, have made the abolition of the death penalty a requirement of membership.

See also EUROPEAN CHARTER OF FUNDAMENTAL RIGHTS OF THE EUROPEAN UNION; EUROPEAN PARLIAMENT; EXTRADITION; INTERNATIONAL SOCIETY FOR HUMAN RIGHTS; LIFE, RIGHT TO; RIGHTS INTERNATIONAL.

CARE INTERNATIONAL. Founded in 1945 to provide relief to survivors of World War II, this confederation of agencies (formally known as the Cooperative for Assistance and Relief Everywhere) has evolved into one of the world's largest private international humanitarian organizations that delivers relief assistance and emergency aid in some 60 countries to survivors of war and natural disasters. The longer-term developmental work of CARE places special emphasis on women and children in community-based efforts to improve basic **education**, prevent the spread of **HIV/AIDS**, increase access to clean **water** and sanitation, expand economic opportunity and protect natural resources.

CARITAS INTERNATIONALIS. Confederation of 164 Roman **Catholic Church** relief and social service organizations dedicated to human advancement and development. From its modest beginnings in 1897, the organization has expanded its operations to over 200 countries. The current focus of its work is on peace and reconciliation, emergencies, economic justice, **climate change**, **HIV/AIDS** and women and migration.

CARNEGIE COUNCIL. Independent New York–based foreign policy **think tank** founded in 1914 by steel magnate Andrew Carnegie to promote moral leadership and find alternatives to armed conflict through greater international understanding and justice. Its current primary concerns focus on four themes: ethics, war and peace, global social justice, and religion in politics. The Council's activities include agenda-setting forums, bringing together professional, educators, students and journalists and the publication of a quarterly scholarly journal, *Ethics and International Affairs*. *See also* CARNEGIE COUNCIL ON ETHICS AND INTERNATIONAL AFFAIRS.

CARNEGIE COUNCIL ON ETHICS AND INTERNATIONAL AFFAIRS. New York–based **think tank** aimed to be the foremost voice of ethics in international affairs through agenda-setting forums and the provision of educational opportunities and information resources for teachers and students, journalists, international affairs professionals, and concerned citizens. The Council's flagship publication is a quarterly scholarly journal, *Ethics and International Affairs*, which was launched in 1987. *See also* CARNEGIE COUNCIL.

CARNEGIE ENDOWMENT FOR INTERNATIONAL PEACE. Foreign-policy multinational, global **think tank** created in 1910 by Andrew Carnegie. Based in Washington, D.C., this organization is dedicated to the advancement of international cooperation and the promotion of the active international engagement by the **United States**. In 1914, the Endowment published an influential "Report of the International Commission to Inquire into the Causes and Conduct of the Balkan Wars" and assisted in the creation of The Hague Academy of International Law. Socioeconomic issues of concern to the organization include development, global trade, **globalization**, global financial questions and migration.

CARPET BOMBING. Air attacks to treat a large area as a single military objective without regard to the civilian population residing in it. The first instances of carpet bombing occurred during the Spanish Civil War. It was subsequently used extensively against German and Japanese civilian population centers for a variety of purposes, including the destruction of the enemy's industries, weakening the morale of the population and retaliating for similar previous attacks during World War II. The bombings of London, Rotterdam, Dresden, Hamburg, Tokyo, Hiroshima and Nagasaki are prominent instances. The subject matter was by and large sidestepped at the Nuremberg and Tokyo tribunals. The 1977 Additional Protocol I to the Geneva Convention prohibits the bombardment of areas with a large concentration of civilians. *See also* VIETNAM WAR.

CARTAGENA DECLARATION ON REFUGEES (1984). Standards' setting document adopted by a group of governmental experts and eminent jurists from the region dealing with the legal and humanitarian problems affecting Central American **refugees**. The declaration significantly broadened the definition of a refugee set out in the 1951 **United Nations Convention Relating to the Status of Refugees** to include individuals who fled their countries when their lives were threatened by endemic violence, foreign aggression, internal conflicts, massive **violation of human rights** or other circumstances which have seriously disturbed public order. *See also* 1969 ORGANIZATION OF AFRICAN UNITY CONVENTION GOVERNING THE SPECIFIC ASPECTS OF REFUGEE PROBLEMS IN AFRICA; SOFT LAW.

CARTER CENTER. Founded in 1982 by former **United States** President **Jimmy Carter** and former First Lady Rosalynn Carter, this non-profit organization carries out a wide range of research, mediation and development assistance activities designed to advance human rights, alleviate human suffering and promote **democracy** worldwide. Supported by individual, **foundation**, corporate and governmental donations, the Center is active in some 70 countries and has a current annual operating budget of $36 million.

CARTER, JIMMY (1924–). The 39th president of the United States (1977–81) and recipient of the 2002 **Nobel Peace Prize**. During his tenure as president, he sought to put a stronger emphasis on human rights in U.S. foreign policy. Upon leaving office, he has remained active in international human rights efforts, acting as a mediator notably in North Korea, Haiti and Bosnia and as an impartial observer of national elections. In 1982, he founded the **Carter Center**, a **non-governmental organization** that works to advance human rights.

CASSIN, RENE (1887–1976). Distinguished French jurist who received the **Nobel Peace Prize** in 1968 for the key role he played in the drafting of the **Universal Declaration of Human Rights** as he served on the **United Nations Commission of Human Rights**. A member of the **European Court of Human Rights** from 1959 to 1965, he became its president from 1965 to 1968. *See also* CCJO RENE CASSIN.

CASTE. System of social stratification primarily found in India rooted in Hindu life and religion but also observable in other parts of the world whereby members of society are grouped into different hereditary categories enjoying differential responsibilities and privileges. In India, individuals may belong to the priests, warriors, traders or laborers castes. Some, known as Dalits, may be excluded altogether from the caste system. In spite of considerable improvements in their socioeconomic conditions brought about by national affirmative legislation and social initiatives, the Dalits still represent approximately 15 percent of the Indian total population. *See also* DISCRIMINATION.

CATHOLIC CHURCH. The world's largest Christian church led by the pope and defining its mission as spreading the gospel of Jesus Christ. Church membership exceeds a billion people and according to Vatican figures there are over 400,000 priests in the world. The Church conception of the common good leads to both an embrace of human rights and **democracy** and a rejection of certain aspects of their secular versions. Catholic social teaching is grounded in the ideas of human **dignity** and **solidarity** which were articulated in an 1891 encyclical but can be traced back to the writings of Catholic thinkers and concepts found in the Bible. Human beings, having been created in the image of God, have a fundamental right to life and its necessities. This entails individual rights to **health, education** and **employment**, including a right to productive work, to decent and fair wages, to safe working conditions and to form trade unions. Drawing from the principle of solidarity, the Church has advocated for greater attention to the concerns and developmental needs of the Global South. Considering that life begins at conception, the Church has rejected contraception and abortion and lobbied in international gathering against recognition of **reproductive rights**. In the past two decades, information has surfaced documenting patterns of sexual abuse of minors by members of the clergy. The issue has generated intense media coverage and triggered legal actions and public debates in a number of countries including the **United States**, Ireland, Germany and Australia. In the fall of 2011, a **non-governmental organization** seized the **International Criminal Court** alleging that the pope and a number of senior Vatican officials had committed a **crime against humanity** by failing to prevent or punish perpetrators of sexual violence. *See also* CARITAS INTERNATIONALIS; JOHN-PAUL II.

CAUCUS. Term derived from practices prevailing in **United States** politics, notably in regard to the functioning of Congress and political parties, referring to meetings that bring together individuals with shared affinities or ethnicity for the purpose of defining a group position on matters of public policy. In regard to international human rights, the term refers primarily to meetings of **civil society** organizations intended to formulate common strategies in the international arena or international organizations.

CCJO RENE CASSIN. Jewish **non-governmental organization** founded in 1946 and named after **Rene Cassin**, one of the authors of the **Universal**

Declaration of Human Rights. CCJO Rene Cassin has undertaken extensive **campaigns** on **refugee** rights, the prevention of **genocide**, religious freedom and racial equality and carries out **human rights education** programs. It has consultative status with the **United Nations Economic and Social Council**.

CELEBICI, FURUDZINA, DEALALIC CASES (1998). Watershed judgments of the **International Criminal Tribunal for the Former Yugoslavia** which, based on the **Akayesu case**'s definition of rape, recognized rape as a violation of the Laws and Customs of War and as a basis of **torture** under the **Geneva Conventions**. *See also* GENDER-BASED VIOLENCE.

CENTER FOR CONSTITUTIONAL RIGHTS (CCR). United States **non-governmental organization** dedicated to the advancement and protection of the **civil and political rights** guaranteed by the U.S. Constitution and the **Universal Declaration of Human Rights**. The Center was founded in 1966 by lawyers representing civil rights activists in the South. At home, CCR has used **litigation** in **racial discrimination**, gender and economic justice cases. CCR pioneered the use of the **Alien Tort Statute** to prosecute in U.S. courts human rights abuses committed abroad and has created a body of law that helps to hold foreign officials and corporations accountable to the public. In addition, it has brought cases against U.S. officials in foreign courts under the principle of **universal jurisdiction**. Drawing on the assumption that the United States must recognize and incorporate the norms of international law into its domestic justice system, the CCR has fought against what it views as the illegal expansion of executive power in the "**war on terror**" filing cases on behalf of individuals detained without **due process** and challenged immigration sweeps, ghost detentions, **extraordinary rendition** and the practice of **torture**.

CENTER FOR ECONOMIC AND SOCIAL RIGHTS. Non-**governmental organization** primarily concerned with promoting through **advocacy** and **research** a human rights culture that integrates the rights to health, **housing**, education, **food**, a healthy **environment** and **work** and more generally economic security, social equality and political freedom in human rights practice in a way consistent with the integrated vision of the 1948 **Universal Declaration of Human Rights**. An important contribution of the Center is its work on the development of new methodologies for measuring and **monitoring** economic and social rights compliance. *See also* NIGER DELTA CONFLICT.

CENTER FOR EUROPEAN POLICY STUDIES. One of the most experienced and authoritative **think tanks** operating in the **European Union**. Based in Brussels, the Center serves as a forum for debate on EU affairs and carries out reputable in-house research in consultation with an extensive network of partner institutes throughout the world. In the context of its work on justice and home affairs, the center deals with **asylum** and **migrant workers** questions.

CENTER FOR GENDER AND REFUGEE STUDIES. California-based **non-governmental organization** (NGO) providing free technical assistance, training and resources to the attorneys and NGOs who represent women **asylum** seekers fleeing gender-related harm. The organization has been involved in groundbreaking **litigation** cases. It tracks and monitors asylum decision cases and uses this information to inform its legal and **advocacy** work and influence the development of national policy. The Center's website contains useful information about gender asylum cases, decisions by immigration judges, the Board of Immigration Appeals, and U.S. Federal Court of Appeals and international gender asylum case law. *See also* CAPACITY BUILDING; DOMESTIC VIOLENCE; FEMALE GENITAL MUTILATION.

CENTER FOR HUMAN RIGHTS AND GLOBAL JUSTICE. Research center attached to the Law School of New York University established to conduct policy-oriented research feeding into ongoing policy debates relating to human rights. Some of the major project areas which the Center has focused on include detainees and the "**war on terror**," **discrimination** and national security, **economic, social and cultural rights**, **extra-judicial executions**, and **transitional justice**. Its reports on **extraordinary rendition**, **forced disappearances**, and detainee abuse have been cited in the **Council of Europe**'s major report on secret flights and prisons in Europe. Likewise, a report that focused on human rights abuses against the Dalits (so-called untouchables) in Nepal has been used by the head of the **United Nations** human rights monitoring mission in Nepal. The Center has also given testimony before the **Inter-American Commission on Human Rights** and the **United Nations Commission on Human Rights** on the rights of migrant **domestic workers** in the United States and on the role of the UN peacekeeping force in Haiti. A joint project with **Human Rights Watch** and **Human Rights First** provides a comprehensive accounting of credible allegations of **torture** and abuse of persons in U.S. custody in Iraq, **Afghanistan** and the **Guantanamo Bay Detention Camp**. Its preliminary findings have been brought to the attention of the **United Nations Committee against Torture**.

CENTER FOR HUMAN RIGHTS AND THE ENVIRONMENT.
Argentine organization set up to promote greater access to justice and guarantee human rights for victims of environmental degradation or due to non-sustainable management of natural resources. The Center seeks to achieve these objectives through litigation and legal advisory assistance, **advocacy, capacity building**, the empowerment of victims and research and publications. It is especially active in the areas of **water, corporate social responsibility** and the linkages between **poverty**, the **environment** and human rights.

CENTER FOR INTERNATIONAL DEVELOPMENT AND CONFLICT MANAGEMENT (CIDCM). Policy-oriented, interdisciplinary research and training center located at the University of Maryland in the United States which focuses its work on conflict **prevention**, the interplay between conflict and development and the creation of conditions that enable societies to create sustainable futures for themselves. Several large data collection projects reside at CIDCM including the International Crisis Behavior project, which gathers data on all international crises since the end of World War I, the **Minorities at Risk Project** which monitors the status of politically active communal groups around the world and the Polity Project which tracks regime characteristics for independent states from 1800 to the present.

CENTER FOR JUSTICE AND ACCOUNTABILITY (CJA). Non-**governmental organization** created in 1998 with initial funding from **Amnesty International** and the United Nations Voluntary Fund for Victims of **Torture** to represent torture survivors in their legal efforts to seek truth, justice and redress. Invoking the **Alien Tort Statute** and the principle of **universal jurisdiction**, CJA has brought cases against individual human rights abusers in the **United States** and Spain and filed cases against human rights violators from Bosnia, **Chile**, China, **El Salvador, Guatemala**, Haiti, **Honduras, Indonesia** and Somalia. CJA has authored or signed onto **amicus curiae** ("friend of the court") briefs in human rights cases filed with appellate courts and the U.S. Supreme Court, including those that deal with the treatment of prisoners at the **Guantanamo Bay Detention Camp** and **Abu Ghraib**. The group complements its legal work with the provision of psychosocial services to torture survivors and their communities. *See also* LITIGATION.

CENTER FOR JUSTICE AND INTERNATIONAL LAW (CEJIL).
Non-governmental organization with consultative status before the **Organization of American States**, the **United Nations** and observer status

before the **African Commission on Human and People's Rights**. Founded in 1991 by a group of **human rights defenders**, the thrust of the activities of CEJIL is to provide free legal counseling and act as representatives of the victims seeking **redress** in the **Inter-American Commission on Human Rights** and the **Inter-American Court of Human Rights**.

CENTER FOR MIGRATION STUDIES (CMS). Non-profit and **non-governmental organization** founded in 1964 to support and undertake **research** and to provide a forum for debate on international migration. It organizes conferences and forums on international migration, including the Annual National Legal Conference on Immigration and Refugee Policy. The CMS's specialized library is one of the most comprehensive libraries worldwide on migration, **refugees** and ethnic groups. The CMS also publishes the *International Migration Review*, a leading peer-reviewed scholarly journal specialized in this subject.

CENTER FOR MINORITY RIGHTS DEVELOPMENT (CEMIRIDE). Kenyan-based **advocacy non-governmental organization** concerned with the rights of **minorities** and **indigenous peoples** in Africa. CEMIRIDE receives funding from multilateral organizations such as the **International Labour Organization** and the **United Nations Development Programme** and bilateral donor agencies of the **United States**, the Netherlands and Denmark.

CENTER FOR REPRODUCTIVE RIGHTS. U.S. global legal **advocacy** organization dedicated to **reproductive rights**, with expertise in both U.S. constitutional and **international human rights law**. Created in 1992, the Center documents abuses, litigates cases in national courts and participates actively in **United Nations** and regional bodies to expand women's access to reproductive health care, including birth control, safe abortion, prenatal and obstetric care, and unbiased information. The center also encourages legal scholarship and teaching on reproductive health and human rights. *See also* LITIGATION.

CENTER FOR VICTIMS OF TORTURE (CVT). Non-partisan **United States**–based organization which provides medical, psychiatric and psychological care, as well as social work and physical therapy to approximately 200 survivors of **torture** each year and trains 3,500 health care, social services and education professionals in working with survivors of torture. The CVT is active in Africa, notably Sierra Leone, **Liberia** and the **Democratic Republic of the Congo**. The CVT's research department collects data on the effects of torture and survivors' lives after treatment. It also works actively with states and national and international institutions to shape public policy in support of torture survivors.

CENTRAL INTELLIGENCE AGENCY (CIA). **United States** civilian government agency created in 1947 whose primary functions are to collect information on foreign governments and individuals and to advise senior policymakers. In addition to intelligence gathering, analysis and reporting, the CIA carries out overt and covert operations. In 2012, it had a budget of $38.5 billion. Throughout its existence, the CIA has been mired in political controversies that linked it to cases of **torture**, **extraordinary rendition**, targeted killings and assassinations, the funding and training of **armed groups** and the overthrow of democratically elected governments. *See also* COLD WAR; GUATEMALA; NATIONAL ENDOWMENT FOR DEMOCRACY; OPERATION CONDOR.

CENTRE ON HOUSING RIGHTS AND EVICTIONS (COHRE). Geneva-based international **non-governmental organization** founded in 1994 with offices in the Netherlands, Brazil, the **United States**, Australia, Cambodia, Sri Lanka, Ghana and Switzerland. Its purpose is to ensure the full enjoyment of the human **right to adequate housing** for everyone, everywhere, including preventing forced evictions of persons, families and communities from their homes or lands. COHRE has **consultative status** with the **United Nations Economic and Social Council** and the **Organization of American States**. It also enjoys participatory status with the **Council of Europe** and observer status with the **African Commission on Human and People's Rights**. COHRE's international activities rely on a mix of tools including alliances and partnerships with community-level organizations, **fact finding**, **investigations**, **advocacy**, **litigation**, petitions to global and regional organizations and the provision of training.

CHANG, P. C. Chinese professor, philosopher and diplomat who played a pivotal role in the drafting of the **Universal Declaration of Human Rights**.

CHATAM HOUSE. London-based research organization formally known as the Royal Institute of International Affairs, which was established in 1920 "to analyse and promote the understanding of major international issues and current affairs." Regarded as one of the world's leading **think tanks**, the Institute produces more than 40 reports, briefing papers and books each year on a wide range of subjects, including the highly respected journal *International Affairs*. Its current programs focus on energy, **environment**

and resource **governance**, international economics and regional and security studies (which encompasses global **health** security).

CHECHNYA. Forcibly incorporated into czarist Russia in the 19th century, irredentist movements have repeatedly sought to win independence for the region, triggering two wars in 1994–96 and 1999–2000. Russian forces have regained control. A controversial referendum in 2003 approved a new constitution that granted Chechnya more autonomy within the Russian Federation. Parliamentary elections in 2005 resulted in the victory of pro-Kremlin political forces. The Russian government claims that constitutional order has been reestablished and has withdrawn the bulk of its military presence. But sporadic fighting continues in the mountains and southern regions of the republic. Both sides of the conflict have committed grievous **violations of human rights**. Russian forces have been accused of widespread abuses including arbitrary arrests, extortion, **torture**, **forced disappearances** and murder. Chechen fighters have also committed abuses against civilians as they have launched deadly terrorist attacks on Russian sites.

Western criticism of Russian tactics and human rights violations has been silenced in the wake of the 11 September 2001 attacks on the **United States**, and since then Russia has portrayed Chechen rebels as part of a global terror network of Muslim fundamentalists. Throughout the conflict, **civil society** organizations have expressed concern about the climate of impunity that prevails and called on the Russian legal system to bring to justice perpetrators of human rights violations. Only a few cases of disappearance, torture and ill treatment have reached the courts, thus prompting Chechens to turn to the **European Court of Human Rights** as the Russian judicial system has failed to show real commitment to investigate cases. *See also* ARMED CONFLICT; CIVILIANS, PROTECTION OF; COUNCIL OF EUROPE; DEATH SQUADS; INTERNATIONAL SOCIETY FOR HUMAN RIGHTS; SELF-DETERMINATION; TERRORISM.

CHEMICAL WEAPONS. Type of weapons, munitions or other devices using toxic non-living chemicals to cause death, temporary incapacitation, or permanent harm to humans or animals. Their use is prohibited by humanitarian law because of their indiscriminate and excessively injurious effects. The Hague Declaration of 1899 and The Hague Convention of 1907 forbade the use of "poison or poisonous weapons" in warfare. The 1925 Geneva Protocol prohibits the use of both chemical and chemical weapons. The more recent 1997 Chemical Weapons Convention prohibits the development acquisition and stockpiling of chemical weapons, their direct or indirect transfer and their use of military preparation for use. Protocol I,

Article 35 of the Geneva Convention bans methods or means of warfare that are intended or may be expected to cause widespread long-term and severe damage to the **environment**.

In spite of these prohibitions, chemical weapons have been used in international as well as internal conflicts, notably in the course of Italy's invasion of Ethiopia in 1935, the 1937 Japanese attack on China, and the 1980–88 Iran-Iraq war. Iraq's military campaigns against its Kurdish minorities is well documented, but there are also uncorroborated allegations of the use of such weapons by South African–backed forces in Mozambique, by contestants in the conflict between **Azerbaijan** and Armenia, by Turks against Kurds, and in the Sudan civil war. *See also* AL-ANFAL CAMPAIGN; BIOLOGICAL WEAPONS; CIVILIANS, PROTECTION OF; KURDISH QUESTION; VIETNAM WAR; WAR CRIMES; WEAPONS OF MASS DESTRUCTION.

CHILD LABOR. *See* WORLD CONFEDERATION OF LABOR.

CHILD RIGHTS INFORMATION NETWORK (CRIN). Global information **network** registered in Great Britain to monitor children's rights worldwide. CRIN is a useful source of data on national and international children rights, laws and practices. It promotes strategic **litigation** to advance children's rights and has heavily lobbied the **United Nations Human Rights Council** to introduce a **complaints** mechanism for children under the **United Nations Convention on the Rights of the Child**. *See also* LOBBYING; MONITORING OF HUMAN RIGHTS.

CHILD SOLDIERS. *See* CHILDREN IN ARMED CONFLICT; SLAVERY.

CHILDREN. *See* CHILD RIGHTS INFORMATION NETWORK; CHILDWATCH INTERNATIONAL RESEARCH NETWORK; CHILDREN IN ARMED CONFLICTS; CHILDREN TRAFFICKING; COALITION TO STOP THE USE OF CHILDREN; COMMITTEE ON THE RIGHTS AND WELFARE OF THE CHILD; CONVENTION ON THE PROTECTION OF CHILDREN AGAINST SEXUAL EXPLOITATION AND SEXUAL ABUSE; CORPORAL PUNISHMENT; DECLARATION OF THE RIGHTS OF THE CHILD; DECLARATION ON THE PROTECTION OF WOMEN AND CHILDREN IN EMERGENCY AND ARMED CONFLICTS; DEFENCE FOR CHILDREN INTERNATIONAL; EUROPEAN PARLIAMENT; FEDERATION INTERNATIONALE TERRE DES HOMMES; FORCED LABOR; FORUM FOR FACT-FINDING DOCUMENTATION AND

ADVOCACY; FUNDAMENTAL GUARANTEES; GRANT, JAMES P.; INHUMAN OR DEGRADING TREATMENT OR PUNISHMENT; INTER-AMERICAN CHILDREN INSTITUTE; INTERNATIONAL BUREAU FOR CHILDREN'S RIGHTS; INTERNATIONAL FEDERATION TERRE DES HOMMES; INTERNATIONAL LABOUR ORGANIZATION; INTERNATIONAL PROGRAMME ON THE ELIMINATION OF CHILD LABOUR; INTERNATIONAL SAVE THE CHILDREN ALLIANCE; LEAGUE OF NATIONS; MACHEL, GRAÇA; NORDIC COMMITTEE FOR HUMAN RIGHTS; OXFAM INTERNATIONAL; SAVE THE CHILDREN INTERNATIONAL; SLAVERY; SPECIAL COURT FOR SIERRA LEONE; UNITED NATIONS CONVENTION FOR THE SUPPRESSION OF THE TRAFFIC IN PERSONS AND OF THE EXPLOITATION OF THE PROSTITUTION OF OTHERS; UNITED NATIONS CONVENTION ON THE REDUCTION OF STATELESSNESS; UNITED NATIONS CONVENTION ON THE RIGHTS OF THE CHILD; UNITED NATIONS DEVELOPMENT PROGRAMME; WAR CHILD; WOMEN IN PEACE AND SECURITY; WOMEN'S REFUGEE COMMISSION; WORLD SUMMIT FOR CHILDREN.

CHILDREN IN ARMED CONFLICT. An estimated 200,000 to 300,000 children—aged between 14 and 18—are serving as soldiers for both government armed forces or government-backed paramilitary groups, militias and self-defense units and militias and a wide range of ethnic, religious, clan-based, factional armed groups opposed to central government rule (or fighting one another over territory and natural resources) in conflict-affected countries across the world. Many adolescents enlist voluntarily. Research shows, however, that they do so as a means of survival in war-torn societies where social structures have collapsed or because of poverty, lack of work and educational opportunities. Large numbers of children are also abducted or recruited by force. Girl soldiers are especially vulnerable as they are not only involved in combat but also subjected to rape and other forms of **sexual violence**.

Since the **World Summit for Children** in 1990, the **United Nations** has increasingly sought to draw international attention to the predicament of children affected by armed conflict. Acting on a recommendation of the **United Nations Committee on the Rights of the Child** and at the request of the **United Nations General Assembly**, the **United Nations secretary-general** appointed in 1993 an independent expert, Ms. **Graça Machel**, former minister of education of Mozambique to study the impact of armed conflict on children. In response to her report published in 1996, the General Assembly authorized the appointment of a special representative of the secretary-general to act as a public advocate and moral voice on behalf of children whose rights and well-being have been and are being violated in the context of armed conflict. In several resolutions, the **United Nations Security Council** has repeatedly condemned the use of children in armed conflicts. In one of its latest initiatives, the Council established a **monitoring** and reporting mechanism on children and armed conflicts within the UN Secretariat. The Council has also increasingly paid attention to the need to strengthen programs supporting the disarmament, demobilization and reintegration of child soldiers into their community in countries emerging from conflict. UN organizations like the **United Nations Children's Fund** provide life skills training, education, health care and counseling to former child soldiers. These programs generally lack funds and adequate resources.

Many of the Council's actions have been prodded by international and national **non-governmental organizations** such as the **Coalition to Stop the Use of Children** which have emerged in the past two decades advocating for and securing the release of children from armed forces and other armed groups. These civil society organizations have played an important role in the criminalization and regulation of the use of children in armed conflicts. There is now a significant body of international humanitarian and human rights law covering child soldiers (not always in a consistent manner though). The 1977 Additional Protocols to the Fourth **Geneva Convention** and the 1989 **United Nations Convention on the Rights of the Child** both use a 15-year minimum age for recruitment and participation in hostilities. A 2000 Optional Protocol to the Convention enjoins state parties to take all feasible measures to ensure that members of their armed forces who have not attained the age of 18 do not take a direct part in hostilities. The **African Charter on the Rights and Welfare of the Child** calls upon state parties to take all necessary measures to ensure that no child under 18 shall take a direct part in hostilities and to refrain in particular from recruiting any child.

Under the Statute of the **International Criminal Court**, the conscripting or enlisting of children under 15 into national armed forces or armed groups or using them to participate actively in hostilities is a war crime coming under the jurisdiction of the Court. In its verdict, the Court found a national of the **Democratic Republic of the Congo** (DRC) guilty of having committed the war crimes of enlisting and conscripting children under the age of 15 years and using them to participate actively in hostilities in the DRC between September 2002 and August 2003. In spite of these normative and jurisprudential breakthroughs, the UN secretary-general could still document grave violations against children in 19 "situations of concern," from **Afghanistan, Angola, Burundi**, Chad, **Cote d'Ivoire**, the DRC, Haiti, Iraq, Lebanon, Occupied Palestinian Territories and Israel, **Liberia**, Somalia,

Sudan and **Uganda** to **Myanmar**, Nepal, Sri Lanka, the **Philippines** and **Colombia**. His report to the Security Council also explicitly cited 40 "parties," both state and **non-state actors**, for the commission of grave violations against children. *See also* HUMAN RIGHTS WATCH; INTERNATIONAL FEDERATION TERRE DES HOMMES; INTERNATIONAL SAVE THE CHILDREN ALLIANCE; WAR CHILD.

CHILDREN TRAFFICKING. Form of **human trafficking** which the Protocol to Prevent, Suppress and Punish Trafficking in Persons to the **United Nations Convention against Transnational Organized Crime** defines as the recruitment, transportation, transfer, harboring or receipt of a child for the purpose of exploitation even without evidence of force, fraud, deception or coercion. The Protocol clarifies that "exploitation" means "exploitation of the prostitution of others or other forms of sexual exploitation, **forced labor** or services, **slavery** or practices similar to slavery, servitude, or the removal of organs." Other international instruments such as the **United Nations Convention on the Rights of the Child** and the Inter-American Convention on International Traffic in Minors, make it clear that the exploitation of children may take forms others than sexual exploitation and include such activities as illicit international adoptions, trafficking for early marriage and recruitment as child soldiers, among others. The **International Labour Organization**'s Worst Forms of Child Labor Convention of 1999 (Convention 182) classifies child trafficking among "forms of slavery or practices similar to slavery" that are to be eliminated as a matter of urgency. Most trafficked children end up in child domestic labor, commercial sexual exploitation, agricultural work, drug couriering, organized begging, child soldiering and exploitative or slavery-like practices in the informal economy and recommends that it be made a criminal offense. In spite of these elaborate normative instruments, an estimated 1.2 million children are trafficked each year. The scale of the phenomenon is attributable in part to the fact that trafficking in children often involves exploitation of the parents' extreme **poverty**.

See also CHILDREN IN ARMED CONFLICT; CONVENTION ON THE PROTECTION OF CHILDREN AGAINST SEXUAL EX-PLOITATION AND SEXUAL ABUSE; GENDER-BASED VIOLENCE; INTERNATIONAL BUREAU FOR CHILDREN'S RIGHTS; INTER-NATIONAL PROGRAMME ON THE ELIMINATION OF CHILD LABOUR; LEAGUE OF NATIONS.

CHILDWATCH INTERNATIONAL RESEARCH NETWORK. Global non-profit non-governmental **network** of institutions collaborating in child research for the purpose of promoting and improving the rights of children and their well-being. Based in Norway, Childwatch was set up in the wake of the adoption of **United Nations Convention on the Rights of the Child**.

CHILE. In spite of a relatively long tradition of democratic institutions and respect for the **rule of law**, increasing political polarization and big powers' covert outside intervention led to the overthrow of the democratically elected socialist president Salvador Allende in 1973. The military coup orchestrated by General **Augusto Pinochet** ushered in the launching of free market policies derived from the prescriptions of American economists who believed that they would be the most effective bulwark against Marxism. The economic role of the state was sharply reduced. Subsidies and price controls were scrapped, tariffs were reduced and a liberal foreign investment regime was instituted. Trade union power was curbed and state-owned industries returned to the private sector and the social security system was privatized. Long heralded for having restored Chile's economic progress, these policies were emulated for some time by many countries in the region. They have now come under increasing criticism and are being partially reversed for having encouraged untrammeled foreign competition and unequal distribution of wealth.

At the same time, all political dissidence was ruthlessly suppressed. The elimination of the opposition, especially "leftist opposition," was an overriding concern of the regime. The press was censored, labor strikes were banned, political parties outlawed and opponents—real and imagined— hunted down by the secret police. A 2011 report of a commission investigating human rights abuses updated the findings of previous commissions and identified over 40,000 victims, forcibly disappeared, killed or tortured. A small number of military officers were convicted in the 1990s for human rights abuses, and the number of those under investigation and convictions on charges of **forced disappearances**, **extra-judicial executions** and **torture** has significantly risen over time. But overall, Chile remains a case study in delayed accountability as a result of a 1978 **amnesty** law, inconsistent and narrow rulings of judicial bodies and the priority given by successive democratic governments to truth processes over prosecutions. Advances in posttransitional justice in Chile have been achieved more at the insistence of private actors rather that state authorities. *See also* DEATH SQUADS; KISSINGER, HENRY; OPERATION CONDOR; TRUTH AND RECONCILIATION COMMISSIONS; UNIVERSAL JURISDICTION.

CHINA. *See* ASIAN VALUES; CUBA; CULTURAL RELATIVISM; CULTURAL REVOLUTION; DALAI LAMA; DEMOCRATIC KAMPUCHEA; FEMALE INFANTICIDE; GREAT LEAP FORWARD; KIM IL SUNG; KISSINGER, HENRY; LABOR BONDAGE; MAO

ZEDONG; MYANMAR; SEX TRAFFICKING; SIERRA CLUB; SUHARTO; SYRIA; TIANANMEN SQUARE PROTESTS; TIBET; WOMEN IN PEACE AND SECURITY.

CHOIKE. This project of the Instituto del Tercer Mundo, a **non-governmental organization** (NGO) in special consultative status with the **United Nations Economic and Social Council** based in Montevideo, Uruguay, is, in effect, a portal dedicated to improving the visibility of the work done by NGOs and social movements from the South. It serves as a platform where citizen groups can disseminate their work and at the same time enrich it with information from diverse sources, which is presented from the perspective of Southern civil society.

CITIZENSHIP. The term denotes a link between an individual and the state and refers to the rights and duties of the members of a nation state or city. Originally, as understood in 18th-century documents such as the American Declaration of Independence, the enjoyment of human rights was tied to citizenship. Now sociologists attribute three major components to the idea: a "civil citizenship" which encapsulates individual freedoms; a "political citizenship" which grants rights to participation in the political process; and a "social citizenship" which grants rights to enjoy an appropriate standard of living. Citizenship is synonymous to nationality, although they may have different meanings under national law. The Maastricht Treaty innovated in introducing the concept of citizenship of the **European Union** which adds to but does not replace national citizenship. Under the terms of the treaty, a citizen of the European Union is guaranteed a general right of non-**discrimination**, a limited right of free movement and residence in member states of the European Union and a number of political rights. *See also* NATIONALITY, RIGHT TO; STATELESSNESS; UNITED NATIONS CONVENTION RELATING TO THE STATUS OF STATELESS PERSONS.

CIVICUS. International alliance of **civil society** organizations dedicated to strengthening citizen action and civil society throughout the world. CIVICUS programs are designed to promote the rights of **freedom of association** and **freedom of expression** of citizens so that they may be able to participate in the full range of civic political, economic, cultural, educational, religious in their communities and nations. The group's core projects focus on the state of civil society in more than 50 countries, gender equality, the legitimacy, transparency and accountability of civil society organizations, good governance and the **Millennium Development Goals** as a framework for civil society action.

CIVIL AND POLITICAL RIGHTS. Class of rights also known as "**first-generation rights**" or "negative rights" because they were the first rights to emerge historically to protect individuals against the power and encroachments of the state. Civil rights include protection from all forms of **discrimination** as well as individual entitlements such as freedom of thought, speech, **religion** and **association**. Political rights encompass the rights of the accused, including the right to a **fair trial**; **due process**; the right to seek **redress** or a legal **remedy**; and rights of participation in civil society and politics such as freedom of association, the right to assemble, the right to petition and the right to vote. First enunciated in the **Universal Declaration of Human Rights**, civil and political rights have been codified in particular in the **International Covenant on Civil and Political Rights** and the **European Convention for the Protection of Human Rights and Fundamental Freedoms**. *See also* AMERICAN CONVENTION ON HUMAN RIGHTS; AMERICAN DECLARATION OF THE RIGHTS AND DUTIES OF MAN.

CIVIL SOCIETY. While there is no universally accepted definition of the term, civil society refers broadly to a set of very diverse voluntary, non-profit institutions, organizations and behaviors which are situated between the government and business or the force-backed structures of a state and the commercial institutions of the market and coalesce around shared interests, purposes and values. According to the **United Nations Office of the High Commissioner for Human Rights**, the actors involved include **non-governmental organizations**, associations, victim groups; coalitions and **transnational advocacy networks** concerned about women's rights, children's rights, environmental rights; community-based groups representing **indigenous peoples** or **minorities**; faith-based groups such as churches and religious groups; trade unions and professional associations; **social movements** (peace movements, student movements, pro-democracy movements; and professionals contributing directly to the enjoyment of human rights (humanitarian workers, lawyers, doctors and medical workers). *See also* CAMPAIGNS.

CIVIL WAR. *See* AFGHANISTAN; ALGERIAN CIVIL WAR; ANGOLA; ARMED CONFLICT; THE BALKANS; BIAFRA; BURUNDI; COLOMBIA; COTE D'IVOIRE; CROATIA, WAR OF INDEPENDENCE; DARFUR CONFLICT; DEMOCRATIC REPUBLIC OF THE CONGO; EL SALVADOR; FRANCO, FRANCISCO; GENEVA CONVENTIONS; GREECE; GUATEMALA; INDONESIA; LIBYA; MYANMAR; NORTHERN IRELAND; PHILIPPINES; RWANDA; SIERRA LEONE CIVIL WAR; SYRIA; UGANDA.

CIVILIANS, PROTECTION OF. Term referring to measures that must be taken by states, organized armed groups and humanitarian organizations to protect the safety, dignity and integrity of civilians in times of war as called for under **international humanitarian law** (IHL), **refugee** law, and **international human rights law**. The subject has gained increasing salience in the deliberations and decisions of the **United Nations Security Council** as the **United Nations** was increasingly involved in internal armed conflicts. The matter was first discussed in the Council in 1989. Since then, the **United Nations secretary-general** regularly reports to the Council on the protection of civilians in armed conflict and, in turn, the Council has adopted numerous resolutions on the subject. In addition to country-specific resolutions, the Council has endorsed measures aimed at protecting women, children and humanitarian workers and against sexual exploitation. In its resolutions, statement and missions to conflict regions, the Council has had recourse to a wide array of measures ranging from calls on parties to observe IHL, to imposing **sanctions** on those violating IHL to authorizing action to hold individuals accountable for serious violations of IHL.

See also CARPET BOMBING; INTERNATIONAL CRIMINAL COURT; PHYSICIANS FOR HUMAN RIGHTS; PROTECTED PERSONS; REFUGEE LAW; "RESPONSIBILITY TO PROTECT"; UNITED NATIONS ASSISTANCE MISSION IN AFGHANISTAN; UNITED NATIONS MISSION IN SIERRA LEONE; UNITED NATIONS MISSION IN THE CENTRAL AFRICAN REPUBLIC AND CHAD; UNITED NATIONS OPERATION IN BURUNDI; WORLD WAR II.

CLAIM. Legal demand asserted by an individual alleging that he or she is entitled to a **remedy** for injury caused by an offender (a state, a government official, a **transnational corporation**) and giving rise to a legally enforceable right or judicial or quasi-judicial action. Individuals initiating a legal action before a court with a view to obtaining legal remedy and **redress** through a court ruling are called complainants or plaintiffs.

CLIMATE CHANGE. Changes in weather patterns related to global warming include a contraction of snow-covered areas and shrinking of sea ice, sea level rises and higher water temperatures, increased frequency of hot extremes and heat waves, heavy precipitation events and increases in areas affected by drought and increased intensity of tropical cyclones, typhoons and hurricanes. Studies by the Intergovernmental Panel on Climate Change, among others, have documented and warned that these changes may result in hundreds of millions of people suffering from **hunger**, malnutrition, **water** shortages, floods, droughts, heat stress, diseases triggered by extreme weather events, loss of livelihoods and permanent displacement. The poor, women, children and other vulnerable groups are likely to be most seriously impacted, and there is already talk about the growing number of environmental **refugees**.

But there is considerable uncertainty as to the extent these effects qualify as **violations of human rights** in a strict legal sense. The 1972 Declaration adopted by the **United Nations Conference on Human Environment** acknowledges the interdependence and interrelatedness of human rights and the **environment**. The **United Nations Committee on Economic, Social and Cultural Rights** has opined that the right to adequate **food** requires the adoption of "appropriate economic, environmental and social policies" and that the right to **health** extends to its underlying determinants, including a healthy environment. But only the **United Nations Convention on the Rights of the Child** among universal human rights treaties refers to a specific right to a safe and healthy environment. In a 2008 resolution, the first one on the subject, the **United Nations Human Rights Council** noted that "climate change-related effects have a wide range of implications . . . for the enjoyment of human rights" and "affirmed" that "human rights obligations and commitments have the potential to inform and strengthen international and national policy-making in the area of climate change, promoting policy coherence, legitimacy and sustainable outcomes." *See also* CARITAS INTERNATIONALIS; FRIENDS OF THE EARTH INTERNATIONAL; INTERNATIONAL COUNCIL ON HUMAN RIGHTS POLICY; WORLD FEDERATION OF UNITED NATIONS ASSOCIATIONS; WORLDWATCH INSTITUTE.

CLONING, HUMAN. Process of artificially creating an identical copy of the DNA of an organism. Therapeutic cloning involves cloning adult cells for use in medicine. Reproductive cloning would involve making cloned humans. The various forms of cloning are controversial. Advocates of cloning argue that cloning may be used for organ replacement, as a solution to infertility, for genetic research and to obtain specific traits in organisms. Opponents assert that cloning could be detrimental to genetic diversity, could invite fraudulent malpractice and is inconsistent with human **dignity**. The debate on human cloning focused mainly on reproductive cloning and freedom of scientific research. In 2005, the **United Nations General Assembly** abandoned its five-year-long efforts to elaborate an international convention against the reproductive cloning of humans and instead adopted a nonbinding declaration calling for the ban of all forms of human cloning contrary to human dignity. The **European Charter of Fundamental Rights of the European Union** explicitly prohibits reproductive human cloning. *See also* LIFE, RIGHT TO.

COALITION AGAINST TRAFFICKING IN WOMEN (CATW). Umbrella **non-governmental organization** bringing together regional networks, individuals and groups devoted to combating sexual exploitation in all its forms such as pornography, **sex tourism**, and mail order bride selling but especially prostitution and trafficking in women and children. CATW seeks to achieve its objectives through **research**, education and participation in national and international processes. CATW has **consultative status** with the **United Nations Economic and Social Council**. *See also* HUMAN TRAFFICKING.

COALITION FOR INTERNATIONAL JUSTICE (CIJ). International **non-governmental organization** supporting the international war crimes tribunals for **Rwanda** and the former Yugoslavia, and justice initiatives in **Timor-Leste**, Sierra Leone, and Cambodia. CIJ initiates and conducts **advocacy** and public education **campaigns**, targeting decisionmakers in Washington, D.C., and other capitals, the media, and the public. In the field, CIJ provides practical assistance on legal, technical, and outreach matters to the tribunals and other justice initiatives. In 2005, the CIJ issued an authoritative comprehensive statistical analysis of the death toll in Darfur which asserted that 400,000 people in Darfur had died since the conflict began, a figure most humanitarian and human rights groups now use. *See also* INTERNATIONAL CRIMINAL TRIBUNAL FOR RWANDA; INTERNATIONAL CRIMINAL TRIBUNAL FOR THE FORMER YUGOSLAVIA.

COALITION FOR THE INTERNATIONAL CRIMINAL COURT (CICC). Global network of over 2,500 **non-governmental organizations** set up in 1995 for the initial purpose of supporting the establishment of an **International Criminal Court** (ICC). The CICC did make significant and important contributions at all stages of the process, and its role was formally recognized by a resolution adopted by the Assembly of States Parties in September 2003. The groups making up the CICC now advocate for a fair, effective and independent International Criminal Court and **campaign** for the universal ratification of the Rome Statute of the ICC and the **incorporation** of the crimes under the Rome Statute into domestic legislation. *See also* ADVOCACY.

COALITION TO STOP THE USE OF CHILDREN. London-headquartered international network of **non-governmental organizations** including **Amnesty International, Defence for Children International, Human Rights Watch, International Federation Terre des Hommes, International Save the Children Alliance**, Jesuit Refugee Service, and the Quaker United Nations Office which was formed in 1998 to prevent the recruitment and use of children as soldiers, to secure their demobilization and to ensure their rehabilitation and reintegration into society. The Coalition played an instrumental role in the negotiation, adoption and entry into force of the Optional Protocol to the **United Nations Convention on the Rights of the Child** on the involvement of **children in armed conflicts** and has formed national coalitions in 35 countries worldwide and regional coalitions in Africa, Latin America, the Middle East and Southeast Asia. It is actively involved in the work of such intergovernmental bodies as the **United Nations Security Council**, the **European Union**, the **United Nations Committee on the Rights of the Child** and the **International Labour Organization**. The Coalition conducts and publishes research on children in armed conflicts including periodic "Child Soldiers Global Reports" which provide comprehensive country-by-country information on child recruitment and use worldwide.

COBO, JOSE MARTINEZ. Ecuadorian lawyer and diplomat. He is the author of a landmark study on the problems of **indigenous peoples** which he prepared at the request of and submitted to the United Nations Sub-Commission on Prevention of Discrimination and Protection of Minorities of the **United Nations Commission on Human Rights** from 1981 to 1984. The work addressed a wide range of human rights issues concerning indigenous peoples, including a definition of indigenous peoples, the elimination of discrimination, and the promotion of basic human rights principles, as well as special areas of action in fields such as **health, housing, education**, language, culture, social and legal institutions, employment, land, political rights, religious rights and practices and equality in the administration of justice. Cobo's conclusions and proposals were an important milestone in prodding the international community to intensify its actions to resolve human rights problems facing indigenous peoples. Many are still under consideration and others have been incorporated into the resolutions of intergovernmental human rights bodies. There is little doubt that the study played an important role in sharpening the focus of the United Nations work and in paving the way toward the drafting of a United Nations Declaration on the Rights of Indigenous Peoples. *See also* NORM ENTREPRENEURS.

CODE OF CONDUCT FOR LAW ENFORCEMENT OFFICIALS (1979). Soft law instrument endorsed by the **United Nations General Assembly** in 1979. Grounded in the assumption that those who exercise police power are to respect and protect human dignity and to uphold the human rights of all persons, the Code prohibits **torture** or any act of **corruption** and states that force may be used only when strictly necessary. The Code also sets forth the responsibility to keep personal information confidential and calls for the full protection of the **health** of persons in custody.

CODES OF CONDUCT FOR TRANSNATIONAL CORPORATIONS. Policy standards and guidelines externally generated by government or intergovernmental organizations and to some degree imposed on **transnational corporations** (TNCs) addressing issues relevant to their activities such as their relations in world markets, labor matters (e.g., terms and conditions of work and equality); environmental standards (e.g., emissions, waste or safety in production and transportation); and **health** and safety issues related to individual products (e.g., toys, baby milk substitutes). Most intergovernmental guidelines for TNCs emerged in the 1970s at a time when TNCs were widely criticized for their practices in developing countries. Initial efforts to define a social purpose for TNCs can be traced back to a 1974 resolution of the **United Nations General Assembly** calling for the establishment of a New International Economic Order and to the report of a group of high-level experts which gave rise to intergovernmental negotiations within the United Nations on a UN draft code for TNCs. This bold initiative never went beyond the draft stage.

Negotiations stalled over the legal nature of the code, with Northern countries insisting that it should be purely voluntary and Southern countries arguing that it should be binding. They came to an end altogether in 1992, and the impossibility of reaching a political international agreement on sanctions for noncompliant firms shifted the focus of the debate from mandatory to voluntary codes. Codes of conduct adopted by the **International Labour Organization**, the **World Health Organization** or the **Organization for Economic Co-operation and Development** are instances of that shift. The wave of deregulation and **privatization** which emerged in the late 1980s has rekindled interest in voluntary schemes no longer centered on North-South disparities but on the social and human rights responsibilities of TNCs such as the **United Nations Global Compact**, the **United Nations Principles for Responsible Investment** and the **United Nations "Protect, Respect and Remedy" Framework for Business and Human Rights**. *See also* CORPORATE SOCIAL RESPONSIBILITY.

CODESRIA. Acronym for the Council for the Development of Social Science Research in Africa, an independent pan-African research organization headquartered in Dakar, Senegal. Established in 1973, CODESRIA seeks to promote and facilitate social science **research** and knowledge production in Africa. Some of its work has dealt with human rights issues in Africa.

COLD WAR. Political conflict from roughly from 1946 to 1991 that pitted the **United States** and its **North Atlantic Treaty Organization** allies against the Soviet Union and its Warsaw Pact satellite states. The Cold War never escalated into military action directly involving the superpowers themselves. But their conflict manifested itself through regional collective security arrangements, strategic conventional force deployments, proxy wars, conventional and nuclear arms races and competition for influence in the newly emerging Third World as the process of decolonization gained momentum in the 1950s and 1960s. East-West rivalries had a profound and by and large negative impact on human rights ideas, policies and practices. They polarized human rights supporters into two camps: those embracing **first-generation rights** and those espousing **second-generation rights**, thus paving the way to the adoption of two covenants in implementation of the **Universal Declaration of Human Rights**, an outcome that cast a long shadow over the **universality** and **indivisibility** of human rights.

The competitive relationship between the United States and the USSR severely constrained the capacity of the **United Nations Security Council** and precluded its interventions in situations fraught with **violations of human rights**. The only exception to this pattern were the laboriously agreed-upon **sanctions** that the Council adopted in regard to **apartheid** in South Africa and Southern Rhodesia. Movements in the Soviet bloc, such as those in Hungary and Czechoslovakia, which called for the freedoms stated in the Universal Declaration of Human Rights, were ruthlessly crushed. Concurrently, independence or nationalist movements in the Third World regions and countries were perceived in the West as allied with communist groups and led to covert operations or outright interventions in such countries as **Angola**, **Argentina**, **Brazil**, **Bolivia**, **Chile**, **Colombia**, Congo, Dominican Republic, **Guatemala**, **Indonesia**, Indochina, **Iran**, Mozambique, **Paraguay** and **Uruguay** conducive to massive violations of rights. An unexpected and unintended consequence of the Cold War arising from the superpowers' courting of newly independent countries was to give political impetus to the adoption of the Convention against Racial Discrimination.

See also CENTRAL INTELLIGENCE AGENCY; COUNCIL OF EUROPE; DEMOCRACY; DEMOCRATIC KAMPUCHEA; "DIRTY WAR"; DUVALIER, FRANCOIS; EL SALVADOR; FORCED DISAPPEARANCES; GREECE; HELSINKI FINAL ACT; HONDURAS; INTERDEPENDENCE; KISSINGER, HENRY; OPERATION CONDOR; ORGANIZATION FOR SECURITY AND CO-OPERATION IN EUROPE; PEACE, RIGHT TO; PEACE OPERATIONS; PREVENTION; SANCTIONS; SUHARTO; TIMOR-LESTE; UNITED NATIONS OFFICE OF THE HIGH COMMISSIONER FOR HUMAN RIGHTS; UNITED NATIONS SUB-

COMMISSION ON THE PROMOTION AND PROTECTION OF HUMAN RIGHTS; VIETNAM; WORLD CONFEDERATION OF LABOR.

COLLATERAL DAMAGE. *See* CIVILIANS, PROTECTION OF.

COLLECTIVE RIGHTS. *See* GROUP RIGHTS; THIRD-GENERATION RIGHTS.

COLOMBIA. This South American country has a long tradition of constitutional government, but tensions between the two oldest parties, the Liberal and Conservative parties, fueled by grave social and economic inequalities, have fed recurrent cycles of bloody political violence, notably the Thousand Days War at the turn of the 20th century and a quasi-civil war known as La Violencia, which started in the late 1940s and grew in intensity in the 1990s. The latest conflict that pitted government forces and right-wing **paramilitaries** against left-wing insurgents has been fueled by the lucrative cocaine trade and has only recently subsided with the demobilization of many paramilitary groups in the wake of a highly controversial peace agreement with the government and the guerrillas' loss of the territory they used to control. The progressive criminalization of the conflict, however, has been accompanied by unusual levels of violence.

The government argues that its human rights record has improved, but serious abuses, including those of **international humanitarian law**, persist. The insurgents are responsible for multiple atrocities against **civilians**, including kidnapping and hostage taking, assassinations of elected officials and summary executions. Illegal groups, at times with the acquiescence of security personnel and some government officials, undeterred by an inefficient justice system, have for a long time been involved in **extrajudicial executions**. The war has also triggered a major humanitarian crisis that is largely unknown outside the country which has displaced 2 to 3 million people. Talks between the government and the insurgents have been ongoing for over a year marked by "discretion, realism and seriousness." The two sides reached an agreement on rural development but issues still need to be resolved including the insurgents' participation in politics, their demobilization and judicial treatment and reparations for the victims. *See also* ARMED GROUPS; COLD WAR; DEATH SQUADS; INTERNALLY DISPLACED PERSONS; INTERNATIONAL SOCIETY FOR HUMAN RIGHTS.

COLONIALISM. A broad dictionary definition of the term would state that colonialism is "the policy and practice of a power in extending control over weaker peoples or areas." As such, colonialism has a long history extending as far back as Egyptian, Phoenician, Greek and Roman times. More narrowly understood, colonialism simply refers to the conquest and occupation of overseas territories by European states which began in the 15th century and slowly came to an end by the last decades of the 20th century with the accession to independence of Namibia in 1990 and the Federated States of Micronesia and the Marshall Islands in 1991. Oddly enough, the term is not used or applied to the territorial expansion of such countries as Russia and China. Colonialism has taken not always mutually exclusive forms of settler, exploitative and plantation colonies. Whatever its modalities, the encounter of colonizers with the native populations has had a pervasive short- and long-term impact on both, including the spread of local epidemics of extraordinary virulence, the transformation of ecological systems, the emergence of unequal social relations, land dispossession, hunger and famine, enslavement and technological and infrastructural advances and the creation of new modern state institutions.

There is a continuing debate among colonizers and colonized about the positive or negative effects of colonialism in the medium and longer term. The debate actually started at the onset of the colonization process. But the human toll of colonialism and decolonization has been horrendous, some observers estimating that some 50 million died in Asia and Africa from 1900 to independence. Not surprisingly, there have been demands for **apologies** and **reparations**—by and large unheeded—which have intermittently surfaced, notably in **United Nations** fora.

See also ALGERIAN WAR OF INDEPENDENCE; BOER WARS; CONGO FREE STATE; DECLARATION ON SOCIAL PROGRESS AND DEVELOPMENT; DECLARATION ON THE GRANTING OF INDEPENDENCE TO COLONIAL PEOPLES AND COUNTRIES; DECOLONIZATION; GERMAN SOUTH WEST AFRICA; INDIA, PARTITION OF; INDIGENOUS PEOPLES; INDONESIA; INTERNATIONAL MILITARY TRIBUNAL FOR THE FAR EAST; MANDATES; MERCENARY; NATIVE AMERICANS; SELF-DETERMINATION; SOUTHERN RHODESIA; UNITED NATIONS TRUSTEESHIP SYSTEM; VIETNAM; WORLD CONFERENCE AGAINST RACISM.

"COMFORT WOMEN." Euphemistic expression referring to women from Korea, China, the Philippines, Thailand, Vietnam, and other Japanese occupied territories who were forced into sexual slavery by the Japanese military during World War II. Estimates of the total number of women involved vary widely ranging from 400,000 (by Chinese scholars) to a low of

20,000 (by some Japanese historians). Probably a more reliable figure is in the vicinity of 200,000, but the numbers are still hotly debated as the matter is politically highly charged in Japan and East Asian countries. Initially the Japanese government denied any official involvement, declaring in 1990 that the brothels were run by private contractors. The discovery of incriminating documents in the archives of Japan's defense agency forced the government to recant and to formally recognize in 1993 that the Japanese military had been involved in the establishment and management of the "comfort stations."

In 1995 Japan set up an Asia Women's Fund funded by private donations for material compensation to surviving comfort women to be accompanied by a signed **apology** from the prime minister. Because of the unofficial nature of the fund, many victims rejected these payments and still seek an official apology and compensation. The issue was rekindled in 2007 when the Japanese prime minister stated that there was no evidence of coercion by the military in the recruitment of comfort women. That same year, the lower houses of the Dutch and Canadian Parliament, the **United States** House of Representatives and the **European Parliament** all passed resolutions urging the Japanese government to formally acknowledge its historical and financial responsibility. Reacting to the U.S. House of Representatives resolution, Prime Minister Shinzo Abe labeled it "regrettable." *See also* DENIAL; IMPUNITY; WAR CRIMES.

COMMAND RESPONSIBILITY. Principle according to which civilian or military superiors may be held individually responsible for crimes committed by their subordinates or for failing to prevent or punish them. Much of the debate surrounding the doctrine focuses on the level of knowledge a commander must possess before a court will consider him or her responsible for crimes committed by a subordinate. The principle was first applied by the German Supreme Court in the **Leipzig war trials** after World War I. The Charter of the Nuremberg Tribunal extended it to "leaders, organizers, instigators and accomplices" involved in the planning and commission of **crimes against peace**, **war crimes** and **crimes against humanity**. The 1977 Additional Protocol to the 1949 **Geneva Conventions** is the first international treaty to codify the principle of command responsibility.

Subsequently, the concept has been developed significantly in the jurisprudence of the **International Criminal Tribunal for the Former Yugoslavia** (ICTY) whose statute stipulates that crimes "committed by a subordinate does not relieve his superior of criminal responsibility if he knew or had reason to know that the subordinate was about to commit such acts or had done so and the superior failed to take the necessary and reasonable measures to prevent such acts or to punish the perpetrators." The statute of the **International Criminal**

Court (ICC) also provides that military commanders are individually responsible for crimes committed by forces under their effective command. In the context of the **"war on terror,"** legal observers have argued that high-ranking officials of President **George W. Bush**'s administration could be held responsible of war crimes under the principle of command responsibility. It should be noted that the statutes of the ICTY, the **International Criminal Tribunal for Rwanda**, and the ICC refer to "superior responsibility," suggesting that the doctrine may also apply to paramilitary or irregular commanders and civilian leaders. *See also* ARMENIAN GENOCIDE; BLASKIC CASE; KARADZIC, RADOVAN; MUSEMA CASE; SPECIAL COURT FOR SIERRA LEONE ; TIMOR-LESTE.

COMMITTEE OF CONCERNED SCIENTISTS. American **non-governmental organization** of scientists, physicians, engineers and scholars devoted to the recognition, advancement and preservation of the human rights of scientists. The Committee monitors the rights of scientists, especially their freedom to exchange scholarly information, data and personnel, and their freedom of research, inquiry, publication and travel to and from scholarly and scientific meetings. It also documents **violations of the human rights** and scientific freedom of scientists all over the world, protests directly toward repressive governments and urges similar action by professional societies and individual scientists, publicizes human rights abuses and maintains close contact with members of the **United States** Congress and the executive branch of government to secure their support and intervention for imperiled colleagues. *See also* FREEDOM OF EXPRESSION.

COMMITTEE OF MINISTERS OF THE COUNCIL OF EUROPE. Governmental decision-making body of the **Council of Europe** comprising the ministers of foreign affairs (or their representatives) from the Council's states parties. As the "guardian" of the Council's fundamental values, the Committee monitors the compliance of members states with their **treaty** obligations. One of the Committee's functions is to monitor and ensure states' compliance with the rulings of the **European Court of Human Rights**.

COMMITTEE ON THE ADMINISTRATION OF JUSTICE (CAJ). **Non-governmental organization** established in 1981 to monitor and ensure compliance by the British government of its international human rights law responsibilities in **Northern Ireland**. To achieve this objective, CAJ submits reports to **United Nations** and European human rights bodies. CAJ is affiliated with the **International Federation for Human Rights** and was the recipient in 1998 of the **Council of Europe**'s Human Rights Prize.

COMMITTEE ON THE RIGHTS AND WELFARE OF THE CHILD. Expert group monitoring the implementation of the **African Charter of the Rights and Welfare of the Child** empowered to review reports by state parties on measures they have adopted to enforce the provisions of the Charter and to assess progress regarding how the rights are being protected. The Committee also has broad investigative powers. *See also* INVESTIGATION.

COMMONWEALTH HUMAN RIGHTS INITIATIVE (CHRI). International **non-governmental organization** founded in 1987 by a number of Commonwealth associations devoted to the practical realization of human rights in the countries of the **Commonwealth of Nations**. CHRI's objectives are to promote awareness of and adherence to internationally recognized human rights instruments, as well as domestic instruments supporting human rights in Commonwealth member states. Through reports and periodic fact-finding missions, CHRI draws attention to progress and setbacks in human rights in Commonwealth countries and advocates for approaches and measures to prevent human rights abuses. CHRI is accredited to the Commonwealth. Since 2002 and 2005, respectively, it holds observer status with the **African Commission on Human and People's Rights** and consultative status with the **United Nations Economic and Social Council**.

COMMONWEALTH OF INDEPENDENT STATES (CIS). Regional organization bringing together Russia and the former Soviet republics. The CIS has coordinating functions in trade, finance and security. It has also promoted cooperation on democratization. Since 2002, CIS has monitored a number of national elections. *See also* COMMONWEALTH OF INDEPENDENT STATES CONVENTION ON HUMAN RIGHTS AND FUNDAMENTAL FREEDOMS; DEMOCRACY.

COMMONWEALTH OF INDEPENDENT STATES CONVENTION ON HUMAN RIGHTS AND FUNDAMENTAL FREEDOMS. Signed in 1995 and in force since 1998, this convention purports to protect the civil, political and economic and social rights of nationals of the countries members of the **Commonwealth of Independent States** (CIS). The CIS Convention has been criticized for offering less protection than the **European Convention for the Protection of Human Rights and Fundamental Freedoms** (ECHR) both with regards to the scope of its contents and with regard to the powers of the enforcing body. For instance, Article 11 of the CIS Convention states that everyone shall have the right to freedom of expression but also stipulates that "the exercise of these freedoms, since it carries with it duties and responsibilities, may be subject to such formalities, conditions and restrictions as are prescribed by law and are necessary in a democratic society, in the interests of national security, public safety or public order or for the protection of the rights and freedoms of others." The **monitoring** of the execution of the Convention is assigned to a Commission composed of state parties' appointed representatives. Concern about the compatibility of the two Conventions prompted the **Council of Europe** to reaffirm the primacy and supremacy of the ECHR and its Court of Human Rights for all member states of the Council of Europe and to call upon those Council of Europe member or applicant states which are also members of the CIS not to sign or ratify the CIS Convention on Human Rights. *See also* ABKHAZIA.

COMMONWEALTH OF NATIONS. Intergovernmental organization bringing together countries which were (with two exceptions) formerly part of the British Empire. States members of the Commonwealth are supposed to be guided by a 1971 Declaration which called upon them to cooperate in order to promote **democracy**, human rights, good **governance**, the **rule of law**, individual liberty, free trade, multilateralism and world peace. The organization has occasionally suspended several members (Fiji, Nigeria, Pakistan, Zimbabwe) "for serious violations" of these principles. But in recent years, it has been increasingly criticized for its failure to more forcefully censure its members who violated human rights or democratic norms. *See also* COMMONWEALTH HUMAN RIGHTS INITIATIVE.

COMMUNICATION. Term officially used by the **United Nations Human Rights Council Advisory Committee**, the **United Nations Committee on the Elimination of All Forms of Racial Discrimination** and the **United Nations Committee on the Elimination of All Forms of Discrimination against Women** to refer to **complaints** brought to any of these **treaty** bodies by individuals alleging violations of their human rights. *See also* AFRICAN COMMITTEE ON THE RIGHTS AND WELFARE OF THE CHILD; SOCIAL SECURITY, RIGHT TO; WORLD ORGANIZATION AGAINST TORTURE.

COMMUNISM. Term referring to the writings of Karl Marx, **Vladimir Lenin**, **Josef Stalin** and **Mao Zedong** among others or to a system of social and political organization derived from their precepts involving the abolition of private property and the control of economic and social activities by a one party–based government. Communism has been blamed for the killing of almost 100 million people in the 20th century. *See also* DEMOCIDE; RUMMEL, RUDOLPH JOSEPH.

COMMUNITY-BASED ORGANIZATIONS. Non-profit groups with widely varying structures and modes of organization driven by community residents (often on a voluntary basis) in all aspects of its governance, staffing, issue concerns and practical activities and providing health, educational, social welfare services to neighborhoods and local residents. *See also* CIVIL SOCIETY.

COMPLAINTS. Also known as **applications communications** or petitions, complaints are procedures most often created pursuant to human rights treaties, covenants, or conventions enabling individuals to claim that their rights have been violated by a state party to that treaty. The objectives of complaint procedures are either to identify broad **violations of human rights** affecting a large population or to **redress** specific grievances. The latter may result in legally enforceable **remedies** involving reprimanding government policies and practices and ordering governments to compensate the victim.

Specific treaties providing forums for filing individual complaints include all the regional human rights regimes laid down in the **African Charter on Human and People's Rights**, the **European Convention for the Protection of Human Rights and Fundamental Freedoms**, and the **American Convention on Human Rights**. At the global level, the First Optional Protocol to the **International Covenant on Civil and Political Rights**, the **United Nations Convention against Torture**, the Optional Protocol of the **United Nations Convention on the Elimination of All Forms of Discrimination against Women**, the **International Convention on the Elimination of All Forms of Racial Discrimination**, the **International Convention on the Protection of the Rights of All Migrant Workers and Their Families**, the Optional Protocol to the **United Nations Convention on the Rights of Persons with Disabilities** and the **International Convention for the Protection of All Persons from Enforced Disappearance** allow individuals to petition the "treaty bodies" overseeing their implementation. There are also procedures for complaints which fall outside of the regional human rights regimes and the United Nations treaty body system. These include the **special procedures** of the **United Nations Commission on Human Rights** (now the **United Nations Human Rights Council**) and the **United Nations Commission on the Status of Women** and the 1235 and **1503 Procedures** established under resolutions of the **United Nations Economic and Social Council**. Also relevant here, in the context of **self-determination**, is the authority granted by the **United Nations Charter** to the now defunct **United Nations Trusteeship System** to accept and examine petitions concerning the trust territories. The Special Committee on Decolonization set up in 1961 to oversee the implementation of **United**

Nations General Assembly Resolution 1514 may receive petitions from individuals and groups and, with the permission of the administering state, conduct onsite visits.

There are now only 16 non-self-governing territories, most of them small island possessions of Great Britain and the **United States**. A Committee on Conventions and Recommendations established by the executive board of the **United Nations Educational, Scientific and Cultural Organization** in 1978 may consider petitions alleging violations of human rights in the fields of education, science, culture and information. Another specialized agency of the United Nations, the **International Labour Organization**, has over time developed an elaborate system of reporting and petitions by workers and employees organizations as part of the monitoring and supervising of the labor conventions it adopted.

See also ADMISSIBILITY REQUIREMENTS; AFRICAN COMMISSION ON HUMAN AND PEOPLE'S RIGHTS; AFRICAN COMMITTEE ON THE RIGHTS AND WELFARE OF THE CHILD; DANISH INSTITUTE FOR HUMAN RIGHTS; ENFORCEMENT; EUROPEAN COMMITTEE ON SOCIAL RIGHTS; EUROPEAN OMBUDSMAN; EUROPEAN SOCIAL CHARTER; INQUIRY PROCEDURES; INTER-AMERICAN COMMISSION ON HUMAN RIGHTS; INTERIM MEASURES; INTERSTATE COMMUNICATIONS; NIGER DELTA CONFLICT; OMBUDSMAN; SPECIAL RAPPORTEURS; UNITED NATIONS COMMITTEE AGAINST TORTURE; UNITED NATIONS COMMITTEE ON ECONOMIC, SOCIAL AND CULTURAL RIGHTS; UNITED NATIONS COMMITTEE ON THE ELIMINATION OF RACIAL DISCRIMINATION; UNITED NATIONS COMMITTEE ON THE PROTECTION OF THE RIGHTS OF ALL MIGRANT WORKERS AND THEIR FAMILIES; UNITED NATIONS COMMITTEE ON THE RIGHTS OF THE CHILD; UNITED NATIONS HUMAN RIGHTS COMMITTEE; UNITED NATIONS WORKING GROUP ON ARBITRARY DETENTION.

COMPLEMENTARITY PRINCIPLE. Basic international criminal law and international jurisprudence tenet whereby international judicial bodies can only exert **jurisdiction** or authority in cases where national bodies are unavailable or have proved to be ineffective. The key purpose of the principle is to act as a spur to domestic justice. *See also* DOMESTIC REMEDIES; EXHAUSTION REQUIREMENT.

CONCENTRATION CAMPS. Term first used in reference to camps set up by the British army during the 1899–1902 **Boer War**. Their purpose was to regroup and confine civilian populations in one place in order to keep them under surveillance and to prevent them from providing any assistance to the Boer insurgents. In so doing, the British drew from and vastly expanded on the system of internment used by Spain in its struggle against **Cuban** insurgents and the **United States** in the **Philippine-American War** (1888–1913). Nazi Germany operated over 300 concentration camps in which it interned or murdered political prisoners, criminals, homosexuals, the mentally ill, slave laborers, gypsies and Jews. *See also* DEPORTATION; ETHNIC CLEANSING; GULAG; HOLOCAUST; KARADZIC, RADOVAN; MAU MAU UPRISING.

CONCLUDING OBSERVATIONS. State reporting procedures in **United Nations treaty bodies** normally begin with a brief introduction by a representative of the reporting state followed by comments and questions by the Committees' members. After listening to answers and explanations provided for by the reporting state, the Committees' members present their own assessment of the state report orally and may request additional information. The whole process, on average, lasts six to nine hours and comes to an end with the issuance of "concluding observations" or "concluding comments" which are first discussed in closed sessions with the reporting state representatives and then published in the Committees' annual reports to the **United Nations General Assembly** (or the **United Nations Economic and Social Council** for the **United Nations Committee on Economic, Social and Cultural Rights**). The "observations" are always organized around the following headings: introduction; positive aspects; factors and difficulties impeding the implementation of the human rights treaty; principal subjects of concern; and suggestions and recommendations.

See also UNITED NATIONS COMMITTEE AGAINST TORTURE; UNITED NATIONS COMMITTEE ON THE ELIMINATION OF ALL FORMS OF DISCRIMINATION AGAINST WOMEN; UNITED NATIONS COMMITTEE ON THE ELIMINATION OF RACIAL DISCRIMINATION; UNITED NATIONS COMMITTEE ON THE RIGHTS OF THE CHILD; UNITED NATIONS HUMAN RIGHTS COMMITTEE.

CONFERENCE OF NON-GOVERNMENTAL ORGANIZATIONS IN CONSULTATIVE RELATIONSHIP WITH THE UNITED NATIONS. Independent, international association of **non-governmental organizations** (NGOs) founded in 1948 to facilitate the participation of NGOs in **United Nations** debates and policy-making processes.

CONGO. *See* DEMOCRATIC REPUBLIC OF THE CONGO.

CONGO FREE STATE. Area now known as the **Democratic Republic of the Congo** which was awarded by the 1885 Berlin Congress to King Leopold II of Belgium as his privately owned kingdom. Under King Leopold's personal rule, a brutal regime was instituted to compel indigenous tribes to procure slave labor for the gathering and exploitation of rubber, ivory and other natural resources. The system relied on the enforcement of quotas by means ranging from mass killings and the taking of hostages to the burning of entire villages to torture, rape and mutilation. The atrocities were exposed in the European and American press, triggering public outcry and diplomatic pressures which eventually led the Belgian Parliament to annex the Congo as a colony of Belgium in 1908. In the absence of a census (the first one was conducted in 1924), estimates of the death toll vary considerably, but many observers noted the steep reduction of the population of the Congo at the beginning of colonial rule and the beginning of the 19th century. The *Encyclopaedia Britannica* cites a total population decline of 8 to 30 million. *See also* COLONIALISM; CONGO REFORM ASSOCIATION; GENOCIDE.

CONGO REFORM ASSOCIATION. Modeled after abolitionist organizations and operating through chapters in the **United States**, Great Britain and several European countries, this grassroots and direct **advocacy** movement was created in 1904 to draw attention to and mobilize political support against the gross **violations of human rights** committed in the **Congo Free State**. One of the Association founders, Edmund Morel, was nominated for the **Nobel Peace Prize** in 1924. A number of prominent writers such as Joseph Conrad (*Heart of Darkness*), Anatole France, Arthur Conan Doyle and Mark Twain wrote novellas in support of the Association.

CONSORTIUM OF MINORITY RESOURCES (COMIR). Internet-based cooperative project bringing together a number of **non-governmental organizations** such as the European Academy, European Roma Rights Center, **Human Rights Watch,** the International Helsinki Federation for Human Rights, **Minority Rights Group International** and the International World Organization against Torture acting as a clearinghouse of information and activities relevant to Europe (the **Organization for Security and Co-operation in Europe** region) in support of the democratic **governance** of multiethnic and multinational societies. COMIR's major initiatives include a virtual library, coordinated mailing lists, a meta-search engine across founders' websites, a Minority Rights Practitioners Resource Pack, a best practice database, curriculum development and **advocacy** training.

CONSORTIUM ON GENDER, SECURITY AND HUMAN RIGHTS.
Umbrella organization set up in 2002 bringing together scholars from five
leading academic centers and programs in the Boston area for the purpose
of integrating the study of women and gender into work on human rights,
security and armed conflict. The five centers involved in the Consortium are
the Women and Public Policy program at the Kennedy School of Government,
Harvard University, which focuses on gender issues in **peacebuilding** and
international security; the Center for Gender in Organizations at the Simmons
School of Management, which deals with organizational practices and human
rights; the Center for Human Rights and Conflict Resolution at the Fletcher
School of Law and Diplomacy, which is concerned with human rights and
justice in situations of conflict prevention and postsettlement peacebuilding;
the Carr Center for Human Rights at the Kennedy School of Government,
Harvard University, which emphasizes changing norms of conflict and
human rights, including postconflict traumas; and the Program on Peace and
Justice at Wellesley College, which researches human rights from the ground
up, with a focus on gender issues, particularly violence against women. *See
also* THINK TANKS.

CONSTITUTIONS. Set of laws often codified in written document (notable
exceptions include Israel and Great Britain) which defines the fundamental
political principles and structures, procedures and distribution of power
within a national state. Drawing from and relying on sources of **international
human rights law** and custom, most national constitutions also guarantee
certain rights to the people and establish independent judiciaries to oversee
their implementation. But, not infrequently, actual practice by government
officials belies the principles and procedures laid down in constitutional
documents.

CONSTRUCTIVISM. Drawing from a sociology of knowledge, this
approach to international relations argues contrary to the assumptions of
realism and **liberalism** that humans generate knowledge and meaning
from their experiences. Neither international structures nor **states'** identities
and interests—especially their sovereignty—are givens. Rather, they are
constructed and evolve through the social practice, socialization and
interaction of a multiplicity of actors. States are prominent in these processes.
But **non-state actors** are also drawn into them, notably **non-governmental
organizations**, transnational **advocacy** networks, **social movements**, and
epistemic communities or issue-specific transnational expert networks. By
assigning a central place to identities and interests in international relations
and arguing that such ideas and processes form a structure of their own, which

in turn impact upon international actors, constructivists show how human rights norms and international organizations are integral parts of international political processes and enjoy a significant though not necessarily complete autonomy. *See also* SPIRAL MODEL OF HUMAN RIGHTS CHANGE.

CONSULTATIVE STATUS. Arrangements made for the participation of **non-governmental organizations** (NGOs) in the proceedings of intergovernmental bodies of international organizations such as the **United Nations**, the **Council of Europe** or the **Organization for Security and Co-operation in Europe** or international conferences pertaining to their access to grounds and facilities, involvement in formal and informal discussions and deliberations, access and use of documentation services, appropriate seating and accommodations provisions. Article 71 of the **United Nations Charter** stipulates that the **United Nations Economic and Social Council** (UN-ECOSOC) "may make suitable arrangements for consultation with non-governmental organizations which are concerned with matters within its competence." A 1968 resolution of the Council amended in 1996 defines the criteria and rights associated with consultative status for NGOs. In the immediate years following the founding of the United Nations, there were only approximately 50 NGOs in consultative status with the UN-ECOSOC. There are currently close to 3,000.

See also AMNESTY INTERNATIONAL; CENTRE ON HOUSING RIGHTS AND EVICTIONS; CHOIKE; CONSUMERS INTERNATIONAL; DECEMBER 18; DEFENCE FOR CHILDREN INTERNATIONAL; EUROPE-THIRD WORLD CENTRE; FEDERATION INTERNATIONALE TERRE DES HOMMES; GLOBAL POLICY FORUM; INTERNATIONAL ASSOCIATION OF DEMOCRATIC LAWYERS; INTERNATIONAL FEDERATION FOR HUMAN RIGHTS; INTERNATIONAL LAW ASSOCIATION; INTERNATIONAL LEAGUE FOR HUMAN RIGHTS; INTERNATIONAL MOVEMENT AGAINST ALL FORMS OF DISCRIMINATION AND RACISM; INTERNATIONAL REHABILITATION COUNCIL FOR TORTURE VICTIMS; INTERNATIONAL SOCIETY FOR HUMAN RIGHTS; INTERNATIONAL TRAINING CENTRE ON HUMAN RIGHTS AND PEACE TEACHING; INTERNATIONAL WORK GROUP FOR INDIGENOUS AFFAIRS; MINORITY RIGHTS GROUP INTERNATIONAL; THIRD WORLD INSTITUTE.

CONSUMERS INTERNATIONAL (CI). World federation of some 220 consumer groups in 115 countries set up to help protect and promote the rights of consumers everywhere, especially their rights of access to basic essential goods and services; adequate food, clothing, shelter, **health** care, **education,** public utilities, water, sanitation and a healthy environment, their right to be informed and to participate in the making and execution of consumer government policies, and their right to **redress** and compensation. Drug marketing and **intellectual property rights, corporate social responsibility** and standards are at the center of CI's current activities. An earlier instance of its actions is its participation in the direct action initiated in protest against the promotion of breast milk substitutes in developing countries.

CI has official representation in many global bodies, including the **United Nations Economic and Social Council** and related **United Nations** agencies and commissions, the **United Nations Conference on Trade and Development,** the **United Nations Children's Fund,** the **United Nations Educational, Scientific and Cultural Organization,** the **World Health Organization,** the Codex Alimentarius Commission, the International Organization for Standardization and the International Electrotechnical Commission. CI is also active at the **World Trade Organization** and, at the regional level, in such organizations as the Community for West African States, the **Organization for Economic Co-operation and Development,** the Latin American Parliament, the Pan American Health Organization and the Association of Southeast Asian Nations.

CONVENTION. Term virtually synonymous with the more generic term of "**treaty**" but used to convey the idea that the instrument was negotiated under the auspices of an international or regional organization and involved the participation of a large number of states.

CONVENTION AGAINST DISCRIMINATION IN EDUCATION (1960). Negotiated under the auspices of the **United Nations Educational, Scientific and Cultural Organization** (UNESCO) and a cornerstone of its Education for All movement, this Convention aims at preventing **discrimination** in **education** and promoting equal treatment in education. It entered into force in 1962, 15 years before the **International Covenant on Economic, Social and Cultural Rights,** which posits that education is a human rights entitlement. The Convention provides a normative framework and essential elements of the right to education, with international obligations while addressing many aspects of discrimination in education including the issues of separate schools based on language, gender and religion, and of private schools. It puts forward the fundamental principles of equality of educational opportunities, non-discrimination, *quality* education, parental choice of education and freedom in education and enjoins states parties to make primary education free and compulsory, secondary education in its different forms generally available and accessible to all and higher education equally accessible to all on the basis of individual capacity. The Convention is monitored by UNESCO and has been widely used in the jurisprudence of national courts. *See also* MILLENNIUM DEVELOPMENT GOALS; MINORITIES; UNITED NATIONS CONVENTION ON THE RIGHTS OF THE CHILD.

CONVENTION FOR THE PROTECTION AND ASSISTANCE OF INTERNALLY DISPLACED PERSONS IN AFRICA. Draft treaty adopted under the aegis of the **African Union** in 2009 designed to "[e]stablish a legal framework for preventing internal displacement, and protecting and assisting internally displaced persons in Africa." Based on the United Nations' "Guiding Principles on Internal Displacement," the Convention seeks to "[p]romote and strengthen regional and national measures to prevent or mitigate, prohibit and eliminate root causes of internal displacement as well as provide for durable solutions." The Convention has weak **accountability** mechanisms and it is still under ratification. *See also* INTERNALLY DISPLACED PERSONS.

CONVENTION FOR THE PROTECTION OF HUMAN RIGHTS AND DIGNITY OF THE HUMAN BEING WITH REGARD TO THE APPLICATION OF BIOLOGY AND MEDICINE. Drawing from the assumption of the primacy of the interests of human beings over the interests of science and society, this 1999 legally binding treaty lays down a series of principles and prohibitions concerning **bioethics**, medical research, consent, rights to private life and information and organ transplants. The Convention bans all forms of discrimination based on a person's genetic makeup and allows predictive genetic tests only for medical purposes, genetic engineering only for preventive, diagnostic or therapeutic reasons and only where it does not aim to change the genetic makeup of a person's descendants.

CONVENTION FOR THE SAFEGUARDING OF INTANGIBLE CULTURAL HERITAGE (2003). First raised by Bolivia in 1973 and debated for 40 years in numerous expert meetings and regional conferences, this **United Nations Educational, Scientific and Cultural Organization** (UNESCO) convention is the first multilateral instrument for the safeguarding of the intangible cultural heritage (i.e., "the practices, representations, expressions, knowledge, skills—as well as the instruments, objects, artifacts and cultural spaces associated therewith—that communities, groups and, in some cases, individuals recognize as part of their cultural heritage"). By "safeguarding," the Convention means "measures aimed at ensuring the viability of the intangible cultural heritage, including the identification, documentation, research, preservation, protection, promotion, enhancement, transmission, particularly through formal and non-formal education, as well as the revitalization of the various aspects of such heritage."

The other purposes of the Convention are to ensure respect for the intangible cultural heritage of the communities, groups and individuals concerned and raise awareness at the local, national and international levels of the importance of the intangible cultural heritage. Criteria and procedures have been developed for the establishment of an inventory of the elements constituting the intangible cultural language including oral traditions and expressions, languages, stories, art styles, music, dances, traditional craftsmanship, knowledge and practices concerning nature and the universe, rituals and festive events, religious beliefs which are not directly embodied in material things which are vulnerable to loss and destruction. The Convention does reflect the **globalization**, driven by growing concerns for preserving cultural diversity, and can be viewed as an extension of UNESCO's long-standing interest in protecting the world's artistic treasures. It can also be construed as a manifestation of the simmering discontent engendered by **intellectual property rights** practices that favor individual or corporate actors over the folk traditions of **indigenous peoples**. *See also* CULTURAL RIGHTS.

CONVENTION GOVERNING THE SPECIFIC ASPECTS OF REFUGEE PROBLEMS IN AFRICA (1969). Treaty negotiated under the aegis of the Organization of African Unity with a view to take account of the special characteristics of Africa in regard to **refugees**. The Convention thus considerably broadens the definition of the 1951 **United Nations Convention Relating to the Status of Refugees** by including people who were compelled to leave their countries not only as a result of persecution (or a fear of it) but also because of external aggression, foreign occupation and domination and events seriously disturbing public order. The Convention also acknowledges that non-state groups may trigger and bring about **persecution**.

CONVENTION ON THE ABOLITION OF SLAVERY (1926). Multilateral treaty negotiated under the auspices of the **League of Nations** which outlawed the **slave trade** and **slavery** "in all its forms." The Convention defined slavery as "the status or condition of a person over whom any or all of the powers attaching to the right of ownership are exercised." It further defined slave trade as "all acts involved in the capture, acquisition or disposal of a person with intent to reduce him to slavery; all acts involved in the acquisition of a slave with a view to selling or exchanging him; all acts of disposal by sale or exchange of a slave acquired with a view to being sold or exchanged, and, in general, every act of trade or transport in slaves." The Convention also highlighted the phenomenon of **forced labor**, stipulating that "forced labour may only be exacted for public purposes" and requiring states parties "to prevent compulsory or forced labour from developing into conditions analogous to slavery." The Convention incorporated in its definition various forms of slavery that had been identified by a League of Nations body in 1924 such as serfdom, practices restrictive of the liberty of the person, or tending to acquire control of the person in conditions analogous to slavery, for example, the acquisition of girls by purchase disguised as payment of dowry, the adoption of children, of either sex, with a view to their virtual enslavement, or the ultimate disposal of their persons and all forms of pledging or reducing to servitude of persons for debt or other reason.

A 1956 **Supplementary Convention on the Abolition of Slavery, the Slave Trade, and Institutions and Practices Similar to Slavery** obliges state parties to abolish slavery and practices and institutions entailing servitude "where they still exist and whether or not they are covered by the definition of slavery contained in Article 1 of the Slavery Convention." Numerous appeals to redefine slavery in the context of today's world have gone unheeded. But it is generally agreed that practices involving restrictions on an individual's right to freedom of movement, control over his or her personal belongings, the absence of informed consent and a full understanding of the nature of a relationship between the parties concerned and threats of violence all constitute slavery. Important normative work has taken place within the framework of a Working Group on Contemporary Forms of Slavery operating under the authority of the **United Nations Commission on Human Rights** (now the **United Nations Human Rights Council**). The 1926 Slavery Convention did not establish procedures for reviewing the incidence of slavery in states' parties. Slavery and slavery-related practices are now monitored by a number of **United Nations treaty bodies** such as the **United Nations Human Rights Committee** and the **United Nations Committee on the Rights of the Child** as well as the institutions overseeing the implementation of the **International Labour Organization**'s conventions dealing with forced labor, **migrants** and child labor. *See also* ANTI-SLAVERY INTERNATIONAL.

CONVENTION ON THE PROTECTION AND PROMOTION OF THE DIVERSITY OF CULTURAL EXPRESSION (2005). The product of two years of sometimes acrimonious negotiations, this controversial treaty, concluded under the auspices of **United Nations Educational, Scientific and Cultural Organization**, establishes a series of rights and obligations, at both the national and international levels, aimed at protecting and promoting cultural diversity and in particular the creation, production, distribution or dissemination, access and enjoyment of cultural expressions. One hundred and forty-eight countries voted in favor. The **United States** and **Israel** opposed it, while four countries (Australia, Nicaragua, Honduras and Liberia) abstained. Supporters of the treaty viewed it as a victory for free expression and claimed that it would help governments protect national cultural identities and traditions from the homogenizing pressures of globalization and foreign competition. Opponents feared that the treaty might circumvent the **World Trade Organization**'s rules on the elimination of subsidies and liberalization of tariffs and that it could be used as a pretext for government censorship and arbitrary protection from free trade and curb the flow of goods, services and ideas, especially films, music, radio, books, television programming and other cultural goods, which the Convention presents as expressions of cultural identity rather than global trade products. *See also* CULTURAL RIGHTS; FREEDOM OF EXPRESSION.

CONVENTION ON THE PROTECTION OF CHILDREN AGAINST SEXUAL EXPLOITATION AND SEXUAL ABUSE. Treaty adopted and opened for signature in 2007 by the **Council of Europe**. Focusing on the principle of the best interests of the child, the Convention aims at preventing sexual exploitation and sexual abuse of children, protecting child victims of sexual offenses and prosecuting perpetrators. Its provisions deal with preventive and protective measures; assistance to child victims and their families; intervention programs or measures for child sex offenders; criminal offenses, including several new offenses, such as child grooming; child-friendly procedures for **investigation** and **prosecution**; and recording and storing of data on convicted sex offenders. The Convention provides for a **monitoring** mechanism. *See also* HUMAN TRAFFICKING; UNITED NATIONS CONVENTION ON THE RIGHTS OF THE CHILD.

CORPORAL PUNISHMENT. Infliction of physical pain for the purpose of retribution, disciplining or deterring attitudes and behavior deemed to be unacceptable. Judicial corporal punishment—a criminal sentence imposed by a court of law—remains a feature of many national legal systems. Treaty bodies, notably the **United Nations Human Rights Committee**, have found it a practice amounting to "cruel, inhumane and degrading treatment or punishment." They have been more disposed to accept limited corporal punishment of children by parents or schools. *See also* CAIRO DECLARATION ON HUMAN RIGHTS IN ISLAM; UNITED NATIONS CONVENTION AGAINST TORTURE AND OTHER CRUEL, INHUMAN OR DEGRADING TREATMENT AND PUNISHMENT.

CORPORATE RESPONSIBILITY REPORTING. Ongoing program of the **United Nations Conference on Trade and Development** (UNCTAD) addressing a variety of issues in corporate accounting and reporting with a view to promoting increased transparency and financial disclosure. UNCTAD's work in this area takes place within the broader international context of work carried out by other international organizations including the **Organization for Economic Co-operation and Development**'s "Guidelines for Multinational Enterprises," the **International Labour Organization**'s "Tripartite Declaration" and the **United Nations Global Compact**. Specifically, UNCTAD's efforts, in partnership with member states, academic institutions, and enterprises, have focused on promoting development of corporate responsibility indicators in annual reports through high-level summits, technical workshops and research projects focused on corporate reporting. *See also* CORPORATE SOCIAL RESPONSIBILITY.

CORPORATE SOCIAL RESPONSIBILITY (CSR). Also known as corporate responsibility, corporate citizenship, responsible business, sustainable responsible business, the term, as defined by the **World Business Council for Sustainable Development**, means "the continuing commitment by business to behave ethically and contribute to economic development while improving the quality of life of the workforce and their families as well as of the local community and society at large." CSR refers to a variety of built-in mechanisms of corporate self-regulation put in place in the past two decades by private corporations to promote their adherence to national and international human rights norms and standards. Proponents argue that CSR is sound business practice with a marked impact on human rights protection. Critics counter that CSR, without internationally defined restrictions on **transnational corporations**, is merely a set of self-serving public relations.

See also ACCOUNTABILITY; ACTION FOR SOUTHERN AFRICA; ALIEN TORT STATUTE; BUSINESS AND HUMAN RIGHTS RESOURCE CENTRE; CENTER FOR HUMAN RIGHTS AND THE ENVIRONMENT; CODES OF CONDUCT FOR TRANSNATIONAL CORPORATIONS; CONSUMERS INTERNATIONAL; CORPORATE RESPONSIBILITY REPORTING; CORPWATCH; CORRUPTION; DRAFT NORMS ON THE RESPONSIBILITIES OF TRANSNATIONAL CORPORATIONS AND OTHER BUSINESS ENTERPRISES WITH REGARD TO HUMAN RIGHTS; ENVIRONMENT, RIGHT TO A HEALTHY; EQUATOR PRINCIPLES; EXTRACTIVE INDUSTRIES TRANSPARENCY INITIATIVE; GLOBAL POLICY FORUM; GLOBAL WITNESS; ILO TRIPARTITE DECLARATION OF PRINCIPLES CONCERNING MULTINATIONAL ENTERPRISES AND SOCIAL POLICY; INSTITUTE

FOR HUMAN RIGHTS AND BUSINESS; INTERFAITH CENTER ON CORPORATE RESPONSIBILITY; INTERNATIONAL COMMISSION OF JURISTS; INTERNATIONAL FEDERATION FOR HUMAN RIGHTS; INTERNATIONAL LABOUR ORGANIZATION; KIMBERLEY PROCESS CERTIFICATION SCHEME; REVENUE WATCH; UNITED NATIONS CONFERENCE ON TRADE AND DEVELOPMENT CORPORATE RESPONSIBILITY REPORTING; UNITED NATIONS GLOBAL COMPACT; UNITED NATIONS "PROTECT, RESPECT AND REMEDY" FRAMEWORK FOR BUSINESS AND HUMAN RIGHTS; WORLD BUSINESS COUNCIL FOR SUSTAINABLE DEVELOPMENT; WORLD FEDERALIST MOVEMENT; WORLD SOCIAL FORUM.

CORPWATCH. Initially known as the Transnational Resource and Action Center, this media **non-governmental organization** monitors, investigates, publicizes and organizes campaigns against corporate **violations of human rights**, environmental crimes, fraud and **corruption** through investigative journalism, public education and networking. Thus, CorpWatch has drawn attention to working conditions in Nike's operations in Vietnam and on the corporate practices of the Enron Corporation prior to its collapse. CorpWatch currently investigates **transnational corporations** that profit from the wars in **Afghanistan** and Iraq and the **"war on terrorism."**

CORRUPTION. There is no universally agreed upon definition of what constitutes corruption nor is there any consensus about what specific acts should be included or excluded from its manifestations. The **United Nations,** the **Council of Europe** and the **Organization for Economic Development and Co-operation** (OECD) merely establish a range of corrupt offenses. An OECD Convention established the offense of bribery of foreign public officials as corruption. The Council of Europe added trading in influence and bribing domestic public officials. The 2003 **United Nations Convention against Transnational Organized Crime** covers embezzlement, misappropriation of property and obstruction of justice and obligates state parties to implement a wide and detailed range of anti-corruption measures. The purpose of these rather weak instruments is to promote prevention, the criminalization and law enforcement, international cooperation, technical assistance and information exchange. The UN Convention establishes asset recovery as one of its "fundamental principles" and lays out a framework, in both civil and criminal laws, for tracing, freezing, forfeiting and returning funds obtained through corrupt activities. The provision on asset recovery was a prime concern of **developing countries** where high-level corruption is a common phenomenon. A network of some 300 civil society organizations was created in 2006 to promote the ratification, implementation and monitoring of the Convention.

See also ABACHA, SANI; BOKASSA, JEAN-BEDEL; CORPWATCH; DEMOCRATIC REPUBLIC OF THE CONGO; DUVALIER, JEAN-CLAUDE; DUVALIER, FRANCOIS; FUJIMORI, ALBERTO; GOVERNANCE; HERITAGE FOUNDATION; INDONESIA; INTERNATIONAL COUNCIL ON HUMAN RIGHTS POLICY; MARCOS; FERDINAND; MOBUTU SESE SEKO; NGUEMA, FRANCISCO MACIAS; NIGER DELTA CONFLICT; ORGANIZATION OF AMERICAN STATES; PRIVATIZATION; REVENUE WATCH; STROESSNER, ALFREDO; SUHARTO; TRANSNATIONAL CRIME; TRANSPARENCY INTERNATIONAL.

COTE D'IVOIRE. Former French colony which became independent in 1960. Close to the West and France in particular, the country entered a period of political instability in the late 1990s, experiencing a coup in 1999 and a civil war that broke out in 2002. The armed conflict was triggered by economic setbacks that can be traced back to the 1980s which intensified ethnic rivalries and caused tensions with foreign migrant workers in the northern part of the country. A **United Nations**–prodded political agreement between the government and the rebels who were in control of the northern part of Cote d'Ivoire brought a precarious return to peace. Presidential elections that should have been held in 2005 finally did take place in 2010. Their outcome was contested by the outgoing President Laurent Gbagbo who had lost to his opponent Alassane Ouattara, thus leading to the establishment of parallel governments and another round of violence. The fighting was marked by widespread **violations of human rights** by both sides and massive displacements of population within and outside the country which were documented by the human rights component of the **United Nations Operation in Cote d'Ivoire** and a **fact-finding** international commission dispatched by the **United Nations Human Rights Council**.

Echoing positions taken by the **Economic Community of West African States** and the **African Union**, the **United Nations Security Council** adopted a resolution recognizing Alassane Ouattara as the winner of the elections. UN and French forces took military action against the Gbagbo regime. The capture of Gbagbo and close associates put an end to the hostilities. With the assistance of the **United Nations Office of the High Commissioner for Human Rights**, transitional justice institutions and a Dialogue **Truth and Reconciliation Commission** have been set up with a view to facilitate national reconciliation and foster social cohesion. Accused of murder, rape and other forms of sexual violence, persecution and other inhumane acts, the former president of Cote d'Ivoire has been incarcerated in the Netherlands awaiting trial by the **International Criminal Court.**

COUNCIL OF EUROPE. Set up in 1949 by the Treaty of London, this is the first regional international organization that was established to promote European integration with a particular emphasis on the promotion and protection of human rights, **democracy** and the **rule of law.** Initially comprising 10 states (Belgium, Denmark, France, Ireland, Italy, Luxembourg, the Netherlands, Norway, Sweden and Great Britain), the Council membership vastly expanded in the wake of the end of the **Cold War** and the democratic transitions in Eastern and Central Europe. Located in Strasbourg, the Council now integrates nearly all states of Europe (there are now 47 members). Prerequisites for membership include acceptance of the rule of law and the active protection of human rights and fundamental freedoms.

In fact, the Council of Europe has developed the most advanced system for the international protection of human rights. The cornerstone of the system is the **European Court of Human Rights**, established in accordance with the 1950 **European Convention for the Protection of Human Rights and Fundamental Freedoms** negotiated under the aegis of the Council. Other international human rights instruments and bodies developed through the Council include the **European Committee for the Prevention of Torture**, the Convention on Action against Trafficking in Human Beings, the Convention on the Protection of Children against Sexual Exploitation and Sexual Abuse, the **European Social Charter**, the **European Charter for Regional or Minority Languages**, and the **Framework Convention on the Protection of National Minorities**. The Parliamentary Assembly, the Council's legislative body, has evolved a system of **special rapporteurs** with the mandate to prepare parliamentary reports on specific subjects. Recent reports on secret detentions in Europe and **extraordinary rendition** flights through Europe have received considerable attention. Other Assembly rapporteurs have played an instrumental role in the abolition of the death penalty in Europe, the political and human rights situation in **Chechnya**, disappeared persons in Belarus and **freedom of expression** in the media. Since 1999, the Parliamentary Assembly elects a commissioner for human rights for a nonrenewable term of six years.

See also COMMITTEE ON THE ADMINISTRATION OF JUSTICE; COUNCIL OF EUROPE COMMISSIONER FOR HUMAN RIGHTS; COUNTERTERRORISM; EUROPEAN COMMISSION AGAINST RACISM AND INTOLERANCE; EUROPEAN CONVENTION FOR THE PREVENTION OF TORTURE AND INHUMAN OR DEGRADING TREATMENT OR PUNISHMENT; INTERNATIONAL REHABILITATION

COUNCIL FOR TORTURE VICTIMS; INTERNATIONAL SOCIETY FOR HUMAN RIGHTS.

COUNCIL OF EUROPE COMMISSIONER FOR HUMAN RIGHTS. Office established in 1999 by the **Committee of Ministers of the Council of Europe** with the broad mandate to identify shortcomings in the human rights law and practices of the Council's member states, to promote the implementation of human rights standards and education in awareness of human rights and to encourage the creation of national human rights institutions. The Commissioner reports regularly to the Committee of Ministers and the Parliamentary Assembly on individual states' human rights policies and issues opinions with remedial recommendations on specific national legislative shortcomings. *See also* FACT FINDING.

COUNCIL ON FOREIGN RELATIONS. Prestigious and influential American **think tank** founded in 1921 to act as "a resource for its members, government officials, business executives, journalists, educators and students, civic and religious leaders, and other interested citizens in order to help them better understand the world and the foreign policy choices facing the **United States** and other countries." Headquartered in New York City, the Council, which has some 5,000 members, carries out a wide range of activities. It convenes meetings that bring together senior government officials, members of Congress, global leaders, and prominent thinkers to discuss and debate major international issues and supports a studies program composed of about 50 adjunct and full-time scholars, as well as 10 in-resident recipients of yearlong fellowships who produce numerous articles, reports and books on virtually all significant issues on the international agenda. The Council publishes *Foreign Affairs*, a prominent journal in international affairs.

COUNTERTERRORISM. Practices, techniques and tactics used by governments, militaries and police to prevent, deter and respond to potential terrorist threats and or attacks. Counterterrorism policies generally involve a sharp increase in standard police and domestic intelligence, and many countries—Canada, the **United States**, Great Britain, France, Australia, Russia and the **European Union**, among others—have adopted legislation on phone tapping, police surveillance, encryption technology, detention of migrants, control of the Internet, **freedom of movement** and the monitoring of financial transfers. These measures have received the imprimatur of or were taken in implementation of binding **United Nations Security Council** resolutions (notably Resolution 1373 of 28 September 2001) requiring all states to prevent **terrorism** and report on the steps they take to do so.

Critics argue that these measures have led to abuses of power and **violations of human rights** such as restrictions on dissent, breaches of the principle of non-**discrimination**, prolonged, incommunicado detention without judicial review, **extra-judicial executions**, and **extraordinary rendition** to countries known to practice **torture**. They also point out that they are self-defeating in the fight against terrorism. In their view, counterterrorism policies, at both the national and international levels, would be more effective if they incorporated built-in human rights protection mechanisms. Counterterrorism may also be embedded in broader security strategies to suppress armed insurgencies, as has been the case in Latin American countries in the 1970s and 1980s. In such cases, counterterrorism practices have been accompanied by massive violations of human rights. *See also* ARGENTINA; BRAZIL; COLOMBIA; COURT OF JUSTICE; HABEAS CORPUS; INTERNATIONAL COMMISSION OF JURISTS; KADI CASE; ORGANIZATION FOR SECURITY AND CO-OPERATION IN EUROPE; PERU; PRIVACY, RIGHT TO; REMEDY; STATE TERRORISM; UNITED NATIONS SUB-COMMISSION ON THE PROMOTION AND PROTECTION OF HUMAN RIGHTS; URUGUAY.

COUNTRY-BASED MECHANISMS. *See* NATIONAL HUMAN RIGHTS INSTITUTIONS.

COURT OF JUSTICE (CJ). Judicial arm of the **European Union** (EU) originally known as the European Court of Justice, which was established in 1952 as part of the European Coal and Steel Community. Its functions have evolved over time with the process of European integration, but its basic concern is to ensure compliance by the 27 members of the EU to the rules laid down in the treaties of the European Union and that they uniformly apply EU legislation. Direct access to the Court by individuals is severely restricted because national courts are primarily responsible for adjudicating matters related to the European Union and only national Courts of Final Appeal can make the discretionary decision to refer a question of EU law to the CJ. The CJ rulings, however, have often been portrayed (with dismay by some) as major steps toward greater European integration.

Although the Court draws from and is guided by the "fundamental rights enshrined in the general principles of Community law," the constitutional traditions common to the European Union's member states and the human rights treaties they have ratified, the Court has only occasionally ventured into human rights issues. The situation may change when the uncertain and ambiguous status of the **European Convention for the Protection of Human Rights and Fundamental Freedoms** is further clarified with the implementation of the **Lisbon Treaty**. Notwithstanding the fact that there is no clear list of rights that could be deemed to be legally binding on the European Union, the Court has issued landmark decisions on **counterterrorism**. In 2006, the CJ determined that the European Union had overstepped its authority by agreeing to give the **United States** personal details about airline passengers on flights to America. In 2008, it ruled that a EU regulation implementing a counterterrorism resolution of the **United Nations Security Council** that had placed an appellant on a list whose funds were to be frozen on suspicion of financing terrorism did not sufficiently respect fundamental rights, notably his right to be heard, his right to property, and his right to an effective legal **remedy**. *See also* KADI CASE.

CRIMES AGAINST HUMANITY. As generally understood in **international law**, crimes against humanity refer to specific acts of violence such as murder, **torture** and enforced disappearances that are the product of **persecution** of an identifiable group of persons. Such crimes are considered **non-derogable rights** of international law and as such are subject to **universal jurisdiction**; they allow no immunity from prosecution or **amnesty**, even to heads of state, and are not subject to statutes of limitation and do not recognize "obedience to superior's orders" as a defense. No statutory limitations apply to crimes against humanity under the terms of the 1970 **United Nations** Convention on the Non-Applicability of Statutory Limitations to War Crimes and Crimes against Humanity and the 1974 European Convention on the Non-Applicability of Statutory Limitation to Crimes against Humanity and War Crimes.

See also AL-ANFAL CAMPAIGN; ALIEN TORT STATUTE; APARTHEID; AUSSARESSES, PAUL; BARBIE, KLAUS; BURUNDI; COMMAND RESPONSIBILITY; CRIMES AGAINST PEACE; DEMJANJUK, JOHN; DEPORTATION; EXTRADITION; FORCED DISAPPEARANCES; GLOBAL ACTION TO PREVENT WAR; HUMAN RIGHTS WATCH; IENG SARY; INTERNATIONAL CONVENTION ON THE SUPPRESSION AND PUNISHMENT OF THE CRIME OF APARTHEID; INTERNATIONAL CRIMINAL COURT; INTERNATIONAL CRIMINAL TRIBUNAL FOR RWANDA; INTERNATIONAL CRIMINAL TRIBUNAL FOR THE FORMER YUGOSLAVIA; INTERNATIONAL MILITARY TRIBUNAL FOR THE FAR EAST; INTERNATIONAL MILITARY TRIBUNAL FOR THE PROSECUTION AND PUNISHMENT OF THE MAJOR WAR CRIMINALS OF THE EUROPEAN AXIS; *JUS COGENS*; KAMBANDA, JEAN; KIM IL SUNG; MILOSEVIC, SLOBODAN; MLADIC, RATKO; MUSEMA CASE; NUREMBERG PRINCIPLES; PAPON, MAURICE; SPECIAL COURT FOR SIERRA LEONE; STERILIZATION; TRANSNATIONAL CRIME;

UGANDA; UNIVERSAL JURISDICTION; WAR CRIME TRIBUNALS; WAR CRIMES; WORLD CONFERENCE AGAINST RACISM.

CRIMES AGAINST PEACE. Also known as crimes of **aggression**, crimes against peace was the first charge made against the Nazis in the 1945 Charter of the Nuremberg Tribunal. As the Charter defined them, such crimes involved the "planning, preparation, initiation or waging of a war of aggression or a war in violation of international treaties, agreements or assurance." Until then (and notwithstanding the fact that the victorious Allied Powers in 1918 had toyed with the idea of bringing **Kaiser Wilhelm** to trial for having led his country to war), starting a war was not regarded as an international criminal offense. The 1928 **Kellog-Briand Pact** had only outlawed war and made aggression an illegal act for states. The idea of prosecuting government officials with the crime of starting World War II was therefore immediately controversial and prompted charges of double standards, "victors" justice and retroactive application of criminal law. This debate has not subsided, essentially because defining aggression has, to this day, remained an elusive undertaking.

One of the key conditions for membership in the **United Nations** is that state members of the organization must, as provided for in the **United Nations Charter**, give up the use of force and rely on peaceful methods for settlement of their disputes. Germany's invasion of Poland in 1939, North Korea's invasion of South Korea in 1950, and Iraq's invasion of Kuwait in 1990 would seem to constitute fairly unambiguous cases fitting the definition of aggression found in a 1974 resolution of the **United Nations General Assembly**. But in other cases, states disagree over a whole range of politically charged issues. Who should take the lead in determining whether acts of aggression have occurred: the **United Nations Security Council**, the **International Criminal Court** (ICC), or some other body? The five permanent members of the Council predictably argue that the Council should determine when an act of aggression has taken place. Less powerful countries and **non-governmental organizations** as well aver that this "politicizes" the process and puts too much control in a handful of powerful countries.

Where is the line separating "guilty" from "not guilty" individuals to be drawn since wars are typically planned by many individuals in state bureaucracies? What is a "manifest violation" of the UN Charter? On these points, countries remain divided, and they bicker as to whether there should be higher thresholds depending on the intended purpose behind the act of aggression. Growing concerns about the spread of weapons of mass destruction, the multiplication of failed or weak states, **terrorism** and the inconclusive debates about an "emerging" norm of a right of intervention for humanitarian purposes have further dimmed prospects for reaching a collective sense of moral and political clarity about subject matter in ways reminiscent of the interminable (and unsettled) disputes that flared in the 1950s and 1960s about whether colonialism constituted an act of aggression. These conceptual and operational uncertainties, in addition to the aloofness of the big powers that show little inclination to accept norms that might constrain the exercise of their power, explain why the Rome Statute of the ICC, while granting jurisdiction to the Court over the crime of aggression, allows it to exert this power only after an agreement has been reached on a definition that should also be consistent with the UN Charter. These negotiations are still unfolding. *See also* COMMAND RESPONSIBILITY; INTERNATIONAL MILITARY TRIBUNAL FOR THE FAR EAST; NUREMBERG PRINCIPLES.

CROATIA, WAR OF INDEPENDENCE (1991–1995). Armed conflict between forces loyal to the government of Croatia, which had declared its independence from Yugoslavia, with the assistance of local Serb forces. While Serbia and Croatia never declared war on each other, Serbia was directly and indirectly involved in the war through the provision of manpower, funding and material support. The war ended with a total Croatian victory causing around 20,000 deaths and 500,000 refugees and displaced persons. Both sides committed well-documented **war crimes** against civilians and prisoners of war. As of 2011, the **International Criminal Tribunal for the Former Yugoslavia** has convicted seven officials from the Serb/Montenegrin side and two from the Croatian side. *See also* MILOSEVIC, SLOBODAN.

CRUEL, INHUMAN OR DEGRADING TREATMENT OR PUNISHMENT. *See* TORTURE.

CUBA. Ever since it gained independence from Spain in 1902, Cuba has most of the time been ruled by authoritarian or dictatorial regimes which have been criticized and condemned for serious **violations of human rights**. Human rights **non-governmental organizations** have been particularly critical of the Fidel Castro regime, singling out the high number of political executions (estimated to be between 15,000 and 17,000 from 1858 to 1987) and a wide array of abuses including **torture**, arbitrary imprisonment, unfair trials and restrictive measures on **freedom of movement, association** and **expression**. The recent transfer of power from Fidel Castro to his brother Raul in 2006 has not brought about significant changes. Since 1990, in the **United Nations Human Rights Council**, Cuba has had to fend off efforts led by the **United States** to censure its human rights record. Some members of the Council back the criticism, but others portray it as a manipulation of human rights issues designed to justify the isolation of the island and the decades-old embargo imposed by the United States. Not surprisingly, Cuba has joined forces with such countries as Russia, China and Pakistan in taking positions inimical to Western views and policies on human rights issues and in emphasizing the primacy of the principle of noninterference in the domestic affairs of **United Nations** members. See also ANGOLA; SEX TOURISM.

CULTURAL PROPERTY. The Hague Convention for the Protection of Cultural Property in the Event of Armed Conflict of 1954 defined cultural property as covering "irrespective of origin or ownership: (a) movable or immovable property of great importance to the cultural heritage of every people, such as monuments of architecture, art or history, whether religious or secular; archaeological sites; groups of buildings which, as a whole, are of historical or artistic interest; works of art; manuscripts, books and other objects of artistic, historical or archaeological interest; as well as scientific collections and important collections of books or archives or of reproductions of the property defined above; (b) buildings whose main and effective purpose is to preserve or exhibit . . . movable cultural property . . . such as museums, large libraries and depositories of archives." The Convention prohibits acts of hostility directed against historic monuments' works of art or places of worship and their use for military purposes.

Massive violations of cultural rights nevertheless often occur in countries occupied in the course of international armed conflicts, as was the case in Iraqi-occupied Kuwait in 1990–91 and in the wake of the **United States** invasion of Iraq in 2003. A **United Nations Educational, Educational and Scientific Organization** convention bans the illicit import, export and transfer of ownership of cultural property. The convention lets museums acquire objects that were outside their countries of origin before 1970 (the date of entry in force of the convention) but many countries—Egypt, Greece, Italy, Turkey, among others—have demanded with varying degrees of success the return of artifacts removed from their borders. *See also* CULTURAL RIGHTS; ETHNIC CLEANSING; INTERNATIONAL COVENANT ON ECONOMIC, SOCIAL AND CULTURAL RIGHTS; PROPERTY, RIGHT TO.

CULTURAL RELATIVISM. Assertion that human values are not universal but vary considerably from one culture to another. The definition of human rights accordingly hinges on different cultural, ethnic and religious traditions. One of the essential premises of the doctrine is that the basic unit of society is the group or the community rather than the individual possessing inalienable rights and being driven by the pursuit of self-interest. Such key human rights notions as individualism and freedom of choice and equality are alien to cultural relativism and, in any case, in the absence of "common definitional standards," human rights cannot be truly universal and will remain culture bound. The doctrine usually goes hand in hand with reassertions of **state sovereignty** and leads to the rejection of human rights **advocacy** as a interference in domestic affairs or forms of Western imperialism. *See also* AFRICAN CHARTER ON THE RIGHTS AND WELFARE OF THE CHILD; ARAB CHARTER ON HUMAN RIGHTS; ASIAN VALUES; BANGKOK DECLARATION; CAIRO DECLARATION ON HUMAN RIGHTS IN ISLAM; INDIVISIBILITY; ORGANIZATION OF ISLAMIC COOPERATION.

CULTURAL REVOLUTION (1966–1975). Term referring to the struggle for power within the Communist Party of the People's Republic of China which mobilized large sections of Chinese society and brought the country to the brink of civil war. Millions are believed to have died or been imprisoned in the chaos that gripped China for close to 10 years. The Party officially repudiated the Cultural Revolution in 1981, blaming it in part on **Mao Zedong**.

CULTURAL RIGHTS. Probably the least understood and developed of the rights protected under international human rights law. The problem arises in part because of the complexity and varying understandings of the term "culture." Culture embraces all aspects of life of an individual and a community. It is also linked to one's sense of individual and collective identity and perennial questions of power and dominance. The phenomenon of **globalization** has also had a deep impact on cultural values. Cultural rights thus intersect (and at times conflict) with numerous other individual rights such as freedom of thought, **freedom of religion**, **education**, **food**, **health**, and **adequate housing** as well as collective rights including the rights of **minorities**, women and **indigenous peoples**.

Not surprisingly, while cultural rights are enshrined in numerous legal instruments, none of them provides a concise definition of culture. The **Universal Declaration of Human Rights** simply asserts that "everyone has the right freely to participate in the cultural life of the community, to enjoy the arts and to share in scientific advancement and its benefits" and "the right to the protection of the moral and material interests resulting from any scientific, literary or artistic production of which he is the author."

The **International Covenant on Economic, Social and Cultural Rights** (ICESCR) is hardly more expansive as it says in part that state parties recognize the right of everyone: "(a) to take part in cultural life; (b) to enjoy the benefits of scientific progress and its applications; (c) to benefit from the protection of the moral and material interests resulting from any scientific, literary or artistic production of which he is the author." Other relevant international principles or declarations include the **United Nations Convention on the Punishment and Prevention of the Crime of Genocide**, which has been interpreted to forbid the deliberate destruction of a people's culture. The **Declaration on the Right to Development** posits that the right to development is an inalienable human right by virtue of which every person and all peoples are entitled to participate in, contribute to, and enjoy economic, social, cultural and political development. At the regional level, the **African Charter on Human and People's Rights** and the **American Declaration of the Rights and Duties of Man** also recognize cultural rights.

The practical test of state compliance with the ICESCR's sanctioned right to enjoy one's culture has been evidenced in that a community's culture is not suffering from state oppression. In the ***Lovelace v. Canada*** case, the **United Nations Human Rights Committee** found Canadian law in violation of the ICESCR because it contributed to "the loss of the cultural benefits of living in an Indian Community, the emotional ties to home, family, friends and neighbors, and the loss of cultural identity." In regard to the right to profess and practice religion, the provision or prohibition of religious instruction in schools, the existence of places of worship for the community, and the absence of laws prohibiting religious rites and acts have been used as guideposts to measure state observance of the Covenant.

See also CONVENTION FOR THE SAFEGUARDING OF INTANGIBLE CULTURAL HERITAGE; CONVENTION ON THE PROTECTION AND PROMOTION OF THE DIVERSITY OF CULTURAL EXPRESSIONS; CULTURAL PROPERTY; DECLARATION ON THE RIGHTS OF PERSONS BELONGING TO NATIONAL OR ETHNIC, RELIGIOUS AND LINGUISTIC MINORITIES; EUROPEAN CHARTER FOR REGIONAL OR MINORITY LANGUAGES; FRAMEWORK CONVENTION ON THE PROTECTION OF NATIONAL MINORITIES; SELF-DETERMINATION.

CUSTOMARY INTERNATIONAL LAW (CIL). One of the main sources of international law in addition to **treaties**. The term essentially refers to informal unwritten rules which become binding because they are adhered to out of practice. When enough states have begun to behave as though it were approximating a law, it becomes law "by use." Unlike treaty rules that result from formal negotiations and explicit acceptance through the ratification process, rules of customary law arise out of behavioral regularity and expressed or inferred acknowledgments of legality. Evidence of state "practice" may be found in official policy statements, official manuals on legal questions, executive decisions, press releases, court decisions, legislative acts, the opinions of legislative advisers, diplomatic correspondence, and votes on resolutions relating to legal questions in the **United Nations General Assembly**. A customary rule becomes law when there is a shared conviction that an action is carried out because it is a legal obligation. For example, laws of war were long a matter of customary law before they were codified in the **Geneva Conventions** and other treaties.

The vast majority of the world's governments accept in principle the existence of customary international law, although there are many differing opinions as to what rules are contained in it. CIL is particularly important in areas where multilateral treaties of a general scope have yet to be negotiated. Such is the case, for instance, of state **immunity** and **state responsibility**. CIL is also important in human rights because many states are not parties to existing treaties. The prohibition of **genocide**, **slavery** or **slave trade**, causing **forced disappearances**, consistent patterns of gross internationally recognized **violations of human rights**, **racial discrimination**, **torture**, and prolonged arbitrary detentions are core human rights subjects considered to be governed in part by CIL. But to the extent that state obligations are linked to usage, the determination of a customary rule may be a very difficult and contentious process. There are ongoing disputes in particular about the kind of evidence, whose practice and for how long can be cited to support the existence of a customary rule. These unresolved issues, in part, account for the fact that the human rights field has increasingly been dominated by multilateral treaties that have codified customary standards and rules and developed new ones in international conferences. *See also* TRANSNATIONAL CRIME.

D

DAES, ERICA-IRENE. Greek legal scholar and diplomat who represented her country in a number of subsidiary bodies of the **United Nations General Assembly** and the **United Nations Economic and Social Council**. She chaired and for almost two decades (1984–2002) served as **special rapporteur** of the United Nations Working Group on Indigenous Populations of the **United Nations Commission on Human Rights** where the **Declaration on the Rights of Indigenous Peoples** was negotiated. In that capacity, she provided representatives of indigenous peoples unprecedented access, voice and presence in the **United Nations**. *See also* NORM ENTREPRENEURS.

DALAI LAMA (1935–). Current leader of Tibetan Buddhism who won the **Nobel Peace Prize** in 1989. He is well known for his lifelong advocacy for Tibet's **self-determination**.

DANISH INSTITUTE FOR HUMAN RIGHTS (DIHR). One of the largest and most widely respected **national human rights institutions** set up in 1987 in accordance with the so-called **Paris Principles**. The work of the DIHR includes **research**, analysis, information, education, documentation, and **complaints** handling, as well as a large number of national and international programs.

DARFUR CONFLICT (2003–). Ongoing struggle pitting insurgent groups against the Sudanese government and militia groups which they accuse of oppressing non-Arab Sudanese of the region in favor of Sudanese Arabs. The rebellion has been met by the deployment of troops, indiscriminate air strikes and the arming of local Arab militias conducting a scorched earth policy. Over 5 million people have been affected by the conflict, which has triggered mass displacements and coercive migrations creating a huge humanitarian crisis. Estimates of fatalities vary between over 150,000 and half a million, 80 percent of these due to disease. The response of the international community to what many portray as a "**genocide** in slow motion" has been erratic and piecemeal, contrasting sharply with the loud calls from **advocacy non-**

governmental organizations such as the Genocide Intervention Network and the Save Darfur Coalition for an armed humanitarian intervention.

The **United Nations Security Council** is divided, and Western powers lack the political will to intervene forcefully. A precarious ceasefire monitored by an overstretched United Nations peacekeeping operation prevails, while an arms embargo imposed by the Security Council is widely believed to have been repeatedly breached. In 2005, the Council (with the **United States** and China abstaining) formally referred the situation in Darfur to the **International Criminal Court** (ICC). In 2007, the ICC issued arrest warrants against the former minister of state for the interior of Sudan and militia leader for **crimes against humanity** and **war crimes**. On 14 July 2008, the prosecutor filed charges of war crimes, genocide, crimes against humanity and murder against Omar al-Bashir, Sudan's incumbent president. The **African Union** has publicly stated its opposition to the actions of the ICC, and some analysts believe that the ICC indictment could harm the peace efforts. *See also* AFRICAN UNION-UNITED NATIONS HYBRID OPERATION IN DARFUR; HUMAN RIGHTS FIRST.

DEATH SQUADS. Armed paramilitary units carrying out kidnapping, **torture**, **forced disappearances** and **extra-judicial executions** which gained notoriety in Central and South American countries in the 1970s and 1980s. Their activities, targeted at insurgents and political opponents of military, dictatorial and totalitarian regimes, often had the tacit or express support of state authorities and foreign powers, especially in the context of the **Cold War**. They were conducted in such a way as to hide the killers' identity and preclude any **accountability**. Historical instances of atrocities committed by death squads occurred during the Irish War of Independence, the Spanish civil war, the **Algerian civil war**, the Shah Mohammad Reza Pahlavi's rule in Iran (1941–79) and the Soviet occupation of **Afghanistan** in the 1980s. Death squads were notoriously active in **Argentina** and **Chile** under military rule and the civil wars of **El Salvador** (1980–92), **Guatemala** (1960–96), **Honduras**, Lebanon (1975–90), **Peru** and the former Yugoslavia. The incidence of **violations of human rights** by death squads appears to have declined in recent years, but cases have been reported in **Chechnya**, the **Democratic Republic of the Congo, Colombia**, Iraq and Sudan. *See also* DARFUR CONFLICT; SREBRENICA; STATE TERRORISM; SUHARTO.

DECEMBER 18. Brussels-based non-profit organization dedicated to the promotion and protection of the rights of migrants worldwide on the basis of existing international and regional human rights instruments and mechanisms. This **non-governmental organization** with consultative status at the **United Nations Economic and Social Council** draws its name from the day of adoption of the **International Convention on the Protection of the Rights of All Migrant Workers and Members of Their Families** by the **United Nations General Assembly**. Originally, an international multilingual portal site for information on the human rights of migrants, December 18 has evolved into a resource center on the subject.

DECISIONS. Term utilized by the **United Nations Committee against Torture** to refer to its findings on the merits of individual **complaints**.

DECLARATION. Formal statement, announcement of intent and aspirations which may represent an agreement among state signatories on broad standards but which remains legally nonbinding. **United Nations global conferences** have produced numerous such "declarations" by participating governments. The **United Nations General Assembly** also often issues influential but legally nonbinding declarations, at least until they are translated into **conventions**. One possible exception is the 1948 **Universal Declaration of Human Rights** which has over the years gained a binding character as **customary international law**. In a narrower and more strictly legal sense, a declaration is a statement made by a state when signing a treaty defining the legal effect or expressing their understanding of certain provisions of the treaty. In such cases, a declaration is tantamount to a **reservation**.

See also BEIJING DECLARATION AND PLATFORM OF ACTION; CAIRO DECLARATION ON HUMAN RIGHTS IN ISLAM; DECLARATION OF COMMITMENT ON HIV/AIDS; DECLARATION OF THE RIGHTS OF THE CHILD; DECLARATION ON HUMAN RIGHTS DEFENDERS; DECLARATION ON PRINCIPLES OF INTERNATIONAL LAW CONCERNING FRIENDLY RELATIONS AND COOPERATION AMONG STATES; DECLARATION ON SOCIAL JUSTICE FOR A FAIR GLOBALIZATION; DECLARATION ON SOCIAL PROGRESS AND DEVELOPMENT; DECLARATION ON TERRITORIAL ASYLUM; DECLARATION ON THE ELIMINATION OF ALL FORMS OF INTOLERANCE AND OF DISCRIMINATION BASED ON RELIGION AND BELIEF; DECLARATION ON THE ELIMINATION OF ALL FORMS OF RACIAL DISCRIMINATION; DECLARATION ON THE ELIMINATION OF DISCRIMINATION AGAINST WOMEN; DECLARATION ON THE ELIMINATION OF VIOLENCE AGAINST WOMEN; DECLARATION ON THE GRANTING OF INDEPENDENCE TO COLONIAL PEOPLES AND COUNTRIES; DECLARATION ON THE HUMAN RIGHTS OF INDIVIDUALS WHO ARE NOT NATIONALS OF THE COUNTRY IN WHICH THEY LIVE; DECLARATION ON THE PROTECTION

OF ALL PERSONS FROM BEING SUBJECTED TO TORTURE AND OTHER CRUEL, INHUMAN OR DEGRADING TREATMENT OR PUNISHMENT; DECLARATION ON THE PROTECTION OF ALL PERSONS FROM ENFORCED DISAPPEARANCE; DECLARATION ON THE PROTECTION OF WOMEN AND CHILDREN IN EMERGENCY AND ARMED CONFLICTS; DECLARATION ON THE RIGHT TO DEVELOPMENT; DECLARATION ON THE RIGHTS OF DISABLED PERSONS; DECLARATION ON THE RIGHTS OF INDIGENOUS PEOPLES; DECLARATION ON THE RIGHTS OF MENTALLY RETARDED PERSONS; DECLARATION ON THE RIGHTS OF PERSONS BELONGING TO NATIONAL OR ETHNIC, RELIGIOUS AND LINGUISTIC MINORITIES; HUMAN RIGHTS DEFENDERS; SOFT LAW; UNITED NATIONS GLOBAL CONFERENCES.

DECLARATION OF COMMITMENT ON HIV/AIDS (2001). Program of international action adopted by a special session of the **United Nations General Assembly** to fight the **HIV/AIDS** pandemic. Grounded on an implicit acknowledgment of the **right to health,** the document established a number of goals for the achievement of specific quantified and time-bound targets, including reductions in HIV infection among infants and young adults; improvements in HIV/AIDS education, health care and treatment; and improvements in orphan support.

DECLARATION OF HUMAN DUTIES AND RESPONSIBILITIES (1998). Aspirational, normative document prepared under the auspices of the **United Nations Educational, Scientific and Cultural Organization** and the **United Nations Office of the High Commissioner for Human Rights** highlighting the notion that the fulfillment, realization and effective enjoyment of the rights enshrined in the **Universal Declaration of Human Rights** and subsequent international human rights treaties posit the existence of an implicit system of duties and responsibilities. Drafted by a group of experts, scientists, artists and philosophers representing all the regions of the world under the chairmanship of **Richard Goldstone**, the Declaration reflected a growing concern regarding the lack of political will of governments for enforcing globally human rights norms and standards.

DECLARATION OF INDEPENDENCE (1776). In 1774, representatives of Great Britain's 13 colonies convened in what they called a Continental Congress to protest British policies. Two years later, they voted for independence from Britain issuing a stirring manifesto—the Declaration of Independence—which listed their grievances against the British king and proclaimed their right to secede from Great Britain. The Declaration was a remarkable document in both political and philosophical terms. Drawing from the theories of "**natural rights**" of John Locke and Montesquieu, the drafters of the Declaration boldly asserted as a "self evident truth" that men were endowed with certain unalienable rights, including life, liberty, and the pursuit of happiness, that governments were set up to protect and promote these rights, and that since they had been abridged by the British Crown, American colonists could legitimately sever their political bonds with Great Britain. This was a revolutionary assertion in the world of 1776 in which kings claimed a right to rule by divine right. As such, the Declaration had a far-reaching impact in hastening the coming of the French Revolution and inspiring rebellion against Spanish rule in Latin America. *See also* BILL OF RIGHTS, UNITED STATES; DECLARATION OF THE RIGHTS OF MAN AND THE CITIZEN; UNITED STATES; UNIVERSAL DECLARATION OF HUMAN RIGHTS; SELF-DETERMINATION.

DECLARATION OF THE RIGHTS AND DUTIES OF MAN. First international human rights instrument of a general nature adopted in 1948 together with the Charter of the **Organization of American States** by the Ninth International Conference of American States. The Declaration sets forth a catalog of civil, political and economic, social and cultural rights that prefigures those enshrined in the **Universal Declaration of Human Rights** endorsed by the United Nations a few months later. Both the **Inter-American Court of Human Rights** and the **Inter-American Commission on Human Rights** have relied on the Declaration as a basis for their human rights case rulings.

DECLARATION OF THE RIGHTS OF MAN AND THE CITIZEN (1789). The first step toward writing a constitution, this manifesto, adopted by France's Constituent Assembly in 1789, served as the Preamble to the Constitution of 1791. Drawing in part from the 1689 English Bill of Rights and the 1776 **United States Declaration of Independence**, the French Declaration set forth the principles that guided the French Revolution and the fundamental rights of French citizens. Repudiating the key organizational principle of the pre-revolutionary monarchical regime—that people are born into special classes and enjoy special rights for that reason—the Declaration put forward the notion that "all men are born free and equal in rights" and that all citizens are to be guaranteed the rights of "liberty, property, security, and resistance to oppression." Social distinctions can be founded only on the "common utility." It also provided for freedom of speech and religion and equality before the law. The Declaration's emphasis on the notion of universal rights and that rights pertain to human nature itself makes it a precursor to the **Universal Declaration of Human Rights** and postwar human rights international instruments.

DECLARATION OF THE RIGHTS OF THE CHILD (1959). Building upon a 1924 Geneva Declaration adopted by the **League of Nations** which acknowledged for the first time the existence of rights specific to children and the responsibility of adults toward children, this resolution of the **United Nations General Assembly** endorsed the idea that "The child is recognized, universally, as a human being who must be able to develop physically, mentally, socially, morally, and spiritually, with freedom and dignity." It also approved a number of principles which would be reaffirmed in the 1990 **United Nations Convention on the Rights of the Child.** Disputes over when childhood starts and ends, in effect about abortions, at that time prevented the adoption of a legally binding document.

DECLARATION ON HUMAN RIGHTS DEFENDERS. Resolution of the **United Nations General Assembly** adopted in 1998 after 14 years of protracted negotiations which provides for the support and protection of **human rights defenders** in the context of their work. As the full name of the Declaration indicates (its formal title is Declaration on the Right and Responsibility of Individuals, Groups and Organs of Society to Promote and Protect Universally Recognized Human Rights and Fundamental Freedoms), the draft articulates existing rights in a way that makes it easier to apply them to the practical role and situation of human rights defenders. The Declaration outlines some specific duties of states and the responsibilities of everyone with regard to defending human rights, in addition to explaining its relationship with national law.

Thus, the Declaration provides specific protections to human rights defenders, including the rights (a) to conduct human rights work individually and in association with others, form associations and **non-governmental organizations**; (b) to meet or assemble peacefully; (c) to seek, obtain, receive and hold information relating to human rights; (d) to develop and discuss new human rights ideas and principles and to advocate their acceptance; (e) to submit to governmental bodies and agencies and organizations concerned with public affairs criticism and proposals for improving their functioning and to draw attention to any aspect of their work that may impede the realization of human rights; (f) to make **complaints** about official policies and acts relating to human rights and to have such complaints reviewed; (g) to attend public hearings, proceedings and trials in order to assess their compliance with national law and international human rights obligations; (h) to have unhindered access to and communication with non-governmental and intergovernmental organizations; (i) to benefit from an effective **remedy**; (j) to exercise the lawful exercise of the occupation or profession of human rights defender; (k) to receive effective protection under national law in reacting against or opposing, through peaceful means, acts or omissions attributable to the State that result in violations of human rights; and (l) to solicit, receive and utilize resources for the purpose of protecting human rights (including the receipt of funds from abroad).

On the other hand, states have a responsibility to implement and respect all the provisions of the Declaration. In addition, each state has a responsibility and duty to protect, promote and implement all human rights; to ensure that all persons under its jurisdiction are able to enjoy all social, economic, political and other rights and freedoms in practice; to adopt such legislative, administrative and other steps as may be necessary to ensure effective implementation of rights and freedoms; to provide an effective remedy for persons who claim to have been victims of a **violation of human rights**; to conduct prompt and impartial investigations of alleged violations of human rights; to take all necessary measures to ensure the protection of everyone against any violence, threats, retaliation, adverse discrimination, pressure or any other arbitrary action as a consequence of his or her legitimate exercise of the rights referred to in the Declaration; to promote public understanding of civil, political, economic, social and cultural rights; to ensure and support the creation and development of independent national institutions for the promotion and protection of human rights, such as **ombudsmen** or human rights commissions; and to promote and facilitate the teaching of human rights at all levels of formal education and professional training. The Declaration is not, in itself, a legally binding instrument. However, the principles and rights that it enumerates are based on and derived from human rights standards enshrined in other legally binding international instruments such as the **International Covenant on Civil and Political Rights**. *See also* INTERNATIONAL FEDERATION FOR HUMAN RIGHTS; SOFT LAW.

DECLARATION ON PRINCIPLES OF INTERNATIONAL LAW CONCERNING FRIENDLY RELATIONS AND COOPERATION AMONG STATES. Declaration adopted by the **United Nations General Assembly** in 1970 on the occasion of the 25th anniversary of the entry into force of the **United Nations Charter**. One of the principles thus proclaimed is that states "shall cooperate in the promotion of universal respect for, and observance of, human rights, and fundamental freedoms for all, and in the elimination of all forms of **racial discrimination** and all forms of religious intolerance." *See also* INTERNATIONAL LAW; SOFT LAW.

DECLARATION ON SOCIAL JUSTICE FOR A FAIR GLOBALIZA-TION (2008). Statement adopted by the International Labour Conference reaffirming the strategic objectives of the **International Labour Organization** (promotion of fundamental principles and rights at work, employment, social protection and social dialogue) in the context of **globalization**. The declaration was an outgrowth of a 2004 report of a commission of experts which had concluded that the benefits of globalization were unequally distributed. In the commission's view, there had been a strong bias toward liberalizing trade and production. More focus should be put on promoting "decent work." This meant stimulating full employment, respecting fundamental labor standards and promoting social protection and social dialogue. The global goal should be to narrow the gap between rich and poor and to combat **poverty**. *See also* SOFT LAW.

DECLARATION ON SOCIAL PROGRESS AND DEVELOPMENT. Normative resolution enacted by the **United Nations General Assembly** in 1969 asserting in a nutshell that extreme **poverty** is a denial of human rights. More specifically, defining social progress and development as "the continuous raising of the material and spiritual standards of living of all members of society," the Declaration posits that everyone has "the right to live in dignity and freedom and to enjoy the fruits of social progress and should, on their part, contribute to it." The realization of this right, the Declaration further states, requires "the immediate and final elimination of all forms of inequality, exploitation of peoples and individuals, **colonialism** and racism" and "the recognition and effective implementation of civil and political rights as well as of economic, social and cultural rights without any discrimination" through the attainment of a number of goals including "the elimination of poverty; the assurance of a steady improvement in levels of living and of a just and equitable distribution of income." The Declaration was reaffirmed by the 1995 **World Summit for Social Development** and has been used as the legal justification of a wide number of international human rights **treaties**. *See also* SOFT LAW.

DECLARATION ON TERRITORIAL ASYLUM. Adopted by the **United Nations General Assembly** in 1967, this **soft law** instrument supplements Article 14 of the **Universal Declaration of Human Rights** (UDHR). It provides that **asylum** granted by a state, in the exercise of its sovereignty, to persons entitled to invoke Article 14 of the UDHR, including persons struggling against colonization, shall be respected by all other states. It rests with the state granting asylum to evaluate the grounds for asylum. Where states find difficulty in granting or continuing to grant asylum, they, individually or jointly or through the **United Nations**, shall consider, in the spirit of international solidarity, appropriate measures to lighten the burden on that state. No person entitled to invoke Article 14 of the UDHR shall be subjected to measures such as retention at the frontier or, if he has already entered the territory in which he seeks asylum, expulsion or compulsory return to any state where he may be subjected to persecution. *See also* REFUGEES.

DECLARATION ON THE ELIMINATION OF ALL FORMS OF INTOLERANCE AND OF DISCRIMINATION BASED ON RELIGION AND BELIEF (1981). Adopted without a vote after 19 years of protracted negotiations and debate which pitted East against West and aroused resistance from Muslim states on a right initially recognized in the **Universal Declaration of Human Rights**, this normative **soft law** instrument asserts that intolerance and **discrimination** based on religion or belief are an "affront to human **dignity**" and that the right to freedom of religion or belief includes the right (a) "[t]o worship or assemble in connection with a religion or belief, and to establish and maintain places for these purposes"; (b) "[t]o establish and maintain appropriate charitable or humanitarian institutions"; (c) "[t]o make, acquire and use to an adequate extent the necessary articles and materials related to the rites or customs of a religion or belief; (d) "[t]o write, issue and disseminate relevant publications in these areas"; (e) "[t]o teach a religion or belief in places suitable for these purposes"; (f) "[t]o solicit and receive voluntary financial and other contributions from individuals and institutions"; (g) "[t]o observe days of rest and to celebrate holidays and ceremonies in accordance with the precepts of one's religion or belief"; and (h) "[t]o establish and maintain communications with individuals and communities in matters of religion and belief at the national and international levels." The Declaration is the only international instrument concerned with the practice of a religion or belief. It is not legally binding but it "does have certain legal effects and exerts a high degree of expectation of obedience by members of the international of the international community to the extent that it may be eventually considered as stating rules of customary law." Criticisms of the Declaration highlight the fact it does not define the term "religion" and sidelines the controversial issue of the right of a person to change religion. Since 1980, a **special rapporteur** appointed by the **United Nations Human Rights Council** monitors existing or emerging obstacles to the enjoyment of the right of **freedom of religion** and presents recommendations on ways and means to overcome such obstacles. *See also* INTERNATIONAL ASSOCIATION FOR RELIGIOUS FREEDOM; MINORITIES.

DECLARATION ON THE ELIMINATION OF ALL FORMS OF RACIAL DISCRIMINATION. Nonbinding human rights resolution adopted by the **United Nations General Assembly** in 1963 foreshadowing the **International Convention on the Elimination of All Forms of Racial Discrimination** of 1965. Article 1 of the Declaration posits that **discrimination** on the basis of race, color or ethnicity is "an offence to human dignity" and condemns it as a violation of the principles underlying the **United Nations Charter**, a **violation of human rights** and a threat to peace and security. Article 2 calls on states, institutions, groups and individuals not to discriminate on the basis of race in human rights. It also calls on states to end support for discrimination and to take affirmative action where necessary to correct it. *See also* MINORITIES; SOFT LAW.

DECLARATION ON THE ELIMINATION OF DISCRIMINATION AGAINST WOMEN (1967). Nonbinding resolution of the **United Nations General Assembly** proclaiming that **discrimination** against women and denying or limiting their equality of rights with men is "fundamentally unjust and constitutes an offence against human **dignity**." The Declaration is an important precursor of the binding **United Nations Convention on the Elimination of All Forms of Discrimination against Women**. *See also* SOFT LAW.

DECLARATION ON THE ELIMINATION OF VIOLENCE AGAINST WOMEN (1993). Resolution of the **United Nations General Assembly** recognizing "the urgent need for the universal application to women of the rights and principles with regard to equality, security, liberty, integrity and dignity of all human beings." Articles 1 and 2 of the Declaration offer the most widely used (though controversial) definition of violence against women which encompasses "(a) physical, sexual and psychological violence occurring in the family, including battering, sexual abuse of female children in the household, dowry-related violence, marital rape, **female genital mutilation** and other traditional practices harmful to women, non-spousal violence and violence related to exploitation; (b) physical, sexual and psychological violence occurring within the general community, including rape, sexual abuse, sexual harassment and intimidation at work, in educational institutions and elsewhere, **human trafficking** in women and forced prostitution; (c) physical, sexual and psychological violence perpetrated or condoned by the State, wherever it occurs." Many view the Declaration as an instrument complementing and enhancing the **United Nations Convention on the Elimination of All Forms of Discrimination against Women** (UN-CEDAW). In 1992, the **treaty body** monitoring the implementation of the Convention adopted General Recommendation 19, which requires national reports to the UN-CEDAW Committee to include statistical data on the incidence of violence against women, information on the provision of services for victims, and legislative and other measures taken to protect women against violence. *See also* GENDER-BASED VIOLENCE; SOFT LAW.

DECLARATION ON THE GRANTING OF INDEPENDENCE TO COLONIAL PEOPLES AND COUNTRIES. Resolution adopted by the **United Nations General Assembly** in 1960 asserting that the subjection of peoples to alien subjugation, domination, and exploitation constitutes a denial of fundamental human rights, is contrary to the **United Nations Charter**, and is an impediment to the promotion of world peace and cooperation. The declaration proclaims that all peoples have the right to **self-determination**. At the same time, the General Assembly underlines the overriding principle of respect for territorial integrity, thus suggesting that self-determination applies only to non-self-governing territories and European colonies. *See also* SOFT LAW.

DECLARATION ON THE HUMAN RIGHTS OF INDIVIDUALS WHO ARE NOT NATIONALS OF THE COUNTRY IN WHICH THEY LIVE (1985). Nonbinding resolution of the **United Nations General Assembly** defining the term "alien" as any individual who is not a national of the state in which he or she is present. The Declaration avers that all aliens shall enjoy a wide range of civil rights, as well as the right to safe and healthy working conditions, fair wages, and equal remuneration for work of equal value; the right to join trade unions and other associations; and the right to **health** protection, medical care, social security, **education**, rest, and leisure. No alien shall be deprived of his or her lawfully acquired assets, and aliens shall be free at any time to communicate with the consulate or diplomatic mission of the state of which they are nationals. *See also* INTERNATIONAL CONVENTION ON THE PROTECTION OF THE RIGHTS OF ALL MIGRANT WORKERS AND MEMBERS OF THEIR FAMILIES; MIGRANT WORKERS; SOFT LAW.

DECLARATION ON THE PROTECTION OF ALL PERSONS FROM BEING SUBJECTED TO TORTURE AND OTHER CRUEL, INHU-MAN OR DEGRADING TREATMENT OR PUNISHMENT (1975). Nonbinding resolution of the **United Nations General Assembly** which foreshadows the 1984 **United Nations Convention against Torture and Other Cruel, Inhuman or Degrading Treatment and Punishment** by asserting the obligation of states to take effective measures to prevent **torture** and other similar treatments or punishments from being practiced within its jurisdiction. The Declaration also enjoined states to criminalize all acts of torture or those which constitute participation, complicity, incitement or an attempt to commit torture and to provide means of redress and compensation to victims of torture. *See also* SOFT LAW.

DECLARATION ON THE PROTECTION OF ALL PERSONS FROM ENFORCED DISAPPEARANCE (1992). Nonbinding statement adopted by the **United Nations General Assembly** recognizing the practice of "forced disappearances" as a violation of the rights of **due process**, to **liberty** and security of person, and freedom from **torture**. The Declaration exhorts states to prevent disappearances by upholding **habeas corpus** and other due process rights, ensuring access to all detention facilities and maintaining a central registry of all detainees. It also calls upon states to diligently investigate disappearances and hold their perpetrators accountable. In 2006, the General Assembly adopted the draft of a binding treaty on disappearances. This convention entered into force in 2010.

See also INTERNATIONAL CONVENTION FOR THE PROTECTION OF ALL PERSONS FROM ENFORCED DISAPPEARANCE; SOFT LAW; UNITED NATIONS WORKING GROUP ON THE PROTECTION OF ALL PERSONS FROM ENFORCED DISAPPEARANCES.

DECLARATION ON THE PROTECTION OF WOMEN AND CHILDREN IN EMERGENCY AND ARMED CONFLICTS (1974). **United Nations General Assembly** Declaration stating that attacks on civilians, "especially on women and children, who are the most vulnerable members of the population," shall be prohibited and that states involved in **armed conflicts** shall make all efforts "to spare women and children from the ravages of war . . . and to prohibit **torture**, punitive measures, or degrading treatment of civilians." The General Assembly also requested states to criminalize belligerents who engage in acts of torture, imprisonment, mass arrests, collective punishment, and destroy homes and forcibly evict civilian population from their homes. *See also* INTERNATIONAL HUMANITARIAN LAW; SOFT LAW.

DECLARATION ON THE RIGHT TO DEVELOPMENT. Declaration adopted by the **United Nations General Assembly** in 1986 asserting that development is an inalienable human right. By virtue of that right, every person and all peoples are entitled to participate in, contribute to, and enjoy a pattern of economic, social, cultural, and political development in which all human rights and fundamental freedoms can be fully realized. The right to development also implies the realization of the right of peoples to **self-determination**, including their full sovereignty over all their natural wealth and resources. The declaration was reaffirmed in the Vienna Declaration of the 1993 **World Conference on Human Rights**, but political and conceptual controversies along North-South lines have stymied attempts to turn it into a binding treaty. *See also* MILLENNIUM DEVELOPMENT GOALS; SOFT LAW.

DECLARATION ON THE RIGHTS OF DISABLED PERSONS (1975). Nonbinding, normative statement adopted by the **United Nations General Assembly** meant to serve as a framework for domestic law. The declaration asserts that persons with disabilities are entitled to exercise their civil, political, social, economic and cultural rights on an equal basis as others, notably their rights of equality before the law, nondiscrimination, equal opportunity, independent living and full integration in society. In 2006, the General Assembly approved a binding **United Nations Convention on the Rights of Persons with Disabilities** articulating the same principles. *See also* SOFT LAW.

DECLARATION ON THE RIGHTS OF INDIGENOUS PEOPLES (2007). After more than 20 years of contentious debates and negotiations, the **United Nations Human Rights Council** adopted by a recorded vote the draft of this Declaration which sets forth minimum standards for the survival, dignity and well-being of **indigenous peoples** and determines, in particular, that they have a right to **self-determination** (i.e., a right to autonomy or self-government, which excludes scenarios of secessions or independence). The Declaration accordingly states that indigenous peoples have a right to participate fully in the political, social and cultural life of the states they live in as well as the right to participate in decision making in matters of concern to them. In the same vein, states must consult indigenous people's representative institutions in order to obtain their free, prior and informed consent before adopting any legislative or administrative measures in which they might have a stake. In regard to the particularly sensitive issues of natural resources, the Declaration recognizes the right of indigenous peoples to own, use, develop and control the lands, territories and resources they have traditionally occupied or used. By the same token, indigenous peoples have a right to seek **redress** for the traditional lands, territories and resources that have been confiscated, occupied, used or damaged without their free, prior and informed consent.

The Declaration required approval by the **United Nations General Assembly** and it faced stiff political resistance as it was the target of inconsistent criticisms and objections from numerous quarters. Some governments (former colonial powers) feared they might become the target of compensation claims for past wrongs as the Declaration tacitly recognized that indigenous peoples have been the victims of major injustices during periods of territorial expansion, **colonialism** and imperialism. Others saw, in the Declaration's insistence on the need to recognize indigenous peoples' unique identities, a blanket endorsement of the principle of self-determination and, thus, a threat to the territorial integrity of their fragile states. Still others were concerned that by acknowledging the collective rights of indigenous peoples over land and resources, the Declaration might be used as a legal tool to deny access to and current ownership and exploitation of valuable natural resources (in fact, many countries such as India, Brazil, Thailand and Malaysia have been accused by **civil society** organizations of participating, in conjunction with **transnational corporations**, in "bio-piracy" whereby biological resources used by communities have been patented away, leaving local peoples unable to use their own local resources). Finally, several governments objected that, by granting special rights to indigenous peoples, the Declaration could legitimize discriminatory practices, entailing the creation of "different classes of citizens."

The Declaration was heralded by indigenous peoples as a major symbolic breakthrough in the efforts against discrimination, racism and economic and political marginalization or exploitation, but whether states have the capacity and political will to translate its broad and vague prescriptions into actual policies remains to be seen. So controversial are some of its provisions that the Declaration does not even define what constitutes an indigenous people, although it obliquely uses the criterion of self-identification by stating that "indigenous peoples have the right to determine their own identity or membership in accordance with their customs and traditions." *See also* ABORIGINAL PEOPLES IN CANADA; CORPORATE RESPONSIBILITY REPORTING; DAES, ERICA-IRENE; DECLARATION ON THE RIGHTS OF PERSONS BELONGING TO NATIONAL OR ETHNIC, RELIGIOUS AND LINGUISTIC MINORITIES; SOFT LAW; UNITED NATIONS WORKING GROUP ON THE RIGHTS OF INDIGENOUS PEOPLES.

DECLARATION ON THE RIGHTS OF MENTALLY RETARDED PERSONS (1971). Declaration adopted by the **United Nations General Assembly** proclaiming that a mentally retarded person has, to the maximum degree of feasibility, the same rights as other human beings: the right to proper medical care and physical therapy, **education**, training, rehabilitation, and guidance; the right to economic security and to perform productive work; and the right, when necessary, to a qualified guardian and to protection from exploitation, abuse, and degrading treatment. Whenever mentally retarded persons are unable to exercise all their rights in a meaningful way or if it should become necessary to restrict or deny them, the procedure used must contain proper safeguards against abuse. *See also* SOFT LAW.

DECLARATION ON THE RIGHTS OF PERSONS BELONGING TO NATIONAL OR ETHNIC, RELIGIOUS AND LINGUISTIC MINORITIES (1992). Prompted by rising ethnic tensions in Europe and other continents, the **United Nations General Assembly**, after 10 years of protracted negotiation, adopted this **soft law** instrument with the aim of prohibiting discrimination. Inspired by and building upon Article 27 of the **International Covenant on Civil and Political Rights**, the Declaration requires states to protect the existence and identities of **minorities** and calls upon states to encourage the promotion of national or ethnic, cultural, religious and linguistic identities. Under the Declaration, minorities have the right to practice their religion, enjoy their culture and use their own language in both public and private settings without any kind of discrimination. Article 3 of the Declaration guarantees persons belonging to minorities the right to exercise their rights individually and in community with others without discrimination. *See also* CULTURAL RIGHTS; DECLARATION ON THE RIGHTS OF INDIGENOUS PEOPLES; DISCRIMINATION; EQUALITY; FORUM ON MINORIY ISSUES; MINORITIES; UNITED NATIONS SUB-COMMISSION ON THE PROMOTION AND PROTECTION OF HUMAN RIGHTS.

DECOLONIZATION. Process whereby in the course of a few decades—haltingly beginning in the 1930s and gaining full momentum in the post–World War II era—over 80 former European colonies gained independence. At present, there are only a handful of non-self-governing territories across the globe, home to nearly 2 million people. As a political force, decolonization had a dual impact on the international human rights agenda. In the first place, the struggle for decolonization placed issues of national sovereignty and **self-determination** at the center of the agenda of international organization, most especially the **United Nations**. Two, once independent, **developing countries** were critical of global economic arrangements and regimes and demanded a restructuring of the world economy in the universal language of a human right to development or collective economic and social rights rather than individual civil and political rights. In effect, the decolonization process exacerbated the global political debate about hierarchies of human rights which had begun with the onset of the **Cold War**. *See also* BOER WARS; DECLARATION ON THE GRANTING OF INDEPENDENCE TO COLONIAL PEOPLES AND COUNTRIES; HUMAN RIGHTS PRINCIPLES.

DEFENCE FOR CHILDREN INTERNATIONAL (DCI). Founded in 1979 and headquartered in Geneva, this **non-governmental organization** brings together national sections located in some 45 countries carrying out **lobbying, research, networking** and **advocacy** work primarily around issues of juvenile justice and child labor and providing technical assistance and **capacity building** to its national constituent organizations. The movement played an important role in the drafting and ratification process of the **United Nations Convention on the Rights of the Child**. DCI has **consultative status** with the **United Nations Economic and Social Council** and the **Council of Europe**, and working relations with the **United Nations Educational, Scientific and Cultural Organization**, the **United Nations Children's Fund** and the **International Labour Organization**.

DEL PONTE, CARLA (1947–). Swiss attorney who gained a reputation as an independent and controversial figure for her prosecutorial work against drug traffickers, money launderers and banking scandals. In 1999, she was selected by **United Nations** Secretary-General **Kofi Annan** to take the position of prosecutor for the **International Criminal Tribunal for the Former Yugoslavia** (ICTY) and the **International Criminal Tribunal for Rwanda** (ICTR). The hostility of the Rwandan government to the work of ICTR prompted the **United Nations Security Council** (UN-SC) to split the post of prosecutor of the two tribunals, thus allowing Del Ponte to focus on the ICTY. In that capacity, she made the controversial decision (endorsed by the UN-SC) not to open an investigation into allegations that the **North Atlantic Treaty Organization**'s (NATO) military intervention had involved serious violations of the **Geneva Conventions**, thus blunting Russian criticisms that ICTY was a puppet of NATO.

With U.S. support, she was able to obtain the arrest and transfer to The Hague of **Slobodan Milosevic**, the first time ever that a head of state was being brought to judgment for international crimes. She also expanded Milosevic's initial indictment to cover allegations of **genocide** and **crimes against humanity**. In 2004, after having gathered the testimonies of 296 witnesses, she brought the prosecutorial phase of the trial to a conclusion. All throughout her tenure, Del Ponte was under intense political cross-pressures and loudly complained about Serbia's uncooperative stance, which she later chronicled in her memoirs. She resigned at the end of 2007. Her 2008 book, *The Hunt*, created an international uproar by publicizing evidence that the Kosovo Albanians had been smuggling human organs of kidnapped Serbs after the end of the Kosovo war.

DEMJANJUK, JOHN (1920–2012). Ukrainian American who went through decades of legal wrangling and controversies for his wartime activities. He was stripped of his U.S. nationality and deported to **Israel** to stand trial for **war crimes** after being identified by Israeli **Holocaust** survivors as a guard in the Treblinka and Sobibor Nazi extermination camps. Convicted of **crimes against humanity**, his death sentence was overturned in 1993 by the Israeli Supreme Court after new evidence surfaced casting doubt on the validity of the charges brought against him. Returning to the United States in 1993, his citizenship was restored in 1998. In 2001, Demjanjuk was charged again, this time on the grounds that he had served as a guard in Polish and German camps. In 2009, he was deported to Germany to stand trial. He was convicted by a German court as an accessory to murder and sentenced to five years in prison. He died stateless and without a criminal record, while his sentence was being reviewed by an appellate court. *See also* NATIONALITY, RIGHT TO; STATELESSNESS.

DEMOCIDE. Concept coined (or rather revived) by political scientist **Rudolph J. Rummel** who noted that the term **genocide** narrowly referred to the intentional murder by government of people due to their national, ethnic, racial or religious group membership as spelled out in the 1948 United Nations Convention against Genocide, thus leaving out the politically motivated killing of people by the government. Rummel accordingly used democide as a broader notion encompassing forms of government murder not covered by the term genocide such as the **Ukraine famine**. *See also* DEMOCRATIC KAMPUCHEA.

DEMOCRACY. System of government based on the principles of popular sovereignty (i.e., the idea that the people govern themselves and the notions of individual **dignity**, **equality before the law** and widespread participation in the making of public decisions by majority rule). The end of the **Cold War** triggered a "wave of democratization" and gave legitimacy to the view that achieving democracy is a desirable end. Democracy has thus become a criterion for membership in international organizations and for justifying the actions of international organizations in regard to **electoral assistance**, the promotion of domestic good **governance**, development, and the use of force. For instance, one of the objectives of the **European Union** Common Foreign and Security Policy is the development and consolidation of democracy, the **rule of law** and respect for human rights, which it seeks to achieve through declarations, demarches, and resolutions and interventions in the United Nations as well as the incorporation of human rights and democracy clauses in nearly all of its cooperation agreements with third parties.

There is a growing body of evidence supporting the view that democratic political systems are reliable protectors of human rights, and in turn a growing number of scholars have argued that there should be a human right to democracy. The foundations of such a right can be found in a number of international human rights instruments. Article 21 of the **Universal Declaration of Human Rights** provides that "the will of the people shall be the basis of the authority of government." The **International Covenant on Civil and Political Rights** asserts the right of every citizen to take part in the conduct of public affairs directly or through freely elected representatives. The **European Convention for the Protection of Human Rights and Fundamental Freedoms** and the **American Convention on Human Rights** contain similar provisions. In a 1996 **General Comment**, the **United Nations Human Rights Committee** established a checklist of conditions for "genuine periodic elections." In 1999, the **United Nations Commission on Human Rights** adopted a fiercely contested resolution affirming rights to democratic governance. Opposition to the resolution came from developing countries which feared that a right to democracy might validate foreign interventions in their domestic affairs.

See also AFRICA INSTITUTE OF SOUTH AFRICA; EAST AFRICAN COURT OF JUSTICE; EBADI, SHIRIN; EQUALITY BEFORE THE LAW; FRIEDRICH-EBERT FOUNDATION; GREECE; HUMAN RIGHTS INSTITUTE OF SOUTH AFRICA; INTERNATIONAL CENTRE FOR HUMAN RIGHTS AND DEMOCRATIC DEVELOPMENT; INTERNATIONAL FOUNDATION FOR ELECTORAL SYSTEMS; INTER-PARLIAMENTARY UNION; NATIONAL ENDOWMENT FOR DEMOCRACY; ORGANIZATION OF AMERICAN STATES; PARLIAMENTARIANS FOR GLOBAL ACTION; TRANSITIONAL JUSTICE.

DEMOCRATIC KAMPUCHEA. Official name of Cambodia when the country was under the government of Pol Pot and his Khmer Rouge between 1975 and 1979. With material support from China and Vietnam and presenting themselves as a peace-oriented party, the Khmer Rouge seized power after waging a successful insurgency against the Cambodian government whose policies they deemed too favorable to the **United States'** war aims in Vietnam. Perhaps inspired by China's radical **Great Leap Forward** and in a bid to create an agrarian utopia, the Khmer Rouge immediately undertook turning the country into a nation of peasants free of Western "corruption" and "parasitism." One of their first initiatives was to forcefully remove most of the urban population into the countryside as part of a social transformation scheme which involved giving priority to agricultural self-sufficiency and the immediate collectivization of the countryside. Civil servants, police and military officers, having served under the previous regime, and educated people were hunted down and sent to re-education centers or labor camps or summarily executed. Religious and minority communities were ruthlessly persecuted. The human toll was staggering; as many as 2 million Cambodians—about 25 to 30 percent of the entire population—perished as a result of starvation, overwork and political executions.

A Vietnamese military intervention—to a large extent triggered by the brutal treatment of the Vietnamese minority by the Khmer Rouge—toppled the regime in 1979 and led to the taking over of a new administration of former Khmer Rouge under the control of Hanoi. In the meantime, Pol Pot and the remnants of his armed forces took refuge near the Thai border and were able to keep the country in a state of insecurity. Ironically, the **Cold War** fed internal instability and turmoil for another decade and prevented the pursuit of justice for the mass killings. China, the United States and other Western countries were opposed to any expansion of Vietnamese and Soviet influence in the Indochinese peninsula. Claiming that the government of Cambodia was a puppet state propped up by Vietnam, they refused to recognize it as the legitimate government of Cambodia and assured the continuing seating of the exiled Khmer Rouge in the **United Nations**.

A comprehensive political settlement among all the powers involved was achieved only in 1991, making possible the dispatch of a United Nations peacekeeping force—the **United Nations Transitional Authority in Cambodia** (UNTAC)—with the broad mandate to end violence in the country and establish a democratic government through new elections. UNTAC was terminated in 1995, having completed its assigned political tasks. Vietnam has disengaged from direct intervention into Cambodian affairs, and the Khmer Rouge no longer poses a political and military threat as its armed elements laid down their arms in exchange for immunity from prosecution. Since then, the Cambodian government, headed by a former Khmer Rouge cadre installed with Vietnamese support in the 1980s, has been reluctant to hold the Khmer Rouge accountable, thereby delaying the establishment of a **Special Tribunal for Cambodia** until 2003 to try its surviving leaders. *See also* DEMOCIDE; GENOCIDE; HUMANITARIAN INTERVENTION; IENG SARY; TRANSITIONAL JUSTICE.

DEMOCRATIC REPUBLIC OF THE CONGO (DRC). Formerly known in chronological order as the **Congo Free State**, Belgian Congo, Congo-Leopoldville, Congo-Kinshasa, Zaire, the DRC won its independence from a predatory and abusive colonialism in 1960 and has since been the scene of brutal ethnic fighting and attempted secessions, cronyism and **corruption** during the long dictatorial rule of President **Mobutu Sese Seko**, political strife and an internationalized civil war between 1996 and 2003 in which more than

5 million people were killed. Despite the signing of peace accords, fighting continues in the east of the country, which is sustained by the proliferation of armed militias and supported by external powers, notably **Rwanda**, which fight government forces to control lucrative mineral resources.

A **United Nations** peacekeeping force (at one point the largest ever undertaken by the organization) has been deployed in the DRC for 10 years with the mandate to protect civilians and help with the reconstruction of the country. It has played a significant role in organizing democratic elections and has launched military operations against various rebel groups. But there are continuing reports of **gender-based violence**, killings and other atrocities committed by both rebels and government troops as documented in a 2010 UN-commissioned report which also claims that the rebels are supported by an international crime network. A number of **non-governmental organizations** have also warned that the UN peacekeepers may have been complicit in atrocities against civilians. The international community has frequently denounced human rights abuses and the humanitarian disaster engendered by the kaleidoscopic conflicts that have engulfed the DRC. But, overall, its response is another instance of too little too late. *See also* ENCAMPMENT; IMPUNITY; INTERNATIONAL CRIMINAL COURT; RWANDAN GENOCIDE; SEXUAL VIOLENCE; UNITED NATIONS ORGANIZATION MISSION IN THE DEMOCRATIC REPUBLIC OF THE CONGO.

DENG, FRANCIS (1938–). Sudanese lawyer, scholar, diplomat and UN official. From 2007 to 2012, he was the **United Nations** special adviser on the prevention of **genocide**. He previously had served as a representative of the **United Nations secretary-general** on **internally displaced persons** (IDPs) from 1992 to 2004. In that capacity, he developed at the request of the **United Nations Commission on Human Rights** a set of nonbinding **Guiding Principles on Internal Displacement** designed to provide broad protections for IDPs. An increasing number of states, UN agencies and regional and **non-governmental organizations** have been using these standards in their activities for IDPs.

DENIAL. Common practice of governments which come under criticism for **violations of human rights**. Their kaleidoscopic language varies from case to case as well as in time and place ranging from blanket statements that the accusations are "unfounded" to assertions that the information is "biased," grossly exaggerated or "politically motivated" and that it emanates from "outside agitators." Failing these, there is always the *ultima ratio* argument that such criticisms constitute inappropriate interventions in the domestic affairs of a sovereign state, masking far more reprehensible human rights practices by the accuser. But the official discourse is always designed to demonstrate that the events never took place. This line of reasoning may be in the short run an integral part of what academics describe as the "**spiral model of human rights change**." More disquieting perhaps are attempts by governments or private individuals acting under the guise of scholarship to simply erase the knowledge of gross violations of human rights from social collective memories. Cases in point of such denials include, among others, the **Armenian genocide**, the Soviet-induced **Ukraine famine** (1932–33), the atrocities committed by Japan prior to and during **World War II** in China and the Nazi genocidal enterprise against the Jews in the same period.

Confronting deniers of grievous violations of rights poses a delicate balancing act between protecting their right to **freedom of expression** and the protection of the people being targeted, especially in the **United States** where the First Amendment to the U.S. Constitution places virtually no limit on free speech. Other countries, notably in Europe, have adopted laws punishing genocide denial and the European Court on Human Rights has generally ruled against deniers' complaints about limitations of their freedoms because their discourse aimed at the destruction of others' rights and freedoms. And of course, there are situations like Turkey's, where asserting that the Ottoman authorities did engage in a genocide against the Armenians is an onslaught on Turkish identity and, as such, a criminal offense punishable of prison terms. *See also* "COMFORT WOMEN"; HOLOCAUST.

DENUNCIATION. International law practice whereby a state party to a **treaty** may announce the termination of its obligations. The Vienna Convention on the Law of Treaties states that "termination of a treaty, its denunciation or the withdrawal of a party, may take place only as a result of the application of the provisions of the treaty." If a treaty does not provide for denunciation, withdrawal or termination, "it is not subject to denunciation or withdrawal unless it is established that the parties intended to admit the possibility of denunciation or withdrawal or a right of denunciation or withdrawal may be implied by the nature of the treaty." Several human rights treaties do not contain denunciation or termination clauses. In one of its **General Comments**, the United Nations Committee on Civil and Political Rights opined that the **International Covenant of Civil and Political Rights** is not the type of treaty which by nature implies a right of denunciation.

DEPORTATION. Narrowly defined, the term refers to the expulsion by a national executive agency of foreigners whose presence has been determined to be undesirable because they committed serious crimes, are considered a threat to the country, entered the country illegally, or are wanted in another country. The demands of **asylum seekers** for **refugee** status may be denied by a receiving country and eventually lead to their deportation. The practice of deporting individual criminals to penal colonies such as in Australia and Guyana by Great Britain and France, respectively, is different and is known as "transportation." More broadly, deportation means the forcible resettlement of individuals or large groups of people either to a different part of a country or to another country altogether. The term "population transfer" is used interchangeably if ethnic or religious groups are involved.

Instances of deportations in modern history include the expulsion of Acadians from Nova Scotia in the 18th century and the removal of Native American tribes under the Andrew Jackson administration in the **United States** in the 1830s. The 20th century was witness to massive deportations of a scale unknown until then. Citing security concerns, the government of Russia had by 1917 deported 300,000 Germans and half a million Jews from areas near the front. Deportations continued under Soviet rule such as the 1919–20 *dekossackization* campaign during the civil war and the 1930–33 deportation of relatively affluent peasants (*kulaks*). The approach and outbreak of **World War II** gave rise to yet another wave of deportations of "undesirables" targeted at ethnic or national groups in which 40,000 ethnic Germans and Poles were expelled from Ukrainian border regions and 170,000 Koreans were deported from the Far East to Kazakhstan and Uzbekistan. Approximately 800,000 Koreans, Poles, Germans, Greeks, Finns, Latvians, Estonians, Afghans and Iranians were arrested, deported or executed from 1935 to 1938. In the wake of the Soviet occupation of the Baltic states 380,000 people were deported in the early months of 1940. After the German invasion in 1941, entire nationalities (Kalmyks, Karachai, Chechens, Ingush, Balkars, Crimean Tatars, Crimean Greeks, Meskhetian Turks, Kurds, and Khemshils) accused of collaboration were deported to Central Asia 1943 and 1944.

Individual or mass deportations were defined as **war crimes** and **crimes against humanity** by the Nuremberg Tribunal. Yet the victorious Allies, while condemning the practice of "Germanizing" occupied or annexed territories, followed the same practices in Czechoslovakia, Hungary, Romania and Yugoslavia. For a variety of reasons, including retribution, a desire to create ethnically homogeneous nation states, distrust or enmity toward German communities, invalidating possible German territorial claims, more than 14 million Germans (1 to 2 million of which perished) were forced to flee or were expelled from Central and Eastern European countries and Russia after World War II. These expulsions took place concurrently with the forced resettlement of millions of Poles, Romanians, Ukrainians, Hungarians and Jews.

The 1949 **Geneva Conventions** explicitly forbid the forcible transfers of protected persons in conditions of war. Also forbidden is the common practice of an occupying power to deport or transfer parts of its own civilian population into the territory that it occupies. The evacuation of populations can be justified only for the security of the populations involved or imperative military reasons. The statute of the **International Criminal Court** also defines deportation as a war crime and a crime against humanity.

See also BARBIE, KLAUS; BOSNIA-HERZEGOVINA WAR; ETHNIC CLEANSING; GENOCIDE; GULAG; INTERNALLY DISPLACED PERSONS; KOREMATSU, FRED TOYOSABURO; LABOR CAMPS; MINORITIES; PAPON, MAURICE; PASHA, TALAT; POPULATION EXCHANGE; STALIN, JOSEF; TURKEY.

DERECHOS HUMAN RIGHTS. Founded in 1995, this is an **Internet-based non-governmental organization** promoting human rights through public education, investigations of violations of human rights, assistance to human rights victims and the development of human rights legal instruments. Derechos draws its membership from Latin America, the **United States** and Europe. Most of its work focuses on Latin America. Derechos Human Rights, together with its sister organization **Equipo Nizkor**, is a member of the **World Organization against Torture** and the **Coalition to Stop the Use of Children**.

DEREGULATION. Elimination or simplification of government rules and regulations perceived as unnecessary, inefficient and wasteful constraints on the operation of market forces. The objective is to reduce government interventions in the conduct of business activities in a move toward the free market. *See also* GLOBALIZATION; PRIVATIZATION.

DEROGATION. Literally, to derogate means to deviate from what is expected or to take away from. In human rights practice, a derogation is the suspension of the application of a right which is allowed only in certain narrowly defined situations. The **International Covenant on Civil and Political Rights**, for example, stipulates that "In time of **public emergency** which threatens the life of the nation and the existence of which is officially proclaimed, the States Parties to the present Covenant may take measures derogating from their obligations under the present Covenant to the extent strictly required by the exigencies of the situation, provided that such measures are not inconsistent with their other obligations under international law and do not involve discrimination solely on the ground of race, color, sex, language, religion or social origin." Other regional human rights treaties contain similar provisions. The **European Convention for the Protection of Human Rights and Fundamental Freedoms** allows derogation in times of war or other public emergencies threatening the life of the nation. The **American Convention on Human Rights** allows derogation in times of "war, public danger, or other emergency that threatens the independence or security of a State Party." The **African Charter** contains no emergency clause and, presumably, allows no derogation from the rights it enshrines.

Treaty-based derogation clauses generally require adherence to procedural requirements and consistency with the state's other international law obligations. Certain rights, however, such as the **right to life** and the right to freedom from **torture** and other cruel, inhuman or degrading treatment or punishment, may never be suspended under any circumstances. *See also* NON-DEROGABLE RIGHTS.

DETENTION. *See* ARBITRARY DETENTION.

DEVELOPING COUNTRIES. Group of countries of Africa, Asia and Latin America also labeled Third World countries or the Global South sharing in varying degrees of inadequate physical infrastructures, a relatively low standard of living and high population growth, sharp social inequalities and weak governance structures. Most of them have won their independence over the past half century and face the overlapping challenges of poverty, hunger and disease, human and civil rights abuses, ethnic and regional conflicts, and mass displacement of **refugees**. Collectively and in multilateral fora, they have forcefully articulated policy positions grounded in the principles of sovereignty and nonintervention, **self-determination** and giving priority to socioeconomic **second-generation** and **solidarity rights**. *See also* APARTHEID; DECLARATION ON THE RIGHT TO DEVELOPMENT; DECOLONIZATION; STRUCTURAL ADJUSTMENT PROGRAMS; UNITED NATIONS CONFERENCE ON TRADE AND DEVELOPMENT.

DEVELOPMENT, RIGHT TO. *See* DECLARATION ON THE RIGHT TO DEVELOPMENT; HUMAN RIGHTS BASED APPROACH TO DEVELOPMENT; INSTITUTE OF DEVELOPMENT STUDIES; STRUCTURAL ADJUSTMENT PROGRAMS.

DIGNITY, RIGHT TO. Term used in philosophy, religion, medicine, law and human rights to suggest that an individual has an innate right to respect, autonomy and ethical treatment. The notion of human dignity is mentioned in numerous national constitutions, is at the heart of the major international human rights instruments and is often used in relation to oppressed or vulnerable persons and groups. But it is nowhere defined. For example, the **Universal Declaration of Human Rights** simply proclaims in its opening article that "All human beings are born free and equal in dignity and rights. They are endowed with reason and conscience and should act towards one another in a spirit of brotherhood." The **International Covenant on Civil and Political Rights** and the **International Covenant on Economic, Social and Cultural Rights** state that "these rights [contained in the Covenants] derive from the inherent dignity of the human person." Similar language may be found in the **American Convention on Human Rights** and the **African Charter on Human and People's Rights**.

The **European Charter of Fundamental Rights of the European Union** attached to the **Lisbon Treaty** is clearer in the sense that it makes the protection of dignity an explicit commitment of the European Union and links it to the right to life, the right to physical and mental integrity, the prohibition of **torture** and inhuman or degrading treatment or punishment, and the prohibition of **slavery, forced labor** and **human trafficking** (Art. 5). In recent decades, the right to dignity has also been brought up in political debates related to **bioethics**, human genetic engineering, **human cloning** and end of life care. In a new twist in the use of the human dignity concept, the **United Nations Human Rights Council** recently adopted a nonbinding resolution viewed by many as an abridgement of **freedom of expression** stating that "defamation of religions is a serious affront to human dignity leading to a restriction on the freedom of religion of their adherents and incitement to religious hatred and violence."

See also CAIRO DECLARATION ON HUMAN RIGHTS IN ISLAM; CATHOLIC CHURCH; DECLARATION ON THE ELIMINATION OF ALL FORMS OF INTOLERANCE AND OF DISCRIMINATION BASED ON RELIGION AND BELIEF; DECLARATION ON THE ELIMINATION OF DISCRIMINATION AGAINST WOMEN; DEMOCRACY; EUROPEAN CONVENTION ON HUMAN RIGHTS AND BIOMEDICINE; HUNGER PROJECT; INTERNATIONAL HUMANITARIAN LAW; POVERTY; PRIVACY, RIGHT TO; UNITED NATIONS CONVENTION FOR THE SUPPRESSION OF THE TRAFFIC IN PERSONS AND OF THE EXPLOITATION OF THE PROSTITUTION OF OTHERS; UNITED NATIONS DECLARATION ON HUMAN CLONING; UNIVERSAL DECLARATION ON BIOETHICS AND HUMAN RIGHTS; UNIVERSAL DECLARATION ON THE HUMAN GENOME AND HUMAN RIGHTS.

"DIRTY WAR." Term most frequently used to refer to the state-sponsored violence carried out by the military government of **Argentina** between 1976 and 1983 against leftist guerrillas, the political opposition, trade unionists and

students to restore social order and eliminate individuals deemed to be political subversives. In a more generic way, the term stands for situations of **armed conflict** (mostly internal) that involve a high proportion of civilian deaths and egregious **violations of human rights** such as **torture**, kidnapping, murder and sexual crimes. Health scientists have developed a Dirty War Index, which "systematically identifies rates of particularly undesirable or prohibited, i.e., 'dirty,' war outcomes inflicted on populations during armed conflict."
See also ALGERIA; CHILE; COLD WAR; COLOMBIA; DEMOCRATIC REPUBLIC OF THE CONGO; EL SALVADOR; EQUIPO NIZKOR; GUATEMALA; PERU; STATE TERRORISM; TIMOR-LESTE.

DISABLED PEOPLE'S INTERNATIONAL. Network of national organizations of **disabled persons**, established in 1981 and headquartered in Canada to promote the human rights of disabled people, their economic and social integration and the development of support organizations. It played an important role in the development, adoption and implementation of the **United Nations Convention on the Rights of Persons with Disabilities**.

DISABLED PERSONS. The **United Nations Convention on the Rights of Persons with Disabilities** defines disabilities as including "those who have long-term physical, mental, intellectual or sensory impairments which in interaction with various barriers may hinder their full and effective participation in society on an equal basis with others." So defined, it is estimated that 15 percent of the world's population has a disability and over two-thirds of persons with disabilities live in **developing countries**, where the gap in primary school attendance rates between children with disabilities and others ranges from 10 to 60 percent. Significant improvements have been brought about in the overall predicament of disabled persons at least in a number of Northern countries. In spite of more than three decades of normative and awareness activities, little progress has been made in mainstreaming disability concerns into the activities of international organizations.
See also DISCRIMINATION; INCLUSION INTERNATIONAL; INTER-AMERICAN CONVENTION ON THE ELIMINATION OF ALL FORMS OF DISCRIMINATION AGAINST PERSONS WITH DISABILITIES; RAOUL WALLENBERG INSTITUTE; REHABILITATION INTERNATIONAL; WORLD BLIND UNION; WORLD COUNCIL OF CHURCHES; WORLD FEDERATION OF THE DEAF; WORLD FEDERATION OF THE DEAFBLIND.

DISCRIMINATION. Distinguishing between people on the basis of their race, culture, ethnic origin, nationality, sexual orientation, physical handicap, or characteristics other than individual merit. Treating people differently on such impermissible or arbitrary criteria is considered a **violation of human rights**. The term was given a comprehensive definition in the **United Nations Convention on the Elimination of All Forms of Discrimination against Women**.

See also AFFIRMATIVE ACTION; ALIENS, TREATMENT OF; APARTHEID; BAHA'IS; BERBERS; BRAZIL; BUSINESS AND HUMAN RIGHTS RESOURCE CENTRE; CASTE; DECLARATION ON THE ELIMINATION OF ALL FORMS OF INTOLERANCE AND OF DISCRIMINATION BASED ON RELIGION AND BELIEF; DECLARATION ON THE ELIMINATION OF DISCRIMINATION AGAINST WOMEN; DECLARATION ON THE RIGHTS OF INDIGENOUS PEOPLES; DISABLED PERSONS; DOMESTIC WORKERS; EQUALITY; FAIR TRIAL, RIGHT TO; FRIEDRICH-EBERT FOUNDATION; INDIGENOUS PEOPLES; INTERNATIONAL LEAGUE AGAINST RACISM AND ANTISEMITISM; *LOVELACE V. CANADA*; MIGRANT WORKERS; MINORITIES; NATIONALITY, RIGHT TO; NON-DISCRIMINATION; ORGANIZATION FOR SECURITY AND CO-OPERATION IN EUROPE; PHYSICIANS FOR HUMAN RIGHTS; RIGHTS INTERNATIONAL; ROMA/GYPSIES; SEXUAL ORIENTATION; DECLARATION ON THE ELIMINATION OF ALL FORMS OF RACIAL DISCRIMINATION WORK, RIGHT TO.

DOCTRINE OF NECESSITY. Precept used to provide a constitutional justification to extra-legal acts committed by state agents. The doctrine was first enunciated by Pakistan's chief justice in a 1954 ruling which validated the government's illegal use of emergency powers. It has been invoked in a number of Commonwealth states and Nepal.

DOMESTIC JURISDICTION. One of the principal corollaries of states' sovereignty and equality, the notion of domestic jurisdiction implies the exclusive competence of a state over its territory and population and a duty of nonintervention of other states in its internal affairs. The concept is encapsulated in Article 2.7, the so-called "domestic jurisdiction" of the **United Nations Charter** which stipulates that "nothing . . . shall authorize the United Nations to intervene in matters which are essentially within the domestic jurisdiction of any state." The interpretation of this provision has given rise to interminable disputes about what is meant by the phrase "to intervene," what is to be understood by a state's "domestic affairs," who decides the validity or lack of validity of the competence of the organization and how the prohibition is to be made consistent with the duty of states to cooperate in the promotion of human rights as stated in Articles 55 and 56 of the Charter. By and large, actual state practice in international organizations has incrementally but significantly eroded the political and legal weight of the domestic jurisdiction argument as a shield for preventing international debates and recommendations in response to **violations of human rights.** The argument is most frequently made by states whose human rights record is under criticism. *See also* DOMESTIC REMEDIES; "RESPONSIBILITY TO PROTECT"; STATE SOVEREIGNTY.

DOMESTIC REMEDIES. National administrative and judicial procedures which can be used by alleged victims of **violations of human rights** to seek protection or to obtain **redress** for past abuses. Human rights law jurisprudence makes access to international enforcement mechanisms conditional upon the provision of sufficient evidence showing that domestic remedies have been exhausted, are unavailable, ineffective or unreasonably delayed and that the state has failed to correct the violation or to carry out justice. *See also* ADMISSIBILITY REQUIREMENTS; DOMESTIC JURISDICTION; EXHAUSTION REQUIREMENT.

DOMESTIC VIOLENCE. Data gathered by such organizations as the **United Nations Children's Fund** and the **World Health Organization** suggest that domestic violence is a serious problem around the world, affecting most particularly women. It is estimated that between one-quarter and one-half of all women in the world have at some point been abused by intimate partners. Forms of domestic violence can include physical violence, sexual violence, economic control, and psychological assault. For a long time, the view prevailed that domestic violence was a matter of private concern and that it was exclusively part of certain ethnic or racial communities, or as unique to certain classes, within their societies. The principle of state responsibility for private acts has been increasingly recognized in international circles through the normative work of **United Nations global conferences**, the **United Nations Committee on the Elimination of All Forms of Discrimination against Women**, the **Special Rapporteur** on Violence against Women and the **Council of Europe**. Case law emanating from the **European Court of Human Rights** and the **Inter-American Court of Human Rights** have strengthened this expanding body of **soft law**. According to a recent UN study, 89 countries had adopted some legislation on domestic violence, and a growing number of states had instituted national plans of action. Marital rape is a prosecutable offence in over 100 countries, and 90 countries had enacted laws on sexual harassment. But still, according to the same study, in 102 countries, there were no specific legal provisions against domestic violence, and marital rape was not a prosecutable offence in at least 53 nations. *See also* EQUALITY NOW; GENDER-BASED VIOLENCE; INTER-AMERICAN CONVENTION ON THE PREVENTION, PUNISHMENT AND ERADICATION OF VIOLENCE AGAINST WOMEN.

DOMESTIC WORKERS. Persons working within the employer's household providing housekeeping services such as care for children or elderly persons, cooking, cleaning, food shopping, and the like. Recent estimates by the **International Labour Organization** (ILO) place the number of domestic workers at around 50 million, but experts in the field believe that the number could be twice as high. The overwhelming majority of domestic workers are women and many are **migrant workers**. Of these, at least 10 million children work as domestic servants. Countries importing domestic workers include most Middle Eastern countries, Hong Kong, Singapore, Malaysia and Taiwan. Domestic workers come from such poverty-stricken countries as the Philippines, Thailand, Indonesia, India, Bangladesh, Pakistan, Sri Lanka and Ethiopia. The conditions of domestic workers vary considerably, but they all share a common predicament of vulnerability which often veers into exploitation and servitude. In 2011, the ILO adopted a Convention Concerning Decent Work for Domestic Workers, setting minimum labor standards for domestic workers. *See also* CENTER FOR HUMAN RIGHTS AND GLOBAL JUSTICE; DISCRIMINATION; INTERNATIONAL TRADE UNION CONFEDERATION.

DRAFT ARTICLES ON THE RESPONSIBILITY OF STATES FOR INTERNATIONALLY WRONGFUL ACTS (2001). **Soft law** instrument developed by the **International Law Commission** after 45 years of protracted negotiations. The Draft Articles lay down the broad conditions under which an act of state qualifies as internationally wrongful. A state can be held responsible for the breach of an international obligation as well as the circumstances under which actions of officials, private individuals and other entities may be attributed to the state. An international crime may result from serious breaches of (a) an international obligation of essential importance for the maintenance of international peace and security (i.e., **aggression**); (b) an international obligation of essential importance for safeguarding the right of **self-determination** of peoples (i.e., colonial domination); (c) an international obligation of essential importance for safeguarding the human being (i.e., **slavery**, **genocide** and **apartheid**); (d) an international obligation of essential importance for the safeguarding and preservation of the human **environment**. A state can be held responsible only if a causal connection is established between the injury and its official act of commission or omission. Breaches of international obligations create duties of cessation, nonrepetition and **reparation**. *See also* INTERNATIONAL LAW; SET OF PRINCIPLES FOR THE PROTECTION AND PROMOTION OF HUMAN RIGHTS THROUGH ACTION TO COMBAT IMPUNITY; STATE RESPONSIBILITY; VIOLATION OF HUMAN RIGHTS.

DRAFT DECLARATION ON PRINCIPLES OF HUMAN RIGHTS AND THE ENVIRONMENT. Statement adopted in 1994 by an international group of experts convened at the invitation of the Sierra Club Legal Defense Fund—in cooperation with the Association Mondiale pour l'Ecole, Instrument de Paix and the Société Suisse pour la Protection de l'Environnement—on behalf of the **United Nations Special Rapporteur** on Human Rights and the Environment for the United Nations Sub-Commission on Prevention of Discrimination and Protection of Minorities (known from 1999 to 2006 as the **United Nations Sub-Commission on the Promotion and Protection of Human Rights**). The Draft Declaration addresses the linkages between human rights and the **environment** and stresses that accepted environmental and human rights principles embody the right of everyone to a secure, healthy and ecologically sound environment. The Draft Declaration also spells out the corresponding duties of individuals, governments, international organizations and **transnational corporations**.

DRAFT NORMS ON THE RESPONSIBILITIES OF TRANSNA-TIONAL CORPORATIONS AND OTHER BUSINESS ENTERPRISES WITH REGARD TO HUMAN RIGHTS. Set of ethics guidelines for **transnational corporations** (TNCs) adopted in 2003 by the **United Nations Sub-Commission for the Promotion and Protection of Human Rights**. Drawing from a little-noticed provision of the **Universal Declaration of Human Rights**, the draft describes TNCs as "organs of society" affecting a wide range of human rights and asserts that, as such, they are responsible for promoting and securing them. The Draft Norms spell out a number of legal obligations of TNCs derived from existing human rights, labor and environmental standards, provide guidelines for companies operating in conflict zones and propose mandatory reporting by companies and periodic **United Nations** monitoring and verification of corporate compliance. After a contentious debate pitting human rights advocates supporting a legally binding treaty approach to the Draft Norms and opponents who argued that the Draft was insufficiently precise and unenforceable by governments and corporate interests, the **United Nations Commission on Human Rights** did not endorse the proposal of its subsidiary expert group. The same debate flared up in the follow-up work of Professor **John Ruggie** who was asked by the UN secretary-general to develop a conceptual and policy framework clarifying the human rights responsibilities of TNCs under international law. *See also* CORPORATE SOCIAL RESPONSIBILITY; UNITED NATIONS "PROTECT, RESPECT AND REMEDY" FRAMEWORK FOR BUSINESS AND HUMAN RIGHTS.

DRONES. Unmanned combat air vehicles that have been increasingly relied upon in recent years, especially in the context of the so-called "**war on terror**." Since 2004, the United States has launched over 300 such attacks on targeted individuals in Pakistan, killing over 3,000 people. The Israeli Defence Forces are also known to have a large fleet of drones and to have used them in strikes against Palestinian targets. In 2009, the United Nations **special rapporteur** on extrajudicial, summary or arbitrary executions presented a report to the **United Nations General Assembly** in which he argued that the use of drones should be regarded as a breach of **international law**. In a recently published report, **Human Rights Watch** (HRW) also warned that "fully autonomous weapons could not meet the requirements of **international humanitarian law**." Critics such as HRW focus on the difficulty in assigning **accountability** to a person and the likelihood of civilian casualties. A UN panel is currently investigating what it called the "exponential rise" in drone strikes used in counterterrorist operations "with a view to determining whether there is a plausible allegation of unlawful killing." *See also* EXTRA-JUDICIAL EXECUTIONS.

DUBLIN CONVENTION (1990). Agreement adopted by the members of the **European Union**—it entered into force in 1997 and was supplemented by a 2003 "regulation"—for the purpose of preventing **asylum** claims in multiple states members of the European Union and reducing the number of asylum seekers, who are shuttled from member state to member state. The Dublin system determines the EU member responsible to examine an application for asylum seekers seeking international protection under the 1951 **United Nations Convention Relating to the Status of Refugees**. Most of the time, the responsible EU member state is the state through which the asylum seeker first entered the European Union. The implementation of this policy has been strengthened by the creation of an EU-wide computerized fingerprint database for unauthorized entrants to the European Union.

DUE PROCESS RIGHTS. Procedural requirements that states must respect in criminal and civil matters involving government action that may deprive an individual of his or her life or freedom. The concept of due process originates in English Common Law and has found its fullest expression in the American

Bill of Rights (1787). Due process rights include freedom from unreasonable searches and seizures, freedom from double jeopardy, or being tried more than once for the same crime; the right to a speedy and public trial by an impartial jury; the right to be told of the crime being charged; the right to cross-examine witnesses; the right to be represented by an attorney; freedom from cruel and unusual punishment; and the right to demand that the state prove any charges beyond a reasonable doubt. These due process rights were recognized in the **Universal Declaration of Human Rights** and are protected by the **International Covenant on Civil and Political Rights**, the **European Convention for the Protection of Human Rights and Fundamental Freedoms**, the **American Convention on Human Rights** and the **African Charter on Human and People's Rights**. Many measures taken by states in **counterterrorism—torture** and ill treatment, **extraordinary rendition**, the use of exceptional courts, indefinite detentions without charges—as well as some of the practices of the **United Nations Security Council** have elicited criticism and controversy as they are inconsistent with due process rights. *See also* ARBITRARY DETENTION; FAIR TRIAL, RIGHT TO; FORCED DISAPPEARANCES; GENEVA CONVENTIONS; GUANTANAMO BAY DETENTION CAMP.

DUNANT, JEAN HENRI (1828–1910). Swiss businessman and social activist. A passionate humanitarian throughout his life, he was the driving force behind the creation of the **International Committee of the Red Cross** and inspired the 1864 **Geneva Conventions**. In 1901 he was awarded the **Nobel Peace Prize**.

DUTIES. *See* DUTY BEARERS; RIGHTS HOLDERS.

DUTY BEARERS. Within the framework of the human rights discourse, the term refers to states, governments, national and local authorities, public officials and service providers which are obligated to take appropriate steps and measures to promote the realization and fulfillment of the entitlements of **rights holders**. While it is understood that states are primarily responsible for ensuring the enjoyment of human rights, there is considerable uncertainty as to whether the category of "duty bearers" also includes **non-state actors** such as **transnational corporations**. *See also* ACCOUNTABILITY.

DUVALIER, FRANCOIS (1907–1971). Also known as "Papa Doc" (he trained as a medical doctor), Duvalier won the 1957 elections in Haiti. After an attempted coup in 1958, he purged the army, set up a personal militia (the Tonton Macoutes), formed a group of bodyguards known as the Presidential

Guard and proceeded to declare himself president for life in 1964. Presenting himself as a bulwark against communism, external pressures for the liberalization of the regime foundered after Fidel Castro's taking of power in Cuba. Duvalier thus ruled Haiti until his death in 1971, tightening his grip on power through **corruption**, reliance on private armies, murder, exile and extortions. Estimates of the number of political opponents killed during Duvalier's regime run as high as 30,000. *See also* COLD WAR; DUVALIER, JEAN-CLAUDE.

DUVALIER, JEAN-CLAUDE (1951–). Dictator of Haiti who succeeded his father **Francois "Papa Doc" Duvalier** when he died in 1971 and remained in power until his overthrow by a popular uprising in 1986. His rule was far more benign that his father's as Jean-Claude had a marked preference for ceremonial functions and a playboy lifestyle rather than government work. But, by the same token, he gave free rein to a clique of hard-line Duvalierist cronies who dominated Haitian politics while indulging himself in fraudulent schemes and misappropriations of public funds. He lives in exile in France. Efforts to bring him to justice have been unsuccessful. *See also* IMPUNITY.

E

EARLY WARNING. Process of gathering information and **fact finding** for identifying, measuring and assessing risks early enough in order to allow decision makers to develop and implement preventive steps and measures. Academic studies, **think tanks**, government agencies, international organizations and numerous **non-governmental organizations** have developed systems of early warning alerts for gross **violations of human rights** relying on indicators of short- or long-term (i.e., "structural) conditions conducive to violations of human rights such as instances of physical violence, sporadic massacres, **forced disappearances**, forcible transfers of populations, extreme social and economic polarization, denial of **due process**, degrees of **freedom of expression** and **association**. Considerable attention has been given in particular to the identification of factors enhancing the likelihood of mass atrocities and **genocide** designed to facilitate the implementation of specific preventive measures.

It is also understood that the institutionalization of early warning mechanisms must be accompanied by targeted programs of **prevention**, the development of a capacity for military rapid response, the establishment of international judicial institutions and, in a longer-term perspective, the promotion of **democracy**, freedom, and pluralist tolerance. Early warning is undoubtedly a necessary first step toward prevention. But with the possible exception of the cases of Macedonia (1992 and 2001) and, to a lesser extent, **Timor-Leste**, early warnings have not triggered early and effective responses as the experiences of **Democratic Kampuchea** (1975), **Bosnia-Herzegovina** (1992), **Rwanda** (1994) and **Darfur** (2003–) among many others, amply attest. More disquieting perhaps is that efforts to institutionalize multilateral mechanisms of early warning have generally elicited political resistance, especially from the great powers.

See also BENCHMARKING; FORUM ON EARLY WARNING AND EARLY RESPONSE; GLOBAL ACTION TO PREVENT WAR; INTERNATIONAL ALLIANCE TO END GENOCIDE; INTERNATIONAL CAMPAIGN TO END GENOCIDE; INTERNATIONAL CRISIS GROUP; MONITORING OF HUMAN RIGHTS; OFFICE FOR RESEARCH AND THE COLLECTION OF INFORMATION; ORGANIZATION FOR

SECURITY AND CO-OPERATION IN EUROPE; PEACE OPERATIONS; REFUGEES INTERNATIONAL; RWANDAN GENOCIDE.

EARTH RIGHTS INTERNATIONAL. Non-governmental organization with offices in the **United States** and Southeast Asia focusing its work at the intersection of human rights and the **environment** which it defines as "earth rights." Earth Rights activities involve **fact finding**, legal actions against perpetrators of earth rights abuses, training for grassroots and community leaders and **advocacy** campaigns.

EAST AFRICAN COURT OF JUSTICE. Judicial organ of the East African Union established under the East African Community Treaty (EACT). It became operational in 2001. The Court does not have a specific human rights jurisdiction, but the EACT does call member states to abide by the principles of good **governance**, including adherence to the principles of **democracy**, the **rule of law**, social justice and the maintenance of universally accepted standards of human rights (cf. Art. 7.2) and to recognize, promote and protect human and people's rights in accordance with the provisions of the **African Charter on Human and People's Rights** (cf. Art. 6). Other relevant provisions of the EACT include Article 104 on the free movement of persons, labor and services and Articles 121 to 122 on women in development and business. The Court has not yet adjudicated human rights questions, but, in a 2006 case, it did assert that it will take into account the above-enumerated principles. Natural and legal persons may bring cases against member states. *See also* LITIGATION.

EAST TIMOR TRIBUNAL. *See* SPECIAL PANELS OF THE DILI DISTRICT COURT; TIMOR-LESTE.

EBADI, SHIRIN (1947–). Iranian lawyer and human rights activist who was awarded the **Nobel Peace Prize** in 2003 for her pioneering efforts for **democracy** and human rights, especially women's and children's rights in **Iran**.

ECHEVERRIA, LUIS (1922–). President of Mexico from 1970 to 1976 who embarked on a far-reaching program of populist reforms involving the nationalization of the mining and electrical industries, the redistribution of private land to peasants in some states and the imposition of limits on foreign investment. At the **United Nations**, he sponsored radical proposals such as the Charter of Economic Rights and Duties of States which posited the absolute sovereignty of **developing countries** over their natural resources and legitimized their right to nationalize the assets of foreign **transnational**

corporations. In 2006, an appeals court cleared the way for his arrest and trial on **genocide** charges in connection with the deaths and disappearances of hundreds of students, leftist dissidents and guerrillas in the late 1960s and early 1970s. A federal court dismissed those charges in 2009.

ECOCIDE. Neologism coined in the early 1970s to refer to the large-scale deliberate destruction of the natural **environment** or the excessive use of the ecosystem. The term has been used in relation to environmental damage caused by the use of defoliants in the course of the notable American intervention in Vietnam (1964–75) or the burning of oil wells by retreating Iraqi forces in the Gulf War (1990–91). Other acts of war associated with "ecocide" could also conceivably include the use of **weapons of mass destruction**, attempts to provoke natural disasters, the leveling of forests, attempts at climate modification and the forced, permanent displacement of species for military objectives. The 1977 Environmental Modification Convention (ENMOD) prohibits the military's use of environmental techniques. The 1993 **United Nations Convention on Biological Diversity** also bans some forms of weather modification. Attempts to recognize ecocide as an international **crime against peace** alongside **genocide** and **crimes against humanity** have so far come to naught. *See also* LIFE, RIGHT TO.

ECONOMIC COMMUNITY OF WEST AFRICAN STATES (ECOWAS). Regional organization of 15 countries established in 1975 for the purpose of promoting economic integration in "all fields of economic activity, particularly industry, transport, telecommunications, energy, agriculture, natural resources, commerce, monetary and financial questions, social and cultural matters." Under a 2005 protocol providing that ECOWAS has jurisdiction "to determine cases of **violations of human rights** that occur in any member state," the Community Court of Justice handed down a historic judgment in 2008 that found Niger in violation of its international obligation to protect a woman claimant from **slavery**. This was the first slavery case ever to be won in an international judicial body. The case was supported by **Anti-Slavery International** and a staffer of the **International Centre for the Legal Protection of Human Rights** acted as co-counsel to the victim. Earlier, the Court had ordered the government of the Gambia to release a journalist who had been missing for two years and was believed to be in government custody. The Gambia ignored the judgment. *See also* LITIGATION; UNITED NATIONS OBSERVER MISSION IN LIBERIA.

ECONOMIC, SOCIAL AND CULTURAL RIGHTS. So-called **second-generation rights** that concern the production, development, and management of materials for the necessities of life. The **Universal Declaration of Human Rights** states that everyone has the right to **social security**, the right to **work**, the right to rest and leisure, the right to an **adequate standard of living**, the right to **education** and the right to freely participate in the cultural life of the community (Arts. 22–27). These rights have been codified in such treaties as the **International Covenant on Economic, Social and Cultural Rights**, the **European Social Charter**, the **American Convention on Human Rights** as amended by the 1988 Protocol of San Salvador and the **African Charter on Human and People's Rights**. The **International Labour Organization** and the **United Nations Educational, Scientific and Cultural Organization** have also been active in the development of international **treaties** covering work and education.

Although economic, social and cultural rights are often explicitly acknowledged in national constitutions, there is considerable controversy among states about whether second-generation rights are bona fide rights, calling for specified state responsibilities or more realistically and simply aspirational goals. Overall, the Covenant treats them as standards to be progressively achieved. The **United Nations Committee on Economic, Social and Cultural Rights**, which monitors the implementation of the Covenant, has issued a number of very important **General Comments** clarifying the contours of specific rights and the obligations of states in their realization. *See also* AMERICAN DECLARATION OF THE RIGHTS AND DUTIES OF MAN.

EDUCATION, RIGHT TO. Individual entitlement enshrined in several international human rights instruments including the **Universal Declaration of Human Rights** (Art. 26), the **International Covenant on Economic, Social and Cultural Rights** (Art. 14), the 1960 **United Nations Educational, Scientific and Cultural Organization Convention against Discrimination Education**, the 1990 **United Nations Convention on the Rights of the Child** and the 1981 **United Nations Convention on the Elimination of All Forms of Discrimination against Women**. The legal standards emphasize two major components of the right to education: broadening the access to education for everyone on the basis of equality and nondiscrimination, and freedom to choose the kind (public or private institutions) and content (religious and moral) of education. In one of its **General Comments**, the **United Nations Committee on Economic, Social and Cultural Rights** has established that states have an obligation to enhance the availability, accessibility, acceptability and adaptability of education. The constitutions of several countries include provisions on the right to education.

See also AMERICAN CONVENTION ON HUMAN RIGHTS; CENTER FOR ECONOMIC AND SOCIAL RIGHTS; CULTURAL RIGHTS; EUROPEAN CHARTER OF FUNDAMENTAL RIGHTS OF THE EUROPEAN UNION; FRIEDRICH-EBERT FOUNDATION; INTERNATIONAL CONFERENCE ON POPULATION AND DE-VELOPMENT; MILLENNIUM DEVELOPMENT GOALS; ORGAN-IZATION FOR SECURITY AND CO-OPERATION IN EUROPE; OXFAM INTERNATIONAL; PUBLIC GOODS; SOROS, GEORGE.

EGYPT. For a long time an autonomous vassal state of the Ottoman Empire, Egypt came under the influence of British rule in the 1880s and did not achieve independence until 1922. Ruled by a monarchy until 1952, the country came under the sway of a military dictatorship with a one-party state following a coup engineered by Colonel Gamal Abdel Nasser. Egypt has since been ruled autocratically by military leaders, first by Nasser (until his death in 1970) then by Anwar Sadat from 1971 to his assassination in 1981 and then by Hosni Mubarak from 1981 until his forced resignation in the wake of the **"Arab Spring"** that swept the region and the country.

After more than a year of interim government, elections were held in 2012 which brought Islamist Mohamed Morsi to power. For three decades, Egypt has been in a state of **public emergency** since 1981, thus allowing the government to restrict freedom of expression and of movement and to imprison anyone indefinitely if they are considered a threat to national security. **Non-governmental organizations** (NGOs) have also documented numerous cases of torture and police abuses and discrimination against religious minorities. At its 2010 **Universal Periodic Review** by the United Nations Human Rights Council, Egypt was urged to put an end to the state of emergency, to adopt a moratorium on capital punishment, to investigate allegations of torture, to take further steps to fight violence against women, to prosecute those involved in incitement to religious hatred and violence, to eliminate legal provisions and policies discriminating on a religious basis, to take steps to guarantee an open and free press including on the Internet, and to amend legislation inhibiting NGO activities. Whether regime change has brought significant improvements in human rights conditions remains to be seen. The United Nations High Commissioner for Human Rights publicly questioned the haste with which Egypt's largely Islamic Constituent Assembly approved the final draft of a new constitution and its subsequent adoption by referendum, underlining the fact that the circumstances put the credibility of the process into doubt and contributed to perpetuating political turmoil. Other critics have opined that many of the provisions in the constitution are not consistent with international human rights norms, one of them being that while guaranteeing equality before the law, it does not explicitly prohibit discrimination on the grounds of gender, sexual orientation, and religion. On 3 July 2013, the military removed the duly elected President Morsi and suspended the constitution after ongoing public protests.

EICHMANN, ADOLF (1906–1962). Prime designer and planner of the "Final Solution," during **World War II**, the mass deportation of Jews to ghettos and extermination camps in Nazi-occupied Eastern Europe. Seized by **Israeli** operatives in **Argentina** where he was hiding after the end of the war, he was tried by an Israeli court, convicted of **crimes against humanity** and **war crimes** and executed in 1962. Throughout his trial, Eichmann pleaded that he had merely been following orders and that he was protected under the **Act of State Doctrine.** *See also* HOLOCAUST.

EL SALVADOR. Central American country which was engulfed in a brutal civil war from 1980 to 1992, pitting the military-led government against a coalition of left-wing guerrilla groups. Political factors accounting for the violence include decades of military rule, fraudulent elections, the suppression of political opposition and the control of an economic-landed elite opposed to land reform. For a long time, the military regimes were supported by the **United States**, which viewed the armed insurgency as an attempt to destabilize the region to the benefit of the Soviet Union. About 75,000 people died in the war, which was also marked by grievous **violations of human rights** involving summary killings, kidnapping and **torture**, most of them attributable, according to a **Truth and Reconciliation Commission** set up at the end of the war, to the Salvadoran army, private military groups and **death squads.** More evidence of **war crimes** has emerged, enabling groups and individuals to circumvent an **amnesty** law still in force and to seek **remedies** in national foreign courts against former government officials. *See also* ARIAS, OSCAR; COLD WAR; STATE TERRORISM.

ELDERLY PERSONS. The rights of elderly persons derive from their special vulnerability to abuse and **ill treatment** and can be broken down into three main categories: protection in terms of satisfying their basic human needs and access to heath care; participation, recognizing that there must be a greater acknowledgment of their role in society; and image, shielding elderly persons from negative societal perceptions which may lead to discrimination. Article 25 of the **Universal Declaration of Human Rights** does establish that everyone has the right to a standard of living adequate for the **health** and well-being of himself and of his family, including "the right to security in the event of unemployment, sickness, disability, widowhood, old age or other lack of livelihood in circumstances beyond his control."

But in contrast with women, children, the **disabled** and other vulnerable social groups, special consideration for the rights of elderly persons is only now being attended to by international human rights instruments as exemplified by the 1988 Additional Protocol to the **American Convention on Human Rights** in the Area of Economic, Social and Cultural Rights (Arts. 9–12, 17–18), the 1998 Additional Protocol to the **European Social Charter** (Part II, Art. 4) and the 2000 **European Charter of Fundamental Rights of the European Union** (Arts. 3, 24, 34). A number of recommendations of the **Council of Europe** also acknowledge the special entitlements of elderly persons. The salience of issues related to the elderly is likely to increase in the near and long-term future in light of current demographic trends. According to the **United Nations**, one of every 10 persons is now 60 years or older; and it is projected by 2050, the ratio will be one of five, and by 2150, one of three.

ELECTORAL ASSISTANCE. Originally, the term referred primarily to the observation and supervision of electoral activities. As such, the practice can be traced as far back as to the plebiscite overseen by the **League of Nations** on the disposition of the territories of Upper Silesia in 1921. In the same vein, in the late 1940s, shortly after its founding, the **United Nations** observed elections on the Korean peninsula. Throughout the 1960s and 1970s, the United Nations Trusteeship Council monitored and oversaw some 30 plebiscites, referenda and elections. As elections have increasingly been viewed as an essential ingredient of democratic transitions and the implementation of peace agreements, the scope of activities falling under electoral assistance has been considerably broadened to encompass the provision of technical assistance to help states build credible and sustainable national electoral systems. Capacity-building assistance thus may deal with the design, mechanisms, and effects of different electoral systems, legal and administrative regulations conducive to free and fair elections, the role, functions, organization and funding of electoral management bodies, the delimiting of electoral districts, civic education, voter registration systems, the logistics of voting operations, required personnel resources, regulations relating to parties and candidates, vote counting and the use of information technologies.

During the 1990s, the United Nations organized landmark elections in **Timor-Leste**, Mozambique, and **El Salvador** and, more recently, has provided technical and logistical assistance in **Afghanistan, Burundi**, the **Democratic Republic of the Congo**, Iraq, Nepal, Sierra Leone and Sudan. Other international organizations are actively involved in electoral assistance, notably the **European Union**, the **Organization for Security and Co-operation** in Europe, the **Organization of American States**, the International Organization for Francophonie, and the Southern African Development Community, among others. They all often operate in partnership with bilateral donor country agencies or with **non-governmental organizations** specializing in elections, such as the Association of European Election Officials, the **Carter Center**, the Electoral Institute of Southern Africa, the **International Foundation for Electoral Systems** and the National Democratic Institute.

See also INTERNATIONAL CENTRE FOR HUMAN RIGHTS AND DEMOCRATIC DEVELOPMENT; INTERNATIONAL FOUNDATION FOR ELECTORAL SYSTEMS; UNITED NATIONS MISSION IN BOSNIA AND HERZEGOVINA; UNITED NATIONS OBSERVER MISSION IN LIBERIA; UNITED NATIONS OPERATION IN BURUNDI; UNITED NATIONS OPERATION IN COTE D'IVOIRE; UNITED NATIONS OPERATION IN MOZAMBIQUE; UNITED NATIONS ORGANIZATION MISSION IN THE DEMOCRATIC REPUBLIC OF THE CONGO; UNITED NATIONS STABILIZATION MISSION IN THE DEMOCRATIC REPUBLIC OF THE CONGO; UNITED NATIONS TRANSITION ASSISTANCE GROUP; UNITED NATIONS TRANSITIONAL AUTHORITY IN CAMBODIA.

EMANCIPATION PROCLAMATION (1863). Executive order issued by President Abraham Lincoln during the American Civil War proclaiming the freedom of slaves in the rebellious states of the Confederation. Subsequently, the Amendment 13 to the Constitution in 1865 made **slavery** illegal throughout the country.

EMBARGO. *See* SANCTIONS.

EMERGENCY, STATE OF. *See* PUBLIC EMERGENCY.

EMPLOYMENT. *See* WORK, RIGHT TO.

ENCAMPMENT. Recent practice of host governments requiring **refugees** to live in designated camps. Not infrequently, refugees are also restricted in their movements in and out of the camps, thus leading to social pathologies ranging from substance abuse, violence, abuses of women and children, crime, and **terrorism** to **corruption** and criminality, which in turn lead to violations of the rights spelled out in the 1951 **United Nations Convention Relating to the Status of Refugees**. Protracted refugee situations, for instance in the **Democratic Republic of the Congo**, are known to contribute to the forced recruitment of children from the camps.

ENFORCEMENT. Dictionary definitions posit that enforcement means "to give force to," "to carry out effectively," "compel," or "to effect or gain by force." By these standards, talking about human rights enforcement is at best a misnomer and at worst misleading to the extent that the implementation of human rights norms relies for the most part on voluntary compliance by states. In fact, the word "enforce" does not appear in any international human rights instruments and is superseded by such terms as "promote" and "protect." The effectiveness of even the most coercive mechanisms in place—criminal justice institutions and the **sanctions** regimes authorized by the **United Nations Security Council**—ultimately depends on the willingness of states to cooperate. Insofar as international human rights institutions must rely on the willingness of governments to incorporate international human rights standards within their domestic policies, enforcing human rights involves the interplay of institutions designed to encourage states to voluntarily change their practices through dialogue, moral condemnations and exposure. This is done primarily through such "soft law" mechanisms as **monitoring**, **fact finding** and **investigating**, individual **complaints**, **state reporting** procedures supplemented by the various modes of action of national and international **civil society**.

ENSLAVEMENT. *See* BONDED LABOR; CHILDREN TRAFFICKING; "COMFORT WOMEN"; FORCED LABOR; HUMAN TRAFFICKING; INTERNATIONAL CRIMINAL COURT; INTERNATIONAL CRIMINAL LAW; INVOLUNTARY SERVITUDE; LABOR CAMPS; MAIL-ORDER BRIDES; SLAVE TRADE; SEX TOURISM; SEX TRAFFICKING; TRAFFICKING IN HUMAN ORGANS; WAR CRIMES.

ENVIRONMENT, RIGHT TO A HEALTHY. A deteriorating environment impacts the quality of life of humans and affects their rights to **life**, **health**, **work** and **education**, among others. Moreover, environmental degradation caused by economic activities is often accompanied by violations of civil and political rights as it may intersect with issues of ethnic identity, social inequality and discrimination. Most of the main international human rights instruments were drafted before environmental issues reached the global agenda, and the 1948 **Universal Declaration of Human Rights** makes no reference to the environment. Likewise, the right to an adequate environment is only subsumed and implicit in other rights provided for in the right to an **adequate standard of living** and the right to health enshrined in the **International Covenant on Economic, Social and Cultural Rights** and the right to life in the **International Covenant on Civil and Political Rights**.

It was not until the 1972 Stockholm Conference on the Environment that the right to a healthy environment was explicitly recognized in a **soft law** instrument. The Stockholm Declaration states that "Man has the fundamental right to freedom, equality and adequate conditions of life, in an environment of a quality that permits a life of dignity and well being, and he bears a solemn responsibility to protect and improve the environment for present and future generations." In 1990, the **United Nations General Assembly** adopted a resolution recognizing that all individuals are entitled to live in an environment adequate for their health and well-being. The norm was reiterated in the Rio Declaration endorsed by the 1992 UN Conference on Environment and Development. Concurrently, a number of international treaties have delineated the contours of state responsibilities, including the 1985 Vienna Convention for the Protection of the Ozone Layer, the 1987 Montreal Protocol on Substances that Deplete the Ozone Layer, the 1989 **Basel Convention on the Control of Transboundary Movements of Hazardous Wastes and Their Disposal**, the 1992 Framework Convention on Climate and the 1992 Convention on Biological Diversity. These agreements seek to regulate the conduct of **states** toward one another in regard to environmental issues, and many of them have established dispute resolution mechanisms.

Exceptionally, a number of human rights instruments do specifically mention environmental issues in their texts. Article 24 of the **United Nations Convention on the Rights of the Child** provides that state parties shall take appropriate measures to combat disease and malnutrition "through the provision of adequate nutritious foods and clean drinking water taking into consideration the dangers and risks of environmental pollution." The **International Labour Organization**'s **ILO Convention Concerning Indigenous and Tribal Peoples in Independent Countries** provides that special measures are to be adopted for safeguarding the environment of such peoples consistent with their freely expressed wishes. Articles 21 and 24 of the **African Charter on Human and People's Rights** stipulate respectively that "all peoples shall freely dispose of their wealth and natural resources" and "shall have the right to a general satisfactory environment." The **Council of Europe** is contemplating an additional protocol to the **European Convention for the Protection of Human Rights and Fundamental Freedoms** which would guarantee the right to live in a healthy environment.

At the national level, a number of countries—South Africa, Indonesia, South Korea, Mexico, India among others—have enacted constitutions and laws recognizing the right to a healthy environment and providing for implementation measures such as effective spatial planning management systems, participatory environmental impact policy assessment, monitoring environmental systems, and access to information and public or citizen complaint mechanisms. **National human rights institutions** have been involved in efforts to protect the right to a healthy environment, and there have been successful domestic court cases guaranteeing the right to a healthy environment in various countries. Increasingly, environmental issues are brought to the attention of UN human rights mechanisms. In response to a **complaint** presented by the United States–based **Sierra Club** Legal Defense Fund on behalf of Ecuadorian indigenous populations, which challenged a proposal by a U.S. oil company to build an access road in a national park, the United Nations Sub-Commission on the Prevention of Discrimination and Protection of Minorities appointed a **special rapporteur** to study the relation between the environment and human rights in 1989. In 1995, the **United Nations Commission on Human Rights** established a special rapporteur to monitor the adverse effects of the movement and dumping of toxic and dangerous products and wastes on the enjoyment of human rights.

Litigation has been an important instrument used by **non-governmental organizations** to promote the right to a healthy environment. The **Inter-American Commission on Human Rights** accepted in 2004 a request for precautionary measures to protect the life and health of members of a rural community in **Peru** affected by toxic waste from mining operations. In a more recent case, the Commission was petitioned to rule on measures to be taken in relief from violations resulting from global warming caused by acts and omissions of the United States in the Arctic region that affected the Inuits' rights to "the benefits of culture, to property, to the preservation of health, life, physical integrity, security, and a means of subsistence, and to residence, movement, and inviolability of the home." Another example of litigation is the case that arose in 2006 from the illegal dumping of toxic waste in Abidjan, **Cote d'Ivoire**, in violation of the Basel Convention.

See also ARTICLE 19, THE INTERNATIONAL CENTRE AGAINST CENSORSHIP; BUSINESS AND HUMAN RIGHTS RESOURCE CENTRE; CENTER FOR ECONOMIC AND SOCIAL RIGHTS; CENTER FOR HUMAN RIGHTS AND THE ENVIRONMENT; CORPORATE SOCIAL RESPONSIBILITY; DRAFT DECLARATION ON PRINCIPLES OF HUMAN RIGHTS AND THE ENVIRONMENT; EARTH RIGHTS INTERNATIONAL; ENVIRONMENTALLY INDUCED MIGRANTS; EUROPEAN PARLIAMENT; GREENPEACE INTERNATIONAL; INDIGENOUS PEOPLES; INDIVISIBILITY; MONTREAL PROTOCOL ON SUBSTANCES THAT DEPLETE THE OZONE LAYER; NIGER DELTA CONFLICT; PRECAUTION, PRINCIPLE OF; PRIVACY, RIGHT TO; PUBLIC GOODS; RAINFOREST ACTION NETWORK; UNITED NATIONS CONFERENCE ON HUMAN ENVIRONMENT; UNITED

NATIONS CONFERENCE ON HUMAN SETTLEMENTS; UNITED NATIONS CONVENTION ON BIOLOGICAL DIVERSITY; UNITED NATIONS CONVENTION TO COMBAT DESERTIFICATION; UNITED NATIONS FRAMEWORK CONVENTION ON CLIMATE CHANGE; VIETNAM WAR; WORLD COMMISSION ON ENVIRONMENT AND DEVELOPMENT; WORLD COUNCIL OF CHURCHES; WORLDWATCH INSTITUTE.

ENVIRONMENTALLY INDUCED MIGRANTS. Euphemistic term used in **United Nations** parlance to refer to individuals who have been externally or internally displaced from their traditional habitat, temporarily or permanently, "because of a marked environmental disruption (natural and/or caused by people) that jeopardized their existence and/or seriously affected the quality of their life." Such disturbances may include droughts, desertification, sea level rises, hurricanes and the like. The **International Federation of Red Cross and Red Crescent Societies** estimated that more people are displaced because of environmental disasters than war. They reckon that 25 million people may now be classified as environmentally induced **migrants**, a large proportion of them being women and children. Academic studies and the Intergovernmental Panel on Climate Change suggest that their number may reach 150 million by 2050. There is nevertheless considerable debate about whether such persons qualify as "**refugees**" who could claim protection under the 1951 **United Nations Convention Relating to the Status of Refugees** or constitute a separate category ("climigrants"?) calling for new international human rights legal instruments. *See also* ENVIRONMENT, RIGHT TO A HEALTHY.

EPISTEMIC COMMUNITY. Scholarly term referring to informal global networks of professionals with recognized knowledge in a particular issue area and who share identical value orientations and policy agenda. By supporting and promoting the dissemination of ideas at the national and international levels and providing knowledge to decision makers, epistemic communities may contribute to the emergence of new human rights standards and the development of rules and regulations. A typical instance of an epistemic community would be the loose network of scholars and practitioners which has coalesced around the notion of a "**Responsibility to Protect**" and endeavored to promote it in **United Nations**' fora. *See also* INTERNATIONAL COMMISSION ON INTERVENTION AND STATE SOVEREIGNTY; INTERNATIONAL HUMANITARIAN LAW INITIATIVE RESEARCH.

EQUALITY. The belief that all men and women are equal in rights is a relatively new idea that began to gain momentum in 18th-century Europe with the Enlightenment movement. Since the end of **World War II**, it has become an axiomatic assumption of international human rights advocates. By definition, universal rights should and must be applied to all without any distinction. Drawing from such seminal texts as the **United States**'s **Declaration of Independence** and the French **Declaration of the Rights of Man and the Citizen**, the 1948 **Universal Declaration of Human Rights**, in strikingly similar language, unequivocally states that "everyone is entitled to all the rights and freedoms set forth in this Declaration, without distinction of any kind, such as race, color, sex, language, political and other opinion, national or social origin, property, birth or other status" (Art. 2). The **International Covenant on Civil and Political Rights** (Art. 2.1), the **International Covenant on Economic, Social and Cultural Rights** (Art. 2.2), the **European Convention for the Protection of Human Rights and Fundamental Freedoms** (Art. 14), the **American Convention on Human Rights** (Art. 1), the **African Charter on Human and People's Rights** (Art. 2), the **Commonwealth of Independent States Convention on Human Rights and Fundamental Freedoms** (Art. 2-2), and the **Arab Charter on Human Rights** (Art. 2) all have similar provisions.

Not infrequently, the practice and policies of states are at variance with the principle of de jure equality—of persons before the law, equality of opportunity, equality to education and social services, among others. In a 1935 advisory opinion, the **Permanent Court of International Justice** opined that "equality between members of the majority and minority must be effective and genuine equality." Lapses in state practices explain why the goal of equality in international human right instruments is pursued through the prohibition of **discrimination**. Recent human rights instruments, in this regard, have considerably enlarged the scope of the prohibitions of discrimination, extending it to disability, age, sexual orientation, genetic features and membership in a national minority, as was done in Article 21 of the **European Charter of Fundamental Rights of the European Union**. The **United Nations Convention on the Elimination of All Forms of Discrimination against Women** as well as the practice of the **United Nations Human Rights Committee** have confirmed that there is no inconsistency between affirmative action and international human rights. The elimination of group inequalities was the mainspring of efforts to eliminate **apartheid** and to encourage **self-determination** in colonial countries and territories. *See also* EQUALITY BEFORE THE LAW; EUROPEAN UNION.

EQUALITY BEFORE THE LAW. The **Universal Declaration of Human Rights** avers that "everyone has the right to recognition everywhere as a person before the law." An extension of the concept is that everyone has the right to **equality** before courts of law. Any restriction on the right to sue or access to courts could constitute a form of **discrimination**. In a 1989 **General Comment**, the **United Nations Human Rights Committee** provides guidance on the prohibition of discrimination before the law, stating that the term should imply "any distinction, exclusion, restriction or preference which is based on any ground such as race, color, sex, language, religion or other opinion, national or social origin, property, birth or other status, and which has the effect of nullifying or impairing recognition, enjoyment or exercise by all persons, on an equal footing, of all rights and freedoms." *See also* DEMOCRACY; FAIR TRIAL, RIGHT TO; RULE OF LAW.

EQUALITY NOW. International **non-governmental organization** created in 1992 to protect the rights of women through public awareness campaigns and the provision of support to local grassroots groups. Equality Now has focused its activities on domestic violence, rape, **female genital mutilation**, trafficking and **reproductive rights**. *See also* ADVOCACY; PILLAY, NAVANETHEM; SEXUAL VIOLENCE.

EQUATOR PRINCIPLES. Set of voluntary guidelines developed by leading private banks on the basis of policies and guidelines of the World Bank and the International Finance Corporation. The principles enjoin participating banks to provide loans for projects that have been formulated in a socially responsible manner and according to sound environmental management practices. *See also* CORPORATE SOCIAL RESPONSIBILITY.

EQUIPO NIZKOR. Non-governmental organization affiliated with **Derechos Human Rights** involved in data gathering and dissemination on violations of human rights mostly in Latin America. The group has produced numerous articles on the "**dirty wars**" of South America.

EQUITAS—INTERNATIONAL CENTER FOR HUMAN RIGHTS EDUCATION. Canadian **non-governmental organization** (NGO) established in 1967 by Canadian scholars, jurists and human rights advocates to promote human development through educational programs. Its training programs, originally targeted at Canadian students, has evolved into a widely respected international undertaking involving 100 participants from some 60 countries every year. Their thematic focus is on training for NGO trainers, human rights education in the school system, the protection of women,

migrant workers, children and minorities, the creation of independent
national human rights institutions and the promotion of economic, social
and cultural rights. *See also* CAPACITY BUILDING; HUMAN RIGHTS
EDUCATION.

ESCR-NET. Highly decentralized structure progressively set up since 2000
by activists of human rights organizations to promote a greater recognition
and acceptance of economic, social and cultural rights as a means to
reducing **poverty** and inequality. The network involves a wide range of
non-governmental organizations (NGOs), social movements and activists
throughout the world coalescing around regional and national coordinating
focal points. Its purposes are to foster the development of monitoring and
advocacy tools, joint advocacy at the global or local level, and information
sharing about emerging issue areas in human rights in order to strengthen the
efforts of local communities in defending their rights and becoming part of
a larger movement demanding accountability for economic injustice by state
and non-state decision makers. As an international network, ESCR-NET
could not incorporate as an NGO but instead became juridically speaking the
project of a **United States** nonprofit public charity with a secretariat currently
based in New York.

ETHNIC CLEANSING. Recently coined term focusing on the purpose
of what has been conventionally described as population transfers or
deportations. A commission of experts reporting to the **United Nations
Security Council** on ethnic cleansing in the former Yugoslavia defined it as
"rendering an area ethnically homogeneous by using force or intimidation
to remove persons of given groups from the area." The practice, stated the
commission's report, entailed reliance on criminal acts such as murders,
torture, arbitrary detentions and arrests, **extra-judicial executions**, rapes
and sexual assaults, the confinement of civilian populations, deliberate
military attacks or threats of attacks on civilians and civilian areas and the
wanton destruction of property. In its final 1996 report, the commission
added the crimes of mass murder, the mistreatment of civilian prisoners or
prisoners of war, the use of civilians as human shields and the destruction of
cultural property.

Perpetrators of such actions are subject to individual criminal responsibility,
and military and political leaders who participated in making and implementing
the policy are also susceptible to charges of **genocide** and **crimes against
humanity**, in addition to grave breaches of the **Geneva Conventions**.
Instances of ethnic cleansing include the 1915 **Armenian genocide**, the
expulsion of Greeks from Turkey and Turks from Greece in 1922–23, the

systematic murder of Jews in Europe by Nazi Germany, the removal of ethnic Germans from several European countries at the end of **World War II**, and the forced transfers of populations within the Soviet Union under **Josef Stalin**'s rule. More than 1.5 million people were forcibly driven from their homes during the breakup of the former Yugoslavia. *See also* ABKHAZIA; ALGERIAN WAR OF INDEPENDENCE; ARAB ISRAELI CONFLICT; BOSNIA-HERZEGOVINA WAR; FORCED MIGRATION; HOLOCAUST; INTERNATIONAL CRIMINAL COURT; MINORITIES; NAGORNO-KARABAKH.

EURO-MEDITERRANEAN HUMAN RIGHTS NETWORK. A **network** of more than 80 human rights organizations, institutions and individuals established in 1997 as a follow up to the launching of Euro-Mediterranean Partnership, a wide framework of political, economic and social cooperation between the **European Union** and countries of the Southern Mediterranean subsequently strengthened by the 2003 European Neighborhood Policy and the 2004 EU Strategic Partnership with the Mediterranean and the Middle East. Operating in 30 countries in the Euro-Mediterranean region, the network seeks to promote democratic values, the development of democratic institutions of the **rule of law** and women's rights and gender through **advocacy**, country studies and training material for **human rights education**. The protection of the human rights of Palestinians in the **Arab Israeli conflict** is a key substantive concern of the network. *See also* DEMOCRACY; PALESTINIAN CENTRE FOR HUMAN RIGHTS.

EUROPE. *See* AMSTERDAM TREATY; CENTER FOR EUROPEAN POLICY STUDIES; COMMITTEE OF MINISTERS OF THE COUNCIL OF EUROPE; COMMONWEALTH OF INDEPENDENT STATES; COMMONWEALTH OF INDEPENDENT STATES CONVENTION ON HUMAN RIGHTS AND FUNDAMENTAL FREEDOMS; CONVENTION ON THE PROTECTION OF CHILDREN AGAINST SEXUAL EX-PLOITATION AND SEXUAL ABUSE; COUNCIL OF EUROPE; COUNCIL OF EUROPE COMMISSIONER FOR HUMAN RIGHTS; DUBLIN CONVENTION; EUROPEAN CHARTER FOR REGIONAL OR MINORITY LANGUAGES; EUROPEAN CHARTER OF FUNDAMENTAL RIGHTS OF THE EUROPEAN UNION; EUROPEAN COMMISSION AGAINST RACISM AND INTOLERANCE; EUROPEAN COMMITTEE FOR THE PREVENTION OF TORTURE; EUROPEAN CONVENTION FOR THE PREVENTION OF TORTURE AND INHUMAN OR DEGRADING TREATMENT OR PUNISHMENT; EUROPEAN CONVENTION FOR THE PROTECTION OF HUMAN RIGHTS AND FUNDAMENTAL

FREEDOMS; EUROPEAN OMBUDSMAN; EUROPEAN PARLIAMENT; EUROPEAN RESEARCH CENTRE ON MIGRATION AND ETHNIC RELATIONS; EUROPEAN ROMA RIGHTS CENTER; EUROPEAN SOCIAL CHARTER; EUROPE-THIRD WORLD CENTRE; EUROPEAN UNION; ORGANIZATION FOR SECURITY AND CO-OPERATION IN EUROPE; UNITED NATIONS INTERIM ADMINISTRATION MISSION IN KOSOVO; UNITED NATIONS MISSION FOR THE REFERENDUM IN WESTERN SAHARA; UNITED NATIONS MISSION IN BOSNIA AND HERZEGOVINA; UNITED NATIONS MISSION IN THE CENTRAL AFRICAN REPUBLIC; UNITED NATIONS OBSERVER MISSION IN GEORGIA.

EUROPE-THIRD WORLD CENTRE (CETIM). Geneva-based research and study center in **consultative status** with the **United Nations Economic and Social Council** advocating alternative development policies departing from prevailing Western models, which it views as conducive to the marginalization of a growing number of people in the South as a result of a crushing debt burden, the dismantling of social welfare systems, unemployment, deforestation and pollution and the standardization and loss of identity associated with the process of globalization and its recurring crises. CETIM is especially critical of the policies of the **Bretton Woods Institutions**, the **World Trade Organization** and of the dominant role of **transnational corporations**. Its documentation archives are open to researchers and students on request.

EUROPEAN CHARTER FOR REGIONAL OR MINORITY LANGUAGES. Document adopted in 1992 under the auspices of the **Council of Europe** that entered into force in 1998. The Charter is designed to protect and promote regional and **minority** languages as a threatened aspect of Europe's cultural heritage and enable speakers of a regional or minority language to use it in private and public life. The Charter's overriding purpose is cultural and thus sets out the main objectives and principles that states undertake to apply to all regional or minority languages existing within their national territory and contains a series of concrete measures designed to facilitate and encourage the use of specific regional or minority languages in public life. The Charter does not establish a list of European languages but, as defined by the Charter, "regional or minority languages" are languages (a) traditionally used within a given territory of a state by nationals of that state who form a group numerically smaller than the rest of the state's population (languages spoken by recent immigrants for other states are thus excluded); (b) significantly different from the majority or official language(s) of that state (thus excluding mere local dialects of the official or majority language); and (c) which have a territorial basis (and are therefore traditionally spoken by populations of regions or areas within the state) or are used by linguistic minorities within the state as a whole (thereby including such languages as Catalan, Yiddish and Romany, which are used over a wide geographic area). The complexity of the definition is a vivid reflection of the political sensitivities associated with the legal status of regional and minority languages, a significant factor contributing to the low number of ratifications. *See also* CULTURAL RIGHTS; FRAMEWORK CONVENTION ON THE PROTECTION OF NATIONAL MINORITIES; EUROPEAN COMMISSION AGAINST RACISM AND INTOLERANCE; EUROPEAN COURT OF HUMAN RIGHTS.

EUROPEAN CHARTER OF FUNDAMENTAL RIGHTS OF THE EUROPEAN UNION (EChFR). Originally an annex to the 2001 Nice Treaty and therefore not legally binding, the Charter was included in the **Lisbon Treaty** and became, after considerable tribulations, a source of obligation for **European Union** members when the Lisbon Treaty came into effect in 2009. Organized into six headings—"**dignity**," freedoms, "**equality**," solidarity, citizens' rights, and justice—the Charter's provisions are noteworthy for prohibiting **capital punishment** and the **cloning** of human beings. Along with Denmark and the Czech Republic, Great Britain has negotiated opt outs. Under the Charter, the European Union must act and legislate consistently with the Charter and the EU's courts are bound to strike down EU legislation which contravenes it. The 55 articles of the EChFR list political, social, and economic rights for EU citizens. Their purpose is to ensure that EU regulations and directives are not inconsistent with the **European Convention for the Protection of Human Rights and Fundamental Freedoms** (ECHR).

The Charter is based on the ECHR, the jurisprudence of the **Court of Justice** and the provisions of preexisting EU law. The rights covered in the Charter include civil and political rights—dignity, **life**, the prohibition of **torture**, **slavery** and capital punishment—and the rights to liberty, **privacy**, marriage, thought, **expression**, **association**, **education**, **work**, **property** and **asylum**. The Charter also includes economic and social rights such as the rights of collective bargaining, fair working conditions, protection against unjustified dismissal and access to **health** care. Special mention is made of the rights of children and the **elderly** and persons with disabilities.

A separate section covers the rights of EU citizens such as the right to vote in election to the European Parliament and to move freely within the European Union. It also includes several administrative rights such as a right to good administration, to access documents and to petition the **European Parliament** and to contact the European **ombudsman**. The penultimate section of the Charter concerned with justice issues reaffirms the rights to an effective **remedy**, a fair trial, to the presumption of innocence, the principle of legality, nonretrospectivity and double jeopardy.

EUROPEAN COMMISSION AGAINST RACISM AND INTOLER-ANCE. Independent expert body established in 1993 by the **Council of Europe** to monitor manifestations of racism, xenophobia, **anti-Semitism** and intolerance in the Council member countries. The Commission publishes country-by-country **monitoring** reports, formulates general policy recommendations and develops close ties with **civil society** organizations. *See also* FACT FINDING.

EUROPEAN COMMISSION ON HUMAN RIGHTS. *See* EUROPEAN CONVENTION FOR THE PROTECTION OF HUMAN RIGHTS AND FUNDAMENTAL FREEDOMS.

EUROPEAN COMMITTEE FOR THE PREVENTION OF TORTURE (CPT). Body of independent experts elected by the **Committee of Ministers of the Council of Europe**. Acting as a preventive arm of the **European Convention for the Prevention of Torture and Inhuman or Degrading Treatment or Punishment**, the Committee has the power to make unannounced visits to places of detention of the member states of the Council of Europe (prisons and juvenile detention centers, police stations, holding centers for immigration detainees and psychiatric hospitals) to "examine the treatment of persons deprived of their liberty with a view to strengthening, if necessary, the protection of such persons from **torture** and from inhuman or degrading treatment or punishment." The Committee also has the right to interview in private detained persons and to enter into contact with anyone else whom it deems able to provide relevant information. At the end of each visit, the CPT prepares a confidential report with conclusions and recommendations which serve as a basis for a "dialogue" with the national authorities intended to strengthen the protection of detained persons from **ill treatment**. The CPT may, in rare cases, make unilateral "public statements" when it has clear evidence of a practice of torture and when states under investigation refuse to publish its report.

Over the years, the CPT has developed standards relating to the treatment of persons deprived of their liberty on such topics as police custody, imprisonment, training of law enforcement personnel, health care services in prisons, foreign nationals detained under aliens legislation, involuntary placement in psychiatric establishments and juveniles and women deprived of their liberty. As of 2012, the CPT had undertaken 328 visits (198 periodic visits plus 130 ad hoc visits) and published 274 reports.

EUROPEAN COMMITTEE ON SOCIAL RIGHTS. Body of independent experts appointed by the **Committee of Ministers of the Council of Europe** monitoring the implementation of the **European Social Charter** by its state parties. The Committee assesses the conformity of national laws and practices with the Charter through an examination of periodic state reports and by acting upon collective **complaints**. In respect of national reports, the Committee adopts "conclusions." In regard to collective complaints, it adopts "decisions." As of May 2009, the Committee had dealt with 57 collective complaints from national trade unions and **non-governmental organizations** like the **Centre on Housing Rights and Evictions**, the **European Roma Rights Centre**, the **World Organization against Torture**, the **International Commission of Jurists** and the **International Federation for Human Rights**. In 2011, the Committee registered 12 new complaints, declared 11 of them admissible and adopted decisions on the merits of four.

EUROPEAN CONVENTION FOR THE PREVENTION OF TORTURE AND INHUMAN OR DEGRADING TREATMENT OR PUNISHMENT (ECPT). Article 3 of the **European Convention for the Protection of Human Rights and Fundamental Freedoms** provides that "No one shall be subjected to torture or to inhuman or degrading treatment or punishment." This provision inspired and guided the adoption in 1987 of the ECPT which provides nonjudicial preventive mechanisms for the protection of detainees in countries that are members of the **Council of Europe**. It is based on a system of visits by the **European Committee for the Prevention of Torture**. The Convention has been ratified by all members of the Council of Europe with no **reservations**, declarations or objections. The European Convention was used as a model for the 2002 Optional Protocol to the **United Nations Convention against Torture and Other Cruel, Inhuman or Degrading Treatment and Punishment**. *See also* INTERNATIONAL COMMISSION OF JURISTS.

EUROPEAN CONVENTION FOR THE PROTECTION OF HUMAN RIGHTS AND FUNDAMENTAL FREEDOMS. First comprehensive human rights treaty which also established the first international **complaint** procedure and the first international court to adjudicate human rights matters. Negotiated under the auspices of the **Council of Europe**, the Convention was meant to be a response to the atrocities of **World War II** and to constitute a major step toward regional integration and the institutionalization of shared democratic values as deterrents to future conflicts. Another important consideration at the time, in the context of the **Cold War**, was to consolidate the unity of non-communist countries. Persisting concerns over sovereignty and a general reluctance to unduly institutionalize the norm of state **accountability** precluded agreement over more radical proposals, and the drafters of the Convention eventually followed the model set forth in early drafts of the **International Covenant on Civil and Political Rights**.

The Convention entered into force in 1953 when it received the ratifications of the then 10 members of the Council of Europe. As a result of the breakup of the Soviet Union, the number of states parties has expanded to 47. The original Convention set forth a short list of fundamental civil and political rights derived from the **Universal Declaration of Human Rights** (**right to life**, prohibition of **torture**, prohibition of **slavery** and **forced labor**, right to liberty and security, right to a fair trial, no punishment without law, right to respect for private and family life, freedom of thought, conscience and religion, **freedom of expression**, **freedom of association** and assembly, right to marry, right to an effective **remedy**, prohibition of **discrimination**). The Convention also establishes international enforcement mechanisms consisting of two independent bodies—the European Commission on Human Rights and the **European Court of Human Rights** which dealt with individual and interstate petitions. At the request of the **Committee of Ministers of the Council of Europe**, the Court may also give advisory opinions concerning the interpretation of the Conventions and its protocols. Both the court's jurisdiction and the individual petition procedure, however, were optional.

The Commission had sole authority to receive and screen individual complaints, undertake **fact finding**, attempt a friendly settlement or refer cases to the Court. The "normal" procedure thus envisaged was a typical system of **interstate communications** or complaints. This modest system has since undergone revolutionary change. Several protocols adopted by the Council of Europe have significantly expanded the list of protected rights, adding to the original list a right to property, a right to **education** and a right to regular, free and fair elections, freedom from imprisonment for civil debts, freedom of movement and residence and freedom to leave any country. Other protocols bar the forced exile of nationals and the collective expulsion of aliens, abolish **capital punishment**, and augment the non-discrimination guarantees. More importantly, Protocol 11 adopted in 1998 overhauled the supervisory mechanisms initially set up by the Convention by eliminating the Commission and providing for a full-time Court with compulsory jurisdiction over interstate and individual complaints. *See also* DEMOCRACY; EQUALITY; EUROPEAN CHARTER OF FUNDAMENTAL RIGHTS OF

THE EUROPEAN UNION; EUROPEAN CONVENTION ON HUMAN RIGHTS AND BIOMEDICINE; FRAMEWORK CONVENTION FOR THE PROTECTION OF NATIONAL MINORITIES; MINORITIES.

EUROPEAN CONVENTION ON HUMAN RIGHTS AND BIOMEDICINE (1999). Also known as the Oviedo Convention after Oviedo, Spain, where it was signed, this is the only binding legal instrument creating relatively precise international minimum standards for the protection of individuals against new developments in the biologic and medical fields and their possible misuse. The Convention negotiated under the umbrella of the **Council of Europe** draws from the key human rights principles of protecting the **dignity**, identity and integrity of the human being and existing fundamental rights documents, in particular the **European Convention for the Protection of Human Rights and Fundamental Freedoms**. Its key objective is to ensure that the interests of the individual prevail over the interests of society and science and to provide equal access to **health** care services.

In particular, the Convention seeks to regulate such individual aspects as the protection of the patients' autonomy within the meaning of their "informed consent," protective provisions for minors and persons with a mental disorder, access to medical data, predictive genetic tests, interventions on the **human genome**, medical research on persons, organ and tissue removal from living donors for transplantation purposes and the use of human body substances. Additional protocols ban **human cloning**, organ transplants and biomedical research. *See also* BIOETHICS; DIGNITY, RIGHT TO; HEALTH, RIGHT TO; LIFE, RIGHT TO; UNITED NATIONS DECLARATION ON HUMAN CLONING; UNIVERSAL DECLARATION ON BIOETHICS AND HUMAN RIGHTS; UNIVERSAL DECLARATION ON THE HUMAN GENOME AND HUMAN RIGHTS.

EUROPEAN COURT OF HUMAN RIGHTS (ECtHR). Judicial body exerting jurisdiction over alleged **violations of human rights** and freedom spelled out in the **European Convention for the Protection of Human Rights and Fundamental Freedoms**. The Court may receive **complaints** ("**applications**") from any individual (or their relatives) and **non-governmental organizations** (NGOs) "within the jurisdiction" of the states parties to the Convention. Nationals or non-nationals may therefore apply. To be admissible, applications must be submitted only after exhaustion of all available domestic civil, criminal or administrative **remedies**. They will be considered only "6 months from the date on which the final domestic decision was taken." Applicants must be represented by a lawyer and the Convention makes provision for legal aid. States parties and NGOs may intervene before the court and submit **amicus curiae** briefs. In urgent cases and to avoid irreparable harm to the victim of an alleged violation, the Court may recommend **interim measures**. The **Committee of Ministers of the Council of Europe** supervises the execution of the Court's judgments.

Any state party to the ECtHR can sue another contracting state in the Court for alleged breaches of the Convention, but this procedure has practically fallen into desuetude. The 1998 revision of the Convention allowing individual applicants to submit their cases directly to the Court has led to an exponential growth of the Court's caseload and the Court now is overburdened with cases. Over the past half century the Court has delivered more than 12,000 judgments obliging governments to amend legislation and administrative practices in such areas as treatment while detained, **freedom of expression**, respect for private and **family** life, forced evictions, arbitrary killings, **forced disappearances**, **torture** and the lack of internal remedies. The Court can order that compensation be paid because of a breach of the Convention. Although less than 10 percent of the applications received by the Court meet its admissibility requirements, the judgments handed down by the Court, frequently intrusive and controversial, have been met with a remarkably high degree of compliance. *See also* ILL TREATMENT; INHUMAN OR DEGRADING TREATMENT OR PUNISHMENT; JUDICIARY, INDEPENDENCE OF; KATYN FOREST MASSACRE; NORTHERN IRELAND; RIGHTS INTERNATIONAL; SEXUAL ORIENTATION.

EUROPEAN COURT OF JUSTICE. *See* COURT OF JUSTICE.

EUROPEAN OMBUDSMAN. Position created by the 1993 Maastricht Treaty. Elected by the **European Parliament**, the incumbent investigates any **European Union** institution (except the **Court of Justice**) on the grounds of maladministration: administrative irregularities, unfairness, discrimination, abuse of power, failure to reply, refusal of information or unnecessary delay. The procedure may be initiated by any EU citizen or resident or company registered in a EU country. Each year the ombudsman receives about 3,000 to 4,000 **complaints**.

EUROPEAN PARLIAMENT (EP). Legislative arm of the **European Union** whose members are directly elected for a five-year term by citizens of the EU state members. The EP shares its legislative power with the Council and the Commission of the European Union, but its authority has been progressively expanded and it exerts considerable indirect influence through non-binding resolutions and committee hearings. Its Committee on Petitions (established since 1987) can receive appeals from any citizen or resident of the European Union or any company or organization headquartered in one of the EU member states, involving possible infringements of their rights in the application of European laws in such areas as the **environment, privacy,** social affairs and **freedom of movement.**

Each year, the Committee hears some 1,500 cases which it tries to resolve through mediation in cooperation with national, regional and local authorities. The Committee on Foreign Affairs, Human Rights, Common Security and Defence Policy works on the development of EU guidelines on human rights on such matters as **torture, capital punishment,** violence against women, the protection of children's rights and **children in armed conflict** and **human rights defenders.** It also may make recommendations pertaining to the inclusion of human rights clauses in EU agreements with third countries and publishes an annual report on human rights in the world. Another committee concerned with women's rights and gender equality seeks to promote women's rights in the European Union and third countries.

EUROPEAN RESEARCH CENTRE ON MIGRATION AND ETHNIC RELATIONS. European **think tank** located in Utrecht University, the Netherlands, carrying policy-oriented **research** and instruction and **capacity building** in the fields of international migration and ethnic relations within the European context. The Centre focuses its activities on environmental change and forced migration, the structural and cultural dimensions of the inclusion of immigrants and their descendants into European host societies and nationalism and ethnic conflict.

EUROPEAN ROMA RIGHTS CENTER. International public interest law organization engaged since its establishment in 1996 in activities aimed at combating anti-Romani **racism** and human rights abuses of **Roma** through strategic **litigation,** international **advocacy, research** and policy development, and human rights training of Romani activists.

EUROPEAN SOCIAL CHARTER. Council of Europe treaty adopted in 1961 and amended in 1999 which recognizes a wide array of economic, social and cultural rights including the right to work, the right to just conditions of work, the right to safe and healthy working conditions, the right to a fair remuneration, the right to bargain collectively, the right to **social security,** the right to benefit from social welfare services, the rights to social and legal protection, free movement of persons and non-**discrimination.** As such the Charter complements the **European Convention for the Protection of**

Human Rights and Fundamental Freedoms which guarantees civil and political rights. The rights set out in the Charter are protected by a system of states parties reporting yearly to the **European Committee on Social Rights**, a committee of independent experts who assesses whether situations in the countries concerned are in conformity with the Charter in law and practice.

Since the entry into force of an Additional Protocol in 1998, certain **nongovernmental organizations** enjoying participatory status with the Council of Europe and may lodge **complaints** with the Committee and may declare state parties to be in violation of the Charter. So far, the Committee has received some 60 complaints about a wide range of topics including the length of service of mobilized civilian populations, the right of armed forces to organize and bargain collectively, the prohibition of corporal punishment against children within the family, in secondary schools and other institutions that take care of children, the entitlement of illegal immigrants to medical assistance, discrimination in employment, child labor, the housing conditions for **Roma** (standards of permanent dwellings, temporary housing and the forced evictions) and their right to **health** care, restriction to the right to strike and the impact of lignite mining on the **environment** and on the health of the population living in the main lignite mining regions. *See also* EDUCATION, RIGHT TO; HOUSING, RIGHT TO ADEQUATE.

EUROPEAN UNION. Economic and political organization of 27 members which traces its origins to the 1957 six-country–based European Economic Community (EEC). Several treaties—especially the 1993 Maastricht, 1997 Amsterdam and 2009 **Lisbon Treaty**—have allowed the organization to enhance its powers and to acquire, in some areas, elements of a quasi-supranational authority. The Rome Treaty, which established the European Community, did not specifically protect human rights, although it did prohibit discrimination among EEC nationals, established the right of **freedom of movement** for workers in the Community and called for equal pay for equal work for men and women.

Subsequent treaties have profoundly altered the situation. They now aver that the European Union is "founded on the values of respect for human **dignity**, freedom, **democracy**, **equality**, the **rule of law** and respect for human rights, including the rights of persons belonging to minorities . . . in a society in which pluralism, non-discrimination, tolerance, justice, solidarity and equality between women and men prevail." The Lisbon Treaty has given effect to the 2001 **European Charter of Fundamental Rights of the European Union** and membership in the European Union is conditional upon becoming a party to the **European Convention for the Protection of Human Rights and Fundamental Freedoms** (ECHR) and the abolition of **capital punishment**. The Treaty also provides for the accession of the European Union to the ECHR.

See also CITIZENSHIP; COUNTERTERRORISM; COURT OF JUSTICE; EUROPEAN OMBUDSMAN; EUROPEAN PARLIAMENT; EUROPEAN SOCIAL CHARTER; UNITED NATIONS INTERIM ADMINISTRATION MISSION IN KOSOVO; UNITED NATIONS MISSION IN THE CENTRAL AFRICAN REPUBLIC AND CHAD.

EUTHANASIA. Practice of intentionally ending a life in order to relieve pain or suffering. Also called "mercy killing" or "assisted suicide" and, so defined, euthanasia has nothing to do with the Nazi program that gave authority to certain midwives and physicians to destroy "life unworthy of life" focusing first on newborn and very young children and later expanded to include anyone with symptoms of mental retardation or physical deformity. In part as a result of the aging of societies, euthanasia is a growing political and moral issue. Voluntary euthanasia is legal in some countries (such as Belgium and the Netherlands), and physician aid in dying is legal in four states in the **United States**. Non-voluntary euthanasia is illegal in all countries. *See also* LIFE, RIGHT TO.

EVANS, GARETH (1944–). Australian lawyer and politician who also served his country as foreign minister. He played a key role in brokering the **United Nations** peace plan for Cambodia and in bringing to a conclusion the negotiations over the international Chemical Weapons Convention. He co-chaired, with Mohamed Sahnoun of Algeria, the **International Commission on Intervention and State Sovereignty** whose 2001 report coined the groundbreaking concept of a "**Responsibility to Protect.**" From 2000 to 2009, he was the president of the **International Crisis Group**, a group devoted to conflict prevention. *See also* NORM ENTREPRENEURS.

EVENTS-BASED DATA. Method used to count and chart reported acts of omission or commission that constitute or may lead to **violations of human rights** against groups and individuals such as **extra-judicial executions**, **arbitrary detention** and arrests, cases of **torture**. This type of measuring of human rights is one of the prime activities of **non-governmental organizations** in tracking developments in the human rights situation of individual countries. *See also* MONITORING OF HUMAN RIGHTS.

EXHAUSTION REQUIREMENT. International law doctrine requiring that individual claimants first seek relief and **remedies** in a forum where the harm occurred (i.e., in the courts of a national state). Only when such means of **redress** have been exhausted or have proved ineffectual or unavailable can a claimant turn to an international judicial or quasi-judicial body for redress. Human rights instruments generally follow the international law standard and incorporate an exhaustion requirement. The **European Convention for the Protection of Human Rights and Fundamental Freedoms** provides that "[t]he Court may only deal with the matter after all **domestic remedies** have been exhausted, according to the generally recognised rules of international law." Similarly, Article 41 of the **American Convention on Human Rights** requires that "the remedies under domestic law have been pursued and exhausted in accordance with generally recognized principles of international law." The **International Covenant on Civil and Political Rights** refers to exhaustion of local remedies "in conformity with the generally recognized principles of international law." The exhaustion requirement is in effect a corollary of the **complementarity principle** and severely restricts the number of human rights claims acted upon by international judicial and quasi-judicial bodies. *See also* ADMISSIBILITY REQUIREMENTS.

EXTERNAL DEBT CRISIS. Until recently, this might have referred only to the long-standing and contentious issue of the indebtedness of countries of the Southern Hemisphere which has pitted them against their creditor Northern countries for more than four decades. Attention is now more focused on Europe's attempts to grapple with the sovereign debts of some of its members. The former problem emerged in many **developing countries** in the early 1980s and can be traced back to domestic economic mismanagement, higher oil prices in 1973–74 and 1979–80, high interest rates, declining export prices and volumes associated with the global recession of 1981–82.

The subsequent increasing integration of the world economy, changing conceptions of development now more focused on market-oriented prescriptions and the tensions on world commodity markets and the economic and financial turmoil of the past few years have tended to perpetuate and aggravate the crisis.

A number of impoverished countries have recently received partial or full cancellation of loans from foreign governments or international financial institutions. But the combined stock of developing countries' external debt, which was estimated to exceed $600 billion in 1980, has, according to **United Nations** figures, climbed to $4 trillion. The servicing of the debt represented 2.8 percent of GDP in 1980. It now exceeds 5 percent. The current average external debt to export ratio of developing countries is 82.4 percent.

These figures suggest the existence of an enormous drain of resources operating for the past decades from South to North. They have prompted calls emanating from **non-governmental organizations** and United Nations bodies for more drastic debt relief measures on the grounds that indebtedness-locked developing countries—especially the poorest among them—in a self-perpetuating cycle of poverty aggravation, blocked their development on the periphery of the world economy, contributed to deteriorations in living standards and adversely impacted the capacity of governments to fulfill their human rights obligations. Since 1998, a United Nations **special rapporteur** has been tasked by the **United Nations Commission on Human Rights** to analyze and assess the effects of foreign debt and the policies adopted to address them on the full enjoyment of all human rights, in particular, economic, social and cultural rights in developing countries. The latest incumbent has developed Guiding Principles on Foreign Debt and Human Rights which are being considered by the **United Nations Human Rights Council**. *See also* INTERNATIONAL MONETARY FUND; JUBILEE DEBT COALITION.

EXTRACTIVE INDUSTRIES TRANSPARENCY INITIATIVE (EITI). Voluntary scheme bringing together governments, investor companies, **civil society** groups and international organizations designed to strengthen the transparency and **accountability** of **governance** in the extractive sectors of countries rich in oil, gas and minerals on the basis of globally developed standards entailing the publication and verification of company payments and government mineral resources revenues. Launched in 2002, the EITI now involves some 30 mineral producing countries and a number of **non-governmental organizations** such as **Global Witness** and the Revenue Watch Institute. It has also received the support of the World Bank and the **International Monetary Fund**. The secretariat of the EITI is located in Oslo, Norway. *See also* CORPORATE SOCIAL RESPONSIBILITY; REVENUE WATCH; SOFT LAW; TRANSNATIONAL CORPORATIONS.

EXTRADITION. Legal process whereby a state surrenders an alleged offender to another state so that the latter can prosecute him or her. The procedure is normally based on bilateral agreements. Extradition may take place only if the actions of the accused constitute a crime within the jurisdiction of the courts of both the requested and requesting states (the so-called double criminality requirement). Offenses of a political nature precludes extradition. States that have ratified the second optional protocol to the **International Covenant on Civil and Political Rights** (ICCPR), other abolitionist states that are parties to the ICCPR, and states party to Protocol 6 of the **European Convention for the Protection of Human Rights and Fundamental Freedoms** cannot extradite without gaining assurances from the requesting state that it may not seek to impose **capital punishment** on the extradited offender. International instruments on **torture**, **terrorism**, hijacking and piracy require contracting states to extradite alleged offenders for trial unless the host state or the state of nationality decides to try the individuals concerned. The Statute of the **International Criminal Court** requires states to arrest on request specified individuals before surrendering them to the Court. *See also* CAPITAL PUNISHMENT; EXTRAORDINARY RENDITION; GENOCIDE; IMMUNITY; INTERNATIONAL CRIMINAL COURT; UNITED NATIONS CONVENTION AGAINST TRANSNATIONAL ORGANIZED CRIME; UNIVERSAL JURISDICTION.

EXTRA-JUDICIAL EXECUTIONS. Killing of a person by government police, military or paramilitary organizations without proper judicial proceeding and **due process** protections. Such killings, which often target leading political, trade union, dissidents, religious, and social figures, are in principle illegal but frequently occur in the context of internal conflicts, guerrilla warfare, counterinsurgency or **counterterrorism** practices. Efforts to prevent extra-judicial killings extend as far back as 1982 with the creation of a **special rapporteur** by the **United Nations Commission on Human Rights**.

See *also* ALGERIAN CIVIL WAR; ALGERIAN WAR OF INDEPENDENCE; ALIEN TORT STATUTE; ALSTON, PHILIP; ARGENTINA; ARMED GROUPS; BANGLADESH LIBERATION WAR; BRAZIL; CENTER FOR HUMAN RIGHTS AND GLOBAL JUSTICE; CHECHNYA; CHILE; DEATH SQUADS; DRONES; EL SALVADOR; ETHNIC CLEANSING; EXTRAORDINARY RENDITION; FORCED DISAPPEARANCES; HONDURAS; KOSOVO; LIFE, RIGHT TO; MYANMAR; PERU; PHILIPPINES; PUBLIC EMERGENCIES; SRI LANKA CIVIL WAR; STATE TERRORISM; UNIVERSAL JURISDICTION.

EXTRAORDINARY RENDITION. Rendition refers to the apprehension and handing over of persons or property by one state jurisdiction to another after legal proceedings and in accordance with the law and the treaties binding the states involved. **Extradition** is a common type of rendition. Extra-legal rendition is known as extraordinary rendition. And has been used, in particular, by the **Central Intelligence Agency** under President **George W. Bush** and involved the transfer of suspected terrorists to countries known to employ interrogation techniques rising to the level of **torture**. An estimated 150 people are believed to have been rendered between 2001 and 2005. Critics argue that the U.S. program was unethical, unconstitutional and violated international human rights and humanitarian law, notably the **Geneva Conventions** and the **United Nations Convention against**

Torture. Official investigations in Europe (not by organs of the **Council of Europe**) into alleged secret detention centers and unlawful interstate transfers revealed that several member states of the Council of Europe and their intelligence agencies had tolerated these illegal actions on their territories. One of the first decisions of the Barack Obama administration was to order the discontinuation of extraordinary renditions. *See also* CENTER FOR CONSTITUTIONAL RIGHTS; CENTER FOR HUMAN RIGHTS AND GLOBAL JUSTICE; COUNTERTERRORISM; FORCED DISAPPEARANCES; GUANTANAMO BAY DETENTION CAMP; "WAR ON TERROR."

F

FACT FINDING. Processes whereby information is investigated, collated, corroborated and publicized on human rights situations for the purpose of establishing and verifying the accuracy of the facts surrounding allegations of human rights problems and issues. Fact finding may consist of observing and reporting on what is happening as it occurs. It may also deal with the elucidation of facts about events which took place in the past. States, international organizations and their secretariats, judicial and quasi-judicial bodies, **non-state actors**, especially **non-governmental organizations**, all carry out more or less formalized fact-finding activities in widely different formats and modalities. Most of them result in the issuance of reports designed to meet a wide variety of objectives including raising awareness, preventing **violations of human rights** and **international humanitarian law**, influencing human rights policy debates and outcomes, conveying the truth and ensuring accountability and seeking the punishment of perpetrators. By and large, human rights fact-finding procedures have not been standardized in regard to issues such as accuracy, impartiality, sources protection or funding. They frequently proceed from political considerations and turn into substitutes for de facto inaction in the face of the commission of human right violations.

See also ARAB ORGANIZATION FOR HUMAN RIGHTS; CENTRE ON HOUSING RIGHTS AND EVICTIONS; COUNCIL OF EUROPE COMMISSIONER FOR HUMAN RIGHTS; EARTH RIGHTS INTERNATIONAL; ENFORCEMENT; EUROPEAN COMMISSION AGAINST RACISM AND INTOLERANCE; GOLDSTONE REPORT; HABITAT INTERNATIONAL COALITION; HUMAN RIGHTS INSTITUTE; HUMAN RIGHTS WATCH; INDEPENDENT INTERNATIONAL COMMISSION ON KOSOVO; INQUIRY PROCEDURES; INTERNATIONAL COMMISSION OF JURISTS; INTERNATIONAL FEDERATION FOR HUMAN RIGHTS; INTERNATIONAL LABOUR ORGANIZATION; INVESTIGATION; KURDISH HUMAN RIGHTS PROJECT; OFFICE FOR RESEARCH AND THE COLLECTION OF INFORMATION; PHYSICIANS FOR HUMAN RIGHTS; SPECIAL RAPPORTEURS; UNITED NATIONS

WORKING GROUP ON ARBITRARY DETENTION; WOMEN'S REFUGEE COMMISSION.

FAILED STATE. Although there is no universally accepted definition of the term, it is generally understood that a failed state is a state whose central government exerts little practical control over its territory and is unable to perform its security and public service functions. An American **think tank** and the magazine *Foreign Policy* publish an annual index of failed states relying on social, economic and political indicators including demographic pressures, massive movements of **refugees** and **internally displaced persons**, a legacy of vengeance-seeking group grievances, uneven economic development along group lines, sharp or severe economic decline, endemic **corruption**, the progressive deterioration of public services, widespread **violations of human rights**, the rise of factional elites and intervention of other states.

FAIR TRIAL, RIGHT TO. One of the cornerstones of the **rule of law** incorporating a number of principles including the right to recognition as a person and equality before the law and the freedom from **discrimination**, the presumption of innocence, the right to a public trial, a speedy determination of the law, an adequate defense, the right to appeal and compensation in the event of a mistrial. These principles have been elaborated in **General Comment** 13 of the **United Nations Human Rights Committee** and they have received considerable attention at the regional level, especially in the comprehensive jurisprudence of the **European Court of Human Rights**. *See also* DUE PROCESS RIGHTS; EQUALITY BEFORE THE LAW; RECOGNITION, RIGHT TO.

FAMILY, RIGHT TO A. The right to establish a family is enshrined in most international and regional human rights instruments (the **Universal Declaration of Human Rights**, Art. 16; **International Covenant on Civil and Political Rights**, Art. 23; the **International Covenant on Economic, Social and Cultural Rights**, Art. 10; **International Convention on the Elimination of All Forms of Racial Discrimination**, Art. 5; **United Nations Convention on the Elimination of All Forms of Discrimination against Women**, Art. 16, the **American Convention on Human Rights**, Art. 17, the **Arab Charter on Human Rights**, Art. 33 and the **European Convention for the Protection of Human Rights and Fundamental Freedoms** [ECHR], Art. 12). The right entails in particular the right to procreate and adopt children and is thus incompatible with any compulsory or discriminatory family planning schemes. It might be potentially invoked in connection with the issue of whether individuals have a right to access new techniques of reproductive medicine. The definition of a family, however, has been a recurrent source of controversy to the extent that family rights relate closely to issues of taxation, property and **nationality** which are traditionally considered culturally defined matters of internal law as underlined by the high number of **reservations** entered in the instruments of **ratification** of the **United Nations Convention on the Elimination of All Forms of Discrimination against Women**.

The more uniform cultural traditions prevailing in Europe explain why the **European Court of Human Rights** (ECHR) has developed in its jurisprudence a more precise definition of the family. Its case law recognizes marital and extramarital relationships between men and women as family ties. Homosexual couples can only invoke the right to respect of private life. The ECHR also emphasized that family life must be based on genuine relationships and close personal ties. The Court's jurisprudence as well as UN treaty **monitoring** bodies have addressed questions related to the removal of parents' guardianship rights over children, the custody of children after divorce or separation and a father's right of access to a child born out of wedlock. Both the ECHR and the **United Nations Human Rights Committee** have also addressed the issue of family unity in the area of immigration law. *See also* INTER-AMERICAN CHILDREN INSTITUTE; MARRY, RIGHT TO; NON-DEROGABLE RIGHTS; NORDIC COMMITTEE FOR HUMAN RIGHTS; PRIVACY, RIGHT TO; REPRODUCTIVE RIGHTS; RIGHTS INTERNATIONAL; STERILIZATION; TRUTH, RIGHT TO THE.

FAMILY CARE INTERNATIONAL (FCI). **Non-governmental organization** founded in 1986 seeking cooperation within governments, professional groups, and international agencies to improve maternal **health** at the global, regional, and country levels through the exchange of information and experience, building the capacity of local partners in developing countries, and the development of training material. The FCI works within the comprehensive, rights-based approach to sexual and reproductive health endorsed by the international community at recent United Nations conferences, safe motherhood and **HIV/AIDS** with particular attention to unsafe abortions, **gender-based violence** and family planning. In 2008, the FCI was the recipient of the United Nations Population Award. *See also* REPRODUCTIVE RIGHTS.

FAMILY PLANNING. *See* REPRODUCTIVE RIGHTS.

FEDERATION INTERNATIONALE DES DROITS DE L'HOMME. *See* INTERNATIONAL FEDERATION FOR HUMAN RIGHTS.

FEDERATION INTERNATIONALE TERRE DES HOMMES. Swiss **non-governmental organization** founded in 1960 for the purpose of providing support to underprivileged children who were not receiving assistance from relief agencies. Guided by the **United Nations Convention on the Rights of the Child**, Terre des Hommes now advocates, mobilizes political will and carries out field projects in some 70 countries to improve living conditions of disadvantaged children. It enjoys **consultative status** with the United Nations, the **United Nations Children Fund**, the **International Labour Organization** and the **Council of Europe**.

FEMALE GENITAL MUTILATION (FGM). Procedure involving the partial or total removal of the external female genitalia for a variety of cultural and religious reasons. Most of the girls and women who have undergone genital mutilation live in Africa and some Asian and Middle Eastern countries. They are also increasingly found in Europe, Australia, Canada and the United States, primarily among immigrants from these countries. The number of girls and women who have undergone FGM is estimated to range from 120 to 140 million. It is believed that each year, a further 3 million girls are at risk of undergoing FGM. Usually performed by traditional practitioners with crude instruments and without anesthetics, FGM has adverse **health** consequences ranging from severe pain, shock, hemorrhage, urine retention, ulceration of the genital region and injury to adjacent tissue. Hemorrhage and infection can cause death.

For nearly 30 years, the issue has been discussed in the **United Nations General Assembly**, the **United Nations Commission on the Status of Women**, the now defunct **United Nations Commission on Human Rights** and its successor body, the **United Nations Human Rights Council** where efforts to prohibit female circumcision were often perceived as interference in social and cultural practices. A number of **non-governmental organization** networks such as the **Inter-African Committee on Traditional Practices Affecting the Health of Women** have provided the impetus for individual attention to the issue. United Nations global conferences (notably the 1994 and 1995 conferences on population and women respectively) have widely condemned the practice and called upon member states to prohibit it. Several international human rights conventions (the **International Covenant on Civil and Political Rights**, the **United Nations Convention on the Elimination of All Forms of Discrimination against Women** and the **United Nations Convention on the Rights of the Child**) include provisions that can be applied to FGM, and the expert bodies overseeing their implementation have encouraged states parties to increase their efforts to combat the practice.

At the regional level, a 2003 Protocol to the **African Charter on the Rights and Welfare of the Child** has also called for the elimination of harmful traditional customs and practices. A number of states have launched **advocacy** and awareness raising **campaigns**, enacted legislation banning or criminalizing female circumcision as a form of violence or a **violation of the human rights** of women and children and taken other supportive measures. Major challenges nevertheless remain, including weak enforcement, inadequate financial resources, insufficient awareness and commitment and the persistence of the belief that the practice is a private and family issue that should not be brought into the public arena for discussion and action. New approaches are thus being developed (for example by the **United Nations Children's Fund** and **United Nations Population Fund**) that are both culturally sensitive and address the practice as a human rights violation through the involvement of highly visible opinion makers and community and religious leaders. *See also* CAIRO CONFERENCE ON POPULATION AND DEVELOPMENT; CULTURAL RELATIVISM; EQUALITY NOW; INTER-AFRICAN COMMITTEE ON TRADITIONAL PRACTICES AFFECTING THE HEALTH OF WOMEN; NO PEACE WITHOUT JUSTICE.

FEMALE INFANTICIDE. Abortion of a fetus ("foeticide") or killing of an infant because it is female. This long-standing practice is as old as many civilizations and probably accounts for millions of gender-selective deaths. Female infanticide is often officially outlawed, but its persistence reflects the low status accorded to women in many societies and it is still widespread in a number of Third World countries, notably China, India and Japan, some of the most populous countries in the world. There are no overall statistics on the numbers of girls who die annually from infanticide. The unreliability and ambiguity of much of the available data are further justification for cautiousness. But the number of "missing girls" may be as high as 60 million fewer than demographic trends had forecast, and demographers have documented significant imbalances in the gender distribution of many national populations. An unintended consequence of female infanticide has been to encourage the transnational trade in kidnapped and enslaved women. *See also* FEMICIDE; GENDERCIDE; REPRODUCTIVE RIGHTS.

FEMICIDE. Culturally driven social practices leading to various forms of murder of women including sexual murder; the killings of prostitutes; **honor killings, female infanticide** and dowry deaths. The causes and risks factors of this type of violence have been linked to gender inequalities, discrimination, economic disempowerment and, more generally, a cultural environment involving the acceptance of acts of violence against women and the indifference or benign neglect of government authorities. *See also* GENDERCIDE.

FEMINISM. Political movement which originated in Great Britain and the **United States** at the end of the 19th century and initially focused on the promotion of equal marriage, contract and property rights for women. Thereafter, feminist activism has progressively broadened its agenda to include the right of women's suffrage and, now, the defense of equal political, social and economic opportunities for women. One of the major contributions of feminism to human rights has been not only to promote greater gender equality but also to question and open large breaches in the conventional divide of the social world into the private and public spheres, long viewed by advocates of human rights as the cornerstone of the **universality** and inalienability of rights. As feminists argue, maintaining that distinction simply leads to ignoring egregious and systematic violations of women's rights.

Milestones in the process of enhancing women's rights were a series of **United Nations Global Conferences** which started in 1975 and the adoption in 1979 of the **United Nations Convention on the Elimination of All Forms of Discrimination against Women.** Greater attention is now being given to protecting women's rights to bodily integrity and, in particular, to such issues as **domestic violence, gender-based violence,** and **reproductive rights.** Feminism has been criticized for reflecting the viewpoint of Western white, educated, middle class women but it is increasingly espoused by women around the world. *See also* FOURTH WORLD CONFERENCE ON WOMEN.

FINTA, IMRE (1911–2003). Hungarian police commander during **World War II**, Finta emigrated to Canada in 1948 and acquired Canadian nationality in 1956. Accused of assisting the Nazis in the deportation of over 8,000 Jews, he was prosecuted under Canada's war crimes legislation but was acquitted in 1990 on the grounds that he was following orders and was only responsible for transporting Jews. Thereafter, the Canadian government dealt with alleged war criminals first by stripping them of their Canadian nationality and then deporting them to the countries where the crimes were alleged to have been committed. *See also* COMMAND RESPONSIBILITY; HOLOCAUST.

FIRST-GENERATION RIGHTS. Set of individual rights that are fundamentally **civil and political rights** such as freedom of speech, **freedom of religion**, the right to a **fair trial** and voting rights. *See also* COLD WAR; GENERATION OF RIGHTS; SECOND-GENERATION RIGHTS; THIRD-GENERATION RIGHTS; VASAK, KAREL.

FOOD, RIGHT TO. Individual and collective right stated in the **International Covenant on Economic, Social and Cultural Rights** (ICESR, Art. 11(1)) and also enshrined in several international human rights bodies, notably the **United Nations Convention on the Rights of the Child** (Art. 24 (2)) and of the Additional Protocol to the **Geneva Conventions** Relating to the Protection of Victims of International and Non-International Armed Conflicts (Art. 54(1)(2)). A **United Nations special rapporteur** has defined the right to food as an inherent right "in all people, to have regular, permanent and unrestricted access, either directly or by means of financial purchases, to quantitatively and qualitatively adequate and sufficient food corresponding to the cultural traditions of people to which the consumer belongs, and which ensures a physical and mental, individual and collective fulfilling and dignified life free of fear." In a 1999 **General Comment**, the **United Nations Committee on Economic, Social and Cultural Rights** clarified that the states' obligations under the right to food were to "respect, protect and fulfill each person's access to food."

The obligation to *fulfill* incorporates both an obligation to *facilitate* and an obligation to *provide*. The obligation to *respect* existing access to adequate food requires states parties to refrain from taking any measures that result in preventing such access. The obligation to *protect* requires measures by the state to ensure that enterprises or individuals do not deprive individuals of their access to adequate food. The obligation to *fulfill* (facilitate) means that the state must proactively engage in activities intended to strengthen people's access to and utilization of resources and means to ensure their livelihood, including **food security**. Finally, whenever an individual or group is unable, for reasons beyond their control, to enjoy the right to adequate food by the means at their disposal, states have the obligation to *fulfill* (provide) that right directly. This obligation also applies to persons who are victims of natural or other disasters.

Under the ICESR, states' parties pledge to take steps "individually and through international assistance and cooperation" to bring about the progressive realization of social, economic and cultural rights. National constitutions generally acknowledge at least implicitly that the state has a responsibility to secure adequate living conditions for everybody in the form, for example, of **agrarian reform** and minimum wage legislation or the payment of a lump sum for the purchase of food. In a landmark 2001 case, the **African Commission on Human and People's Rights** found that the Nigerian government had violated the Ogoni community's rights to **health**, a healthy **environment**, **housing** and food under the **African Charter on Human and People's Rights** for allowing or contributing to the widespread contamination of soil, water and air; the destruction of homes; the burning of crops and killing of farm animals. Yet, by and large, even benign national policies do not necessarily translate into legal guarantees to be free from hunger. Agrarian reform measures, an indispensable tool of food security, have frequently been deficient. Likewise, at the international level, few states explicitly accept the existence of a right to food. This is why the 2004 Guidelines adopted by the **Food and Agriculture Organization** to provide further guidance to states and stakeholders working toward a better implementation of the right to food at national level remain purely voluntary and nonbinding.

See also AMERICAN CONVENTION ON HUMAN RIGHTS; CENTER FOR ECONOMIC AND SOCIAL RIGHTS; FOOD FIRST INFORMATION AND ACTION NETWORK; GRASSROOTS INTERNATIONAL; HUNGER PROJECT; INTELLECTUAL PROPERTY RIGHTS; PUBLIC GOODS; SEN, AMARTYA; SOCIAL SECURITY, RIGHT TO; SOFT LAW; WORK, RIGHT TO; UNITED NATIONS CONFERENCE ON HUMAN SETTLEMENTS; UNITED NATIONS CONVENTION TO COMBAT DESERTIFICATION; UNIVERSAL DECLARATION ON THE ERADICATION OF HUNGER AND MALNUTRITION.

FOOD AND AGRICULTURAL ORGANIZATION (FAO). United Nations specialized agency which, since its creation in 1945, has served as a forum for policy debate, a source of knowledge and information and an instrument to help countries modernize and improve agricultural, forestry and fisheries practices and ensure good nutrition and **food security** for all. FAO's Strategic Framework 2000–2015 calls for the organization to take into full account "progress made in further developing a rights-based approach to food security in carrying out its mission and helping to build a food-secure world for present and future generations." *See also* AGRARIAN REFORM; HUMAN RIGHTS BASED APPROACH TO DEVELOPMENT; INTERNATIONAL CONFERENCE ON AGRARIAN REFORM AND RURAL DEVELOPMENT.

FOOD FIRST INFORMATION AND ACTION NETWORK (FIAN). International **non-governmental organization** acting in defense of a **right to food** and "**food sovereignty**." FIAN claims to have around 3,300 members with sections in a dozen countries. Its **advocacy** activities focus primarily on small farmers and landless peoples. A typical activity of FIAN is to organize "action alerts" in situations involving violations of the right of food (evictions of farmers from their land, for example).

FOOD SECURITY. According to the **Food and Agricultural Organization** (FAO), food security prevails when all people, at all times, have physical and economic access to sufficient, safe and nutritious food to meet their dietary needs and food preferences for an active and healthy life. Global per capita food production has been increasing substantially for the past several decades, but many countries experience recurring food shortages and distribution problems. Over a billion people are currently undernourished and chronically hungry due to a wide range of factors including varying degrees of **poverty** and inequality, population growth, climate change, water shortages, loss of agricultural land, declining shares of Official Development Assistance devoted to agriculture, poor **governance**, and rising world commodity prices. The FAO has held four "Summits," in 1974, 1996, 2002 and 2009, which adopted time-bound targets for the reduction of global undernourishment that have been largely ignored. Under current trends, it is not expected that the target of halving the number of undernourished people will be met at the earliest before the mid-2040s.

See also AGRARIAN REFORM; FOOD, RIGHT TO; FOOD FIRST INFORMATION AND ACTION NETWORK; FOOD SOVEREIGNTY; KIM IL SUNG; SEN, AMARTYA; UNIVERSAL DECLARATION ON THE ERADICATION OF HUNGER AND MALNUTRITION.

FOOD SOVEREIGNTY. Policy framework increasingly touted by small farmers, peasants, **indigenous peoples**, women, rural youth and environmental organizations as an alternative to the narrower concept of **food security**. According to the **Food First Information and Action Network**, food security places "the perspective and needs of the majority at the heart of the global food policy agenda and embraces not only the control of production and markets, but also the right to **food**, people's access to and control over land, **water** and genetic resources, and the use of environmentally sustainable approaches to production." The approach is "a persuasive and highly political argument for refocusing the control of food production and consumption within democratic processes rooted in localized food systems."

Food security thus rests on a number of interrelated principles and assumptions. First, access to safe, nutritious and culturally appropriate food in sufficient quantity and quality should be a constitutionally guaranteed and protected right; second, the concrete realization of this right requires genuine **agrarian reform** in order to give landless and farming people ownership and control of the land; third, natural resources should be managed in a sustainable way and biodiversity protected from restrictive **intellectual property rights**; fourth, national policy should give priority to domestic production and self-sufficiency in order to prevent imports from displacing local producers; fifth, speculative capital should be regulated and multinational agro-businesses controlled by means of binding codes of conduct; sixth, smallholder farmers should be granted direct and active decision-making on food and rural issues at the national and international levels. In late 2008, Ecuador enshrined food security in its constitution.

FORCED DISAPPEARANCES. Term used when people vanish because they have been secretly seized, imprisoned or killed by the government or other organizations. The Spanish language equivalent (*desaparecidos*) explicitly refers to persons who disappeared in South American countries in the 1970s and 1980s. Forced (or enforced or involuntary) disappearances have been a long-standing practice of abusive governments. Millions disappeared in the Soviet Union during the Great Purge of the 1930s. During **World War II**, Nazi Germany initiated a *Nacht und Nebel* policy involving the use of secret police forces in occupied countries which hunted down dissidents and partisans.

During the **Cold War**, disappearances occurred in Latin American regimes as part of their self-proclaimed struggle against "leftists" and "terrorists." Throughout the 1960s, 1970s and 1980s, security forces, paramilitary **armed groups** and shady **death squads** in **Argentina, Brazil, Chile, El Salvador, Guatemala, Honduras**, Nicaragua, **Paraguay**, the **Philippines** and **Uruguay** secretly kidnapped, tortured and killed thousands of political opponents. Dozens of people disappeared in the course of **Northern Ireland**'s "Troubles" in the 1970s. Iraq and Sri Lanka are the countries with the highest number of disappearances between 1980 and 2003 as documented by the **United Nations Working Group on the Protection of All Persons from Enforced Disappearances**, a watchdog of the **United Nations Commission on Human Rights**. Disappearances continue to take place in such countries torn by civil wars or irredentist insurgencies as **Colombia** and the Russian Federation.

The practice has been condemned and it was prohibited by the 1992 **Declaration on the Protection of All Persons from Enforced Disappearance** and the 2006 **International Convention for the Protection of All Persons from Enforced Disappearance**. The Rome Statute of the **International Criminal Court** identifies disappearances as a **crime against humanity** and defines it as "the arrest, detention or abduction of persons by, or with the authorization, support or acquiescence of a state or political organization, followed by a refusal to acknowledge that deprivation of freedom or to give information on the fate or whereabouts of those persons, with the intention of removing them from the protection of the law for a prolonged period of time."

Incommunicado detention does not necessarily constitute "disappearance" under international law, but the **International Covenant on Civil and Political Rights** requires its state parties to treat prisoners "with humanity and with respect for the inherent **dignity** of the human person." The United Nations Human Rights Committee has also commented that its parties must guarantee the effective protection of detained persons and make public their names as well as their place of detention.

Under international human rights law, disappearances infringe upon a whole range of human rights, especially the right to recognition as a person before the law, the right to **liberty** and the security of the person, the right not to be subjected to **torture** and the right to **life**. Disappearances can also involve serious violations of norms and rules dealing with the treatment of prisoners. The Committee has also dealt with a number of **complaints** involving forced disappearances. Legal claims of forced disappearances have been adjudicated since the 1980s by the **Inter-American Court of Human Rights** and, more recently, by the **European Court of Human Rights**. The onset of the "**war on terror**" has rekindled the practice of disappearances, fueling fresh political and legal controversy.

See also AL-ANFAL CAMPAIGN; ARBITRARY DETENTION; CENTER FOR HUMAN RIGHTS AND GLOBAL JUSTICE; CHECHNYA; "DIRTY WAR"; EGYPT; EXTRA-JUDICIAL EXECUTIONS; EXTRAORDINARY RENDITION; HONDURAS; INTER-AMERICAN CONVENTION ON FORCED DISAPPEARANCES OF PERSONS; LIBERTY, RIGHT TO; LIBYA; OPERATION CONDOR; ORGANIZATION OF AMERICAN STATES; STATE TERRORISM; SYRIA; TRUTH, RIGHT TO THE; TURKEY; UNITED NATIONS WORKING GROUP ON THE PROTECTION OF ALL PERSONS FROM ENFORCED DISAPPEARANCES; UNIVERSAL JURISDICTION; WORLD ORGANIZATION AGAINST TORTURE.

FORCED EVICTIONS. In one of its **General Comments**, the **United Nations Committee on Economic, Social and Cultural Rights** has defined forced evictions as "the permanent or temporary removal against their will of individuals, families and/or communities from the homes and/or land which they occupy, without the provision of, and access to, appropriate forms of legal or other protection." The Committee has further opined that forced evictions breach the rights enshrined in the **International Covenant on Economic, Social and Cultural Rights**, notably the right to adequate **housing**, may lead to further violations of **civil and political rights**, such as the **right to life**, the right to the security of the person, the right to non-interference with **privacy**, **family** and home, and the right to the peaceful enjoyment of possessions. The obligations of governments include a responsibility to enact legislation against forced eviction and the provision of legal **remedies** and compensation. If forced evictions are

274 • FORCED LABOR

deemed necessary, they should be carried out "in accordance with general principles of reasonableness and **proportionality**. Surveys published by **non-governmental organizations** such as the **Centre on Housing Rights and Evictions** show, however, that governments, international agencies such as the World Bank and **transnational corporations** are often actively involved in the physical removal of people from their homes. *See also* HABITAT INTERNATIONAL COALITION; UNITED NATIONS SUB-COMMISSION ON THE PROMOTION AND PROTECTION OF HUMAN RIGHTS.

FORCED LABOR. For the purposes of international human rights law, the 1930 Forced Labor Convention of the **International Labour Organization** (ILO) defines forced labor as "all work or service which is exacted from any person under the menace of any penalty and for which the said person has not offered himself voluntarily." So defined, the concept of forced labor covers a wide range of phenomena including **slavery**, slavery-like practices such as serfdom, **human trafficking** for labor or sexual exploitation, **migrant workers** trapped in debt **labor bondage**, women and girls forced into prostitution, children working in sweatshops with little pay, farm and rural debt bondage, the abuse of **domestic workers**, labor exacted by a state or by agencies of a state, other than as a punishment for a criminal offence (labor camps, prison labor). A 1957 ILO convention enjoins its parties to suppress and not to make use of any form of forced or compulsory labor, and most countries have adopted legislation that deals with forced labor as a serious criminal offense. But it is believed that at least 12.3 million people around the world are trapped in forced labor conditions, more than 2.4 million have been trafficked, 9.8 million are exploited by private agents and 2.5 million are forced to work by the state or rebel groups. A recent study by the organization avers that the victims of forced labor lose an estimated 20 billion every year in unpaid earnings.

    See also ALIEN TORT STATUTE; CHILDREN TRAFFICKING; CORPORATE SOCIAL RESPONSIBILITY; EUROPEAN CONVENTION FOR THE PROTECTION OF HUMAN RIGHTS AND FUNDAMENTAL FREEDOMS; GULAG; INTERNATIONAL TRADE UNION CONFEDERATION; LIBERTY, RIGHT TO; MYANMAR; SIERRA CLUB.

FORCED MIGRATION. The **International Organization for Migration** defines forced migration as the non-voluntary movement of people who wish to escape an armed conflict, violence, the violation of their rights or a natural or man-made disaster. The term has also been applied to **refugee** movements, the forced exchange of populations among states or **human trafficking.** *See also* ETHNIC CLEANSING.

FORD FOUNDATION. Private **foundation** based in New York created in 1936 by the Edsel and Henry Ford family. It is one of the most important foundations in the world, with assets of $10 billion and approved grants exceeding $400 million in 2011. **Poverty** reduction, the promotion of **democracy** and the advancement of the arts have been long-standing objectives of the foundation. Its current priorities are democratic government and **accountability**, **freedom of expression**, sustainable development, **reproductive rights**, and the expansion of educational opportunities. Specifically, in regard to human rights, the foundation focuses its funding on racial and ethnic **minorities** and **indigenous peoples**, **migrant**'s rights, the reform of civil and criminal justice, the advancement of economic and social rights, the protection of women's rights and the protection of people affected by **HIV/AIDS**.

FORUM 18. Norwegian news service of Christian obedience reporting on threats and actions against **freedom of religion**, especially in the republics of the former Soviet Union. Forum 18 issues daily and weekly news summaries which may be freely subscribed to on the Internet. It also holds public hearings to make available research on serious violations.

FORUM FOR FACT-FINDING DOCUMENTATION AND AD-VOCACY (FFDA). Indian human rights monitoring and **advocacy** organization founded in 1995 which focuses on the issues of displacement, violence against women and children, **torture**, and attacks on **minorities** and **indigenous peoples**.

FORUM ON EARLY WARNING AND EARLY RESPONSE. International coalition of **non-governmental organizations**, governmental agencies and academic institutions established in 1987 promoting coordinated preventive and peace-building responses to violent conflict through **research** and analysis in Africa and Eurasia. *See also* EARLY WARNING; PREVENTION.

FORUM ON MINORITY ISSUES. Successor body to the **United Nations Working Group on Minorities** set up by the **United Nations Human Rights Council** in 2007 to provide, under the guidance of the Council, a platform for promoting dialogue and cooperation on issues pertaining to national or ethnic, religious and linguistic **minorities**, as well as thematic contributions and expertise to the work of the independent expert on minority issues. The Forum is expected to identify and analyze best practices, challenges, opportunities and initiatives for the further implementation of the **Declaration on the Rights of Persons Belonging to National or Ethnic, Religious and Linguistic Minorities**. The Forum meets twice a year and draws a large participation from representatives of member states, concerned **United Nations** bodies, governmental organizations, regional organizations and mechanisms in the field of human rights, **national human rights institutions** and other relevant national bodies, academics and experts on minority issues and **non-governmental organizations** (NGOs). A typical session of the Forum involves over 500 individuals, including more than 80 minority political actors and representatives of some 90 NGOs.

FOUNDATIONS. Non-governmental entities established by endowment as not-for-profit corporations or charitable trusts whose typical function is to make grants to unrelated organizations, institutions or individuals for scientific, educational, cultural and other purposes. Private foundations like **George Soros's Open Society Institute** or the **Ford Foundation** derive their money from a family, an individual or a corporation. Public foundations draw their resources from various sources, including individuals and government agencies. Their activities touch on virtually all spheres of human activities with direct or indirect consequences for the promotion of human rights including **education**, civil rights, crime prevention, the protection of the **environment, health, employment, food,** nutrition, **housing,** public safety, community improvement, **capacity building.** *See also* FRIEDRICH-EBERT FOUNDATION; GLOBAL FUND FOR WOMEN; NON-GOVERNMENTAL ORGANIZATIONS; NORWEGIAN REFUGEE COUNCIL.

FOURTEEN POINTS. *See* WILSON, WOODROW.

FOURTH WORLD CONFERENCE ON WOMEN (1995). Fourth in a series of **global conferences** organized by the **United Nations** (the three previous conferences were held in Mexico City [International Women's Year, 1975], Copenhagen [1980] and Nairobi [1985]). The meeting which was held in Beijing 4–15 September 1995 brought together 189 governments and more than 5,000 representatives of 2,100 **non-governmental organizations** and dealt with a broad array of issues related to the advancement and empowerment of women, women and poverty, women and decision-making, the girl-child and **gender-based violence**. The Beijing Declaration and Platform for Action adopted by the Conference is a strongly worded normative document emphasizing that the elimination of inequality and

discrimination against women in private and public life must be understood as an integral part of the realization of universal human rights and calling for a renewed commitment to the standards of **equality** between men and women that required changes in values, attitudes, practices, priorities and institutions at the local, national, regional and global levels. *See also* INTERNATIONAL CONFERENCE ON POPULATION AND DEVELOPMENT; GENDER MAINSTREAMING; SOFT LAW.

FRAMEWORK CONVENTION ON THE PROTECTION OF NATIONAL MINORITIES (1994). Regional international convention elaborated by the **Council of Europe** which remains, as of today, the only legally binding multilateral instrument devoted to the protection of national **minorities**. The Convention which entered into force in 1998 reaffirms the broad principles of protection of minorities (non-**discrimination**, **equality**, and the promotion and preservation of their culture, religion and traditions) and spells out their individual and collective rights (**freedom of association**, **freedom of religion** and assembly, use of minority language, **education**, participation in economic, social, cultural and political life, among others). It also establishes a system of **accountability** by states parties which are required to submit periodic reports containing full information on the measures they take to give effect to the principles of the Convention. Country visits complement these monitoring procedures.

See also CULTURAL RIGHTS; EUROPEAN CHARTER FOR REGIONAL OR MINORITY LANGUAGES; EUROPEAN CONVENTION FOR THE PROTECTION OF HUMAN RIGHTS AND FUNDAMENTAL FREEDOMS; STATE REPORTING.

FRANCE. *See* ALGERIAN WAR OF INDEPENDENCE; AUSSARESSES, PAUL; BARBIE, KLAUS; *BATTLE OF ALGIERS*; BOKASSA, JEAN-BEDEL; COUNTERTERRORISM; HARKIS; HONOR KILLING; INTERNATIONAL MILITARY TRIBUNAL FOR THE FAR EAST; INTERNATIONAL MILITARY TRIBUNAL FOR THE PROSECUTION AND PUNISHMENT OF THE MAJOR WAR CRIMINALS OF THE EUROPEAN AXIS; NO-FLY ZONE; PAPON, MAURICE; TOUVIER, PAUL; VIETNAM WAR; WOMEN IN PEACE AND SECURITY; WORLD WAR I PEACE TREATIES.

FRANCO, FRANCISCO (1892–1975). Head of state of Spain from 1936 to his death. He came to power in the wake of a bitter and bloody civil war which he won with the support of Fascist Italy and Nazi Germany (some 200,000 executions were carried out by both sides during the war). Thereafter,

Franco maintained a tight grip over the country, relying on repressive and authoritarian measures ranging from summary executions and the use of **capital punishment**, to **torture**, imprisonment, **forced labor** and censorship. Amid considerable controversy and lingering resistance by large segments of the population who benefited from the economic gains achieved during Franco's rule, Spain gradually and gingerly evolved back to **democracy** after his demise. It was not until 2004 that the government set up a Commission to repair the dignity and restore the memory of the victims of Francoism. Three years later, legislation was enacted to officially recognize the crimes committed against civilians during the Francoist rule and mandating a search for mass graves under state supervision. In 2006, a Commission of the **European Parliament** unanimously adopted a resolution condemning the "multiple and serious **violations**" **of human rights** committed in Spain by the Franco regime between 1939 and 1975.

FRASER INSTITUTE. Canadian **think tank** founded in 1974 and headquartered in Vancouver which conducts **research** on "the impact of competitive markets and government intervention on the welfare of individuals." While it describes itself as "an independent international research and educational organization," the Institute has been variously labeled politically conservative and right-wing libertarian. It has also been embroiled in controversies for its close ties with the logging and tobacco industries. It is best known for its annual Economic Freedom of the World index, which ranks the countries of the world according to their degrees of economic freedom. *See also* MONITORING OF HUMAN RIGHTS.

FREEDOM HOUSE. American, governmentally funded **research** institute located in Washington, D.C., focused on the promotion of liberal **democracy** in the world. Founded in 1941, Freedom House supported the Marshall Plan and the establishment of the **North Atlantic Treaty Organization**. It was critical of McCarthyism in the 1950s but backed the United States civil rights movement in the 1960s. During the 1980s, it lent its support to the Solidarity movement in Poland and the democratic opposition in the Philippines. Since 1978, Freedom House produces a yearly report assessing the degree of democracy and levels of political rights and civil liberties in individual countries. It also issues annual reports on press freedom and governance. Freedom House has aroused criticisms (which it disputes) that it favors American definitions of human rights and acts as an "anticommunist propaganda institution." *See also* MONITORING OF HUMAN RIGHTS; THINK TANKS.

FREEDOM NOW. All volunteer, non-profit, non-partisan organization which facilitates legal representation for arbitrarily detained individuals. Freedom Now focuses on high-impact cases. For example, in 2006, it filed a petition to the **United Nations Working Group on Arbitrary Detention** on behalf of **Aung San Suu Kyi** demanding her release from house arrest.

FREEDOM OF ASSEMBLY. *See* FREEDOM OF ASSOCIATION.

FREEDOM OF ASSOCIATION. Also sometimes used interchangeably with "freedom of assembly," the term refers to the right of individuals to express, promote, pursue and defend common interests. Assembling and protesting in public places, establishing and freely joining associations are instances of freedom of association. As such, the right is explicitly recognized as a fundamental right by the **Universal Declaration of Human Rights** (Art. 20), the **International Covenant on Civil and Political Rights** (Art. 21), the **European Convention for the Protection of Human Rights and Fundamental Freedoms** (Art. 11) and the **American Convention on Human Rights** (Art. 15). The right is also enshrined in the constitutions of liberal democratic regimes. In the context of the international labor movement, freedom of association means the right of workers to organize and collectively bargain. Overall, respect for freedom of association has close links with political participation, elections, the formation of **civil society** organizations and political parties, more generally, with democratic governance. Government restrictions constraining or limiting the activities of civil society organizations are useful indicators of governments respect for human rights. They are common currency in **public emergencies**.

See also ALIENS, TREATMENT OF; CIVICUS; DEMOCRACY; EUROPEAN CHARTER OF FUNDAMENTAL RIGHTS OF THE EUROPEAN UNION; FREEDOM OF EXPRESSION; ORGANIZATION FOR SECURITY AND CO-OPERATION IN EUROPE; WORK, RIGHT TO; INTERNATIONAL LABOUR ORGANIZATION.

FREEDOM OF EXPRESSION. "Participatory" political rights of seeking, communicating and imparting ideas and information. In the language of Article 19 of the **Universal Declaration of Human Rights** (UDHR), "Everyone has the right to freedom of opinion and expression; this right includes freedom to hold opinions without interference and to seek, receive and impart information and ideas through any media and regardless of frontiers." The right is also recognized by the **International Covenant on Civil and Political Rights** (ICCPR, Art. 19), the **European Convention for**

the **Protection of Human Rights and Fundamental Freedoms** (Art. 10), the **American Convention on Human Rights** (Art. 13) and the **African Charter on Human and People's Rights** (Art. 9). It is also enshrined in most national constitutions. The drafters of the UDHR primarily understood freedom of expression as a tool for the full exchange of information both within and among nations. But in practice, freedom of expression is closely linked to other rights, including linguistic rights, **minority** rights, **freedom of association**, freedom of the press, **freedom of religion**, right to **privacy**, and freedom from state interference in correspondence and personal property and rights related to **health** matters and **education**.

Freedom of expression may conflict with other rights and human rights instruments and acknowledge that there are legitimate limits on its exercise. As the ICCPR states, the right "carries with it special duties and responsibilities" (Art. 19-3). In one of its **General Comments**, the **United Nations Human Rights Committee** observed that restrictions on freedom of expression must be prescribed by law and in furtherance of specified overriding objectives. There is considerable controversy about exactly how the Committee's language should be interpreted, but common potentially acceptable restrictions—the boundaries of which remain in dispute—relate to **public emergencies**, national security, propaganda for war or national, racial, or religious hatred, public health and morality, the rights and reputations of others.

Advocates of freedom of expression are increasingly concerned by the possibility of abuses arising from government-sponsored censorship, monitoring and surveillance of the **Internet** as well as gathering and use of electronic data (fingerprints, DNA and other biometric data, credit ratings, among others). Since 1999 and until 2010, the **United Nations** has adopted resolutions condemning "defamation of religion." Sponsored by Islamic states, their stated intent was to combat "Islamophobia" and the linkages made in some Western media between Islam and **terrorism** and **violations of human rights**. Critics of the resolutions argued that they legitimized the adoption of domestic blasphemy laws and constituted hardly veiled attacks on freedom of expression. In 2011, the **United Nations Human Rights Council** passed a resolution recognizing freedom of religious beliefs, thus seemingly abandoning the concept of religious defamation.

See also ARTICLE 19, THE INTERNATIONAL CENTRE AGAINST CENSORSHIP; BLASPHEMY; CAIRO DECLARATION ON HUMAN RIGHTS IN ISLAM; CIVICUS; COMMITTEE OF CONCERNED SCIENTISTS; CONVENTION ON THE PROTECTION AND PROMOTION OF THE DIVERSITY OF CULTURAL EXPRESSION; COUNCIL OF EUROPE; EUROPEAN CHARTER OF FUNDAMENTAL RIGHTS OF THE EUROPEAN UNION; HATE SPEECH; INFORMATION,

RIGHT TO; INTER-AMERICAN DECLARATION ON FREEDOM OF EXPRESSION; INTERNATIONAL CENTRE FOR HUMAN RIGHTS AND DEMOCRATIC DEVELOPMENT; INTERNATIONAL FEDERATION OF JOURNALISTS; INTERNATIONAL FREEDOM OF EXPRESSION EXCHANGE; INTERNATIONAL LEAGUE AGAINST RACISM AND ANTISEMITISM; OPEN SOCIETY INSTITUTE; ORGANIZATION FOR SECURITY AND CO-OPERATION IN EUROPE; PORNOGRAPHY; REPORTERS WITHOUT BORDERS; RIGHTS INTERNATIONAL; SOROS, GEORGE; THIRD WORLD INSTITUTE.

FREEDOM OF INFORMATION. *See* FREEDOM OF EXPRESSION; UNITED NATIONS SUB-COMMISSION ON THE PROMOTION AND PROTECTION OF HUMAN RIGHTS.

FREEDOM OF MOVEMENT. The right to freedom of movement includes the freedom to choose a residence in one's own country and is recognized by the **International Covenant on Civil and Political Rights** (ICCPR, Art. 12(1)), the **American Convention on Human Rights** (Art. 22), the **African Charter on Human and People's Rights** (Art. 12) and the **European Convention for the Protection of Human Rights and Fundamental Freedoms** (Art. 2). Freedom of movement thus implies protection against forced displacement or relocation and includes the right to leave one's country. These rights may be restricted by law and under permissible conditions to protect national security, public order, public health or the rights of others. Dealing with the ICCPR prescription that none can be arbitrarily deprived of the right to enter one's own country, the **United Nations Human Rights Committee** has emphasized in one of its **General Comments** that this right in effect prohibits expulsion or punishment by exile and a right to return for **refugees** seeking voluntary repatriation. *See also* COUNTERTERRORISM; DEPORTATION; EUROPEAN PARLIAMENT.

FREEDOM OF OPINION. *See* FREEDOM OF EXPRESSION.

FREEDOM OF RELIGION. One of the fundamental rights recognized in the 1948 **Universal Declaration of Human Rights**, freedom of religion is protected by the **International Covenant on Civil and Political Rights**, the **International Convention on the Elimination of All Forms of Racial Discrimination** (Art. 18) and the **United Nations General Assembly's Declarations on the Elimination of All Forms of Intolerance and of Discrimination Based on Religion and Belief** (1981) and the **Declaration on the Rights of Persons Belonging to National or Ethnic, Religious and Linguistic Minorities** (1992).

As far back as 1962, the **United Nations General Assembly** (UN-GA) adopted a non-binding resolution which demanded the rescission of discriminatory laws perpetuating religious intolerance. In 1981, the UN-GA adopted a "Statement" defining intolerance and discrimination based on religion or belief as "any distinction, exclusion, restriction or preference based on religion or belief and having as its purpose or as its effect nullification or impairment of the recognition, enjoyment or exercise of human rights and fundamental freedoms on an equal basis." Since 1981, an independent expert appointed by the **United Nations Commission on Human Rights** has been tasked to identify existing and emerging obstacles to the exercise of the right of freedom of religion.

Work on a draft convention was also initiated at that time but has only yielded a nonbinding declaration. The inability of the international community to come up with a stronger instrument in part relates to the fact that religious freedom is exercisable only in concert with other rights, notably the right to **freedom of assembly** and **freedom of expression**. It may also conflict or infringe on these and other human rights and clash with prevailing practices. State legislation varies considerably ranging from the nondenominational practices of Western democracies to those of Islamic states that confer an inherent degree of superiority to Sharia Law. As such, freedom of religion carries with it the potential for controversies, civil strife and ideological conflicts as evidenced by the breakup of the former Yugoslavia or the polarized discussions that have taken place in United Nations fora in the past decade over the question of "defamation of religion." In the wake of the publication of the "Mohammed caricatures" in the European press, the Organization of Islamic Conference has tabled resolutions "combating defamation of religions," which has elicited considerable controversy with Western countries, objecting that the notion of defamation can be used to justify arbitrary limitations on the exercise of other rights, in particular the right to freedom of expression.

Every year, the UN-GA adopts resolutions on the subject. In one of its most recent resolutions, the UN-GA reaffirmed that freedom of religion and belief and freedom of expression are interdependent.

In a 1992 **General Comment** mapping out the contours of the right to freedom of religion, the **United Nations Human Rights Committee** argued that the right encompassed the right to have the religion or conviction of one's choice, the freedom to manifest one's religion "individually or in community with others and in public or private," the prohibition of religious hatred and the freedom to establish and maintain places of worship. Another component of the right is the prohibition of all discrimination based on religion or conviction. In the view of the Committee, governments would then have a responsibility to protect the existence and the religious identity of minorities.

See also ALIENS, TREATMENT OF; BLASPHEMY; CULTURAL RELATIVISM; CULTURAL RIGHTS; FORUM 18; INTERNATIONAL ASSOCIATION FOR RELIGIOUS FREEDOM; INTERNATIONAL SOCIETY FOR HUMAN RIGHTS; ORGANIZATION FOR SECURITY AND CO-OPERATION IN EUROPE; SHARIA LAW; SOFT LAW; SPECIAL RAPPORTEURS.

FRIEDRICH-EBERT FOUNDATION. Named after the social democratic leader and first democratically elected president of the country, this German **foundation** headquartered in Bonn was originally created to work against **discrimination** of workers in the area of **education**. Dissolved under the Nazi regime and reinstituted in 1946, the Foundation has evolved into a charitable organization devoted to "the advancement of democratic education." Its student aid department has sponsored more than 12,000 grantee students schooled "in the spirit of **democracy** and pluralism." Since the 1960s, the Foundation has also worked in the area of development aid, supporting democracy and freedom movements in South Africa, Greece, Spain and Portugal.

FRIENDS OF THE EARTH INTERNATIONAL (FOEI). Federation of some 70 autonomous national grassroots environmental groups mobilizing over 2 million members and supporters around the world. Originally largely based in North America and Europe, the membership of Friends of the Earth International is now heavily weighted toward groups in the developing world. FOEI focuses on environmental issues in their social, political, developmental and human rights contexts. Challenging the current model of economic liberalism and "corporate globalization" and promoting solutions that will help to create environmentally sustainable and socially just societies, FOEI organizes campaigns involving local communities, **indigenous peoples**, farmers movements, trade unions and human rights groups on urgent environmental and social issues, especially, **climate change**, deforestation, genetically modified organisms, and what it views as the excessive power and deleterious environmental and human rights impact of **transnational corporations** and international institutions like the **World Trade Organization** and the World Bank.

FUJIMORI, ALBERTO (1938–). President of **Peru** from 1990 to 2000. Spurred on by the **International Monetary Fund**, he initiated a radical program of free market economic reforms, removing subsidies, privatizing state-owned companies, liberalizing foreign investment and reducing the role of the state in virtually all spheres of the economy. This shock therapy ended the rampant hyperinflation which had brought the Peruvian economy to near collapse but also generated considerable hardship for ordinary Peruvians. At the same time, Fujimori granted broad powers to the military to eliminate the threat of a Marxist-Leninist and Maoist insurgency which controlled more than 60 percent of the country in the early 1990s. In 1992, with the support of the military, Fujimori dissolved the Peruvian Congress and courts and seized dictatorial powers, arguing that the legislative and judiciary had been hindering security forces in their fight against the rebels. He was re-elected for a second term in 1995, by and large on the basis of his claim to have crushed the insurgency and restored macroeconomic growth.

He resigned in 2000 and fled to Japan amid widespread and mounting charges of **corruption**. Arrested during a visit in Chile in November 2005, Fujimori was extradited to face criminal charges in Peru in 2007. The same year, he was convicted of ordering an illegal search and seizure. In 2009, he was convicted of **violations of human rights** and sentenced to 25 years in prison for his role in killings and kidnappings committed by government controlled **death squads** during the civil war. *See also* PRIVATIZATION.

FUNDAMENTAL GUARANTEES. Minimum standards of protection applying to individuals in times of peace, situations of **internal disturbances** and tensions and during **armed conflicts**. Certain rights established by international conventions—the so-called **non-derogable rights**—may never be infringed or amended. Article 3 common to the four **Geneva Conventions** spells out the fundamental guarantees that must be provided to all persons who are not or are no longer taking part in hostilities in international and noninternational conflicts. They are further elaborated in two optional protocols. Additional Protocol I applies to victims of international armed conflicts and lists a number of acts absolutely prohibited in all circumstances, including violence to life, **health** or physical or mental well-being, in particular murder, **torture** of any kind, whether physical or mental, corporal punishment and mutilation; outrages upon personal **dignity**, in particular humiliating and degrading treatment, enforced prostitution and any form of indecent assault; and the taking of hostages and collective punishments. Additional Protocol II focuses on the protection of victims of noninternational conflicts and prohibits collective punishments, taking hostages, acts of **terrorism**, outrages upon personal dignity, **slavery** and pillage. Optional Protocol II also provides for special protections for children. *See also* EXTRA-JUDICIAL EXECUTIONS; PROTECTED PERSONS; PUBLIC EMERGENCIES.

G

GACACA COURTS. Informal traditional communal assemblies presided by local elders to settle village or familial disputes about such issues as theft, land rights and property damage. They have been used since 2005 as a means to relieve Rwanda's justice system overwhelmed by the number of alleged perpetrators involved in the 1994 **genocide**. From 1996 to 2006, only 10,000 suspects had been tried out of some 120,000 people held in jails on charges of genocide, **war crimes** and **crimes against humanity**. *Gacaca* courts operate in public, allowing villagers to speak for or against the defendants. They are intended to operate as mechanisms for delivering justice, providing the basis for settlements and promoting reconciliation by encouraging collaboration between deciders and the village community and placing justice partially into the hands of the victims. The system, however, has come under criticism for encouraging false accusations and the intimidation of witnesses and its lack of legal protection of the accused. *See also* INTERNATIONAL CRIMINAL TRIBUNAL FOR RWANDA; RWANDAN GENOCIDE; TRANSITIONAL JUSTICE.

GARZON, BALTHAZAR (1955–). Spanish judge who sat on the country's central criminal court. In that capacity, he investigated major criminal cases in Spain arising from **terrorism**, organized crime and money laundering. He set a major precedent when in 1998, under the doctrine of **universal jurisdiction**, he issued an international warrant for the arrest of former Chilean President General **Augusto Pinochet** for the death and torture of Spanish nationals during his tenure in office. Close to the Socialist government, he came under attack, was suspended and was tried on charges of having overstepped his functions and "prevarication" after he launched investigations of crimes by the **Francisco Franco** regime that were amnestied by a sweeping 1977 law. Found guilty of some of these charges, Judge Garzon no longer practices law in Spain.

GENDER-BASED VIOLENCE. In one of its **General Recommendations**, the **United Nations Committee on the Elimination of All Forms of Discrimination against Women** (UN-CEDAW) has defined gender-based violence as "violence that is directed against a woman because she is a woman, or violence that affects women disproportionately." Acts of violence against women occur both in the public and private spheres, cut across boundaries of age, race, culture, wealth and geography and may include physical, sexual and psychological violence. The most common form of violence experienced by women globally is intimate partner violence. Other forms of violence include harmful **traditional practices** such as female infanticide or **female genital mutilation, honor killings** forced marriage, **femicide**, sexual violence by nonpartners, sexual harassment in the workplace, educational institutions and in sports, human trafficking and forced prostitution, custodial violence against women, forced sterilization and sexual violence in armed conflict settings.

Wider attention to the phenomenon has emerged primarily in the wake of the United Nations Decade for Women (1975–85) through the interaction between women's advocacy around the world and United Nations initiatives, notably the work of the UN-CEDAW, the normative declarations emerging from the **United Nations global conferences** devoted to women and population, resolutions of the United Nations, the **United Nations Security Council** and **United Nations General Assembly** (UN-GA) and the jurisprudence of international criminal courts. Violence against women is now widely viewed as a form of **discrimination** and a violation of women's human rights, calling for holistic and multisectoral responses in criminal justice, **health**, development, humanitarian, and peace building and security sectors as reflected in a nonbinding declaration adopted by the UN-GA in 2013.

There are a number of international and regional human rights treaties addressing gender-based violence, complemented by an extensive array of **soft laws** in the form of **declarations** and resolutions adopted by international and regional bodies providing detailed guidance for remedial action. Human rights UN **treaty** bodies address the issue in their work under individual **complaints** and inquiry procedures. There is also a rapidly expanding body of jurisprudence at the international and regional levels, and case law has been established by the European and Inter-American human rights systems and by **war crime tribunals**.

In this process, international organizations have focused their work on data collection and research, awareness raising, communication and dissemination of good practices and resource mobilization. They have also endeavored to eliminate **human trafficking** and to prevent sexual exploitation, highlighted the role of violence as an obstacle for development and, more generally, sought to strengthen the capacity of states to prevent, punish and eliminate violence against women. In 1992, CEDAW adopted General Recommendation 19, which requires national reports to the CEDAW to include statistical data on the incidence of violence against women, information on the provision of services for victims, and legislative and other measures taken to protect women against violence in their everyday lives, such as harassment at the workplace, abuse in the family and sexual violence.

See also AKAYESU CASE; ASSOCIATION OF AFRICAN WOMEN FOR RESEARCH AND DEVELOPMENT; BANGLADESH LIBERATION WAR; BRAZIL; CELEBICI, FURUDZINA, DEALALIC CASES; DECLARATION ON THE ELIMINATION OF VIOLENCE AGAINST WOMEN; DEMOCRATIC REPUBLIC OF THE CONGO; DOMESTIC VIOLENCE; FORUM FOR FACT-FINDING DOCUMENTATION AND ADVOCACY; GENEVA CONVENTIONS; GUATEMALA; INTER-AMERICAN CONVENTION ON THE PREVENTION, PUNISHMENT AND ERADICATION OF VIOLENCE AGAINST WOMEN; INTERNATIONAL CONVENTION ON THE PROTECTION OF THE RIGHTS OF ALL MIGRANT WORKERS AND MEMBERS OF THEIR FAMILIES; INTERNATIONAL CRIMINAL COURT; PHYSICIANS FOR HUMAN RIGHTS; PROTOCOL TO THE AFRICAN CHARTER ON HUMAN AND PEOPLE'S RIGHTS ON THE RIGHTS OF WOMEN IN AFRICA; UNITED NATIONS ASSISTANCE MISSION IN AFGHANISTAN; UNITED NATIONS CONVENTION ON THE ELIMINATION OF ALL FORMS OF DISCRIMINATION AGAINST WOMEN; UNITED NATIONS CONVENTION ON THE RIGHTS OF THE CHILD; UNITED NATIONS SUB-COMMISSION ON THE PROMOTION AND PROTECTION OF HUMAN RIGHTS.

GENDER DEVELOPMENT INDEX. Measure of the standard of living in a country developed by the **United Nations Development Programme** in its annual **Human Development Report**. Its objective is to highlight inequalities between men and women in regard to life expectancy, **health**, knowledge and decent standards of living. *See also* GENDER EMPOWERMENT MEASURE; MONITORING OF HUMAN RIGHTS.

GENDER DISCRIMINATION. In broad terms, **discrimination** entails the prejudicial treatment of an individual because of his or her membership in a certain group or social category. Gender discrimination specifically refers to socially constructed ideas and perceptions of men and women. Such beliefs and attitudes vary between countries and may or may not carry any legal implications. Research shows, for example, that a large number of countries around the world continue to consider homosexuality illegal and several carry the death penalty for homosexual activity. But the overall trend in recent decades has been to consider any adverse actions taken by one person against another that would not have occurred had the person been of another sex, an illegal and justiciable **violation of human rights** as evidenced by the growing (though uneven and grudging) acceptance of social and group rights.

See also CULTURAL RELATIVISM; EDUCATION, RIGHT TO; HOUSING, RIGHT TO ADEQUATE; HEALTH, RIGHT TO; INTERNATIONAL CONVENTION ON THE ELIMINATION OF ALL FORMS OF RACIAL DISCRIMINATION; UNITED NATIONS CONVENTION ON THE ELIMINATION OF ALL FORMS OF DISCRIMINATION AGAINST WOMEN; WORK, RIGHT TO.

GENDER EMPOWERMENT MEASURE. Set of indicators developed by the **United Nations Development Programme** measuring inequalities between men and women in three areas: political participation and decision making, economic participation and decision making and power over economic resources. See also MONITORING OF HUMAN RIGHTS.

GENDER MAINSTREAMING. Notion that emerged from the **United Nations** development and human rights community and was formally articulated in 1995 at the **Fourth World Conference on Women** in Beijing. The **United Nations Economic and Social Council** has defined gender mainstreaming as the process of "assessing the implications for women and men of any planned action, including legislation, policies or programmes, in all areas and at all levels. It is a strategy for making women's as well as men's concerns and experiences an integral dimension of the design, implementation, monitoring and evaluation of policies and programmes in all political, economic and societal spheres so that women and men benefit equally and inequality is not perpetuated. The ultimate goal is to achieve gender **equality**." An instance of mainstreaming may be found in a 2000 resolution of the **United Nations Security Council** which called for an enhanced female participation in the prevention, management and resolution of conflict. In practice, making the goal of gender equality central to all public policy activities has proved both challenging and elusive. The strategy requires holistic approaches taking into account the interconnected causes that create unequal relations between men and women. It also calls for a profound rethinking of policy ends and means, prioritizing gender equality objectives and shifts in institutional and organizational cultures. See also WOMEN IN PEACE AND SECURITY.

GENDER-SPECIFIC CLAIM. Assertion as a right or demand of the recognition of a right in response to forms of discrimination or persecution that are specific to or more likely to happen to women including, for example, **female genital mutilation**, forced abortion and sterilization, **domestic violence** or access to contraception. The matter has gained increasing salience in cases of **asylum**-seeking women, leading some to argue that the special problems experienced by **refugee** women and girls, who constitute the majority of the world's refugees, face harsh treatment at home due to their having transgressed the social mores of their societies of origins and should be protected more directly than other groups by including gender considerations in the international definition of a refugee. Fears that a formal debate on refugee definition might eventually lead to more restrictive provisions have stymied efforts to amend the 1951 **United Nations Convention Relating to the Status of Refugees**. In practice, however, some national courts have displayed a growing willingness to broaden the Convention's enumerated grounds to which a claim to persecution must be related by including gender-based considerations. *See also* REFUGEE DETERMINATION PROCESS.

GENDERCIDE. Neologism derived from the concept of "**genocide**." By analogy, the term means the deliberate extermination of persons of a specific sex (or gender). Mass rape and **infanticide** are instances of gendercides targeted at women. The deliberate killing in July 1995 of some 7,000 men in the silver-mining town of **Srebrenica** after having been separated from women is another example of gendercide. *See also* FEMALE INFANTICIDE; FEMICIDE; REPRODUCTIVE RIGHTS.

GENERAL COMMENTS. Statements periodically issued by a **United Nations treaty body** that are meant to provide authoritative guides for states on how to implement and interpret specific points of procedure or substance of the conventions to which they are a party. The **United Nations Committee on Economic, Social and Cultural Rights**, the **United Nations Human Rights Committee**, the **United Nations Committee against Torture** and the **United Nations Committee on the Rights of the Child** have published General Comments. The **United Nations Committee on the Elimination of All Forms of Racial Discrimination** and the **United Nations Committee on the Elimination of All Forms of Discrimination against Women** have produced similar statements that are known as "general recommendations." The **United Nations Office of the High Commissioner for Human Rights** puts out recurrent compilations of general comments and observations. Such comments—essentially driven by liberal interpretations of human rights norms—frequently elicit considerable unease if not resistance among governments. They are considered a source of **soft law** in human rights jurisprudence.

See also AMNESTIES; ARBITRARY DETENTION; CLIMATE CHANGE; DEMOCRACY; DENUNCIATION; DEROGATION; EDUCATION, RIGHT TO; EQUALITY BEFORE THE LAW; FAIR TRIAL, RIGHT TO; FOOD, RIGHT TO; FORCED EVICTIONS; FREEDOM OF EXPRESSION; FREEDOM OF MOVEMENT; FREEDOM OF RELIGION; GENDER-BASED VIOLENCE; HEALTH, RIGHT TO; HOUSING, RIGHT TO ADEQUATE; INTELLECTUAL PROPERTY RIGHTS; INTERIM MEASURES; JUDICIARY, INDEPENDENCE OF; LIFE, RIGHT TO; POVERTY; PUBLIC EMERGENCIES; RECOGNITION, RIGHT TO; RESERVATIONS TO TREATIES; SOCIAL SECURITY, RIGHT TO.

GENERATION OF RIGHTS. Mode of classification of types of human rights developed by **Karel Vasak** who established a purely analytical distinction between **first-, second-,** and **third-generation rights.** First-generation rights are liberty rights corresponding to the **civil and political rights** enshrined in the **International Covenant on Civil and Political Rights.** Second-generation rights are **economic, social and cultural rights** found in the **International Covenant on Economic, Social and Cultural Rights.** Third-generation rights, also known as fraternity, solidarity or **group rights** which relate to communal aspects of human beings and are provided in such normative instruments as the Declaration on the Rights of Peoples to Peace and the **Declaration on the Right to Development.** This typology was not meant to suggest that one generation of human rights sprang from a previous one in a linear historical process. Nor did it imply that one category of rights was more important than the other. Rather, each generation of rights was understood to be cumulative, overlapping, **indivisible** and interdependent.

GENEVA CONVENTIONS (1949). Set of four **treaties** and three additional protocols updating previous instruments agreed upon in 1864, 1906 and 1929 establishing basic standards of international humanitarian law for the conduct of warfare, the treatment of victims of war and the protection of civilians in zones of war. The protections of the Conventions apply to all cases of international conflict including declared wars, "police actions," armed conflict against colonial domination and foreign occupation. Common Article 3 posits that certain minimum rules of war apply to non-international **armed conflicts.** The Conventions have been ratified by 194 states and enjoy virtual universal acceptance. They call for the prevention and punishment of individuals responsible for "grave breaches" of its provisions. These breaches include willful killing, **torture** or inhumane treatment, including biological experiments, willfully causing great suffering or serious injury to body or **health**, compelling someone to serve in the forces of a hostile power, willfully depriving someone of the right to a fair trial if accused of a **war crime**, taking of hostages, extensive destruction and appropriation of property not justified by military necessity and carried out unlawfully and wantonly, unlawful **deportation**, transfer, or confinement. States parties must enact and enforce legislation penalizing any of these crimes.

See also ABU GHRAIB PRISON; ARAB ISRAELI CONFLICT; BOSNIA-HERZEGOVINA WAR; CARPET BOMBING; COMMAND RESPONSIBILITY; DUE PROCESS RIGHTS; FUNDAMENTAL GUARANTEES; GUANTANAMO BAY DETENTION CAMP; HUMAN EXPERIMENTATION; HUMANITARIAN ASSISTANCE, DENIAL OF; INTERNATIONAL COMMITTEE OF THE RED CROSS; INTERNATIONAL HUMANITARIAN LAW; LIFE, RIGHT TO; MERCENARY; MILOSEVIC, SLOBODAN; POPULATION EXCHANGE; SAFE ZONES; SEXUAL VIOLENCE; TADIC, DUSAN; UNIVERSAL JURISDICTION.

GENOCIDE. Term coined by Polish scholar **Raphael Lemkin** who constructed it from the ancient Greek prefix *genos-* (family, tribe or race) and Latin suffix *-cide* (*occidere* or *cideo*, to massacre). The word, which in effect drew from the mass killing of Armenians during World War I in the Ottoman Empire and the **Holocaust** perpetrated by the Nazis during **World War II**, was meant to convey the idea of a coordinated set of actions designed to destroy the life foundations of a group or the group itself. Genocide was legally defined in the **United Nations Convention on the Punishment and Prevention of the Crime of Genocide**. It is an international crime defined in the same language under the statutes of the **International Criminal Tribunal for the Former Yugoslavia**, the **International Criminal Tribunal for Rwanda** and the **International Criminal Court**.

Considerable controversy, nevertheless, clouds the meaning of exactly which acts constitute genocide rather than simply criminal or inhuman behavior, especially since the use of the term carries with it, under the terms of the Convention, specific state obligations. For some, genocide means the mass murder by governments of people because of their national, ethnic, racial, religious or cultural backgrounds as well as government killings of political opponents (in which case they prefer the term of **democide**). For others, non-lethal practices such as the deliberate spread of contagious diseases, the forcible transfer of children or **infanticide** also qualify as genocide. Not surprisingly, charges of genocide often elicit **denials** and are accompanied by fierce disputes over and clashing interpretations of the significance of the facts at hand.

Whatever definition one may wish to use, events approximating the characteristics of genocides—large-scale massacres, pillage, rape, **torture**— appear to be a recurrent occurrence of the modern and contemporary world with precedents extending back to biblical and medieval times. Historians thus point to the savagery of the Crusades, the slaughters that accompanied the rise of the Mongol empire in the 12th and 13th centuries, the human toll of **slavery** and the virtual destruction of Native American populations in the New World by conquering and colonizing Europeans. More recent instances of deliberate killings of entire groups have taken place in **German South West Africa** (1904–07), the **Congo Free State** (1880–1920), the Ottoman Empire, Korea under Japanese rule (1920–45), Russia under czarist and Soviet rule and Germany during the Nazi regime. Since the end of World War II, mass killings tantamount to genocide have taken place in Bangladesh (1971), **Burundi** (1972), Cambodia (1975–79), Bosnia (1992–95), **Rwanda** (1994) and the **Darfur conflict** in Sudan (2003–).

See also AL-ANFAL CAMPAIGN; ARMENIAN GENOCIDE; BANGLADESH LIBERATION WAR; BARAYAGWIZA CASE; BIAFRA; BOSNIA-HERZEGOVINA WAR; CRIMES AGAINST HUMANITY; CROATIA, WAR OF INDEPENDENCE; ETHNIC CLEANSING; GENDERCIDE; GLOBAL ACTION TO PREVENT WAR; GUATEMALA; HUMAN RIGHTS WATCH; INDIGENOUS PEOPLES; INTERNATIONAL ALLIANCE TO END GENOCIDE; INTERNATIONAL CAMPAIGN TO END GENOCIDE; INTERNATIONAL COURT OF JUSTICE; INTERNATIONAL MILITARY TRIBUNAL FOR THE PROSECUTION AND PUNISHMENT OF THE MAJOR WAR CRIMINALS OF THE EUROPEAN AXIS; KAMBANDA, JEAN; KARADZIC, RADOVAN; KATYN FOREST MASSACRE; LIFE, RIGHT TO; MENCHU, RIGOBERTA; MENGHISTU, HAILE MARIAM; MILOSEVIC, SLOBODAN; MINORITIES; MLADIC, RATKO; MUSEMA CASE; PREVENT GENOCIDE INTERNATIONAL; SEXUAL VIOLENCE; TIBET; UNIVERSAL JURISDICTION.

GEORGIA. *See* ABKHAZIA; MINORITIES; SELF-DETERMINATION; SOUTH OSSETIA.

GERMAN SOUTH WEST AFRICA. Colony of the German empire from 1884 until 1917 when its administration was transferred to South Africa under the **League of Nations' mandates** system. After a long military struggle against South Africa and repeated interventions by the **United Nations General Assembly**, South African control came to an end in 1990 and the former colony became independent under the name of Namibia.

Several uprisings broke out against German rule between 1893 and 1904. All were ruthlessly squashed, leading to the deaths of 25,000 to 100,000 indigenous Herero, Ovambo and Nama tribesmen, half of the estimated population at the turn of the century. A 1985 report prepared by a **special rapporteur** for the United Nations Sub-Commission on the Prevention of Discrimination and Protection of Minorities labeled it one of the first instances of **genocide** of the 20th century. In 2004, the German government issued an **apology** but ruled out financial compensation for the victims' descendants. *See also* COLONIALISM.

GERMANY. *See* GERMAN SOUTH WEST AFRICA; HOLOCAUST; HONOR KILLING; INTERNATIONAL MILITARY TRIBUNAL FOR THE PROSECUTION AND PUNISHMENT OF THE MAJOR WAR CRIMINALS OF THE EUROPEAN AXIS; LUSTRATION; POPULATION EXCHANGE; SEX TRAFFICKING; STATE TERRORISM; UNIVERSAL JURISDICTION.

GIRCA (Gypsy International Recognition and Compensation Action). Swiss-based association founded in 2000 with the goals to promote respect for the interests, culture, language and human rights of **Roma/Gypsies** and to seek compensation for the crimes committed against them under Nazi rule between 1933 and 1945. In 2002, GIRCA filed a suit against IBM arguing that IBM machines were designed to enable the Nazis to track their victims. In 2006, the Swiss Supreme Court dismissed the lawsuit because too much time had elapsed. *See also* LITIGATION.

GLOBAL ACTION TO PREVENT WAR. Transnational **network** of organizations dedicated to reducing global levels of conflict by focusing on actions promoting advances in **early warning**, prevention of **armed conflict**, nonviolent means of conflict resolution, peacekeeping and peacemaking, transparency and other confidence-building measures, disarmament, and the implementation of criminal law regarding **genocide** and **crimes against humanity**.

GLOBAL ALLIANCE AGAINST TRAFFIC IN WOMEN. Alliance of over 80 **non-governmental organizations** in more than 50 countries active in the promotion of the rights of trafficked persons and **migrant** women. The membership includes organizations that provide direct assistance to trafficked persons, policy and research organizations, self-organized groups of women with direct experience of **human trafficking** or migration into the informal sector and community development organizations. The International Secretariat of the Alliance was established in 1994 in Bangkok, Thailand.

GLOBAL CENTER FOR THE RESPONSIBILITY TO PROTECT. Academic institution set up in 2008 with the support of a number of governments and **non-governmental organizations** such as the **International Crisis Group, Human Rights Watch** and **Oxfam** for the purpose of promoting the operationalization of the norm of a "**responsibility to protect**" through **advocacy** and policy-oriented **research.** *See also* EPISTEMIC COMMUNITY.

GLOBAL FUND FOR WOMEN. American non-profit grant-making **foundation** that advances women's human rights worldwide. The Fund makes grants to women-led organizations that promote the economic security, **health,** safety, **education** and leadership of women and girls. Since its establishment in 1987, the Fund has contributed some $60 million to approximately 3,500 women's organizations in 166 countries.

GLOBAL JUSTICE CENTER. Human rights **non-governmental organization** focused on the promotion of legal tools enabling activists, lawyers and judges to enforce laws and treaties which give women rights to political power in legislatures, policy reform campaigns, courts, media and in international forums such as the United Nations, international criminal courts, peace-keeping missions, ceasefire negotiations, and peace treaty processes.

GLOBAL LAWYERS AND PHYSICIANS. Non-profit **non-governmental organization** (NGO) created in 1996 which works at the local, national, and international levels in collaboration and partnerships with individuals, NGOs, intergovernmental organizations, and governments on the health-related provisions of the **Universal Declaration of Human Rights** and the **International Covenants on Civil and Political Rights** and **Economic, Social and Cultural Rights**, with a focus on **health** and human rights, patient rights, and **human experimentation**.

GLOBAL NETWORK OF WOMEN PEACE BUILDERS. Launched in 2010, this coalition of women's groups and civil society organizations, in partnership with the **International Civil Society Action Network**, advocates action for the full implementation of **United Nations Security Council** Resolutions 1325 and 1820 on **Women in Peace and Security** at the local, national, regional and international levels. The network aims at consolidating and strengthening efforts in bridging the gap between policy discussions at the international level and action for policy implementation on the ground. It also operates as a platform for information sharing among its members.

GLOBAL POLICY FORUM (GPF). **Non-governmental organization** in consultative status with the **United Nations** founded in 1991 to monitor policy making at the United Nations, educate and mobilize for global citizen action and advocate on key issues of international peace and justice. GPF **monitors** the proceedings of the **United Nations Security Council** and organizes frequent informal meetings with ambassadors and senior UN officials. GPF also organizes conferences on socioeconomic issues covering such topics as **corporate social responsibility**, the **United Nations Global Compact**, financing for development and the reform of the **International Monetary Fund**. GPF carries out useful original policy-oriented **research** which it disseminates through a variety of reports and a sizable website. *See also* ADVOCACY; CAPACITY BUILDING.

GLOBAL RIGHTS. Non-governmental organization founded in 1978 and headquartered in Washington, D.C., it is primarily concerned with training of local activists and lawyers in the development of legal advocacy and legal strategies and the application of international human rights standards in their domestic polities. Global Rights has been involved in a wide range of countries including **Afghanistan**, Algeria, Bosnia and Herzegovina, Brazil, **Burundi**, **Colombia**, the **Democratic Republic of the Congo**, India, **Liberia**, Mongolia, Morocco, Nigeria, Sierra Leone, and Tunisia. Each year, the organization hosts delegations of global activists at sessions of the **United Nations Human Rights Council** to facilitate their advocacy efforts. *See also* CAPACITY BUILDING; LITIGATION.

GLOBAL SOUTH. *See* DEVELOPING COUNTRIES.

GLOBAL SURVIVAL NETWORK. Small, non-profit organization that carries out investigations, public media campaigns, and global networking to expose and address flagrant violations of environmental and human rights regulations, especially **human trafficking** in women.

GLOBAL WITNESS. London-based **non-governmental organization** established in 1993 and carrying out **investigations** of corporate **accountability** in resource exploitation and management. Global Witness's groundbreaking work on the trafficking of diamonds that fueled conflict in the **Democratic Republic of the Congo, Liberia** and Sierra Leone led to the adoption of the so-called **Kimberley Process Certification Scheme** (KPCS). While still **monitoring** the KPCS and advocating for its strengthening, Global Witness also investigates money laundering, tax evasion and organized crime.

GLOBALIZATION. Term often equated to internationalization, economic liberalization or Westernization. In a broader sense, it refers to a worldwide process driven by a combination of political, economic, technological and sociocultural factors which are accompanied by an intensification of cross-border transactions and flows of services, goods, labor and capital, leading, in turn, to a greater interpenetration of national states, markets, communications, ideas and cultures. The overall impact of globalization on the promotion and protection of human rights remains in dispute. Some argue that it fosters development, **democracy**, personal empowerment, and better global governance. Critics respond that it has weakened the capacity of states to meet their human rights duties because some of their sovereign functions (especially their social welfare functions) were eroded, lost or ceded to global markets or **transnational corporations**. There is little doubt, however, that the costs and benefits of globalization have not been evenly distributed and that the process has exacerbated inequalities of wealth, consumption, and power within and between countries. At the same time, because globalization entails a large degree of de-territorialization of social activities, it has facilitated the emergence of cosmopolitan transnational movements networks operating in an increasingly cosmopolitan and interconnected international environment.

See also AGREEMENT ON TRADE-RELATED ASPECTS OF INTELLECTUAL PROPERTY RIGHTS; BRETTON WOODS INSTITUTIONS; CONVENTION ON THE PROTECTION AND PROMOTION OF THE DIVERSITY OF CULTURAL EXPRESSION; CULTURAL RIGHTS; HUMAN TRAFFICKING; INSTITUTE OF DEVELOPMENT STUDIES; INTERNATIONAL LABOUR ORGANIZATION; MIGRANT WORKERS; PRIVATIZATION; STRUCTURAL ADJUSTMENT PROGRAMS; UNITED NATIONS SUB-COMMISSION ON THE PROMOTION AND PROTECTION OF HUMAN RIGHTS; WORLD SOCIAL FORUM.

GOLDSTONE REPORT. Outcome of a **fact-finding** mission headed by Judge **Richard Goldstone** mandated by the **United Nations Human Rights Council** to investigate all alleged **violations of human rights** and **international humanitarian law** committed during the December 2008 to January 2009 war between **Israel** and Hamas in the Gaza Strip. Released in September 2009, the report concluded that both Israel and Hamas were responsible for serious violations of international human rights and humanitarian law, which might amount to **war crimes** and possible **crimes against humanity**. The Council endorsed the report amid bitter controversies as it was rejected by Hamas, derided by Israel as "a mockery of history" and by and large ignored by the **United Nations Security Council**. The issuance of the report made no apparent dent in the dreadful human rights or humanitarian situation in the Gaza Strip and further polarized the political protagonists involved. Two years later, Judge Goldstone published an op ed in a Washington newspaper seemingly backtracking on some of the report's conclusions. *See also* ARAB ISRAELI CONFLICT; INVESTIGATION.

GOLDSTONE, RICHARD (1938–). Eminent South African former judge who, as a commercial lawyer, served for 17 years on the Transvaal Supreme Court from 1980 to 1989 and the Appellate Division of the Supreme Court of South Africa from 1990 to 1994 where he issued key rulings that undermined **apartheid**. In the run-up to South Africa's first democratic elections, he headed a commission that investigated political violence in South Africa between 1991 and 1994. The work of the commission is widely credited for having helped smooth the country's peaceful transition into democratic rule. Goldstone served as chief prosecutor of the United Nations' **International Criminal Tribunal for the Former Yugoslavia** and for the **International Criminal Tribunal for Rwanda** from August 1994 to September 1996. He prosecuted a number of groundbreaking war crimes suspect cases, notably those of Bosnian Serb political and military leaders **Radovan Karadzic** and **Ratko Mladic**. In that capacity, he effectively resisted attempts to include a blanket **amnesty** clause in the Dayton peace negotiations and gave prosecutorial direction to the tribunal, thus enhancing its legitimacy in the face of widespread skepticism.

After completing his two-year term as prosecutor for the ad hoc tribunals, Goldstone returned to South Africa to take up his seat on the Constitutional Court. He retired from the Court in 2003 after having participated in a number of precedent setting decisions on the right of prisoners to vote, extradition issues and the provision of **HIV/AIDS** treatment to pregnant mothers. During his tenure, he was a member of the International Panel of the Commission of Enquiry into the Activities of Nazism in Argentina (1997) and chair of the **Independent International Commission on Kosovo** (from August 1999 until December 2001). In 2009, Goldstone led the **fact-finding** mission created by the **United Nations Human Rights Council** to investigate international human rights and humanitarian law violations related to the Gaza War. *See also* GOLDSTONE REPORT.

GOVERNANCE. Broad term which refers to the physical management of power and policy making (i.e., the process of decision making and the process by which decisions are implemented). Governance can be applied to different contexts such as corporate governance, international (or global) governance, national governance, and local governance. The focus is always on "the complex of formal and informal institutions, mechanisms relationships, and processes between and among states, markets, citizens and organizations, both inter- and non-governmental, through which collective interests on the global plane are articulated, rights and obligations are established, and differences are mediated."

"Good governance," understood as governance being consensus-oriented, accountable, transparent, responsive, equitable and inclusive, effective and efficient and responsive to the present and future needs of society, has become an important yardstick of respect for human rights. Measuring it, however, has proved to be an inherently controversial and political exercise. The World Bank, among others, has developed aggregate and individual indicators for more than 200 countries for six dimensions of governance: **accountability**, political stability and lack of violence, government effectiveness, regulatory quality, rule of law and control of corruption.

See also AFRICA INSTITUTE OF SOUTH AFRICA; DEMOCRACY; EAST AFRICAN COURT OF JUSTICE; INSTITUTE FOR INTERNATIONAL LAW AND JUSTICE; INSTITUTE OF DEVELOPMENT STUDIES; RAOUL WALLENBERG INSTITUTE; UNITED NATIONS DEVELOPMENT PROGRAMME; UNITED NATIONS INTEGRATED MISSION IN TIMOR-LESTE; UNITED NATIONS MISSION IN AFGHANISTAN.

GRANT, JAMES P. (1922–1995). American children's advocate who first served in various capacities in the **United States** Department of State and the U.S. Agency for International Development and became the third executive director of the **United Nations Children's Fund** from 1980 until 1995. Throughout his tenure he promoted the use of vaccinations and diarrhea treatment to reduce child mortality. He was one of the main architects of the 1990 **World Summit for Children**. *See also* NORM ENTREPRENEURS.

GRASSROOTS INTERNATIONAL. Non-governmental organization supporting, through grant making, education and **advocacy**, grassroots initiatives of peasants and family farmers, women and indigenous groups to protect their right to land, **water** and **food**. Since its establishment in 1983, Grassroots International has worked in the Middle East, Asia, Africa, and the Americas. *See also* CAPACITY BUILDING; INDIGENOUS PEOPLES.

GREAT BRITAIN. *See* BOER WARS; BRITISH INSTITUTE OF HUMAN RIGHTS; CHATAM HOUSE; CHILD RIGHTS INFORMATION NETWORK; COUNTERTERRORISM; DEPORTATION; EUROPEAN CHARTER OF FUNDAMENTAL RIGHTS OF THE EUROPEAN

UNION; FEMINISM; HONOR KILLING; INDIA, PARTITION OF; INTERNATIONAL MILITARY TRIBUNAL FOR THE FAR EAST; INTERNATIONAL MILITARY TRIBUNAL FOR THE PROSECUTION AND PUNISHMENT OF THE MAJOR WAR CRIMINALS OF THE EUROPEAN AXIS; INTERNATIONAL SAVE THE CHILDREN ALLIANCE; NO-FLY ZONE; NORTHERN IRELAND; SLAVERY; UNITED NATIONS RELIEF AND WORKS AGENCY FOR PALESTINE REFUGEES IN THE NEAR EAST; UNIVERSAL JURISDICTION; WOMEN IN PEACE AND SECURITY; WORLD WAR I PEACE TREATIES.

GREAT LEAP FORWARD. Economic policy launched by **Mao Zedong** in 1957 with the goal of increasing steel and agricultural production and speeding up the growth of socialism. Special communes relying on collective labor and mass mobilization were established to attain these objectives. Steel production did increase significantly, but chaos in the communes and adverse climatic conditions resulted in a widespread famine believed to have killed 20 to 30 million individuals.

GREECE. Mediterranean country which traces its origins to the civilization of ancient Greece and prides itself in being the cradle of civilization and the birthplace of **democracy**. Part of the Roman Empire and the Byzantine Empire, Greece was conquered by the Ottoman Turks in 1456 and remained under Turkish rule for almost four centuries. In 1832, Turkey recognized the independence of Greece in the wake of a war that had involved major European powers. Greece obtained parts of Macedonia and Epirus and Western Thrace in the 1912–13 Balkan Wars. It fought World War I on the victorious Allies' side and received the remnants of European Turkey (Eastern Thrace and the Dodecanese) at the 1919 peace conference. With the tacit support of some of the Allies, Greece invaded Asia Minor in 1921 but was defeated by Turkish forces. The 1923 Treaty of Lausanne redrew the Greco-Turkish frontier in Europe, and a separate agreement provided for a massive compulsory exchange of populations. Under the nominal supervision of the **League of Nations**, about 1.5 million Greeks of Asia Minor were resettled in Greece and about 800,000 Turks and 80,000 Bulgarians were transferred from Greece to their respective countries.

Following the Asia Minor catastrophe, Greece was ruled by a dictatorship and, after liberation from Nazi occupation, experienced a bitter civil war between communist and anticommunist forces. Continuing political turbulence led to a coup d'etat in 1967 by the military, which again brought to the fore human rights issues. In response to a complaint filed by the Netherlands and Scandinavian countries, the European Commission on Human Rights conducted an **investigation** which documented "beyond doubt" that officials of the regime had inflicted **torture** and ill treatment on political prisoners and failed to take any effective steps to investigate allegations of these acts. Widely denounced by campaigns orchestrated by **non-governmental organizations** such as **Amnesty International** and discredited at home for its brutal repressive rule, the military regime collapsed in the wake of the Turkish invasion of Cyprus which it had, in effect, instigated. *See also* COLD WAR; INTERSTATE COMMUNICATIONS; SEX TRAFFICKING.

GREENPEACE INTERNATIONAL. Independent grassroots global **non-governmental organization** based in Amsterdam campaigning to protect and conserve the **environment** and to promote peace. Active since the early 1970s, Greenpeace has 2.8 million supporters worldwide and has national as well as regional offices in some 40 countries. Its activities focus on **climate change** and energy, the defense and protection of forests and the oceans, socially and ecologically responsible farming, the elimination of toxic chemicals and the elimination of nuclear weapons.

GROOTBOOM DECISION (2000). The new constitution adopted by South Africa immediately after the end of **apartheid** made provision for a right to adequate **housing**. In this landmark ruling, the country's highest court declared the government in breach of its constitutional obligations and ordered it to implement policies and programs, providing at a minimum adequate housing to people living in intolerable or crisis situations. The case was heralded by academics and human rights activists as demonstrating the justiciability of economic and social rights. *See also* LIMBURG PRINCIPLES ON THE IMPLEMENTATION OF THE INTERNATIONAL COVENANT ON ECONOMIC, SOCIAL AND CULTURAL RIGHTS.

GROUP RIGHTS. Rights deemed to be held by a group rather than its members individually. In contrast to individual rights, which may be considered universal to all people because they are human, group rights are group differentiated. A commonly asserted group right is the right possessed by a nation or people to be self-determining. Other similar rights include the right of a group to have its own **culture**, language or **religion** respected or supported by state authorities. Another possible understanding of group rights are the rights accorded to a particular group within a society but not to the larger society within which the group exists. For example, special rights may be conferred upon children, women, **indigenous peoples**, **migrant workers**, or **minorities**. Still another definition of group rights derives from the idea that a right can be a group right if it is a right to a **public good** like clean air.

Some critics of group rights argue that giving standing to groups may lead to empowering collectivities to wield disproportionate power over the rights of the individuals making up the group. Others are skeptical of the claim that groups may have rights because such rights as a right to **peace** are so amorphous as to preclude any clear operational definition and identification of the bearers and providers of rights. Still others draw attention to the political disruptiveness which may arise from a recognition of group rights, a case in point being the right of **self-determination** which if applied in a systematic and consistent manner would in effect destroy the state system. Because of their conceptual fuzziness and the fierce political controversies that they trigger, few group rights have been codified into binding **international human rights law**. Most of the time, **soft law** prevails as aspirations prevail over obligations. *See also* AFRICAN CHARTER ON HUMAN AND PEOPLE'S RIGHTS; AFRICAN CHARTER ON THE RIGHTS AND WELFARE OF THE CHILD; THIRD-GENERATION RIGHTS.

GUANTANAMO BAY DETENTION CAMP. Detention and interrogation facility established in 2002 in southern **Cuba** used to house suspected terrorists captured by **United States** forces mainly in **Afghanistan** and Iraq who were deemed to be "unlawful combatants." The camp held 779 men in 2002. By 2012, the number had dwindled to 167. Most detainees have been held without the right to legal counsel, denied the protections of the **Geneva Conventions** and investigated through practices defined by some observers as **torture**. Since its establishment, the facility has thus been the target of criticism both at home and abroad, from leaders of other countries, **non-governmental organizations** such as the American Bar Association, **Amnesty International**, the **Center for Constitutional Rights**, the **Center for Justice and Accountability, Human Rights Watch, Physicians for Human Rights** and **United Nations** bodies including the **United Nations Committee on Human Rights**, the **United Nations Committee against Torture** and the United Nations **special rapporteur** on rights in **counterterrorism**.

The **International Committee of the Red Cross** inspected the camp in 2004 and its confidential report leaked to the press concluded that "the construction of such a system, whose stated purpose is the production of intelligence, cannot be considered other than an intentional system of cruel, unusual and degrading treatment and a form of torture." In 2008, the U.S. Supreme Court ruled that detainees should be allowed to be heard by federal courts. The debate over the disposition of detention camp has been a politically charged controversy in the United States centered around national security concerns. Congressional restrictions have forced the Barack Obama administration to retreat from its promise to close it and to try suspected terrorists in regularly constituted federal courts. *See also* DUE PROCESS RIGHTS; *HAMDI ET AL. v. RUMSFELD, SECRETARY OF DEFENSE, ET AL.*; PUBLIC EMERGENCIES; RUMSFELD, DONALD.

GUATEMALA. Central American country which became independent in 1821. Until recently, Guatemala was ruled by a series of dictators supported by American multinational companies. **Cold War** concerns also prompted the **United States** to intervene in the country's domestic politics. In 1954, the democratically elected President Jacobo Arbenz Guzmán, who considered himself a socialist and envisaged to implement a radical land reform, was overthrown by a coup widely believed to have been orchestrated by the **Central Intelligence Agency**. From 1960 to 1996, the country was plunged into a bloody civil war triggered by extreme social inequality and widespread poverty among its indigenous population, the Maya, who make up about half the population. The war pitted leftist, mostly Maya, insurgents against the army which waged a vicious campaign to eliminate the guerrillas. More than 200,000 people—most of them civilians—were killed or disappeared. Over 450 Mayan villages were destroyed and some 1 million people were displaced.

According to the **United Nations**–sponsored **truth and reconciliation commission** (the Commission for Historical Clarification), which was set up at the end of the conflict, most of these atrocities were committed by government forces and state-sponsored **armed groups** directly supervised and trained by U.S. security advisers. In certain areas, the truth commission considered that the Guatemalan state had engaged in **genocide** against particular ethnic groups. The peace accord brokered by the United Nations which brought the war to an end called upon the establishment of a state based on the rule of law. But moves to bring those responsible for atrocities to account have been slow and haphazard. **Impunity** continues to prevail notwithstanding the fact that the head of the military junta which took power in 1982 was found guilty of genocide by a Guatemalan court in 2013 (the court's ruling was overturned on a technicality by the Guatemalan Constitutional Court). The structural causes of the conflict—extreme social inequalities— remain by and large untouched. In addition, like many of its neighbors, the country has become a major corridor for drug smuggling and is now plagued by high levels of violent crime. *See also* AMNESTIES; APOLOGIES; ARIAS, OSCAR; DEATH SQUADS; FORCED DISAPPEARANCES; INDIGENOUS PEOPLES; MENCHU, RIGOBERTA; UNITED NATIONS VERIFICATION MISSION IN GUATEMALA.

GUERRILLAS. *See* ARMED GROUPS.

GUIDELINES ON INTERNATIONAL HUMAN RIGHTS FACT FINDING VISITS AND REPORTS. Set of procedural methods issued in 2009 by the International Bar Association's Human Rights Institute and the **Raoul Wallenberg Institute** for **non-governmental organizations** designed to enhance the objectivity and reliability in the conduct of their **fact-finding** visits and compilation of reports. The product of several years of work, the Guidelines were produced to fill a gap arising from the absence of international standards for human rights fact-finding reporting. The gap was underscored by the fact that many of these reports are frequently referred to by governments, international organizations as well as courts and tribunals. *See also* SOFT LAW.

GUIDING PRINCIPLES ON INTERNAL DISPLACEMENT. Based on international humanitarian and human rights law, these guidelines serve as an international standard to guide governments, international organizations and all other relevant actors in providing assistance and protection to **internally displaced persons** (IDPs). They identify the rights of IDPs and provide protection against arbitrary displacement, offer a basis for protection and assistance during displacement, and set forth guarantees for safe return, resettlement and reintegration. Although they are not binding, the Principles have gained a degree of authority. The 2005 World Summit in New York recognized the Guiding Principles as "an important international framework for the protection of internally displaced persons." They have been formally acknowledged by the Organization of African Unity (now the **African Union**). The **Economic Community of West African States** has called on its member states to disseminate and apply them. The **Organization for Security and Co-operation in Europe** (OSCE) has labeled the principles "a useful framework for the work of the OSCE." The **Council of Europe** has urged its member states to incorporate them into domestic laws. An increasing number of states have developed national policies based on the Principles. *See also* DENG, FRANCIS; INCORPORATION; SOFT LAW.

GULAG. Originally an acronym standing for Chief Directorate of Corrective Labor Camps and Colonies, the branch of the Soviet Union state security which operated the penal system of camp-style detention facilities established by **Vladimir Lenin** in 1919. The term "Gulag" has come to refer to the various types of camps and colonies which made up the system of Soviet **forced labor** as well as the whole repressive system put in place under Soviet rule.

Located mainly in the remote regions of Siberia and the far north, the Gulag camps housed common criminals along with political enemies and dissenters, former aristocrats, businessmen, large landowners, members of national minorities and officials accused of **corruption**, sabotage and embezzlement. Over 450 camp complexes came into existence in the course of the Soviet Union's existence, thus playing an important role in the growth of the Soviet economy. The Gulag population expanded significantly under **Josef Stalin**'s rule and the drive toward industrialization. It reached its apex in the early 1950s and declined rapidly after Stalin's death, although forced labor camps continued to exist into the Mikhail Gorbachev period. Conditions in the camps varied across time and place but generally were harsh. According to estimates based on archival documents, 18 to 20 million people were held prisoner throughout the period of Stalinism. Declassified archival figures suggest that roughly 1.6 million inmates died from 1930 to 1956. *See also* CONCENTRATION CAMPS; SOLZHENITSYN, ALEXANDER.

GYPSIES. *See* ROMA/GYPSIES.

HABEAS CORPUS. Latin meaning "you may have the body," the term refers to a legal action ordering that a person deprived of his or her liberty be brought to a court so that it can be determined whether or not that person is imprisoned lawfully and should be released from custody. *See also* COUNTERTERRORISM; DECLARATION ON THE PROTECTION OF ALL PERSONS FROM ENFORCED DISAPPEARANCE; *HAMDI ET AL. v. RUMSFELD, SECRETARY OF DEFENSE ET AL.*; LIBERTY, RIGHT TO.

HABITAT. *See* UNITED NATIONS HUMAN SETTLEMENTS PROGRAMME.

HABITAT INTERNATIONAL COALITION (HIC). Independent, international, non-profit alliance of some 400 organizations and individuals working in the area of human settlements which sprang out of the 1972 **United Nations Conference on the Human Environment** in Stockholm. Initially focused on pressuring governments to implement the recommendations adopted by the 1976 **United Nations Conference on Human Settlements**, HIC subsequently initiated diverse **fact-finding** missions to denounce violations of the right to **housing** in Santo Domingo, Seoul, Hong Kong, Panama, Managua, **Israel** and the Occupied Palestinian Territories; Rio de Janeiro, Kobe, Istanbul and Lima. It has played a major **civil society** role at international meetings on housing, such as at the Istanbul Conference on Human Settlements (1996) and at the World Urban Forums in Nairobi (2002).

The broad objectives of this **non-governmental organization** (NGO) are to win recognition and the promotion of everyone's right everywhere to a secure place to live in peace and dignity and to defend the human rights of the homeless, poor and inadequately housed. To attain these objectives, the HIC carries a wide array of activities which include, in addition to fact-finding missions, **campaigns** for housing rights and against **forced evictions**, the coordination of NGO conferences on housing and **land rights**, the facilitation of exchanges of information, expertise and strategies, the publication of public information and **advocacy** material, research and **capacity building**. The Coalition has produced several reference documents promoted by NGOs, such as the World Charter for the Right to the City, which aims to support movements for decent housing in urban centers.

HABRE, HISSENE (1942–). Ruler of Chad, a former French colony, from 1982 to 1990 when he was ousted from power and fled to Senegal where he still lives. His one-party regime, long supported by France and the **United States** as a bulwark against Libya, was marked by widespread atrocities, many of them targeted at ethnic groups. A 1992 **truth and reconciliation commission** accused Habre of 40,000 political killings and 200,000 cases of systematic **torture**, and human rights organizations have nicknamed him "Africa's Pinochet." Indicted in Senegal in 2000, national courts ruled that he could not be tried there. In September 2005, a Belgian judge acting under the principle of **universal jurisdiction** charged Habre of **crimes against humanity, war crimes** and torture and asked for his extradition. Two months later, the Senegalese government arrested Habre but has yet to bring him to trial. In 2006, the **United Nations Committee against Torture** ruled that Senegal was in violation of its treaty obligations for failing to bring Habre to justice, and the **African Union** called on Senegal to prosecute him "in the name of Africa." In early February 2008, Belgium filed a case with the **International Court of Justice** asking the Court to rule that Senegal had violated the **United Nations Convention against Torture** and was bound to prosecute Habre or, failing that, to extradite him to Belgium. In a 2012 decision, the Court determined that Senegal must either prosecute the former Chadian president or extradite "without further delay." *See also* BRODY, REED.

HAITI. *See* DUVALIER, JEAN-CLAUDE; DUVALIER, FRANCOIS; HUMANITARIAN INTERVENTION; SEXUAL VIOLENCE.

HAMDI ET AL. v. RUMSFELD, SECRETARY OF DEFENSE, ET AL. **(2004).** **United States** Supreme Court decision which reversed the dismissal of **habeas corpus** petition brought on behalf of Mr. Hamdi, a U.S. national being held indefinitely as an "illegal enemy combatant." The Court ruled that as a U.S. citizen, Mr. Hamdi had the right to challenge his detention before a judge. See also COUNTERTERRORISM; PUBLIC EMERGENCIES.

HARD LAW. Shorthand terminology referring to the obligations of states arising from international **treaties** and customary international law. *See also* SOFT LAW.

HARKIS. Algerian Muslims who served as auxiliaries to the French army during the **Algerian war of independence**. It is believed that, by 1962, there were over 200,000 Harkis fighting for the French army. Branded as collaborators by Algerian nationalists, 50,000 to 150,000 were killed when **Algeria** won its independence. Some 90,000 were able to find refuge in France where they were held in "temporary" internment camps until the 1970s. The French government has since recognized their political and civil rights, but Harkis still remain a neglected and unassimilated group of **refugees**.

HATE SPEECH. Term referring in law to any form of communication which involves the disparagement of persons or groups on the basis of such characteristics as race, color, ethnicity, gender, disability, **sexual orientation**, nationality and religion and may lead to intimidation or violence against them. International human rights law obligates states to restrict **freedom of expression** in circumstances involving propaganda for war or for inciting national, racial, or religious hatred. The United Nations Genocide Convention prohibits incitement to genocide and the **International Criminal Tribunal for Rwanda** convicted the mayor of a Rwandan township on those grounds. The **International Covenant on Civil and Political Rights** states that "any advocacy of national, racial or religious hatred that constitutes incitement to discrimination, hostility or violence shall be prohibited by law" (Art. 20). Under the **International Convention on the Elimination of All Forms of Racial Discrimination** (CERD), the dissemination of ideas or theories of superiority of race, color, or ethnic origins is to be prohibited and punished by the law (Art. 4). A considerable number of countries specifically exclude hate speech from the constitutional protection of free speech. The **United States**, the only country in the developed world where hate speech is legal, entered a **reservation** to Article 4 of the CERD upon ratification to protect the constitutional right of its nationals to speak freely, regardless of content. *See also* AKAYESU CASE.

HEALTH, RIGHT TO. The constitution of the **World Health Organization** (WHO) asserts that the enjoyment of the highest attainable standard of health is one of the fundamental rights of every human being without distinction of race, religion, political belief, economic or social condition. Several global and regional human rights **treaties** explicitly set forth a right to health including the **Universal Declaration of Human Rights** (1948, Art. 25), the **International Covenant on Economic, Social and Cultural Rights** (Art. 12), the **United Nations Convention on the Elimination of All Forms of Discrimination against Women** (Art. 12.2), the **United Nations Convention on the Rights of the Child** (Arts. 23 and 24), the **European Social Charter** (1961, Art. 11), the **African Charter on Human and People's Rights** (Art.

16), the **African Charter on the Rights and Welfare of the Child** (Art. 14), the **American Declaration on the Rights and Duties of Man** (Art. 33) and the Additional Protocol to the American Convention on Human Rights in the Area of Economic, Social and Cultural Rights (the Protocol of San Salvador, 1988, Art. 10).

The WHO 1978 Declaration of Alma-Ata on Primary Health Care enjoined states to progressively develop comprehensive health care systems to ensure effective and equitable distribution of resources for maintaining health, and WHO subsequently designed a plan, "Health for All by the Year 2000" consisting of a series of goals and programs to achieve minimum levels of health for all, which still remain relevant in the context of the **Millennium Development Goals**, the 1994 Program of Action of the **International Conference on Population and Development** and the 1995 Beijing Platform of Action of the Fourth World Conference on Women. In a 2000 **General Comment**, the **United Nations Committee on Economic, Social and Cultural Rights** clarified the contents of state obligations, stressing, in accordance with the principle of **indivisibility**, that the **realization** of the rights to health entailed not only the timely and appropriate provision of health care but also the creation of conditions conducive to ensure access to health care for all, such as access to safe and potable **water** and adequate sanitation, an adequate supply of safe **food**, nutrition and **housing**, healthy occupational and environmental conditions, and access to health-related education and information, including on sexual and reproductive health.

The right to health is also enshrined in numerous national constitutions all over the world and reflected in national legislation. The right to health may have won virtually universal normative recognition, but persisting levels of poverty and inequality for large segments of the world population underline the gap between aspirational goals and practice.

See also AMERICAN CONVENTION ON HUMAN RIGHTS; BUSINESS AND HUMAN RIGHTS RESOURCE CENTRE; CENTER FOR ECONOMIC AND SOCIAL RIGHTS; CULTURAL RIGHTS; EUROPEAN CHARTER OF FUNDAMENTAL RIGHTS OF THE EUROPEAN UNION; FAMILY CARE INTERNATIONAL; GLOBAL LAWYERS AND PHYSICIANS; INFORMATION, RIGHT TO; INTELLECTUAL PROPERTY RIGHTS; INTER-AMERICAN CONVENTION ON THE PREVENTION, PUNISHMENT AND ERADICATION OF VIOLENCE AGAINST WOMEN; INTERNATIONAL LABOUR ORGANIZATION; LIFE, RIGHT TO; NUCLEAR WEAPONS; PHYSICIANS FOR HUMAN RIGHTS; UNITED NATIONS CONFERENCE ON HUMAN SETTLEMENTS; UNIVERSAL DECLARATION ON BIOETHICS AND HUMAN RIGHTS; WORK, RIGHT TO.

HELSINKI FINAL ACT (1975). Declaration that emerged from the 1975 Conference on Security and Cooperation in Europe. Attended by 35 states including the **United States**, the Soviet Union and most European countries and designed to reduce **Cold War** tensions, the Conference paved the way to the establishment of the **Organization for Security and Co-operation in Europe**. The Declaration posited 10 principles to guide future relations between the participants to the conference: sovereign equality, respect for the rights inherent in sovereignty; refraining from the threat or use of force; inviolability of frontiers; territorial integrity of states; peaceful settlement of disputes; non-intervention in internal affairs; respect for human rights and fundamental freedoms, including freedom of thought, conscience, religion or belief; equal rights and **self-determination** of peoples; cooperation among states; and fulfillment in good faith of obligations under international law. Politically, the conference in effect legitimized the frontiers which had emerged from **World War II**. One of its unintended consequences was the emergence of **Human Rights Watch**, which was created in 1978 to support groups formed throughout the Soviet Union to monitor its compliance with the Helsinki Accords. *See also* HUMAN DIMENSION MECHANISM.

HERITAGE FOUNDATION. Influential American **think tank** founded in 1973 and based in Washington, D.C., whose stated mission is to "formulate and promote conservative public policies based on the principles of free enterprise, limited government, individual freedom, traditional American values, and a strong national defense." In partnership with the *Wall Street Journal*, Heritage publishes an annual "Index of Economic Freedom" measuring a country's freedom in terms of property rights and freedom from government regulation. Other parameters factored into the development of this index include **corruption** in government, barriers to international trade, tax rates, government expenditures, **rule of law**, regulatory burdens on banking, and labor and black market activities. *See also* MONITORING OF HUMAN RIGHTS.

HIGH COMMISSIONER FOR HUMAN RIGHTS (UN). *See* UNITED NATIONS OFFICE OF THE HIGH COMMISSIONER FOR HUMAN RIGHTS.

HIGH COMMISSIONER ON NATIONAL MINORITIES. *See* ORGANIZATION FOR SECURITY AND CO-OPERATION IN EUROPE.

HIV/AIDS. Globally, some 34 million people are believed to be living with HIV at the end of 2011. The burden of the epidemic, however, varies considerably between regions and countries, Sub-Saharan Africa being the most severely affected with nearly 1 in 20 adults living with HIV and accounting for 69 percent of all people with HIV. Worldwide, during the past decade, the incidence of HIV infection among adults fell by more than 25 percent, and the number of people newly infected continues to decrease. Human rights are inextricably linked with the spread and impact of HIV on individuals and communities around the world in the dual sense that a lack of respect for human rights fuels the spread and exacerbates the impact of the disease, while at the same time HIV undermines progress in the realization of human rights. That link is apparent in the disproportionate incidence of the disease among vulnerable groups, especially women and children living in **poverty** who face stigmatization and **discrimination.**

States' obligations to promote and protect HIV-related human rights are defined in provisions of existing international treaties dealing notably with the right to **life**; the right to **liberty** and security of the person; the right to the highest attainable standard of mental and physical **health**; the right to non-discrimination, equal protection and **equality before the law**; the right to **freedom of movement**; the right to seek and enjoy **asylum**; the right to **privacy**; the right to **freedom of expression** and opinion and the right to freely receive and impart **information**; the right to freedom of association; the right to marry and found a **family**; the right to **work**; the right to equal access to **education**; the right to an **adequate standard of living**; the right to **social security**, assistance and welfare. These linkages are acknowledged in a 2011 political **declaration** adopted by the **United Nations General Assembly** which seeks to reverse the spread of the pandemic and contribute to the achievement of the **Millennium Development Goals** through the provision of universal access to HIV prevention, treatment, care and support.

See also ACTION FOR SOUTHERN AFRICA; CARITAS INTERNATIONALIS; DECLARATION OF COMMITMENT ON HIV/AIDS; FAMILY CARE INTERNATIONAL; FORD FOUNDATION; GOLDSTONE, RICHARD; INTERNATIONAL FEDERATION TERRE DES HOMMES; OXFAM INTERNATIONAL; UNITED NATIONS DEVELOPMENT PROGRAMME.

HOLOCAUST. Mass murder of 6 million European Jews (two-thirds of the 9 million Jews who resided in Europe at the time) organized by the Nazis in German occupied territories during **World War II**. The persecution and **genocide** (the term did not exist at that time) proceeded in several stages as soon as the Nazis took power in 1933, beginning with the enactment of discriminatory laws, followed by the establishment of **concentration camps**, the mass shootings of Jewish populations by specialized units in the conquered territories of Eastern Europe and the rounding up of Jews in ghettos before their transport to extermination camps. Memories of the Holocaust shaped the response of the international community to Jewish demands for statehood in the British Mandate of Palestine. An acrimonious debate has erupted in recent years pitting those who argue that the Holocaust is a unique instance of genocide against those who maintain that there are similar instances of the same phenomenon which may be found in the killing of Armenians during World War I, the crimes committed by the communist regimes in the Soviet Union and **Democratic Kampuchea** and the atrocities committed in **Rwanda** in 1994.

See also ARMENIAN GENOCIDE; BARBIE, KLAUS; DARFUR CONFLICT; DEMJANJUK, JOHN; EICHMANN, ADOLF; FINTA, IMRE; ISRAEL; KATYN FOREST MASSACRE; LEMKIN, RAPHAEL; UKRAINE FAMINE; WORLD CONFERENCE AGAINST RACISM.

HOMOSEXUALS. *See* SEXUAL ORIENTATION.

HONDURAS. For most of the 20th century, the country has been ruled by military leaders who became presidents through rigged elections or coups (1932, 1948, 1955, 1963, 1975, 1978). The return to civilian government in 1982 did not put an end to **violations of human rights** as an intelligence military unit, with **United States** training and support, embarked on a campaign of assassinations and torture of political opponents to the government. According to figures published by **Amnesty International**, 184 people were "disappeared" between 1980 and 1992. In a 1988 decision dealing with a Honduras **forced disappearance** case, the **Inter-American Court of Human Rights** established an important precedent by ruling that, under the terms of the **Inter-American Convention on Human Rights**, states have an obligation to respect the human rights of individuals and to guarantee the enjoyment of these rights and that they must accordingly "prevent, investigate and punish any violation of the rights recognized in the Convention."

Concerns about human rights have been rekindled after a military-backed group of civilians forced out the democratically elected president in 2009. **Non-governmental organizations** have reported attacks on the independence of the judiciary and public prosecutors and threats against journalists, **human rights defenders** and political activists. The findings of a **truth and reconciliation commission** established in 2011 documenting cases of excessive police or army force and selective killings by government agents have so far gone unheeded. The country is also plagued by sporadic rural violence triggered by long-simmering land conflicts and violent crime associated with drug trafficking organizations involved in the transport of cocaine from South American to the United States. *See also* COLD WAR; DEATH SQUADS; IMPUNITY.

HONOR KILLING. Social practice defined by **Human Rights Watch** as "acts of violence, usually murder, committed by male family members against (most of the time) female family members, who are held to have brought dishonor upon the family." A woman can be targeted by (individuals within) her family for a variety of reasons, including refusing to enter into an arranged marriage, being the victim of a sexual assault, seeking a divorce—even from an abusive husband—or (allegedly) committing adultery. The mere perception that a woman has behaved in a way that "dishonors" her family is sufficient to trigger an attack on her life.

Honor killings have been reported in **Egypt**, Jordan, Lebanon, Morocco, Pakistan, Syria, Turkey, and Yemen. They have also occurred in Northern countries with large migrant communities such as France, Germany and Great Britain. According to estimates of the **United Nations Population Fund**, the annual number of honor killing victims may be as high as 5,000. In reports to the **United Nations Human Rights Council**, the **special rapporteur** on violence against women has described honor killings as an indicator of **femicide** and called upon states' parties to the **United Nations Convention on the Elimination of All Forms of Discrimination against Women** to develop more effective preventive and remedial penal, civil and administrative sanctions.

HOSTAGES. The 1979 United Nations Convention against the Taking of Hostages defines a hostage taker as "any person who seizes or detains and threatens to kill or to continue to detain another person . . . in order to compel a third party, namely a State, an international inter-governmental organization, a natural or juridical person, or a group of persons, to do or abstain from doing any act as an explicit or implicit condition for the release of the hostage." **International humanitarian law** prohibits taking and executing hostages in times of war and considers such acts as **war crimes** which can be tried before any national court under the **universal jurisdiction** principle. *See also* CIVILIANS, PROTECTION OF; GENEVA CONVENTIONS.

HOUSING, RIGHT TO ADEQUATE. Second-generation right founded at the international level in the **Universal Declaration of Human Rights** and given explicit legal recognition in the **International Covenant on Economic, Social and Cultural Rights** (ICESCR). Similar provisions can be found in the **International Convention on the Elimination of All Forms of Racial Discrimination**, the **United Nations Convention on the Elimination**

of All Forms of Discrimination against Women, the United Nations Convention on the Rights of the Child, the International Convention on the Suppression and Punishment of the Crime of Apartheid, and the United Nations Convention Relating to the Status of Refugees. It is also codified in the European Social Charter and African instruments for the protection of children and women.

A considerable number of countries have recognized the right to adequate housing as a basic human right and have either incorporated it in their constitutions or enacted legislation to realize it. A case in point is the constitution of South Africa, which, after asserting that everyone has the right to have access to adequate housing, also stipulates that the state must take reasonable legislative and other measures, within its available resources, to achieve its progressive realization. The South African constitution also provides that no one may be evicted from their home, or have their home demolished, without an order of court made after considering all the relevant circumstances and that no legislation may permit arbitrary evictions.

While reviewing reports submitted by states parties to the Covenant, the United Nations Committee on Economic, Social and Cultural Rights has affirmed that states do have a clear obligation to protect the right to adequate housing, and in two of its comments, the Committee has clarified the scope and meaning of the right which, in its view, involves the following components: legal security of tenure, availability of services, materials, facilities and infrastructure, affordability, habitability, accessibility and cultural adequacy. The UN special rapporteur on the right to housing has further emphasized that the realization of the right to adequate housing was intimately linked to the realization of other basic human rights, such as the right to life, the right to protection of one's private life, of one's family and one's home, the right to not be subjected to inhuman or degrading treatment, the right to land, the right to food, the right to water and the right to health. He has also insisted that its realization is tied to respect of the fundamental principles of non-discrimination and gender equality.

Housing rights are determinate and justiciable and there are judicial and quasi-judicial means of redress at the national, regional and international levels. In countries where the right to adequate housing is legally established, individual claims may be placed before administrative or court instances. Regional-level redress mechanisms may be found in the African Court of Human and People's Rights, the African Commission on Human and People's Rights, the Inter-American Court and Commission on Human Rights, the European Committee on Social Rights and the European Court of Human Rights. The main mechanisms available at the international level for the protection of the right to adequate housing are the

UN special rapporteur on the right to adequate housing, who reports to the **United Nations Human Rights Council** on the realization and violations of the right throughout the world and the ICESCR, which monitors the implementation of the Covenant on the basis of periodic states reports. Housing rights issues have also been occasionally dealt with by other **United Nations treaty bodies** including the **United Nations Committee on the Elimination of Racial Discrimination, United Nations Committee against Torture**, the **United Nations Committee on the Elimination of All Forms of Discrimination against Women**, the **United Nations Committee on the Rights of the Child**, the **United Nations Human Rights Committee** and the **United Nations Committee on the Protection of the Rights of All Migrant Workers and Their Families**.

In practice, achieving the progressive realization of the right to housing remains a far off distant objective. The latest *State of the World's Cities* published by UN Habitat documents high levels of slum prevalence in the cities of the developing world especially in Sub-Saharan Africa, with its concomitant baggage of overcrowding and lack of access to safe drinking water, sanitation, and durable housing structures and secure tenure to shelter. Violations by commission or omission are not infrequent, triggered or aggravated by, as the UN special rapporteur repeatedly stressed, land and property speculation; expropriations and **forced evictions**; rural exodus and the growth of slums; discrimination against vulnerable groups, including women, children, **refugees**, migrants, the elderly and the disabled; and the negative effects of the **privatization** of public services.

See also ARAB ASSOCIATION FOR HUMAN RIGHTS; CAPABILITY APPROACH:CENTER FOR ECONOMIC AND SOCIAL RIGHTS; CENTRE ON HOUSING RIGHTS AND EVICTIONS; CULTURAL RIGHTS; GROOTBOOM DECISION; INDIVISIBILITY; INTERNATIONAL CENTRE FOR HUMAN RIGHTS AND DEMOCRATIC DEVELOPMENT; MILLENNIUM DEVELOPMENT GOALS; PRIVACY, RIGHT TO; ROMA/ GYPSIES; UNITED NATIONS HUMAN SETTLEMENTS PROGRAMME; UNITED NATIONS SUB-COMMISSION ON THE PROMOTION AND PROTECTION OF HUMAN RIGHTS.

HUMAN DEVELOPMENT REPORT (HDR). Independent annual report commissioned and prepared under the auspices of the **United Nations Development Programme**. Published since 1990, HDR has considerably altered conventional views about development and contributed to a paradigm shift in development thinking, refocusing attention from economic growth and national accounting onto expanding the individual's capabilities and opportunities and people-centered policies. Another contribution of the report has been to develop new indices which are useful to measure differential levels of development (the "human development" index), poverty (the "human poverty" index) and gender inequalities (the "gender-related development" index and the **gender empowerment measure**"). *See also* SEN, AMARTYA.

HUMAN DIMENSION MECHANISMS. Set of procedures in the **Organization for Security and Co-operation in Europe** allowing member states to raise questions relating to the human rights situation of other member states and to establish ad hoc missions of independent experts to investigate and assist in the resolution of these problems. Between 1992 and 2011, the procedure has been used seven times. *See also* HELSINKI FINAL ACT; INVESTIGATION.

HUMAN EXPERIMENTATION. Experimentation on humans is an important tool for the advancement of medical and public **health** knowledge which may be acceptable as long as it is conducted on consenting persons for socially useful purposes. Medical experiments have a long and by and large unchartered history but the large-scale, unrestricted and state-sanctioned practices of Nazi and Japanese doctors before and during **World War II** triggered a process of standards setting through the development of ethical codes protecting humans involved in experimentation and the banning of impermissible forms of medical experimentation in international humanitarian and human rights law.

The **Geneva Conventions** prohibit medical or scientific experiments which are not necessitated by the medical treatment of protected persons. The **International Covenant on Civil and Political Rights** stipulates, in Article 7, that "no one shall be subjected to **torture** or to cruel, inhuman or degrading treatment or punishment. In particular, no one shall be subjected without his free consent to medical or scientific experimentation." The 1998 Rome Statute of the **International Criminal Court** defines torture or inhuman treatment, including biological experiments and willfully causing great suffering, or serious injury to body or health as grave breaches of the Geneva Conventions and "**war crimes**." Subjecting persons who are in the power of an adverse party to physical mutilation or to medical or scientific experiments of any kind which are neither justified by the medical, dental, or hospital treatment of the person concerned, nor carried out in his or her interest, and which cause death to or seriously endanger the health of such person or persons is also a serious violations of the laws and customs applicable in international armed conflict. *See also* GLOBAL LAWYERS AND PHYSICIANS.

HUMAN GENOME. The full complement of genes within an organism or in an individual.

See also BIOETHICS; EUROPEAN CONVENTION ON HUMAN RIGHTS AND BIOMEDICINE; UNITED NATIONS DECLARATION ON HUMAN CLONING; UNIVERSAL DECLARATION ON BIOETHICS AND HUMAN RIGHTS; UNIVERSAL DECLARATION ON THE HUMAN GENOME AND HUMAN RIGHTS.

HUMAN RIGHTS BASED APPROACH TO DEVELOPMENT (HRBA). Development strategy grounded on the assumption that human rights standards contained in, and principles derived from, the **Universal Declaration of Human Rights** and other international human rights instruments should guide development cooperation as well as the process of programming, planning, design, goal setting, implementation, monitoring and evaluation in all sectors such as **food security, health, education, governance,** nutrition, **water** and sanitation, **HIV/AIDS, work** and **labor** relations and social and economic security, including the achievement of the **Millennium Development Goals.**

By anchoring development policies as well as international cooperation for development into a system of rights, HRBA focuses attention on the need to eliminate inequalities, **redress** discriminatory practices related to gender, **minorities, indigenous peoples** and, more generally, unjust distributions of power that impede the development process as well as the **realization** of individual and group rights. From this perspective, HRBA is portrayed as a means toward better and more sustainable human development outcomes such as improved girls' education, ensuring women's equal access to land, and the importance of civil and political rights and participation for good governance. While few openly take exception with such prescriptions, HRBA has nevertheless proved virtually as controversial as the right to development concept because it highlights the entitlements of rights holders and calls for corresponding obligations of **duty bearers** (i.e., states and their governments).

See also DECLARATION ON THE RIGHT TO DEVELOPMENT; FOOD AND AGRICULTURAL ORGANIZATION; INTERNATIONAL LABOUR ORGANIZATION; INTERNATIONAL PROGRAMME ON THE ELIMINATION OF CHILD LABOUR; OXFAM INTERNATIONAL; UNITED NATIONS CHILDREN'S FUND; UNITED NATIONS EDUCATIONAL, SCIENTIFIC AND CULTURAL ORGANIZATION; UNITED NATIONS HIGH COMMISSIONER FOR REFUGEES; UNITED NATIONS HUMAN SETTLEMENTS PROGRAMME; UNITED NATIONS POPULATION FUND; WORLD HEALTH ORGANIZATION.

HUMAN RIGHTS COMMISSIONS. Generic term referring to international, national or subnational bodies set up to investigate and protect human rights. There are national commissions in countries such as Australia, Canada, Great Britain, **Greece**, India, Indonesia, Republic of Korea, Malaysia, Mauritius, Mexico, Mongolia, Nepal, New Zealand, Nigeria, **Northern Ireland**, Pakistan, **Peru**, Sri Lanka, Thailand and Uganda.

See also AFRICAN COMMISSION ON HUMAN AND PEOPLE'S RIGHTS; ASIAN HUMAN RIGHTS COMMISSION; INTER-AMERICAN COMMISSION ON HUMAN RIGHTS; TRUTH AND RECONCILIATION COMMISSIONS; UNITED NATIONS HUMAN RIGHTS COUNCIL.

HUMAN RIGHTS DEFENDERS (HRDs). "Individuals, groups and associations . . . contributing to . . . the effective elimination of all **violations of human rights** and fundamental freedoms of peoples and individuals" in their national state or region. Human rights defenders perform a wide variety of tasks as they may investigate, gather information regarding and report on human rights violations, assist victims of human rights abuses, endeavor to end **impunity** for violations of human rights, encourage governments to fulfill their human rights obligations, contribute to the material implementation of human rights treaties or provide **human rights education** and training targeted at judges, lawyers, police officers, soldiers or human rights monitors. Human rights defenders often work closely with human rights **non-governmental organizations** such as **Human Rights Watch** in their **investigations** and **monitoring of human rights** conditions throughout the world. Not infrequently, human rights defenders are subject to abusive and suppressive actions by governments. In 1998, the **United Nations General Assembly** adopted a Declaration on Human Defenders which recognized not only the importance and legitimacy of their work but also their need for better protection.

See also ASIAN CENTER FOR HUMAN RIGHTS; CENTER FOR JUSTICE AND INTERNATIONAL LAW; DECLARATION ON HUMAN RIGHTS DEFENDERS; EUROPEAN PARLIAMENT; INTERNATIONAL SERVICE FOR HUMAN RIGHTS; ORGANIZATION FOR SECURITY AND CO-OPERATION IN EUROPE; PEACE BRIGADES INTERNATIONAL; SOFT LAW; UNITED NATIONS STABILIZATION MISSION IN THE DEMOCRATIC REPUBLIC OF THE CONGO; WORLD ORGANIZATION AGAINST TORTURE.

HUMAN RIGHTS EDUCATION. The importance of human rights education has long been recognized by the international community. The

Universal Declaration of Human Rights invites governments to strive "by teaching and education to promote respect" for human rights and freedoms. The same idea was prominently emphasized by the 1993 **World Conference on Human Rights.** The **United Nations Educational, Scientific and Cultural Organization** (UNESCO) has had a long-standing interest in promoting human rights education through the development of national and local capacities, development of learning material and publications and advocacy activities. UNESCO was also instrumental in persuading the **United Nations General Assembly** to launch a "Decade for Human Rights Education" extending from 1995 to 2004. At the end of the Decade, the Assembly proclaimed the World Programme for Human Rights Education to seek to promote a common understanding of the basic principles and methodologies of human rights education and provide a concrete framework for action and strengthen partnerships and cooperation from the international level down to the grass roots. These activities are all grounded in the assumption that human rights education and learning is a strong instrument for conflict prevention, the prevention of **human rights violations** and that it is an essential ingredient in processes of postconflict transformation and consolidation.

From the standpoint of the **United Nations,** the core elements of human rights education include emphasizing the universal character of human rights, strengthening respect for human rights and fundamental freedoms, **capacity building** for society and the empowerment of the individual or groups to make full use of their human rights, intensifying efforts against **discrimination,** racism, xenophobia and related intolerance, ensuring gender equality and enabling participation in democratic processes. A significant number of **non-governmental organizations** like **Amnesty International** and the **Human Rights Education Associates** promote human rights education through their programs. Several schools in individual countries offer human rights education as part of their curriculum.

That being said, an evaluation carried out at the midpoint of the UN Decade showed that while states had proclaimed their support for human rights education, few, if any, had developed or implemented relevant national programs. One of the major obstacles confronting human rights education advocates is a perennial lack of resources both at the national and international levels.

See also ADVOCATES FOR HUMAN RIGHTS; BRITISH INSTITUTE OF HUMAN RIGHTS; CAIRO INSTITUTE FOR HUMAN RIGHTS STUDIES; CCJO RENE CASSIN; EQUITAS—INTERNATIONAL CENTER FOR HUMAN RIGHTS EDUCATION; FRIEDRICH-EBERT FOUNDATION; HUMAN RIGHTS EDUCATION ASSOCIATES; INTER-

AFRICAN COMMITTEE ON TRADITIONAL PRACTICES AFFECTING THE HEALTH OF WOMEN; INTER-AMERICAN INSTITUTE OF HUMAN RIGHTS; INTERNATIONAL CENTRE FOR HUMAN RIGHTS AND DEMOCRATIC DEVELOPMENT; INTERNATIONAL NGO COALITION FOR AN O.P. TO THE ICESCR; INTERNATIONAL SERVICE FOR HUMAN RIGHTS; INTERNATIONAL TRAINING CENTRE ON HUMAN RIGHTS AND PEACE TEACHING; MANDAT INTERNATIONAL; MINORITY RIGHTS INTERNATIONAL; OPEN SOCIETY INSTITUTE; PEOPLE'S MOVEMENT FOR HUMAN RIGHTS LEARNING; PREVENT GENOCIDE INTERNATIONAL; RAOUL WALLENBERG INSTITUTE; RIGHTS INTERNATIONAL; UNITED NATIONS HUMAN RIGHTS COUNCIL ADVISORY COMMITTEE; UNITED NATIONS TRANSITIONAL AUTHORITY IN CAMBODIA; WOMEN'S INTERNATIONAL LEAGUE FOR PEACE AND FREEDOM.

HUMAN RIGHTS EDUCATION ASSOCIATES (HREA). International **non-governmental organization** promoting human rights learning, the training of activists and professionals, the development of educational materials and programming; and community building through online technologies. The services provided by HREA include assistance in curriculum and materials development, training of professional groups, research and evaluation and networking human rights advocates and educators. *See also* HUMAN RIGHTS EDUCATION.

HUMAN RIGHTS FIRST (HRF). New York-based **non-governmental organization** (formerly known as the Lawyers Committee for Human Rights) set up in 1987 with a long-standing concern for the rights of **refugees**, **human rights defenders** and a fuller participation of the **United States** in the international human rights regime. More recently, HRF has dealt with the human rights implications of the "**war on terror**," discriminatory practices in Europe and **war crimes** and **crimes against humanity** in places like **Darfur**. Illustrative activities of HRF include its pro bono representation program, **litigation** in American courts and **advocacy** with Congress and the sitting administration on behalf of refugees.

Along with the **American Civil Liberty Union** and **Human Rights Watch**, HRF initiated legal proceedings against Defense Secretary **Donald Rumsfeld** on behalf of four Iraqis and four Afghans previously detained by the U.S. military. Human Rights First has also worked on other issues. It has brought together major **Internet** providers and human rights groups to develop principles on free expression and **privacy**. In its annual Hate Crime Survey, it examines anti-bias and nondiscrimination laws in the countries of the **Organization for Security and Co-operation in Europe**, documents hate crime violence, and assesses government responses. In 2008, HRF issued a detailed study documenting how China's close economic and military ties with the government of Sudan violated the sanctions imposed by the **United Nations Security Council** and helped sustain mass atrocities in Darfur.

HUMAN RIGHTS INSTITUTE. Subsidiary body of the London-based **International Bar Association** set up in 1995 to promote and protect international human rights standards through a variety of means, including the training of lawyers, judges and prosecutors in human rights law and international humanitarian law, especially in postconflict countries or countries where basic state infrastructures may have been eroded; **fact-finding** missions; making representations to national authorities worldwide where individuals or the independence of the **judiciary** has been threatened; media and **advocacy** campaigns; and providing long-term technical assistance to underresourced bar associations and law societies. *See also* CAPACITY BUILDING.

HUMAN RIGHTS INSTITUTE OF SOUTH AFRICA. Non-govern-mental **organization** which offers professional services toward the promotion of a human rights culture, peace and **democracy**. Since 1993, the Institute offers human rights training courses, disseminates human rights information and conducted research and does **advocacy** in South Africa and on the continent of Africa. *See also* CAPACITY BUILDING.

HUMAN RIGHTS INTERACTIVE NETWORK. United States California-based **non-governmental organization** dedicated to the promotion of and respect for human rights worldwide. It produces and funds websites like the Internet Guide to Human Rights which provides introductory information about human rights and its related areas such as international development, disaster relief, consumer awareness and identifies comprehensive links to organizations, government agencies and academic institutions throughout the world.

HUMAN RIGHTS INTERNET (HRI). **Non-governmental organization** set up in 1976 in the **United States** and now headquartered in Ottawa, Canada, to facilitate the exchange of information within the worldwide human rights community through the use of modern communication technologies. HRI communicates by phone, fax, mail and the **Internet** with more than 5,000 organizations and individuals around the world working for the advancement of human rights. It also carries out and disseminates widely human rights

research and produces useful human rights resources including databases and directories in digital, hard copy and microfiche formats.

HUMAN RIGHTS PRINCIPLES. Normative assumptions underpinning the language of human rights. These include the ideas that human rights are universal and inalienable; **indivisible**; interdependent and interrelated. Rights are equal in importance and none can be enjoyed without the others. Rights are protected by the rule of law and may provide the basis for legitimate claims against governments accountable to international standards. *See also* ACCOUNTABILITY; EQUALITY; GENERATION OF RIGHTS; INTERDEPENDENCE; NON-DISCRIMINATION; RULE OF LAW; UNIVERSALITY OF RIGHTS.

HUMAN RIGHTS WATCH (HRW). Major international **non-governmental organization** which traces its origins to the Helsinki Final Act. Headquartered in New York, HRW conducts **fact-finding** missions, **research** and **advocacy campaigns** on perceived **human rights violations** on such issues as **abortion** rights, gay rights, the safety of civilians in war, child labor, **genocide**, **war crimes** and **crimes against humanity**, **torture**, **extra-judicial executions** and **human trafficking** in women and girls. Each year HRW publishes more than 100 reports on the 70 or so countries that it monitors and compiles annual reports providing an authoritative overview of the worldwide state of human rights. It was instrumental in drawing attention to violations of human rights in Central America in the 1980s and in Iraq a decade later. HRW played a key role in the international campaign that led to the adoption of the 1996 Ottawa Convention prohibiting the use of antipersonnel mines and has vigorously campaigned against the use of **children in armed conflicts**. In 2008, HRW was awarded the United Nations Human Rights Prize. *See also* AL-ANFAL CAMPAIGN; BRODY, REED; CONSORTIUM OF MINORITY RESOURCES; DRONES; INVESTIGATION; MONITORING OF HUMAN RIGHTS; NEIER, ARYEH.

HUMAN SECURITY. The **United Nations Development Programme** defines the term as the "the liberation of human beings from those intense, extensive, prolonged, and comprehensive threats to which their lives and freedom are vulnerable." The approach, drawn from and expanding on by **Amartya Sen**, identifies **poverty** and unemployment, pressures on the **environment**, hunger and malnutrition, disease in addition to foreign occupation and military intervention as threats to human security and posits that the prime function of states is to contain and avert them. From this perspective, human security relates to human rights in the sense that respect for people's basic rights creates conditions favorable to human security. *See also* "RESPONSIBILITY TO PROTECT."

HUMAN TRAFFICKING. There is considerable controversy about the definition of the term, but human trafficking involves three core elements: the recruitment, transportation, transfer, harboring or receipt of persons; the threat of or use of force, deception, coercion, abuse of power or position of vulnerability; and exploitation. Trafficking in human beings is in essence a method of obtaining slaves. Victims are recruited through deception, sale by family members, intimidation and outright coercion. In its latest estimates, the **United Nations** reckoned that nearly 2.5 million people from 127 different countries are being trafficked into 137 countries around the world and, according to the **International Labour Organization**, human trafficking generates a global annual profit of over $30 billion. The majority of trafficking victims are between 18 and 24 years of age, most of them experiencing physical or sexual violence during trafficking. The most common form of trafficking is sexual exploitation as the victims are predominantly women and girls (paradoxically, for countries where the information is available, women make up the largest proportion of traffickers).

A number of international instruments seek to prevent and protect the victims of human trafficking. At the regional level and within the framework of the **Council of Europe**, a 2005 Convention on Action against Trafficking in Human Beings provides for a Group of Experts on Action against Trafficking in Human Beings which monitors the implementation of the Convention through country reports. A Convention on the Protection of Children against Sexual Exploitation and Sexual Abuse is designed specifically to protect children. The **European Court of Human Rights** has passed judgments concerning trafficking in human beings which violated obligations under the **European Convention for the Protection of Human Rights and Fundamental Freedoms**. The **Organization for Security and Co-operation in Europe** has an anti-trafficking mechanism aimed at raising public awareness of the problem and prompting governments to take action.

At the global level, the Protocol to Prevent, Suppress and Punish Trafficking in Persons, especially Women and Children attached to the **United Nations Convention against Transnational Organized Crime** defines trafficking in persons as "the recruitment, transportation, transfer, harboring or receipt of persons, by means of the threat or use of force or other forms of coercion, of abduction, of fraud, of deception, of the abuse of power or of a position of vulnerability or of the giving or receiving of payments or benefits to achieve the consent of a person having control over another person, for the purpose of exploitation. Exploitation shall include, at a minimum, the exploitation of the prostitution of others or other forms of sexual exploitation, **forced labor** or services, **slavery** or practices similar to slavery, servitude or the removal of organs." A recently published United Nations—Global Report on Trafficking in Persons—based on data gathered from 155 countries, shows that in the past few years, the number of states seriously implementing the Protocol has more than doubled, but too many countries still lack the necessary legal instruments or political will.

See also CHILDREN TRAFFICKING; COALITION AGAINST TRAFFICKING IN WOMEN; CONVENTION ON THE PROTECTION OF CHILDREN AGAINST SEXUAL EXPLOITATION AND SEXUAL ABUSE; DECLARATION ON THE ELIMINATION OF VIOLENCE AGAINST WOMEN; GLOBAL ALLIANCE AGAINST TRAFFIC IN WOMEN; GLOBAL SURVIVAL NETWORK; HUMAN RIGHTS WATCH; KOSOVO; LABOR BONDAGE; LIBERTY, RIGHT TO; SEX TRAFFICKING; TRANSNATIONAL CRIME; UNITED NATIONS CONVENTION FOR THE SUPPRESSION OF THE TRAFFIC IN PERSONS AND OF THE EXPLOITATION OF THE PROSTITUTION OF OTHERS; UNITED NATIONS INTERIM ADMINISTRATION MISSION IN KOSOVO.

HUMANITARIAN ASSISTANCE, DENIAL OF. Situations in **armed conflicts** preventing directly affected groups from receiving emergency material aid (food, water, clothing, medicines, fuel, shelter, hospital equipment) or the services of humanitarian personnel that are essential to their survival. The jurisprudence of **war crime tribunals** suggests that the deliberate and intentional withholding of humanitarian assistance may constitute crimes under **international humanitarian** and **international human rights law**. *See also* GENEVA CONVENTIONS.

HUMANITARIAN INTERVENTION. Legal doctrine which calls for the use of force by a state or group of states or an international organization to protect the nationals of a particular state from widespread deprivations of internationally recognized human rights, including **genocide** and **crimes against humanity**. The idea is not new since it can be traced back to and draws from earlier "just war" doctrines associated with the writings of Saint Augustine, Saint Thomas Aquinas and Grotius and the widespread practice of European powers throughout the 19th century to intervene in areas under the control of the Ottoman Empire. But in its modern context, the idea of humanitarian intervention runs counter to the basic **United Nations Charter** paradigm that states are prohibited from using force against other states unless they are acting in self-defense and with the authorization of the **United Nations Security Council** (UN-SC).

Throughout the **Cold War** no state practice emerged in support of the doctrine, and in the rare instances of interventions that appeared to protect human rights, the intervening states typically justified their use of force as an exercise in self-defense as was the case with Tanzania's intervention in **Uganda** in 1979. In the same context, the **United Nations General Assembly** condemned armed interventions like Vietnam's invasion of Cambodia in 1978 against the Khmer Rouge. With the demise of the Cold War, the UN-SC has on numerous occasions determined that humanitarian crises and **violations of human rights** constituted threats to international security, justifying the use of force. In December 1992 the UN-SC authorized a U.S.-led intervention in Somalia to end a civil conflict that threatened the lives of hundreds of thousands of Somalis. In June 1994 the Council authorized France's intervention in **Rwanda** to end the genocide between the Tutsis and Hutus. A month later, the Council authorized a U.S.-led intervention in Haiti to reverse a military coup that had ousted democratically elected president Jean-Bertrand Aristide. The **North Atlantic Treaty Organization** (NATO) led armed intervention in **Kosovo** in 1999 was prompted by Russian and Chinese vetoes in the UN-SC and was still justified by several governments on the basis of the doctrine of humanitarian intervention.

In the wake of the controversies triggered by the Kosovo war, a number of scholars and experts acting under the umbrella of the **International Commission on Intervention and State Sovereignty** have endeavored to develop criteria governing humanitarian intervention. In the framework of what they labeled the **"Responsibility to Protect"** (R2P), the authors of the Commission's report identified three major criteria governing the use of force for humanitarian purposes: first, there must be a just cause for the intervention (i.e., serious and irreparable harm occurring or likely to occur to human life). By "harm" the Commission meant "large scale loss of life, actual or apprehended, with genocidal intent or not, which is the product either of deliberate state action, or state neglect or inability to act, or a failed state situation" or "large scale 'ethnic cleansing', actual or apprehended, whether carried out by killing, forced expulsion, acts of terror or rape." Second, the primary purpose of the intervention should be to put an end to human suffering. Third, the scale, modalities and duration of the armed intervention should be proportionate to the scope of the humanitarian objectives. Fourth, all non-military options should be explored and deemed ineffective. Fifth, states participating in a collective intervention should secure the consent of the UN-SC.

In mapping out these criteria, the intent of the Commission was to give a halo of legality and legitimacy to the doctrine of humanitarian intervention. The UN-SC and the General Assembly have formally endorsed the R2P concept. But notwithstanding the claims of the vigorous campaign of **non-governmental organizations** and academic scholars, the disputes generated by the NATO-led armed intervention against Libya in 2011 and the concurrent inaction of the UN-SC in the face of the grievous violations of human rights committed by the government in Syria all underline the ambiguities and fragility of the acceptance of the doctrine of humanitarian intervention among states. *See also* DEMOCRATIC KAMPUCHEA; INDEPENDENT INTERNATIONAL COMMISSION ON KOSOVO.

HUMANITY. *See* CRIMES AGAINST HUMANITY; DIGNITY, RIGHT TO.

HUNGER PROJECT. Global non-profit organization founded in 1977 against the background of the rising debate about world hunger triggered by the first Rome World Food Conference sponsored by the United Nations. The group currently operates in Africa, South Asia and Latin America through three essential activities: mobilizing village clusters at the grassroots level to build self-reliance, empowering women as key change agents, and forging effective partnerships with local government. Its strategies are built upon such principles as human **dignity**, gender **equality** and empowerment. *See also* CAPACITY BUILDING; FOOD, RIGHT TO.

HUSSEIN, SADDAM (1937–2006). President of Iraq from July 1979 to April 2003 when he was ousted from power by the **United States** and its allies during the 2003 invasion of the country. Cognizant of the fact that Iraq was split along deep social, ethnic, and religious fault lines, Saddam Hussein actively sought to broaden his Baath Party's appeal after taking power by espousing a secular pan-Arabist ideology, economic modernization and Arab socialism. Using the country's oil revenues, Saddam Hussein fostered the modernization of the Iraqi economy and society. At the same time, however, his regime rapidly evolved into an authoritarian and ruthless state security system designed to suppress any form of political dissent deemed threatening, such as those of religious or ethnic groups which sought independence or greater autonomy. Thus, arbitrary arrests, **torture** and **extra-judicial executions** became common practice as tools of societal control and instruments for the elimination of real or suspected political opponents.

The regime displayed a similar disregard for human rights in its foreign policies. During the 1980–88 war with **Iran**, Iraq used chemical weapons against Iranian forces in the Southern Front and Kurdish separatists in the north of the country who were suspected to be trying to open a second front with the assistance of Iran. Iraq's military defeat in the 1990 Persian Gulf War triggered social and ethnic unrest in the Kurdish north and Shi'a southern and central parts of Iraq. The uprisings were ruthlessly crushed and as many 300,000 people are believed to have been killed in 1991.

Accused by the United States as having developed **weapons of mass destruction** and supporting international terrorism, Iraq was invaded by U.S.-led troops in March 2003. The regime fell quickly and Saddam Hussein went into hiding. On 13 December 2003, he was captured by American forces. Six months later, on 30 June 2004, he and a number of other senior Baathist officials were handed over to the interim Iraqi government to stand trial for **war crimes, crimes against humanity** and **genocide** committed in particular in the violent campaigns against the Kurds in the North during the Iran-Iraq war and against the Shiites in the south in 1991 and 1999. On 18 July 2005, Saddam Hussein was charged by the **Supreme Iraqi Criminal Tribunal** for his role in the killings of 148 Shiite Muslims from a village where assassins tried to kill him in 1982. Found guilty and sentenced to death, he was executed on 30 December 2006. At his death, Saddam Hussein was in the midst of another trial, charged with genocide and other crimes related to the 1987–88 military crackdown that led to the massacre of an estimated 180,000 Kurds in northern Iraq. *See also* AL-ANFAL CAMPAIGN; IMPUNITY; KURDISH QUESTION.

HUTU-TUTSI CONFLICTS. *See* BURUNDI; RWANDA; UGANDA.

HYBRID COURTS. *See* AD HOC INTERNATIONAL COURTS.

I

IENG SARY (1925–2013). Senior member of the Khmer Rouge and deputy prime minister and foreign minister of **Democratic Kampuchea** from 1975 to 1979. He was arrested in 2007 in Phnom Penh on charges of **genocide**, **war crimes** and **crimes against humanity**. Tried by the **Special Tribunal for Cambodia**, the court could not complete the judgment because of his death. *See also* IMPUNITY.

ILO CONVENTION CONCERNING INDIGENOUS AND TRIBAL PEOPLES IN INDEPENDENT COUNTRIES (1989). Adopted by 328 votes for, 1 against and 49 abstentions and ratified by only a few countries, this convention remains the sole binding international instrument devoted to the defense and strengthening of indigenous rights at the national, regional and international levels. It departs significantly from the integrationist and assimilationist thrust of an earlier convention with its emphasis on the need to recognize, protect and promote **indigenous peoples'** distinct identity, traditions, customs and their right to determine their own way and pace of economic and social development. In this regard, the Convention clearly states that indigenous and tribal peoples have rights to the land they traditionally occupy. A clause of the Convention stipulates that economic activities—logging, agribusiness or mining projects—must be based on "prior consultation" with indigenous peoples and "must be carried out in good faith and in a form appropriate to the circumstances, with the objective of achieving agreement or consent to the proposed measures." So far, the Convention has been ratified by only 22 states. *See also* DECLARATION ON THE RIGHTS OF INDIGENOUS PEOPLES; SELF-DETERMINATION; UNITED NATIONS PERMANENT FORUM ON INDIGENOUS ISSUES.

ILO TRIPARTITE DECLARATION OF PRINCIPLES CONCERNING MULTINATIONAL ENTERPRISES AND SOCIAL POLICY. Voluntary standards negotiated between workers' and employers' organizations and governments, adopted in 1977 and revised in 2000 and 2006 within the **International Labour Organization** (ILO). The Declaration provides guidance on the private sector's responsibilities regarding employment, skills development, conditions of work, living standards and industrial relations and, in effect, sets up a complaint procedure in respect to national law and practice and ILO conventions and recommendations that may be initiated by a government member of the ILO and national or international organizations of employers or workers. Since 1981, the ILO has handled only a handful of complaints. *See also* CORPORATE SOCIAL RESPONSIBILITY; TRANSNATIONAL CORPORATIONS; SOFT LAW.

ILL TREATMENT. The **United Nations Convention against Torture and Other Cruel, Inhuman or Degrading Treatment and Punishment**, the **International Covenant on Civil and Political Rights** and the Fourth **Geneva Convention** all prohibit ill treatment. None of these instrument defines the term, but case law and literature suggest that the intensity of suffering and the purpose underlying the methods used differentiate **torture** from ill treatment. International human rights law imposes an absolute prohibition on both torture or ill treatment which states may not derogate from even in **public emergencies**. The **United Nations Human Rights Committee** makes no distinction between the prohibitions of torture and ill treatment, leaving open the determination of which cases fall into one category or the other. In contrast, the **European Court of Human Rights** does make a distinction between the two prohibitions while holding both of them equally absolute. *See also* INHUMAN OR DEGRADING TREATMENT OR PUNISHMENT.

IMMUNITY. General rule of **international law** whereby high-ranking state officials are deemed to enjoy immunity from civil suits and criminal prosecution initiated in other states. The principle, as enshrined in the 1961 Vienna Convention on Diplomatic Relations and the 1963 Vienna Convention on Consular relations, is a reflection of the sovereign equality of states and is designed to allow them and their representatives to engage in international relations. Functional immunities cover the activities carried out by state representatives in their official capacity as long as they are in office and even after they leave office. Personal immunities cover all activities of the officials but cease to apply upon completion of their official duties.

Recent developments in international criminal justice have considerably eroded the rule. The statutes of the **International Military Tribunal for the Prosecution and Punishment of the Major War Criminals of the European Axis** and the **International Military Tribunal for the Far East**, the 1948 **United Nations Convention on the Punishment and Prevention of the Crime of Genocide,** and the 1950 so-called **Nuremberg Principles** already indicated that individuals committing **crimes against humanity, war crimes** and acts of **genocide** could be individually responsible for them.

The idea that no state office is entitled to functional or personal immunities is enshrined in the statutes of the **International Criminal Tribunal for the Former Yugoslavia**, the **International Criminal Tribunal for Rwanda** and the **Special Court for Sierra Leone**. It is reiterated in the wording of Article 27 of the Rome Statute of the **International Criminal Court** (ICC). The same provision enjoins states parties to amend their national legislation accordingly in order to enable them to comply with ICC orders for arrest or surrender. The **Augusto Pinochet** case highlights this evolution and shows that the moment accused officials leave office, they become liable to be prosecuted for crimes committed before or after their term of office in a personal capacity.

But there is greater uncertainty as to whether the rejection of official immunity also applies to proceedings before national jurisdictions. In a 2002 case (*Democratic Republic of the Congo v. Belgium*), the **International Court of Justice** ruled that the issuance of a warrant for the arrest of the minister of foreign affairs of the **Democratic Republic of the Congo** by a Belgian investigating judge violated international law. Likewise, there are continuing legal and political disputes as to which dignitaries enjoy immunities, the nature and scope of "acts committed in a private capacity" and the immunity of state representatives in civil actions filed against them for monetary damages. *See also* INHUMAN OR DEGRADING TREATMENT OR PUNISHMENT; PEREMPTORY NORMS; STATE RESPONSIBILITY.

IMPUNITY. The **Set of Principles for the Protection and Promotion of Human Rights Through Action to Combat Impunity**, submitted to the **United Nations Commission on Human Rights** in 2005 by one of its independent experts, defines impunity as "the impossibility, *de jure* or *de facto*, of bringing the perpetrators of violations to account—whether in criminal, civil, administrative or disciplinary proceedings—since they are not subject to any inquiry that might lead to their being accused, arrested, tried and, if found guilty, sentenced to appropriate penalties, and to making reparations to their victims." In essence, impunity refers to offenders who escape retribution and punishment for an offense that inflicted harm on someone and, more generally, from the failure to bring perpetrators of **violations of human rights** to justice. It is a denial of the right to a **remedy**. Impunity may arise from **corruption**, patronage, outright denial, the suppression of evidence, intimidation, tradeoffs through deal making, the weakness of judicial bodies, or the continued protection of the perpetrators by special jurisdictions, **amnesty** laws and **immunities**. The incidence of impunity appears to have declined somewhat in recent decades with the establishment of international judicial institutions, the creation of **truth and**

reconciliation commissions in nations emerging from civil conflict, the repeal of amnesty laws and the increasing reliance of victims on **litigation**.

See also ABACHA, SANI; AMIN, IDI; AUSSARESSES, PAUL; BANGLADESH LIBERATION WAR; BOLIVIA; BRAZIL; "COMFORT WOMEN"; COMMAND RESPONSIBILITY; DUVALIER, JEAN-CLAUDE; GUATEMALA; HONDURAS; IENG SARY; IMPUNITY WATCH; LEMAY, CURTIS; MARCOS, FERDINAND; MENGHISTU, HAILE MARIAM; MOBUTU SESE SEKO; NANKING MASSACRE; PAPON,MAURICE;PARAGUAY;PASHA,TALAT;PRIVATEMILITARY COMPANIES; SHARON, ARIEL; SUHARTO; TIANANMEN SQUARE PROTESTS; TUDJMAN, FRANJO; UNITED NATIONS CONVENTION ON THE NON-APPLICABILITY OF STATUTORY LIMITATIONS TO WAR CRIMES AND CRIMES AGAINST HUMANITY; UNITED NATIONS VERIFICATION MISSION IN GUATEMALA; "WAR ON TERROR."

IMPUNITY WATCH. Online interactive website run by students at Syracuse University College of Law in New York (United States) and operating as a law review, message board, and blog. Launched in 2007, Impunity Watch monitors and seeks to raise awareness about state violations of fundamental human rights such as *forced labor* or the sexual exploitation of individuals, the denial of access to *food* and *water* and acts of *genocide*. *See also* IMPUNITY; INTERNET.

INALIENABILITY. *See* UNALIENABLE RIGHTS.

INCLUSION INTERNATIONAL (II). One of the largest international disability **non-governmental organizations**, founded in 1982 and located in London, officially recognized by the **United Nations**. This global federation of over 200 family-based organizations based in more than 115 countries advocates for the rights of intellectually **disabled persons** worldwide. II works with international agencies including the **World Health Organization**, the **United Nations Educational, Scientific and Cultural Organization**, the World Bank, the **International Labour Organization** and the **United Nations Children's Fund** to promote policies, practices and investment strategies conducive to the integration of disabled persons into their communities.

INCORPORATION. Process whereby, under **international law**, countries which are parties to a **treaty** pass domestic legislation to give effect to the obligations to which they have agreed. In a few countries (the Netherlands, for instance), treaties become automatically effective without incorporation. The practice of most countries, however, especially in regard to international human right treaties, is to rely on a system requiring that treaties be incorporated into domestic law. *See also* INTERNALIZATION.

INDEPENDENT INTERNATIONAL COMMISSION ON KOSOVO. High-level **fact-finding** body established on the initiative of Swedish Prime Minister Goran Persson, Justice **Richard Goldstone** of South Africa and Carl Tham, secretary-general of the Olof Palme International Center in Stockholm. The report examines key developments prior to, during, and after the **Kosovo** war, including systematic **violations of human rights** in the region and assesses the effectiveness of diplomatic efforts to prevent the war, the legality of the **North Atlantic Treaty Organization**'s bombing campaign against Yugoslavia, and the progress of the **United Nations** in postconflict reconstruction. One of the commission's primary conclusions was that the intervention was illegal but legitimate: "it was illegal because it did not receive prior approval from the **United Nations Security Council**. However, the . . . intervention was justified because all diplomatic avenues had been exhausted and because the intervention had the effect of liberating the majority population of Kosovo from a long period of oppression under Serbian rule." *See also* HUMANITARIAN INTERVENTION.

INDIA, PARTITION OF. The subcontinent of India encompasses the territory of modern India, Pakistan and Bangladesh. Its history as well as its tribulations under British colonialism have been shaped, to a considerable extent, by the extraordinary variety of customs, languages and ethnic groups that it encompasses as well as by the interplay of Buddhism, Hinduism and Sikhism (which all originate from the Indian subcontinent) and Islam which established itself in India at the end of the 12th century. The British made their first permanent inroads into India in 1612 when they established a trading post in Surat. For the next 250 years, British power was exerted through the East India Company, to which Queen Elizabeth I had granted a monopoly of British trade with the Far East. The East India Company was dissolved and India was brought under direct control of the British Crown in the wake of the suppression of the Indian Mutiny in 1857. The rest of the 19th century witnessed the height of British power in the subcontinent, although nationalist opposition continued to simmer and developed in earnest after World War I.

The Indian National Congress (INC), created in 1885, comprised Hindus, Muslims and Sikhs all united in their demands for equal opportunity and freedom from colonial rule. Throughout the 1920s, the three religious groups bonded in support of the nonviolent mass resistance advocated by Mahatma Gandhi. But as the British conceded more political power and fairer representation to the Hindu-dominated INC, Muslim leaders felt that the INC was beginning to dictate decision making in British India. Sentiment grew among them that Muslims should have their own state and, in 1940, the All-India Muslim League under Muhammed Ali Jinnah declared its desire for a separate state of Pakistan ("the Land of the Pure"). Subsequent relations between the two religious groups further deteriorated, and growing inter-ethnic unrest spread throughout India.

The failure of the Congress–League coalition to govern the country prompted both parties and the British to agree to partition. India remained independent, being partitioned into the Republic of India and Pakistan on 14–15 August 1947, respectively. During this period of partition, nearly 12 million Hindus, Muslims and Sikhs, the largest **forced migration** ever recorded in modern history, crossed the newly established borders to join other Muslims in Pakistan and Hindus and Sikhs in India. As violence escalated, especially in the Punjab, more than 1 million people perished in inter-ethnic violence. India and Pakistan have since then fought three wars over the disputed province of Kashmir. *See also* BANGLADESH LIBERATION WAR; COLONIALISM; POPULATION EXCHANGE; SELF-DETERMINATION.

INDICATORS. *See* MONITORING OF HUMAN RIGHTS.

INDIGENOUS AUSTRALIANS. These are a broad variety of communities with differing modes of subsistence, cultures and languages sharing nevertheless a sense of collective identity derived from their common distant ancestry with the first inhabitants of the Australian continent. It is estimated that between 250,000 and 1 million people lived in Australia when the first British colonizers arrived at the end of the 18th century. By the early 20th century, the indigenous population had dramatically declined to between 50,000 and 90,000 as a result of the impact of disease and the spread of white settlers' industries and concomitant loss of land. There are now approximately half a million indigenous people representing 2.5 percent of the Australian total population. Indigenous Australians have long faced outright legal discrimination but have since the 1960s won increasing recognition of their civil and political rights. They still face conditions of deprivation and marginalization reflected in levels of poverty, unemployment and criminality significantly higher that the general population. *See also* INDIGENOUS PEOPLES.

INDIGENOUS PEOPLES. Variously known as Aborigines, Native Peoples, First Nations, Autochtonous and Fourth World, indigenous peoples, as defined by a seminal study prepared at the request of and issued for the United Nations Sub-Commission on the Prevention of Discrimination and Protection of Minorities between 1981 and 1984, "indigenous communities, peoples and nations are those which, having a historical continuity with the pre-invasion and pre-colonial societies that developed on their territories, consider themselves distinct from other sectors of the societies now prevailing in those territories, or parts of them. They form at present non-dominant sectors of society and are determined to preserve, develop, and transmit to future generations their ancestral territories, and their ethnic identity, as the basis of their continued existence as peoples, in accordance with their own cultural patterns, social institutions, and legal systems." In a similar vein, the **International Labour Organization** (ILO) defines indigenous peoples as "both tribal peoples whose social, cultural and economic conditions distinguish them from other sections of the national community and whose status is regulated wholly or partially by their own customs or traditions or by special laws or regulations, and to peoples who are regarded as indigenous on account of their descent from the populations which inhabit the country at the time of conquest or colonization."

The term thus essentially refers to non-dominant groups which have historical links to communities that preexisted **colonialism** or invasion by other peoples and are culturally distinctive and distanced from the state, society and economy they live in. Precise estimates are not altogether reliable, but it is believed that there are currently 350 to 370 million indigenous peoples throughout the world including over 5,000 distinct peoples in over 70 countries. Notwithstanding the wide variety of their historical experience, all indigenous populations have suffered dramatic declines, and only a handful of them are undergoing a recovery. Some of them, as a result of the impact of epidemic diseases, displacement, conflict and exploitation, have become extinct or still currently face possible extinction. Most others remain threatened in their interactions with the rest of society and share common human rights issues regarding their inferior civil, economic and political status, de facto economic and social **discrimination**, the preservation of their culture, language and traditions, the degradation of their natural **environment** by intrusive and predatory groups and the ownership and exploitation of their natural resources.

Indigenous peoples have only recently been recognized as a special category of individuals requiring protection under **international human rights law**. Article 27 of the **International Covenant on Civil and Political Rights** protects the rights of ethnic, religious and linguistic **minorities**. A

1957 ILO Convention was concerned with the "protection and integration" of indigenous populations in independent states. Widely criticized for its paternalistic undertones, this Convention was replaced after considerable dispute over the term "Peoples" by another ILO convention in 1989. The Vienna Declaration and Programme of Action adopted by the 1993 **World Conference on Human Rights** makes a number of references to indigenous peoples and recognizes, in particular, the "inherent **dignity** and the unique contribution of indigenous people to the development and plurality of society."

These issues are now aired in the **United Nations Permanent Forum on Indigenous Issues** which was set up in 2000 by the **United Nations Economic and Social Council** as one of its subsidiary bodies. The **United Nations General Assembly** has launched two international decades for the periods of 1995–2004 and 2005–15, respectively, seeking to increase the Organization's commitment to the promotion and protection of indigenous peoples. In 2006, the **United Nations Human Rights Council** adopted the draft of a **Declaration on the Rights of Indigenous Peoples** which won grudging acceptance by the United Nations General Assembly.

See also ABORIGINAL PEOPLES IN CANADA; BOLIVIA; CENTER FOR MINORITY RIGHTS DEVELOPMENT; COBO, JOSE MARTINEZ; COLONIALISM; CONVENTION FOR THE SAFEGUARDING OF INTANGIBLE CULTURAL HERITAGE; CORPORATE SOCIAL RESPONSIBILITY; CULTURAL RIGHTS; DAES, ERICA-IRENE; FORUM FOR FACT-FINDING DOCUMENTATION AND ADVOCACY; FRIENDS OF THE EARTH INTERNATIONAL; GENOCIDE; GROUP RIGHTS; ILO CONVENTION CONCERNING INDIGENOUS AND TRIBAL PEOPLES IN INDEPENDENT COUNTRIES; INDIGENOUS AUSTRALIANS; INDIGENOUS PEOPLES' CENTER FOR DOCUMENTATION, RESEARCH AND INFORMATION; INTELLECTUAL PROPERTY RIGHTS; INTER-AMERICAN INDIAN INSTITUTE; INTERNATIONAL MOVEMENT AGAINST ALL FORMS OF DISCRIMINATION AND RACISM; INTERNATIONAL WORK GROUP FOR INDIGENOUS AFFAIRS; MENCHU, RIGOBERTA; MINORITY RIGHTS GROUP INTERNATIONAL; NATIVE AMERICANS; PROPERTY, RIGHT TO; RAOUL WALLENBERG INSTITUTE; RIGHTS AND DEMOCRACY; SURVIVAL INTERNATIONAL; UNITED NATIONS CONVENTION ON BIOLOGICAL DIVERSITY; UNITED NATIONS VERIFICATION MISSION IN GUATEMALA; UNITED NATIONS WORKING GROUP ON THE RIGHTS OF INDIGENOUS PEOPLES; UNREPRESENTED NATIONS AND PEOPLES ORGANIZATION; WORLD CONFERENCE AGAINST RACISM; WORLD COUNCIL OF CHURCHES; WORLD COUNCIL OF INDIGENOUS PEOPLES.

INDIGENOUS PEOPLES' CENTER FOR DOCUMENTATION, RESEARCH AND INFORMATION. Swiss nonprofit organization supporting the rights of **indigenous peoples** by acting as an information clearinghouse and the provision of technical services to indigenous peoples organizations participating in the sessions of international bodies such as the **United Nations Human Rights Council** in Geneva and the **United Nations Permanent Forum on Indigenous Issues** in New York.

INDIVIDUAL RECOURSE. Legal actions that can be taken by individuals to obtain a **remedy** to a **violation of human rights**. *See also* COMMUNICATION; COMPLAINTS; LITIGATION.

INDIVISIBILITY. Basic principle of the human rights discourse postulating that, because they derive from the dignity of the person, all human rights have equal status. Accordingly, neither can human rights be ranked on a hierarchy of importance nor can they be realized without realizing all of them. A practical and politically controversial consequence of the notion of indivisibility is that states cannot pick and choose among rights. *See also* ASIAN VALUES; CULTURAL RELATIVISM; ENVIRONMENT, RIGHT TO A HEALTHY; HUMAN RIGHTS PRINCIPLES; UNIVERSAL DECLARATION OF HUMAN RIGHTS; UNIVERSALITY OF RIGHTS; WORLD CONFERENCE ON HUMAN RIGHTS.

INDONESIA. Archipelagic nation which won its independence from the Netherlands in 1949. It is now the world's fourth most populous country with hundreds of distinct native and linguistic groups, the largest being the politically dominant Javanese. The country's identity was forged by its history of **colonialism** and rebellion against it as well as its resistance to Japanese occupation during **World War II** (a **United Nations** report issued after independence stated that 4 million died as a result of famine and **forced labor** during Japan's occupation). Indonesia rapidly evolved toward an authoritarian rule which sought to maintain an uneasy balance between a conservative coalition of military, religious and liberal groups and, at that time, the largest communist political party in the world. The Communist Party was blamed for a failed 1965 attempted coup. In the army-led repression which followed, it is estimated that from 500,000 to as many as 1 million "communists" were killed. Leftist loyalists were removed from the government. Press censorship was instituted. As many as 750,000 people were arrested and 55,000 to 100,000 accused of being communists may have been held in jail for several years. About 500,000 people are believed to have died.

The "New Order" which emerged from the violence with the support of the **United States** has been widely accused of **corruption** and the suppression of political opposition and secessionist attempts in **Timor-Leste** and the province of **Aceh**. Regime change beginning in 1989 allowed the country to make significant strides toward greater stability and **democracy**, but serious human rights concerns remain. No significant steps were taken to hold Indonesian military forces accountable for the **abuses** committed in Timor-Leste prior to and at the time of the runup to a referendum on independence. **Non-government organizations** are critical of the criminal justice system for its incapacity to deal with cases of **torture**, **ill treatment** of detainees and the use of excessive force against protesters by security forces. They also draw attention to the persistence of severe restrictions on **freedom of expression** and the violence and discriminatory practices faced by religious **minorities**. *See also* SPECIAL PANELS OF THE DILI DISTRICT COURT; SUHARTO.

INFANTICIDE. Intentional killing of infants. Not uncommon in the past, the practice is unlawful everywhere but subsists in some countries for a variety of economic, social, cultural reasons, notably China and India, where the victims are primarily female children. *See also* FEMALE INFANTICIDE; GENDERCIDE; GENOCIDE; LIFE, RIGHT TO.

INFORMATION, RIGHT TO. Derived from the right of **freedom of expression**, this right provides that individuals have a basic human right to demand information held by government bodies. In turn, such entities are legally required to respond and to provide the information unless there is a compelling reason to turn the request down. The right to information is generally recognized at the national level in constitutional provisions or national legislation. The **United Nations**, the **Organization of American States**, the **Council of Europe** and the **African Union** have all developed standards or set up mechanisms authoritatively recognizing the fundamental and legal nature of the right to freedom of information. The precise contours of the right has been elucidated through evolving state practice as well as the studies of **United Nations special rapporteurs** and **non-governmental organizations** such as **Article 19**; freedom of information legislation would be guided by the principle of maximum disclosure and laws inconsistent with the principle amended or repealed, public bodies should be under an obligation to publish key information and actively promote open government, exceptions to the right of access to information should be clearly drawn and subject to strict "harm and public interest" tests, requests for information should be processed rapidly and an independent review of any refusal should be available and individuals releasing information on wrongdoing should be protected. *See also* FORCED DISAPPEARANCES; ENVIRONMENT, RIGHT TO A HEALTHY; PRIVACY, RIGHT TO.

INHUMAN OR DEGRADING TREATMENT OR PUNISHMENT. Although there is no universally accepted definition of what constitutes "inhuman or degrading treatment and punishment," the expression is widely understood to imply a lesser degree of severity and intensity and cruelty than **torture**. Violence against women and children can be viewed as an instance of the term. In the same vein, complainants have successfully argued in the **United Nations Human Rights Committee** and the **European Court of Human Rights** that lengthy periods of retentions following a sentence of death may be akin to inhuman treatment (the so-called death row phenomenon). In their jurisprudence, treaty monitoring bodies have tended to condemn judicial corporal punishment, although they have been more inclined to accept the corporal punishment of children. *See also* ILL TREATMENT.

INQUIRY PROCEDURES. Process of gathering evidence to determine whether allegations of **violations of human rights** by a state party to a human rights treaty are substantiated. The **United Nations Convention against Torture** empowers the **United Nations Committee against Torture** (UN-CtteeAT) to receive and consider—in a confidential procedure—allegations of the systematic practice of **torture** in countries which are states parties to the Convention. If these allegations are substantiated, UN-CtteeAT invites the state party concerned to respond to them. It may also designate one or more of its members to undertake a confidential inquiry, which may include a visit to the country concerned. The UN-CtteeAT may thereafter make public a summary account of the results. Under this procedure, the Committee has completed inquiries involving **Egypt**, Mexico, **Peru**, Sri Lanka and **Turkey**. Under the Optional Protocol to the **United Nations Convention on the Elimination of All Forms of Discrimination against Women**, the **United Nations Committee on the Elimination of All Forms of Discrimination against Women** may likewise initiate inquiries addressing grave and systematic violations resulting from acts of omission by the states parties concerned. In contrast to individual **complaints** which it does not preclude, the inquiry procedure cannot lead to a recommendation for individual remedy. *See also* FACT FINDING; INTERNATIONAL CONVENTION FOR THE PROTECTION OF ALL PERSONS FROM ENFORCED DISAPPEARANCE.

INSTITUTE FOR FOOD AND DEVELOPMENT POLICY. *See* FOOD FIRST INFORMATION AND ACTION NETWORK.

INSTITUTE FOR GLOBAL COMMUNICATIONS. Founded in 1987, this **non-governmental organization** acts together with several partners as an information and communications service provider at several United Nations–sponsored world conferences. It manages four information networks for non-profit activist organizations: PeaceNet, EcoNet, WomensNet, and Anti-RacismNet. Each of these networks offers headlines of breaking news in the field as well as "action alerts" for people who want to be involved. The site contains chat rooms, event calendars, and advocacy tips of interest primarily to the site's activist audience as well as a subject directory of member websites related to activism and advocacy. *See also* INTERNET.

INSTITUTE FOR GLOBAL POLICY. Founded in 1983 by the **World Federalist Movement** with which it remains affiliated, the Institute carries out **research** on human security, international justice, the **prevention** of armed conflict and the protection of **civilians** with an emphasis on the democratization of international and regional organizations and the development and global application of international law.

INSTITUTE FOR HUMAN RIGHTS AND BUSINESS. Think tank promoting business accountability and responsibility through **research**, on thematic issues at the interface of internationally proclaimed human rights and private sector activity, awareness raising reports and policy briefs and **capacity-building** work.

INSTITUTE FOR HUMAN RIGHTS AND DEVELOPMENT IN AFRICA. African **non-governmental organization** established in 1998 in Banjul, The Gambia. It endeavors to strengthen human rights protection in Africa by offering pro bono legal counsel for victims of human rights **abuses,** by conducting training and other **capacity-building** efforts on the African Human Rights System and other human rights issues and publishing and distributing information on the African Human Rights System. *See also* LITIGATION.

INSTITUTE FOR INTERNATIONAL LAW AND HUMAN RIGHTS. Research, capacity-building and **advocacy** institution embedded in De Paul University College of Law (United States). Founded in 1990, the Institute designs and manages projects on postconflict justice, conducts scholarly research on **international criminal law**, **international humanitarian law** and human rights and **rule of law** issues.

INSTITUTE FOR INTERNATIONAL LAW AND JUSTICE. Academic body pertaining to the New York School of Law carrying out **research,**

scholarship, teaching and outreach work, in close connection with the policy activities of the **United Nations**, **non-governmental organizations**, law firms, and industry. The Institute's research and scholarship is organized through three affiliated thematic centers and programs: the Center for Human Rights and Global Justice, the Jean Monnet Center for International and Regional Economic Law and Justice, and the Program in the History and Theory of International Law. The Institute also runs cross-cutting research projects among these affiliates, including work on global **governance** and **accountability**, legal issues in United Nations security and development operations, financing of development projects, international arbitration, private military firms, intelligence, and **rule of law** issues especially relating to states at risk.

INSTITUTE FOR WAR AND PEACE REPORTING. Washington, D.C.–based international network founded in 1991 for media development supporting training and **capacity-building** programs for local journalism. The institute operates in two dozen conflict-prone or postconflict countries such as **Afghanistan**, **Chechnya**, **Iran**, Iraq, Pakistan, **Philippines**, Uzbekistan, Zimbabwe.

INSTITUTE OF DEVELOPMENT STUDIES. Highly respected British **think tank** founded in 1966 and located in University of Sussex. Hosting approximately 100 researchers, 70 knowledge services staff, 65 support staff and about 200 students at any one time, the Institute's **research** program focuses on **globalization**, **governance**, knowledge technology and society, participation, power and society and vulnerability and **poverty** reduction. Its broadly stated objective is to contribute to academic debates on human rights in a development context, engage with policymakers, **advocacy** organizations and donors on key issues, and influence the practice of implementing rights agendas in development programs.

INTELLECTUAL PROPERTY RIGHTS. Human rights and intellectual property rights have for a long time evolved independently. They intersected for the first time in the **Universal Declaration of Human Rights** in the sense that the Declaration recognized intellectual property rights as a human right. The **International Covenant on Economic, Social and Cultural Rights** elaborates on the elusive language of the Declaration by stating that "everyone has the right freely to participate in the cultural life of the community, to enjoy the arts and to share in scientific advancement and its benefits." The Covenant also stipulates that "everyone has the right to the protection of the moral and material interests resulting from any scientific, literary or artistic production of which he is the author." It also imposes three sets of obligations on states parties: to undertake the steps necessary for the conservation, development, and diffusion of science and culture; to respect the freedom indispensable for scientific research and creative activity; and to recognize the benefits to be derived from encouragement and development of international contacts and cooperation in the scientific and cultural fields.

How to achieve a proper balance between the rights of inventors and creators and the interests of the wider society has proved politically elusive. The former assert a human rights justification for the expansion of legal protections, the latter rely on human rights arguments as counterweights to the expansion of intellectual property in areas touching on **freedom of expression**, public **health**, **education**, **privacy**, agriculture, and the rights of **indigenous peoples**. The entry into force in 1995 of the **World Trade Organization's Agreement on Trade-Related Aspects of Intellectual Property Rights** (TRIPS Agreement) and the proliferation of increasingly strict intellectual property rules at the bilateral, regional and multilateral levels, especially patents and copyrights, have rekindled the debate over the impact of intellectual property rights over the realization of human rights and, in particular, the capacity of states (primarily states from the Global South) to meet their human rights obligations such as the obligation to ensure access to affordable medicines, adequate **food** and educational materials.

In one of its **General Comments**, the **United Nations Committee on Economic, Social and Cultural Rights** has taken the still politically divisive position that intellectual property rights are not human rights. At the same time, the Committee argued that the scope of protection of the right "to benefit from the protection of the moral and material interests resulting from any scientific, literary or artistic production of which he is the author" (Art. 15.1 of the Covenant) extended to indigenous communities and cultural minorities but excluded legal persons. *See also* CONSUMERS INTERNATIONAL; CONVENTION FOR THE SAFEGUARDING OF INTANGIBLE CULTURAL HERITAGE; FOOD SOVEREIGNTY.

INTER-AFRICAN COMMITTEE ON TRADITIONAL PRACTICES AFFECTING THE HEALTH OF WOMEN. Non-governmental organization created in 1984 which focuses its activities on the elimination of harmful practices affecting the health of children and women, notably **female genital mutilation**. Headquartered in Addis-Ababa, the Committee has branches in some 28 African countries, a liaison office in Geneva and affiliates in Europe, Canada, the United States and Japan. Its modus operandi relies on **education** and government authorities **lobbying** to achieve social values and legislative change.

INTER-AMERICAN CHILDREN INSTITUTE (IIN). Originally set up in 1927, the IIN became a specialized organization of the **Organization of American States** in 1948. Under the terms of its Charter, IIN is responsible for "promoting the study of issues relating to children and the family in the Americas, as well as for designing technical instruments that will contribute to solving the problems affecting them."

INTER-AMERICAN COMMISSION OF WOMEN. Originally established in 1928 at the Sixth International Conference of American States in Havana, **Cuba**, the Commission is now a specialized agency of the **Organization of American States**. Its objectives are to promote and improve the rights and status of women throughout the Americas. Since its inception, the Commission has pressed governments to address and improve women's rights. It played a key role in the development and negotiation of the Inter-American Convention on the Prevention, Punishment, and Eradication of Violence against Women. In force since 1995, the Convention is noteworthy for defining violence against women as a **violation of human rights** and for the emphasis it places on the duty of states to address the issue. *See also* INTER-AMERICAN CONVENTION ON THE PREVENTION, PUNISHMENT AND ERADICATION OF VIOLENCE AGAINST WOMEN.

INTER-AMERICAN COMMISSION ON HUMAN RIGHTS (IACmHR). Headquartered in Washington, D.C., the IACmHR is an autonomous organ of the **Organization of American States** (OAS) responsible together with the **Inter-American Court of Human Rights** for the promotion and protection of human rights in the Latin American region. The IACmHR was set up in 1959 and began operations two years later. Its seven members are elected by the General Assembly of the OAS in their personal capacity. Under the terms of its mandate derived from the OAS Charter, the **American Declaration of the Rights and Duties of Man** and the **American Convention on Human Rights**, the IACmHR carries out onsite visits to observe the general human rights situation in a country or to investigate specific situations and make recommendations to governments. Between 1961 and 2012, the IACmHR has undertaken more than 100 such onsite visits.

Since 1965, the IACmHR has been authorized to provide recourse to individuals who have suffered violations of their rights. It may examine **complaints** or petitions regarding specific cases of **violations of human rights**, and it has the power to request information from the governments concerned to investigate the facts and to refer the case to the Inter-American Court of Human Rights. Up until 1997, the IACmHR had received thousands of **petitions**, which have resulted in 12,000 cases which have been processed or are currently being processed. The IACmHR has also been given authority to deal with matters related to the obligations undertaken by state parties to all human rights conventions adopted in the Latin American regional framework with the exception of the Convention on Persons with Disabilities which created a separate supervisory committee. In the first 15 years or so of its existence, the IACmHR made in loco visits and country reports the main focus of its work, thus establishing and publicizing human rights issues and seeking or prompting change through negotiation. For instance, a 1980 report of the IACmHR brought to light the Argentine military government record on disappeared persons in the late 1970s. The IACmHR has since given greater priority to individual petitions, with some of them referred to the Inter-American Court of Human Rights for final and binding decision. *See also* ARBITRARY DETENTION; FORCED DISAPPEARANCES; INTER-AMERICAN DECLARATION ON FREEDOM OF EXPRESSION; INVESTIGATION; LITIGATION; RIGHTS INTERNATIONAL.

INTER-AMERICAN CONVENTION ON FORCED DISAPPEAR-ANCES OF PERSONS. Regional human rights instrument adopted in 1994 (in force in 1996) which defines **forced disappearance** as "the act of depriving a person or persons of his or their freedom, in whatever way, perpetrated by agents of the state or by persons or groups of persons acting with the authorization, support, or acquiescence of the state, followed by an absence of information or a refusal to acknowledge that deprivation of freedom or to give information on the whereabouts of that person, thereby impeding his or her recourse to the applicable legal **remedies** and procedural guarantees." The Convention enjoins state parties not to practice, permit, or tolerate the forced disappearance of persons, even in states of emergency or suspension of individual guarantees; to punish within their jurisdictions, those persons who commit or attempt to commit the crime of forced disappearance of persons and their accomplices and accessories; to cooperate with one another in helping to prevent, punish, and eliminate the forced disappearance of persons; and to take legislative, administrative, judicial, and any other measures necessary to comply with the commitments undertaken in this Convention. The Convention makes forced disappearances an extraditable offense.

INTER-AMERICAN CONVENTION ON THE ELIMINATION OF ALL FORMS OF DISCRIMINATION AGAINST PERSONS WITH DISABILITIES. This regional human rights instrument was adopted in 1999 and entered into force two years later. It is designed to prohibit discrimination against **disabled persons** and to promote their full integration within society through appropriate supportive legislation and other measures enabling disabled persons to have better access to buildings, methods of communication, recreation, offices, and homes. A committee composed of representatives of the states parties monitors the implementation of the Convention.

INTER-AMERICAN CONVENTION ON THE PREVENTION, PUNISHMENT AND ERADICATION OF VIOLENCE AGAINST WOMEN (1995). First regional human rights treaty focused exclusively on **gender-based violence** and explicitly prohibiting **domestic violence**. The Convention broadly defines violence against women "to include physical, sexual and psychological violence: a) that occurs within the family or domestic unit or within any other interpersonal relationship, whether or not the perpetrator shares or has shared the same residence with the woman, including, among others, rape, battery and sexual abuse." The convention also requires states parties to condemn, prevent and punish violence against women and calls on governments to undertake progressively specific positive measures to address the root causes of gender-based violence, such as mass education programs to counter gender stereotypes, as well as to create protective and social services for victims of violence.

Domestic violence is increasingly recognized as a critical public **health** problem by organizations like the Pan American Health Organization and the **Inter-American Commission of Women** of the **Organization of American States**, and some 30 countries in the region have enacted laws against domestic violence. But enforcement by police and the judicial system remains a major problem, and national surveys indicate that a large number of cases of violence against women remain unreported.

INTER-AMERICAN CONVENTION TO PREVENT AND PUNISH TORTURE (IACPPT, 1985). Regional human rights instrument developed through the **Organization of American States**. To date, 17 states have ratified it and three have signed but not yet ratified. The IACPPT expands on the provisions of the **American Convention on Human Rights** which bans **torture** in less detail by requiring states to take effective measures to prevent the use of torture within their borders and mandating them to extradite persons accused of torture. One interesting aspect of the IACPPT is that it defines torture more broadly than the **United Nations Convention against Torture**: "the use of methods upon a person intended to obliterate the personality of the victim or to diminish his physical or mental capacities, even if they do not cause physical pain or mental anguish."

INTER-AMERICAN COURT OF HUMAN RIGHTS. Autonomous judicial body created in 1979 as a result of the entry into force of the **American Convention on Human Rights.** Together with the **Inter-American Commission on Human Rights,** the Court's function is to ensure compliance with the obligations imposed by the Convention on its states parties. It is located in San Jose, Costa Rica. The judges are elected by the state parties by secret ballot and by a vote of the General Assembly of the **Organization of American States** (OAS). In accordance with the provisions of the Convention, the Court has adjudicatory and advisory jurisdiction. The Court may hear and rule on specific cases of human rights referred to it either by the Commission or a state party to the Convention which has accepted its contentious jurisdiction (to date, 21 states have done so).

In contrast to the European human rights regime, nationals of the states parties to the Convention do not have direct access to the Court. They must first lodge their complaints to the Commission which will rule on the **admissibility** of the case and may forward it to the Court only after the Commission has failed to resolve the issue with the concerned state in a noncontentious manner. In regard to the advisory function of the Court, any member state of the OAS may consult the Court on the interpretation of the Convention or of other treaties on the protection of human rights in the American states. This right of consultation extends to some of the organs of the OAS. At the request of any member state of the OAS, the Court may issue opinions on the compatibility of any of its domestic laws with the Convention's provisions. Between 1997 and 2010, the Court issued 169 judgments and granted 632 **interim measures.** *See also* CENTER FOR JUSTICE AND INTERNATIONAL LAW; FORCED DISAPPEARANCES; LIFE, RIGHT TO; LITIGATION; RIGHTS INTERNATIONAL; URUGUAY.

INTER-AMERICAN DECLARATION ON FREEDOM OF EX-PRESSION. Normative, aspirational statement adopted in 2000 by the **Inter-American Commission on Human Rights.** Portrayed by the Commission as a "fundamental document for the defense of freedom within the inter-American system," the Declaration lays down a number of key principles asserting in particular that access to information held by the state is a fundamental right of individuals and that states are obligated to guarantee it. Another principle states that "prior censorship, interference, or direct or indirect pressure on any expression, opinion, or information disseminated by any oral, written, artistic, visual, or electronic means of communication should be prohibited by law." Still another principle defines assassination, kidnapping, intimidation, and threats directed at journalists as actions that "place severe constraints on freedom of expression." *See also* FREEDOM OF EXPRESSION; SOFT LAW.

INTER-AMERICAN INDIAN INSTITUTE. Specialized body of the **Organization of American States** headquartered in Mexico City whose primary purpose is to promote **research** and training, contributing to the development of indigenous communities. *See also* CAPACITY BUILDING; INDIGENOUS PEOPLES.

INTER-AMERICAN INSTITUTE OF HUMAN RIGHTS (IIDH). Independent international academic institution, created in 1980 under an agreement between the **Inter-American Court of Human Rights** and the Republic of Costa Rica. Guided by the principles of representative **democracy**, the **rule of law**, ideological pluralism and respect for the fundamental human rights, the IIDH seeks to consolidate democracy in the Americas through **human rights education, research**, political mediation, programs for training, technical assistance in the field of human rights, and the dissemination of knowledge by means of specialized publications. It has evolved into an important world center for teaching and academic research on human rights, also serving as a facilitator of dialogue among **non-state actors** of the human rights movement and government authorities. *See also* CAPACITY BUILDING.

INTER-STATE COMPLAINT. Procedure available under most human rights **treaties** (albeit on an optional basis) under which any state party may bring a **complaint** against another for not fulfilling its obligations under the treaty. Originally considered to be a major component of an effective international human rights **monitoring** and **accountability** system, these procedures (deliberately "statist" in the sense that they rule out any involvement of individuals and **non-governmental organizations**) were designed to enhance the protection of human rights by pressuring governments violators of human rights to accept "friendly solutions" negotiated in closed meetings of state representatives. They have never been used in the **United Nations'** treaty bodies established under the **International Covenant on Civil and Political Rights**, the **United Nations Convention against Torture**, the **International Convention on the Elimination of Racial Discrimination**, the **United Nations Convention on the Elimination of All Forms of Discrimination against Women** and the United Nations Convention on Migrant Workers. The equivalent procedure under the **European Convention for the Protection of Human Rights and Fundamental Freedoms** has been very sparingly used, notably against Great Britain, Greece and Turkey in cases revolving around conditions of detention imposed by the governments in situations of **"public emergency"** and the use of **torture** by state officials. Likewise, the inter-state complaint procedure provided for by the constitution of the **International Labour Organization** has been virtually ignored.

INTERACTION COUNCIL. Established in 1983 as an independent international organization to mobilize the experience, energy and international contacts of statesmen having held the highest office in their own countries. The Interaction Council thus informally brings together on a regular basis more than 30 former heads of state or government—serving in their individual activities and developing recommendations on, and practical solutions in, three priority areas: peace and security, the revitalization of the world economy and the promotion of universal ethical standards.

INTERDEPENDENCE. One of the basic **human rights principles** stressing that the realization of political rights depends on economic, social and cultural rights (and vice versa). The idea of the interdependence of rights is implied in the **Universal Declaration of Human Rights** but floundered on the politics of the **Cold War**. It was nevertheless reaffirmed by the 1993 **World Conference on Human Rights** and made explicit in most of human rights instruments. For example, in its preamble, the **United Nations Convention on the Elimination of All Forms of Discrimination against Women** states that the eradication of **racial discrimination** and other forms of subordination is "essential to the full enjoyment of the rights of men and women." The UN committee that oversees implementation of the **International Convention on the Elimination of All Forms of Racial Discrimination** has adopted General Recommendation 25 on Gender Related Dimensions of Racial Discrimination, which calls upon states parties to include information on gender aspects of racial discrimination in their reports to the Committee on the Elimination of Racial Discrimination.

INTERFAITH CENTER ON CORPORATE RESPONSIBILITY (ICCR). International coalition of faith-based institutional investors including denominations, religious communities, pension funds, health care corporations, foundations, asset management companies, colleges, and dioceses seeking to change unjust or harmful corporate policies and obtain economic justice through a variety of instruments including sponsoring shareholder resolutions, meetings with management and screening their investments, conducting public hearings, publishing special reports and letter writing campaigns. ICCR grew out of opposition to the **Vietnam War** in the **United States**, the production of **nuclear weapons**, foreign military sales, **apartheid** in South Africa and discrimination and segregation. Today, ICCR members seek to promote environmental justice, access to capital, access to pharmaceuticals and health care, **accountability** of corporate governance structures and an end to global warming and sweatshop abuses. *See also* CORPORATE SOCIAL RESPONSIBILITY.

INTERIGHTS. *See* INTERNATIONAL CENTER FOR THE LEGAL PROTECTION OF HUMAN RIGHTS.

INTERIM MEASURES. Decision (also known as precautionary measure) whereby a **United Nations treaty body** or a human rights judicial body may ask a state party to take temporary measures in order to avoid irreparable harm that might be caused to a complainant before the merits of his or her case can be determined. Interim measures are similar to injunctive rulings under domestic law. The **European Court of Human Rights** has ordered interim measures in order to prevent imminent deportations or extraditions. So have the **International Court of Justice** and the **Inter-American Court of Human Rights**, not always with much effectiveness. *See also* PRECAUTION, PRINCIPLE OF.

INTERNAL DISPLACEMENT MONITORING CENTRE (IDMC). International body established in 1998 by the Norwegian Refugee Council to monitor conflict-induced internal displacement worldwide and contribute to improving national and international capacities to protect and assist persons displaced within their own country as a result of conflicts or violations of human rights. Based in Geneva, the IDMC runs an online database providing comprehensive information and analysis on internal displacement in some 50 countries. The IDMC also carries out training activities designed to enhance the capacity of local actors to respond to the needs of **internally displaced persons**. *See also* CAPACITY BUILDING; MONITORING OF HUMAN RIGHTS.

INTERNAL DISTURBANCES. Situations such as riots, isolated and sporadic acts of violence, in which the level of violence within a state has not reached an intensity qualifying it as an **armed conflict**. In such cases, humanitarian law is not applicable and governments may adopt exceptional measures allowing them to derogate from certain responsibilities and that constrain public liberties. Human rights considered **non-derogable rights**, however, remain enforceable and continue to protect individuals. *See also* GENEVA CONVENTIONS.

INTERNALIZATION. Process, otherwise known in **international law** parlance as **incorporation**, whereby human rights standards are embedded into domestic law. The practice first entails the procedure of treaty **ratification** through which a state in effect surrenders a degree of sovereignty and allows international scrutiny subject to possible **reservations**. Also of particular significance is the role of national courts in utilizing, relying on and enforcing international human rights standards in their rulings. For example, in a number of rulings, the U.S. Supreme Court reasoned that the **Geneva Convention** required that "unlawful combatants" should have the ability to challenge their detention. *See also HAMDI ET AL. v. RUMSFELD, SECRETARY OF DEFENSE, ET AL.*

INTERNALLY DISPLACED PERSONS (IDPs). "Persons or groups of persons who have been forced or obliged to flee or to leave their homes or places of habitual residence, in particular as a result of or in order to avoid the effects of **armed conflict**, situations of generalized violence, **violations of human rights** or natural or human-made disasters, and who have not crossed an internationally recognized State border." There are no accurate figures for IDPs because of constant changes in populations and under-reported developments, but the total number of IDPs is estimated to range from 20 to 25 million. Updated country data can be found at the website of the **Internal Displacement Monitoring Center**. Two-thirds of all IDPs are women and children. Countries with significant number of IDPs include **Angola**, **Burundi**, **Colombia**, Cyprus, the **Democratic Republic of the Congo**, Ethiopia, Iraq, Sudan, **Uganda** and the West Bank and Gaza Strip. Unlike **refugees** who are entitled to international protection and help under the 1951 **United Nations Convention Relating to the Status of Refugees** because they have crossed international boundaries, IDPs do not receive the same legal protection from the international community.

Under international law, national governments retain primary responsibility for their security and well-being and, notwithstanding the fact that they are often unable or unwilling to provide such protection, any attempt by external bodies to prescribe to national governments how they should treat their own citizens has been seen as a violation of the principle of sovereignty. IDPs thus remain exposed to violence and other human rights **abuses** during their displacement and, frequently, have no or only very limited access to **food**, **work**, **education** and **health** care. Large numbers of IDPs are caught in desperate situations amid fighting or in remote and inaccessible areas cut off from international assistance, while others have been forced to live away from their homes for many years, or even decades, because the conflicts that caused their displacement remained unresolved.

Their predicament has prompted calls for a reformulation of the principle of sovereignty as a "**responsibility to protect**" and a moral imperative to stop gross abuse of citizens by their governments through coercive means. An example of military intervention for humanitarian purposes would be the 1998 **Kosovo** war. In the absence of a specific global international legal instrument applying to them, the **United Nations Office of the High Commissioner for Human Rights** has issued non-binding **Guiding Principles on Internal Displacement** based on refugee instruments and acts as an ad hoc lead on IDPs matters. Since 2004, a **special rapporteur** of the **United Nations Human Rights Council** monitors the predicament of IDPs.

See also ABKHAZIA; AZERBAIJAN; CONVENTION FOR THE PROTECTION AND ASSISTANCE OF INTERNALLY DISPLACED PERSONS IN AFRICA; DENG, FRANCIS; INTERNATIONAL INSTITUTE OF HUMANITARIAN LAW; SOFT LAW; UNITED NATIONS INTERIM ADMINISTRATION MISSION IN KOSOVO; UNITED NATIONS MISSION IN THE CENTRAL AFRICAN REPUBLIC AND CHAD; UNITED NATIONS MISSION IN THE REPUBLIC OF SOUTH SUDAN; UNITED NATIONS OPERATION IN BURUNDI; UNITED NATIONS OPERATION IN MOZAMBIQUE; UNITED NATIONS STABILIZATION MISSION IN HAITI; UNITED NATIONS TRANSITIONAL AUTHORITY IN CAMBODIA; WOMEN'S REFUGEE COMMISSION.

INTERNATIONAL ACCOUNTABILITY PROJECT (IAP). Advocacy **non-governmental organization** campaigning to promote global norms and standards of accountability, environmental sustainability and participation at international financial institutions on behalf of local communities in developing countries threatened by development projects financed by such institutions as the World Bank and the Asian Development Bank which might uproot or impoverish them.

INTERNATIONAL ALERT (IA). London-based **non-governmental organization** set up in 1986 by a number of human rights advocates increasingly concerned about the growing incidence of ethnic conflicts and genocidal situations in the late 1980s. The group's underlying rationale is that the denial of human rights often leads to internal **armed conflicts** which, in turn, further undermine efforts to protect individual and collective rights and to promote sustainable development. IA has since evolved into a leading **peacebuilding** and **advocacy** organization with activities in the Great Lake region of Africa, West Africa, the Caucasus, the Andean region of South America, Sri Lanka, Nepal and the Philippines.

INTERNATIONAL ALLIANCE TO END GENOCIDE. Coalition of **non-governmental organizations** (NGO) headquartered in Washington,

D.C., concentrating its consciousness raising, coalition building and **advocacy** work on predicting, preventing, stopping, and punishing **genocide** and other forms of mass murder. The Alliance focuses on four goals: the provision of public information on the nature of genocide and creation of the political will to prevent and end it; the creation of an effective **early warning** system for the **United Nations Security Council**, the **North Atlantic Treaty Organization** and other regional alliances, the establishment of a United Nations' and regional rapid response force; and the effective punishment of individuals who committed genocide. The Alliance has its own NGO early warning system called Genocide Watch.

INTERNATIONAL ARMED CONFLICT. *See* ARMED CONFLICT.

INTERNATIONAL ASSOCIATION OF REFUGEE LAW JUDGES. **Non-governmental organization** established in 1997 "to foster recognition that protection from persecution on account of race, religion, nationality, membership in a particular social group, or political opinion is an individual right established under **international law**, and that the determination of **refugee** status and its cessation should be subject to the **rule of law**." Toward this end, the Association endeavors to promote a common understanding of refugee law and principles through the convening of conferences, the sharing of information, **research** and the production of training material. *See also* CAPACITY BUILDING.

INTERNATIONAL ASSOCIATION FOR RELIGIOUS FREEDOM (IARF). Interfaith **non-governmental organization** founded in 1900 and based in London to promote religious freedom worldwide. Over 90 faith groups representing Buddhism, Christianity, Hinduism, Islam, Shinto and Zoroastrianism are affiliated with the IARF. Guided by Article 18 of the **Universal Declaration of Human Rights** and the 1981 **United Nations' Declaration on the Elimination of All Forms of Intolerance and of Discrimination Based on Religion and Belief**, the activities of the group have three core objectives: to eliminate or prevent oppressive interference or discrimination by the state, government or society's institutions on the grounds of religion or belief; to promote mutual understanding, respect and the promotion of harmony, or at least "tolerance," between communities or individuals of different religions or beliefs; and to ensure that the practices of religious communities uphold the fundamental dignity and human rights of their members and others. *See also* FREEDOM OF RELIGION.

INTERNATIONAL ASSOCIATION OF DEMOCRATIC LAWYERS (IADL). Non-governmental organization with **consultative status** to the **United Nations Economic and Social Council** and represented at the **United Nations Educational, Scientific and Cultural Organization** and the **United Nations Children's Fund** established in 1946 with the broad mandate to achieve the aims set out in the **United Nations Charter.** The IADL brings together activist lawyers and judges interested in promoting the principle of **equality** among peoples, the rights of all peoples to **self-determination**, the elimination of **colonialism** and imperialism and the peaceful settlement of disputes. Through its campaigns and in arguments before UN bodies and international courts (the **European Court of Human Rights**, the **Inter-American Court of Human Rights**) challenging the doctrine of "**domestic jurisdiction**" (United Nations Charter, Art. 2.7), the Association has contributed to a greater acceptance of the right to self-determination and the protection of national human rights. In 2001, the IADL and the **International Centre for Trade Union Rights** entered into an agreement providing for the establishment of an **International Commission for Labor Rights** to investigate and provide assistance to victims of labor rights abuses and violations of national and international law. *See also* INVESTIGATION.

INTERNATIONAL ASSOCIATION OF LAWYERS AGAINST NUCLEAR ARMS (IALANA). Non-governmental organization focusing its work on the prevention of nuclear war, the elimination of **nuclear weapons**, the strengthening of international law and encouraging the peaceful resolution of international conflicts. In conjunction with the International Peace Bureau and the International Physicians for the Prevention of Nuclear War, IALANA led a worldwide campaign (the so-called World Court Project) which resulted in the 1996 ruling of the **International Court of Justice** asserting that the threat or use of nuclear weapons was generally illegal, and that states had an obligation to conclude negotiations on their elimination. *See also* INTERNATIONAL LAW; WEAPONS OF MASS DESTRUCTION.

INTERNATIONAL ASSOCIATION OF WOMEN JUDGES. Non-governmental organization bringing together some 4,000 women judges from some 100 countries for the purpose of advancing the rights of women through the judicial system and to protect and empower women throughout the world. In operation since 1991, the Association seeks to promote women's access to the courts and to increase the number of women judges at all levels. It also conducts legal research on gender equality and human rights and acts as a mechanism for the exchange of information on issues of concern to women.

INTERNATIONAL BANK FOR RECONSTRUCTION AND DEVELOPMENT (IBRD). Commonly known as the World Bank, the IBRD, together with its sister institution, the **International Monetary Fund** (IMF), was created at the end of **World War II**. Its purpose was to promote the stability of the international economy through reconstruction and development. The World Bank should more accurately be described as the World Bank Group because in addition to the IBRD itself, it also includes the International Development Association (IDA), which gives no-interest loans to the world's poorest developing countries, the International Finance Corporation, which finances private sector investments, the Multilateral Investment Guarantee Agency, which provides guarantees to foreign investors against commercial risks, and the International Center for the Settlement of Investment Disputes, a dispute settlement mechanism.

The Bank is headquartered in Washington, D.C. It has 184 member states, operates in some 100 countries and has a staff of 10,000, one-third of them working in the field. It views itself as a "banker," a "loan facilitator," a "donor" and a development "adviser." Although technically a "specialized agency" of the **United Nations**, it does not consider itself bound by UN policies and decisions. In fact, the Bank's governance differs fundamentally from the United Nations in the sense that it is governed by the principle of "one dollar, one vote" rather than the "one country-one vote" rule followed by the United Nations. The World Bank lends between $20 and $28 billion annually to **developing countries**. Most recent Bank lending to developing countries by IBRD/IDA totaled just under $47 billion. The Bank provides loans and grants for productive sectors (rural development, fisheries and mining); for infrastructure projects (roads, dams, water and sanitation works, and power plants) and for human development including **education, health,** nutrition and population. About 40 percent of its lending is committed to structural adjustment programs and sector reform in its borrowing countries.

Human rights are not part of the mandate of the Bank (and for that matter the IMF) and the Bank has taken the position that its decisions were driven by developmental and economic concerns as called for in its founding documents, which also proscribe any interference into the internal affairs of its members. Yet its activities have affected the lives and livelihood of millions in developing countries and have had repercussions on the creation of conditions for the attainment of human rights. Human rights groups, **civil society** organizations, and UN critics have drawn attention to World Bank projects which have disrupted **indigenous peoples'** communities, forcibly displaced millions of poor people and causing widespread environmental damage. While still resisting the idea that its policies and projects should be based on **international human rights law**, the Bank has in effect demonstrated increased concern for human rights. The Bank has made **poverty** reduction, together with the tools to achieve it, its overriding priority. It has also put particular emphasis on the notion of good **governance** and embraced the **Millennium Development Goals** and, in so doing, it has, at least rhetorically, increasingly integrated human rights concerns—the right to development, the right to be free from poverty, the right to education and health, women's rights, and environmental rights—into the rationale and justification of its policies and projects.

In this regard, and in response to previous serious breaches of human rights, the Bank has drawn up Operational Directives that recognize human rights protection such as those on involuntary resettlement (1990), poverty reduction (1991), and indigenous peoples (1994). Established by the Bank in August 1993, a three-person Inspection Panel has been in operation since August 1994 reviewing requests for inspection by an affected party in the territory of the borrowing state. Heralded as a step toward greater **accountability** for the human rights consequences of the Bank's activities, the purpose of these requests is to demonstrate that locally impacted people's "rights or interests have been or are likely to be affected by an action or omission of the Bank as a result of a failure of the Bank to follow its operational policies and procedures." To date, however, only some 60 such requests have been reviewed by the Panel, most of them dealing with the environmental consequences of large-scale infrastructural projects. *See also* FRIENDS OF THE EARTH INTERNATIONAL; INTERNATIONAL ACCOUNTABILITY PROJECT; STRUCTURAL ADJUSTMENT PROGRAMS.

INTERNATIONAL BAR ASSOCIATION (IBA). The world's leading organization of international legal practitioners, bar associations and law societies acting as a clearinghouse for the exchange of information among its constituent members through conferences and publications. Established in 1947 and based in London, the IBA supports the independence of the **judiciary** and the right of lawyers to practice their profession without interference. Through its **Human Rights Institute**, it also supports the human rights of lawyers worldwide.

INTERNATIONAL BILL OF HUMAN RIGHTS. Statement in a constitution of human or civil rights that lists protections against interferences by governments. The expression also refers to the body of international human rights law encapsulated by the **Universal Declaration of Human Rights**, the **International Covenant on Civil and Political Rights** and the **International Covenant on Economic Social and Cultural Rights**. *See also* BILL OF RIGHTS, UNITED STATES.

INTERNATIONAL BUREAU FOR CHILDREN'S RIGHTS. Canadian international **non-governmental organization** founded in 1994 to contribute to the realization of children's rights through **advocacy**, coalition building, the sharing of good practices and the provision of legal expertise. The Bureau focuses its activities on **children trafficking**, child sex tourism and war-affected children. It also produces country profiles on the status of implementation of the **United Nations Convention on the Rights of the Child** by its state parties. *See also* MONITORING OF HUMAN RIGHTS.

INTERNATIONAL CAMPAIGN TO BAN LANDMINES (ICBL). Coalition of some 1,400 women, children, veterans, religious groups, environmental, human rights, arms control, peace and development **non-governmental organizations** established in 1992 to press for the elimination of anti-personnel mines. The ICBL was awarded the **Nobel Peace Prize** in 1997 for the key role that it played at the national, regional and international levels in the elaboration and entry in force of the Ottawa Treaty banning the production and use of anti-personnel mines. Through its network of researchers, the ICBL **monitors** the implementation of the treaty and **lobbies** governments for its universal ratification. In addition to its **advocacy** activities, the ICBL also carries out humanitarian mine action programs in support of affected communities. *See also* CAMPAIGNS.

INTERNATIONAL CAMPAIGN TO END GENOCIDE. Loose international coalition of **non-governmental organizations** and individuals dedicated to creating the international institutions and the political will to end **genocide**. Headquartered near Washington, D.C., the Campaign provides public information on the nature of genocide and has created an **early warning** system to alert the **United Nations Security Council**, the **North Atlantic Treaty Organization** and other regional alliances to potential ethnic conflicts and genocide.

INTERNATIONAL CENTER FOR TRANSITIONAL JUSTICE. Located in New York City, this **non-governmental organization** provides assistance to societies emerging from civil strife by addressing their legacies of massive human rights violations and building inclusive and democratic state institutions. The Center advises state institutions and policymakers at the local, national and international levels, works with victims' groups and civil society organizations with a justice agenda and carries out and disseminates research on **transitional justice**. Instances of recent work undertaken by the Center include the provision of technical assistance to Argentine prosecutors in helping to organize and prioritize public information about pending prosecutions for abuses during the "**dirty war**," training local activists in documenting human rights abuses in Burma, helping victims from rural communities in **Peru** to engage with government on their demands for reparations and researching lessons learned. *See also* PEACEBUILDING.

INTERNATIONAL CENTRE FOR CRIMINAL LAW REFORM AND CRIMINAL JUSTICE POLICY. Canadian independent non-profit institute founded in 1991 to promote the **rule of law**, human rights, **democracy** and good **governance** through technical cooperation projects, **research**, training and **capacity building**, and **advisory services** in the fields of criminal law, criminal justice and crime prevention. The Centre has been working, among others, on development of the reporting procedures and tools on implementation of the **United Nations Convention against Transnational Organized Crime**. *See also* THINK TANKS.

INTERNATIONAL CENTRE FOR HUMAN RIGHTS AND DEMOCRATIC DEVELOPMENT. Montreal-based **non-governmental organization** set up in 1985 by an act of the Canadian Parliament. Its purpose is to "promote, advocate and defend the democratic and human rights set out in the **International Bill of Human Rights**," notably the right to an adequate standard of living; the rights of persons to not be subjected to **torture** or to cruel, inhuman or degrading treatment or punishment, the rights of freedom of opinion and **freedom of expression** and the right to vote and be elected at periodic, genuine elections in pluralistic political systems." More specifically, the Centre supports programs to strengthen laws and democratic institutions, principally in **developing countries**. One of its principal concerns is to "end **human rights violations** committed against Palestinians in the West Bank, Gaza Strip and East Jerusalem." *See also* DEMOCRACY.

INTERNATIONAL CENTRE FOR THE LEGAL PROTECTION OF HUMAN RIGHTS (INTERIGHTS). Also known as Rights and Democracy, this **non-governmental organization** based in London is devoted to the protection of human rights and freedom primarily through strategic **litigation** (i.e., by bringing or supporting cases in critical areas where there is either a potential for human rights standards to be developed or where existing standards are under threat, especially in regard to economic and social rights, equality and security and the rule of law). INTERIGHTS represents individual applicants before international and regional human rights bodies or acts as an adviser. In some cases, INTERIGHTS intervenes as a third party. The Centre complements its litigation work through legal capacity building and standards-setting activities and by publishing and disseminating legal information. The Centre has consultative status with the **United Nations Economic and Social Council**, the **Council of Europe** and the **African Commission on Human and People's Rights**. It is also accredited with the Commonwealth secretariat and is authorized to present collective **complaints** under the **European Social Charter**.

INTERNATIONAL CENTRE FOR TRADE UNION RIGHTS (ICTUR). Self-described as "an organizing and campaigning body with the fundamental purpose of defending and improving the rights of trade unions and trade unionists throughout the world." Based in London, ICTUR basically offers legal research and consultancy services and is commissioned to produce special reports of particular interest to trade unions. One of its main publications is the quarterly journal *International Union Rights*. ICTUR has accredited status with the **United Nations** and the **International Labour Organization**. *See also* WORK, RIGHT TO.

INTERNATIONAL CIVIL SOCIETY ACTION NETWORK (ICAN). **Civil society** organization founded in 2006 to strengthen women's participation and influence in conflict prevention, social justice, coexistence, and **peacebuilding** efforts, in situations of closed political space and conflict-affected states. ICAN collects and disseminates information on the situation of women in conflict-affected countries and provides training to locally based organizations in transitional and conflict-affected countries on such thematic issues as security sector reform, constitutional issues, **transitional justice**), and technical skills (e.g., organizational management, fundraising, consensus building, conflict resolution). ICAN also advocates in support of women's inclusion in the peacebuilding process. One of its main projects is to assess whether and how various actors (**United Nations**, donors, national governments, **non-governmental organizations**) have endeavored to include women and to ensure gender sensitivity in the language of peace accords. *See also* ADVOCACY; CAPACITY BUILDING; GLOBAL NETWORK OF WOMEN PEACE BUILDERS.

INTERNATIONAL COALITION FOR THE RESPONSIBILITY TO PROTECT (ICR2P). Recently created umbrella group bringing together **non-governmental organizations** from all regions of the world to strengthen the normative consensus for the concept of a "Responsibility to Protect" and press for strengthened national capacities to prevent and halt genocide, war crimes, ethnic cleansing and crimes against humanity. The ICR2P includes such groups as Act for Peace (Sydney, Australia), Centre for Media Studies and Peace Building (Monrovia, Liberia), Citizens for Global Solutions

(Washington, D.C.), Coordinadora Regional de Investigaciones Económicas y Sociales (Buenos Aires, Argentina), East Africa Law Society (Arusha, Tanzania), Genocide Alert (Cologne, Germany), Global Action to Prevent War, **Human Rights Watch**, Initiatives for International Dialogue (Davao City, Philippines), International Refugee Rights Initiative (New York and Uganda), Kofi Annan International Peacekeeping Training Centre (Accra, Ghana), **Oxfam International**, International Réseau de Développement et de Communications de la Femme Africaine (Bamako, Mali), West Africa Civil Society Forum (Abuja, Nigeria), West Africa Civil Society Institute (Accra, Ghana), Women's Refugee Commission (New York), World Federalist Movement-Institute for Global Policy (New York and The Hague) and the **World Federation of United Nations Associations** (New York and Geneva).

INTERNATIONAL CODE OF CONDUCT FOR PRIVATE SECURITY SERVICE PROVIDERS. Voluntary guidelines endorsed in 2010 by 58 **private military companies** committing to adhere to international human rights principles and support the **rule of law** while also protecting the interests of their clients. The Code provides guidance on how to ensure that fundamental human rights are protected in conflict situations, as well as general guidance on transparency and **accountability**. *See also* SOFT LAW.

INTERNATIONAL COMMISSION FOR LABOR RIGHTS. Founded in 2002, this New York–based non-profit organization coordinates the pro bono work of a global network of lawyers committed to advancing workers' rights through legal **research**, **advocacy** and cross-border collaboration. The network brings together more than 300 lawyers from around the world who respond to requests for legal advice, expert opinions, information on political realities country by country, and concrete experiences with different legal and political fora. The Commission also convenes delegations of lawyers, at the request of individual unions and global federations, to investigate allegations of labor rights violations. Their reports form the basis of domestic **litigation** and international complaints. *See also* INTERNATIONAL ASSOCIATION OF DEMOCRATIC LAWYERS; WORK, RIGHT TO.

INTERNATIONAL COMMISSION OF JURISTS. One of the oldest **non-governmental organizations** created in 1952 to work toward the establishment and implementation of international human rights standards. The Commission itself consists of 60 eminent judges and lawyers. Mary Robinson was its president from 2009 to 2010. ICJ operates through **inquiry** commissions, trial observations, **fact-finding** missions, public denunciations and quiet diplomacy. It was instrumental in exposing human rights abuses in

Chile following the 1973 military coup and in exposing atrocities committed in **Uganda** under the rule of **Idi Amin**. It also played an important role in the process leading to the adoption of the **African Charter on Human and People's Rights** and the **European Convention for the Prevention of Torture** and the creation of the **International Criminal Court**. Two of its most recent studies critically examined the impact of **counterterrorism** laws on human rights at the United Nations in New York and patterns of corporate complicity in gross **violations of human rights**.

See also AL HAQ; CORPORATE SOCIAL RESPONSIBILITY; EUROPEAN COMMITTEE ON SOCIAL RIGHTS; LIMBURG PRINCIPLES ON THE IMPLEMENTATION OF THE INTERNATIONAL COVENANT ON ECONOMIC, SOCIAL AND CULTURAL RIGHTS; PALESTINIAN CENTRE FOR HUMAN RIGHTS; ROBINSON, MARY; STANDARDS' SETTING; YOGYAKARTA PRINCIPLES ON THE APPLICATION OF INTERNATIONAL HUMAN RIGHTS LAW IN RELATION TO SEXUAL ORIENTATION AND GENDER IDENTITY.

INTERNATIONAL COMMISSION ON INTERVENTION AND STATE SOVEREIGNTY. Blue ribbon commission founded by **Gareth Evans** and **Mohamed Sahnoun** with the financial and political support of the government of Canada to explore whether a moral responsibility to intervene overrode respect for **state sovereignty** in situations of man-made or natural humanitarian emergencies. The report of the Commission, "The **Responsibility to Protect**," issued in December 2001, in essence argued that sovereign states have a responsibility to protect their own citizens. If they are unwilling or unable to do so, the broader community of states would have a right of **humanitarian intervention** to put an end to gross and systematic **violations of human rights**.

INTERNATIONAL COMMITTEE OF THE RED CROSS (ICRC). Private humanitarian organization founded in 1863 by **Jean Henri Dunant** whose mission is now explicitly defined by the **Geneva Conventions** and recognized and accepted by the states party to the Conventions. Its mission is to provide protection and assistance to victims of international and non-international conflicts or internal disturbances. As the guardian of the Conventions, the ICRC promotes the understanding and dissemination of international humanitarian law. The Conventions also empower the ICRC to visit places of internment, to receive complaints based on alleged breaches of **international humanitarian law** in **armed conflicts** and to search for missing persons. It may also act as a "Protecting Power" and, in that role, the tasks of the ICRC are to **monitor** and safeguard the interests of the parties to a conflict. The ICRC is located in Geneva, Switzerland, and has observer status at the **United Nations**. It was awarded the **Nobel Peace Prize** in 1917, 1944 and 1963.

See also ABU GHRAIB PRISON; ARAB ISRAELI CONFLICT; GUANTANAMO BAY DETENTION CAMP; INTERNATIONAL FEDERATION OF RED CROSS AND RED CRESCENT SOCIETIES; INTERNATIONAL HUMANITARIAN LAW; INTERNATIONAL HUMANITARIAN LAW INITIATIVE RESEARCH; INTERNATIONAL RED CROSS AND RED CRESCENT MOVEMENT; NATIONAL RED CROSS AND RED CRESCENT SOCIETIES.

INTERNATIONAL CONFEDERATION OF FREE TRADE UNIONS (ICFTU). International trade unions organization set up in 1949 at the prodding of non-communist national trade union federations which alleged communist domination of the **World Federation of Trade Unions**. It was dissolved and merged into the **World Confederation of Labor** in 2006 to form the **International Trade Union Confederation**. The ICFTU produced an annual report documenting violations by governments, industries and military and police forces against trade unions.

INTERNATIONAL CONFERENCE ON AGRARIAN REFORM AND RURAL DEVELOPMENT. Organized jointly by the **Food and Agricultural Organization** and the government of Brazil, this global conference was held in Porto Alegre, Brazil, 7–10 March 2006 and resulted in the adoption of a program of action which sought to promote a better understanding of desirable and appropriate policies and practices for securing and improving access to the land by the poor and promoting **agrarian reform** to alleviate **poverty** and **hunger**. *See also* FOOD, RIGHT TO.

INTERNATIONAL CONFERENCE ON POPULATION AND DEVELOPMENT. Global conference sponsored by the **United Nations** held in Cairo, Egypt, 5–13 September 1994 which dwelled on a wide range of issues and their linkage with development including immigration, infant mortality, birth and family planning and the education of women. The Programme of Action adopted by the conference, which was attended by some 20,000 delegates from governments, United Nations agencies and **non-governmental organizations**, endorsed a number of quantitative objectives related to universal **education** and infant, child and maternity mortality to be achieved by 2015 (these targets are among the **Millennium Development Goals**). After considerable debate and in spite of the opposition of the Holy See and several Islamic and Catholic countries, the Cairo Plan of Action asserts the right of women to have access to reproductive and sexual health services including family planning and counseling, prenatal care, safe delivery, the prevention of abortion and sexually transmitted diseases. The text also calls for an end to **female genital mutilation**. See also ABORTION; HEALTH, RIGHT TO; REPRODUCTIVE RIGHTS.

INTERNATIONAL CONVENTION AGAINST APARTHEID IN SPORTS. Under the terms of this convention adopted by the **United Nations General Assembly** in 1985 and in force since 1988, states parties strongly condemn **apartheid** and undertake to pursue immediately its elimination in all its forms from sports. They also commit themselves to not permit their sports bodies, teams and individual sportsmen to have contact with a country practicing apartheid. See also DISCRIMINATION.

INTERNATIONAL CONVENTION FOR THE PROTECTION OF ALL PERSONS FROM ENFORCED DISAPPEARANCE. Adopted by the **United Nations General Assembly** (UN-GA) in 2006 after five years of negotiations, this human rights treaty will take effect when it is ratified at least by 20 countries. Its provisions significantly expand upon those of the non-binding **Declaration on the Protection of All Persons from Enforced Disappearance** proclaimed in 1992 by the UN-GA. The oversight mechanisms that it sets up should also supersede the functions of the United Nations Working Group on Enforced or Involuntary Disappearances operating since 1980 under the authority of the **United Nations Commission on Human Rights**. The Convention establishes an absolute right not to be subjected to **forced disappearance** and enjoins states to prohibit and criminalize the practice in their national legislation.

Defining disappearances as the abduction or deprivation of liberty of a person by state authorities, followed by the denial of those authorities to disclose their fate or whereabouts, the Convention describes these acts as crimes and, if widespread or systematic, **crimes against humanity** subject to international criminal prosecution. It also includes provisions related to the criminal responsibility of subordinates and superiors, to national and international preventive measures, extradition and international cooperation. Some of the states' legal obligations in regard to prevention include the prohibition of secret detention, the deprivation of liberty, except in officially recognized and supervised places of detention equipped with a detailed register of the detainees and **non-derogable rights** to **habeas corpus** and to obtain information on detainees. Under the terms of the Convention, victims and their families have a right to the truth and to form organizations and associations to fight against disappearances. Like other UN human rights treaties, the Convention sets up a Committee on Enforced Disappearances which will monitor state parties compliance, consider individual and inter-state complaints and have the power to carry out humanitarian functions now undertaken by the United Nations Working Group on Enforced Disappearances. When constituted, the Committee will have the authority to carry out field **inquiries** and the ability to bring to the attention of the UN-GA situations of widespread and systematic practice of enforced disappearances. *See also* COMMAND RESPONSIBILITY; INTERNATIONAL FEDERATION FOR HUMAN RIGHTS.

INTERNATIONAL CONVENTION ON THE ELIMINATION OF ALL FORMS OF RACIAL DISCRIMINATION (1965). Building on a Declaration adopted in 1963 by the **United Nations General Assembly** at the prodding of the growing majority of newly independent Third World countries in the organization, this convention asserts that government policies based on racial superiority or hatred violate fundamental human rights and endanger friendly relations among peoples, cooperation among nations, and international peace and security.

Under the Convention, state parties are pledged to engage in no act or practice of **racial discrimination** against individuals, groups of persons or institutions; to amend or repeal laws and regulations which create or perpetuate racial discrimination; to prohibit racial discrimination by persons, groups and organizations; and to encourage integrationist or multiracial organizations and movements and other means of eliminating barriers between races, as well as to discourage anything which tends to strengthen racial division. The Convention requires states parties to eradicate racial discrimination and the crime of **apartheid** and to criminalize the incitement of racial hatred. The **United States** attached a **reservation** to its 1994 ratification stating that the treaty's restrictions on freedom of speech and freedom of assembly were inconsistent with the First Amendment to the Constitution of the United States. The Convention provides for a committee of experts to monitor the implementation of the treaty by its state parties. As of 2011, the Convention had 175 parties and 86 signatories. *See also* AFFIRMATIVE ACTION; UNITED NATIONS COMMITTEE ON THE ELIMINATION OF ALL FORMS OF RACIAL DISCRIMINATION.

INTERNATIONAL CONVENTION ON THE PROTECTION OF THE RIGHTS OF ALL MIGRANT WORKERS AND THEIR FAMILIES (2003). To date, the most comprehensive treaty on the rights of all **migrant workers** and their families, emphasizing the fundamental notion that all migrants—legal or undocumented—should have access to a minimum degree of protection. The Convention acknowledges the role of migrant workers in the world economy (it is currently estimated that there are over 175 million migrants in the world and the flows of migrant workers earnings exceed the level of Official Development Assistance) and defines their rights and protection at all stages of the migratory process from preparation for migration and departure to transit and the entire period of stay and remunerated employment in the receiving countries to return and resettlement in their countries of origin. In this regard, the Convention covers previously neglected categories of migrant workers including frontier workers, seasonal workers, seafarers, workers on offshore installations, and self-employed workers.

The rights enshrined in the convention include a right to safety and security, **equality before the law** and **due process**, non-**discrimination**, cultural identity, just working conditions, **education**, **health** care, **adequate housing** and **family** reunion. The Convention spells out the obligations and responsibilities of states which host migrant workers and, like other **United Nations treaty bodies**, sets up a monitoring mechanism based on periodic states parties' reports to a committee of experts. This treaty body may also receive **communications (complaints)** from one state party against another and complaints from individuals. Adopted by the **United Nations General Assembly** on 18 December 1990, the Convention did not become effective until 2003, and although it synthesizes over 30 years of often acrimonious discussions, not a single migrant worker–receiving state has yet ratified it. Since 1999, a **special rapporteur** set up by the **United Nations Commission on Human Rights** has examined ways and means to overcome the obstacles existing to the full and effective protection of the human rights of migrant workers. *See also* DECEMBER 18; INTERNATIONAL LABOUR ORGANIZATION; INTERNATIONAL ORGANIZATION FOR MIGRATION; MINORITIES; UNITED NATIONS EDUCATIONAL, SCIENTIFIC AND CULTURAL ORGANIZATION.

INTERNATIONAL CONVENTION ON THE SUPPRESSION AND PUNISHMENT OF THE CRIME OF APARTHEID. Adopted and opened for signature in 1973 by the **United Nations General Assembly**, it entered into force in 1976. The convention defines **apartheid** as "inhuman acts committed for the purpose of establishing and maintaining domination by one racial group of persons over any other racial group of persons and systematically oppressing them." Such acts include denial of the right to life and liberty, the imposition of living conditions designed to destroy the group, legislative measures to prevent the group's participation in national life, the division of the population along racial lines, and the exploitation of the group's labor force. Their commission, under the terms of the Convention which also defines apartheid as a **crime against humanity**, could entail individual responsibility and **accountability**. Over 100 countries—none of them Western countries—have acceded or ratified the Convention. *See also* INTERNATIONAL CRIMINAL COURT; MINORITIES.

INTERNATIONAL COUNCIL OF WOMEN (ICW). Worldwide **non-governmental organization** created in 1888 in the United States by Susan Anthony to promote equal rights for men and women and eliminate discrimination based on birth, race, sex, language or religion. Active in some 70 countries, the ICW also supports efforts to achieve peace through negotiation, arbitration and conciliation and to encourage the integration of women in development and their participation in public policy. The ICW worked closely with the **League of Nations**. It now has consultative status with numerous bodies of the **United Nations**.

INTERNATIONAL COUNCIL ON HUMAN RIGHTS POLICY. Set up in 1994 and bringing under its umbrella leading human rights activists and eminent personalities from academia, social movements, inter-governmental organizations and other communities of practice, this independent **non-governmental organization** closed down in 2011 as a result of continuing financial difficulties. It leaves behind a rich body of original policy-oriented cross-cutting **research** which was carried out by global research teams and disseminated through outreach and policy **advocacy** initiatives. **Climate change**, **corruption**, crime, foreign aid, **national human rights institutions**, migration, military intervention, racism, the role of the media, **sexual orientation**, and **terrorism** are some of the themes and projects which were on the Council research agenda. This material has been archived at the library of the Graduate Institute of International and Development Studies in Geneva, Switzerland.

INTERNATIONAL COURT OF JUSTICE. Successor body of the **League of Nations**' Permanent Court of International Justice and one of the **United Nations** principal organs tasked with the function of settling legal disputes submitted to it by states and to give advisory opinions on legal questions at the request of the **United Nations General Assembly** or the **United Nations Security Council** or by another UN organ or specialized agency authorized by the United Nations General Assembly. In recent years, the Court has devoted increasing attention to human rights issues but, historically speaking, because of its mandate and composition, human rights matters have not been a significant part of its docket. Furthermore, in the human rights cases that it has dealt with—**self-determination**, **reservations** to human rights treaties, the application of human rights instruments to the Israeli occupied territories, and allegations of **genocide** by one state against another—the Court has primarily been guided less by human rights norms and standards than **international law** and custom. *See also* ARAB ISRAELI CONFLICT; HABRE, HISSENE; IMMUNITY; INTERNATIONAL ASSOCIATION OF LAWYERS AGAINST NUCLEAR ARMS; KOSOVO; NATIONALITY, RIGHT TO; NUCLEAR WEAPONS; OBLIGATION *"ERGA OMNES"*; SREBRENICA.

INTERNATIONAL COVENANT ON CIVIL AND POLITICAL RIGHTS (ICCPR). Human rights treaty derived from the **Universal Declaration of Human Rights** which entered into force in 1976. Together with the **International Covenant on Economic, Social and Cultural Rights** which it complements, the ICCPR constitutes what is known in human rights parlance as the **International Bill of Human Rights**. The Covenant obligates states' parties to protect and preserve basic human rights related to **self-determination**; a person's physical integrity (against things such as execution, **torture**, and arbitrary arrest); procedural fairness in law (**rule of law**, rights upon arrest, trial, basic conditions that must be met when imprisoned, rights to a lawyer, impartial process in trial); **equality** between men and women; individual freedom of belief, speech, association, freedom of the press, right to hold assembly and political participation (organize a political party and vote). The Covenant also requires governments to take administrative, judicial and legislative measures in order to protect the rights enshrined in the treaty, and its implementation by states parties is monitored by a **United Nations Human Rights Committee** (UN-HRCttee), an expert **United Nations treaty body** which considers periodic reports submitted by member states on their compliance with the treaty. Two Optional Protocols in force since 1976 and 1991, respectively, complement the Covenant. The first protocol sets up a mechanism enabling individuals in member states to submit **complaints** (also known as **communications**) which are reviewed by the UN-HRCttee. The second protocol abolishes the use of **capital punishment** but allows countries to make a **reservation** allowing for its use for the most serious crimes of a military nature, committed during wartime. A large majority of states of the world are parties to the covenant (161 as of this writing) and most have introduced national legislation in conformity with its provisions. Notable countries which have not ratified the ICCPR include Malaysia, **Myanmar**, Pakistan, Qatar, **Saudi Arabia**, Singapore, and United Arab Emirates. A lesser number have ratified the first Optional Protocol and only 35 had joined the Second Optional Protocol. More disquieting is the large number of reservations entered by major states such as the **United**

States, which have rendered ineffective the Covenant rights that would require changes in national law. *See also* HUMAN EXPERIMENTATION; INCORPORATION; JUDICIARY, INDEPENDENCE OF; LIFE, RIGHT TO; STATE REPORTING; UNITED NATIONS GENERAL ASSEMBLY.

INTERNATIONAL COVENANT ON ECONOMIC, SOCIAL AND CULTURAL RIGHTS (ICESCR). Together with its sister covenant, the **International Covenant on Civil and Political Rights** (ICCPR), it now forms part of the **International Bill of Human Rights**. Originally, it was envisaged that the ICCPR and the ICESCR would constitute a single convention implementing the **Universal Declaration of Human Rights**. Continuing differences on the relative importance attached by East and West to negative civil and political rights versus positive economic, social and cultural rights instead led to two distinct treaties. The ICESCR proclaims the right of all peoples to **self-determination**, including the right to freely pursue their economic, social and cultural development and to freely dispose of their natural wealth and resources. Acknowledging that the enjoyment of some of the rights might be difficult in practice to achieve in a short period of time, the Covenant establishes the principle of the "progressive realization . . . without **discrimination** of any kind as to race, color, sex, language, religion, political or other opinion, national or social origin, property, birth or other status" of the following rights: the right to **work** (Art. 6), the right to fair conditions of employment (Art. 7), the right to join and form trade unions (Art. 8), the right to **social security** (Art. 9), the right to protection of the **family** (Art. 10), the right to an **adequate standard of living**, including the right to **food**, clothing, and housing (Art. 11), the right to **health** (Art. 12), the right to **education** (Art. 13) and the right to **culture** (Art. 15).

A body of independent experts, the **United Nations Committee on Economic, Social and Cultural Rights** (UN-CtteeESCR), established by the **United Nations Economic and Social Council** in 1985, monitors the implementation of the Covenant by its states parties. All states parties are required to submit regular reports to the Committee outlining the legislative, judicial, policy and other measures they have taken to implement the rights affirmed in the Covenant. The Committee examines each report and addresses its concerns and recommendations to the state party in the form of "concluding observations." An Optional Protocol adopted by the **United Nations General Assembly** in late 2008 allows the Committee to consider **complaints** from individuals. Several recurring problems have shaped the functioning of the Committee. The broad and vague language of the Covenant has prompted the Committee to issue **General Comments** which have provided greater and increasingly authoritative interpretive clarity as to the intent, meaning and content of the rights it purports to protect, and elucidated the understanding of the rights and obligations within the Covenant. So far, the Committee has produced some 20 comments on a wide range of rights and on such important issues as the reporting of states parties, the nature of states parties obligations, the role of **national human rights institutions**, gender **equality**, the domestic application of the Covenant and the impact of UN **sanctions** on the welfare of vulnerable groups. Considerable delays have marred the operation of the states parties' reporting system, at times forcing the Committee to consider national situations without official documentation. The UN-CtteeESCR also took in the early 1990s the unprecedented step of officially inviting "all concerned bodies and individuals to submit relevant and appropriate documentation to it," in effect broadening the scope of the reporting system to non-state parties and, in particular, legitimizing the participation of **non-governmental organizations**.

INTERNATIONAL CRIME CONGRESSES. Continuing a practice which started in 1872 and expanded under the **League of Nations**, the **United Nations** decided in 1950 to convene international congresses every five years on crime control matters. The first United Nations Congress was held in 1955 in Geneva, the latest one in 2010 in Brazil. These quinquennial meetings have resulted in the formation of a significant body of **soft law**—"minimum standards," "guidelines," "model treaties," "codes of conduct"—which has contributed to shaping international and domestic policies and promoted novel thinking and approaches to the administration of national criminal justice systems. Some of the important instruments progressively developed in this **standards-setting** process include the Standard Minimum Rules for the Treatment of Prisoners (1977), the Code of Conduct for Law Enforcement Officials (1979), the Principles of Medical Ethics Relevant to the Role of Health Personnel Particularly Physicians in the Protection of Prisoners and Detainees against Torture and Other Cruel, Inhuman, or Degrading Treatment of Punishment (1982), the Declaration of the Basic Principles of Justice for Victims of Crime and Abuse of Power (1985), the Standard Minimum Rules for the Administration of Juvenile Justice (Beijing Rules, 1985), the Body of Principles for the Protection of All Persons Under Any Form of Detention or Imprisonment (1988), the Principles on the Effective Prevention and Investigation of Extra Legal Arbitrary and Summary Executions (1989), the Basic Principles on the Role of Lawyers and Prosecutors (1990), the Basic Principles on the Use of Force and Firearms by Law Enforcement Officials (1990), the Standard Minimum Rules for Non-Custodial Measures (Tokyo Rules, 1990), the United Nations Guidelines for the Prevention of Juvenile Delinquency (1990), the International Code of Conduct for Public Officials

(1996), and the Model Strategies and Practical Measures on the Elimination of Violence against Women in the Field of Crime Prevention and Criminal Justice (2009).

INTERNATIONAL CRIMES. Serious offenses prohibited under **international humanitarian law** and **international human rights law**. Instances of international crimes include **aggression**, **war crimes**, **crimes against humanity**, grave breaches of the provisions of the four **Geneva Conventions** of 1949 in situations of internal of international **armed conflict**, and **terrorism**. Other crimes defined by international conventions include the theft of **cultural property** and the crime of **apartheid**. International criminal law offenses may be prosecuted in international criminal tribunals such as the **International Criminal Court**. They are more frequently enforced in domestic military or civilian courts, but many of them are subject to **universal jurisdiction**. *See also* COMMAND RESPONSIBILITY; STATE RESPONSIBILITY.

INTERNATIONAL CRIMINAL COURT (ICC). The first permanent international tribunal, the ICC was created by treaty, the Rome Statute, which was signed in 1998 and entered into force on 1 July 2002. On that date, the Court began operations. By 2012, 121 nations were parties to the Statute. The Court has the power to try persons accused of the most serious international crimes (i.e., **genocide**, **crimes against humanity**, **war crimes** and **crimes against peace**) when final agreement has been reached on its definition.

The Rome Statute defines genocide as any of the following acts committed with intent to destroy, in whole or in part, a national, ethnic, racial or religious group: killing members of the group; inflicting serious harm on members of the group (including **torture** and rape); deliberately inflicting conditions calculated to bring about the group's destruction (such as withholding food or medicine); or preventing births within the group or forcibly transferring children of the group to another group. Drawing on international instruments, notably, the **United Nations Convention against Torture**, the Rome Statute defines crimes against humanity as any of the following acts when committed as part of a widespread or systematic attack directed against any civilian population: murder, torture, or enslavement (including trafficking of women and children); extermination (including withholding food and medicine); deportation or forcible transfer of population (**ethnic cleansing**); imprisonment or confinement in violation of fundamental rules of international law; rape, sexual slavery, enforced prostitution, forced pregnancy, or enforced sterilization; persecution against any identifiable group based on gender, political affiliation, race, nationality, ethnicity, culture, or religion; or **forced disappearance** of persons. Based on the **Geneva Conventions**, the Rome Statute includes the following war crimes: conscripting or enlisting children under age 15 into armed forces; taking hostages; intentionally directing attacks against civilians not participating in hostilities; intentionally directing attacks against peacekeepers and humanitarian aid workers; deliberately impeding relief supplies; use of poison gas; and rape, sexual slavery, enforced prostitution, forced pregnancy, or enforced sterilization.

The Court does not have **universal jurisdiction**. It may only exercise jurisdiction if the accused is a national of a state party or a state otherwise accepting the jurisdiction of the Court; if the crime took place on the territory of a state party or a state otherwise accepting the jurisdiction of the Court; or if the **United Nations Security Council** has referred the situation to the prosecutor, irrespective of the nationality of the accused or the location of the crime. In addition, the Court's jurisdiction is further limited by a number of provisions of its Rome Statute. It is a court of last resort as it is designed to complement national courts in the sense that it may exert its jurisdiction only when national courts are genuinely unwilling or unable to carry out the investigation or prosecution of a person accused of the crimes defined in the Rome Statute. The UN Security Council can vote to block any investigation or prosecution. Finally, in order to be consistent with the principle of the non-retroactivity of the law, the Court may not try crimes which took place before 1 July 2002.

The Office of the Prosecutor is currently conducting seven investigations, all of them in Africa (**Democratic Republic of the Congo**, **Uganda**, Central African Republic, Darfur, Sudan, Kenya, **Libya** and **Cote d'Ivoire**). The Court has indicted 29 persons, issued arrest warrants for 20 individuals and summonses for nine others. Five individuals are in custody and 10 remain at large. The first trial conducted by the ICC began in January 2009. The defendant was a former Congolese warlord charged with enlisting and conscripting children under the age of 15 as soldiers and using them to participate actively in combat between September 2002 and August 2003. He was found guilty and sentenced to 14 years in prison. A second trial was concluded in 2012 and the judgment is pending.

See also ACCESS TO JUSTICE; AGGRESSION; APARTHEID; CHILDREN IN ARMED CONFLICT; COALITION FOR THE INTERNATIONAL CRIMINAL COURT; COMPLEMENTARITY PRINCIPLE; CRIMES AGAINST PEACE; DARFUR CONFLICT; HUMAN EXPERIMENTATION; INTERNATIONAL COMMISSION OF JURISTS; INTERNATIONAL HUMANITARIAN LAW; INTERNATIONAL LAW COMMISSION; LORD'S RESISTANCE ARMY; NO PEACE WITHOUT

JUSTICE; PROPORTIONALITY; RETRIBUTIVE JUSTICE; SEXUAL VIOLENCE; SLAVERY; STATUTORY LIMITATIONS; WOMEN'S CAUCUS FOR GENDER JUSTICE; WOMEN'S INITIATIVE FOR GENDER JUSTICE; WORLD FEDERALIST MOVEMENT.

INTERNATIONAL CRIMINAL LAW (ICL). Component of **international law** concerned with **international crimes**. In sharp contrast with international law, which regulates inter-state relations and ignores individuals as a subject of law, international criminal law applies to persons deemed to have incurred criminal responsibility for their acts. From this standpoint, ICL is essentially a postwar development. The Treaty of Versailles did call for the creation of an international tribunal to try **Kaiser Wilhelm II**, and a number of national trials of violators of **laws of war** were conducted in Germany and Turkey. The major precedent setting the stage for the development of ICL was the constitution of the Nuremberg Tribunal at the end of **World War II**.

The main sources of ICL include customary **international law, peremptory norms**, the Hague Conventions, the **Geneva Conventions**, the Nuremberg Charter, the **Nuremberg Principles**, the **United Nations Charter**, the United Nations Convention against Genocide and the **United Nations Convention against Torture**. The following are considered violations of the ICL: **crimes against humanity, crimes against peace, apartheid, genocide**, piracy, the slave trade and **war crimes**. The main judicial bodies involved in the administration of the ICL include the **International Criminal Court**, the **International Criminal Tribunal for the Former Yugoslavia**, the **International Criminal Tribunal for Rwanda**, the **Special Tribunal for Cambodia**, the **Special Court for Sierra Leone**, the war crimes court in **Kosovo**, the **Special Panels of the Dili District Court** and the **Special Tribunal for Lebanon**. *See also* COMMAND RESPONSIBILITY; RAOUL WALLENBERG INSTITUTE; STATUTORY LIMITATIONS; TIMOR-LESTE; UNIVERSAL JURISDICTION.

INTERNATIONAL CRIMINAL TRIBUNAL FOR RWANDA (ICTR). International court established after much indecision by the **United Nations Security Council** (UN-SC) in 1994 for the prosecution of persons responsible for **genocide, crimes against humanity** and **war crimes**, defined as violations of Common Article Three and Additional Protocol II of the **Geneva Conventions** (dealing with war crimes committed during internal conflicts) that were committed between 1 January 1994 and 31 December 1994 in Rwanda or nearby states.

The ICTR began its first trial of Jean-Paul Akayesu in 1998. So far, the tribunal has completed 50 trials and convicted 29 accused persons. Another

370 PERSONS · INTERNATIONAL CRIMINAL TRIBUNAL FOR THE FORMER YUGOSLAVIA

11 trials are in progress, 14 individuals are awaiting trial in detention and 13 others are still at large, some suspected to be dead. The work of the court has drawn both praise and criticism. In a number of landmark cases, the ICTR has set new standards of international justice, notably in regard to rape and **sexual violence**, and it has not hesitated to convict former high-level civilian and military officials. Critiques point to the considerable delays that have plagued the proceedings of the ICTR. The UN-SC had originally envisaged that the court should complete its investigations by the end of 2004, wrap up all trial activities by the end of 2008, and complete all work in 2010. The Council has set up international mechanisms to address outstanding issues that might emerge from the closing of the ICTR. **Non-governmental organizations** have also pointed to the ICTR's failure to address war crimes committed by the Tutsi minority and to deal with officials of Western governments for giving alleged perpetrators of the genocide a safe haven in their countries. *See also* AKAYESU CASE; BARAYAGWIZA CASE; GOLDSTONE, RICHARD; INTERNATIONAL CRIMINAL LAW; KAMBANDA, JEAN; MUSEMA CASE; PILLAY, NAVANETHEM.

INTERNATIONAL CRIMINAL TRIBUNAL FOR THE FORMER YUGOSLAVIA (ICTY). After determining in 1992 that those who committed or ordered the commission of grave breaches of the **Geneva Conventions** were individually responsible for such breaches, the **United Nations Security Council**, acting under Chapter VII of the **United Nations Charter**, established a year later an international tribunal to prosecute persons responsible for serious violations of **international humanitarian law** that took place on the territory of the former Yugoslavia during the breakup of the country. The Council also asked **United Nations Secretary-General** Boutros Boutros Ghali to prepare a statute of the future ICTY in 60 days, which the Council endorsed without changes. Unlike the **International Criminal Court** and as is the case for the **International Criminal Tribunal for Rwanda** (ICTR), the ICTY is an **ad hoc international court** created as an enforcement measure under Chapter VII whose lifespan is linked to the restoration and maintenance of international peace and security in the former territories of Yugoslavia as determined by the Council. Non-compliant or non-collaborative states can in principle be referred to the Security Council for sanction.

A unique feature of the ICTY (and, for that matter, the ICTR), is that the jurisdiction of the ICTY is concurrent with that of national courts, and the tribunal has primacy over national courts (i.e., at any stage of the procedure, it may formally request national courts to defer competence). The Tribunal has indicted 161 individuals (ranging from common soldiers to generals, police commanders and prime ministers), sentenced 64 and acquitted 11. **Slobodan Milosevic**, the former president of the Federal Republic of Yugoslavia, died before the end of his trial.

See also ARBOUR, LOUISE; BLASKIC CASE; CELEBICI, FURUDZINA, DEALALIC CASES; COMMAND RESPONSIBILITY; CROATIA, WAR OF INDEPENDENCE; GOLDSTONE, RICHARD; INTERNATIONAL CRIMINAL LAW; KARADZIC, RADOVAN; MLADIC, RATKO; NEIER, ARYEH; SREBRENICA; TUDJMAN, FRANJO.

INTERNATIONAL CRISIS GROUP (ICG). Independent, non-profit, **non-governmental organization** founded in 1995 working through field-based analysis and high-level **advocacy** to prevent and resolve deadly conflict. Based on information and assessments from the field, the group which has a permanent staff of 154 worldwide produces analytical reports, bulletins and briefing papers containing practical recommendations targeted at key international decision makers. The ICG raises funds from governments, charitable foundations, companies and individual donors. The ICG was led by its founder **Gareth Evans** from 2000 to 2009. Its current president is **Louise Arbour**. *See also* EARLY WARNING; RESEARCH.

INTERNATIONAL DISABILITY ALLIANCE (IDA). Network of eight global and three regional **non-governmental organizations** of persons with disabilities established in 1999 to promote the implementation of the **United Nations Convention on the Rights of Persons with Disabilities**. *See also* DISABLED PEOPLE'S INTERNATIONAL; INCLUSION INTERNATIONAL; REHABILITATION INTERNATIONAL; WORLD BLIND UNION; WORLD FEDERATION OF THE DEAFBLIND; WORLD FEDERATION OF THE DEAF.

INTERNATIONAL FEDERATION FOR HUMAN RIGHTS (FIDH). One of the oldest **non-governmental organization** (NGO) in the field of human rights. Created in 1922, the Federation brings together 164 member organization from over 100 countries. Its self-assigned core mandate is to promote respect for all the rights set out in the **Universal Declaration of Human Rights**, the **International Covenant on Civil and Political Rights**, and the **International Covenant on Economic, Social and Cultural Rights**. Together with the **World Organization against Torture**, the Federation has been working for the implementation of the UN **Declaration on Human Rights Defenders** and the protection of human rights defenders in such organizations as the **Council of Europe** and the **Organization for Security and Co-operation in Europe** through **fact finding**, trial observation missions and the provision of training for local NGOs. The FIDH actively campaigned for the establishment of the **International Criminal Court** (ICC) and has since its creation investigated violations of human rights and transmitted the first applications by victims to participate in proceedings before the ICC.

Through **litigation**, the FIDH has sought to strengthen the social responsibilities of **transnational corporations** and played an instrumental role in securing public commitments from Carrefour (one of the giants among worldwide retailers) to comply with international human rights standards. In defense of women's rights, the FIDH has submitted **shadow reports** to the **United Nations Committee on the Elimination of All Forms of Discrimination against Women** and launched campaigns in the Middle East and North Africa. It has also initiated and supported key proceedings before domestic courts, regional and international bodies in cases concerning arbitrary measures and practices in the fight against **terrorism**. The FIDH played a significant role in the finalization of the **International Convention for the Protection of All Persons from Enforced Disappearances**. It enjoys **consultative status** with the United Nations, the **United Nations Educational, Scientific and Cultural Organization** and the **Council of Europe**. The FIDH has the status of observer with the **African Commission on Human and People's Rights**. *See also* CORPORATE SOCIAL RESPONSIBILITY; INVESTIGATION.

INTERNATIONAL FEDERATION OF JOURNALISTS (IFJ). First founded in 1926, relaunched in 1946 and again, in its present form, in 1952, the Federation now represents around 500,000 members in more than 100 countries. Its main office is in Brussels, Belgium. The IFJ promotes international action to defend press freedom and social justice through strong, free and independent trade unions of journalists. *See also* FREEDOM OF EXPRESSION.

INTERNATIONAL FEDERATION OF RED CROSS AND RED CRESCENT SOCIETIES. Umbrella organization of the National Societies which was founded in 1919. Based in Geneva, it coordinates the projects of National Societies and in particular their relief assistance missions responding to large-scale emergencies (such as earthquakes, epidemics, etc.) and provides them with operational support. *See also* INTERNATIONAL COMMITTEE OF THE RED CROSS; NATIONAL RED CROSS AND RED CRESCENT SOCIETIES.

INTERNATIONAL FEDERATION TERRE DES HOMMES (IFTDH). Federation of 11 national **non-governmental organizations** guided by the principles and provisions of the **United Nations Convention on the Rights of the Child** and involved in **advocacy** and field projects designed to improve the living conditions of disadvantaged children in such fields as **child trafficking**, the economic exploitation of children, child soldiers and children affected by **HIV/AIDS**. The IFTDH has consultative status with the **United Nations**, the **United Nations Children's Fund**, the **International Labour Organization** and the **Council of Europe**.

INTERNATIONAL FOUNDATION FOR ELECTORAL SYSTEMS (IFES). Independent, **non-governmental organization** headquartered in Washington, D.C., providing professional support to electoral **democracy**. Through field work, applied **research**, training and **advocacy**, the IFES promotes citizen participation, transparency, and **accountability** in political life and **civil society**. Since its founding in 1987, the IFES has worked in more than 100 countries. It is funded by bilateral and multilateral agencies such as the United States Agency for International Development and the **United Nations**. The IFES also receives funding from private corporations, individuals and **foundations**. *See also* CAPACITY BUILDING; ELECTORAL ASSISTANCE.

INTERNATIONAL FREEDOM OF EXPRESSION EXCHANGE. Virtual global network bringing together some 70 **non-governmental organizations** that monitor free expression violations worldwide and defends journalists, writers and others who are persecuted for exercising their right to **freedom of expression**. *See also* INTERNET; REPORTERS WITHOUT BORDERS.

INTERNATIONAL GAY AND LESBIAN HUMAN RIGHTS COMMISSION. International **non-governmental organization** dedicated to human rights **advocacy** on behalf of people who experience discrimination or abuse on the basis of their actual or perceived **sexual orientation**, gender identity or expression. The group focuses its activities on governmental violations of the right to **privacy**, the decriminalization of homosexuality and the promotion of legislation protecting the free expression of gender identity.

INTERNATIONAL HUMAN RIGHTS LAW. Branch of **international law** specifically intended to promote and protect human rights at the international, regional and local levels. Like international law, its sources are found in binding international **treaties** and **customary international law**. Other nonbinding "**soft law**" instruments are recognized as sources of obligation. Human rights law regulates the relationship between states and individuals, laying down obligations that states are bound to respect (i.e., they must put into place domestic measures compatible with their treaty duties, refrain from interfering with or curtailing the enjoyment of human rights and take measures to facilitate the enjoyment of basic rights). *See also* INCORPORATION; INTERNATIONAL HUMANITARIAN LAW.

INTERNATIONAL HUMANITARIAN LAW (IHL). Body of laws (also known as the "law of **armed conflict**") regulating the conduct of warfare and relief actions within the context of an international conflict. The 1949 **Geneva Conventions** and their 1977 additional protocols constitute the heart of IHL. The Conventions enjoin the parties to a conflict to distinguish between civilian population and combatants in order to spare the latter and their property. Attacks may be made solely against military objectives. Captured combatants and civilians must be protected against all acts of violence or reprisal. The wounded and sick must be collected and cared for. Medical personnel and medical establishments, transports and equipment must be spared. The use of weapons or methods of warfare that may cause unnecessary losses or excessive suffering is prohibited. Common Article 3 of the Conventions establishes a minimum level of protection to be provided in times of "non-international" (i.e., civil wars) armed conflicts and imposes an absolute prohibition on the following acts: violence to life and person, in particular murder of all kinds, mutilation, cruel treatment and **torture**; taking of **hostages**; outrages upon personal **dignity**, in particular humiliating and degrading treatment; and the passing of sentences and the carrying out of executions without previous judgment by a regularly constituted court.

The Geneva Conventions require the ratifying parties to repress grave breaches of the conventions, which are classified as **war crimes** under statutes of the **International Criminal Court**. Grave breaches to the Conventions include such acts as willful killing, torture or inhuman treatment, including biological experiments; willfully causing great suffering or serious injury to body or health; compelling one to serve in the forces of a hostile power; and willfully depriving one of the right to a fair trial. The taking of hostages; the extensive destruction and appropriation of **property** not justified by military necessity and carried out unlawfully and wantonly; and the unlawful **deportation**, transfer, or confinement of population also constitute "grave breaches" of the Fourth Geneva Convention relative to the protection of **civilians** in armed conflicts.

See also COMMAND RESPONSIBILITY; CRIMES AGAINST HUMANITY; DECLARATION ON THE PROTECTION OF WOMEN AND CHILDREN IN EMERGENCY AND ARMED CONFLICTS; FUNDAMENTAL GUARANTEES; INTERNATIONAL COMMITTEE

OF THE RED CROSS; INTERNATIONAL HUMAN RIGHTS LAW; INTERNATIONAL HUMANITARIAN LAW INITIATIVE RESEARCH; INTERNATIONAL INSTITUTE OF HUMANITARIAN LAW; *JUS AD BELLUM/JUS IN BELLO*; MERCENARY; NATIONAL RED CROSS AND RED CRESCENT SOCIETIES; NUCLEAR WEAPONS; OCCUPATION; PRECAUTION, PRINCIPLE OF; PROPORTIONALITY; PROTECTED PERSONS; REFUGEE LAW; SAFE ZONES.

INTERNATIONAL HUMANITARIAN LAW INITIATIVE RESEARCH. Harvard University program set up in 2002 to promote a scientific approach to emerging challenges in the implementation of **international humanitarian law** (IHL). Designed to complement the activities of the **International Committee of the Red Cross** and international **non-governmental organizations**, the program seeks to develop and support an international network of scholars, policymakers and humanitarian practitioners and to serve as a central resource for operational work conducive to the strengthening of IHL through publications, advisory services and expert meetings. *See also* CAPACITY BUILDING; EPISTEMIC COMMUNITY.

INTERNATIONAL HUMAN RIGHTS LAW INSTITUTE. Nonprofit **research**, training and **advocacy non-governmental organization** founded in 1990 and registered in Washington, D.C., and Brussels. Staffed with diplomats, parliamentarians, human rights activists, and attorneys, the Council endeavors to help states in transition to **democracy** develop the capacity to strengthen the **rule of law** and build respect for human rights. It has carried out programs in the Middle East, South Asia, Africa, and Central and Eastern Europe. *See also* CAPACITY BUILDING.

INTERNATIONAL INSTITUTE OF HUMANITARIAN LAW (IIHL). Private, independent **non-governmental organization** (NGO) set up in 1970 and located in San Remo, Italy, concerned with humanitarian law and issues. IIHL, in cooperation with NGOs, academic institutions and international organizations such as the **International Committee of the Red Cross**, the **United Nations High Commissioner for Refugees** and the **United Nations Office of the High Commissioner for Human Rights**, conducts a broad range of activities including courses on **refugees** and migration law and **internally displaced persons**. The institute also organizes annual roundtables which serve as an informal forum to practitioners and policymakers for examining topical humanitarian problems, assessing relevant legal instruments and identifying policy solutions. IIHL has consultative status with the **United Nations Economic and Social Council** and the **Council of Europe**.

INTERNATIONAL LABOUR ORGANIZATION (ILO). Set in 1919 at the Paris Peace Conference to promote labor rights and improved labor conditions, the ILO became one of the **United Nations** Specialized Agencies at the end of **World War II**. Driven by humanitarian, political and social considerations, its original constitution may be viewed as the first instance of an international arrangement designed to secure individual freedoms. A 1944 Declaration adopted by the ILO reaffirmed that peace could not be achieved without social justice. Today, the organization firmly sees itself as a body "which seeks the promotion of social justice and internationally recognized human and labor rights."

Standards' setting has been the ILO's main task since its creation. The Conventions and Recommendations that it has adopted over time are known as the International Labour Code and cover a wide array of labor rights such as the right to organize, the rights of labor unions, **freedom of association**, collective bargaining, abolition of **forced labor** and child labor, equality of treatment and opportunity, conditions of work, labor administration, **social security** and safety and **health** at work. The ILO has in recent years considerably broadened the scope of its work to include children rights, gender equality and **indigenous peoples** rights. It has devoted increasing attention to the need to ensure the accountability of **transnational corporations** for labor rights and to mitigate the negative social consequences of **globalization**.

Standards' setting is accompanied by an elaborate supervisory system which includes periodic reports by states having ratified labor conventions by independent experts, investigations by independent commissions of inquiry, complaints lodged by governments, **fact finding**, conciliation and recourse to the **International Court of Justice**. A procedure put in place in 1950 relating to freedom of association allows governments, employers or workers' organizations to submit complaints against a member state even if that state has not ratified the relevant convention.

The ILO has an extensive program of technical assistance supporting its standards' setting and supervisory activities in such areas as vocational training and rehabilitation, employment policy, labor administration, social security, labor statistics and occupational health and safety. A particularly distinctive feature of the organization is its tripartite structure which gives government, employers and workers' organizations an equal voice in the ILO decision-making processes. The ILO, however, does not have an individual **complaint** procedure, and it gives only limited access to **non-governmental organizations**.

See also CAPACITY BUILDING; CORPORATE SOCIAL RESPONS-IBILITY; DECLARATION ON SOCIAL JUSTICE FOR A FAIR GLOBALIZATION; DOMESTIC WORKERS; ILO CONVENTION

CONCERNING INDIGENOUS AND TRIBAL PEOPLES IN INDEPENDENT COUNTRIES; ILO TRIPARTITE DECLARATION OF PRINCIPLES CONCERNING MULTINATIONAL ENTERPRISES AND SOCIAL POLICY; INTERNATIONAL PROGRAMME ON THE ELIMINATION OF CHILD LABOUR; INTERNATIONAL TRADE UNION CONFEDERATION; RIGHTS AND DEMOCRACY.

INTERNATIONAL LAW. Body of rules governing relations between independent states. As articulated in a 1927 ruling of the Permanent Court of International Justice, "the rules of law binding upon states therefore emanate from their own free will as expressed in conventions [**treaties**] or by usages [customary state practice]."

See also AGGRESSION; CRIMES AGAINST HUMANITY; CRIMES AGAINST PEACE; DECLARATION ON PRINCIPLES OF INTERNATIONAL LAW CONCERNING FRIENDLY RELATIONS AND COOPERATION AMONG STATES; HARD LAW; INTERNATIONAL BAR ASSOCIATION; INTERNATIONAL COURT OF JUSTICE; INTERNATIONAL HUMAN RIGHTS LAW; INTERNATIONAL HUMANITARIAN LAW; INTERNATIONAL LAW COMMISSION; *JUS AD BELLUM/JUS IN BELLO*; *JUS COGENS*; OBLIGATION *"ERGA OMNES"*; PERMANENT COURT OF INTERNATIONAL JUSTICE; RESERVATIONS TO TREATIES; SOFT LAW; STATE RESPONSIBILITY; STATE SOVEREIGNTY.

INTERNATIONAL LAW ASSOCIATION (ILA). International **non-governmental organization** founded in 1873 and based in London for "the study, clarification and development of international law, both public and private, and the furtherance of international understanding and respect for international law." The ILA has **consultative status** with a number of **United Nations** specialized agencies. The ILA pursues its objectives primarily through the work of International Committees which undertake **research** and prepare reports on selected areas of international law in the form of statements of the law; draft treaties or conventions; an elaboration of a code or rules or principles of international law; or review of recent developments of law or practice. Current topics being explored include cultural heritage, the **International Criminal Court**, biotechnology, sustainable development, international trade, Islamic law and **international law**, non-state actors, the proliferation of **nuclear weapons** and the rights of **indigenous peoples**. Previous research areas of international law include the **accountability** of international organizations, the formation of customary international law, **internally displaced persons**, human rights law and practice, **refugees**

procedures, the transnational enforcement of environmental law and water resources law.

INTERNATIONAL LAW COMMISSION. Expert committee established in 1948 by the **United Nations General Assembly** and tasked, under its authority, to codify and progressively develop **international law**. Criticized for its slow and ponderous work style and the narrow focus of most of its work, the Commission has nevertheless considered and produced draft conventions and other documents on core topics of international law including the law of treaties, the law of the sea, diplomatic and consular relations, the creation of an **international criminal court** and **state responsibility**. *See also* DRAFT ARTICLES ON THE RESPONSIBILITY OF STATES FOR INTERNATIONALLY WRONGFUL ACTS; UNITED NATIONS CONVENTION RELATING TO THE STATUS OF STATELESS PERSONS.

INTERNATIONAL LAW INSTITUTE. Independent, non-profit educational body founded in 1955 as part of Georgetown University in Washington, D.C., to provide training and technical assistance for practical solutions to the legal, economic and financial problems of **developing countries**. The Institute has regional centers in **Uganda**, Nigeria, **Egypt**, Chile and Hong Kong. Its training programs cover a wide range of subjects including procurement, **privatization**, arbitration and mediation, negotiating and implementing trade agreements, **World Trade Organization** rights and obligations, project management, legislative drafting, judicial administration, corporate governance. *See also* THINK TANKS.

INTERNATIONAL LEAGUE AGAINST RACISM AND ANTISEMITISM. Non-governmental organization established in France in 1926 to fight racism and **anti-Semitism** in the country. The League has participated in several prominent national court cases through the years, notably the **Klaus Barbie** trial in 1987. In 2000, it successfully brought charges against Yahoo! for selling Nazi memorabilia on its online auction service. In the past few years, the League has broadened its international action by opening offices abroad and extending the scope of its interventions by working on **discrimination**, citizenship and disadvantaged young people. *See also* FREEDOM OF EXPRESSION.

INTERNATIONAL LEAGUE FOR HUMAN RIGHTS. New York–headquartered human rights **non-governmental organization** which traces its origins to La Ligue Française pour la Défense des Droits de l'Homme et du Citoyen, founded in France back in the late 19th century. Through its global network of more than 300 human rights advocates, journalists and government officials, the League draws attention to urgent international **violations of human rights** and cases. Since 1947, the League has had **consultative status** in the **United Nations Economic and Social Council**. It also regularly attends the meetings of the **United Nations Commission for Human Rights** (now the United Nations Council of Human Rights) and the **United Nations Committee on the Elimination of All Forms of Discrimination against Women**.

INTERNATIONAL MILITARY TRIBUNAL FOR THE FAR EAST. Patterned along the model of the Nuremberg Tribunal, this court was set up by the victorious Allies to try the principal government and military leaders of the empire of Japan (28 in all) for **crimes against peace, war crimes** and **crimes against humanity** committed during **World War II**. Victimized countries (Australia, China, France, Great Britain, the Netherlands, the **Philippines** and the **United States**) conducted separate trials involving a far greater number of defendants. The tribunal functioned from 1946 to 1948 and convicted 23 defendants, seven of who were sentenced to death and 16 to life imprisonment. The Tribunal, like the Nuremberg Tribunal, faced similar criticisms of "victor's justice." Most of the charges were ex post facto. The tribunal was funded and staffed by Americans. The prosecution was led by an American lawyer. The emperor and members of the imperial family were not prosecuted. In a secret deal, members of Japan's bacteriological and chemical warfare unit were granted immunity in exchange for sharing information on biological weapons with American authorities. The sentences of several defendants were later reduced. The sitting Indian justice in the Tribunal filed separate dissenting rulings and argued that Western **colonialism** and the use of the atom bomb by the United States should have been prosecuted. *See also* INTERNATIONAL MILITARY TRIBUNAL FOR THE PROSECUTION AND PUNISHMENT OF THE MAJOR WAR CRIMINALS OF THE EUROPEAN AXIS.

INTERNATIONAL MILITARY TRIBUNAL FOR THE PROSECU-TION AND PUNISHMENT OF THE MAJOR WAR CRIMINALS OF THE EUROPEAN AXIS. Until **World War II**, **war crimes** trials had been held by national courts and had focused on relatively minor defendants for isolated and well-established violations of the laws of war as had been the case for Imperial Germany and the Ottoman Empire in the aftermath of World War I. The massive atrocities committed by Germany during World War II prompted the victorious Allies (after considerable haggling among themselves) to create an international military tribunal to prosecute well-known Nazi officials and military leaders on three counts: conspiracy to commit aggressive war (i.e., the planning, preparation, initiation or waging of a war of **aggression**, or a war in violation of international treaties, agreements or assurances, or participation in a common plan or conspiracy for the accomplishment of any of the foregoing); war crimes (i.e., murder, **ill treatment** or deportation into slave labor or for any other purpose of the civilian population of or in an occupied territory, murder or ill treatment of prisoners of war or persons on the seas, the killing of hostages, the plunder of public or private property, the wanton destruction of cities, towns or villages, or devastation not justified by military necessity); and **crimes against humanity** (i.e., murder, extermination, enslavement, **deportation**, and other inhuman acts committed against any civilian population, before or during the war, or persecutions on political, racial or religious grounds in execution of or in connection with any crime within the jurisdiction of the Tribunal, whether or not in violation of the domestic law of the country where perpetrated).

The Court met in Nuremberg, Germany, and was made up of representatives of the **United States**, Great Britain, the Union of Soviet Socialist Republics and France, each country taking charge of prosecuting the defendants on one of the four counts. Twenty-two defendants made it to the trial. Eleven of them received the death penalty, eight were sentenced to prison terms and three were acquitted. The trial was controversial from the outset, leading some observers to labeling it as "victor's justice." Indeed, there was no full-fledged legal precedent to the constitution of an international penal institution. The notion that individuals could be held personally accountable and prosecuted for acts committed in their official capacity under **international law** was hotly contested. Most of the charges brought against the defendants were not considered crimes under international law prior to their commission. Finally, the unpunished Allies' bombings of civilian populations in Dresden, Hamburg and Tokyo, not to mention the nuclear attacks on Hiroshima and Nagasaki, elicited criticisms of double standards.

However imperfect the Nuremberg trials may have been, the Nazi defendants were provided with a modicum of **due process** and the ideals and principles upon which they rested—especially the notion that individuals are responsible for what they do in power and can be held accountable for committing serious crimes under international law—were formally incorporated into international law following adoption by the **United Nations General Assembly** of the **Nuremberg Principles** in 1950. The tribunal served as a model for the **International Military Tribunal for the Far East** and the 1960 **Adolf Eichmann** trial. It also paved the way toward the establishment of the UN **International Criminal Tribunal** for the **Former Yugoslavia** and the **International Criminal Tribunal for Rwanda** in the 1990s and, more importantly, the creation, in 1998 of a permanent **International Criminal Court** empowered to prosecute internationally recognized international crimes committed *after* the beginning of its operation. *See also* AMNESTIES; COMMAND RESPONSIBILITY; KATYN FOREST MASSACRE; LEIPZIG WAR TRIALS; LEMKIN, RAPHAEL.

INTERNATIONAL MONETARY FUND (IMF). International organization set up together with the **International Bank for Reconstruction and Development** (IBRD) in 1944 at the Bretton Woods Conference. Its purpose was and remains to promote international monetary cooperation and orderly exchange arrangements in support of economic growth and full employment. Over the years, the IMF has also become a major instrument in the provision of temporary financial and technical assistance to countries experiencing balance of payment problems. The policies of the IMF are grounded on a neoliberal, market-oriented philosophy which it shares with the IBRD. In this regard, the IMF's conditionalities attached to its loans in the form of **Structural Adjustment Programs** together with its reluctance to forgive a substantial part of the **external debt** of **developing countries** have led to criticisms that it induces recipient governments to flaunt their treaty-based human rights obligations and "banks on the poor." Mandatory state budget cuts are usually accompanied by the reduction or abolition of subsidies for **food, education** and **health**. Interest rate increases, local currency devaluations and **privatization** make the price of essential services skyrocket. The decentralization of fiscal responsibility has in effect meant transferring vital governmental functions to local authorities with little if any capacity to do so. While the IMF has softened the bluntness of its conditionality, it has more firmly than the World Bank rejected any obligation in the field of human rights. *See also* FUJIMORI, ALBERTO; PUBLIC GOODS.

INTERNATIONAL MOVEMENT AGAINST ALL FORMS OF DISCRIMINATION AND RACISM (IMADR). Founded in 1988 by one of Japan's largest minorities, the Buraku people, this Japan-based non-profit, **non-governmental organization** in **consultative status** with the **United Nations Economic and Social Council** has grown into a global network of individuals and minority groups with regional committees and partners in Asia, Europe, North America and Latin America and is devoted to the elimination of **racial discrimination**. Through grassroots empowerment, action-oriented **research**, information sharing and **advocacy** campaigns, IMADR endeavors to strengthen international human rights protection mechanisms for the elimination of discrimination and racism and to uphold the rights of **indigenous peoples** and **minorities**. Related objectives focus on the elimination of exploitative migration and trafficking of women and children and of racial discrimination in the administration of justice. *See also* CHILDREN TRAFFICKING.

INTERNATIONAL NETWORK FOR ECONOMIC, SOCIAL AND CULTURAL RIGHTS (ESCR-Net). International human rights network seeking to strengthen economic, social and cultural rights by working with activists and practitioners worldwide in joint actions, enhancing communications and building solidarity across regions. ESCR-Net has developed a useful case law database on economic and social and cultural rights. *See also* INTERNET; LITIGATION.

INTERNATIONAL NGO COALITION FOR AN O.P. TO THE ICESCR. Broad array of grassroots activists, **community-based organizations**, international **non-governmental organizations** and regional networks promoting ratification of the Optional Protocol to the **International Covenant on Economic, Social and Cultural Rights** (ICESCR). The Coalition develops and disseminates information and material for **advocacy** purposes, engages in public **human rights education** and develops strategies for states' ratification of the Protocol. Members of the Coalition commit to sharing resources, strategies and information about their own activities. A steering committee comprised of national, regional and international organizations provides overall direction. The Committee includes **Amnesty International**, the **Centre on Housing Rights and Evictions**, **International Network for Economic, Social and Cultural Rights**, the **Food First Information and Action Network**, the **International Commission of Jurists**, the **International Federation of Human Rights**, the **International Women's Rights Action Watch** Asia-Pacific, and the Inter-American Platform of Human Rights, Democracy and Development. *See also* INTERNET.

INTERNATIONAL ORGANIZATION FOR MIGRATION (IOM). Intergovernmental organization set up (under a different name) in 1951 to assist with the resettlement of European **refugees** after **World War II**. It has progressively broadened its mandate from a logistics to a migration agency, designed, in cooperation with governments and **civil society**, to "promoting humane and orderly migration for the benefit of all" through the provision of services to governments and migrants in need, be they refugees, **displaced persons** or other uprooted people. The IOM was involved in the crises of Hungary (1956), Czechoslovakia (1968), Chile

(1973), the Vietnamese **Boat People** (1975), Kuwait (1990), **Kosovo** and **Timor-Leste** (1999) and the Asian tsunami and the Pakistan earthquake of 2004–5. In addition, the IOM has often organized elections for refugees out of their home country, as was the case in the 2004 Afghan elections and the 2005 Iraqi elections. The IOM currently works in the areas of migration management: migration and development, facilitating migration, regulating migration, and addressing forced migration. Cross-cutting activities include the promotion of international migration law, policy debate and guidance, protection of migrants' rights, migration **health** and the gender dimension of migration. The IOM Constitution gives explicit recognition to the link between migration and economic, social and cultural development as well as to the right of **freedom of movement** of persons, but its operational principle and policy of "orderly migration" has prompted criticisms by migrant organizations and **non-governmental organizations** that in effect it supports or encourages practices such as **deportations**, militarized border controls or detention centers. *See also* MIGRANT WORKERS.

INTERNATIONAL PEACE INSTITUTE (IPI). Originally known as the International Peace Academy, this **think tank** located in New York was created in 1970 initially for the purpose of training military and civilian professionals in United Nations **peacekeeping**. The institute today has broadened its **research** and **advocacy** activities to encompass the prevention and settlement of conflicts between and within states. The IPI provides policy advice and insights to international and national policymakers on a wide-ranging number of issues with human rights implications including **terrorism**, fragile states, **transnational crime, weapons of mass destruction**, peace and justice, the privatization of security, small arms and light weapons, biosecurity and **United Nations Security Council** reform. The IPI is actively involved in the implementation of the norm of a **responsibility to protect**.

INTERNATIONAL PLANNED PARENTHOOD FEDERATION (IPPF). Global **non-governmental organization** with the broad aims of promoting sexual and reproductive health and advocating the right of individuals to make their own choices in family planning. First formed in 1952 in Bombay, India, it now consists of more than 172 member associations which provide family planning services, sexual health and abuse prevention training and education. To achieve these goals, the IPPF works in close cooperation with the **World Health Organization**, the **United Nations Development Programme**, the **United Nations Children's Fund**, the **United Nations Population Fund**, and the **Organization for Economic Co-operation and Development**. The IPPF is a prominent pressure group in the

European Union and the **United Nations Economic and Social Council**. As an advocate of free access to contraception and safe abortion services, the IPPF has come into conflict with the Roman **Catholic Church** and the conservative **United States** Republican administrations of Presidents Ronald Reagan and **George W. Bush**. *See also* REPRODUCTIVE RIGHTS.

INTERNATIONAL PROGRAMME ON THE ELIMINATION OF CHILD LABOUR (IPEC). Program launched by the **International Labour Organization** (ILO) in 1992 with the overall objective to eliminate child labor through **capacity-building** projects and the promotion a worldwide movement to combat child labor. The IPEC is active in some 90 countries. Its priority targets derive from the 1990 ILO Convention on the worst forms of child labor (No. 182) which aims at the elimination of all forms of **slavery** or practices similar to slavery, the sale of children and **children trafficking**, debt bondage and serfdom and forced or compulsory labor, including forced or compulsory recruitment of children for use in armed conflict and the use, procuring or offering of a child for prostitution, for the production of **pornography** or for pornographic performances. *See also* CHILDREN IN ARMED CONFLICT.

INTERNATIONAL RED CROSS AND RED CRESCENT MOVE-MENT. International movement of some 100 million volunteers operating in the framework of three distinct independent organizations: the **National Red Cross and Red Crescent Societies**; the **International Federation of Red Cross and Red Crescent Societies**; and the **International Committee of the Red Cross**. The three components of the movements meet every four years and share the same basic objectives of protecting human life and health, ensuring respect for all human beings and to prevent and alleviate human suffering on the basis of the principles of humanity, impartiality, neutrality, independent, voluntary service, unity and universality.

INTERNATIONAL REHABILITATION COUNCIL FOR TORTURE VICTIMS (IRCT). International health professional **non-governmental organization** based in Denmark which promotes and supports the rehabilitation of **torture** victims and works for the prevention of torture in some 70 countries. The activities of the IRCT include awareness raising about the rehabilitation needs of torture victims, assistance in the establishment of treatment facilities, and the production of information documenting the impact and consequences of torture. The IRCT has **consultative status** with the **United Nations Economic and Social Council** and participatory status with the **Council of Europe**.

INTERNATIONAL RESCUE COMMITTEE (IRC). Leading international **advocacy**, relief and humanitarian **non-governmental organization** which traces its origins to a 1942 merger of the International Relief Association set up by Albert Einstein in 1933 to help opponents of Adolf Hitler with the Emergency Rescue Committee which rescued European refugees trapped in Vichy France. The Committee operates in over 25 countries providing shelter, clean water, health care, and education to people displaced by natural disasters or armed conflict. The IRC also gives longer-term assistance to **refugees** and issues authoritative reports on humanitarian questions. Its recent studies have documented the deteriorating social conditions or refugees in war-torn Iraq and the devastating impact of the civil war on civilians in the **Democratic Republic of the Congo**.

INTERNATIONAL SAVE THE CHILDREN ALLIANCE. Umbrella international organization bringing together national Save the Children **non-governmental organizations** dedicated to the provision of emergency relief as well as long-term development assistance to children worldwide who suffer from **poverty**, disease, injustice and violence. This global network of some 30 national nonprofit organizations was founded in 1977 and is, since 1997, headquartered in London. The Alliance traces its origins back to Save the Children Fund, a group set up in 1919 in Great Britain to raise money and send emergency aid to children suffering as a result of wartime food and supplies shortages. Together with a number of other similar organizations working for children, the Fund subsequently distributed emergency relief to children in several countries, especially in the wake of the 1921 Russian famine and the 1919–22 Greco-Turkish war. At the same time, the Fund evolved into a worldwide movement also promoting the rights of children. Its **advocacy** efforts culminated in the adoption in 1924 by the **League of Nations** of a Declaration of the Rights of the Child, a step that would eventually lead to the 1989 **United Nations Convention on the Rights of the Child**.

During **World War II**, the humanitarian work of Save the Children was mainly focused on Great Britain. After the war, Save the Children's activities first shifted to the European continent and then progressively expanded to Africa, Asia and the Middle East. The Alliance now has projects in over 100 countries. Its long-standing children's rights-based approach still shapes its humanitarian and development work. **Research** and advocacy for children's rights—to **food, shelter, health** care, **education** and freedom from violence, abuse and exploitation—are important components of its activities. The Alliance and its national constituents speak out for children and seek to secure legislative and policy changes aimed at ending harmful practices and secure respect for children rights. In this regard, they played a key role in the preparation and adoption of the UN Convention and they have been instrumental in the global campaign undertaken since the late 1990s against the use of **children in armed conflicts.**

INTERNATIONAL SERVICE FOR HUMAN RIGHTS (ISHR). Established in 1984 by members of a number of **non-governmental organizations** in Geneva, this worldwide **network** of human rights activists provides information and support and training to **human rights defenders** through analytical reports on **United Nations** and other international and regional human rights mechanisms, training on how to use international and regional norms and procedures and strategic advice for **lobbying.** Since 1988, ISHR publishes the *Human Rights Monitor,* which features comprehensive detailed and analytical reviews of UN human rights meetings in Geneva and New York. *See also* CAPACITY BUILDING; YOGYAKARTA PRINCIPLES ON THE APPLICATION OF INTERNATIONAL HUMAN RIGHTS LAW IN RELATION TO SEXUAL ORIENTATION AND GENDER IDENTITY.

INTERNATIONAL SOCIETY FOR HUMAN RIGHTS (ISHR). International **non-governmental** organization with **consultative status** with the **Council of Europe** and the **United Nations Economic and Social Council.** Based in Germany, the ISHR has monitored the situation of human rights in **Chechnya, Colombia, Cuba,** Georgia and Vietnam and published reports about them. It has also campaigned for **freedom of religion,** the **International Criminal Court** and the abolition of inhumane forms of **capital punishment.** *See also* MONITORING OF HUMAN RIGHTS.

INTERNATIONAL TRADE UNION CONFEDERATION (ITUC). World's largest international trade union organization with a membership of 175 million workers in over 50 countries and territories. The ITUC works closely with the **International Labour Organization** and other **United Nations** specialized agencies. Promoting workers rights and interests, the ITUC focuses its activities on the global economy, child labor, **forced labor,** climate change, **domestic workers,** the global economy, migration, women and youth. *See also* INTERNATIONAL CONFEDERATION OF FREE TRADE UNIONS; WORK, RIGHT TO.

INTERNATIONAL TRAINING CENTRE ON HUMAN RIGHTS AND PEACE TEACHING (CIFEDHOP). International **non-governmental organization** with **consultative status** to the **United Nations,** the **United Nations Educational, Scientific and Cultural Organization,**

the **International Labour Organization** and the **Council of Europe**. Operational since 1984 and headquartered in Geneva, CIFEDHOP provides training for teachers in college and primary, secondary and vocational schools in **human rights education**. *See also* CAPACITY BUILDING.

INTERNATIONAL WOMEN'S RIGHTS ACTION WATCH (IWRAW). Global **network** of individuals and organizations set up in 1985 at the Third World Conference on Women in Nairobi, Kenya, to promote recognition of women's human rights under the **United Nations Convention on the Elimination of All Forms of Discrimination against Women** to monitor its implementation. The activities of IWRAW have expanded to encompass **advocacy** for women's human rights under all the international human rights **treaties**.

INTERNATIONAL WOMEN'S RIGHTS PROJECT. Project of the University of Victoria, British Columbia, Canada, and non-profit organization incorporated in Canada and South Africa. Founded in 1998, the project works in partnership with **civil society** organizations, **research** institutions, donors, universities, and individuals to provide research, **capacity building**, and an exchange of knowledge and learning on women's rights. Studies recently published relate to the impact of the **United Nations Convention on the Elimination of All Forms of Discrimination against Women**, violence against women, women and constitutions, women and **HIV/AIDS**, women's peace and security and the "**Responsibility to Protect**."

INTERNATIONAL WORK GROUP FOR INDIGENOUS AFFAIRS (IWGIA). Non-governmental organization supporting **indigenous peoples'** quest for human rights, **self-determination**, right to territory, control of land and resources, cultural integrity, and the right to development. The group's activities combine the production of documentation and publication, political **lobbying** with field work focused on organizational empowerment building, promotion and protection of **land rights**, awareness creation about the human rights situation of indigenous peoples and community **capacity building** and mobilization. Funded primarily by the Nordic Ministries of Foreign Affairs and the **European Union**, the Group holds **consultative status** with the **United Nations Economic and Social Council** and is an observer to the Arctic Council.

INTERNET. According to the International Telecommunication Union, the total number of Internet users worldwide exceeds 2 billion. Because it is an interactive medium which allows for the sharing as well as the making of information, the use of the Internet can be a powerful instrument in the realization of a wide range of human rights and in promoting active citizen participation in public affairs. The ability that the Internet offers to communicate, organize and publicize was underlined throughout the so-called **Arab Spring** which has recently jolted the Middle East. Not surprisingly, governments have sought to restrict access to the Internet through the criminalization of online expression, measures taken to prevent certain content from reaching end users, the targeting of individuals who seek, receive and impart politically sensitive information via the Internet and the imposition of conditionalities on Internet service providers. Legislative and judicial bodies in a small number of countries have pronounced access to the Internet a human right. In a recent report, the **United Nations special rapporteur** on the promotion and protection of the right to **freedom of expression** and opinion has argued that facilitating and ensuring universal access to the Internet should be a priority for all states.

See also ANTI-DEFAMATION LEAGUE; CONSORTIUM OF MINORITY RESOURCES; DERECHOS HUMAN RIGHTS; HUMAN RIGHTS INTERNET; IMPUNITY WATCH; INSTITUTE FOR GLOBAL COMMUNICATIONS; INTERNATIONAL FREEDOM OF EXPRESSION EXCHANGE; INTERNATIONAL NETWORK FOR ECONOMIC, SOCIAL AND CULTURAL RIGHTS; INTERNATIONAL NGO COALITION FOR AN O.P. TO THE ICESCR; MANDAT INTERNATIONAL; NETWORK; PORNOGRAPHY; PREVENT GENOCIDE INTERNATIONAL; PRIVACY, RIGHT TO; WORLD SUMMIT ON THE INFORMATION SOCIETY.

INTER-PARLIAMENTARY UNION (IPU). Intergovernmental organization of parliaments of sovereign states established in 1889 (originally it was an organization made up of individual parliamentarians). The IPU is headquartered in Geneva and enjoys observer status at the **United Nations**. Its overall mandate is to foster contacts among parliaments and parliamentarians and to contribute to strengthening representative institutions. The IPU regularly debates human rights questions during its statutory Assemblies (called Conferences until 2003), the Standing Committees of which are entirely devoted to issues relating to **democracy** and human rights.

INTERSTATE COMMUNICATIONS. Standard procedure of human rights **treaties** allowing human rights treaty bodies to receive **complaints** from a state party regarding violations of convention obligations by another state party. The procedure has rarely been used as a matter of practice because states are reluctant to have recourse to it. *See also* EUROPEAN

CONVENTION FOR THE PROTECTION OF HUMAN RIGHTS AND FUNDAMENTAL FREEDOMS; GREECE; UNITED NATIONS TREATY BODIES.

INTERVENTION, RIGHT OF. *See* HUMANITARIAN INTERVENTION.

INTIFADA (1987–1993, 2000–2005). Arabic for "shaking off" but translated into English as "uprising" or "resistance." As such, the term refers to such uprisings as those that have occurred in Bahrain (1965 and 1990s), Spanish Sahara (1970 and 2005) and Lebanon (2005), among others. Most frequently, it is understood as a shorthand description of Palestinian civil disobedience and resistance to **Israeli** rule in Gaza, the West Bank and East Jerusalem from 1987 to 1993 and 2000 to 2005, respectively. Triggered by local incidents, both were the product of Palestinian disillusionment with the leadership of Arab states and the Palestinian Liberation Organization and long-simmering resentment against the perceived deepening of the military occupation. An estimated 1,000 Palestinians and 160 Israelis were killed in the first intifada, which was also characterized by extensive intra-Palestinian violence directed at alleged Israeli collaborators. The human toll of the second intifada was heavier, an Israeli human rights group reckoning that it cost more than 4,000 lives. Over 3,000 were killed by security forces in the West Bank and Gaza, and more than 1,000 Israelis were killed by terrorist attacks. The Palestinian side denounce Israeli measures of extra-judicial targeted killings, property destruction, movement restrictions, arbitrary detention, **torture** and **ill treatment**, and forced transfers as violations of international human rights and humanitarian law. The Israeli authorities justify these practices in the name of security and **counterterrorism**.

INVESTIGATION. Procedure widely used by global or regional inter-governmental human rights bodies and **non-governmental organizations** designed to gather objective evidence to corroborate the existence of violations of human rights. The process normally unfolds along four phases: (a) the receipt or reporting of complaints of rights violations; (b) the inquiry proper, which entails a detailed follow-up of the facts; (c) reporting of the outcome of the **fact-finding** phase to the bodies which mandated the investigation with recommendations for compensating the injury or for rectifying the situation if it is found that the complaints or allegations were confirmed; and (d) the final decision made by mandating bodies. The process outlined above most closely corresponds to the experience of UN peace operations which have a human rights **monitoring** component in the field. There are wide variations in the actual modalities and outcomes of investigations.

See also AFRICAN COMMITTEE ON THE RIGHTS AND WELFARE OF THE CHILD; ASIAN CENTER FOR HUMAN RIGHTS; ASIAN HUMAN RIGHTS COMMISSION; BRODY, REED; CENTRE ON HOUSING RIGHTS AND EVICTIONS; ENFORCEMENT; EUROPEAN PARLIAMENT; GLOBAL WITNESS; GOLDSTONE REPORT; HUMAN RIGHTS DEFENDERS; HUMAN RIGHTS WATCH; INTER-AMERICAN COMMISSION ON HUMAN RIGHTS; INTERNATIONAL ASSOCIATION OF DEMOCRATIC LAWYERS; NATIONAL HUMAN RIGHTS INSTITUTIONS; OXFAM INTERNATIONAL; PEACE OPERATIONS; PHYSICIANS FOR HUMAN RIGHTS; SABRA AND SHATILA MASSACRE; SPECIAL RAPPORTEURS; SRI LANKAN CIVIL WAR; UNITED NATIONS HUMAN RIGHTS COUNCIL; UNITED NATIONS MISSION OF SUPPORT IN EAST TIMOR; UNITED NATIONS OBSERVER GROUP IN EL SALVADOR; UNITED NATIONS OPERATION IN MOZAMBIQUE; UNITED NATIONS TRANSITIONAL AUTHORITY IN CAMBODIA; UNITED NATIONS WORKING GROUP ON ARBITRARY DETENTION; UNITED NATIONS WORKING GROUP ON THE PROTECTION OF ALL PERSONS FROM ENFORCED DISAPPEARANCES.

INVOLUNTARY SERVITUDE. Any type of **slavery, peonage,** or compulsory non-consensual labor for the satisfaction of debts and more generally, a worker's inability to quit because of threats to use force or imprisonment. *See also* SEX TRAFFICKING.

IRAN. Although the constitution of Iran in force under the Shah's regime from 1925 to its downfall in 1979 provided for a constitutional monarchy which introduced electoral reforms in the 1960s, extending suffrage to all members of society, including women, political dissent throughout this period was stifled through reliance on an omnipresent secret police, administrative detentions, **torture** and **extra-judicial executions.** The human rights record of the country has hardly improved and has been condemned by Iranian nationals, international human rights activists and **non-governmental organizations, United Nations** bodies, including the **United Nations Human Rights Council** (UNHCR) and the **United Nations General Assembly.** Criticism has singled out the use of restrictions and harsh punishments grounded on Islamic law and such actions as torture, rape, the harassment and beating of dissenters and demonstrators and the killing of political prisoners. Government officials respond that they are not bound to follow "the West's interpretation of human rights" and that they are the targets of "biased propaganda" of enemies of Islam. Be that as it may, in 2011, after a contentious debate, the UNHRC appointed a **special rapporteur** to examine, advise and publicly report on the human rights situation in Iran. *See also* KURDISH HUMAN RIGHTS PROJECT.

IRAQ. *See* ABU GHRAIB PRISON; AL-ANFAL CAMPAIGN; CHEMICAL WEAPONS; CRIMES AGAINST HUMANITY; IMPUNITY; HUSSEIN, SADDAM; KURDISH HUMAN RIGHTS PROJECT; KURDISH QUESTION; SAFE ZONES; STATE TERRORISM; SUPREME IRAQI CRIMINAL TRIBUNAL; WAR CRIMES.

IRREGULARS. *See* ARMED GROUPS; MERCENARY.

ISLAM. *See* CULTURAL RELATIVISM; SHARIA LAW.

ISRAEL. The 1948 Declaration of the Establishment of the State of Israel posits, among other things, that the state of Israel "will ensure complete equality of social and political rights irrespective of religion, race or sex" and "will guarantee **freedom of religion**, conscience, language, education and culture." Notwithstanding the fact that Israel is a Jewish state and that problems have arisen in regard to the treatment of ethnic and religious **minorities** and Arab citizens, by and large the country ranks high on the ratings of political and civil liberties and ratings of **non-governmental organizations** (NGOs) such as **Freedom House**, the Economic Intelligence Unit, **Reporters Without Borders** and **Transparency International** relating to religious freedom, **due process rights**, **freedom of expression** and the media, and gender equality. Israeli practices in the territories that it currently occupies, however, have elicited considerable criticism by governments, international organizations, **United Nations treaty bodies** as well as NGOs. Such criticisms have focused attention on Israel's settlements policy, the building of a wall inside the West Bank, collective punishments, targeted killings and cases of **torture**, reliance on administrative detention procedures and the application of disproportionate force. The Israeli government has repeatedly stated that it observes the humanitarian laws contained in the Fourth **Geneva Convention** in the occupied territories and that neither the **International Covenant on Civil and Political Rights** nor the **International Covenant on Economic, Social and Cultural Rights** is applicable.

See also ANTI-DEFAMATION LEAGUE; ANTI-SEMITISM; ARAB ISRAELI CONFLICT; ARBOUR, LOUISE; CONVENTION ON THE PROTECTION AND PROMOTION OF THE DIVERSITY OF CULTURAL

EXPRESSION; DEMJANJUK, JOHN; DRONES; GOLDSTONE REPORT; HOLOCAUST; INTERNATIONAL COURT OF JUSTICE; INTIFADA; SABRA ANDS SHATILA MASSACRE; SHARON, ARIEL; UNITED NATIONS RELIEF AND WORKS AGENCY FOR PALESTINE REFUGEES IN THE NEAR EAST; UNIVERSAL PERIODIC REVIEW; WORLD CONFERENCE AGAINST RACISM.

J

JAPAN. *See* "COMFORT WOMEN"; DENIAL; FEMALE INFANTICIDE; FORCED LABOR; INTERNATIONAL MILITARY TRIBUNAL FOR THE FAR EAST; SEX TRAFFICKING; WORLD WAR I PEACE TREATIES.

JAPANESE DETENTION CAMPS. *See* KOREMATSU, FRED TOYOSABURO.

JOHN-PAUL II (1920–2005). Pope of the Roman **Catholic Church** from 1978 to his death. He is praised for having contributed to the fall of communism in his native Poland and to have significantly improved relations between the Church and Islam, Judaism and the Eastern Orthodox Church. He has been criticized though for conservative positions on social issues relating to **reproductive rights**, contraception and **abortion** and gender roles.

JUBILEE DEBT COALITION. Coalition of national organizations (also known as Jubilee Debt Campaign) formed as a successor organization to Jubilee 2000 which calls for the cancellation of the poorest countries' **external debt** and the alleviation of **poverty** (the concept of Jubilee refers to the practice described in the Old Testament whereby every 50 years, people sold into slavery, or land sold due to bankruptcy, were redeemed). The Coalition focuses its activities on the organization of worldwide **campaigns** designed to mobilize public opinion and influence governmental decision makers in creditor countries.

JUDICIALIZATION. *See* ADJUDICATION.

JUDICIARY, INDEPENDENCE OF. Enshrined in Article 14 of the **International Covenant on Civil and Political Rights**, this principle is deemed to be essential to ensuring the impartiality of justice. In one of its **General Comments**, the **United Nations Human Rights Committee** (UN-HRCttee) has asserted that the independence of the judiciary should be established not only in regard to such criteria as the rules and procedures governing the appointment and dismissal of judges, the terms and conditions of service of judges, the qualifications and training of judges, procedural, specific and legal guarantees available to defendants but also to the actual independence of the judiciary from the executive and legislative branches of government. A considerable volume of jurisprudence on these subjects has emanated from the **European Court of Human Rights** suggesting that the appearance of bias may be sufficient to give rise to individual **complaints**. In that context, the reliance of military courts and tribunals has prompted the UN-HRCttee to opine that they pose "serious problems as far as the equitable, impartial and independent administration of justice is concerned" and to seek further clarification from states in their reports to the Committee on the safeguards they have put in place to protect civilians in such judicial bodies (General Comment 13). *See also* GUANTANAMO BAY DETENTION CAMP; HUMAN RIGHTS INSTITUTE; INTERNATIONAL BAR ASSOCIATION.

JURISDICTION. Authority granted to a legal entity to deal with or make pronouncements on legal matters. The term may refer to a geographic area of authority as is the case in regard to the territory of a state, in which case, jurisdiction is determined by the site of the crime (territorial jurisdiction). Jurisdiction may also be exercised by a state whose nationals commit particularly nefarious offenses on the territory of another state (nationality principle). Finally, jurisdiction can also refer to the capacity of courts or court-like bodies to hear and decide on cases brought to them by claimants. Normally, the relationship between the jurisdiction of national and international courts is expressly based on the **complementarity principle**. Only rarely are international tribunals empowered to prevail over national courts as is the case for the **International Criminal Tribunal for the Former Yugoslavia** and the **European Court of Human Rights**. *See also* ACT OF STATE DOCTRINE; ALIEN TORT STATUTE; STATE SOVEREIGNTY; UNIVERSAL JURISDICTION.

JUS AD BELLUM/JUS IN BELLO. Latin for "right to war" and "justice in war." The former refers to the branch of **international law** that defines the legitimate reasons for a state to engage in war. The key normative source of *jus ad bellum* is Articles 2 and 51 of the **United Nations Charter** which, respectively, state that "all members shall refrain in their international relations from the threat or the use of force against the territorial integrity or political independence of any state, or in any other manner inconsistent with the purposes of the **United Nations**" and that "nothing in the present Charter shall impair the inherent right of individual or collective self-defense if an armed attack occurs against a Member of the United Nations." In contrast, *jus in bello* is concerned with the legally permissible practices that the parties engaged in warfare must respect. This body of law is described as **international humanitarian law**.

JUS COGENS. Set of principles of **international law** that are considered universal and **non-derogable** and, therefore, apply to all states. As such, *jus cogens* is closely related to the notion of **universal jurisdiction**. There is considerable controversy about the origins of the concept and, more importantly, the criteria that are required for a legal norm to become *jus cogens*. But it is generally accepted that the prohibitions on the aggressive use of force, **war crimes**, **genocide**, **crimes against humanity**, **slavery**, **racial discrimination**, piracy and **torture** constitute *jus cogens* norms. As a consequence, provisions of **treaties** contradicting *jus cogens* rules may be rendered null and void. In the same vein, while certain human rights treaties allow states parties to derogate from their obligations in times of public emergencies, governments may do so under certain conditions and may never infringe upon non-derogable rights. *See also* OBLIGATIONS *"ERGA OMNES"*; PEREMPTORY NORMS.

JUST WAR. Military ethics doctrine grounded in early Roman and Catholic teachings dealing with the justification of how and why wars are fought. From this perspective, a just war can only be waged as a last resort; all non-violent options must have been exhausted before the use of force; a war is just only if it is waged by a legitimate authority; a just war can only be fought to **redress** a wrong suffered; a war can only be just if it is fought with a reasonable chance of success; the violence used in the war must be proportional to the injury suffered and the weapons used in war must discriminate between combatants and non-combatants. Interest in the doctrine has been rekindled by the ambiguities of the **United Nations Charter** on the principle of the non-use of force and the need to legitimize armed **humanitarian interventions**. *See also* "RESPONSIBILITY TO PROTECT."

K

KADI CASE (2008). Landmark ruling of the European **Court of Justice** which struck down a regulation adopted by the Commission of the **European Union** in implementation of a **United Nations Security Council** decision that had placed the appellant (Mr. Kadi) on a list of individuals whose funds were frozen because of suspicion of financing **terrorism**. The Court determined that the regulation did not sufficiently respect certain fundamental rights of the appellant, namely his right to be heard, his right to property, and his right to an effective legal **remedy**.

KAISER WILHELM II (1859–1941). Last German emperor and king of Prussia who ruled from 1888 until 1918 when he abdicated and took refuge in the Netherlands. Notwithstanding his love for the cultural trappings of militarism, support for the German military establishment and industry, ambitions for the German empire to be a world power and the encouragements he gave to the Austro-Hungarian empire to pursue a hard line with Serbia, there is now a consensus among historians that Kaiser Wilhelm played a far more nuanced and complex role than was widely assumed by his contemporaries in the 1914 summer events which led to the outbreak of World War I. At the time, however, the emperor was viewed—especially by the French—as personally responsible for unleashing the conflict, and the 1919 Versailles Treaty between Germany and the Allies provides for his prosecution "for a supreme offence against international morality and the sanctity of treaties." His trial never took place as the Netherlands refused to extradite him. *See also* LEIPZIG WAR TRIALS; WORLD WAR I PEACE TREATIES.

KAMBANDA, JEAN (1955–). Prime minister of the caretaker government during the **Rwandan genocide**, Kambanda was arrested in 1997 in Nairobi, Kenya, and immediately transferred to Arusha to the **International Criminal Tribunal for Rwanda**. He was convicted of all charges against him and condemned to life imprisonment in 1998 for **genocide**, agreement to commit genocide, public and direct incitation to commit genocide, aiding and abetting genocide and **crimes against humanity**. Kambanda is serving his sentence in Mali.

KARADZIC, RADOVAN (1945–). Former Bosnia Serb politician on trial in the **International Criminal Tribunal for the Former Yugoslavia** (ICTY). Indicted by the ICTY in 1996 for **war crimes** and **genocide** committed against Bosnian Muslims and Bosnian Croats during the **Bosnia-Herzegovina War** (1992–95), he evaded capture until 2008 when he was arrested and extradited to the Netherlands. He is accused, as commander of the Bosnian Serb armed forces and head of the Republika Srpska, to have initiated the siege of **Sarajevo**, taken **United Nations** personnel **hostage**, imprisoned non-Serbs in **concentration camps**, and ordered the **Srebrenica** massacre. *See also* COMMAND RESPONSIBILITY.

KATYN FOREST MASSACRE. Mass killing of an estimated 22,000 Polish nationals carried out by the Soviet Union secret police in April and May 1940. The victims included 8,000 prisoners of war, 6,000 police officers and members of the intelligentsia. The mass graves were discovered by the German army in 1943 but demands by the Polish government for an **investigation** by the **International Committee of the Red Cross** were brushed aside and the matter was not litigated at the Nuremberg Trials. Soviet authorities denied any responsibility until 1990 when they formally expressed "profound regret" and admitted Soviet secret police responsibility. In November 2010, the Russian State Duma approved a declaration blaming **Josef Stalin** and other Soviet officials for having personally ordered the massacre. The legal description of the Katyn remains a matter of dispute between the Russian government and Polish authorities who describe it as a case of **genocide** and demand more thorough investigations and a complete disclosure of Soviet documents. Complaints of relatives of the victims were declared admissible by the **European Court of Human Rights** in 2011.

KELLOG-BRIAND PACT (1928). Multilateral agreement signed by 15 nations which condemned "recourse to war for the solution of international controversies" and called upon its signatories to settle their disputes by peaceful means. The treaty—still in force—has not made significant contributions to international order. But it provided the legal basis for the notion of **crimes against peace** and the principle of the non-use of force found in Article 2 of the **United Nations Charter**.

KHMER ROUGE. *See* DEMOCRATIC KAMPUCHEA.

KIM IL SUNG (1912–1994). Leader of North Korea from its founding in 1948 until his death when he was succeeded by his son Kim Jong-il. All throughout this period, Kim exerted dictatorial powers, presiding over a

Soviet-style command economy and establishing an extensive personality cult. By the end of the 1970s and in the wake of China's economic reforms, North Korea began to encounter increasing economic difficulties. The collapse of communism in Eastern Europe and the Soviet Union further compounded North Korea's isolation. Droughts coupled with an outdated economic infrastructure, inadequate government revenues and the impact of international sanctions over North Korea's **nuclear weapons** program have since crippled the country's **food security**. One million North Koreans are believed to have died of starvation during Kim's rule. The country can function only by means of massive injections of multilateral humanitarian health and food assistance. Over 6 million people are still considered at risk, and studies by the World Food Programme and the **United Nations Children's Fund** suggest that malnutrition has left more than 40 percent of North Korean children physically stunted and in danger of intellectual impairment. In the view of some observers, "The state's culpability in this vast misery elevates the North Korean famine to a **crime against humanity**." Since 2003, the United Nations has adopted resolutions condemning the country's dismal human rights record. In 2011, the **United Nations General Assembly** urged the government to end its "systematic, widespread and grave violations of human rights" which included **arbitrary detentions** and public executions.

KIMBERLEY PROCESS CERTIFICATION SCHEME (KPCS). Voluntary and self-policing international governmental procedure established in 2003 to certify the origin of rough diamonds with member countries pledging not to import or export rough diamonds originating from conflict zones controlled by forces or factions opposed to legitimate and internationally recognized governments. Under the KPCS, participating countries must also ensure that rough diamonds are not used to fund military action in opposition to those governments or in contravention of the decisions of the **United Nations Security Council**. The system was put in place following the issuance of a report in 2000 documenting the strong links between the illicit diamond trade, Third World conflicts and **violations of human rights**, notably in **Angola**. The scheme has made it more difficult for "blood diamonds" to reach international markets, but it has been criticized by **civil society** organizations such as **Global Witness** for ignoring the noncompliance of a number of member countries and for neglecting cutting and polishing centers which can be used as entry points for conflict diamonds into international markets.

KING, MARTIN LUTHER, JR. (1929–1968). American clergyman and civil rights leader. His philosophy of nonviolent resistance inspired by

Gandhi spearheaded mass protest campaigns which brought him worldwide attention and led to the adoption in 1964 of sweeping national legislation banning de jure discriminatory practices in the **United States**. *See also* RACIAL DISCRIMINATION.

KISSINGER, HENRY (1923–). Political scientist and diplomat who served as national security adviser to U.S. President Richard Nixon (1969–73) and secretary of state to both Nixon and President Gerald Ford (1973–77). In these capacities, he played an instrumental role in the rapprochement between the **United States** and the People's Republic of China and the termination of the **Vietnam War**. As a *realpolitik* advocate in the **Cold War**, Kissinger opposed left-wing governments and endeavored to maintain friendly relations with right-wing military regimes. In this context, he has become the focal point of criticism by human rights groups who have accused him of **war crimes** including the indiscriminate mass killing of civilians in the Vietnam War, collusion in mass murder in the **Bangladesh liberation war**, the planning of the overthrow of the Salvador Allende government in **Chile**, the killing of a senior Chilean military officer and enabling **genocide** in **Timor-Leste**. In 2001, he was summoned to testify by French and Argentinian judges making separate investigations into his possible involvement in **Operation Condor**. *See also* UNIVERSAL JURISDICTION.

KOREA, NORTH. *See* KIM IL SUNG.

KOREMATSU, FRED TOYOSABURO (1919–2005). In the wake of the Japanese attack on Pearl Harbor on 6 December 1941, there was widespread concern in the **United States** about yet another possible immediate attack against the West Coast. In March 1942, invoking "military necessity" and ostensibly to protect against possible sabotage and espionage, the administration of Franklin Delano Roosevelt authorized, with the approval of the U.S. Congress, the deportation of all American citizens of Japanese ancestry on the West Coast to "resettlement camps" and "havens of refuge" constructed by the government in desertic and remote areas of Arizona, Arkansas, California, Colorado, Utah and Wyoming. Fred Korematsu was one of the 120,000 Japanese Americans affected by the Roosevelt executive order. He refused to submit to the **deportation** orders, went into hiding and was eventually caught, tried and convicted in federal court. His case ended up in the U.S. Supreme Court which ruled in December 1944 that compulsory exclusion, though constitutionally suspicious, was justified under circumstances of "emergency and peril." A commission set up in 1980 by President Jimmy Carter to investigate the internment of Japanese Americans during **World War II** concluded that the deportation orders were the result of "race prejudice, war hysteria, and a failure of political leadership." In 1988, Congress formally apologized and granted personal compensation to each survivor detainee. *See also* APOLOGIES; PUBLIC EMERGENCIES.

KOSOVO. Former province of the Federal Republic of Yugoslavia (FRY), with a population comprising a majority of ethnic Albanians, which sought to gain its independence in the late 1990s. An armed insurgency launched in early 1996 provoked a violent response of Serbian police and Yugoslav military, which in turn led to the launching of an air campaign by the **North Atlantic Treaty Organization** (NATO) on the FRY. The NATO intervention was justified as a **humanitarian intervention**. But it has remained controversial because it did not receive the authorization of the **United Nations Security Council**. A Russian-sponsored resolution affirming that NATO's "unilateral use of force constitutes a flagrant violation of the **United Nations Charter**" failed to win adoption. Estimates of the war casualties range from 12,000 to over 13,000 deaths, with a significant number of **war crimes** and **crimes against humanity** committed by all sides in the conflict.

The province was administered by the **United Nations Interim Administration Mission in Kosovo** (UNMIK) until 2008, when it unilaterally proclaimed its independence. The status of its Serbian minority remains unresolved, and the new country has not received universal recognition. In the same year, in its **concluding observations** on a report submitted by UNMIK, the **United Nations Committee on Economic, Social and Cultural Rights** opined that the armed conflict in 1998–99 and the uncertainty about the final status of Kosovo have since 1999 adversely affected the enjoyment in Kosovo of the rights recognized in the **International Covenant on Economic, Social and Cultural Rights**. In 2010, at the request of Serbia, the **International Court of Justice** issued an advisory opinion determining that Kosovo's declaration of independence did not violate international law. *See also* INDEPENDENT INTERNATIONAL COMMISSION ON KOSOVO; INTERNATIONAL CRIMINAL TRIBUNAL FOR THE FORMER YUGOSLAVIA; MILOSEVIC, SLOBODAN; NO-FLY ZONE.

KURDISH HUMAN RIGHTS PROJECT (KHR). London-based **non-governmental organization** focusing its work on protecting the human rights of the Kurdish **minorities** in **Iran**, Iraq, **Syria** and **Turkey** through **advocacy** and training, **fact finding** and trial observation missions and **research**. Central to the work of KHR is its strategic use of **litigation** in the **European Court of Human Rights** where it brings cases on behalf of victims and survivors of **extra-judicial executions, forced disappearances,**

torture, unfair trials, censorship and other abuses and **violations of human rights**. *See also* KURDISH QUESTION.

KURDISH QUESTION. There are probably about 25 to 35 million Kurds worldwide. They share a common language and are mostly Sunni Muslims. They are the largest ethnic group without a state of their own. In the wake of U.S. President **Woodrow Wilson**'s call for **self-determination**, the question of the creation of a Kurdish state did come up at the 1919 Paris Peace Conference. A Kurdish delegation was present, but its claims for statehood quickly fell into oblivion as a result of discord among the victorious Allies and, above all, the rise of Turkish nationalism under the leadership of Mustafa Kemal Ataturk. Consequently, about 15 million Kurds now live in **Turkey**, 6 million in **Iran**, 5 million in Iraq and up to 1.5 million in **Syria**. Close to a million Kurds live in Europe, half of them in Germany.

Kurdish national aspirations have become of major political and human rights issue in Turkey and to a lesser extent in Syria and Iran. In the late 1980s, in the course of the Iran-Iraq war, the Kurdish minority in Iraq was the target of vicious military campaigns organized by the **Saddam Hussein** regime. Following the 1991 Gulf War, the Kurdish areas of Northern Iraq became virtually independent as they were protected from further attacks by a **no-fly zone** patrolled by the **United States** and Great Britain. The political status of the region within the new Iraqi state has evolved into a major contentious issue. More recently, the Kurds in northern Syria have gained a degree of autonomy. *See also* AL-ANFAL CAMPAIGN; KURDISH HUMAN RIGHTS PROJECT; MINORITIES; SUPREME IRAQI CRIMINAL TRIBUNAL.

L

LABOR. *See* LEAGUE OF NATIONS; WORK, RIGHT TO.

LABOR BONDAGE. According to **Anti-Slavery International**, "a person enters debt bondage when their labor is demanded as a means of repayment of a loan or of money given in advance. Usually, people are tricked or trapped into working for no pay or very little pay (in return for such a loan), in conditions which violate their human rights. Invariably, the value of the work done by a bonded laborer is greater that the original sum of money borrowed or advanced." Defined as such, debt bondage is prohibited by the **United Nations** 1956 Supplementary **Convention on the Abolition of Slavery**. But it has a long history extending back to the widespread practice of indenture service of European settlers arriving in Colonial America. Discrimination, prejudice, local customs, the absence of credit security or bankruptcy mechanisms or formal title to the land all combine to perpetuate the persistence of the phenomenon. Debt bondage may be legally banned but it continues to be very common in such countries as **Bolivia**, **Brazil**, China, **Peru**, the **Philippines**, Pakistan and India. A conservative estimate by Anti-Slavery International places the total number of bonded workers in the world in the range of 10 to 20 million. *See also* DOMESTIC WORKERS; HUMAN TRAFFICKING.

LABOR CAMPS. Detention facilities for convicted criminals but also political prisoners, people from conquered or occupied territories, members of persecuted minorities and prisoners of war who are forced to engage in labor. As such, labor camps are prisons as well as particular modern forms of **slavery**. Labor camps were an established feature of Czarist Russia's judicial system. Other notorious historical instances include the **Gulag** camps run by the Soviet Union until their official closing in 1960, the use of 12 million forced laborers by Nazi Germany with the complicity of such major companies as Daimler, Deutsche Bank, Siemens, Volkswagen, Krupp, BASF and BMW, the enslavement of 10 million Chinese workers in Manchukuo and North China and 4 to 10 million "manual laborers" in South East Asia by the Japanese military. The death rate in Japanese wartime labor camps could be as high 80 percent.

At the end of **World War II**, some 4 million German prisoners of war were used by the victorious Allies as "reparation labor." More recently, the Khmer Rouge in **Democratic Kampuchea** relied on labor camps to resettle urban populations into rural areas. Under the statute of the **International Criminal Court**, enslavement, **deportation** or forcible transfers of population, imprisonment and other severe deprivation of physical liberty in violation of fundamental rules of international law are likewise considered **crimes against humanity**.

LAND RIGHTS. Land rights, particularly in developing countries, are inextricably linked with a host of human rights and, in particular, the right to **food**. In many instances, the right to land is also bound with a community's identity, its livelihood and thus its very survival. Feudal exploitation, **colonization** and the increasing control of the state over natural resources, encroachment by private and commercial interests and the process of **globalization** have over time collided with the right to ancestral domain, collective ownership of land, customary land rights and the concept of "time immemorial" possession, thus compounding the problem and explaining why access to land and landlessness frequently trigger social unrest and political conflicts. National legal systems generally try to reconcile the right of private ownership with a growing concern—still more rhetorical than real—for access, use, possession and occupation of land.

At the international level, land rights have only recently been addressed from a human rights perspective. A number of international human rights instruments acknowledge the right to own property, notably the **Universal Declaration of Human Rights** (Art. 17), the First Protocol to the **European Convention for the Protection of Human Rights and Fundamental Freedoms**, the **American Convention on Human Rights** (Art. 21), and the **African Charter on Human and People's Rights** (Art. 14). Land rights matters have been more directly addressed in a number of **soft law** instruments, especially the **Declaration on Social Progress and Development** adopted by the **United Nations General Assembly** in 1969, which recognizes the social function of property, including land, and calls for forms of land ownership that ensure equal rights to property for all. Also relevant here is a 1962 **International Labour Organization** Convention on Social Policy which covers measures to improve the standard of living for agricultural producers, including control of the alienation of land to nonagriculturalists, regard for customary land rights and the supervision of tenancy arrangements. The 1989 **ILO Convention Concerning Indigenous**

and Tribal Peoples in Independent Countries, a key instrument in the evolution of concepts of land rights in international law, recognizes the special relationship between **indigenous peoples** and their lands, requires states to adopt special measures of protection on their behalf, provides safeguards against the arbitrary removal of indigenous people from their traditional land, with procedural guarantees and includes other provisions related to the transmission of land rights and respect for customary procedures. The **United Nations Convention on the Elimination of All Forms of Discrimination against Women** focuses on and recognizes women's land rights and calls states parties "to take all appropriate measures to eliminate discrimination against women in rural areas in order to ensure, on the basis of **equality** of men and women, that they participate in and benefit from rural development and, in particular . . . ensure to such women the right . . . to have access to agricultural credit and loans, marketing facilities, appropriate technology and equal treatment in land and **agrarian reform** as well as in land resettlement schemes" (Art. 14).

Land rights activists have focused their efforts on legal change and reform and exposing or opposing the negative effects of dam construction, "land grabs" by foreign governments or companies and plantations and mining projects that entail large-scale displacement or dispossession. Such campaigns have underlined the importance of a broad range of larger (and often intractable issues) including the development priorities of governments, official **corruption** and the role of **non-state actors** such as the World Bank, the **International Monetary Fund** and **transnational corporations**. Ultimately, questions of land rights hinge on considerations of non-**discrimination** and **reparative justice**. A case in point is South Africa, which has acknowledged its history of conquest and dispossession, of forced removal and racially skewed land distribution by providing in its constitution a right to **redress** and restitution. *See also* HABITAT INTERNATIONAL COALITION; INTERNATIONAL WORK GROUP FOR INDIGENOUS AFFAIRS.

LATIN AMERICA. *See* AMERICAN CONVENTION ON HUMAN RIGHTS; AMERICAN DECLARATION OF THE RIGHTS AND DUTIES OF MAN; BORDABERRY, JUAN MARIA; BRAZIL; CARTAGENA DECLARATION ON REFUGEES; CHILE; CHOIKE; COBO, JOSE MARTINEZ; COLOMBIA; CUBA; DECLARATION OF THE RIGHTS AND DUTIES OF MAN; DERECHOS HUMAN RIGHTS; "DIRTY WAR"; EQUIPO NIZKOR; GUANTANAMO BAY DETENTION CAMP; GUATEMALA; HONDURAS; INTER-AMERICAN CHILDREN INSTITUTE; INTER-AMERICAN COMMISSION OF WOMEN; INTER-AMERICAN COMMISSION ON HUMAN RIGHTS; INTER-AMERICAN

CONVENTION ON FORCED DISAPPEARANCES OF PERSONS; INTER-AMERICAN CONVENTION ON THE ELIMINATION OF ALL FORMS OF DISCRIMINATION AGAINST PERSONS WITH DISABILITIES; INTER-AMERICAN CONVENTION ON THE PREVENTION, PUNISHMENT AND ERADICATION OF VIOLENCE AGAINST WOMEN; INTER-AMERICAN CONVENTION TO PREVENT AND PUNISH TORTURE; INTER-AMERICAN COURT OF HUMAN RIGHTS; INTER-AMERICAN DECLARATION ON FREEDOM OF EXPRESSION; INTER-AMERICAN INDIAN INSTITUTE; INTER-AMERICAN INSTITUTE OF HUMAN RIGHTS; ORGANIZATION OF AMERICAN STATES; PARAGUAY; PEONAGE SYSTEM; UNITED NATIONS OBSERVER GROUP IN EL SALVADOR; URUGUAY; VIDELA, JORGE RAFAEL.

LAWS OF WAR. Body of **international law** delineating the acceptable justifications for engaging in war and setting limits on the conduct of warfare.

See also AGGRESSION; ARMED CONFLICT; CARPET BOMBING; CIVILIANS, PROTECTION OF; CONCENTRATION CAMPS; CRIMES AGAINST PEACE; DRONES; ETHNIC CLEANSING; EXTRA-JUDICIAL EXECUTIONS; GENDER-BASED VIOLENCE; GENEVA CONVENTIONS; HUMAN EXPERIMENTATION; INTERNATIONAL HUMANITARIAN LAW; *JUS AD BELLUM/JUS IN BELLO*; JUST WAR; LEIPZIG WAR TRIALS; MASSACRES; NON-DEROGABLE RIGHTS; OCCUPATION; PRECAUTION, PRINCIPLE OF; PROPORTIONALITY; PROTECTED PERSONS; SAFE ZONES; WAR CRIMES.

LAWYERS COMMITTEE FOR HUMAN RIGHTS. *See* HUMAN RIGHTS FIRST.

LEAGUE OF ARAB STATES (LAS). Informally named the Arab League, this regional organization was created on 1945 by seven Arab states enjoying independence at the time (**Egypt**, Iraq, Lebanon, **Saudi Arabia**, **Syria**, Jordan, Yemen). Its membership, which is based on culture rather than geographical proximity, has expanded to 22 members: **Algeria** (which joined in 1962), Bahrain (1971), Comoros (1993), Djibouti (1977), Kuwait (1961), Libya (1953), Mauritania (1973), Morocco (1958), Oman (1971), Qatar (1971), Somalia (1974), Southern Yemen (1967), Sudan (1956), Tunisia (1958), and the United Arab Emirates (1971). The Palestine Liberation Organization was admitted in 1976.

Designed to "draw closer the relations between member States and co-ordinate collaboration between them, to safeguard their independence and sovereignty, and to consider in a general way the affairs and interests of the

Arab countries," the League has spawned a number of related specialized agencies that have brought a degree of functional cooperation among its member states in such matters as civil aviation, social and economic development, educational, cultural, and scientific affairs. Inter-Arab rivalries and conflicts and conflicting **Cold War** allegiances, however, have precluded further economic integration and stymied the League's political, military and collective security objectives.

None of the members of the Arab League can be said to have a stellar human rights record and, notwithstanding its common public stands and pronouncements on behalf of Palestinian rights (particularly, their right to **self-determination**), the organization has by and large remained an ineffective body for the promotion and protection of international human rights. The constituting Charter of the League makes no mention of human rights. The human rights institutions set up within the League such as the Permanent Arab Commission of Human Rights are essentially powerless. On the occasion of its 50th anniversary, the League endorsed an **Arab Charter on Human Rights** which was subsequently revised in 2003. But the draft Charter recognizes human rights only within the context of cultural-, religious- or civilization-based specificities and it is still not in force, having yet to receive a sufficient number of ratifications. On the whole, the collective position of the League on international human rights issues has been influenced by the priority that it has consistently given to the principles of **state sovereignty** and non-interference. It is on these grounds that the Arab League denounced what it called biased campaigns launched by some international non-governmental human rights organizations against Algeria when the country was engulfed in its 1992–98 civil war. In the same spirit, the League has counseled international patience and provided diplomatic support to Sudan in the **Darfur** crisis while some of its members sitting for the **United Nations Security Council** (voting in the name of Arab countries) either sought to water down or to derail forceful Council resolutions. *See also* PERMANENT ARAB COMMISSION ON HUMAN RIGHTS.

LEAGUE OF NATIONS. International organization set up in the wake of World War I for the broad purpose of promoting international cooperation and achieving peace and security. Its Covenant, the League's founding document, was signed in June 1919 and it has as many as 58 members but, despite the efforts of **Woodrow Wilson**, the **United States** did not join the organization. The words "human rights" do not appear in the Covenant but a number of principles are explicitly or implicitly stated including the right of **self-determination**, "freedom of conscience and religion, subject on to the maintenance of public order and morals," "the prohibition of abuses

408 • LEIPZIG WAR TRIALS

such as the **slave trade**, the arms traffic and the liquor traffic," "fair and human conditions of labor for men, women and children," the supervision of **treaties** to suppress "traffic in women and children, and the traffic in opium and other dangerous drugs," the improvement of **health**, the prevention of disease and the mitigation of suffering." The League played a limited yet path-breaking role in the prohibition of **slavery**, the protection of religious and linguistic **minorities** and the promotion of labor rights. The **mandates** system put in place by the League introduced the novel idea that colonial powers were accountable for their treatment of indigenous populations in their colonial possessions. The **state reporting** procedures that it also instituted for colonial powers foreshadow those established by the **United Nations** and **United Nations treaty bodies**. *See also* CHILDREN TRAFFICKING; DECLARATION OF THE RIGHTS OF THE CHILD; HUMAN TRAFFICKING; INTERNATIONAL COUNCIL OF WOMEN; INTERNATIONAL CRIME CONGRESSES; INTERNATIONAL LABOUR ORGANIZATION; OFFICE INTERNATIONAL NANSEN POUR LES REFUGIÉS; REFUGEES; UNITED NATIONS TRUSTEESHIP SYSTEM; WORLD WAR I PEACE TREATIES.

LEIPZIG WAR TRIALS (1920–1922). On 25 January 1919, the victorious Allies set up a Commission to study the violations of **international law** chargeable to Germany and its allies. The Commission's majority report declared that most **war crimes** could be tried in military tribunals or ordinary criminal courts of the injured nations. At the same time, they declared that some charges (for example, offenses against civilians and soldiers of the Allied nations) could be tried before an international tribunal whose judges would be appointed by the Allied government. This "High Tribunal" could determine its own procedures and apply "the principles of the law of nations as they result from the usages established among civilized peoples, from the laws of humanity and from the dictates of public conscience." The recommendations of the Commission were not adopted by the Peace Conference as the American and Japanese delegations objected that there was no precedent in state practice for the creation of an international criminal court and failure to prevent violations of the laws and customs of war did not, in any event, constitute a criminal act. The Treaty of Versailles thus made no provision for an international criminal court, but Article 227 does call for the creation of a "special tribunal" composed of five judges appointed by the **United States**, Great Britain, France, Italy, and Japan to try the former Kaiser who had taken refuge in Holland.

Under Article 228 of the Versailles Treaty, the German government recognized the right of the Allies "to bring before military tribunals persons accused of having committed acts in violation of the laws and customs of war." The Allies submitted to the German government a list of 900 alleged war criminals which included ex-Chancellor Theobald von Bethmann Hollweg and other high-placed offenders accused of murder, arson, theft, pillage, wanton destruction, bombardment of open towns, sinking of hospital ships without warning and similar offenses. Altogether only 12 men were tried by the Criminal Senate of the German Imperial Court of Justice, most of them were on minor charges leading to light and desultory punitive sentences. *See also* KAISER WILHELM II; WORLD WAR I PEACE TREATIES.

LEMAY, CURTIS (1906–1990). United States air force general who participated in air combat operations against Germany during **World War II**. Transferred to the Pacific in July 1944, he directed all strategic air operations against Japan. Concluding that the techniques and tactics of daylight, high altitude, precision bombing, developed for use in Europe against the Luftwaffe were unsuited in the Pacific theater, LeMay switched to massive low-altitude, nighttime attacks with incendiary clusters, magnesium bombs, white phosphorus bombs and napalm on Japanese cities and military targets. Asked later about the morality of this brutal campaign, LeMay opined that if the United States had lost the war, he would have been tried as a war criminal. *See also* WAR CRIMES.

LEMKIN, RAPHAEL (1900–1959). International legal scholar of Polish origin. Born of Jewish parents, he and his brother were the only members of his family to survive the **Holocaust** and he had already been particularly disturbed by the slaughter of Armenians by Turks during World War I. Wounded while fighting the Nazis outside Warsaw, Lemkin eventually escaped to Sweden in 1940. There he compiled a seminal analysis of the legal instruments that had been used by the Nazis to systematically kill entire groups of people and coined the term of **genocide**. His work was used as a basis for determining the charges that were brought against Nazi leaders at the **International Military Tribunal for the Prosecution and Punishment of Major War Criminals of the European Axis** where he served as legal adviser to the U.S. chief prosecutor. Lemkin subsequently played a key role in the drafting, adoption and ratification of the 1948 **United Nations Convention on the Punishment and Prevention of the Crime of Genocide** which established genocide as a crime under **international law** in war and peace times. *See also* ARMENIAN GENOCIDE.

LENIN, VLADIMIR (1870–1924). Russian revolutionary, leader of the Communist Party who headed the Soviet state from 1917 when he seized power from the enfeebled government to his death in 1924. He withdrew Russia from World War I, muzzled opposition parties, censored the press, set up a secret service, formed the Red Army and requisitioned grain from the peasantry in order to fight secessionist and counterrevolutionary insurgencies and foreign interventions. The six-year-long civil war claimed 2 million combat fatalities, an equal number of deaths from epidemics and 5 million from famine, a death toll that exceeded Russian losses during World War I. To rebuild the country's industry and agriculture, Lenin initiated the short-lived New Economic Policy which was reversed by **Josef Stalin**'s collectivization of the economy. *See also* GULAG.

LESBIAN, GAY, BISEXUAL, AND TRANSGENDER. *See* SEXUAL ORIENTATION.

LIBERALISM. Scholarly approach to the study of international relations stressing that human rights are an extension of natural and inalienable individual and personal rights which it pertains to states to protect. State-embedded institutions and regimes (i.e., informal rules) at the national and international levels are key instruments for protecting and **monitoring** rights. So defined, liberalism is closely associated with the promotion of **democracy** and good governance. Elaborating on these premises, a number of observers have recently advanced the idea that if states fail to protect human rights, they may forfeit their sovereignty. *See also* LIMITED GOVERNMENT; "RESPONSIBILITY TO PROTECT"; RULE OF LAW; STATE SOVEREIGNTY.

LIBERTY, RIGHT TO. Article 3 of the **Universal Declaration of Human Rights** asserts that "everyone has the right to life, liberty and **security** of person." The right is enshrined in all major human rights instruments, including the **International Covenant on Civil and Political Rights** (Art. 8), the **European Convention for the Protection of Human Rights and Fundamental Freedoms** (Art. 4), the **American Convention on Human Rights** (Art. 6) and the **African Charter on Human and People's Rights** (Art. 5). **Habeas corpus** is an integral part of the right to liberty, and human rights laws essentially seek to establish procedural guarantees and minimum standards for individuals who are deprived of their liberty against arbitrary state actions. *See also* ARBITRARY DETENTION; COUNTERTERRORISM; FORCED DISAPPEARANCES; FORCED LABOR; HUMAN TRAFFICKING; PUBLIC EMERGENCIES; SLAVERY.

LIBERIA. Formally founded in 1847 by former slaves from the **United States**, Liberia was one of the founding members of the **United Nations**. It began to modernize in the 1940s but tensions between the American and Liberian leadership and native ethnic groups triggered in 1980 the beginning of political and economic instability and two civil wars which left a quarter of a million dead, displaced a million others in neighboring countries and spawned countless atrocities and human rights violations. A peace deal achieved in 1995 led to the election of **Charles Taylor** as president in 1997. During Taylor's tenure, Liberia became known for its use of blood diamonds and illegal timber to fund the **Sierra Leone civil war**. Taylor was overthrown in 2003 and under yet another peace agreement among the wearying parties, the **United Nations Security Council** authorized the dispatch of a peacekeeping force to provide security and monitor the peace accord. The same year an interim government took over and presidential elections were held in 2005, leading to the election of Ellen Johnson Sirleaf, the first female president in the African continent. In 2006, the government set up a **truth and reconciliation commission** to address crimes committed during the civil war. Sirleaf was reelected in 2011. She was awarded the 2011 **Nobel Peace Prize** with two other women "for their non-violent struggle for the safety of women and for women's rights to full participation in peace-building." *See also* SPECIAL COURT FOR SIERRA LEONE; UNITED NATIONS OBSERVER MISSION IN LIBERIA.

LIBYA. A rare case of decolonization successfully brokered by the **United Nations**, Libya became independent in 1951. This Italian colony was initially ruled by a monarchy until it was overthrown by a military coup in 1969 engineered by Colonel Muammar Gaddafi. The new regime did make significant strides in promoting the economic and social development of the country and it had all the trapping of a direct "people's democracy." Its human rights record, however, was repeatedly criticized by United Nations bodies, notably the **United Nations Human Rights Council** (HRC) and the **United Nations Committee on the Elimination of All Forms of Racial Discrimination** as well as governments and **non-governmental organizations**. Persisting concerns were voiced about restrictions on **freedom of expression**, assembly, **association** and **religion**, arbitrary arrests, **forced disappearances**, prisons conditions, allegations of **torture**, **discrimination** against **minorities** and foreign workers. Simmering discontent, fueled by regime change in Tunisia and **Egypt**, morphed into a full-fledged civil war which led to the demise of the regime and the death of Colonel Gaddafi. The violence of the conflict and the use of military and **mercenaries**

against civilians prompted condemnations by the **League of Arab States** and the **African Union**. Libya was suspended from membership in the HRC by a unanimous vote of the **United Nations General Assembly**. In a parallel unprecedented move, the **United Nations Security Council** invoked the principle of the **responsibility to protect**, imposed strict targeted sanctions on Libya, authorized the use of force by the **North Atlantic Treaty Organization** and referred members of the Gaddafi regime to the **International Criminal Court** for investigation into allegations of brutalities against civilians. Libya is currently in a phase of political transition. *See also* NO-FLY ZONE; SAFE ZONES.

LIFE, RIGHT TO. Undoubtedly the most fundamental of human rights in the sense that all rights depend on the pre-existence of life. As the **United Nations Human Rights Committee** (UN-HRCttee) put it in one of its **General Comments**, it is "the supreme right from which no derogation is permitted even in time of **public emergency**." The right to life is enshrined in all major human rights instruments, including the **Universal Declaration of Human Rights** (Art. 3), the **International Covenant on Civil and Political Rights** (Art. 6), the **European Convention on the Protection of Human Rights and Fundamental Freedoms** (Art. 2), the **African Charter on Human and People's Rights** (Art. 4) and the founding document of the **Commonwealth of Independent States** (Art. 2). All of these instruments place a positive obligation on the state to protect life through the maintenance of law and order and the shielding of individuals against criminal behavior. States also have an obligation to fully investigate any deprivation of life.

Both the **Inter-American Court of Human Rights** and the **European Court of Human Rights** (ECtHR) have found a number of governments to be in violation of the right to life for failing to investigate individuals who were in their custody, the Court's reasoning being that lack of information over a period of years could create a reasonable presumption that detainees had been executed without proper trial and their bodies concealed. Likewise, the UN-HRCttee and the ECtHR have recognized the right of states to use lethal force but only under narrowly defined circumstances, such as the need to prevent a greater loss of life or to quell a riot or insurrection. In situations of international **armed conflicts**, non-combatants and wounded members of the armed services are protected by the **Geneva Conventions**. International law proscribes the use of **chemical and biological weapons** and landmines. Mass exterminations of sections of the population are gross violations of the right to life and may constitute the international crime of **genocide**.

See also ABORTION; AMERICAN CONVENTION ON HUMAN RIGHTS; CAPITAL PUNISHMENT; CLONING, HUMAN; EUTHAN-

ASIA; EXTRA-JUDICIAL EXECUTIONS; FEMICIDE; FORCED DISAPPEARANCES; INFANTICIDE; NON-DEROGABLE RIGHTS; NUCLEAR WEAPONS; SECURITY, RIGHT TO; UNIVERSAL DECLARATION ON BIOETHICS AND HUMAN RIGHTS.

LIMBURG PRINCIPLES ON THE IMPLEMENTATION OF THE INTERNATIONAL COVENANT ON ECONOMIC, SOCIAL AND CULTURAL RIGHTS (1986). Interpretative guidelines adopted by a group of legal experts at a meeting sponsored by the **International Commission of Jurists** and the Universities of Maastricht and Cincinnati seeking to clarify the nature and scope of state obligations under the **International Covenant on Economic, Social and Cultural Rights** (ICESCR). Overall, the document seeks to demonstrate that the ICESCR is sufficiently concrete to be implemented. It also provides criteria about what constitute **violations** and abuses of economic, social and cultural rights. The Principles also blur the distinction between **first-** and **second-generation rights**, suggesting instead that both categories of rights call upon states to "respect," "protect" and "fulfill" rights. By "respect," the authors of the draft mean that a state must prevent violations of economic, social and cultural rights by third parties. "Protecting" and "fulfilling" require states to take appropriate measures toward the full realization of economic, social and cultural rights. Failure to do so, however, would constitute a violation.

LIMITED GOVERNMENT. One of the basic principles underpinning the practice of human rights, the notion of limited government entails the idea that government power should be restrained by the **rule of law** and organized in such a manner as to promote and preserve individual rights. *See also* DEMOCRACY; GOVERNANCE; LIBERALISM; NATURAL RIGHTS.

LISBON TREATY (2009). Treaty signed by the members of the **European Union** in 2007 amending the 1992 Maastricht Treaty on European Union and the 1957 Treaty establishing the European Community. The Lisbon Treaty modifies some of the decision-making procedures and institutions of the European Union, strengthening in particular the powers of the **European Parliament**. It also incorporates the **European Charter of Fundamental Rights of the European Union**, thus making it legally binding. In addition, the treaty makes specific references to the respect of human **dignity**, human rights and equality, includes a horizontal clause on non-**discrimination** stating that the European Union should combat discrimination in the definition and implementation of all its policies and activities as well as a social clause requiring the Union to take account of employment, social protection and the fight against social exclusion in the development and implementation of its policies. *See also* AMSTERDAM TREATY.

LITIGATION. Legal method of settling human rights issues through national or international courts of law which are suitably empowered to hear the case. The process involves individuals—or **non-governmental organizations** acting on their behalf—bringing charges of **violations of human rights** before international courts of law against their state authorities and seeking declaratory judgments imposing a temporary or permanent injunction to prevent deleterious acts, enforcing a right, providing **remedies** or awarding damages. Access to international courts is subject to more or less rigorous conditions of **admissibility**. One of these conditions, shared by all human rights regimes, is for the plaintiff to have exhausted all available means of **redress** in his or her home state.

See also AFRICAN COMMISSION ON HUMAN AND PEOPLE'S RIGHTS; AFRICAN COURT ON HUMAN AND PEOPLE'S RIGHTS; ARAB ORGANIZATION FOR HUMAN RIGHTS; ARTICLE 19, THE INTERNATIONAL CENTRE AGAINST CENSORSHIP; CENTER FOR CONSTITUTIONAL RIGHTS; CENTER FOR GENDER AND REFUGEE STUDIES; CENTER FOR HUMAN RIGHTS AND THE ENVIRONMENT; CENTER FOR JUSTICE AND INTERNATIONAL LAW; CENTER FOR REPRODUCTIVE RIGHTS; CENTRE ON HOUSING RIGHTS AND EVICTIONS; CHILD RIGHTS INFORMATION NETWORK; EAST AFRICAN COURT OF JUSTICE; ECONOMIC COMMUNITY OF WEST AFRICAN STATES; EUROPEAN COURT OF HUMAN RIGHTS; EUROPEAN ROMA RIGHTS CENTER; GIRCA; GLOBAL RIGHTS; HUMAN RIGHTS FIRST; INSTITUTE FOR HUMAN RIGHTS AND DEVELOPMENT IN AFRICA; INTER-AMERICAN COMMISSION ON HUMAN RIGHTS; INTER-AMERICAN COURT OF HUMAN RIGHTS; INTERNATIONAL ASSOCIATION OF LAWYERS AGAINST NUCLEAR ARMS; INTERNATIONAL CENTRE FOR THE LEGAL PROTECTION OF HUMAN RIGHTS; INTERNATIONAL COMMISSION FOR LABOR RIGHTS; INTERNATIONAL FEDERATION FOR HUMAN RIGHTS; INTERNATIONAL NETWORK FOR ECONOMIC, SOCIAL AND CULTURAL RIGHTS; KURDISH HUMAN RIGHTS PROJECT; PALESTINIAN CENTRE FOR HUMAN RIGHTS; RIGHTS INTERNATIONAL.

LOBBYING. Attempts by individuals, organized groups, or corporations to influence directly or indirectly the outcomes of the public policymaking process. Targets of lobbying efforts may be members of national legislatures, regulatory agencies or judicial bodies or, at the international level, officials of international bodies or members of national delegations participating in international conferences. But the modalities of lobbying vary widely ranging from the provision of information to building personal and informal relationships with decision makers, to generating support through grassroots mobilization and media campaigns.

See also ADVOCACY; ARTICLE 19, THE INTERNATIONAL CENTRE AGAINST CENSORSHIP; ASIAN CENTER FOR HUMAN RIGHTS; CHILD RIGHTS INFORMATION NETWORK; INTER-AFRICAN COMMITTEE ON TRADITIONAL PRACTICES AFFECTING THE HEALTH OF WOMEN; INTERNATIONAL CAMPAIGN TO BAN LANDMINES; INTERNATIONAL CAMPAIGN TO END GENOCIDE; INTERNATIONAL WORK GROUP FOR INDIGENOUS AFFAIRS; OXFAM INTERNATIONAL; SHADOW REPORTS; SPIRAL MODEL OF HUMAN RIGHTS CHANGE; WOMEN'S INTERNATIONAL LEAGUE FOR PEACE AND FREEDOM.

LORD'S RESISTANCE ARMY (LRA). Armed group formed in 1987 in the Acholi ethnic region of Northern **Uganda** in the context of the larger armed resistance of some Acholi people against the central government who felt that they were marginalized and discriminated. The group comprises less that 500 combatants, but it also operates in several adjacent states (South Sudan, **Democratic Republic of the Congo** and Central African Republic) with practices that include the recruitment of children, rapes, killing and maiming, and sexual slavery. In 2005, the **International Criminal Court** issued a warrant for the arrest of its leader, Joseph Kony, and four other LRA commanders, but they have not, to date, been captured or brought to trial.

LOVELACE V. CANADA **(1981).** International precedent-setting ruling of the **United Nations Human Rights Committee**. Acting on an individual **complaint** procedure established by the Optional Protocol to the **International Covenant on Civil and Political Rights**, the Committee determined that Canada's Indian Act provision which denied women who were married to non-Indian spouses equal access to, and enjoyment of, reserved lands (and not vice versa) was discriminatory on the basis of sex. *See also* CULTURAL RIGHTS; INDIGENOUS PEOPLES.

LUMUMBA, PATRICE (1925–1961). Congolese nationalist leader who helped win the independence of the Republic of the Congo from Belgium in June 1960. Elected prime minister, his government was within weeks deposed in a coup. In the political turmoil that engulfed the country (the president dismissed his prime minister, the province of Katanga sought to secede and the Congolese army under **Mobutu Sese Seko** intervened), Lumumba was imprisoned and murdered under circumstances suggesting that his assassination had been supported or condoned by the governments of the **United States** and Belgium. *See also* IMPUNITY.

LUSTRATION. Term derived from Latin meaning purification rituals referring to a form of **transitional justice** implemented by the European governments of countries emerging from communist rule at the end of the **Cold War**. The objectives of the practice, which have been utilized in the Czech Republic, Slovakia, Hungary, Macedonia, Albania, Bulgaria, the Baltic States (Lithuania, Latvia, and Estonia), Germany, Poland, and Romania, were to deal with past human rights abuses or injustices which had occurred under communist or to regulate the participation of former communists in the civil service or political positions of successor states.

M

MACHEL, GRAÇA (1945–). Mozambican government official and tireless advocate of women and children's rights of Mozambican nationality. She was the United Nations–appointed expert in charge of the groundbreaking 1996 United Nations Report on the Impact of Armed Conflict on Children, which drew attention to the plight of children in civil wars. In 1995, she was awarded the **Nansen** Medal in recognition of her humanitarian work for **refugee** children.

MAIL-ORDER BRIDES. Practice which can be traced back to women who in the 18th and 19th centuries moved to the **United States** by listing themselves in catalogs and were selected by men for marriage. Nowadays, women meet their spouses through the use of catalogs, agencies, advertisements and the **Internet**. Marriage agencies and mail-order bride publications are legal in almost all countries. To the extent that mail-order brides entail the connecting of financially secure men and women from impoverished countries, it may lead to abusive situations and conditions of involuntary servitude. *See also* SEX TRAFFICKING.

MALIK, CHARLES HABIB (1906–1987). Lebanese statesman and educator who represented his country at the 1945 San Francisco Conference. He subsequently served as a rapporteur for the **United Nations Commission on Human Rights** between 1947 and 1950, after which he succeeded **Eleanor Roosevelt** as chairman of the Commission. He remained in that post and was ambassador to the **United States** and the **United Nations** until 1955. Malik is recognized as one of the driving forces behind the shaping of the **Universal Declaration of Human Rights**. His natural law views are directly visible in Article 16, which refers to the family as "the natural and fundamental group unit of society."

MANDAT INTERNATIONAL. International **non-governmental organization** (NGO) in consultative status with the **United Nations**. Also known as the International Cooperation Foundation, Mandat International is based in Geneva and focuses its activities on facilitating the participation of NGO representatives in international conferences and meetings. It carries out educational programs, manages a documentation center and maintains several multilingual information websites with legal research engines on **international human rights** and **humanitarian law**. *See also* INTERNET.

MANDATES. System put in place by the Covenant of the **League of Nations** whereby territories formerly held by Germany and the Ottoman Empire were parceled out among the victors subject to the League's supervision. The Covenant stipulated that certain "advanced nations" serving as "Mandatories on behalf of the League" would promote the "well being and development" of the peoples living in these territories as a "sacred trust of civilization." These territories were all considered not to be ready for self-government but differed in terms of their political development and economic conditions and were thus grouped in three different categories. Class "mandate A" like Iraq and Palestine were considered to be "provisionally recognized subject to the rendering of administrative advice and assistance by a Mandatory until such time as they are able to stand alone." Class B territories (**Burundi,** Togo) were governed without explicit provision for independence. Class C mandates (Nauru, Samoa, and South West Africa) were "administered under the laws of the Mandatory as integral portions of its territory." A standing commission of the League received and examined annual reports by the Mandatory Powers and was empowered to receive individual petitions.

A forerunner of the **United Nations trusteeship system** under the **United Nations Charter**, the mandate system sought to reconcile the principle of **self-determination** proclaimed in President **Woodrow Wilson**'s Fourteen Points, with the political reality of the resolve of European powers to retain and aggrandize their colonial possessions. It may nevertheless be viewed as the first manifestation of the goal to bring colonial territories under some form of international supervision pending the abrogation of the colonial system. *See also* COLONIALISM; STATE REPORTING; SYRIA.

MANDELA, NELSON (1918–2013). South African anti-**apartheid** activist. Arrested in 1964 and convicted of sabotage, he served 27 years in prison, becoming the leading symbol of South Africa's oppressed black majority. Released in 1990, Mandela helped lead the peaceful transition toward multiracial democracy and majority rule in South Africa, for which he was awarded the **Nobel Peace Prize** in 1993 (jointly with President F. W. de Klerk). From 1994 to 1999, he served as South Africa's first democratically elected president.

MAO ZEDONG (1893–1976). Communist leader of the People's Republic of China (PRC) from the establishment of the PRC in 1949 to his death. He is credited by some for having reestablished central control over China after decades of turmoil and civil war. These achievements must be measured against the ghastly human toll of the sweeping land reform that he initiated after taking power, the class warfare against so-called capitalist elements which followed, the forced collectivization of peasants into communes, the "Great Leap Forward" which caused the world's largest recorded famine and the intra-party conflict known as the **Cultural Revolution**. The exact number of those who perished is not known. The "prudent" estimate offered by Professor Rudolph Rummel is 35 million.

MARCOS, FERDINAND (1917–1989). Dictator who ruled the **Philippines** from 1965 to 1986. His tenure was marked by widespread corruption, political repression and **violations of human rights**. A study by a U.S. military historian cites over 3,000 **extra-judicial executions**, 35,000 **torture** victims and 70,000 incarcerations during Marcos's 20-year rule. Public outrage triggered by suspicion of Marcos's involvement in the assassination in 1983 of Benigno Aquino, his primary political opponent, led to his removal from power and exile in Hawaii. After it was discovered that Marcos and his wife had moved billions of embezzled public funds to the **United States**, class action suits were brought before U.S. courts against Marcos and his daughter on charges of executions, torture and disappearances. A circuit court awarded $2 billion to the plaintiffs, but its ruling was reversed by the U.S. Supreme Court. *See also* IMPUNITY.

MARRY, RIGHT TO. The right to marry and the related right to found a **family** are recognized in numerous instruments: the **Universal Declaration of Human Rights** (Art. 16); the **International Covenant on Civil and Political Rights** (Art. 23); the **International Covenant on Economic, Social and Cultural Rights** (Art. 10); the **International Convention on the Elimination of All Forms of Racial Discrimination** (Art. 5); the **United Nations Convention on the Elimination of All Forms of Discrimination against Women** (Art. 16), the (Inter) **American Convention on Human Rights** (Art. 17), the **Arab Charter on Human Rights** (Art. 33) and the **European Convention for the Protection of Human Rights and Fundamental Freedoms** (Art. 12). All of these guarantee the right to marry on the basis of free consent thus reinforcing a 1962 **United Nations** Convention on Consent to Marriage, Minimum Age for Marriage and Registration for Marriages, which also calls upon states to specify a minimum age for marriage and establishes an appropriate system for registering marriages. This guarantee thus prohibits any form of forced marriage but also polygamy and discriminatory restrictions such as the prohibition of marriage between members of different ethnic groups. Controversies, however, have arisen in regard to criteria for marriage on such issues as age, dissolution of marriage, remarriage, and whether marriage is restricted to a union between a male and female. These matters are generally considered to fall within the competency of governments as long as there is no discrimination involved. So far, no right to divorce can be derived from the right to marry.

See also EUROPEAN CHARTER OF FUNDAMENTAL RIGHTS OF THE EUROPEAN UNION; MAIL-ORDER BRIDES; NATIONALITY, RIGHT TO; UNITED NATIONS CONVENTION ON CONSENT TO MARRIAGE, MINIMUM AGE FOR MARRIAGE AND REGISTRATION OF MARRIAGES; UNITED NATIONS CONVENTION ON THE NATIONALITY OF MARRIED WOMEN.

MASS GRAVES. Defined by a **United Nations special rapporteur** as locations where three or more bodies of victims of summary or arbitrary, or **extra-judicial executions** who did not die in combat or armed confrontations are buried. Mass graves are investigated for the purpose of identifying the dead for return to their families and documenting physical evidence that may be used in judicial proceedings against individual suspected of **genocide**, **war crimes** or **crimes against humanity**. Extensive forensic investigations were held in the wake of **World War II**. After a hiatus of four decades, investigations resumed in the mid-1990s, with exhumations carried out in countries emerging from conflict or civil wars such as **Afghanistan**, **Argentina**, Bangladesh, Cambodia, **Chile**, Congo, **El Salvador**, **Guatemala**, **Indonesia**, Iraq, Nepal, **Peru**, Sierra Leone, Sri Lanka and **Timor-Leste**.

MASSACRES. Incidents involving, in the language of the *Oxford English Dictionary*, "the indiscriminate and brutal slaughter of people or (less commonly) animals; carnage, butchery, slaughter in numbers." The victims are usually civilians or non-combatants, including men, women, children or elderly people. They may also involve disarmed soldiers. Notorious instances of massacres include the killing of Polish officers in **Katyn** in February 1940, hostage executions during **World War II**, the targeted murder of Bengalis during the **Bangladesh liberation war** in 1971, the **Sabra and Shatila massacre** in Lebanon (1982), in which more than 1,000 Palestinians were killed by the Christian Lebanese militia, the crushing of the **Tiananmen Square protests** in 1989 by the Chinese army and the 1995 killing of Bosnian men and boys in **Srebrenica** by Serbian paramilitary units. The list is by no means exhaustive as massacres are common in civil war situations. The use of the term is of course contested by one of the parties involved, usually the perpetrators whose aims range from the intent of subjugating what remains of a community or eliminating it altogether. *See also* GENOCIDE; MY LAI MASSACRE; NANKING MASSACRE; PASHA, TALAT; RWANDA.

MAU MAU UPRISING. Anti-colonialist insurgency that took place in Kenya from 1952 to 1960. The revolt which involved an anti-colonial group dominated by Kikuyus, the country's largest ethnic group, was squashed by the British military but arguably set the stage for Kenyan independence in 1963. The conflict was marked by extreme violence and has been described as "a story of atrocity and excess on both sides." Mau Mau militants committed numerous wanton killings and the British killed some 20,000 Mau Mau. Over a million Kikuyus were forcibly relocated in "protected villages" which were tantamount to **concentration camps**. More than 1,000 Mau Mau suspects were dealt with by **capital punishment**, more than double the number of individuals executed by the French during the **Algerian war of independence**.

MEASURING. *See* BENCHMARKING; EVENTS-BASED DATA; GENDER DEVELOPMENT INDEX; GENDER EMPOWERMENT MEASURE; INVESTIGATION; MONITORING OF HUMAN RIGHTS; STANDARD-BASED MEASURES; SURVEY DATA.

MEDECINS SANS FRONTIERES (MSF)/DOCTORS WITHOUT BORDERS. Independent international medical humanitarian organization delivering emergency aid to people affected by **armed conflicts**, epidemics and man-made disasters. Founded in 1971, Doctors without Borders fields close to 4,000 medical and non-medical professionals working along with over 20,000 locally hired staff. Although it is not, strictly speaking, a human rights advocate, Doctors without Borders combines the provision of medical care with a commitment to speaking out against the causes of human suffering. MSF volunteers thus raise their concerns of the people they assist with government officials, the **United Nations** and other international bodies, the general public and the media. MSF was awarded the **Nobel Peace Prize** in 1999 in recognition of the organization's pioneering humanitarian work.

MEDIA. *See* INSTITUTE FOR WAR AND PEACE REPORTING; INTERNATIONAL COUNCIL ON HUMAN RIGHTS POLICY; INTERNATIONAL FREEDOM OF EXPRESSION EXCHANGE; WOMEN BUILDING PEACE.

MEDIA CAMPAIGNS. *See* ADVOCACY.

MENCHU, RIGOBERTA (1959–). Guatemalan activist of Quiché-Mayan ethnic origins who won the **Nobel Peace Prize** in 1992 for her campaigns against **violations of human rights** committed by Guatemalan armed forces during the country's 1960–96 civil war. Since the end of the war, she has become a champion of the rights of **indigenous peoples** in **Guatemala** and around the world. She also tried, unsuccessfully, to have a number of Guatemalan political and military leaders tried by Spanish courts for **genocide** against the Mayan people in Guatemala. *See also* UNIVERSAL JURISDICTION.

MENDEZ, JUAN (1944–). Argentine human rights lawyer, advocate and educator who started his career as a labor lawyer defending workers imprisoned for political activity. Arrested in 1975 by the military regime, he was held in detention for 18 months and subjected to **torture**. He was released and expelled from Argentina after being declared a "prisoner of conscience" by **Amnesty International**. In the **United States**, where he gained **asylum**, he has worked for the Lawyers Committee for Civil Rights, **Human Rights Watch** and the **International Center for Transitional Justice** while teaching in various universities. From 2004 to 2007, he was special adviser on the prevention of genocide to UN Secretary-General **Kofi Annan**. In 2010, The **United Nations Human Rights Council** selected him for a three-year term as **special rapporteur** on torture and cruel, inhuman and degrading treatment or punishment. *See also* NORM ENTREPRENEURS.

MENGHISTU, HAILE MARIAM (1937–). Initially head of a collective military dictatorship which deposed Emperor Haile Selassie in 1974 and proclaimed a socialist state, Menghistu assumed full power as president of Ethiopia in 1977. His Marxist-style government implemented socialist reforms, instituting state controls over the economy and nationalizing landlords' and churches' property. From 1977 through early 1978, thousands of political opponents were tortured or killed in a purge called the Red Terror. Droughts and famine subsequently affected some 8 million people and left 1 million dead. During this period Ethiopia also fought against Eritrean secessionists as well as Somali rebels. Approximately 1.5 million Ethiopians are believed to have died under Menghistu's rule. Drought and famine, the implosion of the Soviet Union from which the regime received considerable economic and military assistance and ethnically driven insurgencies, eventually contributed to Menghistu's fall in 1991. Menghistu fled to Zimbabwe where he still resides. In 2006, an Ethiopian court convicted him of **genocide** in absentia and sentenced him to life imprisonment for his role in the Red Terror. *See also* IMPUNITY.

MERCENARY. According to Protocol I to the 1949 **Geneva Conventions** relating to the protection of victims of international conflict, a mercenary is an individual taking part in an **armed conflict** who is not a national or a party to the conflict and is "motivated to take part in the hostilities by the desire for private gain." Additional criteria of definition include the ideas that a mercenary is especially recruited locally or abroad to fight in an armed conflict and has not been sent by a state which is not party to the conflict on official duty as a member of its armed forces. Mercenaries are not entitled to prisoner-of-war status, although a state may grant them equivalent treatment if it so desires. Some countries prohibit their nationals from fighting in foreign wars unless they are under the control of their own national armed forces. International concern about mercenaries initially arose as a result of the participation of mercenaries in a number of decolonization struggles, notably in the Congo crisis (1960–65), the **Biafra** war (1967–70) and **Angola** in the 1970s and 1980s.

The involvement of mercenaries in internal African politics prompted the **United Nations General Assembly** to adopt in 1989 an International Convention against the Recruitment, Use, Financing and Training of Mercenaries. The Convention relies on but also broadens the Geneva Conventions' definition by stating that a mercenary is a non-national recruited to overthrow a government or otherwise undermine the constitutional order or territorial integrity of a state. Several legal observers, including a **United Nations special rapporteur** active from 1987 until 2005 when he was replaced by a working group tasked with examining the use of mercenaries "as a means of violating human rights and impeding the exercise of the right of peoples to **self-determination**," have opined that neither the Geneva protocol nor the UN Convention address adequately the use of **private military companies** by sovereign states. *See also* ARMED GROUPS; COLONIALISM; LIBYA.

MEXICO. *See* ECHEVERRIA, LUIS; MINORITIES.

MIDDLE EAST. *See* AL-ANFAL CAMPAIGN; AL HAQ; AL MEZAN CENTER FOR HUMAN RIGHTS; ALGERIA; ALGERIAN CIVIL WAR; ALGERIAN WAR OF INDEPENDENCE; ARAB ASSOCIATION FOR HUMAN RIGHTS; ARAB CHARTER ON HUMAN RIGHTS; ARAB COMMISSION ON HUMAN RIGHTS; ARAB ISRAELI CONFLICT; ARAB LAWYERS UNION; ARAB ORGANIZATION FOR HUMAN RIGHTS;

"ARAB SPRING"; CAIRO DECLARATION ON HUMAN RIGHTS IN ISLAM; CAIRO INSTITUTE FOR HUMAN RIGHTS STUDIES; EGYPT; ORGANIZATION OF ISLAMIC COOPERATION; PERMANENT ARAB COMMISSION ON HUMAN RIGHTS; UNITED NATIONS RELIEF AND WORKS AGENCY FOR PALESTINE REFUGEES IN THE NEAR EAST.

MIGRANT RIGHTS INTERNATIONAL (MRI). Advocacy **non-governmental organization** and global alliance bringing together **migrant workers** associations and migrant rights, human rights, trade unions and faith-based groups active at the local, national, regional or international level. Originally founded in 1994 and formally renamed MRI in 2000, its stated purpose is to promote the protection and fulfillment of the full range of human rights of migrants around the world and to foster unity and the inclusion of migrant voices at all levels of policy making.

MIGRANT SMUGGLING. The Protocol against the Smuggling of Migrants by Land, Sea and Air attached to the **United Nations Convention against Transnational Organized Crime** defines the smuggling of migrants as the procurement, for financial or other material benefit, of illegal entry of a person into a state of which that person is not a national or resident. It differs from **human trafficking** in that it involves the consent of the migrants and ends with their arrival at their destination. There are no data reliable enough to paint an accurate picture of the number of people smuggled each year, but it is widely admitted that migrant smuggling affects almost every country in the world and that it is an increasingly expanding, lucrative and deadly business. The Protocol requires states to criminalize the smuggling of migrants and the enabling of a person to remain in a country illegally, as well as aggravating circumstances that endanger lives or safety or entail inhuman or degrading treatment of migrants. Concrete steps taken by international organizations generally focus on assisting states in bringing their legislation in line with the Protocol and in developing effective criminal justice responses to migrant smuggling. *See also* FORCED LABOR; GLOBAL ALLIANCE AGAINST TRAFFIC IN WOMEN; MIGRANT WORKERS.

MIGRANT WORKERS. The **International Convention on the Protection of the Rights of All Migrant Workers and Members of Their Family** defines a migrant worker as "a person who is engaged or has been engaged in a remunerated activity in a State of which he or she is not a national." The motivations for leaving one's country range from seeking out gainful employment to getting a better education to fleeing persecution. The term may accordingly refer to a wide array of different groups including students,

asylum seekers, **refugees**, undocumented workers from abroad or any worker moving from one seasonal job to another. In popular parlance, it is used to designate workers involved in lower wage fields. International migration has become an intrinsic feature of the **globalization** of the world economy, and it is currently estimated that the number of migrants crossing international borders has grown steadily over the past decades to approximately 200 million (i.e., 3 percent of the world population). Migratory flows are likely to further swell due to differential demographic trends in an aging North and a youthful South.

The linkages between migration and human rights have increasingly become a politically sensitive issue in many countries with undertones of **racial discrimination** and xenophobia which underline the growing relevance of the UN Convention on migrant workers and the **United Nations Convention Relating to the Status of Refugees**, the two key legal instruments that affirm the rights of migrants to **due process**, family reunification, and non-discrimination, among others. Two conventions adopted under the aegis of the **International Labour Organization** in 1949 and 1975 are concerned with the labor-related rights of migrant workers.

See also ALIENS, TREATMENT OF; CENTER FOR EUROPEAN POLICY STUDIES; DECLARATION ON THE HUMAN RIGHTS OF INDIVIDUALS WHO ARE NOT NATIONALS OF THE COUNTRY IN WHICH THEY LIVE; DISCRIMINATION; FORCED LABOR; GLOBAL ALLIANCE AGAINST TRAFFIC IN WOMEN; HUMAN TRAFFICKING; INTERNATIONAL CONFERENCE ON POPULATION AND DEVELOPMENT; INTERNATIONAL ORGANIZATION FOR MIGRATION; MIGRANT RIGHTS INTERNATIONAL; MIGRANT SMUGGLING; MIGRATION POLICY GROUP; MINORITIES; PLATFORM FOR INTERNATIONAL COOPERATION ON UNDOCUMENTED MIGRANTS; UNITED NATIONS DEVELOPMENT PROGRAMME; UNITED NATIONS EDUCATIONAL, SCIENTIFIC AND CULTURAL ORGANIZATION; UNITED NATIONS HUMAN RIGHTS COUNCIL; UNITED NATIONS OFFICE OF THE HIGH COMMISSIONER FOR HUMAN RIGHTS; WORLD CONFERENCE AGAINST RACISM; WORLD CONFERENCE ON HUMAN RIGHTS.

MIGRATION POLICY GROUP (MPG). Self-described European "think and do tank" seeking to promote change resulting in open and inclusive societies by stimulating well-informed European debate and action on migration, equality and diversity and enhancing European cooperation between and among governmental agencies, **civil society** organizations and the private sector. Established in 1995 and located in Brussels, MPG has four primary activities focused on gathering, analyzing and sharing information, creating opportunities for dialogue and mutual learning, mobilizing and engaging stakeholders in policy debates and establishing, inspiring and managing expert networks. *See also* THINK TANKS.

MILLENNIUM DEVELOPMENT GOALS (MDGs). Set of development objectives to be achieved by 2015 contained in a "Millennium Declaration" adopted by the **United Nations General Assembly** in 2000. The MDGs address key dimensions of well-being—**poverty**, **hunger**, primary **education**, gender equality, maternal and child mortality, **HIV/AIDS**, environmental sustainability—and call for global partnerships to achieve these objectives in development aid, trade, debt relief and technology transfer. In that sense, they can be viewed as conditions for the achievement of social and economic rights as well as a framework of **accountability** for human rights. Yet, with the possible exception of **health** and the right to development, they have been rarely invoked in the work of UN deliberative bodies. Perhaps more telling is the fact that the MDGs are not cast in a human rights framework. Whether human rights considerations should be mainstreamed into the development goals to be embraced by the international community for the period extending beyond 2015 is a divisive issue pitting Northern against Southern countries.

See also DECLARATION; INTERNATIONAL CONFERENCE ON POPULATION AND DEVELOPMENT; FOOD, RIGHT TO; HOUSING, RIGHT TO ADEQUATE; RUGGIE, JOHN G.; UNITED NATIONS DEVELOPMENT PROGRAMME; WORLD FEDERATION OF UNITED NATIONS ASSOCIATIONS; WORLD SUMMIT FOR SOCIAL DEVELOPMENT.

MILOSEVIC, SLOBODAN (1941–2006). President of Serbia from 1989 to 1997 and then president of the Federal Republic of Yugoslavia until 2000 when he resigned in the wake of demonstrations triggered by contested presidential elections. One of the key figures during the Yugoslav wars of the 1990s and the 1999 **Kosovo** war, he was indicted in 1999 by the **International Criminal Tribunal for the Former Yugoslavia** for **crimes against humanity** in Kosovo. He was also charged of violating the laws and customs of war and grave breaches of the **Geneva Conventions** in Croatia and Bosnia and **genocide** in Bosnia. Extradited in 2001, he stood trial in The Hague but died after five years in prison before the conclusion of the trial. *See also* ARBOUR, LOUISE; BOSNIA-HERZEGOVINA WAR.

MINORITIES. Ethnic, linguistic, cultural or religious groups with a distinctive collective identity that differs, in varying degrees, from that of the majority population of the states they live in. Virtually all states nowadays have one or more such minorities, and relations among minorities and between minorities and majorities are often prone to tension. Such tensions are related to the existence of structures, systems or attitudes that have the effect of either perpetuating the marginalization of minority communities from decision making or of unfairly benefiting majority or dominant groups in the economic, social and political life of the country. It is not uncommon for the identity aspirations of minorities to escalate to "low-level intensity conflicts" or outright armed insurgencies, especially when they are perceived by governments as a threat to the economic, social and political fabric of the national society.

As minority groups may be targets of violence and **discrimination**, human rights norms call upon governments to refrain from such violence and to provide protections against it. From this vantage point, the notion of minority protection is an old one which may be traced as far back as to the rights of aliens recognized in antiquity. First attempts to protect minorities, especially religious minorities, can be found in the 1555 Peace of Augsburg and the 1598 Edict of Nantes. By the 19th century, a number of multilateral treaties, for instance the 1815 Final Act of the Congress of Vienna, incorporated minority protection clauses. The drastic redrawing of national frontiers which took place in the wake of the collapse of the Ottoman and Austro-Hungarian empires at the end of World War I (no less than 30 million people were transformed into minorities in new or enlarged states) and the growing salience of the principle of **self-determination** ushered in a new era of minority protection. In their peace treaties with the Allied and Associated Powers, Czechoslovakia, Greece, Poland, Romania and the Serb-Croat-Slovene State were obligated, under the supervision of the **League of Nations**, to secure the civil, political, economic and cultural rights of their minorities. Several other states—Albania, Estonia, Iraq, Latvia and Lithuania—made unilateral declarations assuming similar obligations when they were admitted into the League.

The system fell into desuetude with the rise of authoritarian regimes and minority issues received scant attention at the San Francisco Conference as the emphasis shifted from minority protection to the promotion of individual rights. Minority protection, however, has resurfaced as a human rights concern first as a result of the emergence of a large number of new and weak states out of the remnants of European colonial empires but also with the revival of nationalisms in the wake of the implosion of the Soviet Union and the end of the **Cold War**. The present minority rights regime provides a framework to ensure that a specific group which is in a vulnerable, disadvantaged or marginalized position in society is able to achieve equality and is protected from persecution.

One of the major tenets of the **Universal Declaration of Human Rights** is that all human beings are born free and equal in **dignity** and rights. Members of minorities either individually or collectively as a group accordingly have the right to be protected from any form of discrimination and persecution. They are also entitled to the equal protection of the law and may freely enjoy their own culture, practice their own religion and use their own language. In this context, the 1966 **International Covenant on Civil and Political Rights** commits its participating states to respecting and protecting their people's rights "without distinction of any kind, such as race, color, sex, language, political or other opinion, national or social origin, property, birth, or social status." Article 27 of the Covenant states that persons belonging to ethnic, religious, or linguistic minorities "shall not be denied the right, in community with other members of their group, to enjoy their own culture, to profess and practice their own religion, or to use their own language."

Other global human rights instruments codifying minority rights include the 1948 **United Nations Convention on the Punishment and Prevention of the Crime of Genocide,** the **United Nations Convention Relating to the Status of Refugees** (1950), the **International Convention on the Elimination of All Forms of Racial Discrimination** (1965), the **International Convention on the Suppression and Punishment of the Crime of Apartheid** (1976), the **United Nations Convention on the Elimination of All Forms of Discrimination against Women** (1979), the **Declaration on the Elimination of All Forms of Intolerance and of Discrimination Based on Religion and Belief** (1981), the **International Convention against Apartheid in Sports** (1985), the **United Nations Convention on the Rights of the Child** (1989), the **Declaration on the Rights of Persons Belonging to National or Ethnic, Religious and Linguistic Minorities** (1992) and the **International Convention on the Protection of the Rights of Migrant Workers and Members of Their Families** (2003). In 2005, the **United Nations Commission on Human Rights** requested the **United Nations High Commissioner for Human Rights** to appoint an independent expert on minority issues to promote the implementation of the Declaration to complement and enhance the work of **United Nations** bodies and mechanisms addressing minority rights and issues, notably the **United Nations Working Group on Minorities**. Several regional human rights instruments provide for minority protection mechanism, including, in Europe, the 1949 **European Convention for the Protection of Human Rights and Fundamental Freedoms** (Art. 14) and its Protocol 12 of 2000 (which provides for a general prohibition of discrimination), the 1995 **Framework Convention on the Protection of National Minorities**) and the 1992 **European Charter for Regional or Minority Languages**, and, in

Africa, the **African Charter on Human and People's Rights** (Art. 18) and the 1990 **African Charter on the Rights and Welfare of the Child** (Art. 26). In 1992, the **Organization for Security and Co-operation in Europe** (known then as the Conference on Security and Co-operation in Europe) created the post of high commissioner on national minorities to assist in the resolution of ethnic tensions that might endanger peace, stability and friendly relations among its participating states.

See also ABKHAZIA; ACEH; ADVOCATES FOR HUMAN RIGHTS; APARTHEID; BAHA'IS; BERBERS; BIAFRA; CENTER FOR INTERNATIONAL DEVELOPMENT AND CONFLICT MANAGEMENT; CONSORTIUM OF MINORITY RESOURCES; CULTURAL RIGHTS; DECLARATION ON THE ELIMINATION OF ALL FORMS OF RACIAL DISCRIMINATION; FORUM FOR FACT-FINDING DOCUMENTATION AND ADVOCACY; FORUM ON MINORITY ISSUES; INDIGENOUS PEOPLES; INTERNATIONAL MOVEMENT AGAINST ALL FORMS OF DISCRIMINATION AND RACISM; KURDISH QUESTION; MIGRANT WORKERS; MINORITIES AT RISK PROJECT; MINORITY RIGHTS GROUP INTERNATIONAL; MYANMAR; PERMANENT COURT OF INTERNATIONAL JUSTICE; ROMA/GYPSIES; SPECIAL PROCEDURES; TIBET; UNITED NATIONS DEVELOPMENT PROGRAMME; UNITED NATIONS SUB-COMMISSION ON THE PROMOTION AND PROTECTION OF HUMAN RIGHTS; UNREPRESENTED NATIONS AND PEOPLES ORGANIZATION.

MINORITIES AT RISK PROJECT (MAR). Long-standing **research** project based at the University of Maryland in the **United States** which monitors and analyzes conflicts involving politically active communal groups in countries with a current population of at least 500,000. The project is designed to provide information in a standardized format for comparative research, early warning and policy advice for the protection of **minorities**. *See also* CENTER FOR INTERNATIONAL DEVELOPMENT AND CONFLICT MANAGEMENT.

MINORITY RIGHTS GROUP INTERNATIONAL (MRG). London-based international **non-governmental organization** set up in the 1960s. It is dedicated to the protection and promotion of the basic rights of non-dominant ethnic, religious and linguistic communities which are among the poorest and most marginalized groups in society, lack access to political power, face discrimination and human rights abuses, and have "development" policies imposed upon them. MRG publishes reports, training manuals and briefing papers on a broad range of issues concerning the rights of **minorities** and

indigenous peoples, runs training events on international minority rights standards and **advocacy** techniques, organizes forums where minorities and indigenous peoples can meet with decision makers and members of majority communities and promotes the implementation of international standards for minority and indigenous groups by maintaining a presence at international forums at the **United Nations** and in the **European Union**. MRG has **consultative status** with the **United Nations Economic and Social Council** and observer status with the **African Commission on Human and People's Rights**. *See also* CAPACITY BUILDING.

MLADIC, RATKO (1942–). Senior military commander of the Bosnian Serb Army during the 1992–95 war in Bosnia. He has been indicted on charges of **genocide, war crimes** and **crimes against humanity** by the **International Criminal Tribunal for the Former Yugoslavia** for his role in the 1992–95 siege of Sarajevo and the 1995 massacre of some 7,000 men and boys at **Srebrenica**. Sheltered by Serb security forces and family, he remained at large until 2011 when he was arrested and transferred to The Hague where he is standing trial. His arrest was considered one of the conditions for Serbia's membership in the **European Union**. *See also* BOSNIA-HERZEGOVINA WAR.

MOBUTU SESE SEKO (1930–1997). Ruler of Zaire, the former Belgian Congo, for over 30 years until his violent overthrow in 1996. Staunch anti-communist, Mobutu received considerable political and economic support from the West and was able to stay in power in spite of his dismal human rights record, disastrous mismanagement of the economy and the pervasive **corruption** of his regime. According to **Transparency International**, Mobutu and his family embezzled over $5 billion. *See also* DEMOCRATIC REPUBLIC OF THE CONGO; IMPUNITY; LUMUMBA, PATRICE.

MONITORING OF HUMAN RIGHTS. Process involving the systematic tracking of the actions of institutions, organizations or governmental bodies for the purpose of determining the extent of enjoyment of human rights and whether governments comply with their human rights obligations. Typical monitoring activities include gathering information about particular incidents (assassinations, **forced disappearances**), observing single events (elections, trials, demonstrations), visiting places of detention and **refugee** camps, and discussions with government authorities to obtain information and to pursue **remedies**. Such reports typically look at what governments are doing as well as at the results of their actions on the basis of results and process-based indicators and **benchmarks**. Results indicators (also known as outcome indicators) focus on the core content of a right and allow for an evaluation of the quality of fulfillment of that right (i.e., the proportion of children who died of a disease that might have been prevented by immunization). Process indicators measure the extent to which a state meets and complies with its human rights obligations (i.e., in regard to the right to **education**, improved access to preschool education as measured by the percentage of eligible urban and rural children enrolled in preschool education).

Benchmarking is the logical next step in human rights monitoring, especially in regard to socioeconomic rights. Benchmarks are quantitative or qualitative targets linked to specific timeframes which provide a basis for measuring and assessing the "progressive realization" of a right. Human rights monitoring is a mainstay practice of activists and **non-governmental organizations**. For instance, **Freedom House**, a U.S.–based civil and political rights advocate, publishes annual reports on freedom of the press, conditions in the postcommunist world and surveys of **governance**, and corruption and transparency in countries in transition. International organizations can also be involved. Monitoring is in fact one of the principal functions of the **special rapporteurs** of international organizations and a large number of UN peacekeeping operations. Likewise, governments participate in the process for a variety of purposes related to their foreign policy objectives. The **United States** Department of State publishes an annual *Country Reports on Human Rights Practices* which is submitted to the U.S. Congress assessing the status of internationally recognized civil, political and workers rights in all foreign countries.

See also ARTICLE 19, THE INTERNATIONAL CENTRE AGAINST CENSORSHIP; CENTER FOR ECONOMIC AND SOCIAL RIGHTS; CHILD RIGHTS INFORMATION NETWORK; CHILDREN IN ARMED CONFLICT; EARLY WARNING; ENFORCEMENT; EUROPEAN COMMISSION AGAINST RACISM AND INTOLERANCE; FACT FINDING; EVENTS-BASED DATA; FRASER INSTITUTE; GENDER DEVELOPMENT INDEX; GENDER EMPOWERMENT MEASURE; GLOBAL POLICY FORUM; GOLDSTONE REPORT; HUMAN RIGHTS DEFENDERS; HUMAN RIGHTS FIRST; HUMAN RIGHTS WATCH; INTERNAL DISPLACEMENT MONITORING CENTRE; INTERNATIONAL BUREAU FOR CHILDREN'S RIGHTS; INTERNATIONAL CAMPAIGN TO BAN LANDMINES; INTERNATIONAL COMMITTEE OF THE RED CROSS; INTERNATIONAL SOCIETY FOR HUMAN RIGHTS; INVESTIGATION; PEACE OPERATIONS; PLATFORM FOR INTERNATIONAL COOPERATION ON UNDOCUMENTED MIGRANTS; PREVENTION; SPECIAL PROCEDURES; SPECIAL RAPPORTEURS; STATE REPORTING; TRANSPARENCY INTERNATIONAL; UNITED NATIONS ASSIST-

ANCE MISSION IN AFGHANISTAN; UNITED NATIONS COMMISSION ON THE STATUS OF WOMEN; UNITED NATIONS COMMITTEE ON ECONOMIC, SOCIAL AND CULTURAL RIGHTS; UNITED NATIONS COMMITTEE ON THE ELIMINATION OF ALL FORMS OF DISCRIMINATION AGAINST WOMEN; UNITED NATIONS COMMITTEE ON THE ELIMINATION OF ALL FORMS OF RACIAL DISCRIMINATION; UNITED NATIONS COMMITTEE ON THE PROTECTION OF THE RIGHTS OF ALL MIGRANT WORKERS AND THEIR FAMILIES; UNITED NATIONS COMMITTEE ON THE RIGHTS OF THE CHILD; UNITED NATIONS HUMAN RIGHTS COMMITTEE; UNITED NATIONS HUMAN SETTLEMENTS PROGRAMME; UNITED NATIONS INTERIM ADMINISTRATION MISSION IN KOSOVO; UNITED NATIONS MISSION FOR THE REFERENDUM IN WESTERN SAHARA; UNITED NATIONS MISSION IN THE REPUBLIC OF SOUTH SUDAN; UNITED NATIONS OBSERVER GROUP IN EL SALVADOR; UNITED NATIONS OBSERVER MISSION IN GEORGIA; UNITED NATIONS OBSERVER MISSION IN LIBERIA; UNITED NATIONS OFFICE OF THE HIGH COMMISSIONER FOR HUMAN RIGHTS; UNITED NATIONS OPERATION IN COTE D'IVOIRE; UNITED NATIONS OPERATION IN MOZAMBIQUE; UNITED NATIONS ORGANIZATION MISSION IN THE DEMOCRATIC REPUBLIC OF THE CONGO; UNITED NATIONS TREATY BODIES; UNITED NATIONS VERIFICATION MISSION IN GUATEMALA; UNITED NATIONS WORKING GROUP ON THE PROTECTION OF ALL PERSONS FROM ENFORCED DISAPPEARANCES; UNIVERSAL PERIODIC REVIEW; WOMEN'S INTERNATIONAL LEAGUE FOR PEACE AND FREEDOM.

MONTREAL PROTOCOL ON SUBSTANCES THAT DEPLETE THE OZONE LAYER (1987). International **treaty** designed to reduce and eventually eliminate the emissions of man-made ozone-depleting substances. The Protocol has been amended seven times since 1987. The amendments established mechanisms for transfer of technology and financing and added chemicals to the list of those ozone-depleting substances that should be phased out. The treaty has been hailed as an example of exceptionally successful international cooperation. *See also* ENVIRONMENT, RIGHT TO A HEALTHY.

MOTHERS OF THE PLAZA DE MAYO. Association of Argentine mothers which sprang out of chance meetings in public demonstrations as they were searching for their children who disappeared during the military dictatorship between 1976 and 1983. Through weekly and annual marches, these activists sought to break the veil of silence that surrounded government atrocities during the "**dirty war**" and pressed the military dictatorship and successor democratic governments for full disclosure and an end to the **impunity** of former military and civilian officials suspected of having been involved in cases of **torture, extra-judicial executions** or **forced disappearances**. *See also* ARGENTINA.

MULTINATIONAL CORPORATIONS. *See* TRANSNATIONAL CORPORATIONS.

MUSEMA CASE. The defendant in this case was the head of a civilian tea factory who actively participated in the commission of crimes during the **Rwanda** genocide. The **International Criminal Tribunal for Rwanda** found him guilty on 27 January 2000 of **genocide** and of **crimes against humanity** and imposed a life sentence. The ruling is notable for its determination that the doctrine of **command responsibility** could be extended to and applied to civilian enterprises.

MY LAI MASSACRE. Tragic episode which took place on 16 March 1968 during the **Vietnam War** and involved the mass murder of civilians, a majority of whom were women, children and elderly people by a unit of the **United States** army. The number of victims remains uncertain, ranging from 347 to 504. Twenty-six U.S. soldiers were initially charged with criminal offenses but only one was convicted and served three years of an original life sentence. The reduction of that sentence on the grounds that the convicted officer had merely obeyed orders was viewed by many as a reversal of the standards set forth at the **International Military Tribunal for the Prosecution and Punishment of the Major War Criminals of the European Axis** and **International Military Tribunal for the Far East**. *See also* IMPUNITY.

MYANMAR. Formerly known as Burma, this Southeast Asia country of roughly 50 million has a long history of human rights abuses committed by its ruling military regime. Myanmar achieved independence from Great Britain in 1948, but after 14 years of attempted democracy, conflicts involving communist, religious and ethnic **minorities** brought Burma to the verge of civil war and prompted the military to seize power. Fears of a resumption of full-scale armed insurgencies account for the continuing grip of the military over the country, and there is general agreement that the regime, at least until recently, has been one of the world's most repressive regimes. Human rights organizations like **Amnesty International** and **Human Rights Watch** repeatedly denounced the dictatorship clampdown on **freedom of expression** or of **assembly**. There have been reports of **torture** and ill treatment of political prisoners, **extra-judicial executions** and the kidnapping and recruiting of children into the army.

Intermittent military operations against ethnic minorities combined with higher rates of poverty have triggered massive waves of **refugees** into Thailand and displaced perhaps half a million people within the country. Perhaps more disquieting there have been allegations of genocidal targeting of certain ethnic groups.

Transnational corporations have been criticized for profiting from the dictatorship's favors. In this regard, the **International Labour Organization** has frequently censured Burma for its **forced labor** practices. In 1997, 13 Burmese villagers filed suit under the **Alien Tort Statute** alleging **violations of human rights** against Unocal, a giant California oil multinational corporation. The villagers claimed that the military junta had forced people to work using tactics such as murder and rape. In December 2004, Unocal agreed to settle the case out of court. The details of the settlement are not known but are believed to include direct compensation and "substantial assistance" to improve the villagers' living conditions.

Economic **sanctions** by the **United States** and the **European Union** and **United Nations** mediation efforts have for a long time failed to nudge the military into a dialogue with pro-democracy leaders as Myanmar's neighbors, China, India, Singapore and Thailand, are more concerned to secure their long-term access to the country's oil and gas resources and have taken a stance of non-interference and turned a blind eye to human rights violations. In fact, twice, in 2007 and 2010, Russia and China vetoed draft resolutions before the **United Nations Security Council** pressuring the junta to respect human rights and begin a democratic transition through sanctions. Since the transition to a new government in August 2011, the country's human rights situation appears to be improving. Political dissidents have been freed or allowed to return home from exile. Restrictions on civil liberties have been relaxed. A National Human Rights Commission has been set up and the opposition was allowed to win a presence in the parliament. Continuing ethnic tensions and flare ups involving the Buddhist and Muslim communities, however, underline the fragility of the changes. *See also* AUNG SAN SUU KYI; SIERRA CLUB.

MYRDAL, KARL GUNNAR (1898–1987). Swedish economist, politician, and **Nobel Peace Prize** laureate. He is the author of *An American Dilemma*, an influential sociological, anthropological and economic study on race relations in the **United States** since the Civil War. Published in 1944, the book highlighted the wide gap between the country's human rights ideals and practice for the black population. *See also* RACIAL DISCRIMINATION.

NAGORNO-KARABAKH. Autonomous region with a predominantly ethnic Armenian population set up by the Soviets at the end of World War I within **Azerbaijan**. Ethnic Armenian-Azeri tensions smoldered throughout the Soviet period and exploded into violence with the breakup of the Soviet Union. In late 1991, Armenian separatists proclaimed the independence of the enclave. Low-level violence which had started in 1988 turned into large-scale warfare between Azerbaijani and ethnic Armenian forces backed by Armenia, eventually leaving 30,000 people dead and displacing 1 million. A Russian-brokered ceasefire was signed in 1994 and, since the end of the war, Armenia and Azerbaijan have been holding inconclusive peace talks mediated by the **Organization for Security and Co-operation in Europe** on the region's status. Karabakh remains under de facto ethnic Armenian control as fleeing Azeris have been unable to return and ethnic Armenians now account for virtually the entire population. In spite of objections by Azerbaijan, a referendum was held in the region in December 2006 approving a new constitution and proclaiming the existence of Karabakh as a sovereign state. Technically, Armenia and Azerbaijan are still at war over the disputed territory. The self-styled "Republic of Nagono-Karabakh" which absorbed 20 percent of Azerbaijan has not been recognized by any government. *See also* ETHNIC CLEANSING; SELF-DETERMINATION.

NAMING AND SHAMING. First utilized by **Human Rights Watch** against the Soviet Union, this strategy is now widely used by individuals, **non-governmental organizations** and international bodies as a means to enforce human rights norms. Naming and shaming involves the public exposure of violations of human rights through information gathering and disseminating, direct exchanges with policymakers, media coverage and other means of publicity. The expectation is that tarnishing the public reputation and images of governments, **transnational corporations** and other violators of human rights will lead to their complying with human rights norms and standards.

NANKING MASSACRE. Mass atrocities committed by the Japanese military after the fall of Nanking (then China's capital city) on 13 December

1937 during the second Sino-Japanese war. The carnage, which involved looting, massive property destruction, the killing of civilians and soldiers and the rape of perhaps up to 80,000 women, lasted for six weeks and led to the deaths of 150,000 to 300,000 non-combatants (the numbers are disputed, with Chinese observers claiming the highest death toll while Japanese critics minimize civilian casualties or even dispute that the massacres ever occurred). The top-ranking military officer of the Japanese armed forces was tried by the **International Military Tribunal for the Far East**. Found guilty of **war crimes**, he was sentenced to death and executed in 1948. However, under an accord concluded by General Douglas MacArthur and Emperor Hirohito, Prince Yasuhiko Asaka, the emperor's uncle, who exerted supreme authority over the invading Japanese forces, was never prosecuted. *See also* IMPUNITY; MASSACRES.

NANSEN, FRIDTJOF (1861–1930). Norwegian scientist, explorer and diplomat who won the **Nobel Peace Prize** in 1923 for his humanitarian work as high commissioner for refugees of the **League of Nations**. He played an instrumental role in the return of prisoners of war from Russia, in alleviating the deadly famine which struck Russia in 1921–22 and in the population exchange between **Greece** and **Turkey** called for in the 1923 Lausanne Treaty. He designed in 1922 the so-called "Nansen passport," the first internationally recognized identity card issued by the League for stateless **refugees**. Some 450,000 Nansen passports were issued by the League until its demise. National authorities and the **United Nations** now issue similar documents variously known as certificates of identity, refugee travel documents and laissez passers. *See also* NATIONALITY, RIGHT TO; STATELESSNESS.

NATIONAL ENDOWMENT FOR DEMOCRACY (NED). Think tank founded in 1983 by the U.S. Congress to promote **democracy** through cash grants funded primarily by annual congressional appropriations. Headquartered in Washington, D.C., NED also supports other projects such as the *Journal of Democracy*, a World Movement for Democracy, an International Forum for Democratic Studies, a Network of Democracy Research Institutes, and a Center for International Media Assistance. It has been frequently criticized for interfering in foreign countries and acting as a de facto cover to the continuation of prohibited **Central Intelligence Agency** activities.

NATIONAL HUMAN RIGHTS INSTITUTIONS (NHRI). National quasi-governmental or statutory institutions with various powers and degrees of independence and commonly known as human rights commissions, **ombudsmen**, *defensores del pueblo*, and procurators for human rights. NHRIs are set up to protect and promote human rights and may receive and investigate **complaints** on **violations of human rights**. There are some 110 such bodies, not all compliant with the **United Nations** standards set out in the 1993 **Paris Principles**. *See also* DANISH INSTITUTE FOR HUMAN RIGHTS; INVESTIGATION; RAOUL WALLENBERG INSTITUTE.

NATIONAL RED CROSS AND RED CRESCENT SOCIETIES. Entities established in the territory of states' party to the **Geneva Conventions**, carrying out humanitarian work in their home countries on the basis of the principles of **international humanitarian law** and the statutes of the **International Committee of the Red Cross** (ICRC). There are at present 186 National Societies recognized by the ICRC that belong to the **International Federation of Red Cross and Red Crescent Societies**. National societies serve as medical auxiliaries to the authorities. In peacetime, they provide emergency medical services, especially in cases of natural disasters. In situations of warfare, they may act as auxiliaries of military medical services. *See also* HEALTH, RIGHT TO.

NATIONALITY, RIGHT TO. The **Universal Declaration of Human Rights** states that "no one shall be arbitrarily deprived of his nationality nor denied the right to change his nationality." The right to nationality has been further elaborated in the **International Convention on the Elimination of All Forms of Racial Discrimination**, which guarantees the right to everyone, without distinction as to race, color, nationality or ethnic origin, to **equality** before the law. The **United Nations Convention on the Nationality of Married Women** (1957) and the 1979 **United Nations Convention on the Elimination of All Forms of Discrimination against Women** (Art. 9) seek to ensure that women enjoy equal rights to acquire, change or retain nationality. The **United Nations Convention on the Rights of the Child** (Arts. 7 and 8) establishes the right of children to be registered and to acquire a nationality from birth. The 2006 Convention on the Avoidance of **Statelessness** in relation to State Succession provides for detailed rules to be applied by states with a view to preventing, or at least reducing to the extent possible, cases of statelessness arising from state succession.

At the regional level, the **African Commission on Human and People's Rights**, the **European Convention for the Protection of Human Rights and Fundamental Freedoms** and the **Inter-American Commission on Human Rights** all posit a right to nationality and prohibit the arbitrary deprivation of nationality or the right to change it. Two key international conventions, the 1954 **United Nations Convention Relating to the Status of Stateless Persons** and the 1961 **United Nations Convention on the Reduction of Statelessness** complement this global and regional legal architecture but few states have ratified them.

While international law is unambiguous in affirming the existence of a right to nationality and emphasizing the need for special protection of vulnerable groups vis-à-vis this right, by and large it provides little guidance on the procedures and criteria that states should follow in establishing bonds of nationality between the state and an individual and the awarding of citizenship. The jurisprudence of the **International Court of Justice** and of regional human rights courts simply suggests the broad principle that nationality should derive from "genuine and effective links" as demonstrated by such parameters as "the habitual residence of the individual concerned . . . the center of his interests, his family ties, his participation in public life, attachment shown by him for a given country and inculcated into his children." Stateless persons thus face a legal void similar to those confronting **internally displaced persons**, conducive, in spite of the modest and limited efforts of agencies like the **United Nations High Commissioner for Refugees**, to uncertainty and arbitrariness. Not surprisingly, the problem of disenfranchised groups and individuals being left without nationality which affects in particular **refugee** populations has intensified in recent years with the breakup of the Soviet Union, the spread of civil wars and the rise of ethnic tensions worldwide. *See also* CITIZENSHIP; DECLARATION ON THE HUMAN RIGHTS OF INDIVIDUALS WHO ARE NOT NATIONALS OF THE COUNTRY IN WHICH THEY LIVE; DEMJANJUK; JOHN; FAMILY, RIGHT TO A; MINORITIES; NANSEN, FRIDTJOF; NON-DEROGABLE RIGHTS; OPEN SOCIETY INSTITUTE; TRUTH, RIGHT TO THE.

NATIVE AMERICANS. Indigenous peoples now living within the boundaries of the **United States**, Alaska and Hawaii. Warfare, killing at the hands of European colonists, forced displacement, enslavement, assimilation and, above all, epidemic diseases brought from Europe led to a rapid decline in the Native American population. There are now some 2.7 million Native Americans. They have a unique relationship with the U.S. government as members of "sovereign nations" with treaty rights.

NATURAL RIGHTS. In contrast to legal rights which are based on a society's customs and laws like the right to vote, natural rights are considered to be inherent in every individual because of their human nature. Natural rights are thus beyond the authority of any government. While it is widely admitted that humans have a natural right to **life**, there are nevertheless disagreements about exactly what other rights could be considered as such. This has prompted some to argue that the idea of natural rights is simply a political tool. *See also* CULTURAL RELATIVISM; DECLARATION OF INDEPENDENCE; LIBERALISM; LIMITED GOVERNMENT; UNALIENABLE RIGHTS.

NECESSITY, DOCTRINE OF. Controversial doctrine used to justify extra-legal conduct and actions which violate the law and produce harm by state actors on the grounds that they avert greater evils and preserve political stability, the **rule of law** and **democracy** in the long term. The principle whereby "that which is otherwise not lawful is made lawful by necessity" has been invoked in countries affected by civil strife and **terrorism**. *See also* PEREMPTORY NORMS; PUBLIC EMERGENCY.

NEIER, ARYEH (1937–). American human rights activist who fled Germany in 1939. Now president of the Open Society Foundation, he first worked for 15 years with the **American Civil Liberties Union** where he led efforts to protect the civil rights of prisoners and fought for the abolition of **capital punishment**. In 1978, in the wake of the 1975 Helsinki Conference, he participated in the foundation of Helsinki Watch which later evolved into **Human Rights Watch** (HRW). He headed HRW for 12 years and in that capacity endeavored to bring together human rights law and humanitarian law in monitoring and investigating human rights abuses in Latin America, especially **El Salvador**, and **Guatemala** and the former Yugoslavia. A long-time advocate of the creation of **war crime tribunals**, he played an important role in the establishment of the **International Criminal Tribunal for the Former Yugoslavia**.

NETWORK. Social structure composed of individuals or **non-governmental organizations** connected to one another by ties of interdependency and commonality derived from shared knowledge, beliefs, orientations and political objectives. The use of the term in regard to human rights **civil society** groups suggests a prevalence of loose and informal relationships.

See also CHILD RIGHTS INFORMATION NETWORK; CHILD-WATCH INTERNATIONAL RESEARCH NETWORK; EURO-MEDITERRANEAN HUMAN RIGHTS NETWORK; GLOBAL ACTION TO PREVENT WAR; GLOBAL NETWORK OF WOMEN PEACE BUILDERS; GLOBAL SURVIVAL NETWORK; INSTITUTE FOR WAR AND PEACE REPORTING; INTER-AFRICAN COMMITTEE ON TRADITIONAL PRACTICES AFFECTING THE HEALTH OF WOMEN;

INTERNATIONAL NGO COALITION FOR AN O.P. TO THE ICESCR; INTERNATIONAL SERVICE FOR HUMAN RIGHTS; INTERNATIONAL WOMEN'S RIGHTS ACTION WATCH; PARLIAMENTARIANS FOR GLOBAL ACTION; PREVENT GENOCIDE INTERNATIONAL; REHABILITATION INTERNATIONAL.

NGO WORKING GROUP ON WOMEN, PEACE AND SECURITY. Coalition of international **non-governmental organizations** (NGOs), strategically positioned in New York, which was formed in 2000 to advocate for the adoption of resolutions by the **United Nations Security Council** (UN-SC) calling for the full and equal participation of **women in peace and security** efforts. The Group initially worked in support of the adoption of UN-SC Resolution 1325 of 2000 and now focuses on its implementation. Its members include **Amnesty International**; the Consortium on Gender, Security and Human Rights; Femmes Africa Solidarité; Global Action to Prevent War; Global Justice Center; **Human Rights Watch**; the International Action Network on Small Arms; **International Alert**; the **International Rescue Committee**; the International Women's Program at the Open Society Institute; United Methodist Women's Division, General Board of Global Ministries–United Methodist Church; Women's Refugee Commission; Women's Action for New Directions and Women's International League for Peace and Freedom.

NGUEMA, FRANCISCO MACIAS (1924–1979). First president of Equatorial Guinea from 1969 until his violent overthrow by his nephew Obiang Gguema in 1979. Under his dictatorial rule, widespread **violations of human rights** caused a third of the population to flee to other countries. The violence, unpredictability and anti-intellectual nature of his regime have prompted frequent comparisons with the Pol Pot regime in **Democratic Kampuchea**. Obiang Gguema still rules the country and has been criticized by human rights groups for continuing widespread human rights abuses and for suppressing political opposition. Off-shore large oil and gas deposits discovered in the mid-1990s have driven a spectacular growth of the country's economy. **Transparency International** ranks Equatorial Guinea as one of the top-ten world's most **corrupt** states.

NIGERIA. *See* ABACHA, SANI; BIAFRA; NIGER DELTA CONFLICT.

NIGER DELTA CONFLICT. "Low intensity" conflict pitting since the early 1990s the Nigerian federal government against a number of minority ethnic groups in the southern part of the country. Perceived injustices arising from the degradation of the **environment** caused by the unbridled activities of multinational oil companies and coupled with the inaction of a central government more concerned about maintaining law and order and safeguarding levels of oil production for export than to bring about a better redistribution of energy revenues and **redress** the grievances of impoverished people displaced by environmental damage have fueled sporadic violent forms of resistance. Clashes with government forces, sabotage of oil installations, hostage-taking and lethal bombings have been met with harsh military responses.

In 2001, a Nigerian **non-governmental organization** (NGO), the Social and Economic Rights Action Center, and a U.S. NGO, the **Center for Economic and Social Rights,** filed a **complaint** before the **African Commission on Human and People's Rights** accusing the Nigerian government of being complicit with the Shell oil company in the destruction of the **land, housing** and **water** resources of one of the ethnic groups involved in the rebellion. The Commission concluded that the government of Nigeria had the obligation of respecting and safeguarding the rights of these groups and protecting them from the activities of national and international oil companies. Two years ago, an **amnesty** offer, accompanied by cash payouts to armed militants and a proposal to give oil-producing communities a 10 percent stake in government oil ventures, has brought about a precarious calm which may be shattered by the potent mix of **poverty**, government **corruption** and environmental damage which underlie the violence and discontent in the region.

According to a recent study of the United Nations Environmental Programme, the environmental restoration of the region could prove to be the world's most wide-ranging and long-term oil cleanup exercise ever undertaken if contaminated drinking water, land and creeks and other ecosystems are to be brought back to productive health. *See also* ABACHA, SANI; CORPORATE SOCIAL RESPONSIBILITY; SELF-DETERMINATION; SIERRA CLUB; TRANSNATIONAL CORPORATIONS.

NOBEL PEACE PRIZE. One of the five Nobel Prizes awarded each year in Norway in December to individuals who have "done the most or the best work for fraternity between nations, for the abolition or reduction of standing armies and for the holding and promotion of peace congresses." Over the years, the prize has been awarded to human rights and humanitarian activists: **Fridtjof Nansen** (1922), **Rene Cassin** (1968), Desmond Tutu (1984), **Aung San Suu Kyi** (1991), **Rigoberta Menchu** (1992), Jody Williams (1997), **Shirin Ebadi** (2003); labor leaders: Léon Jouhaux (1951); political leaders: **Jimmy Carter** (2002); **non-governmental organizations: Amnesty International** (1977) and **Medecins Sans Frontieres** (1999); humanitarian organizations: the **Office International Nansen pour les Réfugiés** (1938), the **International Committee of the Red Cross** (1917, 1944 and 1963); United Nations organizations: the **United Nations Children's Fund** (1965), the **International Labour Organization** (1969) and the Office of the **United Nations High Commissioner for Refugees** (1981); the United Nations, jointly with UN Secretary-General **Kofi Annan** (2001) and one of its secretary-generals: Dag Hammarskjöld (1961). *See also* WALESA, LECH.

NO-FLY ZONE. Designated territory or area over which aircraft are not allowed to fly. Patrolled by military aircraft that have the authority to shoot down unauthorized planes, the purpose of a no-fly zone is generally to prevent massive **violations of human rights** and to protect civilian populations. As an instance of the use of force, no-fly zones should abide by the standards of **international law** and normally require approval by the **United Nations Security Council** (UN-SC). The **United States**, Great Britain and France imposed two no-fly zones after the Gulf War as part of a humanitarian effort to protect Shi'a Muslims in the south and Kurds in the north. In the course of the **Bosnia-Herzegovina war**, the UN-SC passed resolutions prohibiting unauthorized military aircraft in Bosnian airspace which were implemented by the **North Atlantic Treaty Organization** (NATO). In 1999, NATO imposed a no-fly zone over **Kosovo** as a prelude to an air assault on Serbian forces. In 2011, NATO policed a no-fly zone over **Libya** mandated by the UN-SC to prevent attacks on civilian targets. The legality of no-fly zones remains a contentious subject. Their effectiveness appears to hinge on a number of factors including unified command structures, clear policy objectives and regional support. *See also* HUMANITARIAN INTERVENTION; KURDISH QUESTION; REGIONAL ARRANGEMENTS; "RESPONSIBILITY TO PROTECT."

NO PEACE WITHOUT JUSTICE. International **non-profit organization** founded in 1993 and working in three main areas: the strengthening of the international criminal justice system and particularly the legitimacy, credibility and effectiveness of the **International Criminal Court**; building up the strategic capacity of women's rights advocates and field practitioners working on **female genital mutilation**; and bolstering **democracy** in the Middle East and North Africa.

NON-BINDING. Character of a type of resolution adopted by human rights deliberative bodies expressing their approval of a norm, principle, policy or practice but which cannot progress or gel into a law or obligation. **United Nations General Assembly** resolutions are non-binding. In contrast, the **United Nations Security Council** makes binding decisions. *See also* DECLARATION; SOFT LAW.

NON-DEROGABLE RIGHTS. Several international human rights **treaties** allow states to suspend or restrict certain human rights guarantees. Such **derogation** clauses recognize the right of states to avoid exceptional, irreparable damage resulting from **public emergencies** such as war, civil unrest or natural catastrophes. At the same time, human rights treaties and **customary international law** do stipulate that some rights may never be suspended under any circumstances. Under the **International Covenant on Civil and Political Rights** (ICCPR), the right to **life** (Art. 6); the prohibition of **torture** (Art. 7); the prohibition of **slavery** and servitude (Art. 8, para. 1 and 2); the prohibition of detention for debt (Art. 11); the prohibition of retroactive criminal laws (Art. 15); the recognition of legal personality (Art. 16); and freedom of thought, conscience, religion and belief (Art. 18) may never be suspended. Under the **European Convention for the Protection of Human Rights and Fundamental Freedoms**, the prohibition of torture, slavery, servitude and retroactive criminal laws and the right to life are non-derogable rights. The list of non-derogable rights found in the **American Convention on Human Rights** is similar to the ICCPR's but it also includes the right to participate in government, rights of the child and the family, rights to a name and **nationality** and judicial guarantees essential for the protection of non-derogable rights. It should be noted that a number of human rights treaties, notably the **United Nations Convention against Torture** and the **Geneva Conventions** and their two Additional Protocols do not allow derogations. *See also* ARMED CONFLICT; INTERNATIONAL CONVENTION FOR THE PROTECTION OF ALL PERSONS FROM ENFORCED DISAPPEARANCE; OBLIGATION *"ERGA OMNES"*; PEREMPTORY NORMS.

NON-DISCRIMINATION. Cross-cutting principle in **international human rights law** which underlies all major international human rights **treaties** such as, for example, the **International Convention on the Elimination of All Forms of Racial Discrimination** and the **United Nations Convention on the Elimination of All Forms of Discrimination against Women** (CEDAW). The principle, which is also enshrined in the **United Nations Charter**, applies to everyone and to all rights and prohibits any form of exclusion or rejection based on such categories as age, gender, race, color, ethnicity, language or national origins. It is a consequence and extension of the principle of **equality**, as stated in Article 1 of the **Universal Declaration of Human Rights**: "All human beings are born free and equal in dignity and rights."

A typical legal definition of non-discrimination can be found in Article 1 of CEDAW which states: "For the purposes of the present Convention, the term 'discrimination against women' shall mean any distinction, exclusion or restriction made on the basis of sex which has the effect or purpose of impairing or nullifying the recognition, enjoyment or exercise by women, irrespective of their marital status, on a basis of equality of men and women, of human rights and fundamental freedoms in the political, economic, social, cultural, civil or any other field." It should be noted that the same convention also posits that "adoption by States Parties of temporary special measures aimed at accelerating de facto equality between men and women shall not be considered discrimination as defined in the present Convention, but shall in no way entail as a consequence the maintenance of unequal or separate standards; these measures shall be discontinued when the objectives of equality of opportunity and treatment have been achieved" (Art. 4). *See also* HUMAN RIGHTS PRINCIPLES; RAOUL WALLENBERG INSTITUTE.

NON-GOVERNMENTAL ORGANIZATIONS (NGOs). There is no generally accepted definition of an NGO, but it is widely understood that NGOs share at least four broad characteristics: (a) they bring together individuals sharing common objectives within a legally constituted entity which may variously operate at the local, provincial, regional, international or global level(s); (b) they are private organizations (i.e., they are independent from direct government control); (c) they only seek to influence public policy decision making rather than take power as political parties do; (d) they are not-for-profit organizations and are therefore distinct from private sector corporations. In brief, NGOs are "independent voluntary associations of people acting together on a continuous basis, for some common purpose, other than achieving government office, making money or illegal activities."

Defined as such, NGOs in the field of human rights work on **advocacy** campaigns, promote, develop and set human rights standards and norms, **monitor** human rights violations and provide a wide range of advisory, informational, educational, **capacity building** and legal services. NGOs played a key role in securing a provision in the **United Nations Charter**, institutionalizing their participation in the **United Nations Economic and Social Council** (ECOSOC). In 1948, there were only 48 NGOs that had been granted such "consultative" status whereby they are allowed to attend meetings of ECOSOC and its subsidiary bodies, circulate documentation and make formal statements. By the latest count, there are now over 3,200 NGOs in consultative status with ECOSOC. Other international organizations such as the **European Union** have developed similar arrangements. But the growing role, influence and impact of NGOs in the practice of human rights can best be measured by their extensive involvement in multilevel informal processes extending from community action to their boisterous but not inconsequential involvement in **United Nations global conferences**.

See also ADVOCACY; ADVOCATES FOR HUMAN RIGHTS; AL HAQ; AL MEZAN CENTER FOR HUMAN RIGHTS; AMERICAN JEWISH COMMITTEE; AMERICAN SOCIETY OF INTERNATIONAL LAW; AMNESTY INTERNATIONAL; ANTI-DEFAMATION LEAGUE; ANTI-RACISM INFORMATION SERVICE; ANTI-SLAVERY INTERNATIONAL; ARAB ASSOCIATION FOR HUMAN RIGHTS; ARAB LAWYERS UNION; ARAB ORGANIZATION FOR HUMAN RIGHTS; ARTICLE 19, THE INTERNATIONAL CENTRE AGAINST CENSORSHIP; ASIAN CENTER FOR HUMAN RIGHTS; ASIAN HUMAN RIGHTS COMMISSION; ASSOCIATION FOR THE PREVENTION OF TORTURE; BUSINESS AND HUMAN RIGHTS RESOURCE CENTRE; CCJO RENE CASSIN; CARE INTERNATIONAL; CARITAS INTERNATIONALIS; CENTER FOR CONSTITUTIONAL RIGHTS; CENTER FOR ECONOMIC AND SOCIAL RIGHTS; CENTER FOR GENDER AND REFUGEE STUDIES; CENTER FOR JUSTICE AND ACCOUNTABILITY; CENTER FOR MIGRATION STUDIES; CENTER FOR MINORITY RIGHTS DEVELOPMENT; CENTER FOR REPRODUCTIVE RIGHTS; CENTER FOR VICTIMS OF TORTURE; CENTRE FOR HOUSING RIGHTS AND EVICTIONS; CHILD RIGHTS INFORMATION NETWORK; CHOIKE; COALITION AGAINST TRAFFICKING IN WOMEN; COALITION FOR INTERNATIONAL JUSTICE; COALITION FOR THE INTERNATIONAL CRIMINAL COURT; COMMONWEALTH HUMAN RIGHTS INITIATIVE; CORPORATE REASONABILITY REPORTING; CORPWATCH; DECEMBER 18; DERECHOS HUMAN RIGHTS; EARTH RIGHTS INTERNATIONAL; EQUALITY NOW; EQUIPO NIZKOR; EQUITAS—INTERNATIONAL CENTER FOR HUMAN RIGHTS EDUCATION; EUROPEAN ROMA RIGHTS CENTER; FAMILY CARE INTERNATIONAL; FEDERATION INTERNATIONALE TERRE DES HOMMES; FOOD FIRST INFORMATION AND ACTION NETWORK; FORUM FOR FACT-FINDING DOCUMENTATION AND ADVOCACY; FORUM ON EARLY WARNING AND EARLY RESPONSE; FREEDOM NOW; GIRCA; GLOBAL ALLIANCE AGAINST TRAFFIC IN WOMEN; GLOBAL CENTER FOR THE RESPONSIBILITY TO PROTECT; GLOBAL JUSTICE CENTER; GLOBAL LAWYERS AND PHYSICIANS; GLOBAL POLICY FORUM; GLOBAL RIGHTS; GLOBAL WITNESS; GRASSROOTS INTERNATIONAL; HABITAT INTERNATIONAL COALITION; HUMAN RIGHTS FIRST; HUMAN RIGHTS INSTITUTE; HUMAN RIGHTS INSTITUTE OF SOUTH AFRICA; HUMAN RIGHTS

INTERACTIVE NETWORK; HUMAN RIGHTS INTERNET; HUMAN RIGHTS WATCH; HUNGER PROJECT; INDIGENOUS PEOPLES' CENTER FOR DOCUMENTATION, RESEARCH AND INFORMATION; INCLUSION INTERNATIONAL; INSTITUTE FOR HUMAN RIGHTS AND DEVELOPMENT IN AFRICA; INTER-AFRICAN COMMITTEE ON TRADITIONAL PRACTICES AFFECTING THE HEALTH OF WOMEN; INTERNATIONAL ACCOUNTABILITY PROJECT; INTERNATIONAL ALERT; INTERNATIONAL ALLIANCE TO END GENOCIDE; INTERNATIONAL ASSOCIATION FOR REFUGEE LAW JUDGES; INTERNATIONAL ASSOCIATION FOR RELIGIOUS FREEDOM; INTERNATIONAL ASSOCIATION OF DEMOCRATIC LAWYERS; INTERNATIONAL ASSOCIATION OF LAWYERS AGAINST NUCLEAR ARMS; INTERNATIONAL ASSOCIATION OF WOMEN JUDGES; INTERNATIONAL BAR ASSOCIATION; INTERNATIONAL BUREAU FOR CHILDREN'S RIGHTS; INTERNATIONAL CAMPAIGN TO BAN LANDMINES; INTERNATIONAL CAMPAIGN TO END GENOCIDE; INTERNATIONAL CENTER FOR TRANSITIONAL JUSTICE; INTERNATIONAL CENTRE FOR HUMAN RIGHTS AND DEMOCRATIC DEVELOPMENT; INTERNATIONAL CENTRE FOR HUMAN RIGHTS AND DEMOCRATIC DEVELOPMENT; INTERNATIONAL CENTRE FOR THE LEGAL PROTECTION OF HUMAN RIGHTS; INTERNATIONAL CENTRE FOR TRADE UNION RIGHTS; INTERNATIONAL CIVIL SOCIETY ACTION NETWORK; INTERNATIONAL COALITION FOR THE RESPONSIBILITY TO PROTECT; INTERNATIONAL COMMISSION FOR LABOR RIGHTS; INTERNATIONAL COMMISSION OF JURISTS; INTERNATIONAL COUNCIL OF WOMEN; INTERNATIONAL COUNCIL ON HUMAN RIGHTS POLICY; INTERNATIONAL CRISIS GROUP; INTERNATIONAL FEDERATION OF HUMAN RIGHTS; INTERNATIONAL FEDERATION OF JOURNALISTS; INTERNATIONAL FEDERATION TERRE DES HOMMES; INTERNATIONAL GAY AND LESBIAN HUMAN RIGHTS COMMISSION; INTERNATIONAL HUMAN RIGHTS LAW INSTITUTE; INTERNATIONAL INSTITUTE OF HUMANITARIAN LAW; INTERNATIONAL LAW ASSOCIATION; INTERNATIONAL LEAGUE AGAINST RACISM AND ANTISEMITISM; INTERNATIONAL LEAGUE FOR HUMAN RIGHTS; INTERNATIONAL MOVEMENT AGAINST ALL FORMS OF DISCRIMINATION AND RACISM; INTERNATIONAL PLANNED PARENTHOOD FEDERATION; INTERNATIONAL REHABILITATION COUNCIL FOR TORTURE VICTIMS; INTERNATIONAL RESCUE COMMITTEE; INTERNATIONAL SAVE THE CHILDREN ALLIANCE; INTERNATIONAL SERVICE

FOR HUMAN RIGHTS; INTERNATIONAL SOCIETY FOR HUMAN RIGHTS; INTERNATIONAL TRAINING CENTRE ON HUMAN RIGHTS AND PEACE TEACHING; INTERNATIONAL WORK GROUP FOR INDIGENOUS AFFAIRS; KURDISH HUMAN RIGHTS PROJECT; MANDAT INTERNATIONAL; MEDECINS SANS FRONTIERES/DOCTORS WITHOUT BORDERS; MIGRANT RIGHTS INTERNATIONAL; NO PEACE WITHOUT JUSTICE; NORDIC COMMITTEE FOR HUMAN RIGHTS; OXFAM INTERNATIONAL; PALESTINIAN CENTRE FOR HUMAN RIGHTS; PEACE BRIGADES INTERNATIONAL; PEOPLE'S MOVEMENT FOR HUMAN RIGHTS LEARNING; PHYSICIANS FOR HUMAN RIGHTS; PLATFORM FOR INTERNATIONAL COOPERATION ON UNDOCUMENTED MIGRANTS; PREVENT GENOCIDE INTERNATIONAL; RAINFOREST ACTION NETWORK; REDRESS; REFUGEES INTERNATIONAL; REPORTERS WITHOUT BORDERS; REVENUE WATCH; RIGHTS AND DEMOCRACY; RIGHTS INTERNATIONAL; RUCKUS SOCIETY; SAVE THE CHILDREN INTERNATIONAL; SHADOW REPORTS; SIERRA CLUB; SOFT LAW; SURVIVORS INTERNATIONAL; THIRD WORLD INSTITUTE; UNIVERSAL HUMAN RIGHTS NETWORK; UNREPRESENTED NATIONS AND PEOPLES ORGANIZATION; WAR CHILD; WOMEN BUILDING PEACE; WOMEN'S INITIATIVE FOR GENDER JUSTICE; WOMEN'S INTERNATIONAL LEAGUE FOR PEACE AND FREEDOM; WOMEN'S REFUGEE COMMISSION; WORLD BLIND UNION; WORLD FEDERATION OF THE DEAFBLIND; WORLD FEDERATION OF THE DEAF; WORLD FEDERATION OF UNITED NATIONS ASSOCIATIONS; WORLD JUSTICE PROJECT; WORLD ORGANIZATION AGAINST TORTURE.

NON-INTERNATIONAL ARMED CONFLICT. *See* ARMED CONFLICT.

NON-*REFOULEMENT*. Basic principle of international **refugee** law codified in the 1951 **United Nations Convention Relating to the Status of Refugees** which prohibits the forced repatriation of an individual seeking refugee status to the country where he or she originates from. The principle has frequently been flouted. A contentious debate has been triggered by the common practice of some states—for example, the **United States** and Italy—to intercept on the high seas vessels suspected of transporting potential refugees thus preventing them from reaching a safe haven and to apply there for **asylum**. *See also* UNITED NATIONS HIGH COMMISSIONER FOR REFUGEES.

NON-STATE ACTORS. Term used to designate actors in the international arena that are not states (e.g., **non-governmental organizations, think tanks, private military companies,** terror networks, **armed groups, transnational corporations**). Non-state actors may play a critical role in heightening human security. They may also pose serious threats to human rights. A growing area of concern is the absence of mechanisms of **accountability** of non-state actors with regard to **violations of human rights.**

NON-TREATY-BASED MECHANISMS. Human rights protection instruments based on the constitution or charter of an intergovernmental human rights forum or on decisions taken by the assembly or a representative body of the forum in question. The European Commission against Racism and Intolerance under the **Council of Europe** is an example of a regional non-treaty-based mechanism. In the context of the **United Nations,** non-treaty-based mechanisms are referred to as charter-based mechanisms, such as the **United Nations Human Rights Council** and its **Special Procedures,** the **1503 Procedure,** and the **Universal Periodic Review.** *See also* UNITED NATIONS TREATY BODIES.

NORDIC COMMITTEE FOR HUMAN RIGHTS. Created in 1996 and located in Sweden, this international, **non-governmental organization** seeks to strengthen respect for basic human rights and fundamental freedoms in the Nordic countries and most especially the rights and freedoms of private individuals and their families based on the United Nations Declaration of Human Rights, the **European Convention for the Protection of Human Rights and Fundamental Freedoms** and the **United Nations Convention on the Rights of the Child.** The Committee submits yearly reports of suspected violations of families' rights to United Nations human rights organs, to the European Commission on Human Rights and to the **United Nations Committee on the Rights of the Child.** Through **monitoring** and **advocacy,** it endeavors to bring about changes in Nordic countries' policies adversely affecting private and family life.

NORM ENTREPRENEURS. Generic term which may refer to a wide variety of actors—individuals, **non-governmental organizations,** government or intergovernmental organizations officials, private **foundations,** academics—which individually or collectively through networking can be said to have played an important role in enlisting and mobilizing political support for the creation or enforcement of human rights standards.
See also ARIAS, OSCAR; BELO, BISHOP CARLOS-FELIPE XIMENES; BRODY, REED; BURGER, JAN HERMAN; COBO, JOSE MARTINEZ;

DAES, ERICA-IRENE; DUNANT, JEAN-HENRI; EVANS, GARETH; GRANT, JAMES P.; JOHN-PAUL II; KING, MARTIN LUTHER, JR.; MENDEZ, JUAN; NEIER, ARYEH; RAMOS-HORTA, JOSE; RUGGIE, JOHN G.; SPIRAL MODEL OF HUMAN RIGHTS CHANGE; STANDARDS' SETTING; WILLIAMS, JODY.

NORTH ATLANTIC TREATY ORGANIZATION (NATO). Collective security military organization set up in the context of the **Cold War** to counter Soviet threats to Western Europe. With the demise of the Cold War, NATO has morphed into an organization devoted to the promotion of **democracy** and conflict prevention through consultation and cooperation among its 28 members on defense and security issues. Under the terms of its constitutive treaty, a **United Nations' mandate** or in cooperation with other countries and other international organizations, it has the capacity to undertake "crisis management operations." During the **Bosnia-Herzegovina war**, NATO carried out several air strikes and enforced a **no-fly zone** under UN mandate. In 1999, it waged an 11-week-long bombing campaign against the Federal Republic of Yugoslavia in an effort to put an end to Serbian atrocities in **Kosovo**. NATO subsequently deployed forces in Albania to deliver humanitarian aid to Kosovo refugees and in Macedonia to disarm Albanian militias. During the 2011 Libyan civil war and, this time with the authorization of the **United Nations Security Council**, several NATO members enforced a no-fly zone over **Libya** to protect civilian populations. *See also* INDEPENDENT INTERNATIONAL COMMISSION ON KOSOVO; "RESPONSIBILITY TO PROTECT."

NORTH KOREA. *See* KIM IL SUNG.

NORTHERN IRELAND (1960s–1998). Ethno-political conflict which pitted the mainly Protestant Unionist community that believed it should remain part of the United Kingdom of Great Britain and Northern Ireland against the Catholic community that wished to join the Republic of Ireland. The "Troubles," as the period is known locally to refer to targeted killings, armed robberies, bombings and arsons, were an outgrowth of decades-long **discrimination** against the Catholic minority over **education**, **housing** and jobs. From the late 1960s to 1998, despite the Belfast Good Friday Agreement between the British and Irish governments which was endorsed by most Northern Irish political parties and paved the way toward the establishment of the current power sharing arrangements, the violence involved **paramilitary** groups and British security forces resulting in over 3,000 deaths and 30,000 injured. The conflict was marked by widespread

violations of human rights. A 1971 Parliamentary report documented the use of certain techniques by the Northern Ireland and British governments—wall standing, hooding, subjection to noise, deprivation of sleep and deprivation of food and drink—and labeled them as illegal and recommended that they be discontinued. In 1978, the **European Court of Human Rights** ruled that these techniques "did not occasion suffering of the particular intensity and cruelty implied by the word **torture** . . . [but] amounted to a practice of inhuman and degrading treatment in breach of the European Convention on Human Rights." A 2006 report issued by the Irish government asserted that undercover British security forces had colluded with loyalist paramilitaries in a number of attacks. Hundreds of individuals found guilty of **terrorism** have or are attempting to have their cases reopened, alleging that their confessions were forced by intimidation or ill treatment. *See also* COMMITTEE ON THE ADMINISTRATION OF JUSTICE; FORCED DISAPPEARANCES; STATE TERRORISM.

NORWEGIAN REFUGEE COUNCIL. Established in 1946 under the name Aid to Europe, to assist **refugees** in Europe after **World War II**, this 2,000 staff-strong independent, private **foundation** cooperates closely with the **United Nations** and other organizations around the world as well as in Norway to assist and protect people who have been forced to flee their countries, or their homes within their country, due to war or conflict. The humanitarian assistance provided by the Council to refugees, **internally displaced persons** and returnees focuses on home and school building, the distribution of **food** and non-food relief items, information counseling and legal assistance, camp management and **education**.

NUCLEAR WEAPONS. Strategic and tactical weapons of mass destruction deriving their power from the energy released by fission or fusion of atomic nuclei. The control of nuclear weapons and nuclear disarmament has been on the agenda of the international community since the inception of the **United Nations**, and negotiations on arms control and disarmament measures have generally been divorced from human rights considerations. A 1983 resolution of the **United Nations General Assembly** did "resolutely, unconditionally and for all time, condemn(s) nuclear war as being contrary to human conscience and reason, as the most monstrous crime against peoples and as a violation of the foremost human right—the right to **life**." That same year, the **World Health Organization** adopted a resolution asserting that "nuclear weapons constitute the greatest immediate threat to the health and survival of mankind." In a guarded and somewhat cryptic advisory opinion referring to the notion of **proportionality**, the **International Court of**

Justice determined in 1996 that it could not conclude definitely whether the threat or use of nuclear weapons would be lawful or unlawful even in an extreme circumstance of self-defense, but that it would be generally contrary to the rules of international law applicable in **armed conflict** and in particular the principles and rules of **international humanitarian law**. No international treaty has been adopted banning nuclear weapons, although the United Nations and some member states like the United States have endeavored to keep them out of the hands of a number of countries like North Korea and **Iran**.

NULLUM CRIMEN, NULLA POENE SINE PRAEVIA LEGE. Latin for "no crime, no punishment without a previous law." Legal maxim positing that the existence of a crime rests on a preexisting rule of law. The principle has been incorporated into **international criminal law** in the wake of the criticisms that had been targeted at the **International Military Tribunal for the Prosecution and Punishment of the Major War Criminals of the European Axis**. It is for that reason that the **International Criminal Court** may not deal with situations which took place prior to the entry into force of its statute in 2002.

NUREMBERG PRINCIPLES. In response to Nazi and Japanese atrocities committed in the course of **World War II**, the victorious Allies set two international military tribunals in Nuremberg and Tokyo—the **International Military Tribunal for the Prosecution and Punishment of the Major War Criminals of the European Axis** and the International Military Tribunal for the Far East—where high-level officials and private citizens faced trial for **crimes against peace**, **war crimes** and **crimes against humanity**. As reflected in the statutes of the tribunals, the trials rested on a number of principles, the most important of them being (a) that individuals should be held accountable for the most serious international crimes; (b) the fact that criminal justice was part of international law; and (c) that state leaders and their accomplices were and are not entitled to **immunity**. Their basic premise was that no person, no matter what his or her office, stood above international law.

At the request of the **United Nations General Assembly**, these principles were formalized in a 1950 document prepared by the **International Law Commission**. In an earlier resolution adopted at its first session in 1946, the Assembly had determined that the principles of the Charter of the Nuremberg Tribunal and its judgment were principles of **international law**. The Nuremberg Principles are anchored in the national criminal law of many countries and are enshrined in the statutes of the ad hoc criminal tribunals set up after the end of the **Cold War** as well as the **International Criminal Court.**

NUREMBERG TRIBUNAL. *See* INTERNATIONAL MILITARY TRIBUNAL FOR THE PROSECUTION AND PUNISHMENT OF THE MAJOR WAR CRIMINALS OF THE EUROPEAN AXIS; NUREMBERG PRINCIPLES.

O

OBLIGATION "*ERGA OMNES*." Latin for "in relation to everyone and toward all." In international law, *erga omnes* rights refer to obligations owed by states toward the community of states as a whole rather than individual states because all states share a common interest protecting certain critical rights and in preventing their breach. In a 1970 ruling (the Barcelona Traction case), the **International Court of Justice** clarified that "an essential distinction should be drawn between the obligations of a State towards the international community as a whole, and those arising vis-à-vis another State in the field of diplomatic protection. By their very nature, the former are the concern of all States. In view of the importance of the rights involved, all States can be held to have a legal interest in their protection; they are obligations *erga omnes*." Such obligations derive, for example, in contemporary **international law**, from the outlawing of acts of **aggression** and **genocide**, and also from the principles and rules concerning the basic rights of the human person, including protection from **slavery** and racial **discrimination**. Some of the corresponding rights of protection have entered into the body of general international law, others are conferred by international instruments of a universal or quasi-universal character. *See also JUS COGENS*; NON-DEROGABLE RIGHTS; PEREMPTORY NORMS.

OCCUPATION. In **international humanitarian law**, a territory is considered "occupied" when it comes under the de facto authority of a foreign army. The **Geneva Conventions** spell out the rights and duties of occupying forces and the civilian population. Occupying powers have an obligation to provide adequate provisions of food and medical supplies which are essential to survival of the civilian population. Requisitions are permissible if they do not affect the satisfaction of the needs of the civilian population. Transfers and deportations of population are prohibited and so is the destruction of personal property or real estate unless necessary for the conduct of military operations. Member of organized resistance must, under certain conditions, be treated as prisoners of war. *See also* ARAB ISRAELI CONFLICT; DETENTION; FUNDAMENTAL GUARANTEES;

HUMANITARIAN ASSISTANCE, DENIAL OF; PAPON, MAURICE; PROTECTED PERSONS; WAR CRIMES.

OCCUPIED PALESTINIAN TERRITORIES. *See* ARAB ISRAELI CONFLICT; OCCUPATION.

OECD REVISED GUIDELINES FOR MULTINATIONAL EN-TERPRISES. The only multilaterally endorsed set of voluntary ethical principles and standards for **transnational corporations** (TNCs) operating in or from the 33 countries of the **Organization for Economic Co-operation and Development** (OECD) covering information disclosure, employment and industrial relations, **environment, corruption,** consumer interests, science and technology, competition, and taxation. First agreed on in 1976 at a time when there was a growing public concern about **violations of human rights** by TNCs and revised subsequently several times, the Guidelines called for the establishment on an ad hoc basis of quasi-judicial panels to review **complaints** lodged by **civil society** actors. They were last updated in 2011 but have fallen into relative disuse. *See also* CORPORATE SOCIAL RESPONSIBILITY; SOFT LAW.

OFFICE FOR RESEARCH AND THE COLLECTION OF IN-FORMATION. Entity established in 1987 within the United Nations Secretariat to assist the secretary-general in the exercise of his **fact finding,** preventive diplomacy and good office functions. The specific tasks assigned to the Office, the members of which reported directly to the secretary-general, were to assess global trends; to prepare country, regional, and issue-related profiles, to provide **early warning** of developing situations requiring the secretary-general's attention; to maintain current regional information in data systems using inside and outside data banks; to monitor factors related to possible **refugee** flows and comparable emergencies and to carry out ad hoc research and assessments for the immediate needs of the secretary-general. The quiet but persisting opposition of the United States and the Soviet Union to the project led to the abolition of the Office by Secretary-General Boutros Boutros Ghali in 1992. The fact-finding and early warning work of the office, however, continues to be conducted in a very decentralized and informal manner in many of the departments making up the UN Secretariat.

OFFICE INTERNATIONAL NANSEN POUR LES RÉFUGIÉS. **League of Nations** institution that provided material and political support to **refugees** from 1930 (following the death of **Fridtjof Nansen**) until its dissolution in 1939. It was awarded the **Nobel Peace Prize** in 1938.

OFFSHORE PROCESSING. Practice whereby the **refugee determination** status of **asylum seekers** by a receiving country is carried out outside of its national borders, thus preventing them from invoking national refugee legislation and virtually ruling out their resettlement in this country.

OMBUDSMAN. Official appointed by a national government or legislature or an international organization typically charged with investigating and resolving **complaints** through binding or non-binding recommendations or mediation. **National human rights institutions** frequently act as ombudsmen. The **United Nations** and the **European Union** have instituted posts of ombudsmen. *See also* DECLARATION ON HUMAN RIGHTS DEFENDERS; EUROPEAN CHARTER OF FUNDAMENTAL RIGHTS OF THE EUROPEAN UNION; EUROPEAN OMBUDSMAN.

OPEN SOCIETY INSTITUTE. Private operating and grant-making **foundation** created in 1993 by investor and philanthropist **George Soros**. Originally set up to support foundations in Central and Eastern Europe and the former Soviet Union, the Institute has broadened its initiatives promoting public policies supportive of justice, **education**, public **health** and the protection and improvement of the lives of people in marginalized communities. One of its programs combines **litigation**, legal **advocacy**, technical assistance, and the dissemination of knowledge to secure advances in such areas as anti-**corruption**, **equality** and citizenship, freedom of information and **freedom of expression**, international justice, and national criminal justice. *See also* HUMAN RIGHTS EDUCATION; NATIONALITY, RIGHT TO; REVENUE WATCH.

OPERATION CONDOR. Covert transnational military network of intelligence and secret services of the military governments of **Argentina, Bolivia, Brazil, Chile**, Ecuador, **Paraguay**, and **Uruguay** which developed in the mid-1970s to eliminate Marxist influence in the region and targeted "terrorists" and political opponents in exile. The campaign involved the use of **torture, forced disappearances** and executions and other illegal activities which reached out to such countries as France, Italy, Portugal, Spain and the **United States**. Operation Condor came to an end with the demise of the Argentinian dictatorship in 1983. Records uncovered by the Truth and Justice Commission set up in 2004 in Bolivia documented the secret establishment of the network in 1975 as well as the existence of a joint information center at the headquarters of the Chilean secret police in Santiago. Notwithstanding spectacular cases such as the assassination of a former foreign minister of the Chilean Salvador Allende government who was killed by a car bomb explosion in Washington, D.C., in 1976, the total number of victims is still unknown. Bringing the perpetrators to justice has been a long and tortuous process that is still unfolding, varying in depth and range from one country to another. *See also* BORDABERRY, JUAN MARIA; PINOCHET, AUGUSTO; STROESSNER, ALFREDO; VIDELA, JORGE RAFAEL.

OPINIONS. Terminology used by the **United Nations Committee on the Elimination of All Forms of Racial Discrimination** to refer to its findings on the merits of individual **complaints**.

OPTIONAL PROTOCOL. Less formal than a **treaty** or a **convention** but with the same legal value, a protocol is an agreement which generally amends, supplements or clarifies any subject dealt with in an existing multilateral treaty. It may deal with something in the original treaty, address a new and emerging concern or add a procedure for the operation and enforcement of the treaty (i.e., an individual **complaints** procedure). To the extent that a protocol places additional obligations, the parties to the parent treaty may not necessarily endorse protocols attached to the original treaty, hence the adjective "optional" often attached to the term to underline the fact that states must independently ratify a protocol for it to become binding on them. For instance, the **United Nations Convention on the Rights of the Child** has 193 state parties but its two optional protocols on the involvement of **children in armed conflicts** and the sale and prostitution of children, respectively, have received a far lower number of ratifications. *See also* RATIFICATION; RESERVATIONS TO TREATIES.

ORGANIZATION FOR ECONOMIC CO-OPERATION AND DEVELOPMENT (OECD). Paris-based international organization set up in 1948 under the name of Organization for European Economic Cooperation for the purpose of assisting in the distribution of American financial aid for the recovery and reconstruction of Europe in the wake of **World War II**. In 1961, the organization was turned into an instrument of coordination among its member states to promote policies contributing to economic growth and the expansion of world trade in the context of free market and democratic practices. Although its membership has been extended to a few non-European states, the OECD remains an organization of high-income countries and has been criticized by **civil society** groups and **developing countries** for being so. In regard to human rights, it has produced a number of conventions (for instance on corruption and bribery) and **soft law** instruments such as the **OECD Revised Guidelines on Multinational Enterprises**.

ORGANIZATION FOR SECURITY AND CO-OPERATION IN EUROPE (OSCE). Regional organization which traces its origins to the creation of the Conference on Security and Co-operation in Europe (CSCE) in the early 1970s. Serving as a multilateral forum for dialogue and negotiation between East and West, the CSCE reached agreement on the **Helsinki Final Act** in 1975. Until 1990, the CSCE functioned mainly as a series of meetings and conferences. With the end of the **Cold War**, it developed permanent institutions and operational capabilities and changed its name to the OSCE in 1994.

The OSCE has 57 members in Europe, central Asia and North America. It functions as a primary instrument for **early warning**, conflict prevention, crisis management and post-conflict rehabilitation and carries out several field operations in southeastern Europe, Eastern Europe, the Caucasus and Central Asia. It addresses a wide range of security-related concerns, including arms control, confidence- and security-building measures, election observation, human rights, national **minorities**, democratization, **counterterrorism** and economic and environmental activities. The OSCE's human rights activities focus on such priorities as **freedom of religion** and movement, preventing **torture** and **human trafficking**.

The OSCE monitors and reports on the human rights situation in each of its participating states, particularly in the areas of freedom of assembly and **freedom of association**, the right to liberty and to a fair trial, and in the use of **capital punishment**. It provides training and **education** across the field of human rights, including for government officials, law-enforcement officers, **human rights defenders** and students. The organization also deals with issues relating to the protection of human rights in the global fight against **terrorism** and combating racism, **discrimination** and related forms of intolerance.

Of particular significance among the bodies comprising the OSCE is the Office of the High Commissioner on National Minorities, an office established in 1992 for the purpose of identifying and seeking an early resolution to ethnic tensions. The Office cannot address individual cases but has been credited with contributing to the peaceful resolution of a number of minorities conflicts in the emerging democracies of Eastern Europe. Also important is the Representative on Freedom of the Media which was set up in 1997 and operates from Vienna. The office is designed to "provide rapid response to serious non-compliance with OSCE commitments and principles in respect of **freedom of expression** and free media." Its functions are advisory rather than judicial. *See also* CONSORTIUM OF MINORITY RESOURCES; HUMAN DIMENSION MECHANISM.

ORGANIZATION OF AFRICAN UNITY. *See* AFRICAN UNION.

ORGANIZATION OF AMERICAN STATES (OAS). Regional organization created in 1948, the origins of which can be traced back to the 1890 First International Conference of American States. It now comprises the **United States**, Canada, and 33 states of Central and South America and the Caribbean and it has its headquarters in Washington, D.C. Its purposes are to maintain and strengthen peace and security on the continent and to promote, "by cooperative action," its members' economic, social, and cultural development. Successive amendments to the Charter have been adopted with a view to strengthen the work of the OAS in raising living standards, ensuring social justice and achieving economic development and integration among the nations of the Western Hemisphere. A 1992 amendment assigns to the OAS the eradication of extreme **poverty** as one of its basic objective. The same amendment also calls for the suspension of any member if its democratically elected government has been forcibly overthrown.

The OAS has been the source of numerous human rights norms and **treaties** for ratification by its member states, such as the 1948 **American Declaration of the Rights and Duties of Man**, the 1969 **American Convention on Human Rights** and its additional **protocols** of 1988 and 1990 on economic, social and cultural rights and the abolition of **capital punishment**, the 1987 **Inter-American Convention to Prevent and Punish Torture**, the 1994 **Inter-American Convention on the Prevention, Punishment and Eradication of Violence against Women**, the 1994 **Inter-American Convention on Forced Disappearances of Persons**, the 1999 **Inter-American Convention on the Elimination of All Forms of Discrimination against Persons with Disabilities** and the 2000 **Inter-American Declaration on Freedom of Expression**.

The General Assembly of the OAS, together with the states parties to the **American Convention on Human Rights**, elect the judges of the **Inter-American Court of Human Rights** and adopts its budget. The Assembly also loosely oversees the activities of the OAS specialized economic and social agencies and related bodies concerned with human rights including the Inter-American Juridical Committee, the **Inter-American Commission of Women**, the **Inter-American Children's Institute** and the **Inter-American Indian Institute**.

The OAS's record in the implementation of this impressive array of international legal instruments has been more lackluster and arises from the persisting ambivalence of its state members toward the human rights institutions set up through the Organization. The political culture of the Organization places a premium on the norm of non-intervention. National democratic experiments have often been cut short by recurring waves of authoritarianism and military rule accompanied by frequent states of emergencies with their attendant large-scale practices of **torture, forced disappearances** and **extra-judicial executions**. Weak national judicial institutions, widespread **corruption**, economic crises and persisting large income inequalities have also provided fertile grounds for repeated **human rights violations**. *See also* DEMOCRACY; INTER-AMERICAN COMMISSION ON HUMAN RIGHTS; INTER-AMERICAN CONVENTION ON FORCE DISAPPEARANCES OF PERSONS; INTER-AMERICAN INSTITUTE OF HUMAN RIGHTS.

ORGANIZATION OF ISLAMIC CONFERENCE. *See* ORGANIZATION OF ISLAMIC COOPERATION.

ORGANIZATION OF ISLAMIC COOPERATION (OIC). International organization created in 1969 (called, until 2011, the Organization of Islamic Conference) bringing together Muslim countries for the purpose of enhancing their cooperation in political, economic, social and cultural affairs and safeguarding their common interests. In 1990, the OIC endorsed the **Cairo Declaration on Human Rights in Islam** as an instrument designed to guide its member states in matters of human rights. The Declaration asserts that "[a]ll the rights and freedoms stipulated in this Declaration are subject to the Islamic Shari'ah" and that "[t]he Islamic Shari'ah is the only source of reference for the explanation or clarification of any of the articles of this Declaration." In 2008, the OIC formally revised its charter. The new draft makes no reference to the Cairo Declaration and appears to be embracing the values of the **Universal Declaration of Human Rights**. But, until recently, the OIC has taken a lead role in the United Nations Council on Human Rights (UN-CHR) in condemning the publication of cartoons in Western media which it deems offensive to the Muslim faith. It has also sought to prevent the Council from debating the notion of **sexual orientation** which it has denounced as contrary to "the fundamental teachings of various religions, including Islam." At the same time, while being invariably critical of Israel's practices in the Palestinian occupied territories, the OIC has endeavored to shield its member countries from criticism in the UN-CHR, especially in the context of the **Universal Periodic Review**. *See also* CULTURAL RELATIVISM.

OTTOMAN EMPIRE. *See* TURKEY.

OXFAM INTERNATIONAL. International confederation comprising 13 independent **non-government organizations** in Australia, Belgium, Canada, France, Germany, Great Britain, Hong Kong, Ireland, the Netherlands, New Zealand, Quebec, Spain and the **United States** dedicated to fighting **poverty** and related injustice around the world. A small Oxfam International secretariat is based in Oxford, and the secretariat runs advocacy offices in Washington, D.C., New York, Brussels and Geneva. The name "Oxfam" is derived from the Oxford Committee for Famine Relief, founded in Britain during **World War II**. This group of Oxford citizens campaigned for grain ships to be sent through the Allied naval blockade to provide relief for women and children in enemy-occupied **Greece**.

Poverty eradication has been an overriding concern for Oxfam. Under the strategic plan for 2007–12, Oxfam placed particular emphasis in its **human rights–based approach** on the need to address growing inequality and to empower people living in poverty, particularly women, as a prerequisite to achieving rights-based aims: the right to a sustainable livelihood, the right to basic social services, the right to **life** and security, the right to be heard and the right to an identity. To achieve these objectives and in cooperation with over 3,000 partner organizations from some 100 countries, Oxfam carries out development programs focusing on issues such as **education**, gender, **HIV/AIDS** and human rights, humanitarian emergency work (Oxfam has a recognized expertise in **water** and sanitation), **research** and **lobbying** and popular campaigning.

P

PALESTINIAN CENTRE FOR HUMAN RIGHTS (PCHR). Established in 1995 by a group of Palestinian lawyers and human rights activists and based in Gaza City, PCHR's stated purposes are to protect human rights, promote the **rule of law**, develop democratic institutions and culture within Palestinian society and support efforts aimed at enabling the Palestinian people to exert its right of **self-determination** and independence. The Centre thus conducts **research**, investigates allegations of **human rights violations** and provides legal aid and counseling. The Centre has consultative status with the **United Nations Economic and Social Council** and is an affiliate of the **International Commission of Jurists**, the **International Federation for Human Rights**, the **Euro-Mediterranean Human Rights Network**, the **Arab Association for Human Rights** and the International Legal Assistance Consortium. See also DEMOCRACY; INVESTIGATION.

PALESTINIAN OCCUPIED TERRITORIES. *See* ARAB ISRAELI CONFLICT.

PAPON, MAURICE (1910–2007). Prominent high-ranking French civil servant, politician and government official. During **World War II**, he was secretary-general for police of the Prefecture of Bordeaux and, in that capacity, between 1942 and 1944, authorized the **deportation** of Jews to Germany. As the tide of war turned, he developed contacts with Resistance leaders who vouched for him after the Liberation. After the war, Papon rose through the bureaucracy to various top security positions, eventually reaching senior ministerial positions after 1968. It was not until 1981 that details about his past during the Nazi **occupation** began to emerge, leading to his trial and, after a very long investigation, conviction for **crimes against humanity** in 1998. He was released before the term of his 10-year sentence on grounds of health. *See also* IMPUNITY; PROSECUTION.

PARAGUAY. Latin American country plagued by a long history of political instability, military rule, a civil war and a war against **Bolivia**.

From 1954 to 1989, it came under the dictatorial rule of General **Alfredo Stroessner**. A Truth and Justice Commission set up in 2004 reported 19,862 arbitrary detentions, 18,772 cases of **torture**, at least 59 victims of summary executions, 336 **forced disappearances** and a total of more than 120,000 victims of the Stroessner regime. The Commission attributed these violations to the state authorities' fight against internal subversion, communism and **terrorism**. The Commission also concluded that Stroessner was responsible for 60 cases of **human rights violations**. The country returned to civilian government in 1993 but judicial inquiries into past human rights violations have been delayed or obstructed. **Non-governmental organizations** have highlighted the persistence of human rights issues related to the treatment of **indigenous populations**, police and security forces abuses, violence against women and **human rights defenders**. *See also* COLD WAR; IMPUNITY; TRANSITIONAL JUSTICE.

PARAMILITARIES. Group of civilians organized in a military fashion acting as a civil force or in support of military forces. Such groups may conduct armed operations against a ruling or an occupying power. Paramilitary groups are the parties considered to be most responsible for violent forms of **human rights violations** in a large number of internal conflicts. *See also* ARMED GROUPS; COLOMBIA; EL SALVADOR; GUATEMALA; NORTHERN IRELAND.

PARIS PRINCIPLES. Non-binding guidelines adopted in 1992 by the **United Nations Commission on Human Rights** on the role, composition, status and functions of the **national human rights institutions** (NHRIs). The guidelines emphasize the need to respect the independence of NHRIs, to empower them with the capacity to monitor and advise governmental authorities on specific **human rights violations** and to enable them to relate to regional and international institutions. *See also* MONITORING OF HUMAN RIGHTS; SOFT LAW.

PARLIAMENTARIANS FOR GLOBAL ACTION (PGA). Non-profit, non-partisan international **network** of over 1,300 legislators from more than 100 elected parliaments. Set up in 1978 and headquartered in Washington, D.C., PGA seeks to promote joint action by parliamentarians on global issues. Initially concerned with nuclear disarmament, the organization has progressively broadened the range of its activities, dealing now with the promotion of **democracy**, conflict prevention and management, international law and human rights.

PARTICIPATORY RIGHTS. Political rights in essence empower citizens to vote in free elections and to stand for election. Such rights cannot be realized unless individuals also enjoy the right of free access to information, **freedom of expression**, assembly and **association**.

See also AFRICAN CHARTER ON HUMAN AND PEOPLE'S RIGHTS; AMERICAN CONVENTION ON HUMAN RIGHTS; EUROPEAN CONVENTION FOR THE PROTECTION OF HUMAN RIGHTS AND FUNDAMENTAL FREEDOMS; INTERNATIONAL COVENANT ON CIVIL AND POLITICAL RIGHTS; UNITED NATIONS COMMITTEE ON THE ELIMINATION OF ALL FORMS OF RACIAL DISCRIMINATION; UNITED NATIONS CONVENTION ON THE RIGHTS OF THE CHILD; UNIVERSAL DECLARATION OF HUMAN RIGHTS.

PASHA, TALAT (1874–1921). Ottoman statesman who, together with Djemal Pasha and Enver Pasha, effectively ruled the Ottoman government from 1913 to the end of World War I. As minister of interior affairs in 1915, he ordered the **deportation** of the Armenians from the empire's eastern provinces to Syria, thus setting in motion atrocities resulting in the destruction of two-thirds of the Armenian community in Turkey. He resigned from his subsequent position as prime minister (Grand Vizier) one week before the capitulation of the Ottoman government and fled to Berlin. A Turkish military court found him responsible for the **massacres** committed against the Armenians and sentenced him to death in absentia. He was assassinated by an Armenian who blamed him for massacres that took place in his village. *See also* ARMENIAN GENOCIDE; GENOCIDE; IMPUNITY; TURKEY.

PEACE, RIGHT TO. **Solidarity right** of the **third generation of human rights** advocated mainly by **civil society** organizations and grounded in the assumption that equity and social justice would eliminate the need for violence. From this perspective, individuals and groups have not only a right to life without violence but also the right to positive peace (i.e., life without conditions such as malnutrition, disease, and **poverty**. Another frequently advanced argument is that unless humanity enjoys peace, it cannot exercise its **first-** and **second-generation rights**. Doctrinally, the right to peace may be inferred from the prohibition of the use of force and the mandate for peaceful resolution of conflicts contained in the **United Nations Charter** (Art. 2, para. 4 and Art. 33). Article 28 of the **Universal Declaration of Human Rights** provides that "everyone is entitled to a social and international order in which the rights and freedoms set forth in this Declaration can be fully realized." A 1984 Declaration of the **United Nations General Assembly** (UN-GA) asserted, in the **Cold War** context of the nuclear arms race, that the "preservation of the right of peoples to peace and the promotion of its implementation constituted a fundamental obligation of each State."

The end of the Cold War and increasing attention to the notion of **human security** have led the UN-GA to adopt further resolutions on the subject. The **United Nations Commission on Human Rights** in 2002 adopted a resolution affirming "that all States should promote the establishment, maintenance and strengthening of international peace and security and, to that end, should do their utmost to achieve general and complete disarmament under effective international control, as well as to ensure that the resources released by effective disarmament measures are used for comprehensive development, in particular that of the developing countries." The right to peace now figures on the agenda of the **United Nations Human Rights Council.** In 2010, the Council requested its Advisory Committee to draft, in consultation with member states, civil society, academic and all relevant stakeholders a draft declaration on the right of peoples to peace. *See also* GROUP RIGHTS; NUCLEAR WEAPONS; PUBLIC GOODS; WEAPONS OF MASS DESTRUCTION.

PEACE BRIGADES INTERNATIONAL (PBI). International grassroots **non-governmental organization** which sends teams of volunteers providing non-violent "protective accompaniment" to **human rights defenders** threatened by political violence in conflict areas. PBI has sent teams to several countries, including Nicaragua during the Contra war, the Balkans (1994–2001), **El Salvador** (1987–92), **Guatemala** (1983–99 and again in 2003–), Sri Lanka (1989–98), Haiti (1995–2000), and North America (1992–99, in Canada and the **United States**). They have ongoing projects in **Colombia,** Guatemala, **Indonesia,** Mexico and Nepal.

PEACE OPERATIONS. Multilateral tool for conflict prevention and resolution initially developed during the **Cold War.** Then known as "peacekeeping," the technique involved the deployment of unarmed or lightly armed military personnel for the purpose of observing a cease-fire agreement or acting as a buffer between consenting states. The first peacekeeping operations—the United Nations Truce Supervision Organization and the United Nations Military Observer Group in India and Pakistan—were launched in 1948. Important subsequent operations cast in essentially the same mold were implemented in Egypt (1956, 1973), the Congo (1960–64) and Cyprus (1964). Peacekeeping operations have also been carried out by regional organizations such as the **North Atlantic Treaty Organization,** the **Economic Community of West African States,** the **African Union,** the **European Union** or ad hoc "coalitions of the willing."

With the end of the Cold War, peacekeeping has morphed into "multidimensional" "peace operations" reflecting a fundamental change in its practice. Peace operations now generally refer to missions with military and non-military components that are dispatched by the **United Nations Security Council** to states emerging from internal conflict with a wide variety of short- and medium-term functions involving not only the maintenance of peace and security but the reconciliation of former combatants, the protection of civilians, the disarmament, demobilization and reintegration of former combatants, the organization of elections, the restoration of the **rule of law**, and the resettlement of **refugees** and **internally displaced persons**. Their longer-term objective is to lay down the foundation of lasting peace in a society that will have the capacity of sustaining itself when the internationals have left.

From that perspective, peace operations are concerned with state institution building, the promotion of **democracy**, reconstruction and development. On the assumption that the **realization of human rights** is an essential ingredient of conflict **prevention** and sustainable peace, most peace operations are now tasked to monitor, document, investigate and report on the local human rights situation and to assist in building national human rights capacity and institutions. A number of them have child protection advisers.

See also AFRICAN UNION-UNITED NATIONS HYBRID OPERATION IN DARFUR; DARFUR CONFLICT; INVESTIGATION; MONITORING OF HUMAN RIGHTS; PEACEBUILDING; UNITED NATIONS ASSISTANCE MISSION IN AFGHANISTAN; UNITED NATIONS INTEGRATED MISSION IN TIMOR-LESTE; UNITED NATIONS INTERIM ADMINISTRATION MISSION IN KOSOVO; UNITED NATIONS MISSION IN BOSNIA AND HERZEGOVINA; UNITED NATIONS MISSION IN THE REPUBLIC OF SOUTH SUDAN; UNITED NATIONS MISSION OF SUPPORT IN EAST TIMOR; UNITED NATIONS OBSERVER GROUP IN EL SALVADOR; UNITED NATIONS OPERATION IN BURUNDI; UNITED NATIONS OPERATION IN COTE D'IVOIRE; UNITED NATIONS OPERATION IN MOZAMBIQUE; UNITED NATIONS ORGANIZATION MISSION IN THE DEMOCRATIC REPUBLIC OF THE CONGO; UNITED NATIONS STABILIZATION MISSION IN HAITI; UNITED NATIONS STABILIZATION MISSION IN THE DEMOCRATIC REPUBLIC OF THE CONGO; UNITED NATIONS TRANSITIONAL ADMINISTRATION IN EAST TIMOR; UNITED NATIONS TRANSITION ASSISTANCE GROUP; UNITED NATIONS TRANSITIONAL ADMINISTRATION IN EAST TIMOR; UNITED NATIONS TRANSITIONAL AUTHORITY IN CAMBODIA; UNITED NATIONS VERIFICATION MISSION IN GUATEMALA; WOMEN IN PEACE AND SECURITY.

PEACEBUILDING. Widely used but ill defined term which was highlighted by **United Nations Secretary-General** Boutros Boutros Ghali in his 1992 Agenda for Peace. In essence, the term refers to a broad range of activities initiated with the support of the international community in societies emerging from civil conflict for the purpose of bringing about structural and relational transformations that will create conditions of sustainable and durable peace. Such activities purport to build governance structures and institutions and effective dispute resolution mechanisms and to strengthen the capacity of **non-governmental organizations** and legal and human rights institutions. The emphasis of the United Nations has been on structural transformation, with particular attention to institutional reform.

See also CONSORTIUM ON GENDER, SECURITY AND HUMAN RIGHTS; INTERNATIONAL ALERT; INTERNATIONAL CENTER FOR TRANSITIONAL JUSTICE; INTERNATIONAL CIVIL SOCIETY ACTION NETWORK; PEACE OPERATIONS; UNITED NATIONS PEACEBUILDING COMMISSION; WOMEN IN PEACE AND SECURITY.

PEACEKEEPING. *See* INTERNATIONAL PEACE INSTITUTE; PEACE OPERATIONS.

PEONAGE SYSTEM. Term derived from the Spanish "peon" referring to an unskilled laborer or farm worker bound in **involuntary servitude** to a landlord creditor. Peonage was widely practiced in South America after Spanish conquerors forced poor natives to work in mines and plantations. It was also common in the South of the **United States** after the Civil War. In **Peru** a peonage system existed from the 16th century until **land reform** in the 1950s. *See also* BONDED LABOR; SLAVERY.

PEOPLE'S MOVEMENT FOR HUMAN RIGHTS LEARNING. Formerly known as the People's Movement for Human Rights Education, it is an international service organization founded in 1988 to develop, publish and disseminate demand-driven human rights training manuals and teaching materials. *See also* HUMAN RIGHTS EDUCATION; NON-GOVERNMENTAL ORGANIZATIONS.

PEREMPTORY NORMS. Or *jus cogens*, from the Latin meaning "compelling law." Principle in **international law** positing that here are rules and standards from which no exception or **derogation** can be made. Under the **Vienna Convention on the Law of Treaties**, any treaty that conflicts with a peremptory norm is void. The principle clashes with the tenet of state **sovereignty** which underlines the consensual nature of states' legal obligations. For this reason, there is no clear international consensus regarding precisely which norms are *jus cogens*. Nor is there any agreement how a norm reaches the status of a peremptory norm. But while states may reserve the right to determine what constitutes *jus cogens*, it is generally accepted since the Nuremberg Trials that *jus cogens* includes the prohibition of **genocide**, **torture**, maritime piracy, **slavery** and the slave trade, and wars of **aggression**. **International criminal law** has since **World War II** considerably expanded the scope and range of peremptory norms regarding violations of the **laws of war** and **crimes against humanity**. States are considered to have a duty to prosecute and extradite suspected perpetrators. Defendants, including former heads of states, may no longer invoke statutes of limitations or **immunity**. "Obedience to superior orders" is no longer an acceptable defense. Individuals suspected of such crimes fall under the principle of **universal jurisdiction**. *See also* NECESSITY, DOCTRINE OF; NON-DEROGABLE RIGHTS; NUREMBERG PRINCIPLES; OBLIGATION *"ERGA OMNES."*

PERMANENT ARAB COMMISSION ON HUMAN RIGHTS. Subsidiary body of the **League of Arab States** set up in 1968 to advise the League on ways and means whereby its member states could protect human rights. The Commission has been primarily concerned with publicizing the human rights situation of Arabs living in Israeli-occupied territories. *See also* ARAB ISRAELI CONFLICT.

PERMANENT COURT OF INTERNATIONAL JUSTICE. Legal arm of the **League of Nations** from 1922 to 1940. In the course of its brief history, the court heard a total of 66 cases and rendered 27 **advisory opinions** and 32 judgments. A number of these decisions relate to the rights of **minorities** in Poland and Albania and the 1923 **population exchange** between **Greece** and **Turkey**. The court was formally dissolved in 1945 and replaced, with the establishment of the United Nations, by the **International Court of Justice**. *See also* INTERNATIONAL LAW.

PERSECUTION. Key element in the recognition of **refugee** status and the disposition of **asylum** claims. The 1951 **United Nations Convention Relating to the Status of Refugees** does not define the concept of persecution. Nor does it clarify whether persecution must emanate from a state or **non-state actors**. Practice and national jurisprudence suggest that persecution embraces all serious **violations of human rights** and that recognition of refugee status is justified when persecution is perpetrated by non-state actors under circumstances indicating that the state was unable or unwilling to provide effective protection. The statute of the **International**

Criminal Court (ICC) has in part filled the legal gap by defining persecution as "the intentional and severe deprivation of fundamental rights contrary to international law by reason of the identity of the group or collectivity." The ICC statute also establishes that gender may be grounds for fearing persecution. It includes "persecution against any identifiable group or collectivity on political, racial, national, ethnic, cultural, religious, gender . . . or other grounds that are universally recognized as impermissible under international law" as a crime against humanity. *See also* BLASKIC CASE; CONVENTION GOVERNING THE SPECIFIC ASPECTS OF REFUGEE PROBLEMS IN AFRICA; ROMA/GYPSIES; SEXUAL ORIENTATION; UNITED NATIONS HIGH COMMISSIONER FOR REFUGEES.

PERU. Latin American country with a long history of violence which culminated, in the past two decades of the 20th century, in a bloody conflict pitting the government against two guerrilla groups of Maoist communist leanings, Shining Path and the Tupac Amaru Revolutionary Movement. Draconian measures introduced in the 1990s at the prodding of President **Alberto Fujimori** eventually curbed the activities of the insurgents but the struggle led to the deaths of approximately 70,000 people and was marked by grievous **violations of human rights** by both sides. A **truth and reconciliation commission** established in 2001 to investigate human rights abuses that took place in the 1980s and 1990s concluded that while the majority of the atrocities committed during that period was the work of the insurgents, the Peruvian armed forces were also responsible for the destruction of villages and the murder of *campesinos* suspected of supporting them. The Commission thus called for the punishment of all perpetrators and compensation for individuals and communities affected by the conflict and its recommendations are slowly and partially being implemented.

Collective **reparations** and individual reparations programs were launched in 2007 and 2010, respectively. There have been high-profile prosecutions, most notably those which led to the conviction of former President Fujimori, his secret police chief and a number of senior military and intelligence officials who ran paramilitary **death squads** on human rights and **corruption** charges. But most perpetrators remain unpunished as a result of the military continued obstruction of judicial investigations. Persisting discrimination against indigenous populations and ethnic minorities and failure to apply and enforce labor laws continue to provoke sporadic violence involving local communities and security forces. In 2011, the Peruvian Parliament adopted legislation compelling private companies to consult indigenous communities before going ahead with major projects such as mines. *See also* APOLOGIES; LABOR BONDAGE.

PETITION. *See* COMPLAINTS.

PHILIPPINES. Multiparty democracy with an elected president, a bicameral legislative body and a buoyant **civil society** confronted by the interrelated challenges of a long-standing and deeply rooted dynastic political culture, **corruption**, severe income inequalities and long running low-intensity communist and separatist insurgencies in the southern part of the country. **Non-governmental organizations** and United Nations human rights investigators have documented cases of **arbitrary detentions**, unlawful **extra-judicial executions** by elements of the security services and political killings, including killings of journalists and vigilantism by a variety of state and **non-state actors**. In 2010, the government set up a truth and reconciliation commission to investigate allegations of human rights violations by the previous administration. But the majority of extrajudicial killings and forced disappearances remain unsolved and the actions of senior military commanders have not been investigated. Meanwhile, separatist groups have been linked to the killings of soldiers and police officers in armed encounters as well as bombings that have caused civilian casualties. A peace deal between the government and the main Muslim rebel group in late 2012 could bring an end to more than four decades of fighting. *See also* ARMED GROUPS; LABOR BONDAGE; MARCOS, FERDINAND; PHILIPPINE-AMERICAN WAR; SEX TOURISM.

PHILIPPINE-AMERICAN WAR (1888–1913). When the 1898 Treaty of Paris was signed, bringing to an end the Spanish American War, the **United States** purchased the **Philippines** from Spain. Philippine insurgents, however, had proclaimed their independence six months earlier, and when the treaty was signed, they were besieging Manila and actually controlled most of the country. Hostilities between arriving American occupation troops and Filipino insurgents flared up in February 1899 escalating into a decade-long ferocious war that pitted a large American expeditionary corps against weaker and ill-equipped Filipinos. The conflict thus increasingly shifted to guerrilla warfare and led to a cycle of violence in which hit-and-run bloody raids and ambushes triggered large-scale reprisals including scorched earth campaigns and the forced relocation of civilians into "protected zones" by U.S. troops. Officially declared over in 1902, the insurgency dragged on for another 10 years. By then over 4,000 American soldiers and some 20,000 Filipino fighters had perished. The civilian toll was much heavier, estimates of civilian deaths ranging from 250,000 to 1 million as a result of war, malnutrition and disease. *See also* CONCENTRATION CAMPS; WAR CRIMES.

PHYSICIANS FOR HUMAN RIGHTS. Non-governmental organization founded in 1986 by a small group of doctors who conduct **fact-finding investigations** and **research** on **human rights violations** and their **health** effects in over 40 countries. One of the first missions of the group was to testify on behalf of doctors and human rights activists in **Chile** who were working against the regime of **Augusto Pinochet**. The focus of its investigations is now on atrocities against **civilians** during **armed conflict, gender-based violence, torture** and lack of access to health care due to racial, ethnic and gender **discrimination**.

PILLAY, NAVANETHEM (1945–). South African lawyer currently serving as United Nations high commissioner for human rights. A long-standing anti-**apartheid** activist, she helped expose the use of **torture** and secured the right for political prisoners to have access to lawyers. Co-founder of **Equality Now**, she played an instrumental role in the inclusion in South Africa's constitution of a clause barring **discrimination** on the grounds of race, religion and **sexual orientation**. After a brief tenure on South Africa's Supreme Court in 1995, she served for eight years as a judge on the **International Criminal Tribunal for Rwanda**. In 2003, she began a six-year term judgeship on the **International Criminal Court** from which she resigned in 2008 to take her UN commissioner post. *See also* AKAYESU CASE.

PINOCHET, AUGUSTO (1915–2006). Commander in chief of the army and leader of a four-man junta which led, with **United States** support, a successful military coup in 1973 against **Chile**'s democratically elected socialist president Salvador Allende. The coup followed months of political unrest, hyperinflation, recession and labor strife which were caused, in the military's view, by a coalition of socialists and communists in control of government. Asserting that Chile needed "an authoritarian government that had the capacity to act decisively," Pinochet soon reduced the rest of the junta to a purely ceremonial role and ruled the country under a system of institutional terror, which lasted until 1990 when he voluntarily relinquished the presidency. In that period, the country experienced an era of robust economic growth, but its human rights record made it an international pariah.

After the handover of power, Pinochet remained head of the armed forces, casting himself in the role of "protector of democracy." But in a dramatic turnaround, he was arrested in 1998 in a London clinic where he had gone for back surgery after a Spanish judge in Madrid issued a warrant for his arrest to face charges of crimes against humanity under the rule of **universal jurisdiction**. A 16-month legal battle ensued, ending with the decision to send him back to Chile in March 2000 on the grounds that he was too old and ill to stand trial. In subsequent years, Chilean judges stripped Pinochet of his legal **immunities** and he faced an increasing number of **human rights violations** charges as well as accusations of tax evasion, fraud and other financial improprieties. Repeated attempts to bring him to justice nevertheless ran aground on the argument that his physical and mental ailments made him unfit to stand trial. *See also* OPERATION CONDOR; STATE TERRORISM.

PLATFORM FOR INTERNATIONAL COOPERATION ON UN-DOCUMENTED MIGRANTS. **Non-governmental organization** based in Brussels, promoting respect for the human rights of undocumented **migrants** in Europe by **monitoring** and reporting relevant developments within European institutions. The group issues a newsletter produced in seven languages and circulated to a network of more than 2,400 **civil society** organizations and individuals.

POGROMS. Russian term originally used to designate planned (if not tolerated by state authorities) or spontaneous large-scale mob violence in 19th-century Imperial Russia that was targeted at Jewish communities and could involve looting, the physical destruction of property, sexual crimes and sheer mass killing. Anti-Jewish rioting was common in czarist Russia (2 million Jews fled the Russian empire between 1880 and 1914), but many pogroms also took place in the course of the 1917 Revolution and the civil war which followed, leading to the death of an estimated 70,000 to 250,000 civilian Jews. Pogroms were also frequent in Central and Eastern Europe. The concept has also been applied in a more generic sense to similar incidents against **minorities** in different countries.

POPULATION EXCHANGE. Transfers of populations explicitly or tacitly agreed to by two more states. Instances of population exchanges in the 20th century include the agreement reached by **Turkey** and **Greece** in the 1923 Convention Concerning the Exchange of Greek and Turkish Populations attached to the Treaty of Lausanne which Turkey and Greece signed in the wake of Greece's failed invasion of Turkey's Anatolian mainland and Turkey's repudiation of the Treaty of Sevres of 1920. Within the framework of the Convention, over 1 million Greeks and approximately 500,000 Turks were forced to relocate. Nearly 20 million people in Europe were expelled, transferred or exchanged between 1944 and 1951 in the wake of the Yalta Agreements. A large-scale population exchange between India and Pakistan took place in the months immediately following the 1947 Partition. The bulk of the population exchange took place in the west, especially in the Punjab region. Involuntary population transfers are now considered violations of international law. The 1949 Fourth **Geneva Convention** prohibits mass movement of people out of or into occupied territories. *See also* DEPORTATION; INDIA, PARTITION OF; OCCUPATION.

PORNOGRAPHY. Explicit portrayal of sexual acts for the purpose of sexual arousal and erotic satisfaction through a variety of means including books, magazines, photos, sound recording, films, video and the **Internet.** With the notable exception of the prohibition of the sexual exploitation of children in pornography, there is no universally accepted standard of public morality and the legal status of pornography varies considerably over time and from country to country as governments enjoy a considerable margin of discretion in determining the scope of permissible behavior. *See also* FREEDOM OF EXPRESSION; UNITED NATIONS CONVENTION ON THE RIGHTS OF THE CHILD.

PORTUGAL. *See* ANGOLA; TIMOR-LESTE.

POVERTY. According to the **International Bank for Reconstruction and Development**, poverty is defined as "pronounced deprivation in well being" (i.e., low incomes and the inability to acquire the basic goods and services necessary for survival with human **dignity**). Other dimensions of poverty include low levels of **health** and **education**, poor access to clean **water** and sanitation, inadequate physical security, lack of voice, and insufficient capacity and opportunity to better one's life. Under the influence of **Amartya Sen's** writings and the work of the **United Nations Development Programme**, poverty has been increasingly understood as a denial of choices and opportunities to achieve well-being or "the absence or inadequate realization of certain basic freedoms, such as the freedoms to avoid hunger, disease and illiteracy."

From the standpoint of this **capability approach**, to reduce poverty requires empowering the poor, recognizing the centrality of **accountability** in poverty reduction strategies (PRS), eliminating inequality and **discrimination** and ensuring the participation of the poor in the formulation, implementation and **monitoring** of PRS. There are accordingly close links between PRS and the **realization** of socioeconomic rights. In the language of the **United Nations Committee on Economic, Social and Cultural Rights**, the "rights to work, an adequate standard of living, housing, food, health and education . . . lie at the heart of the Covenant [and] have a direct and immediate bearing upon the eradication of poverty."

See also BUSINESS AND HUMAN RIGHTS RESOURCE CENTRE; INSTITUTE OF DEVELOPMENT STUDIES; JUBILEE DEBT COALITION; MILLENNIUM DEVELOPMENT GOALS; ORGANIZATION OF

AMERICAN STATES; OXFAM INTERNATIONAL; UNITED NATIONS DEVELOPMENT PROGRAMME.

PRECAUTION, PRINCIPLE OF. International humanitarian law precept which requires all fighting parties to take preventative measures to ensure that civilian populations and civilian objects are spared. In the field of environmental law, the principle calls upon states and **non-state actors** to anticipate, prevent and mitigate the causes of environmental damage. *See also* CLIMATE CHANGE; ENVIRONMENT, RIGHT TO A HEALTHY.

PRECAUTIONARY MEASURES. *See* PRECAUTION, PRINCIPLE OF.

PREVENT GENOCIDE INTERNATIONAL (PGI). Global education and **advocacy network** established in 1998 with a view to eliminating the crime of **genocide**. PGI relies on the use of the **Internet** as a way of bringing together a transnational network of local, national and international organizations and individuals around the world speaking out and capable of mobilizing the general public against ongoing or probable episodes of genocide.

PREVENTION. The spread and recurrence of humanitarian crises in the post–**Cold War** era and their devastating impact on security and development has led to an increasing recognition of the importance of prevention (i.e., proactive measures and practices designed to defuse tensions before they reach the stage of violence leading to **human rights violations** and massive humanitarian crises is both desirable and cost-effective). **Think tanks** and **non-governmental organizations** on **United Nations**–related issues have also been actively sponsoring conferences and seminars and issuing publications that feed into the policy debate. This ongoing debate clearly shows that the prevention of human rights violations is a complex matter that includes a wide range of topics ranging from mediation to the development of **early warning** and **monitoring** systems to the training of peacekeepers and to programs designed to strengthen **civil society**.

The conversation originally focused on the effectiveness of peacekeeping operations and traditional diplomatic measures. Its parameters have been broadened considerably and now encompass longer-term efforts to assist **developing countries** in enhancing durable structures conducive to peace and democratic stability and the targeted use of development cooperation. The debate has also shifted from theoretical considerations to the search for concrete policies and the development of practical tools for the prevention of humanitarian crises as evidenced by the creation of a United Nations **Peacebuilding** Commission in 2005.

Yet, preventing human rights violations and humanitarian crises remains an elusive notion both conceptually and operationally. Conflicts continue to flare up with deadly consequences. Precise details about how conflict prevention is to be done, under what circumstances and by whom are clouded with considerable uncertainty. States remain reluctant to take decisive steps toward preventive measures, and international organizations are often stymied by their constituents weary of embarking on policies fraught with high risks and costs. The **United Nations Convention on the Punishment and Prevention of the Crime of Genocide** contains rudimentary and by and large neglected preventive components. In its jurisprudence, the **International Court of Justice** has determined that the prohibition of **genocide** is a **peremptory norm** of **international law** and acknowledged that the principles underlying the Convention are principles which are recognized by civilized nations binding on states. **United Nations treaty bodies**, notably the **United Nations Human Rights Committee**, the **United Nations Committee on Economic Social and Cultural Rights**, the **United Nations Committee on the Rights of the Child**, and the **United Nations Committee on the Elimination of All Forms of Racial Discrimination** have endorsed preventive action procedures including limitations on **freedom of expression** and **association** which may be used to prevent the incitement of racial hatred or violence. *See also* UNITED NATIONS CONVENTION AGAINST TRANSNATIONAL ORGANIZED CRIME; WOMEN IN PEACE AND SECURITY.

PRIVACY, RIGHT TO. Fundamental human right recognized by numerous national constitutions and international human rights instruments including the **Universal Declaration of Human Rights** (Art. 12), the **International Covenant on Civil and Political Rights** (Art. 17), the **International Convention on the Protection of the Rights of All Migrant Workers and Their Families** (Art. 14) and the **United Nations Convention on the Rights of the Child** (Art.16). Article 8 of the **European Convention for the Protection of Human Rights and Fundamental Freedoms** guarantees the right to respect for private and **family** life, one's home and correspondence. The **American Declaration of the Rights and Duties of Man** and the **American Convention on Human Rights** (Art. 11) also contain provisions pertaining to the right to privacy.

In essence, the right to privacy refers to the prevention of intrusions into a person's physical and mental space. Relevant treaty provision and case law suggest that the right to privacy has at least three dimensions. First, the right to privacy includes the idea of a secure space for individual self-determination and development without external interference. This entails freedom from state surveillance, a right to privacy in the media, the right to make choices about one's own body, the entitlement to protection of one's name, respect for intimate relationships between individuals and the right to protection of a person's honor and reputation. **United Nations treaty bodies** have not determined conclusively whether abortion falls within the sphere of privacy, and the **European Court of Human Rights** (ECHR) has repeatedly left the question open. Second, the right to privacy implies non-interference with correspondence and modern means of communication, the main contentious issue here being the permissibility of restricting correspondence by and with persons in custody. Third, the right to privacy includes respect for the home and protection against interference such as searches, **forced evictions** or the destruction of **housing** by state authorities. In a number of cases which began in the 1990s, the ECHR has established a link between the right to privacy, the right to a healthy **environment** and environmental pollution and determined that breaches of the right to respect the home also include physical breaches such as noise, emissions, smells and other forms of interference.

As the level of information generated by individuals has dramatically increased as a result of advances in medical research, information technology and financial transactions, there have been growing concerns about the protection of privacy related to the use of identity cards, biometrics, surveillance of communications and **Internet** and mail interception. Such concerns have been heightened by government **counterterrorism** policies and practices.

See also EUROPEAN CHARTER OF FUNDAMENTAL RIGHTS OF THE EUROPEAN UNION; EUROPEAN PARLIAMENT; HUMAN RIGHTS FIRST; INTELLECTUAL PROPERTY RIGHTS; INTERNATIONAL GAY AND LESBIAN HUMAN RIGHTS COMMISSION; RIGHTS INTERNATIONAL.

PRIVATE MILITARY COMPANIES (PMCs). Also known as security contractors, private military contractors, private security contractors or, as they call themselves, private military corporations, private military firms, private security providers, or military service providers, PMCs have been defined as "corporate bodies that specialize in the provision of military skills—including tactical combat, operations, strategic planning, intelligence gathering and analysis, operational support, troop training, and technical assistance." By and large a phenomenon of the post–**Cold War** era and of the **privatization** of tasks long considered the monopoly of state authorities, PMCs have proliferated and operate in some 50 countries. It is believed that the PMC industry is now worth over $100 billion a year. The involvement of PMCs in combat activities has led to documented instances of **violations of human rights** which raise complex issues of **accountability**

and responsibility that have been met with relative **impunity** in the current domestic and international legal landscapes. *See also* ARMED GROUPS; INTERNATIONAL CODE OF CONDUCT FOR PRIVATE SECURITY SERVICE PROVIDERS; MERCENARIES.

PRIVATIZATION. Process of transferring the ownership of a business, enterprise or public service from the public sector to the private sector. More generally, the term refers to the transfer of a government function to the private sector. Proponents and critics of privatization argue about matters of economic efficiency, **corruption** and **accountability**. From a human rights perspective, privatization has been shown to lead, at least in the short and medium term, to a greater concentration of wealth as well as a higher incidence of **poverty** and social deprivation. *See also* CHILE; DEREGULATION; FUJIMORI, ALBERTO; GLOBALIZATION; INTERNATIONAL LAW INSTITUTE; PERU; PRIVATE MILITARY COMPANIES; STRUCTURAL ADJUSTMENT PROGRAMS; WATER, RIGHT TO.

PROCEDURAL REQUIREMENTS. *See* ADMISSIBILITY REQUIRE-MENTS.

PROJECT ON INTERNATIONAL COURTS AND TRIBUNALS. Internationally based undertaking sponsored by New York University and the University of London combining academic **research** with concrete action aimed at facilitating the work of international courts and tribunals and developing the legal skills of potential actors, in particular, in developing countries and economies in transition. *See also* CAPACITY BUILDING.

PROPERTY, RIGHT TO. The assertion that individuals have a right to property has from the outset been controversial. The **Universal Declaration of Human Rights** does recognize the existence of the right, but the two United Nations covenants remain silent on the subject, partly because of a lack of consensus between East, West and South over the question of compensation in cases of nationalization or expropriation. Some aspects of the right to property are obliquely recognized by the **International Covenant on Economic, Social and Cultural Rights** in the context of the realization of the right to **food** and **housing** (Art. 11), the right to a court hearing in civil disputes and the right to **privacy** and **family** life under the **International Covenant on Civil and Political Rights** (Arts. 14 and 17). Regional human rights conventions do not protect the freedom to acquire property but do protect its continued possession. The **European Court of Human Rights** has produced a large body of jurisprudence on this subject. It should be noted that the **Inter-American Court of Human Rights** has a rich jurisprudence on the protection of the collective property of **indigenous peoples**.

In contrast to human rights law, **international humanitarian law** does provide for direct protection of the property rights falling under the category of "**protected persons**" in times of **armed conflicts**. Pillage is a war crime under the **Geneva Conventions**. In addition, the Conventions prohibit the destruction of private property in occupied territories and attacks on civilian objects. They also provide safeguards for the personal property of prisoners of war and civilian internees. *See also* EUROPEAN CHARTER OF FUNDAMENTAL RIGHTS OF THE EUROPEAN UNION; INTELLECTUAL PROPERTY RIGHTS.

PROPORTIONALITY. Principle of **international humanitarian law** asserting that the effects of the means and methods of warfare being used may not be disproportionate to the military advantage being sought. Military operations should accordingly cause damage or lead to casualties that are strictly necessary or unavoidable. Acts that are excessive in relation to concrete and direct military advantages anticipated are considered **war crimes** under the statute of the **International Criminal Court** and fall under its jurisdiction. *See also JUS AD BELLUM/IN BELLUM*; NUCLEAR WEAPONS; PUBLIC EMERGENCIES.

PROSECUTION. "[T]he institution and continuance of a criminal suit involving the process of pursuing formal charges against an offender to final judgment." Thus defined, the idea that individuals can be held accountable and responsible for the most egregious **violations of human rights** before an international court of law and should be subject to criminal punishment is not new, but it is only in the past two decades or so that it has gained significant political traction. The 1919 Treaty of Versailles and the 1920 Treaty of Sevres were the first international **treaties** recognizing individual responsibility for crimes committed against **international law**. Trials were held in the wake of **World War II** in Nuremberg and Tokyo. Throughout the postwar period, universal instruments have been developed explicitly requiring prosecution. These include the United Nations Convention against Genocide, the **United Nations Convention against Torture**, the **Convention on the Abolition of Slavery**, the **International Convention against Apartheid in Sports**, the **International Convention on the Elimination of All Forms of Racial Discrimination** and the more recent **International Convention for the Protection of All Persons from Enforced Disappearances**. The end of the **Cold War** gave new impetus to the establishment of **war crime tribunals**

and the **International Criminal Court** (ICC), and their jurisprudence has yielded increasingly exact definitions of international crimes which have been, in effect, codified in the statute of the ICC.

Concurrently, a significant number of prosecutions have been conducted in domestic judicial systems on the basis of the principles of territorial, passive personality or **universal jurisdiction** principles. But the acceptance of states to bring to trial their own nationals has widely fluctuated. In many postconflict states, transitional governments granted **amnesties** to former rulers and those amnesties which were overturned required years, if not decades, of efforts. In other cases (**Cote d'Ivoire** and Sudan, for instance), it is sometimes argued that criminal punishment threatens peace and reconciliation. Most frequently, prosecutions are utilized in conjunction with other **transitional justice** mechanisms.

See also ARGENTINA; BARBIE, KLAUS; BRAZIL; CHILE; DEMJANJUK, JOHN; EICHMANN, ADOLF; IMMUNITY; IMPUNITY; KAISER WILHELM; JURISDICTION; KOSOVO; LEIPZIG WAR TRIALS; MY LAI MASSACRE; PAPON, MAURICE; PINOCHET, AUGUSTO; RWANDA; SANCTIONS; TIMOR-LESTE; TOUVIER, PAUL; TRUTH AND RECONCILIATION COMMISSIONS.

PROTECTED PERSONS. Categories of individuals who, under **international humanitarian law** regulating international conflict, have special rights in terms of protection and assistance. These include the wounded and sick in armed forces in the field and at sea, medical and religious personnel, wounded and sick civilians, parliamentarians, personnel of civil defense organizations, relief personnel, the civilian population, persons detained, interned or otherwise deprived of liberty, the population of occupied territories, and women and children. In situations of internal armed conflict, all individuals must benefit from the minimum **fundamental guarantees**. The civilian population and objects indispensable to their survival, persons deprived of their liberty for reasons related to the conflict, wounded and sick civilians and medical and religious personnel enjoy the same entitlements. *See also* ARMED CONFLICT; CIVILIANS, PROTECTION OF; GENEVA CONVENTIONS; PROPERTY, RIGHT TO.

PROTOCOL. *See* OPTIONAL PROTOCOL.

PROTOCOL TO THE AFRICAN CHARTER ON HUMAN AND PEOPLE'S RIGHTS ON THE RIGHTS OF WOMEN IN AFRICA. Also known as the Maputo Protocol (where is was signed in 2003), this addendum to the **African Charter on Human and People's Rights** elaborates on the principle of nondiscrimination enunciated in the Charter by guaranteeing comprehensive rights to women including the rights to take part in the political process and to social and political **equality** with men. It also entitles women to control their reproductive health and calls for an end to **female genital mutilation**. These last two provisions elicited considerable opposition from Christian and Muslim groups. Only four African states have neither signed nor ratified the Protocol. *See also* GENDER-BASED VIOLENCE; REPRODUCTIVE RIGHTS.

PROVISIONAL MEASURES. *See* INTERIM MEASURES.

PUBLIC EMERGENCIES. International human rights law (notably the **International Covenant on Civil and Political Rights** [Art. 4], the **European Convention for the Protection of Human Rights and Fundamental Freedoms** [Art. 17] and the **American Convention of Human Rights** [Art. 27]) recognizes that under exceptional circumstances which threaten the life of the nation such as **armed conflicts**, natural catastrophes and violent civil unrest, states may derogate from their obligations (i.e., they may suspend human rights). In **General Comments** 4 and 29, the **United Nations Human Rights Committee** clarified that the validity of these exceptional measures hinges on a number of requirements. Any emergency must be serious, of concern to the international community, declared publicly and registered with an international body. **Derogations** must be limited only to the exigencies of the situation in accordance with the principle of **proportionality**. They must be absolutely necessary to achieving a time-bound specific goal. In no case can they involve the suspension of **non-derogable** rights such as the right to **life** and freedom from **torture** and **slavery**. Derogations are subject to monitoring by an international or regional body. In its jurisprudence, notably two cases involving the Great Britain and Greece, the **European Court of Human Rights** clarified that public emergencies must "be actual or imminent." Their effects "must involve the whole nation," the continuance of the organized life of the community must be threatened and the crisis or danger must be exceptional. The purpose of the derogation regime is to strike a balance between the protection of individual human rights and the protection of the nation in times of crises. In practice, such a balance has proved elusive.

See also ABROGATION OF RIGHTS; ALGERIAN WAR OF INDEPENDENCE; AMERICAN CIVIL LIBERTIES UNION; COUNTERTERRORISM; EGYPT; FUJIMORI, ALBERTO; *HAMDI ET AL. v. RUMSFELD, SECRETARY OF DEFENSE, ET AL.*, KOREMATSU, FRED TOYOSABURO; LIBERTY, RIGHT TO; NECESSITY, DOCTRINE OF; PERU; SYRIA; TURKEY.

PUBLIC GOODS. Products which "all enjoy in common in the sense that each individual's consumption of that good leads to no substraction from any other individual's consumption of that good." Under the terms of this definition, peace and national defense and clean air may be said to be public goods. More specifically, in terms of public policy, public goods carry with them "benefits that are strongly universal in terms of countries . . . people . . . and generations." The prevention of deadly conflict, health and the eradication of disease, financial stability, **refugee** and **migrant workers** protection, mental sustainability and the preservation of the global commons can be viewed as public goods. From that perspective, access to such goods and services as basic **education**, a healthy **environment**, **food** and **water**, primary **health** care and sanitation is indispensable to the fulfillment of socioeconomic rights and can provide the basis for human rights claims inasmuch as they may require government intervention in the market to ensure their provision. *See also* DEVELOPMENT, RIGHT TO; GROUP RIGHTS.

R

RACIAL DISCRIMINATION. The historic experiences of **colonialism**, the German **Holocaust** and **apartheid** have contributed to making race an especially odious reason for treating persons differently and shaped the prohibition of racial discrimination formulated in the **International Convention on the Elimination of All Forms of Racial Discrimination** which forcefully posits that people should not be impeded from enjoying their guaranteed rights on account of their color, origin or descent. The notion of race may, in some situations, be defined on observable physical or biological characteristics but, frequently, determining whether discrimination is solely based on race becomes difficult as race is a social construct, with the outcome of collective ascription typically referring to individuals viewed as different and inferior primarily because of particular cultural attributes.

Not surprisingly, in its jurisprudence, the **United Nations treaty body** that **monitors** the convention has broadened its understanding of racism to the self-identification of the individuals concerned and has thus considered the cases of groups not contemplated at the time of the drafting of the Convention such as the **Romas** in Bulgaria, Germany and the Czech Republic, Tibetans in China, Aborigines in Australia, immigrants in France and Italy, and the Hutus and Tutsis in **Rwanda** and **Burundi**. But the Committee has upheld very few individual **complaints** of alleged **violations of human rights**.

See also CENTER FOR CONSTITUTIONAL RIGHTS; INTERNATIONAL MOVEMENT AGAINST ALL FORMS OF DISCRIMINATION AND RACISM; KING, MARTIN LUTHER, JR.; MYRDAL, KARL GUNNAR; ORGANIZATION FOR SECURITY AND CO-OPERATION IN EUROPE; WORLD CONFERENCE AGAINST RACISM.

RAINFOREST ACTION NETWORK. Described as "some of the most savvy environmental agitators in the business," this American **non-governmental organization**, founded in 1985 and based in San Francisco, primarily focuses its activities on the planning and coordination of public campaigns to leverage public opinion and consumer pressure against **transnational corporations'** practices that are destructive to the **environment**

and, in particular, of the rainforests and the human rights of those living in and around those forests. *See also* INDIGENOUS PEOPLES.

RAMOS-HORTA, JOSE (1949–). Founder of the Revolutionary Front for an Independent East Timor who led the resistance against the Indonesian annexation and occupation of East Timor. He played a key role in the negotiations which led to independence. In 1996, he shared the **Nobel Peace Prize** with his compatriot Bishop **Ximenes Belo** for his "sustained efforts to hinder the oppression of a small people." Ramos also served as foreign minister and prime minister of his country when it became independent as **Timor-Leste**. He was elected to the presidency in 2007.

RAND CORPORATION. This well-respected American **think tank** began operation in 1946 and was turned into a non-profit organization in 1948 and is based in Santa Monica, California. Its purpose is "to further and promote scientific, educational and charitable purposes, all for the public welfare and security of the **United States**." RAND's **research** agenda revolves around the priorities of the nation. Its international research programs currently focus on a wide range of cross-cutting issues, including global economies and trade, space and maritime security, diplomacy, global **health** and **education**, national building and regional security and stability. RAND also analyzes the policies and effectiveness of international organizations such as the **United Nations**, the **North Atlantic Treaty Organization**, the **European Union**, and the Association of South East Asian Nations and, in that context, has produced a number of studies of national human rights practices.

RAOUL WALLENBERG INSTITUTE. Named after the Swedish diplomat who undertook humanitarian work in Hungary at the end of **World War II**, the mission of this independent institution is to promote respect for human rights through academic **education, research** and training. Its full name is the Raoul Wallenberg Institute on Human Rights and Humanitarian Law and it is located in Lunds, Sweden. The institute offers graduate as well as undergraduate human rights study programs. Its research carried out with various bodies of the United Nations, including the **United Nations Office of the High Commissioner for Human Rights**, the **United Nations Development Programme**, the **United Nations High Commissioner for Refugees** and the **International Bank for Reconstruction and Development**, deals with a wide range of topics such as the administration of justice, business and human rights, democratic **governance** and **rule of law, international humanitarian law, indigenous peoples, international criminal law, non-discrimination, reproductive rights, disabled persons**

and **national human rights institutions** among others. A major component of the **capacity-building** programs the Institute provides is training for key persons and the transfer of knowledge and skills to target institutions.

RAPE. *See* GENDER-BASED VIOLENCE.

RATIFICATION. Process by which a national constitutionally designated body—normally a legislative organ—confirms the government signature of a **treaty**. Completion of this process signals that a state accepts to be bound by the provisions of a treaty. *See also* RESERVATIONS.

REALISM. School of thought in international relations studies highlighting the anarchic nature of an international society grounded on the primacy of sovereign **states**. From this perspective, states are guided by their national interests rather than universal moral or ethical values. Great powers typically invoke human rights considerations when this serves their interests or when they wish to hide the pursuit of narrow self-interests. For instance, universal standards were used by European imperial powers in the 19th century to justify their colonial enterprises. In the same vein, realist observers argue, **democracy** promotion can be viewed as a tool for the consolidation of a state hegemony. In any event, international human rights institutions have little autonomy; they are created at the will of states and can operate only as long as their activities are consistent with the interests of the powerful. *See also* CONSTRUCTIVISM; SPIRAL MODEL OF HUMAN RIGHTS CHANGE.

REALIZATION OF HUMAN RIGHTS. A human right is realized when individuals enjoy the freedoms covered by that right and their enjoyment of the right is secure. A person's human rights are realized if sufficient social arrangements are in place to protect him or her against threats to his or her enjoyment of the freedoms covered by those rights. *See also* STANDARD-BASED MEASURES; STRUCTURAL ADJUSTMENT PROGRAMS; UNITED NATIONS GLOBAL CONFERENCES; VIOLATION OF HUMAN RIGHTS.

RECOGNITION, RIGHT TO. Closely related to the right to **life** is the notion that everyone has the right to recognition as a person before the law. This right is enshrined in the **Universal Declaration of Human Rights** (Art. 6), the **International Covenant on Civil and Political Rights** (Arts. 16 and 26), the **American Convention on Human Rights** (Art. 5) and the **African Charter on Human and People's Rights** (Art. 5). Recognition as a person before the law first means legal capacity (i.e., the capacity of individuals to enter into legal obligations and to have access to courts of law). From this standpoint, this entitlement is arguably as important as the right to life as its total or partial denial precludes the exercise of other rights as evidenced by the predicament of **indigenous peoples, minorities** and **refugee** or **asylum seekers** sometimes attest when they seek to engage with national law. Children, however, are fully recognized as persons in spite of the fact that they do not have full legal capacity. The **United Nations Committee on the Rights of the Child** has endeavored to raise the age of criminal responsibility to 18, but the subject remains highly controversial.

A corollary of the right to recognition as a person is the prohibition of **discrimination** which the **United Nations Human Rights Committee** in a 1989 **general comment** has defined as "any distinction, exclusion, restriction or preference which is based on any ground of race, color, sex, language, religion or other opinion, national or social origin, property, birth or other status . . . which has the effect of nullifying or impairing recognition, enjoyment or exercise by all persons, on an equal footing, of all rights and freedoms." *See also* FAIR TRIAL, RIGHT TO; RULE OF LAW.

REDRESS. The *Merriam-Webster Dictionary* defines redress as "to set right," "to make up for," "to remove the cause of (a grievance or a complaint)." From a substantive viewpoint, redress involves compensation for pecuniary or non-pecuniary losses. National and international legal practice and jurisprudence suggest that at a minimum, redress requires, depending on the case, restitution or compensation and a right to the **truth**. *See also* ACCOUNTABILITY; REMEDY; REPARATIONS.

REDRESS (NGO). London-based human rights **non-governmental organization** founded in 1992 which seeks to obtain **reparation** for victims of **torture** and to make accountable those who perpetrate or are complicit in acts of torture. To achieve these objectives, Redress provides legal advice and assists torture survivors to gain access to national courts and international human rights institutions such as the **Inter-American Commission on Human Rights** and the **United Nations Human Rights Committee**, promotes the development and implementation of national and international legal civil and criminal remedies and increases awareness about the use of torture and the need of measures to provide **redress**, notably through country reports. *See also* REMEDIES; VIOLATION OF HUMAN RIGHTS.

REFUGEE DETERMINATION PROCESS. Practice of the Office of the **United Nations High Commissioner for Refugees** (UNHCR) whereby it determines whether an individual seeking **asylum** meets the criteria contained in the 1951 UN Refugee Convention qualifying him or her as a **refugee**. Precise definitions can be found in the *Handbook on Procedures and Criteria for Determining Refugee Status*, reissued in 2012 by the UNHCR. The procedure may result in the voluntary return to one's homeland, resettlement in third countries or local integration. *See also* GENDER-SPECIFIC CLAIM; INTERNATIONAL ASSOCIATION FOR REFUGEE LAW JUDGES; OFFSHORE PROCESSING; REFUGEE LAW; UNITED NATIONS CONVENTION RELATING TO THE STATUS OF REFUGEES.

REFUGEE LAW. International rules and procedures designed to protect persons seeking **asylum** and those who have been recognized as **refugees** from persecution. This body of law in part overlaps with the legal regime applicable to the protection of **civilians** in **armed conflicts** under **international humanitarian law**. The main sources of global refugee law are **customary international law**, **peremptory norms** and international **treaties** including the 1951 **United Nations Convention Relating to the Status of Refugees** and its 1967 Protocol and the **United Nations Convention against Torture**. These are complemented by several regional instruments. The **European Convention for the Protection of Human Rights and Fundamental Freedoms** requires that detention be based on clear laws and allows for appeals procedures. Regional international organizations—the Asian-African Legal Consultative Committee, the Organization of African Unity, the **Organization of American States**, the **European Union** and the **Council of Europe**—have also developed further standards of refugee protection through treaties and declarations.

See also BANGKOK PRINCIPLES ON STATUS AND TREATMENT OF REFUGEES; CARTAGENA DECLARATION ON REFUGEES; CONVENTION GOVERNING THE SPECIFIC ASPECTS OF REFUGEE PROBLEMS IN AFRICA; REFUGEE DETERMINATION PROCESS.

REFUGEES. Under the terms of the 1951 **United Nations Convention Relating to the Status of Refugees**, refugees are persons who seek refuge in a foreign country because of war and violence or out of fear of persecution on account of race, religion, **nationality**, and membership in a particular social group or of a political opinion. This definition differs markedly from earlier definitions that prevailed in the years following World War I under the **League of Nations** which tended to describe refugees in terms of their nationality as "Assyrians," "Turks," "Greeks" or "Armenians." The term **persecution** has evolved so as to mean threats to life, bodily harm, **torture,** prolonged **detention**, repeated interrogations and arrests and internal exile. It does not cover conditions such as **poverty** or natural disasters. The **United**

Nations High Commissioner for Refugees (UNHCR) issued in 1979 an authoritative *Handbook on Procedures and Criteria for Determining Refugee Status* under the 1951 Convention and the 1967 Protocol Relating to the Status of Refugees which still provides widely accepted guidance on the interpretation of this definition. Individuals who have applied for refugee status but have not yet obtained it are known as **asylum seekers**.

National government agencies of the host country determine whether or not a person is a refugee, a process that frequently entails inconsistency, denial of **due process** and arbitrariness. Applicants for refugee status must have crossed an international border and be outside the country of their nationality. If they have not, they are considered **internally displaced persons** (IDPs) who, as such, do not qualify for the protections provided for in the 1951 Refugee Convention. States' parties to the UN refugee convention are obligated not to return a refugee to a country of territory where he or she would be at risk of persecution. The principle is known as **non-*refoulement*** and is widely considered part of international customary law. The 1984 **United Nations Convention against Torture** also prohibits the forcible removal of persons to a country where there is a real risk of torture.

International **refugee law** sets out the rights to which refugees are entitled. The 1951 Convention stipulates all refugees must be granted identity papers and travel documents that allow them to travel outside the country and receive the same treatment as nationals of the receiving country with regard to their free exercise of religion and religious education, free access to the courts, access to elementary education and to public relief and assistance, protection provided by social security, protection of industrial property and literary, artistic and scientific work and equal treatment by taxing authorities. As of October 2008, there were 144 states parties to the Convention. By the end of 2010, over 40 million people—15.4 refugees and 27.5 million IDPs—were receiving protection or assistance by UNHCR.

See also ABKHAZIA; ADVOCATES FOR HUMAN RIGHTS; ALIENS, TREATMENT OF; BANGKOK PRINCIPLES ON STATUS AND TREATMENT OF REFUGEES; CCJO RENE CASSIN; CARTAGENA DECLARATION ON REFUGEES; DEPORTATION; ENCAMPMENT; ENVIRONMENTALLY INDUCED MIGRANTS; EUROPEAN CON-VENTION FOR THE PROTECTION OF HUMAN RIGHTS AND FUNDAMENTAL FREEDOMS; FREEDOM OF MOVEMENT; GENDER-SPECIFIC CLAIM; HARKIS; INTERNATIONAL INSTITUTE OF HUMANITARIAN LAW; INTERNATIONAL RESCUE COMMITTEE; NORWEGIAN REFUGEE COUNCIL; OFFSHORE PROCESSING; RACIAL DISCRIMINATION; REFUGEE DETERMINATION PROCESS; RIGHTS INTERNATIONAL; SABRA AND SHATILA MASSACRE; UNITED

NATIONS CONVENTION ON THE REDUCTION OF STATELESSNESS; UNITED NATIONS HUMAN RIGHTS COMMITTEE; UNITED NATIONS INTERIM ADMINISTRATION MISSION IN KOSOVO; UNITED NATIONS MISSION IN THE CENTRAL AFRICAN REPUBLIC AND CHAD; UNITED NATIONS MISSION IN THE REPUBLIC OF SOUTH SUDAN; UNITED NATIONS OPERATION IN BURUNDI; UNITED NATIONS OPERATION IN MOZAMBIQUE; UNITED NATIONS RELIEF AND WORKS AGENCY FOR PALESTINE REFUGEES IN THE NEAR EAST; UNITED NATIONS TRANSITIONAL AUTHORITY IN CAMBODIA; WORLD CONFERENCE AGAINST RACISM.

REFUGEES INTERNATIONAL (RI). Early-warning and **advocacy non-governmental organization** seeking to generate increases in resources and policy changes by government and United Nations agencies to improve conditions for **refugees** and **internally displaced persons**. RI primarily acts as a witness to the suffering of the displaced and refugees, interviewing and reporting on war-affected populations in the field in such conflict zones as the Darfur region of Sudan, Ethiopia, Bangladesh, **Liberia**, Haiti, **Uganda**, Cambodia, and the Thai–Burma border.

REGIONAL ARRANGEMENTS. Undefined terminology found in a separate chapter of the **United Nations Charter** concerned with the maintenance of international peace and security. The Charter simply states that the **United Nations Security Council** (UN-SC) may rely on such "regional arrangements" for its enforcement actions and that these "arrangements" may themselves take enforcement actions under the authority of the UN-SC. Regional arrangements only emerged after the establishment of the **United Nations**, most of them, such as the **North Atlantic Treaty Organization** (NATO) and the Warsaw Pact coming into existence against the backdrop of the **Cold War**. With the demise of the Cold War, NATO security and military functions have been linked to the achievements of human rights objectives as was the case in **Kosovo** and, more recently, **Libya**. Regional arrangements for the protection of human rights may be found in the proliferation of international organizations of a regional character in the postwar period which have their own regional mechanisms and mechanisms such as the **African Union**, the **Economic Community of West African States**, the **European Union**, the **League of Arab States**, the **Organization of Security and Co-operation in Europe** and the **Organization of American States**.

REHABILITATION INTERNATIONAL (RI). Global **network** of 1,000 members and affiliated organizations from nearly 100 nations founded in

1922 to promote the rights of people with disabilities. Its overall objective is to empower **disabled persons** and provide sustainable solutions for a more inclusive and accessible society. One of the key players in the field of disability, RI developed the International Symbol of Access, a widely recognized symbol for disability worldwide. It was instrumental in the genesis, development and adoption of the **United Nations Convention on the Rights of Persons with Disabilities.**

RELIGION. *See* FREEDOM OF RELIGION.

RELIGIOUS DISCRIMINATION. *See* DECLARATION ON THE ELIMINATION OF ALL FORMS OF INTOLERANCE AND OF DISCRIMINATION BASED ON RELIGION AND BELIEF; FREEDOM OF RELIGION; UNITED NATIONS HUMAN RIGHTS COMMITTEE.

REMEDY. The term has two components: one procedural, the other substantive. In the first sense, remedy refers to the processes thereby a right is enforced by courts, administrative agencies or any other competent body. This is what Article 8 of the **Universal Declaration of Human Rights** refers to when it posits that "Everyone has the right to an effective remedy by the competent national tribunals for acts violating the fundamental rights granted him by the constitution or by law." Similar provisions are found in regional human rights instruments. The second meaning of the term focuses attention on the outcome of these processes (i.e., the relief that is afforded to victims of violations of rights). The **Basic Principles and Guidelines on the Right to a Remedy and Reparation for Victims of Gross Violations of International Human Rights Law and Serious Violations of International Humanitarian Law** adopted by the **United Nations General Assembly** in 2005 embraces the two concepts by stating that the right to a remedy entails equal and effective **access to justice**, adequate, effective and prompt **reparation** for harm suffered, access to relevant information concerning violations and reparation mechanisms and access to justice. In principle, there should be a remedy for the violation of every right. Practice in regard to compensation, rehabilitation, reparation, deterrence and punishment, both at the national and international levels, of course, varies considerably. *See also* ACCOUNTABILITY; ADMISSIBILITY REQUIREMENTS; DUE PROCESS RIGHTS; EUROPEAN COURT OF HUMAN RIGHTS; KADI CASE; LITIGATION; REDRESS; STATUTORY LIMITATIONS; TRUTH, RIGHT TO THE; "WAR ON TERROR."

RENDITION. *See* EXTRAORDINARY RENDITION.

REPARATIONS. In human rights legal parlance, reparations are broadly understood as compensation for an abuse, injury or the harm suffered by an individual or a group as a result of the violation of their rights. The corollary of the right of a victim to receive reparation is the duty of the party responsible for the injury to provide **redress**. The United Nations **Basic Principles and Guidelines on the Rights to a Remedy and Reparation for Victims of Gross Violations of International Human Rights Law and Serious Violations of International Humanitarian Law** describes five formal categories of reparations: restitution, compensation, rehabilitation, satisfaction, and guarantees of non-repetition. Reparations can thus be symbolic as well as material, ranging from financial compensation to formal **apologies** to the provision of special services. In a 1928 international court case, the **Permanent Court of International Justice** called the obligation of states to make reparations for an unlawful act "a general principle of international law" and part of "a general conception of law" (*Factory at Chorzów [Germany v. Poland]*).

The legal underpinning of the right to an effective **remedy** and the duty to provide reparation can now be found in numerous human rights instruments including the **Universal Declaration of Human Rights** (Art. 8), the **International Covenant on Civil and Political Rights** (Art. 2), the **International Convention on the Elimination of All Forms of Racial Discrimination** (Art. 6), and the **United Nations Convention against Torture** (Art. 14) among others. Reparations can be sought by individuals through national courts or international judicial or quasi-judicial bodies. They can also be developed and implemented as governments' policies. More specifically, and in the light of the traditional law of state responsibility, human rights law and international criminal law, claimants have five possible routes: (a) acting on their behest, the state of **nationality** of the victims can bring a claim against the state responsible for the wrong; (b) the victims may take the responsible state before an international human rights tribunal; (c) the victims may act against the responsible state in national judicial or administrative bodies; (d) the victims may initiate proceedings in an international criminal court; and (e) the victims may make a claim against the individual perpetrators in a national civil or criminal proceeding. In nearly all situations, under the doctrine of exhaustion of local remedies, reparations must first be claimed in national administrative or judicial bodies before being brought to an international body.

Reparations programs have been proposed or implemented in **Argentina, Brazil**, Cambodia, Canada, **Colombia, Democratic Republic of the Congo, El Salvador**, Germany, Ghana, **Guatemala**, Haiti, Iraq, Japan, Malawi, **Liberia**, South Africa, Kenya, **Timor-Leste**, and the **United States**. The

United Nations Human Rights Council recently established a mandate for a **special rapporteur** on the promotion of truth, justice, reparation and guarantee of non-recurrence.

See also COLONIALISM; "COMFORT WOMEN"; DRAFT ARTICLES ON THE RESPONSIBILITY OF STATES FOR INTERNATIONALLY WRONGFUL ACTS; REPARATIVE JUSTICE; SET OF PRINCIPLES FOR THE PROTECTION AND PROMOTION OF HUMAN RIGHTS THROUGH ACTION TO COMBAT IMPUNITY; SLAVERY; STATUTORY LIMITATIONS; TRANSITIONAL JUSTICE; TRUTH, RIGHT TO THE; WORLD CONFERENCE AGAINST RACISM.

REPARATIVE JUSTICE. Modality of **transitional justice** focused on remedying past suffering and loss. The issuance of official **apologies** and the awarding of compensation or **restitution** are two key methods in bringing about **reparation**. *See also* INTERNATIONAL CRIMINAL LAW; KOREMATSU, FRED TOYOSABURO; PERU; RESTORATIVE JUSTICE; RETRIBUTIVE JUSTICE.

REPORTERS WITHOUT BORDERS (RWB). International **non-governmental organization** advocating freedom of the press and freedom of information. RWB was founded in 1985 and is based in France. Guided by Article 19 of the 1948 **Universal Declaration of Human Rights**, which states that everyone has "the right to freedom of opinion and expression" as well as the right to "seek, receive and impart" information and ideas "regardless of frontiers," RWB compiles and publishes an annual ranking of countries based on its assessment of their press freedom records. *See also* ARTICLE 19, THE INTERNATIONAL CENTRE AGAINST CENSORSHIP; FREEDOM OF EXPRESSION.

REPRODUCTIVE RIGHTS. Category of rights linked to sexual reproduction and reproductive **health** and enshrined in a number of legally binding international treaties notably, the **International Covenant on Civil and Political Rights**, the **International Covenant on Economic, Social and Cultural Rights**, the **United Nations Convention on the Elimination of All Forms of Discrimination against Women** and the **United Nations Convention on the Rights of the Child**. Specifically protected reproductive rights relate to the right to **life** and survival, the right to **liberty** and security of the person, the right to voluntarily **marry** and establish a **family**, the right to decide the number and spacing of one's children, the right to the highest attainable standard of health, the right to benefit from scientific progress and the right to receive and impart information.

Advocates of reproductive rights have also argued that there is a close connection between achieving reproductive health and **poverty** eradication and a number of **United Nations** conferences, especially the 1994 **International Conference on Population and Development** and the 1995 **Fourth World Conference on Women** in Beijing, China, have stressed that reproductive rights are a cornerstone of sustainable development which, in turn, hinges on women's empowerment and gender equality. Relevant national policies, legislation and practices about the right to reproduce such as compulsory sterilization or forced contraception as well as the right not to reproduce (i.e., support for access to birth control and abortion) and the rights to **privacy**, medical coverage, contraception, sex education, family planning and protection from discrimination and **gender-based violence** are monitored by **United Nations treaty bodies** and other regional institutions such as the **European Court of Human Rights**. The **United Nations Population Fund** is the world's largest multilateral source of funding for population and reproductive health programs.

See also ABORTION; ALAN GUTTMACHER INSTITUTE; ARTICLE 19, THE INTERNATIONAL CENTRE AGAINST CENSORSHIP; BEIJING DECLARATION AND PLATFORM OF ACTION; CATHOLIC CHURCH; CENTER FOR REPRODUCTIVE RIGHTS; EQUALITY NOW; FAMILY CARE INTERNATIONAL; FEMALE GENITAL MUTILATION; FEMALE INFANTICIDE; INTERNATIONAL PLANNED PARENTHOOD FEDERATION; MILLENNIUM DEVELOPMENT GOALS; PROTOCOL TO THE AFRICAN CHARTER ON HUMAN AND PEOPLE'S RIGHTS ON THE RIGHTS OF WOMEN IN AFRICA; RAOUL WALLENBERG INSTITUTE; SOFT LAW; UNITED NATIONS COMMISSION ON THE STATUS OF WOMEN; WOMEN'S REFUGEE COMMISSION.

RESEARCH. In the broadest sense of the term, research in human rights practice entails the systematic gathering and studying of information and facts for the purpose of identifying and documenting rapidly developing violations of human rights or longer-term human rights issues, reporting on them and, often, advocating for change in policies and practices. Interviews, field missions, reviews of media reports, analysis of domestic legislation, international law and policy papers, academic reports and civil society studies are the main tools of human rights research carried out by government or non-governmental actors. Satellite technology has been increasingly relied on to gather information from societies closed to investigators because of insecurity or restrictions imposed by the authorities.

See also ADVOCATES FOR HUMAN RIGHTS; AFRICA INSTITUTE OF SOUTH AFRICA; AL HAQ; ALAN GUTTMACHER INSTITUTE;

ASIAN CENTER FOR HUMAN RIGHTS; BRITISH INSTITUTE OF HUMAN RIGHTS; CENTER FOR ECONOMIC AND SOCIAL RIGHTS; CENTER FOR HUMAN RIGHTS AND GLOBAL JUSTICE; CENTER FOR MIGRATION STUDIES; COALITION AGAINST TRAFFICKING IN WOMEN; CODESRIA; EUROPE-THIRD WORLD CENTRE; EUROPEAN RESEARCH CENTRE ON MIGRATION AND ETHNIC RELATIONS; EUROPEAN ROMA RIGHTS CENTER; FRASER INSTITUTE; FREEDOM HOUSE; GLOBAL CENTER FOR THE RESPONSIBILITY TO PROTECT; HUMAN RIGHTS INTERNET; HUMAN RIGHTS WATCH; INSTITUTE FOR GLOBAL POLICY; INSTITUTE FOR HUMAN RIGHTS AND BUSINESS; INSTITUTE FOR INTERNATIONAL LAW AND HUMAN RIGHTS; INSTITUTE FOR INTERNATIONAL LAW AND JUSTICE; INSTITUTE OF DEVELOPMENT STUDIES; INTER-AMERICAN INDIAN INSTITUTE; INTER-AMERICAN INSTITUTE OF HUMAN RIGHTS; INTERNATIONAL ASSOCIATION OF REFUGEE LAW JUDGES; INTERNATIONAL CENTRE FOR CRIMINAL LAW REFORM AND CRIMINAL JUSTICE POLICY; INTERNATIONAL CENTRE FOR TRADE UNION RIGHTS; INTERNATIONAL COMMISSION FOR LABOR RIGHTS; INTERNATIONAL COMMISSION OF JURISTS; INTERNATIONAL COUNCIL ON HUMAN RIGHTS POLICY; INTERNATIONAL CRISIS GROUP; INTERNATIONAL FEDERATION FOR HUMAN RIGHTS; INTERNATIONAL FOUNDATION FOR ELECTORAL SYSTEMS; INTERNATIONAL HUMAN RIGHTS LAW INSTITUTE; INTERNATIONAL LAW ASSOCIATION; INTERNATIONAL MOVEMENT AGAINST ALL FORMS OF DISCRIMINATION AND RACISM; INTERNATIONAL PEACE INSTITUTE; INTERNATIONAL RESCUE COMMITTEE; INTERNATIONAL SAVE THE CHILDREN ALLIANCE; IN-TERNATIONAL WOMEN'S RIGHTS PROJECT; KURDISH HUMAN RIGHTS PROJECT; MINORITIES AT RISK PROJECT; MINORITY RIGHTS GROUP INTERNATIONAL; OXFAM INTERNATIONAL; PHYSICIANS FOR HUMAN RIGHTS; PROJECT ON INTERNATIONAL COURTS AND TRIBUNALS; RAND CORPORATION; RAOUL WALLENBERG INSTITUTE; RUMMEL, RUDOLPH JOSEPH; THINK TANKS; THIRD WORLD INSTITUTE; TRANSNATIONAL INSTITUTE; UNITED NATIONS CHILDREN'S FUND; UNITED NATIONS HUMAN SETTLEMENTS PROGRAMME; UNITED NATIONS OFFICE OF THE HIGH COMMISSIONER FOR HUMAN RIGHTS; WOMEN'S REFUGEE COMMISSION; WORLD FEDERATION OF UNITED NATIONS ASSOCIATIONS.

RESERVATIONS TO TREATIES. Unilateral statements (also known as **declarations** or understandings, derogations, or objections) by the states parties to a **treaty** signaling that they will not accept or wish to modify a particular legal obligation arising from that treaty. Some treaties may expressly forbid any reservations but, under **international law** (more specifically, the 1969 Convention on the Law of Treaties), they are now generally accepted as state practice as long as they are not inconsistent with the goals and purposes of the treaty. Other states parties to the same treaty have the option to accept, object to or oppose those reservations. Numerous states have made reservations to human rights treaties, thereby rekindling the debate about their admissibility. A case in point are the reservations adopted by the **United States** when it ratified the **United Nations Convention on the Punishment and Prevention of the Crime of Genocide** and the **International Covenant on Civil and Political Rights** in 1986 and 1992, respectively, which many nations view as voiding key provisions of both treaties (one of these reservations stipulated that the United States could not act upon the obligations contained in the Convention if such actions were prohibited by the U.S. Constitution). Since 1994, the **International Law Commission** has been trying to elaborate guidelines for the validity of reservations against human rights treaties. In their **General Comments**, several United Nations **treaty bodies** have articulated the view that governments have only limited grounds for justifying their reservations to human rights treaties.

See also ADVISORY OPINION; INTERNATIONAL CONVENTION ON THE ELIMINATION OF ALL FORMS OF RACIAL DISCRIMINATION; INTERNATIONAL COURT OF JUSTICE; SAUDI ARABIA; STATUTORY LIMITATIONS; UNITED NATIONS CONVENTION ON THE ELIMINATION OF ALL FORMS OF DISCRIMINATION AGAINST WOMEN; VIENNA CONVENTION ON THE LAW OF TREATIES.

"RESPONSIBILITY TO PROTECT" (R2P or RtoP). Normative principle first articulated by the **International Commission on Intervention and State Sovereignty** in a report published in 2001 highlighting that governments under the doctrine of **state sovereignty** have a primary obligation to protect their people. If they are unwilling or unable to do so, the international community would acquire the right to prevent atrocities and abuses of human rights, to react if such abuses do occur and to rebuild structures and institutions after an intervention in order to prevent their recurrence. The emphasis of the report is on **prevention** (i.e., a set of policies which include measures for building state capacity and supporting the **rule of law** and mechanisms for remedying grievances). The use of force is only a last resort.

The concept was formally endorsed by the 2005 United Nations World Summit. Two years later, the **United Nations General Assembly** approved the creation of a post of special adviser on the responsibility to protect to explore ways and means to operationalize the idea. These may not be more than pyrrhic victories for the promoters of R2P who are basically **non-governmental organizations** and academic groups outside the United Nations. A few governments have adopted various domestic policies to prevent atrocity crimes, including the appointment of national R2P Focal Points. But within the United Nations, which remains anchored on the traditional principle of the sovereign equality of states, the theme of a "just cause" for preemptive humanitarian intervention elicits deep political unease as well as fears that R2P could provide the pretext or rationale for unilateral armed interventions by big powers.

See also EVANS, GARETH; GLOBAL CENTER FOR THE RESPONSIBILITY TO PROTECT; HUMAN SECURITY; HUMANITARIAN INTERVENTION; INTERNATIONAL COALITION FOR THE RESPONSIBILITY TO PROTECT; INTERNATIONAL CRISIS GROUP; INTERNATIONAL PEACE INSTITUTE; LIBYA; NO-FLY ZONE; SAHNOUN, MOHAMED; SYRIA; WORLD FEDERALIST MOVEMENT.

RESTITUTION. Form of **restorative justice** measures seeking to reestablish the situation that existed prior to **violations of human rights** and humanitarian law. These include a wide array of courses of action ranging from returning a lost asset (such as restoration of liberty, citizenship, return of property), to monetary compensation for economically assessable damage, to medical and psychological care as well as legal and social services to guarantees of non-repetition. The notion of restitution is closely linked to the idea of **state responsibility**, and its principles have been developed in the context of interstate relations as reflected in the **Draft Articles on the Responsibility of States for Internationally Wrongful Acts** adopted in 2001 by the **United Nations' International Law Commission**. The Articles have yet to receive the imprimatur of the **United Nations General Assembly**.

In the meantime, it has been suggested that the duty of states to make reparations for violations of human rights has attained the status of **customary international law** and that **international human rights law** and **international humanitarian law** enshrine the idea that individuals enjoy remedial rights, including a right to restitution. In this regard, the **International Covenant on Civil and Political Rights**, the **International Convention on the Elimination of All Forms of Racial Discrimination**, the **United Nations Convention on the Rights of the Child** and the **United Nations Convention against Torture and Other Cruel, Inhuman** or **Degrading Treatment and Punishment** do create a general duty to make appropriate reparations for violations of human rights. States have nevertheless generally paid scant (and late) attention to reparations for human rights abuses, especially when restitution claims are related to historical injustices or were connected to armed conflicts involving dispossession driven by **ethnic cleansing**. It was only in the late 1980s that Canada and the **United States** adopted legislation granting personal compensation to Canadian and American citizens of Japanese ancestry who had been placed in internment camps following the 1941 attack on Pearl Harbor. A possible exception to this pattern is the very comprehensive system of reparations introduced by the Federal Republic of Germany for compensating victims of Nazi persecution.

Restitution is probably more likely to be achieved in regard to violations of **property** rights, such as illegal or arbitrary expropriations. The **European Court of Human Rights** has occasionally ordered states to return seized properties. In a 2001 landmark case underlining the importance of international human rights mechanisms in matters related to large-scale dispossession affecting an entire community, the **Inter-American Court of Human Rights**, in the Awas Tingni case, found that Nicaragua had violated the rights to property and judicial protection of the members of the Mayagna (Sumo) community of Awas Tingni and ordered the government to enforce its historical title on its ancestral land and resources.

See also BASIC PRINCIPLES AND GUIDELINES ON THE RIGHT TO A REMEDY AND REPARATION FOR VICTIMS OF GROSS VIOLATIONS OF INTERNATIONAL HUMAN RIGHTS LAW AND SERIOUS VIOLATIONS OF INTERNATIONAL HUMANITARIAN LAW; KOREMATSU, FRED TOYOSABURO.

RESTORATIVE JUSTICE. Procedure used in the **transitional justice** processes aimed at reconciling victims and perpetrators of **violations of human rights** in order to restore a shared sense of community. **Truth and reconciliation commissions** are a commonly used restorative mechanism. *See also* *GACACA* COURTS; INTERNATIONAL CRIMINAL LAW; REPARATIVE JUSTICE; RETRIBUTIVE JUSTICE.

RETRIBUTIVE JUSTICE. One possible approach to **transitional justice** designed to punish the perpetrators of **violations of human rights** by means of **prosecution** in a public trial. Such prosecutions may be carried out by national courts. If government authorities are unwilling or unable to do so, the international community may set up ad hoc international courts or tribunals which would be disbanded once they have completed their task. Instances of such mechanisms include the **International Criminal Tribunal for the Former Yugoslavia**, the **International Criminal Tribunal for Rwanda**

and the **Special Court for Sierra Leone**. An alternative scenario is to have recourse to the **International Criminal Court**. *See also* INTERNATIONAL CRIMINAL LAW; RESTORATIVE JUSTICE; REPARATIVE JUSTICE; WAR CRIME TRIBUNALS.

RETURNEES. *See* UNITED NATIONS CONVENTION RELATING TO THE STATUS OF REFUGEES.

REVENUE WATCH. Non-profit policy organization promoting through expertise, funding and technical assistance transparency, **accountability** and effectiveness in the management of oil, gas and mineral resources of some 20 producing countries often affected by conflict, **poverty** and **corruption**. Originally launched in 2002 as a program of the **Open Society Institute** and with financial support of the Bill and Melinda Gates Foundation, the William and Flora Hewlett Foundation, Revenue Watch has operated independently since 2006. Much of its work focuses on building and strengthening **civil society**'s capacity in producing countries and developing partnerships with governments and industry. One of its notable activities has been the development, implementation and internationalization of the **Extractive Industries Transparency Initiative**. *See also* CORPORATE SOCIAL RESPONSIBILITY; GLOBALIZATION.

RIGHTS AND DEMOCRACY. Originally known as the International Centre for Human Rights and Democratic Development, this organization was created by Canada's Parliament in 1988 to encourage and support the universal values of human rights and the promotion of democratic institutions and practices around the world. Inaugurated in 1990, Rights and Democracy focuses its activities on the development of democratic practices, institutions and culture at the national and regional levels, economic and social rights and the rights of **indigenous peoples** and women. Rights and Democracy receives the bulk of its funding from Canada's Department of Foreign Affairs and International Trade. It has **consultative status** with the **United Nations Economic and Social Council** and is on the **International Labour Organization**'s Special List of **non-governmental organizations**. It also has observer status with the **African Commission on Human and People's Rights**. *See also* DEMOCRACY.

RIGHTS HOLDERS. In the language of human rights advocates, all individuals or groups or communities within a particular jurisdiction who are entitled to make a rights claim against **duty bearers**. *See also* NON-DISCRIMINATION.

RIGHTS INTERNATIONAL. United States–based **non-governmental organization** set up in 1994 by human rights lawyers and international policy analysts to litigate cases of **violations of human rights** in international human rights institutions such as the **Inter-American Commission on Human Rights** and the **Inter-American Court of Human Rights**, the **European Court of Human Rights** and the **African Commission on Human and People's Rights**. Rights International appears before such bodies both as lawyers for its clients and as amicus. The cases involve a wide range of human rights, including **capital punishment, family** and **privacy** rights, **freedom of expression**, humanitarian and international criminal law, legal access and assistance, preventive detention, race and gender **discrimination, refugee** and **asylum** law, and **torture**. Rights International also organizes continuing legal education programs on international human rights law practice and publishes texts and casebooks for scholars, practitioners, and students of international human rights law, with a particular focus on the increasingly large body of case law emanating from international tribunals. *See also* ASSOCIATION FOR THE PREVENTION OF TORTURE; LITIGATION.

ROBINSON, MARY (1944–). President of Ireland from 1990 to 1997 and **United Nations high commissioner for human rights** from 1997 to 2002. As UN Commissioner, Robinson was a tireless promoter of human rights, assigning priority to principled **advocacy** over consensus building in the functions of her office. Within the organization, she pressed for mainstreaming human rights concerns in all the activities of the **United Nations**. She was unabashedly critical of member states **violations of human rights**, censuring Ireland's treatment of immigrants as a form of **bonded labor**, China's treatment of its Tibetan minority and the United States' **counterterrorism** policies for their human rights abuses. Sustained pressure by the United States which intensified in the wake of the 2001 **World Conference against Racism** in effect forced her out of office. In 2004, **Amnesty International** awarded her its Ambassador of Conscience Award for work in promoting human rights. In 2002, she founded Realizing Rights, an advocacy **non-governmental organization** seeking to integrate human rights standards, gender equality and enhanced accountability in global governance and policy making. From 2009 to 2010, she was the head of the **International Commission of Jurists**.

ROMA/GYPSIES. Nomadic communities variously known as Tsigans, Gitanos, Gypsies and Zigeuners originally from Northern India and, since the 14th century, now living throughout Europe. There are currently some 8.5 million Roma/Gypsies in Europe, two-third of them concentrated in Central and Eastern Europe. Roma/Gypsies speak many dialects but share common cultural and ethnic characteristics and, most particularly, a common history of **discrimination** and persecution which continues to this day. Widely perceived as outcasts unable to fit into the settled structures of society because of their distinct nomadic lifestyle, Roma communities have been the targets of discriminatory policies, ranging from bans imposed on their nomadic lifestyle or strictly controlled residency requirements, to the outlawing of their languages and traditions, to forced assimilation and outright **persecution**. Up to half a million Romas died in **concentration camps** in Nazi Germany.

In theory, Roma most of the time now enjoy the same formal rights as any other citizens. In practice, they are still the targets of negative stereotyping and violent attacks by the public. They remain an "underclass" living in poverty with its host of attendant problems including low life expectancy, disease, and rates of unemployment higher than the rest of society. Over the past quarter of century, efforts have been made through the **United Nations** and various European institutions—notably the **Council of Europe**, the **European Union** and the **Organization for Security and Cooperation in Europe**—to improve the Romas' legal and social situation. But their status under **international human rights law** remains uncertain as they are variously classified as immigrants, **migrant workers**, **asylum seekers** and displaced persons under international law rather than defined as bona fide members of **minorities**. *See also* EUROPEAN ROMA RIGHTS CENTER; EUROPEAN SOCIAL CHARTER.

ROOSEVELT, ELEANOR (1884–1962). First Lady of the **United States** from 1933 to 1945 who assumed the role of New Deal, women and civil rights advocate throughout Franklin D. Roosevelt's tenure as president. In 1945, President Harry S. Truman appointed her as a delegate to the **United Nations General Assembly**. Subsequently, she served as the first chairperson of the **United Nations Commission on Human Rights** and played an instrumental role, along with **Rene Cassin**, John Humphrey, and **Charles Habib Malik** among others in the drafting of the **Universal Declaration of Human Rights**.

RUCKUS SOCIETY. The objective of this **non-profit organization** is to provide "environmental, human rights, and social justice organizers with the tools, training, and support needed to achieve their goals." In brief, the group trains activists in "direct action" and "guerrilla communication" techniques (i.e., "police confrontation strategies," "street blockades," "urban climbing and rappelling," "using the media to your advantage") in support of "historically marginalized communities" such as "youth, women, people of color, **indigenous people** and immigrants, poor and working class people, lesbian, gay, bisexual, gender queer, and transgendered people." American multinational corporations, the **Bretton Woods Institutions** and the **World Trade Organization** have been among the main targets of the Society's activities. It has proven to be a more controversial defender of human rights than other non-governmental organizations.

RUGGIE, JOHN G. (1944–). Distinguished and influential American political scientist who has served the United Nations in various capacities in the past two decades. As a senior aide of **United Nations Secretary-General Kofi Annan**, he oversaw the launching of the Global Compact and secured **United Nations General Assembly** approval of the **Millennium Development Goals**. From 2005 to 2011, as special representative of the United Nations secretary-general for business and human rights from 2005 to 2011, he was the architect of the **United Nations "Protect, Respect and Remedy" Framework for Business and Human Rights**. *See also* NORM ENTREPRENEURS.

RULE OF LAW. Human rights principle closely related to the notion of **accountability**, stressing that government decisions should be made in accordance with known principles or laws. There is considerable controversy as to whether the rule of law implies a judgment about the "justness" of the law or simply refers to the existence of specific procedures which must be respected by governments. A 1959 international meeting of judges, lawyers and law professors sponsored by the **International Commission of Jurists** issued a declaration stating that the rule of law implies certain rights and freedoms, an independent judiciary, and social, economic and cultural conditions conducive to human **dignity**.

Another **non-governmental organization**, the **World Justice Project**, has identified four core elements of the rule of law: governments and their agents must be accountable under the law; the laws must be clear, publicized, stable, fair, and protect fundamental rights, including the security of persons and property; the process by which the laws are enacted, administered, and enforced must be accessible, fair, and efficient; and access to justice must be provided by competent, independent, and ethical adjudicators, attorneys or representatives and judicial officers with adequate resources and reflecting the makeup of the communities they serve. On the basis of these criteria, the World Justice Project has developed an index measuring the accountability of governments under the law and whether legal institutions protect individual human rights and allow individuals access to justice.

Since 1992, rule of law questions have been discussed by the **United Nations General Assembly**. The **United Nations Security Council** has held a number of thematic debates on the subject, resulting in resolutions or statements emphasizing the importance of the rule of law in the context of women, **peace** and **security, children in armed conflicts** and the **protection of civilians** in armed conflict. The rule of law is an important component of the agenda of the **United Nations Peacebuilding Commission**. The Vienna Declaration and Programme of Action adopted by the 1993 Vienna **World Conference on Human Rights** called for including the rule of law in **human rights education** programs.

See also EAST AFRICAN COURT OF JUSTICE; EQUALITY BEFORE THE LAW; EURO-MEDITERRANEAN HUMAN RIGHTS NETWORK; EUROPEAN UNION; FAIR TRIAL, RIGHT TO; HERITAGE FOUNDATION; INTERNATIONAL ASSOCIATION FOR REFUGEE LAW JUDGES; INTERNATIONAL HUMAN RIGHTS LAW INSTITUTE; LIBERALISM; NECESSITY, DOCTRINE OF; PALESTINIAN CENTRE FOR HUMAN RIGHTS; RAOUL WALLENBERG INSTITUTE; RECOGNITION, RIGHT TO; TRANSITIONAL JUSTICE; UNITED NATIONS DEVELOPMENT PROGRAMME; UNITED NATIONS INTERIM ADMINISTRATION MISSION IN KOSOVO; UNITED NATIONS MISSION IN BOSNIA AND HERZEGOVINA; UNITED NATIONS MISSION IN THE REPUBLIC OF SOUTH SUDAN; WORLD FEDERALIST MOVEMENT; WORLD JUSTICE PROJECT.

RUMMEL, RUDOLPH JOSEPH (1932–). American political scientist who has devoted his **research** to documenting and quantifying collective forms of mass violence and wars. The author of two dozen scholarly books, he coined the term **democide**—meaning murder by government—arguing that the death toll from democide in the past century far exceeded the death toll from war. In his writings, he has also developed the interrelated (and controversial) idea that **democracies** are the least likely forms of government to kill their citizens and that they virtually never wage war among themselves. *See also* DEMOCRATIC KAMPUCHEA; GENOCIDE.

RUMSFELD, DONALD (1932–). American businessman and politician who served as secretary of defense under both President Gerald Ford from 1975 to 1977 and President George W. Bush from 2001 to 2006. In that latter capacity, he planned and executed the U.S.-led invasions of **Afghanistan** and Iraq. He also defended the Bush administration's claim to detain "enemy combatants" without the protection of the **Geneva Conventions**. But in a 2004 landmark case (***Hamdi v. Rumsfeld***), the U.S. Supreme Court ruled that Mr. Hamdi was a U.S. citizen and could not be held indefinitely without having the capacity to challenge his detention in court. A U.S. Senate panel determined that Rumsfeld should be held personally responsible for the **Abu Ghraib** torture and prisoner abuse scandal and the UN **special rapporteur** on **torture** stated at the **United Nations Human Rights Council** in January 2009 that Rumsfeld and others should be prosecuted for **war crimes** because they had authorized the use of interrogation methods amounting to torture on prisoners at the **Guantanamo Bay Detention Camp**. **Litigation** efforts by former Guantanamo Bay detainees seeking compensatory damages for torture and arbitrary detention authorized by Rumsfeld and the military chain of command in violation of the U.S. Constitution the Geneva Conventions and the **Alien Tort Statute** have been unsuccessful. *See also* HUMAN RIGHTS FIRST; UNIVERSAL JURISDICTION.

RUSSELL-SARTRE TRIBUNAL. Panel of world-renowned intellectuals constituted in 1966 by Bertrand Russell and Jean-Paul Sartre to investigate and document possible **war crimes** by the **United States** in the course of its military intervention in **Vietnam**. After hearings held in Stockholm and Copenhagen, the "tribunal" concluded in 1967 that the United States had committed acts of **aggression** and that its armed forces had subjected the civilian population to inhuman treatment in violation of international law. The panel's work received considerable international attention but was dismissed by the United States as a biased show trial.

RUSSIAN FEDERATION. *See* ABKHAZIA; ANGOLA; BANGLADESH LIBERATION WAR; BIAFRA; COLD WAR; COUNTERTERRORISM; CUBA; DEPORTATION; FORCED DISAPPEARANCES; GULAG; INTERNATIONAL MILITARY TRIBUNAL FOR THE FAR EAST; INTERNATIONAL MILITARY TRIBUNAL FOR THE PROSECUTION AND PUNISHMENT OF THE MAJOR WAR CRIMINALS OF THE EUROPEAN AXIS; KATYN FOREST MASSACRE; KOSOVO; LENIN, VLADIMIR; MENGHISTU, HAILE MARIAM; MYANMAR; NAGORNO-KARABAKH; POGROMS; SEX TRAFFICKING; SOLZHENITSYN, ALEXANDER; SOUTH OSSETIA; STALIN, JOSEF; STATE TERRORISM; SYRIA; UKRAINE FAMINE; UNITED NATIONS SUB-COMMISSION ON THE PROMOTION AND PROTECTION OF HUMAN RIGHTS; WOMEN IN PEACE AND SECURITY.

RWANDA. Former **mandate** of the **League of Nations** and Trust Territory of the **United Nations** administered by Belgium which became independent in 1960 in the wake of a UN supervised referendum. After independence, government-sponsored Hutu gangs carried out periodic **pogroms** of Tutsis, prompting many to take refuge in neighboring countries (6,000 to 16,000 Tutsi members of the ruling class were killed between 1962 and 1964). By the 1990s, there were some 1 million refugees scattered about mostly in **Uganda** and **Burundi**. A group of them formed the backbone of an armed insurgency under the umbrella of the Rwandan Patriotic Front (RPF) which in 1990 crossed into Rwanda and launched a guerrilla offensive. The Hutu government of Juvenal Habyarimana responded by orchestrating an anti-Tutsi radio campaign, secretly training informal armed gangs and unleashing massacres of Tutsis. The insurgency nevertheless kept gaining strength and Habyarimana was compelled to accept a peace accord with power-sharing arrangements supervised by a United Nations peacekeeping force (the **United Nations Assistance Mission in Rwanda**).

The assassination of President Habyarimana triggered the long planned mass killing of the Tutsi and moderate Hutu. The **genocide** came to an end only when the RPF, led by Paul Kagame, the country's present ruler, routed the Rwandan army and seized power. Post-genocide Rwanda still struggles with the legacy of the genocide and faces daunting challenges of reconciliation and reconstruction. The Kagame government initially concentrated much of its efforts on suppressing a powerful Hutu counterinsurgency originating from refugee camps located in the **Democratic Republic of the Congo**. High-level members of the government and armed forces are being tried by the **International Criminal Tribunal for Rwanda**. Lower-level leaders and people are being prosecuted by Rwanda. Tensions between Hutus and Tutsis still fester not far below the surface, and human rights organizations have criticized the Kagame government for clamping down on any opposition by equating dissent to government policies with genocidal ideology. *See also* RWANDAN GENOCIDE.

RWANDAN GENOCIDE. One of the most abhorrent large-scale ethnicity-driven atrocities of the second half of the 20th century. In the course of a mere 100 days, from 6 April to mid-July 1994, Hutu militiamen slaughtered some 800,000 to 1 million Tutsis and moderate numbers of Hutus, one-tenth of the entire population of the country. By any standard, this was the worst act of bloody violence in a long string of recurring **massacres** of Tutsis which shook **Rwanda** after winning its independence from Belgium. The **genocide** was triggered by the assassination of Rwandan President Juvenal Habyarimana and Cyprien Ntaryamira, the president of **Burundi** (both Hutus) who died when the plane carrying them was shot down on 6 April 1994 as it prepared to land in Kigali. There is still much uncertainty about who should bear responsibility for the assassinations. Be that as it may, there is considerable evidence confirmed by information which came to light in the proceedings of the **International Criminal Tribunal for Rwanda** (ICTR) that the killings were well organized.

By and large, the international community remained indifferent to the unfolding drama. **Early warnings** by the military commander of the UN force in Rwanda that plans were being made for the extermination of the Tutsis were downplayed, and his request for reinforcements went unheeded by the **United Nations** Secretariat in New York. Key members of the **United Nations Security Council** opposed any involvement of the United Nations on the grounds that the crisis was an "internal affair." Only in late April 1994 did the Council finally recognize that something approximating a genocide was being committed in Rwanda and authorized the dispatch of 5,500 troops to be provided by African countries. Squabbling over costs, however, delayed their deployment, leading the Security Council, at France's prodding, to authorize on 22 June 1994 French forces to set up a "safe zone" (the so-called Zone Turquoise) throughout southwestern Rwanda to ensure "the security and protection of displaced persons, **refugees** and civilians in danger in Rwanda." While it may have saved lives and stopped the killing, Operation Turquoise remains controversial. It has been criticized in particular for having been initiated only six weeks after the beginning of the genocide, for undermining the **mandate** of the revamped **United Nations Assistance Mission in Rwanda** and for allowing the continuation of Tutsi killings in the area under the control of French troops. It has also been portrayed as a hardly veiled attempt by France to prop up the Hutu regime and to protect the perpetrators of genocide. In 2006, victims of the genocide initiated court action in France against the French army alleging that French soldiers in Operation Turquoise had committed atrocities and assisted Hutu militias in identifying their victims.

In any event, the genocide did come to an end when the Tutsi-dominated expatriate insurgency led by Paul Kagame's Rwandan Patriotic Front ousted the Hutu government and seized power in July 1994, thus triggering yet another exodus of, this time, 2 million Hutus who feared retribution and took refuge in Burundi, Tanzania, **Uganda** and western Zaire. The presence of such a large number of Rwandan refugees along the border of the **Democratic Republic of the Congo** (DRC) has been a major source of regional instability. It is at the roots of the military conflicts which engulfed half a dozen countries in a five-year-long protracted armed conflict which officially ended in 2003 and killed nearly 4 million people. It continues to be a source of tensions between Rwanda and the DRC. According to

Rwandan government estimates, 2 million individuals participated in the genocide. The principal perpetrators are being tried by the ICTR. Thousands of other genocide suspects have been brought to justice in Rwandan courts and, since 2001, in *Gacaca* **courts**, a participatory village justice system used to address the enormous backlog of cases. *See also* ARTICLE 19, THE INTERNATIONAL CENTRE AGAINST CENSORSHIP; SAFE ZONES; SEXUAL VIOLENCE.

S

SABRA AND SHATILA MASSACRE (1982). Large-scale killing of Palestinian and Lebanese civilians carried out by Christian Lebanese militias in **refugee** camps surrounded by Israeli forces in the midst of the Lebanese civil war. The exact number of victims is still disputed and ranges from around 700 or 800 to 3,500. Several commissions were set up to investigate the **massacre**, all coming to different conclusions. An independent commission chaired by Sean McBride concluded that the Israeli forces or government was directly or indirectly responsible. A Lebanese inquiry cleared the Lebanese armed forces. An Israeli investigation found that Israeli military personnel were aware that a massacre was in progress. Insofar as they had failed to prevent it, **Israel** bore indirect responsibility for the killings. **Ariel Sharon**, then minister of defense, resigned in the wake of publication of the Commission's findings. In 2001, he was elected prime minister of Israel.

SAFE ZONES. Also known as corridors of tranquility, humanitarian corridors, neutral zones, safe havens, protected areas and **no-fly zones**, safe zones are areas set aside where people not involved in the fighting can find a degree of safety and refuge. The **Geneva Conventions** provide for the establishment of hospitals and safe zones to protect the wounded, the sick, the elderly, children, and pregnant women from the effects of war. The **United Nations Security Council**, in the discharge of its responsibility of maintaining peace and security, has occasionally designated safe zones to protect civilians from attack with varying degrees of effectiveness as was the case in the **Bosnia-Herzegovina war** (1994), Iraq (1990), **Libya** (2011), and the **Rwandan genocide** (1994) among others. *See also* SREBRENICA.

SAHNOUN, MOHAMED. Senior Algerian diplomat who served as his country's ambassador to Morocco, the **United States**, France, Germany, and the **United Nations**. He also served in various capacity at the Organization of African Unity and the **League of Arab States**. At the United Nations, he also was a special representative of the secretary-general to Somalia and for the Great Lakes region of Africa. He was a member of the World Commission on

Environment and Development (the Brundtland Commission). He co-chaired the **International Commission on Intervention and State Sovereignty**, whose report, "**The Responsibility to Protect**," was published in December 2001.

SANCTIONS. Term generally defined under international law as "a broad range of reactions adopted unilaterally or collectively by the states against the perpetrator of an internationally unlawful act in order to ensure respect for and performance of a right or obligation." There are various forms of sanctions including exclusion, suspension, expulsion from an international organization, the severance of diplomatic relations, the complete or partial interruption of communications, economic measures (typically a ban on trade, possibly limited to certain sectors such as armaments, or with certain exceptions such as food and medicine), international **prosecution** and the use of force. Under Chapter VII of the **United Nations Charter**, the **United Nations Security Council** (UN-SC) can take enforcement measures to maintain or restore international peace and security.

During the **Cold War**, the UN-SC only took sanctions against Rhodesia and South Africa. Since then, the UN-SC has with increasing frequency relied on sanctions against a number of countries including **Afghanistan, Angola, Burundi, Cote d'Ivoire**, the **Democratic Republic the Congo**, Ethiopia and Eritrea, Haiti, **Iran**, Iraq, **Liberia, Libya, Myanmar**, North Korea, **Rwanda**, Sierra Leone, Somalia, Sudan, **Syria**, and Yugoslavia. The comprehensive sanctions that the UN-SC took against Iraq in 1990 were widely criticized for their harmful humanitarian impact and the deterioration of human rights conditions in the country. Concerns have also been voiced about the negative impact that sanctions can have on the economy of third countries.

Since then, the UN-SC has shifted its focus from comprehensive to more selective measures, abandoning the general use of trade sanctions and relying instead on targeted measures such as financial asset freezes, travel bans, aviation sanctions, commodity boycotts and arms embargoes. So-called smart sanctions have thus been applied to "conflict diamonds" in African countries, where wars have been funded in part by the trade in illicit diamonds for arms and related material. In the wake of the terrorist attacks of 11 September 2001, the UN-SC has mandated the application of these targeted tools to disable terrorist networks. In turn, the UN-SC's **counterterrorism** decisions have generated considerable unease within the human rights community and triggered criticisms that the UN-SC's practices were developed without regard to **due process** rights. Academic studies have shown that economic sanctions tend to increase levels of state repression in non-democracies but have no effect in democracies.

Within the framework of its Common Foreign and Security Policy (CFSP), the European Union applies sanctions or restrictive measures in pursuit of the specific CFSP objectives set out in the Treaty on **European Union** or in implementation of the UN-SC decisions. Such restrictive measures are designed to bring about a change in activities or policies such as violations of international law or human rights or policies that do not respect the rule of law or democratic principles. They may target governments of third countries, or non-state entities and individuals (such as terrorist groups and terrorists). *See also* APARTHEID; DARFUR CONFLICT; ENFORCEMENT; KADI CASE.

SARAJEVO. Capital city of Bosnia and Herzegovina which was besieged, from 5 April 1992 to 29 February 1996, by military forces of the self-proclaimed Republika Srpska and the Yugoslav People's Army during the **Bosnia-Herzegovina war.** An estimated 10,000 people were killed or went missing in the city, including over 1,500 children. Five times as many people were wounded, including nearly 15,000 children. In 2002, the **International Criminal Tribunal for the Former Yugoslavia** convicted and sentenced two Serb generals to life imprisonment and 33 years imprisonment, respectively, for **crimes against humanity** involving, in particular, the indiscriminate shelling and sniper terror campaign that they carried out during the siege. *See also* KARADZIC, RADOVAN; MLADIC, RATKO.

SAUDI ARABIA. Largest state in the Arab world after Algeria founded in 1932 by Abdul Aziz Ibn Saud. The kingdom's primary source of law is Islamic **Sharia Law** and its interpretation by cleric judges and royal decrees. Significant changes have been introduced in the past decade, but the country's human rights practices remain the target of criticisms, notably by **United Nations treaty bodies** and **non-governmental organizations**. Human rights issues that have had attention to include the absence of **due process** protection in criminal procedures, the severity of punishments, the use of the **capital punishment**, religious discrimination and the treatment of women and **migrant** labor. Saudi Arabia was one of two countries which did not vote in favor of the **Universal Declaration of Human Rights**. It has ratified a number of human rights **treaties** but with sweeping **reservations**, upholding the superiority of Sharia Law.

SAVE THE CHILDREN INTERNATIONAL. Humanitarian international umbrella **non-governmental organization** coordinating 29 national organizations serving over 120 countries that promote children's rights, provide relief and help support children in **developing countries**. Formerly known as the Save the Children Alliance and tracing its origins to the original Save the Children organization founded in London in 1919, Save the Children International played a key role in the adoption of the **United Nations Convention on the Rights of the Child** and promotes policy changes aimed at improving the living conditions of children and giving more rights to young people. Its current priorities are to advocate for increased infant and child survival rates, bring quality **education** to conflict-ridden areas and help to protect children from the effects of war.

SECOND-GENERATION RIGHTS. Category of rights which includes essentially **equality** rights. Their existence hinges on the assumption that certain basic goods should be equally available to all people and that the enjoyment of **civil and political rights** is anchored in favorable conditions of well-being and welfare, notably in the areas of **education, housing, health** care, **social security, food** and **work.** These rights are found in such instruments as the **International Covenant on Economic, Social and Cultural Rights,** the **European Social Charter** and other regional human rights **treaties.** They are also called "positive" rights in the sense that they enjoin states, as **duty bearers,** to act in their progressive **realization.** *See also* COLD WAR; DEVELOPING COUNTRIES; VASAK, KAREL.

SECURITY, RIGHT TO. The right to **liberty** and security of the person is enshrined in the **International Covenant on Civil and Political Rights** (Art. 9), the Inter-American Convention on Human Rights (Art. 7), the **Arab Charter on Human Rights** (Art. 14) and the **European Convention for the Protection of Human Rights and Fundamental Freedoms** (Art. 5). The fulfillment of this right derives from the state's responsibility to maintain law and order and to investigate and prosecute criminal loss of life. The **United Nations Human Rights Committee** has ruled that the right to security of person is violated if a state knowingly declines to afford protection to a person notwithstanding the existence of a serious threat to his or her life from third parties. In the same vein, the **European Court of Human Rights** has determined that the right to **life** is violated if a state does not take sufficient steps to protect the life of an individual who had been murdered after receiving death threats. *See also* ACCESS TO JUSTICE.

SECURITY COUNCIL REPORT. Independent not-for-profit organization in affiliation with Columbia University's Center on International Organization. Founded with the encouragement of former **United Nations Secretary-General Kofi Annan**, and with financial support from Canada, Norway and a number of U.S. **foundations,** the group provides factual information and analysis on the activities of the **United Nations Security Council**. It also publishes regular reports on the Council's current or prospective agenda, supplemented by Update Reports on breaking news.

SELF-DETERMINATION. Doctrine first enunciated by President **Woodrow Wilson** asserting the right of a people to govern themselves. It received a degree of recognition in the **mandates** system of the **League of Nations**. It is one of the founding principles of the **United Nations Charter** and is fully recognized in the **International Covenant on Civil and Political Rights** and the **International Covenant on Economic, Social and Cultural Rights**. Its interpretation, however, has been a constant source of political disputes as demands for self-determination have a variety of meanings. Self-determination has thus been variously viewed as the right of a people to independence, the right of a population of a state to determine their form of governance, the right of a state to territorial integrity and to non-violation of its boundaries and the right of a minority within or across state boundaries to special rights. Furthermore, there is no agreement as to the meaning of the term "people."

United Nations practice has led to a (long contested) consensus that self-determination applies to people under colonial rule. But the United Nations rarely separates the principle of self-determination from the overriding principle of respect for territorial integrity. As sovereign states have been unwilling to recognize self-determination as a right leading to secession and deny that it could be used to justify territorial claims, inconsistencies abound. The breakup of Czechoslovakia was a peaceful exercise in self-determination in stark contrast to the experience of the former Yugoslavia. Hong Kong and Macao reverted to the People's Republic of China without consultation of the inhabitants of these territories. South West Africa became independent under the name of Namibia only after the white South African regime collapsed. **Western Sahara** has no identifiable territorial boundaries and remains subject to dispute and counter-claims by the local population, Algeria and Morocco. The realization of the cultural, social and economic international self-determination of **indigenous peoples** and **minorities** in Europe has yet to become a reality.

See also ABKHAZIA; ABORIGINAL PEOPLES IN CANADA; ACEH; AFRICAN COMMISSION ON HUMAN AND PEOPLE'S RIGHTS; APARTHEID; ARAB ISRAELI CONFLICT; BIAFRA; CHECHNYA; CULTURAL RIGHTS; DALAI LAMA; DECLARATION OF INDEPENDENCE; DECLARATION ON THE GRANTING OF INDEPENDENCE TO COLONIAL PEOPLES AND COUNTRIES; DECLARATION ON THE RIGHTS OF INDIGENOUS PEOPLES; DEVELOPING COUNTRIES; ILO CONVENTION CONCERNING

INDIGENOUS AND TRIBAL PEOPLES IN INDEPENDENT COUN-
TRIES; INDIA, PARTITION OF; INTERNATIONAL ASSOCIATION
OF DEMOCRATIC LAWYERS; KOSOVO; KURDISH QUESTION;
MERCENARY; NAGORNO-KARABAKH; NATIVE AMERICANS;
PALESTINIAN CENTRE FOR HUMAN RIGHTS; SOUTH OSSETIA; SRI
LANKA CIVIL WAR; TIMOR-LESTE; UNITED NATIONS GENERAL
ASSEMBLY; UNITED NATIONS MISSION FOR THE REFERENDUM
IN WESTERN SAHARA; UNITED NATIONS TRUSTEESHIP SYSTEM.

SEN, AMARTYA (1933–). Influential development economist born in
India. In a seminal study on the Bengal famine of 1943 in which 3 million
died, he presented data demonstrating that the catastrophe had occurred
not because of a lack of food supplies but because a number of social and
economic factors, such as declining wages, unemployment, rising food
prices, and poor food distribution systems, had prevented particular groups
of people including rural landless laborers and urban service providers from
having access to these supplies. Out of this work evolved the groundbreaking
capability approach which challenged prevailing conventional wisdom
about development thinking and exerted considerable influence in the
formulation of the **Human Development Report** published by the **United
Nations Development Programme**.

SERVITUDE. *See* SLAVERY.

**SET OF PRINCIPLES FOR THE PROTECTION AND PROMOTION
OF HUMAN RIGHTS THROUGH ACTION TO COMBAT IMPU-
NITY. Soft law** instrument adopted by consensus by the **United Nations
General Assembly** in 2005 after 15 years of consultations and negotiation
following its initiation by the United Nations Sub-Commission on the
Prevention of Discrimination and Protection of Minorities in 1989 (now
known as the **United Nations Sub-Commission on the Promotion and
Protection of Human Rights**). Weaving together the related issues of
state responsibility, **reparations** and **impunity**, the principles affirm the
obligations of states in connection with gross violations of **international
human rights law** and serious violations of **international humanitarian
law** including, in particular, the obligations to prevent **violations of human
rights**, to investigate, prosecute and punish perpetrators, to provide access
to justice and to afford full **reparation** to victims. The principles lay down
guidelines qualifying national practices in regard to **universal jurisdiction**,
extradition, statutes of limitations and judicial assistance. They also spell out
a broad range of material and symbolic forms of monetary and non-monetary

reparation. The principles have provided "appropriate guidance" to the **International Criminal Court** in some of its procedural decisions as well as serving as the basis for the more elaborate and specific rights of victims to obtain reparations spelled out in the **International Convention for the Protection of All Persons from Enforced Disappearance**.

SEX DISCRIMINATION. *See* SEXUAL ORIENTATION.

SEX TOURISM. The World Tourism Organization, a specialized agency of the **United Nations**, defines sex tourism as "trips organized from within the tourism sector, or from outside this sector but using its structures and networks, with the primary purpose of effecting a commercial sexual relationship by the tourist with residents at the destination." Countries such as **Brazil**, Costa Rica, **Cuba**, the Dominican Republic, Kenya, the Netherlands, the **Philippines**, and Thailand have become preferred destinations for sex tourists. As long as it does not involve child prostitution or non-consensual **sex trafficking**, sex tourism is not necessarily illegal and falls under the local laws applying to prostitution.

SEX TRAFFICKING. Recruitment, transportation (within national or across international borders), transfer, harboring, or receipt of persons for the purposes of commercial sexual exploitation. Sex trafficking is accomplished by means of fraud, deception, threat of or use of force, abuse of a position of vulnerability, and other forms of coercion. Victims of trafficking are forced into various forms of commercial sexual exploitation including prostitution, **pornography**, stripping, live sex shows, **mail-order brides**, military prostitution and **sex tourism**. Victims of sex trafficking can be women or men, girls or boys, but the majority are women and girls. Worldwide, it is estimated that there are roughly 1.4 million victims of commercial sexual servitude, both transnational and within countries. According to the **United Nations Children's Fund**, over 1 million children enter the sex trade every year. Countries of origin include Albania, Belarus, Bulgaria, China, Lithuania, Nigeria, Romania, the Russian Federation, Thailand and Ukraine, and countries of destination Germany, **Greece, Israel**, Italy, Japan, the Netherlands, Thailand, **Turkey** and the **United States**. *See also* CHILDREN TRAFFICKING; HUMAN TRAFFICKING; INVOLUNTARY SERVITUDE; UNITED NATIONS CONVENTION AGAINST TRANSNATIONAL CRIME.

SEXUAL ORIENTATION. Attitudes toward non-conventional forms of sexual behavior and homosexuality in particular have widely fluctuated over time and space ranging from temporary social tolerance to more dominant patterns of disapproval leading to surveillance, legal discrimination, outright **persecution** and, in their most virulent manifestations, killings and extermination. At present, the legal position of homosexuals varies significantly from country to country—from constitutionally recognized freedom to legal **discrimination** on the basis of sexual orientation to laws making homosexual acts punishable by death. Even in countries where homosexuals enjoy a degree of legal protection, there are ongoing politically divisive controversies over same-sex marriages, partnerships, civil unions, hate crime and the like.

There is, however, a discernible trend toward greater protection of homosexuals as a group. Domestic courts in many countries have, with increasing frequency, granted **asylum** on the basis of persecution against homosexuals. Likewise, **international human rights law** is slowly recognizing the rights of homosexuals. The non-discrimination provisions of international human rights instruments as well as the statute of the **International Criminal Court** do not refer to sexual orientation, but rulings by the **United Nations Human Rights Committee** and the **European Court of Human Rights** in the early 1990s, grounded on the right to **privacy**, have led to changes in national legislation which criminalize consensual homosexual activity.

In 2011, the **United Nations Human Rights Council** adopted its first resolution condemning discrimination on the grounds of sexual orientation. Introduced by South Africa, the resolution passed with 23 votes in favor, 19 opposed and three abstentions amid strong criticism by Islamic nations, Nigeria and Pakistan saying the resolution had "nothing to do with fundamental human rights." A follow-up report issued in December 2011 by the **United Nations Office of the High Commissioner for Human Rights** documented violations of the rights of lesbian, gay, bisexual and transgender people (LGBT) and called for the repeal of laws criminalizing homosexuality; equitable ages of consent; comprehensive laws against discrimination based on sexual orientation; prompt investigation and recording of hate crime incidents; and other measures to ensure the protection of LGBT rights. *See also* CULTURAL RELATIVISM; INTERNATIONAL COUNCIL ON HUMAN RIGHTS POLICY; INTERNATIONAL GAY AND LESBIAN HUMAN RIGHTS COMMISSION; ORGANIZATION OF ISLAMIC COOPERATION.

SEXUAL VIOLENCE. Wide range of sexual acts encompassing not only forced penetration but also non-penetrative sexual offenses such as forced nudity, forced marriage, rape, enslavement and prostitution. As such, sexual violence has occurred, notably in **armed conflicts**, as far back as antiquity and has long been regarded as an inevitable consequence of war. It still persists today. It has been estimated, for instance, that 20,000 women were raped in the conflict triggered by the breakup of the former Yugoslavia between 1991 and 1995. In 1994, 250,000 to 500,000 women were raped in the four-month-long **Rwandan genocide**. The number of male victims of sexual violence in armed conflict may be less visible but remains quite significant. A string of sex scandals in recent years involving accusations of trafficking, rape and related crimes has tarnished the image and reputation of United Nations peacekeeping missions from Bosnia to the **Democratic Republic of the Congo** to Haiti.

As a result of a number of developments, notably the landmark 1998 **Akayesu** judgments of the **International Criminal Tribunal for Rwanda**, sexual abuses suffered by men, women and children are now prohibited by international law. Building upon the 1949 **Geneva Convention**, ad hoc criminal courts have issued rulings charging and convicting individuals of sexual violence as constituent elements of **genocide** or **crimes against humanity** and **war crimes**. The statute of the **International Criminal Court** (ICC) classifies "rape, sexual slavery, forced pregnancy, enforced sterilization, or any other form of sexual violence of comparable gravity" as crimes against humanity or war crimes. A large number of arrest warrants issued by the ICC involve charges of crimes of sexual violence. In 2008, the **United Nations Security Council** conducted a thematic discussion of the subject and determined that rape and sexual violence are crimes against humanity and a component of genocide. *See also* CELEBICI, FURUDZINA, DEALALIC CASES; "COMFORT WOMEN"; EQUALITY NOW; ETHNIC CLEANSING; INTERNATIONAL CRIMINAL TRIBUNAL FOR THE FORMER YUGOSLAVIA; SIERRA LEONE CIVIL WAR.

SHADOW REPORTS. Widespread practice of **non-governmental organizations** (NGOs) whose purpose is to supplement, present alternative information to or "shadow" the official periodic reports national governments are required to submit under treaties to human rights global or regional **monitoring** bodies. Shadow reports generally consist of critical commentaries on the entire report from a government. Organized according to the articles of the particular treaty, they are frequently the product of a collective and coordinated undertaking by many **civil society** organizations. Alternatively, shadow reports may simply aim at specific aspects of a government report. NGOs use shadow reports to **lobby United Nations treaty bodies** (such as the **United Nations Committee on the Elimination of All Forms of Discrimination against Women**), including the **United Nations Human Rights Council**, and thematic or country-specific **special rapporteurs**, charter-based bodies (such as the **United Nations Commission on the Status**

of Women) and the **United Nations Office of the High Commissioner for Human Rights** (UN-OHCHR). NGOs are also active in regional human rights–concerned organizations such as the **Council of Europe**.

Many NGOs such as the **Amnesty International**, the **Center for Reproductive Rights**, the **International Women's Rights Action Watch**, and **Human Rights Watch** have issued step-by-step procedural guides and manuals to help civil society organizations produce shadow reports assessing a country's de jure and de facto compliance with **international human rights law**. Additionally, the UN-OHCHR publishes handbooks and manuals as part of a Professional Training Series which is intended "to increase awareness of international standards" and "serve as practical tools for organizations that provide human rights education to professional groups."

SHARIA LAW. Set of principles derived from the Quran and traditions gathered from the Prophet Muhammad meant to provide the guideposts for the "way" Muslims should live. As a source of religious and common and civil law, Sharia Law touches on virtually all aspects of life including crime, politics, economics, banking, business, contracts, family, sexuality, hygiene, and social issues. Opinions differ widely as to whether Sharia Law is consistent with the principles and injunctions of modern human rights. Some draw attention to the subservient status of women in Muslim countries as evidence of Sharia Law conflicts with the norm of gender **equality**. Others argue that early Islamic jurists in medieval times had introduced legal concepts such as **equality before the law**, social solidarity and human **dignity** that anticipated similar modern notions and were in fact unknown at that time in Europe. The debate often strays into doctrinal and political disputes about the **universality of rights** and is likely to continue unabated because Sharia norms lend themselves to conflicting interpretations by scholars, judges and politicians.

See also CAIRO DECLARATION ON HUMAN RIGHTS IN ISLAM; CULTURAL RELATIVISM; FREEDOM OF RELIGION; LIFE, RIGHT TO; SAUDI ARABIA; UNITED NATIONS CONVENTION ON THE ELIMINATION OF ALL FORMS OF DISCRIMINATION AGAINST WOMEN.

SHARON, ARIEL (1928–). Controversial **Israeli** general and politician who served as prime minister from 2001 until 2006 when he suffered a crippling stroke. Sharon was the chief architect of the 1982 Israeli invasion of Lebanon and was criticized for allowing Lebanese Christian forces into Palestinian refugee camps in West Beirut and held responsible for the subsequent massacre of civilians. A government investigative body found that he bore an "indirect responsibility," specifically "for having disregarded the prospect of acts of vengeance and bloodshed by the Phalangists against the population of the **refugee** camps and for having failed to take this danger into account." Sharon subsequently resigned from his post but remained in the government as minister without portfolio. *See also* SABRA AND SHATILA MASSACRE.

SIERRA CLUB. United States environmental **non-governmental organization** created in 1892 by John Muir with 1.3 million members and supporters. Its current mission is to promote the responsible use of the Earth's ecosystems and resources through national campaigns relying extensively on volunteers' work. Sierra Club takes the position that **environmental** rights are human rights. Of priority to the Sierra Club are the right to organize to protect the environment and the right to have access to full and accurate information about the environment. The Sierra Club's strategy is thus to focus public attention on oppressive conditions leading to such **violations of human rights** and to pressure governments and states and **transnational corporations** which it holds complicit in the violation of environmental rights. The Sierra Club has, for instance, encouraged international criticism of **Myanmar**'s ruling military regime for continuing to use **forced labor** in the country's teak forests. The Sierra Club has also been critical of Shell's oil exploitation in the **Niger Delta conflict** and of China's Three Gorges Dam Project, the largest hydroelectric project ever attempted in the world, which will displace over 1 million people and submerge 100,000 hectares of cropland.

SIERRA LEONE CIVIL WAR (1991–2002). Civil war triggered through an attempt by the student-led Revolutionary United Front which crossed the eastern border of Sierra Leone from **Liberia** in an attempt, with **Libyan** support, to overthrow the central government widely viewed as corrupt and ineffective. The war dragged on for a decade fed by coups of a divided and politicized military, the thuggery and nepotism of government leaders, the rebels' control of the country's diamond mining, the involvement of **mercenaries**, foreign interventions (notably by Nigeria and Liberia) and externally induced economic shocks provoked by the conditionalities of the **International Monetary Fund**. Several peace agreements were broken and a **United Nations Security Council** peacekeeping force—the **United Nations Mission in Sierra Leone** (UNAMSIL)—nearly collapsed, prompting a decisive intervention of British troops which stabilized the situation and led to a permanent ceasefire in 2000.

An estimated 150,000 people died in the 11-year civil war. More than half the country was rendered homeless, 600,000 **refugees** (over 10 percent of the population) fled to neighboring countries, more than 200,000 women were raped, and about 1,000 civilians suffered amputations. A **truth and reconciliation commission** operated from November 2002 to October 2004. Its final report includes the names of individual perpetrators, but many of its recommendations to ensure accountability and reparation for the abuses committed during the civil war have still not been put into effect. In March 2003, the **Special Court for Sierra Leone** issued its first indictments for **war crimes** committed during the civil war. In 2012, the Court found former Liberian President Charles Taylor guilty of delivering shipments of arms and ammunition to Sierra Leone insurgents.

UNAMSIL has disarmed and demobilized more than 75,000 ex-fighters, including child soldiers. It organized the country's first ever free and fair presidential, parliamentary and local government elections. The country nevertheless still faces daunting challenges. The central government is stable but politics are still fragmented along regional and ethnic lines, and the implementation of enacted progressive human rights legislation remains weak. The economy remains dependent on donor funds. A disproportionate share of income from diamond mining still ends up in private hands. Thousands remain unemployed. Peace has yet to produce the economic and social dividends that will address the root causes of the war and lead to a culture of human rights. The **United Nations Office of the High Commissioner for Human Rights** has been involved in Sierra Leone since 1998 as part of successive UN missions, conducting **monitoring**, **capacity building**, technical assistance and training sensitization activities.

SLAVE TRADE. Records of slave trading go as far back as ancient Greece and earlier. Slave trading has thus been going on for centuries, but the modern slave trade flourished in the early Middle Ages especially between Muslim traders and Western African kingdoms. As the Crusades brought to a virtual halt the Muslim trade of African slaves, Europeans took over and began transporting African slaves to their American colonies. The number of Africans thus deported to the Americas by the Europeans from the 1600s to the early 1900s range from 10 to 15 million. Some historians estimate that between 11 and 18 million African slaves crossed the Red Sea, Indian Ocean, and Sahara Desert from 650 AD to 1900 AD. With the outlawing of **slavery** in all countries, the slave trade has not altogether disappeared. It went underground and morphed into what is euphemistically called **human trafficking**.

SLAVERY. Economic reasons (the introduction of labor-saving devices in farming and industrial production) combined with a growing sense that slavery was morally repugnant fueled throughout the 18th and 19th centuries an increasingly powerful political movement which led to the progressive abolition of slavery worldwide. The adoption of the 1926 **Convention on the Abolition of Slavery** under the auspices of the **League of Nations** was an important turning point in this process. That convention was complemented by a 1956 Supplementary Convention outlawing and banning slavery worldwide, including child slavery. Article 4 of the 1948 **Universal Declaration of Human Rights** and Article 8 of the 1966 **International Covenant on Civil and Political Rights** explicitly banned slavery. Article 7(2)(c) of the Rome Statute of the **International Criminal Court** characterizes "enslavement" as a **crime against humanity** falling within the jurisdiction of the Court. The most recent reference to slavery in an international instrument is in the Protocol to Prevent, Suppress and Punish Trafficking in Persons, Especially Women and Children (Trafficking Protocol), supplementing the **United Nations Convention against Transnational Organized Crime** which criminalizes **human trafficking** "for the purpose of exploitation" including, "at a minimum, the exploitation of the prostitution of others, or other forms of sexual exploitation, **forced labor** or services, slavery or practices similar to slavery, servitude or the removal of organs." "Chattel slavery" has therefore virtually disappeared today and would be considered either illegal or unlawful and punished by imprisonment in nearly all societies.

Nevertheless, two centuries after the **United States** and the British Empire banned the **slave trade**, millions of people are still subjected to slavery-like practices in which individuals are held against their will under the control of another, a group, a **non-state actor** or a state. Such contemporary forms of slavery include child labor, **peonage**, servile concubinage, **bonded labor**, child soldiers and trafficking in humans as contemporary forms of slavery that continue to flourish as a result of discrimination, social exclusion, and vulnerability exacerbated by **poverty**. Forced labor which the **International Labour Organization** defines as "all work or service which is extracted from any person under the menace of any penalty and for which the said person has not offered himself voluntarily" is also considered a form of slavery. If this broader definition is accepted, then according to some estimates, there are 27 to 200 million people living today in virtual slavery throughout the world and producing a gross economic product of $13 billion annually.

In recent years, there have been demands for **apologies** and financial reparations from former Western colonial or slave trading nations to the descendants of Black African slaves. **Anti-Slavery International**, for example, has called for measures of **reparation** toward the communities and countries which have been impoverished by the Trans-Atlantic slave trade. In 2000, a self-appointed World Reparation Truth Commission concluded its meeting in Ghana calling for $777 trillion against the United States, Canada and Great Britain for "unlawful removal and destruction of Petitioners" mineral and human resources from the African continent from 1503 to the end of the colonial era in the 1950s and 1960s. The descendants of black American slaves sued Lloyd's of London in 2004 for insuring ships used in the slave trade in the 18th and 19th centuries. These demands, which were particularly intense during the 2001 UN-sponsored **World Conference against Racism**, Racial Discrimination, Xenophobia and Related Intolerance in Durban, South Africa, have remained by and large unheeded.

See also ARAB CHARTER ON HUMAN RIGHTS; CHILDREN TRAFFICKING; ECONOMIC COMMUNITY OF WEST AFRICAN STATES; EUROPEAN CHARTER OF FUNDAMENTAL RIGHTS OF THE EUROPEAN UNION; EUROPEAN CONVENTION FOR THE PROTECTION OF HUMAN RIGHTS AND FUNDAMENTAL FREEDOMS; INTERNATIONAL CRIMINAL LAW; LABOR CAMPS; MAIL-ORDER BRIDES; PEREMPTORY NORMS; SEX TOURISM; SEX TRAFFICKING; SPECIAL COURT FOR SIERRA LEONE; TRAFFICKING IN HUMAN ORGANS; UNITED NATIONS SUB-COMMISSION ON THE PROMOTION AND PROTECTION OF HUMAN RIGHTS; UNIVERSAL JURISDICTION.

SOCIAL FORUM. Initiative of the **United Nations Sub-Commission on the Promotion and Protection of Human Rights** designed to provide an arena within the **United Nations** allowing for the participation of a broad range of state and **non-state actors**, especially grassroots organizations which are not in **consultative status** with the **United Nations Economic and Social Council**. The Social Forum started functioning in 2002 focusing on the interaction between economic, social, cultural and political rights as it examined such issues as **poverty**, international trade, finance and economic policies. It continues to operate under the new **United Nations Human Rights Council** with the same broad mandate to promote "social cohesion based on the principles of social justice, equity and solidarity." The Forum meets once a year and has addressed such themes as the negative impact of economic and financial crisis on efforts to combat poverty, best practices of states in implementing social security programs from a human rights perspective, international assistance and cooperation in combating poverty and the implications of **climate change** for the enjoyment of human rights. *See also* NON-GOVERNMENTAL ORGANIZATIONS.

SOCIAL MOVEMENTS. Although they vary widely in their demands and operation, social movements are essentially large informal groupings of individuals or organizations which seek to influence the political process with a focus on political and social issues such as women's rights, gay rights, civil rights, the abolition of **capital punishment** and the **environment**. The spread of democracy, mass **education** and the development of communication technologies—the press and the **Internet**—have all fostered the growth of social movements. Considerable attention has been given in recent years to the phenomenon of social networking and its role in the formation and mobilization social movements, as highlighted by the 2009–10 **Iranian** election protests and the subsequent political changes brought about by the "**Arab Spring**" in a number of Arab countries. *See also* CIVIL SOCIETY; NON-GOVERNMENTAL ORGANIZATIONS.

SOCIAL SECURITY, RIGHT TO. Social security may be defined as "the prevention, by social means, of very low standards of living irrespective of whether these are the result of chronic deprivation or temporary adversity" arising from such factors as unemployment, ill health, disability, maternity or old age. As such, the right to social security is enshrined in the **International Covenant on Economic, Social and Cultural Rights** (ICESCR) and provisions of the **United Nations Convention on the Elimination of All Forms of Discrimination against Women**, the **United Nations Convention on the Rights of the Child**, conventions of the **International Labour Organization** (ILO) and the **European Social Charter**. At the national level, social security rights may be protected through a combination of constitutional provisions, legislative measures or judicial oversight. The nature of a state's international obligations in realizing the right to social security varies from one treaty to the next.

In a series of **communications** decided by the **United Nations Human Rights Committee** under the First Optional Protocol to the **International Covenant on Civil and Political Rights** and rulings of the **European Court of Human Rights**, the right to social security is believed to imply comprehensiveness of coverage and access, adequate levels of benefits, non-discriminatory practices and respect for procedural rights. The ICESCR has commented that states' parties to the Covenant should adopt "deliberate, concrete and targeted" legislative, financial, administrative, educational and social measures with a view to achieving progressively the full realization of the right to social security. States should generally avoid "any deliberate retrogressive measures" resulting in a reduction of coverage or level of benefits. Compliance with international standards is overseen through the reporting systems of the ILO and the ICESCR. Individual and collective **complaints** mechanism are available under the European Social Charter and the Optional protocol to the ICESCR. *See also* UNITED NATIONS CONFERENCE ON HUMAN SETTLEMENTS.

SOFT LAW. Quasi-legal instruments that have no **binding** force but may influence the behavior of states, **non-state actors** and individuals. Instances of soft law include most resolutions and **declarations** of the **United Nations General Assembly** (such as the **Universal Declaration of Human Rights**), statements of principles, and codes of conduct such as the **United Nations "Protect, Respect and Remedy" Framework for Business and Human Rights** and plans of action adopted by **United Nations global conferences.** Soft law may be a convenient instrument to overcome the resistance of states to enter into treaty obligations. It may also be a first step in the process of **treaty** making, as evidenced by the fact that most global international human rights treaties have been preceded by the adoption of declarations. Alternatively, it may also be part of the broader process of **customary law** formation as soft law instruments are used by **non-governmental organizations,** national courts and other civil society actors to pressure their governments.

See also BASIC PRINCIPLES AND GUIDELINES ON THE RIGHT TO A REMEDY AND REPARATION FOR VICTIMS OF GROSS VIOLATIONS OF INTERNATIONAL HUMAN RIGHTS LAW AND SERIOUS VIOLATIONS OF INTERNATIONAL HUMANITARIAN LAW; BEIJING DECLARATION AND PLATFORM OF ACTION; CARTAGENA DECLARATION ON REFUGEES; CODE OF CONDUCT FOR LAW ENFORCEMENT OFFICIALS; DECLARATION ON PRINCIPLES OF INTERNATIONAL LAW CONCERNING FRIENDLY RELATIONS AND COOPERATION AMONG STATES; DECLARATION ON SOCIAL PROGRESS AND DEVELOPMENT; DECLARATION ON THE ELIMINATION OF ALL FORMS OF INTOLERANCE AND DISCRIMINATION BASED ON RELIGION AND BELIEF; DECLARATION ON THE HUMAN RIGHTS OF INDIVIDUALS WHO ARE NOT NATIONALS OF THE COUNTRY IN WHICH THEY LIVE; DECLARATION ON THE GRANTING OF INDEPENDENCE TO COLONIAL PEOPLES AND COUNTRIES; DECLARATION ON THE RIGHTS OF PERSONS BELONGING TO NATIONAL OR ETHNIC, RELIGIOUS OR LINGUISTIC MINORITIES; DRAFT ARTICLES ON THE RESPONSIBILITY OF STATES FOR INTERNATIONALLY WRONGFUL ACTS; EXTRACTIVE INDUSTRIES TRANSPARENCY INITIATIVE; GUIDELINES ON INTERNATIONAL HUMAN RIGHTS FACT FINDING VISITS AND REPORTS; GUIDING PRINCIPLES ON INTERNAL DISPLACEMENT; ILO TRIPARTITE DECLARATION OF PRINCIPLES CONCERNING MULTINATIONAL ENTERPRISES AND SOCIAL POLICY; INTER-AMERICAN DECLARATION ON FREEDOM OF EXPRESSION; INTERNATIONAL CODE OF CONDUCT FOR PRIVATE SECURITY SERVICE PROVIDERS; OECD

REVISED GUIDELINES FOR MULTINATIONAL ENTERPRISES; PARIS PRINCIPLES; SET OF PRINCIPLES FOR THE PROTECTION AND PROMOTION OF HUMAN RIGHTS THROUGH ACTION TO COMBAT IMPUNITY; THIRD-GENERATION RIGHTS; UNIVERSAL DECLARATION ON BIOETHICS AND HUMAN RIGHTS; UNIVERSAL DECLARATION ON THE ERADICATION OF HUNGER AND MALNUTRITION; UNIVERSAL DECLARATION ON THE HUMAN GENOME AND HUMAN RIGHTS; YOGYAKARTA PRINCIPLES ON THE APPLICATION OF INTERNATIONAL HUMAN RIGHTS LAW IN RELATION TO SEXUAL ORIENTATION AND GENDER IDENTITY.

SOLIDARITY RIGHTS. Category of rights also labeled group rights or **third-generation rights** which relates to such communal aspects of humans as the right to development, the right to **peace**, the right to ownership of the common heritage of mankind and the recognition of **minority** groups, social identity and cultural issues. Advocates of solidarity rights argue that these rights are grounded on the **United Nations Charter** and, in particular, on Article 28 of the **Universal Declaration of Human Rights** which provides that everyone is entitled to social and international order in which the rights and freedoms set forth in the Declaration can be fully realized. These views are hotly contested and, by and large, solidarity rights are the least institutionalized. *See also* DEVELOPING COUNTRIES.

SOLZHENITSYN, ALEXANDER (1918–2008). Russian novelist, dramatist and historian whose novels—notably *The Gulag Archipelago* and *One Day in the Life of Ivan Denisovich*—spread knowledge about the Soviet forced labor camp system in the West. *See also* GULAG.

SOMALIA. *See* UNITED NATIONS OPERATION IN SOMALIA.

SOROS, GEORGE (1930–). Hungarian American investor, businessman and philanthropist known for his **advocacy** of liberal and progressive causes. He has created a network of **foundations** supporting projects promoting the development of open societies in post-Soviet states (primarily in Central Europe), human rights, **freedom of expression** and access to public **health** and **education**. To date, Soros is believed to have given away over $8 billion.

SOUTH AFRICA. *See* APARTHEID; BIAFRA; GERMAN SOUTH WEST AFRICA; GROOTBOOM DECISION; MANDELA, NELSON; TRUTH AND RECONCILIATION COMMISSIONS; TUTU, DESMOND.

SOUTH ASIAN ASSOCIATION FOR REGIONAL COOPERATION CONVENTION ON PREVENTING AND COMBATTING TRAFFICKING IN WOMEN AND CHILDREN FOR PROSTITUTION. Regional **treaty** seeking to promote cooperation among the states parties to the South Asian Association for Regional Cooperation (SAARC) so that they may more effectively deal with the various aspects of prevention, interdiction and suppression of **human trafficking** in women and children; repatriation and rehabilitation of victims of trafficking and preventing the use of women and children in international prostitution networks, particularly where the SAARC member countries are the countries of origin, transit or destination.

SOUTH OSSETIA. Former Soviet autonomous administrative region (oblast) which broke away, with Russian support, from Georgia when the country became independent in 1991. The conflict was triggered by the Georgian government's insistence on the use of Georgian as the only administrative language throughout the country and the South Ossetian minority's demand for greater autonomy including the use of Ossetian as the only language of their state. The violence in 1991 provoked the outflow of 60,000 to 100,000 **refugees** into North Ossetia or into Georgia proper. At present, only 15 percent of the Ossetian population lives in South Ossetia as a precarious military and political stalemate prevails monitored by a peacekeeping force of the **Organization for Security and Cooperation in Europe** since 1992. The secessionist government of South Ossetia is widely considered to be an integral part of Georgia and has not been recognized in particular by the **United Nations**, the **European Union**, the **Organization for Security and Cooperation in Europe**, the **Council of Europe** and the **North Atlantic Treaty Organization.** *See also* ABKHAZIA; MINORITIES; SELF-DETERMINATION.

SOUTHERN AFRICAN DEVELOPMENT COMMUNITY TRIBUNAL. Judicial organ of the Southern African Development Community (SADC) established in 2000 in Windhoek, Namibia, and operational since 2005. The Court's primary function is to ensure adherence to and the proper interpretation of the SADC Treaty, its Protocols and other instruments concluded by SADC members among themselves. It does not have a specific human rights jurisdiction, but the SADC Treaty does allude to human rights which would fall under the purview of the Tribunal. In addition, as SADC members have signed the 2003 Charter of Fundamental Social Rights, which "embodies the recognition by governments, employers and workers in the Region of the universality and indivisibility of basic human rights proclaimed in instruments such as the **United Nations Universal Declaration of**

Human Rights, the **African Charter on Human and Peoples' Rights**, the Constitution of the **International Labour Organization** and other relevant international instruments," the Tribunal could conceivably exercise jurisdiction over human rights–based claims.

SOUTHERN RHODESIA. British colony which proclaimed its independence in 1965. The Commonwealth and the **United Nations** condemned the move initiated by the white minority which was opposed to an immediate transfer to black majority rule. The **United Nations Security Council** imposed economic and diplomatic **sanctions** against the regime on the grounds that its declaration of independence had been "made by a racist minority." Yielding to pressure, Rhodesia reverted to British control for a brief period during which multiracial elections were held, eventually leading to the independence of the country in 1980 under the name of Zimbabwe. *See also* SELF-DETERMINATION.

SOVEREIGN IMMUNITY. Judicial doctrine whose origins may be traced to the medieval English principle that a monarch can do no wrong, asserting that a government cannot be sued without its consent and is immune from civil suit or criminal prosecution. The tenets of the doctrine apply primarily to court actions growing out of a state's commercial activities, but they have been significantly eroded by the growing acceptance of **peremptory** human rights norms. Questions of sovereign immunity, however, continue to arise in cases under the **Alien Tort Statute** in regard to the ability of plaintiffs to sue a foreign state directly or its agents. *See also* ACCESS TO JUSTICE; ACT OF STATE DOCTRINE; IMMUNITY; STATE RESPONSIBILITY.

SOVEREIGNTY. *See* STATE SOVEREIGNTY.

SPAIN. *See* AMNESTIES; FRANCO, FRANCISCO; GARZON, BALTHAZAR; UNIVERSAL JURISDICTION.

SPECIAL COURT FOR SIERRA LEONE. Hybrid court established by agreement between the government of Sierra Leone and the **United Nations** to "try those who bear greatest responsibility" for the **war crimes** and **crimes against humanity** committed in Sierra Leone after 30 November 1996 during the **Sierra Leone civil wa**r. The court has indicted 13 individuals and convicted and sentenced eight of them. Two indictees died before they could be sentenced. Another two are at large, one of them presumed dead. The trial of **Charles Taylor** has just been completed. In landmark rulings creating major legal precedents in international criminal law, the Court convicted some of the defendants on charges related to conscripting children under the age of 15 years into the armed forces or groups and subjecting them to sexual **slavery** and forced marriage.

SPECIAL PANELS OF THE DILI DISTRICT COURT. Also called the East Timor Tribunal. Hybrid court created in 2000 by the **United Nations Transitional Administration in East Timor** (UNTAET) to try "serious criminal offences"—including murder, rape, and torture —which took place in East Timor in 1999. The Special Panels sat from 2000 to 2006. They were dissolved shortly after the termination of the United Nations Mission of Support in East Timor (UNMISET) which had taken over from UNTAET in 2002. The Panels indicted close to 400 people, tried 88 accused persons, convicted 84 and acquitted four. But when they ceased functioning, there were still 514 outstanding cases for which investigations had been conducted but no indictments issued and 50 cases for which no investigations had yet been conducted. These cases which were not tried include 828 cases of alleged murder, 60 cases of alleged rape, and over 100 cases of alleged **torture** or other serious violence.

The judicial process has been described as a "virtual textbook case of how not to create, manage and administer a 'hybrid' justice process." The Panels were handicapped by a crippling lack of resources, an unclear mandate, inadequate recruitment and ineffective oversight by UNTAET. In a significant number of cases, some defendants were in effect denied **due process**. In addition, the work of the Special Panels was cut short by the decision of the **United Nations Security Council** on 20 May 2005 to terminate the UNMISET of which it was a part. Lack of political will in the Council and the refusal of the government of **Indonesia** to hand over to East Timor or the United Nations Indonesian suspects compounded the problems with the resulting failure to bring to trial high-ranking individuals and the conviction of only lowly Timorese perpetrators. The former defense minister and commander of the Indonesian armed forces was charged in 2004 with **command responsibility** for murder, deportation and **persecution** committed in the context of widespread and systematic attacks on the civilian populations but the Timorese government refused to request the International Criminal Police Organization to issue an international warrant for his arrest.

Indonesia brought to trial 18 officers of its armed forces in an ad hoc human rights court created in response to international pressure. The court convicted six of them. But five of the convictions were reversed on appeal (the conviction which was not overturned was that of the militia's leader who was the only Timorese national on trial). *See also* IMPUNITY; INTERNATIONAL CRIMINAL LAW; RETRIBUTIVE JUSTICE; TIMOR-LESTE.

SPECIAL PROCEDURES. Mechanisms set up over the years by the **United Nations Commission on Human Rights** to examine, **monitor**, advise and report on allegations of **violations of human rights** either in specific countries or on thematic issues. The **United Nations** may, finally, offer advisory services to nations that request it in the form of educational and informational assistance, seminars, training courses, and clinics as well as advice from experts to states designed to help them observe a high level of human rights protection. One of the first decisions of the new **United Nations Human Rights Council** was to initiate a review of all special procedures with a view to improving and rationalizing them.

See also 1503 PROCEDURE; UNITED NATIONS HUMAN RIGHTS COUNCIL ADVISORY COMMITTEE; UNITED NATIONS WORKING GROUP ON MINORITIES; UNITED NATIONS WORKING GROUP ON THE PROTECTION OF ALL PERSONS FROM ENFORCED DISAPPEARANCES.

SPECIAL RAPPORTEURS. Independent human rights experts and investigators appointed by an international organization with the mandate to examine, monitor, advise and publicly report on human rights problems. The first such mechanism was established in 1967 by the **United Nations Commission on Human Rights** to investigate **apartheid**-related issues in South Africa. The number of special rapporteurs has since considerably expanded. There are now some 40 special rapporteurs operating under the authority of the **United Nations Human Rights Council** (UN-HRC). Variously known as independent experts, working groups or special representatives of the secretary-general, some of them focus their work on individual countries, and others are tasked with thematic mandates.

At present, there are special rapporteurs dealing with **Burundi**, Cambodia, the **Democratic Republic of the Congo**, Haiti, **Liberia**, **Myanmar**, North Korea, the Palestinian territories, Somalia, Sudan and **Iran**. The thematic mandates currently covered include **adequate housing**, contemporary forms of **slavery**, **cultural rights**, **education**, the effects of foreign debt on human rights, extrajudicial, summary or arbitrary executions, right to **food**, freedom of peaceful assembly, **freedom of expression**, **freedom of religion** or beliefs, **human rights defenders**, independence of judges and lawyers, **minority** issues, racism and **racial discrimination**, physical and mental **health**, violence against women, **terrorism** and human rights, human rights and access to safe **water**, human rights and international **solidarity**, human rights and **transnational corporations**, human rights and the illicit treatment of toxic waste, **indigenous peoples**, **internally displaced persons**, and migrants.

Special rapporteurs also exist in regional organizations. The **Organization of American States'** special rapporteurs, acting under the aegis of the **Inter-American Commission on Human Rights**, are concerned with freedom of expression, migrant workers and the rights of women. Within the framework of the **African Commission on Human and People's Rights** of the **African Union,** there are special rapporteurs on extra-judicial arbitrary summary executions, freedom of expression, human rights defenders, prisons and conditions of detention, **asylum seekers** and internally displaced persons and women in Africa.

Special rapporteurs are typically appointed for three-year renewable terms. They carry out a wide range of preventive, protective and **advocacy** human rights functions: studies and reports on individual countries or rights issues, **fact-finding** missions, issuing urgent appeals, developing rights standards, acting as intermediaries on behalf of victims of rights abuse and generally raising public awareness. In 2009, special rapporteurs submitted 136 reports to the UN-HRC and 24 reports to the **United Nations General Assembly**, carrying out 73 investigative missions to 51 countries and territories. These activities, which must be undertaken with the consent and cooperation of the governments involved (only half of the missions cited above were conducted with the approval of the governments concerned), are often a source of intense political disputes which resurface when the terms of special rapporteurs come up for renewal and may lead to their termination or the abolition of their functions. *See also* AGREEMENT ON TRADE-RELATED ASPECTS OF INTELLECTUAL PROPERTY RIGHTS; COBO, JOSE MARTINEZ; COUNCIL OF EUROPE.

SPECIAL TRIBUNAL FOR CAMBODIA. Established in 2003 through an agreement between the **United Nations** and the government of Cambodia, this hybrid trial court, consisting of three Cambodian and two foreign judges, is tasked with trying former Khmer Rouge leaders accused of mass killings and other crimes between 1975 and 1979 during Pol Pot's rule. Under the terms of the agreement, the tribunal deals with senior Khmer Rouge leaders and those who were most responsible for crimes and serious violations of Cambodian penal law, **international humanitarian law** and custom and international conventions recognized by Cambodia, that were committed from 17 April 1975 to 6 January 1979. The jurisdiction of the tribunal— formally known as the Extraordinary Chambers in the Courts of Cambodia— is the crime of **genocide** as defined in the 1948 **United Nations Convention on the Punishment and Prevention of the Crime of Genocide, crimes against humanity** as defined in the 1988 Rome Statute of the **International Criminal Court** and grave breaches of the 1949 **Geneva Conventions**.

Whether the court will bring some measure of justice to the survivors of Cambodia "killing fields" remains to be seen. The agreement came after five years of protracted negotiations with a foot-dragging government. Administrative delays over the shape and structure of the Court further delayed the constitution of the Court. **United States'** support of Khmer Rouge exiles and of their continuing seat in the United Nations stymied earlier efforts to achieve justice for the mass killings. Many likely defendants have already died (notably Pol Pot) and the others are in their late 70s or early 80s. Human rights groups also argue that the Cambodian government is reluctant to try former Khmer Rouge officials who switched alliance toward the end of the conflict, exerts undue influence through its national judges and that the tribunal is not able to function with impartiality. In 2007, seven officials of the Khmer Rouge regime were arrested on charges of crimes against humanity and genocide: Khieu Samphan, the former head of state, former foreign minister Ieng Sari and his wife, Ieng Thirith, the social affairs minister, Pol Pot's second in command, Nuon Chea and Kang Ke, the head of a notorious prison where thousands were detained, tortured and summarily executed. So far, only one case has been ruled upon. *See also* IMPUNITY; INTERNATIONAL CRIMINAL LAW; RETRIBUTIVE JUSTICE.

SPECIAL TRIBUNAL FOR LEBANON (STL). Ad hoc international court established in 2007 by an agreement between the **United Nations** and the government of Lebanon pursuant to a 2006 resolution of the **United Nations Security Council** (UN-SC) to "prosecute persons responsible for the attack on 14 February 2005 resulting in the death of sitting Prime Minister Rafiq Hariri and in the death or injury of other persons." The STL is a "hybrid court" in that it comprises both Lebanese and international judges and will apply national law. It was initially set up for a period of three years but it may continue its work beyond that date depending on the scope of the investigation. For security reasons, it sits in The Hague.

This is the first time that a UN-sponsored court has tried a "terrorist" crime committed against a high-level specific person. The STL has provoked considerable political controversy and tensions among Lebanon's rival political groups as an initial UN investigation implicated senior Lebanese and Syrian officials and members of Hezbollah. **Syria** has argued that the decision of the UN-SC violated the sovereignty of Lebanon and stressed that it retained jurisdiction over possible Syrian suspects. The first indictments were released in 2011. *See also* INTERNATIONAL CRIMINAL LAW; RETRIBUTIVE JUSTICE.

SPEECH, FREEDOM OF. *See* FREEDOM OF EXPRESSION.

SPIRAL MODEL OF HUMAN RIGHTS CHANGE. Attempt by American constructivist scholars to describe the process whereby human rights norms impact and change a state's domestic and international human rights policies. Transnational **advocacy networks** and international organizations play a key role in this process. First, they raise awareness about the activities of human rights norm violators. Second, they mobilize and empower domestic opposition at the national and international levels. Third, these pressures may, after denial and rejection, lead governments to embrace human rights norms at least rhetorically. The model rests on the assumption that human rights norms are first articulated by **"norm entrepreneurs"** (individuals, groups or international organizations) and then "cascade" or spread progressively through a process of socialization and internalization, thus gaining progressive acceptance which can be measured through a number of indicators such as the ratification by governments of international human rights **treaties** and conventions, the institutionalization of human rights norms in national constitutions and domestic law, the establishment of mechanisms enabling citizens to complain about **violations of human rights** and the actual practices of government officials now guided by human rights norms and principles. See also CONSTRUCTIVISM; DENIAL.

SREBRENICA. Silver-mining town of Bosnia-Herzegovina which before the 1992–95 war was predominantly Muslim with a large Serb minority. During the conflict, the **United Nations Security Council** declared the town to be a **"safe zone"** for Muslims. Bosnian Serbs laid siege to Srebrenica and took control of it in July 1995. In the following days, between 13 and 19 July, Serb military and para-military forces separated civilian men from women and killed 7 to 8 thousands Bosnian Muslims. The **International Criminal Tribunal for the Former Yugoslavia** (ICTY) convicted in 2001 a Bosnia Serb general of **genocide** and sentenced him to 46 years in prison for not preventing the **massacre**. In a 2007 judgment, the **International Court of Justice** found that Serbia was neither directly responsible nor complicit for the genocide, but it did determine that Serbia had committed a breach of the United Nations Convention against Genocide by failing to prevent it and for not cooperating with the ICTY. See also BOSNIA-HERZEGOVINA WAR; DEATH SQUADS; KARADZIC, RADOVAN; MLADIC, RATKO.

SRI LANKAN CIVIL WAR (1983–2009). Conflict which pitted the Sri Lanka government against the armed separatist insurgency of the Liberation Tigers of Tamil-speaking Eelam for 25 years. The war was rooted in the ethnic/religious/socioeconomic divide between the mainly ethnic Sinhala-speaking, largely Buddhist majority and the ethnic Tamil largely Hindu minority. The rebels were fighting to carve out a homeland in the northern part of the country. An estimated 80,000 to 100,000 people died during the war, with both sides being accused of **violations of human rights** and atrocities and the Tamil Tigers being branded as a terrorist organization by over 30 countries for its ruthless attacks against police, military and civilian targets and use of suicide bombers. The war came to a brutal end with the complete military defeat of the Tigers after several failed peace efforts and amid allegations of **war crimes** committed by the Sri Lankan military and the Liberation Tigers involving attacks on civilians and civilian buildings, executions of combatants and prisoners and **forced disappearances**. The final stages of the war also created 300,000 **internally displaced persons**.

A panel of experts appointed by the **United Nations secretary-general** found "credible allegations" of war crimes and **crimes against humanity** and called for an independent international inquiry. A special session of the **United Nations Human Rights Council** ended in a stalemate as the Sri Lankan government denied any wrong doing and opposed any international **investigation**. A government-sponsored Lessons Learnt and Reconciliation Commission (LLRC) subsequently concluded that the Sri Lankan military had not deliberately targeted civilians and blamed Sinhalese and Tamil politicians for the civil war. **Non-governmental organizations** have taken issue with these findings and criticized the LLRC's limited mandate, alleged lack of independence and failure to meet minimum international standards or offer protection to witnesses. It is widely believed that the military victory of the government will prove to be a pyrrhic victory as long as Sinhalese-dominated political parties do not acknowledge and address the need for a more inclusive and democratic society and polity. *See also* TRUTH AND RECONCILIATION COMMISSIONS.

STALIN, JOSEF (1878–1953). Adopted name of Joseph Vissarionovich Dzhugashvili, translating into "Man of Steel." Stalin rose to power as general secretary of the Communist Party of the Soviet Union's Central Committee from 1922 until his death. Through his control of the party, Stalin in effect exerted de facto dictatorial powers over the country throughout these years. His economic and social policies are credited either with transforming the Soviet Union from a predominantly peasant society into a major world industrial power or to having significantly accelerated that historical process. These accomplishments, however, were achieved at a staggering human cost. In 1928, Stalin replaced **Vladimir Lenin**'s New Economic Policy with five-year plans entailing a crash collectivization of the agricultural sector and the rapid industrialization of the country. An estimated 25 million farmers were forced onto state farms and land collectivization contributed to a famine between 1932 and 1934 that killed perhaps 6 to 8 million in the key agricultural regions of the Soviet Union, especially the Ukraine, Kazakhstan and North Caucasus.

To further consolidate his power, Stalin "purged" the Communist Party of all real or imagined opponents, branding them as "opportunists" or "counter-revolutionary infiltrators" and subjecting them to measures ranging from banishment to labor camps to executions after show trials. According to Soviet nuclear physicist Andrei Sakharov, more than half the party members (1.2 million) were arrested between 1936 and 1939. Half of them were executed or perished in the **Gulag**. Shortly before, during and immediately after **World War II**, Stalin ordered large-scale **deportations** which deeply affected the ethnic map of the country. Nearly 7 million (Armenians, Bulgarians, Chechens, Ingush, Crimean Tatars, Finns, Greeks, Ukrainians, Volga Germans, Latvians, Lithuanians, Estonians, Poles, and Jews) are believed to have been deported to Siberia and the Central Asian republics between 1941 and 1949. Historians still quarrel about the number of victims of Stalin's regime, their estimates ranging from a low of 3 million to as high as 60 million. Recent studies suggest a probable figure somewhere between 15 and 20 million. *See also* KATYN FOREST MASSACRE; UKRAINE FAMINE.

STANDARD-BASED MEASURES. Technique used to measure government practice on the protection of human rights by integrating **events-based data** on an ordinal scale. **Freedom House**, for instance, has developed a scale derived from press reports and country sources for civil and political liberties state practices ranging from 1 (full protection) to 7 (full violation). Similar standard-based measures have been developed in regard to political terror and torture, the degree to which states sign, ratify and enter reservations to international human rights treaties. More complex methodologies drawing on administrative and socioeconomic statistics have led to the development of aggregate measures which provide insight into the realization of human rights. The Human Development Index featured in the **Human Development Report** is a scale combining weighted measures of literacy rates, infant mortality rates, gross enrollment ratio and per capita gross national product. Other indexes have measured levels of gender equality or empowerment, **democracy** and good **governance**, physical quality of life, the satisfaction of basic needs, among others. *See also* MONITORING OF HUMAN RIGHTS.

STANDARDS' SETTING. Formal and informal processes involving **states**, international organizations, judicial and quasi-judicial bodies and **non-state actors (non-governmental organizations, norm entrepreneurs)** which lead to the adoption of international binding human rights treaties or instruments, creating legal obligations or non-binding documents recommending desirable norms of conduct and policy. New standards are usually created in order to fill a gap in protection. This gap may be normative, for instance in regard to special groups like women, children, migrants who need more detailed protection. There may also be "application gaps" (i.e., in situations where an international instrument cannot apply in particular situations as was the case in regard to disappeared persons who were protected by the **Geneva Conventions** only in situations of armed conflicts). "Supervisory" gaps may arise when there is no mechanism for **monitoring** and enforcing state compliance of its treaty obligations. *See also* INTERNATIONAL CENTRE FOR THE LEGAL PROTECTION OF HUMAN RIGHTS; INTERNATIONAL CRIME CONGRESSES; INTERNATIONAL LABOUR ORGANIZATION; SOFT LAW; UNITED NATIONS GLOBAL CONFERENCES.

STANDING. Legal right to initiate a lawsuit. For a long time, under **international law**, only states had *locus standi*, a practice which continues in regard to the **International Court of Justice**. Developments in the law of human rights have considerably altered this situation, drawing from and expanding on the preexisting practice of a right to petition before investigative bodies under the regimes for the protection of **minorities** instituted by the **League of Nations** and carried over by the **United Nations** in the context of the trusteeship system. The constitutive instruments of international judicial or quasi-judicial bodies allow access to entities other than states, albeit in varying degrees and according to differing modalities.

United Nations treaty bodies allow "communications" by individuals. The **Council of Europe** created the first international court before which individuals have automatic and direct standing. Individuals can take a case to the **Inter-American Court of Human Rights** only indirectly through the intervention of the Commission. The **European Court of Human Rights**, the **Inter-American Commission on Human Rights**, the **African Commission on Human and People's Rights**, the recently established African Court of Justice and, to a certain extent, the **European Court of Justice** grant legal standing to **non-governmental organizations**, allowing them to submit applications, present amicus briefs or participate in their proceedings. To initiate a lawsuit, a party must demonstrate that there was injury (i.e., invasion of a legally protected right), that the injury can be traced back to actions of the defendant and that there is a reasonable prospect of obtaining relief as a result of a favorable ruling. *See also* COMPLAINTS.

STATE. Compulsory political organization with a centralized government enjoying a monopoly of the legitimate use of force over a defined territory and exercising internal and external sovereignty over a permanent population within a defined territory. State institutions normally include administrative bureaucracies, legal and judicial systems, a military and a police force. The international community now comprises around 200 sovereign states, most of them being represented in the **United Nations**. But the emergence of states is a relatively recent development which grew out of the imposition by force of a culture and set of laws over diverse nations of European medieval societies.

In human rights language, a state is viewed as a **duty bearer** responsible for the provision, protection and enjoyment of human rights in society. The boundaries between state and society are not always easily identifiable. Various processes of population movements, emigration, immigration and population transfers account for the fact that states and nations—groups of individuals sharing common customs, language, origins, ancestry and history—do not always coincide. Likewise, it is not uncommon for some states to lack the capacity to exert de facto control of their claimed territories or the resources to contribute to the **realization of human rights**. *See also* TREATY.

STATE IMMUNITY. *See* IMMUNITY.

STATE PARTY. Country that has acceded or ratified a **treaty** and is legally bound by the provisions of that treaty.

STATE REPORTING. With the notable exception of the 1948 **Genocide Convention** and the 1956 **Supplementary Convention on the Abolition of Slavery** virtually all universal and regional human rights **treaties** create special organs of independent experts (the so-called **United Nations treaty bodies**) to monitor the implementation of the treaties by their **state parties**. All treaty bodies play this role on the basis of periodic reports of the states parties to the treaty. Normally, states must submit an initial report, usually one year after joining, and then periodically every four or five years. In addition to the government report, the treaty bodies may receive information from **non-governmental organizations**, United Nations agencies, other intergovernmental organizations, academic institutions and the press. After examining this information together with the state's report and on the basis of the "dialogue" that follows with the representatives of the reporting state, the treaty bodies make known their concerns and recommendations, referred to as **concluding observations**, in a public document. In order to meet their reporting obligations, state parties must include in their reports information on the constitutional, legal and practical measures they have taken to ensure conformity of national law with each substantive human rights provisions of the treaty.

Initially, this reporting system was widely perceived as a relatively pro-forma exercise but, over the years, it has evolved into a much more expansive task fraught with increasing challenges ranging from delays in submission or consideration of reports, non-reporting and duplication of reporting requirements among treaty bodies and also complaints and criticisms by participants, opponents and the press.

See also CHILDREN IN ARMED CONFLICT; ENFORCEMENT; INVESTIGATION; MANDATES; MONITORING OF HUMAN RIGHTS; UNITED NATIONS COMMITTEE AGAINST TORTURE; UNITED NATIONS COMMITTEE ON ECONOMIC, SOCIAL AND CULTURAL RIGHTS; UNITED NATIONS COMMITTEE ON THE ELIMINATION OF ALL FORMS OF DISCRIMINATION AGAINST WOMEN; UNITED NATIONS COMMITTEE ON THE ELIMINATION OF RACIAL DISCRIMINATION; UNITED NATIONS COMMITTEE ON THE PROTECTION OF THE RIGHTS OF ALL MIGRANT WORKERS AND THEIR FAMILIES; UNITED NATIONS COMMITTEE ON THE RIGHTS OF THE CHILD.

STATE RESPONSIBILITY. Principle of **international law** governing the conditions under which a **state** can be held accountable for a breach of its obligations. Originally, the concept of state responsibility referred only to state responsibility for injuries to aliens. The development of **international human rights law**, which applies to all individuals, including aliens, has contributed to the emergence of a general regime of state legal responsibility now encapsulated in the Articles on the Responsibility of States for Internationally Wrongful Acts, a project that the **International Law Commission** had been working on for 40 years and was finally adopted by the **United Nations General Assembly** in 2001 (only after the notion of state crimes was excised from the draft). Under this **soft law** instrument, by commission or omission, "every internationally wrongful act of a State entails the international responsibility of that State."

An internationally wrongful act must be attributable to the state (not private individuals) and constitute a breach of an international obligation of the state which is essential to the protection of the fundamental interests of the international community and, in that sense, is recognized as a crime by that community. International crime may arise from a serious breach of obligations of the prohibition of **aggression**, **slavery**, **genocide** and **apartheid**, the safeguarding of **self-determination** of peoples and the preservation of the human environment. States are responsible for the actions of their officials and organs and, as a general rule, not for the acts of private individuals. The conduct of an insurrectional movement which becomes the new government of a state is considered an act of that state.

States are under an obligation to make full **reparation** for the injury caused by the internally wrongful act in the form of restitution, compensation or satisfaction. But a causal connection must be established between the injury and an official act of commission or omission. This poses increasingly significant issues of **fact finding**, interpretation and practical clarification in the light of the large-scale **privatization** of governments' traditional functions and the growing role of **non-state actors**, notably, terrorist networks, **transnational corporations** and **non-governmental organizations**. *See also* IMMUNITY; SET OF PRINCIPLES FOR THE PROTECTION AND PROMOTION OF HUMAN RIGHTS THROUGH ACTION TO COMBAT IMPUNITY; STATE SOVEREIGNTY.

STATE SOVEREIGNTY. The meaning of the term has been widely discussed, debated and questioned over time and its definition has likewise considerably evolved. Since the mid-17th century it basically refers to the legal attribute of a state to exert supreme authority within a territory. Holders of authority, whether constitutional rulers, dictators, juntas or theocracies, must possess authority (i.e., "the right to command and correlatively the right to be obeyed") based on some principle of legitimacy, natural law, a divine mandate, hereditary law, a constitution, or even international law. The territorial dimension of sovereignty is closely linked to the idea that national policies must be indigenously determined and that nations should freely determine their political status. In **international law**, these precepts mean that interferences in other states' governing practices are illegitimate, and that all states are juridically equal, enjoy rights of membership in international organizations and may only voluntarily enter into mutually acceptable **treaties** placing limits on their sovereignty.

While sovereignty is a quintessential feature of statehood enshrined in Chapter 1 of the **United Nations Charter**, in practice, its exercise has never been absolute. It is commonplace to hear arguments to the effect that **globalization** and the emergence of global threats have eroded state sovereignty. In any event, it was always understood that the sovereignty of a state was closely connected to its ability to act in the best interests and for the welfare of its subjects. The idea has resurfaced in recent years under the guise of a **"responsibility to protect."** Furthermore, external interventions have in the past and still today continue to be justified on the basis of alternative principles, some of them based on human rights (religious toleration, **minority** rights, **self-determination**) others on the more prosaic realities of power (e.g., the collapse of domestic authority structures or governance failures) and the need to maintain international peace and security. *See also* BIAFRA; CULTURAL RELATIVISM; DEVELOPING COUNTRIES;

DOMESTIC JURISDICTION; RULE OF LAW; TREATY; UNITED NATIONS SECURITY COUNCIL; UNIVERSAL JURISDICTION.

STATE TERRORISM. Narrowly defined, the term is meant to convey the idea that unlawful acts of violence against civilians such as **torture**, terror bombings, kidnapping and other forms of intimidation, unfair trials and **extra-judicial executions** can be tolerated, encouraged or carried out by national governments and their army, police, state supported militias or other organizations. The purpose of state **terrorism** is to repress, intimidate and control the state's own population as a whole or private groups or individuals viewed as dangerous to the state. Examples of state terrorism include the archetypical cases of the reign of terror instituted by the Jacobin government during the French Revolution and police state measures employed by the Soviet Union beginning in the 1920s, and by Germany's Nazi regime in the 1930s and 1940s. More recent examples include the use of violence by Latin American military regimes in the 1970s, Saddam Hussein's repression of Kurdish upheavals in **Iraq**, or the suppression of democratic protestors in **Syria**. A variant of state terrorism (but in this case labeled "state-sponsored terrorism") can be found in situations where governments provide supplies, training, and other forms of support to insurgencies and non-state terrorist organizations. Some would cite as a possible example of state sponsorship of terrorism, the support which Hamas and Hezbollah receive from states of the region. Notwithstanding their potential for massive **violations of human rights**, all of these situations trigger unending politically charged and inconclusive debates. *See also* ARGENTINA; COUNTERTERRORISM; DEATH SQUADS; OPERATION CONDOR; NORTHERN IRELAND.

STATELESSNESS. Condition of persons who are not considered nationals by any **state**. The phenomenon of statelessness was more common before the 20th century but the **United Nations Office of the High Commissioner for Refugees** presently estimates that there may still be as many of 12 million stateless people in the world (there are no reliable statistics in part due to the fact that there is no agreement about who exactly is a stateless person). While it may be possible to become stateless by voluntarily renouncing citizenship, most of the time, however, because the acquisition of **nationality** is a sovereign prerogative of states, individuals are most likely to lose their nationality in periods of state collapse, state transformation or state creation. As states cease to exist, individuals may fail to get **citizenship** in their successor states. Changes in citizenship laws may lead to the denial of citizenship to ethnic **minorities**. Legal differences between countries or failure to register the birth of a child may also result in the same outcome. Although the 1957 **United Nations Convention on the Nationality of Married Women** prohibits the automatic acquisition of the husband's citizenship, in many countries, women may lose their citizenship upon marriage to foreigners or are unable to pass on their citizenship to their children.

Climate change could conceivably wipe out small island countries, potentially leaving their entire populations stateless. Individuals deprived of citizenship face a whole range of problems, amounting to a denial of their political, economic, social and cultural rights as they are unable, for example, to establish a legal residence, travel, work in the formal economy, send children to school, have access to basic **health** services and purchase or own property. *See also* DEMJANJUK, JOHN; NANSEN, FRIDTJOF; UNITED NATIONS CONVENTION ON THE REDUCTION OF STATELESSNESS; UNITED NATIONS CONVENTION RELATING TO THE STATUS OF STATELESS PERSONS.

STATEWATCH. British non-profit voluntary group set up in 1991 bringing together lawyers, academics, journalists, researchers and community activists providing news, analyses and documentation that can be freely accessed on the state of civil and political liberties in the **European Union**.

STATUTORY LIMITATIONS. Also known as "prescriptions," statutory limitations prohibit state authorities from investigating or prosecuting a crime after a certain period of time. Balancing the need for retribution with the right to a fair trial accounts for the enactment of statutes of limitations in national legal systems, with it being understood that exceptions or extensions may be recognized for certain crimes such as the sexual abuse of children which may be reported only years after their commission. The increasing number of unpunished crimes of **World War II** in the postwar period and **Israel**'s prosecution of **Adolf Eichmann** in 1962 focused attention on the possibility that statutory limitations might prevent the prosecution of suspected war criminals. It is in that spirit that the **United Nations General Assembly** adopted in 1968 the Convention on the Non-Applicability of Statutory Limitations to War Crimes and Crimes against Humanity, which declares that "[n]o statutory limitation shall apply [to these crimes] . . . irrespective of the date of their commission" (Art. 1) and calls upon states ratifying the Convention to "undertake to adopt, in accordance with their respective constitutional processes, any legislative or other measures necessary to ensure that statutory or other limitations shall not apply to the prosecution and punishment of the(se) crimes . . . and that, where they exist, such limitations shall be abolished" (Art. 4). The words "irrespective of the date of their commission" in Article 1 underline the possible retroactive application of the 1968 Convention to crimes having taken place before its ratification.

Some states have filed declarations (i.e., **reservations**) stating that the Convention applies only with respect to crimes committed after its entry into force. Others have supported the retroactivity of the Convention. In the meantime, the **Council of Europe** adopted in 1974 a convention on the non-applicability of statutory limitations whose provisions are identical to the UN Convention and which entered into force in 2003. Concurrently, the norm of imprescribability has gained increasing acceptability within national legal systems as is the case of a 1964 French law which made the trial of **Klaus Barbie** possible. It is now enshrined in the 1998 Rome Statute of the **International Criminal Court**. *See also* ARGENTINA; BRAZIL; INTER-AMERICAN COURT OF HUMAN RIGHTS; URUGUAY.

STERILIZATION. Surgical operation in medicine intended to terminate the possibility of reproduction in men or women. The procedure may be used for eugenic or therapeutic reasons. It may also be a mode of fertility control. In all cases, sterilization must be performed voluntarily. Forced sterilization occurs when a person is sterilized without his or her knowledge or is not given an opportunity to provide consent. Forced or coerced sterilization is a grave **violation of human rights** and medical ethics. The **European Court of Human Rights** has produced an extensive jurisprudence underlining that sterilization is in violation of the prohibition of inhuman or degrading treatment and **discrimination**, the right to respect for private and **family** life and the right to found a family. Under the statute of the **International Criminal Court**, enforced sterilization is categorized as a **crime against humanity**. *See also* ABORTION; LIFE, RIGHT TO; REPRODUCTIVE RIGHTS.

STROESSNER, ALFREDO (1912–2006). President of **Paraguay** for eight consecutive terms from 1958 until 1988 when he was ousted by a military coup. His regime was criticized for widespread **corruption** and the use of **torture** and kidnappings against the political opposition and indigenous populations. A staunch anti-communist, he participated in **Operation Condor** with Chilean President **Augusto Pinochet** and Argentinian President **Jorge Rafael Videla**. *See also* COLD WAR.

STRUCTURAL ADJUSTMENT PROGRAMS (SAPs). Lending policies of the **International Bank for Reconstruction and Development** and the **International Monetary Fund** which are intended to promote economic growth and efficiency in **developing countries**. Attached to these loans are conditionalities calling for the implementation by recipient countries of free market policies that result in the minimization of the role of the state in the economy and society. SAPs usually require reductions in the size and structure of government expenditures to achieve a balanced budget, the **privatization** of state-owned industries, the dismantlement of state controls over the public sector and the restructuring of economic sectors to conform to liberalized trade rules. To the extent that the net effect of SAPs, at least in the short and medium terms, is to make the quality and availability of essential **food, health** and **education** services virtually unaffordable to low-income groups, they have been criticized for their negative impact on the **realization** of economic and social rights and triggered calls by such organizations as the **United Nations Children's Fund** and the **International Labour Organization** to implement SAPs "with a human face" (i.e., programs accompanied by measures softening the bluntness of their adverse social consequences). *See also* GLOBALIZATION.

SUBSTANTIVE REQUIREMENTS. *See* ADMISSIBILITY REQUIRE-MENTS.

SUDAN. *See* DARFUR CONFLICT; INTERNATIONAL COURT OF JUSTICE; INTERNATIONAL CRIMINAL COURT; UNITED NATIONS MISSION IN THE REPUBLIC OF SOUTH SUDAN.

SUHARTO (1921–2008). Indonesian dictator who ruled the country for 32 years until 1998 when he was driven out of office by widespread rioting and the political chaos triggered by the 1997–98 Asian financial crisis. Born in central Java, Suharto joined the Indonesian nationalist forces and fought against the Dutch during the 1945–50 war of independence. Steeped in anti-communism, a stance which won him the economic and diplomatic support of several Western governments in the era of the **Cold War**, he seized power from Sukarno, the country's independence leader and first president, in the wake of an aborted coup in 1965 which resulted in the killing of six senior anti-communist generals. The New Order to Indonesia, which Suharto subsequently instituted, brought about a measure of national unity in a fractious country of 200 million people comprising no less than 300 ethnic groups speaking 250 languages and spread over more than 17,000 islands extending over a 3,500-mile archipelago.

Whereas Sukarno had built close relations with China, Suharto cultivated a close relationship with the **United States** which remained a strong ally throughout the Cold War. He liberalized the economy and succeeded in attracting billions in foreign investment which enabled the country to experience rapid economic growth until the Asian financial crisis of the late 1990s. The end of the Cold War, however, has brought to increasing light an appalling human rights and governance record. In the military crackdown which followed the 1965 coup, the army which Suharto controlled whipped up a campaign of violence at people—many of them of Chinese ancestry—who were suspected of being communists. **Death squads** organized by the army in the early 1980s are believed to have killed 4,000 to 9,000 petty criminals and political operatives. In 1975, Suharto ordered the invasion and annexation of East Timor and oversaw a brutal counterinsurgency campaign that lasted 24 years and killed 200,000 of the former Portuguese colony's population of 700,000. **Corruption** and nepotism were also rampant throughout Suharto's three-decade long rule. **Transparency International** has charged that Suharto and his family embezzled more money than any other world leader, amassing as much as $35 billion in state funds by siphoning money from state charities, controlling state enterprises and receiving kickbacks for governmental contracts. *Forbes* magazine rates the assets of the Suhartos as among the world's 12 largest. Half-hearted efforts to prosecute Suharto started in 2000 but have been dropped after court-appointed doctors ruled him unfit to stand trial. In July 2007, prosecutors filed a civil suit which is still pending, seeking $1.1 billion in damages for embezzling, and an investigation was announced in six cases of human rights abuses in the 1960s. *See also* IMPUNITY; TIMOR-LESTE.

SUPPLEMENTARY CONVENTION ON THE ABOLITION OF SLAVERY, THE SLAVE TRADE, AND INSTITUTIONS AND PRACTICES SIMILAR TO SLAVERY (1956). International human rights **treaty** complementing the 1926 Slavery Convention as well as the 1930 Forced Labor Convention by banning debt bondage, serfdom, servile marriage and child servitude. *See also* INVOLUNTARY SERVITUDE; SLAVERY.

SUPREME IRAQI CRIMINAL TRIBUNAL. Court established under Iraqi national law to try Iraqi nationals accused of **genocide, crimes against humanity** and **war crimes** committed between 1968 and 2003. It also has powers to hear cases on squandering national resources and the use of force against another Arab country in contravention of the **United Nations Charter**. The court was responsible for the trials of **Saddam Hussein**, Ali Hassan al-Majid (also known as "Chemical Ali"), former vice president Taha Yassin Ramadan, former deputy prime minister Tariq Aziz and other former senior officials in the deposed Ba'athist regime. It ruled that the killings of Kurdish men from the Barzani tribe by the Ba'ath regime in the 1980s, the

Anfal campaign and the 1988 chemical attack on the city of Halabja were acts of **genocide**. Many international human rights groups have criticized the court for the role that the **United States** played in its creation, financing and operation and expressed the view that former Iraqi officials should have been tried by an international tribunal. Objections have also been raised about the Tribunal's reliance on and imposition of **capital punishment**.

SURVEY DATA. Information gathered through a wide variety of techniques from a representative sample of individuals with a view to making inferences about a broader set of people. There is a growing body of academic **research** dealing with a broad range of topics including among others levels of support for **democracy**, patterns of **corruption**, citizens attitudes and perceptions toward human rights and the like. *See also* EVENTS-BASED DATA; MONITORING OF HUMAN RIGHTS; STANDARD-BASED MEASURES.

SURVIVAL INTERNATIONAL (SI). London-based international **non-governmental organization** concerned with the protection of **indigenous peoples'** rights worldwide. It was founded in 1969 in the wake of media uncovering of **massacres**, land theft and indiscriminate killings taking place in Brazilian Amazonia. SI has since sought to influence government and corporate policies through education work, **advocacy** and **campaigns** designed to mobilize national and international public.

SURVIVORS INTERNATIONAL (SI). Non-profit organization dedicated to providing essential psychological and medical services to survivors of **torture** who have fled from around the world to the San Francisco Bay Area. SI aims to help survivors put the pieces back together by providing the support they need to reestablish healthy and productive lives after their experiences of torture. The group claims to serve more than 2,000 clients from 96 different countries.

SYRIA. Former **mandate** of the **League of Nations** under French administration, Syria gained independence in 1946 as a parliamentary republic. In effect, the country has been governed by a single party for the past 60 years or so. A state of **public emergency** proclaimed as far back as 1963 has given free rein to authoritarian rulers backed up by security forces with sweeping unchecked powers. Under the rule of President Hafez al-Assad and his son Bashar al-Assad who took the reins of power upon the death of his father in 2000, the regime has imposed severe restrictions on **freedom of expression** and **freedom of association** and assembly. Ethnic minorities (notably a sizable Kurdish minority) face discrimination. **Non-governmental organizations** have blamed the authorities of widespread practices of arbitrary **detention**, **torture** and **forced disappearances**. What began in the spring of 2011 as spontaneous protestations against nearly five decades of single party rule has turned into a full-fledged civil war between forces loyal to the government and increasingly well-armed and -organized insurgents bent on ousting it. As of July 2013, the death toll was estimated at 100,000 and was still rising rapidly. Half of these deaths were civilians and the vast majority were caused by government armed forces, equipped with modern weapons and aircraft, as opposed to the less well-armed rebels.

According to the United Nations, about 1.2 million Syrians have been displaced within the country and hundred of thousands have fled to neighboring countries. Human rights non-governmental organizations have documented numerous and serious **violations of human rights**, the vast majority of them committed by government forces. In several special sessions, on the basis of investigative report which it ordered, the **United Nations Human Rights Council** has condemned the acts of violence of the Syrian regime. It also ordered an investigation into the commission of possible **war crimes**. Vetoes by Russia and China have prevented the **United Nations Security Council** from taking forceful action on the basis of the principle of a **responsibility to protect**. *See also* KURDISH HUMAN RIGHTS PROJECT; KURDISH QUESTION; STATE TERRORISM.

T

TADIC, DUSAN (1955–). In late May 1992, Serb forces attacked and overran Bosnian Muslim and Croat population centers in the Prijedor municipality of Bosnia and Herzegovina and subsequently confined thousands of Muslims and Croats in three **concentration camps**. Accused of having participated in attacks on and the seizure, murder and maltreatment of Bosnian Muslims and Croats both within and outside the camps, Tadic became the first person since **World War II**'s Nuremberg and Tokyo trials to be convicted of **war crimes** by an international court. In 1997, the **International Criminal Tribunal for the Former Yugoslavia** found him guilty of grave breaches of the 1949 **Geneva Conventions** (Art. 2 of the Statute—willful killing; **torture** or inhuman treatment; willfully causing great suffering or serious injury to body or health), **crimes against humanity** (Art. 5 thereof—murder), and violations of the **laws of war** (Art. 3 thereof—murder). Tadic is currently serving a 20-year prison sentence. *See also* ARMED CONFLICT.

TAYLOR, CHARLES (1943–). President of **Liberia** from 1997 to 2003. He came to power after a protracted bloody armed struggle as the leader of the National Patriotic Front of Liberia, a rebel group which had fought to overthrow the government since 1989. In turn, he left office after new rebel forces now battling him had come close to entering the Liberian capital. Granted political asylum in Nigeria, Taylor was transferred to the custody of the **Special Court for Sierra Leone** where he faced trial. Charged with 11 counts of **war crimes** and **crimes against humanity**, he was found guilty in April 2012 on all charges including terror, murder and rape and sentenced to 50 years in prison.

TERRORISM. Although there is no universally agreed upon definition of the term, it is commonly understood that terrorism refers to acts of violence that target civilians in the pursuit of ideological or political objectives. A 1994 non-binding declaration of the **United Nations General Assembly** elaborates by stating that terrorism includes "criminal acts intended or calculated to provoke a state of terror in the general public, a group of persons or particular persons for political purposes" and that such acts "are in any circumstances unjustifiable, whatever the considerations of a political, philosophical, ideological, racial, ethnic, religious or other nature that may be invoked to justify them." In the wake of the 11 September 2001 attacks on the **United States**, the **United Nations Security Council** posited that terrorism was a collective security threat and that its suppression was an essential element in the maintenance of international peace and security.

From a human rights perspective, terrorism, with its frequent links with **transnational crime**, is widely viewed as a phenomenon threatening the **dignity** and security of everyone, adversely affecting the **rule of law**, undermining pluralistic societies and destabilizing legitimately constituted **states**. It is also recognized that governments have a **responsibility to protect** their nationals from possible violations by private actors, including terrorist acts. **Counterterrorism** measures adopted in the past decade, however, have often been inconsistent with human rights principles and law.

See also INTERNATIONAL COUNCIL ON HUMAN RIGHTS POLICY; INTERNATIONAL PEACE INSTITUTE; LIFE, RIGHT TO; NON-DEROGABLE RIGHTS; ORGANIZATION FOR SECURITY AND CO-OPERATION IN EUROPE; STATE TERRORISM; TORTURE; TRANS-NATIONAL CRIME; TURKEY; UNITED NATIONS SUB-COMMISSION ON THE PROMOTION AND PROTECTION OF HUMAN RIGHTS.

THINK TANKS. Organizations variously known as institutes, councils, centers, corporations, foundations, bureaus and the like which primarily conduct applied **research**, provide policy advice to decision makers and may also engage in **advocacy**. Although they generally bring together public officials, academics, interest groups, and the media, the rapidly expanding constellation of thinks tanks defies simple classification. Some of them have a broad agenda, others a narrower focus on limited areas such as security, military strategy, disarmament, development, business, science and technology, medicine or the environment. Some are fiercely independent while others are de facto arms of governments.

Some have large budgets and staff; others are one-person operations. A recent study reckons that there are some 5,000 think tanks in the world, one-third of them in the **United States**. Important think tanks active in the field of human rights include such organizations as the Carter Center, the European Human Rights Center, **Freedom House** and the **International Peace Institute**. Numerous **non-governmental organizations** such as **Amnesty International**, **Human Rights Watch** and **Human Rights First** also have large-scale research programs.

See also ACCOUNTABILITY; AFRICA INSTITUTE OF SOUTH AFRICA; AMERICAN JEWISH COMMITTEE; CARNEGIE COUNCIL;

CARNEGIE COUNCIL ON ETHICS AND INTERNATIONAL AFFAIRS; CARNEGIE ENDOWMENT FOR INTERNATIONAL PEACE; CENTER FOR EUROPEAN POLICY STUDIES; CHATAM HOUSE; CONSORTIUM ON GENDER, SECURITY AND HUMAN RIGHTS; COUNCIL ON FOREIGN RELATIONS; DANISH INSTITUTE FOR HUMAN RIGHTS; EUROPEAN RESEARCH CENTRE ON MIGRATION AND ETHNIC RELATIONS; FRASER INSTITUTE; FRIEDRICH-EBERT FOUNDATION; HERITAGE FOUNDATION; INSTITUTE FOR GLOBAL POLICY; INSTITUTE FOR HUMAN RIGHTS AND BUSINESS; INSTITUTE OF DEVELOPMENT STUDIES; INTERNATIONAL CENTRE FOR CRIMINAL LAW REFORM AND CRIMINAL JUSTICE POLICY; INTERNATIONAL CRISIS GROUP; INTERNATIONAL LAW INSTITUTE; INTERNATIONAL PEACE INSTITUTE; MIGRATION POLICY GROUP; NATIONAL ENDOWMENT FOR DEMOCRACY; RAND CORPORATION; RAOUL WALLENBERG INSTITUTE; TRANSNATIONAL INSTITUTE; TRANSPARENCY INTERNATIONAL; UNITED STATES INSTITUTE OF PEACE; WORLDWATCH INSTITUTE.

THIRD-GENERATION RIGHTS. Category of rights in the scheme developed by Karel Vasak which concern group or collective rather than individual rights and whose **realization** is predicated upon affirmative and negative interventions and duties of the state. For example, the right to a healthy **environment** concerns an entire national society and hypothetically entails the obligation of governments to not only adopt the necessary measures to achieve its full realization but also to refrain from interfering directly or indirectly with its enjoyment and to prevent third parties such as **transnational corporations** from interfering in any way.

Third-generation rights have been understood to extend to the recognition of **minority** groups, social identity and cultural issues, the right of **self-determination**, the right to **peace**, the right to development, sovereignty over natural resources, and a right to intergenerational equity and sustainability. This category of rights is probably the most controversial development of the past few decades in the field of human rights, some arguing that it is merely an attempt to cloak a political agenda and goals in human rights language. It is also the least anchored and institutionalized in international human right law. *See also* FIRST-GENERATION RIGHTS; GROUP RIGHTS; SECOND-GENERATION RIGHTS; SOFT LAW.

THIRD WORLD INSTITUTE (ITEM). Latin American **non-governmental organization** in **consultative status** with the **United Nations Economic and Social Council**. It was created in 1989 and has its headquarters in

Montevideo, Uruguay. Its formal name is Instituto del Tercer Mundo. ITEM's stated purposes are to contribute to the construction of democratic, equitable and environmentally sustainable societies, to promote respect for human rights, in particular **freedom of expression** and free access to information and to conduct policy-oriented **research** on the problems affecting Third World countries.

TIANANMEN SQUARE PROTESTS. Protests which began in April 1989 at the initiative of students and intellectuals, thereafter joined by workers and ordinary citizens in and around Tiananmen square in Beijing, China. Demonstrators demanded the **rule of law, freedom of association, expression** and the press and denounced corruption. The area was forcefully cleared up on 4 June by the army. The actual death toll is not known but is estimated to be around 2,600. Hundreds of protesters were thereafter hunted down, arrested and jailed or imprisoned in labor camps. Demands for **accountability** have until now been unheeded.

TIBET (1950–). Himalayan northern province of the People's Republic of China (PRC) adjacent to India. Nicknamed "the roof of the world" or "the land of snows" for its long-standing remoteness and isolation, Tibet was incorporated into the PRC after a military intervention in 1950 and the conclusion of an agreement, a year later, between the Chinese authorities and the Dalai Lama, then Tibet's formal feudal ruler. The treaty empowered the Chinese government to handle Tibet's external affairs and guaranteed that China would not alter the existing political systems in Tibet or interfere with the status functions and powers of the Dalai Lama. The agreement also stipulated that Tibet would enjoy regional autonomy, that religion and custom would be respected and that all internal reforms would be effected only after consultations with leading Tibetans.

The nature of Tibet's political status vis-à-vis China has ever since been the subject of bitterly clashing views. For some (primarily Tibetan exiles), Tibet emerged from its obscure history as a distinctly Buddhist kingdom in the seventh and eighth centuries and remained, on the whole, independent until its forcible integration into the PRC in 1950. This Chinese invasion was an act of unprovoked aggression, and the 1951 treaty turning Tibet into a "national autonomous region" of China under the traditional rule of the Dalai Lama was a treaty imposed by the threat of the use of force and, therefore, legally void. The Chinese's subsequent attempt to impose a radical agrarian reform which broke up the monastic estates; the bloody repression of the unrest that these policies triggered, forcing in 1959 the Dalai Lama to take refuge in India; the restrictions and obstacles placed on the free exercise of religion; and the use of the Tibetan language (distantly connected to Chinese), the destruction of cultural sites and introduction of secular education, and the import of Chinese settlers tilting the ethnic balance against the native Tibetans are some of the facets of a deliberate policy purposely designed to deny the Tibetan people of their right to **self-determination**.

Since the restoration of Chinese rule, medieval feudal serfdom has been eliminated and big strides have been made in the development of an economic infrastructure and promotion of **education**, culture, public **health** and higher standards of living. Chinese authorities also reject the accusations that over 1.2 million Tibetans have perished in genocidal violence perpetrated since the 1950s and that the territory is being settled with the Chinese people. In this regard, independent observers point to gaps in Chinese census data that lend credence to assertions that 200,000 to 400,000 Tibetans may have perished since the establishment of Chinese rule. Be that as it may, the Tibetan issue was discussed in the **United Nations** on several occasions during the **Cold War**. In 1959, 1961 and 1965, the **United Nations General Assembly** adopted, with **United States** support, tersely worded resolutions calling for the cessation of practices destructive of the Tibetan people's distinctive cultural and religious life and depriving them of their fundamental human rights and freedoms including their right to self-determination. United States support, however, evaporated as the country moved toward formal recognition of the PRC. Foreign governments continue to make occasional protests about aspects of the PRC rule in Tibet. But they recognize China's sovereignty over Tibet, and none has recognized the Dalai Lama government in exile in India. *See also* FREEDOM OF RELIGION; MINORITIES.

TIMOR-LESTE. Southeast Asian country occupying the eastern half of the island of Timor. A Portuguese colony since 1702 known as East Timor, Timor-Leste became independent in 2002 after close to 25 years of brutal Indonesian occupation and amid conditions of extreme violence. In the wake of the change in government which followed the demise of the Antonio Salazar dictatorship, Portugal embarked on a policy of decolonization and, in 1974, sought to establish a provisional government and a popular assembly that would determine the status of East Timor. But civil war broke out between those who favored independence and those who advocated integration with **Indonesia**. More focused on the decolonization problems posed by **Angola** and Mozambique and unable to control the situation, Portugal withdrew from East Timor.

East Timor unilaterally declared its independence. A few days later, however, Indonesia invaded and occupied East Timor, alleging that the East Timorese independence movement was infiltrated by communists and had received support from the People's Republic of China. The Indonesian military invasion and subsequent annexation had apparently received the tacit approval of **United States** President Gerald Ford and Secretary of State **Henry Kissinger** who viewed pro-Western Indonesia as a bulwark against the Soviet Union in the **Cold War.** The integration of East Timor into Indonesia as its 27th province was never recognized by the **United Nations** and, nominally, the territory remained a "non-self governing territory" under Portuguese administration. Both the **United Nations Security Council** and the **United Nations General Assembly** repeatedly called upon Indonesia to withdraw and successive secretaries-general held regular talks with Indonesia and Portugal aimed at resolving the status of the territory. These mediating efforts succeeded only in 1998 when Indonesia proposed a limited autonomy for East Timor within Indonesia and agreed to entrust the **United Nations secretary-general** with organizing and conducting a "popular consultation" in order to ascertain whether the East Timorese people accepted or rejected the special autonomy proposed by Indonesia.

A UN-sponsored referendum was held on 30 August 1999, resulting in an overwhelming vote in favor of full independence. Indonesia relinquished control of the territory as a UN peacekeeping operation, the **United Nations Transitional Administration in East Timor** (UNTAET) took over the administration of East Timor. UNTAET was abolished on 20 May 2002. Most of its functions were passed on to the East Timor government, and East Timor became a full member of the United Nations on 27 September 2002. The 1999 UN-supervised popular consultation was marred by violent clashes instigated primarily by the Indonesian military with the assistance of Timorese militias organized, financed, trained, equipped and assisted by the Indonesian armed forces. The intervention of an Australian-led peacekeeping operation quelled the violence, but many East Timorese were killed and as many as 500,000 were displaced from their homes, with about half leaving the territory. In 2000, UNTAET created Special Panels composed of international and Timorese judges to try those responsible for "serious crimes" such as **war crimes, genocide,** and **crimes against humanity** committed during the 1999 vote.

Between 1975 and 1999, the Indonesian army waged a brutal war against East Timorese insurgents. Estimates of the death toll arising from attacks on civilians, hunger and disease range from 100,000 according to a report of a **truth and reconciliation commission** set up to investigate human rights violations committed between 1974 and October 1999 to 200,000 according to **Amnesty International** figures. *See also* RAMOS-HORTA, JOSE; SELF-DETERMINATION; SPECIAL PANELS OF THE DILI DISTRICT COURT; SUHARTO.

TOKYO TRIBUNAL. *See* INTERNATIONAL MILITARY TRIBUNAL FOR THE FAR EAST.

TORTURE. Deliberate infliction of severe pain—psychological or physical—designed to control, punish, coerce and obtain confessions. Physical torture may include such atrocities as severe beatings to the head and genitals, burning of the skin with cigarettes and torches, suspension by arms or legs, near suffocation, electric shocks, and multiple rapes and other sexual violations. Methods of psychological torture range from prolonged isolation, seeing or hearing others tortured, sexual humiliation, confinement in small places or crowded cells to mock executions. Torture is a form of cruel, inhuman or degrading **ill treatment** that is now almost universally considered an extreme **violation of human rights**. Under **international law** and **international human rights law**, freedom from torture is a **non-derogable right** which may not be infringed or restricted by states. The Statute of the **International Criminal Court** defines torture as a **war crime** or a **crime against humanity**. The 1949 **Geneva Convention** prohibited torture in all times and all circumstances.

Fleeing from torture or fear of it is a legitimate grounds for seeking **asylum**. The 1951 **United Nations Convention Relating to the Status of Refugees** posits that no state party may "expel or return (refouler) a refugee in any manner whatsoever to the frontiers of territories where his life or freedom would be threatened on account of his race, religion, nationality, membership of a particular social group or political opinion." In this context, the 1984 **United Nations Convention against Torture and Other Cruel, Inhuman, or Degrading Treatment and Punishment** affirms that "no State party shall expel, return (refouler) or extradite a person to another State where there are substantial grounds for believing that he would be in danger of being subjected to torture."

Other international human rights instruments banning torture include the **Universal Declaration of Human Rights** (Art. 5), the **International Covenant on Civil and Political Rights** (Art. 7), the **European Convention for the Prevention of Torture and Inhuman or Degrading Treatment or Punishment** (Art. 3), the **American Convention on Human Rights** (Art. 5), the **African Charter on Human and People's Rights** (Art. 5) and the **Inter-American Convention to Prevent and Punish Torture**. In practice, torture continues to be used with the express or implicit consent or acquiescence of public officials. According to human rights organizations reports, over 120 countries in the world today routinely use torture to control their citizens.

See also ABU GHRAIB PRISON; AFRICAN COMMISSION ON HUMAN AND PEOPLE'S RIGHTS; ALGERIAN WAR OF INDEPENDENCE; AMNESTY INTERNATIONAL; ASSOCIATION FOR THE PREVENTION

OF TORTURE; CENTER FOR HUMAN RIGHTS AND GLOBAL JUSTICE; CENTER FOR VICTIMS OF TORTURE; CENTRAL INTELLIGENCE AGENCY; CHILE; CORPORAL PUNISHMENT; DECLARATION ON THE PROTECTION OF ALL PERSONS FROM BEING SUBJECTED TO TORTURE AND OTHER CRUEL, INHUMAN OR DEGRADING TREATMENT OR PUNISHMENT; EUROPEAN CHARTER OF FUNDAMENTAL RIGHTS OF THE EUROPEAN UNION; EUROPEAN COMMITTEE FOR THE PREVENTION OF TORTURE; EUROPEAN CONVENTION FOR THE PREVENTION OF TORTURE AND INHUMAN OR DEGRADING TREATMENT OR PUNISHMENT; EUROPEAN COURT OF HUMAN RIGHTS; EUROPEAN PARLIAMENT; EXTRADITION; EXTRAORDINARY RENDITION; FORCED DISAPPEARANCES; FORUM FOR FACT-FINDING DOCUMENTATION AND ADVOCACY; FUNDAMENTAL GUARANTEES; GUANTANAMO BAY DETENTION CAMP; HUMAN RIGHTS WATCH; INDIVIDUAL RECOURSE; INHUMAN OR DEGRADING TREATMENT OR PUNISHMENT; INQUIRY PROCEDURES; INTER-AMERICAN COURT OF HUMAN RIGHTS; INTERNATIONAL CENTRE FOR HUMAN RIGHTS AND DEMOCRATIC DEVELOPMENT; INTERNATIONAL HUMANITARIAN LAW; INTERNATIONAL REHABILITATION COUNCIL FOR TORTURE VICTIMS; NORTHERN IRELAND; ORGANIZATION OF AMERICAN STATES; PARAGUAY; PEREMPTORY NORMS; PHYSICIANS FOR HUMAN RIGHTS; REDRESS; RIGHTS INTERNATIONAL; STATE TERRORISM; TURKEY; UNITED NATIONS COMMITTEE AGAINST TORTURE; UNITED NATIONS HUMAN RIGHTS COMMITTEE; UNIVERSAL JURISDICTION; URUGUAY; "WAR ON TERROR"; WORLD ORGANIZATION AGAINST TORTURE.

TOUVIER, PAUL (1915–1996). French Nazi collaborator and assistant to **Klaus Barbie**. Sentenced to capital punishment *in abstentia*, for treason and collusion with the enemy, he went into hiding for several years, benefiting from the assistance of the **Catholic Church** hierarchy. He obtained a presidential pardon in 1971, but two years later a complaint was filed against him charging him with **crimes against humanity**. After years of legal arguments, trials and appeals, a warrant for his arrest was issued in 1981. He disappeared again until his arrest in 1989. In 1994, he was convicted of complicity to commit crimes against humanity in the murder of seven Jews and sentenced to life imprisonment. *See also* PROSECUTION.

TRADE AND HUMAN RIGHTS. *See* AGREEMENT ON TRADE-RELATED ASPECTS OF INTELLECTUAL PROPERTY RIGHTS;

BUSINESS AND HUMAN RIGHTS RESOURCE CENTRE; CONVENTION ON THE PROTECTION AND PROMOTION OF THE DIVERSITY OF CULTURAL EXPRESSION; WORLD TRADE ORGANIZATION.

TRADITIONAL PRACTICES. All communities share beliefs and cultural practices for periods often spanning for generations which help sustain and nurture their existence and maintenance. Because they so intimately fall within the private domain of the family and take on an aura of morality in the eyes of those practicing them, the international community has been wary about treating the adverse consequences of a number of traditional practices as a subject warranting international and national scrutiny. Such practices include, for instance, **female genital mutilation**, child marriage, forced isolation in the home, exchange marriages and **honor killings**, the various taboos which prevent women from controlling their own fertility, nutritional taboos and traditional birth practices, son preference, **female infanticide**, early pregnancies and dowry price and the maltreatment of older women and widows in particular.

Adding to the sensitivity of these questions, religious leaders reinforce these harmful customs by invoking their interpretations of holy scriptures. Yet some of these practices indeed can be viewed as violations of a women's right to **health**, **life**, **dignity** and personal integrity. The **United Nations Convention on the Elimination of All Forms of Discrimination against Women** enjoins its states parties "to take all appropriate measures, including legislation, to modify or abolish existing laws, regulations, customs and practices which constitute discrimination against women." The elimination of discriminatory sociocultural and economic inequalities that reinforce women's subordinate place in society is a particularly problematic challenge at the national level. At the international level, the dispute between advocates of change and supporters of the status quo has morphed into a contentious debate over the **universality of rights**. The **United Nations Human Rights Council**, after bitter discussions spanning over several years, recently adopted a resolution asserting that a better understanding and appreciation of traditional values of dignity, freedom and responsibility contributed to promoting and protecting human rights.

TRAFFICKING IN HUMAN ORGANS. Modality of trade involving human organs—like kidney, liver, cornea and lung—for transplantation. **Human trafficking** for the purpose of organ removal is prohibited by the Protocol to Prevent, Suppress and Punish Trafficking in Persons, Especially Women and Children attached to the **United Nations Convention against Transnational Organized Crime**. But the global demand for live transplants has grown exponentially in recent decades, triggering the expansion of a shadowy organ trading business facilitated by **poverty** and discrimination, inadequate national legislations, widespread corrupt practices and a general lack of public awareness on the extent of the trade. Organ sellers are frequently exploited and deceived in black markets, a situation that led some to call for the regulation of the market. Human rights groups generally oppose the legalization of human organ trading. *See also* SLAVERY.

TRAINING. *See* ADVISORY SERVICES; CAPACITY BUILDING.

TRANSITIONAL JUSTICE. Process whereby national societies emerging from brutal internal strife address past **violations of human rights** including the pursuit of accountability, truth and **reparation**, the preservation of peace and the building of **democracy** and the **rule of law**. Allowing for the specificity of local situations, strategies to achieve these sometimes inconsistent objectives entail a wide combination of **retributive, restorative** and **reparative justice** such as individual criminal **prosecutions**, vetting and dismissals, reparations programs, **truth and reconciliation commissions**, security system reform and memorialization efforts at the national or international level.

    See also APOLOGIES; CENTER FOR HUMAN RIGHTS AND GLOBAL JUSTICE; INTERNATIONAL CENTER FOR TRANSITIONAL JUSTICE; INTERNATIONAL CIVIL SOCIETY ACTION NETWORK; INTERNATIONAL CRIMINAL COURT; INTERNATIONAL CRIMINAL LAW; INTERNATIONAL CRIMINAL TRIBUNAL FOR RWANDA; INTERNATIONAL CRIMINAL TRIBUNAL FOR THE FORMER YUGOSLAVIA; KOSOVO; LUSTRATION; RESTITUTION; SPECIAL COURT FOR SIERRA LEONE; UNIVERSAL JURISDICTION.

TRANSNATIONAL ADVOCACY NETWORKS (TANs). Mode of organization (also called transnational social movements) bringing together internationally linked national and international **non-governmental organizations**, citizens associations and trade union activists which coalesce around such global issues as women's rights, the **environment, peace**, Third World debt and development. Through the use of telecommunications and transportation technologies, TANs seek to generate public interest and support for global causes through highly publicized **campaigns** targeting the policies and practices of international organizations or seeking democratic intergovernmental regime changes. The anti-**slavery** and labor movements of the 19th and 20th centuries are early instances of TANs. More recent examples include the Jubilee 2000 campaign against Third World debt, the anti-landmine campaign or the recurring demonstrations against **globalization** and the **Bretton Woods Institutions**. *See also* ADVOCACY; COALITION FOR INTERNATIONAL JUSTICE; COALITION FOR THE INTERNATIONAL CRIMINAL COURT; COALITION TO STOP THE USE OF CHILDREN; INTERNATIONAL CAMPAIGN TO BAN LANDMINES.

TRANSNATIONAL CORPORATIONS (TNCs). Earlier, often known as multinational corporations, TNCs have been defined as "an economic entity or a group of economic entities operating in two or more countries, whatever the legal framework, the country of origin or the country or countries of activity, whether its activity is considered individually or collectively." Transnational corporations are legal persons in private law with multiple territorial implantations but with a single center for strategic decision making. As economic agents, TNCs employ a tiny share of the world's total labor force, but they control and orient huge amounts of capital and a large proportion of the world gross product. The volume of business of several TNCs is greater than the gross domestic product (GDP) of the 100 poorest developing countries. Walmart has revenues that would make it on par with the GDP of the 25th largest economy in the world.

Many view TNC investment as the engine behind **globalization**. But their impact on economic development and human rights is controversial. Some argue that TNCs are a driving force of beneficial changes and modernization, while others assert that, on balance, they remain profit-seeking conglomerates paying little attention to the social welfare implications of their actions. In any event, inevitably, the activities of TNCs have led to situations affecting the enjoyment and the **realization** of human rights. Monopolistic or oligopolistic behavior by TNCs can have an adverse impact on the right of **self-determination** of peoples. TNCs sometimes rely on poor and discriminatory wages and arbitrary hiring policies and turn a blind eye to working conditions. They may also make use of special economic zones set up by governments to induce foreign investment to prevent the organization of unions. There are documented cases of chemical poisoning of land and water and forced expropriation of land. Corporate control of **intellectual property rights** has led to situations threatening people's access to food and land.

Oddly enough though, while they may cause harm and loss, with the exception of serious crimes or acts of negligence, TNCs cannot legally be deemed to violate human rights because international human rights concerns the relationship of the state to the individual, not the relationship between individuals. Human rights activists, however, have relied on the doctrine that states are responsible for **violations of human rights** that result from their failure to exercise due diligence in controlling the behavior of **non-state**

actors. Existing jurisprudence at the national, regional and international levels has brought, at least in principle, a degree of **accountability**. In the **United States**, the 1789 Alien Tort Claims Act was used by litigants to seek redress for torts in U.S. courts. In 2001, in a case involving the activities of oil corporations in Nigeria's Delta region, the **African Commission on Human and People's Rights** found that the government of Nigeria was responsible for the protection of the environment, **health** and livelihood of the Ogoni people living there.

The **European Court of Human Rights** has issued rulings condemning governments for authorizing TNCs to operate without adequate safeguards against health risks and the destruction of local ecosystems. In a 1990 **General Comment**, the **United Nations Committee on Economic, Social and Cultural Rights** opined that states should draw up a range of legislative measures criminalizing all activities by TNCs which violate economic, social and cultural rights. Commenting on the report of Surinam to the **International Covenant on Civil and Political Rights** in 2004, the **United Nations Human Rights Committee** criticized the government for granting logging and mining concessions without due regard to the welfare of **indigenous peoples** and invited it to take remedial measures. Concurrently, under pressure from **non-governmental organizations** and social movements, a number of non-binding instruments have been enacted laying down the basis for a broad legal framework for **corporate social responsibility**.

In 1976, the **Organization for Economic Co-operation and Development** (OECD) adopted loose *Guidelines for Multinational Enterprises* operating in or from OECD countries which cover such matters as employment and industrial relations, **environment**, information disclosure, combating bribery, consumer interests, science and technology, competition, and taxation. In regard to human rights, the Guidelines simply call upon TNCs to "respect the human rights of those affected by their activities consistent with the host government's obligations and commitments." A year later, the **International Labour Organization** approved the *Tripartite Declaration of Principles Concerning Multinational Enterprises and Social Policy* which recommends to governments, to employers' and workers' organizations and to TNCs, voluntary observance of principles dealing with employment, training, working and living conditions as well as professional relations. The latest additions to this catalog of **soft law** instruments are the **United Nations Global Compact** and the **United Nations "Protect, Respect and Remedy" Framework for Business and Human Rights**.

See also ALIEN TORT STATUTE; BUSINESS AND HUMAN RIGHTS RESOURCE CENTRE; CODES OF CONDUCT FOR TRANSNATIONAL CORPORATIONS; CORPORATE SOCIAL

RESPONSIBILITY; CORPWATCH; DECLARATION ON THE RIGHTS OF INDIGENOUS PEOPLES; DRAFT NORMS ON THE RESPONSIBILITIES OF TRANSNATIONAL CORPORATIONS AND OTHER BUSINESS ENTERPRISES WITH REGARD TO HUMAN RIGHTS; EQUATOR PRINCIPLES; FOOD SECURITY; FRIENDS OF THE EARTH INTERNATIONAL; HIV/AIDS; KIMBERLEY PROCESS CERTIFICATION SCHEME; MYANMAR; NIGER DELTA CONFLICT; OECD REVISED GUIDELINES FOR MULTINATIONAL ENTERPRISES; PRIVATIZATION; RAINFOREST ACTION NETWORK; RUGGIE, JOHN G.; SIERRA CLUB; STRUCTURAL ADJUSTMENT PROGRAMS; UNITED NATIONS CONFERENCE ON TRADE AND DEVELOPMENT CORPORATE RESPONSIBILITY REPORTING; UNITED NATIONS PRINCIPLES FOR RESPONSIBLE INVESTMENT; UNITED NATIONS SUB-COMMISSION ON THE PROMOTION AND PROTECTION OF HUMAN RIGHTS; WORLD BUSINESS COUNCIL FOR SUSTAINABLE DEVELOPMENT; WORLD TRADE ORGANIZATION; WORLD SOCIAL FORUM.

TRANSNATIONAL CRIME. Term commonly used by law enforcement officials and scholars to refer to the planning and execution of illegal activities involving groups or networks of individuals operating in more than one country. **Globalization**, the expansion of financial markets and technological change, the weakening of government institutions in some countries and the resurgence of ethnic and regional conflicts have, among other factors, contributed to the expanding and growing global reach of international crime since the end of the **Cold War**. Examples of transnational crimes include **human trafficking**, the smuggling and trafficking of goods (weapons, drugs), **terrorism**, cyber crime, money laundering and government **corruption**. The phenomenon is widely viewed as a major threat to international security, development and human rights as it can undermine **democracies**, destabilize societies, disrupt the functioning of markets and drain national assets. Under certain circumstances, transnational crimes may constitute breaches of customary international law and **crimes against humanity**. The **United Nations Convention against Transnational Organized Crime** encapsulates an effort to combat a problem now no longer viewed as a domestic one but one of global proportions requiring an international response. *See also* INTERNATIONAL PEACE INSTITUTE; UNITED NATIONS INTERIM ADMINISTRATION MISSION IN KOSOVO.

TRANSNATIONAL INSTITUTE. Independent, international **think tank** engaged in a broad range of **research**, policy **advocacy** and **civil society**

networking activities from its Amsterdam headquarters. Four of the Institute's current programs have important human rights implications. A Drugs and Democracy program examines connections between illicit drugs and wider issues of demilitarization, democratization, public **health** promotion and **poverty** reduction. A New Politics program focuses on alternative modes of participatory **democracy**, political organization, urban **governance** and rural democratization. An Environmental Justice project monitors the negative impact of pollution trading upon environmental, social and economic justice and works to develop community-led responses to it. A Water Justice project looks into ways and means to promote participatory, public sector **water** as the most viable means to achieve the goal of water for all.

TRANSPARENCY INTERNATIONAL (TI). Created in 1993 and headquartered in Germany but operating through more than 70 national chapters, this **think tank** produces, in collaboration with anti-corruption **civil society** organizations, surveys and indices, global reports, country studies, toolkits, working papers and expert briefs documenting, **monitoring** and publicizing corporate and political corruption. Since 1995, TI has issued an annual Corruption Perceptions Index (CPI); it also publishes an annual Global Corruption Report, a Global Corruption Barometer and a Bribe Payers Index. The CPI ranks nations on the prevalence of **corruption** within each country, based on surveys of businesspeople. Instances of its substantive work include thematic issues related to access to information, climate governance, the **water** sector, defense and security, **education**, **health**, humanitarian assistance, the judiciary and the protection of whistleblowers.

TREATY. Also known as protocols, covenants, **conventions**, or accords, treaties are formal written agreements willingly concluded between **states** which create obligations for the governments that are parties to them. Treaties, however, are binding only on those states that have consented to be bound by them. In accordance with the norm of **state sovereignty**, any state party to a treaty may, when signing, ratifying or acceding to it, unilaterally enter **reservations** excluding or modifying some of its legal obligations. Treaties (together with **customary international law** and other **soft law** instruments) form the backbone of **international human rights law** that defines the responsibilities of states in the promotion and protection of the human rights of individuals and groups. One of these obligations is for governments to put into place domestic measures and legislation compatible with their treaty commitments.

A human rights treaty typically contains three parts: a list of rights; a specification of the obligations of the parties in regard to the rights enumerated in the treaty; and a system to monitor compliance with the agreement. *See also* ACCESSION; ADOPTION; INCORPORATION; INTERNATIONAL LAW; RATIFICATION.

TREATY BODIES. *See* UNITED NATIONS TREATY BODIES.

TRIPS. *See* AGREEMENT ON TRADE-RELATED ASPECTS OF INTELLECTUAL PROPERTY RIGHTS.

TRUTH, RIGHT TO THE. In human rights practice, truth implies something that can be verified and implies an obligation to say what happened. National practice, as suggested by court rulings and the functioning of **truth and reconciliation commissions**, has increasingly recognized the importance of the right to the truth in relation to **forced disappearances** derived from a right to mourning, the right to justice, the need for historical clarification, societal healing and the prevention of future **violations of human rights**. The right to truth is not explicitly stated in any international human rights instruments but it can be derived from **customary international law** and has been characterized as one of the "emerging principles of **international law**." The **United Nations Human Rights Committee** has acknowledged that the right to the truth is linked to the protection of the family and that it is an indispensable means to bring to an end or to prevent the psychological torture of families of victims of forced disappearances.

The right to the truth has also been associated to the rights of children to preserve their identity, **nationality**, name and family relations guaranteed in the **United Nations Convention on the Rights of the Child**. Human rights regional courts have also inferred a right to the truth from the rights to be free from **torture** and the rights to effective **remedies** and investigation. In a case involving **El Salvador**, the **Inter-American Commission on Human Rights** has endorsed the right "to know the full, complete and public truth as to the events that transpired, their specific circumstance and who participated in them" as "part of the right to **reparation** for human rights violations." *See also* INTERNATIONAL CONVENTION FOR THE PROTECTION OF ALL PERSONS FROM ENFORCED DISAPPEARANCE; REDRESS.

TRUTH AND RECONCILIATION COMMISSIONS (TRCs). Bodies established to investigate and make publicly known human rights abuses committed over a period of time in a given country. TRCs have been set up in such countries as **Argentina**, **Bolivia**, **Brazil**, Chad, **Chile**, Ecuador, **El Salvador**, Fiji, Germany, Ghana, **Guatemala**, Haiti, **Liberia**, Morocco, Nepal, Nigeria, Panama, **Paraguay**, **Peru**, the **Philippines**, Serbia and

Montenegro (formerly the Federal Republic of Yugoslavia), Sierra Leone, South Africa, South Korea, Sri Lanka, **Timor-Leste**, **Uganda**, **Uruguay** and Zimbabwe. Their mandates, organizational arrangements, methods of work and procedures vary considerably. But TRCs are generally authorized, sponsored and financed by national governments or international organizations at the end of a civil conflict (a few human rights **non-governmental organizations** have at times adopted TRC roles in countries still in political transition). Their immediate objective is to provide a framework for the victims and perpetrators of human rights violations to air and give evidence of **violations of human rights**. Ultimately, by making recommendations on steps to be taken to prevent the reoccurrence of such abuses, the TRCs' longer-term purpose is to promote national reconciliation and to contribute to the emergence and consolidation of legitimate and democratic political regimes and policies. *See also* TRUTH, RIGHT TO THE.

TUDJMAN, FRANJO (1922–1999). First democratically elected president of the State of Croatia in 1990. Reelected in 1992 and 1997, Tudjman remained in power until his death. Croatia's declaration of independence in 1991 triggered a Serbian military intervention and occupation which were rolled back in 1995 by Croatian forces. In the course of these military operations, 200,000 Serbians were forcibly removed to neighboring Serbia and Bosnia and Herzegovina. Tudjman's role in that military campaign was scrutinized by the **International Criminal Tribunal for the Former Yugoslavia** but the investigation never led to formal charges. *See also* IMPUNITY.

TURKEY. The current political regime of Turkey came into existence in 1923. The intent of the founders of modern Turkey was to create a "pure Turkish nation" out of the ruins of the multiethnic and multicultural Ottoman Empire. The population transfer with Greece in 1922–23 has been viewed by historians as a step toward achieving such a homogeneous society. Early on, this policy clashed with the nationalist aspirations of the Kurdish minority, which had been first acknowledged and then sidelined by the Great Powers at the end of World War I. When confronted with increasingly vocal and violent demands for **self-determination**, the new Turkish state has primarily relied on assimilation and repression. In essence, its response has been to portray Kurdish claims as a threat to the integrity of the state and acts of **terrorism**. The Kurdish language was banned in 1924. Until the 1960s, Turkish Kurdistan was declared a prohibited zone for foreigners. Martial law in Turkish Kurdistan was imposed in 1978 in response to armed rebellion and replaced after a coup in 1980 by a state of siege and in 1987 a state of emergency. Today, the state of emergency has been officially lifted, but the existence of "temporary security zones" testify to the volatility of the political situation.

According to data produced by a Turkish **non-governmental organization**, between 1990 and 2008, there were more than 5,000 political killings, 840 cases of **forced disappearances** and thousands of **arbitrary detentions**. Other serious violations of human rights involve the use of **torture** and mass **deportations**. The tense standoff that prevails in the region reflects in part the willingness of the government to heed **European Union** pressures for greater respect of human rights as a condition for Turkey's membership in the European Union. The fact that from 1959 to 2009 the **European Court of Human Rights** delivered no less than 2,295 judgments finding Turkey responsible for serious violations of the **European Convention for the Protection of Human Rights and Fundamental Freedoms** may have also been a contributing factor. *See also* ARMENIAN GENOCIDE; HONOR KILLING; KURDISH HUMAN RIGHTS PROJECT; KURDISH QUESTION; PASHA, TALAT; SEX TRAFFICKING.

TUTU, DESMOND (1931–). South African religious leader. Ordained in 1961, he became in 1975 the first black Anglican dean of Johannesburg. In his capacity as general secretary of the South African Council of Churches from 1978 to 1984, he was an outspoken opponent of **apartheid**. In 1984, he was awarded the **Nobel Peace Prize** for his nonviolent advocacy of reform. In 1986, he was elected archbishop of Cape Town. From the end of his tenure and until 2003, he headed a **truth and reconciliation commission** investigating human rights abuses during the apartheid era.

U

UGANDA. Former British colony which became independent in 1962, the country has since then gone through repeated periods of gross **violations of human rights**, under the **Idi Amin** regime (1971–79) and the rule of Milton Obote (1980–86) as well as the current Yoweri Museveni regime (1986–). Political instability has been fed by ethnic, religious and regional politics and grievances as each regime sought to impose its rule with an iron fist and each regime change involved bloody civil conflict accompanied by grievous human rights abuses and **crimes against humanity**. Gross abuses of human rights in the Museveni era have been centered in the Acholiland region in the north of the country where rebel groups such as the **Lord's Resistance Army** (LRA) have been fighting the government. The still-unfolding conflict has claimed the lives of an estimated 100,000 civilians and displaced 1.5 million people with both sides responsible for serious violations of human rights and humanitarian law.

At the request of the Ugandan government, the **International Criminal Court** (ICC) opened an investigation into Northern Uganda in 2004 and, a year later, issued warrants for the LRA leaders on charges ranging from the mutilation of civilians to the forced abduction of and sexual abuse of children. At the same time, the government has issued **amnesties** to those willing to demobilize and disarm, and some have expressed the fear that the ICC prosecution might jeopardize so far inconclusive peace talks with the rebels. It remains to be seen whether all parties responsible for abuses, including Ugandan army commanders, are ever brought to justice. *See also* INTERNATIONAL COMMISSION OF JURISTS; TRUTH AND RECONCILIATION COMMISSIONS.

UKRAINE FAMINE (1932–33). Beginning in 1929, the Soviet government ordered the collectivization of all privately owned farmlands and livestock in the Ukraine, a region known for being the breadbasket of Europe. By mid-1932, systematic terror campaigns were targeted at wealthy farmers who owned 24 or more acres of land or employed farm workers known as Kulaks. Mass **deportations** (10 million people are believed to have been removed to "special settlements" in Siberia) virtually broke down local resistance as nearly three-quarters of the farms in the Ukraine were forcibly collectivized. These measures, compounded by mandatory quotas of foodstuffs earmarked for export to generate cash for financing **Josef Stalin**'s five-year plans and military buildup, resulted in widespread famine. By the end of 1933, nearly 7 million people (roughly 25 percent of the population of the Ukraine) had perished. By and large, the reaction of the international community was one of **denial**. In 1934, the Soviet Union was admitted to the **League of Nations**.

UNALIENABLE RIGHTS. Rights which are present in all human beings, are not contingent upon the laws or beliefs of any particular culture or government and cannot be taken away, denied or transferred. The concept was central in the justification of the American and the French revolutions. One of the best known references to the concept can be found in the American **Declaration of Independence**. It is reaffirmed in secular language (i.e., without a creator god granting such rights) in the **Universal Declaration of Human Rights** and all other major human rights instruments. Governments pay lip service to this core principle of the human rights language but do not always respect it. *See also* ABROGATION OF RIGHTS; DEROGATION; LIFE, RIGHT TO; NATURAL RIGHTS; PEREMPTORY NORMS.

UNITED NATIONS. International organization founded in 1945 after **World War II** to replace the **League of Nations** with the stated aims to encourage and facilitate interstate cooperation in support of the maintenance of peace and security, the promotion of human rights and development and strengthening of international law. Headquartered in New York and Geneva but with offices around the world, notably Vienna and Nairobi, the membership of the United Nations has grown from 51 to 193 **states** at present. It is financed from assessed and voluntary contributions from its member states. As provided for in the **United Nations Charter**, its principal organs are the **United Nations Security Council** (UN-SC), the **United Nations General Assembly** (UN-GA), the **United Nations Economic and Social Council**, the United Nations Trusteeship Council (now inactive), the Secretariat headed by a **United Nations secretary-general** and the **International Court of Justice**.

Like most other international organizations, the United Nations develops and implements a broad range of policies which vary considerably depending on the degree of obligation that they carry or of "coercion" that is built into them. In regard to human rights, the United Nations has been primarily a mechanism for the making of normative policies (i.e., prescriptive statements of action in support of desirable goals and aspirational ways of doing things). Its "legislative bodies" (notably the UN-GA and, under its authority, the **United Nations Human Rights Council**) "produce non-binding resolutions," "recommendations," "directives" and the like, which do not necessarily rest on a widely shared consensus and generate intense competition among contending groups to win the collective recognition of the legitimacy of their claims. Non-coercive techniques used by the UN legislative bodies also include deliberations, **fact finding**, **investigations** and mediation. The United Nations also produces regulatory policies which place restrictions on individuals and institutions and may entail a degree of coercion by prohibiting unacceptable forms of behavior and requiring mandatory alternate ones. Short of the use of force, the UN-SC may impose **sanctions** such as arms, commodities and oil embargoes, travel bans, partial assets' freezes to economic blockades and more comprehensive measures in support of human rights.

The **United Nations specialized agencies** are primarily involved in the making of distributive policies intended to identify rules and regulations pertaining to the provision of such services as education, highway, **health**, **food**, and public safety to segments of the population. The **Bretton Woods Institutions** typically produce redistributive policies which entail transfers of resources from one group of states to another. The human rights significance of both distributive and redistributive policies differs considerably from one agency to another.

UNITED NATIONS ASSISTANCE MISSION IN AFGHANISTAN (UNAMA, 2002–). "Integrated" peacekeeping mission of the **United Nations** set up in 2002 by the **United Nations Security Council** to assist the Afghan government's efforts in the areas of security, governance and economic development. UNAMA's human rights mandate is to "monitor the situation of civilians, to coordinate efforts to ensure their protection, to promote accountability and to assist in full implementation of the fundamental freedoms and human rights provisions of the Afghan Constitution and international treaties to which **Afghanistan** is **state party**, in particular those regarding the full enjoyment by women of their human rights." Its strategy is to "embed" human rights in the country through targeted **research**, reporting, **advocacy** and engagement in strategic partnerships and dialogue with government, military, international and **civil society** actors and communities across Afghanistan in four priority areas: **civilian protection**; **gender-based violence**; peace and reconciliation; and conditions of detention. The mission currently has 66 human rights staff deployed throughout the country at the regional and provincial levels.

UNITED NATIONS ASSISTANCE MISSION FOR RWANDA (UNAMIR, 1993–1996). United Nations **peace operation** set by the **United Nations Security Council** (UN-SC) to facilitate the implementation of peace accords that had brought to an end to the Rwanda civil war. UNAMIR's original mandate was to assist in ensuring the security of the capital city of Kigali; **monitor** the ceasefire agreement, including establishment of an expanded demilitarized zone and demobilization procedures; monitor the security situation during the final period of the transitional government's mandate leading up to the elections; assist with landmine clearance; and assist in the coordination of humanitarian assistance activities in conjunction with relief operations. The mandate of UNAMIR was amended several times in light of the deterioration of the security situation and the resumption of hostilities between the Hutus and Tutsis which eventually led to the **genocide**. To the extent that UNAMIR was unable—or more accurately, never empowered by the UN-SC—to prevent the Rwandan genocide, it is widely regarded as a major failure.

UNITED NATIONS CHARTER. After considerable bickering among delegations at the San Francisco Conference of June 1945 and notwithstanding the unease of some governments, notably the **United States**, which was concerned about possible interference of the United Nations into its domestic affairs, it was finally agreed—to a large extent owing to pressures by **nongovernmental organizations**—to give a prominent place to human rights in the Charter. The Preamble states boldly: "We the peoples of the United Nations [are] determined to reaffirm faith in fundamental human rights, in the dignity and worth of the human person, in the equal rights of men and women and of nations large and small."

There are subsequently no less than six references to human rights and fundamental freedoms in the operative provisions of the Charter (Arts. 13, 55, 56, 62, 68, 76). Under Article 1-1, one of the four purposes of the new organization is to "achieve international cooperation in solving international problems of an economic, social, cultural, or humanitarian character, and in promoting and encouraging respect for human rights and for fundamental freedoms for all without distinction as to race, sex, language, or religion." Article 55 asserts that, "with a view to the creation of conditions of stability and well being which are necessary for peaceful and friendly relations among nations," the United Nations "shall promote . . . universal respect for, and observance of, human rights and fundamental freedoms for all without distinction as to race, sex, language, or religion."

Article 68 requires the **United Nations Economic and Social Council** to set up commissions in the human rights and economic and social fields, an injunction which led to the establishment in 1946 of the **United Nations Commission on Human Rights** by the Council. At the same time, the Charter cautions that "nothing . . . shall authorize the United Nations to intervene in matters which are essentially within the **domestic jurisdiction** of any state." There have since been recurring debates and controversies about the scope of what constitutes an acceptable role for the United Nations in the field of human rights, a predicament aggravated by the fact that the Charter leaves undefined the terms "human rights" and "promote." *See also* *JUS AD BELLUM/JUS IN BELLO*; NON-DISCRIMINATION; REGIONAL ARRANGEMENTS; STATE SOVEREIGNTY; UNITED NATIONS CHARTER-BASED BODIES; UNITED NATIONS TREATY BODIES.

UNITED NATIONS CHARTER-BASED BODIES. Institutions which derive their existence and functions from provisions contained in the provisions of the **United Nations Charter**. In the field of human rights, current UN Charter-based bodies include the **United Nations Human Rights Council** and its predecessor body **United Nations Commission on Human Rights** and their subsidiaries, the **Universal Periodic Review** Working Group, and the Advisory Committee of the **United Nations Sub-Commission on the Promotion and Protection of Human Rights** under the Commission regime.

See also INTERNATIONAL COURT OF JUSTICE; UNITED NATIONS COMMISSION ON THE STATUS OF WOMEN; UNITED NATIONS ECONOMIC AND SOCIAL COUNCIL; UNITED NATIONS GENERAL ASSEMBLY; UNITED NATIONS SECRETARY-GENERAL; UNITED NATIONS SECURITY COUNCIL; UNITED NATIONS TREATY BODIES.

UNITED NATIONS CHILDREN'S FUND (UNICEF). Humanitarian agency set by the **United Nations General Assembly** in 1946 to provide **food**, clothing and **heath** care to European children affected by **World War II**. In 1951, the Assembly extended UNICEF's mandate indefinitely and the agency began a global campaign against yaws, a disfiguring disease affecting millions of children that can be cured with penicillin. For more than a decade, UNICEF remained focused on child health care issues, but the agency progressively enlarged the range of its concerns as it increasingly sought to address the needs of the whole child (i.e., **education**, starting with support to teacher training and classroom equipment in newly independent countries).

In the wake of the 1981 World Health Assembly's adoption of the International Code of Marketing of Breast Milk Substitutes in order to encourage breastfeeding, UNICEF promoted life-saving low-cost techniques: growth monitoring, oral rehydration therapy, breastfeeding and immunization.

At the same time, UNICEF sponsored **research** that started altering the conceptual map of decision makers. Its Innocenti Centre study on Adjustment with a Human Face prompted a global debate on how to protect children and women from the adverse effects of **structural adjustment programs** and reforms taken to reduce national debt in poor countries. The impact of war on children was the focus of the **Graça Machel** report, a study supported by UNICEF. When the **United Nations Convention on the Rights of the Child** (UN-CRC) was adopted, UNICEF shifted more definitely from being an institution active in development and responsive to emergencies to a human rights–based organization and to an implementing agent of the Convention. The thrust of its activities is no longer limited to meeting the needs of children but also includes the recognition and **realization** of their rights. The close links of the Convention with UNICEF are acknowledged in Article 45 of the Convention, which empowers UNICEF to provide expert advice and submit reports on the implementation of the Convention. In effect, the UN-CRC has become for UNICEF a planning and programming tool which guides its cooperative and **advocacy** program, the development of partnerships as well as a **benchmark**, a set of references against which it can measure progress in its work.

UNITED NATIONS COMMISSION OF HUMAN RIGHTS. Subsidiary body of the **United Nations Economic and Social Council** (UN-ECOSOC) established in 1946 by the UN-ECOSOC in accordance with Article 69 of the **United Nations Charter**. Its functions, mandate, and composition were decided after lengthy negotiations. The original idea was to have a small body tasked with the formulation of an international bill of rights, the status of women, freedom of information, the protection of **minorities**, the prevention of **discrimination** and any matter likely to impair friendly relations among nations. Governments ruled out the last envisaged competence, and the Commission was never empowered to assist the **United Nations Security Council** in determining whether a **violation of human rights** could amount to a breach of international peace and security. Eventually, the Commission was authorized to carry out **standards' setting** activities and to consider "any matter concerning human rights," a mandate broad enough to allow it to incrementally expand the scope of its work over time.

The Commission's membership was enlarged several times, from nine members in 1946 to 53 prior to being dissolved in 2006, elected by UN-ECOSOC for three-year renewable terms and with due consideration to geographic representation: 15 seats for the African group, 12 for Asia, 5 for Eastern Europe, 11 for Latin America and the Caribbean and 10 for Western European and other groups. The Commission held six-week-long annual sessions in March–April in Geneva, drawing some 3,000 participants (member-states delegations, observer governments and **non-governmental organizations**). Its non-binding resolutions (subject to the approval of UN-ECOSOC and the **United Nations General Assembly**) were adopted, most of the time, by consensus after an intense process of formal and informal bargaining among governments strongly influenced by the **lobbying** of non-governmental organizations and the discreet prodding of UN officials.

Standards' setting was for a long time (especially during the **Cold War**) the most important function of the Commission. Its notable accomplishments were the **International Covenant on Civil and Political Rights** and the **International Covenant on Economic, Social and Cultural Rights**, the **United Nations Convention against Torture**, the **Declaration on the Right to Development** and the **United Nations Convention on the Rights of the Child**.

Concurrently, and beginning in the mid-1950s, the Commission launched programs of technical assistance, **capacity building** and **advisory services** on an ever-growing range of areas to states willing to enhance and bring their domestic institutions in line with their human rights obligations. These activities are now a major component of the work of the **United Nations Office of the High Commissioner for Human Rights**. The Commission was never designed to respond to human rights violations. But, eventually, and in a remarkably inchoate and incremental manner, it progressively overrode its "no power doctrine" in line with Article 2.7 of the Charter which bars the United Nations from intervening in matters falling essentially within the jurisdiction of national states. The impetus for the change came from the growing number of developing nations admitted in the United Nations which coalesced around the issues of **apartheid** and racial discrimination and pushed these issues to the forefront of the Organization over the objections of Western powers fearful of their own human rights records in regard to race relations at home or in their colonies. These pressures led to the establishment of the 1235 and **1503 Procedures**, which, in turn, paved the way to the creation of the Commission's **special procedures** with powers of **investigation**, reporting and recommendation. The process began in 1963 when the Commission mandated a mission to investigate human rights violations in Vietnam and continued thereafter with other missions in Southern Africa (1967) and Latin America (forced disappearances in 1980, summary executions in 1982 and torture 1985).

Perhaps in a long-term perspective the most impressive achievement of the Commission may have been to legitimize the idea that human rights are no longer the exclusive concern of national governments. Its successes, however, were the product of a disjointed political process which inevitably generated repeated accusations of bias, selectiveness and double standards. Issues of bloc voting and regional alliances and membership further undermined the credibility and authority of the Commission and eventually led to its dissolution. Interestingly though, all the functions of the Commission— standards' setting, forum for dialogue and discussion, space for civil society participation, instrument of monitoring human rights worldwide and responding to human rights abuses, provider of technical assistance—have been taken over by the **United Nations Human Rights Council.**

See also AGREEMENT ON TRADE-RELATED ASPECTS OF INTELLECTUAL PROPERTY RIGHTS; BASIC PRINCIPLES AND GUIDELINES ON THE RIGHT TO A REMEDY AND REPARATION FOR VICTIMS OF GROSS VIOLATIONS OF INTERNATIONAL HUMAN RIGHTS LAW AND SERIOUS VIOLATIONS OF INTERNATIONAL HUMANITARIAN LAW; COBO, JOSE MARTINEZ; CONVENTION ON THE ABOLITION OF SLAVERY; DENG, FRANCIS; DRAFT NORMS ON THE RESPONSIBILITIES OF TRANSNATIONAL CORPORATIONS AND OTHER BUSINESS ENTERPRISES WITH REGARD TO HUMAN RIGHTS; ENVIRONMENT, RIGHT TO A HEALTHY; EXTERNAL DEBT CRISIS; IMPUNITY; MALIK, CHARLES HABIB; PARIS PRINCIPLES; PEACE, RIGHT TO; SPECIAL RAPPORTEURS; UNITED NATIONS HUMAN RIGHTS COUNCIL; UNITED NATIONS SUB-COMMISSION ON THE PROMOTION AND PROTECTION OF HUMAN RIGHTS; UNITED NATIONS WORKING GROUP ON ARBITRARY DETENTION; UNITED NATIONS WORKING GROUP ON THE PROTECTION OF ALL PERSONS FROM ENFORCED DISAPPEARANCES.

UNITED NATIONS COMMISSION ON THE STATUS OF WOMEN (UN-CSW). Functional commission of the **United Nations Economic and Social Council** (ECOSOC) established in 1946 as a mechanism to promote, report on and monitor issues relating to the political, economic, civil, social and educational rights of women. Composed of 45 member states of the United Nations elected by ECOSOC on the basis of equitable geographic distribution, the Commission meets annually. The **Declaration on the Elimination of Discrimination against Women** endorsed by the **United Nations General Assembly** in 1967 and the **United Nations Convention on the Elimination of All Forms of Discrimination against Women** (CEDAW) of 1979 were drafted and agreed upon under the auspices of the UN-CSW. The Commission monitors the implementation of the **Beijing Declaration and Platform of Action** adopted by the 1995 **Fourth World Conference on Women** and, in that capacity, has played a key role in broadening acceptance of women's **reproductive rights** and in mainstreaming gender perspectives in UN activities. The terms of the reference of the Commission were further enlarged in 1996 to include the identification of emerging issues, trends and new approaches to issues affecting equality between women and men. Since the 1980, UN-CSW has had the authority to received individual **complaints** thus supplementing and augmenting the **1503 Procedure** and the **communications** allowed under an **Optional Protocol** to the CEDAW. *See also* GENDER-BASED VIOLENCE; MONITORING OF HUMAN RIGHTS.

UNITED NATIONS COMMITTEE AGAINST TORTURE. Body of 10 independent experts **monitoring** the implementation of the **United Nations Convention against Torture and Other Cruel, Inhuman or Degrading Treatment and Punishment** by its states parties. The Committee began to function on 1 January 1988, six months after the entry into force of the Convention, adopted by the **United Nations General Assembly** on 10 December 1984. The Committee meets in Geneva and normally holds two sessions per year and exerts its monitoring functions through three modalities. First, the Committee examines periodic state reports and addresses its concerns and recommendations to the state party in the form of "**concluding observations.**" For instance, after a two-day hearing on the **United States** second periodic report in 2006, the Committee made public its objection to the U.S. contention that the law of **armed conflict** precluded the application of the Convention. Taking the position that the prolonged detention of hundreds of persons without charge at the **Guantanamo Bay Detention Camp** "constituted per se a violation of the Convention," the Committee called upon the United States to cease to detain any person at Guantanamo and close this detention facility, permit access by the detainees to judicial process or release them as soon as possible.

Second, the Committee may, under certain circumstances, consider individual **complaints** or communications from individuals claiming that their rights under the Convention have been violated. The Committee had dealt with some 450 individual complaints against two dozen countries and found Australia, Austria, Canada, France, the Netherlands, Serbia, Spain, Sweden, Switzerland, Tunisia and Venezuela in violation of the Convention.

Third, in accordance with the 2002 Optional Protocol to the Convention (in force since 2006), the Committee may initiate regular visits to places where people are deprived of their liberty, in order to prevent torture and other cruel, inhuman or degrading treatment or punishment. This system of inspections, to be overseen by a Subcommittee on Prevention of **Torture** and Other Cruel, Inhuman or Degrading Treatment or Punishment, was modeled after the system which has been in place in Europe since 1987.

Finally, the Committee publishes its interpretation of the content of human rights provisions, known as "**General Comments**," on thematic issues. In a 2007 General Comment on the principles underlying the Convention's prohibition of torture, the Committee stressed "the absolute and **non-derogable** character of this prohibition" and recalled that under the provisions of the Convention, no exceptional circumstances whatsoever may be invoked by a state party to justify acts of torture in any territory under its jurisdiction. Such circumstances, in addition to those spelled out in the Convention (i.e., state of war, internal political instability or other public emergency) also encompass "any threat of terrorist acts or violent crime as well as armed conflict, international or non-international." The Committee in effect rejected "absolutely" any efforts by states to justify torture and **ill treatment** as a means to protect public safety or avert emergencies in these and all other situations and, in the same vein, averred that amnesties or other impediments which preclude or indicate unwillingness to provide prompt and fair prosecution and punishment of perpetrators of torture or ill treatment violated the principle of non-derogability. *See also* DECISIONS; EXTRAORDINARY RENDITION; INQUIRY PROCEDURES; STATE REPORTING.

UNITED NATIONS COMMITTEE ON ECONOMIC, SOCIAL AND CULTURAL RIGHTS (UN-CtteeESCR). Body of independent experts set up in 1985 by the **United Nations Economic and Social Council** to **monitor** the implementation of the **International Covenant on Economic, Social and Cultural Rights** by its states parties. Like all other **United Nations treaty bodies**, the UN-CtteeESCR reviews and makes "**observations**" on periodic reports by states parties. An Optional Protocol to the Covenant now under ratification will empower the Committee to receive individual complaints. The Committee also issues widely respected "**General Comments**," providing interpretations of key provisions of the Covenant. Thus the Committee has offered its views on the nature and scope of the rights to **social security**, **work, water, health, education, food** and **housing**. Other topics explored by the Committee include the nature of states parties obligations, reporting by state parties, the role of **national human rights institutions** in the protection of economic, social and cultural rights, the domestic application of the Covenant, the relationship between economic **sanctions** and respect for economic, social and cultural rights, the economic social and cultural rights of **elderly persons** and **disabled persons**.

See also ADEQUATE STANDARD OF LIVING, RIGHT TO; ARAB ASSOCIATION FOR HUMAN RIGHTS; CLIMATE CHANGE; FORCED EVICTIONS; INTELLECTUAL PROPERTY RIGHTS;

KOSOVO; LIMBURG PRINCIPLES ON THE IMPLEMENTATION OF THE INTERNATIONAL COVENANT ON ECONOMIC, SOCIAL AND CULTURAL RIGHTS; POVERTY; PREVENTION; SELF-DETERMINATION; STATE REPORTING.

UNITED NATIONS COMMITTEE ON THE ELIMINATION OF ALL FORMS OF DISCRIMINATION AGAINST WOMEN. Body of 23 independent experts elected by the states parties to the **United Nations Convention on the Elimination of All Forms of Discrimination against Women** to **monitor** its implementation. For that purpose, the Committee reviews states parties' recurrent reports and addresses its concerns and recommendations in the form of **concluding observations**. Under the provisions of a 2000 Optional Protocol to the Convention, the Committee may receive **complaints** (or communications) from individuals or groups of individuals claiming **violations of human rights** protected by the Convention. It may also initiate inquiries into situations of grave and systematic abuses of women's rights. As of 2011, the Committee had adopted 17 decisions on 27 complaints and conducted one inquiry into **femicide** in Cuidad Juarez, Mexico.

The Committee also formulates general recommendations (known for other similar committees as "**General Comments**") on issues which it believes warrant more attention by states parties. As of 2010, the Committee had made 26 general recommendations on a wide variety of problems including **gender-based violence**, **female genital mutilation**, women and **HIV/AIDS**, equality in **marriage** and **family** relations, and women **migrant workers**. The Committee has also issued guidelines for more rigorous and extensive states reports and for reducing the high incidence of states parties **reservations** to the Convention. *See also* ARAB ASSOCIATION FOR HUMAN RIGHTS; DOMESTIC VIOLENCE; INQUIRY PROCEDURES; PREVENTION.

UNITED NATIONS COMMITTEE ON THE ELIMINATION OF ALL FORMS OF RACIAL DISCRIMINATION. Expert body monitoring the implementation of the **International Convention on the Elimination of All Forms of Racial Discrimination** by its states parties. Like all other **United Nations treaty bodies**, the Committee exerts its function through a review and evaluation of reports submitted periodically by states parties. In addition, the Committee can also initiate an **early warning** procedure to prevent and respond to violations of the Convention. Using such criteria of early warning as the presence of a pattern of escalating racial hatred and violence, racist propaganda or appeals to racial intolerance, notably by public officials;

significant flows of **refugees** or displaced persons resulting from **racial discrimination**; or encroachment on the lands of **minority** communities, the Committee has issued statements or adopted resolutions in relation to more than 20 states parties.

Recent warnings have been addressed to Guyana, **Israel**, Laos, Sudan on Darfur, New Zealand and Suriname. Under the terms of the Convention, the Committee may receive individual **complaints**. As of 2011, the Committee had received 45 such complaints and ruled that 17 of them were inadmissible, 10 disclosed a violation and 14 disclosed no violation. Concurrently, the Committee has issued from time to time **General Comments** or general recommendations (i.e., legal interpretations of the provisions of the Convention). Some of the subject matters dealt with by the Committee include the prevention of racial discrimination in the administration and functioning of criminal justice systems, the rights of non-citizens, discrimination against **Roma**, gender-related dimensions of racial discrimination, the rights of **indigenous peoples**, refugees and **internally displaced persons**, and the right to **self-determination**. *See also* ANTI-RACISM INFORMATION SERVICE; MONITORING OF HUMAN RIGHTS; PREVENTION.

UNITED NATIONS COMMITTEE ON THE PROTECTION OF THE RIGHTS OF ALL MIGRANT WORKERS AND THEIR FAMILIES. **United Nations treaty body** of independent experts elected for a term of four years by states parties to the **International Convention on the Protection of the Rights of All Migrant Workers and Members of Their Families**. The Committee started operations in 2004 but its functioning has been hampered by a slow rate of **ratifications** and by the fact that none of the migrant-receiving states has ratified the Convention. The Committee has begun **monitoring** the implementation of the Convention by its states parties by reviewing and commenting on their reports. Once fully operational (a minimum of 10 states must approve this procedure laid down in Art. 77 of the Convention), it will also be able to consider individual **complaints**.

UNITED NATIONS COMMITTEE ON THE RIGHTS OF THE CHILD (CRC). **United Nations treaty body** of independent experts **monitoring** the implementation of the **United Nations Convention on the Rights of the Child** and its two optional protocols on the involvement of **children in armed conflicts** and the sale of children, child prostitution and child pornography by their state parties. The Committee reviews reports by states parties on measures they have taken to give effect to their treaty obligations and to the Committee's **concluding observations** thereon. The Committee is not empowered to receive individual **complaints** although child rights issues have surfaced in other treaty bodies that have that authority. The CRC, however, organizes from time to time "days of general discussions" and does issue **General Comments**, spelling out its legal interpretation of thematic issues of concern to children. Topics thus covered by the Committee have included the rights of indigenous children, the rights of children with disabilities, children's rights in juvenile justice, the rights of the child to protection from corporal punishment and other cruel or degrading forms of punishment, the treatment of unaccompanied and separated children outside of their country of origin, adolescent health, **HIV/AIDS** and the rights of the child and the aims of **education**. *See also* COALITION TO STOP THE USE OF CHILDREN; PREVENTION.

UNITED NATIONS CONFERENCE ON THE HUMAN ENVIRONMENT (1972). International conference convened under **United Nations** auspices in Stockholm widely credited for having placed international environmental issues on the agenda of the international community. The meeting endorsed a declaration of 26 principles concerning the **environment** and development and an action plan with 109 recommendations which, in essence, called for "a major reorientation of man's values and redeployment of his energies and resources" to roll back environmental degradation and addressed such problems as global climatic change, marine pollution, access to clean **water**, population growth, the dumping of toxic wastes, and the preservation of biodiversity. *See also* UNITED NATIONS HUMAN SETTLEMENTS PROGRAMME.

UNITED NATIONS CONFERENCE ON HUMAN SETTLEMENTS (1976). United Nations global conference held in Vancouver which drew attention to the consequences of rapid urbanization, especially in the developing world. The declaration which it adopted avers that "the improvement of the quality of life of human beings is the first and most important objective of every human settlement policy. These policies must facilitate the rapid and continuous improvement in the quality of life of all people, beginning with the satisfaction of the basic needs of **food**, shelter, clean **water**, employment, **health**, **education**, training, **social security** without any discrimination as to race, color, sex, language, religion, ideology, national or social origin or other cause, in a frame of freedom, **dignity** and social justice." Delegations also acknowledged that "the right of free movement and the right of each individual to choose the place of settlement within the domain of his own country should be recognized and safeguarded." *See also* HABITAT INTERNATIONAL COALITION; UNITED NATIONS HUMAN SETTLEMENTS PROGRAMME.

UNITED NATIONS CONFERENCE ON THE ENVIRONMENT AND DEVELOPMENT. United Nations global conference held in Rio de Janeiro, Brazil, from 3 to 14 June 1992 which sought to reconcile the environmental concerns of Northern industrial countries with the priority given by Southern countries to the elimination of poverty. Widely attended (172 governments and some 2,400 representatives of **non-governmental organizations** participated), the conference focused on such controversial issues as patterns of production and consumption, alternative sources of energy and the growing scarcity of **water**. It resulted in the adoption of a number of prescriptive **soft law** documents such as the Rio Declaration on Environment and Development, Agenda 21 and the Forest Principles. By the end of the meeting, two important legally binding agreements—the Convention on Biological Diversity and the Framework Convention on Climate Change—were opened for signature. Neither of these instruments relies on or frames states' obligations in human rights language. But they have been used by civil society groups and international organizations as a basis for arguing that the **realization** of human rights requires a recognition of their **indivisibility**. Follow-up "summits" in 2002 and 2012 have yielded few if any new tangible results.

UNITED NATIONS CONFERENCE ON TRADE AND DEVELOP-MENT (UNCTAD). Organ of the **United Nations General Assembly** established in 1964 at the prodding of **developing countries** which believed that existing institutions like the General Agreement on Tariffs and Trade (since then replaced by the **World Trade Organization**), the **International Monetary Fund** and the World Bank were not properly designed to deal with their concerns. The organization's goals are to "maximize the trade, investment and development opportunities of developing countries and assist them in their efforts to integrate into the world economy on an equitable basis." For a long time, UNCTAD was considered the progenitor of the redistributive prescriptions contained in the New International Economic Order. It has since the 1990s significantly recalibrated its work along neo-liberal lines, but its primary objective is to formulate policies relating to all aspects of development including trade, aid, transport, finance and technology. *See also* UNITED NATIONS CONFERENCE ON TRADE AND DEVELOPMENT CORPORATE RESPONSIBILITY REPORTING; POVERTY.

UNITED NATIONS CONFERENCE ON TRADE AND DEVELOP-MENT CORPORATE RESPONSIBILITY REPORTING. Program launched in 2001 by the **United Nations Conference on Trade and Development** within the broader context of work by other international organizations on various aspects of **corporate social responsibility**. This particular activity entails high-level meetings, technical workshops and research projects, bringing together governments, academic institutions and enterprises for the purpose of promoting the development of corporate responsibility indicators in annual reports. *See also* TRANSNATIONAL CORPORATIONS.

UNITED NATIONS CONVENTION AGAINST TORTURE AND OTHER CRUEL, INHUMAN OR DEGRADING TREATMENT AND PUNISHMENT. International human rights instrument negotiated and adopted in 1984 under the auspices of the **United Nations**. It entered into force in 1987. To date, the Convention has been ratified by 145 states and signed by another nine. The Convention defines **torture** as "any act by which severe pain or suffering, whether physical or mental, is intentionally inflicted on a person" for such purposes as obtaining information or a confession, punishing an individual for an act that he or she or a third person committed, intimidating or coercing an individual or a third person and any reason based on **discrimination** of any kind. Such pain and suffering must have been inflicted, instigated or acquiesced to by a person acting in an official capacity to be deemed violations of international law. The pain and suffering must also be "severe" to qualify as torture, but the Convention gives no guidance on the level of severity required, a state of affairs that has led to contradictory (and conveniently flexible) definitions of what constitutes torture.

Under the terms of the Convention, torture is such a grave offense that no **state party** to the Convention may authorize or tolerate it, even in the most exceptional circumstances, including a state or threat of war, internal political instability and any other **public emergencies**. The Convention requires states to take effective measures to prevent torture within their borders and forbids them to expel **asylum seekers** to their home country if there is reason to believe that they will be tortured. Finally, it provides for the establishment of a **United Nations Committee against Torture** with broad powers of examination and **investigation** to monitor the implementation of the Convention by its state parties. An Optional Protocol to the Convention which entered into force in 2006 sets up a system of regular inspections of prisons and detention centers in every country adhering to the Protocol. The purpose is to seek evidence of torture directed against prison inmates, prisoners of war, refugees and other detainees. The Protocol has elicited less enthusiasm as it has been ratified only by 35 states and signed by 61.

See also ABU GHRAIB PRISON; ASSOCIATION FOR THE PREVENTION OF TORTURE; BURGER, JAN HERMAN; DECLARATION ON THE PROTECTION OF ALL PERSONS FROM BEING SUBJECTED TO TORTURE AND OTHER CRUEL, INHUMAN OR DEGRADING

TREATMENT OR PUNISHMENT; EUROPEAN CONVENTION FOR THE PREVENTION OF TORTURE AND INHUMAN OR DEGRADING TREATMENT OR PUNISHMENT; EXTRAORDINARY RENDITION; INQUIRY PROCEDURES; INTER-AMERICAN CONVENTION TO PREVENT AND PUNISH TORTURE; UNIVERSAL JURISDICTION.

UNITED NATIONS CONVENTION AGAINST TRANSNATIONAL ORGANIZED CRIME. Main international instrument adopted by the **United Nations General Assembly** in force since 2003 which calls for the domestic criminalization of organized crime activities and the adoption of new frameworks for mutual legal assistance, extradition, law enforcement cooperation and technical assistance and training. The Convention is supplemented by three protocols targeting specific areas and manifestations of organized crime. A 2003 Protocol to Prevent, Suppress and Punish Trafficking in Persons, Especially Women and Children, seeks to promote international cooperation in the investigation and prosecution of trafficking in persons cases and to protect and assist the victims of **human trafficking** with full respect for their human rights. The 2004 Protocol against the Smuggling of Migrants by Land, Sea and Air provides an agreed upon definition of **migrant smuggling** and aims at preventing and combating that while protecting migrants' rights against the worst forms of exploitation. The 2005 Protocol against the Illicit Manufacturing of and Trafficking in Firearms, Their Parts and Components and Ammunition requires that state parties adopt legislative measures criminalizing the illegal manufacturing of, and trafficking in, firearms, to establish a system of government authorizations or licensing of firearms and to set up mechanisms for the marking and tracing of firearms. *See also* CHILDREN TRAFFICKING; INTERNATIONAL CENTRE FOR CRIMINAL LAW REFORM AND CRIMINAL JUSTICE POLICY; PREVENTION; TRAFFICKING IN HUMAN ORGANS.

UNITED NATIONS CONVENTION FOR THE SUPPRESSION OF THE TRAFFIC IN PERSONS AND OF THE EXPLOITATION OF THE PROSTITUTION OF OTHERS. Adopted by the **United Nations General Assembly** in 1949 and in force since 1951, this treaty consolidated and superseded earlier international agreements concluded on this issue since 1904. Declaring that prostitution and **human trafficking** are incompatible with the **dignity** and worth of the human and endanger the welfare of the individual, the family and the community, the Convention requires states parties to take measures to prevent prostitution and provide rehabilitation and social reintegration of its victims. The 2000 Protocol to Prevent, Suppress and Punish Trafficking in Persons, Especially Women and Children, supplementing the **United Nations Convention against Transnational Organized Crime**, broadens the definition of "trafficking in persons" to include a range of cases where humans are exploited by organized criminal groups. *See also* SEXUAL VIOLENCE.

UNITED NATIONS CONVENTION ON BIOLOGICAL DIVERSITY (1992). International treaty aimed at conserving biological diversity as well as encouraging sustainable, fair and equitable use and benefits of genetic resources. It requires its **states parties** to create national strategies, plans and programs for conserving biodiversity and to integrate biodiversity conservation into national economic planning. Parties to the Convention are also required to take specific measures, including creating protected area systems, establishing means of managing modified organisms, and preventing or controlling alien species. It recognizes the importance of indigenous peoples' traditions, lifestyles and knowledge with respect to biodiversity conservation. *See also* AGREEMENT ON TRADE-RELATED ASPECTS OF INTELLECTUAL PROPERTY RIGHTS; ENVIRONMENT, RIGHT TO A HEALTHY.

UNITED NATIONS CONVENTION ON CONSENT TO MARRIAGE, MINIMUM AGE FOR MARRIAGE AND REGISTRATION OF MARRIAGES. Treaty agreed upon in the **United Nations General Assembly** which entered into force in 1964. The Convention reaffirms the consensual nature of marriages and requires the parties to establish a minimum age by law. These provisions were reiterated in the 1979 **United Nations Convention on the Elimination of All Forms of Discrimination against Women**. *See also* MARRY, RIGHT TO.

UNITED NATIONS CONVENTION ON THE ELIMINATION OF ALL FORMS OF DISCRIMINATION AGAINST WOMEN (UN-CEDAW). Landmark convention often referred to as an international bill of rights for women which came into effect on 3 September 1981. UN-CEDAW, which was created in the **United Nations Commission on the Status of Women**, broadly defines what constitutes **discrimination** against women as "any distinction, exclusion or restriction made on the basis of sex which has the effect or purpose of impairing or nullifying the recognition, enjoyment or exercise by women, irrespective of their marital status, on a basis of **equality** of men and women, of human rights and fundamental freedoms in the political, economic, social, cultural, civil or any other field." It also requires governments to undertake a series of measures to end and prevent discrimination against women by incorporating the principle of equality of men and women in their constitutional and legal systems, abolishing all discriminatory laws and adopting appropriate ones prohibiting discrimination against women. In this regard, a particularly striking provision of the Convention is its injunction that governments take all appropriate measures to eliminate customs and practices which constitute discrimination against women.

The Convention has been ratified by most members of the United Nations (only a handful of states including the **United States** have not ratified it). But instruments of ratification have been accompanied by a record number of **reservations**, many of them from Islamic countries which view the UN-CEDAW principle of gender equality as inconsistent with **Sharia Law.** UN-CEDAW was complemented by a 1999 Optional Protocol allowing individual **complaints**. The implementation of the Convention is monitored by the **United Nations Committee on the Elimination of All Forms of Discrimination against Women** which has not hesitated, in its review of **state parties'** reports, to admonish states parties in breach of their obligations and to make politically sensitive recommendations in such matters as the decriminalization of prostitution, **reproductive rights** and **female genital mutilation.**

See also AFFIRMATIVE ACTION; FAMILY, RIGHT TO A; INQUIRY PROCEDURES; UNITED NATIONS CONVENTION ON CONSENT TO MARRIAGE, MINIMUM AGE FOR MARRIAGE AND REGISTRATION OF MARRIAGES; UNITED NATIONS CONVENTION ON THE NATIONALITY OF MARRIED WOMEN; UNITED NATIONS CONVENTION ON THE POLITICAL RIGHTS OF WOMEN.

UNITED NATIONS CONVENTION ON THE NATIONALITY OF MARRIED WOMEN (1957). Adopted at a time when many states still had discriminatory practices which frequently led women to lose their **nationality** in favor of that of their husband, this convention aims at protecting the right of married women to retain their nationality. Notwithstanding **marriage,** divorce or a change in the nationality of the husband during marriage, married women are entitled to retain their citizenship of birth and may acquire their husband's nationality if they choose to do so. This right of women to retain citizenship after marriage has been further reaffirmed in Article 9 of the 1979 **United Nations Convention on the Elimination of All Forms of Discrimination against Women.** *See also* STATELESSNESS.

UNITED NATIONS CONVENTION ON THE NON-APPLICABILITY OF STATUTORY LIMITATIONS TO WAR CRIMES AND CRIMES AGAINST HUMANITY. The Convention provides that no state party may enact and apply national statutory limitations legislation to **war crimes** and **crimes against humanity** as defined by the Charter of the Nuremberg International Military Tribunal, the **Geneva Conventions**, the Convention against **Apartheid** and the **United Nations Convention on the Punishment and Prevention of the Crime of Genocide**. Its purpose is to ensure that the punishment of such crimes is not prevented by statutory limitations in regard to prosecution and enforcement of the punishment. It entered into force in 1970. *See also* IMPUNITY.

UNITED NATIONS CONVENTION ON THE POLITICAL RIGHTS OF WOMEN (1952). Drawing from the **Universal Declaration of Human Rights** which declares that everyone has the right to participate in the government of his or her country and to access public service (Art. 21), this convention commits state parties to allow women to vote and hold public office on equal terms with men and without discrimination on the basis of sex. *See also* UNITED NATIONS CONVENTION ON THE ELIMINATION OF ALL FORMS OF DISCRIMINATION AGAINST WOMEN.

UNITED NATIONS CONVENTION ON THE PUNISHMENT AND PREVENTION OF THE CRIME OF GENOCIDE. Adopted by the **United Nations General Assembly** in 1948, the convention enjoins its state parties (currently 140) to prevent and punish actions of **genocide**. It entered into force in 1951. The drafters of the Convention were inspired by the work and lobbying of **Raphael Lemkin** and they rather narrowly defined the term ignoring for instance references to "cultural genocide" (opposed by the **United States**) and the inclusion of "political groups" (politicide) as a protected category (opposed by the Soviet Union). Under Article 2 of the Convention, genocide may be "any of the following acts committed with intent to destroy, in whole or in part, a national, ethnic, racial or religious group, such as: (a) killing members of the group; (b) causing serious bodily or mental harm to members of the group; (c) deliberately inflicting on the group conditions of life calculated to bring about its physical destruction in whole or in part; (d) imposing measures intended to prevent births within the group and (e) forcibly transferring children of the group to another group." Article 3 defines the crimes that can be punished under the convention: genocide, conspiracy to commit genocide, direct and public incitement to commit genocide, attempt to commit genocide and complicity in genocide.

Overall, the provisions of the treaty on punishment have proven more effective than those on prevention. The language of the treaty is vague on the specific mechanisms, policies and procedures that states must take to prevent genocide. It is more specific in regard to punishment as it lists five specific charges and conditions for extradition. The Convention also makes it clear that individuals may be punished whether or not they are public officials, that contracting parties must enact legislation outlawing genocide and that persons committing genocide must be brought to trial in a domestic or international court.

Implementation of the Convention has been plagued by disputes over the place of intentionality, the meaning of "partial" destruction of a group, how genocide relates to other **crimes against humanity**, how parties to the Convention should respond to genocide where it occurred, and how genocide should be prosecuted. In 1998, the **International Criminal Tribunal for Rwanda** convicted of genocide the former mayor of a small town in Rwanda and the former head of the country. In a 2007 ruling of the **International Court of Justice**, Serbia was the first state to be found in breach of the Convention for having failed to prevent the 1995 **Srebrenica** genocide and for failing to try or transfer persons accused of genocide to the **International Criminal Tribunal for the Former Yugoslavia**. *See also* PREVENTION.

UNITED NATIONS CONVENTION ON THE REDUCTION OF STATELESSNESS (1961). Originally intended to be a Protocol to the **United Nations Convention Relating to the Status of Refugees** covering persons who were not **refugees**, this international legal instrument seeks to resolve some of the problems associated with **statelessness**. It defines ways in which persons who would otherwise be stateless can acquire or retain **nationality** notably in cases arising from a change of civil status, residence abroad, or the voluntary renunciation of nationality. It also stipulates that children should be granted the nationality of the state party in which a parent has citizenship and prohibits **states parties** from depriving people of their nationalities on racial, ethnic, religious, or political grounds. Under its terms, however, states are under no obligation to grant nationality to stateless persons entering their territory unless they have strong ties with the state and cannot acquire nationality elsewhere. No specific body comparable to the **United Nations treaty bodies** monitors the implementation of the Convention and, as of 2011, only 40 states had ratified or acceded to it. To that extent, the Convention remains primarily an aspirational document.

UNITED NATIONS CONVENTION ON THE RIGHTS OF PERSONS WITH DISABILITIES. Global human rights instrument adopted by the **United Nations General Assembly** in 2006 which came into force two years later. Regarded by some as addressing the needs of a "minority" group and by others as a **discrimination** treaty, the intent of the Convention is to promote, protect and ensure the full enjoyment of human rights by **disabled persons**

and their full equality under the law in regard to access to justice, **education**, **health**, **work** and employment and standards of living. An Optional Protocol which entered into force in 2012 allows **state parties** to recognize the competence of a United Nations Committee on the Rights of Persons with Disabilities to consider **complaints** from individuals. Disability rights' **non-governmental organizations**, notably the **International Disability Alliance**, played a key role in the gestation and elaboration of the Convention, contributing to the shift from welfare to rights in dealing with disability. *See also* DECLARATION ON THE RIGHTS OF DISABLED PERSONS; REHABILITATION INTERNATIONAL.

UNITED NATIONS CONVENTION ON THE RIGHTS OF THE CHILD. Comprehensive human rights treaty adopted by the **United Nations General Assembly** in 1989 after a decade of negotiations influenced by strong **lobby** groups which argued, as had been the case of women's rights, that more precise norms were needed and that some important children's rights were in fact not covered by existing treaties. The Convention is rooted in a number of key values about the treatment of children and their protection and participation in society, all linked by common principles: **non-discrimination**; devotion to the best interests of the child; the right to **life**, survival and development; and respect for the views of the child. The Convention spells out the basic human rights that children everywhere have the right: to survival; to develop to the fullest; to protection from harmful influences, abuse and exploitation; and to participate fully in family, cultural and social life. It also sets standards in health care and welfare, **education**, leisure and culture, and legal, civil and social services.

Under the Convention, **states parties** commit themselves to protect these rights and to develop and undertake actions and policies guided by the best interests of the child. A group of experts, the **United Nations United Nations Committee on the Rights of the Child**, monitors state compliance with the Convention. Two **optional protocols** complement the Convention. The first one, on the involvement of **children in armed conflict**, establishes 18 as the minimum age for compulsory recruitment and requires states to do everything they can to prevent individuals under the age of 18 from taking a direct part in hostilities. The second Protocol, on the sale of children, child prostitution and child **pornography**, draws special attention to the criminalization of these serious violations of children's rights and emphasizes the importance of fostering increased public awareness and international cooperation in efforts to combat them. The Convention has been ratified by virtually the entire membership of the **United Nations** (with the notable exceptions of Somalia and the **United States**), reflecting the wide consensus upon which it rests.

However, it has indirectly triggered major controversies over the interpretation of Article 4 which stipulates that states parties "shall undertake such measures to the maximum extent of their available resources and, where needed, within the framework of international cooperation." Questions, for example, have been raised in various international fora about the scale of the resources to be made available for child-related services. Specifically, to what extent can or should national budgets be trimmed in periods of recession? How do programs of **structural adjustment** relate to and impact the rights of the child? What priority should donor countries give to child-related programs in their overall development policies? The issue of **privatization** of public services has also been and remains part of this still ongoing debate.

See also AFRICAN CHARTER ON THE RIGHTS AND WELFARE OF THE CHILD; ALSTON, PHILIP; CHILD RIGHTS INFORMATION NETWORK; CHILDREN TRAFFICKING; CLIMATE CHANGE; COALITION TO STOP THE USE OF CHILDREN; CONVENTION ON THE PROTECTION OF CHILDREN AGAINST SEXUAL EXPLOITATION AND SEXUAL ABUSE; DECLARATION OF THE RIGHTS OF THE CHILD; DEFENCE FOR CHILDREN INTERNATIONAL; FOOD, RIGHT TO; HEALTH, RIGHT TO; HOUSING, RIGHT TO ADEQUATE; INTERNATIONAL BUREAU FOR CHILDREN'S RIGHTS; INTERNATIONAL FEDERATION TERRE DES HOMMES; INTERNATIONAL SAVE THE CHILDREN ALLIANCE; MINORITIES; NATIONALITY, RIGHT TO; REPRODUCTIVE RIGHTS; UNITED NATIONS CHILDREN'S FUND.

UNITED NATIONS CONVENTION RELATING TO THE STATUS OF REFUGEES (1951). Multilateral treaty providing a legal definition of a **refugee.** Under the Convention, **internally displaced persons,** environmentally displaced persons and economic migrants are not considered refugees. Individuals who have committed crimes against peace, **war crimes, crimes against humanity** or serious political crimes outside the country of refuge do not qualify either. Refugees are required to respect the laws and regulations of the host state. **States parties** to the Convention agree to cooperate with the **United Nations High Commissioner for Refugees** in the exercise of its functions and to inform the **United Nations secretary-general** about the legislation they have adopted in implementation of the Convention. Another one of their obligations is the granting of a right to an alien who is not subject to the granting of a similar treatment by the alien's country of **nationality.**

See also 1969 ORGANIZATION OF AFRICAN UNITY CONVENTION GOVERNING THE SPECIFIC ASPECTS OF REFUGEE PROBLEMS

IN AFRICA; CARTAGENA DECLARATION ON REFUGEES; ENVIRONMENTALLY INDUCED MIGRANTS; GENDER-SPECIFIC CLAIM; PERSECUTION; REFUGEE DETERMINATION PROCESS; UNITED NATIONS CONVENTION ON THE REDUCTION OF STATELESSNESS; UNITED NATIONS CONVENTION RELATING TO THE STATUS OF STATELESS PERSONS.

UNITED NATIONS CONVENTION RELATING TO THE STATUS OF STATELESS PERSONS. One of the primary universal instruments on **statelessness** complementing the 1961 **United Nations Convention on the Reduction of Statelessness**. Prepared by the **International Law Commission** and adopted in 1954 by a Conference of Plenipotentiaries convened by the **United Nations Economic and Social Council**, the Convention defines a stateless person as a person not considered a national (or citizen) under the law of any state. Its basic purpose is to help ensure that stateless persons enjoy fundamental rights and freedoms without **discrimination** by regulating their legal rights, access to work and welfare and urging state parties to facilitate their assimilation and naturalization. As of 2012, there were only 76 state parties to the Convention. *See also* NATIONALITY, RIGHT TO.

UNITED NATIONS CONVENTION TO COMBAT DESERTIFI-CATION. International **treaty** adopted in 1994 seeking to encourage international cooperation for the protection of land and soil on dryland regions and desertification, affected communities through innovative local programs and supportive international partnerships and awareness-raising, education, and training programs both in developing and developed countries. *See also* ENVIRONMENT, RIGHT TO A HEALTHY; FOOD, RIGHT TO.

UNITED NATIONS DECLARATION ON HUMAN CLONING (2005). **Soft law** instrument adopted by a recorded vote of the **United Nations General Assembly** which calls upon governments to "prohibit all forms of human cloning inasmuch as they are incompatible with human **dignity** and the protection of human life" and to refrain from any genetic engineering techniques "that may be contrary to human dignity." The Declaration also invited member states to "take into account the pressing global issues such as **HIV/AIDS**, tuberculosis and malaria, which affect in particular the **developing countries**" when financing medical research. *See also* BIOETHICS; EUROPEAN CONVENTION ON HUMAN RIGHTS AND BIOMEDICINE; HEALTH, RIGHT TO; LIFE, RIGHT TO; UNIVERSAL DECLARATION ON BIOETHICS AND HUMAN RIGHTS; UNIVERSAL DECLARATION ON THE HUMAN GENOME AND HUMAN RIGHTS.

UNITED NATIONS DEVELOPMENT PROGRAMME (UNDP). Development agency of the **United Nations** created in 1965 providing expert advice, training, and grant support to developing countries. The Programme is guided by the **Millennium Development Goals** and focuses on **poverty** reduction, social development, **HIV/AIDS**, the empowerment of women, democratic **governance**, energy and the environment. Since 1990, the UNDP has published its annual **Human Development Report**, a cornerstone of international debate and discussions about development. The UNDP was one of the first UN agencies to mainstream human rights considerations in its development work as evidenced by its activities in the field which target disadvantaged or marginalized groups (women, children, **minorities, migrant workers,** people with HIV/AIDS), bridge social justice and development, encourage people's participation, address governance issues such as **corruption,** the **rule of law** and **accountability** and seek to strengthen the human rights capacity of national legislative and judicial institutions.

UNITED NATIONS ECONOMIC AND SOCIAL COUNCIL (UN-ECOSOC). One of the principal intergovernmental bodies of the **United Nations** entrusted with the task of coordinating the economic and social work of the UN specialized agencies and the subsidiary bodies (eight functional commissions, five regional economic commissions and numerous programs and funds) which report to it. In regard to human rights and under Article 62 of the **United Nations Charter,** the Council may initiate reports, studies and recommendations "for the purpose of promoting respect for, and observance of human rights and fundamental freedoms for all." In addition, the Council can establish new subsidiary bodies. Under Article 71 of the Charter, it is responsible for making suitable arrangements for consultations with **non-governmental organizations.**

In spite of its apparent broad and impressive formal powers, UN-ECOSOC has never been able to play the coordinating role that the drafters of the Charter expected it to play. Its record in the field of human rights is, at best, mixed. The Council was the progenitor of the 1235 and **1503 Procedures,** and in 2000 it did set up a new body—the **United Nations Permanent Forum on Indigenous Issues**—which provides a limited political space for the consideration of **indigenous peoples'** concerns within the United Nations. On the other hand, the Council has not been in a position to build policy bridges between human rights and broader economic and social development concerns. In fact, not infrequently, its actions have run counter to its Charter-mandated responsibility to promote human rights. For example, it was the Council which decided shortly after the establishment of the

United Nations Commission on Human Rights (UN-CHR) to make it a body made up of government representatives rather than individual experts as originally envisaged, thus setting the stage for what was decried later as the politicization of the Commission. The creation of a **United Nations Human Rights Council**, which replaced the UN-CHR, that reports directly to the **United Nations General Assembly**, may in the long term further weaken the Council in the promotion of human rights. It remains, in any case, that the center of gravity of the UN work in human rights has always revolved around its subsidiary bodies such as the UN-CHR and the **United Nations Commission on the Status of Women** rather than UN-ECOSOC itself. *See Also* CONSULTATIVE STATUS; SOCIAL FORUM; UNITED NATIONS WORKING GROUP ON MINORITIES.

UNITED NATIONS EDUCATIONAL, SCIENTIFIC AND CULTURAL ORGANIZATION (UNESCO). United Nations specialized agency established to advance science, learning, education and culture. Its founding document specifically mandates UNESCO to promote international cooperation "to further universal respect for justice, for the **rule of law** and for the human rights and fundamental freedoms which are affirmed for the peoples of the world, without distinction of race, sex, language or religion, by the Charter of the United Nations." Within this broad framework, UNESCO has acted as an incubator of international human rights norms and treaties in regard to the right to **education** and to participate in cultural life, the right of **freedom of expression** and opinion, the right to seek, receive and distribute information and the right to enjoy the benefits of scientific progress, access to information, cultural diversity and gender **equality**.

The Organization considers the right to education a fundamental human right as reflected in the goals that it has enjoined the international community to achieve by 2015 in its 2000 "Education for All" initiative: expanding early childhood care and education, providing compulsory free primary education, increasing learning opportunities for youths and adults, improving adult literacy by 50 percent, and eliminating gender inequalities in schooling. UNESCO's normative work also includes its promotion of cultural and linguistic diversity and of freedom of the press in countries in transition and zones of conflict as well as its efforts to bridge the "digital divide" between developed and developing countries. In the field of science and technology, UNESCO played an active role in the adoption of the Universal Declaration on the Human Genome and Human Rights in 1977 and the International Declaration on Human Genetic Data in 2003.

Under a procedure authorized by UNESCO's governing body in 1978, UNESCO may receive individual **complaints** about violations of human rights. Most of the cases that reached UNESCO concerned the release of detained persons before completion of their sentence and allowing individuals to return to their countries from exile or to resume their employment. A large number of them have been satisfactorily resolved, but this little known procedure has been rarely used (between 1978 and 2003 there were 508 cases) and has fallen into desuetude.

See also CONVENTION AGAINST DISCRIMINATION IN EDUCATION; CONVENTION FOR THE SAFEGUARDING OF INTANGIBLE CULTURAL HERITAGE; CONVENTION ON THE PROTECTION AND PROMOTION OF THE DIVERSITY OF CULTURAL EXPRESSION; UNIVERSAL DECLARATION ON BIOETHICS AND HUMAN RIGHTS; UNIVERSAL DECLARATION ON THE HUMAN GENOME AND HUMAN RIGHTS.

UNITED NATIONS FRAMEWORK CONVENTION ON CLIMATE CHANGE (1992). International treaty agreed on at the **United Nations Conference on the Environment and Development** which requires parties to achieve "stabilization of greenhouse gas concentrations in the atmosphere at a level that would prevent dangerous anthropogenic interference with the climate system." Its key objective is to protect the climate system and mitigate against the adverse effects of climate change. In this regard, the Convention recognizes that the **state parties** "have a right to, and should, promote sustainable development." The treaty itself is considered non-binding and calls for "updates" (called "protocols") that would set mandatory emission limits. The Kyoto Protocol is the principal update of the Framework Convention. See also ENVIRONMENT, RIGHT TO A HEALTHY.

UNITED NATIONS GENERAL ASSEMBLY (UN-GA). One of the principal organs of the **United Nations,** consisting of representatives of all member states. The Assembly formally stands at the apex of the United Nations. It considers and approves the reports of its subsidiary bodies including the **United Nations Economic and Social Council** and the **United Nations Human Rights Council.** It has a final say in the adoption of the Organization's budget. It may consider all matters of concern to the United Nations, including "international cooperation in solving international problems of an economic, social, cultural or humanitarian character and in promoting and encouraging respect for human rights and for fundamental freedoms for all without distinction as to race, sex, language, or religion." Each year, in the course of its annual sessions, it considers a broad array of human rights issues: social development, crime **prevention** and criminal justice, drug control, the advancement of women, children's rights,

indigenous peoples, **refugees**, racism, **self-determination**, country human rights situations, among others.

In spite of its broad authority, the Assembly has exerted little leadership in scrutinizing human rights situations and **monitoring** the implementation of human rights standards. With the notable exceptions of **apartheid**, the **Declaration on the Right to Development**, the Second Protocol of the **International Covenant on Civil and Political Rights** on **capital punishment** and **decolonization** issues, where it has been active in drafting human rights instruments on its own, the Assembly has generally dealt with human rights questions in a fragmented and selective manner and by and large contented itself to give its imprimatur to what emerged from its subsidiary machinery.

See also AGGRESSION; BASIC PRINCIPLES AND GUIDELINES ON THE RIGHT TO A REMEDY AND REPARATION FOR VICTIMS OF GROSS VIOLATIONS OF INTERNATIONAL HUMAN RIGHTS LAW AND SERIOUS VIOLATIONS OF INTERNATIONAL HUMANITARIAN LAW; CODE OF CONDUCT FOR LAW ENFORCEMENT OFFICIALS; CODES OF CONDUCT FOR TRANSNATIONAL CORPORATIONS; DECLARATION; GERMAN SOUTH WEST AFRICA; HUMAN RIGHTS DEFENDERS; HUMAN RIGHTS EDUCATION; HUMANITARIAN INTERVENTION; INTERNATIONAL LAW COMMISSION; MILLENNIUM DEVELOPMENT GOALS; SOFT LAW; SPECIAL RAPPORTEURS; STATUTORY LIMITATIONS.

UNITED NATIONS GLOBAL COMPACT. "Voluntary corporate citizenship initiative" launched by **United Nations Secretary-General Kofi Annan** in 2000. The scheme brings together private companies which pledge to mainstream human rights, labor standards, **environment**, and anti-**corruption** norms and standards in their policies. Specifically, companies wishing to join the Compact must make it and its principles an integral part of their business strategy, day-to-day operations, and organizational culture. They must incorporate the Compact's principles in their decision making, contribute to broad development objectives (including the **Millennium Development Goals**) through partnerships and integrate in their annual report (or in a similar public document, such as a sustainability report) a description of the ways in which it implements the principles and supports broader development objectives (also known as the Communication on Progress). Participating companies must also advance the Global Compact and the case for responsible business practices through **advocacy** and active outreach to peers, partners, clients, consumers and the public at large. They are also encouraged to share case studies of good practices and participate in policy dialogues.

The Global Compact, however, has no robust built-in or external oversight mechanism for assessing the implementation, disclosure, and promotion of its universal principles. The number of participants in the Global Compact exceeds 7,000 organizations from more than 135 countries and is growing at a rate of some 100 additional participants per month. Some 1,000 companies were dropped from the Compact in 2008 for failure to meet their annual mandatory reporting requirement. *See also* CORPORATE SOCIAL RESPONSIBILITY; SOFT LAW; TRANSNATIONAL CORPORATIONS.

UNITED NATIONS GLOBAL CONFERENCES. Long-standing practice of multilateral diplomacy which started under the **League of Nations** and gained momentum within the framework of the **United Nations** as they evolved from narrowly focused, functional meetings from the early 1950s to a series of widely publicized gatherings attended by high-level representatives and several thousand other participants in the 1990s. Criticized by various constituencies for being too politicized or too large and unwieldy to set an international agenda, the frequency of UN-sponsored global conferences has significantly slowed down, giving way to less formal and more modest follow-up processes within UN institutions, the so-called "Plus 5s," "Plus 10s" and "Plus 20s." Such meetings have dealt primarily with global development and social issues—**population**, **food**, **hunger**, **water**, urbanization, the **environment**, sustainable development, women, children, aging, crime and, less frequently, peace and security issues such as disarmament and arms trafficking. The UN organized two conferences focused on human rights in 1968 and 1993.

UN global conferences vary considerably in scope and modalities. But, essentially, their key purpose is to promote global participation, consultation, **standards' setting** and policy formation. Their outcomes take the form of "**Declarations**" and "Plans of Action," which although non-binding, may have a strong moral and political value in the sense that they appear to confer a stamp of collective legitimacy to norms guiding practical programs and activities at the state level. As "town meetings of the world," UN global conferences can thus serve as incubators of ideas, raise elite consciousness, identify emerging issues and nurture public support for solutions to global issues. **Civil society** organizations play a key role in most of these meetings as they organize parallel conferences to discuss the major issues or participate alongside government representatives, serving on national delegations and presenting position papers.

See also CAIRO CONFERENCE ON POPULATION AND DEVELOPMENT; FOURTH WORLD CONFERENCE ON WOMEN; INTERNATIONAL CONFERENCE ON AGRARIAN REFORM AND

RURAL DEVELOPMENT; INTERNATIONAL CONFERENCE ON POPULATION AND DEVELOPMENT; INTERNATIONAL CRIME CONGRESSES; NON-GOVERNMENTAL ORGANIZATIONS; UNITED NATIONS CONFERENCE ON THE HUMAN ENVIRONMENT; UNITED NATIONS CONFERENCE ON HUMAN SETTLEMENTS; UNITED NATIONS CONFERENCE ON THE ENVIRONMENT AND DEVELOPMENT; WOMEN'S CAUCUS FOR GENDER JUSTICE; WORLD CONFERENCE AGAINST RACISM; WORLD CONFERENCE ON HUMAN RIGHTS; WORLD SUMMIT FOR CHILDREN; WORLD SUMMIT FOR SOCIAL DEVELOPMENT; WORLD SUMMIT ON THE INFORMATION SOCIETY.

UNITED NATIONS HIGH COMMISSIONER FOR REFUGEES (UN-HCR). Successor organization to the International Refugee Office established in 1950 by the **United Nations General Assembly** to protect **refugees** and to promote durable solutions to their problems. Since its creation, the agency has helped millions of people. UN-HCR currently assists about 34 million persons in more than 110 countries. The primary purpose is to safeguard the rights and well-being of refugees and to ensure that everyone can exercise his or her right to seek **asylum** and find safe refuge in another state, with the option to return home voluntarily, integrate locally or resettle in a third country.

In practical terms, the evolving nature of refugee flows over time has led to considerable changes in the original mandate of the agency. While UN-HCR still deals with individual cases of **persecution**, it has increasingly been involved in the protection of and assistance to groups of refugees fleeing persecution, civil strife or massive **violations of human rights**. The agency has also acquired the additional role of coordinating material assistance for refugees and returnees in less developed countries. Finally, UN-HCR has increasingly been called on to assist **internally displaced people** who have not crossed an international border but are in a refugee-like situation inside their own country. In more than five decades, the agency has helped an estimated 50 million people. It has a staff of around 6,689 people in 116 countries.

See also ALIENS, TREATMENT OF; BIAFRA; BOAT PEOPLES; CARTAGENA DECLARATION; CCJO RENE CASSIN; HARKIS; INTERNAL DISPLACEMENT MONITORING CENTRE; MYANMAR; NATIONALITY, RIGHT TO; STATELESSNESS; UNITED NATIONS OFFICE OF THE HIGH COMMISSIONER FOR HUMAN RIGHTS; UNITED NATIONS RELIEF AND WORKS AGENCY FOR PALESTINE REFUGEES IN THE NEAR EAST.

UNITED NATIONS HUMAN RIGHTS COMMITTEE. Body of 18 independent experts **monitoring** the implementation of the **International Covenant on Civil and Political Rights** by its **states parties**. The functions of the Committee are threefold: to "study and provide" **general comments** on periodic states' reports on "measures they took to give effect to the rights recognized in the Covenant and the progress made in the enjoyment of those rights"; to receive inter-state **complaints**; and, under the First Optional Protocol of the Covenant, to receive individual complaints. The Committee holds three sessions a year, each three weeks long, in New York and Geneva (twice). Its proceedings are public and are often attended by representatives of interested UN agencies and international and national **non-governmental organizations**.

Following their initial reports, states now submit their periodic reports normally every five years, although the Committee may occasionally request ad hoc special reports. State reports are structured on the basis of indicative guidelines prepared by the Committee, and they must provide information on national applicable procedures for seeking enforcement or **remedies** for the rights covered by the Covenant. The current practice of the Committee is to issue "**concluding observations**" assessing a state's human rights situation in the light of the information provided by the state, the answers it gave to questions posed by members of the Committee during the examination of its report and any other information obtained by the Committee. The observations of the Committee are non-binding but are reproduced in the Committee report to the **United Nations General Assembly**.

Over the years, the Committee has considerably broadened its mandated activities by issuing "**General Comments**" not only on particular aspects of state reports but also on its own interpretation of specific provisions of the Covenant. Thus, the Committee has criticized state reports for their incomplete coverage, undue emphasis on formal arrangements and delays in their timely submission. More importantly, the Committee's comments often provide useful and authoritative guidance on human rights legal issues such as the principles that apply to the making of **reservations** (General Comment 24), the nature of legal obligations imposed on state parties to the Covenant (General Comment 31); and the legality of the **derogations** invoked by states in situations of emergencies (General Comment 29). The number of individual complaints has increased considerably in the past two decades but remains low due to the stiff standards of admissibility set out by the Optional Protocol. To date, the Committee has received 1,777 "communications" with respect to 82 countries and determined, in 489 of them, that there had been a violation. The worst offenders appear to be Jamaica, Uruguay, Australia and Spain. There are at present some 400 cases pending.

The complaint procedure of the Committee has evolved into a quasi-judicial process: complainants may use legal representation and the committee may request a state to take **interim measures** (i.e., the suspension of a death sentence) without prejudice to the merits of the complaints or pending a decision on its admissibility, which may take 18 months. But neither the opinions of the Committee nor its requests for interim measures are legally binding. They do nevertheless carry with them considerable normative weight and often prompt states to provide necessary remedies. Since 1990, the Committee has monitored state compliance with its decisions.

See also ACCESS TO JUSTICE; ARBITRARY DETENTION; CORPORAL PUNISHMENT; CULTURAL RIGHTS; DEMOCRACY; DENUNCIATION; DEROGATION; EQUALITY BEFORE THE LAW; FAIR TRIAL, RIGHT TO; FORCED DISAPPEARANCES; FREEDOM OF EXPRESSION; FREEDOM OF MOVEMENT; FREEDOM OF RELIGION; ILL TREATMENT; INHUMAN OR DEGRADING TREATMENT OR PUNISHMENT; JUDICIARY, INDEPENDENCE OF; LIFE, RIGHT TO; *LOVELACE V. CANADA*; PUBLIC EMERGENCIES; RECOGNITION, RIGHT TO; REDRESS; SECURITY, RIGHT TO; SELF-DETERMINATION; SEXUAL ORIENTATION; SOCIAL SECURITY, RIGHT TO; TRUTH, RIGHT TO THE.

UNITED NATIONS HUMAN RIGHTS COUNCIL (UN-HRC). Intergovernmental body established in 2006 by the **United Nations General Assembly** to replace the **United Nations Commission on Human Rights** which had come under intense criticism for having a membership which included nations with poor human rights records, for inconsistencies and double standards in its policy recommendations and for its general ineffectiveness in the face of blatant violations. After over a year of protracted negotiations, the Council adopted an "institution-building package" which provides the general framework of its current work. That package essentially maintains the **complaints** procedures developed by the Commission. It also retains the previous system of expert advice on thematic human rights issues, the previous **United Nations Sub-Commission on the Promotion and Protection of Human Rights** being superseded by a **United Nations Human Rights Council Advisory Committee** with roughly similar functions. One-third of the council's members can call for the convening of special sessions, which virtually makes the Council a standing body able to address emerging issues on short notice. The most innovative feature of the Council's work is the newly instituted **Universal Periodic Review**, a common system whereby the Council scrutinizes at regular intervals the human rights records of all countries members of the **United Nations**.

The functioning of the Council since its inception does not seem to have significantly departed from the practices of the Commission. The new Council is slightly smaller than the Commission, with 47 members instead of 53, and its membership is based on a modified principle of geographic distribution. The political center of gravity has in fact shifted to a majority of 26 nations from Asia and Africa, with human rights conceptions at odds with those in Western European and North American states, which are entitled to only seven seats under the new system. Membership in the Council is open to all UN members. The founding resolution of the General Assembly stipulates that each council member must be elected individually by a majority of the Assembly, with account being taken of the candidate's contribution and respect of human rights standards. But countries with dubious human rights credentials are still able to circumvent these criteria.

By and large the convening of special sessions (13 have so far been held) remains primarily driven by political considerations—legitimizing or de-legitimizing, blaming, justifying policy demands and the like—rather than a genuine concern for devising ways and means to protect human rights. Critiques of the **special procedures** have become a regular feature of the Council's sessions. The Advisory Committee has lost the power of initiative that the Sub-Commission had enjoyed. The General Assembly carried out a perfunctory assessment of the work of the Council five years after its launching.

See also 1503 PROCEDURE; BLASPHEMY; CLIMATE CHANGE; CONVENTION ON THE ABOLITION OF SLAVERY; CUBA; DEMOCRACY; EXTERNAL DEBT CRISIS; FORUM ON MINORITY ISSUES; FREEDOM OF EXPRESSION; FREEDOM OF RELIGION; GOLDSTONE REPORT; INDIGENOUS PEOPLES; ORGANIZATION OF ISLAMIC COOPERATION; PEACE, RIGHT TO;. SEXUAL ORIENTATION; SOCIAL FORUM; SPECIAL RAPPORTEURS; TRADITIONAL PRACTICES; UNITED NATIONS WORKING GROUP ON ARBITRARY DETENTION.

UNITED NATIONS HUMAN RIGHTS COUNCIL ADVISORY COMMITTEE. Human rights charter body of the United Nations established in 2006 to replace the **United Nations Sub-Commission on the Promotion and Protection of Human Rights**. Composed of 18 experts, the Committee functions as a **think tank** for the **Human Rights Council**. Its work has focused on questions related to the right to **food**, missing persons and the development of a UN Declaration on Human Rights Education and Training and principles and guidelines for the elimination of **discrimination** against persons affected by leprosy and their family members. *See also* PEACE, RIGHT TO.

UNITED NATIONS HUMAN SETTLEMENTS PROGRAMME (UN-HABITAT). United Nations program established in implementation of a resolution of the first UN-sponsored global conference on human settlements held in Vancouver in 1976. Its original mandate was to deal with the effects of urbanization and massive urban growth on human well-being. UN-Habitat's mission has been redefined in the wake of a second UN-sponsored global conference held in Istanbul in 1996 and the adoption of the **Millennium Development Goals** (target 11 of goal 7 aims at improving the lives of at least 100 million slum dwellers by 2020). Overall, its purpose is to promote socially and environmentally sustainable towns and cities and achieve the goal of providing adequate shelter for all.

UN-Habitat is primarily a technical and operational body dealing with the downside of urbanization through **monitoring** and **research**, **capacity building** and financing for **housing** and urban development. But the agency considers itself guided by human rights considerations (i.e., by such norms and principles as sustainable urban development, adequate shelter for all, improvements in the lives of slum dwellers, access to safe **water** and sanitation, social inclusion and environmental protection). For example, by "shelter for all," UN-Habitat means affordable shelter for all groups in all types of settlements, meeting the basic requirements of affordability, tenurial security, structural stability and infrastructural support, with convenient access to employment and community services and facilities. UN-Habitat works in close cooperation with the **United Nations Office of the High Commissioner for Human Rights** and the **United Nations Human Rights Council special rapporteur** on adequate housing.

UNITED NATIONS INTEGRATED MISSION IN TIMOR-LESTE (UNMIT, 2006–2012). The latest in a series of **United Nations** missions deployed in **Timor-Leste** since 1999, UNMIT was a multidimensional, integrated **peace operation** established by the **United Nations Security Council** after the political, humanitarian and security crisis which rocked the country in 2006. Its mandate was to support the government in "consolidating stability, enhancing a culture of democratic **governance**, and facilitating political dialogue among Timorese stakeholders, in their efforts to bring about a process of national reconciliation and to foster social cohesion."

UNITED NATIONS INTERIM ADMINISTRATION MISSION IN KOSOVO (UNMIK, 1999–). Established by the **United Nations Security Council** in the wake of the **North Atlantic Treaty Organization** armed intervention and dispatch of the multinational Kosovo Force, UNMIK originally was vested with the sweeping mandate to provide Kosovo with a "transitional administration while establishing and overseeing the development of provisional democratic self-governing institutions to ensure conditions for a peaceful and normal life for all inhabitants in Kosovo." Under the terms of the resolution, UNMIK was expected to perform basic civilian administrative functions; promote the establishment of substantial autonomy and self-government in Kosovo; facilitate a political process to determine Kosovo's future status; coordinate humanitarian and disaster relief of all international agencies; support the reconstruction of key infrastructure; maintain civil law and order; promote human rights; and ensure the safe and unimpeded return of all **refugees** and **internally displaced persons** (IDPs) to their homes in Kosovo. In effect, the Security Council placed Kosovo under UN trusteeship. These functions were significantly changed after Kosovo's declaration of independence in 2008. Some of them have been taken over by the **European Union**, especially those concerned with the **rule of law**, the police, the judiciary and customs. But UNMIK's main strategic objective still remains the promotion of security, stability and respect for human rights in Kosovo through engagement with all its ethnic communities.

Whether UNMIK has achieved (or is achieving) its stated objectives remains a subject of controversy. The country's economic infrastructure is still in tatters and, according to some international organizations, it has become a major destination country for women and young girls trafficked into forced prostitution. Tensions between the Albanian majority and the Serb minority run high, and ethnic violence outbreaks are not infrequent. The IDPs problem is still unresolved as many displaced Serbs claim that they are the victims of **discrimination** and are afraid to return to their homes.

UNITED NATIONS MISSION FOR THE REFERENDUM IN WESTERN SAHARA (MINURSO, 1991–). UN Peacekeeping Operation established by the **United Nations Security Council** (UN-SC) in accordance with settlement proposals between Morocco and the Frente Popular para la Liberación de Saguia el-Hamra y de Río de Oro (Frente POLISARIO) which had been vying for control over the contested territory of **Western Sahara** since Spain relinquished it in 1975. The settlement plan provided for a transitional period for the preparation of a referendum that would enable the people of Western Sahara to choose between independence and integration with Morocco. MINURSO has since then monitored a shaky ceasefire and was expected to organize and conduct a referendum.

The MINURSO mandate has been repeatedly extended since 1991 as the it has been unable to overcome Moroccan resistance and manipulation of the process of **self-determination** (with the tacit support of France in the

UN-SC). In spite of reports of civilian abuses, the UN-SC has not mandated MINURSO to initiate programs of human rights **monitoring**.

UNITED NATIONS MISSION IN BOSNIA AND HERZEGOVINA (UNMIBH, 1995–2002). Peace operation mandated by the **United Nations Security Council** to contribute to the establishment of the **rule of law** in Bosnia-Herzegovina by assisting in reforming and restructuring the local police into a multi-ethnic force and revamping the judicial system. UNMIBH was also empowered to investigate **violations of human rights** by law enforcement agents and implement corrective measures.

UNITED NATIONS MISSION IN HAITI (UNMIH, 1993–1996). Peacekeeping operation of the **United Nations** set up to oversee the return to civilian rule in Haiti after the ousting of the military, which had seized power from the democratically elected president Jean-Bertrand Aristide. Its mandate was to professionalize the armed forces, create a separate police force and establish an environment conducive to free and fair elections.

UNITED NATIONS MISSION IN SIERRA LEONE (UNAMSIL, 1999–2005). Created by the **United Nations Security Council** in 1999 to assist in the implementation of an agreement that brought to an end the **Sierra Leone civil war**, UNAMSIL was entrusted with a number of security tasks, notably overseeing the adherence of all parties to the ceasefire and the disarmament and demobilization of combatants. In addition, it was intended to facilitate the delivery of humanitarian assistance and to support the operations of UN civilian officials, including the special representative of the secretary-general and his staff, human rights officers and civil affairs officers. In this regard, UNAMSIL was mandated to protect **civilians** under imminent threat of physical violence "within its capabilities and areas of deployment."

UNITED NATIONS MISSION IN THE CENTRAL AFRICAN RE-PUBLIC AND CHAD (MINURCAT, 2007–2010). UN civilian and police operation authorized by the **United Nations Security Council** mandated together with a **European Union** military force (EUFOR) to promote human rights and provide protection to **refugees** from Darfur and internally displaced Chadians against the activities of armed groups based in eastern Chad and Darfur. The mandate of MINURCAT was first scaled down and eventually abandoned in 2010. *See also* CIVILIANS, PROTECTION OF.

UNITED NATIONS MISSION IN THE REPUBLIC OF SOUTH SUDAN (UNMISS, 2011–). United Nations' peace operation established by the **United Nations Security Council** to support implementation of the Comprehensive Peace Agreement signed by the government of Sudan and the Sudan People's Liberation Movement/Army on 9 January 2005, which brought the Sudanese civil war to an end. UNMISS is tasked to facilitate and coordinate, within its capabilities and in its areas of deployment, the voluntary return of **refugees** and **internally displaced persons** and **humanitarian assistance** to assist the parties in the mine action sector and to contribute toward international efforts to protect and promote human rights in the Sudan. *See also* MONITORING OF HUMAN RIGHTS.

UNITED NATIONS MISSION OF SUPPORT IN EAST TIMOR (UNMISET, 2002–2005). Successor **United Nations' peace mission** to the **United Nations Transitional Administration in East Timor** (UNTAET) which came into existence when East Timor became independent as **Timor-Leste**. Its mandate was to provide assistance to core administrative structures in the country and to contribute to the maintenance of its external and internal security. It was extended until 2005 and replaced by a downsized operation, the United Nations Office in Timor-Leste. The functions assigned to UNMISET included the continuation of investigations begun by UNTAET into **violations of human rights** believed to have been committed in East Timor by Indonesian and pro-Indonesian military forces in 1999. *See also* SPECIAL PANELS OF THE DILI DISTRICT COURT.

UNITED NATIONS OBSERVER MISSION IN EL SALVADOR (ONUSAL, 1991–1995). First **United Nations' peace operation** established by the **United Nations Security Council** fully incorporating human rights concerns within its mandate. Set up to verify the implementation of the agreements that brought to an end a decade civil war between the government and the Frente Farabundo Martí para la Liberación Nacional, ONUSAL monitored the ceasefire and related measures, the reform and reduction of the armed forces, the creation of a new police force, the reform of the judicial and electoral systems, human rights practices, land tenure and other economic and social issues. *See also* MONITORING OF HUMAN RIGHTS.

UNITED NATIONS OBSERVER MISSION IN GEORGIA (UNOMIG, 1993). Established by the **United Nations Security Council** (UN-SC) to verify compliance with a ceasefire agreement between the government of Georgia and the authorities of **Abkhazia** in Georgia, the mandate of this peacekeeping operation was to investigate reports of ceasefire violations and to attempt to resolve such incidents with the parties involved. It was also entrusted with the task of reporting **violations of human rights**. Lack of consensus among the permanent members of the UN-SC over the mandate of UNOMIG led to its dissolution in 2009. *See also* MONITORING OF HUMAN RIGHTS.

UNITED NATIONS OBSERVER MISSION IN LIBERIA (UNOMIL, 1993–1997). United Nations' peace operation launched by the **United Nations Security Council** to support the efforts of the **Economic Community of West African States** in Liberia during the first Liberian civil war (1989–96). Its mandate was to monitor the implementation of peace agreements between the Liberian parties, facilitate humanitarian assistance, investigate **violations of human rights** and monitor the electoral process. It was superseded in 2003 by the United Nations Mission in Liberia. *See also* ELECTORAL ASSISTANCE; MONITORING OF HUMAN RIGHTS.

UNITED NATIONS OFFICE OF THE HIGH COMMISSIONER FOR HUMAN RIGHTS (UN-OHCHR). The idea of such an office dates as far back as the creation of the **United Nations**, but it did not come to fruition until after the end of the **Cold War** in 1993 in the wake of the **World Conference on Human Rights**. Based in Geneva with a Liaison Office in New York, which has recently been strengthened by the establishment of a senior post, the Office is mandated to perform an exceptionally broad range of responsibilities. It is expected to promote universal enjoyment of all human rights by giving practical effect to the will and resolve of the world community as expressed by the United Nations; to promote international cooperation for human rights, to stimulate and coordinate action for human rights throughout the United Nations system; to promote universal ratification and implementation of international standards; to assist in the development of new norms; to support the work of human rights organs and treaty-monitoring bodies; to respond to serious **violations of human rights**; to undertake preventive human rights action and human rights field activities and operations; to promote the establishment of national human rights infrastructures; and to provide **education**, information **advisory services** and **capacity-building** assistance in the field of human rights.

This dizzying array of functions has not, however, been matched by a corresponding commitment of financial resources by UN member states. UN-OHCHR is funded both from the United Nations regular budget and voluntary contributions from member states, intergovernmental organizations, foundations and individuals. The regular budget funding of the Office has gradually increased, but the human rights programs receive only 3 percent of the regular budget of the United Nations Secretariat. UN-OHCHR has had to supplement its resources with voluntary contributions which, in 2011, amounted to some $110 million. According to UN-OHCHR figures, the Office's total estimated resource requirements for the 2012–13 biennium were $448 million! Perhaps more troublesome is the fact that these functions are contradictory. All too often the incumbents have had to walk on a tightrope, switching roles between quiet diplomacy or swashbuckling activism and serving governments or acting as a shield against those very same governments. Inevitably, their actions have sometimes elicited sharp political disavowals or rebukes, compelling them to leave their posts as the cases of **Mary Robinson** and **Louise Arbour** show.

The most influential development since the creation of the Office, which now has a staff of 859 persons, has been its growing emphasis on field work. The Office has 11 country offices and seven regional offices around the world, including a workforce of some 240 international human rights officers serving in UN **peace operations**. This network provides a wide range of services including support to national human rights institutions, follow-up on implementation of human rights bodies recommendations, **monitoring of human rights** situations, delivering technical assistance in legislative reform, human rights education, administration of justice, advice on ratifying treaties, constitutional reform, training of armed forces, electoral assistance, training of law enforcement officials, preparation of national human rights plans, among others. The outreach work of the commissioner includes educational and training activities, awareness raising campaigns, research and publications. *See also* SEXUAL ORIENTATION.

UNITED NATIONS OPERATION IN BURUNDI (ONUB, 2004–2006). Having determined that the situation in **Burundi** continued to pose a threat to international peace and security in the region, the **United Nations Security Council** established the ONUB to help implement efforts to bring about national reconciliation in the country. ONUB was tasked with contributing to the creation of a security environment, allowing for the provision of humanitarian assistance to facilitate the voluntary return of **refugees** and **internally displaced persons** and to contribute to the successful holding of elections. It was also authorized to use "all necessary means" to ensure the respect of ceasefire agreements, carry out disarmament and protect **civilians** under imminent threat of physical violence. The mission was terminated in 2006 and many of its functions were transferred to a scaled-down United Nations Integrated Office in Burundi.

UNITED NATIONS OPERATION IN COTE D'IVOIRE (UNOCI, 2004–). Peace operation authorized by the **United Nations Security Council** in 2004. It replaced a peacekeeping force set up by the Council a year earlier. Its original objective was to monitor and facilitate the implementation of the peace agreement signed by the government and insurgents in 2003 which aimed at ending the Ivoirian civil war. Its specific tasks were to disarm the militias, monitor the arms embargo imposed by the Security Council and support the organization of free, transparent and fair elections. ONUCI was also tasked with promoting and protecting human rights with special attention to violence committed against women and children and to investigate violations with a view to ending **impunity**. Prior to the elections, ONUCI organized training workshops on rules to enforce law and order in line with international human rights norms and standards. In the wake of the 2010 presidential elections and the five-month-long armed struggle which followed, ONUCI's activities are geared toward strengthen the authority of the new Ivoirian government. *See also* COTE D'IVOIRE; ELECTORAL ASSISTANCE; MONITORING OF HUMAN RIGHTS.

UNITED NATIONS OPERATION IN MOZAMBIQUE (ONUMOZ, 1992–1994). Set up by the **United Nations Security Council** in 1992, this **peace operation** was intended to monitor and verify the implementation of a ceasefire agreement between the Mozambican government and the insurgency of the Resistência Nacional Moçambicana. In addition to supervising the separation and demobilization of the combatants, monitoring the withdrawal of foreign forces and disbanding of private and irregular armed groups, ONUMOZ provided technical assistance in the elections called for in the peace agreement and coordinated humanitarian assistance operations, in particular those relating to **refugees, internally displaced persons**, demobilized military personnel and affected local population. It had a civilian component entrusted with **monitoring of human rights** in prisons and police stations and to **investigate** complaints.

UNITED NATIONS OPERATION IN SOMALIA (UNOSOM, 1992– 1994). Late in 1990, Somalia collapsed into clan warfare and civil war. Anarchy and mass starvation ensued, prompting the **United Nations Security Council** (UN-SC) to set up a peacekeeping operation to monitor a ceasefire in Mogadishu, the capital of Somalia, to provide protection and security for **United Nations** personnel, equipment and supplies at the seaports and airports in Mogadishu and escort deliveries of humanitarian supplies from there to distribution centers in the city and its immediate environs. As the situation continued to deteriorate, the Council authorized in December 1992 the formation of the Unified Task Force (UNITAF), a multinational force organized and led by the **United States** to use "all necessary means" to establish a secure environment for humanitarian relief operations in Somalia.

In mid-1993, UNITAF was brought under the authority of a second successor peacekeeping operation, UNOSOM II, whose mandate, as determined by the UN-SC, was to take appropriate action, including enforcement measures, to establish throughout Somalia a secure environment for humanitarian assistance. To that end, UNOSOM II was to complete, through disarmament and reconciliation, the task begun by UNITAF for the restoration of peace, stability, law and order. UNOSOM II's attempts to implement disarmament led to repeated clashes and violence. In October, a U.S.-ordered and led military operation attempted to capture the senior aides of one of the most powerful local clan leaders. The operation ended in bloodshed, prompting President Bill Clinton to order the withdrawal of U.S. troops. By March 1994, all U.S. troops had been withdrawn. Other troop-contributing nations followed suit. By the late spring of 1994, UNOSOM had effectively been terminated.

UNITED NATIONS ORGANIZATION MISSION IN THE DEMOCRATIC REPUBLIC OF THE CONGO (MONUC, 1999–2010). Initially set up by the **United Nations Security Council** (UN-SC) to observe and report on compliance with the provisions of a peace accord between the **Democratic Republic of the Congo** (DRC) and five regional states that had been involved in the Congolese civil war, the mandate of this **peace operation** was rapidly expanded to include, under Chapter VII of the **United Nations Charter**, multiple related additional tasks ranging from the protection of UN personnel, facilities, installations and equipment to ensuring the security and freedom of movement of its personnel and to protecting **civilians** under imminent threat of physical violence. Over the years, the 20,000 civilian and military strong personnel of MONUC monitored ceasefires between foreign and Congolese forces, brokered local truces, disarmed and repatriated thousands of foreign armed combatants and assisted in the transition to **democratic** rule by facilitating in 2006 the first democratic elections in 49 years held in the country.

Some 20,000 ex-combatants have been demobilized or integrated into the Congolese army, but the process is incomplete, and heavily armed rebels continue to challenge state authority in the eastern provinces of Kivu. The exploitation of the DRC's rich mineral wealth has funded insurgencies and continues to fuel internal and regional insecurities. Rape and **gender-based violence** have been used as weapons of war with **impunity** by all sides of the conflict, including peacekeepers. Ethnic differences and land disputes remain unresolved. The central government's reach has limited impact beyond Kinshasa and **corruption** is endemic. In May 2010, at the request of the Congolese government, the UN-SC agreed to withdraw 2,000 troops and replaced MONUC with the United Nations Organization Stabilization Mission in the Democratic Republic of the Congo. The new mission has been authorized to use all necessary means to carry out its mandate relating, among other things, to the protection of civilians, humanitarian personnel and **human rights defenders** under imminent threat of physical violence and to support the government of the DRC in its stabilization and peace consolidation efforts.

UNITED NATIONS PEACEBUILDING COMMISSION. Subsidiary intergovernmental organ of the **United Nations General Assembly** and the **United Nations Security Council** set up in 2005 with a view to supporting reconstruction efforts in countries emerging from conflict through the development of integrated **peacebuilding** strategies, drawing on the UN experience in such matters as conflict prevention, mediation, peacekeeping, respect for human rights, the **rule of law**, humanitarian assistance and long-term development. At present, Burundi, the Central African Republic, Guinea, Guinea-Bissau, Liberia and Sierra Leone are on the agenda of the Commission.

UNITED NATIONS PERMANENT FORUM ON INDIGENOUS ISSUES. First proposed by the 1993 **World Conference on Human Rights** in Vienna, this subsidiary body of the **United Nations Economic and Social Council** (UN-ECOSOC) was established in 2000 and first met in 2002. The Permanent Forum consists of 16 independent experts (eight of them nominated by governments and the other eight by **indigenous peoples**) appointed by the president of the UN-ECOSOC. Its mandate is to discuss indigenous issues (including economic and social development, culture, environment, **education**, **health** and human rights), provide expert advice and recommendations to the UN-ECOSOC and the programs, funds and agencies of the **United Nations** system and to raise awareness about indigenous issues and help integrate and coordinate activities in the UN system. *See also* INDIGENOUS PEOPLES' CENTER FOR DOCUMENTATION, RESEARCH AND INFORMATION; UNITED NATIONS SUB-COMMISSION ON THE PROMOTION AND PROTECTION OF HUMAN RIGHTS.

UNITED NATIONS POPULATION FUND (UNFPA). United Nations agency set up in 1969 originally to finance population stabilization projects. Its mandate has considerably evolved over time and is now embedded in developmental and human rights concerns. UNFPA's stated main goals are to promote universal access to reproductive health and universal primary **education**, reduce maternal and infant mortality and increase life expectancy.

To achieve these objectives, ultimately designed to reduce the incidence of **poverty**, UNFPA integrates human rights standards in its programming procedures. *See also* GENDER MAINSTREAMING; REPRODUCTIVE RIGHTS.

UNITED NATIONS PRINCIPLES FOR RESPONSIBLE INVEST-MENT (UNPRI). Set of voluntary and aspirational guidelines developed by leading institutional investors in coordination with the United Nations Environment Programme and the **United Nations Global Compact** to serve as a basis for the integration of environmental, social and corporate considerations into investment activities. The stated underlying rationale of the scheme, which includes recommendations ranging from financial reporting and transparency to active promotion and implementation, is to achieve more sustainable markets and eventually better investment returns and to "better align investors with broader objectives of society." As of October 2010 over 800 investment institutions from 45 countries have become signatories. Each year, UNPRI's asset owners and investment manager signatories fill out an online questionnaire whose aggregated results are published in a yearly document. *See also* CORPORATE SOCIAL RESPONSIBILITY; SOFT LAW; TRANSNATIONAL CORPORATIONS.

UNITED NATIONS "PROTECT, RESPECT AND REMEDY" FRAMEWORK FOR BUSINESS AND HUMAN RIGHTS. Broad set of normative guidelines providing the foundations for mapping out and giving effect over time to the human rights responsibilities of states, companies and other social actors. The proposal, developed by the **United Nations secretary-general**'s Special Representative **John Ruggie** after three years of extensive research and consultations with governments, business and **civil society**, was endorsed by the **United Nations Human Rights Council** in 2008. The "Framework" rests on three "pillars": the state's responsibility to protect against human rights abuses by third parties, including business, through appropriate policies, regulation and adjudication; the corporate responsibility to respect human rights (i.e., the obligation to act with due diligence to avoid infringing on the rights of others and to address adverse impacts that occur); and greater access by victims to effective judicial and non-judicial **remedies**.

In 2011, the special representative offered "Guiding Principles" for the implementation of the "framework" which the Council also endorsed. The expectation is that these **soft law** instruments will eventually be viewed as authoritative global reference points on business and human rights. These normative standards have been widely endorsed by businesses, governments and investors, but they have received a mixed reception by civil society organizations, some of them arguing that they do not require states to put in place effective regulatory measures to prevent and punish companies abusing the rights of individuals and communities in other countries. In the same vein, critics point out that the Guiding Principles do not specify whether states should require companies to undertake human rights due diligence and do not explicitly recognize the right to remedy as a human right.

See also BUSINESS AND HUMAN RIGHTS RESOURCE CENTRE; CODES OF CONDUCT FOR TRANSNATIONAL CORPORATIONS; CORPORATE SOCIAL RESPONSIBILITY; DRAFT NORMS ON THE RESPONSIBILITIES OF TRANSNATIONAL CORPORATIONS AND OTHER BUSINESS ENTERPRISES WITH REGARD TO HUMAN RIGHTS; TRANSNATIONAL CORPORATIONS.

UNITED NATIONS PROTECTION FORCE (UNPROFOR, 1992–1995). Peacekeeping operation authorized by the **United Nations Security Council** (UN-SC) to ensure the demilitarization of designated areas in Croatia, the mandate of UNPROFOR was subsequently extended several times to Bosnia and Herzegovina to protect the airport of Sarajevo, support the delivery of humanitarian relief, monitor the **no-fly zones** and **safe zones** and assist civilian refugees when required by the **International Committee of the Red Cross**. UNPROFOR forces were brought under the **North Atlantic Treaty Organization**–led Implementation Force, which was tasked with implementing the Dayton Accords. Although severely undermanned, poorly equipped, constrained by restrictive UN-SC mandates in relation to its assigned duties and confronted by a proliferation of warring parties and paramilitary units outside regular chains of commands, UNPROFOR did perform useful humanitarian functions but was unable to prevent numerous exactions and in particular the Serb attack on **Srebrenica**.

UNITED NATIONS RELIEF AND WORKS AGENCY FOR PALESTINE REFUGEES IN THE NEAR EAST (UNWRA). Relief and human development agency established in 1949 to provide assistance to Palestinians uprooted as a result of the 1948 **Arab Israeli conflict**. The beneficiaries of UNWRA originally included persons who had resided in the British **Mandate** of Palestine between June 1946 and May 1948 and who lost their homes and means of livelihood as a result of the war. They now include their descendants. Currently, UNWRA provides **health** care, **education**, social services and emergency aid to some 4 million registered **refugees** scattered in and out of recognized camps located in Jordan, Lebanon, Syria, the West Bank and the Gaza Strip. It also runs micro-credit programs aimed at alleviating **poverty** and supporting economic development. UNWRA operations are funded by voluntary contributions.

The agency's annual budget is approved by the **United Nations General Assembly** and approximates half a billion U.S. dollars, the largest donors being the **United States**, the European Commission, Sweden, Norway and Great Britain. In the past 10 years or so, UNWRA has increasingly been involved in emergency operations work designed to mitigate the impact of curfews, closures and blockades imposed by Israeli authorities on the refugee population in the West Bank and Gaza Strip. Many governments have praised the work of the agency, but relations between UNWRA and **Israel** have often been strained, with Israeli authorities blaming the UNWRA for supporting, in effect, **terrorism** and militancy.

UNITED NATIONS SECRETARY-GENERAL (UN-SG). Under Article 7 of the **United Nations Charter**, the United Nations Secretariat is one of the six "principal organs of the United Nations." The Secretariat consists of international civil servants performing administrative, budgetary and servicing functions. It is headed by a secretary-general who is, in the language of Article 97 of the Charter, "the chief administrator of the Organization." Appointed for five-year terms, the UN-SG is elected by the **United Nations General Assembly** upon recommendation of the **United Nations Security Council**, the responsibilities of the UN-SG are only sketchily spelled out in the Charter. According to the UN website, the UN-SC's roles entail acting as "diplomat and advocate, civil servant and CEO" of the Organization. The vagueness of this language has left room for considerable interpretations in the roles assigned to the UN-SG, which range from "general" to sheer "secretary." In a long-term perspective, the office has acquired a gravitas and a political weight far exceeding the anticipation of the drafters of the Charter. In practice, the UN-SG not only prepares the agendas of major UN organs and services their meetings; but the UN-SG also draws up and puts into effect the budget of the Organization, supervises its day-to-day operations and serves as ceremonial head. Much of the time of the UN-SG is also devoted to good offices, missions and mediation. In addition, UN-SGs may suggest new programs and activities and offer political and normative leadership by invoking the values and moral authority of the United Nations. In this last respect, involvement and effectiveness in the field of human rights have widely fluctuated from one incumbent to the next depending on their personal skills and inclinations, organizational qualities and the constraints of the political environment. The **Cold War**, by and large, stymied the efforts of the ebullient Trygve Lie of Norway (1946–52), the self-effacing U-Thant of Burma (1961–71) and Javier Perez de Cuellar (1982–91) and the politically ambitious Kurt Waldheim of Austria (1972–81). Dag Hammarskjöld of Sweden, who served from 1953 until his death in 1961, had a clear preference for behind-the-scenes "quiet diplomacy" and a focus on peacekeeping. In contrast, Boutros Boutros Ghali (1992–96) and Kofi Annan (1997–2006) boldly asserted their leadership and endeavored to give a prominent place to human rights in the work of the United Nations. However, both fell out of grace with the great powers and failed to secure another term. Current Secretary-General Ban Ki-moon of South Korea took office on 1 January 2007 and was re-elected, unopposed, to a second term on 21 June 2011.

UNITED NATIONS SECURITY COUNCIL (UN-SC). One the principal organs of the **United Nations** tasked with the "primary responsibility to maintain international peace and security" (Art. 24). The Charter makes no reference to human rights in its provisions dealing with the functions and mode of operation of the Council. The prevailing norms of **state sovereignty** and non-intervention combined with the threat of vetoes did indeed prevent the UN-SC throughout the **Cold War** from establishing links between peace and security and the promotion and protection of human rights. Throughout this period, in only three major instances—all related primarily to the right of **self-determination**—did a majority of the members of the UN-SC, including its permanent members, deemed it fit to intervene (i.e., in the cases of **Western Sahara**, **Apartheid** in South Africa and the unilateral proclamation of independence of **Southern Rhodesia**).

The practice of the UN-SC has considerably evolved since the end of the Cold War. Beginning with the establishment of the UN **peace operation** in South West Africa (Namibia) in 1989, the UN-SC has shown a growing inclination to define internal human rights violations and humanitarian concerns as "threats to international peace and security," as was the case in Iraq in 1991 with the creation of "safe havens," Somalia and the former Yugoslavia with the dispatch of the **United Nations Operation in Somalia** and the **United Nations Protection Force** in 1992–93 to provide military protection to the delivery of humanitarian relief and, more recently, the deployment of the **United Nations Operation in Burundi** (2004–06) and the **United Nations Mission in the Republic of South Sudan** (2005–). As UN peacekeeping operations have morphed into "peace operations," weaving peacemaking, peacekeeping, and **peacebuilding** with peace enforcement and long-term prevention, virtually all the new peace operations now set up by the UN-SC have a human rights component.

Concurrently, the UN-SC has used the language of human rights and, occasionally, the use of force to support **democracy** as in Haiti (1994), **Burundi** (1996), **Liberia** (1996) and Guinea Bissau (2000) and elements of democratization such as free and fair elections, participation in public life and adequate political representation. It has also invoked Chapter VII of the **United Nations Charter** to find violations of **international humanitarian law** notably in regard to the use of child soldiers and violence against civilians in **armed conflicts**. Finally, in response to **genocide**, violations of the laws of war and **crimes against humanity**, the UN-SC set up the **International Criminal Tribunal for the Former Yugoslavia**, the **International Criminal Tribunal for Rwanda** and the **Special Court for Sierra Leone** and has referred cases to the **International Criminal Court**. These developments are noteworthy but should not be overstated. They should not be viewed as a paradigm shift in the work of the UN-SC. While the UN-SC now routinely considers gross violations of human rights, political constraints have not disappeared and often lead to double standards and inconsistencies, a continuing failure to address human rights issues in a preventive manner and outright cases of omissions.

See also AFRICAN UNION; AFRICAN UNION-UNITED NATIONS HYBRID OPERATION IN DARFUR; AGGRESSION; ARAB ISRAELI CONFLICT; BANGLADESH LIBERATION WAR; CHILDREN IN ARMED CONFLICT; CIVILIANS, PROTECTION OF; COUNTERTERRORISM; DARFUR CONFLICT; ENFORCEMENT; GENDER MAINSTREAMING; GOLDSTONE REPORT; HUMAN RIGHTS FIRST; HUMANITARIAN INTERVENTION; INTERNATIONAL CRIMINAL COURT; INTERNATIONAL PEACE INSTITUTE; KIMBERLEY PROCESS CERTIFICATION SCHEME; KOSOVO; LIBYA; NO-FLY ZONE; REGIONAL ARRANGEMENTS; SAFE ZONES; SANCTIONS; SEXUAL VIOLENCE; SPECIAL TRIBUNAL FOR LEBANON; SREBRENICA; SYRIA; TIMOR-LESTE; UNITED NATIONS ASSISTANCE MISSION IN AFGHANISTAN; UNITED NATIONS ASSISTANCE MISSION FOR RWANDA; UNITED NATIONS INTEGRATED MISSION IN TIMOR-LESTE; UNITED NATIONS INTERIM ADMINISTRATION MISSION IN KOSOVO; UNITED NATIONS MISSION FOR THE REFERENDUM IN WESTERN SAHARA; UNITED NATIONS MISSION IN BOSNIA AND HERZEGOVINA; UNITED NATIONS MISSION IN HAITI; UNITED NATIONS MISSION IN SIERRA LEONE; UNITED NATIONS MISSION IN THE CENTRAL AFRICAN REPUBLIC AND CHAD; UNITED NATIONS MISSION OF SUPPORT IN EAST TIMOR; UNITED NATIONS OBSERVER GROUP IN EL SALVADOR; UNITED NATIONS OBSERVER MISSION IN GEORGIA; UNITED NATIONS OBSERVER MISSION IN LIBERIA; UNITED NATIONS OPERATION IN COTE D'IVOIRE; UNITED NATIONS OPERATION IN MOZAMBIQUE; UNITED NATIONS ORGANIZATION MISSION IN THE DEMOCRATIC

REPUBLIC OF THE CONGO; UNITED NATIONS STABILIZATION MISSION IN HAITI; UNITED NATIONS STABILIZATION MISSION IN THE DEMOCRATIC REPUBLIC OF THE CONGO; UNITED NATIONS TRANSITION ASSISTANCE GROUP; UNITED NATIONS TRANSITIONAL ADMINISTRATION IN EAST TIMOR; UNITED NATIONS TRANSITIONAL AUTHORITY IN CAMBODIA; UNITED NATIONS VERIFICATION MISSION IN GUATEMALA; WOMEN IN PEACE AND SECURITY.

UNITED NATIONS SPECIALIZED AGENCIES. International organizations linked to the **United Nations** through special agreements. cooperating with one another and with various United Nations organs. There are now 17 such agencies. Along with the United Nations, they are often referred to collectively as the "United Nations system." Their activities range from **standard's setting**, the formulation of policies and the provision of technical assistance in virtually all areas of economic and social development. The specialized agencies formally report every year to the **United Nations Economic and Social Council**, but in effect they are autonomous as they have their own budgets and governing bodies. Their principles, goals and rules are supposed to be supportive of those of the United Nations. The **World Health Organization** and the **International Labour Organization**, for instance, have mainstreamed human rights norms and principles into their activities. Others, however, because of the technicality of their mandates (civil aviation, maritime transportation, telecommunications) or the ideological underpinnings of their work, have virtually ignored human rights norms or carried out activities which some view as inimical to the realization of human rights. *See also* FOOD AND AGRICULTURAL ORGANIZATION; INTERNATIONAL MONETARY FUND; UNITED NATIONS EDUCATIONAL, SCIENTIFIC AND CULTURAL ORGANIZATION.

UNITED NATIONS STABILIZATION MISSION IN HAITI (MINUSTAH, 2004–). Peace operation authorized by the **United Nations Security Council** to assist the Haitian government in ensuring public safety and public order and restoring the rule of law in the country. The mandate of MINUSTAH was expanded after the 2010 earthquake and now encompasses support for relief and reconstruction operations. Reforming and strengthening the country's criminal justice institutions system, professionalizing the Haitian national police, training counter-narcotics agents, protecting **internally displaced persons** and providing logistical support for presidential and parliamentary elections have been some of the main tasks of MINUSTAH.

The Mission has been beset by repeated controversies and challenges. Some critics view it as a hardly veiled attempt to install in power a government more favorable to the **United States**, France and Canada than the populist president Jean-Bertrand Aristide. Others underline its relative neglect of the socioeconomic problems facing Haiti, which have been compounded by the earthquake and contribute to the persistence of crime and violence. Human rights advocates have also publicized several instances of violations human rights and **gender-based violence** by MINUSTAH troops. A cholera epidemic that has killed more than 7,050 Haitians and sickened more than 531,000, or 5 percent of the population, appears to have been ignited by Nepalese UN peacekeeping troops. *See also* ELECTORAL ASSISTANCE.

UNITED NATIONS STABILIZATION MISSION IN THE DE-MOCRATIC REPUBLIC OF THE CONGO (MONUSCO, 2010–). **Peace operation** authorized by the **United Nations Security Council** (UN-SC) which took over from an earlier UN mission, the **United Nations Organization Mission in the Democratic Republic of the Congo**. The new mission can take all necessary means to protect civilians, humanitarian personnel and **human rights defenders** and to support the government in its stabilization and consolidation efforts. The MONUSCO is also mandated to monitor the implementation of an arms embargo imposed by the UN-SC in 2009. At the request of the government, the MONUSCO may also provide technical and logistical support for the organization of national and local elections. *See also* ELECTORAL ASSISTANCE.

UNITED NATIONS STANDARD MINIMUM PRISON RULES. Soft **law** instrument adopted by the **United Nations** in 1955 representing generally accepted good principles and practices for the treatment of prisoners and the management of criminal justice institutions on such matters as accommodations, education and treatment, medical services and work. More than 100 countries worldwide have relied on these standards and norms in writing their national law and policies. *See also* AMNESTY INTERNATIONAL; ARBITRARY DETENTION.

UNITED NATIONS SUB-COMMISSION ON THE PREVENTION OF DISCRIMINATION AND PROTECTION OF MINORITIES. *See* INDIGENOUS PEOPLES; UNITED NATIONS COMMISSION ON HUMAN RIGHTS; UNITED NATIONS SUB-COMMISSION ON THE PROMOTION AND PROTECTION OF HUMAN RIGHTS.

UNITED NATIONS SUB-COMMISSION ON THE PROMOTION AND PROTECTION OF HUMAN RIGHTS. Known until 1999 as the

Sub-Commission on the Prevention of Discrimination and Protection of Minorities, the research and analysis activities into new and contentious human rights issues of this subsidiary expert body of the **United Nations Commission on Human Rights** have contributed significantly to expanding our understanding of human rights. Its creation was suggested by the Soviet Union in a move intended to counter a U.S. proposal for the establishment of a subcommission on freedom of information and the press. The Sub-Commission eventually came together in 1947 tasked with the responsibility to undertake studies and make recommendations to the Commission concerning the prevention of discrimination of any kind relating to human rights and fundamental freedoms and the protection of racial, national, religious and linguistic minorities.

In spite of its inauspicious **Cold War** beginnings and notwithstanding the deep divisions of governments over minority rights, the Sub-Commission played a key role in the inclusion of a provision on minority rights in the **International Covenant on Civil and Political Rights** (Art. 27) and the development of the 1977 **Declaration on the Rights of Persons Belonging to National or Ethnic, Religious and Linguistic Minorities**. In 1971, it also sponsored a landmark study on the protection of minorities. The Sub-Commission was active for a while in the development of the 1235 and **1503 Procedures**, but the main focus of its work, with the assistance of "working groups," was on a range of human rights concerns expanding well beyond the subject of minorities: the human rights aspects of the administration of justice, **public emergencies**, criminal justice systems, military tribunals, incarcerated women, **gender-based violence**, extreme **poverty**, **transnational corporations**, **housing** and **forced eviction**, the rights of non-citizens, contemporary forms of **slavery** and **terrorism** and **counterterrorism**. The relations of the independent-minded Sub-Commission and the politically driven Commission were always tense if not contentious, and there was no dearth of proposals to change its relationship with its parent body, ranging from placing it on an equal footing with the Commission to abolishing it to changing its name. It was eventually replaced by the **United Nations Human Rights Council Advisory Committee** in 2006 under the authority of the **United Nations Human Rights Council**.

See also AGREEMENT ON TRADE-RELATED ASPECTS OF INTELLECTUAL PROPERTY RIGHTS; COBO, JOSE MARTINEZ; CULTURAL RIGHTS; DRAFT DECLARATION ON PRINCIPLES OF HUMAN RIGHTS AND THE ENVIRONMENT; DRAFT NORMS ON THE RESPONSIBILITIES OF TRANSNATIONAL CORPORATIONS AND OTHER BUSINESS ENTERPRISES WITH REGARD TO HUMAN RIGHTS; SET OF PRINCIPLES FOR THE PROTECTION AND

PROMOTION OF HUMAN RIGHTS THROUGH ACTION TO COMBAT IMPUNITY; SOCIAL FORUM; UNITED NATIONS WORKING GROUP ON MINORITIES; UNITED NATIONS WORKING GROUP ON THE RIGHTS OF INDIGENOUS PEOPLES; UNREPRESENTED NATIONS AND PEOPLES ORGANIZATION.

UNITED NATIONS TRANSITION ASSISTANCE GROUP (UNTAG, 1989–1990). One of the first **United Nations peace operations** designed to assist in the political process leading to the independence of South West Africa as Namibia. The role of UNTAG was to supervise free and fair elections, the disarmament of the insurgents and the withdrawal of the South African troops, the repeal of discriminatory laws, the release of political prisoners, the return of **refugees** and the maintenance of law and order. *See also* ELECTORAL ASSISTANCE.

UNITED NATIONS TRANSITIONAL ADMINISTRATION IN EAST TIMOR (UNTAET, 2000–2002). Integrated, multi-dimensional peace operation established by the **United Nations Security Council** which was responsible for the administration of East Timor during its transition to independence as **Timor-Leste**. Its mandate was to provide security and maintain law and order throughout the territory of East Timor; to establish an effective administration; to assist in the development of civil and social services; to ensure the coordination and delivery of humanitarian assistance, rehabilitation of humanitarian assistance and development assistance; to support **capacity building** for self-government; and to assist in the establishment of conditions for sustainable development. UNTAET was also tasked to develop a functioning judicial and legal system and, in that context, established a **Special Panel of the Dili District Court** to serve as a de facto international tribunal to prosecute Indonesian and pro-Indonesian East Timorese persons responsible for the mass killings in 1999 and other serious **violations of human rights**.

UNITED NATIONS TRANSITIONAL AUTHORITY IN CAMBODIA (UNTAC, 1992–1993). Peace operation set up by the **United Nations Security Council** to ensure implementation of the October 1991 Paris Agreements which brought to an end decades of civil strife and foreign interventions in Cambodia. For the first time ever, the United Nations took over the administration of an independent state to supervise the ceasefire and to "kick start" the rehabilitation of the country. Its mandate was to oversee military security and maintain law and order, restore peace and civil government and organize and conduct elections, repatriate and resettle **refugees** and **internally displaced persons**, assist in landmine clearance, rehabilitate essential infrastructure and assist in economic reconstruction and development. The human rights component of the mission focused on encouraging the country to ratify relevant international human rights instruments, conducting **human rights education** campaigns and investigating allegations of human rights abuses. The elections held in May 1993 were deemed free and fair by the United Nations. UNTAC was subsequently withdrawn in the fall after the proclamation of a new constitution. *See also* DEMOCRATIC KAMPUCHEA; ELECTORAL ASSISTANCE; INVESTIGATION.

UNITED NATIONS TREATY BODIES. Committees of independent experts set up by a human rights **treaty** also known as "treaty-monitoring bodies" because they are tasked with overseeing and following up on the implementation of the human rights obligations of the states parties to that treaty. There are now 10 human rights treaty bodies: the **United Nations Human Rights Committee** which monitors the implementation of the **International Covenant on Civil and Political Rights** and its optional protocols; the **United Nations Committee on Economic, Social and Cultural Rights** which monitors implementation of the **International Covenant on Economic, Social and Cultural Rights**; the **United Nations Committee on the Elimination of All Forms of Racial Discrimination** which monitors the implementation of the **International Convention on the Elimination of All Forms of Racial Discrimination**; the **United Nations Committee on the Elimination of All Forms of Discrimination against Women**, which monitors the implementation of the **United Nations Convention on the Elimination of All Forms of Discrimination against Women**; the **United Nations Committee against Torture**, which monitors the implementation of the **United Nations Convention against Torture and Other Cruel, Inhuman or Degrading Treatment and Punishment**; the **United Nations Committee on the Rights of the Child**, which monitors implementation of the Convention on the Rights of the Child and its optional protocols; and the United Nations Committee on Migrant Workers, which monitors the implementation of the **International Convention on the Protection of the Rights of All Migrant Workers and Members of Their Families**; the Committee on Enforced Disappearances, which monitors the **International Convention for the Protection of All Persons from Enforced Disappearance**; and the Committee on the Rights of Disabled Persons, which monitors the **United Nations Convention on the Rights of Persons with Disabilities**. The functions of treaty bodies include the consideration of state parties' periodic reports, the review and disposition of individual **complaints** or **communications** and the publication of **General Comments** on the states' practice of their constituting treaties. *See also* AMICUS CURIAE; INTERIM MEASURES; MONITORING OF HUMAN RIGHTS; STATE REPORTING.

UNITED NATIONS TRUSTEESHIP SYSTEM. Arrangements called for by the **United Nations Charter** which replaced the **League of Nations' Mandates** system. Its purpose was to promote the welfare of native inhabitants and to advance them toward self-government or independence. Its operation was supervised by a Trusteeship Council, which reviewed annual reports from the administering powers, considered petitions from inhabitants of the territories and made periodic inspection tours. All the former mandates of the League (with the exception of South West Africa) were placed under the Trusteeship system and became independent or self-governing by the mid-1970s. The Trusteeship Council is currently inactive and there have been proposals to either abolish it or to turn it into an institution concerned with the protection of the **environment**. *See also* SELF-DETERMINATION.

UNITED NATIONS VERIFICATION MISSION IN GUATEMALA (MINUGUA, 1994–2004). Civilian, humanitarian and military mission of the **United Nations** established in the wake of an agreement between the government and leftist guerrillas which brought to an end the country's 30-year civil war. The mission was initially launched by the **United Nations General Assembly** (UN-GA) which authorized the deployment of more than 250 experts in human rights, legal matters, indigenous affairs and policing with a mandate for institution and confidence building and to verify compliance with the terms of the agreement. MINUGUA was strengthened by the dispatch of 145 peacekeepers by the **United Nations Security Council** in 1997. In its final report, the head of the Mission cited the persistence of problems with the criminal justice system, continued racism against the country's indigenous peoples majority, **corruption** and **poverty** and social inequalities. Following the departure of MINUGUA in 2004, the government agreed to the establishment of a field office of the **United Nations Office of the High Commissioner for Human Rights**. In its own reports to the UN-GA, the High Commissioner has repeatedly warned about "long-standing gaps" in the enjoyment of human rights such as high levels of insecurity, **impunity**, discrimination and **gender-based violence** in **indigenous populations**.

UNITED NATIONS WORKING GROUP ON ARBITRARY DETENTION. One of the United Nations **"special procedures"** created to monitor **violations of human rights** and currently under the purview of the **United Nations Human Rights Council** (UN-HRC), this UN body of independent experts was set up in 1991 by the former **United Nations Commission on Human Rights** to **investigate** under its purview (now under the purview of its successor body, the UN-HRC) allegations of **arbitrary detention** which may be in violation of **international human rights law**. Toward that end, the Working Group may seek and receive information from government and intergovernmental and **non-governmental organizations** and from the individuals concerned, their families or their representatives. It may also conduct **fact-finding** country visits (upon the invitation of the government), receive individual **complaints** and send urgent appeals to governments to ascertain the whereabouts and condition of those allegedly detained and issue "deliberations" or comments on pertinent questions of principles arising from its consideration of individual cases submitted to it. Each year, the Working Group submits a report on its activities to the UN-HRC in which it expresses its observations on the different institutions, (legal) insufficiencies, policies, and judicial practices which, in its opinion, are the cause for arbitrary deprivation of liberty. The opinions adopted by the Working Group on individual cases and summaries of its field visits are annexed to its annual report. The Working Group has carried out fact-finding missions **Argentina**, Australia, Bahrain, Belarus, Bhutan, Canada, China, Ecuador, Great Britain, **Honduras**, **Indonesia**, **Iran**, Latvia, Mexico, Nepal, Nicaragua, **Peru**, Romania, South Africa, and Vietnam. Between 1991 and the end of 1997, the Working Group had declared the detention of 1,331 persons to be arbitrary and the detention of 19 others to be not arbitrary; it decided to file 335 cases, with the detainees having been freed by the time the Working Group considered their case. In 2010, the Working Group issued 33 opinions, covering detentions in 23 countries concerning 98 people; it also sent 102 urgent appeals to 56 countries, covering questions about 2,826 individuals, of whom 23 were released from detention. *See also* LIBERTY, RIGHT TO.

UNITED NATIONS WORKING GROUP ON MINORITIES. From its inception in 1995 when it was established by the **United Nations Economic and Social Council** until its dissolution in 2007 and replacement by a **Forum on Minority Issues**, the Working Group on Minorities was the only arena where minority representatives could engage formally or informally in a political dialogue with states. In the course of the 12 sessions that it held during its existence, this subsidiary body of the **United Nations Sub-Commission on the Promotion and Protection of Human Rights** has contributed to a greater awareness of the differing perspectives on minority issues. It has also produced a wealth of information on the conceptualization of the rights of persons belonging to **minorities** and good practices and other measures for the promotion and protection of minorities on a wide range of topics such as multicultural and intercultural education, recognition of the existence of minorities, their participation in public life and inclusive development, and conflict prevention.

UNITED NATIONS WORKING GROUP ON THE PROTECTION OF ALL PERSONS FROM ENFORCED DISAPPEARANCES. Independent group of experts established in 1980 by the **United Nations Commission on Human Rights** to assist families in determining the fate and whereabouts of disappeared relatives. For this purpose, the Working Group receives and examines reports on **forced disappearances** submitted by relatives of missing persons or human rights organizations acting on their behalf. It meets in private meetings but regularly invites representatives of governments, **non-governmental organizations**, family members and witnesses. After ascertaining the admissibility of these reports, the Working Group transmits the cases to the government concerned, requesting it to carry out **investigations** and to inform the Working Group of the results. It remains seized of the cases until they are resolved. The Working Group's mandate is purely humanitarian as it functions essentially as a channel of communication between the families of missing persons and the governments concerned. The Working Group may also act on the basis of an urgent action procedure under which the chairperson is authorized to act on reported cases of disappearances which occurred between the group sessions (the Working Group meets three times a year).

Since the adoption in 1992 of the **United Nations' Declaration on the Protection of All Persons from Enforced Disappearance**, the Working Group has also been monitoring states' compliance with the Declaration. To date, the Working Group has dealt with over 50,000 cases which arose in some 90 countries. This function will devolve to the **United Nations treaty body** monitoring the International Convention for the Protection of All Persons from Enforced Disappearance when the Convention enters into force. *See also* SPECIAL PROCEDURES.

UNITED NATIONS WORKING GROUP ON THE RIGHTS OF INDIGENOUS PEOPLES. Subsidiary expert body of the United Nations Sub-Commission on the Prevention of Discrimination and Protection of Minorities set up by the **United Nations Economic and Social Council** in 1982. Assigned to review developments pertaining to the promotion and protection of human rights and fundamental freedoms of **indigenous peoples**, the Working Group focused its work on the elaboration of the draft of a

United Nations' Declaration on the Rights of Indigenous Peoples. *See also* DAES, ERICA-IRENE.

UNITED STATES. Drawing from its revolutionary experience, national experience of limited government and domestic culture of adversarial two-party politics, the United States has been for a long time a prime mover in the promotion of respect for human rights and the **rule of law**. The references to human rights in the **United Nations Charter** were American-inspired and the United States played a key role in the elaboration and adoption of the **Universal Declaration of Human Rights**. As reflected in the Country Reports on Human Rights Practices published annually by the U.S. Department of State, the United States places particular emphasis on the "integrity of the person" (i.e., individual civil and political rights rather than economic, social and cultural rights or **solidarity rights**). In international fora such as the **United Nations Human Rights Council** and its predecessor body the **United Nations Commission on Human Rights**, U.S. government representatives tend to advance both country-specific resolutions which cite states that abuse human rights by name and thematic resolutions highlighting **"first-generation"** standards, ideals and objectives.

Critics point to the "exceptionalism" underlying these public positions, drawing attention in particular to the fact that the United States does not support human rights treaties if they interfere with U.S. **state sovereignty**, alter the balance between the states and the federal government and are deemed either inconsistent with the U.S. Constitution or inimical to the values of free enterprise. In addition, the handful of human rights **treaties** that have been ratified by the U.S. Senate contain **reservations** highlighting that they are not self-executing or create a basis for **litigation** by individuals in domestic courts. Since the terrorist attacks on U.S. soil of 11 September 2001, the country has been operating within the framework of what is variously described as "crisis government," a "state of exception" or a "constitutional dictatorship," which has been accompanied by the adoption of legislative and administrative measures circumscribing individual rights and freedoms and resorting to practices such as indefinite detention, **torture, extraordinary rendition**, long considered to be prohibited under any circumstances under **international customary law**. At the same time, throughout the **Cold War**, strategic concerns prevailed over human rights considerations, leading successive administrations to lend their political, diplomatic and military support to military or dictatorial regimes in Latin America and Africa which committed grievous **violations of human rights**.

See *also* ABU GHRAIB PRISON; ACT OF STATE DOCTRINE; AFGHANISTAN; ALIEN TORT STATUTE; AMERICAN CIVIL

LIBERTIES UNION; ANGOLA; APOLOGIES; BANGLADESH LIBERATION WAR; BASIC PRINCIPLES AND GUIDELINES ON THE RIGHT TO A REMEDY AND REPARATION FOR VICTIMS OF GROSS VIOLATIONS OF INTERNATIONAL HUMAN RIGHTS LAW AND SERIOUS VIOLATIONS OF INTERNATIONAL HUMANITARIAN LAW; BIAFRA; BILL OF RIGHTS, UNITED STATES; BOAT PEOPLES; CARTER, JIMMY; CENTRAL INTELLIGENCE AGENCY; CONVENTION ON THE PROTECTION AND PROMOTION OF THE DIVERSITY OF CULTURAL EXPRESSION; COUNCIL ON FOREIGN RELATIONS; COUNTERTERRORISM; CUBA; DECLARATION OF INDEPENDENCE; DEPORTATION; DRONES; EMANCIPATION PROCLAMATION; GUANTANAMO BAY DETENTION CAMP; GUATEMALA; *HAMDI ET AL. v. RUMSFELD, SECRETARY OF DEFENSE, ET AL.*; HATE SPEECH; HUSSEIN, SADDAM; INDONESIA; INTERNATIONAL CONVENTION ON THE ELIMINATION OF ALL FORMS OF RACIAL DISCRIMINATION; INTERNATIONAL COVENANT ON CIVIL AND POLITICAL RIGHTS; INTERNATIONAL MILITARY TRIBUNAL FOR THE FAR EAST; INTERNATIONAL MILITARY TRIBUNAL FOR THE PROSECUTION AND PUNISHMENT OF THE MAJOR WAR CRIMINALS OF THE EUROPEAN AXIS; INTERNATIONAL PLANNED PARENTHOOD FEDERATION; KING, MARTIN LUTHER, JR.; KISSINGER, HENRY; KOREMATSU, FRED TOYOSABURO; LEAGUE OF NATIONS; LEMAY, CURTIS; LIBERIA; LUMUMBA, PATRICE; MARCOS, FERDINAND; MONITORING OF HUMAN RIGHTS; MYRDAL, KARL GUNNAR; NATIONAL ENDOWMENT FOR DEMOCRACY; NATIVE AMERICANS; NO-FLY ZONE; ORGANIZATION OF AMERICAN STATES; PHILIPPINE-AMERICAN WAR; PUBLIC EMERGENCIES; RAND CORPORATION; REPARATIONS;RESTITUTION;ROOSEVELT,ELEANOR;RUMSFELD, DONALD; RUSSELL-SARTRE TRIBUNAL; SEX TRAFFICKING; SLAVERY; SUHARTO; SUPREME IRAQI CRIMINAL TRIBUNAL; TERRORISM; THINK TANKS; UNITED NATIONS OPERATION IN SOMALIA; UNITED NATIONS RELIEF AND WORKS AGENCY FOR PALESTINE REFUGEES IN THE NEAR EAST; UNITED NATIONS SUB-COMMISSION ON THE PROMOTION AND PROTECTION OF HUMAN RIGHTS; UNIVERSAL JURISDICTION; URUGUAY; VIETNAM WAR; "WAR ON TERROR"; WILSON, WOODROW; WORLD CONFERENCE AGAINST RACISM; WORLD WAR I PEACE TREATIES.

UNITED STATES INSTITUTE OF PEACE (USIP). Established by an act of the U.S. Congress in 1984 as an independent, non-partisan, federal institution, the stated mission of this Washington, D.C.-based **think tank** is "to prevent and resolve violent international conflicts, promote post-conflict stability and democratic transformations, and to increase peace building capacity, tools, and intellectual capital worldwide." Its activities include projects promoting the **rule of law**, strengthening **civil society** and state building.

UNIVERSAL DECLARATION OF HUMAN RESPONSIBILITIES (1997). The idea of human responsibilities is a corollary and counterbalance to the philosophical idea of human rights. It refers in essence to the universal duties and tasks of individuals regardless of jurisdiction, ethnicity, nationality, religion or gender. Perhaps the most well-known scheme of universal responsibilities that has been proposed (within the framework of the **United Nations Educational, Scientific and Cultural Organization**) is that of the InterAction Council, an international council of former heads of state which has been working on the matter since 1987. In the group's view, "If one person or government seeks to maximize freedom but does it at the expense of others, a larger number of people will suffer. If human beings maximize their freedom by plundering the natural resources of the earth, then future generations will suffer." To complement the **Universal Declaration of Human Rights** with a Human Rights Declaration of Responsibilities would, in the group's view, bring freedom and responsibility into balance and contribute to reconciling antagonistic political views. *See also* DECLARATION OF HUMAN DUTIES AND RESPONSIBILITIES.

UNIVERSAL DECLARATION OF HUMAN RIGHTS (UDHR). Path-breaking resolution adopted by the **United Nations General Assembly** in 1948 after two years of intense negotiations in the **United Nations Commission on Human Rights**. As envisaged by its drafters, the Declaration was to reflect "recognition of the inherent **dignity** and . . . equal and inalienable rights of all members of the human family" and through that recognition provide "the foundation of freedom, justice and peace in the world." Short, inspirational and energizing, the Declaration opens with the ringing statement that "All human beings are born free and equal in dignity and rights. They are endowed with reason and conscience and should act towards one another in a spirit of brotherhood." It subsequently lists rights which today would be thought as **second-generation** as well as **first-generation rights** (17 of the 30 articles of the Declaration can be regarded as relating, respectively, to civil and political rights and eight to economic and social rights).

But the Declaration does not make the distinction nor does it rank them in order of importance, thus underlining their **indivisibility**. In this regard,

Article 3, which gives every human being the right to **life**, liberty, and security of person, and Article 27, which establishes a right to an **adequate standard of living**, are probably the core of the substantive provisions in the Declaration. The Declaration, however, makes no reference to the so-called **third-generation rights** and is silent on the **environment** (although environmental rights may be implied from rights such as the right to life and to an adequate standard of living). Article 28, which emphasizes the responsibility of the whole international community for seeking and putting into place arrangements of both a civil and political as well as an economic and social kind that allow for the full realization of human rights, has received only scant attention and has not been given legally binding force in the two Covenants.

Until 1976, when the **International Covenant on Civil and Political Rights** and the **International Covenant on Economic, Social and Cultural Rights** codified into law its provisions, the Declaration was the sole quasi-legal international standard of achievement for human rights. Today the Universal Declaration, along with the Covenants, make up the International Bill of Rights. The Declaration is, strictly speaking, only a **soft law** instrument. Reaching agreement on it was strenuous and initially triggered overt political resistance (six Soviet bloc countries, South Africa and **Saudi Arabia** abstained when it was put to a vote). Nevertheless, the Declaration has achieved international stature and progressively evolved into an influential statement of human rights standards which even its architects— **Eleanor Roosevelt, Charles Malik, Rene Cassin**, John Humphrey and **P. C. Chang**—might not have expected.

The UDHR is widely viewed as a virtual extension of the **United Nations Charter**, and nearly all international human rights instruments adopted subsequently by the **United Nations** or regional organizations elaborated or built upon the principles it laid down. The UDHR has informed national constitutions and international treaties, establishing international organizations such as the **Council of Europe** and the Organization of African Unity. Virtually all of the provisions of the UDHR have become a part of **international customary law** as national and international courts invoke them as a basis for their rulings. *See also* DECLARATION OF INDEPENDENCE; DECLARATION OF THE RIGHTS OF MAN AND THE CITIZEN.

UNIVERSAL DECLARATION ON BIOETHICS AND HUMAN RIGHTS (2005). Non-binding instrument negotiated under the auspices of the **United Nations Educational, Scientific and Cultural Organization** seeking to promote the establishment of universal ethical principles for the development and application of scientific and technological advances affecting men and women. Its core principle is that "human **dignity**, human rights and fundamental freedoms are to be fully respected." Specific provisions deal with the notions of prior informed consent, confidentiality, non-**discrimination**, international cooperation, respect for cultural diversity and pluralism, the protection of future generations, the **environment**, the biosphere and biodiversity, and benefit sharing.

See also BIOETHICS; EUROPEAN CONVENTION ON HUMAN RIGHTS AND BIOMEDICINE; HEALTH, RIGHT TO; LIFE, RIGHT TO; UNITED NATIONS DECLARATION ON HUMAN CLONING; UNIVERSAL DEC-LARATION ON THE HUMAN GENOME AND HUMAN RIGHTS.

UNIVERSAL DECLARATION ON THE ERADICATION OF HUNGER AND MALNUTRITION. Broad policy statement adopted by the 1974 World Food Conference convened by the **United Nations General Assembly** to develop policy responses to the world food problems which had particularly affected the Sahelian region. One of the outcomes of the conference was this declaration, which proclaims the inalienability of the right of every individual to be free from hunger and malnutrition in order to develop fully and maintain their physical and mental faculties and calls upon governments to work together for higher **food** production and a more equitable and efficient distribution of food between countries and within countries. *See also* FOOD SECURITY; SOFT LAW.

UNIVERSAL DECLARATION ON THE HUMAN GENOME AND HUMAN RIGHTS (1997). Adopted under the aegis of the **United Nations Educational, Scientific and Cultural Organization**, this **soft law** instrument seeks to ensure that human rights are fully respected in the application of scientific and technological advances, particularly those which relate to the human genome. Prior-informed consent, confidentiality of data, **reparation**, protection of public **health**, benefit sharing, freedom of research, and international cooperation are the key principles which should guide public policies. The Declaration also asserts that genetic discrimination should be prohibited, along with any "practices which are contrary to human **dignity**, such as reproductive cloning of human beings" and that states ensure that technologies are not used for non-peaceful purposes. *See also* BIOETHICS; EUROPEAN CONVENTION ON HUMAN RIGHTS AND BIOMEDICINE; LIFE, RIGHT TO; UNIVERSAL DECLARATION ON BIOETHICS AND HUMAN RIGHTS.

UNIVERSAL HUMAN RIGHTS NETWORK. Washington, D.C.-based group which maintains a resource data base of practitioners, policymakers and academics who are recruited in civilian peacekeeping missions and share the conviction that they must uphold the principles of the **Universal Declaration of Human Rights**.

UNIVERSAL JURISDICTION. Legal doctrine allowing national courts to try cases over persons whose alleged crimes were committed outside the boundaries of the prosecuting state regardless of nationality and country of residence. The reasoning is that the crimes committed are considered threats against all states and can therefore be prosecuted by any state. The concept is not new as it was used throughout the 19th century in regard to the punishment of piracy and slavery. But since the Augusto Pinochet case, governments have shown an increased willingness to use the principle against individuals, including former high-ranking government officials suspected of having committed genocide, crimes against humanity, extra-judicial executions, war crimes, torture and forced disappearances. More than a dozen states including Australia, Austria, Belgium, Canada, Denmark, France, Germany, Great Britain, **Israel**, Mexico, the Netherlands, Senegal, Spain, Switzerland and the **United States**, have conducted **investigations**, initiated prosecutions or completed trials on the basis of universal jurisdiction.

The doctrine, however, remains controversial. Some argue that it provides the legal basis for states to give effect to their moral duty to take action against gross **violations of human rights**. Others maintain that it is a breach in the principle of **state sovereignty**. The establishment of the **ad hoc international courts** and the **International Criminal Court** softened the edge of this doctrinal and political debate. In addition, the **United Nations Convention against Torture** and the Inter-American Convention of Human Rights require their state parties to prosecute or extradite individuals suspected of torture. It is also widely recognized under **customary international law** that even states that are not parties to these **treaties** may exercise universal jurisdiction over cases of torture. In an April 2006 resolution, the **United Nations Security Council** reaffirmed "the provisions of paragraphs 138 and 139 of the 2005 World Summit Outcome Document regarding the **responsibility to protect** populations from genocide, war crimes, ethnic cleansing and crimes against humanity."

See also CENTER FOR CONSTITUTIONAL RIGHTS; CENTER FOR JUSTICE AND ACCOUNTABILITY; EICHMANN, ADOLF; GARZON, BALTHAZAR; GENEVA CONVENTIONS; HABRE, HISSENE; HOSTAGES; INTERNATIONAL CRIMES; *JUS COGENS*; KISSINGER, HENRY; PEREMPTORY NORMS; WORLD FEDERALIST MOVEMENT.

UNIVERSAL PERIODIC REVIEW (UPR). Procedure established by the **United Nations Human Rights Council** (UN-HRC) in 2007 to review and assess the extent to which members of the organization meet their human rights obligations as set out in the **United Nations Charter**, the **Universal Declaration of Human Rights**, human rights instruments to which the state is party, voluntary pledges and commitments made by the state and applicable **international humanitarian law**. The review is based on information provided by the state under review, independent human rights experts and groups, **United Nations treaty bodies, non-governmental organizations** and **national human rights institutions**. The UPR is designed to ensure equal treatment for every country when its human rights situation is assessed. Its stated ultimate aim is to improve the human rights situation in all countries and address violations of human rights.

While the UPR procedure is unique and unprecedented, it has built-in limitations which became apparent when implementation started in 2008. First, member states of the **United Nations** are scrutinized once in a four-year cycle. Thus 48 states come under review each year, which means in practice that the Council only devotes a few hours every four years to its evaluation of a state's human rights record. Also, the UPR remains state driven and controlled. The "interactive discussions" between the state under review and other UN member states have been tame, bland, or formal and have generally shunned controversial subjects. The result of each review is an "outcome report" containing a summary of "interactive dialogue," responses by the state under review and recommendations by states which the state under review may accept or reject. Presumably, the following round of reviews will determine whether states have duly complied. What happens during the intervening interim four years, however, is unclear. Equally uncertain is when, how and to what extent the UN-HRC might be willing to address cases of persistent non-cooperation with the UPR mechanism. In this regard, all members of the United Nations have so far been willing to come under the UPR. In this respect, **Israel** has recently flagged its unwillingness to participate in the second UPR cycle.

UNIVERSALITY OF RIGHTS. Notion suggesting that all members of humanity without exception as to race, religion, class, gender, group, beliefs, convictions or any other distinction enjoy the same rights. All members of the human family are endowed with the same rights precisely because they are human. A corollary of this idea is that all people should be treated equally and should be able to enjoy the same rights as anyone else. So defined, the universality of rights is taken as an axiomatic and "self-evident truth" by human rights advocates. But it has come under attack by proponents of the doctrine of "**cultural relativism**," leading some observers to argue instead for the "relative universality" of internationally recognized human rights. *See also* INDIVISIBILITY; WORLD CONFERENCE ON HUMAN RIGHTS.

UNREPRESENTED NATIONS AND PEOPLES ORGANIZATION (UNPO). Created in 1991, this **non-governmental organization** is based in The Hague and seeks to promote the rights of **indigenous peoples** and **minorities** by assisting them in their efforts to participate in international meetings through training programs, briefings and the provision of technical and **advisory services.** UNPO, in particular, assists its members in presenting their cases to **United Nations** bodies such as the **United Nations Human Rights Council**, the United Nations Sub-Commission on the Prevention of Discrimination and Protection of Minorities and the **United Nations Permanent Forum on Indigenous Issues.**

URUGUAY. Now a constitutional republic with an elected president, a bicameral legislature and a multiparty system, this Latin American country had to deal with leftist guerrilla movements in the 1960s which led to the proclamation of a state of emergency in 1968, the suspension of civil liberties in 1972 by President Juan Maria Bordaberry and the taking over of power by the military from 1973 to 1985. Around 180 Uruguayan nationals are known to have been killed during that period either in the country itself or in neighboring countries (a large number of them were never found). Cases of **torture** committed by security forces trained in policing and interrogation techniques by U.S. operatives have also been documented. Progress in prosecuting and punishing those responsible for serious human rights abuses has been slowed by a 1986 **amnesty** law. Presidential initiatives classifying abuses committed by the military and police forces as **crimes against humanity** and rulings by the **Inter-American Court of Human Rights** have made it possible to circumvent the amnesty law, to initiate new **investigations** and to hold a number of senior military and police officials accountable on charges of homicide, **forced disappearances** and torture. *See also* TRUTH AND RECONCILIATION COMMISSIONS.

USE OF FORCE. *See* AGGRESSION; DECLARATION ON PRINCIPLES OF INTERNATIONAL LAW CONCERNING FRIENDLY RELATIONS AND COOPERATION AMONG STATES; DEMOCRACY; HUMANITARIAN INTERVENTION; *JUS AD BELLUM/JUS IN BELLO*; JUST WAR; KELLOG-BRIAND PACT; NO-FLY ZONE; PEACE OPERATIONS; REGIONAL ARRANGEMENTS; SANCTIONS; UNITED NATIONS CHARTER; UNITED NATIONS SECURITY COUNCIL.

V

VAN BOVEN, THEO (1934–). Dutch jurist and professor of law. He led the United Nations Secretariat Division for Human Rights for many years and subsequently served as United Nations **special rapporteur** on the right to reparation to victims of gross violations of human rights (1986–91) and special rapporteur on **torture** (2001–04). He was a main progenitor of the **Basic Principles and Guidelines on the Right to a Remedy and Reparation for Victims of Gross Violations of International Human Rights Law and Serious Violations of International Humanitarian Law**.

VASAK, KAREL. Czech-born French jurist and international official. He worked for the **Council of Europe**, the **United Nations Educational, Scientific and Cultural Organization** and the World Tourism Organization and was the first secretary-general of the Strasbourg-based International Institute of Human Rights founded by **Rene Cassin**. Inspired by the three themes of the French Revolution (liberty, equality, fraternity), Vasak is credited with having coined the simplified but useful idea of "**generation of rights**" as a template for organizing our understanding of human rights.

VIDELA, JORGE RAFAEL (1925–). Leader of a military junta which overthrew President Isabel Peron in 1976 for the stated purpose of putting an end to the violent and bloody attacks, kidnappings, **torture** and assassinations that pitted Marxist groups against right-wing paramilitary groups since the death of President Juan Peron in 1974. Videla was the effective president of Argentina until 1981 when he relinquished power. Under his rule, civil liberties were suspended, the judiciary was abolished and labor unions and strikes were banned. The Argentine military was given full power to arrest, detain and eliminate all terrorists and political opponents and an estimated 9,000 to 30,000 people are believed to have been subject to **forced disappearances**, detention and torture.

With the restoration of democracy in 1983, Videla was tried and found guilty of numerous killings, torture and other **violations of human rights** and sentenced to life imprisonment. In 1990, after serving five years of his sentence, he was pardoned, together with several former members of the military regime, by President Carlos Menem. In 2006, the pardon granted by President Menem was ruled unconstitutional, thus opening the possibility of further judicial actions against Videla. On 22 December 2010, Videla was found responsible for the deaths of 31 prisoners following the military coup and sentenced to life in prison. Two years later, he was convicted of systematic kidnapping of children during his tenure and sentenced to 50 years in prison. *See also* AMNESTIES; "DIRTY WAR"; OPERATION CONDOR; PINOCHET, AUGUSTO; STROESSNER, ALFREDO.

VIENNA CONVENTION ON THE LAW OF TREATIES (1980). Negotiated under the aegis of the **International Law Commission** of the **United Nations**, this treaty in essence is a restatement of **international customary law** and codifies state practice in regard to the making and effects of **treaties**. The principal matters covered in the Convention are conclusion and entry into force of treaties, including **reservations** and provisional application of treaties; observance, application and interpretation of treaties, including treaties and third states; amendment and modification of treaties; invalidity, termination and suspension of the operation of treaties; and the consequences of the invalidity, termination or suspension of the operation of a treaty.

VIETNAM WAR (1946–1975). Long-winding and bloody conflict which began as a colonial insurgency against France (1946–54) and subsequently morphed into a **Cold War** issue involving the **United States**. Conservative estimates reckon that 4 million Vietnamese on all sides were killed, wounded or missing during the period 1965–75 alone. This translates into one of 30 Indochinese killed, one of 12 wounded and one of five made a **refugee**. There were numerous cases of **massacres**, atrocities and **torture** committed by all sides in the conflict. Between 1961 and 1967, the U.S. air force sprayed 12 million gallons of concentrated herbicides affecting an estimated 13 percent of South Vietnam's land and impacting succeeding generations. Suits filed against the United States and several chemical companies were rejected by U.S. federal courts in 2007 on the grounds that "Agent Orange and similar U.S. herbicides cannot be considered poisons banned under international rules of war" and that the lack of large-scale research made it impossible to show what caused the illnesses. *See also* BOAT PEOPLES; ECOCIDE; ENVIRONMENT, RIGHT TO A HEALTHY; KISSINGER, HENRY; MY LAI MASSACRE; RUSSELL-SARTRE TRIBUNAL.

VIEWS. Terminology used by the United Nations Committee on Civil and Political Rights and the **United Nations Committee on the Elimination of**

All Forms of Discrimination against Women to refer to their findings on the merits of individual **complaints**. *See also* DECISIONS; OPINIONS.

VIOLATION OF HUMAN RIGHTS. Human rights instruments—national, regional or international—create entitlements, and the beneficiaries of these entitlements are individuals or groups of individuals. As human rights are enforceable toward the **state**, it follows that the fulfillment of state obligations arising from national constitutional arrangements or international **treaties** lies with states and their agents. Doctrine, practice and jurisprudence acknowledge that human rights guarantees entail three types of negative and positive obligations on the part of government: an obligation to respect, through lack of state interference in the enjoyment of rights; an obligation to protect from threats emanating from breaches by state agents, agents of third states or private actors; and an obligation to fulfill (i.e., to ensure that human rights are realized in practice as comprehensively as possible).

As a rule of thumb, a human rights violation may be said to occur whenever states fail, by omission or commission, to meet any of these obligations. Violations thus occur when a law, policy or practice removes existing human rights protections or contravenes, transgresses or ignores obligations attributable to state authorities. They may also occur when governments fail to achieve a required standard of conduct or result. This is particularly relevant to the progressive realization of so-called **second-generation rights** which requires states to satisfy "minimum essential levels" of economic, social and cultural rights irrespective of the availability of resources.

See also BASIC PRINCIPLES AND GUIDELINES ON THE RIGHT TO A REMEDY AND REPARATION FOR VICTIMS OF GROSS VIOLATIONS OF INTERNATIONAL HUMAN RIGHTS LAW AND SERIOUS VIOLATIONS OF INTERNATIONAL HUMANITARIAN LAW; BENCHMARKING; DENIAL; DEROGATION; "DIRTY WAR"; DISCRIMINATION; DOMESTIC JURISDICTION; DRAFT ARTICLES ON THE RESPONSIBILITY OF STATES FOR INTERNATIONALLY WRONGFUL ACTS; DUTY BEARERS; EARLY WARNING; EVENTS-BASED DATA; FACT FINDING; FAILED STATE; FEMALE GENITAL MUTILATION; GENDER DISCRIMINATION; GENDER MAINSTREAMING; HONDURAS; INDIVIDUAL RECOURSE; INQUIRY PROCEDURES; INTERNATIONAL COMMISSION ON INTERVENTION AND STATE SOVEREIGNTY; INVESTIGATION; KIMBERLEY PROCESS CERTIFICATION SCHEME; LIMBURG PRINCIPLES ON THE IMPLEMENTATION OF THE INTERNATIONAL COVENANT ON ECONOMIC, SOCIAL AND CULTURAL RIGHTS; LITIGATION; MONITORING OF HUMAN RIGHTS; NATIONAL HUMAN RIGHTS INSTITUTIONS; NO-

FLY ZONE; NON-STATE ACTORS; PREVENTION; REALIZATION OF HUMAN RIGHTS; REDRESS; REMEDY; REPARATIVE JUSTICE; RESTITUTION; RESTORATIVE JUSTICE; RETRIBUTIVE JUSTICE; RIGHTS HOLDERS; SPIRAL MODEL OF HUMAN RIGHTS CHANGE; STATE TERRORISM; STERILIZATION; TRADITIONAL PRACTICES; TRANSITIONAL JUSTICE; TRUTH, RIGHT TO THE; TRUTH AND RECONCILIATION COMMISSIONS; UNITED NATIONS OFFICE OF THE HIGH COMMISSIONER FOR HUMAN RIGHTS.

VIOLENCE AGAINST WOMEN. *See* GENDER-BASED VIOLENCE.

W

WALESA, LECH (1943–). Charismatic Polish trade union leader and human rights activist turned politician who played a key role in the demise of the communist regime in Poland. A co-founder of the Solidarity trade union movement, he successfully challenged repressive government policies (he was arrested several times, martial law was imposed and Solidarity was outlawed) and his efforts led to a 1989 agreement with the government that paved the way for semi-free elections in the same year and a Solidarity-led government. In 1990, Walesa was elected to the newly established post of president. He ran again in 1995 but narrowly lost the election. In 1993, he was awarded the **Nobel Peace Prize**.

WAR CHILD. Network of independent **non-governmental organizations** (NGOs) seeking to alleviate the suffering of children in war zones by bringing material aid, assisting in their evacuation into **refugee** camps and initiating rehabilitation programs. War Child also provides funding and logistical support to other NGOs and, in cooperation with the media and entertainment industries, promotes awareness of the problems facing **children in armed conflicts** and mobilizes public support on their behalf.

WAR CRIME TRIBUNALS. International courts of law established to try individuals accused of **war crimes** and **crimes against humanity** sponsored by an organization like the **United Nations** or a state. They are a form of **retributive justice** and as such are expected to act as a deterrent to further violations of human rights and assist in the transition from repressive regimes to stable democracy by helping members of society come to terms with past atrocities and demonstrating the usefulness of the **rule of law**.
See also INTERNATIONAL CRIMINAL COURT; INTERNATIONAL CRIMINAL TRIBUNAL FOR RWANDA; INTERNATIONAL MILITARY TRIBUNAL FOR THE FAR EAST; INTERNATIONAL CRIMINAL TRIBUNAL FOR THE FORMER YUGOSLAVIA; INTERNATIONAL MILITARY TRIBUNAL FOR THE PROSECUTION AND PUNISHMENT OF THE MAJOR WAR CRIMINALS OF THE EUROPEAN AXIS;

NEIER, ARYEH; SPECIAL COURT FOR SIERRA LEONE; SPECIAL PANELS OF THE DILI DISTRICT COURT; SPECIAL TRIBUNAL FOR CAMBODIA; SPECIAL TRIBUNAL FOR LEBANON.

WAR CRIMES. Punishable offenses under international law for violations of the laws of war by any military or civilian person. The 1949 **Geneva Conventions** (GC) are the legal basis of the conduct of warfare. They provided the basis for the listing of war crimes enumerated in the statute of the **International Criminal Court.** These include, first, grave breaches of the GC, such as willful killing or causing great suffering or serious injury to body or health, **torture** or inhuman treatment, unlawful wanton destruction or appropriation of property, forcing a prisoner of war to serve in the forces of a hostile power, depriving a prisoner of war of a fair trial, unlawful **deportation**, confinement or transfer and **hostage** taking. In situations of international armed conflicts, the following are considered war crimes: directing attacks against civilians, humanitarian workers or UN peacekeepers, killing a surrendered combatant, misusing a flag of truce, the settlement of occupied territory, deporting inhabitants of an occupied territory, using poisonous gas, using civilian shields and using **children in armed conflicts.** Murder, cruel or degrading treatment and torture, directing attacks against civilians, humanitarian workers and UN peacekeepers, hostage taking, summary executions, pillage and rape, sexual slavery, forced prostitution or forced pregnancy all constitute war crimes in situations of non-international conflicts. A 1968 UN Convention and a 1974 European Convention prohibited states from enacting **statutory limitations** on the prosecution of war crimes.

See also AL-ANFAL CAMPAIGN; ALIEN TORT STATUTE; BIOLOGICAL WEAPONS; "COMFORT WOMEN"; CROATIA, WAR OF INDEPENDENCE; DEMJANJUK, JOHN; GOLDSTONE, RICHARD; HUMAN EXPERIMENTATION; HUMAN RIGHTS WATCH; INTERNATIONAL MILITARY TRIBUNAL FOR THE FAR EAST; INTERNATIONAL MILITARY TRIBUNAL FOR THE PROSECUTION AND PUNISHMENT OF THE MAJOR WAR CRIMINALS OF THE EUROPEAN AXIS; KARADZIC, RADOVAN; LEIPZIG WAR TRIALS; LEMAY, CURTIS; MLADIC, RATKO; NUREMBERG PRINCIPLES; PHILIPPINE-AMERICAN WAR; PROPORTIONALITY; SRI LANKA CIVIL WAR; UNIVERSAL JURISDICTION; WAR CRIME TRIBUNALS.

"WAR ON TERROR." Term coined under the presidency of **George W. Bush** meant to refer to the mix of political and military policies developed by the **United States** and its allies in response to the terrorist attacks of 11 September 2001 and the military, legal and ideological threat which they perceived as emanating from Islamic **terrorism**, Islamic militants and regimes and organizations. The Barack Obama administration has discontinued use of the term, preferring instead the use of the expression "Overseas Contingency Operation." The stated objective of the "war on terror" was to protect nationals of the United States and its allies and dismantle terrorist cells in the United States and abroad, but these policies have proved to be highly contentious. Critics argue that national legislative and administrative measures enacted by governments have removed restrictions on government powers and contributed to an erosion of civil liberties and **violations of human rights** and **international humanitarian law** by allowing the use of **forced disappearances**, cruel, inhuman and degrading treatment, prolonged incommunicado detention as well as other forms of indefinite and **arbitrary detention** and acts amounting to **torture** and **extraordinary rendition** in secret prisons. They also point to the spread of a climate of **impunity** for past human rights violations and the absence of **redress** and **remedy** for victims. *See also* ARMED CONFLICT; CENTER FOR HUMAN RIGHTS AND GLOBAL JUSTICE; DRONES.

WATER, RIGHT TO. Water is a limited natural resource as well as a **public good** fundamental to **life** and **health**. In addition, according to **United Nations** data, nearly 900 million people lack access to clean water and more than 2.6 billion people lack access to basic sanitation. Yet, the right to water has only recently received international recognition in a 2010 resolution of the **United Nations General Assembly** which explicitly recognized a human right to clean drinking water and have access to sanitation. Prior to that, a right to water was firmly rooted in **international humanitarian law** and considered part of the right to an **adequate standard of living**. In 2002, the **United Nations Committee on Economic, Social and Cultural Rights** issued a non-binding **comment** affirming that access to water was a human right because water was indispensable for leading a life in human **dignity** and a prerequisite for the realization of other human rights.

The right to water is thus mentioned as such in the **United Nations Convention on the Elimination of All Forms of Discrimination against Women** (Art. 14), the **United Nations Convention on the Rights of the Child** (Art. 24) and the **United Nations Convention on the Rights of Persons with Disabilities** (Art. 28), the **African Charter on the Rights and Welfare of the Child** (Art. 14) and the **Protocol to the African Charter on Human and People's Rights on the Rights of Women in Africa** (Art. 15). In contrast, the **International Covenant on Economic, Social and Cultural Rights**, the **European Social Charter** and the American Convention on Human Rights in the Area of Economic, Social and Cultural Rights remain silent on the subject. States' obligations include a duty to take measures with a view to ensuring access to water of all individuals under their jurisdiction and to refrain from interfering with an individual's use of water in his or her territory or that of a neighboring state by polluting water resources or endangering access to water through the construction of infrastructural projects. States must also enact effective regulatory systems in order to prevent private company practices which might compromise equal, affordable and physical access to sufficient, safe and acceptable water. Human rights law jurisprudence, however, does not go as far as prohibiting the **privatization** of water infrastructure. *See also* CENTER FOR HUMAN RIGHTS AND THE ENVIRONMENT; GRASSROOTS INTERNATIONAL; OXFAM INTERNATIONAL; SOFT LAW; UNITED NATIONS CONFERENCE ON HUMAN SETTLEMENTS.

WEAPONS OF MASS DESTRUCTION (WMD). Types of weapons— **biological, chemical** and **nuclear**—which have the capacity for large-scale, indiscriminate physical and personal harm and destruction. Such concerns originally focused on inter-state conflicts but have shifted to their possible utilization by **non-state actors** in the wake of the 11 September 2001 terrorist attacks on the **United States**. The threat and possible use of WMDs by state and non-state actors have a direct bearing on the enjoyment of all human rights and in particular the right to **peace**, the right to **life** and the right to **health**. But in practice, the connection, loudly emphasized by **non-governmental organizations**, has been overlooked by governments as they have paid primary attention to the national security implications of WMDs. In 2004, the **United Nations Security Council** adopted a binding resolution mandating all UN member states to take and enforce effective measures against the proliferation of WMDs. *See also* INTERNATIONAL ASSOCIATION OF LAWYERS AGAINST NUCLEAR ARMS; INTERNATIONAL PEACE INSTITUTE.

WESTERN SAHARA. Spanish colony since the late 19th century until 1966 when Spain relinquished its control following the adoption by the **United Nations General Assembly** of a resolution calling for the organization of a referendum on **self-determination**. Morocco and Mauritania took over the territory as soon as Spain bowed out, and war ensued with the Sahrawi national liberation movement Polisario Front, which proclaimed the Sahrawi Arab Democratic Republic. A ceasefire agreement brokered by the **United Nations** brought the armed conflict to an end in 1991. But most of the territory and its rich natural resources are under Moroccan control (Mauritania gave up its claim on the territory in 1979).

Polisario is backed by Algeria and has gained membership in the **African Union**. Morocco is supported by some African states and most members of the **League of Arab States**. The presence of a UN peacekeeping force helps maintain a precarious peace, but a negotiated settlement has proved elusive as Morocco has endeavored to tilt the demographic balance in its favor through population transfers. Meanwhile, the conflict has resulted in a major humanitarian problem and has been accompanied by severe human rights **abuses**. *See also* UNITED NATIONS MISSION FOR THE REFERENDUM IN WESTERN SAHARA.

WILLIAMS, JODY (1950–). American teacher and human rights activist who received the **Nobel Peace Prize** for her campaign in support of an international treaty banning anti-personnel landmines which was eventually signed in Ottawa in 1997. She made pioneering use of fax and email to mobilize transnational political support for the treaty.

WILSON, WOODROW (1856–1924). Leading American scholar and politician scholar who served as president of Princeton University (1902–10) and governor of New Jersey (1911–13) before being elected for two terms to the presidency of the **United States** in 1912 and 1916. As president, he steered through the U.S. Congress the 1913 Revenue Act instituting a federal progressive income tax and, during his second term, a constitutional amendment establishing women's suffrage. Elected on a peace platform, he eventually prodded Congress to declare war on Germany and Austria. In a 1919 speech to the joint chambers of Congress, he outlined his views of a postwar settlement. The so-called Fourteen Points, a blend of idealistic internationalism focused on making the "world safe for democracy" and pragmatic economic and commercial interests, evolved into a broad framework for postwar peace in Europe, centering on free trade, open agreements, **democracy** and **self-determination**.

WOMEN. *See* ADVOCATES FOR HUMAN RIGHTS; ARAB CHARTER ON HUMAN RIGHTS; ASSOCIATION FOR WOMEN'S RIGHTS IN DEVELOPMENT; CAIRO DECLARATION ON HUMAN RIGHTS IN ISLAM; CARITAS INTERNATIONALIS; CENTER FOR GENDER AND REFUGEE STUDIES; DECLARATION ON THE ELIMINATION OF DISCRIMINATION AGAINST WOMEN; DECLARATION ON THE ELIMINATION OF VIOLENCE AGAINST WOMEN; DECLARATION ON THE PROTECTION OF WOMEN AND CHILDREN IN EMERGENCY AND ARMED CONFLICTS; DOMESTIC VIOLENCE; EQUALITY NOW; EURO-MEDITERRANEAN HUMAN RIGHTS NETWORK;

EUROPEAN PARLIAMENT; FEMALE GENITAL MUTILATION; FEMALE INFANTICIDE; FEMICIDE; FEMINISM; FORUM FOR FACT-FINDING DOCUMENTATION AND ADVOCACY; FOURTH WORLD CONFERENCE ON WOMEN; GENDER-BASED VIOLENCE; GENDER DEVELOPMENT INDEX; GENDER DISCRIMINATION; GENDER EMPOWERMENT MEASURE; GENDER MAINSTREAMING; GENDER-SPECIFIC CLAIM; GENDERCIDE; GLOBAL ALLIANCE AGAINST TRAFFIC IN WOMEN; GLOBAL FUND FOR WOMEN; GLOBAL JUSTICE CENTER; GLOBAL NETWORK OF WOMEN PEACE BUILDERS; GLOBAL POLICY FORUM; GLOBAL RIGHTS; GLOBAL SURVIVAL NETWORK; HONOR KILLING; HUNGER PROJECT; INFANTICIDE; INHUMAN OR DEGRADING TREATMENT OR PUNISHMENT; INTER-AFRICAN COMMITTEE ON TRADITIONAL PRACTICES AFFECTING THE HEALTH OF WOMEN; INTER-AMERICAN COMMISSION OF WOMEN; INTER-AMERICAN CONVENTION ON THE PREVENTION, PUNISHMENT AND ERADICATION OF VIOLENCE AGAINST WOMEN; INTER-AMERICAN CONVENTION ON THE PREVENTION, PUNISHMENT AND ERADICATION OF VIOLENCE AGAINST WOMEN; INTERNATIONAL ASSOCIATION OF WOMEN JUDGES; INTERNATIONAL CIVIL SOCIETY ACTION NETWORK; INTERNATIONAL CONFERENCE ON POPULATION AND DEVELOPMENT; INTERNATIONAL COUNCIL OF WOMEN; INTERNATIONAL PLANNED PARENTHOOD FEDERATION; INTERNATIONAL WOMEN'S RIGHTS ACTION WATCH; INTERNATIONAL WOMEN'S RIGHTS PROJECT; LEAGUE OF NATIONS; *LOVELACE V. CANADA*; MAIL-ORDER BRIDES; MINORITIES; NATIONALITY, RIGHT TO; NGO WORKING GROUP ON WOMEN, PEACE AND SECURITY; NO PEACE WITHOUT JUSTICE; OXFAM INTERNATIONAL; PROTOCOL TO THE AFRICAN CHARTER ON HUMAN AND PEOPLE'S RIGHTS ON THE RIGHTS OF WOMEN IN AFRICA; REPRODUCTIVE RIGHTS; RIGHTS AND DEMOCRACY; SEX TOURISM; SEX TRAFFICKING; SEXUAL VIOLENCE; SLAVERY; STERILIZATION; UNITED NATIONS COMMISSION ON THE STATUS OF WOMEN; UNITED NATIONS CONVENTION FOR THE SUPPRESSION OF THE TRAFFIC IN PERSONS AND OF THE EXPLOITATION OF THE PROSTITUTION OF OTHERS; UNITED NATIONS CONVENTION ON CONSENT TO MARRIAGE, MINIMUM AGE FOR MARRIAGE AND REGISTRATION OF MARRIAGES; UNITED NATIONS CONVENTION ON THE ELIMINATION OF ALL FORMS OF DISCRIMINATION AGAINST WOMEN; UNITED NATIONS CONVENTION ON THE NATIONALITY OF MARRIED WOMEN;

UNITED NATIONS CONVENTION ON THE POLITICAL RIGHTS OF WOMEN; UNITED NATIONS DEVELOPMENT PROGRAMME; UNITED NATIONS SUB-COMMISSION ON THE PROMOTION AND PROTECTION OF HUMAN RIGHTS; WOMEN BUILDING PEACE; WOMEN IN PEACE AND SECURITY; WOMEN'S CAUCUS FOR GENDER JUSTICE; WOMEN'S FUNDING NETWORK; WOMEN'S INITIATIVE FOR GENDER JUSTICE; WOMEN'S INTERNATIONAL LEAGUE FOR PEACE AND FREEDOM; WOMEN'S REFUGEE COMMISSION.

WOMEN BUILDING PEACE. London-based global information and communication network enabling **non-governmental organizations** to engage in the review process of the 1995 **Beijing Declaration and Platform of Action** with a special focus on women and the media. It is funded by bilateral donor agencies and a consortium of UN agencies.

WOMEN IN PEACE AND SECURITY. The idea that sustainable peace entails a gender perspective and respect for human rights in all peace and security, conflict **prevention** and management and **peacebuilding** initiatives of the **United Nations** and depends on the full participation of women in all decision making to prevent violent conflict and to protect all civilians has progressively emerged from the praxis of peacekeeping and the normative agenda setting of **United Nations Global Conferences** on women. It gained further legitimacy with the adoption of Resolution 1325 by the **United Nations Security Council** in 2000. The resolution addresses the "disproportionate and unique impact of armed conflict on women, recognized the under-valued and under-utilized contributions women make to conflict prevention, peacekeeping, conflict resolution and peace-building, and stressed the importance of their equal and full participation as active agents in peace and security." Specifically, it calls for increasing the political participation of women at all levels of decision-making mechanisms, protecting the rights of women and children during wars and **armed conflict** with due attention to their special needs, including women in peace talks, conflict resolution, and peace-building and post-conflict reconstruction and rehabilitation efforts and **gender mainstreaming** in **peace operations** and the security sector. Resolution 1325 was adopted unanimously and has been repeatedly reaffirmed by the Council.

Since 2001, a group of (15 to 20) "Friends of 1325" has been established at the initiative of Canada and meets very two or three months with UN senior officials to broaden support among UN member states for Resolution 1325. Some countries—Canada, Chile, Denmark, France, Mexico, Namibia and Great Britain—are very active in the promotion of issues under the scope of Resolution 1325. But others like Algeria, China and Russia are weary about the Council's expansion of its activities into areas that they feel are the domain of other UN organs or other international fora. Some members of the Council have been reluctant to engage in public debates about incidents involving instances of sexual exploitation by UN peacekeepers while others—troop-contributing countries—may find proposed measures such as the inclusion of more women in their military forces difficult to implement. Nevertheless, gender perspectives appear to be increasingly, if not systematically, incorporated in the Security Council's planning, implementation and monitoring of UN peace operations. At the same time, in the field, violations of **international humanitarian law** by parties to armed conflicts continue. *See also* GLOBAL NETWORK OF WOMEN PEACE BUILDERS; NGO WORKING GROUP ON WOMEN, PEACE AND SECURITY; WOMEN'S CAUCUS FOR GENDER JUSTICE; WOMEN'S FUNDING NETWORK.

WOMEN'S CAUCUS FOR GENDER JUSTICE. Network of individuals and groups which grew out of a number of **United Nations Global Conferences** in the early 1990s with the objective of integrating gender concerns into the jurisdiction of the **International Criminal Court** (ICC). The caucus was actively involved in the international campaign for ratification of the Statute of the Court and now focuses on strengthening the capacity of women in the use of the ICC as a means of **redress**.

WOMEN'S FUNDING NETWORK. Collaborative scheme originating from the **United States'** women's movement which was launched in 1985 and has since grown into a worldwide network of over 155 women's funds with collective assets of close to half a billion dollars making grants of over $160 million a year for projects in support of women and girls.

WOMEN'S INITIATIVE FOR GENDER JUSTICE. International women's human rights **non-governmental organization** based in The Hague advocating for inclusion of gender-based crimes in the **investigations** and **prosecutions** of the **International Criminal Court** (ICC) and the rights of women victims or survivors of **armed conflict** throughout the justice process. The group has been granted **amicus curiae** status before the ICC since the Court's inception.

WOMEN'S INTERNATIONAL LEAGUE FOR PEACE AND FREEDOM (WILPF). International **non-governmental organization** with national sections and secretariats in Geneva and New York. Founded in 1915, WILPF's activities revolve around peace, disarmament and gender-related issues. It **lobbies** governments at the international, national and local levels, seeks to connects communities with the international scene through its national sections, participates in and collaborates and networks with international institutions and global movements, develops reference, education and action tools through websites, conferences, seminars and publications and **monitors** and contributes to the work of the **United Nations**. Its consultative status at the United Nations enables it to follow the proceedings of the **United Nations Human Rights Council**, the **Universal Periodic Review** and the work of the **United Nations treaty bodies**. *See also* HUMAN RIGHTS EDUCATION.

WOMEN'S REFUGEE COMMISSION. Originally founded in 1989 as the Women's Commission for Refugee Women and Children, this **non-governmental organization**, affiliated with and legally part of the **International Rescue Committee**, is based in New York. The Commission identifies critical problems that affect displaced women, children and young people, documents best practices through **research** and **fact-finding** missions and proposes ways and means to improve humanitarian assistance in such areas as **reproductive rights** services, educational and vocational opportunities and sustainable livelihoods for displaced women and children. In the **United States**, the Commission advocates for the fair treatment of women, children and families who seek **asylum** in the country. The Commission produced in 2009 a comprehensive guide to assist field-based programmers and practitioners in designing and implementing economic interventions for **internally displaced persons**.

WORK, RIGHT TO. First of the specific rights recognized by the **International Covenant on Economic, Social and Cultural Rights** (ICESCR) which it defines as "the right of everyone to the opportunity to gain his living by work." The ICESCR also stipulates that "the full **realization** of this right shall include technical and vocational guidance and training programmes." The right to work deals exclusively with access to work (i.e., as a means to earn an **adequate standard of living** through wage labor or other freely chosen socially acceptable means including self-employment. From this vantage point, the obligations of states are to respect, protect and fulfill each individual's access to work. Closely related to the right to work are rights at work or labor rights which protect a person who sells his or her labor. These rights include the right to safe and dignified working conditions; the right to work that is freely chosen or accepted; the right to adequate remuneration; the right to a limited workday and remunerated periods of rest; the right to equal pay for work of equal value; and the right to equal treatment.

The scope and contents of these rights are defined and regulated primarily through the conventions adopted by the **International Labour Organization** and have been, at least theoretically, incorporated in national and administrative systems. The right to dignified working conditions is closely linked to the prohibition against **slavery**, servitude and **forced labor**, the right to form trade unions and to strike, the right to equal pay for work of equal value and the prohibition of sexual harassment and other forms of employment **discrimination**.

See also AMERICAN CONVENTION ON HUMAN RIGHTS; BUSINESS AND HUMAN RIGHTS RESOURCE CENTRE; CENTER FOR ECONOMIC AND SOCIAL RIGHTS; EUROPEAN CHARTER OF FUNDAMENTAL RIGHTS OF THE EUROPEAN UNION; EUROPEAN SOCIAL CHARTER; INTERNATIONAL CENTRE FOR TRADE UNION RIGHTS; INTERNATIONAL COMMISSION FOR LABOR RIGHTS; INTERNATIONAL CONFEDERATION OF FREE TRADE UNIONS; MIGRANT WORKERS; UNIVERSAL DECLARATION OF HUMAN RIGHTS.

WORKING GROUPS. *See* SPECIAL PROCEDURES

WORLD BANK. *See* INTERNATIONAL BANK FOR RECONSTRUCTION AND DEVELOPMENT.

WORLD BLIND UNION (WBU). Non-political, non-religious, **nongovernmental organization**, set up in 1984 which brings together approximately 600 organizations representing over 160 million blind and partially sighted persons in 178 member countries. The WBU is primarily an **advocacy** organization rather than a provider of services. Its work includes **capacity building**, leadership development, Braille literacy, and empowerment for women, children and **indigenous people**, the development and sharing of tools and resources and speaking on behalf of the blind and those with low vision at the international level to organizations such as the **United Nations** and its agencies. *See also* DISABLED PERSONS; WORLD FEDERATION OF THE DEAFBLIND.

WORLD BUSINESS COUNCIL FOR SUSTAINABLE DEVELOPMENT (WBCSD). Global association bringing together some 200 private companies active in 30 countries and 20 major industrial sectors related to energy, climate, development and ecosystems and serving as a platform for the exploration of sustainable development issues and the sharing of knowledge, experiences and best practices with states and **non-state actors**. According to its mission statement, the WBCSD is an "advocate of market based solutions to development and **environment** challenges" and "believes that the leading companies of the future will be those that align profitable business ventures with the needs of society and thereby contribute to a more sustainable world." *See also* CORPORATE SOCIAL RESPONSIBILITY; TRANSNATIONAL CORPORATIONS.

WORLD COMMISSION ON ENVIRONMENT AND DEVELOP-MENT (WCED). High-level panel of politicians and experts named after its chair, Gro Harlen Brundtland, constituted in 1983 to address growing concern "about the accelerating deterioration of the human **environment** and natural resources and the consequences of that deterioration for economic and social development." Its report published in 1987 coined the influential concept of sustainable development, that is, "development that meets the needs of [the] present without compromising the ability of future generations to meet their own needs." The definition draws attention to two ideas: (a) the need to accord overriding priority to meeting the essential needs of the world's poor; and (b) factoring into development policies the limitations imposed by the state of technology and social organization on the environment's capacity to meet present and future needs.

WORLD CONFEDERATION OF LABOR (WCL). International labor organization set up in 1920 in The Hague initially catering to Roman **Catholic Church** constituencies. The activities of the Confederation were severely disrupted by the rise of totalitarian governments in the 1930s and its secretariat was destroyed by the Nazis World War II. During the **Cold War**, the WLC experienced difficulties reestablishing its presence in Eastern Europe and eventually reoriented its activities toward Third World countries, dealing with such issues as human rights and international labor standards, child labor, women workers, **migrant workers** and the informal economy. With **globalization** increasingly underlining the problems arising from a fragmented labor movement around the world, the WCF merged with the **International Confederation of Free Trade Unions** to form the **International Trade Union Confederation** in 2006.

WORLD CONFERENCE AGAINST RACISM (2001). Formally known as the World Conference against Racism, Racial Discrimination, Xenophobia and Related Intolerance, this United Nations–sponsored conference was held in Durban, South Africa, from 31 August to 8 September 2001 and addressed inconclusively a number of politically sensitive issues connected with racism, **racial discrimination** and xenophobia including **slavery**, migrants, **refugees** and **asylum seekers**, and discrimination on the basis of gender and caste and **indigenous peoples**. Bitter controversy plagued the proceedings of the meeting about the Middle East conflict and the **Israeli** treatment of Palestinians, indigenous rights and the **Holocaust**. African countries unsuccessfully pressed for **apologies** and **reparations** from countries responsible for slavery. The **United States** and **Israel** withdrew from the conference over a draft resolution likening Zionism to racism. Over 3,000 **non-governmental organizations** participated in a parallel conference, thus providing a forum to victims of racism and intolerance for the articulation of their grievances. The "Declaration" and "Program of Action" adopted by the conference reflect a general concern over the richness of human diversity, but political consensus could not be achieved over concrete and practical measures. Of note, however, is the Declaration's identification of slavery and the slave trade as **crimes against humanity**. An equally divisive and inconclusive follow-up conference was held in 2009 in Geneva which was boycotted by 10 Western countries. A "high-level" meeting of the **United Nations General Assembly** held in September 2011 to mark the 10th anniversary of the Declaration went by and large unnoticed. *See also* ROBINSON, MARY.

WORLD CONFERENCE ON HUMAN RIGHTS (1993). Largest ever global conference to be held on human rights issues under the aegis of the **United Nations**. Attended by representatives of 171 countries and some 800 **non-governmental organizations**, the conference was criticized for sidetracking any discussion of ongoing **violations of human rights** and adopting a **declaration** and program of action viewed by some as a "well crafted but empty exhortation." The outcome of the conference was indeed a reminder of the persistence of the deep political rift pitting Western and non-Western countries over the **universality** of human rights. In spite of its ambiguities, however, from a normative standpoint, the Declaration did sanction the **interdependence** and **indivisibility** of human rights, thus bridging the gap engendered by the **Cold War** between political and civil rights on the one hand and economic, social and cultural rights on the other. It also gave greater prominence to the rights of **minorities**, women, children and indigenous peoples. It also called for strengthening the UN human rights work through greater funding and the establishment of a new office, the **United Nations Office of the High Commissioner for Human Rights**. *See also* CULTURAL RELATIVISM.

WORLD COUNCIL OF CHURCHES (WCC). Humanitarian ecumenical Geneva-based organization founded in 1948 bringing together "a worldwide fellowship of . . . global, regional and sub-regional, national and local churches seeking unity, a common witness and Christian service." The Roman **Catholic Church** does not belong to the Council. The activities of the WCC focus on the **environment, indigenous peoples, disabled persons, racism,** women and children.

WORLD COUNCIL OF INDIGENOUS PEOPLES. Dissolved in 1996 because of internal dissentions, the Council was the first international body to advocate for the preservation and protection of the political, economic, social and cultural rights of **indigenous peoples** and, in particular, for their right to **self-determination** regarding their land and resources.

WORLD FEDERALIST MOVEMENT (WFM). Worldwide organization bringing together groups and individuals supporting the establishment of a system of democratic global institutions accountable to the citizens of the world. WFM has thus promoted the ideas of a more representative **United Nations Security Council**, a World Court with compulsory jurisdiction and judicial review authority and a democratically elected **United Nations General Assembly** standing as a functional equivalent of a world parliament. One of the key advocacy activities of WFM has been its efforts to strengthen international justice and the **rule of law**. The WFM played an important role in the establishment of the **International Criminal Court** and has campaigned for a fuller reliance on and utilization of the normative principles of **universal jurisdiction**, **corporate responsibility** and a **responsibility to protect**. *See also* INSTITUTE FOR GLOBAL POLICY.

WORLD FEDERATION OF THE DEAF (WFD). International advocacy **non-governmental organization** established in 1951. Headquartered in Helsinki, with a membership of associations in 130 countries worldwide, its current activities focus on improving the status of national sign languages, better education and improved access to information and services for deaf peoples. WFD has consultative status in the **United Nations** system, including the **United Nations Economic and Social Council**; the **United Nations Educational, Scientific and Cultural Organization**; the **International Labour Organization**; and the **World Health Organization** to whom it provides expert advice. It also co-operates closely with the **United Nations Office of the High Commissioner for Human Rights**. *See also* WORLD BLIND UNION; WORLD FEDERATION OF THE DEAFBLIND.

WORLD FEDERATION OF THE DEAFBLIND (WFDB). International non-governmental organization comprised of national organizations or groups of deafblind persons and of deafblind individuals worldwide. Created in 1997 and located in Sweden, the Federation's purposes are is to serve as a forum of exchange of knowledge and experiences among deafblind persons and to obtain inclusion and full participation of deafblind persons in all areas of national societies. *See also* DISABLED PERSONS; WORLD BLIND UNION; WORLD FEDERATION OF THE DEAF.

WORLD FEDERATION OF TRADE UNIONS (WFTU). Successor body to the International Federation of Trade Unions established in 1945 to bring together trade unions across the world in a single international organization. Western trade unions withdrew from the WFTU in 1949 as a result of disputes over support for the Marshall Plan to form the **International Confederation of Free Trade Unions**. Portrayed throughout the **Cold War** as a Soviet front organization, the role of the Federation further declined after the demise of communist regimes in Eastern Europe and Russia. It now devotes its work to organizing regional federations of unions in the Third World while continuing to advocate for full **employment, social security, health** protection, and trade union rights. Meanwhile, the International Confederation of Free Trade Unions was dissolved in 2006, merging with the **World Confederation of Labor** to form the **International Trade Union Confederation** which brings together 175 million workers from over 300 organizations in the world.

WORLD FEDERATION OF UNITED NATIONS ASSOCIATIONS (WFUNA). Umbrella **non-governmental organization** in consultative status with the **United Nations Economic and Social Council** bringing together a network of national United Nations Associations from over 100 member countries of the **United Nations**. Created in 1946 with the overall purpose of promoting **research**, information and education about the goals of the **United Nations Charter** and the work of the organization, WFUNA has served as a forum for global dialogue on human rights, disarmament, and development issues. Its current priorities focus on the **Millennium Development Goals, climate change,** human rights, peace and conflict resolution and bridging the digital divide. *See also* ADVOCACY.

WORLD HEALTH ORGANIZATION (WHO). United Nations **specialized agency** established in 1948 to promote the attainment by all peoples of the highest level of **health**. The agency understands "health" as a state of complete physical, mental and social well-being not merely as the absence of disease. WHO's specific areas of work include the coordination of international efforts to prevent and control outbreaks of infectious diseases, such as malaria, tuberculosis, swine flu, SARS and **HIV/AIDS**, support for the development and distribution of safe and effective vaccines, pharmaceutical diagnostics, and drugs, the conduct of health research in communicable diseases, non-communicable conditions and injuries and the provision of assistance in the development of national health research systems. Since 2005 WHO has applied a human rights approach in its work guided by the findings of the **United Nations Committee on Economic and Social Rights (General Comment** 14) as it endeavors to advance the right to health in international law and the development process. In this context, WHO cooperates closely with the United Nations **special rapporteur** on the right to health. *See also* ABORTION; NUCLEAR WEAPONS.

WORLD JUSTICE PROJECT (WJP). Originally launched by the American Bar Association, this **non-governmental organization** has become a multinational entity whose goal is to strengthen the **rule of law** through the convening of global and regional meetings of world leaders and the provision of seed grants for rule of law projects. The WJP has developed an index combining a variety of indicators measuring adherence to the rule of law in over 200 countries.

WORLD ORGANIZATION AGAINST TORTURE (OMTC). Coalition of **non-governmental organizations** fighting primarily against **arbitrary detention**, **torture**, summary executions, and **forced disappearances**. The OMTC provides victims of torture with the first medical, legal or social assistance, focusing on specific categories of vulnerable peoples such as women, children and **human rights defenders**. In the framework of its activities, OMTC also submits individual **communications** and alternative reports to the special mechanisms of the **United Nations** and actively collaborates in the development of international norms for the protection of human rights. One of its major contributions is a large-scale study of the causes of violence that relied on cross-national human rights measurements.

WORLD SOCIAL FORUM (WSF). Self-described as "an opened space— plural, diverse, non-governmental and non-partisan—that stimulates the decentralized debate, reflection, proposals building, experiences exchange and alliances among movements and organizations engaged in concrete actions towards a more solidary, democratic and fair world . . . permanent space and process to build alternatives to neo-liberalism." This loose organization was set up in 2001 and meets annually in Brazil. Its purpose is to coordinate world **campaigns** against "corporate **globalization**" and develop alternative policies promoting an equal distribution of economic resources. *See also* CORPORATE SOCIAL RESPONSIBILITY; TRANSNATIONAL CORPORATIONS.

WORLD SUMMIT FOR SOCIAL DEVELOPMENT (1995). Widely attended **United Nations Global Conference** devoted to social development issues. Over 14,000 participants were in attendance, including governmental delegations from 186 countries, some 2,300 representatives from 811 **non-governmental organizations** (NGOs), and over 2,800 journalists. In addition, some 12,000 NGO representatives and others held a parallel "Forum." By focusing on the long-neglected social dimensions of development, the Summit is credited with having refocused political attention on the reduction of **poverty**, the goal of full employment and the fostering of social integration as overriding objectives of development. Many of the "commitments" agreed to at the conclusion of the meeting foreshadow the **Millennium Development Goals** endorsed five years later by the **United Nations General Assembly**. Insofar as the issues dealt with by the Summit intersect with the economic and social rights recognized in the **Universal Declaration of Human Rights** and the **International Covenant on Economic, Social and Cultural Rights**, it was a step toward the mainstreaming of human rights into development thinking and policies. *See also* DECLARATION ON SOCIAL PROGRESS AND DEVELOPMENT.

WORLD SUMMIT FOR CHILDREN. High-level **United Nations Global Conference** held at **United Nations** headquarters in New York from 29–30 September 1990 shortly after the adoption of the **United Nations Convention on the Rights of the Child** for the purpose of setting a broad agenda to improve the well-being of children in the areas of **health**, **education**, nutrition and human rights. The conference was the brainchild of **James P. Grant**, then head of the **United Nations Children's Fund**. The main outcome of the Summit was the adoption of a World Declaration on the Survival, Protection and Development of Children and a Plan of Action which included targeted reductions in infant and maternal mortality, child malnutrition and illiteracy, as well as targeted increases in access to basic services for health and family planning, education, water and sanitation. These normative goals have had a remarkable mobilizing power, creating new partnerships among governments, **non-governmental organizations**, the media, **civil society** and international organizations. The Summit was thereafter used as a model for the organization of other UN global conferences throughout the 1990s. *See also* CHILDREN IN ARMED CONFLICT.

WORLD SUMMIT ON THE INFORMATION SOCIETY (WSIS).
United Nations Global Conference held in two phases. The first one was
hosted by the government of Switzerland in Geneva from 10 to 12 December
2003 and the second by Tunisia from 16 to 18 November 2005. The main
objective of these meetings was to formulate policies to bridge the so-called
digital divide separating rich from poor countries. The Summit yielded few
tangible results as it focused primarily on **Internet** governance problems and
paid scant attention to the human rights dimensions of access to information
and knowledge. In fact the conveners were sharply criticized by **civil society**
organizations for hosting the meeting in a country with a less than stellar
human rights record. *See also* FREEDOM OF EXPRESSION.

WORLD TRADE ORGANIZATION (WTO). Successor organization
to the postwar General Agreement on Tariffs and Trade (GATT) which
began operations in 1995. The main purpose of the WTO is to supervise
the liberalization of international trade by providing a framework for trade
negotiations and a dispute resolution system for concluded agreements. Some
critics argue that the WTO's operation is biased toward rich countries and
multinational corporations, thus harming smaller countries which have less
negotiation power. Others claim that the WTO does not pay enough attention
to **health, labor, environment** and human rights issues arising from the free
trade and deregulation arrangements it promotes.

See also AGREEMENT ON TRADE-RELATED INTELLECTUAL
PROPERTY RIGHTS; CONVENTION ON THE PROTECTION AND
PROMOTION OF THE DIVERSITY OF CULTURAL EXPRESSION;
FRIENDS OF THE EARTH INTERNATIONAL; INTELLECTUAL
PROPERTY RIGHTS; INTERNATIONAL LAW INSTITUTE; PUBLIC
GOODS.

WORLD WAR I PEACE TREATIES. World War I formally came to
an end with the signing of peace treaties between the so-called Allied and
Associated powers and the Central Powers: Germany (Versailles, 28 June
1919); Austria (Saint Germain, 10 September 1919); Bulgaria (Neuilly, 27
November 1919), Hungary (Trianon, 4 June 1920), and Turkey (Sèvres, 10
August 1920). (In the wake of Ataturk's resistance and military defeat of
Greece in 1922, the Sevres Treaty was renegotiated and superseded by the
24 July 1923 Lausanne Treaty.) All of these treaties contained provisions
calling for the trial by national military tribunals of individuals suspected
of violations of the laws and customs of war. None of them were fully
implemented in the political turmoil which followed the war.

The Versailles Treaty does contain a clause requiring the establishment of a special tribunal composed of Judges appointed by the **United States**, Great Britain, France, Italy, and Japan to try the German emperor on charges of having committed a supreme offense against international morality and the sanctity of treaties. The former emperor took refuge in the Netherlands. The Dutch government refused to extradite him and the international tribunal was never constituted. *See also* KAISER WILHELM II; LEIPZIG WAR TRIALS.

WORLD WAR II. Undoubtedly the deadliest military conflict in modern history in absolute terms if not in terms of deaths relative to the size of the world population. Over 60 million people were killed, two-thirds of them civilians. Famine, disease, population transfers, **persecution** and crimes against humanity and strategic bombing are among the main causes of the high rate of civilian casualties. Violations of the laws of war and **crimes against humanity** were committed by virtually all the major parties to the conflict. Over 57 percent of Russian prisoners of war held by Germany died. Major German and Japanese cities were firebombed. Between March and August 1945, 63 Japanese cities were consumed by fire, killing more than 1 million civilians. Some 1.4 million women were raped in East Prussia, Pomerania and Silesia alone at the end of the war.

See also INTERNATIONAL MILITARY TRIBUNAL FOR THE FAR EAST; INTERNATIONAL MILITARY TRIBUNAL FOR THE PROSECUTION AND PUNISHMENT OF THE MAJOR WAR CRIMINALS OF THE EUROPEAN AXIS; LEMAY, CURTIS; OXFAM INTERNATIONAL; PAPON, MAURICE.

WORLDWATCH INSTITUTE. Globally focused environmental **think tank** based in Washington, D.C., whose mission is to develop and disseminate data, analyses and strategies to create environmentally sound societies that can meet basic human needs and the challenges of **climate change**, resource degradation, **population** growth and **poverty**. Its research is disseminated in over 20 languages through print and online media. The Worldwatch Institute's flagship annual *State of the World* is an indispensable resource for policymakers, academics and the broad public. *See also* ENVIRONMENT, RIGHT TO A HEALTHY.

X

XENOPHOBIA. *See* WORLD CONFERENCE AGAINST RACISM.

Y

YOGYAKARTA PRINCIPLES ON THE APPLICATION OF INTERNATIONAL HUMAN RIGHTS LAW IN RELATION TO SEXUAL ORIENTATION AND GENDER IDENTITY. Set of principles relating to **sexual orientation** and gender identity developed by a group of human rights experts in 2006 convened by the **International Commission of Jurists** and the **International Service for Human Rights**. These non-binding normative prescriptions call upon governments, regional intergovernmental organizations, **civil society** and the United Nations to address human rights violations and abuses endured by lesbian, gay, bisexual and transgender people such as sexual assault, rape, **torture**, **extra-judicial executions**, arbitrary arrest and imprisonment, denial of free speech and assembly and **discrimination**. *See also* SOFT LAW.

YUGOSLAVIA. *See* ARTICLE 19, THE INTERNATIONAL CENTRE AGAINST CENSORSHIP; BOSNIA-HERZEGOVINA WAR; ETHNIC CLEANSING; GENDER-BASED VIOLENCE; INTERNATIONAL CRIMINAL TRIBUNAL FOR THE FORMER YUGOSLAVIA; MILOSEVIC, SLOBODAN.

Appendix 1

International Human Rights Standards: Implementation Mechanisms

Individual Complaints		Reporting Procedures	
Treaty bodies	**Other bodies**	**Treaty bodies**	**Other bodies**
National level	**National level**	**National level**	**National level**
• National courts • Internationally established national courts (Bosnia; East Timor)	• Truths commissions	• National human rights institutions	• National human rights institutions
Regional level	**Regional level**	**Regional level**	**Regional level**
• ECHR, ACHR, ACHPR	• ACmHR	• ESC and other European treaties	• European Commission against Racism
• Interstate complaints: ECHR, ACHR, ACHPR	• OSCE	• ACHPR • Special American treaties	
Global level	**Global level**	**Global level**	**Global level**
• Communications: ICCPR, ICESR, CEDAW, CERD, CAT, ICRMW, CPAPED	• Human Rights Council • Special rapporteurs • CSW • UNESCO; ILO	• State reports: ICESCR, ICCPR, CERD, CAT, CEDAW, CRC, ICRMW, CPAPED, CRPD	• Human Rights Council: UPR • ILO
Treaty bodies	**Other bodies**		
National level	**National level**	**National level**	**National level**
• Visits under CAT	• National human rights institutions; Truth commissions	• Domestic criminal law • Obligation to prosecute under HR treaties • Incorporation of ICL • Hybrid courts	• Political process

(continued)

Individual Complaints		Reporting Procedures	
Regional level	**Regional level**	**Regional level**	**Regional level**
• Visits under ECPT	• Country reports of ACmHR • OSCE (Minorities Commissioner) • European Council of Europe: Commission against racism • Special rapporteurs (OAS, AU)	• Ad hoc criminal courts	
Global level	**Global level**	**Global level**	**Global level**
• CtteeAT, CtteeERD, CtteeEDAW, etc.	• UN thematic/ country rapporteurs • UN peace operations • ICRC visit system • ILO; UNESCO	• ICC	• Nonmilitary sanctions • Military sanctions • Peace operations

Adapted from Walter Kalin and Jorg Kunzli, *The Law of International Human Rights Protection*, New York: Oxford University Press, 2009, pp. 204–5.

Appendix 2

Human Rights Architecture at the United Nations

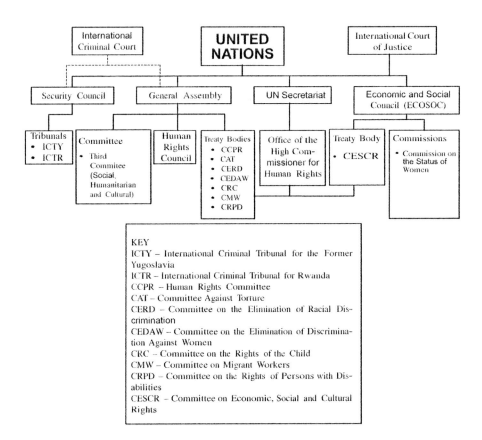

```
                International        UNITED         International Court
                Criminal Court     NATIONS          of Justice

      Security Council   General Assembly    UN Secretariat    Economic and Social
                                                               Council (ECOSOC)
```

Tribunals	Committee	Human Rights Council	Treaty Bodies	Office of the High Commissioner for Human Rights	Treaty Body	Commissions
• ICTY • ICTR	• Third Commitee (Social, Humanitarian and Cultural)		• CCPR • CAT • CERD • CEDAW • CRC • CMW • CRPD		• CESCR	• Commission on the Status of Women

KEY
ICTY – International Criminal Tribunal for the Former Yugoslavia
ICTR – International Criminal Tribunal for Rwanda
CCPR – Human Rights Committee
CAT – Committee Against Torture
CERD – Committee on the Elimination of Racial Discrimination
CEDAW – Committee on the Elimination of Discrimination Against Women
CRC – Committee on the Rights of the Child
CMW – Committee on Migrant Workers
CRPD – Committee on the Rights of Persons with Disabilities
CESCR – Committee on Economic, Social and Cultural Rights

Appendix 3

Structure of the UN Human Rights Council

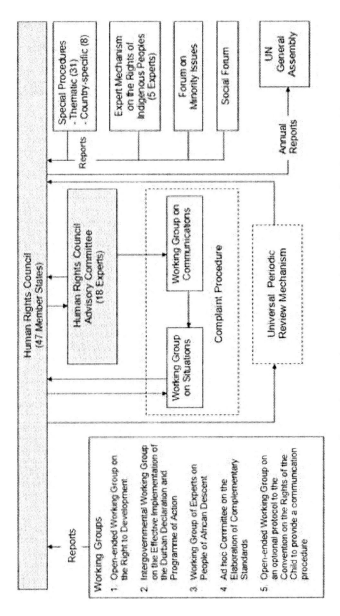

Source: www.claiminghumanrights.org/scheme_hrc.html?&L=1%2F%3Foption%3D

Appendix 4

UN 1503 Complaint Procedure

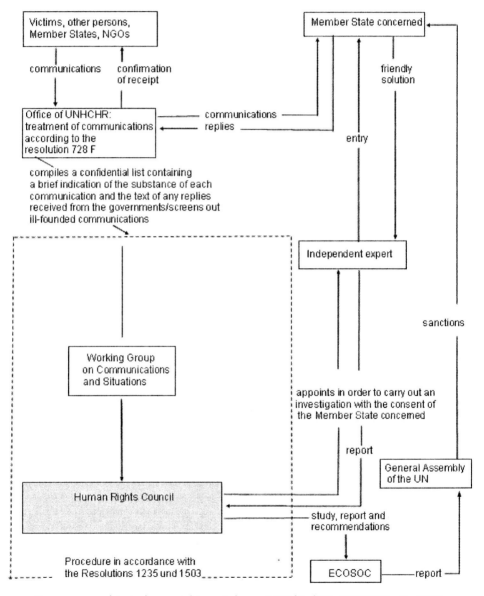

Source: www.claiminghumanrights.org/scheme_1503.html?&L=1%2F%3Foption%3D

The 1503 Procedure is confidential and examines the human rights situation within a state. The Council therefore does not decide on individual cases. The individuals or NGOs who file a complaint will not be informed about the steps taken. Generally, they receive, as the only answer, a letter confirming the reception of the complaint. Anonymous complaints are not accepted.

The complaint procedure allows an examination of such complaints which reveal the existence of a *consistent pattern of gross and reliably attested violations of human rights and fundamental freedoms*. Once the Council has received several individual cases which form a consistent pattern of gross systematic human rights violations which are reliably proved, it can decide to examine the situation of the human rights in the country concerned.

A communication is admissible unless:

- It has manifestly political motivations and its object is not consistent with the UN Charter, the Universal Declaration of Human Rights and other applicable instruments in the field of human rights law; or
- It does not contain a factual description of the alleged violations, including the rights which are alleged to be violated; or
- Its language is abusive. However, such communication may be considered if it meets the other criteria for admissibility after deletion of the abusive language; or
- It is not submitted by a person or a group of persons claiming to be the victim of violations of human rights and fundamental freedoms or by any person or group of persons, including NGOs acting in good faith in accordance with the principles of human rights, not resorting to politically motivated stands contrary to the provisions of the UN Charter and claiming to have direct and reliable knowledge of those violations. Nonetheless, reliably attested communications shall not be inadmissible solely because the knowledge of the individual author is secondhand, provided they are accompanied by clear evidence; or
- It is exclusively based on reports disseminated by mass media; or
- It refers to a case that appears to reveal a consistent pattern of gross and reliably attested violations of human rights already being dealt with by a special procedure, a treaty body or other United Nations or similar regional complaints procedure in the field of human rights; or
- The domestic remedies have not been exhausted, unless it appears that such remedies would be ineffective or unreasonably prolonged.

The complaint must comprise:

- The name of the author of the complaint (i.e., the name of the person(s) or organization(s) who file(s) the complaint). The claimant has to be precise if he or she wishes the case to be treated anonymously. However, despite all the precautions taken by the United Nations, a state can still ascertain the claimants' identity (due to the facts mentioned in the complaint or by other means).

- The complaint must expose the existence of a consistent pattern of gross and reliably attested violations of human rights and fundamental freedoms.
- A description of the facts, comprising the identification of the victims and suspects of the violation, accompanied by a detailed description of the events when the violation took place. This description must reveal the existence of a consistent pattern of violations.
- Apparent evidence, such as written declarations on the facts by the victims, their families or witnesses of the violation, or a medical report indicating the consequences of the violation. The evidence can be included in the complaint itself or attached to it.
- The complaint must indicate the rights which have been violated. It must clearly indicate the article(s) of the Universal Declaration of Human Rights which the claimant considers to be violated.
- It must further indicate the purpose of the complaint (i.e., the reason for which it was filed). This purpose could be, for example, the wish for an intervention of the United Nations to terminate the violation.
- The complaint should demonstrate the exhaustion of all available remedies within the country.

The correspondence and inquiries relying on the complaint procedure should be directed to:

Office of United Nations High Commissioner for Human Rights
Human Rights Council Branch-Complaint Procedure Unit
OHCHR—Palais Wilson
United Nations Office at Geneva
CH-1211 Geneva 10, Switzerland
Fax: (41 22) 917 90 11
E-mail: CP@ohchr.org

The claimant could be informed about the course of his/her request (i.e., whether it has been accepted by the working groups and how they decided on it).

Sources: www.claiminghumanrights.org/hrc_complaints.html; www.ohchr.org/EN/HRBodies/HRC/Pages/Complaint.aspx

Appendix 5

UN Special Procedures Manual: Excerpts

Most Special Procedures provide for the relevant mandate-holders to receive information from different sources and to act on credible information by sending a communication to the relevant Government(s) in relation to any actual or anticipated human rights violations which fall within the scope of their mandate.

Communications may deal with cases concerning individuals, groups or communities, with general trends and patterns of human rights violations in a particular country or more generally, or with the content of existing or draft legislation considered to be a matter of concern.

Communications do not imply any kind of value judgment on the part of the Special Procedure concerned and are thus not per se accusatory. They are not intended as a substitute for judicial or other proceedings at the national level. Their purpose is to obtain clarification in response to allegations of violations and to promote measures designed to protect human rights.

The Quick Response Desk (QRD) of OHCHR coordinates the sending of communications by all mandates. Information available to the Office is provided to relevant mandate-holders in order to ascertain whether they wish to take action on them. In the case of an affirmative response a draft communication is prepared and circulated for approval. The Quick Response Desk also provides information on any previous action taken in relation to the case in question.

Mandate-holders are encouraged to send joint communications whenever this seems appropriate. Communications by thematic mandate-holders in relation to a State for which a country rapporteur exists shall be prepared in consultation with the latter. Where agreement between the thematic and country Special Procedures cannot be reached the advice of the Coordination Committee shall be sought.

OHCHR desk officers and relevant United Nations field offices should also be consulted, to the extent feasible, in the preparation of communications concerning the areas of their responsibility. In order to ensure necessary coordination they should also be provided with copies of any relevant communications which have been sent.

Each communication must be expressly authorized by the relevant mandate-holder(s). Communications usually take the form of a letter transmitted by the OHCHR to the Permanent Representative of the country concerned to the Office of the United Nations in Geneva. In the absence of such representation the letter shall be transmitted to the relevant Permanent Representative at United Nations Headquarters in New York, or to the Ministry of Foreign Affairs of the country or countries concerned.

In communications sent to Governments, the source is normally kept confidential in order to protect against reprisals or retaliation. An information source may, however, request that its identity be revealed.

In light of information received in response from the Government concerned, or of further information from other sources, the mandate-holder will determine how best to proceed. This might include the initiation of further inquiries, the elaboration of recommendations or observations to be published in the relevant report, or other appropriate steps designed to achieve the objectives of the mandate.

All communications sent and responses received thereon are confidential until such time as they are published in the relevant report of the mandate-holder or the mandate-holder determines that the specific circumstances require action to be taken before that time. Periodic reports issued by the Special Procedures should reflect the communications sent by the mandate-holder and the governments' responses thereto. They may also contain observations of the mandate-holders in relation to the outcome of the exchange of views. The names of alleged victims are reflected in the reports, although exceptions may be made in relation to children and other victims of violence in relation to whom publication would be problematic.

Source: www2.ohchr.org/english/bodies/chr/special/docs/Manual_English_23jan.pdf

Appendix 6

Procedure for Individual Complaints to the UN Human Rights Committee

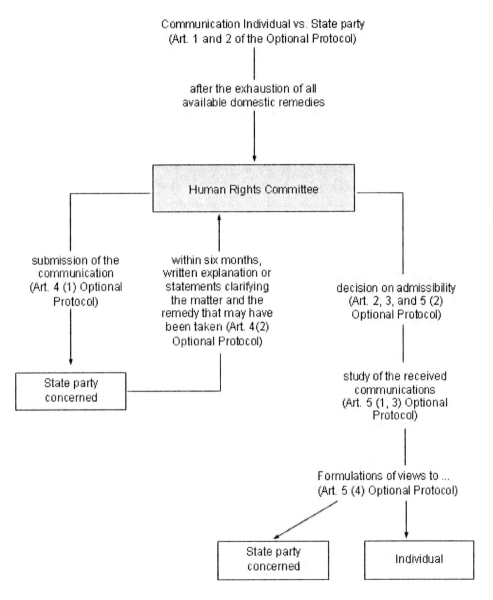

Communication Individual vs. State party
(Art. 1 and 2 of the Optional Protocol)

after the exhaustion of all
available domestic remedies

Human Rights Committee

submission of the
communication
(Art. 4 (1) Optional
Protocol)

within six months,
written explanation or
statements clarifying
the matter and the
remedy that may have
been taken (Art. 4(2)
Optional Protocol)

decision on admissibility
(Art. 2, 3, and 5 (2)
Optional Protocol)

State party
concerned

study of the received
communications
(Art. 5 (1, 3) Optional
Protocol)

Formulations of views to ...
(Art. 5 (4) Optional Protocol)

State party
concerned

Individual

Adapted from Claiming Human Rights, www.claiminghumanrights.org/iccpr_scheme_state_reports
.html?&L=...i%20te%20sera%20surement%20utile%29%2F%2F%3Fpage%3D..%2F..%2F..%2F..%2F

Appendix 7

State Party Reporting to the UN Committee on Economic, Social and Cultural Rights

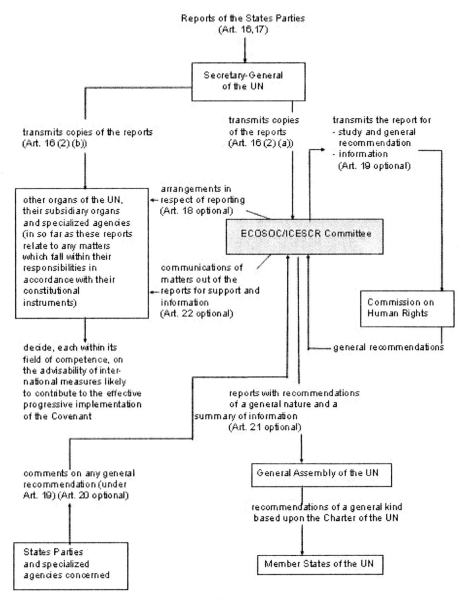

Reports of the States Parties
(Art. 16, 17)

Secretary-General
of the UN

transmits copies of the reports
(Art. 16 (2) (b))

transmits copies
of the reports
(Art. 16 (2) (a))

transmits the report for
- study and general
  recommendation
- information
  (Art. 19 optional)

other organs of the UN,
their subsidiary organs
and specialized agencies
(in so far as these reports
relate to any matters
which fall within their
responsibilities in
accordance with their
constitutional
instruments)

arrangements in
respect of reporting
(Art. 18 optional)

ECOSOC/ICESCR Committee

communications of
matters out of the
reports for support and
information
(Art. 22 optional)

Commission on
Human Rights

decide, each within its
field of competence, on
the advisability of international measures likely
to contribute to the effective
progressive implementation
of the Covenant

general recommendations

reports with recommendations
of a general nature and a
summary of information
(Art. 21 optional)

comments on any general
recommendation (under
Art. 19) (Art. 20 optional)

General Assembly of the UN

recommendations of a general kind
based upon the Charter of the UN

States Parties
and specialized
agencies concerned

Member States of the UN

Source: Adapted from Claiming Human Rights www.claiminghumanrights.org/icescr_scheme _state_reports.html?&L=ofefghqitmbv

Appendix 8

State Reporting to UN Committee on the Elimination of All Forms of Racial Discrimination

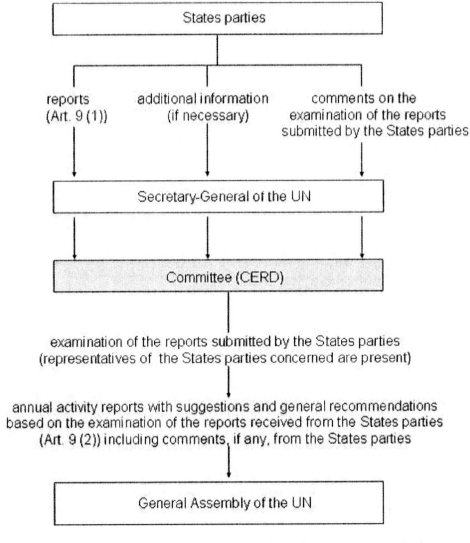

Source: Adapted from Claiming Human Rights www.claiminghumanrights.org/cerd_scheme
_state_reports.html?&L=1%20%28site%20qui%20te%20sera%20surement%20utile%29)

Appendix 9

UNESCO Individual Complaint Procedure: Procedure of 104 EX/Decision 3.3

Protected rights: Rights falling under the competence of UNESCO and the UDHR

- Right to education (Article 26)
- Right to participate in cultural life and to share scientific advancement (Article 27)
- Right to information, including freedom of opinion and expression (Article 19)
- Freedom of thought, conscience and religion (Article 18)
- Right to freedom of association (Article 20)

Procedure:

Individuals, groups of individuals and NGOs can submit individual complaints to the UNESCO Committee on Conventions and Recommendations if they are direct victims or if they have a sufficient connection to the claimed violation. Protected persons include teachers, students, researchers, artists, writers and journalists. The procedure is entirely confidential.

Complainants must submit a short letter to the Secretariat of UNESCO stating violations of human rights protected by the Organization. The Secretariat then acknowledges receipt of the letter and requests its author to complete a form that will constitute his or her "communication." The communication is then forwarded to the government concerned and examined by UNESCO's Committee on Conventions and Recommendations which will review its admissibility.

To be admissible a communication must meet the following conditions:

- must not be anonymous
- must not be manifestly ill-founded and must be accompanied by sufficient evidence
- must not constitute an abuse of the right to submit communications

- must not be based exclusively on information disseminated through the mass media
- must be submitted within a reasonable time limit following the facts or the knowledge of the alleged facts
- must indicate whether attempts have been made to exhaust all available domestic remedies and what these decisions by national jurisdiction are.

In the course of its review, the Committee meeting in private sessions may hear from representatives of the State concerned. Its decisions are communicated to the state and the author of the communication. These decisions are not subject to appeal but may be re-examined in the light of new information received.

Source: www.claiminghumanrights.org/unesco_procedure.html

Appendix 10

Complaint Procedure of the International Labour Organization

MAIN PROTECTED RIGHTS

The complaint procedure is governed by Articles 26 to 34 of the ILO Constitution and covers all rights protected under the Constitution and the Conventions adopted by the ILO Conference. Most particularly:

- Freedom of Association and of Collective Bargaining (Conventions No. 87 and No. 98)
- Prohibition of Forced Labour (Conventions No. 29 and No. 105)
- Elimination of Discrimination in Respect of Employment and Occupation (Conventions No. 100 and No. 111)
- Abolition of Child Labour (Conventions No. 138 and No. 182)

PROCEDURE

Complaint procedures against a member state not observing a convention to which it is a party cannot be filed by individual but may be initiated by another Member State also having ratified the same convention, any delegate to the ILO Conference the employers or the workers, and the ILO Governing Body.

Complaints are handled by the ILO Governing Body which may appoint a Commission of Inquiry which will examine the merits of the complaint, investigate the facts and formulate remedial measures.

If a state refuses to comply with the recommendations of the Commission, the Governing Body may take measures on the basis of Article 33 of the ILO Constitution which provides that "in the event of any Member failing to carry out within the time specified the recommendations, if any, contained in the report of the Commission of Inquiry . . . the Governing Body may recommend to the Conference such action as it may deem wise and expedient to secure compliance therewith."

Source: www.ilo.org/global/standards/applying-and-promoting-international-labour-standards/complaints/lang--en/index.htm

Appendix 11

Taking a Case to the European Court of Human Rights

WHO CAN SUBMIT TO THE ECHR?

Any individual or group who is/are the direct victim(s) of a human rights violation can bring a case to the ECHR. (Family members may also be considered direct victims.) Non-government human rights organizations that have faced state repression in their work can appeal to the court as victims. Those submitting cases do not need be a national of any of the states that are under the Court's jurisdiction. Legal representation is not required to submit a case, but petitioners' commission may receive the assistance of a lawyer from the beginning. A lawyer can ensure an application is properly formulated and thoroughly articulated.

APPLICATIONS

Applications must contain a brief summary of the facts, an indication of the Convention right(s) the complainant believes has been violated, the remedies already undertaken and copies of the result of such remedies. No documents will be returned and only copies should be sent. Applications must be written in English, French or in an official language of one of the States that have ratified the Convention.

ADMISSIBILITY CRITERIA

Applications must demonstrate the following in order to be considered admissible by the court:

1. An application must concern a violation of the European Convention of Human Rights and Fundamental Freedoms.
2. Individuals or groups who are bringing cases forward must have first exhausted domestic remedies. This usually means that the party submitting the case must have already appealed to the highest court of the

state, and that this court refused to hear the case, took an unreasonably long time processing the case or produced a response unsatisfactory to the interests of human rights. In other words, the state itself must have been given an opportunity to redress the violation through its own institutional means. In cases where domestic remedies have shown themselves to be ineffective, it is not necessary for applicants to appeal to these domestic mechanisms, however, applicants should provide evidence showing the remedy's ineffectiveness.

3. Applications must be submitted within six months "following the last judicial decision in the case."

4. The applicant must be a direct victim of the violation(s) that the application concerns; family to a victim of a human rights violation is considered a direct victim in cases of violation of the right to life. The application must be lodged against a state that has ratified the Convention before the violation took place.

5. According to Protocol 14, an amendment to the European Convention on Human Rights that entered into force in June 2010, those submitting cases must now show the violation caused them "significant disadvantage." The significant disadvantage clause does not apply to cases that were not "duly considered" by domestic courts or cases that require examination in order for the Court to uphold respect for human rights as defined by the convention.

Once the court receives an application, it is reviewed and deemed "admissible," meaning it is approved for further deliberation, or "inadmissible," meaning the case is thrown out. If the Court declares a case inadmissible, the decision is final; however, an applicant may resubmit if further evidence comes to light. Decisions on admissibility must contain reasons, must be made public and cannot be made by a judge from the country in which the case concerns. To be admissible, an application must satisfy several technical and legal requirements.

If a case is "admissible," the Court proceeds to consider the case on its merits. The government of the state that the application has been lodged against is notified, and each party presents additional information and evidence on the alleged violation(s). Applicants may wish to seek the representation of a lawyer at this stage and the Court may provide legal aid to some parties.

If both parties are willing, the Court will oversee a friendly settlement through negotiations with the parties. If ongoing violations related to the case are likely to occur, the Court may order the state to take "provisional measures" to protect the individual(s) during the interim period. Interim measures are most often applied when individuals face deportation or extradition.

For cases that are "repetitive," meaning they are very similar to other cases brought to the Court in the past, a three-judge member committee has the power to decide on cases based on their merits and the well-established case law of the Court. The committee's decisions are final.

Other cases are considered by one of five seven-member Chambers, each of which has a president and vice president and will include the national judge of the state concerned. Often, the Chamber may order a basic remedy, such as compensation, based on the written material provided by both parties and will consider the case closed. Only rare cases are provided a public hearing.

In cases of massive or egregious human rights violations, cases are automatically referred to a 17-judge Chamber, which includes the Court's president and vice president and all of the presidents of the chambers, in addition to 10 rotating judges. The Chambers' decisions on cases are made by a majority vote.

Either party of a case that has been heard by a seven-member Chamber may request an appeal to the Grand Chamber within three months after the judgment. This request is made to a panel of judges from the Grand Chamber and is only granted in exceptional cases. When this referral occurs, the judges who heard the case in the initial Chamber are excluded. Chambers may also relinquish cases to the Grand Chamber when it involves an especially complicated interpretation of the Convention, however, such a relinquishment is unusual. The Grand Chamber judgment is always final; however, applicants may resubmit a case if it contains fresh evidence.

THIRD-PARTY INTERVENTION

Experts, representatives of human rights organizations and others can gain permission from the Court to intervene in the proceedings by filing pleadings or to take part in public hearings. In addition, states that are party to the Convention can intervene in cases where the applicant is a national to that state. The purpose of such intervention is to ensure the proper administration of justice and third-party interveners should thus conduct themselves in a manner that shows no bias. Third-party submissions often include the basic facts of the case and provide additional context or legal interpretation, such as information on the human rights repercussions of a law or legal decision.

Source: www.echr.coe.int/NR/rdonlyres/DD9DE91F-2494-4347-B9B6-C5B 9F89BAC32/0/ENG_SCHEMA.pdf

Appendix 12

Complaint Procedure in the Inter-American Commission and Court on Human Rights

I. COMMISSION

Who May File a Complaint?

Article 44 ACHR: "Any person or group of persons, or any non-governmental entity legally recognized in one or more member states of the Organization, may lodge petitions with the Commission containing denunciations or complaints of violation of this Convention by a State Party."

Admissibility

Exhaustion of domestic remedies: Article 46 ACHR and Article 31 Rules of Procedure of the Inter-American Commission. Admission by the Commission of a petition or communication requires that "the remedies under domestic law have been pursued and exhausted in accordance with generally recognized principles of international law." According to Article 46(2), this rule is not applicable "when: (a) the domestic legislation of the state concerned does not afford due process of law for the protection of the right or rights that have allegedly been violated; (b) the party alleging violation of his rights has been denied access to the remedies under domestic law or has been prevented from exhausting them; or (c) there has been unwarranted delay in rendering a final judgment under the aforementioned remedies."

Time period: Article 46 ACHR. The petition or communication must be lodged "within a period of six months from the date on which the party alleging violation of his rights was notified of the final judgment."

Duplication of procedures at the international level: Article 46 ACHR. Admission by the Commission of a petition or communication requires "that the subject of the petition or communication is not pending in another international proceeding for settlement." According to Article 47, the Commission shall consider any petition or communication inadmissible if "the petition or communication is substantially the same as one previously studied by the Commission or by another international organisation."

Inadmissibility

Article 47 ACHR. The Commission shall consider any petition or communication inadmissible if: "(a) any of the requirements indicated in Article 46 has not been met [see above]; (b) the petition or communication does not state facts that tend to establish a violation of the rights guaranteed by this Convention; (c) the statements of the petitioner or of the state indicate that the petition or communication is manifestly groundless or obviously out of order."

Friendly Settlements

Article 48(1)(f) ACHR: "The Commission shall place itself at the disposal of the parties concerned with a view to reaching a friendly settlement of the matter on the basis of respect for the human rights recognized in this Convention."

Interim Measures

Article 25(1) Rules of Procedure: "In serious and urgent cases, and whenever necessary according to the information available, the Commission may, its own initiative or at the request of a party, adopt precautionary measures to prevent irreparable harm to persons."

II. INTER-AMERICAN COURT OF HUMAN RIGHTS

Who May File a Complaint?

Article 61(1) ACHR. Only a state party and the Inter-American Commission have the right to submit a case to the Court. Individuals may, however, submit cases to the Inter-American Commission (see below). In cases before the Court, alleged victims are allowed to participate in the proceedings submitting their pleadings, motions and evidence, autonomously, throughout the proceedings. They may also request the adoption of provisional measures (Articles 23 and 25 Rules of Procedure).

Admissibility

Exhaustion of domestic remedies: Articles 46 and 47 ACHR. Admission by the Commission requires "that the remedies under domestic law have been pursued and exhausted in accordance with generally recognised principles of international law." This rule shall not be applicable when "(a) the domestic legislation of the state concerned does not afford due process of law for the protection of the right or rights that have allegedly been violated; (b) the party alleging violation of his rights has been denied access to remedies under domestic law or has been prevented from exhausting them; or (c) there has been unwarranted delay in rendering a final judgment under the aforementioned remedies."

Time period: Article 46 ACHR. Admission by the Commission requires "that the petition or communication is lodged within a period of six months from the date on which the party alleging violation of his rights was notified of the final judgment."

Duplication of procedures at the international level: Article 46 ACHR. Admission by the Commission requires "that the subject of the petition or communication is not pending in another international proceeding for settlement."

Interim Measures

Article 63(2) ACHR: "In cases of extreme gravity and urgency, and when necessary to avoid irreparable damage to persons, the Court shall adopt such provisional measures as it deems pertinent in matters it has under consideration. With respect to a case not yet submitted to the Court, it may act at the request of the Commission."

Judgments

Article 63(1) ACHR: "If the Court finds that there has been a violation of a right or freedom protected by this Convention, the Court shall rule that the injured party be ensured the enjoyment of his right or freedom that was violated. It shall also rule, if appropriate, that the consequences of the measure or situation that constituted the breach of such right or freedom be remedied and that fair compensation be paid to the injured party."

Binding force: Article 68 ACHR. "1. The States Parties to the Convention undertake to comply with the judgment of the Court in any case to which they are parties. 2. That part of a judgment that stipulates compensatory damages may be executed in the country concerned in accordance with domestic procedure governing the execution of judgments against the state."

Execution of judgements: The Convention does not establish any institutional role for the political organs of the Organisation of American States to supervise enforcement of the Court's rulings. There is no counterpart, for example, to the Committee of Ministers of the Council of Europe. In the American Convention, only one article refers to the enforcement of judgments. According to Article 65, the Court is obliged to submit an Annual Report to each regular session of the General Assembly of the OAS for its consideration. In this report, the Court "shall specify, in particular, the cases in which a state has not complied with its judgments, making any pertinent recommendations."

Amicus Curiae Briefs

The Court receives amicus curiae briefs regularly, although there is no specific provision regulating their submission.

Inquiry Procedures

Article 45(4) Rules of Procedure. The Court may at any stage of the proceedings "[c]ommission one or more of its members to hold hearings, including preliminary hearings, either at the seat of the Court or elsewhere, for the purpose of gathering evidence."

Friendly Settlements

Article 54 Rules of Procedure: "When the parties to a case before the Court inform it of the existence of a friendly settlement, compromise, or any other occurrence likely to lead to a settlement of the dispute, the Court may strike the case from its list."

Advisory Opinions

Article 64 ACHR: "1. The member states of the Organisation may consult the Court regarding the interpretation of this Convention or of other treaties concerning the protection of human rights in the American states. Within their spheres of competence, the organs listed in Chapter X of the Charter of the Organization of American States, as amended by the Protocol of Buenos Aires, may in like manner consult the Court. 2. The Court, at the request of a member state of the Organization, may provide that state with opinions regarding the compatibility of any of its domestic laws with the aforesaid international instruments."

Source: www.humanrights.is/the-human-rights-project/humanrightscasesand materials/howtocomplain/interamericancommission/

Appendix 13

Paris Principles Relating to the Status of National Human Rights Institutions: Annex to UNGA Resolution 48/134 of 4 March 1994

COMPETENCE AND RESPONSIBILITIES

1. A national institution shall be vested with competence to promote and protect human rights.
2. A national institution shall be given as broad a mandate as possible, which shall be clearly set forth in a constitutional or legislative text, specifying its composition and its sphere of competence.
3. A national institution shall, inter alia, have the following responsibilities:

   (a) To submit to the Government, Parliament and any other competent body, on an advisory basis either at the request of the authorities concerned or through the exercise of its power to hear a matter without higher referral, opinions, recommendations, proposals and reports on any matters concerning the promotion and protection of human rights; the national institution may decide to publicize them; these opinions, recommendations, proposals and reports, as well as any prerogative of the national institution, shall relate to the following areas:

   (i) Any legislative or administrative provisions, as well as provisions relating to judicial organizations, intended to preserve and extend the protection of human rights; in that connection, the national institution shall examine the legislation and administrative provisions in force, as well as bills and proposals, and shall make such recommendations as it deems appropriate in order to ensure that these provisions conform to the fundamental principles of human rights; it shall, if necessary, recommend the adoption of new legislation, the amendment of legislation in force and the adoption or amendment of administrative measures;

   (ii) Any situation of violation of human rights which it decides to take up;

      (iii) The preparation of reports on the national situation with regard to human rights in general, and on more specific matters;

      (iv) Drawing the attention of the Government to situations in any part of the country where human rights are violated and making proposals to it for initiatives to put an end to such situations and, where necessary, expressing an opinion on the positions and reactions of the Government;

(b) To promote and ensure the harmonization of national legislation regulations and practices with the international human rights instruments to which the State is a party, and their effective implementation;

(c) To encourage ratification of the above-mentioned instruments or accession to those instruments, and to ensure their implementation;

(d) To contribute to the reports which States are required to submit to United Nations bodies and committees, and to regional institutions, pursuant to their treaty obligations and, where necessary, to express an opinion on the subject, with due respect for their independence;

(e) To cooperate with the United Nations and any other organization in the United Nations system, the regional institutions and the national institutions of other countries that are competent in the areas of the promotion and protection of human rights;

(f) To assist in the formulation of programmes for the teaching of, and research into, human rights and to take part in their execution in schools, universities and professional circles;

(g) To publicize human rights and efforts to combat all forms of discrimination, in particular racial discrimination, by increasing public awareness, especially through information and education and by making use of all press organs.

COMPOSITION AND GUARANTEES
OF INDEPENDENCE AND PLURALISM

1. The composition of the national institution and the appointment of its members, whether by means of an election or otherwise, shall be established in accordance with a procedure which affords all necessary guarantees to ensure the pluralist representation of the social forces (of civilian society) involved in the promotion and protection of human rights, particularly by powers which will enable effective cooperation to be established with, or through the presence of, representatives of:

(a) Non-governmental organizations responsible for human rights and efforts to combat racial discrimination, trade unions, concerned social and professional organizations, for example, associations of lawyers, doctors, journalists and eminent scientists;
(b) Trends in philosophical or religious thought;
(c) Universities and qualified experts;
(d) Parliament;
(e) Government departments (if these are included, their representatives should participate in the deliberations only in an advisory capacity).

2. The national institution shall have an infrastructure which is suited to the smooth conduct of its activities, in particular adequate funding. The purpose of this funding should be to enable it to have its own staff and premises, in order to be independent of the Government and not be subject to financial control which might affect its independence.
3. In order to ensure a stable mandate for the members of the national institution, without which there can be no real independence, their appointment shall be effected by an official act which shall establish the specific duration of the mandate. This mandate may be renewable, provided that the pluralism of the institution's membership is ensured.

METHODS OF OPERATION

Within the framework of its operation, the national institution shall:

1. Freely consider any questions falling within its competence, whether they are submitted by the Government or taken up by it without referral to a higher authority, on the proposal of its members or of any petitioner;
2. Hear any person and obtain any information and any documents necessary for assessing situations falling within its competence;
3. Address public opinion directly or through any press organ, particularly in order to publicize its opinions and recommendations;
4. Meet on a regular basis and whenever necessary in the presence of all its members after they have been duly convened;
5. Establish working groups from among its members as necessary, and set up local or regional sections to assist it in discharging its functions;
6. Maintain consultation with the other bodies, whether jurisdictional or otherwise, responsible for the promotion and protection of human rights (in particular ombudsmen, mediators and similar institutions);

7. In view of the fundamental role played by the non-governmental organizations in expanding the work of the national institutions, develop relations with the non-governmental organizations devoted to promoting and protecting human rights, to economic and social development, to combating racism, to protecting particularly vulnerable groups (especially children, migrant workers, refugees, physically and mentally disabled persons) or to specialized areas.

ADDITIONAL PRINCIPLES CONCERNING THE STATUS OF COMMISSIONS WITH QUASI-JURISDICTIONAL COMPETENCE

A national institution may be authorized to hear and consider complaints and petitions concerning individual situations. Cases may be brought before it by individuals, their representatives, third parties, non-governmental organizations, associations of trade unions or any other representative organizations. In such circumstances, and without prejudice to the principles stated above concerning the other powers of the commissions, the functions entrusted to them may be based on the following principles:

1. Seeking an amicable settlement through conciliation or, within the limits prescribed by the law, through binding decisions or, where necessary, on the basis of confidentiality;
2. Informing the party who filed the petition of his rights, in particular the remedies available to him, and promoting his access to them;
3. Hearing any complaints or petitions or transmitting them to any other competent authority within the limits prescribed by the law;
4. Making recommendations to the competent authorities, especially by proposing amendments or reforms of the laws, regulations and administrative practices, especially if they have created the difficulties encountered by the persons filing the petitions in order to assert their rights.

Bibliography

CONTENTS

INTRODUCTION

Documentation about human rights practice is a growth industry and its exponential variety and vastness can be overwhelming to the uninitiated. The primary goal of this bibliography is to provide a guide to students, educators, practitioners and general readers to the ever-expanding body of information pertaining to international human rights practice with a focus on primary and secondary English-language publicly accessible sources.

The bibliography is divided into two broad sections. The first one focuses on reference material, a category which includes guides, dictionaries, yearbooks, encyclopedias, texts and treaties, official publications, academic journals, newsletters, think tanks and non-governmental organizations. The second section is of a topical nature covering the practices of state and non-state actors, the functioning and activities of human rights institutions (global and regional), and practice in selected categories of human rights: civil and political rights, slavery and servitude, torture, the treatment of prisoners, genocide, war crimes and crime against humanity, economic and social and cultural rights, group rights and corporate social responsibility. Also featured in this section are matters related to transitional, retributive and restorative justice. At the end of this section, secondary source material is provided on country/regional case studies, and the last section deals with emerging issues and challenges confronting human rights practitioners with particular attention to the impact of globalization-related issues on the realization of human rights, the fractious ongoing and intensifying debate over the universality of human rights, the significance of terrorism for the enjoyment of rights and the implications of the emerging norm of "a responsibility to protect." The bibliography closes with items dealing with baffling substantive questions which so far have received imperfect legal and political remedies.

All throughout and under each of the bibliography's sections, due attention is given to electronic sources of information which are, whenever appropriate and feasible, treated separately. Overall and with due attention to the indispensable "musts" or "classics," priority has been given to publications—all of them in the English language—which have been issued in the past decade or so.

REFERENCE

Dictionaries, Bibliographies, Yearbooks, Encyclopedias and Guides to Research and Practice

Web

An enormous body of information on human rights practice can be found on the Internet. A good place to start is to check library catalogs at WorldCat (www.worldcat.org/) which provides access to more than 10,000 library catalogs. Library catalogs are often available on the web and some of them may be accessed at the Library of Congress (http://lcweb.loc.gov/z3950/

gateway.html#other). Guides to online resources (and written) resources include the United Nations Documentation Research Guide on Human Rights (www.un.org/Depts/dhl/resguide/spechr.htm) and UNBISnet (http://unbisnet .un.org/) both issued by the by the United Nations Dag Hammarskjöld Library.

- The Office of the High Commissioner for Human Rights (UN-HCHR) has developed a Professional Training Series, which includes a number of handbooks and manuals on human rights treaty reporting, monitoring and documentation of specific human rights abuses. Manual No. 7, Training Manual on Human Rights Monitoring, includes an overview of international and humanitarian law, principles of monitoring, guidelines on information gathering and interviewing as well as specific information on monitoring in detention facilities, the rights of refugees and displaced persons, and the rights of children and monitoring during situations of armed conflict. The manual can be accessed in PDF format from the UN-HCHR training and educational materials webpage or chapter by chapter in HTML format from the University of Minnesota, Human Rights Library.
- The Directory of Human Rights Resources on the Internet, launched in 1996 by the American Association for the Advancement of Science and Human Rights, has been replaced by Human Rights Information and Documentation Systems (HURISEARCH, www.hurisearch.org/). This search engine gives access to over 5,000 human rights websites. Since 1990, Human Rights Internet (www.hri.ca/index.aspx) has collected and indexed one of the largest collection of human rights documents. Its microfiche database provides information on the location, mandate, activities and publications of over 300 organizations globally.
- The International Relations and Security Network (ISN) is an open access information service for international relations and security professionals providing access to special reports on key security, defense and international relations issues, including human rights. The site (www.isn.ethz .ch/) also features a digital library offering the full text of research papers, reports and journal articles, all available to download without charge, a comprehensive directory of think tanks, research institutes, NGOs and other organizations. The human rights documents in the world Microfiche Database provide information on the location, mandate, activities and publications of over 300 organizations globally.
- Marci Hoffman, Researching International Human Rights Law (revised August 2010) (www.law.berkeley.edu/library/dynamic/guide .php?id=36) is yet another useful guide available through the web as is the Human Rights Guide at the University of Toronto (http://guides.library .utoronto.ca/internationalhumanrights).

Printed Sources

Alston, Philip, and James Heenan. *Economic, Social and Cultural Rights. A Bibliography.* New York: Cambridge University Press, 2008.

Anheier, Helmut K. *A Dictionary of Civil Society, Philanthropy and the Non-Profit Sector.* New York: Routledge, 2005.

Bouchet-Saulnier, Francoise. *The Practical Guide to Humanitarian Law.* New Edition. Lanham, Md.: Rowman & Littlefield, 2007.

Brown, Bartram S. *Research Handbook on International Criminal Law.* Northampton, Mass.: Edward Elgar, 2011.

Brownlie, Ian, and Guy Goodwin-Gill. *Basic Documents on Human Rights.* Sixth Edition. New York: Oxford University Press, 2010.

Cassese, Antonio. *The Oxford Companion to International Criminal Justice.* New York: Oxford University Press, 2009.

Chaterjee, Deen. *Encyclopedia of Global Justice.* New York: Springer, 2011.

Cheria, Anita Edwin, and Sriprapha Petcharamesree. *A Human Rights Approach to Development: A Source Book.* Bangalore: Published by Books for Change, 2003.

Chiweshe, F. G. *Reference Book on Human Rights Enforcement and Monitoring Mechanisms.* Harare, Zimbabwe: Human Rights Trust of Southern Africa, 2007.

Conde, H. Victor. *A Handbook on International Human Rights Terminology.* Lincoln: University of Nebraska Press, 2004.

Crane, A., et al. (eds.). *The Oxford Handbook of Corporate Social Responsibility.* New York: Oxford University Press, 2008.

Crowther, D., and N. Capaldi (eds.). *The Ashgate Research Companion to Corporate Social Responsibility.* Aldershot: Ashgate, 2008.

Cushman, Thomas (ed.). *Handbook of Human Rights.* New York: Routledge, 2011.

De Beco, Gauthier. *Human Rights Monitoring Mechanisms of the Council of Europe.* New York: Routledge, 2012.

De Greiff, P. (ed.). *The Handbook on Reparations.* New York: Oxford University Press, 2006.

Du Plessis, Max (ed.). *African Guide to International Criminal Justice.* Tswane, SA: Institute for Security Studies, 2008.

Elagab, Omer, and Jeehaan Elagab. *International Law Documents Relating to Terrorism.* New York: Routledge, 2006.

Encyclopedia of Associations. *Encyclopedia of Associations.* International Organizations [serial]. Detroit, Mich.: Gale Research, 1961–.

Europa Publications. *European Foundations and Grant-Making NGOs.* London: Europa Publications, 2004.

Fitzpatrick, Joan M. (ed.). *Human Rights Protection for Refugees, Asylum-Seekers, and Internally Displaced Persons: A Guide to International Mechanisms and Procedures*. New York: Transnational Publishers, 2001.

Fleck, Dieter. *The Handbook of International Humanitarian Law*. Second Edition. New York: Oxford University Press, 2008.

Forsythe, David (ed.). *Encyclopedia of Human Rights*. New York: Oxford University Press, 2009.

Franklin, Bob (ed.). *The New Handbook of Children's Rights: Comparative Policy and Practice*. Second Edition. London: Routledge, 2002.

GCS Yearbook Series. Oxford: Oxford University Press; 2004, onward by London: Sage.

Ghandhi, Sandy. *Blackstone's International Human Rights Documents*. Seventh Edition. New York: Oxford University Press, 2010.

Global Agenda: Issues Before the General Assembly of the United Nations: An Annual Publication of the United Nations Association of the United States of America. Lanham, Md.: University Press of America, 1991–2005, 2009–.

Gorman, Robert F., and Edward S. Mihalkanin. *Human Rights and Humanitarian Organizations*, Second Edition. Lanham, Md.: Rowman & Littlefield, 2007.

Groome, Dermot. *The Handbook of Human Rights Investigation. A Comprehensive Guide to the Investigation and Documentation of Violent Human Rights Abuses*. Northborough, Mass.: Human Rights Press, 2000.

Haynes, Jeffrey (ed.). *Routledge Handbook of Democratization*. New York: Routledge, 2011.

Hollis, Duncan (ed.). *The Oxford Guide to Treaties*. New York: Oxford University Press, 2012.

Hufner, Klaus. *How to File Complaints on Human Rights Violations: A Manual for Individuals and NGOs*. Bonn, Germany: UNO-Verlag, 2010.

Human Rights Watch World Report. New York: Human Rights Watch, 1991–.

Hurst, Hannum (ed.). *Guide to International Human Rights Practice*. Ardsley, N.Y.: Transnational, 2005.

Jacobsen, Anette Faye. *Human Rights Monitoring: A Field Mission Manual*. Leiden: Martinus Nijhoff Publishers, 2008.

Joseph, Sarah, and Adam McBeth (eds.). *Research Handbook on International Human Rights Law*. Northampton, Mass.: Edward Elgar, 2010.

Joseph, Sarah, Katie Mitchell, and Linda Gyorki. *Seeking Remedies for Torture Victims. A Handbook on the Individual Complaints Procedures of the UN Treaty Bodies*. Geneva: OMCT, 2006.

Knight, W. Andy, and Frazer Egerton (eds.). *The Routledge Handbook of the Responsibility to Protect*. New York: Routledge: 2012.

Kolb, Robert, and Gloria Gagglioli (eds.). *Research Handbook on Human Rights and Humanitarian Law.* Herndon, Va.: Edward Elgar Publishing, 2013.

Langley, Winston. *Encyclopedia of Human Rights Since 1945.* Westport, Conn.: Greenwood Press, 1999.

Leckie, Scott, and Anne Gallanger. *Economic, Social and Cultural Rights: A Legal Resource Guide.* Baltimore, Md.: University Press of Pennsylvania, 2006.

MacGinty, Roger (ed.). *Routledge Handbook of Peacebuilding.* New York: Routledge, 2012.

Mackenzie, Ruth, Cesare Romano, and Yuval Shany. *The Manual on International Courts and Tribunals.* Second Edition. New York: Oxford University Press, 2010.

Maddex, Robert L. *International Encyclopedia of Human Rights: Freedoms, Abuses, and Remedies.* Washington, D.C.: CQ Press, 2000.

Marks, Stephen P. *Health and Human Rights: Basic International Documents.* Second Edition. Cambridge, Mass.: François-Xavier Bagnoud Center for Health and Human Rights, Harvard School of Public Health/Harvard University Press, 2006.

Marks, Susan, and Andrew Clapham. *International Human Rights Lexicon.* New York: Oxford University Press, 2005.

Martin, Francisco Forrest, Stephen J. Schnably, Richard Wilson, Jonathan Simon, and Mark Tushnet. *International Human Rights and Humanitarian Law. Treaties, Cases, and Analysis.* New York: Cambridge University Press, 2006.

Martin, Mary, and Taylor Owe (eds.). *Routledge Handbook of Human Security.* New York: Routledge, 2012.

Mateseza, Philliat. *Human Rights Monitoring and Enforcement Mechanisms: A Practical Guide to the United Nations and the African Union Protection Mechanisms.* Harare, Zimbabwe: Human Rights Trust of Southern Africa, 2006.

Murray, Rachel, and Malcolm Evans (eds.). *Documents of the African Commission on Human and Peoples' Rights.* Volume II: *1999–2005.* Oxford: Hart Publishing, 2008.

Office of the High Commissioner for Human Rights. *Manual of Operations of the Special Procedures of the Human Rights Council.* Geneva: United Nations, 2008.

Office of the High Commissioner for Human Rights (in cooperation with the International Bar Association). Professional Training Series No. 9. *Human Rights in the Administration of Justice. A Manual on Human Rights for Judges, Prosecutors and Lawyers.* New York: United Nations, 2003.

O'Flaherty, Michael (ed.). *The Human Rights Field Operation: Law, Theory and Practice*. Burlington, Vt.: Ashgate, 2007.

O'Flaherty, Michael, and George Ulrich (eds.). *The Professional Identity of the Human Rights Field Officer*. Burlington, Vt.: Ashgate, 2010.

Perruchoud, Richard, and Katarina Tomolova (eds.). *Compendium of International Migration Law Instruments*. New York: Cambridge University Press, 2007.

Phelan, Margaret. *Immigration Law Handbook*. Fifth Edition. New York: Oxford University Press, 2007.

Rausch, Colette (ed.). *Combating Serious Crimes in Post Conflict Societies. A Handbook for Policymakers and Practitioners*. Herndon, Va.: United States Institute of Peace Press, 2006.

Redman, Nina. *Human Rights: A Reference Handbook*. Santa Barbara, Calif.: ABC-CLIO, 1998.

Reid, Karen. *A Practitioner's Guide to the European Convention on Human Rights*. Third Edition. London: Sweet & Maxwell, 2008.

Reinisch, August (ed.). *Challenging Acts of International Organizations before National Courts*. New York: Oxford University Press, 2010.

Rummel, Rudolph G. *Statistics of Democide*. Center on National Security and Law, University of Virginia, 1997. Republished by Lit Verlag, Myster, Germany in 1998 and distributed in America by Transaction Publishers.

Sachleben, Mark. *Human Rights Treaties, Considering Patterns of Participation. 1948–2000*. New York: Routledge, 2005.

Schmid, Alex (ed.). *The Routledge Handbook of Terrorism Research*. New York: Routledge, 2011.

Shelton, Dinah (ed.), *Encyclopedia of Genocide and Crimes Against Humanity*. 3 vols. Detroit, Mich.: Macmillan Reference, 2005.

Stidsen, Sills (ed.). *The Indigenous World, 2006*. New Brunswick, N.J.: Transaction Publishers, 2006. (Annual since 2002).

Thoolen, Hans, and Beth Verstappen. *Human Rights Missions: A Study of the Fact-Finding Practice of Non-Governmental Organizations*. Dordrecht: M. Nijhoff, 1986.

Totten, Samuel (ed.). *Genocide at the Millennium. A Critical Bibliographic Review*, Volume 5. Rutgers, N.J.: Transaction Publishers, 2006.

——— (ed.). *The Prevention and Intervention of Genocide. A Critical Bibliographic Review*, Volume 6. Rutgers, N.J.: Transaction Publishers, 2007.

Tully, S. (ed.). *Research Handbook on Corporate Social Responsibility*. Cheltenham: Edward Elgar, 2005.

Union of International Associations. *Yearbook of International Organizations*. Published since 1908. Brussels: Union of International Associations.

United Nations. *Bringing International Human Rights Law Home*. New York: United Nations, 2000.

———. *Handbook on HIV and Human Rights Institutions*. New York: United Nations, 2007.

United Nations Centre for Human Rights. *National Human Rights Institutions: A Handbook on the Establishment and Strengthening of National Institutions for the Promotion and Protection of Human Rights*. Professional Training Series No. 4. New York: United Nations, 1995.

Vega, Constance de la (ed.). *Dictionary of International Human Rights*. Herndon, Va.: Edward Elgar Publishing, 2013.

Visser, W., et al. (eds.). *The A to Z of Corporate Social Responsibility*. Hoboken, N.J.: Wiley, 2007.

Treaties and Texts

Web

Compilations of international human rights instruments are widely available through the international organizations that sponsored them. The website of the United Nations Office of the High Commissioner for Human Rights (OHCHR) (www.ohchr.org/EN/Pages/WelcomePage.aspx) is an essential starting point, especially its Human Rights Bodies section (www.ohchr.org/EN/HRbodies/Pages/HumanRightsBodies.aspx) and its more recent Universal Human Rights Index of United Nations Documents (www.universalhumanrightsindex.org/) which contain information about charter-based bodies as well as the treaty-based bodies.

In regard to the European Convention of Human Rights and the European Social Charter adopted under the aegis of the Council of Europe, the reader will find it useful to consult the websites of the Council (www.coe.int/DefaultEN.asp and human-rights-convention.org/). Documentation on the African Union can be obtained from the official website of the African Union (www.africa-union.org) and that of the Organization of American States (www.oas.org/en/information_center/default.asp).

The conventions and recommendations of the International Labour Organization can be accessed at www.ilo.org/ilolex/english/convdisp1.htm and www.ilo.org/ilolex/english/recdisp1.htm. Information on the United Nations Educational, Scientific and Cultural Organization (UNESCO) can be obtained through the UNESCO Official web server (www.unesco.org/) under the Standard Setting Instruments section. Relevant instruments on refugees and internally displaced persons (IDPs) can be found on the Office of the United Nations High Commissioner of Human Rights (UN-OHCHR) website (www.unhcr.org/cgi-bin/texis/vtx/home).

The Commonwealth Secretariat produces material covering policy issues, case studies and good practice promotion in areas including globalization and multilateral trade issues, export and enterprise development, education, gender, public service management and reform, law and human rights, and issues of concern to small states. These publications are available for purchase through http://publications.thecommonwealth.org/.

Collections of the most important documents on human rights, including several hundred human rights treaties and other primary international human rights instruments, can be accessed at the University of Minnesota Human Rights Library (www1.umn.edu/humanrts/) and Human Rights Network International (www.hrni.org/index_flash.html).

Another useful guide warranting mention here is the *ASIL Guide to Electronic Resources for International Law* (www.asil.org/erghome.cfm) which includes sections on human rights and international criminal law and a guide to researching treaties.

The status of international human rights instruments can be verified in the United Nations Treaty Collection (http://treaties.un.org/Pages/Home.aspx?lang=en) and declarations and reservations at http://treaties.un.org/Pages/UNTSOnline.aspx?id=1.

Researching the jurisprudence of human rights bodies and international criminal courts and tribunals requires having recourse to a combination of search tools available on the organizations' websites, commercial databases such as Lexis and Westlaw and search engines developed by academic entities such as the University of Minnesota (mentioned above) and the World Legal Information Institute or public policy research organizations (see below). The website of Professor A. F. Bayefsky, York University, Toronto, Canada, provides extensive information and data on the application of the UN human rights treaty system by its monitoring treaty bodies (www.bayefsky.com).

Printed Sources

Arnold, Roberta, and Noelle Quenivet (eds.). *International Humanitarian Law and Human Rights Law: Towards a New Merger in International Law*. Leiden: Martinus Nijhoff, 2008.

Baderin, Mashood, and Manisuli Ssenyonjo (eds.). *International Human Rights Law. Six Decades after the UDHR and Beyond.* Burlington, Vt.: Ashgate, 2010.

Belts, Charles R., and Robert E. Goodin (eds.). *Global Basic Rights*. New York: Oxford University Press, 2009.

Ben-Nafali, Orna (ed.). *International Human Rights and International Humanitarian Law*. New York: Oxford University Press, 2011.

Brems, Eva (ed.). *Conflicts Between Rights*. Antwerp: Intersentia, 2008.

Clayton, Gina. *Textbook on Civil Liberties and Human Rights*. New York: Oxford University Press, 2010.

Clayton, Richard, and Hugh Tomlinson. *The Law of Human Rights*. New York: Oxford University Press, 2009.

De Schutter, Olivier. *International Human Rights Law*. New York: Cambridge University Press, 2010.

Edmundson, William A. *An Introduction to Rights*. Cambridge: Cambridge University Press, 2012.

Eide, A., C. Krause, and A. Rosas (eds.). *Economic, Social and Cultural Rights: A Textbook*. Second Edition. Dordrecht: Martinus Nijhoff, 2001.

Fagan, Andrew. *Human Rights. Confronting Myths and Misunderstandings*. Northampton, Mass.: Edward Elgar, 2009.

Forsythe, David. *Human Rights in International Relations*. Third Edition. Cambridge: Cambridge University Press, 2011.

Fredman, Sandra. *Human Rights Transformed*. New York: Oxford University Press, 2008.

Gearty, Conor. *Principles of Human Rights Adjudication.* New York: Oxford University Press, 2004.

Gearty, Conor, and Costas Douzinas. *The Cambridge Companion to Human Rights Law*. New York: Cambridge University Press, 2012.

Gerber, Paula. *Understanding Human Rights. Educational Challenges for the Future.* Herndon, Va.: Edward Elgar Publishing, 2013.

Gibney, Mark. *International Human Rights Law: Returning to Universal Principles*. Lanham, Md.: Rowman & Littlefield, 2008.

Gondek, Michal. *The Reach of Human Rights in a Globalizing World: Extraterritorial Application of Human Rights Treaties*. Antwerp: Intersentia, 2009.

Goodale, Mark. *The Anthropology of Human Rights: Critical Explorations in Ethical Theory and Social Practice*. Philadelphia: University of Pennsylvania Press, 2008.

Goodale, Mark, and Sally Engle Merry (eds.). *The Practice of Human Rights. Tracking Law Between the Global and the Local.* New York: Cambridge, 2007.

Henkin, Louis. *The Age of Rights.* New York: Columbia University Press, 1990.

Ife, Jim. *Human Rights and Social Work: Towards Rights-Based Practice*. Cambridge: Cambridge University Press, 2001.

Ignatieff, Michael. *Human Rights as Politics and Idolatry*. Edited by Amy Gutmann. Princeton, N.J.: Princeton University Press, 2001.

Iriye, Akira, Petra Goedde, and William Hitchcock (eds.). *The Human Rights Revolution. An International History*. New York: Oxford University Press, 2012.

Janis, Mark W., Richard S. Kay, and Anthony W. Bradley. *European Human Rights Law. Text and Materials*. New York: Oxford University Press, 2008.

Jayawickrama, Nihal. *The Judicial Application of Human Rights Law. National, Regional and International Jurisprudence*. New York: Cambridge University Press, 2003.

Jovanovic, Miodrag, and Ivana Krstic (eds.). *Human Rights Today—60 Years of the Universal Declaration*. Utrecht: Boom Eleven International, 2010.

Kalin, Walter, and Jorg Kunzli. *The Law of International Human Rights Protection*. New York: Oxford University Press, 2010.

Keller, Helen, Magdalena Forowicz, and Lorenz Engi. *Friendly Settlements before the European Court of Human Rights*. New York: Oxford University Press, 2010.

Krause, Catarina, and Martin Scheinin (eds.). *International Protection of Human Rights: A Textbook*. Turku, Finland: Abo Akademi University: Institute for Human Rights, 2009.

Kurasawa, Fuyuki. *The Work of Global Justice. Human Rights as Practices*. New York: Cambridge University Press, 2007.

Landman, Todd. *Protecting Human Rights: A Comparative Study*. Washington, D.C.: Georgetown University Press, 2005.

Lauren, Paul Gordon. *The Evolution of International Human Rights: Visions Seen*. Second Edition. Philadelphia: University of Pennsylvania Press, 2003.

Lester, Anthony, David Pannick, and Javan Herberg (eds.). *Human Rights Law and Practice*. New York: NYREV, 2009.

Lijnzaad, Liesbeth. *Reservations to UN Human Rights Treaties, Ratify and Ruin?* The Hague: Martinus Nijhoff, 1995.

Martin, Francisco Forrest, et al. *International Human Rights and Humanitarian Law: Treaties, Cases, and Analysis*. Cambridge: Cambridge University Press, 2006.

Moeckli, Daniel, Sangeta Sha, Sandesh Sivakumaran, and David Harris. *International Human Rights Law*. New York: Oxford University Press, 2010.

Nickel, James W. *Making Sense of Human Rights*. Second Edition. Malden, Mass.: Blackwell, 2006.

Rehman, Javaid. *International Human Rights Law: A Practical Approach*. New York: Longman, 2003.

Reichert, Elisabeth. *Social Work and Human Rights: A Foundation for Policy and Practice*. New York: Columbia University Press, 2003.

Risse, Thomas, Stephen C. Ropp, and Kathryn Sikkink (eds.). *The Power of Human Rights: International Norms and Domestic Change*. Cambridge: Cambridge University Press, 1999.

Shelton, Dinah. *Remedies in International Human Rights Law*. Second Edition. New York: Oxford University Press, 2005.

Simmons, William Paul. *Human Rights Law and the Marginalized Other*. Cambridge: Cambridge University Press, 2011.

Smith, Rhona. *Textbook in International Human Rights*. New York: Oxford University Press, 2009.

Steiner, Henry J., and Philip Alston. *International Human Rights in Context, Law, Politics, Morals*. Third Edition. New York: Oxford University Press, 2007.

Sriram, Chandra Lekha, Olga Martin-Ortega, and Johanna Herman. *War Conflict and Human Rights*. New York: Routledge, 2010.

Stone, Richard. *Textbook on Civil Liberties and Human Rights*. Eighth Edition. New York: Oxford University Press, 2009.

Symonides, Janusz (ed.). *Human Rights: International Protection, Monitoring, Enforcement*. Aldershot: Ashgate Publishing, 2003.

Van Schaack, Elizabeth, and Ronald C. Slye. *International Criminal Law. The Essentials*. New York: Oxford University Press, 2008.

Vincent, Andrew. *The Politics of Human Rights*. New York: Oxford University Press, 2010.

Information Sources on National Human Rights Practice/Experience

Web

Official Publications

To glean reliable information on national human rights practices from official publications may be a challenge. At worst, government-sponsored or -produced material available on official websites tend to be selective and self-congratulatory. At best, they reflect the political and epistemological assumptions and biases of their authors. With this caveat, as a starting point for any inquiry, the researcher may consult Jean L. Sears and Marilyn Moody, *Using Government Information Sources* published by Greenwood (2001). PAIS Archives and PAIS International feature references to government publications.

For the United States, one may consult the U.S. Department of State Country Reports on Human Rights Practices (annual, www.state.gov/g/dri/hr/), the U.S. Department of State Annual Report on International Religious Freedom (http://state.gov/g/dri/irf) and the U.S. Department of State Country reports on Trafficking in Persons (www.state.gov.g/tip/). A new web portal sponsored by the state (www.humanrights.gov) offers hundreds of searchable government reports related to human rights.

The U.S. Agency for International Development has an extensive set of links on Regions & Countries throughout the world, including information on human rights and democracy. The Library of Congress maintains a Country Studies page with studies written pursuant to a handbook program sponsored by the U.S. Army.

International Organizations

With their prudential hyperfactualism, publications of international organizations tend to be elusive and difficult to decipher analytically. For the proceedings and decisions of the United Nations Human Rights Council and the reports of state parties, concluding observations or comments and recommendations and other basic documents issued by the UN treaty bodies, the best source is the website of the United Nations Office of the High Commissioner for Human Rights.

The European Union's work on fundamental human rights is covered in the EU's page European Union, Fundamental Rights (http://ec.europa.eu/ justice_home/fsj/rights/fsj_rights_intro_en.htm).

Equally important in this regard are the websites of the International Court of Justice (www.icj-cij.org/), the International Criminal Court (www.icc-cpi .int/home.html), the International Criminal Tribunal for the Former Yugoslavia (www.un.org/icty/index.html), the International Criminal Tribunal for Rwanda www.ictr.org/), the Special Court for Sierra Leone (www.sc-sl.org/) and the Special Court for Lebanon (www.stl-tsl.org/).

Secondary Sources

Secondary sources will be needed to supplement and augment whatever has been obtained through official publications on human rights conditions in various countries. Newspapers are of course a must for human rights conditions in various countries. On this point, see Online Newspapers (www .onlinenewspapers.com) which provides links to newspapers from all over the world.

Standards-based quantitative information on government respect for human rights can be found from Benetech Human Rights Data Analysis Group (HRDAG; www.hrdag.org/); the Cingranelli-Richards (CIRI) Human Rights Dataset (http://ciri.binghamton.edu/); and the Political Terror Scale (PTS, originally developed by Freedom House and based on country reports of

Amnesty International and the U.S. Department of State; www.freedom house.org/template.cfm?page=1).

Search Engines Sites

The Think Tanks and Civil Societies Program, a non-profit program at the University of Pennsylvania in Philadelphia, Pennsylvania, was established at the Foreign Policy Research Institute in 1989. It researches, catalogs, and maintains a comprehensive database of approximately 6,300 think tanks from 206 countries and territories.

The University of Minnesota Human Rights Library (www1.umn.edu/ humanrts/), Duke University Libraries' NGO Research Guide (http://library .duke.edu/research/subject/guides/ngo_guide/ngo_database.html) and the World Association of Non-Governmental Organizations (WANGO) (www .wango.org/resources.aspx?section=ngodir) together provide a comprehensive source of information on non-governmental world side.

For more pointed thematic investigations, the following (in alphabetical order) may be useful. The list is by no means exhaustive.

The Advancing Science (Servicing Society's Science and Human Rights Program) maintains a database of information on human rights.

AfricaFiles (www.africafiles.org/humanrights.asp) is a network of volunteers from different fields committed to promoting African perspectives and alternative analyses for human rights in Africa. On the website it publishes articles available for download.

African Human Rights Resource Center (www1.umn.edu/humanrts/africa/) is part of the Human Rights Library of the Human Rights Center at the University of Minnesota. This resource center assembles a collection of international human rights materials with a particular focus on Africa.

Amnesty International Online (www.amnesty.org/) is the official Internet site for AI, which features annual country reports and links to other sites.

Annual Review of Population Law (www.hsph.harvard.edu/population/ annual_review.htm) is a database of summaries and excerpts of legislation, constitutions, court decisions, and other official government documents from every country in the world relating to population policies, reproductive health, women's rights, and HIV/AIDS.

Association for Women's Rights in Development (www.awid.org/ Issues-and-Analysis/By-Region) contains news, issues and analyses and tools regarding women's human rights issues, sorted by world regions.

Asylumlaw.org (www.asylumlaw.org) was founded on 1 March 1999 with the purpose of using the Internet to help lawyers and other accredited representatives worldwide prepare asylum cases.

Cornell Law School (www.lawschool.cornell.edu/womenandjustice/ legalresources/index.cfm) provides access to treaties and agreements, statutes and cases related to gender-based violence.

Business and Human Rights Resource Center (www.business-human rights.org/Categories/RegionsCountries/Africa) is a global independent non-profit information clearinghouse for news and links to information about corporate responsibility and human rights issues.

Center for Gender and Refugee Studies (http://cgrs.uchastings.edu/) offers links to a list of recommended resources for country conditions in gender asylum cases and a selection of links to relevant related organizations and web resources.

Centre for Human Rights at the University of Pretoria (www.chr.up.ac .za; www.chr.up.ac.za/centre_publications/ahrlj/ahrlj_contents.html) is one of the most active human rights organization in Africa. It publishes some of the leading reference works on African human rights law like the *African Human Rights Law Journal*, which is available for free download on the website. The website features important human rights documents sorted by country and thematic issue.

Child Rights Information Network (www.crin.org/reg/index.asp) offers detailed information regarding children's rights.

Coalition for an International Criminal Court (www.iccnow.org/) provides access to documents, reports, and current information regarding the ICC.

Derechos—Human Rights (www.derechos.org/) features reports on human rights violations and actions organized by country and by issue with a focus on Latin America.

European Country of Origin Information Network (www.ecoi.net/) provides up-to-date and publicly available country-of-origin information with a special focus on the needs of asylum lawyers, refugee counsels and persons deciding on claims for asylum and other forms of international protection.

Global Compact Critics (http://globalcompactcritics.blogspot.com/ 2010/01/on-its-website-un-global-compact-office.html) is an informal network of organizations and people gathering and sharing information about the Global Compact, partnerships between the United Nations and companies, and corporate accountability.

Global Rights (www.globalrights.org/site/PageServer) includes summaries of activities and downloadable reports on some African countries.

Human Right/Constitutional Rights at Columbia University (www .hrcr.org/).

Human Rights Documentation Center (www.hrdc.net/) is a portal to human rights resources.

Human Rights Network International (HRNI) is a bilingual (English/French) online database on human rights developed by the Free University of Brussels. Accessible free of charge (www.hrni.org), the database includes the full texts of judgments and decisions of the European Court of Human Rights, of the Inter-American Court of Human Rights and of the UN Human Rights Committee, as well as international and regional conventions on human rights, reports of the United Nations or non-governmental organizations, scholarly articles, bibliographic references, and a portal of Internet sites on human rights and a list of actors (NGOs, universities, international organizations) playing a role in this field. HRNI is also developing a network of human rights specialists to encourage and promote research and information exchange.

Human Rights Watch (www.hrw.org/en/publications/reports) contains country reports by issue or country. See also Digest of the Case Law (www.hrw.org/en/reports/2010/01/12/genocide-war-crimes-and -crimes-against-humanity) and World Reports (www.hrw.org/world -report-2010). Earlier World Reports are also available (www.hrw.org/en/node/79288).

ICRC Country Reports (www.icrc.org/eng/operations_country).

Institute for Human Rights and Development in Africa (www.africaninstitute.org) documents past and ongoing cases and decisions of the African Commission for Human and People's Rights, with whom it has observer status. It also publishes and distributes general information on the African human rights system.

Inter-African Union for Human Rights (www.iuhr.org/spip.php) publishes news and country reports (most of it only in French).

Inter-American Commission on Human Rights (www.cidh.org/publi .eng.htm) contains country reports. For selected country reports, see www.wcl.american.edu/pub/humright/digest/inter-american/index.html.

International Centre for the Legal Protection of Human Rights (www .interights.org/africa-programme/index.htm) contains up-to-date news and interpretations of recent decisions of tribunals applying international human rights law and a database.

International Crisis Group (www.crisisgroup.org/home/index.cfm) and its **CrisisWatch Data Base** (www.crisisgroup.org/home/index .cfm?id=2937&l=1) is a monthly bulletin providing succinct regular updates on the state of play in all the most significant situations of conflict or potential conflict around the world.

International Network for Economic and Social Rights ESCR-Net Caselaw Database (www.escr-net.org/caselaw/) is a database on ESCR-related pleadings, commentary and decisions.

Legislationline.org (www.legislationline.org/) is a free online service that compiles international documents and domestic legislation (for OSCE countries) on citizenship, fair trial, migration, independent judiciary, human trafficking.

Minority Rights Information System (http://dev.eurac.edu:8085/mugs2/index.jsp?TopBarItem=Home) features a database providing access to domestic legislation, international documents, case law, country information, reports, and treaties on minority rights-related issues.

Netherlands Institute of Human Rights (http://sim.law.uu.nl/SIM/Dochome.nsf?Open) provides access to databases containing the case law of international supervisory organs.

One World Network (www.oneworldnetwork.com) is an online media gateway built on sources including nongovernmental organizations, development-oriented news services, foundations and research institutions which serves as both a search engine and online community for information or guidance on human rights and sustainable development global issues.

Protection Project (www.protectionproject.org) provides information on trafficking in persons, especially women and children, with a focus on national and international laws and case law.

UN High Commissioner for Refugees maintains a comprehensive database of information on human rights in countries around the world.

University of Minnesota Human Rights, Meta Search Engine for Searching Multiple Human Rights Sites (www1.umn.edu/humanrts/lawform.html)—see in particular its Resources for Researching Country Conditions (www1.umn.edu/humanrts/research/).

Violence Against Women Database (http://webapps01.un.org/vawdatabase/home.action) is a recently set up UN database that provides information "on the extent, nature and consequences of all forms of violence against women, and on the impact and effectiveness of policies and programmes for, including best practices in, combating such violence."

War Crimes Research Office: Basic Documents and Jurisprudence of Internationalized Criminal Courts and Tribunals (https://www.wcl.american.edu/warcrimes/wcro_docs/index.cfm) is a database on the jurisprudence of international criminal courts and tribunals.

Women's Human Rights Resources (www.law-lib.utoronto.ca/Diana/) is probably one of the best resources on women's human rights.

World Bank Countries and Regions (http://web.worldbank.org/WBSITE/EXTERNAL/COUNTRIES/0,,menuPK:3030988~pagePK:180619~piPK:3001866~theSitePK:136917,00.html).

World LII Human Rights Links (www.worldlii.org/catalog/303.html) provides links to many human rights websites around the world arranged by category.

Printed Sources

Akinrinade, Babafemi. *Human Rights and State Collapse in Africa*. Utrecht: Boom Eleven International, 2010.

Alston, Philip. *Promoting Human Rights Through Bills of Rights. Comparative Perspectives*. New York: Oxford University Press, 2000.

Balfour, Rosa. *Human Rights and Democracy in EU Foreign Policy. The Cases of Ukraine and Egypt*. New York: Routledge, 2011.

Banakar, Reza (ed.). *Rights in Context. Law and Justice in Late Modern Society*. Burlington, Vt.: Ashgate, 2011.

Barratt, Bethany Amal. *Human Rights and Foreign Aid. For Love of Money?* New York: Routledge, 2007.

Bartels, Lorand. *Human Rights Conditionality in the EU's International Agreements*. New York: Oxford University Press, 2005.

Bassouini, M. Cherif. *International Extradition. United States Law and Practice*. Fifth Edition. New York: Oxford University Press, 2007.

Beatson, Jack, Stephen Grosz, Tom Hickman, Rabinder Singh, and Stephanie Palmer. *Human Rights: Judicial Protection in the United Kingdom*. London: Sweet and Maxwell, 2008.

Bercusson, Brian (ed.). *European Labour Law and the EU Charter of Fundamental Rights*. Baden-Baden: Nomos Publishers, 2006.

Black, Jan Knippers. *The Politics of Human Rights Protection*. Lanham, Md.: Rowman & Littlefield, 2010.

Blau, Judith, David L. Brunsma, Alberto Moncada, and Catherine Zimmer (eds.). *The Leading Rogue State. The U.S. and Human Rights*. Boulder, Colo.: Paradigm Publishers, 2008.

Brinks, Daniel M. *The Judicial Response to Police Killings in Latin America. Inequality and the Rule of Law*. New York: Cambridge University Press, 2007.

Burke, Roland. Decolonization and the Evolution of International Human Rights. Philadelphia, Pa.: University of Pennsylvania Press, 2010.

Campbell, Tom, and K. D. Ewing. *The Legal Protection of Human Rights. Skeptical Essays*. New York: Oxford University Press, 2011.

Cardenas, Sonia. *Conflict and Compliance: State Responses to International Human Rights Pressure*. Philadelphia: University of Pennsylvania Press, 2007.

Carey, Sabine C., Mark Gibney, and Steven C. Poe. *The Politics of Human Rights. The Quest for Dignity*. New York: Cambridge University Press, 2010.

Cleary, Edward. *Mobilizing for Human Rights in Latin America*. Bloomfield, Conn.: Kumarian Press, 2007.

Commonwealth Secretariat. *Commonwealth Model National Plan of Action of Human Rights.* London: Commonwealth Secretariat, 2008.

———. *Comparative Study on Mandates of National Human Rights Institutions in the Commonwealth.* London: Commonwealth Secretariat, 2008.

Dickson, Brice. *Human Rights and the European Convention: The Effects of the Convention on the United Kingdom and Ireland.* London: Sweet & Maxwell, 1997.

Eldridge, Phil. *Politics of Human Rights in Southeast Asia.* London: Routledge, 2002.

Eryilmaz, M. Bedri. *Arrest and Detention Powers in English and Turkish Law and Practice in the Light of the European Convention on Human Rights.* The Hague: Martinus Nijhoff, 1999.

Fedtke, Jorg, and Dawn Oliver. *Human Rights and the Private Sphere: A Comparative Study.* New York: Routledge, 2007.

Ferdinandusse, W. N. *Direct Application of International Criminal Law in National Courts.* New York: Cambridge University Press, 2006.

Feyter, Koen De, Stephan Parmentier, Christiane Timmerman, and George Ulrich. *The Local Relevance of Human Rights.* New York: Cambridge University Press, 2011.

Forsythe, David P. (ed.). *Human Rights and Comparative Foreign Policy.* Tokyo: United Nations University Press, 2000.

Francioni, Francesco (ed.). *Access to Justice as a Human Right.* New York: Oxford University Press, 2007.

Freedom House. *Countries at the Crossroad 2011. An Analysis of Democratic Governance.* Lanham, Md.: Rowman & Littlefield, 2012.

———. *Freedom in the World 2011. The Annual Survey of Political Rights and Civil Liberties.* Lanham, Md.: Rowman & Littlefield, 2012.

———. *Nations in Transit 2010. Democratization from Central Europe to Eurasia.* Lanham, Md.: Rowman & Littlefield, 2011.

Goodman, Ryan, and Thomas Pegram (eds.). *Human Rights, State Compliance, and Social Change. Assessing National Human Rights Institutions.* New York: Cambridge University Press, 2011.

Hancock, Jan. *Human Rights and US Foreign Policy.* New York: Routledge, 2007.

Harris, David, and Sarah Joseph. *The International Covenant on Civil and Political Rights and United Kingdom Law.* Oxford: Clarendon Press, 1995.

Heinz, Wolfgang, S. Heinz, and Hugo Frühling. *Determinants of Gross Human Rights Violations by State and State-sponsored Actors in Brazil, Uruguay, Chile, and Argentina, 1960–1990.* The Hague: Martinus Nijhoff, 1999.

Hertel, Shareen, and Kathryn Libal (eds.). *Human Rights in the United States.* New York: Cambridge University Press, 2011.

Ignatieff, Michael (ed.). *American Exceptionalism and Human Rights*. Princeton, N.J.: Princeton University Press, 2005.

International Council on Human Rights Policy. *Performance and Legitimacy. National Human Rights Institutions*. Second Edition. Geneva: International Council on Human Rights Policy, 2004 [available at http://hrbaportal.org/wp-content/files/1247496341_8_1_1_resfile.pdf].

Iwasawa, Yuji. *International Law, Human Rights, and Japanese Law: The Impact of International Law on Japanese Law*. Oxford: Clarendon, 1999.

Jayawickrama, Nihal. *The Judicial Application of Human Rights Law. National, Regional and International Jurisprudence*. New York: Cambridge University Press, 2003.

Jen Keller, Helen (ed.). *The Reception of the ECHR in the Member States*. New York: Oxford University Press, 2008.

Landman, Todd. *Protecting Human Rights. A Comparative Study*. Washington, D.C.: Georgetown University Press, 2005.

Leach, Philip. *Taking a Case to the European Court of Human Rights*. Second Edition. New York: Oxford University Press, 2005.

Letsas, George. *A Theory of Interpretation of the European Convention on Human Rights*. New York: Oxford University Press, 2008.

Liang-Fenton, Debra. *Implementing US Human Rights Policy. Agendas, Policies, and Practices*. Washington, D.C.: United States Institute of Peace Press, 2004.

Meijknecht, Anna K. *Minority Protection: Standards and Reality. Implementation of Council of Europe Standards in Slovakia, Romania and Bulgaria*. New York: Cambridge University Press, 2004.

Mertus, Julie A. *Bait and Switch. Human Rights and US Foreign Policy*. New York: Routledge, 2004.

Meydani, Assaf. *The Israeli Supreme Court and the Human Rights Revolution*. New York: Cambridge University Press, 2011.

O'Connell, Donncha (ed.). *60 Years, 30 Perspectives. Ireland and the Universal Declaration of Human Rights*. Dublin: New Island, 2009.

Payaslian, Simon. *United States Policy Toward the Armenian Question and the Armenian Genocide*. New York: Palgrave Macmillan, 2005.

Peerenboom, Randall, Carole J. Petersen, and Albert H. Y. Chen (eds.). *Human Rights in Asia. A Comparative Legal Study of Twelve Asian Jurisdictions, France and the USA*. New York: Routledge, 2006.

Pohjolainen, A.-E. "The Evolution of National Human Rights Institutions—The Role of the United Nations." Danish Institute for Human Rights, 2006, available at www.nhri.net/pdf/Evolution_of_NHRIs.pdf

Politi, Mauro, and Federica Gioia (eds.). *The International Criminal Court and National Jurisdictions*. Burlington, Vt.: Ashgate, 2008.

Ramcharan, Bertrand G. (ed.). *The Protection Role of National Human Rights Institutions.* New York: Cambridge University Press, 2007.

Rhea, Harry M. *The United States and International Criminal Tribunals.* Portland, Oreg.: Intersentia, 2010.

Risse, Thomas, Stephen Ropp, and Kathryn Sikkink (eds.). *The Power of Human Rights: International Norms and Domestic Change.* Cambridge, Mass.: Cambridge University Press, 1999.

Roniger, Luis, and Mario Sznajder. *The Legacy of Human Rights Violations in the Southern Cone. Argentina, Chile, and Uruguay.* New York: Oxford University Press, 1999.

Rosas, Allan (ed.). *International Human Rights Norms in Domestic Law: Finnish and Polish Perspectives.* Helsinki: Finnish Lawyers Publishing, 1990.

Sardar Ali, Shaheen, Savitri Goonesekere, Emilio Garcia Mendez, and Rebecca Rois-Kohn. *Protecting the World's Children. Impact of the Convention on the Rights of the Child in Diverse Legal Systems.* New York: Cambridge University Press, 2007.

Scheinin, Martin (ed.). *International Human Rights Norms in the Nordic and Baltic Countries.* The Hague: Martinus Nijhoff, 1996.

Sen, Purna (ed.). *Human Rights in the Commonwealth. A Status Report.* London: Commonwealth Secretariat, 2009.

——— (ed.). *Child Rights in the Commonwealth. 20 Years of the Convention on the Rights of the Child.* London: Commonwealth Secretariat, 2010.

Shany, Yuval. *Regulating Jurisdictional Relations Between National and International Courts.* New York: Oxford University Press, 2009.

Sikkink, Kathryn. *Mixed Signals. U.S. Human Rights Policy and Latin America.* Ithaca, N.Y.: Cornell University Press, 2006.

Simpson, Brian A. W. *Human Rights and the End of Empire. Britain and the Genesis of the European Convention.* New York: Oxford University Press, 2004.

Slymovics, Susan. *The Performance of Human Rights in Morocco.* Philadelphia: University of Pennsylvania Press, 2005.

Stephens, Beth, and Michael Ratner. *International Human Rights Litigation in U.S. Courts.* Irvington-on-Hudson, N.Y.: Transnational Publishers, 1996.

Thompson-Barrow, Cheryl. *Bringing Justice Home. The Road to Final, Appellate and Regional Court Establishments.* London: Commonwealth Secretariat, 2008.

Viljoen, Frans. *International Human Rights Law in Africa.* New York: Oxford University Press, 2008.

Vincent, Andrew. *The Politics of Human Rights.* New York: Oxford University Press, 2010.

Williams, Andrew. *EU Human Rights Policies. A Study in Irony.* New York: Oxford University Press, 2004.

Williams, George. *Human Rights under the Australian Constitution.* New York: Oxford University Press, 1999.

Wronka, Joseph. *Human Rights and Social Policy in the 21st Century: A History of the Idea of Human Rights and Comparison of the United Nations Universal Declaration of Human Rights with United States Federal and State Constitutions.* Lanham, Md.: University Press of America, 1998.

Academic Journals and Newsletters

The periodical literature available on the Internet or in print is an excellent source of information on human rights practice. Some journals are available full text electronically but many more are available only in print. The Public Affairs Information Service (PAIS International and its retrospective companion PAIS Archive) contains citations to journal articles, books and research reports. The following is a listing of journals and newsletters which deal with human rights and other related subjects.

African Human Rights Law Journal
American Journal of International Law
Asia-Pacific Journal of Human Rights
Australian Journal of Human Rights
Canadian Human Rights Yearbook (Toronto, Canada)
China Rights Forum Journal
Clearing House Review (International Institute for Democracy)
Columbia Human Rights Law Review (New York)
Columbia Journal of Transnational Law
Duke Journal of Comparative & International Law
East African Journal of Peace & Human Rights
European Human Rights Law Review
European Journal of Migration and Law
Forced Migration Review
Harvard Civil Rights–Civil Liberties Law Review
Harvard Human Rights Journal
Health and Human Rights
Helsinki Monitor
Housing and ESC Rights Law Quarterly
Human Rights
Human Rights Case Digest
Human Rights Dialogue
Human Rights Information Bulletin (Council of Europe)

Human Rights Law Journal
Human Rights Law Journal (Arlington, Virginia, USA)
Human Rights Law Review
Human Rights Quarterly Baltimore (Maryland, USA)
Human Rights Review
Human Rights Tribune
ICJE-Bulletin on Counter Terrorism and Human Rights
ICTR Bulletin (International Criminal Tribunal for Rwanda)
IDS Bulletin (Institute of Development Studies)
Indigenous Affairs
ILSA Journal of International and Comparative Law
Indiana Journal o Global Legal Studies
International Affairs
International and Comparative Law Quarterly
International Children's Rights Monitor
International Criminal Law Review
International Committee for Human Rights–Newsletter
International Human Rights Reports
International Journal of Children's Rights
International Journal of Discrimination and the Law
The International Journal of Human Rights (London)
International Journal on Minority and Group Rights
International Journal of Refugee Law (Oxford, UK)
International Journal of Transitional Justice
International Migration
International Migration Journal (IOM)
International Review of Contemporary Law
International Review of the Red Cross
JEMIE–Journal on Ethnopolitics and Minority Issues in Europe
Journal of Genocide Research
Journal of Human Rights
Journal of Human Rights and the Environment
Journal of Human Rights Practice
Journal of Humanitarian Assistance
Journal of International Criminal Justice
Journal of International Economic Law
Journal of International Law and Practice
Journal of International Migration and Integration
Journal of Refugee Studies
Journal of the History of International Law
Law and Practice of International Courts and Tribunals
Leiden Journal of International Law
Migration Policy Practice (IOM)

Muslim World Journal of Human Rights
Netherlands Quarterly of Human Rights (Utrecht, Netherlands)
Newsletter of the Inter-American Institute of Human Rights
New York Law School Journal of Human Rights
Non-state Actors and International Law
Objective: Justice
Pugwash Newsletter
Refugee Survey Quarterly (Geneva, Switzerland)
Religion and Human Rights
Review (International Commission of Jurists)
Revue Trimestrielle des Droits de l'Homme
Revue Universelle des Droits de l'Homme
Roma Rights Quarterly
Security and Human Rights
S.O.S. Torture
South African Journal on Human Rights (Braamfontein, South Africa)
Statewatch
Women's Rights Law Reporter (full text via WestLaw)
WUS Human Rights Bulletin
Yale Human Rights & Development Law Journal

Public Policy Research Organizations

According to one of the latest headcounts, there are more than 6,000 public research organizations in the world, over half of them located in North America and Europe. Variously known as think tanks, research centers or institutes, or foundations, these organizations generate knowledge, analysis and advice on domestic and international issues. The following list is primarily drawn from James G. McGann, "The Global 'Go to Think Tanks'. The Leading Public Policy Research Organizations in the World" (University of Pennsylvania, 2010 retrievable from www.sas.upenn.edu/irp/documents/2009GlobalGoToReportThinkTankIndex_1.31.2010.02.01_000.pdf). By no means comprehensive, it is limited to institutions whose work has a direct or indirect bearing on human rights practice.

African Institute of South Africa
American Enterprise Institute (USA)
Aspen Institute (USA)
Australian Human Rights Centre (University of New South Wales)
Austrian Human Rights Institute (Salzburg, Austria)
Bangladesh Institute of Development Studies (Bangladesh)
Belgrade Centre for Human Rights (Serbia)

British Institute of Human Rights (London, UK)

Brookings Institution (USA)

Carnegie Council for Ethics in International Affairs (USA)

Carnegie Endowment for International Peace (USA)

Carter Center (USA)

Cato Institute (USA)

Cellule de Recherche Interdisciplinaire en Droits de l'Homme (University of Louvain, Belgium)

Center for European Reform (UK)

Center for Global Development (USA)

Center for Human Rights and Conflict Resolution (The Fletcher School, Tufts University, USA)

Center for Humanitarian Dialogue (Switzerland)

Center for Immigration Studies (USA)

Center for Transatlantic Relations (Johns Hopkins University, USA)

Centre d'Etudes et de Recherches Internationales (Paris)

Centre de Recherches et d'Etudes sur les Droits de l'Homme et le Droit Humanitaire (University of Paris Sud, France).

Centre for Human Rights (University of Pretoria, South Africa)

Centre for International and Comparative Human Rights Law (Queen's University Belfast)

Civitas (UK)

Colegio de Bexico (Mexico)

Council on Foreign Relations (USA)

Danish Institute for Human Rights (Copenhagen, Denmark)

Deutsches Institut für Menschenrechte (Berlin, Germany)

Erik Castrén Institute of International Law and Human Rights (University of Helsinki)

European Center for Minority Issues (Germany)

European Roma Rights Center (Hungary)

European Training and Research Centre for Human Rights and Democracy (Austria)

Finnish Institute of International Affairs (Utrikespolitiska institutet—Ulkopoliittinen instituutti)

Foreign Policy Research Institute (USA)

Freedom House (USA)

French Institute of International Relations (France)

Friedrich-Ebert Foundation (Germany)

Heritage Foundation (USA)

Human Rights Centre (University of Essex)

Human Rights Centre of the University of Potsdam (MRZ)

Human Rights Education and Research Network (University of Washington)

Human Rights Institute (University of Latvia)

Icelandic Human Rights Center (Reykjavik, Iceland)

Institute of Commonwealth Studies (London, UK).

Institute for Human Rights, Intellectual Property and Development Trust (Zambia)

Institute for International Law of Peace and Armed Conflict (University of Bochum)

Institute of Human Rights Pedro Arrupe (Duesto University, Spain)

Inter-American Institute of Human Rights (Costa Rica)

International Council on Human Rights Policy (Switzerland)

International Committee for Human Rights (Spain)

International Crisis Group (Belgium)

International Peace Institute (USA)

Irish Centre for Human Rights (National University of Ireland, Galway)

Journal of Human Rights and the Environment

Ludwig Boltzmann Institute of Human Rights (Austria)

Migration Policy Institute (USA)

Netherlands Institute of Human Rights (Utrecht, Netherlands)

Nordic Africa Institute (Upsala, Sweden)

Norwegian Centre for Human Rights (Oslo, Norway)

Open Society Institute (Hungary)

Overseas Development Institute (UK)

Peace Research Institute of Oslo (Norway)

Rand Corporation (USA)

Raoul Wallenberg Institute of Human Rights and Humanitarian Law (Sweden)

Social Science Research Council (USA)

Stockholm International Peace Research Institute (Sweden)

Transparency International (Germany)

United States Institute of Peace (USA)

University of New South Wales, Initiative for Health and Human Rights

The University of Nottingham Human Rights Law Centre (UK)

World Bank Research Department (USA)

World Policy Institute (USA)

Practitioners' Memoirs, Personal Testimonies, Biographies

Albright, Madeleine. *Madam Secretary: A Memoir*. New York, N.Y.: Miramax, 2003.

Annan, Kofi, with Nader Mousavizadeh. *Interventions: A Life in War and Peace*. New York: Penguin, 2012.

Arbour, Louise. *War Crimes and the Culture of Peace*. Toronto: University of Toronto Press, 2003.

Aung San Suu Kyi. *The Voice of Hope*. New York: Seven Stories Press, 1997.
———. *Letters from Burma*. London: Penguin, 1997.
———. *Freedom from Fear and Other Writings: Revised Edition*. New York: Penguin, 1991.
Aussaresses, Paul. *The Battle of the Casbah: Terrorism and Counter-Terrorism in Algeria, 1955–1957*. New York, Enigma Books, 2010.
Bashir, Halima. *Tears in the Desert: A Memoir of Survival in Darfur*. New York: One World/Ballantine, 2008.
Beah, Ishmael. *A Long Way Gone: Memoirs of a Boy Soldier*. New York: Farrar, Straus and Giroux, 2007.
Benson, Mary. *Nelson Mandela: The Man and the Movement*. New York: W.W. Norton, 1986.
Beresford, Quentin. *Rob Riley: An Aboriginal Leader's Quest for Justice*. Canberra: Aboriginal Studies Press, 2006.
Burgos-Debray, Elisabeth (ed.). *I, Rigoberta Menchu. An Indian Woman in Guatemala*. New York: Verso, 1984.
Cohen, Warren I. *Profiles in Humanity. The Battles for Peace, Freedom, Equality, and Human Rights*. Lanham, Md.: Rowman & Littlefield, 2009.
Dallaire, Roméo. *Shake Hands with the Devil: The Failure of Humanity in Rwanda*. New York: Carroll & Graf, 2004.
Dau, John Bul, with Michael S. Sweeny. *God Grew Tired of Us. A Memoir*. Culver City, Calif.: National Geographic, 2007.
De Klerk, Willem. *W. de Klerk: The Man in His Time*. Johannesburg, South Africa: Jonathan Ball, 1991.
Del Ponte, Carla. *Madame Prosecutor. Confrontations with Humanity's Worst Criminals and the Culture of Impunity*. New York: Other Press, 2009.
Egeland, Jan. *A Billion Lives: An Eyewitness Report from the Frontlines of Humanity*. New York: Simon and Shuster, 2008.
Goldstone, Richard J. *For Humanity: Reflections of a War Crimes Investigator*. New Haven, Conn.: Yale University Press, 2000.
———. *Kosovo: An Assessment in the Context of International Law*. New York: Carnegie Council on Ethics and International Affairs, 2000.
Hari, Daoud. *The Translator: A Tribesman's Memoir of Darfur*. New York: Random House, 2008.
Hatzfeld, Jean. *Machete Season: The Killers in Rwanda Speak* (trans. Linda Coverdale). New York: Farrar, Straus and Giroux, 2005.
———. *Lie Laid Bare. The Survivors of Rwanda Speak*. New York: Other Press, 2007.
Holland, Heidi. *The Struggle: A History of the African National Congress*. London: Grafton, 1989.
Hooks, Margaret (ed.). *Guatemalan Women Speak*. Introduction by Rigoberta Menchu Tum. London: Catholic Institute for International Relations, 1991.

Ignatieff, Michael. *Human Rights as Politics and Idolatry*. Princeton, N.J.: Princeton University Press, 2001.

Mandela, Nelson. *Long Walk to Freedom*. Boston: Little, Brown, 1994.

———. *Nelson Mandela Speaks: Forging a Democratic, Non-Racial South Africa*. New York: Pathfinder, 1993.

Mandela, Winnie. *Part of My Soul*. Harmondsworth: Penguin, 1985.

Marker, Jamsheed. *East Timor: A Memoir of the Negotiations of Independence*. Jefferson, N.C.: McFarland, 2003.

Meredith, Martin. *Nelson Mandela: A Biography*. New York: St. Martin's Press, 1998.

Neier, Aryeh. *The International Human Rights Movement: A History*. Princeton, N.J.: Princeton University Press, 2012.

Ogata, Sadako. *The Turbulent Decade: Confronting the Refugee Crises of the 1990s*. New York: Norton, 2005.

Pran, Dith (compiler). *Children of Cambodia's Killing Fields: Memoirs by Survivors*. New Haven, Conn.: Yale University Press, 1997.

Prendergast, John, with Don Cheadle. *The Enough Moment. Fighting to End Africa's Worst Human Rights Crimes*. New York: Three River Press, 2010.

Qisheng, Jiang. *My L:ife in Prison. Memoirs of a Chinese Political Dissident*. Lanham, Md.: Rowman & Littlefield, 2012.

Sampson, Anthony. *Mandela: The Authorized Biography*. New York: Knopf, 1999.

Scheffer, David. *All the Missing Souls. A Personal History of the War Crimes Tribunals*. Princeton, N.J.: Princeton University Press, 2011.

Sharratt, Sara. *Gender, Shame and Sexual Violence. The Voices of Witnesses and Court Members at War Crimes Tribunals*. Burlington, Vt.: Ashgate, 2012.

Solzhenitsyn, Alexander. *The Gulag Archipelago, 1918–1956*. New York: Harper Perennial, 2002.

Traub, James. *The Best Intentions: Kofi Annan and the UN in the Era of America World Power*. New York: Farrar, Straus and Giroux, 2006.

White, Richard Alan. *Breaking Silence: The Case that Changed the Face of Human Rights*. Washington, D.C.: Georgetown University Press, 2004.

Wiesel, Elie. *From the Kingdom of Memory: Reminiscences*. New York: Summit Books, 1980.

TOPICAL/THEMATIC HUMAN RIGHTS PRACTICES

Human Rights Actors: Non-State and State Actors Practice

Alston, Philip (ed.). *Non-State Actors and Human Rights*. New York: Oxford University Press, 2005.

Amutabi, Maurice Nyamanga. *The NGO Factor in Africa: The Case of Arrested Development in Kenya.* New York: Routledge, 2006.

Andreopoulos, George, Zerha F. Kabasakal Arat, and Peter Juviler (eds.). *Non-State Actors in the Human Rights Universe.* Bloomfield, Conn.: Kumarian Press, 2006.

Baehr, Peter, and Monique Castermans-Holleman. The *Role of Human Rights in Foreign Policy.* New York: Palgrave, 2004.

Baker, Gideon, and David Chandler. *Global Civil Society: Contested Futures.* New York: Routledge, 2005.

Basu, Amrita (ed.). *Women's Movements in the Global Era. The Power of Local Feminisms.* Boulder, Colo.: Westview Press, 2010.

Ben Néfissa, Sarah, et al. *NGOs and Governance in the Arab World.* Cairo, New York: American University in Cairo Press, 2005.

Blau, Judith, David L. Brunsma, Alberto Moncada, and Catherine Zimmer (eds.). *The Leading Rogue State: The US and Human Rights.* Boulder, Colo.: Paradigm Publishers, 2009.

Bob, Clifford. *The Marketing of Rebellion: Insurgents, Media, and International Activism.* Cambridge: Cambridge University Press, 2005.

Bouvard, Marguerite Guzman. *Women Reshaping Human Rights: How Extraordinary Activists Are Changing the World.* Wilmington, Del.: SR Books, 1996.

Brysk, Aliso. *Global Good Samaritans: Human Rights as Foreign Policy.* New York: Oxford University Press, 2009.

Burgerman, Susan. *Moral Victories: How Activists Provoke Multilateral Action.* Ithaca, N.Y.: Cornell University Press, 2001.

Cakmak, Cenap. *Transnational Activism in World Politics NGOs and Creation of the ICC; Role of a Loosely Organized Principled Network in the Establishment of a Global Court.* Dissertation, Rutgers University, 2007.

Clapham, Andrew. *Human Rights Obligations of Non-State Actors.* New York: Oxford University Press, 2006.

——— (ed.). *Human Rights and Non-State Actors.* Northampton, Mass.: Edward Elgar Publishing, 2012.

Clark, Ann Marie. *Diplomacy of Conscience. Amnesty International and Changing Human Rights Norms.* Princeton, N.J.: Princeton University Press, 2001.

Clark, John. *Worlds Apart. Civil Society and the Battle for Ethical Globalization.* Bloomfield, Conn.: Kumarian Press, 2003.

Cleary, Edward. *Mobilizing for Human Rights in Latin America.* Sterling, Va.: Kumarian Press, 2007.

Davenport, Christian. *State Repression and the Domestic Democratic Peace.* Cambridge: Cambridge University Press, 2007.

Davenport, Christian, Hank Johnston, and Carol Mueller. *Repression and Mobilization*. Minneapolis: University of Minnesota Press, 2005.

Della, Donatena della, and Sidney Tarrow. *Transnational Protest & Global Activism: People, Passions, and Power.* Lanham, Md.: Rowman & Littlefield, 2004.

Dezalay, Yves (ed.). *Lawyers and the Construction of Transnational Justice.* New York: Routledge, 2011.

Drinan, Robert F. *The Mobilization of Shame: A World View of Human Rights*. New Haven, Conn.: Yale University Press, 2001.

Dupuy, Pierre-Marie, and Luisa Vierucci (eds.). *NGOs in International Law. Efficiency in Flexibility?* Northampton, Mass.: Edward Elgar Publishing, 2008.

Feinberg, Richard, et al. *Civil Society and Democracy in Latin America*. New York: Palgrave Macmillan, 2006.

Forsythe, David. *International Committee of the Red Cross. A Neutral Humanitarian Actor.* New York: Routledge, 2007.

———. *The Politics of Prisoner Abuse: The US and Enemy Prisoners after 9/11*. Cambridge: Cambridge University Press, 2011.

Frost, Mervyn. *Constituting Human Rights. Global Civil Society and the Society of Democratic States*. New York: Routledge, 2006.

Gillies, David. *Between Principle and Practice: Human Rights in North-South Relations*. Montreal: McGill-Queen's University Press, 1996.

Glasius, Marlies. *The International Criminal Court: A GCS Achievement.* London: Routledge, 2005.

Glendon, Mary Ann. *A World Made New: Eleanor Roosevelt and the Universal Declaration of Human Rights.* New York: Random House, 2001.

Hawkesworth, Mary. *Political Worlds of Women. Activism, Advocacy, and Governance in the Twenty-First Century*. Boulder, Colo.: Westview, 2012.

Heinrich, V. Finn (ed.). *Civicus Global Survey of the State of Civil Society.* Volume 1: Country Profiles. Bloomfield, Conn.: Kumarian Press, 2007.

Heinrich, V. Finn, and Lorenzo Fioramonti (eds.). *Civicus Global Survey of the State of Civil Society*. Volume 2. Bloomfield, Conn.: Kumarian Press, 2007.

Hertel, Shareen. *Unexpected Power. Conflict and Change Among Transnational Activists*. Ithaca, N.Y.: Cornell University Press, 2006.

Hodson, Loveday. *NGOs and the Struggle for Human Rights in Europe*. Oxford: Hart Publishing, 2011.

Hopgood, Stephen. *Keepers of the Flame. Understanding Amnesty International*. Ithaca, N.Y.: Cornell University Press, 2006.

Human Rights Watch. *Sudan, Oil and Human Rights*. New York: Human Rights Watch, 2003.

————. *The Lost Agenda: Human Rights and UN Field Operations*. New York: Human Rights Watch, 1973.

Ignatieff, Michael (ed.). *American Exceptionalism and Human Rights*. Princeton, N.J.: Princeton University Press, 2005.

Joachim, Jutta M. *Agenda Setting, the UN, and NGOs. Gender Violence and Reproductive Rights*. Washington, D.C.: Georgetown University Press, 2007.

Jonsson, Christer, and Jonas Tallberg (eds.). *Transnational Actors in Global Governance: Patterns, Explanations and Implications*. New York: Palgrave, 2010.

Kaldor, Mary. *GCS: An Answer to War*. Cambridge: Polity Press, 2003.

Keck, Margaret, and Kathryn Sikkink (eds.). *Activists Beyond Borders: Advocacy Networks in International Politics*. Ithaca, N.Y.: Cornell University Press, 1998.

Khagam, Sanjeev. *Dams and Development. Transnational Struggles for Water and Power*. Ithaca, N.Y.: Cornell University Press, 2004.

Klein, Woody. *Liberties Lost: The Endangered Legacy of the ACLU*. Westport, Conn.: Praeger Publishing, 2006.

Korey, William. *NGOs and the Universal Declaration of Human Rights: "A Curious Grapevine."* New York: Palgrave Macmillan, 2001.

Lindblom, Anna-Karin. *Non-Governmental Organizations in International Law*. New York: Cambridge University Press, 2006.

Ma, Qiusha. *Non-Governmental Organizations in Contemporary China: Paving the Way to Civil Society?* London and New York: Routledge, 2006.

MacKenzie, Heather (ed.). *Democratizing Global Governance: Ten Years of Case Studies and Reflections by Civil Society Activists*. New Delhi: Mosaic Books, 2009.

Maina, Peter Chris. *Human Rights in Africa: A Comparative Study of the African Human and Peoples' Rights Charter and the New Tanzanian Bill of Rights*. Westport, Conn.: Greenwood Press, 1990.

Marchetti, Raffaele, and Nathalie Tocci (eds.). *Civil Society, Conflicts and the Politicization of Human Rights*. Tokyo: United Nations University Press, 2011.

Martens, Kerstin. *NGOs and the United Nations. Institutionalization, Professionalization and Adaptation*. New York: Palgrave, 2006.

McBeth, Adam. *International Economic Actors and Human Rights*. New York: Routledge, 2010.

McCorquodale, Robert. *International Law beyond the States: Essays on Sovereignty, Non-State Actors and Human Rights*. London: Cameron May, 2011.

Médecins Sans Frontières. *In the Shadow of 'Just Wars'. Violence, Politics and Humanitarian Action*. Edited by Fabrice Weissman. Ithaca, N.Y.: Cornell University Press, 2004.

Meydani, Assaf. *The Israeli Supreme Court and the Human Rights Revolution. Courts as Agenda Setters.* New York: Cambridge University Press, 2011.

Miller, Carol. *Lobbying the League: Women's International Organizations and the League of Nations.* Oxford: University of Oxford, 1992.

Muthumbi, Jane W. *Participation, Representation and Global Civil Society. Christian and Islamic Fundamentalist Anti-Abortion Networks and United Nations Conferences.* Lanham, Md.: Lexington Books, 2010.

Nayar, Pramond K. *The Cultural Construction of Rights in India.* New York: Routledge, 2011.

Nelson, Paul J., and Ellen Dorsey. *New Rights Advocacy. Changing Strategies of Development and Human Rights NGOs.* Washington, D.C.: Georgetown University Press, 2008.

Okafor, Obiora Chinedu. *The African Human Rights System, Activist Forces and International Institutions.* New York: Cambridge University Press, 2007.

Payes, Shany. *Palestinian NGOs in Israel: The Politics of Civil Society.* London, 2005.

Peters, Anne, Lucy Koechlin, Till Förster, and Gretta Fenner Zinkernagel (eds.). *Non-State Actors as Standard Setters.* New York: Cambridge University Press, 2009.

Price, Monroe E., and Mark Thompson (eds.). *Forging Peace: Intervention, Human Rights, and the Management of Media Space.* Bloomington: Indiana University Press, 2002.

Rotberg, Robert I., and Thomas G. Weiss (eds.). *From Massacres to Genocide: The Media, Public Policy, and Humanitarian Crises.* Washington, D.C.: Brookings Institution, 1996.

Salamon, Lester M., S. Wojciech Sokolowski, et al. *Global Civil Society. Dimensions of the Nonprofit Sector,* Volume 2. Bloomfield, Conn.: Kumarian Press, 2004.

Salamon, Lester, et al. *Global Civil Society. Dimensions of the Nonprofit Sector,* Volume 1. Bloomfield, Conn.: Kumarian Press, 2004.

Scholte, Jan Aart (ed.). *Building Global Democracy? Civil Society and Accountable Global Governance.* New York: Cambridge University Press, 2011.

Sigal, Leon. *Negotiating Minefields. The Landmines Ban in American Politics.* New York: Routledge, 2006.

Sikkink, Kathryn. *Mixed Signals: US Human Rights Policy and Latin America.* New York: Century Foundation, 2004.

Sluiter, Liesbeth. *Clean Clothes. A Global Movement to End Sweatshops.* New York: Palgrave, 2009.

Snyder, Sarah B. *Human Rights Activism and the End of the Cold War: A Transnational History of the Helsinki Network.* Human Rights in History. New York: Cambridge University Press, 2011.

Stoddard, Abby. *Humanitarian Alert: NGO Information and Its Impact on US Foreign Policy.* Bloomfield, Conn.: Kumarian Press, 2006.

Taylor, Rupert (ed.). *Creating a Better World. Interpreting Global Civil Society.* Bloomfield, Conn.: Kumarian Press, 2004.

Tolley, Howard B., Jr. *The International Commission of Jurists: Global Advocates for Human Rights.* Philadelphia: University of Pennsylvania Press, 1994.

UNICEF. *Protecting the World's Children: Impact of the Convention on the Rights of the Child in Diverse Legal Systems.* New York: Cambridge University Press, 2007.

Willetts, Peter. *Non-Governmental Organizations in World Politics.* New York: Routledge, 2007.

Williams, Phil, and Dimitri Vlassis (eds.). *Combating Transnational Crime.* Portland, Oreg.: Frank Cass Publishers, 2001.

Global and Regional Practice: Instruments and Institutions

United Nations System

Alfreedson, G., and A. Eide (eds.). *The Universal Declaration of Human Rights. A Common Standard of Achievement.* The Hague: Martinus Nijhoff, 1999.

Alston, Philip. *The United Nations and Human Rights. A Critical Appraisal.* New York: Oxford University Press, 2008.

Alston, Philip, and Frederic Megret (eds.). *The United Nations and Human Rights: A Critical Appraisal.* Second Edition. Oxford: Oxford University Press, 2011.

Alston, Philip, and James Crawford (eds.). *The Future of the UN Human Rights Treaty Monitoring.* New York: Cambridge University Press, 2000.

Aspen Institute. *Honoring Human Rights under International Mandates: Lessons from Bosnia, Kosovo and East Timor.* Washington, D.C.: Aspen Institute, 2003.

Barria, Lilian A., and Steven D. Roper (eds.). *The Development of Institutions of Human Rights.* New York: Palgrave, 2010.

Bayefsky, Anne F. *How to Complain to the UN Human Rights Treaty System.* New York: Transnational Publishers, 2003.

———. *The UN Human Rights Treaty System: Universality at the Crossroads.* New York: Transnational Publishers, 2001.

Betts, Alexander, Gil Loescher, and James Milner. *The United Nations High Commissioner for Human Rights (UNHCR). The Politics and Practice of Refugee Protection.* Second Edition. New York: Routledge, 2011.

Carlson, Scott, and Gregory Gisvold, with Andrew Solomon. *Practical Guide to the International Covenant on Civil and Political Rights.* New York: Transnational Publishers, 2003.

Cholewinski, Ryszard, Paul de Guchteneire, and Antoine Pecoud. *Migration and Human Rights. The United Nations Convention on Migrant Workers' Rights.* New York: Cambridge University Press, 2010.

Clark, Roger. *The United Nations Crime Prevention and Criminal Justice Program: Formation of Standards and Efforts at the Implementation.* Philadelphia: University of Pennsylvania Press, 1994.

Conte, Alex. *Defining Civil and Political Rights. The Jurisprudence of the United Nations Human Rights Committee.* Burlington, Vt.: Ashgate, 2009.

Craven, M. C. R. *The International Covenant on Economic, Social and Cultural Rights. A Perspective on its Development.* Oxford: Clarendon Press, 1995.

Freedman, Rosa. *The United Nations Human Rights Council. A Critique and early Assessment.* New York: Routledge, 2013.

Gaeta, Paola (ed.). *The UN Genocide Convention. A Commentary.* New York: Oxford University Press, 2009.

Horowitz, Adam, Lizzy Ratner, and Philip Weiss (eds.). *The Goldstone Report. The Legacy of the Landmark Investigation of the Gaza Conflict.* New York: Perseus, 2011.

Hugues, Steve, and Nigel Hawarth. *International Labor Organization: Coming in from the Cold.* New York: Routledge, 2010.

Joseph, Sarah, Jenny Schultz, and Melissa Castan. *The International Covenant on Civil and Political Rights: Cases, Materials, and Commentary.* New York: Oxford University Press, 2004.

Keller, Helen, and Geir Ulfstein (eds.). *UN Human Rights Treaty Bodies. Law and Legitimacy.* New York: Cambridge University Press, 2012.

Mertus, Julie. *United Nations and Human Rights.* New York: Routledge, 2005.

Morsink, Johannes. *The Universal Declaration of Human Rights: Origins, Drafting, and Intent.* Philadelphia: University of Pennsylvania Press, 2000.

Murray, Rachel. *The Optional Protocol to the UN Convention Against Torture.* New York: Oxford University Press, 2011.

Nolte, Georg (ed.). *Peace through International Law: The Role of the International Law Commission. A Colloquium at the Occasion of Its Sixtieth Anniversary.* Berlin: 2009.

Nowak, Manfred. *The United Nations Convention Against Torture. A Commentary*. New York: Oxford University Press, 2007.

O'Flaherty, Michael, and P. N. Bhagwati. *Human Rights and the UN: Practice Before the Treaty Bodies*. Boston, Mass.: Brill Academic Publishers, 2004.

Quigley, John. *The Genocide Convention. An International Law Analysis*. Burlington, Vt.: Ashgate, 2006.

Ramcharan, Bertrand. *The UN Human Rights Council*. New York: Routledge, 2011.

Ramcharan, B. G. *The Security Council and the Protection of Human Rights*. The Hague: Kluwer Law International, 2002.

Sadat, Leila Nadya. *Forging a Convention for Crimes against Humanity*. New York: Cambridge University Press, 2011.

Schabas, William (ed.). *The Universal Declaration of Human Rights*. 3 volume set. *The Travaux Preparatoires*. New York: Cambridge University Press, 2013.

Schopp-Schkking, Hanna B., and Cees Flinterman (eds.). *The Circle of Empowerment. Twenty-Five Years of the UN Committee on the Elimination of Discrimination against Women*. New York: Feminist Press, 2007.

Sen, Purna (ed.). *Universal Periodic Review of Human Rights. Towards Best Practice*. London: Commonwealth Secretariat, 2009.

Shelton, Dinah. *Regional Protection of Human Rights*. New York: Oxford University Press, 2010.

Shivdas, Meena, and Sarah Coleman (eds.). *Without Prejudice. CEDAW and the Determination of Women's Rights in a Legal and Cultural Context*. London: Commonwealth Secretariat, 2010.

Symonides, Janusz (ed.). *Human Rights: International Protection, Monitoring, Enforcement*. Aldershot: Ashgate, 2003.

Vandenhole, W. *Procedures before the UN Human Rights Committee*. Mortsel, Belgium: Intersentia, 2004.

Wheeler, Ron. "The United Nations Commission on Human Rights, 1982–1997: A Study of Targeted Resolutions." *Canadian Journal of Political Science* 99, no. 32 (1999): 75–102.

Zwart, Tom. *The Admissibility of Human Rights Petitions: The Case Law of the European Commission of Human Rights and the Human Rights Committee*. Dordrecht: M. Nijhoff, 1994.

Zyberi, Gentian. *The Humanitarian Face of the International Court of Justice. Its Contribution to Interpreting and Developing International Human Rights and Humanitarian Law Rules and Principles*. Antwerp: Intersentia, 2008.

Europe

Alston, Philip. *The EU and Human Rights.* New York: Oxford University Press, 1999.

Anagnostou, Dia, and Evangelina Psychogiopoulou (eds.). *The European Court of Human Rights and the Rights of Marginalized Individuals and Minorities in National Context.* Leiden: Martinus Nijhoff Publishers, 2009.

Arold, Nina-Louisa. *The Legal Culture of the European Court of Human Rights.* Leiden: Martinus Nijhoff Publishers, 2009.

Bartels, Lorand. *Human Rights Conditionality in the EU's International Agreements.* New York: Oxford University Press, 2005.

Bates, Ed. *The Evolution of the European Convention on Human Rights. From Its Inception to the Creation of a Permanent Court of Human Rights.* New York: Oxford University Press, 2010.

Christensen, Ane Maria Roddik. *Judicial Accommodation of Human Rights in the European Union.* Copenhagen: Djoef Publishing, 2007.

Christoffersen, Jonas, and Mikael Rask Madsen. *The European Court of Human Rights between Law and Politics.* New York: Oxford University Press, 2011.

Christou, Theodora, and Juan Pablo Raymond (eds.). *European Court of Human Rights: Remedies and Execution of Judgments.* London: British Institute of International and Comparative Law, 2005.

Clements, Luke J. *European Human Rights: Taking a Case under the Convention.* London: Sweet & Maxwell, 1999.

Çoban, Ali Riza. *Protection of Property Rights within the European Convention on Human Rights.* Aldershot: Ashgate, 2004.

Council of Europe. *Reforming the European Convention on Human Rights: A Work in Progress.* Strasbourg: Council of Europe, 2009.

Dembour, Marie Bénédicte. *Who Believes in Human Rights? Reflections on the European Convention.* New York: Cambridge University Press, 2006.

Dickson, Brice. *The European Convention on Human Rights and the Conflict in Northern Ireland.* New York: Oxford University Press, 2010.

Dijk, Pieter van. *Theory and Practice of the European Convention on Human Rights.* The Hague: Kluwer Law International, 1998.

Emberland, Marius. *Exploring the Structure of ECHR Protection.* New York: Oxford University Press, 2006.

Goldhaber, Michael D. *A People's History of the European Court of Human Rights.* New Brunswick, N.J.: Rutgers University Press, 2007.

Greer, Steven. *The European Convention on Human Rights.* New York: Cambridge University Press, 2007.

Harris, David, Michael O'Boyle, Edward Bates, and Carla Bubkley. *Harris, O'Boyle & Warbrick: Law of the European Convention Human Rights.* New York: Oxford University Press, 2009.

Isa, Felipe Gómez, and Koen de Feyter (eds.). *International Protection of Human Rights: Achievements and Challenges.* Bilbao, Spain: University of Deusto, 2006.

Johnson, Paul. *Homosexuality and the European Court of Human Rights.* New York: Routledge, 2012.

Kemp, Walter A. *Quiet Diplomacy in Action: The OSCE High Commissioner on National Minorities.* Boston: Kluwer Law International, 2001.

Krishnamurthy, B., and Geetha Ganapathy-Dore (eds.). *European Convention on Human Rights. Sixty Years and Beyond.* New Delhi, India: New Century Publications, 2012.

Mowbray, Alastair. *The Development of Positive Obligations under the European Convention on Human Rights by the European Court of Human Rights.* Oxford: Hart, 2004.

Peers, Steve, and Angela Ward (eds.). *The EU Charter and of Fundamental Rights: Politics, Law and Polity.* Oxford: Hart, 2004.

Reid, Karen. *A Practitioner's Guide to the European Convention on Human Rights.* Fourth Edition. London: Thompson/Sweet, 2012.

Sikuta, Jan, and Eva Hubalkova. *European Court of Human Rights: Case-Law of the Grand Chamber 1998–2006.* The Hague: Asser Press, 2007.

Sweeney, James A. *The European Court of Human Rights in the Post-Cold War Era.* New York: Routledge, 2012.

Van Dijk, Pieter, Fried Van Hoof, Arjen Van Rijn, and Leo Zwaak (eds.). *Theory and Practice of the European Court of Human Rights.* Mortsel, Belgium: Intersentia, 2006.

White, Robin C. A., and Clare Ovey. *Jacobs, White & Ovey: The European Convention on Human Rights.* Fifth Edition. New York: Oxford University Press, 2010.

Xns, Dimitri. *The Positive Obligations of the State under the European Convention of Human Rights.* New York: Routledge, 2011.

Latin America

Burgorgne-Larsen, Laurence, and Amaya Ubeda de Torres. *The Inter-American Court of Human Rights.* (Translated by Rosalind Greenstein). New York: Oxford University Press, 2011.

Cavallaro, James. "Reevaluating Regional Human Rights. Litigation in the Twenty-First Century: The Case of the InterAmerican Court." *American Journal of International Law* 102, no. 4 (July 2009): 768–822.

Cleary, Edward. *Mobilizing for Human Rights in Latin America.* Herndon, Va.: Kumarian Press, 2007.

Cooper, Andrew F., and Thomas Legler. *Intervention Without Intervening? The OAS Defense and Promotion of Democracy in the Americas*. New York: Palgrave Macmillan, 2006.

Davidson, Scott. *The Inter-American Human Rights System*. Aldershot: Dartmouth, 1997.

Harris, David, and Stephen Livingstone (eds.). *The Inter-American System of Human Rights*. New York: Oxford University Press, 1998.

Pasqualucci, Jo M. *The Practice and Procedure of the Inter-American Court of Human Rights*. Second Edition. Cambridge: Cambridge University Press, 2012.

Serrano, Monica, and Vesselin Popovski. *Human Rights Regimes in the Americas*. Tokyo: United Nations University Press, 2010.

Africa

Abass, Ademola (ed.). *Protecting Human Security in Africa*. New York: Oxford University Press, 2010.

An-Na'im, Abdullahi Ahmed. *Human Rights under African Constitutions: Realizing the Promise for Ourselves*. Philadelphia: University of Pennsylvania Press, 2003.

An-Na'im, Abdullahi Ahmed, and Francis M. Deng (eds.). *Human Rights in Africa: Cross-Cultural Perspectives* Washington, D.C.: Brookings Institution, 1990.

Ankumah, Evelyn A. *The African Commission on Human and People's Rights: Practice and Procedures*. The Hague: Martinus Nijhoff, 1996.

Bösl, A., and Diescho, J. *Human Rights in Africa. Legal Perspectives on Their Protection and Promotion* (foreword by Desmond Tutu). London: Macmillan, 2009.

Evans, Malcolm (ed.). *The African Charter on Human and People's Rights. The System in Practice, 1986–2006*. Second Edition. New York: Cambridge University Press, 2008.

Fatsah, Ouguergouz. *The African Charter on Human Rights and People's Rights: A Comprehensive Agenda for Human Dignity and Sustainable Democracy in Africa*. The Hague: Kluwer Law International, 2003.

Mugwanya, George William. *Human Rights in Africa: Enhancing Human Rights Through the African Regional Human Rights System*. New York: Transnational Publishers, 2003.

Murray, Rachel. *Human Rights in Africa. From the OAU to the African Union*. New York: Cambridge University Press, 2005.

Okafor, Obiora Chinedu. *The African Human Rights System. Activist Forces and International Institutions*. Cambridge, Mass.: Cambridge University Press, 2007.

Viljoen, Frans. *International Human Rights Law in Africa*. Oxford: Oxford University Press, 2007.

Zeleza, Tiyambe and Philip J. McConnaughay. *Human Rights, the Rule of Law and Development in Africa*. Philadelphia: University of Pennsylvania Press, 2004.

Other Regions of the World

Baik, Tae-Ung. *Emerging Regional Human Rights Systems in Asia*. Cambridge: Cambridge University Press, 2012.

Bauer, Joanne, and Daniel Bell. *The East Asian Challenge for Human Rights*. New York: Cambridge University Press, 1999.

Chase, Anthony. *Human Rights, Revolution and Reform in the Muslim World*. Boulder, Colo.: Lynne Rienner, 2012.

Kelsall, Michelle. *The New ASEAN Intergovernmental Commission on Human Rights: Toothless Tiger of Tentative First Step?* Honolulu: East-West Center, 2009.

Monshipouri, Mahmoud. *Human Rights in the Middle East: Frameworks, Goals and Strategies*. New York: Palgrave-Macmillan, 2011.

Nasu, Hitoshi, and Ben Saul. *Human Rights in the Asia-Pacific Region: Towards Institution Building*. New York: Routledge, 2011.

Tan, Hsien-Li. *The Asian Intergovernmental Commission on Human Rights in Southeast Asia*. New York: Cambridge University Press, 2011.

United Nations Development Programme. *The Arab-Human Development Report 2009: Challenges to Human Security in the Arab Countries*. New York: UNDP, 2009.

———. *The Arab-Human Development Report 2005: Towards the Rise of Women in the Arab World*. New York: UNDP, 2006.

Civil and Political Rights

Bailey, Stephen. *Bailey, Harris & Jones: Civil Liberties Cases, Materials and Commentary*. New York: Oxford University Press, 2009.

Barendt, Eric (ed.). *Freedom of the Press*. Burlington, Vt.: Ashgate, 2009.

Birkinshaw, Patrick. *Freedom of Information. The Law, the Practice, the Ideal*. New York: Cambridge University Press, 2001.

Bowen, John R. *Why the French Don't Like Headscarves: Islam, the State, and Public Space*. Princeton, N.J.: Princeton University Press, 2007.

Brooks, Thom (ed.). *The Right to a Fair Trial*. Burlington, Vt.: Ashgate, 2009.

Conte, Alex, and Richard Burchill. *Defining Civil and Political Rights. The Jurisprudence of the United Nations Human Rights Committee*. Second Edition. Burlington, Vt.: Ashgate, 2009.

Cortese, Anthony. *Opposing Hate Speech.* Westport, Conn.: Praeger Publishers, 2006.

Erman, Eva. *Human Rights and Democracy: Discourse Theory and Global Rights Institutions.* Aldershot: Ashgate, 2005.

Evans, Carolyn. *Freedom of Religion under the European Convention on Human Rights.* New York: Oxford University Press, 2001.

Freedom House. *Freedom of the Press 2007. A Global Survey of Media Independence.* Lanham, Md.: Rowman & Littlefield, 2007.

———. *Nations in Transit 2007. Democratization from Central Europe to Eurasia.* Lanham, Md.: Rowman & Littlefield, 2007.

———. *Freedom in the World 2007. The Annual Survey of Political Rights and Civil Liberties.* Lanham, Md.: Rowman & Littlefield, 2007.

———. *Countries at the Crossroads 2007. A Survey of Democratic Governance.* Lanham, Md.: Rowman & Littlefield, 2007.

Gant, Scott. *We're All Journalists Now: The Transformation of the Press and Reshaping of the Law in the Internet Age.* New York: Free Press, 2007.

Gearon, Liam (ed.). *Freedom of Expression and Human Rights. Historical, Literary and Political Contexts.* Sussex: Sussex Academic Press, 2006.

Gibbons, Thomas (ed.). *Free Speech in the New Media.* Burlington, Vt.: Ashgate, 2009.

Guilhot, Nicolas. *The Democracy Makers: Human Rights and the Politics of Global Order.* New York: Columbia University Press, 2005.

Guiora, Amos N. *Freedom from Religion.* New York: Oxford University Press, 2009.

Hare, Ivan, and James Weinstein (eds.). *Extreme Speech and Democracy.* New York: Oxford University Press, 2009.

Herz, Michael, and Peter Molnar (eds.). *The Content and Context of Hate Speech. Rethinking Regulation and Responses.* New York: Cambridge University Press, 2012.

Johnson, David T., and Franklin E. Zimring. *The New Frontier. National Development, Political Change and the Death Penalty in Asia.* New York: Oxford University Press, 2009.

Marshall, Paul A. *Religious Freedom in the World.* Lanham, Md.: Rowman & Littlefield, 2007.

McGoldrick, Dominic. *Human Rights and Religion: The Islamic Headscarf Debate in Europe.* Oxford: Hart Publishing, 2006.

Moran, Christopher, *Classified: Secrecy and the State in Modern Britain.* Cambridge: Cambridge University Press, 2012.

Press, Robert M. *Peaceful Resistance: Advancing Human Rights and Democratic Freedoms.* Burlington, Vt.: Ashgate Publishing, 2006.

Taylor, Paul M. *Freedom of Religion. UN and European Rights Law and Practice.* New York: Cambridge University Press, 2006.

Thierer, Adam, and Brian Anderson. *A Manifesto for Media Freedom.* New York: Encounter Books, 2008.

Slavery and Servitude Including Sexual Exploitation, Forced Labor and Human Trafficking

Abadeed, Adel S. *The Entrapment of the Poor into Involuntary Labor.* Lewiston, N.Y.: Mellen Press, 2008.

Andrees, Beate, and Patrick Belser (eds.). *Forced Labor: Coercion and Exploitation in the Private Economy.* Boulder, Colo.: Lynne Rienner, 2005.

Bales, Kevin. *Understanding Global Slavery. A Reader.* Berkeley: University of California Press, 2005.

Bales, Kevin, and Zoe Trodd (eds.). *To Plead Our Own Cause. Personal Histories by Today's Slaves.* Ithaca, N.Y.: Cornell University Press, 2008.

Beeks, Karen D., and Delila Amir (eds.). *Trafficking and the Global Sex Industry.* Lanham, Md.: Lexington Books, 2006.

Blackburn, Robin. *The Making of New World Slavery.* London: Verso, 1997.

Brown, Louise. *Sex Slaves: The Trafficking of Women in Asia.* London: Virago Press, 2000.

Cameron, Sally, and Edward Newman (eds.). *Trafficking in Humans. Social, Cultural and Political Dimensions.* Tokyo: United Nations University Press, 2008.

Farr, Kathryn. *Sex Trafficking: The Global Market in Women and Children.* New York: Worth Publishers, 2005.

International Labour Office. *The Cost of Coercion. Global Report under the Follow Up to the ILO Declaration on Fundamental Principles and Rights at Work.* Geneva: International Labour Office, 2009.

Kempadoo, Kamala, Jyoti Sanghera, and Bandana Pattanaik. *Trafficking and Prostitution Reconsidered: New Perspectives on Migration, Sex Work and Human Rights.* Boulder, Colo.: Paradigm Publishers, 2005.

LeBreton, Binka. *Trapped. Modern-Day Slavery in the Brazilian Amazon.* Bloomfield, Conn.: Kumarian Press, 2003.

Martinez, Jenny S. *The Slave Trade and the Origins of International Human Rights Law.* New York: Oxford University Press, 2012.

Monzini, Paola. *Sex Traffic: Prostitution, Crime and Exploitation.* Bangkok, Thailand: White Lotus, 2005.

Segreve, Marie, Sanja Milivojevic, and Sharon Pickering. *Sex Trafficking. International Context and Response.* Portland, Oreg.: Willan Publishing, 2009.

Siddharth Kara. *Sex Trafficking: Inside the Business of Modern Slavery.* New York: Columbia University Press, 2008.

Stoecker, Sally, and Louise Shelley (eds.). *Human Traffic and Transnational Crime: Eurasian and American Perspectives.* Lanham, Md.: Rowman & Littlefield, 2005.
UNICEF. *Child Trafficking in Europe. A Broad Vision to Put Children First—Summary.* New York: United Nations, 2008.
Wylie, Gillian, and Penny McRedmond (eds.). *Human Trafficking in Europe. Character, Causes and Consequences.* New York: Palgrave, 2010.
Zheng, Tiantian (ed.). *Sex Trafficking, Human Rights, and Social Justice.* New York: Routledge, 2010.

Torture, Cruel, Inhuman and Degrading Treatment

Aceves, William J. *The Anatomy of Torture: A Documentary History of Filartiga v. Pena-Irala.* New York: Martin's Nijhoff, 2007.
Conroy, John. *Unspeakable Acts, Ordinary People: the Dynamics of Torture—An Examination of the Practice of Torture in Three Democracies.* New York: Knopf, 2000.
Danner, Mark. *Torture and Truth: America, Abu Ghraib, and the War on Terror.* London: Granta, 2005.
Guiora, Amos N. *Constitutional Limits on Coercive Interrogation.* New York: Oxford University Press, 2008.
Jaffer, Jameel, and Amrit Singh. *Administration of Torture. Documentary Record from Washington to Abu Ghraib and Beyond.* New York: Columbia University Press, 2007.
Lazreg, Marnia. *Torture and the Twilight of Empire. From Algiers to Baghdad.* Princeton, N.J.: Princeton University Press, 2008.
Miles, Steven H. *Oath Betrayed: Military Medicine and the War on Terror.* New York: Random House, 2006.
McCoy, Alfred. *A Question of Torture: CIA Interrogation, from the Cold War to the War on Terror.* New York: Metropolitan Books, 2006.
Miles, Steven H. *Oath Betrayed: Military Medicine and the War on Terror.* New York: Random House, 2006.
Rajiva, Lila. *The Language of Empire: Abu Ghraib and the American Media.* New York, N.Y.: Monthly review, 2005.
Rejali, Darius. *Torture and Democracy.* Princeton, N.J.: Princeton University Press, 2007.
Roth, K., and. M. Worden (eds.). *Torture: Does It Make Us Safer? Is It Ever OK?* New York New Press, 2005.
Scott, Craig (ed.). *Torture as Tort: Comparative Perspectives on the Development of Transnational Tort Litigation.* Oxford: Hart, 2001.

Treatment of Prisoners

Aromaa, Kauko, and Terhi Viljanen. *Survey of United Nations and Other Best Practices in the Treatment of Prisoners in the Criminal Justice System.* Proceedings of the workshop held at the Twelfth United Nations Congress on Crime Prevention and Criminal Justice Salvador, Brazil, 12–19 April 2010. Helsinki: Academic Bookshop, 2010.

Bassiouni, M. Cherif (ed.). *The Protection of Human Rights in the Administration of Criminal Justice: A Compendium of United Nations Norms and Standards.* New York: Transnational Publishers, 1994.

Greenberg, Karen. *The Least Worst Place. Guantanamo's First 100 Days.* New York: Oxford University Press, 2010.

McCarthy, Melissa. *Incarceration and Human Rights.* Manchester: Manchester University Press, 2010.

Office of the High Commissioner for Human Rights, in cooperation with the International Bar Association. *Human Rights in the Administration of Justice, a Manual on Human Rights for Judges, Prosecutors and Lawyers.* Professional Training Series, No. 9, 2003, available at www.ohchr.org/Documents/Publications/training9

Rodley, Nigel, with Matt Pollard. *The Treatment of Prisoners under International Law.* Third Edition. New York: Oxford University Press, 2009.

United Nations. *Surveys on Crime Trends and the Operations of Criminal Justice Systems.* Vienna: United Nations [annual].

Genocide, War Crimes and Crimes Against Humanity

Akhavan, Payam. *Reducing Genocide to Law. Definition, Meaning and the Ultimate Crime.* New York: Cambridge University Press, 2011.

Alvarez, Alex. *Genocidal Crimes.* New York: Routledge, 2009.

Annas, George J., and Michael A. Grodin. *The Nazi Doctors and the Nuremberg Code: Human Rights in Human Experimentation.* New York: Oxford University Press, 1992.

Bartov, Omer, Anita Grossmann, and Mary Nolan (eds.). *Crimes of War: Guilt and Denial in the Twentieth Century.* New York: New Press, 2002.

Bassiouni, M. Cherif. *Crimes against Humanity. Historical Evolution and Contemporary Application.* New York: Cambridge University Press, 2011.

Booth, Ken. *The Kosovo Tragedy. Human Rights Dimensions.* Portland, Oreg.: Frank Cass Publishers, 2001.

Browning, Christopher R. *Ordinary Men: Reserve Police Battalion 101 and the Final Solution in Poland.* New York: Harper, 1992.

Chua, Amy. *World on Fire: How Exporting Free Market Democracy Breeds Ethnic Hatred and Global Instability.* New York: Anchor, 2004.

Chirot, Daniel, and Clark McCauley. *Why Not Kill Them? The Logic and Prevention of Mass Political Murder.* Princeton, N.J.: Princeton University Press, 2006.

Courtois, Stephane, et al. *The Black Book of Communism.* Cambridge, Mass.: Harvard University Press, 1999.

Dolot, Miron. *Execution by Hunger. The Hidden Holocaust.* New York: Norton, 1987.

Downes, Alexander B. *Targeting Civilians in War.* Ithaca, N.Y.: Cornell University Press, 2008.

Duffett, J. (ed.). *Against the Crime of Silence: Proceedings of the Russell International War Crimes Tribunal.* New York: O'Hare Books, 1968.

Fournet, Caroline. *The Crime of Destruction and the Law of Genocide. Their Impact on Collective Memory.* Burlington, Vt.: Ashgate, 2007.

Goldhagen, Daniel. *Worse than War. Genocide, Eliminationisim, and the Ongoing Assault on Humanity.* New York: Perseus Books Group, 2010.

Gutman, Roy, and David Rieff (eds.). *Crimes of War: What the Public Should Know.* New York: Norton, 1999.

Hannebel, Thomas, and Thomas Hochmann (eds.). *Genocide Denials and the Law.* New York: Oxford University Press, 2011.

Harff, Barbara. *Early Warning of Communal Conflict and Genocide: Linking Research to International Responses.* Boulder, Colo.: Westview Press, 2003.

Hayner, Priscilla B. *Unspeakable Truths: Confronting State Terror and Atrocity.* New York: Routledge, 2001.

Heidenrich, John G. How to Prevent Genocide: A Guide for Policymakers, Scholars, and the Concerned Citizen. Westport, Conn.: Praeger, 2001.

Henhan, Ralph, and Paul Behrens (eds.). *The Criminal Law of Genocide. International, Comparative and Contextual Aspects.* Burlington, Vt.: Ashgate, 2007.

Human Rights Watch. *Slaughter among Neighbors: The Political Origins of Communal Violence.* New Haven, Conn.: Yale University Press, 1995.

———. *Human Rights in Iraq.* New Haven, CT: Yale University Press, 1990.

———. *Iraq's Crime of Genocide: The Anfal Campaign Against the Kurds.* New Heaven, Conn.: Yale University Press, 1995.

Jones, Adam. *Genocide. A Comprehensive Introduction.* New York: Routledge, 2006.

——— (ed.). *Genocide, War Crimes, and the West: History and Complicity.* London: Zed Books, 2004.

Khatchadourian, Haig. *War, Terrorism, Genocide, and the Quest for Peace.* Lewiston, N.Y.: Mellen Press, 2003.

Kimenyi, Alexandre, and Otis L. Scott. *Anatomy of Genocide State Sponsored Mass Killings in the Twentieth Century.* Lewiston, N.Y.: Mellen Press, 2001.

La Haye, Eve. *War Crimes in Internal Armed Conflicts.* New York: Cambridge University Press, 2010.

Lattimer, Mark (ed.). *Genocide and Human Rights.* Burlington, Vt.: Ashgate, 2007.

Leebaw, Bronwyn. *Judging State-Sponsored Violence, Imagining Political Change.* New York: Cambridge University Press, 2012.

Lemkin, Raphael. *Axis Rule in Occupied Europe; Laws of Occupation—Analysis of Government Proposals for Redress.* Washington, D.C.: Carnegie Endowment for International Peace, 1944.

———. *Key Writings of Raphael Lemkin on Genocide.* Compiled by PreventGenocide.org, www.preventgenocide.org/lemkin. Online selection of Lemkin's core work on genocide.

Lorey, David E., and William H. Beezley. *Genocide, Collective Violence, and Popular Memory: The Politics of Remembrance in the Twentieth Century.* Wilmington, Del.: Scholarly Resources, 2002.

MacDonogh, Giles. *After the Reich: The Brutal History of Allied Occupation.* New York: Basic Books, 2007.

Maguire, Peter. *Facing Death in Cambodia.* New York: Columbia University Press, 2005.

Mahmood, Mamdani. *When Victims Become Killers: Colonialism, Nativism, and the Genocide in Rwanda.* Princeton, N.J.: Princeton University Press, 2001.

Markusen, Eric, and David Kopf. *The Holocaust and Strategic Bombing: Genocide and Total War in the Twentieth Century.* Boulder, Colo.: Westview Press, 1995.

Mertus, Julie A. *War's Offensive on Women. The Humanitarian Challenge in Bosnia, Kosovo, and Afghanistan.* Bloomfield, Conn.: Kumarian Press, 2000.

Mills, Nicolauss, and Kira Brunner (eds.). *The New Killing Fields: Massacre and the Politics of Intervention.* New York: Basic Books, 2002.

Moses, Dirk (ed.). *Colonialism and Genocide.* New York: Routledge, 2006.

Olusoga, David, and Casper W. Erichsen. *The Kaiser's Holocaust: Germany's Forgotten Genocide and the Colonial Roots of Nazism.* London: Faber and Faber, 2010.

Osiel, Mark. *Making Sense of Mass Atrocities.* New York: Cambridge University Press, 2011.

Power, Samantha. *"A Problem from Hell": America's and the Age of Genocide.* New York: Basic Books, 2002.

Radu, Michael S. *The New Insurgencies. Anti-Communist Guerrillas in the Third World.* New Brunswick, N.J.: Transaction Publishers, 1990.

——— (ed.). *Violence and the Latin American Revolutionaries.* New Brunswick, N.J.: Transaction Publishers, 1988.

Renshaw, Layla. *Exhuming Loss. Memory, Materiality and Mass Graves of the Spanish Civil War.* Walnut Creek, Calif.: Left Coast Press, 2011.

Rosenbaum, Alan S. (ed.). *Is the Holocaust Unique? Perspectives on Comparative Genocide.* New Edition. Boulder, Colo.: Westview Press, 2008.

Rummel, Rudolph J. *Death by Government.* New Brunswick, N.J.: Transaction Publishers, 1997.

———. *Power Kills. Democracy as a Method of Nonviolence.* New Brunswick, N.J.: Transaction Publishers, 2002.

Sadat, Leila Nadya (ed.). *Forging a Convention for Crimes against Humanity.* New York: Cambridge University Press, 2011.

Schabas, William A. *Genocide in International Law: The Crime of Crimes.* Cambridge: Cambridge University Press, 2000.

Smith, Karen. *Genocide and the Europeans.* New York: Cambridge University Press, 2010.

Stern, Steve. *Battling for Hearts and Minds: Memory Struggles in Pinochet's Chile, 1973–1988.* Durham, N.C.: Duke University Press, 2006.

———. *Remembering Pinochet's Chile. On the Eve of London 1998.* Durham, N.C.: Duke University Press, 2006.

Stover, Eric. *The Witnesses. War Crimes and the Promise of Justice in The Hague.* Philadelphia, Pa.: University of Pennsylvania Press, 2005.

Taylor, Frederick. *Dresden: Tuesday, February 13, 1945.* New York: HarperCollins, 2004.

Totten, Samuel (ed.). *The Prevention and Intervention of Genocide.* New Brunswick, N.J.: Transaction Publishers, 2007.

Totten, Samuel, and William S. Parsons (eds.). *Century of Genocide. Critical Essays and Eyewitness Accounts.* New York: Routledge, 2008.

Valentino, Benjamin A. *Final Solutions: Mass Killing and Genocide in the Twentieth Century.* Ithaca, N.Y.: Cornell University Press, 2004.

Whitaker, Benjamin. *Revised and Updated Report on the Question of the Prevention and Punishment of the Crime of Genocide (The Whitaker Report).* ECOSOC (United Nations), 2 July 1985, available in full at www.preventgenocide.org/prevent/UNdocs/whitaker

Economic, Social, Cultural and Development Rights

Aaronson, Susan Ariel, and Jamie M. Zimmerman. *Trade Imbalance. The Struggle to Weigh Human Rights Concerns in Trade Policy Making.* New York: Cambridge University Press, 2007.

Aguirre, Daniel. *The Human Right to Development in a Globalized World.* Burlington, Vt.: Ashgate, 2008.

Alston, Philip. *Labour Rights as Human Rights.* New York: Oxford University Press, 2005.

Anton, Donald K., and Dinah L. Shelton. *Environmental Protection and Human Rights.* New York: Cambridge University Press, 2012.

Baderin, M., and R. McCorquodale (eds.). *Economic, Social and Cultural Rights.* Oxford University Press, 2007.

Beyer, Chris, and H. F. Pizer (eds.). *Public Health and Human Rights. Evidence-Based Approaches.* Baltimore, Md.: Johns Hopkins University Press, 2007.

Bilchitz, D. *Poverty and Fundamental Rights. The Justification and Enforcement of Socio-Economic Rights.* New York: Oxford University Press, 2007.

Blau, Judith, and Alberto Moncada. *Freedoms and Solidarities. In Pursuit of Human Rights.* Lanham, Md.: Rowman & Littlefield Publishers, 2007.

Bohning, W. R. (ed.). *Labour Rights in Crisis. Measuring the Achievements of Fundamental Human Rights in the World of Work.* New York: Palgrave Macmillan, 2005.

Bun, Isabella. *The Right to Development and International Economic Law. Legal and Moral Dimensions.* Oxford: Hart Publishers, 2012.

Chapman, A., and S. Russell (eds.). *Core Obligations: Building a Framework for Economic, Social and Cultural Rights.* New York: Intersentia, 2002.

Clapham, A., M. Robinson, C. Mahon, and S. Jerbi (eds.). *Realizing the Right to Health.* Zurich: Rüffer & Rub, 2009.

Coomans, F. *Justiciability of Economic and Social Rights: Experiences from Domestic Systems.* Antwerpen, Oxford: Intersentia, Maastricht Center for Human Rights, 2006.

Cotter, Anne-Marie Mooney. *This Ability. An International Legal Analysis of Disability Discrimination.* Burlington, Vt.: Ashgate, 2007.

Darrow, Mac. *Between Light and Shadow: The World Bank, the International Monetary Fund, and International Human Rights Law.* Oxford: Hart, 2003.

De Shutter, Olivier (ed.). *Economic, Social and Cultural Rights as Human Rights.* Herndon, Va.: Edward Elgar, 2013.

De Schutter, Olivier, and Katilin Cordes (eds.). *Accounting for Hunger. The Right to Food in the Era of Globalization.* Oxford: Hart Publishing, 2011.

Di Dio, Debora, "Development as a Human Right." *Development* 54 (June 2011): 267–268.

Dommem, Caroline. *Trading Rights: Human Rights and the WTO.* London: Zed Books, 2004.

Donders, Yvonne, and Vladimir Volodin (eds.). *Human Rights in Education, Science and Culture. Legal Developments and Challenges.* Burlington, Vt.: Ashgate, 2007.

Dreze Jean, and Sen Amartya. *Hunger and Public Action.* Oxford: Clarendon Press, 1989.

Eidem W. B., and U. Kracht (eds.). *Food and Human Rights in Development.* Antwerpen: Intersentia Press, 2005.

Englund, Harri. *Prisoners of Freedom: Human Rights and the African Poor.* Berkeley, Calif.: University of California Press, 2006.

Evans, Tony. *Human Rights in the Global Economy: Critical Processes.* Boulder, Colo.: Lynne Rienner Publishers, 2011.

Felice, William. *The Global New Deal. Economic and Social Human Rights in World Politics.* Lanham, Md.: Rowman & Littlefield, 2010.

Felner, E. *A New Frontier in Economic and Social Rights Advocacy.* Center for Economic and Social Rights, 2008. Available at http://cesr.org/article.php?id=359

Francioni, Francesco (ed.). *Biotechnologies and International Human Rights.* Portland, Oreg.: International Specialized Book Services, 2007.

Fujita, Sanae. *The World Bank, Asian Development Bank and Human Rights.* Herndon, Va.: Edward Elgar, 2013.

Golay, C. *The Optional Protocol to the International Covenant on Economic, Social and Cultural Rights*, CETIM, 2008. Available at www.cetim.ch/en/documents/report_2.pdf

Harrington, John, and Maria Stuttaford (eds.). *Global Health and Human Rights. Legal and Philosophical Perspectives.* New York: Routledge, 2010.

Harrison, James. *The Human Rights Impact of the World Trade Organization.* Oxford: Hart Publishing, 2007.

Heinicke-Motsch, Karen, and Susan Sycall (eds.). *Building and Inclusive Development Community. A Manual on Including People with Disabilities in International Development Programs.* Bloomfield, Conn.: Kumarian Press, 2004.

Hertel, Shareen, and Lanse Minkler. *Economic Rights: Conceptual, Measurement and Policy Issues.* New York: Cambridge University Press, 2007.

Hestermeyer, Holger P. *Human Rights and the WTO. The Case of Patents and Access to Medicines.* New York: Oxford University Press, 2007.

Hickey, Sam, and Diana Mitlin (eds.). *Rights Based Approaches to Development. Exploring the Potential and the Pitfalls.* Herndon, Va.: Kumarian Press, 2009.

Hodgson, Douglas. *The Human Right to Education.* Aldershot: Ashgate, 1998.

Hunt, Paul. *Reclaiming Social Rights: International and Comparative Perspectives.* Aldershot: Dartmouth Publishing, 1996.

International Commission of Jurists. *Courts and the Legal Enforcement of Economic, Social and Cultural Rights. Comparative experiences of Justi-*

ciability. Human Rights and Rule of Law Series No. 2, 2008. Available at www.icj.org/dwn/database/ESCR.pdf

Johnston, Barbara Rose. *Life and Death Matters. Human Rights, Environment, and Social Justice.* Walnut Creek, Calif.: Left Coast Press, 2011.

Kent, George. *Freedom from Want. The Human Right to Adequate Food.* Washington D.C.: Georgetown University Press, 2005.

———— (ed.). *Global Obligations for the Right to Food.* Lanham, Md.: Rowman & Littlefield, 2007.

Kirkchmeier, Felix. *Right to Development—Where Do We Stand: State of the Debate on the Right to Development.* Geneva: Friedrich Ebert Stiftung, 2006.

Langford, Malcolm, Wouter Vandenhole, Martin Scheinin, and Willem van Genugten. *Global Justice, State Duties. The Extraterritorial Scope of Economic, Social, and Cultural Rights in International Law.* New York: Cambridge University Press, 2012.

Louka, Elli. *Biodiversity and Human Rights: The International Rules for the Protection of Diversity.* New York: Transnational Publishers, 2002.

Minkler, Lanse (ed.). *The State of Economic and Social Human Rights. A Global Overview.* New York: Cambridge University Press, 2012.

Morijn, John. *Reframing Human Rights and Trade. Potential and Limits of a Human Rights Perspective of WTO Law on Cultural and Educational Goods and Services.* Portland, Oreg.: Intersentia, 2010.

Nanda, Ved P., George W. Shepherd, Jr., and Eileen McCarthy-Arnolds (eds.). *World Debt and the Human Condition Structural Adjustment and the Right to Development.* Santa Barbara, Calif.: Greenwood Press, 1992.

Office of the United Nations High Commissioner for Human Rights. *Frequently Asked Questions on Human Rights–Based Approach to Development Cooperation.* New York: United Nations, 2006.

————. *Human Rights and Poverty Reduction: A Conceptual Framework.* New York: United Nations, 2004.

Oxfam America and CARE USA. *Rights Based Approaches.* Boston and Atlanta: Oxfam and CARE, 2007.

Paterson, William B. *The World Trade Organization and Protest Movements. Altering World Order?* New York: Routledge, 2012.

Pogge, Thomas W. *World Poverty and Human Rights.* Malden, Mass.: Blackwell, 2002.

Ramcharan, Bertrand G. (ed.). *Judicial Protection of Economic, Social and Cultural Rights: Cases and Materials.* Leiden: Martinus Nijhoff, 2005.

Riedel, E., and P. Rothen (eds.). *The Human Right to Water.* Berlin: Berliner Wissenschafts Verlag, 2006.

Ross, Sandy. *The World Food Programme in Global Politics.* Boulder, Colo.: Lynne Rienner, 2011.

Salomon, Margot E. *Global Responsibility for Human Rights. World Poverty and the Development of International Law*. New York: Oxford University Press, 2008.

Sen, A. *Poverty and Famines. An Essay on Entitlement and Deprivation*. New York: Clarendon Press, Oxford University Press, 1981.

Sengupta, Arjun, Archa Negi, and Moushimou Basu, et al. (eds.). *Reflections on the Right to Development*. New Delhi: Sage, 2005.

Sepúlveda, M. *The Nature of the Obligations under the International Covenant on Economic, Social and Cultural Right*. New York: Intersentia, 2003.

Sepúlveda, M., T. Van Bannning, G. Gudmundsdóttir, and C. Chamoun. *Universal and Regional Human Rights Protection. Cases and Commentaries*. San José, Costa Rica: University for Peace, 2004.

Skogly, Sigrun I. *The Human Rights Obligations of the World Bank and the International Monetary Fund*. London: Cavendish Publishing, 2001.

Squires, J., M. Langford, and B. Thiele. *The Road to a Remedy. Current Issues in the Litigation of Economic, Social and Cultural Rights*. Sydney: Australian Human Rights Centre, 2005.

Ssenyonjo, Manisulli (ed.). *Economic, Social and Cultural Rights*. Burlington, Vt.: Ashgate, 2011.

Sunstein, Cass R. *The Second Bill of Rights: FDR's Unfinished Revolution and Why We Need It More than Ever*. New York: Basic Books, 2004.

Tobin, John. *The Right to Health in International Law*. New York: Oxford University Press, 2011.

Torremans, Paul (ed.). *Intellectual Property and Human Rights* (enhanced edition of Copyright and Human Rights). Frederick, Md.: Aspen Publishers, 2008.

Ulrich, George, and Louise Krabbe (eds.). *Human Rights in Development: Reparations: Redressing Past Wrongs*. The Hague: Kluwer Law International, 2003.

United Nations Development Programme. *Human Development Report 2000: Human Development and Human Rights*. New York: Oxford University Press, 2000.

Uvin, Peter. *Human Rights and Development*. Bloomfield, Conn.: Kumarian Press, 2004.

Vizard, Polly. *Poverty and Human Rights. Sen's 'Capability Perspective' Explored*. New York: Oxford University Press, 2006.

Williams, Lucy (ed.). *International Poverty Law. An Emerging Discourse*. London: Zed Books, 2006.

Winkler, Inga T. *The Human Right to Water. Significance, Legal Status and Implications for Water Allocation*. Oxford: Hart Publishing, 2012.

Woods, Jeanne M., Hope Lewis, and Ibrahim Gassama (eds.). *Economic, Social and Cultural Rights: International and Comparative Perspectives.* Ardsley, N.Y.: Transnational Publishing, 2004.

World Health Organization. *Human Rights, Health and Poverty Strategies.* Geneva: World Health Organization, 2005.

Zacker, Mark W., and Tania J. Keefe. *The Politics of Global Health Governance.* New York: Palgrave Macmillan, 2008.

Zeleza, Paul Tiyambe, and Philip J. McConnaughay (eds.). *Human Rights, the Rule of Law, and Development in Africa.* Philadelphia: University of Pennsylvania Press, 2004.

Ziegler, Jean, C. Golay, C. Mahon, and S-A Way. *The Fight for the Right to Food. Lessons Learned.* London: Palgrave Macmillan, 2011.

Group Rights

Ahmed, Ishtiaq. *The Politics of Group Rights. The State and Multiculturalism.* Lanham, Md.: University Press of America, 2005.

De Feyter, Koen, and George Pavlakos (eds.). *The Tension Between Group Rights and Human Rights.* Oxford: Hart Publishing, 2008.

Jones, Peter (ed.). *Group Rights.* Burlington, Vt.: Ashgate, 2009.

Lyons, Gene, and James Mayall. *International Human Rights in the 21st Century: Protecting the Rights of Groups.* Lanham, Md.: Rowman & Littlefield, 2003.

Women

Abu-Duhou, Jamileh. *Giving Voices to the Voiceless. Gender-Based Violence in the Occupied Palestinian Territories.* Highclere, Berkshire: Berkshire Academic Press, 2011.

Agosín, Marjorie (ed.). *Women, Gender, and Human Rights: A Global Perspective.* New Brunswick, N.J.: Rutgers University Press, 2001.

Askin, Kelly D., and Dorean M. Koenig (eds.). *Women and International Human Rights Law*, 3 vols. Ardsley, N.Y.: Transnational Publishing, 2000.

Banda, Fareda. *Women, Law and Human Rights: An African Perspective.* Oxford: Hart, 2005.

Chen, Martha Alter (ed.). *Widows in India: Social Neglect and Public Action.* New Delhi: Sage, 1998.

Cook Rebecca J., Bernard M. Dickens, and Mahmoud F. Fathalla. *Reproductive Health and Human Rights: Integrating Medicine, Ethics and Law.* New York: Oxford University Press, 2003.

Edwards, Alice. *Violence against Women under International Human Rights Law.* New York: Cambridge University Press, 2011.

El Saawadi, Nawal. *The Hidden Face of Eve. Women in the Arab World*. Second Edition. London: Zed Books, 2007.

Elson, Diane. *Budgeting for Women's Rights. Monitoring Government Budgets for Compliance with CEDAW*. Bloomfield, Conn.: Kumarian Press, 2006.

Giles, Wenona, and Jennifer Hyndman (eds.). *Sites of Violence: Gender and Conflict Zones*. Berkeley: University of California Press, 2004.

Grown, Caren, Elissa Braustein, and Anju Malhotra (eds.). *Trading Women's Health and Rights? Trade Liberalization and Reproductive Health in Developing Countries*. London: Zed Books, 2006.

Heimer, Karen, and Candace Kruttschnitt. *Patterns of Victimization and Offending*. New York: New York University, 2005.

Hilsdon, Anne-Marie, et al. (eds.). *Human Rights and Gender Politics: Asia-Pacific Perspectives*. London: Routledge, 2000.

Holtmaat, Riki, and Jonneke Naber. *Women's Human Rights and Culture. From Deadlock to Dialogue*. Portland, Oreg.: Intersentia, 2011.

Jain, Devaki. *Women, Development, and the UN: A Sixty-Year Quest for Equality and Justice*. Bloomington: Indiana University Press, 2005.

Jones, Adam (ed.). *Gendercide and Genocide*. Nashville, Tenn.: Vanderbilt University Press, 2004.

Kelly, Sanja, and Julia Breslin (eds.). *Women's Rights in the Middle East and North Africa*. Lanham, Md.: Rowman & Littlefield, 2010.

Khan, Tahira S. *Beyond Honour: A Historical Materialist Explanation of Honour Related Violence*. Oxford: Oxford University Press, 2006.

Knop, Karen (ed.). *Gender and Human Rights*. Oxford: Oxford University Press, 2004.

Kuehnast, Kathleen, Chantal de Jong Oudraat, and Helga Hernes (eds.). *Women & War: Power and Protection in the 21st Century*. Washington, D.C.: United States Institute of Peace, 2011.

Lockwood, Bert B. (ed.). *Women's Rights. A Human Rights Quarterly Reader*. Baltimore, Md.: Johns Hopkins University Press, 2006.

Merry, Sally Engle. *Human Rights and Gender Violence: Translating International Law into Local Justice*. Chicago: University of Chicago Press, 2005.

Mertus, Julie A. *War's Offensive on Women. The Humanitarian Challenge in Bosnia, Kosovo, and Afghanistan*. Bloomfield, Conn.: Kumarian Press, 2000.

Olonisakin, Funmi, Karen Bartes, and Elka Ikpe (eds.). *Women, Peace and Security. Translating Policy into Practice*. New York: Routledge, 2010.

Otto, Dianne (ed.). *Gender Issues and Human Rights*. Northampton, Mass.: Edward Elgar Publishing, 2013.

Peterson, V. Spike, and Anne Sisson Runyan. *Global Gender Issues*. Second Edition. Boulder, Colo.: Westview Press, 1999.

Rehn, Elisabeth, and Ellen Johnson Sirleaf. *Progress of the World's Women 2002, Volume One. Women, War, Peace: The Independent Assessment on the Impact of Armed Conflict on Women and Women's Role in Peace Building*. New York: UNIFEM, 2003.

Schuler, Margaret. *From Basic Needs to Basic Rights: Women's Claim to Human Rights*. Washington, D.C.: Women, Law & Development International, 1995.

Stewart, Ann. *Gender, Law and Justice in the Global Market*. New York: Cambridge University Press, 2011.

Stiglmayer, Alexandra (ed.). *Mass Rape: The War against Women in Bosnia-Herzegovina*. Lincoln: University of Nebraska Press, 1995.

Van Leeuwen, Pleur. *Women's Rights Are Human Rights. The Practice of the Human Rights Committee and the Committee on Economic, Social and Cultural Rights*. Portland, Oreg.: Intersentia, 2010.

Werner, Gunda (ed.). *Road Map to 1325. Resolution for Gender-Sensitive Peace and Security Policies*. Farmington Hills, Mich.: Barbara Budrich Publishers, 2010.

Zoelle, Diana Grace. *Globalizing Concern for Women's Human Rights*. New York: St. Martin's Press, 2000.

Children

Ai, Shahreen Sardar, Savitri Goonesekere, Emilio Garcia Mendez, and Rebeca Rois-Kohn. *Protecting the World Children. Impact of the Convention on the Rights of the Child in Diverse Legal Systems*. New York: Cambridge University Press, 2007.

Alston, Philip. *The Best Interests of the Child: Reconciling Culture and Human Rights*. Oxford: Oxford University Press, 1994.

Apocada, Clair. *Child Hunger and Human Rights*. New York: Routledge, 2010.

Arts, Karin, and Vesselin Popovski (eds.). *International Criminal Accountability and the Rights of Children*. New York: Cambridge University Press, 2006.

Black, Maggie. *Children First: The Story of UNICEF*. Oxford: Oxford University Press, 1996.

Buck, Trevor. *International Child Law*. New York: Routledge, 2005.

Carpenter, Charli (ed.). *Born of War. Protecting Children of Sexual Violence Survivors in Conflict Zones*. Bloomfield, Conn.: Kumarian Press, 2007.

Cohen, Cynthia Price, with Lori Kujawski. *The Jurisprudence on the Rights of the Child*. New York: Transnational Publishers, 2004.

Craig, Gary (ed.). *Child Slavery Now. A Contemporary Reader.* Portland, Oreg.: Policy Press, 2010.

Denov, Myriam S. *Child Soldiers: Sierra Leone's Revolutionary United Front.* New York: Cambridge University Press, 2010.

Drumbl, Mark A. *Reimagining Child Soldiers in International Law and Policy.* New York: Oxford University Press, 2012.

Ensalaco, Mark, and Linda C. Majaka (eds.). *Children's Human Rights. Progress and Challenges for Children Worldwide.* Lanham, Md.: Rowman & Littlefield, 2005.

Grover, Sonja C. *Prosecuting International Crimes and Human Rights Abuses Committed against Children: Leading International Court Cases.* London: Springer, 2010.

Machel, Graça. *The Impact of War on Children: A Review of Progress since the 1996 United Nations Report on the Impact of Armed Conflict on Children.* New York: Palgrave, 2001.

Nesi, Giuseppe, Luca Nogler, and Marco Pertile (eds.). *Child Labour in a Globalized World.* Burlington, Vt.: Ashgate, 2008.

Schoenberger, Karl. *Levi's Children: Coming to Terms with Human Rights in the Global Marketplace.* New York: Atlantic Monthly Press, 2000.

Sen, Purna (ed.). *Child Rights in the Commonwealth. 20 Years of the Convention on the Rights of Children.* London: Commonwealth Secretariat, 2010.

Sloth-Nielsen, Julia (ed.). *Children's Rights in Africa. A Legal Perspective.* Burlington, Vt.: Ashgate, 2008.

Weston, Burns H. (ed.). *Child Labor and Human Rights: Making Children Matter.* Boulder, Colo.: Lynne Rienner Publishing, 2005.

Williams, Jane, and Antonella Invernizzi (eds.). *The Human Rights of Children. From Visions to Implementation.* Burlington, Vt.: Ashgate, 2011.

Migrants

Bacon, David. *Communities without Borders. Images and Voices from the World of Migration.* Ithaca, N.Y.: Cornell University Press, 2006.

Brysk, Allison, and Gershon Shafir. *People Out of Place: Globalization, Human Rights and the Citizenship Gap.* New York: Routledge, 2004.

Calavita, Kitty. *Immigrants at the Margins. Law, Race, and Exclusion in Southern Europe.* New York: Cambridge University Press, 2005.

Cholewinski, Ryszard. *Migrant Workers in International Human Rights Law; Their Protection in Countries of Employment.* New York: Oxford University Press, 1997.

Cholewinski, Ryszard, and Richard Perruchoud (eds.). *International Migration Law. Developing Paradigms and Key Challenges.* New York: Cambridge University Press, 2007.

Cornelius, Wayne A. *Controlling Immigration: A Global Perspective.* Edited by Wayne A. Cornelius, Philip L. Martin, and James F. Hollifield. Stanford, Calif.: Stanford University Press, 1994.

Dauvergne, Catherine. *Making People Illegal. Migration Laws for Global Times.* New York: Cambridge University Press, 2008.

Dembourg, Marie-Benedicte. *Are Human Rights for Migrants? Critical Reflections on the Status of Irregular Migrants in Europe and the United States.* New York: Routledge, 2011.

Ho, Christine, and James Loucky. *Dispossessed People. Establishing Legitimacy and Rights for Global Migrants.* Herndon, Va.: Kumarian Press, 2011.

International Organization for Migration. *Assessing the Costs and Impacts of Migration Policy.* New York: IOM, 2008.

———. *Migration and the Right to Health.* New York: IOM, 2008.

Juss, Satvinder. *International Migration and Global Justice.* Burlington, Vt.: Ashgate, 2007.

Korinek, Kim Marie, and Thomas N. Maloney. *Migration in the 21st Century: Rights, Outcomes, and Policy.* New York: Routledge, 2011.

Korinman, Michel (ed.). *The Long March to the West. Twenty-First Century Migration in Europe and the Greater Mediterranean Area.* Portland, Oreg.: Vallentine Mitchell Publishers, 2007.

Krieken, Peter J. van (ed.). *The Migration Acquis Handbook. The Foundation for a Common European Migration Policy.* New York: Cambridge University Press, 2001.

Layont-Henry, Zig (ed.). *The Political Rights of Migrant Workers in Western Europe.* Thaousand Oaks, Calif.: Sage Publications, 1990.

Lee, T. L. *Statelessness, Human Rights and Gender: Irregular Migrant Workers from Burma in Thailand.* Leiden: Martinus Nijhoff, 2005.

Messina, Anthony M., and Gallya Lahav (eds.). *The Migration Reader: Exploring Politics and Policies.* Boulder, Colo.: Lynne Rienner, 2006.

Perruchoud, Richard, and Katarina Tomolova (eds.). *Compendium of International Migration Law Instruments.* New York: Cambridge University Press, 2007.

Piper, Nicola. *New Perspectives on Gender and Migration: Livelihood, Rights and Entitlements.* New York: Routledge, 2008.

Rosenberg, Clifford. *Policing Paris: the Origins of Modern Immigration Control between the Wars.* Ithaca, N.Y.: Cornell University Press, 2006.

United Nations. Office of the High Commissioner for Human Rights. *The Rights of Non-Citizens.* New York: United Nations, 2006.

Weiner, Myron. *The Global Migration Crisis: Challenge to States and to Human Rights.* New York: HarperCollins College Publishers, 1995.

Weissbrodt, David S. *The Human Rights of Non-Citizens.* New York: Oxford University Press, 2008.

Wilsher, Daniel. *Immigration Detention. Law, History, Politics.* New York: Cambridge University Press, 2011.

Discrimination

Bell, Mark. *Anti-Discrimination Law and the European Union.* Oxford: Oxford University Press, 2002.

———. *Racism and Equality in the European Union.* New York: Oxford University Press, 2009.

Blank, Rebecca M., Marilyn Dabady, and Constance F. Citro (eds.). *Measuring Racial Discrimination.* Washington, D.C.: National Academies Press, 2004.

Cotter, Anne-Marie Mooney. *Race Matters. An International Legal Analysis of race Discrimination.* Burlington, Vt.: Ashgate, 2006.

De Schutter, Olivier. *The Prohibition of Discrimination under European Human Rights Law: Relevance for EU Racial and Employment Equality Directives.* Luxemburg: Office for Official Publications of the European Communities, 2005.

Dickson, Brice. *The European Convention on Human Rights and the Conflict in Northern Ireland.* New York: Oxford University Press, 2010.

Ellis, Soma Ray. *Discrimination and Human Rights.* Markham, Ont.: LexisNexis, Canada, 2001.

Fredman, S. *Discrimination and Human Rights—The Case of Racism.* Oxford: Oxford University Press, 2001.

Goldstein, Melvyn C. *A History of Modern Tibet, 1913–1951. The Demise of the Lamaist State.* Berkeley: University of California Press, 1991.

Hathaway, James C. *Human Rights and Refugee Law.* Herndon, Va.: Edward Elgar Publishing, 2013.

Keane, David. *Caste-Based Discrimination in International Human Rights Law.* Burlington, Vt.: Ashgate, 2007.

Lauren, Paul Gordon. *Power and Prejudice: the Politics and Diplomacy of Racial Discrimination.* Boulder, Colo.: Westview, 1988.

Lerner, N. *Group Rights and Discrimination in International Law.* The Hague: Martinus Nijhoff, 1991.

Louw, Eric P. *The Rise, Fall and Legacy of Apartheid.* New York: Praeger, 2004.

Mjoll Arnardottir, Oddny. *Equality and Non-Discrimination under the European Convention on Human Rights.* New York: Nijhoff, 2003.

Monaghan, Karon, Max Du Plessis, Tajinder Malhi, and Jonathan Cooper. *Race, Religion and Ethnicity Discrimination: Using International Human Rights Law.* London: Justice, 2003.

Taylor, Paul M. *Freedom of Religion: UN and European Human Rights Law and Practice.* Cambridge: Cambridge University Press, 2005.

Van der Vyver, Johan D., and John Witte, Jr. *Religious Human Rights in Global Perspective: Legal Perspectives.* The Hague: Kluwer Law International, 1996.

Weissbrodt, David, and Mary Rumsey (eds.). *Vulnerable and Marginalized Groups and Human Rights.* Herndon, Va.: Edward Elgar, 2013.

Refugees, Asylum, Internally Displaced Persons and Statelessness

Agler, Michel. *On the Margins of the World: The Refugee Experience Today.* Malden, Mass.: Polity Press, 2005.

Amnesty International. *The UN and Refugees' Human Rights: A Manual on How UN Human Rights Mechanisms Can Protect the Rights of Refugees.* London: Amnesty International, 1997.

Benhabib, S. *The Rights of Others: Aliens, Residents, and Citizens.* Cambridge: Cambridge University Press, 2004.

Betts, Alexander (ed.). *Refugees in International Relations.* New York: Oxford University Press, 2010.

Blake, Nicholas, and Raza Husain. *Immigration, Asylum and Human Rights.* Oxford: Oxford University Press, 2003.

Blitz, Brad K., and Maureen Lynch. *Statelessness and the Benefits of Citizenship: A Comparative Study.* Published by the Geneva Academy of International Humanitarian Law and Human Rights and International Observatory on Statelessness, 2009.

Boyle, Francis Anthony. *Palestine, Palestinians & International Law.* Atlanta, Ga.: Clarity Press, 2003.

Dumper, Michael (ed.). *Palestinian Refugee Repatriation. Global Perspectives.* London: Routledge, 2006.

Feller, Erika, Volker Turk, and Frances Nicholson. *Refugee Protection in International Law: UNHCR's Global Consultations on International Protection.* Cambridge: Cambridge University Press, 2003.

Foster, Michelle. *International Refugee Law and Socio-Economic Rights. Refuge from Deprivation.* New York: Cambridge University Press, 2007.

Gammerltoft-Hansen, Thomas. *Access to Asylum.* Cambridge: Cambridge University Press, 2011.

Goodwin-Gill, Guy S. *The Refugee in International Law.* Third Edition. New York: Oxford University Press, 2007.

Haddad, Emma. *The Refugee in International Society. Between Sovereigns.* New York: Cambridge University Press, 2008.

Kneebone, Susan (ed.). *The Refugee's Convention 50 Years on Globalisation and International Law.* Aldershot: Avebury Technical, 2003.

Leckie, Scott (ed.). *Housing and Property Restitution Rights of Refugees and Displaced Persons.* New York: Cambridge University Press, 2007.

Loesher, Gil. *The UNHCR and World Politics: A Perilous Path.* Oxford: Oxford University Press, 2001.

Loesher, Gil, Anna Betts, and James Milner. *UNHCR: The Politics and Practice of Refugee Protection into the 21st Century.* London: Routledge, 2008.

Loesher, Gil, Anna Betts, Edward Newman, and James Milner (eds.). *Protracted Refugee Situations: Political, Security and Human Rights Implications.* Tokyo: United Nations University Press, 2008.

Marrus, Michael R. *The Unwanted: European Refugees from the First World War through the Cold War.* Philadelphia, Pa.: Temple University Press, 2001.

McAdam, Jane (ed.). *Forced Migration, Human Rights and Security.* Oxford: Hart Publishing, 2008.

Morris, Benny. *The Birth of the Palestinian Refugee Problem Revisited.* New York: Cambridge University Press, 2004.

Newman, Edward, and Joanne van Selm (eds.). *Refugees and Forced Displacement: International Security, Human Vulnerability, and the State.* Tokyo: United Nations University Press, 2003.

Ngaruni Kenney, David, and Philip G. Shrag. *Asylum Denied. A Refugee's Struggle for Safety in America.* Berkeley: University of California Press, 2008.

Office of the Special Representative of the Secretary General for Children and Armed Conflict. *The Rights and Guarantees of Internally Displaced Children in Armed Conflict.* Working Paper No. 2. New York: United Nations, 2010.

Pappe, Ilan. *The Ethnic Cleansing of Palestine.* London: Oneworld, 2006.

Peteet, Julie. *Landscape of Hope and Despair. Palestinian Refugee Camps.* Philadelphia: University of Pennsylvania Press, 2009.

Phuong, Catherine. *The International Protection of Internally Displaced Persons.* New York: Cambridge University Press, 2005.

Rabben Linda. *Give Refuge to a Stranger. The Past, Present, and Future of Sanctuary.* Walnut Creek, Calif.: Left Coast Press, 2011.

Sales, Rosemary. *Understanding Immigration and Refugee Policy.* Oxford: Hart Publishing, 2007.

Shaw, J. *The Transformation of Citizenship in the European Union: Electoral Rights and the Restructuring of Political Space.* Cambridge: Cambridge University Press, 2007.

Sidorenko, Olga Ferguson. *The Common European Asylum System. Background, Current State of Affairs, Future Direction.* New York: Cambridge University Press, 2007.

Simeon, James C. *Critical Issues in International Refugee Law. Strategies toward Interpretative Harmony.* New York: Cambridge University Press, 2010.

Somers, Margaret. *Genealogies of Citizenship: Markets, Statelessness, and the Right to Have Rights.* Cambridge: Cambridge University Press, 2008.

Steiner, Niklaus, Mark Gibney, and Gil Loesher (eds.). *Problems of Protection: The UNHCR, Refugees and Human Rights in the 21st Century.* London: Routledge, 2003.

Van Waas, L. *Nationality Matters: Statelessness Under International Law.* Antwerp: Intersentia, 2008.

Weis, Paul. *The Refugee Convention, 1951: The Travaux Preparatoires Analysed, with a Commentary.* Cambridge: Cambridge University Press, 1995.

Weiss, Thomas G., and David A. Korn. *Internal Displacement. Conceptualization and Its Consequences.* New York: Routledge, 2006.

Whittaker, David J. *Asylum Seekers and Refugees in the Contemporary World.* New York: Routledge, 2005.

Zimmermann, Andreas. *The 1951 Convention Relating to the Status of Refugees and Its 1867 Protocol.* New York: Oxford University Press, 2010.

Indigenous Peoples, Minorities and Self-Determination

Anaya, James. *International Human Rights and Indigenous Peoples.* Waltham, Mass.: Aspen Publishers, 2009.

Barker, Joanne (ed.). *Sovereignty Matters: Locations of Contestation and Possibility in Indigenous Struggles for Self-Determination.* Lincoln: University of Nebraska Press, 2005.

Barume, Albert Kwokwo. *Heading Toward Extinction? Indigenous Rights in Africa: The Case of the Twa of the Kahuzi-Biega National Park, Democratic Republic of the Congo.* New Brunswick, N.J.: Transaction Publishers, 2000.

Bryce, James, and Arnold Toynbee. *The Treatment of Armenians in the Ottoman Empire, 1915–1916: Documents Presented to Viscount Grey of Falloden by Viscount Bryce (Uncensored Edition) also Known as The Blue Book.* Reading: Taderon Press, 2000.

Brysk, Alison. *From Tribal Village to Global Village: Indian Rights and International Relations in Latin America.* Stanford, Calif.: Stanford University Press, 2000.

Buchanan, Allen. *Justice, Legitimacy, and Self-Determination: Moral Foundations for International Law (Oxford Political Theory)*. New York: Oxford University Press, 2007.

Castellino Joshua (ed.). *Global Minority Rights*. Burlington, Vt.: Ashgate, 2012.

Castellino, Joshua, and David Keane. *Minority Rights in the Pacific Region. A Comparative Legal Analysis*. New York: Oxford University Press, 2009.

Coates, Ken S. *A Global History of Indigenous Peoples: Struggle and Survival*. Basingstoke: Palgrave Macmillan, 2004.

Cocker, Mark. *Rivers of Blood, Rivers of Gold: Europe's Conquest of Indigenous Peoples*. New York: Grove Press, 2001.

Danspeckgruber, Wolfgang F. (ed.). *The Self-Determination of Peoples: Community, Nation, and State in an Interdependent World*. Boulder, Colo.: Lynne Rienner, 2002.

Dean, B., and J. M. Levi (eds.). *At the Risk of Being Heard: Identity, Indigenous Rights, and Postcolonial States*. Ann Arbor: University of Michigan Press, 2003.

Eversole, Robyn, John-Andrew McNeish, and Alberto D. Cimadamore (eds.). *Indigenous Peoples and Poverty. An International Perspective*. London: Zed Books, 2006.

Fink, Carole. *Defending the Rights of Others. The Great Powers, the Jews, and International Minority Protection, 1878–1918*. Cambridge: Cambridge University Press, 2006.

Gedicks, Al. *Resource Rebels: Native Challenges to Mining and Oil Corporations*. Cambridge, Mass.: South End Press, 2001.

Gewald, Jan-Bart. *Herero Heroes: A Socio-Political History of the Herero of Namibia, 1890–1923*. Athens: Ohio University Press, 2001.

Gilbert, Jérémie. *Indigenous Peoples' Land Rights under International Law. From Victims to Actors*. Cambridge: Cambridge: University Press, 2006.

Gurr, Ted Robert. *Peoples versus States. Minorities at Risk in the New Century*. Herndon, Va.: Institute of Peace Press, 2000.

Hannum, Hurst. *Autonomy, Sovereignty, and Self-Determination: The Accommodation of Conflicting Rights*. Philadelphia: University of Pennsylvania Press, 1996.

Hinton, Martin, Daryle Rigney, and Elliott Johnston. *Indigenous Australians and the Law*. New York: Routledge, 2007.

Hitchcock, Robert K. (ed.). *Genocide of Indigenous Peoples*. Lanham, Md.: Rowman & Littlefield, 2010.

Hocking, Barbara Ann (ed.). *Unfinished Constitutional Business: Rethinking Indigenous Self-Determination*. Canberra: Aboriginal Studies Press, 2005.

Howard, Bradley Reed. *Indigenous Peoples and the State: The Struggle for Native Rights*. DeKalb: Northern Illinois University Press, 2003.

Hsieh, Jolan. *Collective Rights of Indigenous Peoples. Identity-Based Movement of Plain Indigenous in Taiwan*. New York: Routledge, 2006.

Ilona Klimova, Alexander. *The Romani Voice in World Politics: The United Nations and Non-state Actors*. Burlington, Vt.: Ashgate, 2005.

Keane, David. *Caste-based Discrimination in International Human Rights Law*. Burlington, Vt.: Ashgate, 2007.

Kidd, Rosalind. *Trustees on Trial: Recovering the Stolen Wages*. Canberra: Aboriginal Studies Press, 2006.

Kjaer, Anne Lise, and Silvia Adamo (eds.). *Linguistic Diversity and European Democracy*. Burlington, Vt.: Ashgate, 2011.

Knop, Karen. *Diversity and Self-Determination in International Law*. New York: Cambridge University Press, 2002.

Lam, Maivan Clech. *At the Edge of the State: Indigenous Peoples and Self-Determination*. New York: Transnational Publishers, 2000.

Letschert, Rianne M. *The Impact of Minority Rights Mechanisms*. New York: Cambridge University Press, 2006.

Manafy, A. *The Kurdish Political Struggles in Iran, Iraq, and Turkey*. Lanham, Md.: University Press of America, 2005.

Montejo, Victor. *Voices from Exile: Violence and Survival in Modern Maya History*. Norman: University of Oklahoma Press, 1999.

Moorehead, Alan. *The Fatal Impact: The Invasion of the South Pacific, 1767–1840*. New York: HarperCollins, 1990.

Morgan, Rhiannon. *Transforming Law and Institution: Indigenous Peoples, the United Nations, and Human Rights*. Burlington, Vt.: Ashgate, 2011.

Moses, A. Dirk (ed.). *Genocide and Settler Society: Frontier Violence and Stolen Indigenous Children in Australian History*. New York: Berghahn Books, 2004.

Munda, R. D., and S. Bosu Mullick (eds.). *The Jharkhand Movement. Indigenous Peoples' Struggle for Autonomy in India*. New Brunswick, N.J.: Transaction Publishers, 2003.

Niezen, Ronald. *The Origins of Indigenism: Human Rights and the Politics of Identity*. Berkeley, Calif.: University of California Press, 2003.

O'Nions, Helen. *Minority Protection in International Law. The Roma of Europe*. Burlington, Vt.: Ashgate, 2007.

Povinelli, Elizabeth. *The Cunning of Recognition: Indigenous Alterities and the Making of Australian Multiculturalism*. Durham, N.C.: Duke University Press, 2002.

Pritchard, Sarah (ed.). *Indigenous Peoples, the United Nations and Human Rights*. London: Zed Books, 1998.

Pulitano, Elvira (ed.). *Indigenous Rights in the Age of the UN Declaration.* New York: Cambridge University Press, 2012.

Raic, David. *Statehood and the Law of Self-Determination.* The Hague: Kluwer Law International, 2003.

Robertson, Lindsay G. *Conquest by Law. How the Discovery of America Dispossessed Indigenous Peoples of Their Lands.* New York: Oxford University Press, 2005.

Robins, Nicholas. *Native Insurgencies and the Genocidal Impulse in the Americas.* Bloomington: Indiana University Press, 2005.

Roepstorff, Kristina. *The Politics of Self-Determination. Beyond the Decolonization Process.* New York: Routledge, 2012.

Sellers, M. *The New World Order: Sovereign Human Rights and the Self-Determination of Peoples.* Oxford: Berg, 1996.

Roy, Rajkumari Chandra. *Land Rights of the Indigenous Peoples of the Chittagong Hill Tract, Bangladesh.* New Brunswick, N.J.: Transaction Publishers, 2002.

Shoraka, Kirsten. *Human Rights and Minority Rights in the EU: A History.* New York: Routledge, 2010.

Short, Damien. *Reconciliation and Colonial Power. Indigenous Rights in Australia.* Burlington, Vt.: Ashgate, 2008.

Smith, Andrea. *Conquest: Sexual Violence and American Indian Genocide.* Cambridge, Mass.: South End Press, 2005.

Sterio, Milena. *The Right to Self-Determination under International Law. "Selfistans," Secession, and the Rule of the Great Powers.* New York: Routledge, 2012.

Stidsen, Sille (ed.). *The Indigenous World 2006.* Copenhagen: International Working Group for Indigenous Affairs, 2006.

Summers, James. *Peoples and International Law. How Nationalism and Self-Determination Shape a Contemporary Law of Nations.* New York: Martinus Nijhoff, 2007.

Thio, Li-Ann. *Managing Babel: The International Legal Protection of Minorities in the Twentieth Century.* New York: Cambridge University Press, 2005.

Valpy Fitzgerald, Frances Stewart, and Rajesh Venugopal (eds.). *Globalization, Violent Conflict and Self-Determination.* London: Palgrave Macmillan, 2006.

Weller, Marc. *Political Participation of Minorities. A Commentary on International Standards and Practice.* New York: Oxford University Press, 2010.

——. *Universal Minority Rights. A Commentary on the Jurisprudence of International Courts and Treaty Bodies.* New York: Oxford University Press, 2008.

Weller, Marc, and Catherine Noble (eds.). *Political Participation of Minorities. A Commentary on International Standards and Practice*. New York: Oxford University Press, 2010.

Whall, Helena, and Meena Shivdas (eds.). *Indigenous Women's Rights. Challenging Social and Gender Hierarchies*. London: Commonwealth Secretariat, 2008.

Wilkinson, Daniel. *Silence on the Mountain: Stories of Terror, Betrayal, and Forgetting in Guatemala*. Boston: Houghton Mifflin, 2002.

Wilson, James. *The Earth Shall Weep: A History of Native America*. New York: Atlantic Monthly Press, 1998.

Xanthaki, Alexandra. *Indigenous Rights and United Nations Standards. Self-Determination, Culture and Land*. New York: Cambridge University Press, 2007.

York, Geoffrey. *The Dispossessed: Life and Death in Native Canada*. London: Vintage UK, 1990.

Zinn, Annalisa. *Globalization and Self-Determination*. London: Taylor & Francis, 2007.

Culture

Bevan, Robert. *The Destruction of Memory: Architecture at War*. Chicago: University of Chicago Press, 2006.

Edwards, Julie B., and Stephan P. Edwards. *Beyond Article 19: Libraries and Social and Cultural Rights*. Duluth, Minn.: Library Juice Press, 2010.

Francioni, Francesco, and Martin Scheinin. *Cultural Human Rights*. Boston: Nijhoff, 2008.

Kymlicka, Will (ed.). *The Rights of Minority Cultures*. New York: Oxford University Press, 1995.

Langfield, Michele, William Logan, and Mairead Nic Craith. *Cultural Diversity, Heritage, Heritage and Human Rights: Intersections in Theory and Practice*. London: Routledge, 2010.

O'Keefe, Roger. *The Protection of Cultural Property in Armed Conflict*. New York: Cambridge University Press, 2006.

Silverman, Helaine, and D. Fairfield Ruggles. *Cultural Heritage and Human Rights*. New York: Springer, 2007.

Stamatopoulou, Elsa. *Cultural Rights in International Law: Article 27 of the Universal Declaration of Human Rights and Beyond*. Boston: Nijhoff, 2007.

Stiftung, Bertelsmann. *Culture and Conflict in Global Perspective. The Cultural Dimensions of Global Conflicts 1945–2007*. Gutersloh: Bertelsmann Stiftung, 2010.

Disabled/Aging

Bartlett, Peter (ed.). *Mental Disability and the European Convention on Human Rights.* Leiden: Brill, 2006.

Brown, Robert N. *The Rights of Older Persons.* Carbondale: Southern Illinois University Press, 1989.

Clements, Luke, and Janet Read. *Disabled People and the Right to Life. The Protection and Violation of Disabled People's Most Basic Human Right.* New York: Routledge, 2007.

David, Paul. *Article 31: The Right to Leisure, Play and Culture.* Boston: Nijhoff, 2006.

Fleischer, Doris Z., and Frieda Zames. *The Disability Rights Movement: From Charity to Confrontation.* Philadelphia: Temple University Press, 2001.

Haugen, David M., Susan Musser, and Andrea B. DeMott. *Rights of the Disabled.* New York: Facts on File, 2008.

Herr, Stanley S., and Germain Weber. *Aging, Rights and Quality of Life: Prospects for Older People with Developmental Disabilities.* Baltimore: Paul H. Brookes, 1999.

Power, Andrew, Janet Lord, and Allison DeFranco. *Active Citizenship and Disability. Implementing the Personalization of Support.* New York: Cambridge University Press, 2012.

Quinn, Gerard, and Theresia Degener. *United Nations. Human Rights and Disability: The Current Use and Future Potential of United Nations Human Rights Instruments in the Context of Disability.* New York: United Nations High Commissioner for Human Rights, 2002.

Rimmerman, Arie. *Social Inclusion of People with Disabilities. National and International Perspectives.* New York: Cambridge University Press, 2012.

Vanhala, Lisa. *Making Rights a Reality? Disability Rights Activists and Legal Mobilization.* New York: Cambridge University Press, 2011.

Weissbrodt, David, and Mary Rumsey (eds.). *Vulnerable and Marginalized Groups and Human Rights.* Northampton, Mass.: Edward Elgar, 2011.

Transitional Justice and Accountability

Aertsen, Ivo, et al. (eds.). *Restoring Justice after Large-Scale Violent Conflicts: Kosovo, DR Congo and the Israeli-Palestinian Case.* Cullompton: Willan Publishing, 2008.

Arthur, Paige. *Identities in Transition. Challenges for Transitional Justice in Divided Societies.* New York: Cambridge University Press, 2010.

Bassiouni, M. Cherif (ed.). *Post-Conflict Justice.* New York: Transnational Publishers, 2002.

Cobban, Helena. *Amnesty After Atrocity? Healing Nations After Genocide and War Crimes.* Herndon, Va.: Paradigm Publishers, 2006.

Collins, Cath. *Post-Transitional Justice. Human Rights Trials in Chile and El Salvador.* University Park: Pennsylvania State University Press, 2010.

Elster, Jon. *Closing the Books. Transitional Justice in Historical Perspective.* New York: Cambridge University Press, 2004.

——— (ed.). *Retribution and Reparation in the Transition to Democracy.* New York: Cambridge University Press, 2006.

Freeman, Mark. *Truth Commissions and Procedural Fairness.* New York: Cambridge University Press, 2006.

Hayner, Priscilla B. *Unspeakable Truths: Confronting State Terror and Atrocity.* New York: Routledge, 2001.

Horowitz, Adam, Lizzy Ratner, and Philip Weiss (eds.). *The Goldstone Report. The Legacy of a Landmark Investigation of the Gaza Conflict.* New York: Perseus, 2011.

Horowitz, Shale, and Albrecht Schnabel (eds.). *Human Rights and Societies in Transition. Causes, Consequences, Responses.* Tokyo: United Nations University Press, 2004.

Isaac, Tracy, and Richard Vernon (eds.). *Accountability for Collective Wrongdoing.* New York: Cambridge University Press, 2011.

Klinghofer, Arthur Jay, and Judith Apter Klinghofer. *International Citizens' Tribunals: Mobilizing Public Opinion to Advance Human Rights.* New York: Palgrave, 2002.

Kritz, Neil J. (ed.). *Transitional Justice: How Emerging Democracies Reckon with Former Regimes.* Washington, D.C.: United States Institute of Peace Press, 1995.

Lavinia Stan (ed.). *Transitional Justice in Eastern Europe and the Former Soviet Union: Reckoning with the Communist Past.* London: Routledge, 2009.

Lessa, Francesca, and Leigh A. Payne. *Amnesty in the Age of Human Rights Accountability.* New York: Cambridge University Press, 2012.

Lincoln, Jessica. *Transitional Justice, Peace and Accountability. Outreach and the Role of International Courts after Conflict.* New York: Routledge, 2011.

Mallinder, Louise. *Amnesty, Human Rights and Political Transitions.* Oxford: Hart Publishing, 2008.

May, Rachel A., and Andrew K. Milton. *Human Rights and Democratic Transitions in Eastern Europe and Latin America.* Lanham, Md.: Rowman & Littlefield, 2007.

McEvoy, Kieran. *Truth, Transition and Reconciliation: Dealing with the Past in Northern Ireland.* Cullompton: Willan Publishing, 2007.

Miller, Barbara. *The Stasi Files Unveiled. Guilt and Compliance in a Unified Germany.* Rutgers, N.J.: Transaction Publishers, 2004.

Minow, Martha. *Between Vengeance and Forgiveness: Facing History After Genocide and Mass Violence.* Boston: Beacon Press, 1998.

Morison, John (ed.). *Judges, Transition, and Human Rights.* New York: Oxford University Press, 2007.

Olsen, Tricia D., Leigh A. Payne, and Andrew G. Reiter. *Transitional Justice in Balance. Comparing Processes, Weighing Efficacy.* Washington, D.C.: United States Institute of Peace Press, 2010.

Phelps, Teresa Godwin. *Shattered Voices: Language, Violence, and the Work of Truth Commissions.* Philadelphia: University of Pennsylvania Press, 2004.

Popovski, Vesselin, and Monica Serrano (eds.). *After Oppression. Transitional Justice in Latin America and Eastern Europe.* Tokyo: United Nations University Press, 2012.

Rae DeShaw, James. *Peacebuilding and Transitional Justice in East Timor.* Boulder, Colo.: Lynne Rienner, 2009.

Ratner, Steven R., and Jason S. Abrams. *Accountability for Human Rights Atrocities in International Law: Beyond the Nuremberg Legacy.* Second Edition. New York: Oxford University Press, 2001.

Roht-Arriaza, Naomi (ed.). *Transitional Justice in the Twenty-First Century. Beyond Truth versus Justice.* New York: Cambridge University Press, 2006.

Roman, David. *Lustration and Transitional Justice.* Philadelphia: Pennsylvania University Press, 2011.

Rotberg, Robert I., and Dennis. Thompson (eds.). *Truth v. Justice.* Princeton, N.J.: Princeton University Press, 2000.

Rowe, Peter. *The Impact of Human Rights Law on Armed Forces.* Cambridge: Cambridge University Press, 2006.

Smyth, Marie Breen. *Truth Recovery and Justice After Conflict. Managing Violent Pasts.* New York: Routledge, 2007.

Sriram, Chandra Lekha. *Confronting Past Human Rights Violations: Justice vs. Peace in Times of Transition.* New York: Frank Cass, 2004.

Stanley, William. *Enabling Peace in Guatemala: The Story of MINUGUA.* Boulder Colo.: Lynne Rienner, 2010.

Stover, E., and H. M. Weinstein (eds.). *My Neighbour, My Enemy: Justice and Community in the Aftermath of Mass Atrocity.* Cambridge: Cambridge University Press, 2004.

Thakur, Ramesh, and Peter Malcontent (eds.). *From Sovereign Impunity to International Accountability.* Tokyo: United Nations University Press, 2004.

Trindade, Antonio, and Augusto Cancado. *The Access of Individuals to International Justice*. New York: Oxford University Press, 2011.

Wiebelhaus-Brahm, Eric. *Truth Commissions and Transitional Justice. The Impact of Human Rights and Democracy*. New York: Routledge, 2009.

Wilde, Ralph. *International Territorial Administration: How Trusteeship and the Civilizing Mission Never Went Away*. Oxford: Oxford University Press, 2008.

Wilson, Richard. *The Politics of Truth and Reconciliation in South Africa: Legitimizing the Post-Apartheid State*. Cambridge: Cambridge University Press, 2001.

Retributive Justice

Anja Seibert-Fohr. *Prosecuting Serious Human Rights Violations*. New York: Oxford University Press, 2009.

Arendt, Hannah. *Eichmann in Jerusalem: A Report on the Banality of Evil*. New York: Viking Press, 1965.

Bantekas, Ilias. *Principles of Direct and Superior Responsibility in International Humanitarian Law*. Manchester: Manchester University Press, 2002.

Bass, Gary Jonathan. *Stay the Hand of Vengeance: The Politics of War Crimes Tribunals*. Princeton, N.J.: Princeton University Press, 2000.

Baudenbacher, Carl, and Erhard Busek (eds.). *The Role of International Courts*. Frankfurt-am-Main: German Law Publications, 2008.

Beigbeder, Yves. *International Criminal Tribunals, Justice and Politics*. New York: Palgrave, 2011.

Birdsall, Andrea. *The International Politics of Judicial Intervention. Creating a More Just Order*. New York: Routledge, 2011.

Boas, Gideon. *The Milosevic Trial. Lessons for the Conduct of Complex Criminal Proceedings*. New York: Cambridge University Press, 2007.

Borneman, John (ed.). *The Case of Ariel Sharon and the Fate of Universal Jurisdiction*. Princeton, N.J.: Princeton University Press, 2004.

Broomhall, Bruce. *International Justice and the International Criminal Court: Between Sovereignty and the Rule of Law*. New York: Oxford University Press, 2003.

Burbach, Roger. *The Pinochet Affair. State Terrorism and Global Justice*. London: Zed Books, 2006.

Byron, Christine. *War Crimes and Crimes Against Humanity in the Rome Statute of the International Criminal Court*. Manchester: Manchester University Press, 2010.

Cassese, Antonio. *International Criminal Law*. New York: Oxford University Press, 2008.

Cryer, Robert. *The Tokyo International Military Tribunal*. New York: Oxford University Press, 2008.

Darcy, Shane and Joseph Powderly (eds.). *Judicial Creativity at the International Criminal Tribunals*. New York: Oxford University Press, 2011.

Development Dialogue: Dealing with Crimes against Humanity. No. 55. Uppsala: Dag Hammarkjold Foundation, 2011.

Fawthrop, Tom, and Helen Jarvis. *Getting Away with Genocide. Elusive Justice and the Khmer Rouge Tribunal*. Ann Arbor, Mich.: Pluto Press, 2004.

Funk, T. Markus. *Victims' Rights and Advocacy at the International Criminal Court*. New York: Oxford University Press, 2010.

Futamura, Madoka. *War Crimes Tribunals and Transitional Justice. The Tokyo Trial and the Nuremberg Legacy*. New York: Routledge, 2007.

Goldstone, Richard J., and Adam M. Smith. *International Judicial Institutions. The Architecture of International Justice at Home and Abroad*. New York: Routledge, 2009.

Hagan, John. *Justice in the Balkans: Prosecuting War Crimes in the Hague Tribunal*. Chicago: University of Chicago Press, 2003.

Heller, Kevin Jon. *The Nuremberg Military Tribunals and the Origins of International Criminal Law*. New York: Oxford University Press, 2011.

Isaacs, Tracy, and Richard Vernon (eds.). *Accountability for Collective Wrongdoing*. New York: Cambridge University Press, 2011.

Ivkovich, Sanja K., and John Hagan. *Reclaiming Justice. The International Tribunal for the Former Yugoslavia and Local Courts*. New York: Oxford University Press, 2011.

Jurdi, Nidal Nabil. *The International Criminal Court and National Courts. A Contentious Relationship*. Burlington, Vt.: Ashgate, 2011.

Kaleck, Wolfgang, et al. (eds.). *International Prosecution of Human Rights Crimes*. New York: Springer, 2006.

Kamari, Clarke. *Fictions of Justice: The International Court and the Challenge of Legal Pluralism in Sub-Saharan Africa*. New York: Cambridge University Press, 2009.

Kerr, Rachel. *The International Criminal Tribunal for the Former Yugoslavia. An Exercise in Law, Politics, and Diplomacy*. New York: Oxford University Press, 2004.

Khan, Karim A. A., Caroline Buisman, and Chris Gosnell (eds.). *Principles of Evidence in International Criminal Justice*. New York: Oxford University Press, 2010.

King-Irani, Laurie. *Universal Jurisdiction for Humanitarian Crimes*. London: Glass House, 2006.

Kleffner, Jann K. *Complementarity in the Rome Statute and National Criminal Jurisdictions*. New York: Oxford University Press, 2009.

Li, Peter (ed.). *Japanese War Crimes. The Search for Justice.* New Brunswick, N.J.: Transaction Publishers, 2003.

Macedo, Steve (ed.). *Universal Jurisdiction.* Philadelphia: University of Pennsylvania Press, 2004.

Mackenzie, Ruth, Kate Mallson, Penny Martin, and Philippe Sands. *Selecting International Judges. Principles, Process, and Politics.* New York: Oxford University Press, 2010.

Maogoto, Jackson Nyamuya. *War Crimes and Realpolitik: International Justice from World War I to the 21st Century.* Boulder, Colo.: Lynne Rienner, 2004.

Mendes, Errol P. *Peace and Justice at the International Criminal Court. A Court of Last Resort.* Northampton, Mass.: Edward Elgar, 2010.

Mettraux, Guenael. *Perspectives on the Nuremberg Trial.* New York: Oxford University Press, 2008.

Moghalu, Kingsley Chiedu. *Global Justice. The Politics of War Crime Trials.* Westport, Conn.: Praeger, 2006.

Morris, Virginia, and Michael P. Scharf. *An Insider's Guide to the International Criminal Tribunal for the Former Yugoslavia: Documentary History and Analysis.* New York: Transnational Publishers, 1995.

———. *The International Criminal Tribunal for Rwanda.* 2 volumes. New York: Transnational Publishers, 1998.

Parish, Mathew. *Mirages of International Justice. The Elusive Pursuit of a Transnational Legal Order.* Northampton, Mass.: Edward Elgar, 2011.

Peskin, Victor. *International Justice in Rwanda and the Balkans. Virtual Trials and the Struggle for State Cooperation.* New York: Cambridge University Press, 2008.

Politi, Paulo, and Federica Gioia (eds.). *The International Criminal Court and National Jurisdictions.* Burlington, Vt.: Ashgate, 2008.

Ratner, Steven R., Jason S. Abrams, and James L. Bishoff. *Accountability for Human Rights Atrocities in International Law: Beyond the Nuremberg Legacy.* Third Edition. New York: Oxford University Press, 2009.

Reydams, Luc. *Universal Jurisdiction—International and Municipal Legal Perspectives.* Oxford: Oxford University Press, 2003.

Roach, Steven (ed.). *Governance, Order, and the International Criminal Court.* New York: Oxford University Press, 2009.

Röling, B. V. A., and C. F. Rüter (eds.). *The Tokyo Judgment: The International Military Tribunal for the Far East.* Amsterdam: APA-University Press Amsterdam, 1977.

Romano, Cesare P. R., Andre Nollkaemper, and Jann K. Kleffner (eds.). *Internationalized Criminal Courts. Sierra Leone, East Timor, Kosovo, and Cambodia.* New York: Oxford University Press, 2004.

Salter, Michael. *Nazi War Crimes, US Intelligence and Selective Prosecution at Nuremberg. Controversies Regarding the Role of the Office of Strategic Services.* New York: Routledge, 2007.

Sands, Philippe (Ed.). *From Nuremberg to the Hague: The Future of International Criminal Justice.* Cambridge: Cambridge University Press, 2003.

Schabas, William A. *The International Criminal Court. A Commentary on the Rome Statute.* New York: Oxford University Press, 2010.

———. *Unimaginable Atrocities. Justice, Politics and Rights at the War Crime Tribunals.* New York: Oxford University Press, 2012.

———. *The UN International Criminal Tribunals. The Former Yugoslavia, Rwanda and Sierra Leone.* New York: Cambridge University Press, 2006.

Schabas, William A., Ramesh Thakur, and Edel Hughes (eds.). *Atrocities and International Accountability.* Tokyo: United Nations University Press, 2007.

Scheipers, Sibylle. *Negotiating Sovereignty and Human Rights. International Society and the International Criminal Court.* Manchester: Manchester University Press, 2010.

Schiff, Benjamin N. *Building the International Criminal Court.* Cambridge: Cambridge University Press, 2008.

Seibert-Fohr, Anja. *Prosecuting Serious Human Rights Violations.* New York: Oxford University Press, 2009.

Sewall, Sarah B., and Carl Kaysen (eds.). *The United States and the International Criminal Court. National Security and International Law.* Lanham, Md.: Rowman & Littlefield, 2003.

Sluiter, Göran. *The Emerging Practice of International Criminal Court.* Boston: Martinus Nijhoff, 2009.

Sottile, Antoine. *The Problem of the Creation of an International Criminal Court.* Geneva: 1951.

Swart, Bert, Alexander Zahar, and Goran Sluiter (eds.). *The Legacy of the International Criminal Tribunal for the Former Yugoslavia.* New York: Oxford University Press, 2011.

Tochilovsky, Vladimir. *Jurisprudence of the International Criminal Courts and the European Court of Human Rights.* Leiden: Martinus Nijhoff, 2008.

United Nations War Crimes Commission. *History of the United Nations War Crimes Commission.* London: Her Majesty's Stationery Office, 1949.

United Nations War Crimes Commission. *Law Reports of Trials of War Criminals*, 15 volumes. London: Her Majesty's Stationery Office, 1947–1949.

U.S. House of Representatives. *Investigation of the My Lai Incident: Report of the Armed Services Investigating Subcommittee of the Committee of Armed Services, House of Representatives, 91st Congress, 2nd session, under Authority of H.Res. 105.* July 15. Washington, D.C.: U.S. Government Printing Office, 1970.

Van den Wyngaert, Christine, and John Dugard. "Non-Applicability of Statute of Limitations." In *The Rome Statute of the International Criminal Court: A Commentary,* ed. Antonio Cassese, Paola Gaeta, and John R. W. D. Jones, 2 volumes. Oxford: Oxford University Press, 2002.

White, James D., and Anthony J. Marsella (eds.). *Fear of Prosecution: Global Human Rights, International Law and Human Well-Being.* Lanham, Md.: Lexington Books, 2007.

Wilson, Richard Ashby. *Writing History in International Criminal Trials.* New York: Cambridge University Press, 2011.

Wright, Thomas C. *State Terrorism in Latin America: Chile, Argentina, and International Human Rights.* Lanham, Md.: Rowman & Littlefield, 2007.

Zahar, Alexander, and Goran Sluiter. *International Criminal Law. A Critical Restatement.* New York: Oxford University Press, 2007.

Zappala, Salvatore, *International Criminal Trials and Human Rights.* Cary, N.C.: Oxford University Press, 2003.

Zolo, Danilo. *Victors' Justice: from Nuremberg to Baghdad.* New York: Verso, 2009.

Restorative and Reparative Justice

Barkan, Elazar. *The Guilt of Nations: Restitution and Negotiating Historical Injustices.* New York: Norton, 2001.

Brennan, Fernne, and John Packer (eds.). *Colonialism, Slavery, Reparations and Trade: Remedying the Past?* New York: Routledge, 2011.

Lenzerini, Federico (ed.). *Reparations for Indigenous Peoples. International and Comparative Perspectives.* New York: Oxford University Press, 2008.

Reddy, Peter. *Peace Operations and Restorative Justice. Groundwork for Post-Conflict Regeneration.* Burlington, Vt.: Ashgate, 2012.

Rose, Barbara. *Waging War, Making Peace. Reparations and Human Rights.* Walnut Creek, Calif.: Left Coast Press, 2008.

Shelton, Dinah. *Remedies in International Human Rights Law.* New York: Oxford University Press, 2001.

Country, Regional Case Studies

Algeria

Aussaresses, Paul. *The Battle of the Casbah: Counter Terrorism and Torture.* New York: Enigma Books, 2005.

Horne, Alistair. *A Savage War of Peace: Algeria 1954–1962*. London: Macmillan, 1971.

Martinez, Luis. *The Algerian Civil War 1990–1998*. London: Hurst, 1998.

Quandt, William B. *Between Ballots and Bullets: Algeria's Transition from Authoritarianism*. Washington, D.C.: Brookings Institution Press, 1998.

Argentina

Feitlowitz, Marguerite. *A Lexicon of Terror: Argentina and the Legacies of Torture*. New York: Oxford University Press, 1998.

Guest, Iain. *Behind the Disappearances: Argentina's Dirty War Against Human Rights and the United Nations*. Philadelphia: University of Pennsylvania Press, 1990.

Lewis, Paul H. *Guerrillas and Generals: The Dirty War in Argentina*. Westport, Conn.: Greenwood, 2001.

Marchak, M. Patricia. *God's Assassins: State Terrorism in Argentina in the 1970s*. Montreal: McGill-Queen's University Press, 1999.

Robben, Antonius C. G. *Political Violence and Trauma in Argentina*. Philadelphia: University of Pennsylvania Press, 2005.

The Armenian Genocide

Balakian, Peter. *The Burning Tigris: The Armenian Genocide and America's Response*. New York: HarperCollins, 2003.

Bloxham, Donald. *The Great Game of Genocide: Imperialism, Nationalism, and the Destruction of the Ottoman Armenians*. Cambridge: Cambridge University Press, 2005.

Hovannisian, Richard (ed.). *The Armenian Genocide. Cultural and Ethical Legacies*. New Brunswick, N.J.: Transaction Publishers, 2006.

Kennedy, Paul, Antoine Prost, and Emmanuel Sivan (eds.). *America and the Armenian Genocide of 1915*. Cambridge: Cambridge University Press, 2004.

Miller, Donald E., and Lorna Touryan Miller. *Survivors: An Oral History of the Armenian Genocide*. Berkeley, Calif.: University of California Press, 1999.

The Balkan Wars (1991–1999)

Ignatieff, Michael. Virtual War: Kosovo and Beyond. New York: Viking, 2000.

Jones, Adam (ed.). *Genocide, War Crimes, and the West: Ending the Culture of Impunity*. New York: Zed Books, 2003.

Kaplan, Robert D. *Balkan Ghosts: A Journey Through History*. New York: St. Martin's Press, 1993.

King, Iain, and Whit Mason. *Peace at Any Price. How the World Failed Kosovo*. Ithaca, N.Y.: Cornell University Press, 2006.

Mojzes, Paul. *Balkan Genocides. Holocaust and Ethnic Cleansing in the Twentieth Century*. Lanham, Md.: Rowman & Littlefield, 2012.

Tochman, Wojciech. *Like Eating Stone: Surviving the Past in Bosnia*. New York: Atlas, 2008.

Weler, Marc. *Twenty Years of Crisis. The Violent Dissolution of Yugoslavia in International Law*. New York: Oxford University Press, 2011.

Bangladesh 1971

Bhattacharyya, S. K. *Genocide in East Pakistan/Bangladesh: A Horror Story*. Houston: Ghosh Publishers, 1988.

Sisson, Richard, and Leo Rose. *War and Secession: Pakistan, India, and the Creation of Bangladesh*. Berkeley, Calif.: University of California Press, 1990.

Zaheer, Hasan. *The Separation of East Pakistan: The Rise and Realization of Bengali Muslim Nationalism*. New York: Oxford University Press, 1994.

Burundi

Lemarchand, René. *Burundi: Ethnic Conflict and Genocide*. Cambridge: Cambridge University Press, 1996.

Nyankanzi, Edward L. *Genocide: Rwanda and Burundi*. Rochester, Vt.: Schenkman Books, 1998.

Scherrer, Christian P. *Genocide and Crisis in Central Africa: Conflict Roots, Mass Violence, and Regional War*. Westport, Conn.: Praeger, 2002.

Vandeginste, Stef. *Stones Left Unturned. Law and Transitional Justice in Burundi*. Antwerp: Intersentia, 2011.

Cambodia and the Khmer Rouge

Cook, Susan E. *Genocide in Cambodia and Rwanda. New Perspectives*. New Brunswick, N.J.: Transaction Publishers, 2005.

Etcheson, Craig. *After the Killing Fields: Lessons from the Cambodian Genocide*. Westport, Conn.: Praeger Publishers, 2005.

Fawthrop, Tom, and Helen Jarvis. *Getting Away with Genocide? Cambodia's Long Struggle against the Khmer Rouge*. London: Pluto Press, 2004.

Hughes, Caroline. *UNTAC in Cambodia: The Impact on Human Rights*. Singapore: Institute of Southeast Asian Studies, Indochina Program, 1996.

Kiernan, Ben. *Genocide and Resistance in Southeast Asia. Documentation, Denial, and Justice in Cambodia and East Timor.* New Brunswick, N.J.: Transaction Publishers, 2007.

Laban Hinton, Alexander. *Why Did They Kill? Cambodia in the Shadow of Genocide.* Berkeley, Calif.: University of California Press, 2005.

Shawcross, William. *Sideshow: Kissinger, Nixon and the Destruction of Cambodia.* Revised Edition. New York: Cooper Square Press, 2002.

Short, Philip. *Pol Pot: Anatomy of a Nightmare.* New York: Henry Holt, 2005.

Tyner, James. *The Killing in Cambodia: Geography, Genocide and the Unmaking of Space.* Burlington, Vt.: Ashgate, 2008.

Central America

Americas Watch. *El Salvador's Decade of Terror: Human Rights since the Assassination of Archbishop Romero.* New Haven, Conn.: Yale University Press, 1991.

Carmack, Robert M. (ed.). *Harvest of Violence: The Maya Indians and the Guatemalan Crisis.* Norman: University of Oklahoma Press, 1992.

Dunbar-Ortiz, Roxanne. *Blood on the Border: A Memoir of the Contra War.* Cambridge, Ma.: South End Press, 2005.

Johnstone, Ian. *Rights and Reconciliation: UN Strategies in El Salvador.* Boulder, Colo.: Lynne Rienner Publishers, 1995.

Lawyers Committee for Human Rights. *Improvising History: A Critical Evaluation of the United Nations Observer Mission in El Salvador.* New York: LCHR, 1995.

Montgomery, Tommie Sue. *Revolution in El Salvador: From Civil Strife to Civil Peace.* Second Edition. Boulder, Colo.: Westview Press, 1995.

Parera, Victor. *Unfinished Conquest. The Guatemalan Tragedy.* Berkeley: University of California Press, 1993.

Popkin, Margaret. *Human Rights, Development and Democracy: Experience of the UN in Post-Conflict El Salvador.* New York: UNDP, 1993.

———. *Peace without Justice: Obstacles to Building the Rule of Law in El Salvador.* University Park: Pennsylvania State University Press, 2000.

Sanford, Victoria. *Buried Secrets: Truth and Human Rights in Guatemala.* New York: Palgrave Macmillan, 2003.

Stanley, William Deane. *The Protection Racket: Elite Politics, Military Extortion and Civil War in El Salvador.* Philadelphia, Pa.: Temple University Press, 1996.

Taylor, Clark. *Return of Guatemala's Refugees: Reweaving the Torn.* Philadelphia, Pa.: Temple University Press, 1998.

Chechnya

Gall, Carlotta, and Thomas de Waal. *Chechnya: Calamity in the Caucasus.* New York: New York University Press, 1998.

Politkovskaya, Anna. *A Small Corner of Hell: Dispatches from Chechnya.* Chicago: University of Chicago Press, 2003.

Wood, Tony. *Chechnya: The Case for Independence.* New York: Verso Books, 2007.

Chile

Frazier, Leslie Jo. *Salt in the Dans: Memory, Violence, and the Nation-States in Chile, 1890 to the Present.* Durham, N.C.: Duke University Press, 2007.

Hawkins, Darren G. *International Human Rights and Authoritarian Rule in Chile.* Lincoln: University of Nebraska Press, 2002.

Huneeus, Carlos. *The Pinochet Regime.* Boulder, Colo.: Lynne Rienner, 2007.

Munoz, Heraldo. *The Dictator's Shadow": Life under Augusto Pinochet.* New York: Basic Books, 2009.

Spooner, Mary Helen. *Soldiers in a Narrow Land: The Pinochet Regime in Chile.* Berkeley: University of California Press, 1999.

China

Becker, Jasper. *Hungry Ghosts: China's Secret Famine.* London: John Murray, 1996.

Craig, Mary. Tears of Blood: A Cry for Tibet. Washington, D.C.: Counterpoint Press, 2000.

Dikotter, Frank. *Mao's Great Famine: The History of China's Most Devastating Catastrophe, 1958–1962.* New York: Walker Publishing, 2010.

Foot, Rosemary. *The Global Community and the Struggle over Human Rights in China.* New York: Oxford University Press, 2000.

Smith, Warren W. *Tibetan Nation: A History of Tibetan Nationalism and Sino-Tibetan Relations.* Boulder, Colo.: Westview Press, 1996.

Thaxton, Ralph A., Jr. *Catastrophe and Contention in Rural China: Mao's Great Leap Forward Famine and the Origins of Righteous Resistance in Da Fo Village.* Cambridge: Cambridge University Press, 2008.

Yang Jusheng. *Tombstone: The Great Chinese Famine 1958–1962.* New York: Farrar, Straus and Giroux, 2012.

Colombia

Avilés, William. *Global Capitalism, Democracy, and Civil-Military Relations in Colombia.* Albany: SUNY Press, 2006.

Brittain, James J. *Revolutionary Social Change in Colombia: The Origin and Direction of the FARC-EP*. New York: Pluto Press, 2010.

Cuellar, Francisco R. *The Profits of Extermination: Big Mining in Colombia*. Monroe, Me.: Common Courage Press, 2005.

Holmes, Jennifer S., Kevin M. Curtin, and Sheila Amin Gutierrez de Pineres *Guns, Drugs, and Development in Colombia*. Austin: University of Texas Press, 2009.

Hristov, Jasmin. *Blood and Capital: The Paramilitarization of Colombia*. Athens: Ohio University Press, 2009.

Livingstone, Grace. *Inside Colombia: Drugs, Democracy, and War*. New Brunswick, N.J.: Rutgers University Press, 2004.

Scott, Peter Dale. *Drugs, Oil, and War: the United States in Afghanistan, Colombia, and Indochina*. Lanham, Md.: Rowman & Littlefield, 2003.

Simons, Geoff L. *Colombia: A Brutal History*. London: Saqi Books, 2006.

Tate, Winifred. *Counting the Dead: The Culture and Politics of Human Rights Activism in Colombia*. Berkeley: University of California Press, 2007.

Congo

Clark, John F. (ed.). *The African Stakes of the Congo War*. London: Palgrave Macmillan, 2004.

Hochschild, A. *King Leopold's Ghost: A Story of Greed, Terror, and Heroism in Colonial Africa*. Boston: Houghton Mifflin, 1998.

Lemarchand, René. *The Dynamics of Violence in Central Africa*. Philadelphia: University of Pennsylvania Press, 2009.

Prunier, Gerard. *Africa's World War: Congo, the Rwandan Genocide, and the Making of a Continental Catastrophe*. New York: Oxford University Press, 2008.

Stearns, Jason. *Dancing in the Glory of Monsters: The Collapse of the Congo and the Great War in Africa*. New York: Public Affairs, 2011.

Turner, Thomas. *The Congo Wars: Conflict, Myth and Reality*. London: Zed Books, 2007.

East Timor

Cristalis, Irena. *Bitter Dawn: East Timor: A People's Story*. London: Zed Books, 2002.

Fischer, Tim. *Seven Days in East Timor: Ballots and Bullets*. London: Allen & Unwin, 2000.

Ishizuka, Katsumi. *The History of Peace Building in East Timor: The Issues of International Interventions*. New York: Cambridge University Press, 2010.

Nevins, Joseph. *A Not-So-Distant Horror. Mass Violence in East Timor*. Ithaca, N.Y.: Cornell University Press, 2005.

Robinson, Geoffrey. *"If You Leave Us Here, We Will Die": How Genocide Was Stopped in East Timor*. Princeton, N.J.: Princeton University Press, 2010.

Haiti

Fatton, Robert, Jr. *Haiti's Predatory Republic: The Unending Transition to Democracy*. Boulder, Colo.: Lynne Rienner, 2002.

———. *The Roots of Haitian Despotism*. Boulder, Colo.: Lynne Rienner, 2007.

Gibbons, Elizabeth D. *Sanctions in Haiti: Human Rights and Democracy under Assault*. New York: Praeger, 1999.

Shamsie, Yasmine, and Andrew S. Thompson (eds.). *Haiti. Hope for a Fragile State*. Waterloo, Ont.: Wilfrid Laurier University Press, 2006.

Iraq

Bruinessen, Martin van. *Kurdish Ethno-Nationalism Versus Nation-Building States. Collected Articles*. Istanbul: Isis Press, 2000.

Human Rights Watch-Middle East. *Iraq's Crime of Genocide: The Anfal Campaign Against the Kurds*. New Haven, Conn.: Human Rights Watch/Yale University Press, 1994.

Makiya, Kanan. *Republic of Fear: The Politics of Modern Iraq*. Berkeley: University of California Press, 1998.

Randal, Jonathan C. *After Such Knowledge, What Forgiveness? My Encounters with Kurdistan*. Boulder, Colo.: Westview Press, 1999.

Kashmir

Sidhu, Waheguru Pal Singh, Bushra Asif, and Cyrus Samil (eds.). *Kashmir: New Voices, New Approaches*. Boulder, Colo.: Lynne Rienner, 2006.

Kosovo

Judah, Tim. *Kosovo: What Everyone Needs to Know*. New York: Oxford University Press, 2008.

Tatum, Dale C. *Genocide at the Dawn of the Twenty-First Century. Rwanda, Bosnia, Kosovo, and Darfur.* New York: Palgrave, 2010.

Japan

Barenblatt, Daniel. *A Plague upon Humanity: The Secret Genocide of Axis Japan's Germ Warfare Operation.* New York: HarperCollins, 2004.
Chang, Iris. *The Rape of Nanking. The Forgotten Holocaust of World War II.* New York: Basic Books, 1997.
Gold, Hal. *Unit 731 Testimony: Japan's Wartime Human Experimentation and the Post-War Cover-Up.* Tokyo: Yenbooks, 1996.
Li, Peter (ed.). *Japanese War Crimes. The Search for Justice.* New Brunswick, N.J.: Transaction Publishers, 2003.
Tanaka, Yukiko. *Hidden Horrors: Japanese War Crimes in World War Two.* Boulder, Colo.: Westview Press, 1996.
Yoshida, Takashi. *The Making of the "Rape of Nanking": History and Memory in Japan, China and the United States.* New York: Oxford University Press, 2006.

Myanmar (Burma)

Callaghan, Mary P. *Making Enemies: War and State Building in Burma.* Ithaca, N.Y.: Cornell University Press, 2004.
Larkin, Emma. *Everything Is Broken: A Tale of Catastrophe in Burma.* New York: Penguin, 2010.
Pedersen, Morten. *Promoting Human Rights in Burma. A Critique of Western Sanctions Policy.* Lanham, Md.: Rowman & Littlefield, 2007.
Rogers, Benedict. *Than Shwe: Unmasking Burma's Tyrant.* Chiang Mai, Thailand: Silkworm Books, 2010.
Thant, Myint-U. *The River of Lost Footsteps: A Personal History of Burma.* New York: Farrar, Straus and Giroux, 2006.

Palestine

Akram, Susan, Michael Dumper, Michael Lynk, and Iain Scobbie (eds.). *International Law and the Israeli-Palestinian Conflict: A Rights-Based Approach to Middle East Peace.* New York: Routledge,, 2010.
Bowker, Robert P. G. *Palestinian Refugees: Mythology, Identity, and the Search for Peace.* Boulder, Colo.: Lynne Rienner, 2003.
Carter, Jimmy. *Palestine: Peace, Not Apartheid.* New York: Simon and Schuster, 2006.

Esber, Rosemarie M. *Under the Cover of War: The Zionist Expulsion of the Palestinians.* Alexandria, Va.: Arabicus Books & Media, 2008.

Gelber, Yoav. *Palestine 1948.* Portland, Oreg.: Sussex Academic Press, 2006.

Morris, Benny. *1948: A History of the First Arab-Israeli War.* New Haven, Conn.: Yale University Press, 2009.

———. *The Birth of the Palestinian Refugee Problem Revisited.* Cambridge: Cambridge University Press, 2003.

Pappe, Ilan. *The Ethnic Cleansing of Palestine.* London: Oneworld, 2006.

Reiter, Yitzhak. *National Minority, Regional Majority: Palestinian Arabs versus Jews in Israel.* Syracuse Studies on Peace and Conflict Resolution. Syracuse, N.Y.: Syracuse University Press, 2009.

Russia

Applebaum, Anne. *Gulag: A History.* London: Penguin, 2003.

Conquest, Robert. *The Great Terror: A Reassessment.* New York: Oxford University Press, 1990.

———. *The Harvest of Sorrow: Soviet Collectivization and the Terror-Famine.* London: Hutchinson, 1986.

Courtois, Stéphane Courtois, et al. *The Black Book of Communism: Crimes, Terror, Repression.* Cambridge, Mass.: Harvard University Press, 1999.

Madden, Cheryl (ed.). "Holodomor: The Ukrainian Genocide 1932–1933." *Canadian American Slavic Studies* 37, no. 3 (2003) [special issue].

Rummel, Rudolph G. *Lethal Politics: Soviet Genocides and Mass Murders, 1917–1987.* New Brunswick, N.J.: Transaction Publishers, 1990.

Serbyn, Roman, and Gohdan Krawchenko (eds.). *Famine in Ukraine: 1932–1933.* Edmonton: Canadian Institute of Ukrainian Studies, 1986.

Rwanda

Adelman, Howard, and Astri Suhrke (eds.). *The Path of a Genocide. The Rwanda Crisis from Uganda to Zaire.* New Brunswick, N.J.: Transaction Publishers, 2000.

Clark, Phil. *The Gacaca Courts, Post-Genocide Justice and Reconciliation in Rwanda. Justice Without Lawyers.* New York: Cambridge University Press, 2010.

Cook, Susan E. *Genocide in Cambodia and Rwanda. New Perspectives.* New Brunswick, N.J.: Transaction Publishers, 2005.

Daly, M. *Darfur's Sorrow: A History of Destruction and Genocide.* New York: Cambridge University Press, 2007.

Des Forges, Alison. *Leave None to Tell the Story: Genocide in Rwanda*. New York: Human Rights Watch, 1999.

Flint, Julie, and Alex de Waal. *Darfur: A New History of a Long War*. Revised and Updated. London: Zed Books, 2008.

Gourevitch, Philip. *We Wish to Inform You that Tomorrow We Will Be Killed with Our Families: Stories from Rwanda*. New York: Farrar, Straus & Giroux, 1998.

Grünfeld, Fred, and Anke Huiboom. *The Failure to Prevent Genocide in Rwanda: The Role of Bystanders*. Leiden: Martinus Nijhoff, 2007.

Mamdani, Mahmood. *When Victims Become Killers: Colonialism, Nativism, and the Genocide in Rwanda*. Princeton, N.J.: Princeton University Press, 2001.

Melvern, Linda. *Conspiracy to Murder: The Rwanda Genocide and the International Community*. London: Verso, 2004.

Moghalu, Kingsley. *Rwanda's Genocide. The Politics of Global Justice*. New York: Palgrave, 2005.

Peskin, Victor. *International Justice in Rwanda and the Balkans: Virtual Trials and the Struggle for State Cooperation*. Cambridge: Cambridge University Press, 2008.

Prunier, Gérard. *Africa's World War: Congo, the Rwandan Genocide, and the Making of a Continental Catastrophe*. New York: Oxford University Press, 2011.

Report of the Independent Inquiry into United Nations Actions During the 1994 Rwanda Genocide. United Nations Document S/1999/1257. 16 December 1999.

Rittner, Carol, John K. Roth, and Wendy Whitworth (eds.). *Genocide in Rwanda: Complicity of the Churches?* St. Paul, Minn.: Paragon House, 2004.

Scherrer, Christian P. *Genocide and Crisis in Central Africa: Conflict Roots, Mass Violence, and Regional War*. Westport, Conn.: Praeger Publishers, 2002.

Straus, Scott. *The Order of Genocide. Race, Power and War in Rwanda*. Ithaca, N.Y.: Cornell University Press, 2006.

Wallis, Andrew. *Silent Accomplice. The Untold Story of France's Role in the Rwandan Genocide*. London: Tauris, 2006.

Sierra Leone

Hirsch, John. *Sierra Leone: Diamonds and the Struggle for Democracy*. Boulder, Colo.: Lynne Rienner, 2001.

Mustapha, Marda, and Joseph J. Bangura. *Sierra Leone Beyond the Lomé Peace Accord*. New York: Palgrave Macmillan, 2010.

Mutwol, Julius. *Peace Agreements and Civil Wars in Africa: Insurgent Motivations, State Responses, and Third-Party Peacemaking in Liberia, Rwanda, and Sierra Leone*. Amherst, N.Y.: Cambria Press, 2009.

Olonisakin, Funmi. *Peacekeeping in Sierra Leone*. Boulder, Colo.: Lynne Rienner, 2008.

Richards, Paul. *Fighting for the Rain Forest: War, Youth and Resources in Sierra Leone*. Oxford: James Currey, 1996.

Sudan

Babiker, Mohamed. *Application of International Humanitarian and Human Rights Law to the Armed Conflicts of the Sudan*. Antwerpen: Intersentia, 2007.

Collins, Robert O. *Civil Wars and Revolution in the Sudan.* Hollywood City, Calif.: Tsehai Publishers, 2005.

De Waal, Alex. *Famine That Kills: Darfur, Sudan*. Revised Edition. Oxford: Oxford University Press, 2004.

Flint, Julie, and Alex de Waal. *Darfur: A Short History of a Long War*. London: Zed Books, 2006.

Hagan, John, and Wehona Rymond-Richmond. *Darfur and the Crime of Genocide*. Cambridge: Cambridge University Press, 2009.

Mamdani, Mahmood. S*aviors and Survivors. Darfur, Politics, and the War on Terror.* New York: Random House, 2009.

Natsios, Andrew S. *Sudan, South Sudan, and Darfur*. New York: Oxford University Press, 2012.

Prunier, Gerard. *Darfur: The Ambiguous Genocide*. Third Edition. Ithaca, N.Y.: Cornell University Press, 2008.

Rafiqul, Islam M. *The Sudanese Darfur Crisis and Internally Displaced Persons in International Law: The Least Protection for the Most Vulnerable*. New York: Oxford University Press, 2006.

Totten, Samuel. *Investigating Genocide. An Analysis of the Darfur Atrocities*. New York: Routledge, 2006.

Prospects for the Future

General

Baxi, Upendra. *The Future of Human Rights*. Oxford: Oxford University Press, 2006.

Bob, Clifford. *The International Struggle for Human Rights.* Philadelphia: University of Pennsylvania Press, 2009.

Bullard, Alice (ed.). *Human Rights in Crisis*. Burlington, Vt.: Ashgate, 2008.

Gearty, Conor. *Can Human Rights Survive?* New York: Cambridge University Press, 2006.

Goodhart, Michael E., and Anja Mihr. *Human Rights in the 21st Century: Continuity and Change since 9/11*. Houndmills, Basingstoke: Palgrave Macmillan, 2011.

Ignatieff, Michael. *Human Rights as Politics and Idolatry*. Princeton, N.J.: Princeton University Press, 2001.

Keane, David, and Yvonne McDermott (eds.). *The Challenge of Human Rights. Past, Present and Future*. Northampton, Mass.: Edward Elgar, 2012.

Kurazawa, Fuyuki. *The Work of Global Justice. Human Rights as Practices*. New York: Cambridge University Press, 2007.

McNamara, Luke. *Human Rights Controversies*. New York: Routledge, 2007.

Osler, Audrey, and Hugh Starkey. *Teachers and Human Rights Education*. London: Trentham, 2010.

Pinker, Steven. *The Better Angels of Our Nature: Why Violence Has Declined*. New York: Viking, 2011.

Power, Samantha, and Graham Allison. *Realizing Human Rights, Moving from Inspiration to Impact*. New York: St. Martin's Press, 2000.

Ramcharan, Bertrand G. *Prevention Human Rights Strategies*. New York: Routledge, 2010.

Reichert, Elisabeth (ed.). *Challenges in Human Rights. A Social Work Perspective*. New York: Columbia University Press, 2007.

Wellman, Carl. *The Proliferation of Rights: Moral Progress or Empty Rhetoric?* Boulder, Colo.: Westview Press, 1998.

Universal or Culturally Defined?

An-Na'im, Abdullahi A. (ed). *Cultural Transformation and Human Rights in Africa*. London: Zed Books, 2002.

An-Na'im, Abdullahi, and Mashood A. Baderin. *Islam and Human Rights*. Burlington, Vt.: Ashgate, 2010.

Bauer, Joanne R., and Daniel A. Bell (eds.). *The East Asian Challenge for Human Rights*. Cambridge: Cambridge University Press, 1999.

Bell, Lynda S., Andrew J. Nathan, and Ilan Peleg (eds.). *Negotiating Culture and Human Rights*. New York: Columbia University Press, 2001.

Blau, Judith, and Alberto Moncada. *Human Rights. Beyond the Liberal Vision*. Lanham, Md.: Rowman & Littlefield, 2005.

Dalacoura, Katerina. *Islam, Liberalism and Human Rights.* Revised Edition. London: Tauris, 2003.

De Barry, Theodore. *Asian Values and Human Rights: A Confucian Communitarian Perspective.* Cambridge, Mass.: Harvard University Press, 1998.

Franck, Thomas M. "Are Human Rights Universal?" *Foreign Affairs* (January/February 2001): 191–204.

Gillies, David. *Between Principle and Practice: Human Rights in North-South Relations.* Montreal: McGill-Queen's University Press, 1996.

Gregg, Benjamin. *Human Rights as Social Construction.* New York: Cambridge University Press, 2011.

Ibhawoh, Bonny. *Imperialism and Human Rights: Colonial Discourses of Rights and Liberties in African History.* Albany: State University of New York Press, 2007.

Kao, Grace Y. *Grounding Human Rights in a Pluralist World.* Washington, D.C.: Georgetown University Press, 2011.

Kohen, Ari. *In Defense of Human Rights. A Non-Religious Grounding in a Pluralist World.* New York: Routledge, 2007.

Langlois, A. Anthony J. *The Politics of Justice and Human Rights. Southeast Asia and Universalist Theory.* New York: Cambridge University Press, 2001.

Mayer, Ann Elizabeth. *Islam and Human Rights: Tradition and Politics.* Fifth Edition. Boulder, Colo.: Westview Press, 2012.

McGoldrick, Dominic. *Human Rights and Religion. The Islamic Headscarf Debate in Europe.* Portland, Oreg.: Hart Publishing, 2006.

Meijer, Martha (ed.). *Dealing with Human Rights. Asian and Western Views on the Value of Human Rights.* Bloomfield, Conn.: Kumarian Press, 2001.

Monshipouri, Mahmood. *Muslims in Global Politics: Identities, Interests, and Human Rights and Islamism, Secularism, and Human Rights in the Middle East.* Philadelphia: University of Pennsylvania Press, 2009.

Mullally, Siobhan. *Gender, Culture and Human Rights: Reclaiming Universalism.* Oxford: Hart, 2006.

Saeed, Abdullah (ed.). *Islam and Human Rights.* Northampton, Mass.: Edward Elgar, 2012.

Sharma, Arvind. *Are Human Rights Western? A Contribution to the Dialogue of Civilizations.* New York: Oxford University Press, 2006.

Shipouri, Mahmood. *Muslims in Global Politics: Identities, Interests, and Human Rights.* Philadelphia: University of Pennsylvania Press, 2009.

Talbott, William J. *Which Rights Should Be Universal?* New York: Oxford University Press, 2005.

Thierney, Stephen (ed.). *Accommodating Cultural Diversity.* Burlington, Vt.: Ashgate, 2007.

Whelan, Daniel J. *Indivisible Rights. A History*. Philadelphia: University of Pennsylvania Press, 2010.

Wilson, Richard A., and Jon P. Mitchell (eds.). *Human Rights in Global Perspective: Anthropological Studies of Rights, Claims and Entitlements*. New York: Routledge, 2003.

The Challenges of Globalization

General

Benedek, Wolfgang, Koen de Feyter, and Fabrizio Marrella (eds.). *Economic Globalization and Human Rights*. New York: Cambridge University Press, 2007.

Blau, Judith, and Alberto Moncada. *Human Rights. Beyond the Liberal Vision*. Lanham, Md.: Rowman & Littlefield, 2005.

Brysk, Alison (ed.). *Globalization and Human Rights*. Berkeley: University of California Press, 2002.

Brysk, Alison, and Gershon Shafir (eds.). *People Out of Place: Globalization, Human Rights, and the Citizenship Gap*. New York: Routledge, 2004.

Clark, John. *World Apart. Civil Society and the Battle for Ethical Globalization*. Bloomfield, Conn.: Kumarian Press, 2003.

Coicaud, Jean-Marc, Michael W. Doyle, and Anne-Marie Gardner (eds.). *The Globalization of Human Rights*. Tokyo: United Nations University Press, 2003.

De Feyter, Koen. *Human Rights. Social Justice in the Age of the Market*. New York: Palgrave, 2005.

Dine, Janet, and Andrew Fagan (eds.). *Human Rights and Globalization. A Multidisciplinary Perspective on Globalization*. Northampton, Mass.: Edward Elgar, 2008.

Disckinson, Rob, Elena Katselli, Colin Murray, and Ole W. Pedersen (eds.). *Examining Critical Perspectives on Human Rights*. Cambridge: Cambridge University Press, 2012.

Evans, Tony. *Human Rights in the Global Political Economy: Critical Processes*. Boulder, Colo.: Lynne Rienner, 2010.

Falk, Richard. *Human Rights Horizons. The Pursuit of Justice in a Globalizing World*. New York: Routledge, 2000.

Gibney, Matthew (ed.). *Globalizing Rights. The Oxford Amnesty Lectures 1999*. New York: Oxford University Press, 2003.

Goodhart, Michael. *Democracy as Human Rights. Freedom and Equality in the Age of Globalization*. New York: Routledge, 2005.

Lee, Daniel E., and Elizabeth J. Lee. *Human Rights and the Ethics of Globalization*. New York: Cambridge University Press, 2010.

Markets and Rights

Aaronson, Susan Ariel, and Jamie M. Zimmerman. *Trade Imbalance: The Struggle to Weigh Human Rights Concerns in Trade Policymaking.* New York: Cambridge University Press, 2007.

Abouharb, M. Rodwan, and David L. Cingranelli. *Human Rights and Structural Adjustment.* Cambridge and New York: Cambridge University Press, 2007.

Bennett, Belinda (ed.). *Health, Rights and Globalization.* Williston, Vt.: Ashgate, 2005.

Bernier, Louise. *Justice in Genetics. Intellectual Property and Human Rights from a Cosmopolitan Perspective.* Northampton, Mass.: Edward Elgar, 2010.

Brainard, Lael, and Derek Chollet (eds.). *Too Poor for Peace? Global Poverty, Conflict, and Security in the 21st Century.* Washington, D.C.: Brookings Institution, 2007.

Brown, Drusiilla, and Robert M. Stern (eds.). *The WTO and Labor and Employment.* Northampton, Mass.: Edward Elgar, 2007.

Cottier, Thomas, Joost Pauwelyn, and Elisabeth B. Bonanomi. *Human Rights and International Trade.* New York: Oxford University Press, 2005.

Deere, Carolyn. *The Implementation Game. The TRIPs Agreement and the Global Politics of Intellectual Property Reform in Developing Countries.* New York: Oxford University Press, 2008.

Evans, Tony. *Human Rights in the Global Economy.* Boulder, Colo.: Lynne Rienner, 2010.

Gibson, Johanna. *Intellectual Property, Medicine and Health. Current Debates.* Burlington, Vt.: Ashgate, 2009.

——— (ed.). *Patenting Lives. Life Patents, Culture and Development.* Burlington, Vt.: Ashgate, 2008.

Grosheide, Willem (ed.). *Intellectual Property and Human Right.* Northampton, Mass.: Edward Elgar, 2010.

Harding, Christopher, Uta Kohl, and Naomi Salmon. *Human Rights in the Market Place. The Exploitation of Rights Protection by Economic Actors.* Burlington, Vt.: Ashgate, 2008.

Harrison, James. *The Human Rights Impact of the World Trade Organization.* Oxford: Hart, 2007.

Helfer, Laurence R., and Graeme W. Austin. *Human Rights and Intellectual Property. Mapping the Global Interface.* New York: Cambridge University Press, 2011.

Hestermeyer, Holger P. *Human Rights and the WTO. The Case of Patents and Access to Medicines.* New York: Oxford University Press, 2007.

Howard-Hassmann, Rhoda E. *Can Globalization Promote Human Rights.* University Park: Pennsylvania State University Press, 2010.

Joseph, Sarah, David Kinley, and Jeff Waincymer (eds.). *The World Trade Organization and Human Rights. Interdisciplinary Perspectives.* Northampton, Mass.: Edward Elgar, 2010.

Likosky, Michael. *Privatizing Development: Transnational Law Infrastructure and Human Rights.* Leiden: Martinus Nijhoff, 2005.

Muchlinski, Peter T. *Multinational Enterprises and the Law.* Second Edition. New York: Oxford University Press, 2007.

Murphy, Therese. *Technologies and Human Rights.* New York: Oxford University Press, 2009.

Oakley, Justin (ed.). *Bioethics.* Burlington, Vt.: Ashgate, 2009.

Sinha, B. R. K (ed.). *Population, Environment and Development.* New Delhi: New Century Publications, 2009.

United Nations. *Embedding Human Rights in Business Practices.* New York: United Nations, 2008.

Winters, L. Alan (ed.). *The WTO and Poverty and Inequality.* Northampton, Mass.: Edward Elgar, 2007.

The Environment and Climate Change

Anton, Donald K. *Environmental Protection and Human Rights.* New York: Cambridge University Press, 2011.

Brainard, Lael, Abigail Jones, and Nigel Purvis (eds.). *Climate Change and Global Poverty. A Billion Lives in the Balance.* Washington, D.C.: Brookings Institution, 2009.

Bullard, Robert D. *The Quest For Environmental Justice: Human Rights and the Politics of Pollution.* San Francisco: Sierra Club Books, 2005.

Council of Europe. *Manual on Human rights and the Environment: Principles Emerging from the Case-Law of the European Court of Human Rights.* Strasbourg: Council of Europe Publishing, 2006.

Humphreys, Stephen (ed.). *Human Rights and Climate Change.* New York: Cambridge University Press, 2010.

Shelton, Dinah L. (ed.). *Human Rights and the Environment.* Northampton, Mass.: Edward Elgar, 2011.

Woods, Kerri. *Human Rights and Environmental Sustainability.* Northampton, Mass.: Edward Elgar, 2010.

Zarsky, Lyuba (ed.). *Human Rights and the Environment: Conflicts and Norms in a Globalizing World.* London: Earthscan, 2003.

Global Crime

Andreas, Peter, and Ethan Nadelmann. *Policing the Globe. Criminalization and Crime Control in International Relations.* New York: Oxford University Press, 2008.

Edwards, Adam, and Peter Gill (eds.). *Transnational Organized Crime. Perspectives on Global Security.* New York: Routledge, 2006.

Friedrichs, Jorg. *Fighting Terrorism and Drugs.* New York: Routledge, 2007.

Galaguer, Anne T. *The International Law of Human Trafficking.* New York: Cambridge University Press, 2012.

Homes, Leslie (ed.). *Trafficking and Human Rights. European and Asia Pacific Perspectives.* Northampton, Mass.: Edward Elgar, 2010.

Madsen, Frank. *Transnational Organized Crime.* New York: Routledge, 2009.

Rijken, Conny. *Trafficking in Persons. Prosecution from a European Perspective.* New York: Cambridge University Press, 2004.

Shelley, Louise. *Human Trafficking. A Global Perspective.* New York: Cambridge University Press, 2010.

Corporate Responsibility

Frynas, Jedrzej George, and Scott Pegg. *Transnational Corporations and Human Rights.* New York: Palgrave Macmillan, 2003.

Gatto, Alexandra. *Multinational Enterprises and Human Rights. Obligations under EU Law and International Law.* Herndon, Va.: Edward Elgar, 2011.

Henne, Peter. *Human Rights and the Alien Tort Statute: Law, History, and Analysis.* Chicago: American Bar Association, 2009.

Jenkins, Rhys O., Ruth Pearson, and Gill Seyfang (eds.). *Corporate Responsibility and Labour Rights.* Sterling, Va.: Earthscan, 2002.

Kinley, David (ed.). *Human Rights and Corporations.* Burlington, Vt.: Ashgate, 2009.

Korten, David C. *When Corporations Rule the World.* Second Edition. Bloomfield, Conn.: Kumarian Press, 2001.

Leech, Garry. *Crude Interventions. The United States, Oil and the New World (Dis) Order.* London: Zed Books, 2006.

May, S., G. Cheney, and J. Roper (eds.). *The Debate over Corporate Social Responsibility.* New York: Oxford University Press, 2007.

McBeth, Adam, et al. *International Economic Actors and Human Rights Crimes.* New York: Springer, 2007.

McIntosh, M., S. Waddock, and G. Kell (eds.). *Learning to Talk: Corporate Citizenship and the Development of the UN Global Compact.* Shefflield: Greenleaf, 2004.

Mgbeoji, Ikechi. *Global Biopiracy. Patents, Plants, and Indigenous Knowledge.* Ithaca, N.Y.: Cornell University Press, 2006.

Newell, Peter, and Joanna Wheeler (eds.). *Rights, Resources and the Politics of Accountability.* London: Zed Books, 2006.

Rasche, Andreas, and Georg Kell. *The United Nations Global Compact. Achievements, Trends and Challenges.* New York: Cambridge University Press, 2010.

Sagafi-nejad, T., and J. H. Dunning. *The UN and Transnational Corporations: From Code of Conduct to Global Compact.* United Nations Intellectual History Project Series. Bloomington: Indiana University Press, 2008.

Salamon, Lester M. *Rethinking Corporate Social Engagement. Lessons from Latin America.* Sterling, Va.: Kumarian Press, 2010.

Sullivan, Rory, ed. *Business and Human Rights: Dilemmas and Solutions.* Sheffield, UK: Greenleaf, 2003.

Williams, O. F. (ed.). *Peace through Commerce: Responsible Corporate Citizenship and the Ideals of the United Nations Global Compact.* Notre Dame, Ind.: University of Notre Dame Press, 2008.

Zerk, Jennifer A. *Multinationals and Corporate Social Responsibility. Limitations and Opportunities in International Law.* New York: Cambridge University Press, 2006.

The "War on Terror" and Human Rights

Beck, Louise D. *Human Rights in Times of Conflict and Terrorism.* New York: Oxford University Press, 2011.

Brysk, Alison, and Gershon Shafir (eds.). *National Insecurity and Human Rights. Democracies Debate Terrorism.* Berkeley, Calif.: University of California Press, 2007.

Donohue, Laura K. *The Cost of Counterterrorism. Power, Politics, and Liberty.* New York: Cambridge University Pres, 2008.

Dyzenhaus, David (ed.). *Civil Rights and Security.* Burlington, Vt.: Ashgate, 2009.

Eckes, Christina. *EU Counter Terrorist Policies and Fundamental Rights. The Case of Individual Sanctions.* New York: Oxford University Press, 2009.

Forsythe, David. *Politics of Prisoners Abuse. The United States and Enemy Prisoners after 9/11.* New York: Cambridge University Press, 2011.

Ginbar, Yuval. *Why Not Torture Terrorists? Moral, Practical, and Legal Aspects of the 'Ticking Bomb' Justification for Torture.* New York: Oxford University Press, 2010.

Goold, Benjamin J., and Liora Lazarus (eds.). *Security and Human Rights.* Oxford: Hart Publishing, 2007.

Hocking, Jenny, and Colleen Lewis (eds.). *Counter-Terrorism and the Post-Democratic State.* Northampton, Mass.: Edward Elgar, 2008.

Londras, Fiona de. *Detention in the 'War on Terror'. Can Human Rights Fight Back?* Cambridge: Cambridge University Press, 2011.

Marchand, Christophe. *European Trends in the War on Terror.* New York: Oxford University Press, 2010.

Masferrer, Aniceto, and Clive Walker (eds.). *Counter-Terrorism, Human Rights and the Rule of Law.* Herndon, Va.: Edward Elgar, 2013.

Mockhtari, Shadi. *After Abu Ghriab. Exploring Human Rights in America and the Middle East.* Cambridge: Cambridge University Press, 2011.

Moeckli, Daniel. *Human Rights and Non-Discrimination in the War on Terror.* New York: Oxford University Press, 2008.

Monshipouri, Mahmood. *Terrorism, Security, and Human Rights: Harnessing the Rule of Law.* Boulder, Colo.: Lynne Rienner, 2009.

Murphy, Karen. *State Security Regimes and the Right to Freedom of Religion and Belief.* New York: Routledge, 2012.

Orttung, Robert, and Anthony Latta (eds.). *Russia's Battle with Crime, Corruption and Terrorism.* New York: Routledge, 2007.

Plaw, Avery. *Targeting Terrorists. A License to Kill?* Burlington, Vt.: Ashgate Publishing, 2008.

Ramraj, Victor V., Michael Hor, Kent Roach, and George Williams. *Global Anti-Terrorism Law and Policy.* Second Edition. Cambridge: Cambridge University Press, 2012.

Scheinin, Martin (ed.). *Terrorism and Human Rights.* Herndon, Va.: Edward Elgar Publishing, 2013.

Shawcross, William. *Justice and the Enemy: Nuremberg, 9/11, and the Trial of Khalid Sheikh Mohammed.* New York: Public Affairs, 2011.

Sottiaux, Stefan. *Terrorism and the Limitation of Rights. The ECHR and the US Constitution.* Oxford: Hart, 2008.

Tsang, Steve (ed.). *Intelligence and Human Rights in the Era of Global Terrorism.* Palo Alto, Calif.: Stanford University Press, 2008.

Vaughan, Barry, and Shane Kilcommins. *Terrorism and the Rule of Law: Negotiating Justice in Ireland.* Devon, UK: Willian Publishing, 2007.

Weinberg, Leonard, and William Eubank. *Democracy and the War on Terror. Civil Liberties and the Fight against Terrorism.* New York: Routledge, 2012.

Wilson, Richard Ashby. *Human Rights in the 'War on Terror.'* New York: Cambridge University Press, 2005.

To Intervene or Not: Prevention and the Responsibility to Protect

Barnett, Michael N. *Empire of Humanity: A History of Humanitarianism.* Ithaca, N.Y.: Cornell University Press, 2011.

Branch, Adam. *Displacing Human Rights. War and Intervention in Northern Uganda*. New York: Oxford University Press, 2011.

Buchanan, Allen. *Human Rights, Legitimacy, and the Use of Force*. New York: Oxford University Press, 2009.

Chandler, David. *From Kosovo to Kabul: Human Rights and Humanitarian Intervention*. Second Edition. London: Pluto, 2006.

Cooper, Richard H., and Juliette Voinov Kohler (eds.). *Responsibility to Protect: The Global Moral Compact for the 21st Century*. New York: Palgrave Macmillan, 2008.

Crawford, Timothy, and Alan Kuperman (eds.). *Gambling on Humanitarian Intervention: Moral Hazard, Rebellion and Civil War*. New York: Routledge, 2006.

Dorman, Andrew M. *Blair's Successful War: British Military Intervention in Sierra Leone*. Burlington, Vt.: Ashgate, 2009.

Evans, Gareth. *The Responsibility to Protect. Ending Mass Atrocity Crimes Once and for All*. Washington, D.C.: Brookings Institution Press, 2008.

Genser, Jared, and Irwin Cotler. *The Responsibility to Protect*. New York: Oxford University Press, 2011.

Hehir, Aidan. *Humanitarian Intervention. An Introduction*. New York: Palgrave, 2010.

Heinze, Eric. *Waging Humanitarian War: The Ethics, Laws and Politics of Humanitarian Intervention*. Albany: State University of New York Press, 2009.

Hoffman, Peter J., and Thomas G. Weiss. *Sword and Salve. Confronting New Wars and Humanitarian Crises*. Lanham, Md.: Rowman & Littlefield, 2011.

International Commission on Intervention and State Sovereignty. *The Responsibility to Protect*. Ottawa: International Development Research Centre, 2001.

Janzekovic, John. *The Use of Force in Humanitarian Intervention. Morality and Practicalities*. Burlington, Vt.: Ashgate, 2006.

Mani, Rama, and Thomas G. Weiss (eds.). *The Responsibility to Protect*. New York: Routledge, 2011.

Pattison, James. *Humanitarian Intervention and the Responsibility to Protect. Who Should Intervene?* New York: Oxford University Press, 2010.

Rubinstein, Robert A. *Peacekeeping under Fire: Culture and Intervention*. Boulder, Colo.: Paradigm Publishers, 2008.

Serrano, Monica, and Claudio Fuentes (eds.). *The Responsibility to Protect in Latin America. A New Map*. New York: Routledge, 2012.

Stauss, Ekkehard. *The Emperor's New Clothes? The United Nations and the Implementation of the Responsibility to Protect*. Portland, Oreg.: Nomos Publishers, 2009.

Teson, Fernando R. *Humanitarian Intervention: An Inquiry into Law and Morality.* Third Edition. Ardsley, N.Y.: Transnational Publishing, 2005.

Thakur, Ramesh. *The Responsibility to Protect Norms, Laws and the Use of Force in International Politics.* New York: Routledge, 2010.

Tonny-Brems-Knudsen. *Humanitarian Intervention. Contemporary Manifestations of an Explosive Doctrine.* New York: Routledge, 2012.

Van Arsdale, Peter W. *Humanitarians in Hostile Territory. Expeditionary Diplomacy and Aid Outside the Green Zone.* Walnut Creek, Calif.: Left Coast Press, 2010.

Waxman, Matthew C. *Intervention to Stop Genocide and Mass Atrocities: International Norms and US Policy.* Washington, D.C.: Council on Foreign Relations, 2009.

Weiss, Thomas G. *Humanitarian Intervention: Ideas in Action.* Cambridge: Polity Press, 2007.

———. *Military-Civilian Relations: Humanitarian Crisis and the Responsibility to Protect.* Second Edition. Lanham, Md.: Rowman & Littlefield, 2005.

Wheeler, Nicholas. Saving Strangers: Humanitarian Intervention in International Society. Oxford: Oxford University Press, 2000.

Reconstructing War-Torn Societies

Akinrinade, Babafemi. *Human Rights and State Collapse in Africa.* Utrecht, Netherlands: Boom Eleven International, 2010.

Benner, Thorsten, Stephen Mergenthaler, and Philipp Rotmann. *The New World of Peace Operations: Learning to Build Peace.* Oxford: Oxford University Press, 2011.

Brosche, Johan, and Daniel Rothbart. *Violent Conflict and Peacebuilding. The Continuing Crisis in Darfur.* New York: Routledge, 2012.

Buyse, Antoine. *Post-Conflict Housing Restitution. The European Human Rights Perspective with a Case Study on Bosnia.* Antwerp: Intersentia, 2008.

Clark, John F. *The Failure of Democracy in the Republic of Congo.* Boulder, Colo.: Lynne Rienner, 2008.

Doyle, Michael, and Nicholas Sambanis, *United Nations Peace Operations: Making War & Building Peace.* Princeton, N.J.: Princeton University Press, 2006.

Hurwitz, Agnes, and Reyko Huang. *Civil War and the Rule of Law: Society, Development, Human Rights.* Boulder, Colo.: Lynne Rienner, 2008.

Mertus, Julie, and Jeffrey W. Helsing (eds.). *Human Rights and Conflict. Exploring the Links between Rights, Law and Peacebuilding.* Herndon, Va.: Institute of Peace Press, 2006.

Ndulo, Muna. *Security, Reconstruction, and Reconciliation. When the Wars End.* New York: Routledge, 2006.

O'Connor, Vivienne, and Colette Rausch (eds.). *Model Codes for Post-Conflict Criminal Justice.* Volume I: *Model Criminal Code.* Herndon, Va.: United States Institute of Peace Press, 2007.

———— (eds.). *Model Codes for Post-Conflict Criminal Justice.* Volume II: *Model Criminal Procedure.* Herndon, Va.: United States Institute of Peace Press, Forthcoming.

Pouligny, Beatrice, Simon Chesterman, and Albrecht Schnabel (eds.). *After Mass Crime. Rebuilding States and Communities.* Tokyo: United Nations University Press, 2006.

Pugh, Michael, Neil Cooper, and Mandy Turner (eds.). *Whose Peace? Critical Perspectives on the Political Economy of Peacebuilding.* New York: Palgrave Macmillan, 2008.

Otenyo, Eric E. *American Promotion of Democracy in Africa, 1988–2000.* Lewiston, N.Y.: Mellen Press, 2009.

Özerdem, Alpaslan. *Post-War Recovery: Disarmament, Demobilization and Reintegration.* New York: Palgrave Macmillan, 2008.

Sesay, Amadu, et al. *Post-War Regimes and State Reconstruction in Liberia and Sierra Leone.* Dakar, Senegal: Council for the Development of Social Science Research in Africa, 2009.

Stromseth, Jane, David Wippman, and Rosa Brooks. *Can Might Make Rights. Building the Rule of Law after Military Interventions.* New York: Cambridge University Press, 2006.

United Nations. *Good Governance Practices for the Protection of Human Rights.* New York: United Nations, 2008.

Normative Gaps

Africa Rights. *Somalia, Human Rights Abuses by the United Nations Forces.* London: July 1995.

Annas, George J. *American Bioethics: Crossing Human Rights and Health Law Boundaries.* New York: Oxford University Press, 2005.

Azam, Jean-Paul. "On Thugs and Heroes: Why Warlords Victimize Their Own Civilians." *Economics of Governance* 7, no. 1 (2006): 53–73.

Brown, Abbe E. L. *Intellectual Property, Human Rights and Competition.* Herndon, Va.: Edward Elgar, 2013.

Cameron, Lindsey, and Vincent Chetail. *Privatising War. Private Military Companies under Public International Law.* New York: Cambridge University Press, 2013.

Campbell, Greg. *Blood Diamonds: Tracing the Deadly Path of the World's Most Precious Stones*. Boulder, Colo.: Westview, 2004.

Francioni, Francesco (ed.). *War by Contract. Human Rights, Humanitarian Law and Private Contractors*. New York: Oxford University Press, 2011.

Gaultier, L., et al. *The Mercenary Issue at the UN Commission on Human Rights: The Need for a New Approach*. London: International Alert, 2001.

Gordon, Joy. *Invisible War: The United States and the Iraq Sanctions*. Cambridge, Mass.: Harvard University Press, 2010.

Larsen, Mujezinovic, Kjetil. *The Human Rights Treaty Obligations of Peacekeepers*. New York: Cambridge University Press, 2012.

Lujala, Paivi. "A Diamond Curse?: Civil War and a Lootable Resource." *Journal of Conflict Resolution* 49, no. 4 (2005): 538–562.

Mujezinovic Larsen, Kjetil. *The Human Rights Treaty Obligations of Peacekeepers*. New York: Cambridge University Press, 2012.

Musah, A.-F., and J. K. Fayemi (eds.). *Mercenaries: An African Security Dilemma*. London: Pluto Press, 2000.

Rimmer, Matthew, and Ann Kent. *China, the Internet and Human Rights*. Herndon, Va.: Edward Elgar, 2013.

Roche, Douglas. *The Human Rights to Peace*. Ottawa: Novalis, 2003.

Tihola, Mariana. *Accountability under Human Rights Law of Non-State Actors*. East Sussex, UK: Gardners Books, 2010.

United Nations Commission on Human Rights. *The Impact of Mercenary Activities on the Right of Peoples to Self-Determination*. Fact Sheet No. 28. New York: United Nations, 2002.

Wills, Siobhan. *Protecting Civilians. The Obligations of Peacekeepers*. New York: Oxford University Press, 2009.

Zarate, J. C. "The Emergence of a New Dog of War: Private International Security Companies, International Law, and the New World Disorder." *Stanford Journal of International Law* 34 (1998): 75–162.

About the Author

Jacques Fomerand, a native of France, studied law and graduated in political science from the Institut d'Etudes Politiques in Aix en Provence. He completed his graduate studies at the City University of New York, where he earned a PhD in political science with a specialization in comparative government and international organization. Prior to his joining the United Nations in 1977, he taught at the Institut d'Etudes Politiques in Aix-en-Provence, Brooklyn College, City College, and Queens College of the City University of New York and the School of Advanced International Studies of Johns Hopkins University.

At the United Nations, he followed economic and social questions in the Office of the Under-Secretary General of the former Department for International Economic and Social Affairs (DIESA), serving as special assistant to the head of the department. He then was appointed chief of the Inter-Organizational Co-operation Section of DIESA, which was tasked with the function of promoting better coordination among UN bodies in the field of development. In 1992, he joined the United Nations University. When he retired from United Nations service in 2003, he was director of the United Nations University Office in North America. In this capacity, he strengthened the university's links with member states of the United Nations, the United Nations and its system of organizations and the international North American scholarly community. He participated actively in the establishment of the Academic Council on the United Nations System (ACUNS) and in the creation of its journal, *Global Governance.*

Since 2002, he has taught in the United Nations Program of Occidental College and is now the assistant director of the program. He also teaches at John Jay College of Criminal Justice. He has held teaching positions at the School of International Public Affairs of Columbia University, the School of Continuing Education of New York University and the Division of Global Affairs of Rutgers University. He has widely published on matters related to international relations, international organization, human rights and global human security issues at the United Nations. He is the author of *The A to Z of the United Nations.*